Storytelling
Encyclopedia

Storytelling Encyclopedia

Historical, Cultural, and Multiethnic Approaches to Oral Traditions Around the World

General Editor
David Adams Leeming

Project Editor
Marion Sader

Oryx Press
1997

Written and developed by BOOK BUILDERS INCORPORATED

© 1997 by The Oryx Press
4041 North Central at Indian School Road
Phoenix, Arizona 85012-3397

Published simultaneously in Canada

Library of Congress Cataloging-in-Publication Data

Storytelling encyclopedia : historical, cultural, and multiethnic
    approaches to oral traditions around the world / general editor,
David Adams Leeming ; project editor, Marion Sader.
        p. cm.
    Includes bibliographical references and index.
    ISBN 1-57356-025-1 (alk. paper)
    1. Storytelling—Encyclopedias. 2. Tales—Encyclopedias. 3. Oral
tradition—Encyclopedias.   I. Leeming, David Adams, 1937– .
II. Sader, Marion.
GR72.S76 1997
808.5'43—dc21   97-23081
                                                                    CIP

CONTENTS

CONTRIBUTORS

ADVISORS AND CONSULTANTS

Carol Birch   Storyteller, Librarian, Author, and Adjunct Professor
    Weslyan University, Middletown, Connecticut and Southern Connnecticut
    State University

Dr. Emory Elliott   Professor of English; Director, Center of Ideas and Society
    University of California, Riverside

Melissa Heckler   Storyteller, Librarian, Author, and Children's Literature
    Consultant

Jackie Stallcup   Lecturer
    California State Polytechnic University, Pomona

Dr. Jack Zipes   Professor of German Literature; Department of German,
    Scandinavian, and Dutch
    University of Minnesota, Minneapolis

PRINCIPAL CONTRIBUTORS

Wim Coleman   Storyteller; Former Instructor, Writing and Literature
    Drake University

Helane Levine-Keating   Professor of English
    Pace University

Pat Perrin   Former High School Teacher, Humanities, Newport News, Virginia

Allison Singley   Teaching Assistant, English
    University of Connecticut, Storrs

ADDITIONAL CONTRIBUTORS

Kathleen Drowne
  University of North Carolina, Chapel Hill
Matthew Elliott
  University of Maryland
Cathy Goldberg
  University of California, Riverside
Neville Hoad
  Columbia University
Bradley Johnson
  University of Connecticut, Storrs
Tamara Layman
  University of California, Santa Barbara
  Director, Minnesota Historical Society's Folk Festival
Kimberly Lutz
  University of California, Riverside
Julie Nash
  Eastern Connecticut State University, Willamantic
Jason Parker
  University of California, Riverside

PREFACE

One of our primary defining characteristics as human beings is our need to tell stories and to pass those stories along from one person and one generation to another. It is only in recent times that the transmitting of stories has been primarily by way of the written word, and even now the art of oral storytelling is alive and well. More often than not stories have been conveyed by storytellers and mythmakers who have spoken, sung, drawn, danced, and acted out the tales that we somehow require for our emotional and psychological stability. Stories have always been a convenient and entertaining path to our considering and better understanding the nature of our own being. When we hear or read the tale called "Cinderella," we of course enjoy and are thrilled by its fantasy aspect, but, through the tale, we also confront directly the abstract human realities to which we give names such as deprivation, humility, and hope.

The subject of the *Storytelling Encyclopedia* is the whole question of the oral tradition that we call storytelling—its history, its purposes, its cultural dimensions. We recognize that although stories always attempt to address an aspect of our human condition, some stories work better than others; and we know that some storytellers possess in greater quantity than others the "magic" that can carry us into the mysterious and sometimes outrageous world of myth, folktale, legend, epic, and fantasy. We do not pretend to have included all there is to know about storytelling—even good storytelling—in this volume. That would, in any case, have been impossible. We have had to make choices, and choices are nearly always at least somewhat subjective. There are doubtless entries that should have been included that have not been, and there are entries that some might find inappropriate or superfluous. We have, for instance, included several articles on works that are primarily literary rather than oral. These works, however, have been highly influenced by oral storytelling.

Virgil's *Aeneid,* for example, although a written work, developed directly out of Homer's great oral epics.

This is not a dictionary of storytelling, then; it is a selective work, which necessarily reflects the specialized knowledge, the interests, and even the limitations of the writers, editors, and expert consultants who have worked on the project and who have selected what they consider to be a balanced and interesting treatment of the subject at hand.

The editors have tried to be as inclusive as possible, by involving writers and consultants who come from a broad range of disciplines and points of view and by avoiding any single approach. For example, while the *Storytelling Encyclopedia* does not advocate an archetypal approach to fairy tale and myth or a diffusionist one, both approaches have found a place here. Further, we have attempted to take into careful consideration the storytelling traditions of as many cultures and geographical areas as possible. This is by no means a book devoted to or even emphasizing American- or European-based storytelling. It is, as the title suggests, a storytelling *encyclopedia,* which concerns itself with historical, cultural, and multiethnic approaches to oral literature around the world.

Finally, we have made a serious attempt to achieve some balance in our entries among the stories themselves, the best-known storytellers, some of the more important scholars in the field, recurrent themes and motifs, cultural overviews, and particularly significant fictional characters. The readers will find entries on the *Odyssey,* "Rumpelstilzchen," and the *Thousand and One Nights,* as well as on the Japanese sun goddess Amaterasu and the African spider trickster. There are entries on African American, Scandinavian, and Ancient Greek storytelling, as well as entries on the trickster concept, the tall tale, the virgin birth motif, and the hero's quest. Country music, fertility stories, and the cosmic egg are represented, as are scholars Joseph Campbell, Mircea Eliade, and Vladimir Propp.

Some of the entries will be more familiar than others. Most readers will have heard of Homer, Jesse James, and Calamity Jane. Perhaps fewer will recognize figures like the *griot* or the *shaman*, collections like the *Nihongi* or the Navajo creation myth, or characters such as the African heroine Wanjiru or the Indonesian moon-maiden Hainuwele.

Our aim is to introduce the subject of storytelling, as broadly conceived as possible, to those who wish to know more about it and to provide librarians, teachers, students, and the general reader with a comprehensive source book on the subject. With these goals in mind, the editors have created an extensive cross-referencing system by which the reader will be able to make necessary connections between entries. So, for example, the entry on *Mary* is cross referenced to the one on the virgin birth, the *Coyote* entry is tied to the *trickster* entry as a type, the *Amaterasu* entry refers back to the *Sun* entry. (Cross references appear in the entries in SMALL CAPITAL letters.) In moving from one cross reference to another, the reader will obtain an in-depth knowledge of a topic for which the original entry was a beginning.

A book such as this one is long overdue. There have been books on how to tell a story, scholarly books on the nature of story and storytelling, publications of available materials for the teaching and studying of storytelling from particular cultures. And there have been many collections of stories from around the world. But this work is the first complete treatment, in one volume, of the various aspects of the storytelling art.

The first section of the *Storytelling Encyclopedia* is made up of four essays by the primary advisors and consultants to this project. As a mythologist and general editor of this volume, my own essay, "Once Upon a Time," traces storytelling from its origins in rock and cave painting, ritual, and song; it shows how professional storytellers evolved and treated certain universal themes in myth, fable, epic poems, and other genres. Storytellers Melissa Heckler and Carol Birch remind us in their essay "Building Bridges with Stories" that tales, however universal, require cultural details to give them life and that stories create "cultural meaning." They emphasize that stories can build bridges between people and cultures. In their essay, "American Oral Tradition," professor of English, Emory Elliott, and lecturer in English, Jackie Stallcup consider the question of the oral tradition in the United States. They discuss the on-going nature of American storytelling in "urban folklore" and other contemporary forms and provide a valuable overview of the various ethnic and cultural contexts for folklore in America, including the Native American, African American, Hispanic American, Asian American, and European American contexts. Dr. Elliott and Ms. Stallcup pay particular attention, as well, to the role of the woman in American folklore. Finally, Jack Zipes, a fairy-tale and folklore expert, in "The Utopian Tendency of Storytelling: Turning the World Upside Down," discusses storytelling as a response to the innate human desire for redemption, for an improvement in our ways of life and our social relations: "the tendency toward utopia is kept alive through storytelling," he writes.

The main body of the *Encyclopedia* is made up of the more than 700 entries arranged in A-Z format and taken from the many areas of storytelling. It is the writers of these articles, under the direction of the general editor, the project editor, Marion Sader, and the consultants mentioned above, who have contributed most to the *Encyclopedia* and whose names appear at the front of this volume.

The selected bibliography that appears at the end of the book is an alphabetical compilation of the main resources used by the contributors in researching their entries. Because a comprehensive list would be unwieldy and would include some very general reference works, the contributors and editors have selected only those sources from which substantive ideas or comments may have been drawn.

Other selected bibliographic citations may be found at the ends of many of the entries in the main part of the book. These citations point the way to variant or modern editions of tales, including some well-illustrated editions for use in storytelling, and authoritative work to provide deeper or particularly illustrative information on the subject of the entry. Entries that cover major characters, tales, epics, authors/compilers, and creation stories and storytelling traditions generally cite works for further reading.

Whatever their academic disciplines or points of view, the contributors to the *Storytelling Encyclopedia* share a belief that human beings are united, as storytellers and story listeners, in a universal attempt to understand themselves and to celebrate that understanding in what a Native American holy man has called "a vast and wondrous unfolding of creation."

David Adams Leeming

Ammut, Anubis, and Maet   C.M. Dixon, Canterbury

PART ONE

ONCE UPON A TIME

David Adams Leeming

Once upon a time when language and consciousness were sufficiently developed, a human being told a story. Perhaps a wise woman or man looked at the stars in the sky and said, "Those are campfires in the world above" and went on from there.

It is difficult to see a picture from inside of it. For this reason humans make comparisons—they imitate, they represent reality in words and other media, they project existence onto a screen, as it were—so they can better understand it. So it is that nonliterate early people expended significant time and energy, in spite of a very precarious position in a hostile and dangerous world, telling stories—either directly or indirectly. They did so by donning unusual paints and body coverings (costumes) and moving and acting in patterned ways (dance and ritual). They did so by containing incidents and observations in oddly patterned words and consciously altered vocal sounds (poetry and song). And eventually they did so by making up narratives—plots—in words. They did these things because, in a sense, they had to. Storytelling has always been a defining human characteristic. It is an essential element in our apparent purpose for being, which is to understand and articulate life, to make creation conscious of itself.

We can speak of storytelling, then, as a human instinct, a survival impulse like the drives for nourishment, shelter, and procreation. We would not be who we are as a species without the storytelling aspect. As we can say that plants provide oxygen and horses neigh we can say that human beings make up plots.

Aristotle described plot as a narrative pattern with a beginning, a middle, and an end. Humans, unlike other species, see their individual and collective lives in terms of plot—of story and history. The dog, the horse, the plant, the elements live primarily in the present; humans, with their particular form of consciousness, live in an ever-evolving plot of past, present, and future: "Where did we come from, what are we now, what will our end be?" Overall collective plot might be said to be the story of our attempt to make sense of the world and our place in it. Storytelling-plot-making is a universal and timeless aspect of that attempt. It is as if our consciousness leads us to copy in some small way the creator in whose image so many religions tell us we are made, the creator being, for most cultures, the master storyteller, the power that thinks, dreams, or creates out of nothing the story that is creation itself.

So we are all storytellers. "Let me tell you what happened to me today" announces a story. "Once upon a time" heralds a tale told by anyone who remembers or can read one of those ancient tales whose origins are buried in the collective folk past. Some, of course, are better at storytelling than others. Every society that we know of has had what we would call "professional" storytellers: *griots* in West Africa, *shanachies* in the Celtic world, *scops* in the Anglo Saxon, *hakawtis* among the Arabs, troubadors and minstrels in western Europe, and *rhapsodes* in ancient Greece all belong to the ancient guild of the singer of tales. Some societies have treated these people with special reverence. Stories are told, after all, to convey knowledge. It has been assumed by many cultures that a "higher power" uses the storyteller as a medium for the transference of that knowledge and that the story is, therefore, a commodity of great value.

The Seneca Indians tell how a boy was given the first stories by the numinous Storytelling Stone in return for fresh game and other gifts. In Africa the story is told by the Ashanti and others of the spider trickster Anansi. In order to receive a box of stories owned by the sky-god, Nyami, Anansi was required to perform difficult deeds. At the end of that story we find a reason for one of the primary characteristics of orally transmitted tales: when Anansi opens the box in a village square the stories begin to fly away. Anansi catches some of them and so do the villagers, but others fly away "to the four corners of the world" where more people will catch them.

Most of us would grant that stories have a mysterious power all their own, not only to move from place to place in various cultural disguises, but, above all, the power to attract and to captivate. In a recent *New Yorker* article on storytelling, Bill Buford suggests that "strong narrative . . . is, at its most elementary, an act of seduction. . . . It flirts, stimulates an appetite, verges on satisfying it, only to stimulate another, greater appetite—an appetite for more, please, now . . . ; story means pleasure" (1 July 96, p.12). In short, a good story works because it entertains (holds and moves) us, even as it re-creates us by showing us more about ourselves than we knew before.

The first stories told by way of the spoken word, as opposed to cave and rock painting or ritual dance, for instance, were probably what we would call myths. Myths are religious and scientific in the sense that they explore questions like the creation, the afterlife, the arrangement of the cosmos, and the relationship between humans and the "higher powers." As such they are related to or part of what we call the organized "scripture"—the holy books—that developed later. But they are, above all, stories. Myths cover the whole gamut of storytelling themes: love, betrayal, trickery, mistaken identity, death, adultery, journey quests, how things come to be, what the distant future will be, relationships between parents and children. There are comic myths and tragic ones, there are mythic heroes and mythic villains. All cultures have myths.

Most people in the European or European-influenced world have grown up with stories of Zeus and Hera and their family. In India every child knows who Siva and Visnu and the Goddess (Devi) in their many masks are; their stories are told by traveling storytellers, by puppet shows, on television, and even in comic books. The Australian aboriginal storytellers tell myths about the "Dreaming," the means by which, in a mythological past, the world itself with all its special landmarks, animals, and people, was "dreamed" into existence by the divine ancestors. Indian storytellers of North and South America tell how the world was created by tricksters and sky-gods and maidens who fell from the sky. Polynesians tell of the volcano goddess Pele. A close and ancient relative of the myth is the secular tale or folktale. Folktales can take many forms: legends, animal tales, ballads, and so-called fairy tales probably evolved from situations faced by early humans. The memory of a successful hunt led by a particularly brave man might have resulted in time in heroic legend. A particularly gruesome event like the killing of a child by a parent might have been re-created in a tale of a jealous witch who cooks a child for food.

Like myths, folktales are noticeably archetypal. That is, they make use of motifs that express certain concerns and feelings that seem to be part of the psyche of the human race as a whole. Some of these archetypal motifs include the hero, the quest, the enchantress, the search for the father, the wronged woman, the descent to an underworld. The list of archetypal motifs and the forms they take around the world is an endless one, as collators like Antti Aarne and Stith Thompson have shown us. A recognition of the existence of archetypes helps us to see that the Buddha and Paul Bunyan, for example, are related as heroes; that the Native American Kutoyis goes on a quest that has something in common with the quest of the ancient Greek Theseus; that Zeus's being tricked into a sexual encounter with his nagging wife in the *Iliad* can be better understood in light of Samson's being "unmanned" by Delilah in the Bible; that Cinderella, as a wronged maiden whose mistreatment leads to a glorious victory, is an archetypal relative of the Indonesian Hainuwele; and that the descent of Herakles into the underworld has echoes in the visit of the American Indian Waterjar Boy to his ancestors under the water.

Forms of the folktale in so-called Western culture include, among many others, the fairy-tale legends, the Brer Rabbit stories, and the Indian trickster tales of the Americas; heroic stories such as those of the Celtic Tain or the English Robin Hood cycles; animal fables told to convey a moral by the ancient Greek Aesop, by many medieval European writers, and by the seventeenth-century Frenchman Jean de La Fontaine; and the ballad of broken hearts, which still takes form today in such genres as the folk song and in rock and country music. A descendant of the animal tale and the fairy tale is the "Three Little Pigs"- or "Goldilocks"-type story we associate with early childhood bedtime reading.

Folktales of all kinds have been popular all over the world. India has its collection of educative allegorical tales called the *Panchatantra*; the Middle East has its comic tales of Nassredin Hodja and its *Arabian Nights*, including such favorites as "Ali Baba and the Forty Thieves"; Africa has its animal tales. East Asia has its share of folktales as well. Often they are used primarily to educate, as in the case of the Zen *koan* in Japan, which is used to reveal to the novice a new sense of reality, or the pithy teaching tales attributed to the Chinese founder of Taoism, Lao-tsu. The Buddha, too, illustrated his lessons with stories, and so did Jesus in the form we call the parable. The folktale is as ubiquitous as the situation of a parent putting a child to bed, a pretelevision community staving off fear and keeping itself amused around a nighttime fire, learners sitting around a guru, or a group of adults being entertained by a joke at a dinner party.

Myths and folktales have, of course, been collected and written down over the centuries, but their original composition has generally been attributed to the collective "folk" ("the people"). In the case of another early form of storytelling, the epic, specific authorship has always been assigned. We do not know whether a Homer actually existed, but a whole tradition—a folktale in itself—of a blind traveling bard from Asia Minor or the island of Chios (depending on the version) has been associated with the *Iliad* and the *Odyssey*. In India we are told that the author of the *Mahabharata*—eight times as long as the Homeric epics together—was one Vyasa and that the poet Valmiki composed the also very long *Ramayana*. In fact, the authors of the great oral epics are all unknown. The fact that cultures feel the need to attribute authorship to epics such as the Greek and Indian ones is probably related to the emergence in the ancient world of professional storytellers who traveled about like the real or legendary Homer, singing narrative poetry for payment. These poets worked improvisationally with great skill around certain stylistic formulae and well-known basic plots, and, taking pride in their artistic powers to move and inform their audiences, they must have craved recognition of some sort in addition to pay.

The oral epic was usually a celebration of a culture— its religion, its manner of warfare, its values, its history. In this sense it was intended to transmit knowledge. But as it was performed in return for goods or money, it was important that the poem be entertaining, that there be action, love, murder—all the things still required of popular literature. For, it must be remembered, epics were composed and performed mostly for illiterate audiences.

By the time Virgil wrote his *Aeneid* for a Roman audience the situation was entirely different. The epic was written down as it was composed and was intended not to be recited aloud but to be read by the elite. The *Aeneid* is a literary masterpiece—like other later literary epics such as Milton's *Paradise Lost* or Dante's *Divine Comedy*—but it lacks the storytelling spontaneity of the oral epics. It is much more the product of an individual than of the folk tradition.

In any case, literary epic or not, in the periods we call the Middle Ages and Renaissance in Europe and elsewhere storytelling remained much more important to the majority of people than the art of storywriting. This was so in spite of an increase in the availability of the written word and the greater literacy that resulted from the invention of the printing press in the mid-fifteenth century. Throughout the period in question storytelling continued, in fact, to develop as a way of entertaining and transferring knowledge.

Drama was one such area of development. In classical Greece it had achieved a literary status associated with particular known playwrights, but when it reemerged in Europe in the Middle Ages it did so as a highly effective and popular form of anonymously composed Christian folk art. Mystery plays such as *The Second Shepherd's Play* or *Abraham and Isaac*, based—sometimes loosely—on biblical stories, were performed by craft guild amateurs. And morality plays such as *Everyman* and *The Castle of Perseverance*, which conveyed ethical messages, were also anonymously composed, sometimes even for paying audiences. In India there has long been an equivalent to mystery plays in the form of temple dramas centered on religious stories. In Japan, Indonesia, and many other Asian countries several types of popular folk drama still exist, including the highly popular *Barong* play in Bali, connected to the ancient art of ritual dance storytelling. The *Barong* is not unrelated in spirit to the more comic mummer's plays in England.

Another popular form of storytelling in the Middle Ages and Renaissance was the romance. While stories of King Arthur's court and other chivalric tales of love and separation were written down in the period, there continued to be a tradition of troubadors singing them. Non-Western romances, or their equivalents, were also told or sung in parts of the Middle East and Asia. Their offspring may well be the exaggerated romantic movie popular in India today.

The printing press and the written word have had little effect on the storytelling practices of societies to which literacy has come late. In fact, storytelling remained the primary form of narrative transmission for many peoples well into the twentieth century and continues to be for some to this day. And in recent times, storytelling has undergone a revival even in highly literate and industrial societies. After a long period of neglect, for instance, the importance of fairy tale and myth to contemporary society was brought to our attention at the turn of this century by psychiatrists and anthropologists such as Sigmund Freud, Carl Jung, Sir James Frazer, Jane Harrison, Jessie Weston, and Franz Boas, to mention only a few. In still more recent times the task has been taken over by many more thinkers and scholars, including Mircea Eliade and Joseph Campbell, and a large number of professional storytellers who, like the bards of the past, travel from place to place, from school to library to theater, entertaining and teaching through their art. These scholars and storytellers have helped us to rediscover story in our process of keeping in touch with, understanding, and articulating the real world around and within us. That is, in their different ways they have tried to lead us back to the re-creative properties of the story itself and to its importance in our psychic survival. If we lose touch with the story, they rightly tell us, we lose touch with our reason for being.

BUILDING BRIDGES WITH STORIES

Melissa Heckler and Carol Birch

What's a person to do? In the United States, one of the least homogeneous countries in the world, educators are charged with making pluralism work. The task is to teach children to celebrate the diversity of gender, ethnicity, and religion. Children need to develop pride in their own cultural identity, which enables them to deal responsibly and sensitively with the similarities and differences of others. Stories are a natural means to this end. Yet, as the conflicts between cultures intensify, the use of stories by people outside the culture of the story comes under closer scrutiny; educators are also charged with the injunction not to misrepresent or exploit another culture.[1] Perusing the vast list of cultures in a book like this leads back to the question: What *is* a person to do?

The very success of the world and its future depends on the ability of people to accept each other and thrive together. We do not have an answer to solve the "world's" dilemma. What we can offer are suggestions for better representing and communicating the stories of the world's peoples. These suggestions range from simple strategies to more complex models with which to think about storytelling. The longevity of the oral tradition is a testimony to the power of the told story. Stories improve understanding by building bridges of intellectual, emotional, and spiritual connections among peoples. If what is universal in stories is a vast stewpot of broth, then it is the ethnic, geographic and historical, in short cultural details, which season the broth. Jalapeño peppers, cumin seeds, and lemon grasses season food distinctively, so it is flavorful and satisfying to a people. One reason people respond to stories is because stories simultaneously remind people of what is universal while celebrating

---

[1] We wish to thank Lynn Moroney for her expression of the quandary on which this essay is based.

what is unique to a culture. When we are outside a culture, we have to take care not to season the story-stew so inappropriately that it becomes putrid to those it once fed (Birch, *Teacher's* 1).

As a teller of Buddhist tales, storyteller Rafe Martin immerses himself in Buddhist culture, intellectually through research and spiritually through daily practices. However, classroom teachers and librarians simply cannot devote the same quantity and quality of research each time they read or tell a story to children. A simple solution for increasing the number of cultures brought into the classroom seems to be making available books of stories from many cultures. If teachers look at the books in their classrooms, they will discover part of the story they are telling their students. Children in the classroom should be able to find "their" stories on the shelves. Not only their stories, but the stories of those around them.

Unfortunately, it is not simple to find credible versions of stories. Good retellings accurately represent a culture not only in words and graphic images, but also in underlying cultural values and assumptions, metaphors, and speech patterns. We need to seek out authors, illustrators, and editors who do their cultural homework before a book is published.

For example, the book jacket of a Puerto Rican story proclaimed that the illustrator, whose name could not be identified with any specific culture, *listened to salsa music while drawing.* As if what was culturally, geographically, and historically appropriate could be gleaned from listening to a certain type of music!

Even descendants of European cultures must be aware of how many cultural references in European stories have been lost to us. All too often contemporary people dismiss a story like "Rapunzel" as commonplace, lacking depth. Yet, the tale emerged from a culture with extensive knowledge of its local plants. People today do not associate the name Rapunzel with the herb rampion, *campanula rapunculus.* The plant rampion literally grows in a column that splits, if no pollination occurs, into halves that curl like braids.

> Rapunsel does indeed have a tower, does indeed send out a call for the male to come and pollinate her, and does indeed have 'collecting hairs' that allow her to draw up the male into intimate contact with her reproductive organs. (Thompson 31)

What other resonances and metaphoric levels are lost to us?

Similarly a recent picture-book edition of the ancient Irish myth, *The Children of Lir,* appalled Marianne McShane, a storyteller from Ireland. The version by Shiela MacGill-Callahan with illustrations by Gennady Spirin (Dial, 1993) "changes the entire character of the story and strays so far from the meaning and integrity of the original it is barely recognizable as the same tale." In the original version, the children of Lir are changed into swans and condemned to remain in this shape for nine hundred years. There are three boys and one girl, Fionnuala, whose name in translation means "maid of the fair shoulder," symbolic of her role in the story. All that remains of their humanity, for what is nearly an eternity, are their human hearts and voices, enabling them to make the sweetest music. "They are not two sets of twin boys and girls who regain human form one day each year for dancing 'the night away in merry jigs and reels'."

> On a deeper level, the original myth reveals the tensions between the old and new Gods in Ireland; how the coming of Christianity quenched the old pagan beliefs . . . Lir, while still remaining a God, shrinks in size and becomes one of the fairy people. And this is the origin of the Irish fairy

folk—they are the old Gods, now shrunken in size and significance, who dwell today in the fairy forts dotted around the countryside.

Most damaging of all, MacGill-Callahan radically changes the ending to the original story of deeply felt loss and almost unbearable poignancy. In the traditional myth the children of Lir never see their father again after the first three hundred years. The swans regain their human shape as ancient men and women, so feeble and frail they die almost instantly. In the new version the four children are reunited with their father, and the story ends happily with the children again cavorting gaily.

Alas, even the illustrations, lush and beautiful as they appear on the surface, are inaccurate and misleading. For example pictures of stone churches illustrate a period long before the time of Christ. Dotted throughout are pretty thatched cottages, which are wonderful tourist attractions today, but the like of which were never seen in the pre-Christian era. Irish men and women of over 2000 years ago look remarkably like medieval European peasants.

The end result of this insensitive and disrespectful collaboration between author and illustrator is that a myth, revered over the centuries by Irish storytellers as one of the "Three Sorrows of Storytelling," reads in parts like a parody. Even worse, it reads as a late-twentieth-century "New Age" Celtic fantasy. (McShane)

Betsy Hearne addressed the dilemma of the impossibility of knowing everything about every folktale retold in picture-book format. "Cite the Source: Reducing Cultural Chaos in Picture Books" is a seminal piece of writing in which she asks:

How do you tell if a folktale in picture-book format is authentic or true to its cultural background? What picture books have met the challenge of presenting authentic folklore for children? These two questions . . . generate even broader questions: How can an oral tradition survive in print? How do children's books pass on—and play on—folklore?

In part one, she suggests

that the producers of picture-book folktales provide source notes that set these stories in their cultural context; [and] that those of us who select these materials for children judge them, at least in part, on how well their authors and publishers meet this responsibility. (Hearne, Part One 22)

In part two, she states

Folktales belong to all of us, but we do not own them. Like the air we breathe and the earth we stand on, they are ours to take care of for a short while. In recreating a folktale for children in picture-book form, we are borrowing an old story, adding to it, and returning it to the world renewed. That is the ideal scenario, but sometimes more is subtracted from a story than is added.

Achieving a balance between old and new depends on equal respect for *both* old and new, for what we've received and what we have to give, for the "original" source of a story (i.e., where we heard or read it) and for the possibilities of re-creating it . . . . I propose—beyond a standard requirement for source citation—that a text adapted from folklore be judged for its balance of two traditions: the one from which it is drawn and the one that it is entering. (Hearne, Part Two 33)[2]

Once her standards are met, when we find a marvelous story to share with children, it often serves the needs of Hearne's two traditions to read the story aloud with book in hand. For example, Lorenz Graham retold Bible stories in the idiomatic, rhythmic English spoken by the Liberians with whom he worked. Across the divides of time, culture, and geography comes Goliath's challenge to David, "Do you Mommy know you out?" If a Euro-American woman, like one of the authors of this essay, were to tell the story *without the book*, children might wonder why our use of language changed. In speaking this way, they might ask who was this librarian, who regularly told them stories in her own voice, turning into? The point is not that idiomatic language or dialects can never be used, but rather that the presence of the book itself clarifies that the reader is making the *author's* words and voice audible (Birch, "Who Says?" 115).

Questions about the use of dialects cannot be reduced to rules that fit across the board. The issues are much more complex than that. Historically, dialects employed by a person outside the cultural origin of the speech pattern has had negative connotation. Dialects often turn language into an oral, cultural artifact that promotes a static and quaint view of the culture. Story readers and storytellers would do well to consider the following questions that Ruth Crawford Seeger raises in her book *American Folksongs for Children:*

> How important to the song is the pronunciation of the words? What sorts of changes can be allowed without loss of character to the song and without loss to the child of a valuable social and speech experience? . . . Does the use of such stylized expressions as "de," "dat," "gwine"— especially by the educated city singer, to whom they are not natural modes of expression and to whom they signify lower levels of education than his own—tend to be self-conscious, condescending, precious, "cute"? Shall we perhaps just decide to sing the song in a way natural to each of us—not too carefully or precisely—dropping a few final "g's" from the "ings" when the mood strikes us, but not straining after the picturesque? (Seeger 16)

The question of the use of dialect points to even deeper cross-cultural issues. "Straining after the picturesque," on *any* level, suggests that the story does not have power and that only the way it is told gives it potency. For instance, stories from indigenous cultures have been used as examples of primitive, misguided, or quasi-scientific explanations into the origins of the natural world. As Barre Toelken points out the cultural point of a Native American story in which selfish girls turn into birds is not an attempt to explain the origin of birds, but in part to say,

> Whenever you hear the birds' wings beating [as the girls had beaten the berry stems and leaves out of their baskets to make room for more] and see the birds flying past us bringing berries home to their young, you are reminded of your obligations to nature and to family. . . . Tales such as this function far more powerfully to situate a people in its cultural, spiri-

[2]Reprinted, with permission, from *School Library Journal.* Copyright by Cahners Publishing Company, A Division of Reed Elsevier Inc.

11

tual, natural, and geographical contexts than they do to provide puffy "explanations" [of natural phenomena]. (Toelken 49)

Stories operate on many levels in a culture. To use a familiar story, small children might think Little Red Riding Hood mistakes a wolf for her grandmother. The storyteller tells it with the larger recognition that in life people are not always what they seem to be. As children grow into a story and become less literal, they may see other possibilities and lessons in a tale. Telling a story from another culture requires storytellers to grasp more than its most literal and/or simplistic level.

One strategy for using culture responsibly as a curriculum tool is to pursue more actively contact with people from the culture that will be studied. Educators know which assignments repeat each year. Too often the muffled cry (yawn?) can be heard in libraries and teacher lounges across America: "It's time for the local Indians." The reason for the ennui is that educators approach the culture as static, teaching it repetitively and didactically. Beyond the textbooks, beyond the publications used in research, there is always the possibility of learning from members of a Native American community. Many times, there are people who still know and live within local tribal customs. They are the true historians of their culture. If we are encouraging respect for a local indigenous group, it is the teacher's responsibility to foster a learning relationship in which he or she is as much a student as any child in the class. Not all at once, but over a teaching or telling career, a meaningful relationship can emerge. Children can leave third or fourth grade with a more lasting sense of appropriate cultural celebrations—celebrations that do not belittle others.

In a similar vein, cultural artifacts that may hold deep religious significance are not appropriate curriculum tools or playthings. The all too human tendency is to treat one's own religion with reverence, and other religions as 'mere stories.' This is particularly true for the way Euro-American-centered school systems appropriate or act culturally rough with the world view, tools, and creative arts of indigenous peoples.

The strategies discussed here could do a great deal to counteract the tradition of "cultural roughness" and promote cultural respect and zestfulness. For those who wish to delve more deeply into cross-cultural studies and communication through stories, we offer three contemporary research models for storytelling (Heckler 25-29).

Diana Wolkstein faced the challenge of telling stories from an extinct culture when she sought to retell the ancient Sumerian myth of Inanna. Because she loved the story and wished to share it, she contacted the late Sumerian scholar and translator, Samuel Noah Kramer. Line by line, Wolkstein worked with Kramer to recreate the myth for contemporary audiences. Section by section, she gathered friends and read the work in progress. Her audiences responded, telling her what moved them, what they found humorous, sad, and confusing. Wolkstein and Kramer worked and reworked the story fragments to create a piece rooted in the culture of its origin, yet accessible and resonant with more modern sensibilities.

Rebecca Chamberlain, a Euro-American storyteller from the northwest coast of Washington, was apprenticed to Vi Hilbert, a Salish Elder. Chamberlain learned the Salish language and stories as she steeped herself in the culture of the Salish people. She acquired knowledge of their values, grounding her story translations in what she had learned of the principles, dreams, confusions, and conflicts of the original tellers. Her relationship to these stories was also strengthened by growing up in the same geographical area of the Salish. In the folklore of indigenous people, stories can be both a home and a map of the literal landscape, as well as indicative of the way people lived in relation to the land. Chamberlain was eventually given permission to tell these stories.

Melissa Heckler discovered stories of the /Xam Bushman of South Africa, a people extinct since the late 1800s. Her research began in anthropological literature. She also read stories collected in the 1800s by Wilhelm Bleek and his sister-in-law, Lucy Lloyd, and later by Bleek's daughter, Dorothea Bleek. Heckler began retelling these stories, while she continued her research, seeking out new information to fill in cultural gaps. When Heckler found *Nisa: The Life and Words of a !Kung Woman,* by Marjorie Shostak, a seismic shift occurred. Shostak lived and worked with a contemporary group of Bushmen, or San. The appendix of her book listed several of Shostak's colleagues. Suddenly the extinct /Xam had living relatives, a contemporary group of San, the Ju/'hoansi of Namibia. Heckler now had contemporary people to contact. One of the first contacts was anthropologist and folklorist Megan Biesele, whose ground-breaking studies of the Ju/'hoan folklore extends over a quarter of a century. From her, Heckler learned about Ju/'hoan life: childrearing, hunting and gathering, storytelling, humor, kinship ties, etc. Finally, Heckler joined Biesele and the Ju/hoansi in Namibia. There she heard new San stories and, from the teachings of the Ju/hoansi, deepened her knowledge of the ancient tales from these relatives of the /Xam. In exchange for their generosity, Heckler reciprocated by contributing to the creation of in-village literacy programs for the schools.

A year later, Heckler also visited the South Africa home from which /Xam storytellers came. The landscape of the /Xam was completely different than that of the Ju/'hoansi. She saw, firsthand, how the landscape itself was uniquely represented in the stories from each community. The aridity of the two deserts were vastly different. From a distance the desert of the /Xam seemed harsh and dry compared to the semi-arid desert of the Ju/hoansi. The Kalahari landscape seemed lush in comparison; a lushness reflected in their stories.

When the stories first touched Heckler, and she began to retell them, she could not speak with the knowledge gained over the last fifteen years. She will never tell the stories as if she were within the Ju/'hoan culture; to try to do so would be ludicrous at best and quite possibly horrific. What she can do is to tell the stories out of her ongoing relationship with the people from whom she heard them. Her retelling of the stories is informed by research, by contact with the Ju/'hoan, by contact with other scholars in the field, as well as firsthand knowledge of the cultures and the landscapes in which the /Xan lived and the Ju/'hoan live.

The landscape of a story is one of its key elements. Television's sameness and our mall-culture mind-set so dominate our national landscape that we are de-sensitized in our awareness to the differences of landscape and how those differences affect a story. In our appreciation of rascally characters and inventive plots, we often forget how extensively time and place touch nearly every aspect of a story. Consider time and place and you immediately have feelings, assumptions, and images of time of day, climate, topography, food, architecture, clothing, threats to survival, options for work and play, class distinctions of an age, and definitions of good, beauty, and wealth—in short, geography, ethnicity, history, and culture. The king in Norwegian folktales is often in the kitchen opening the door to visitors himself; no Japanese emperor ever would. The power of the sea affects the storyline in tales from around the world, yet the sea of Inuit, Filipino, and Moroccan fishermen can be dramatically different. Though folktales give voice to universal experiences of love, fear, anger, joy, and sorrow, the characters do not walk on air. The characters are more dimensional for their tangible humanity as they walk beside a Navajo hogan, a Bushman's *scherm*, or a squire's estate (Birch, *Teachers* 1).

Learning about a culture is a process that precedes the telling of its tales, and never ends. If we choose to read stories as a means of introducing a culture, then our task is finding credible and responsible versions. If, however, we are going to retell the stories of a people, we become involved in a more complex and dynamic relationship. As our opportunities increase, so do our responsibilities.

The responsibilities extend back to the people from whom the story came as well as to the audience before us. Storytelling is a process involving relationships. People tend to focus on the process of developing performance skills in storytelling. To the uninitiated, storytelling and acting may seem one and the same. Practice, and techniques borrowed from acting, are thought to minimize the problems of beginning storytellers. Yet, the central impulse of the two arts is radically different. In acting the goal is to submerge one's own personality in the portrayal of a character behind an imaginary fourth wall. In storytelling the goal is to speak effectively as oneself, with some directness, and indeed often rather intimately, to the people before you. Performance is not the heart of the storytelling process; relationship is. The teller through both cultural and personal homework brings a story to an audience and builds a bridge relating audience, teller, and story.

In remembering the charge to make pluralism work, there is another and perhaps more familiar model with which to work. The original storytelling unit is the family. A family does not always function harmoniously. When parents and grandparents are wise and compassionate adults, who believe that the family structure works, then friction between siblings becomes safe. It is a positive force. Differences take place within the context of familial relationships, they do not threaten its survival. Friction between children, struggling to recognize their differences and similarities, can help them achieve a fulsome relatedness. Among children within a family, similarities can be as frightening as differences. When pluralism works in a family, then it actually reinforces and makes more flexible the family's tensile strength.

More than being politically correct, more than employing an effective curriculum tool, and more than fulfilling externally imposed values, those of us who accept the charge to make pluralism work in American cultures have to believe passionately in the relatedness of people. Frictions, joys, and shared references help create a family's culture, and cultures are built on families. Pluralism isn't about politics, curriculum, or didacticism. If we bind ourselves to each other, then we strengthen the ties to each other's cultural differences and similarities. Pluralism can and does work. The relationships among all of us contribute to the diastolic pressure at the heart of our unwieldy, democratic process. At its best, this process recognizes that *all* stories contribute to the dynamic, ongoing process of creating cultural meaning.

LITERATURE CITED

Birch, Carol. *Teacher's Guide: The Storytelling Festival.* Williamsburg, VA: Busch Gardens, 1988.

———. "Who Says? The Storyteller as Narrator." *Who Says? Essays on Pivotal Issues in Contemporary Storytelling.* Edited by Carol Birch and Melissa Heckler. Little Rock, AK: August House, 1996. 106–108.

Hearne, Betsy. "Respect the Source: Reducing Cultural Chaos in Picture Books: Part One." *School Library Journal* (July 1993): 22-27.

————. "Respect the Source: Reducing Cultural Chaos in Picture Books: Part Two." *School Library Journal* (August 1993): 33-37.

Heckler, Melissa. "Two Traditions." *Who Says? Essay on Pivotal Issues In Contemporary Storytelling.* Edited by Carol Birch and Melissa Heckler. Little Rock, AK: August House, 1996. 15-34.

McShane, Marianne. Review of *The Children of Lir* by Shiela MacGill-Callahan. Westchester Library System, NY, 1993.

Seeger, Ruth Crawford. *American Folk Songs for Children: In Home, School and Nursery School.* New York: Doubleday, 1948.

Thompson, William Irwin. *Imaginary Landscape: Making Worlds of Myth and Science.* New York: St. Martin's Press, 1989.

Toelken, Barry. "The Icebergs of Folktale: Misconception, Misuse, Abuse." *Who Says? Essays on Pivotal Issues in Contemporary Storytelling.* Edited by Carol Birch and Melissa Heckler. Little Rock, AK: August House, 1996. 35-63.

AMERICAN ORAL TRADITION

Emory Elliott and Jackie Stallcup

Have you heard the story about the man who found a dead mouse in his can of soda? Or the hitchhiker who foretold an earthquake to the driver of a car—then disappeared . . . or the woman who brought home what she thought was a small puppy from a foreign country, only to find after washing it and letting it sleep in her bed that it was a *sewer rat* . . . or the young girl who perfected her bouffant hair-do to the point that she didn't wash it for weeks and then died of spider bites from a nest of black widows who had taken up residence in her hair?

You may have heard that these things happened to your best friend's brother's wife's cousin, or to the sister-in-law of a man you work with, or you might have read about it in the newspaper. You may have even passed a story like this on to other listeners. If so, you have participated in the long, varied, and incredibly rich tradition of American oral narrative. What Jan Brunvand has called "urban folklore"—those incredible stories of modern life that we pass along as true, but which can rarely be traced back to a single source or actual event—is only the latest incarnation of a tradition that started long before Europeans landed on these shores. Folklore, in other words, is not merely an artifact of past cultures; it doesn't only belong to preliterate societies, nor is it solely concerned with past events or what we think of as fantasy or fairy tales. It is a living, breathing tradition with millions of practitioners, even today. What, then *is* folklore, and how are our current "mice-in-a-can-of-soda" tales connected to the witches and devils of the Puritans, the tricksters of various Native American tribes, Brer Rabbit of the African American slaves, and La Llorona, the weeping woman of Hispanic American legend?

Folklore can be defined broadly as including those stories, myths, customs, fictions, beliefs, tales, riddles, jokes, and games that are traded orally within a homogenous group of people, shifting and developing as they are passed along, so that variations are continuously arising. The oral nature of folklore and its consequent variability are essential parts of its definition; when folklore is written down, it loses its vitality and vibrancy. Transcribed exactly as told by a storyteller, it becomes a shadow of itself, bereft of all the "extras" that oral transmission brings: intonation, inflection, building of suspense through manipulation of voice, interaction with audience. Transformed into a printed tale, it becomes a piece of literature, frozen by print so that it can no longer change and develop, and is therefore no longer "of the folk." Folklore, in other words, is not just the words of a story or joke or myth or legend; it is the words inseparable from the teller and the telling. The variations that inevitably arise with oral transmission help make folklore a living, breathing, and growing creation, and this has long allowed folklore to adapt to the ever-changing needs of tellers and listeners. Among these are some very deep and basic cultural desires. At a basic level, storytelling and jesting can add liveliness to a long winter evening and relieve the monotony of shared tasks, such as corn husking or sewing. Stories can knit groups together, helping people to understand they are not alone in their fears and concerns, and they can be used to transmit culture and history, providing a sense of rootedness and of origins. Newcomers to the American continent could also use them to legitimate their claims, while certain Native Americans, on the other hand, added to their repertoire stories about the newcomers after their arrival; not surprisingly, the stories related, among other things, why the Native Americans were superior to the invaders. Oral narratives can also serve as warning (don't talk to strangers, wash your hair regularly) and as explanation (why the world is the way it is). Through storytelling, people are able to share their life experiences with each other, solidify ties within a community, and deal with the problems that they all face. Brunvand's explanation of the popularity of modern urban tales is also suggestive of reasons behind the enduring nature of all folklore. Although the stores are not true in the sense that they did not happen to any one person, they do "tell one kind of truth. They are a unique, unselfconscious reflection of major concerns of individuals in the societies in which the legends circulate" (Brunvand, *The Vanishing Hitchhiker* xii). This held as true for the Puritans who developed a folklore of demons and witches and pacts with the devil as it did for the Hispanic cultures of the Southwest with their stories of saints and weeping, ghostly women, and in fact for all of the various legends, myths, jokes, jests, pranks, and tall tales that make up the history of American folklore. The stories people tell clearly reflect their day-to-day concerns and anxieties and convey what seems to them worthwhile cultural information.

Folklore of most societies includes creation myths, tall tales, legends, animal stories, tales of magic, religious stories, trickster tales, and yarns, as well as songs, ballads, games, dances, food and drink customs, jests, jokes, anecdotes, and pranks, although the general mix varies. In the United States, the mix incorporates worldwide traditions, from those of the indigenous peoples of the Americas, to those of the various immigrant groups who all brought their own folklores along with them. New tales and legends were also created from the blending of these cultures as storytellers tailored tales to the specific stimuli of the "new" world in which they found themselves. As a result, the traditions of Native Americans and various immigrant groups adapted to the new, complex environment that they shared, allowing the development of a rich American tradition that was a marvelous amalgam of new and old, Native American, European, Mexican, African and many other traditions. In fact, writing a history of oral tradition in America is not unlike writing a history of the place itself, as it involves examining the interweaving of a variety of traditions and peoples. Untangling the roots of any tradition so complex and intertwined is beyond the scope of this essay; however, we *can* take a brief look at some of the major sources.

NATIVE AMERICAN

The Americas, of course, were far from a "new," empty, or culturally destitute continent when Europeans arrived here. The various peoples of the Americas formed an array of culturally complex societies encompassing some 100 million people speaking over 850 languages. In North America alone were hundreds of diverse groups, each with their own language and rich oral tradition through which the members received entertainment, learning, and important historical background. In a selection this short, it is impossible to do justice to the folklore created by Native Americans, as it was every bit as complex and varied as that of different European cultures. We can, however, look at a few common characteristics and touch on some of the major types and themes of some of the groups.

Most Native American folklore includes a rich mythology and diverse set of *pourquoi* tales, which purport to explain such things as the origins of their people, their religious beliefs, and certain natural phenomena. Many Native American societies offered tales that were specific to their own circumstances, including stories that accounted for the shape, size, or location of lakes or other landscape elements, and stories that explained things about the animals around them, such as why the squirrel has stripes, why the coyote has a black-tipped nose and tail, and where the various animals in their world came from.

Trickster figures are also common in Native American folklore, going by different names in different areas. The Great Plains trickster is known as Coyote, while woodland tribes tell stories of Manabozho or the Great Hare. In the Pacific Northwest, the tricksters are Bluejay, Mink, and Raven. Many of these characters appear in creation myths or *pourquoi* tales, and in tales told for amusement. They can be greedy, stupid, or boastful, and quite often are themselves caught by their own cleverness. Native American trickster tales sometimes employ obscene motifs, dealing with incest and excrement (Voegelin 798). In fact, many stories of American folklore contain obscene elements. However, as a modern audience of children is often assumed, these elements are often eliminated in modern printings of the tales.

Other functions of Native American folklore include explaining religious beliefs, teaching appropriate behavior, and conveying tribal customs, and work through such forms as prose narratives, songs, chants, speeches, and formulae. These last can be from one to many lines long, either recited or sung, and are considered valuable personal property that can be sold or bequeathed (Voegelin 801). Prose narratives can range in length from extremely brief Great Basin tales, to the sometimes days-long Great Dream tales of the Mohave Indians. For many tribes, tales could only be told at certain times of year, often winter, and were frequently told by practiced storytellers to mixed-gender groups of all ages. Parents and grandparents told tales to children in more informal settings, and small groups of men or women also exchanged stories. Some important cultural information, such as history of sacred bundles or tribal ceremonies, were restricted by custom to a special group of listeners.

With the arrival of European settlers, Native American folklore shifted to reflect this new influence on their environment. Some new tales purported to explain the differences between Native Americans and the invaders, while some storytellers also began to borrow for their repertoire from these new sources. Some of the European tales were taken almost whole, while others were completely recast for suitability in their new environment, becoming European motifs with a Native American setting, cultural background, and thematic emphasis (Voegelin 799).

AFRICAN AMERICAN

The men and women who were enslaved and brought to the Americas carried with them their own rich cultural traditions, including that of storytelling and oral narratives. This process continued to develop and flourish on the slave plantations, with embellishments inspired by their new environment and the storytelling traditions of those who surrounded them. While many stories in African American folklore can be directly traced to African antecedents, many others show signs of European influence.

Among the best known of all African American folklore are the Uncle Remus tales, collected by journalist Joel Chandler Harris and first published in the Atlanta *Constitution*. Harris published the tales collectively in 1880 in *Uncle Remus, His Songs and His Sayings: The Folklore of the Old Plantation,* and later in *Nights with Uncle Remus* and *Brer Rabbit.* Brer Rabbit is a classic trickster figure in these tales, a rascally character playing hoaxes on a host of less cunning creatures who cross his path; sometimes Brer Rabbit comes out on top, but quite often, his schemes backfire so that the joke is on him, such as when he gets stuck to the tar baby. Other tales collected by Harris include *pourquoi* tales such as "Why the Turkey Buzzard is Baldheaded."

As well known as these stories are however, they do not give a complete or even very accurate picture of African American folklore. As a collector of folklore, Harris, as a Euro-American, faced at least two problems. First, he was working in a period in which many white folklorists were invested in perpetuating the myth of the "happy slave," a position suggested by Harris's invented framework of the contented African slave telling nursery stories to white children (Dorson, *American Negro Folktales* 66). And second, the fact that Harris was a white collector of these tales probably affected both *which* tales the informants told, as well as *how* they told them. "Old Master" (or "Old Marster"/"Old Massa") tales, for example, formed another large but less widely known or studied cycle, in which the planter/slave owner was often pitted against John, his slave. The stories generally follow one of a few patterns that hark back to even earlier traditions of Europe, West Africa, and India. In one pattern, John's status is that of "favored slave" of "Master," who is either tripped up by John's cunning (and takes it good-naturedly), or uses John's smarts in wagers with other plantation owners. Another pattern involves pitting master and slave against each other harshly, with slaves stealing from plantation owners and shirking their work whenever they can. In these particular narratives, the cruel nature of the slaveholding relationship is clearly denoted (Dorson, *American Negro Folktales* 124). An African American storyteller relating these stories to a white folklorist in the late nineteenth or early twentieth centuries could certainly have emphasized certain aspects of the stories that would not have been accentuated in a less artificial storytelling environment. Alan Dundes suggests that "the collecting context may well have influenced which tales were told to the extent that some of John's best put-downs of Old Marster were omitted and occasional tales in which John received punishment from Old Marster were included" (Dundes 549). Or the stories were omitted altogether—Harris only included one Old Master tale in all of his collections, and, according to famed folklorist Richard Dorson, "apparently never understood the cycle to which it belonged" (Dorson, *American Negro Folktales* 124).

In a collection of modern retellings of the Uncle Remus stories (written without the black-storyteller/white-child-listener framework), Julius Lester also warns us against assuming that the trickster elements present in both the Brer Rabbit and Old Master cycles are a direct reflection of the position of the black slave storyteller. Too often, these stories are read as an explicit commentary on the master/slave relationship, with the slave sublimating his or her anger towards the slave owner through creating and relating stories that champion the underdog. However, to reduce the stories to a single cause such as this is to obscure their true richness as well as their roots: many of the trickster themes come straight from Africa, where the American slave/owner dynamic did not exist, but where the rabbit as trickster was common, along with other trickster figures such as the tortoise and spider. It's also important to note that the trickster is a prevalent figure in many folklore traditions and that Lester interprets the trickster as a far more complex character than just a simple underdog. Instead, he is the "avatar of a higher morality," a being whose apparently amoral exploitation of other animals' images of themselves keeps us all firmly grounded. "Trickster's function is to keep Order from taking itself too seriously. . . . The tales were not psychological compensation for the obvious lack of power in the slaves' lives. Rather, they represented an extraordinary effort to balance the totalitarian order of the slave system with archetypal disorder, and thereby become whole" (Lester, *More Tales of Uncle Remus* x-xiv).

Other important forms of African American folklore include jokes, proverbs, riddles, folk songs, spirituals, folk beliefs, and "the dozens" or pointed verbal sparring that is often rhymed.

HISPANIC AMERICAN

In the American Southwest, the stories or *cuentos* of Hispanic folklore played a vital role in sustaining people's lives, which were lived out in the often harsh and unforgiving conditions of the desert. As Angel Vigil points out in his collection of Hispanic *cuentos*, the folklore of the Hispanic culture, like most strong folklore traditions, functioned in specifically useful ways, and so flourished. "The shared experience of listening to the stories bound family members together. The religious nature of many of the *cuentos* provided ongoing strength to the religious life in communities seldom visited by priests. The stories allowed older generations to pass on their wisdom and values to succeeding generations. They provided a way for people to make sense of their world and to explain the mysterious events that accompany human life" (Vigil xx).

These stories, legends, and myths were rooted both in the Spanish culture as well as in that of the indigenous peoples of South America. When Spaniards began to arrive in the Americas in the late fifteenth century, the Aztecs were the dominant culture in Mexico, with a complex cosmology unfolded in a rich oral tradition. This included tales that explained natural phenomena and creation stories that placed them as the chosen people who gave life to the sun (Vigil 3). Some of the most powerful Hispanic legends still in wide circulation bear marks of the influence of the Aztecs, including the story of La Llorona, or the Weeping Woman. In some versions of this tale, La Llorona is a mother who has killed her two children; in others, they have died accidentally, or have been lost, and now she roams the earth searching for them, or trying to take living children to replace her dead ones. One possible root of this still widely disseminated tale may be the Aztec story of Cihuacoatl, a pre-Columbian goddess of childbirth and death (Vigil 11).

Traditions that had influenced Spanish oral culture, such as other European tales as well as Arab and Jewish folklore, can also be discerned in Hispanic tales. Other stories of Hispanic culture that have become a part of the folklore of the American Southwest include many that concern religious figures such as Christ, the Virgin Mary, or others; animal tales (complete with rabbit tricksters); and stories that involve transformation or magic.

ASIAN AMERICAN

Among the sources of Asian American folklore were the folklore and proverbs of the immigrant Chinese men who labored to build the western railroads. A number of these stories, collected as part of a WPA project in 1930s Oakland, California, have been retold by Laurence Yep in his book *The Rainbow People*. All but one of these stories are set in China, rather than in America, but each sheds light on the American experiences of the immigrants who told them. One theme that stands out is the difficulty of retaining a sense of restraint when the traditional community and social safety nets are no longer in place: "the older brother argued for a while longer, but he knew he was helpless. At home, there were family and friends to help him hold back his little brother. But in this strange place, he was the only one and he wasn't enough, so he had to let his little brother go on his own way" (Yep 62). Of course, the younger brother comes to grief in this tale, which clearly is intended to encourage thoughtfulness, self-control, and respect for wisdom. The loneliness and isolation of the men who worked here far from their families were integral parts of many of the stories they told; and they may have modified traditional tales in order to make their new experiences clear to the families at home. The tales they told included trickster figures and fools, as well as proverbs that possibly helped both storyteller and listener cope with their new and confusing situations.

As with other traditions that have influenced American folklore, the various Asian folklores are complex and rich, with often familiar motifs, including ancient versions of the familiar "Little Red Riding Hood" and "Cinderella." In particular, an Asian Cinderella, "Yeh-Shen," predates European versions of this tale by a thousand years. Among other themes of Asian folklores are the importance of cooperation, caring for one's parents before oneself, and the dangers of pride (Huck 342). Tales and lore also revolve around such issues as seasons and harvesting, marriage, birth and death; animal stories, tricksters, fools, and *pourquoi* tales can also be found.

BRITISH AND EUROPEAN SOURCES

European and British storytelling traditions also form a strong part of American oral tradition; each wave of immigrants brought over and often clung to their stories, telling them in their new homes and modifying them to deal with new situations. The Puritan settlers brought with them a rich tradition of supernatural and religious tales revolving around witches, pacts with the Devil, providences, judgments, and specters. These were further developed among the young colonies as part of the process of establishing their claims of creating a holy society in part through giving literal embodiment to the oppositions that they faced. As with modern urban legends, the line between fact and fiction was blurred in these stories, and we might argue that it was this folklore, combined with motifs and images from the Afro-Caribbean folk tradition, that fueled the Salem witchcraft crisis of 1692.

Jack tales were another strong British tradition transplanted to America, especially to settlements in the Appalachian mountains, where they are still a powerful part of many storytellers' repertoires. Some of the stories remained virtually intact, while others were greatly modified to encompass the new environment; but many can be traced back to tales and songs that were popular in sixteenth- and seventeenth-century Britain, where Jack was the most popular name for heroes of chapbooks and nursery tales. Scottish and Irish Jacks can also be discerned in American Jack tales (Lindahl xvii). The Jack of the tales is often a trickster figure, and as in other trickster traditions, the stories sometimes involve scatological and obscene elements. Other, less prevalent types of Jack tales include Jack as the underdog, Jack as the younger brother, and occasionally, Jack as the dupe or opponent (Lindahl xxi-xxii).

Germans, among the earliest of European immigrant groups, brought with them proverbs, riddles, rhymes, songs, games, and folk narratives. Among the proverbs are such familiar ones "He takes the bull by the horns," and "Well begun is half done" (Barrick 38–40). The stories collected by the Grimm Brothers and published in 1812 and 1815 also form a significant part of American oral culture, giving us such tales as the "Bremen Town Musicians," "Rapunzel," "Hansel and Gretel," and "Red Riding Hood." In the early German version of "Cinderella," called "Ashenputtel," the wicked stepsisters cut off bits of their feet to fit into the shoe and are punished in the end by having their eyes pecked out by birds—a harsher conclusion than the romanticized renderings familiar to current generations. Finally, the tall tales of Baron Von Munchausen, published in 1785, influenced the development of the tall tale both in Europe and here in America, where it became an important part of the folklore tradition (Barrick 104).

French folklore also strongly influenced American traditions, especially in the Great Lakes area, where the ancient French story of Gargantua was disseminated among the fur traders, who named several landscape features in the area after the bumbling giant. The Cajun and Creole traditions of Louisiana also can be traced back to French folklore. Among the types of oral narrative that thrived in these communities include animal tales, magic tales, lies and tall tales, jokes and historical tales.

Other groups that have influenced American folklore include Swiss, Italian, Scots, Irish, and more recently Lebanese, Syrian, and Vietnamese cultures and many more (Ancelet xxviii). Often, groups of immigrants settled into ethnic enclaves, sometimes by choice, sometimes not, and in these areas in particular, their folklore could flourish and develop into a specifically American tradition. Also, in addition to bringing their own traditions, immigrant groups have also affected American oral narrative in a more oblique way by becoming the butt of ethnic jokes and racist pranks; rude, disreputable, and cruel, they are nonetheless a part of the overall scene, and demonstrate the often rough-and-tumble character of American folklore. These are only part of an antisocial humor that flourished on the frontier and also included gibes at already established minorities, tricks, and pranks to break in greenhorns, and raucous horseplay that apparently allowed the settlers to "laugh in the face of the devil" or make light of the hardships of their new home (Botkin 46). This pattern remains even in our supposedly more enlightened times, in which rumors abound, for example, regarding local pets being turned into stews by recent arrivals from Asian countries; as Jan Brunvand points out in *The Choking Doberman,* these widespread stories have been investigated, with no evidence uncovered of any kind suggesting that they are true in the vast numbers implied (Brunvand, *The Choking Doberman* 122). Instead, the stories suggest the same kind of widespread anxiety about new immigrants that triggered the racist stories, jokes, and general sentiments of earlier times, as well as a certain reluctance to voice that anxiety directly. Couching it in terms of "true" stories not only allows people an outlet for their racist beliefs, but it also reaffirms the "worth" of those beliefs.

AMERICAN TALL TALES

Along with the raucous tales, jokes, and pranks, the tall tale (which relied for comic effect on ridiculous exaggeration told with a completely serious demeanor) also flourished on the frontier. As Ruth Tooze points out in *Storytelling*, "in a young country like the United States, where everything seems bigger and better, the folk tales that flourish best are tall tales of tall heroes, rare mixtures of true achievement and imaginary adventure. . . . Often the story becomes an extreme expression of a powerful compelling desire which seems quite beyond our own powers" (Tooze 10). In other words, the seemingly almost limitless space of the frontier could only be conquered by larger-than-life figures who fit the landscape. Also, through telling tall tales, those who struggled to live on the frontier could make light of the harsh conditions that they faced, using exaggeration to demonstrate their own hardiness and boost their confidence, lightening their burden with comic relief. Out on the Great Plains, for example, the extreme weather conditions prompted the dissemination of many stories; in his book, *Shingling the Fog and Other Plains Lies*, Roger L. Welsch relates the story of a Plains farmer who was asked why the barns didn't have weather vanes. "No sense to it," the farmer replied. "When you want to see which way the wind is blowing, you just look out the window and see which way the barn is leaning" (Welsch 16). The tall tale heroes of the frontier often straddled the line between "good" and "bad," or law-breaking and law-enforcing, and a number were real people around whom folklore gradually was built, such as Davy Crockett. They are often portrayed as the biggest, or the best, or the fastest, or, in later cases, (as with Johnny Appleseed), most enduring and respecting of duty (Botkin 47).

At the same time, the nation was becoming more and more immersed in a commercial print culture, and inevitably, "folklore" was created for specific purposes and passed off as traditional. Loggers rarely tell Paul Bunyan stories, for example, and he may actually have been a creation of lumber advertising men (Botkin 46). Other created heroes include Old Stormalong, King of the Yankee Sailors; Joe Magarac, the original man of steel and hero of Pittsburgh steelworkers; and Febold Feboldson, Nebraska Plainsman. Richard Dorson labeled these stories "fakelore," asserting that tales that did not have roots in a specifically folk and oral tradition could not be folklore by its very definition (Dorson, *American Folklore* 10). However, some of these stories actually did become popular among storytellers, and so passed on into the oral culture; also, the successful creation of these heroes does indeed suggest a desire for them within the American people.

AMERICAN WOMEN

Many of the American tall tales and other forms revolve around men; stories concerning women were far fewer and less well-known. But women there were, after all—we just have to dig a little to find their stories. The Chippewa have the "Star Maiden"; storytellers of the Apache, Ojibwa [also spelled "Ojibway"], and Cheyenne all spoke of warrior women; and a folk song sung by French explorers in nineteenth-century Louisiana Territory told the story of "La Sauvagesse" or "The Girl of the Wilds." Brer Rabbit's female counterpart in African American folklore was called Molly Cottontail and a number of folklore heroes had sisters, wives, or daughters of similar proportions and skills: Mike Fink's daughter Sal, the trickster Coyote's clever sister Fox, Pecos Bill's giant bride Slue-Foot Sue. Robert San Souci collected these and other songs and tales about women in *Cut From the Same Cloth* and comments on the difficulty of unearthing them: "In the past, American society expected women to limit their concerns to home and family—not to put themselves forward as explorers, hunters, warriors or rulers. . . . Tales of such women went against popular thinking and made people uncomfortable. So they were not often told" (San Souci xii).

And what about female storytellers or female storytelling traditions? Men gathered around such public places as the barber shop or local store to spin yarns. Where were the women telling their tales? Scholars have long looked upon the folklore of men as worthy of study, while that of women has been sorely neglected. Recent studies such as a collection of essays edited by Rosan A. Jordan and Susan J. Kalčik have tried to remedy this situation, and in the process have provided some very interesting insights into the world of female-oriented folklore. Jordan's study of Mexican American women's lore, for example, reveals that it abounds with tales of "snakes or lizards sexually assaulting women," or what Jordan terms the "vaginal serpent theme" (Jordan, "The Vaginal Serpent" 27). As with other folklore traditions, one can read into this concern about life; Jordan argues that this theme "reveals much about the sexual fears and fantasies of the Mexican-American women who tell them" (Jordan, "The Vaginal Serpent" 27) and connects these fears with what she traces as the "Hispanic ideal of modest and submissive behavior for women, and dominant, aggressive behavior for males" (Jordan, "The Vaginal Serpent" 26). She also traces evidence of similar tales in African American lore, and in the stories of Ozark women, among other places. Other essays in this collection examine a quilting bee, rug-weaving, and women's Citizen Band radio names.

As Rayna Green points out in *Feminist Theory and the Study of Folklore,* women's oral tradition, passed from mother and grandmother to daughter and granddaughter, functioned in ways similar to that of male-oriented folklore, helping women to cope with their world:

> All the things [Grandmother] told me have been instructive, both in negotiating the small rigors of daily life as well as in the more substantial rigors of work, politics, relationships and ethical behavior. All the ways in which she told me what she had to say gave me a voice, the Word, the power of song and story, the sense of myself as both speaking and spoken for. At the heart of understanding, which is what scholarship is supposed to be about, rests the work and lives of women who, like my grandmother—through their singing, game-playing, altar-making, sewing, talking, bedmaking, storytelling—establish their own versions of their past and present (Green, "It's Okay," 6).

Other essays in this collection emphasize the importance of understanding women's traditions not simply as reaction to men's, but in some cases complementing it, challenging it, and appropriating it. For more information on women's folklore or feminist readings of folklore, see *The Old Wives' Fairy Tale Book* edited by Angela Carter, or *From the Beast to the Blonde* by Marina Warner.

CONTEMPORARY TALES

As with earlier forms, modern folklore varies by region and by ethnic group; urban African Americans have their own cycles of urban tales, for example, and other "folk" groups have also created their own oral traditions. In *Wobblies, Pile Butts and Other Heroes,* Archie Green traces what he calls "laborlore," or the stories, songs, brags, jests, pranks, customs, beliefs, and rituals of men and women at work, and argues that "workers symbolically 'buy back' dignity or identity" with these forms (Green, *Wobblies* 22). College students are rich sources of urban folklore, and hippies of the 1960s gave us what Richard Dorson dubbed "druglore." Many of the stories Dorson's Berkeley students collected in the spring of 1968 were contemporary versions of classic trickster tales, with the druggie as the trickster and the police as the enemy to be fooled. Other druglore includes stories of "freakouts" and local legends, "latrinalia" (folk sayings and parodies of traditional proverbs scribbled on public bathroom walls), and drug-related jokes, riddles, and games (Dorson, *America in Legend* 253-300). We even have what is called "Xerox-lore," or typed and photocopied versions of urban legends; among these are flyers warning of LSD-saturated Mickey Mouse "lick and stick tattoos." Urban legends surrounding the computers that now permeate our lives have recently been circulating, demonstrating our new concerns about modern technology. Many of these deal with computer glitches or viruses that do everything from printing out goofy messages to paralyzing entire systems. Surely, a whole cycle of "Internet-lore" is already flourishing.

And so American oral traditions continue to grow and develop, reflecting our deepest concerns about modern life and helping us to regulate and moderate that which often seems unregulatable—just as stories and their tellers have always done.

LITERATURE CITED

Ames, Russell. "Protest and Irony in Negro Folksong." *Mother Wit from the Laughing Barrel: Readings in the Interpretation of Afro-American Folklore.* Edited by Alan Dundes. New Jersey: Prentice-Hall, 1973. 487-500.

Ancelet, Barry Jean. *Cajun and Creole Folktales: The French Oral Tradition of South Louisiana.* World Folktale Library. New York and London: Garland Publishing, 1994.

Barrick, Mac E., comp. and ed. *German-American Folklore.* The American Folklore Series. Little Rock, AK: August House, 1987.

Botkin, B.A. "American Folklore." *Funk & Wagnalls Standard Dictionary of Folklore, Mythology and Legend.* Edited by Maria Leach and Jerome Fried. 2 vols. New York: Funk & Wagnalls, 1949. 43-48.

Brunvand, Jan Harold. *The Choking Doberman and Other "New" Urban Legends.* New York and London: W. W. Norton, 1984.

———. *The Vanishing Hitchhiker: American Urban Legends and Their Meanings.* New York and London: W. W. Norton, 1981.

Carter, Angela, ed. *The Old Wives' Fairy Tale Book*. New York: Pantheon Books, 1990.

Dorson, Richard M. *America in Legend: Folklore from the Colonial Period to the Present*. New York: Random House, 1973.

————. *American Folklore and the Historian*. Chicago and London: University of Chicago Press, 1971.

————. *American Negro Folktales*. Greenwich, CT: Fawcett Publications, 1967.

Dundes, Alan, ed. *Mother Wit from the Laughing Barrel: Readings in the Interpretation of Afro-American Folklore*. New Jersey: Prentice-Hall, 1973.

Green, Archie. *Wobblies, Pile Butts and Other Heroes: Laborlore Explorations*. Publications of the American Folklore Society, New Series. Urbana and Chicago: University of Illinois Press, 1993.

Green, Rayna. Prologue: "'It's Okay Once You Get It Past the Teeth' and Other Feminist Paradigms for Folklore Studies." *Feminist Theory and the Study of Folklore*. Edited by Susan Tower Hollis, Linda Pershing, and M. Jane Young. Urbana and Chicago: University of Illinois Press, 1993. 1-8.

Huck, Charlotte S., Susan Hepler, and Janet Hickman. *Children's Literature in the Elementary School*. 5th ed. New York: Harcourt Brace Jovanovich, 1993.

Jordan, Rosan A., and Susan J. Kalčik, eds. *Women's Folklore, Women's Culture*. Publications of the American Folklore Society, New Series. 8. Philadelphia: University of Pennsylvania Press, 1985.

————. "The Vaginal Serpent and Other Themes from Mexican-American Women's Lore." *Women's Folklore, Women's Culture*. Edited by Rosan A. Jordan and Susan J. Kalčik. Publications of the American Folklore Society, New Series. 8. Philadelphia: University of Pennsylvania Press, 1985. 26-44.

Lester, Julius. *More Tales of Uncle Remus: Further Adventures of Brer Rabbit, His Friends, Enemies and Others*. New York: Dial, 1988.

————. *The Tales of Uncle Remus: The Adventures of Brer Rabbit*. New York: Dial, 1987.

Lindahl, Carl. Introduction. *Jack in Two Worlds: Contemporary North American Tales and Their Tellers*. Edited by William Bernard McCarthy. Publications of the American Folklore Society. New Series. Chapel Hill and London: University of North Carolina Press, 1994.

San Souci, Robert D. *Cut From the Same Cloth: American Women of Myth, Legend and Tall Tale*. New York: Philomel Books, 1993.

Tooze, Ruth. *Storytelling*. Englewood Cliffs, NJ: Prentice-Hall, 1959.

Vigil, Angel. *The Corn Woman: Stories and Legends of the Hispanic Southwest*. Translated by Jennifer Audrey Lowell and Juan Francisco Marin. Englewood, CO: Libraries Unlimited, 1994.

Voegelin, Erminie W. "North American Indian Folklore." *Funk & Wagnalls Standard Dictionary of Folklore, Mythology and Legend*. Edited by Maria Leach and Jerome Fried. 2 vols. New York: Funk & Wagnalls, 1949. 798-802.

Warner, Marina. *From the Beast to the Blonde: On Fairy Tales and Their Tellers*. New York: Farrar, Straus, Giroux, 1994.

Welsch, Roger. *Shingling the Fog and Other Plains Lies*. Chicago: The Swallow Press, 1972.

Yep, Laurence. *The Rainbow People*. New York: Harper & Row, 1989.

THE UTOPIAN TENDENCY OF STORYTELLING
Turning the World Upside Down

Jack Zipes

It would be misleading to argue that every story told is utopian, or to assert that there is an "essential" utopian nature to storytelling. There is, however, a utopian tendency of telling that helps explain why it is we feel so compelled to create and disseminate tales, and why we are enthralled by particular stories. The tales with this utopian tendency stem from a lack that we feel in our lives, a discernible discontentment, and a yearning for a better condition or world. Paradoxically the happiness of the listeners and readers of utopian tales depends on the unhappiness of the tellers. Without discontent there is no utopia. Without projections of utopia, our world would be a dismal place.

Tomes have been written about utopia, and this is most curious because utopia is allegedly nowhere, a place that has never been seen or experienced. At least this is what Sir Thomas More described in his famous treatise *Utopia,* written first in Latin in 1516 and translated into English in 1551. Utopia is an imaginary island with a perfect social and political system in which everyone is treated fairly. Yet, since this perfect state of government and existence is imaginary, *utopia* has also come to mean an impossible idealistic projection. In fact, More's notion of utopia fostered numerous speculative, philosophical, and political books from the sixteenth century to the present, and it also promoted all kinds of utopias as well as thousands of stories and novels labeled utopian. But utopia's vague and idealistic premises have led many critics to equate it with idealistic dreaming and unrealistic thinking. To be a utopian is frequently to be somebody out of touch with reality.

Nevertheless, there is a more positive way of looking at utopia that links the conception of utopias to reality and hope. In his monumental three-volume work, *The Principle of Hope,* the philosopher Ernst Bloch proposes that our real-life experiences are at the basis of our utopian longings and notions. In our daily lives, which are not exactly what we want them to be, we experience glimpses or glimmerings of another world that urges us on and stimulates our creative drives to reach a more ideal state of being. To be more precise, it is our realization of what is missing in our lives that impels us to create works of art that not only reveal insights into our struggles but also that shed light on alternatives and possibilities to restructure our mode of living and social relations. All art, according to Bloch, contains images of hope that illuminate ways to create a utopian society. Obviously, not every work that presumes to be art is artful. Nor do all art works necessarily contain a utopian tendency. But inspiring and illuminating images of hope can be detected in low and high art, in a Beethoven symphony or in a rock-and-roll song, in a grand Shakespeare production or a state fair. The utopian tendency of art is what propels us to reshape and reform our personal and social lives. In fact, Bloch points out that there are concrete utopias, short-lived experiments that have given real expression to new social and political relations. These concrete utopias set the building blocks for the future, for once hopes are tested and realized, we cannot betray them for long. We can never fully deny what has been concretized. Among his examples are such major events in the world as the American Revolution of 1776, the French Revolution of 1789, and the Russian Revolution of 1917, as well as the Fourier experiments in France and the Brook Farm "commune" in America, all of which have left traces of how we might shape the future. These revolutions and experiments—and there are many more that can be cited—did not entirely succeed because the proper socio-economic conditions to maintain them did not exist. Yet, the very fact that they came into being for a short time reveals a great deal about the validity of our utopian longings that we continue to concretize in different ways.

These longings are recorded in the spoken and written word. They are the source of ancient religions and rituals as well as new cults. The belief in a better and just world has always been with us, and this utopian belief assumes myriad forms. For instance, the belief in miracles and life after death articulated in religious legends and myths stems from utopian longings. Salvation is predicated on the notion of a just world in which the oppressed will be protected by a powerful divinity. Hundreds of thousands of tales in all religious traditions have been spread with hope that we shall be redeemed after this life. But the more interesting utopian tales, in my opinion, focus on the present world. The utopian tendency of sacred stories is clear from the beginning. What is not so evident is how our profane and secular stories have a utopian bent to them and are perhaps more appealing and significant because they restore miraculous power to human beings. In other words, they suggest that ordinary people can take power into their own hands and create better worlds for themselves, if they know how to use their gifts.

In his famous study, *The Morphology of the Folk Tale,* Vladimir Propp demonstrated that the structure of most wonder tales was based on 33 functions, and that if we know how these functions operate, we can grasp the fundamental aspects of any wonder tale and trace its connections to all kinds of variants. Propp maintained that the action of a wonder tale is predicated on the absentation of a member of a family from his home. This person can be a member of the older generation or some young person. Once the protagonist leaves the family there is an interdiction. For instance, in the Grimms's version of "Iron Hans" the boy is told not to touch the water of a pond. Of course, he does, and his hair turns to gold. Inevitably, in most wonder tales, the interdiction is violated, and the protagonist is confronted with a villain who will attempt to prevent the protagonist from compensating for the violation of the interdiction. From this point on, as Propp showed, the plot will depend on such other functions as the acquisition of gifts by the protagonist and the use of these gifts to overcome the villain, leading to an ascension of the throne and/or marriage at the end of the tale.

According to Propp, absentation generally assumes the form of a simple walk into the woods, going off on business, a voyage to visit friends and relatives, a hunting trip, a test between siblings, or a death in the family that causes the members to disperse. In many cases, this is true. Yet, Propp does not explore in depth the meaning of absentation, nor other causes that constitute the utopian tendency of wonder tales—and most wonder tales characteristically have happy endings representing a fulfillment of utopian longings or the anticipation of such fulfillment. That is, there is a sense that a new world opens up to the protagonist. In this respect, wonder tales are *tendentious:* they tend toward illuminating a path through darkness to a more enlightened world or life situation. For Propp, the plot always hinges on absentation and interdiction. Yet, how many wonder tales begin with the protagonist's *desire* to escape abuse, injustice, and horrible circumstances? How many tales relate how the protagonist purposely seeks new surroundings to become king or queen of his or her destiny? Young people in the tales are often beaten, abandoned, cheated, or tested. Leaving home is a significant step because it is an indication that the protagonists are uneasy at home, not at home with themselves, and seek to create a new home. Bloch maintains that home is a futuristic concept because we never have truly experienced home. We have never been in control of history or our own personal destinies. Therefore, we constantly pursue a genuine home that is commensurate with our deep utopian longings.

Stories help us. They help map out the terrain of utopia. They reiterate messages that we sometimes forget. In our most common stories, the utopian tendency is constituted by the actions of an ordinary, quite often naive character who manages to overcome obstacles or an adversary to achieve some kind of success. A good example is the cycle of Jack tales that has spread in the oral and written tradition in England, North America, and elsewhere. In his wonderful collection, *The Jack Tales,* Richard Chase remarks, "it is always through the 'little feller' *Jack* that we participate in the dreams, desires, ambitions, and experiences of a whole people. His fantastic adventures arise often enough among the commonplaces of existence, and he always returns to the everyday life of these farm people of whom he is one" (Chase xi-xii). The most famous of the Jack tales is, of course, "Jack and the Bean Tree," which depicts a resourceful Jack, who literally grows and grows up through his encounter with the giant and manages to gain a treasure in the course of action. There is another tale, "Hardy Hardhead," which is perhaps more interesting because it has many different variants in Europe and contains utopian implications. Here Jack asks his mother to take leave so that he can free a king's daughter who has been bewitched. If he is successful—and many men have died—he can marry the princess. When Jack enters the forest, he meets a "weezedly" old man, who gives him money and a ship that can sail on ground. On his way to meet the ship, he takes on board five men, Hardy Hardhead, Eatwell, Runwell, Harkwell, and Shootwell. These men have talents that will help Jack defeat the witch. He returns home and gives back the money to the old man. The narrator informs us that he does not know whether Jack married the girl, but at least she was no longer bewitched. As for the ship, the narrator confides in us that he knows for a fact that Jack kept it because he's been taken sailing on it several times.

This is a delightful tall tale with many utopian motifs such as the collective action of the six men whose talents are used to liberate an oppressed girl. In the

Grimms's version, "How Six Made their Way through the World," the hero is an ex-soldier, mistreated by a king. He and his five friends defeat the king's daughter in a race and make off with the king's treasures that they share together. In the Italian version, "A Boat for Land and Water," retold by Italo Calvino, the hero is a youngest son. Here, too, he is helped by an old man in the forest, and after the young man completes his task, thanks also to five gifted friends, he builds a palace that houses his father, brothers, and companions, not to mention his bride. The theme of all three tales is liberation through collective action. The implication is that miserable conditions can be changed and evil can be overcome. There is hope for the oppressed, and this hope is carried by ordinary people like Jack, the soldier, and the youngest son. Naturally, they have some extraordinary help, but isn't the miraculous in these tales symbolic of the powers that reside in us, hidden potential that we have not learned how to mine? The magic help from the outside is actually an energy or potential within us that we need to recognize in order to transform ourselves and to pull ourselves up by the bootstraps. The hero receives a call from the outside in the form of an announcement. This call is actually from the future and sends the ordinary protagonist on a mission that will change his life forever, turn his world upside down, and bring more justice to the world around him. The miraculous transformation is a fairy-tale motif that can be found in all types of stories from antiquity to the present and is pervasive in our mass-mediated commercials, where quick slick stories are told on TV and movie screens about beastly men turned into princes by the proper use of the right shampoo, or the scraggly woman who looks like a queen after she uses the right lotion. Drinks, running shoes, beverages, cars are all magic gifts that can change our lives. Here, of course, we see the perversion of the utopian quality of storytelling. Utopia cannot be attained simply on the basis of individual transformation and enrichment. What is needed, as Thomas More long ago pointed out, is social and political change, and there are unusual cycles of tales that address the conception of a paradise on earth such as Atlantis, the Golden Age, *Shangri-La*, and *Cuccagna* (also known in different languages as *Cokagne, Lubberland, Luilekkerland Cocagne*, and *Schlaraffenland*—all connoting the land of milk and honey).

Zedlers Grosses Universal-Lexikon, a German encyclopedia of 1742, defines Schlaraffenland as a utopia that means nowhere. It is not a real, but rather a fictional and moral land. It has been created out of all sorts of intentions. Some Schlaraffenland tales envision a perfect government that does not exist because of the corrupt nature of people in the world and also cannot exist. The storytellers' intention in portraying such a government is to show more clearly and more freely the incomplete nature and foibles of monarchies, aristocracies, and democracies. Others seek to represent the misery and struggles of human life. According to this encyclopedia, this is why storytellers and writers create such countries or islands on which one can have everything without work. For instance, there are images of seas full of wine, streams of beer, forests with fried chicken and fish hanging from the branches. One need only picture Pieter Breugel's famous painting of *The World Turned Upside Down* (1559), also known as *Netherlandish Proverbs*, to imagine what is meant by the Schlaraffenland or Cuccagna as the land of milk and honey. Indeed, Breugel was so intrigued by the stories of *Luilekkerland* that he also painted the *Land of Cockaigne* in 1567.

The excess behavior of the characters in the Cuccagna stories is somewhat disturbing. People eat, sleep, drink, carouse, exchange roles, and turn the world upside down. Chaos seems to be the ruling principle of Schlaraffenland. Yet, there are some historical factors that must be considered if we are to understand why the characters in these tales seem so voracious, boisterous, crude, and lustful. Most of the tales in the Cuccagna, Cocaigne, and Schlaraffenland cycles arose during the sixteenth, seventeenth, and eighteenth centuries, and they are connected to the Carnival, Mardi Gras, and folk traditions when the people were permitted on the day before lent to become "kings for a day." That is, people were allowed to let their hair down and assume the roles of their rulers and oppressors, to dress up and do as they pleased without fear of being punished. In addition, given the great famines during this period, feasting became a major part of the celebration, and to eat to one's content became part of the celebrations. To break all the rules of decorum and to live for pleasure was also a political act, for it was during this time that the daily life and work were becoming more regulated and rationalized. Leisure time was becoming more and more a luxury, and peasants were compelled to treat time more like money. With the rise of the middle classes and mercantilism, the socio-economic system demanded more work and accountability and less time for pleasure.

Perhaps one of the more interesting documents about the "milk and honey" tales is actually a sixteenth-century Italian folk song entitled "A Chapter That Tells about the Existence of a New World found in the Sea Oceano," which was based on different folktales. Probably sung and told by sailors, the narrator begins by reciting how seafarers found a beautiful land in the sea Oceano where nobody ever dies. There is one mountain made out of cheese, and on the top is a kettle a mile wide. In this kettle macaroni is cooked. When the macaroni is ready, it spurts out of the kettle and rolls down the cheese mountain to a house with forks where people can eat as much as they like and drink wine out of the springs. All the trees are filled with cake and cookies, and a river of milk flows through the land. Everything grows there without difficulty: grapes and figs, melons and other fruit. The woods are filled with fried chicken and other game. The weather is so wonderful that clothes are not needed, and all the boys and girls run around naked. For them our decorum is foolish and crazy. Everyone is young and lives for a thousand years. Then they die in their sleep. There are no sicknesses, pain, and suffering. Each person lives cheerfully and enjoys each second of the day. Everyone has what he or she wants, and if some one were to think about working, the others would hang the person and heaven would not save him or her. Everything grows by itself, and the donkeys are tied with sausages. Nobody has anything on his or her mind other than dancing, singing, and making music. The king's name is Bugalosso because he is the fattest lazy person there. In fact, he is so fat that he never moves and never wants to exert himself. Money streams from his rear, and when he spits, he spits out marzipan, and instead of lice, he has fish in his hair. There are no peasants there because everyone is rich. When one wants to sleep, one only has to find a bush equipped with sheets and pillows made out of down. It is not necessary to worry about having too many children to feed, because when it rains, it rains ravioli. The houses are made out of the finest gold, and all the fields are shared and free. What a wonderful land, sings the teller. The sun and moon never set. The people never quarrel or fight. The song ends with the singer commenting something like: "Oh what a beautiful place, Oh what a glorious land! How stupid it is to stay here any longer. I would like to head for this island and live near the beautiful mountain. Whoever wants to go there, I'll tell them the way. He only has to take a ship in Mameluke Harbor and then sail over the sea of lies. And whoever arrives there will be king of those fools."

Despite the wonderful irony of the song, it has a powerful appeal because it articulates the real needs of the common people and illustrates their wishes and desires. Typically, the contours of this utopia are depicted in the extreme so that there is a burlesque and grotesque quality to the narrative. This radical manner of introducing the motif of utopia, also to be found in tall tales and trickster tales, is intended to burst the seams of the status quo and provoke listeners to move ahead in their lives with laughter and optimism. The utopian tendency in storytelling does not accept things as they are and seeks to expose human foibles, hypocrisy, and injustices.

There are many types of utopian tales, and the utopian tendency of ancient tales about paradise has led to the science fiction tales of the present. But the tendency, as the tales reveal, is not simply in the narratives themselves. The tales are articulations of the utopian tendencies within us that we cultivate from childhood to death in our endeavor to seek immortality. One need only watch children at a playground to see how early the utopian tendency in storytelling develops. Left alone to play, children will begin talking to themselves and will invent a magic kingdom and narrative to express their wishes and desires. Or, they will join with other children to act out a story or play a game that has a story line to it. A playground filled with laughing and somewhat "wild" children is not unlike Bruegel's *The World Turned Upside Down* or a land of milk and honey. As they talk and run about, the children seek to grab hold of their lives and map out their destinies, not knowing where they are going, but knowing that there is a land or home out there that will suit them. As Oscar Wilde once said, "A map of the world that does not include Utopia is not worth even looking at, for it leaves out the one country at which Humanity is always landing. And when humanity lands there, it looks out, and seeing a better country, sets sail. Progress is the realisation of Utopia" (Wilde 45). And one might add, the tendency toward utopia is kept alive through storytelling.

LITERATURE CITED

Calvino, Italo. *Italian Folktales.* Translated by George Martin. New York: Harcourt Brace Jovanovich, 1980.

Camporesi, Pietro. "Capitolo qual narra l'essere di un mondo novo trovato nel Mar Oceano," *La maschera di Bertoldo: G.C. Croce e la letteratura carnevalesca.* Turin: Einaudi, 1976. 309-11.

Chase, Richard, ed. *The Jack Tales: Folk Tales from the Southern Appalachians.* New York: Houghton Mifflin, 1943.

Grimm, Jacob, and Wilhelm Grimm. *The Complete Fairy Tales of the Brothers Grimm.* Translated with an introduction by Jack Zipes. New York: Bantam, 1989.

Propp, Vladimir. *The Morphology of the Folktale.* Edited by Louis Wagner and Alan Dundes. Translated by Laurence Scott. 2nd rev. ed. Austin, TX: University of Texas Press, 1968.

Richter, Dieter. *Schlaraffenland: Geschichte einer populären Phantasie.* Cologne: Diederichs, 1984.

Wilde, Oscar. *The Soul of Man under Socialism.* Edited by Robert Ross. London: Humphreys, 1912.

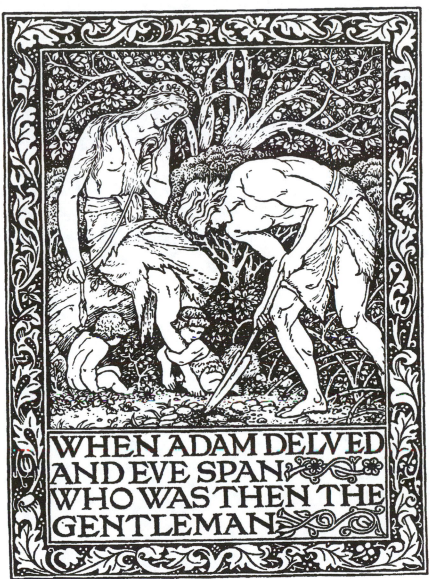

WHEN ADAM DELVED
AND EVE SPAN
WHO WAS THEN THE
GENTLEMAN

PART
TWO

AARDEMA, VERNA (1911–)

Compiler and writer of African American and African FOLKTALES. Born Verna Norberg in New Era, Michigan, in 1911, she received a B.A. from Michigan State University in 1934 and married Albert Aardema in 1936.

Aardema's involvement in folktales began when she had submitted chapter one of a novel to a publisher, but had no idea of what to write for chapter two. In lieu of chapter two, she proposed a collection of African folktales, and thus began a distinguished career of compiling and narrating such stories. Titles include *Tales from the Story Hat, The Sky God Stories, Behind the Back of the Mountain, Why Mosquitoes Buzz in People's Ears* (which received the Caldecott Award), *Ji Nongo Nongo Means Riddles,* and *Bimwili and the Zimwi.* In *Princess Gorilla and a New Kind of Water* (1988), Aardema retells a Mponqwe folktale. *The Lonely Lioness and the Ostrich Chicks* is a 1996 adaptation of a Masai tale.

AARNE, ANTTI (1867–1925)

Finnish folklorist who created the first classification system of international FOLKTALES. Aarne's index of folktale types, *Verzeichnis der Marchentypen* (*The Types of Folktale*), was published in 1910. This index categorized distinguishable tale types to provide a system with which folklorists could locate, identify, and classify various versions of folktales.

Aarne created his index in response to his teacher Kaarle Krohn's suggestion that folktale motifs appeared in related forms in different dialects and languages, in different times and different places (*see* KROHN, KAARLE). After Aarne's death, Krohn asked an American scholar, Stith Thompson, to expand the index and translate it into English (*see* THOMPSON, STITH). The resulting index is often referred to as the *Aarne-Thompson Index.*

The *Aarne-Thompson Index* does not provide a comprehensive analysis of tale origins, but organizes already collected materials into an outlined system. Entries consist of assigned numbers and letters, titles, condensed descriptions of tale types, summaries of the tales, MOTIF numbers, bibliographic references, total number of variants found in national archives, and the countries in which the tales are found. Aarne located as many Northern European folktales as he could and divided them into three categories: ANIMAL tales, ordinary folktales, and humorous tales. Within these categories are further subdivisions based on identities of principal characters, the nature of the tale's content, or selected aspects of the tale's content. For example, animal tales (numbers 1-299) are organized by different kinds of animals in the stories; tale type number 175 is entitled "The TARBABY and the Rabbit." Ordinary folktales, including *marchen*, (numbers 300-1199) are subdivided into magical, romantic, or religious tales. Humorous tales (numbers 1200-1999) are subdivided by the kinds of characters in the stories—for example, numbskulls, married couples, parsons, or liars—and include TALL TALES.

Aarne created 1,940 available spaces for tale entries, but had collected and numbered only 540 by the time of his death. Thompson's completed and expanded index exceeded Aarne's expectations by over 1,000 additional tales, and Thompson expanded the geographical coverage to include all of Europe and Western Asia.

The *Aarne-Thompson Index* is a key resource for collecting, archiving, or doing comparative analysis of Indo-European folktales and their global variants. Folklorists and scholars find this index indispensable for identifying and annotating collected texts and locating parallels already identified in narrative FOLKLORE.

ABANDONED CHILDREN

Children, in stories from many cultures, who have been left to survive on their own. Abandoned children often fare well in FOLKLORE, and are sometimes helped by supernatural beings or raised by ANIMALS.

Typically, children are abandoned because of poverty, illegitimacy, incestuous or super-natural parentage, jealousy, or fear of a prophecy. Some—such as Moses—are abandoned for their own protection (*see* EXODUS). The children usually return later, sometimes for revenge, sometimes with forgiveness and riches.

A familiar example of the abandoned children MOTIF is the story of "Hansel and Gretel," a tale that appears in the GRIMM BROTHERS's collections. At the insistence of their stepmother, but over the objections of their FATHER, Hansel and Gretel are left alone in a forest (*see* STEPMOTHER–WICKED). They find their way to a house made of gingerbread, only to be captured by a WITCH who lives there. The witch forces Gretel to do household chores, while Hansel is fattened to be eaten. Gretel, however, tricks the witch, and traps and roasts her in her own oven. When the children return home, they find that their stepmother has died, but that their father is overjoyed to see them. The children have brought along the witch's jewels, so the family's financial problems are over.

Tales of abandoned children appear in NATIVE NORTH AMERICAN STORYTELLING, the BIBLE, tales in the THOUSAND AND ONE NIGHTS, and in oral storytelling traditions around the world. Feral children— abandoned children raised by animals—include Romulus and Remus, the legendary founders of Rome; Mowgli in Kipling's *Jungle Book* (*see* KIPLING, RUDYARD); and Tarzan in the series of novels by Edgar Rice Burroughs. *See also* CANNIBALISM, CYBELE, HIDING THE CHILD, LOST CHILD, MAUI.

For Further Reading

Manheim, Ralph, trans. *Grimms Tales for Young and Old*. New York: Doubleday, 1977.

ABANDONMENT

Theme occurring in MYTHS and FAIRY TALES concerning the abandonment of a HERO or HEROINE or a lesser character. In *Dictionary of Symbols,* J.E. Cirlot draws a parallel between the symbolism of abandonment and that of DEATH and RESURRECTION. Furthermore, he suggests that, as in the case of THESEUS in the LABYRINTH or the many stories of children lost in the woods, abandonment "imparts to the individual's existence a sense of estrangement." He points out that to feel abandoned is "to lose sight of the eternal light in the human spirit." In the book of Job in the Hebrew BIBLE, for instance, Job feels abandoned by GOD in the face of the injustice of his suffering.

In a story, a character may be abandoned because of age, illness, a physical handicap, or some other form of helplessness. There are factual reasons for such stories. In various cultures, such as certain Native American tribes and nomadic Arabs, the aged were often abandoned as burdensome or economically cumbersome. If food were scarce, the oldest people were the ones whose needs were sacrificed for the health of the rest of the tribe. Infants and children were often abandoned for economic reasons or for reasons of gender. In cultures where girls were considered a liability, as in China, female infants were often left in the wilderness to perish. Twins and triplets, considered unlucky in certain cultures, might also be exposed. Finally, a child might be abandoned because he was somehow dangerous.

In Greek mythology, the new-born Oedipus is supposed to be abandoned in the mountains outside the city of THEBES; his parents, Laius and Jocasta, want him to die because it is prophesied that he will kill his father and marry his mother. In the fairy tale "Hansel and Gretel," the two children are abandoned in the forest when there is not enough food to feed the whole family. When they find their way back home the first time, through Hansel's cleverness, they are abandoned a second time, again with their deaths being the goal of their stepmother (see STEP-MOTHER—WICKED).

While abandonment is often a form of taking a life, it can also be a form of saving life. The biblical story of the birth of Moses, who is born in secret and then hidden, involves his abandonment in a basket in the reeds of the Nile, and here abandonment is a means of saving his life (see CHILD IN THE REEDS, EXODUS).

The abandoned wife is another MOTIF central to the theme of many stories and fairy tales, where the heroine is abandoned by her family and then found by a KING who sees her beauty and worth and marries her. When she has a child, however, she is often abandoned by her husband through pressure from his sister or sister-in-law or another family member, sometimes because she has supposedly borne a monster or murdered her child. In some variants, the abandoned wife then wanders off, finds the WATER OF LIFE, and is restored, as in "The Maiden Without Hands" or "The Handless Maiden." This theme appears all over Europe, in India and Asia, in South America and among Native North Americans, in Chaucer's "The Man of Lawes Tale," in the THOUSAND AND ONE NIGHTS, and in "The Seven Swans." See also ABANDONED CHILDREN.

ABDUCTION

Motif in MYTH and FAIRY TALE connected with rape and MARRIAGE. Abduction in myth and fairy tale often involves a girl or woman who is abducted by a man for the purposes of rape and/or marriage. Resolution of this abduction comes either through freeing oneself, being freed by a savior, or marrying the abductor.

One of the most well-known abduction stories tells how HADES, god of the underworld, seizes the maiden Persephone and carries her to the underworld while her mother, Demeter, searches for her (see PERSEPHONE MYTH). Persephone's abduction can be seen as an explanation of the seasons or as a symbol for every daughter who must leave her mother in order to become a mother herself, and it can be said that on one level, every marriage is a form of abduction from the mother-daughter dyad. In *The Great Mother*, Erich Neumann notes that "Abduction, rape, marriage, death, and separation are the great motifs underlying the Eleusinian mysteries," which were ancient rites in the Greek city of Eleusis that celebrated the reunion of Demeter and Persephone. Another well-known case of abduction is the kidnapping of HELEN OF TROY by the Trojan prince, Paris, which was the cause of the Trojan War and the subject of HOMER'S ILIAD. In marriage celebrations all over the world, mock abductions of the bride are commonplace.

In many myths and FOLKTALES, beautiful women are abducted by ogres, demons, gods, animals, giants, and dwarfs. When the Greek god ZEUS wants the mortal woman Europa, he transforms himself into a bull so that she climbs on his back; he then abducts her by swimming off with her to the cave where he was secretly raised. In Rudyard Kipling's *Jungle Book* (*see* KIPLING, RUDYARD), Mowgli is abducted by the Bander-log. *See also* CRONE, MAIDEN, MOTHER, MOTIF.

For Further Reading

D'Aulaire, Ingri, and Edgar Parin D'Aulaire. *Ingri and Edgar Parin D'Aulaire's Book of Greek Myths.* New York: Dell, 1992.

Neumann, Erich. *The Great Mother.* Translated by Ralph Manheim. Princeton, NJ: Princeton University Press, 1955.

Richardson, I.M. *Demeter & Persephone: The Seasons of Time.* Illustrated. Mahwah, NJ: Troll Associations, 1983.

ACHEBE, CHINUA (1930–)

Nigerian writer of novels, short stories, essays, and poetry. Born in the village of Ogidi in Eastern Nigeria, Achebe studied medicine and literature at the University of Ibadan then worked for a broadcasting company in Lagos. His first novel, *Things Fall Apart*, was published in 1958 and has since been translated into over 50 languages. The novel tells the story of Okonkwo, an important tribesman who must cope with the arrival of British missionaries to his Igbo village in the 1890s. Achebe uses storytelling techniques such as FOLKTALES, PROVERBS, and ANECDOTES that are native to the agrarian, non-literary people he describes, in order to depict the Igbo as a culture rooted firmly in oral traditions. For example, Achebe incorporates the story of the TORTOISE (a TRICKSTER figure in the Igbo oral tradition) into *Things Fall Apart*. Achebe deals with similar themes of colonization, cultural change, and native Nigerian storytelling traditions in *Arrow of God* (1964, revised 1974), the sequel to *Things Fall Apart*. Other works in which Achebe examines the problems and challenges of modern Nigeria include *No Longer At Ease* (1960) and *Anthills of the Savannah* (1987). Achebe's worldwide influence as a writer and storyteller stems from his endeavor to share with the world the stories of native Nigerians and their experiences from the perspective of an insider.

For Further Reading

Achebe, Chinua. *The African Trilogy*. London: Picador, 1988.

Rutherford, Anna, and Kirsten Holst Petersen. *Chinua Achebe: A Celebration*. Oxford: Heineman, 1991.

ACHILLES

Character in classical mythology, often referred to in HOMER'S ILIAD as the greatest and bravest of all Greek HEROES.

Achilles' father is the mortal Peleus, and his mother is the NYMPH Thetis. Thetis dips the infant Achilles in the river Styx in hopes of making him invulnerable, but she holds him by the heel, which remains untouched by the water— thus the origin of the phrase "Achilles' heel," denoting a weak point in a seemingly invulnerable person.

At the beginning of the Trojan War, Achilles is KING of the Myrmidons and the most respected warrior in Greece. Thetis, knowing from a prophecy that her son will die in TROY if he fights there, persuades him to dress in women's clothes and hide in order to avoid joining the Greek army. But Achilles is found out by Odysseus, and he then fights loyally for Greece for the first nine years of the war. After this, Achilles quarrels with AGAMEMNON, king of MYCENAE, over a slave girl. Because of the argument, Achilles refuses to fight any more and the Greeks are nearly defeated. But Achilles returns to the battle once more to avenge the death of his dearest friend, Patroclos.

Achilles slays Patroclos' killer—Hector, the greatest hero of the Trojans—and has Hector's body dragged by a chariot. Achilles is later killed by Paris, Hector's brother, whose arrow is guided by the god APOLLO to Achilles' heel.

Some legends hold that Achilles' ghost now lives in a paradise known as Leuce, where he is happily married to HELEN OF TROY. There he frequently recites passages from Homer for the entertainment of his fellow heroes. Other legends say that Achilles resides in the blessed realm of the Elysian Fields, where he is married to the immortal sorceress Medea.

Achilles is traditionally considered the prototype of the superhuman hero who prefers glory to long life. In view of his cross-dressing to avoid battle, sulking in his tent over a quarrel, and crude treatment of Hector's body, he must also be seen as a hero with human failings.

Stories about Achilles feature several themes popular in FOLKLORE—the hero disguised in woman's clothes (*see* ODYSSEY), heroes with one vulnerability, and magic weapons and/or animals. Heroes with one vulnerability include the Greek warrior Ajax, SIEGFRIED, BALDR, and KRISNA, as well as others in Native American, South African, and European oral traditions. Achilles also has a magic weapon—a spear that can heal wounds it has made—and a talking horse. The horse, Xanthos, reveals that Achilles will be killed by a god and is struck dumb for his prophecy. *See also* ANCIENT GREEK STORYTELLING.

For Further Reading

Graves, Robert. *The Greek Myths.* 2 vols. New York: Penguin Books, 1957.

Hamilton, Edith. *Mythology: Timeless Tales of Gods and Heroes.* New York: Mentor, 1969.

Homer. *The Iliad.* Translated by Robert Fitzgerald. New York: Doubleday, 1974.

ADAM AND EVE

First human beings according to the Hebrew CREATION story in the Book of Genesis (*see* GENESIS, BOOK OF). Created in the image of GOD to replenish and subdue the earth, Adam and Eve inhabit the paradisical Garden of Eden until they are banished because of their disobedience. Having been forbidden by God to eat fruit from the Tree of the Knowledge of Good and Evil, Eve yields to a serpent's persuasions that she try the fruit and convinces Adam to do the same. Attempts to hide from God fail; He banishes them from PARADISE, sentencing them and their descendants to lives of hard work, pain, and DEATH.

The story of Adam and Eve has had a profound effect on the relationships between men and women in Judeo-Christian cultures, most of whom are familiar with some version (often oral), of the story even if they have never read the Old Testament translations. Chapter 2 of Genesis specifies that God created Eve from the rib of Adam to be a "helpmeet" to her husband. This biblical version of the creation of man and woman is the most well-known one, although Chapter 1 contradicts this, stating that the couple were created together. Nonetheless, Eve's subordinate position to her husband and her disobedience have been frequently cited throughout Judeo-Christian history as "evidence" of women's weakness, wickedness, and inferiority. A comparable tale from Greek mythology is that of PANDORA, in which a woman, Pandora, looses all the ills into the world.

The most famous literary adaptation of the myth of Adam and Eve is John Milton's *Paradise Lost,* which perpetuates the hierarchical relationship from God, to the angels, to man, and to woman.

AENEID

Epic poem by the Roman poet Virgil (70 B.C.–19 B.C.) chronicling the HERO Aeneas's departure from TROY and his QUEST to establish a new Troy, Rome. Legends focusing on the journey of Aeneas, son of the Trojan prince Anchises and the Greek goddess APHRODITE, were part of Roman oral tradition. The emperor of Rome commissioned Virgil to create an EPIC poem drawn from these LEGENDS, which Virgil wrote in twelve books c. 29–19 B.C. Clearly influenced by Homer's ILIAD and ODYSSEY, Virgil created an epic with many of the elements of the universal hero ARCHETYPE, especially the three basic rites of passage, which, according to Joseph Campbell in *The Hero with a Thousand Faces,* are "separation—initiation—return."

In the first book of the *Aeneid,* Troy is aflame after being defeated by the Greeks. Aeneas, his family, and his men flee, but Aeneas' wife, Creusa, is killed. Creusa's shade directs Aeneas to journey west to what will eventually become Rome. After their ship wrecks off the coast of North Africa, Aeneas and his companions take temporary refuge with Queen Dido, founder of Carthage.

In the second book, Aeneas recounts to Dido the saga of Troy's downfall, his escape, and the death of his wife. The third book continues Aeneas' account of his adventures as he traveled from Troy to Sicily, his father's death in Sicily, and how he came to Carthage. The fourth book tells of the love between Dido and Aeneas, Aeneas' decision to leave Carthage to pursue his goal, and the suicide by sword of the hurt and angry Dido. In the fifth book, Aeneas and his group return to Sicily, where they honor Aeneas' father, Anchises, by holding funeral games. In the following book, Aeneas, like Odysseus and other heroes, undergoes an initiation in the form of a DESCENT INTO THE UNDERWORLD to visit his father. Also typical of the archetypal hero on his QUEST, who is often guided by a mysterious wise figure, Aeneas is guided by the Sibyl of Cumae, the wise oracle who prophesies from her cave near the entrance to the underworld. After a dangerous journey to the underworld, Aeneas speaks with his father who foretells the eventual power Rome will yield and directs his son in the underlying principles of Roman rule and authority. By Book VII, Aeneas has returned to his journey and arrives at the Italian kingdom of Latinus. Latinus offers his daughter Lavinia as a wife for Aeneas, but Lavinia's mother and Turnus, Lavinia's betrothed, are clearly against the marriage. Turnus, the leader of the Rutuli tribe, decides to make war on Aeneas and his party. Books VIII-XII relate the details of the war between Turnus and Aeneas, and Turnus is finally killed by Aeneas in the final book. Aeneas and Lavinia marry and become the founders of Lavinium. According to Roman mythology, Aeneas's son Ascanius, who escaped with his father from Troy in the *Aeneid*, builds the capital of Lavinium, Alba Longa, around 1152 B.C., after the death of Aeneas. The Roman historian Livy, however, claims that Ascanius was the son of Aeneas and Lavinia. Because of its proximity to Rome, Alba Longa is seen as its precursor, and Julius Caesar was believed to be a descendent of Ascanius.

Virgil looks back to the great oral epics of Greece, the *Iliad* and the *Odyssey*. The first half of his epic, in which Aeneas escapes Troy and searches for the New Troy (Rome), owes much to the adventures of Odysseus. The second half of the epic, in which Aeneas fights his enemies in Italy takes much of its spirit from the *Iliad*, also an epic of war. By following Homer, Virgil continued the traditions of the oral epic, now in written, or literary form. His work, in turn, would influence the epic poets of the Christian middle ages and Renaissance and beyond—poets such as the Italian Dante, who, as the "hero" of his own epic, the *Divine Comedy,* is guided on his journey to the underworld by the now almost sacred figure of Virgil.

For Further Reading

Virgil. *The Aeneid of Virgil*. Translated by Rolfe Humphries. New York: Scribners, 1951.

AESOP

The former slave who popularized the FABLE as a teaching story. Like HOMER, Aesop is a legendary figure who may or may not have actually existed. The story of Aesop's life, itself a fable with many variations, is recounted in some manuscripts of the fables.

Aesop is said to have been a Phrygian slave who lived in the sixth century B.C. He is usually described as dwarfish, dark-skinned, hunchbacked, and ugly. Born dumb, he was given the gift of speech and storytelling skill by the GODDESS Isis in return for a kindness he did for a priestess (*see* ISIS AND OSIRIS). However, Aesop's superior wit did not endear him to those around him. He was traded to a slave dealer, who sold him to a philosopher, Xanthus, who eventually granted him freedom.

Aesop gained fame as a wise man and generally avoided trouble by giving his advice in the form of stories, allowing his listeners to draw their own conclusions. He traveled widely, but when no crowd of admirers greeted him at DELPHI, he insulted the citizens with a tirade against them. In retribution, the Delphians hid a golden bowl from the temple in Aesop's belongings, then accused him of theft. He was tried, found guilty of sacrilege, and hurled over a cliff to his death. As he died, Aesop cursed the Delphians with a prophetic fable. They were later afflicted with famine and pestilence.

Aesop's story and physical description were often revised over the centuries. According to Jayne Elizabeth Lewis in *The English Fable: Aesop and Literary Culture, 1651-1740,* his image was transformed in the seventeenth and eighteenth centuries to become more European, "because he needs to serve the interests of a politically dominant group with access to the classical canon, so . . . [he] has to be well-proportioned and above all Caucasian."

Some of the fables—more properly called *Aesopic* rather than *Aesop's*—were either told long before Aesop's time or were added later. Some stories are as old as the seventh century B.C.

Aesop's collection of fables was passed through the oral tradition long before it was recorded. The original prose versions were eventually turned into verse, translated, enlarged, and adapted to various cultures that became captivated by them. A collection of 200 Aesopic fables was recorded in the fourth century B.C. by the scholar Demetrius of Phalerum in his *Assemblies of Aesopic Tales.*

The earliest surviving collection of Aesop's stories is a Latin version compiled by Phaedrus in the first century A.D. About A.D. 400, 42 of the fables were turned into Latin verse—a prose version of which was later compiled by a Roman, Romulus. These supplied the foundations of versions that were extremely popular throughout the Middle Ages.

With the invention of the printing press, illustrated collections of Aesop's *Fables* became the rage in Europe and England. Over twenty different editions were published in the fifteenth century. The first printed edition in English was by William Caxton in 1484. Retold with innovations by the French author, Jean de la Fontaine, in the seventeenth century, they became a literary standard in France (*see* LA FONTAINE, JEAN DE).

The fables are stories in which ANIMALS speak and behave like humans, serving as examples for humans to consider. However, the meaning of a fable is often ambiguous, and the morals that usually appear at the end of each story vary with cultural perspectives.

For example, the often-used term "sour grapes" is from Aesop's story of "The Fox and the Grapes"—a fox wants to eat some grapes he sees on a vine, but he can not reach them; finally he gives up, deciding that the grapes are sour. In *Aesop Without Morals,* Lloyd W. Daly translates the moral from the Greek as: "Some who can't do what they want because of their own ability blame it on circumstances." According to John J. McKendry in *Aesop: Five Centuries of Illustrated Fables,* Caxton's moral was: "He is wise which faineth not to desire the thing which he may not have."

Nevertheless, we often recognize familiar human behavior in a fable's theme. Daly comments that, "We have only to recall *fishing in muddy waters, out of the frying pan into the fire, the goose that laid the golden eggs, the dog in the manger, the boy who cried wolf, the ant and the grasshopper, the hare and the tortoise,* and *the wolf in sheep's clothing* to realize the proverbial and paradigmatic function the stories serve with us."

Aesop's fable, "The Wolf in Sheep's Clothing," is apparently referred to in the sermon on the mount of Jesus: "Beware of false prophets, which come to you in sheep's clothing, but inwardly they are ravening wolves."

Aesop shares wisdom, physical ugliness, and an unjust execution with the Greek sage Socrates. Teachers of stories can be found in the JATAKA TALES, the MAHABHRATA, the PANCHATANTRA, the Talmud, and the BIBLE. Animal characters are used to illuminate human behavior in stories from many cultures, including COYOTE and the other TRICKSTERS around the world—REYNARD the Fox for example. In his 1986 *Aesop's Forest,* Robert Coover presents a darker view of both the animals and the storyteller. *See also* PARABLES OF JESUS.

For Further Reading

Coover, Robert. *Aesop's Forest.* Santa Barbara: Capra Press, 1986.

Daly, Lloyd W. *Aesop Without Morals: The Famous Fables, and a Life of Aesop.* New York: Thomas Yoseloff, 1961.

Lewis, Jayne Elizabeth. *The English Fable: Aesop and Literary Culture, 1651–1740.* Cambridge: Cambridge University Press, 1996.

Lord, John Vernon, and James Mitchie. *Aesop's Fables.* London: Jonathan Cape, 1989.

McKendry, John J. *Aesop: Five Centuries of Illustrated Fables.* Washington, DC: The Metropolitan Museum of Art, 1964.

AFANAS'EV, ALEKSANDR (1826–1871)

Russian folklorist. Alexander Nikolayevich Afanas'ev was a major collector of Russian FAIRY TALES and FOLKLORE. His many works, published from 1866 on, were among the first to introduce Russian folktales to world literature. His *Russian Fairy Tales*, first translated into English and published in 1945, is still the major source of these tales. Afanas'ev collected variants of the tales, and different stories concerning the Russian WITCH, BABA YAGA, appear in his collection, along with the Russian version of "Cinderella," "Vasilisa the Beautiful."

For Further Reading

Afanas'ev, Aleksandr. *Russian Fairy Tales.* New York: Pantheon, 1945.

———. *Russian Folk Tales.* Translated by Robert Chandler. Illustrated by Ivan Bilibin. Boston: Shambhala, 1980.

AFRICAN AMERICAN STORYTELLING

Oral traditions that can be traced to the beginnings of American slavery, first introduced to this continent by black Africans captured and sold by slave traders. Many of the themes and characters of African American storytelling can be traced back to the African homeland, including GHOSTS, ANIMALS, and the TRICKSTER (*see* AFRICAN STORYTELLING). The African American trickster, Brer Rabbit, for example, is derived from African stories of HARE and other animal tricksters.

Joel Chandler Harris (*see* HARRIS, JOEL CHANDLER) was one of the first writers to attempt to compile stories from the African American oral tradition. His UNCLE REMUS: *His Songs and His Sayings* (1881) is devoted to animal stories, including those of Brer Rabbit. Perhaps the best known of these is the story of the TAR BABY, in which Brer Rabbit attacks a tar doll until he gets hopelessly stuck to it. *Uncle Remus* was followed by other collections that Chandler compiled throughout his life.

Chandler's collections have often been criticized for presenting a simplistic and even sentimental view of the American slave as a mindlessly faithful and cheerful character, particularly as adapted in the 1946 Walt Disney film, *The Song of the South.* Less controversial is THE BOOK OF NEGRO FOLKLORE, edited and compiled by Langston Hughes and Arna Bontemps (*see* HUGHES, LANGSTON; BONTEMPS, ARNA), which also includes stories of Brer Rabbit and other characters.

The above-mentioned works made every effort to capture the rich expressiveness of African American speech. However, as is the case with all oral traditions, no written renditions of these stories can fully convey their spontaneity and immediacy. Improvisation is no small part of the essence of African American storytelling, a component crucial to this tradition that can be traced back to Africa and also to the sermons of African American preachers during the period of slavery. Forbidden to learn to read, enslaved preachers were forced to memorize large portions of the Bible, which they recited to their congregations. Biblical stories were thus retold in the African American vernacular.

The improvisational element has long been present in other African American oral forms as well. These include elaborate games of wit and mental skill such as "Playing the Dozens," in which two people engage in a verbal duel of escalating insults. To the ears of mainstream culture, these oral antics often sound dangerously aggressive and even obscene, particularly now that they have found their way into the mass culture. Such is the case with rap music, which has roots in African American oral storytelling and verbal improvisation. Americans who are frightened by rap's incendiary nature (sometimes real, sometimes illusory) are generally unaware that nothing is new about this genre except its sudden explosion upon the popular scene (*see* RAP SONG).

Indeed, African American storytelling is becoming increasingly prominent in our mass culture. Alex Haley's *Roots* (1976), in which the author traced his ancestry back to Africa, helped pave the way for this upsurge, especially when it broke ratings records as a television miniseries during the 1970s. Since then, many African American film makers have risen to prominence, including John Singleton, Mario van Peebles, and Spike Lee. Film has turned out to be a superb medium for capturing the spontaneous essence of African American storytelling. Lee has been especially innovative in finding a visual equivalent of African American speech rhythms. His groundbreaking film *Do the Right Thing* (1989) is even photographed and edited to reflect the rhythms of such vernacular narrative forms as rap.

In *From Trickster to Badman: The Black Folk Hero in Slavery and Freedom,* John W. Roberts comments, "the path which leads to understanding of the personal attributes and actions of black folk heroes has been one along which survival has been precarious, both individual and collective well-being always in jeopardy, and conflict continuous. Along this path, black folk heroes have traveled as champions of African Americans who have been forced to negotiate the American landscape by being quick of wit and adept at detecting sleight of hand."

For Further Reading

Goss, Linda, and Marian E. Barnes. *Talk That Talk, An Anthology of African American Storytelling.* New York: Simon and Schuster, 1989.

Roberts, John W. *From Trickster to Badman: The Black Folk Hero in Slavery and Freedom.* Philadelphia: University of Pennsylvania Press, 1989.

AFRICAN STORYTELLING

Oral storytelling tradition in Africa. The areas of West, South, East, and Central Africa have a rich oral tradition that has been widely distributed in North America, the West Indies, and South America. Dialects vary from tribe to tribe, depending on the region. There are more than 250,000 African MYTHS, LEGENDS, and FOLKTALES and thousands of proverbs, with the Ashanti tribe alone having at least 36,000. RIDDLES, too, are very popular throughout these regions.

It is difficult to get a true feeling of African FOLKLORE from published collections because language and transmission are so much a part of the oral tradition. As Richard A. Waterman and William R. Bascom observe in *Funk and Wagnall's Standard Dictionary of Folklore, Mythology, and Legend*: "Since the [texts] are verbal rather than written, all forms of folklore, except some of the secret spells used in black magic, involve both the reactions of the audience and the mode of expression of the speaker." (*see* BASCOM, WILLIAM) Each tribe has its storyteller, and storytelling performances regularly involve audience participation. First the storyteller begins with an opening formula, which involves announcing the name of the tale, to which the audience then responds. There is a formal ending to the story that also follows a formula. During the telling of the tale, the audience might interrupt or offer corrections, and many stories include songs that are sung by both storytellers and audience together. Audiences participate by singing and clapping hands, and listeners may reply to a question from the storyteller. Music is an integral part of the act of storytelling, and, Waterman and Bascom tell us, "A good storyteller creates additional occasions for well-liked songs and folktales and used dramatic timing and expressiveness." Depending on the audience's reaction, a tale may be lengthened or shortened. The storyteller is generally skilled in mime and mimicry, and as a raconteur, he or she utilizes the subdialect features of nasality and consonantal variants especially in the telling of ANIMAL-trickster tales. Folktales are generally told at night, heightening the fantasy and adding to the effectiveness of the dramatic techniques employed by the storyteller. In some places, storytelling by day is punished. Some folktales are told in cycles in which one story refers to the one just before it. There is usually a central character who is an animal trickster. In these cycles, two narratives rarely follow the same order.

A story is not memorized and recited word-for-word. As Waterman and Bascom note, "The manner in which a different twist may be given to a story by a slight alteration in a familiar plot comes as no surprise, if the folktale is viewed as a form of verbal art, and if the storyteller is credited with something of the creative imagination of the novelist. . . . Studies in the art of story-telling take into account the creative role of the raconteur."

Typical themes of African stories include GODS, HEROES, TRICKSTERS, and relationships between men and women. Numerous legends and tribal histories exist, and many of them have assumed the character of folklore. Myths exist throughout Africa, with different tribes having their own versions of CREATION stories. Proverbs and riddles are common aspects of the African oral tradition. Many, like the popular TONGUE TWISTER, rely on a knowledge of the language.

Animal trickster tales are the most common type of tale found throughout Africa, with the HARE being the popular trickster of East Africa; the TORTOISE, prevalent among the Aerobe, Edo, and Ibo of Nigeria, also appears in West and East Africa. Liberia's animal trickster, SPIDER, is called ANANSI in Sierra Leone and the Gold Coast. In recounting tales about the spider trickster, the Hausa storyteller lisps whenever the spider speaks and the Aerobe storyteller "speaks down the nose" for the tortoise. The human and divine trickster are also important figures, as in the Zulu tales about Hlakanyana and the Aerobe tales about the deity, Eshu, who is similar to the tortoise. Although a variant of AESOP's fable, "The Tortoise and the Hare," exists, the African tortoise is much more of a trickster figure who triumphs because of brawn and wits rather than steadiness.

A number of folktales that do not focus on trickster figures involve OGRES. In some tales a vegetable or animal agrees to become a barren woman's child. Some tales are known as "dilemma tales," for the stories are unfinished, and no solution is put forth.

Among the best-known of West African tales are "Why We Tell Stories about Spider" and "The Return of Anansi,"from Ghana; and "How Tortoise Won By Losing" and "The Master Trickster," from Nigeria. From East Africa come "The Pauper's Daughter," "The Girl with One Hand," "The Grasshopper and the Fiddle," and the story of the hero "Liongo." Central African tales include "The Two Bundles," "The Unborn Child," and "Ngomba's Balloon." "The Murder of Masiloyane," "Salamone the Orphan," "The Blue Crane," and "Sikjuluma, the Boy Who Did Not Speak" are popular tales of South Africa. *See also* COMPETITION OF LIES.

For Further Reading

Abrahams, Roger. *African Folktales.* New York: Pantheon, 1983.

Berry, Jack. *West African Folktales.* Evanston, IL: Northwestern University Press, 1991.

Scheub, Harold. *The African Storyteller.* Dubuque, IA: Kendall Hunt, 1990.

AFTERLIFE

In different religions, belief in an afterworld or LAND OF THE DEAD. Images of the place humans go after DEATH pervade the oral tradition and religious stories as well as FOLKLORE. Portrayals of the land of the dead take various forms: it may be a place of punishment, such as HELL; it may be more like the underworld of the ancient Greeks, which is portrayed as dark and sad; it may be depicted as HEAVEN or PARADISE; or it may be a more nonphysical state as implied by NIRVANA.

Because humankind witnesses the cyclical nature of the world, there is the tendency to believe that there is life after death. In almost all cultures, the fact that humans are conscious makes it difficult to believe in losing that consciousness forever. The MYTHS of the afterlife provide a way to see the soul survive after death. In most religions that divide the afterlife into hell and heaven, there is the underlying belief that the kind of life one leads on earth is directly related to the rewards or punishments received in the afterlife.

Afterlife depictions include the myth of the Egyptian Osiris and his resurrection (*see* ISIS AND OSIRIS); the various Greek tales of the Elysian Field where heroes go after death and HADES, the underworld to which Persephone is abducted by the god Hades (*see* PERSEPHONE MYTH); the many descriptions of Heaven, Hell, and Purgatory of the Judeo-Christian tradition; the portrait of Heaven and Hell in the *Koran*; the pure land of Buddhism; the San Francisco Peaks where the Hopi KACHINAS live and where those who are rewarded in death go; the three lands of the Central Eskimo peoples, with Qudliven being a happy and pleasurable place, Adlivun the undersea world of punishment, and Adliparmiut the lower region of no return; and the Norse VALHALLA, hall of the chosen slain warriors, Fensalir, for happily married couples, and HEL, the underworld of death.

Stories that depict the DESCENT TO THE UNDERWORLD vividly suggest the nature of the afterlife of that culture. For the Native American Nez Perce tribe, the tale "COYOTE and the Shadow People" depicts the land of the dead as dark when it is dawn in the land of the living and light when it is dark for the living; people appear as shadow-like forms and live in a very large lodge where many fires burn. When the death spirit takes Coyote here so he can try to bring his wife back from the dead, much like the Greek Orpheus who descends to Hades to retrieve his wife, Eurydice, Coyote is delighted to visit with all his friends at the lodge each night (*see* ORPHEUS AND EURYDICE MYTH). However, his instructions from the death spirit require that he take his wife from the lodge and travel over five mountains with his wife before he can touch her; then she will be alive again. As they travel, Coyote's wife is gradually transformed from being practically invisible to looking fully human again. When Coyote sees her in her human form, he cannot resist touching her, although they have not yet crossed the fifth mountain. Like Eurydice, she disappears forever, and Coyote destroys "the practice of returning from death," which the death spirit tried to teach him.

For Further Reading

Ramsey, Jarold, ed. *Coyote Was Going There: Indian Literature of the Oregon Country*. Seattle: University of Washington Press, 1977.

AGAMEMNON

King of MYCENAE and commander-in-chief of the Greek forces during the Trojan War. Agamemnon figures prominently in the action of HOMER'S ILIAD. Though he was long believed to be purely legendary, archeologists have discovered Hittite tablets dating around 1300 B.C. that speak of a historical Mycenaean ruler named Agamemnon. This date corresponds closely with actual events that inspired the story of the Trojan War. The historical Agamemnon is discussed in Michael Wood's richly illustrated book, *In Search of the Trojan War,* a companion to the 1981 BBC television series of the same title.

The Agamemnon of Greek legend is the brother of MENELAOS, whose wife Helen is abducted by Paris and taken to TROY. (*See* HELEN OF TROY). Agamemnon and all the other Greek leaders form an expedition to bring Helen back. However, because Agamemnon has killed a stag sacred to the GODDESS ARTEMIS, the Greek fleet at Aulis is detained by unfavorable winds. As penance, Agamemnon is forced to sacrifice his own daughter, Iphigenia, before the fleet could sail.

The Greeks and Trojans fight indecisively for nine years, then Agamemnon angers the god APOLLO by claiming the daughter of a priest as a spoil of war. Agamemnon agrees to return her to her father, but only after claiming the concubine of ACHILLES for himself. The ensuing quarrel between Agamemnon and Achilles almost leads to a Greek defeat. But after another year of fighting, the Greeks rout and sack Troy. Agamemnon sails for home with his new mistress, Cassandra, the daughter of the Trojan king, Priam.

When Agamemnon reaches Mycenae, he is murdered by his wife Clytemnestra and her lover Aegisthus. Clytemnestra never forgave Agamemnon for Iphigenia's sacrifice. His assassination is the subject of Aeschylus' tragedy *Agamemnon.*

The story of Iphigenia's sacrifice is told in Euripides' tragedy *Iphigenia at Aulis.* A similar incident appears in the BIBLE in the story of Jephthah (Judges, 11:1-12:7), another leader who sacrifices his daughter for the sake of victory in battle. *See also* ANCIENT GREEK STORYTELLING.

For Further Reading

Aeschylus. *Agamemnon.* Translated by Richmond Lattimore. Vol 1, *The Complete Greek Tragedies.* Chicago: University of Chicago Press, 1959.

Evslin, Bernard. *The Trojan War.* Illustrated by Charles Micolaycak. New York: Scholastic, 1971.

Sutcliff, Rosemary. *Black Ships before Troy.* Illustrated by Alan Lee. New York: Delacorte, 1993.

Wood, Michael. *In Search of the Trojan War.* New York: New American Library, 1985.

ALGON AND THE SKY-MAIDEN

A Native American CREATION tale. Found amongst the indigenous peoples of the Algonquian and Iroquois tribes, this creation tale commences with the expulsion of the daughter of the sky-chief, who had been afflicted with an incurable illness, through the heavens, to a world comprised solely of ocean (*see* SKY-MAIDEN). Various marine ANIMALS, including waterfowl, toads, and the Great Turtle, decide that it is time to create the EARTH and construct an island for the sky-maiden to inhabit. In the course of the tale, the sky-maiden recovers from her illness and gives birth to a daughter, who in turn is impregnated by the West Wind while she is digging for potatoes (*see* VIRGIN BIRTH). The daughter of the sky-maiden gives birth to a set of twin boys (Djuskaha and Othagwenda), who, after maturing, decide that it is imperative that they increase the size of the island. Djuskaha creates plants, rivers, and animals that will increase the happiness of future human generations, while Othagwenda creates objects that will prove malevolent to humankind. After this contest of creation, each brother reconfigures the creations of the other after his own respective personality; in the course of this re-creation, Djuskaha kills Othagwenda. Although the tale is interesting in the sense that a matriarch is at the center of the creation of the earth, the tale itself presents a theme common to many creation tales—the struggle for authority between two siblings, as exemplified in the biblical tale of the brothers Cain and Abel. *See also* GENESIS, BOOK OF.

For Further Reading

Bierhorst, John. *The Woman Who Fell from the Sky: The Iroquois Story of Creation.* Illustrated by Robert Andrew Parker. New York: William Morrow, 1993.

Hamilton, Virginia. *In the Beginning: Creation Stories from around the World.* Illustrated by Barry Moser. New York: Harcourt Brace Jovanovich, 1988.

ALI BABA

Hero of the tale "Ali Baba and the Forty Thieves" from the Arabic THOUSAND AND ONE NIGHTS (*see* HERO). The story was not part of the original manuscript but appeared in Antoine Galland's eighteenth-century French collection (*see* GALLAND, ANTOINE). Richard Burton referred to his own 1886 *Supplemental Nights*—which includes the story—as "the most innocent volume of the nights" (*see* BURTON, RICHARD).

Ali Baba, a poor woodcutter, while gathering firewood one day, sees a band of thieves approach a hillside. As Ali Baba watches from hiding, the leader opens and closes a cave with the magic words "Open Sesame" and "Close Sesame." After the robbers leave, Ali Baba uses the words, enters the cave, and finds a large treasure-hall. From it he takes six bags of gold coins.

When Ali Baba's new riches are discovered by his brother, Kassim, Ali Baba offers to share his gold, but Kassim insists on going to the cave himself. But when he sees the treasure room, Kassim is so overwhelmed that he forgets the magic words. The forty thieves discover him and kill him.

Ali Baba finds the hacked-up pieces of his brother's body and brings them home for burial. However, the thieves find Ali Baba. Disguised as an oil merchant transporting large jars—actually filled with thieves—the robber leader asks Ali Baba for hospitality for the night.

Fortunately, Morgiana—a slave girl the family has adopted—discovers the hidden thieves and pours boiling oil on them. She later kills the leader as well. She marries Ali Baba's son, and the family returns to the cave to enjoy its riches.

The theme of hidden treasures shows up in stories from many countries, for example, in the dragon's cave in the epic BEOWULF as does sneaking into an unsuspecting household. In the medieval Welsh *Mabinogion* tales, warriors hide in leather sacks, and during the attack on TROY the Greeks hide in a huge wooden horse in order to get inside the walls of Troy (*see* CELTIC STORYTELLING, ILIAD).

For Further Reading

The Arabian Nights. Retold by Amabel Williams-Ellis. New York: Criterion Books, 1957.

Burton, Richard F. *Supplemental Nights to the Book of the Thousand Nights and a Night.* Vol. 3. Benares: The Kamashastra Society, 1886.

ALLEGORY

A mode of storytelling in which the importance of a secondary level of meaning supersedes the literal or surface level of meaning. Closely related to the FABLE, the PARABLE, and the MYTH, allegories can assume any form or length and frequently appear in the EPIC, the MORALITY PLAY, the ROMANCE, and verse, philosophy, and novels of all kinds. The term *allegory* derives from the Greek *allos*, "other," and *agoria*, "speaking." Thus, *allegoria*, "other-speaking," suggests a method of expression in which characters, places, events, and objects "speak" of a symbolic value different from their own literal meaning. Allegory is an artistic mode that is very often literary in nature, but may also be visual (as in paintings, emblems, and even dramas), musical, or architectural. The most important function of allegory is didactic; allegories attempt to impart some level of wisdom, ideology, or "truth" to the reader, listener, or observer. Personification is the primary vehicle of allegory.

Allegories may represent actual historic personages or occurrences as well as abstract ideas. For example, John Dryden's *Absalom and Achitophel* (1681) is a long poem which uses the biblical story of Absalom's revolt against his father, King David, to portray the political crisis in England when the Duke of Monmouth tried to wrest power from his father, King Charles II. In this instance, specific characters are designed to represent actual historical figures, and the historical meaning of the story takes precedence over the surface plot involving the biblical characters.

Allegories also commonly represent abstract ideas about virtues, vices, and spiritual attitudes in general. Explicit allegories make it very easy for readers to understand the secondary message lying just below the surface level of the text. For example, John Bunyan's PILGRIM'S PROGRESS (1678) uses characters named Christian, Faithful, Mercy, Worldly Wiseman, and others, to represent the average man's journey through life and his attempt to gain entrance to HEAVEN. However, abstract allegories may be much less explicit in their messages.

Allegories may be interpreted on several levels. In the Middle Ages, Christian scholars developed a fourfold theory of allegory in which one first interprets a text literally, then theologically, then tropologically (morally), and then anagogically (spiritually). This fourfold method remains useful in studying allegory, particularly those allegories of a religious nature.

Allegory is a truly ancient storytelling technique that has ancestors in both written and oral texts; its roots can be traced back as far as classical Greek and Roman mythological traditions and ancient Near Eastern poetry. Allegory was an especially favored form of storytelling in the Middle Ages of western civilization because through allegory, a storyteller could impart knowledge of Christian ideology and represent Christian concepts to the masses of nonliterate, uneducated people. Allegory pervades both the Old and New Testaments in the BIBLE, as well as many theological texts in non-Christian, non-western traditions. In fact, allegory has always been a popular method of promoting specific ideologies (both religious and political), and is still commonly used in literature, drama, and film to represent more modern philosophies (democracy, Marxism, etc.). For example, George Orwell's *Animal Farm* (1946), told in the form of a beast fable, is a political allegory of the rise of communism in the first few decades of the Soviet Union. Allegory remains a popular, important, and often subtle storytelling technique to this day; contemporary authors such as Thomas Pynchon (*The Crying of Lot 49, Gravity's Rainbow,* and others), Ishmael Reed (*Mumbo Jumbo*), J. M. Coetzee (*Waiting for the Barbarians, Foe,* and others), Norman Mailer (*Barbary Shore, The Deer Park,* and others), and Stephen King (*The Long Walk, The Running Man,* and others) regularly use allegory as a vehicle to present the political and ideological aspects of their stories.

AMATERASU

Sun GODDESS, the central figure in Shintoism. Amaterasu is considered the deity from which the Japanese imperial family is descended. She is the MOTHER Goddess, responsible for fertility, and the ruler of the other GODS and the universe. Her Ise Naiku shrine is visited by millions of devotees each year. Amaterasu's story is found in the KOJIKI, compiled in A.D. 712, and in the NIHONGI of A.D. 720.

In some versions of the JAPANESE CREATION MYTH, Amaterasu is the child of the deities Izanagi and Izanami. In others, she is born from Izanagi's left eye as he washes his face after visiting his dead wife in the underworld. Amaterasu is such a beautiful child that her parents soon realize she does not belong on the earth. They teach her how to walk up the rainbow so she can live in the HEAVENS. There, she becomes the SUN and sends out her warmth and light to the world.

Many tales are told about Amaterasu. In one, Izanami gives birth to a god almost as beautiful as the Sun Goddess. He is also taught to walk up the rainbow, so he can join Amaterasu. He becomes her husband, the god of the MOON.

In another story, Amaterasu is supposed to marry a very different brother, the storm god SUSA-NO-WO. His temper and manners are coarse, and he is soon thrown out of Amaterasu's house. Annoyed at the disrespect shown to her, the Sun Goddess hides in a cave, plunging the world into darkness. The other deities dance, perhaps obscenely, and laugh together to coax Amaterasu out. They also create the first mirror, which is the lure that finally works.

The sun is also personified in NATIVE NORTH AMERICAN STORYTELLING—occasionally as a female, usually as a male—as well as in other oral traditions. *See also* FERTILITY STORIES.

For Further Reading

Aston, W.G. *Shinto: The Way of the Gods.* London: Longmans, 1905.

Bierlein, J.F. *Parallel Myths.* New York: Ballantine, 1994.

Kojiki. Translated by Donald L. Philippi. Princeton, NJ: Princeton University Press, 1969.

Nihongi: Chronicles of Japan from the Earliest Times to A.D. 697. Translated by W.G. Aston. London: George Allen & Unwin, 1956.

Piggott, Juliet. *Japanese Mythology.* London: Paul Hamlyn, 1969.

ANANSI

Trickster figure, also called SPIDER, of the Ashanti people of Ghana. Stories about Anansi have spread from the Ashanti to other parts of Africa as well as to the American South, the West Indies, and Brazil. The tales of Anansi the Spider are related to other TRICKSTER tales of COYOTE, IKTOME, HARE, and RAVEN of Native North American tribes.

Among the best known of the Anansi tales are "Anansi and the Ear of Corn," "How Anansi Tricked GOD," "Anansi and the Chameleon," "How Anansi Became a Spider," and "Anansi's Box of Stories." Each story reveals Anansi's boastful arrogance and cleverness for which he is at times rewarded and at other times punished.

In "Anansi and the Ear of Corn," Anansi, not yet a spider, is one of "God's Chosen." He first asks God for an ear of corn and promises him one hundred slaves in return. Through his cleverness, he manages to convince several villages to give him corn, a chicken, a corpse, and finally, one hundred of their finest men, whom he then gives to God as slaves. In "How Anansi Tricked God," God tries to disabuse Anansi of his conceit after bringing him the slaves by asking Anansi to bring him, in a sack, what he, God, is thinking of. But Anansi is quick enough to outsmart him. By listening in on God's attendants, Anansi learns that God wants him to bring the SUN and the MOON, which Anansi does. Anansi's reward is to become God's "captain on earth."

Despite his successes with God, Anansi is outsmarted by a chameleon whose field Anansi covets in "Anansi and the Chameleon," and in "How Anansi Became a Spider," Anansi kills a king's prize ram and tries through trickery to pin the blame on a spider. Eventually, the king learns the truth and kicks Anansi, who breaks into many pieces, thus becoming a spider with long legs.

Of these tales, "Anansi's Box of Stories" captures both the spirit of Anansi the trickster as well as the stories that describe the origin of stories and storytelling. Here Anansi would like to buy the Sky-God's box of stories, but the Sky-God's price is high: Anansi must bring him Onini, the python; Osebo, the leopard; Moboro, the hornet; and Mmoatia, the invisible fairy (*see* OSEBO'S DRUM). With the help of his "long-suffering" wife, Aso, who suggests in each case the method to use for catching the four, Anansi is successful, and, one by one, Anansi brings each creature to Nyami, the Sky-God. Nyami gives Anansi a beautifully carved box of stories, which Anansi then opens in front of his wife and the villagers. However, the stories do not stay in the box, but fly all over the world, with Anansi and the villagers catching a few. The storyteller telling the Anansi story is, in effect, one who has caught one of the "flying" stories. An opened magic box also features in the Greek myth of PANDORA, who opens a box and lets sorrows and evil fly into the world.

The figure of Anansi is important to the folklore of the West Indies as well as America, where he plays a role similar to Brer Rabbit. He represents the cunning and crafty trickster who is able to survive, overcome, and prosper because of his wits and cleverness. Anansi is a popular figure in stories told by children in Trinidad; in Surinam and Jamaica Anansi stories are commonly told at funerals and wakes.

For Further Reading

Bierlein, J.F. *Parallel Myths*. New York: Ballantine, 1994.

Haley, Gail E. *A Story—A Story*. New York: Macmillan, 1971.

McDermott, Gerald. *Anansi the Spider: A Tale from the Ashanti*. New York: Henry Holt, 1972.

ANCIENT GREEK STORYTELLING

The history of the storytelling tradition in ancient Greece. Ancient Greece included the area that is today called Greece, parts of Thrace, Asia Minor, and islands in the Aegean and Mediterranean Seas. The language spoken was ancient Greek, belonging to the Indo-European family of languages. Writing came probably around 1500 B.C., when the Greeks started to use the Phoenician alphabet. They recorded on papyrus the works of HOMER, Plato, and Euclid, but the papyrus did not withstand time. The texts we have today had as their source the Egyptian papyrus stored in the great library at Alexandria, for not only did papyrus last longer in the dry Egyptian climate, but Greece came to control Egypt when Alexander the Great built his empire. Many copies of Homer's works existed in the Alexandria library, along with copies of some of the plays of Aeschylus, Sophocles, and Euripedes.

For the ancient Greeks, poetry—whether heroic, lyric, or dramatic—was always recited at religious festivals. An ancient Greek man would not necessarily own a copy of the ILIAD or the ODYSSEY, but he would have memorized long passages of them. As M.I. Finley notes in *The World of Odysseus,* "The mythmaking process had of course begun among the Greeks many centuries earlier, and it went on continuously wherever there were Greeks, always by world of mouth and often ceremonially. . . . As men listened to the narrative, in rituals or on other social occasions, they lived through a vicarious experience."

Both the *Iliad* and the *Odyssey* are heroic poems, oral poems composed orally. The BARDS who composed and recited heroic poems were illiterate, and used chanting and repetition of phrases and lines. As Finley also notes, "The bard composes directly before his audience, he does not recite memorized lines." This required great concentration on the part of both bard and audience. The poet was a highly-esteemed professional with long years of apprenticeship behind him. Most poets were male, as were their audiences, with the exception of the great lyric woman poet Sappho (c. 612 B.C.–575 B.C.), whose largely personal poems were well-respected by Plato, Aristotle, and others.

Many VARIANTS of the Trojan War Cycle of heroic poems existed, just as many versions of the Greek cosmogony and Hesiod's *Theogony* were known. The diffusion of Homer's two poems was oral, with the *Odys-*

sey having a more magical, FAIRY-TALE feel to it, with its disjointed events and wanderings, its HEROES and villains, and its recognition scene upon Odysseus's return home.

Besides the stories Homer included in the *Iliad* and the *Odyssey*, the ancient Greeks had many stories about the GODS and GODDESSES of their PANTHEON, as well as a number of famous myths concerning ICARUS AND DAEDALUS, Daphne and APOLLO, ORPHEUS AND EURYDICE, the HERO THESEUS, Jason and the Argonauts, PROMETHEUS AND THE THEFT OF FIRE, PANDORA'S Box, and the LABORS OF HERAKLES. *See also* QUEST FOR THE GOLDEN FLEECE, TROY.

For Further Reading

Connolly, Peter. *The Legend of Odysseus*. Illustrated. New York: Oxford University Press, 1986.

Farmer, Penelope. *Daedalus and Icarus*. Illustrated by Julek Heller. New York: Harcourt Brace Jovanovich, 1971.

Finley, M.I. *The World of Odysseus*. 1954. Reprint, New York: Meridian Books, 1959.

Lister, Robin, retold by. *The Odyssey*. Illustrated by Alan Baker. New York: Kingfisher, 1994.

William, Marcia. *The Iliad and the Odyssey*. Illustrated. Cambridge, MA: Candlewick Press, 1996.

ANDERSEN, HANS CHRISTIAN
(1805–1875)

Danish author of novels, poems, and plays, but who is known primarily for his children's stories. Andersen composed over 150 original FAIRY TALES between 1835 and 1872, which are collected in his *Fairy Tales and Stories*. His tales, including "The Princess and the Pea," "The Emperor's New Clothes," "The Little MERMAID," "The Steadfast Tin Soldier," "The Little Match Girl," "The Ugly Duckling," "The Swineherd," "The Snow Queen," and "The Red Shoes" have been translated into most modern languages and remain popular throughout the world. The stories were first translated into English in 1846 by Mary Howitt. During his lifetime, Andersen traveled extensively throughout Europe telling his stories to audiences of all ages and walks of life.

His own life story sounds like it could have been taken from one of his tales. Born into the slums of Odense, Denmark, the son of a uneducated mother and a shoemaker father,

Andersen's formal education was minimal. Yet his father was literate and encouraged his highly imaginative son to read and invent dramas with cut-out paper characters. In 1816, after his father's death, Andersen set out for Copenhagen to fulfill his dream of becoming a singer, actor, or dancer. He met with enormous hardships, eventually being forced to leave the Royal Theater of Copenhagen when his voice began to change. However, his years there introduced him to some influential people who raised the money to send Andersen to a grammar school at Slagelse. Constantly bullied and harassed at school, both by other boys and a cruel headmaster, Andersen endured considerable suffering until he was taken out of the school by his sponsor to be tutored privately. He eventually took his degree at Copenhagen University and decided to become a writer.

In 1827, Andersen published his first poem in a Copenhagen journal. Over the years he wrote novels, travel literature, and plays. His novels include *The Improvisator* (1835), *O.T.* (1836), *Only a Fiddler* (1837), *The Two Baronesses* (1848), and *To Be or Not to Be* (1857). His travel writing includes *A Poet's Bazaar* (1842), and *In Spain* (1863). Though he considered himself primarily as a novelist and playwright for adults, it was his children's tales, with their emphasis on tolerance, their sympathetic portrayal of outsiders, and their exposure of pettiness and pomposity that made him the honored guest of numerous European royal courts. Andersen revised his memoirs throughout his life, the standard edition of which is *The Fairy Tale of My Life* (1855).

For Further Reading

Andersen, Hans Christian. *Complete Andersen's Fairy Tales*. New York: Random House, 1987.

ANECDOTE

A short, unelaborated narrative about a single interesting incident. Anecdotes are common in prose and verse as well as in oral storytelling. During the eighteenth century, the term suggested secret or private details of a person's life, exposed in the spirit of gossip; today the term may refer to any brief narrative about a particular episode. Anecdotes may address any subject; they often relate stories of political figures, popular heroes, or other celebrities, but anecdotes also relate more personal stories of family history or individual experiences.

Anecdotes have been popular throughout literary history; ancient examples of anecdotal literature include Plutarch's *Lives* and the *Deipnosophistae* of Athenaeus. The eighteenth and nineteenth centuries witnessed a wide resurgence in the popularity of collected anecdotes; Isaac Disraeli (the father of the English Prime Minister, Benjamin Disraeli), one of the best-known English collectors of anecdotes, published several of the hundreds of books of anecdotage published in the 1700s and 1800s. In 1960, Louis Brownlow published a collection of Civil War anecdotes called *The Anatomy of the Anecdote*. Today, the anecdote is as popular a form of storytelling as ever. Magazines, tabloid television programs, and even the nightly news are full of anecdotes about the lives of Hollywood celebrities, political leaders, the British royal family, and others whose personal lives capture the interest of the general public.

For Further Reading

Brownlow, Louis. *The Anatomy of the Anecdote*. Chicago: University of Chicago Press, 1960.

ANIMAL MASTER

In different Native American tribes and in prehistoric Europe, the medicine man or SHAMAN who knew how to control hunted animals. The task of the animal master was to take control over the hunt to ensure its success. For many Native American tribes, this meant buffalo or bison hunts. The animal master would dress up in buffalo costume and headdress and dance to lure the buffalo to follow him so that the herd would stampede and fall in a chute. With most of the buffalo dead or with broken bones and no means of escape, the tribe could then kill them with their arrows. A very skillful animal master could lure the buffalo even without costume.

In one Blackfoot animal master legend, the hunters are unsuccessful in getting the buffalo to stampede over the cliff into the chute, and the people are starving. A young woman runs to the edge of the cliff and calls to the buffalo, promising that if they come running she will marry one of them. To her surprise, they come her way and tumble off the cliff, A big bull grabs her and makes her keep her promise, but her family misses her when the hunt is over, and her father goes in search of her.

With the help of a handsome bird, the father sends a message to his daughter, who is with the buffalo. The father comes to fetch his daughter, but her buffalo husband smells him, begins bellowing, and induces the other bulls to help him trample her father to death. When the young woman bemoans her father's death, her husband tell her that this is how all buffalo feel as they watch their kin die as they fall over the cliff. However, she can return to her people if she can bring her father back to life. She then sends the bird to find a piece of her father's body, which it brings to her; by covering it with her robe and chanting over it, first his body is restored and then his breath.

The buffalo are very impressed with the power of the woman and her people and agree to let the father and daughter go if they learn the buffalo song and dance, which will restore the buffalo to life. The people promise to teach this ritual, which involves wearing a bull's head and buffalo robe, and when they return, a group of young men of the tribe are taught the buffalo song and dance.

ANIMALS

Subjects of innumerable MYTHS, LEGENDS, and stories the world over. The animal tale is the oldest mode of storytelling, forming the basis of later anthropocentric legends and myths. Even the Greek pantheon shows telltale signs of folkloric animal roots. The demigod Herakles was originally a lion deity, as is hinted by his lion-skin clothing, and the gods ZEUS and APOLLO exhibit residual wolf attributes.

Animals remain at the forefront of NATIVE NORTH AMERICAN STORYTELLING today, partly because Native American religious traditions put a great emphasis on the kinship between humans and animals. SHAMANS train themselves to take the forms of various animals, and Native Americans often have animals as spiritual companions, guides, guardians, or totems (see TOTEMISM). The fact that prehistoric art indicates a similar bond in the Old World between the human and natural world makes it clear that such spiritual traditions form the root of all storytelling about animals—and much subsequent storytelling about humans as well.

Storytellers of many Native American tribes speak of a time when animals and humans were indistinguishable. Frequently, the founders of a tribe were animals of one kind or another. The Dogrib Indians of northern Canada tell of a woman who gave birth to a litter of puppies; half of these remained dogs, while the other half grew up to be the Dogrib's human ancestors. Bears are especially esteemed in Native American folklore, because their humanlike appearance links them to that primordial age when humans and animals were more alike.

Native American TRICKSTER and CULTURE HERO figures are often animals, including such familiar characters as COYOTE and RAVEN. These animals often played a major role—albeit sometimes a bungling one—in the creation of the earth, its creatures, and its physical characteristics. For example, Coyote is said to have created the Columbia River by antagonizing a small stream of water.

Many folktales all over the world deal with MARRIAGES between animals and people. One Indian woman is said to have become a bride to the chief of a bear tribe. Her twin sons grew up to be equally at home among humans and bears. Such stories frequently involve the TRANSFORMATION of animals into people or vice versa. Gaelic folklore abounds with stories of seals who transform themselves into men or women, take human spouses, then eventually become seals again and vanish back into the sea. The stories of Zeus transforming himself into animals in order to seduce mortal women clearly arose out of this sort of FOLKLORE.

Such folkloric traditions constitute the origins of more literary animal stories, including FABLES by AESOP and others. Like true animal folklore, fables often take place in a mythic prehistory when animals talked and behaved like people. But fables are less concerned with explaining the natural world than they are with human nature—particularly its weaknesses and failings. Fables have sometimes been strung together to form beast EPICS, the most famous of which is the Medieval REYNARD the Fox.

European traditions also transmogrophied more plausible animals into extraordinary supernatural beasts, including the part-eagle, part-lion Gryphon; the SPHINX, with her human head attached to an animal's body; and the two-headed snake, Amphisbaena, which is similar to the often two-headed Vision Serpent of the Classic Mayas.

All these traditions are very much alive today. The animated films of Walt Disney are full of animals who talk, sing, and befriend humans. High-tech special effects have recently and vividly brought talking animal characters to live-action movies, as in the popular 1995 film *Babe,* in which an extremely articulate pig proves himself a capable sheepdog.

Animals are still grist for the mill for literary fabulists as well. George Orwell's 1945 novel *Animal Farm* is a kind of twentieth-century beast epic in which an uprising of farm animals symbolizes the worst aspects of Stalinist Russia. And John Gilgun's 1981 collection *Everything That Has Been Shall Be Again* adds an element of reincarnation to the traditional animal fable.

Stories for children featuring animal characters are too numerous to list, but outstanding examples include Kenneth Grahame's *The Wind in the Willows,* A. A. Milne's *Winnie the Pooh,* and E. B. White's *Charlotte's Web. See also* EARTH-DIVER CREATION.

For Further Reading

Erdoes, Richard, and Alfonso Ortiz. *American Indian Myths and Legends.* New York: Pantheon, 1985.

ANUBIS AND BATA

Egyptian story of two brothers. In this violent tale, Anubis and his younger brother Bata work together tilling the fields and tending cattle, but the wife of Anubis wants to do away with Bata. One day when Bata is sent back to the house for seed, Anubis's wife tries to seduce him, but Bata resists, returning to his brother with the seeds but saying nothing. That night, when Anubis returns home, his wife claims that Bata has raped her, and she threatens suicide if he does not kill Bata. So Anubis prepares to kill his brother with a spear. Bata, however, is not only handsome but he is also wise. He anticipates his sister-in-law's treachery, and when he arrives home, he sees Anubis lying in wait for him, and he flees. Being a good man, Bata prays to the SUN god, Ra, as he runs, asking Ra to save him and punish the guilty. Ra answers Bata's prayers by creating a river filled with crocodiles between the two brothers. Bata then tells Anubis that at sunrise, with Ra's appearance, the truth will be told, and Anubis will know from the GODS who is innocent. Indeed, at sunrise Bata tells Anubis the true story of what has transpired, and even though Anubis believes him, Bata emasculates himself to uphold his vow and offer Ra a sacrifice. He then throws his penis in the river, and a fish that is sacred to the sun god swallows it. Bata dies from his wound and Anubis slays his wife and is so miserable that he feeds her remains to the dogs.

This Egyptian tale offers the moral that one should hear both sides of a story before acting. It also resembles tales that portray women as potentially wicked and envious and who will come between two men, in this case, brothers. A similar theme is found in the Greek story of Phaedra, the wife of THESEUS, who uses intrigue and false accusations to turn her husband against his son. Had Theseus listened more carefully to the stories he was told, his son would have been spared.

APACHE CREATION

Various CREATION myths of the five groupings of Apache Indians of the Southwest United States. Because the Apache people are divided in to five groupings—the Jicarilla, the Chiricahua, the Mescalero, the Lipan, and the White Mountain Apaches—their tribes were scattered through Arizona, New Mexico, and Texas, and their different creation myths reflect this separation.

The myths of the Jicarilla of northeastern New Mexico are generally "EMERGENCE CREATION" stories, tied to gestation and birth, and important to puberty rites practiced by Apache girls. In one myth the people and ANIMALS first live in an underworld that resembles "a great swelling womb," but the day animals and the people long for light. Through a game they play, the day animals win the ability to see the rising stars and the SUN. As the sun rises, it reveals to the people and animals that it can see through a hole, and on the other side of the hole is the EARTH. The desire to get through to the other side is eventually accomplished through building mounds and with the help of a buffalo, whose horns provide a ladder. By sending up the sun and MOON for light and the four WINDS to blow away the waters, which finally "break" as in birth, the people and animals emerge from the hole, which becomes the center of the world for the Jicarillas, thanks to the GREAT SPIRIT.

In another Jicarilla "creation from emergence" myth, the basic natural powers are personified by the Hactcin, who resemble the KACHINAS. The Hactcin exist, before creation, in a dark, watery chaos resembling a world womb. People live only as potential in an underworld ruled by Black Hactcin, who makes animals out of clay and gives them life. Eventually Black Hactcin makes the first man as a companion to the animals, and then he makes the first woman as a companion to the man. In one VARIANT, it is the dog that asks Black Hactcin for a companion, which is why man and dog are thereafter so closely connected to each other.

The Mescalero Apaches have a creation myth that is part of a girl's puberty ceremony: when a girl reaches menarche, a sacred lodge is built for her based on the myth. Just as the universe is represented by a circle bisected in four directions, the lodge is held up by four main poles representing the Four Grandfathers that hold up the universe. The Four Grandfathers also represent the four seasons and the FOUR DIRECTIONS. According to the myth, the Great Spirit creates the earth in four days, first creating Father Sun, Mother Earth, Old Man Thunder, Boy Lightning, and the animals, then on the fourth day creates people. Thus, the puberty ceremony takes place over a period of four days and four nights.

Like the Mescaleros, the White Mountain Apache myths tell of Four Grandfathers and a sacred lodge which is, in fact, the universe. The Chiricahua have Hactcin first, a FLOOD, and the presence of the White Man in their myth. Like several of the other myths, the Lipan myth is linked to birth, involves emergence from an underworld, led by Four Grandfathers. The figure of CHANGING WOMAN also appears in this myth.

For Further Reading

Granville, Goodwin. *Myths and Tales of the White Mountain Apaches.* Memoirs of the Apache Society, vol. 33. New York: J.J. Augustin, for the American Folklore Society, 1939.

Leach, Maria. *The Beginning: Creation Myths around the World.* New York: Thomas Crowell, 1956.

APHRODITE

The Greek GODDESS of sexual love. Aphrodite was also celebrated as the goddess of vitality, fertility, and MARRIAGE. Her sacred animal is the goat.

Some accounts of Aphrodite's origins represent a merging of several ancient Hittite legends. In these stories, Aphrodite's father is the Titan Uranos, who is castrated by his son Kronos. Uranos' GENITALS are thrown into the SEA, and from that union Aphrodite is born. She is identified with sea foam, and artworks often depict her borne to the shore of Cyprus on a scallop shell.

In later versions, Aphrodite is a daughter of ZEUS, and Eros, the god of love is her son. She is also given a husband, Hephaistos, the lame craftsman who is destined to be a cuckold. Aphrodite is sometimes the mistress of other deities, including Ares. Another lover is Hermes, with whom she gives birth to Hermaphroditus, a double-sexed person. She gives birth to the Trojan hero Aeneas after her union with a mortal herdsman (*see* AENEID).

Aphrodite has a magic girdle that causes everyone to fall in love with whoever wears it. Occasionally, she is persuaded to loan it to other goddesses—HERA for example.

Like many of the Greek deities, Aphrodite involves herself in the Trojan War. She "starts" the war by allowing Paris to abduct HELEN OF TROY as a reward for giving her the apple meant "for the fairest." When Paris is threatened by the Greek general MENELAUS during the war, Aphrodite wafts Paris back to TROY on a cloud.

However, this goddess was no warrior. When her son Aeneas is wounded on the battlefield, she rushes to his aid, but when the opposing warrior wounds her hand, Aphrodite lets Aeneas fall and makes her way back to Olympus. Zeus tells her to keep her attention on love and stay away from war.

Nevertheless, Aphrodite returns to the battleground again when Aeneas is the only Trojan chief still alive. She urges her son to leave the battlefield and see to his family. Then Aphrodite helps him get his father and son out of the city. She also helps Helen of Troy escape.

Aphrodite falls in love with the mortal Adonis when he is born. She takes him to Persephone and asks the goddess of the underworld to take care of him for her. Persephone agrees. But unfortunately, Persephone herself falls in love with Adonis and refuses to give him back. Finally, Zeus decides that Adonis will spend half of each year with each goddess—autumn and winter with Persephone in the underworld, and spring and summer with Aphrodite (*See also* PERSEPHONE MYTH).

One day, when he is summering with Aphrodite, Adonis is hunting alone and wounded by a boar. Aphrodite hears his moan and flies to his side, but Adonis dies in her arms. Crimson flowers sprang up where the drops of his blood fell on the earth.

In the stories of patriarchal Greece, Aphrodite is portrayed as a loose woman and a threat to marriage. But she is a very different figure in the older oral traditions. In *Lost Goddesses of Early Greece*, Charlene Spretnak (*see* SPRETNAK, CHARLENE) calls Aphrodite "a virgin in the original sense (one-in-herself, not necessarily abstaining from sex but always remaining independent)."

And in *Goddess: Myths of the Female Divine*, David Leeming and Jake Page observe that Aphrodite's "apparent promiscuity, in the Eastern world of her origins, would have been appropriate to an Earth Goddess who is closely related to, if not derived from, earlier goddesses such as Ishtar (INANNA) and Isis." *See also* ODYSSEY, ILIAD, ANCIENT GREEK STORYTELLING.

For Further Reading

D'Aulaire, Ingri, and Edgar Parin D'Aulaire. *Ingri and Edgar Parin D'Aulaire's Book of Greek Myths.* New York: Dell, 1992.

Spretnak, Charlene. *Lost Goddesses of Early Greece: A Collection of Pre-Hellenic Myths.* 4th ed. Boston: Beacon Press, 1992.

Gates, Doris. *Two Queens of Heaven: Aphrodite, Demeter.* Illustrated by Trina Schart Hyman. New York: Puffin Books, 1983.

APOCALYPSE

The end of the world, or a revelation of the world's end, characterized by such cataclysmic events as earthquakes, FLOODS, plagues, and a final judgment of humanity. Stories of the apocalypse are closely related to eschatology, the study of the "end things." Apocalyptic stories take many forms, but all anticipate a general devastation that will bring about the end of an age and, often, the beginning of a new one. Thus many flood stories serve the apocalyptic function of correcting a mistake in the initial CREATION. In the Book of Genesis flood story (*see* GENESIS, BOOK OF), YAHWEH cannot tolerate the sins of humanity and so sends the flood to destroy all living things. In the Mayan POPUL VUH, the creator destroys by flood two early versions of humanity made from mud or wood. The mud and wood beings are not sinful, but they cannot function as the creator had hoped. In this corrective function, apocalyptic stories reflect a human need for cleansing, a desire to purge the creation of evils and begin anew.

In the major religions of the West—Judaism, Islam, and Christianity—this apocalyptic movement demonstrates a linear vision of history. The apocalypse is not a repeated stage in a continuous cycle, but a transition into the ultimate state of being. In Judaism, this transition marks the coming of the messiah who will transform the world. In Islam and Christianity, the emphasis is upon a general

judgment, followed by an eternal paradise for those who have persevered in their faith and conduct. In each case, a new and permanent phase follows the violence of the end times. By contrast, Eastern stories emphasize the dissolution of the world as part of the natural cycle of the universe. In Hindu eschatology, the dissolution of the world constitutes one part of the eternal breathing of the universe. In the unending cycles of life, all have played the roles of KINGS, and all will play the roles of paupers. In this way, apocalyptic mythology of the East lacks the sense of urgency and finality of the West.

Apocalyptic stories exist in the collective expressions of cultures past and present. From the ancient Zoroastrian battle between good and evil to the cyclical movement of history in the poetry of W.B. Yeats (*see* YEATS, WILLIAM BUTLER), humanity seeks answers to the mystery of its own end. Storytellers seek to define a moment or place upon which to set apocalyptic expectations. The ancient Hebrew city of Megiddo, with its adjacent plain of Armageddon, has fueled the imaginations of many storytellers as a symbol for the final confrontation between good and evil, which will hasten the end. Theologians scour prophetic texts in the hope of devising a system to calculate the precise time, place, and nature of the apocalypse. Ultimately, however, the stories that point to the end do not provide explicit directions. Their very ambiguity indicates both a divine secrecy and a human recognition that life is frequently random and unpredictable. The apocalyptic vision may be viewed as a metaphor for the individual life which waxes, wanes, and is extinguished. The inexplicable nature of life finds a voice in the stories of collective destruction in the apocalypse.

In recent history, many apocalyptic stories have moved from the western theme of the end as an act of divine retribution to a more self-imposed catastrophe. These stories, which exist in various forms of literature, film, or music, illustrate modern humanity's ambivalent relationship with a rapidly expanding body of technological innovations. Whether the threat involves nuclear war or self-annihilation through environmental abuses, many stories now look away from a divine source to a reckless humanity as the cause of total destruction. Interestingly, the end of the Cold War did not diminish apocalyptic fears; in fact, those fears appear to have been heightened as the comprehensible threat of the superpowers is replaced by the terrors of the unknown. In recent years apocalyptic stories of alien abductions and invasions have increased dramatically, indicating that the fear of the apocalyptic moment may be based less upon an imminent threat of destruction than upon the psychological need to define an end point to human existence.

Recent scientific investigations have also gained popularity, from the explosive threat of an asteroid collision, to the less immediate theory of entropy in which the earth, no longer infused with energy from a dying SUN, will simply expend its heat. Of the scientific theories, those with a more graphic, conceivable apocalyptic moment seem to have more appeal to the human imagination. Long-term theories such as entropy do not possess the intensity people expect from the final moment of human history. To paraphrase T.S. Eliot, our stories express a desire to end with a bang rather than a whimper. Another reason for the human need for DRAMA in stories of the end arises from our intellectual limitations. The concept of eternity is incomprehensible to the human mind, and the stories we tell grasp at an historical moment that will function as an initiation into the unknown of the coming age.

For Further Reading

Cohn, Normal Rufus Colin. *Cosmos, Chaos, and the World to Come: The Ancient Roots of Apocalyptic Faith.* New Haven: Yale University Press, 1993.

APOLLO

Greek god of healing, light, MUSIC, and archery. He also became popularly regarded as the god who drives the chariot of the SUN across the sky, even though that honor properly belongs to a minor deity named Helios. Apollo is the patron of poets and sometimes of athletes and leader of the Muses. He is the son of the deities ZEUS and Leto. ARTEMIS, GODDESS of the MOON, is his twin sister.

Apollo was originally an Asiatic god, perhaps a god of herding. He became the essence of the values of classical Greece, standing for moderation, self-knowledge, and order. His opposite and complement was DIONYSOS.

Like many of the women Zeus seduced, Apollo's mother, Leto, fled from the jealous wrath of HERA. She hid on the Island of Delos, where Apollo and Artemis were born.

At seven months old, Apollo attacks the serpent Python, his mother's enemy. He follows Python when it flees to DELPHI and hides in the Oracle of Mother EARTH. Boldly, Apollo enters the shrine and kills the Python, then Apollo takes over the shrine and put its priestess into his own service.

One of the best-known stories about Apollo is his futile desire for Daphne, one of the NYMPHS. He falls madly in love with her on first sight, but Daphne has no interest in love or marriage, preferring to spend her time hunting and fishing.

According to some versions of the story, this infatuation is brought about when Apollo foolishly insults Eros. Eros shoots Apollo with an arrow that makes him fall in love with Daphne. Then Eros shoots Daphne with an arrow that makes her avoid love.

Obsessed, Apollo follows Daphne everywhere, pleading with her to be his wife. He also reminds her that he is, after all, a major deity.

Daphne is not impressed with the persistent god, and instead, grows frightened and runs away through the woods. Apollo catches up with her near the river Peneus, who is her FATHER. In despair, Daphne pleads with Peneus for help. Suddenly her body begins to change—her hair turns into leaves, her arms into branches, and her skin into bark. She becomes a laurel tree.

Brokenhearted, Apollo vows that the foliage of the laurel will become sacred to him. That is why the winners of both poetic and athletic contests are crowned with laurel wreaths. In other versions of the story, it is Daphne's mother, Earth, who saves her by turning her into a laurel tree.

In a tale told by Ovid, Apollo falls in love with a Spartan boy, Hyacinthus. When Apollo is teaching him how to throw a discus, the boy is killed—possibly because of the jealousy of the West WIND, who is also infatuated with Hyacinthus. Hyacinth flowers spring up from the dead youth's blood.

Apollo fathered a number of children of nymphs and mortals. Among them is Asklepios, the god of healing. When Asklepios has the nerve to resurrect a dead man, HADES lodges a complaint with Zeus. Zeus kills Asklepios with a thunderbolt. In revenge, Apollo kills the CYCLOPES, the giants who forge Zeus' thunderbolts. To placate Zeus, Apollo works for a year herding sheep. He may well have gained his penchant for moderation from that experience (*see* GODS).

For Further Reading

Graves, Robert. *The Greek Myths.* 2 vols. New York: Penguin Books, 1957.

APOTHEOSIS

Final stage of self-realization in the HERO's journey. Apotheosis for the hero can come in the form of DEATH or ASCENSION to the status of divinity. As David Leeming writes in *Mythology: The Voyage of the Hero*, "The myth of apotheosis is the logical conclusion to the hero's adventures. He is taken out of the cycle of life and given a permanent status in recognition of his inherent divinity—his real self. As he had been miraculously created out of the void, so he must be returned to the creator and that void." Apotheosis comes in different forms for such male and female heroes as the Greek Oedipus, Herakles, and DIONYSOS (*see* LABORS OF HERAKLES); the Judaic Abraham and Moses; the Indian BUDDHA; the Toltec and Aztec QUETZALCOATL; the Celtic King ARTHUR; the Christian MARY and Jesus; and the Italian Christian martyr Saint Agnes.

For Oedipus, who is shown to suffer so greatly in Sophocles' plays *Oedipus the King* and *Oedipus at Colonus*, having found out the truth about himself, his parents, his incestuous marriage, and his children, therefore blinding and exiling himself from his city, his painless death comes in the form of being miraculously taken off by "some attendant from the train of HEAVEN" in a sacred grove near Athens, with the hero THESEUS a witness.

As Sophocles writes, "indeed his end/was wonderful if mortal's ever was."

Like Oedipus, the death of Moses comes as atonement, according to Jewish legend, as GOD receives Moses' soul in Heaven. In Abraham's case, death is his apotheosis, and he is taken to Paradise where he becomes immortal. Buddha's death and apotheosis means the attainment of NIRVANA. Both Herakles and Quetzalcoatl die in fire and are reborn like PHOENIXES as they ascend to Heaven and immortality. King Arthur is taken away by a barge of black-hooded women, three of them queens, while his famous sword, Excalibur, is thrown back into the lake from which a hand reaches out and takes it.

Dionysos, Mary, Jesus, and Agnes all ascend to Heaven as their experience of apotheosis.

As Leeming notes, in being carried off to Heaven, the hero "loses the self to find the self," and "[t]o realize the self in its total reality is to repossess the soul—the world soul of the collective unconscious."

APULEIUS (c. A.D. 124)

A Platonist Latin writer famous for his satirical prose ROMANCE, *The Golden Ass*, or *Metamorphoses*. Lucius Apuleius was born in Numidia, North Africa, and educated in Carthage and Athens, where he was trained as a lawyer. Although he worked in Rome, he spent most of his career in Carthage. His literary works include *De Daemone Socratis* (*On the God of Socrates*) on the subject of invisible spirits, and *The Golden Ass* (c. A.D. 150), his most famous work. Composed in eleven volumes, it is the only complete extant Latin novel. In it, the first-person narrator, a curious and lusty young man named Lucius, relates the story of his wanderings after visiting a sorceress and taking the wrong magic potion: his intention was to be transformed into an owl, but his mistake transforms him into a donkey instead. In the course of his wanderings, he is mistreated by various owners and is privy to the often absurd behavior of humankind. By the end of the tale, Lucius is initiated into the mystery of Isis, where he suffers a "voluntary death" and "approached the realm of death" to acquire his "spiritual birthday"(*see* ISIS AND OSIRIS); Isis also transforms him back into his human shape.

The Golden Ass is especially known for containing "The Myth of Amor [Cupid or Eros] and Psyche," which Apuleius is said to have borrowed from the Greeks. As Erich Neumann notes in *Amor and Psyche: The Psychic Development of the Feminine*, "Like almost all folktales, this one contains mythical substance that was excluded from the mythology recognized by the dominant culture." Apuleius incorporates the tale into his romance by having an old woman relate it to a young girl who had been abducted from her mother by robbers on her wedding day. Trying to console the girl, the old woman tells the story as "an initiation into the feminine destiny of development through suffering," writes Neumann.

Just as Apuleius borrowed from earlier Greek and Latin sources, his work, in turn, influenced Boccaccio, Cervantes, Rabelais, Henry Fielding, and Tobias Smollett, and variants of "The Myth of Amor and Psyche" appear widely in such works as John Milton's *Comus*, John Keats's "Ode to Psyche," Walter Pater's *Marius the Epicurean* (1885), William Morris's *Earthly Paradise* (1868–1870), and, more recently, in C.S. Lewis's novel *Till We Have Faces* (1956). Parallels can also be drawn between the characters of Psyche and CINDERELLA.

For Further Reading

Apuleius, Lucius. *The Golden Ass, or Metamorphoses*. Translated by Robert Graves. New York: Farrar, Strauss, & Giroux, 1951.

Climo, Shirley. "Psyche." *Princess Tales from around the World*. Illustrated by Ruth Sanderson. New York: Harper Collins, 1996.

Eliade, Mircea. *Rites and Symbols of Initiation*. Translated by Willard R. Trask. New York: Harper & Row, 1958.

Haight, Elizabeth H. *Apuleius and His Influence*. 1930. Reprint, New York: Cooper Sq., 1963.

Neumann, Erich. *Amor and Psyche: The Psychic Development of the Feminine*. Translated by Ralph Manheim. Princeton, NJ: Princeton University Press, 1956.

ARCHETYPE

A persuasive idea, image, or symbol that forms part of the collective unconscious. Literally meaning "prototype," or "original pattern from which copies are made," this term applies to things for which there are recognizable universal traits. Plato used the term to define concepts such as beauty, evil, or jealousy by showing examples of them in real life. He pointed out, for example, that jealous people always covet what they did not have, and treat others who possess what they wanted with hostility.

In the nineteenth century, Swiss psychiatrist Carl Jung (1875–1961) adapted the term and applied it to literary criticism, where he recognized recurring types of characters in various sorts of storytelling. Archetypal types of stories exist, such as MYTHS, LEGENDS, and FAIRY TALES, each genre having one or more recognizable trait. A FABLE, for example always teaches a moral lesson, which is usually reiterated at the tale's end.

Common archetypal figures, or stock characters (as they are often called), in the oral storytelling tradition include the DIVINE CHILD, the wicked stepmother, the PRINCE, and, of course, HEROES and villains (*see* STEPMOTHER—WICKED). Though each tale's archetype has characteristics unique to its cultural context, it also has universal traits in common with those of its global counterparts. The archetypal villain in an Old West melodrama, for example, may have a handlebar mustache, a Stetson hat and a Texas twang, thus establishing him as a figure of the Wild West, but he will also be dressed in black—the archetypal color of evil.

Recognizing archetypes provides an integral part of understanding the stories in which they exist, for, even if we read a Russian FOLKTALE with unfamiliar characters and settings, we will connect with, and readily comprehend, the archetypal story plot and characters contained within it. This allows us to both appreciate the tale for the new aspects its Russian version offers and to compare it with global variants, bridging the gap from culture to culture.

ARJUNA

Hero of the Hindu MAHABHARATA. Arjuna is known as one of the five sons of Pandu, but he is actually the son of Indra, the king GOD (*see* INDRA AND THE ANTS). Arjuna undergoes martial training from an early age, and he becomes highly adept at archery under the tutelage of Drona, a celebrated teacher of weapons and warfare. By wining an archery contest, Arjuna is able to wed his cousin DRAUPADI, an avatar of the GODDESS of prosperity.

The climactic episode of Arjuna's life comes in the epic *Bhagavad Gita,* in which humanity battles to an apocalyptic end. Under the guidance of his chariot driver, KRISNA, Arjuna is required to give the signal that will begin the conflict. As the armies line up against one another, Arjuna finds himself unable to justify the bloodshed that will follow. He tells Krisna that he would rather die than kill. To convince him to proceed, Krisna, who is actually the god VISNU in human form, gives Arjuna a "celestial eye," by which he can view Visnu's true form. With the celestial eye, Arjuna gets a glimpse of BRAHMAN, the universal force or idea from which all things come. The vision is beautiful, ghastly, and ultimately too powerful for Arjuna to bear. Upon seeing the brutal, devouring nature of the universe, Arjuna begs Krisna to take the eye from him.

By granting Arjuna this vision, Krisna demonstrates that Arjuna's personal desire to preserve life is irrelevant in contrast with the power of Brahman. Arjuna's obligation is to participate in the game of life, to fulfill his destiny despite his moral sensibilities. The lesson, which brings Arjuna to commence the battle, also teaches the readers of the story to accept the nature of life and the roles in which it casts them (*see also* HERO).

For Further Reading

Campbell, Joseph. *The Masks of God: Oriental Mythology.* New York: Penguin, 1962.

Dowson, John. *A Classical Dictionary of Hindu Mythology and Religion, Geography, History, and Literature.* New York: Routledge, 1979.

Seeger, Elizabeth. *The Five Sons of King Pandu: The Story of the Mahabharata.* Illustrated by Gordon Laite. New York: William R. Scott, 1967.

ARTEMIS

Virgin GODDESS of the hunt and sister of APOLLO in the ancient Greek PANTHEON. Although a virgin, Artemis helps her mother to deliver her twin brother, Apollo. She is thus associated with the contradictory functions of virginity and childbirth. Related to her role in childbirth is Artemis's association with the MOON. The moon, in its cycles of appearance and reappearance, DEATH and REBIRTH, is a symbol of the female principle. This association is probably a remnant of her status as an older, Near Eastern fertility goddess, a theory that is borne out by her depiction as a many-breasted goddess at the temple of Ephesus. Known as Diana in Roman mythology, Artemis is also the protector of animals and the goddess of hunting.

Her seemingly paradoxical roles come together in the story of Actaeon. Actaeon is hunting with his dogs when he spies Artemis bathing with her attendant NYMPHS. The nymphs attempt to shelter Artemis's nakedness from Actaeon's gaze, but Artemis's superior height keeps her in Actaeon's sight. In her embarrassment and anger, she throws water into Actaeon's face and transforms him into a stag. Artemis also puts fear into his heart, and he flees from her, only to be pursued by his own hunting dogs. The dogs catch and tear him apart, and Artemis feels avenged.

Artemis's strong reaction to Actaeon's accidental view of her prompts questions regarding the meaning of the myth. On one level, it is a fertility ritual not unlike those of Actaeon's cousin, DIONYSUS. The ritual dismemberment of the victim brings about, in many mythological systems, the fertility of the land. Enacting the ritual, or even telling the story, restores fertility for the coming year. On another level, Artemis simply reacts to the violation of her virginal status, a status imposed upon her by a patriarchal pantheon. Psychological theories of patriarchy hold that female figures are depicted only in extremes of virginity or eroticism. In the Greek pantheon, Artemis and ATHENA represent the extremes of virginity while Aphrodite represents the eroticized version of the female principle. Athena, like Artemis, is transformed from an association with fertility to a masculine form of violence, namely warfare. In the Greek stories, Athena also guards her virginity closely. In both instances, masculine fear of female reproductive power causes patriarchal power structures to depict female figures in extremes. The power of the fertility cult, over which Artemis once presided, is eliminated by casting her as a violently modest virgin. The story of Artemis and Actaeon demonstrates that, when a male figure threatens to compromise the sexual elements of her nature, he is destroyed.

For Further Reading

Harris, Stephen L., and Gloria Platzner. *Classical Mythology*. Mountain View, CA: Mayfield, 1995.

Pratt, Annis. *Dancing with Goddesses: Archetypes, Poetry, and Empowerment*. Bloomington, IN: Indiana University Press, 1994.

ARTHUR

British KING and leader of the legendary Knights of the Round Table. Historically, Arthur is believed to have been a sixth-century Celtic warrior or king. The sources of the Arthurian legend are in early Celtic oral tradition, although the stories are best known as a cycle of medieval ROMANCES.

Arthur is described as a battle leader in a ninth-century A.D. chronicle by the Welsh cleric, NENNIUS—an account that includes magic and supernatural feats. The LEGEND was already well known in Normandy by 1066, when the Normans conquered Britain.

In about 1135 GEOFFREY OF MONMOUTH developed Arthur's heroic nature in his Latin *History of the Kings of Britain*. Geoffrey's stories include MERLIN, GUINEVERE, SIR GAWAIN, and Mordred. In 1155 the French chronicler Wace made the first mention of the Round Table.

In the twelfth and thirteenth centuries, Arthurian legends were expanded and embroidered under Christian influence, and King Arthur and his knights became great heroes of chivalric romances. French poets on both sides of the English Channel gave the words of wandering storytellers a new literary form, and these tales were retold in all the languages of Europe.

Late in the twelfth century, CHRÉTIEN DE TROYES unified the material into a French narrative, focusing on the deeds of individual knights. He introduced the medieval theme of courtly love in the story of LANCELOT and Guinevere. Around the same time, Layamon, a priest of Worcestershire, wrote Arthurian tales in English for the first time.

Each subsequent storyteller enlarged on the theme of Arthur's survival and return: Nennius was sure the hero could not be permanently dead; Geoffrey described the wounded King's departure for Avalon; Wace cited Merlin's prophecy that Arthur would return; Layamon placed Arthur's sister, Morgan Le Fay, in Avalon to heal the king's wounds. In 1191 the monks of Glastonbury announced the discovery of the bodies of Arthur and Guinevere, possibly to dispel the expectation of Arthur's return.

In 1469, Sir Thomas Malory wrote the *Morte d'Arthur*, which contains the versions of the Arthurian legends most familiar today; William Caxton printed *Morte d'Arthur* for the first time in 1485.

Arthurian characters are referred to by Shakespearean characters, and Arthur is a leading figure in Spenser's *Faerie Queene*. Later, in the nineteenth century, England developed a renewed interest in the Middle Ages and Arthurian legends. Tennyson's *Idyls of the King* was popular in America as well as England. In 1889, Mark Twain published his own version of the adventure: *A Connecticut Yankee in King Arthur's Court*.

Arthur's story contains many elements common to other heroic tales. He was the son of a king, but his parentage was hidden. He was taught by a wise man—the magician Merlin. He was made king after he acquired a magical weapon—the sword Excalibur.

As the legend goes, Arthur accompanies his half-brother to a joust in London. When Sir Kay discovers that he has left his sword behind, Arthur goes to get him a sword that is embedded in a stone. Arthur easily pulls the sword from the stone, a feat many other knights had attempted in vain.

King Arthur gains fame as a warrior and a just ruler. He has the Round Table made so that he and all his knights will be equals when they gathered there. Arthur marries Guinevere, and in the early stories his downfall is due to his wife and the traitor, Mordred. Later romances add the element of illicit love between Guinevere and the knight Lancelot. In either case, Arthur falls victim to treason, is critically wounded in a final battle, and is taken away to the island of Avalon. Some say he still dwells there and will return to lead his people again. In *Mythology: the Voyage of the Hero,* David Leeming comments that "[h]e is taken away, like Oedipus and QUETZALCOATL, as if to another world."

The extraction of a sword from rock appears in the Greek myth of THESEUS and in Norse legends (and Wagnerian operas) about SIEGFRIED. Many of the other knights in medieval romances also had swords with names and magical powers.

Twentieth-century retellings of the Arthurian legend include T.H. White's 1958 *The Once and Future King,* which integrates fantasy and satire of contemporary English mores; John Steinbeck's retelling of Malory's stories in 1976; Mary Stewart's Arthurian novels of the 1970s and 1980s; and Marion Zimmer Bradley's 1982 *The Mists of Avalon,* which presents a fresh perspective by telling the story through the women characters.

Lerner and Loewe had success on Broadway with their 1960 musical, *Camelot.* The Arthurian legends have been popular in movies and on television, including several versions of Twain's novel and the 1965 Disney animated feature, *The Sword in the Stone.*

Magic weapons, special and secret origins, and mystical tutelage, show up in tales of heroes around the world. In recent times they have appeared in Malamud's 1952 novel *The Natural* and the 1984 film, as well as in the *Star Wars* movies. Such elements, as well as Arthurian characters, are also common in many science-fiction/fantasy books, films, and comic books.

As Valerie M. Lagorio and Mildred Leake Day suggest in *King Arthur through the Ages,* "We may experience, consciously or unconsciously, a retrospective nostalgia for the Arthurian Golden Age, with its certain, praiseworthy values and universal truths, the same verities which are threatened in today's world." *See also* CAMELOT, CELTIC STORYTELLING, HOLY GRAIL, PERCIVAL.

For Further Reading

Caxton's Malory: Morte d'Arthur. University of California Press, 1983.

Hopkins, Andrea. *Chronicles of King Arthur.* London: Collins & Brown, 1993.

Lagorio, Valerie M., and Mildred Leake Day. *King Arthur through the Ages.* 2 vols. New York: Garland Publishing, 1990.

Malamud, Bernard. *The Natural.* New York: Harcourt Brace Jovanovich, 1952.

Stewart, Mary. *The Crystal Cave.* New York: William Morrow, 1970.

Tennyson, Alfred. *Idyls of the King.* London: Ticknor and Fields, 1866.

Twain, Mark. *A Connecticut Yankee at King Arthur's Court.* New York: Penguin, 1971.

White, T.H. *The Once and Future King.* New York: Putnam, 1958.

ASBJORNSEN, PETER CHRISTEN (1812–1885)

Norwegian folklorist, writer, and naturalist. As a folklorist, Peter Christen Asbjornsen was fascinated with the FOLKTALES of his native Norway. With his school friend, the poet Jorgen Moe, he collected the four-volume *Norwegian Folk Stories* (1841–44), which was greeted with acclaim all over Europe. In the following year he published the first of his series, *Norwegian Fairy Stories and Folk Legends.* Translations of his *Popular Tales from the Norse* appeared in English in 1858, and *Fairy Tales from the Far North* was translated into English in 1897.

For Further Reading

Asbjornsen, Peter Christen, and Jorgen Moe. *Norwegian Folktales.* Illustrated by Erik Werenskold and Theoodor Kittelsen. New York: Pantheon, 1960.

ASCENSION

In MYTH and LEGEND, the climb to a higher inner spiritual place or HEAVEN. As Mircea Eliade has written, "Whatever the religious context, and whatever the particular form they may take (shamanist or incitation rites, mystic ecstasy, dream-vision, heroic legend), ascensions of all kinds, such as climbing mountains or stairs or soaring upwards through the air, always signify that the human condition is being transcended and that higher cosmic levels are being attained" (*see* ELIADE, MIRCEA). In view of this, the various world-axis symbols—the mountain, the LADDER TO ANOTHER WORLD OR HEAVEN, the tree, the cross, the liana, the rope, the thread of the spider, and the spear—are all connected with ascension.

Ascent to the sky or heaven appears often as a MOTIF in FOLKLORE and storytelling. Among Native North Americans of the North Pacific Coast and the Plateau and Plains areas, a HERO ascends to the sky on a large feather. Sometimes the ascent is achieved through the arrow chain, a motif which also appears in stories from Siberia, Oceania, and South America. In a Mazovian legend, a pilgrim to the holy sepulchre spies a ladder to the sky made of birds' feathers. After three months of climbing, he finally ascends to the Garden of PARADISE.

In many FOLKTALES, ascension to a higher spiritual plain is symbolized by the hero's ascent to the sky to find his father, as in the Fiji tale of the son of Tui Langa, the sky king. Much like the FAIRY TALE of "JACK AND THE BEANSTALK," the Fijian boy places his walking stick in the earth before going to sleep and awakens to find a tree grown in its place. He climbs the tree in order to introduce himself to his father.

ASIAN STORYTELLING

Ancient tradition of MYTHS, LEGENDS, FOLKTALES, and FAIRY TALES, often containing religious themes. Asia encompasses one of the largest regions of the earth, including the nations of China, India, Japan, Korea, Pakistan, Burma, Bangladesh, Tibel, Nepal, Laos, Thailand, and the many island nations of the South Pacific. Because this region is made up of some of the oldest civilizations in human history, a wide diversity of cultures has developed, including hundreds of different ethnic groups and languages, all contributing in their unique way to the cultural and literary traditions of Asia. Most of Asia developed under two main influences, those of China and India, and in many cases, especially after the advent of Buddhism, a combination of Chinese and Indian influences resulted. In many

ways, Asia is one culture made up of many strands of a web of traditions and histories. Even Islam and the connected stories should be considered part of this tradition, since it continues to influence vast regions of Asia. Storytelling and the stories themselves go back thousands of years. Complex mythologies and religious traditions developed, which Asian writers and storytellers used as rich lodes of inspiration, as they do to this day.

India produced the complexity of the Hindu PANTHEON and the HERO-god KRISNA, the stories of the *Bhagavad Gita* and the MAHABHARATA from which it came, the EPIC RAMAYANA, the sacred *Vedas*, *Dhammapada*, and the *Upanishads*. These include stories of conquest, of spiritual endeavor, and of human experience with the phenomenal world. Undoubtedly most of these stories were passed down orally before recorded. BUDDHA told PARABLES almost three hundred years before Jesus of Nazareth, some the very same stories.

In China some basic cultural cornerstones include the stories surrounding Confucius, and the Taoist classics of Lao Tzu and CHUANG TZU use FABLES and stories to develop their precepts. Stories of DRAGONS, originating in China, spread throughout Asia, as did a pantheon of legendary KINGS and heroes intertwined inextricably with authentic history. As in other storytelling cultures, such as Native American and Ancient Greek, China produced a menagerie of ANIMAL myths and stories of mythical beasts.

After Indian Buddhism encountered Confucianism and Taoism in China, the traditions gradually merged to become Chuan Buddhism, eventually better known as the Zen Buddhism of Japan. With the development of Buddhism came thousands of tales of monks and their encounters of Buddhist principles in the mountains of China and Japan.

Some of the earliest writing in human history comes from Asia. The rich culture of Japan, influenced both by Korea and China, produced hundreds of stories of monsters and heroes, such as the tales of "Peach Boy" and "The Golden Boy." The ancient KOJIKI, compiled in A.D. 712, collected tales of the origin of Japan. This cultural background led to such

Japanese classics as *The Tale of Genji* and *Tales of the Heike*. British expatriate Lafcadio Hearn collected and translated numerous Japanese stories in the nineteenth century.

Throughout Asia, writers and storytellers have contributed to a vast literature, and contemporary writers from all Asian countries continue to produce literature in some part derived from this diverse variety of cultural traditions. *See also* BUDDHIST STORYTELLING, CHINESE STORYTELLING, JAPANESE STORYTELLING.

For Further Reading

Murasaki, Shikibu. *Tale of Genji.* New York: Knopf, 1992.

Sakade, Florence. *Peach Boy and Other Japanese Children's Favorite Stories.* Rutland, VT: C.E. Tuttle, 1958.

ATHENA

GODDESS of Greek mythology. In early oral traditions, she was probably a fertility figure, but in the more patriarchal classical Greek stories, she was turned into a virgin goddess—a deity of wisdom and a patroness of the arts and crafts. She was also a battle goddess and the protector of many Greek cities during war, although she preferred to settle disputes peacefully. A gigantic statue of Athena once stood in the Parthenon, her temple at the summit of the Athenian acropolis.

Athena is conceived when ZEUS forces himself on the Titan Metis, a goddess of wisdom and knowledge. An oracle tells him that Metis carries a girl, but if she conceives again, her son will depose Zeus. To forestall this possibility, the god promptly swallows Metis whole. Some time later, he is afflicted with a terrible headache. Hermes splits open Zeus' skull, and out springs Athena, fully armed.

Athena created the olive tree, which was sacred to her. She taught the Greeks crafts, such as weaving and pottery, and invented many tools for farming. She also invented the chariot and the bridle for horses.

Despite her wisdom, Athena occasionally demonstrated jealousy. When Arachne seemed to be a better weaver than Athena, Athena threatened the girl with death. Either from fear or the shame of her defeat in their weaving competition, Arachne killed herself. Athena turned her into a spider—the insect she hated most.

Athena's patronage of Odysseus is described in the ODYSSEY. *See also* ANCIENT GREEK STORYTELLING.

For Further Reading

Graves, Robert. *The Greek Myths.* 2 vols. New York: Penguin Books, 1957.

ATTIS

An emasculated DYING GOD figure of Phrygian mythology whose story recalls those of Osiris, Adonis, and DIONYSOS (*see* ISIS AND OSIRIS, APHRODITE). Many different versions of the Attis story survive, but most share an emphasis upon fertility symbols, emasculation, and the god's birth from, or transformation into, a tree. In an account by Pausanius, Attis's birth reflects his connection to the fertility cults of Greece and Asia Minor.

During one of his frequent amorous pursuits, ZEUS spills some of his semen upon a mountain. The mountain conceives Agdistis, a hermaphroditic being whose capacity for asexual reproduction threatens gods and humans alike. To destroy the threat, the gods employ Dionysos, who ties Agdistis's GENITALS to a tree during sleep. Agdistis awakes and is immediately emasculated. Agdistis's blood spills upon the ground, eventually growing into a fruited tree that the virgin Nana (a manifestation of the GODDESS CYBELE) discovers has miraculously impregnated her. Attis is born and, in several versions of the story, has an incestuous relationship with his mother (*see* INCEST STORIES). While the stories vary widely, in virtually all of them, Attis endures a form of castration and is transformed into a tree.

Attis's miraculous birth from the principles of the EARTH-MOTHER and sky-god, as well as his bloody connection to the EARTH, created a powerful cult mythology which was celebrated throughout the Mediterranean. Ovid and Herodotus both give versions of the story, and the myth became an important component of James Frazer's *The Golden Bough* many centuries later.

For Further Reading

Frazer, James G. *The Golden Bough*. 1890. Reprint, New York: Gramercy, 1981.

Vermaseren, Maarten J. *Cybele and Attis: the Myth and the Cult*. London: Thames and Hudson, 1977.

AUSTRALIAN AND NEW ZEALAND ABORIGINAL STORYTELLING

The history of the storytelling tradition among Australian and New Zealand Aborigines. The Aborigines were the earliest people in Australia and New Zealand. Various local groups and tribes have their own MYTHS and storytellers, yet they all share the idea of "dreamtime" or "dreaming," which is the time of the ancestors and the CREATION of the world at the dawn of time.

Dreamtime, which continues to be a crucial aspect of each Aborigine's identity, refers to the otherworldly realm of the Ancestor Beings who renew and maintain the land and the cyclical seasons—"through a mystical communion with their loving Aboriginal descendants," writes Harvey Arden in *Dreamkeepers*. Thus, Dreaming, the name for an individual's own ancestry, can be traced to one or more of the demigods of Dreamtime. An Aboriginal man will refer to himself by saying, "I'm a Dingo Dreaming Man," with the allusion to the ancestral creator *Dingo*, "who helped shape the landscape in that long-ago time and to whom he bears a special affinity and spiritual relationship. He would never kill or eat a dingo, for he has Dingo Dreaming." As Arden notes, "dreaming species depends, in Aboriginal belief, on the strict performance of the appropriate seasonal rituals—dances, songs-and-story cycles, and so on—that bring them into direct metaphysical contact with ancestor beings."

As part of the Dreaming, Aboriginals go "walkabout," a kind of VISION QUEST or spirit journey where they rigorously follow "preordained routes through their family's own particular inherited portion of Dreaming country along the Tracks of the Ancestors." At each ancestral sacred site, they stop to perform the "prescribed ancient ceremonies," or *corroborees*.

The stories of the epic Dreamtime adventures of the Ancestor Beings are used as mnemonic devices for teaching other Aboriginals a very necessary working knowledge of their own physical environment and how to treat the ANIMALS and plants with whom they share a familial kinship. These Dreamtime stories combine history, moral homilies, and geographical orientation. While in some ways they resemble ancient Greco-Roman myths or the FABLES of AESOP, the Aboriginals see them as sacred PARABLES and crucial roadmaps through the landscape of their home territory.

The role of the Aboriginal storyteller continues to be very important to the Aborigines, and myths are told at the *corroborees*, where the storyteller follows a fixed form in relating a sequence of events. The various sacred spots and totemic centers are referred to as "story places," and they were ostensibly established by the ancestors of the dream time near water holes or in other places along the dream path (*see* TOTEMISM). The myths of the land where an Aborigine lives make that land his or her home in a deep sense, and there is a ritual reenactment of the mythological history done with the accompaniment of music, singing, painting, and DRAMA which energizes the bond between the people, the land, and the ancestors.

Recurrent themes in Aboriginal storytelling include the presence of the RAINBOW SERPENT, though the name changes from region to region, the theme of the SWAN-maiden, the theft of fire kept in a creature's body, and the freeing of hidden water. Myths exist about the constellations of Orion and the Seven Sisters. Various creator figures exist, including DJANGGAWUL AND HIS SISTERS and the WANDJINA. Some of the important myths include "Alinda the Moon-Man," "Wirana's Cave," "The Crow-Man Who Stole Fire," "The First Returning Boomerang," and "Wuriupranili the Sun-Woman."

For Further Reading

Roberts, Ainslie, and Charles P. Mountford. *The First Sunrise: Australian Aboriginal Myths in Paintings with Text*. New York: Taplinger, 1972.

Robinson, Roland E. *Aboriginal Myths and Legends: Age-Old Stories of the Australian Tribes*. Illustrated by Roderick Shaw. London: Paul Hamlyn, 1969.

AVALON *See* CAMELOT

AVESTA

Sacred text of ancient Persia (Iran). The *Avesta*, which means "wisdom," "injunction," or "basic text," is the book containing the earliest form of the Zoroastrian religion through the teachings of the Persian prophet Zarathustra along with myths from pre-Zoroastrian Persian mythology (*see* ZOROASTRIAN CREATION). What is believed to be the original *Avesta* was thought to have been lost in the fourth century B.C., and from the period beginning in the third century B.C. through the sixth century A.D., the Zoroastrian priests, known as *magi,* compiled a new collection of 21 books, or *nasks,* of sacred writing, called the *Zend Avesta*. While some of these writings were drawn from the original *Avesta*, this *Zend Avesta* is more a commentary on sections of the original lost text.

The *Avesta*, which was written in the ancient Avestan language, consists of four sections: *Gathas*, a collection of hymns written by the prophet Zarathustra, although some were thought to have been written earlier; *Yashts*, which includes hymns to individual GODS and some of the earlier Persian myths; *Yasna*, liturgical texts written in both verse and prose; and *Videvdat*, a detailed code of ritual purification. The *Yashts* section of the *Avesta* played an important role in storytelling and the oral tradition, providing a sense of the Zoroastrian PANTHEON and Persian mythology. The Zoroastrian pantheon was divided between good spirits, *ahuras*, led by Ormazd or Ahura Mazdah, and the *daevas* or *divs*, led by Ahriman. As the supreme god of Zoroastrianism, Ahura Mazda was responsible for creating Spenta Mainyu, a beneficent spirit representing light, life, and truth, and Angra Mainyu, the malevolent spirit representing darkness, DEATH, and falsehood. Much of Zoroastrian cosmology depicts the warring between the forces of good and the forces of evil.

The *Yashts* section of the *Avesta* is believed to be the inspiration for the major Persian epic, the *Shah-Namah*, or *Book of* KINGS. A folk epic covering approximately 4,000 years, the *Shah-Namah* is a retelling of an older history, the *Khvatay-namak*, which dates back to mythical times. Drawing on the *Khvatay-namak*, portions of the *Yashts,* and lines from the earlier poet Daqtat, the poet Firdausi (Abo'l-Qasem Mansur) took thirty-five years to compile this epic, which was completed around A.D. 1000.

For Further Reading

Zaehner, R.C. *The Dawn and Twilight of Zoroastrianism*. Oxford: Clarendon Press, 1961.

———. *Zurvan: A Zoroastrian Dilemma*. Oxford: Clarendon Press, 1955.

BAAL

Name for numerous ancient Semitic GODS, usually local agricultural deities, especially of Syria and Palestine; with later theological development, Baal became the Canaanite weather and fertility god. Baal's full name is Baal Hadad. By itself, *baal* means "lord" or "master" and can refer to other gods, but when used without qualification, it almost always refers to Hadad. The name *Hadad* may mean "the thundering one."

Much of today's mythological material about Baal comes from Canaanite cuneiform tablets, dating from the fifteenth century B.C., that were excavated at the ancient site of Ugarit (now Ras Shamra) in Syria beginning in 1929. In the Ugaritic poems from these tablets, Baal is called "strong one," "rider on the clouds," and "Baal PRINCE [of the earth]." The main theme of these poems is Baal's quest for and attainment of kingship over the gods, especially his rivals, Yamm (or Yammu) and Mot, who may have been his brothers. With the help of his sister and consort, Anat, the huntress and blood-thirsty GODDESS of war,

Baal first conquers Yamm (meaning "SEA"), a greedy DRAGON who symbolizes chaos. After this victory, Baal controls the weather and agriculture. With his father's permission, Baal builds a splendid home to which he invites all the gods and goddesses. When Baal realizes the grave error he made by not inviting his brother Mot (meaning "DEATH") to the celebration, he resolves to assuage the furious god by descending to the world below and partaking of Mot's feast. Forgetting that once one eats the food of the dead, he can no longer walk on earth, Baal becomes imprisoned in the underworld. The earth is threatened with sterility because Baal cannot bring rain. The grieving Anat retrieves Baal's corpse from the underworld then attacks Mot, cuts him up, and sows him in the fields. Baal revives but must battle endlessly with the humiliated Mot. Finally, Baal triumphs and resumes his throne while Mot is banished forever to the underworld. The rains and fertility return. This encounter between Baal and Mot regularly recurs, explaining agricultural cycles.

Baal's fierce battle with Yamm, the dragon of the seas, is similar to the great Babylonian god MARDUK's battle with the water deity, Tiamat, in the EPIC *Enuma Elish* (c. 1100 B.C.). Baal and Marduk each rise to power after they defeat their foes from the sea (*see* BABYLONIAN CREATION).

Baal is often represented striding to the right with a club held over his head in his right hand and a lightning bolt in his left hand. Usually, he wears a conical crown with two horns protruding from the front.

In the Old Testament, the cult of Baal detracts the Israelites from following the Hebrew GOD. God instructs Moses to kill those who have aroused his anger by worshipping Baal (Numbers 25:3-5), and Elijah asks the prophets of Baal to invoke their god and then mocks them when Baal does not respond (I Kings 18:25-29).

The story of Baal includes prominent MOTIFS of the DYING GOD and the son-lover, both of which are found in stories from other cultures and frequently are associated with the cycle of vegetation. In the dying god motif, a god-king dies and is in some sense revived if not actually brought back to the living world. Stories about ATTIS, DIONYSOS, Jesus, ODIN, and ISIS AND OSIRIS contain the dying god motif, as do various epics, including the NIBELUNGENLIED and SONG OF ROLAND in the deaths of SIEGFRIED and ROLAND respectively.

The son-lover motif is an aspect of many dying god stories. Often, the god figure is brought back to life in some form by his MOTHER-lover. Baal is the son-lover type to his sister, Anat, as is Osiris to his sister, Isis. Attis is both the son and the lover of his mother, CYBELE. The relationships between the Finnish folk figure LEMMINKAINEN and his mother, who reassembles the body of her dead son, and that of the beautiful Greek youth Adonis and the goddess APHRODITE are further examples of the son-lover motif.

Baal's experience in the underworld and eventual resurrection are common themes in the stories of numerous gods and heroes. In addition to having associations with the cycle of vegetation, Baal's DESCENT TO THE UNDERWORLD can be seen as a metaphor for a psychological descent into the unconscious. His resurrection suggests the achievement of full individuation. Attis, Dionysos, Jesus, and Odin are examples of important figures from various storytelling traditions who descend to death and then reemerge into a new wisdom or wholeness.

For Further Reading

Coogan, Michael D., ed. and trans. *Stories from Ancient Canaan*. Philadelphia, 1978.

"The Poem of Baal." *The Revised English Bible*. Oxford: Oxford University Press, 1989.

BAAL-SHEM STORIES

Group of LEGENDS about the life of Rabbi Israel ben Eliezer (1700–1760), preacher, magician, and founder of Hasidism, a Jewish sect of eastern Europe. Israel ben Eliezer was born in Okopy in the southern Ukraine. He is said to have begun preaching around 1738 after a long period of seclusion in the Carpathian Mountains. He was called the *Baal-Shem,* or the "master of the name," indicating his relationship to the "name" that empowered him to perform what he wished. Some accounts relate that he was a popular healer, writer of amulets, and exorcist of DEMONS — the traditional roles of a Baal-Shem.

The Baal-Shem's powers as a rabbi and a magician attracted many disciples. He saw the supreme goal of religious life as spiritual communion with God. Such a state could be achieved during prayers as well as in the course of mundane, everyday activities. His teachings included the theory that evil can be transformed into goodness by a mystical process of returning it to its original source in the divine world; there, evil is redirected into positive spiritual power. This theory is illustrated in the story of "The Werewolf."

In this story, the child Israel's dying father warns his son of the Adversary, whom the child will confront throughout his life. If the boy stands his ground, he will be victorious in his soul. He must not fear the Adversary.

When Israel is 12, he hires himself as a helper to the community's teacher. He leads a singing procession of pupils from their houses to school and back home. He takes the students on detours through meadows and the forest. The boys' happiness and devotion breaks through the misery and confusion oppressing the earth and reaches to HEAVEN where there is a resplendent reflection.

Adversary appears and finds a charcoal burner, an unsociable person who avoids others. The charcoal burner sometimes changes into a WEREWOLF. In spite of his heart's attempts to resist this bitter compulsion, the charcoal burner is powerless. The Adversary seizes the man's heart and hides it in the earth. Then he puts his own dark heart into the charcoal burner's chest.

The terrifying werewolf appears to Israel and the procession of children one morning at sunrise. Israel remembers his FATHER's words, and when he sees the werewolf again, he confronts it. He seems to enter the werewolf's body. He sees the werewolf's heart, discolored by hatred. The boy grasps the heart, senses its suffering, and places it on the earth which immediately swallows it. Israel returns to the children. They see the charcoal burner lying dead at the edge of the forest. His face has a peaceful expression, and they no longer understand why they feared him.

Another story tells of the conversion of a rabbi who initially strongly opposes the Baal-Shem. Rabbi Jacob Joseph finds three customs of the new sect intolerable: the joy of their feasts, the irregularity of their service, and the gentle sermon that the master delivers after the third Sabbath meal. One day, the Baal-Shem appears in the town of Sharigrod, the home of Rabbi Jacob Joseph, and begins to narrate a story. Soon, the whole town gathers in the marketplace to listen. The story enthralls the synagogue servant and makes him late to unlock the synagogue for the angry rabbi.

Later, one of the Baal-Shem's disciples betroths his daughter to a pupil of Rabbi Jacob Joseph, to the rabbi's distress. To ensure that the rabbi will accompany him to the wedding, the pupil promises not to look at the Baal-Shem's face. When the rabbi learns that the pupil does not plan to keep his promise, he angrily remains in the inn and will not attend the wedding. While attempting to study in his room, Rabbi Jacob Joseph senses that he is being commanded to go to the town of Mesbitz, and when there, he is drawn to the Baal-Shem's house. It seems to grow lighter, then a voice tells the rabbi a story with a message so powerful that he barges through the door of the brightly lit hall and falls at the feet of the Baal-Shem. He becomes a great pupil of the Baal-Shem and preserves the master's teachings in writing for the next generations.

According to modern scholarship, many of the stories told by Hasidism about their leaders are adaptations of Jewish FOLKTALES in which specific leaders (i.e., the Baal-Shem) are presented as the HEROES.

Other groups of stories focusing on the life and teachings of a spiritual leader include tales about the BUDDHA (see JATAKA TALES); the body of legends that surround Zoroaster, the founder of the Persian religion, Zoroastrianism (see AVESTA); the Koran, the holy book of Islam, which contain the teachings of the prophet MUHAMMAD and details about his life; and various books of the BIBLE, such as EXODUS, which describes the life of the prophet Moses, and the New Testament gospels, which relate the life and PARABLES OF JESUS.

For Further Reading

Ben-Amos, Dan, and Jerome R. Mintz, ed. and trans. *In Praise of the Ba'al Shem Tov: The Earliest Collection of Legends about the Founder of Hasidism*. Bloomington, IN, 1970.

Buber, Martin. *The Legend of the Baal-Shem*. Translated by Maurice Friedman. New York: Harper and Brothers, 1955.

BABA YAGA

In Russian FAIRY TALES, the wild woman, WITCH, or hag. Baba Yaga the Bonylegged is a familiar witch in such Russian fairy tales as "Baba Yaga and the Brave Youth," "Vasilisa the Beautiful," "The Virgin Czar," and several stories simply called "Baba Yaga." As a hag who represents Old Mother DEATH as well as nature, Baba Yaga lives in a hut in the forest and is known to devour people. Although people avoid her, surviving an encounter with her is the equivalent of positively overcoming tests or trials in the QUEST of the HERO.

In the fairy tale "Vasilisa the Beautiful," perhaps the most well known of the Baba Yaga tales because it is so similar to the story of "CINDERELLA," Baba Yaga's hut is surrounded by a fence of human bones with posts made of skulls, recalling the necklace of skulls worn by the Hindu goddess KALI. The bolts of the doors are constructed of skeleton's arms and the door locks are actually a skeleton's mouth with teeth sticking out. Vasilisa is sent by her stepmother to Baba Yaga for light after the stepmother lets the flame in their hearth go out, hoping that Vasilisa will be destroyed by her encounter with Baba Yaga (*see* STEPMOTHERS—WICKED). Instead, Vasilisa succeeds in fulfilling the tasks Baba Yaga sets for her with the help of a doll Vasilisa's mother had given her before she died. Because Baba Yaga realizes that Vasilisa is blessed, she gives her a skull with light in it, and when Vasilisa returns home, the glowing skull burns her stepmother and stepsister to ashes. Like Cinderella, Vasilisa ends up marrying the KING. From this tale, Jungian psychoanalyst Marie-Louise von Franz concludes in *The Shadow and Evil in Fairytales* that "Baba-Yaga is not totally evil; she is ambiguous, she is light and dark, good and evil, though here the evil aspect is stressed." Indeed, Baba Yaga is the "Great GODDESS of Nature" as well as the "Goddess of Death" in the sense that death is part of nature.

For Further Reading

Afanas'ev, Aleksandr. *Russian Fairy Tales*. New York: Pantheon, 1945.

Climo, Shirley. "Baba Yaga Bony Legs." *Princess Tales from around the World*. New York: HarperCollins, 1996.

Philip, Neil. *Fairy Tales of Eastern Europe*. Illustrated by Larry Wilkes. Boston: Houghton Mifflin, 1991.

von Franz, Marie-Louise. *The Feminine in Fairy Tales*. Rev. ed. Boston: Shambhala, 1993.

———. *Shadow and Evil in Fairy Tales*. New York: Spring Publications, 1974.

BABYLONIAN CREATION

Comprised of a variety of creation myths originating in different centuries, the best known of which is contained in the EPIC *Enuma Elish,* meaning "when on high." This particular creation story presents several common MOTIFS, including the emergence of order from chaos, the primal waters as source of creation, a war in HEAVEN, the emergence of a KING-GOD (*see* YAHWEH), and the creation of earthly matter from the body of the first MOTHER.

According to the *Enuma Elish*, one of the oldest written creation stories, the sweet, PRIMEVAL WATERS of Apsu, the god of subterranean waters, and the salt waters of Tiamat, a feminine deity and mother of all GODS, mix to form Lahmu and Lahamu, the first generation of gods.

Lahmu and Lahamu produce the gods Anshar and Kishar who are the parents of Anu, the father of Ea, the EARTH and water god, and several other sons. Ea and his brothers band together and surge back and forth on the waters, disturbing Tiamat and Apsu with their unsavory and overbearing ways. Apsu plans to destroy the young gods, but they learn of his plan, and, with the wise Ea as their leader, they kill him.

Ea and the GODDESS Damkina are the parents of the great god Marduk, who is greatly exalted and the loftiest of the gods. Tiamat, in her anger against the young gods for slaying Apsu and making the WINDS that disturb her, creates MONSTERS. The gods are unable to subdue Tiamat and the monsters, and promise Marduk that they will recognize him as king of the universe if he will conquer Tiamat.

When Tiamat opens her mouth to consume Marduk, he drives in the Evil Wind, which distends Tiamat's body. Marduk shoots an arrow that tears her belly, cuts through her insides, and splits her heart. He then crushes her skull and severs her arteries. Marduk splits Tiamat's dead body into two parts: half of her he sets up as the sky and from the rest forms the earth. He makes the SUN's path in Tiamat's stomach and gives her the night to hold. He creates constellations as well as the positions and the responsibilities of the gods. Marduk has Ea create humans from the blood of Kingu, Tiamat's lover.

Other Babylonian creation stories were used for ritual purposes such as the dedications of sacred buildings and purification ceremonies. Marduk continues to be a dominant figure in many of these myths, which often include familiar motifs from the *Enuma Elish* and other Mesopotamian creation stories: primordial waters as a goddess, the sacrificing or division of the first being, and the creation of humans from clay and sacrificed blood. *See also* DISMEMBERMENT OF PRIMORDIAL BEING.

For Further Reading

Green, R.L. "Marduk, the Avenger," *A Book of Myths.* Illustrated by Joan Kiddell-Monroe. New York: Dutton, 1965.

Hamilton, Virginia. *In the Beginning: Creation Stories from around the World.* Illustrated by Barry Moser. New York: Harcourt Brace Jovanovich, 1988.

BADGER

In Japanese folklore, a shape-shifter, transformer, dupe, or friend. There are three types of badgers for the Japanese—*tanuki, mujina,* and *mami*—but the one that appears most frequently in Japanese folklore is *tanuki,* a mischievous shape-shifter that first appears in folktales in the thirteenth century. The Japanese badger figure is sometimes dressed up like a Buddhist priest by the people— his round belly and testicles are exaggerated, and often a wine bottle is put on his back. As a TRICKSTER, the badger is linked with the fox (*see* REYNARD).

In the folktale "The Badger That was a Shamisen Player," a badger is crossing a river when a man catches sight of him. The badger takes a log and puts some weeds on it, and it transforms into the three-stringed musical instrument called a *shamisen.* Then he puts some weeds on another log which becomes a little girl. Finally, the badger transforms himself into a blind woman by putting weeds on his own head. Once disguised as the blind woman, the badger walks off with the *shamisen* in his arms and the little girl leading him. They enter a temple where many people gather around to hear them and are well entertained. The man, who has been watching all the while, is amazed, and goes to the back of the temple to watch through a peephole. Just as he is wondering how all the people can be fooled, he realizes that he is looking into the buttocks of a horse. Clearly, this particular folktale stresses the trickster,

SHAPE-SHIFTING nature of the Japanese badger.

For Further Reading

Dorson, Richard M., ed. *Folk Legends of Japan.* Rutland, VT: Charles E. Tuttle, 1962.

BAKER, AUGUSTA (1911–)

Librarian, broadcaster and storyteller of children's literature. Born in Baltimore, Maryland, in 1911, Augusta Baker received a B.A. in 1933 and a B.S. in Library Sciences in 1934 from the New York College for Teachers.

Baker enjoyed a long association with the New York Public Library (1937–1974), as a children's librarian, assistant coordinator and storytelling specialist, and finally as coordinator of children's services. She lectured at Columbia University as a visiting professor from 1955 to 1979 when she also broadcast a weekly series entitled "The World of Children's Literature." In 1980, she became the storyteller in residence at the University of South Carolina, where she presently resides.

As well as contributing introductions to numerous books on children's literature and compiling many reading lists and pamphlets, she edited many anthologies of children's literature including *Talking Tree* (1955) and *Golden Lynx* (1960). She also edited a scholarly book of essays called *The Black Experience in Children's Books* (1973).

BAKER'S DOZEN

Colonial American FOLKTALE, which centers upon the metamorphosis of a selfish baker into a benevolent contributor to society. In the original tale, Baas, a famous baker, is visited by an uncommonly old woman who wants to purchase a dozen cookies, each bearing an image of SAINT NICHOLAS. When the baker hands the bag of cookies to the woman, she demands one more of the special cookies. Baas, declaring that twelve cookies constitutes a dozen, refuses to grant her request, and rudely escorts her from his shop. In the following days, Baas experiences mysterious episodes of bad luck; for example, his brick oven collapses. On New Year's Eve, Baas, remembering his acerbity toward the old woman, places his hand on a Saint Nicholas cookie, looking for solutions to his problems. Suddenly, Saint Nicholas appears before the startled baker and advises him to remember the spirit of giving indicative of his holiday. The figure of Saint Nicholas is magically replaced by the old woman, and the baker immediately gives her a bag of thirteen cookies and pleasantly wishes her a "Happy New Year." In doing so, the curse is broken. Before the old woman leaves, she makes Baas promise that thirteen will thereafter make a "baker's dozen."

Although this tale is one of the original American colonial tales, it has noticeable connections to some ancient tales. The old woman who demands a "baker's dozen" of cookies operates as a prophetic figure in this tale, professing that someday thirteen powerful states will unite to remind the world of her magical number. Also, the popularity of the Saint Nicholas cookies reflects the duality present in our own society as we incorporate both Christian and pagan customs in the celebration of Christmas.

BALDR

Beautiful, wise, and gracious son of the Norse god ODIN; Baldr's DEATH is the most famous part of his MYTH. He is blonde and so fair of face that light beams from him. His eyebrows are white, and his hair and body are exquisite. Baldr is said to be the wisest, the gentlest, the most merciful, and the most loved of the Norse GODS. The myth of the death of Baldr strongly suggests the MOTIF of the DYING GOD.

According to this myth, the other Norse gods and GODDESSES decide to protect Baldr from all potential danger when they learn of his disturbing DREAMS that suggest his own death. Baldr's mother, Frigg, travels through the nine worlds and gets all the earth-things, sea-things, and sky-things to pledge an oath not to harm her son.

At social gatherings, the gods make sport of testing the power of Baldr's protection, and they throw things at him. Not a single pebble, stick, pointed dart, or stone ever harms Baldr, nor do strikes from axes or slashes from swords.

The mischievous god LOKI observes the gods' pastime and is sickened to see that Baldr is never injured. Loki goes to Frigg disguised as a CRONE, and reports that he saw the gods stoning Baldr and demands to know why. When Frigg explains, the crone asks if there is anything at all that can injure Baldr. Frigg answers that she didn't exact an oath from a small mistletoe bush. Loki immediately gets a branch from the mistletoe bush and shapes it into a dart. He joins the gathering of gods and sidles up to Hod, Baldr's blind brother. Loki convinces Hod that he should show respect to Baldr like the other gods, and he offers to guide Hod's hand as he throws the mistletoe branch at Baldr. As soon as the mistletoe dart strikes Baldr, he falls down dead. The other gods begin to grieve while Loki slips away. Hermod, the messenger of the gods, volunteers to go to HEL, ruler of the Norse underworld, and offer her a ransom for Baldr. All night, the gods and goddesses keep a silent vigil around Baldr's gleaming body. In the morning, four of the gods lift Baldr on their shoulders, and all the gods and goddesses proceed to Baldr's boat, Ringhorn, in which they build his funeral pyre. Baldr's wife, Nanna, collapses with grief and dies. Her body is placed next to her husband's on the boat. Odin places his gold ring, Draupnir, on Baldr's breast. Baldr's horse is killed and put on the pyre. After a sign from Odin, the pyre is lit and then blessed by Thor.

Meanwhile, Hermod rides to the hall of Hel where he sees Baldr sitting on a throne. Hermod begs Hel to let Baldr return with him and tells her of the grief of the gods and goddesses. Hel says that if everything in the nine worlds weeps for Baldr, then she will allow him to return to Asgard, home of the gods. But if even one thing does not weep for him, then he will stay with her.

When Hermod reports Hel's conditions for Baldr's return, the gods send messengers to all corners of the nine worlds, asking all to weep Baldr un-dead. On their way home, the messengers pass a giantess in a cave. She refuses to weep for Baldr, and so he remains with Hel. Everyone guesses that the giantess must be Loki. After RAGNAROK, Baldr and Hod will come from Hel to the new home of the gods (*see also* GIANTS).

The story of Baldr is similar to those about Jesus, ATTIS, DIONYSOS, and Adonis, the exceptionally beautiful Greek youth who is fatally wounded by the tusks of a wild boar and must spend six months of every year in the underworld before returning to APHRODITE. The stories about each of these figures stress their deaths, their DESCENTS TO THE UNDERWORLD, the mourning at their loss, and their subsequent RESURRECTIONS.

For Further Reading

Hodges, Margaret, retold by. *Mistletoe: A Myth of the Vikings*. Boston: Little, Brown, 1974.

BALLAD (ANCIENT AND MODERN)

Folk song that tells a story. Modern ballads are often written down, but originally they were part of a strictly oral tradition that was passed from one singer to another. At one time, ballads were probably danced as well as sung or recited; the word *ballad* comes from the Italian *ballare*, to dance. It is uncertain whether ballads were originally composed by a single person or by a community of people, but through years of repetition by innumerable singers with their own creative interpretations, changes in the tune and even the story of the original ballad often came about. Due to this kind of long-term oral transmission, ballads often exist in multiple forms and are continually shifting and evolving. Ballads appear in the oral traditions of nearly every culture, and are considered one to be one of the earlier forms of literature.

Although the term *ballad* encompasses a diverse genre, there are a few characteristics common to nearly all ballads. Ballads usually present a single dramatic episode in a condensed form, and often begin by stating the climax of the story. Simple, direct language is used, with few surrounding details having to do with characterization, description, or imagery of any kind. The story is usually related by means of swift and intense action and dialogue, with abrupt transitions between stanzas. The narrator is distanced, impersonal, and does not intrude on the story with any personal commentary or bias. Supernatural forces or creatures (such as fairies) often play a major role in the action of the ballad. Although there are some comic ballads, most present a situation that is tragic in some way. Episodes often address issues and themes such as love, death, war, courage, passion, violence, crime, the return of the dead or an absent lover, adultery, jealousy, rivalry, and sometimes historical events or personages. Ballads rarely incorporate a moral theme; instead, they focus entirely on the event that took place and leave the interpretation of that event to the listener.

Ballads make use of several formulaic structures that help the singer remember the song. For example, clichés and common descriptive phrases are often used, such as hair that is "golden" or "nut-brown," wine that is "blood-red," and skin that is "milk-white." Many ballads have refrains, which echo the dominant feeling or detail of the verse. Ballads also may use what is called *incremental repetition,* the repeating of a line or stanza with the addition of action or dialogue that moves the story forward. The most common stanza form, called the ballad stanza, contains four lines of alternating four-stress and three-stress lines. The last syllable of the second and fourth lines nearly always rhyme.

Distinctions have been made between the more traditional folk ballad and the literary ballad. Folk ballads are always anonymous; they are transmitted orally and commonly flourish among illiterate or semi-literate people who live in rural environments. This form of ballad remains popular today in places such as northern Greece, the central Balkans, the West Indies, Iceland, rural Australia, the island of Sicily, the southern Appalachian mountains, and the plains of the American West. Literary ballads are narrative poems that are written down as they are composed; they deliberately imitate the form and language of the traditional ballad. Literary ballads, including John Keats's "La Belle Dame sans Merci" and Samuel Taylor Coleridge's "Rime of the Ancient Mariner," are often longer and more elaborate than traditional folk ballads.

Ballads survive in a more modern popular form as well. Folk singers such as Bob Dylan (*see* DYLAN, BOB) and Joan Baez compose and sing songs in the ballad tradition. Their ballads, however, relate most closely to the tradition of broadside ballads, or street ballads. First made popular in sixteenth-century England, broadside ballads were narrative songs that were printed on one side of a sheet of paper (a "broadside") and sold cheaply. These ballads are associated with more literate, urban populations than are traditional folk ballads; they were sung to a common tune and told the story of a particular current event or issue. Unlike folk ballads, they were not necessarily heroic or tragic; in fact, they often took satirical or comic looks at the news of the day.

Ballads survive in several forms in today's music scene. Contemporary folk music festivals nearly always include the performance of both traditional and modern ballads. The ballad form also appears in popular music, including the songs of Irving Berlin ("Blue Skies," "How Deep is the Ocean," and others), the Beatles ("Hey Jude" and others), Billy Joel, Elton John, and perhaps especially in story-based COUNTRY MUSIC BALLADS AND SONGS.

BANSHEE

Female Gaelic DEATH spirit, whose keening is believed to foretell a death in a family. The word *banshee,* or *bean si* in Gaelic, means "fairy woman." A banshee has long streaming hair and wears a green dress covered by a gray cloak. A single wailing banshee signifies a death of a member of one of the old families, while a group of keening banshees presages the death of a holy or great personage. A banshee's eyes are bright red from constant weeping, and in the Scottish Highlands she is known to wash the grave-clothes of a person who is near death. In Scotland, the banshee is called *bean-nighe,* and believed to be the ghost of a woman who has died in childbirth. The Irish banshee is believed to be more beautiful than the Scottish, who has only one large and protruding front tooth, one nostril, and long, hanging breasts.

A mortal may gain a wish from a banshee by sneaking up on her while she is occupied with her wailing and washing— if one can suck on her long breast, one can declare oneself to be the banshee's foster child, and thus acquire the wish.

Since the banshee can appear as a beautiful woman foretelling death, she is often associated with the White Ladies of other folklore. She appears in many stories told in Ireland and Scotland. *See also* GHOST STORIES.

For Further Reading

Campbell, John Francis. *Superstitions of the Highlands and Islands of Scotland.* Glasgow: J. MacLehose, 1900.

McGowan, Hugh. *Leprechauns, Legends, and Irish Tales.* Illustrated by Peter Haigh. London: Gallancy Children's Paperback, 1988.

BARDS

Poet singers of national or cultural epics. The word *bard* is of distinctly Celtic origin but is commonly used to refer to singing storytellers of diverse backgrounds. Most often, bards were also musicians and accompanied their tales with harps and other instruments. The earliest examples of bards come from HOMER and the Sanskrit scriptures. There are classic accounts of Celtic bards, but the term disappears between the fifth and thirteenth centuries.

By the thirteenth century, bards had become professionalized. In Ireland, the highest ranking bards were called *ollam,* and the mere bard occupied the lowest position in the complex hierarchy of singer historians. The *ollams'* privileges were written into Irish law: the *ollam* were allowed to wear more colors than all but royalty and were followed by a large retinue. An *ollam* would often have his own official chair at court and was in the direct employ of a KING or noble. In Wales, the *pencerdd* enjoyed similar advantages. He was considered one of the king's officers and was given a set share of the spoils of war. Lesser ranked bards tended to be wandering storytellers not connected to particular households. Unlike the *ollam* and *pencerdd,* these bards sang popular folk stories rather than of noble HEROES and kingly conquests.

Early Anglo-Saxons called their bards *scops* and *gleoman*. BEOWULF tells of a *scop* entertaining a chieftain. The *scop* drew upon his experience as a traveler to converse on many topics, but he would also be expected to perform the epic poems. The Norse and Icelandic traditions specifically link the *scops* (called *skalds*) to poetry rather than prose storytelling. By the fourteenth century, the terms "minstrel" and "bard" had replaced the earlier *scop* and *gleoman* in the English language. Minstrels were often skilled acrobats as well as storytellers and increasingly, minstrels became more connected to public meeting places such as church festivals. The types of stories performed changed as minstrels interacted less with the nobility and more with the common folk—the heroic epic was replaced by saints' stories and FOLKTALES.

A strong bardic tradition can be traced throughout Europe. Other forms of bards existed in Africa, the Americas, and Asia. Bards were the primary historians in pre- or semi-literate cultures. However, the significance of bards waned as they were replaced by other mediums of communication. The rise of the printed word allowed history, poetry, and travel accounts to be collected for posterity, making the bards' ritualized memorization redundant. *See also* BALLAD, CELTIC STORYTELLING.

BARING-GOULD, SABINE (1834–1924)

British schoolmaster, writer, and folklorist. As ordained priest of the Church of England and author of over a hundred books, Baring-Gould believed that his most important work was in the field of religious history, in which he published such books as *The Origin and Development of Religious Belief* (1869) and *The Lives of the Saints* (1870). Posterity may have proven him wrong, however, as some of his work in religion has been highly criticized, while his work in FOLKLORE has proven extremely valuable to folklorists. Among these works were numerous collections of folk songs of the West Country of England. In *A Book of the West* (1899), *Collected Folk Songs and Ballads of Devon and Cornwall* (1890),

and *Songs of the West* (1905), Baring-Gould records various songs from the oral tradition of the areas surrounding Devon, where he resided for most of his life. In addition to his folk song collections, Baring-Gould published critical works such as *Curious Myths of the Middle Ages* (1866), where he explores the origins and historical veracity of myths including the tale of William Tell and those of the Wandering Jew (*see* TELL, WILLIAM). In 1865, he explored the mythology of the WEREWOLF in *The Book of Werewolves*.

BASCOM, WILLIAM (1916–1981)

British anthropologist known for analyzing FOLKLORE genres for their function. The search for folklore's purpose in the 1940s and 1950s came to be known as *functionalism*. Bascom defined this search with his extremely influential article entitled "The Four Functions of Folklore." His ideas originated in the teachings of Melville Herskovits (*see* HERSKOVITS, MELVILLE) who had, in turn, been taught by Franz Boas (*see* BOAS, FRANZ). Once folklorists began to question the purpose of the historic geographic method functionalism's popularity increased. The scholars who used this new trend believed that viewing the function of a tale, rather than its origins or patterns of DIFFUSION, gave insight into the culture that produced it.

The first of Bascom's four functions is "escape from reality." He believed that FOLKTALES allow listeners to vicariously leave the weaknesses of their mortal bodies, the restrictions of societal constraints, and the limits of geographical boundaries. These tales often provide tension release by showing the listener a fantasy world where people participate in taboo acts with superhuman form. The second function, often expressed in the form of MYTH, is to "validate and justify" one's culture and RITUALS. Myths are stories that explain how and why worldly objects and events came to be. These tales are told as reminders, reinforcers, and defenders of the status quo. The third function is education. Through the telling of fables the young are taught the morals and values held by the community, while RIDDLES sharpen their wits. The last function is to convince the listener to "maintain conformity" to accepted patterns of behavior. For example, PROVERBS often show disapproval of those who don't conform and provide social approval of those who do. Bascom's functionalist synthesis gave a heightened honor to folklore by deeming it a necessary factor in the maintenance of a culture's stability.

BAUER, CAROLINE FELLER (1935–)

Librarian, puppeteer, storyteller, and television producer. Caroline Feller was born in Washington, DC, in 1935. She obtained a B.A. from Sarah Lawrence College 1957, an M.S. from Columbia in 1958, and a Ph.D. from the University of Oregon in 1971.

From 1958 to 1961, she worked as a children's librarian at the New York Public Library, and in 1966 became an Associate Professor of Library Science at the University of Oregon. For two years in the early seventies, she worked on the adaptation of children's stories for television at KOAP television in Portland, Oregon, and made videos showing how to tell stories.

Her publications include *Children's Literature: A Teletext* (1973), *Handbook for Storytellers* (1977), *Getting it Together with Books* (1974), and *Caroline's Corner* (1978). A member of the Society of American Magicians and Puppeteers of America, Bauer is interested in the visual and performative aspects of storytelling.

BAUMAN, RICHARD (1940–)

Folklore scholar in the 1960s who revolutionized the discipline of FOLKLORE by changing the focus of analysis from text to performance. During the 1960s the field of folklore was saturated with Ph.D. students who asserted new ideas and criticized old. Bauman was one of these new scholars, coined the "Young Turks," who were major critics of the historic geographic method of study. Bauman believed this method, ignoring everything but the written word while mapping and classifying texts according to geographic location in a scientific fashion, isolated texts and elements of texts. He asserted that this item-oriented approach—the study of folklore as a collection of texts with little or no contextual documentation—was incomplete and occasionally misleading. The performance theory looked at the context of the folklore item being studied, including the teller, the tale, the audience, and the occasion. Bauman and his colleagues also noted that due to the inherent nature of performance, each time a tale was told, or a folk song was sung, it was new. Thus, the text is not static and does not exist as a reality on paper, but rather is emergent with interpretation and audience. Because of Bauman's assertions, whole events surrounding storytelling or folk singing were documented, instead of a simple recording of the narration. Bauman's performance theories are best described in *Toward New Perspectives in Folklore,* a work he published with Americo Paredes in 1972 (*see* PAREDES, AMERICO).

BAUSINGER, HERMANN (1927–)

German academic and folklorist. Born in Aalen in 1927, Bausinger achieved his doctorate in 1952. He heads the Ludwig-Uhland Institut für Empirische Kulturwissenschaft (Cultural Studies Institute) and is the author of numerous books on FOLKLORE and more than one hundred essays in specialist journals. His books include *Folkculture in a Technological World,* which explores modern adaptations of residual folk forms and narratives, and *Forms of Folk Poetry,* which outlines the transmutations of forms such as the BALLAD and the FABLE. He is arguably the leading German folklorist of the twentieth century.

BEAR MAN MYTH

Cherokee Indian MYTH of a bear as a resurrected god. In this myth, a hunter tries to kill what appears to him as a wounded bear, but he is unable to kill it for it is a "medicine bear." It has the power to read the thoughts of or talk to a person without actually uttering a word. The hunter follows the bear until the bear turns to him, offering the arrows from his side to the hunter. He then invites the man to come to his home and live with him where there will be sufficient food.

Before the bear takes the hunter to his home, however, he brings him to a council of bears who are meeting in a cave. The bears discuss food shortages and where there is an abundance of acorns and chestnuts. Although they are nervous about the hunter's presence, the bear who accompanies the hunter tells them to leave him alone. Then the bears have a DANCE, and after the dance they attempt to use the hunter's bow and arrows, but they are incapable of making them function. Finally, the bear takes the hunter to his own home where he produces food by rubbing his stomach with his forepaws; every time he rubs he produces huckleberries, blackberries, and chestnuts so the man always has plenty to eat.

The hunter continues to live with the bear all winter. His hair grows long and he begins to grow hair on his body as well. His actions come to resemble those of a bear, but he still walks on two legs like a man. The bear, who can read the thoughts of humans, tells the man that other men will soon be coming to hunt and will kill him (the bear) but will take the hunter home. He directs the hunter to cover the blood of his dismembered body with leaves and to look back at the leaves as the hunter departs with the other men. Indeed, the other hunters arrive, kill the bear, skin him, and cut him up in quarters. They find the long-haired hunter and take him home with them, but first, the hunter covers the bear's blood with leaves. When he looks back at the spot, he sees his friend the bear rise up out of the leaves and return to the woods.

The RESURRECTION of the bear in this myth is similar to the resurrection of the Egyptian god Osiris (*see* ISIS and OSIRIS) and the Blackfoot Indian god, Kutoyis, both of whom first undergo dismemberment. As David Leeming notes, the bear myth "is surely the result of early man's fascination with an ANIMAL which in the winter descended into the earth only to rise again in the spring." This cyclical repetition represents the vegetation cycle as in the Greek myth of Demeter and Persephone (*see* PERSEPHONE MYTH, DISMEMBERMENT OF PRIMORDIAL BEING).

BEAUTY AND THE BEAST

Story of a MARRIAGE between a beast—actually a PRINCE who has been transformed by magic—and a beautiful young woman. The beast is returned to his true appearance by the woman's love. It was first recorded in a sixteenth-century Italian collection of FAIRY TALES and popularized by Charles Perrault (*see* PERRAULT, CHARLES) in the late seventeenth century. The most familiar version, by Madame Leprince de Beaumont, was published in 1757.

Beauty is the youngest daughter of an impoverished merchant. When the father has hopes of regaining his fortune, Beauty's two older sisters demand expensive presents. Beauty asks only for a rose. When the merchant, still poor, stops at a garden to pick the rose, he is accosted by a MONSTER who accuses him of theft. The Beast declares that the unfortunate man must either forfeit his life or give up his daughter. To save her father, Beauty goes to live with the Beast. He treats her well, and she grows fond of him. One day she finds the Beast apparently dead and confesses her love for him. The spell is broken, Beauty and the handsome prince are married, and they live happily ever after.

The story of CUPID AND PSYCHE may have been the foundation for the European version of the tale. Evil sisters are found in many other fairy tales, notably "CINDERELLA." The GRIMM BROTHERS's "Frog Prince" features the undoing of an enchantment through the aid of a beautiful woman.

In some European FOLKTALES, the roles are reversed: a handsome knight breaks the enchantment for an ugly hag often called the "loathly lady," revealing her as a beautiful maiden. One example is a tale from the Arthurian cycle, in which SIR GAWAIN rescues the lady.

In some stories, Beauty is a foundling with a wicked stepmother (*see* STEPMOTHER—WICKED). In early versions, the father is trapped by a promise to give up the first thing that greets him when he returns home, like Jephthah in the BIBLE. The primary fear in early versions is that the Beast will devour the Beauty, but in the MOTHER GOOSE and other versions the focus was changed to the issue of marriage. In a 1740 version by Madame de Villeneuve, Beauty muses about the misfortune of girls compelled to marry rich brutes—a forceful statement for the time.

The Beast is cursed because of his own or another's lust, or because of evil fairies. In the earlier stories, he is vaguely described as repellent and sometimes given an elephant trunk or clanking scales. Still uncouth in nature, he later takes on the more definite form of a serpent, bear, frog, cat, donkey, wolf, pig, or some other ANIMAL.

In *From the Beast to the Blonde,* Marina Warner notes a difference in modern stories. In Jean Cocteau's 1946 film, *"He* does not have to change at all, except in outward shape; *she* has to see past his unsightliness to the gentle and loving human being trapped inside." In the 1987 CBS television series, the Beast does not even change outwardly. And in fact, the Beast of the 1991 Disney movie seems more appealing to many viewers than the handsome prince he becomes.

Italo Calvino (*see* CALVINO, ITALO) tells the story as "Bellinda and the Monster." The theme is pervasive in romances, from Charlotte Bronte's *Jane Eyre* to today's mass-market novels. Nancy Willard's sophisticated 1992 retelling of the tale is set in the early twentieth century and illustrated with woodcuts by Barry Moser. Like many other tales passed down from oral traditions, the story of Beauty and the Beast has been adjusted along with cultural norms. Nevertheless, the resonance of its basic theme has kept the tale alive across the centuries.

For Further Reading

Hearne, Betsy. *Beauties and Beasts.* The Oryx Multicultural Folktale Series. Phoenix: Oryx Press, 1993.

Warner, Marina. *From the Beast to the Blonde: On Fairy Tales and Their Tellers.* New York: Farrar, Straus, Giroux, 1995.

Willard, Nancy. *Beauty and the Beast.* Illustrated by Barry Moser. New York: Harcourt Brace Jovanovich, 1992.

BECHSTEIN, LUDWIG (1801–1860)

German librarian, writer and compiler. After studying pharmacy and medicine, Bechstein studied philosophy, history, and literature in Leipzig and Munich. He then returned to his home town of Meiningen to become the librarian at the ducal library there. In 1848, he founded the Henneberg Antiquarian Society and built up and administered its archive. He wrote poems and historical romances and novels (*Fahrten eines Musikanten,* 3 vols. 1836/7). He is best known as the compiler and publisher of collections of folk sayings and tales—*Deutsches Marchenbuch* (1845)—which built on the work of the GRIMM BROTHERS, but placed greater emphasis on folk wisdom in the form of proverbial sayings.

BENFEY, THEODOR (1809–1881)

German philologist, translator, and folklorist. Benfey was born in 1809 and learned Hebrew early in life. From 1824 to 1828, he studied Classical Philology at Göttingen, Munich, Frankfurt, and Heidelberg, and from 1829 to 1830 , he was a lecturer in Classical Philology at the University of Göttingen. After a brief sojourn in Heidelberg, he returned to Göttingen, where he studied Sanskrit and related languages. From 1861 until his death in 1881, he taught Oriental Philology at Göttingen. He is particularly well-known for his 1859 German translation of PANCHATANTRA. From 1862–1866, he published the periodical *Orient and Occident.* He produced far-reaching work on Sanskrit and Oriental Philology, including a number of dictionaries, and is considered to have laid the groundwork for comparative folklore studies by tracing the westward migration of Indian FOLKTALES.

BEOWULF

Anglo-Saxon EPIC poem; the earliest surviving heroic epic written in English. The poem is regarded as a great masterpiece of Anglo-Saxon literature, but little is known about the author or the circumstances of its composition. Scholars disagree about when the poem was composed; the years between A.D. 700 and A.D. 850 seem to be the most likely approximations, and the surviving *Beowulf* manuscript was written in about A.D. 1000. *Beowulf* is a profoundly important text because it offers rare and valuable insight into the traditions, values, rituals, and culture of the Anglo-Saxons. Although an essentially pagan story, modern scholars recognize the influence of the Christian tradition that had already taken root in England at the time of the epic's creation.

Beowulf is primarily a story of bloody and heroic battles fought against evil forces, but embedded in the accounts of war are examples of honor and virtue that reveal a great deal about cultural ideals in Anglo-Saxon England. The story, set probably in the sixth century, explains that for twelve years a vicious monster named Grendel has terrorized the land and people of Hrothgar, KING of the Danes. In time, a brave and noble warrior, Beowulf of the Geats, arrives in Denmark to rid Hrothgar of his nemesis. The Danes welcome Beowulf with a great celebration, but after the festivities are over, Grendel invades the hall where the soldiers sleep. Beowulf deeply wounds Grendel by twisting his arm off; Grendel flees in terror and pain.

The following night, the monster's vengeful mother appears at the hall and abducts a sleeping warrior. The next day, Hrothgar leads Beowulf and his men to the marsh in which Grendel and his mother live. Beowulf bravely swims to the bottom of the marsh and into the monsters' den. He seizes a sword hanging from the wall and with it slays both the injured Grendel and his mother. Taking the sword and Grendel's severed head, Beowulf swims back up to the surface. On the way, the shaft of the sword disintegrates, but the hilt remains intact. Beowulf presents the sword hilt and the head of the monster as gifts to Hrothgar at a celebratory feast.

Having secured the safety of the Danes, the noble Beowulf returns to his home among the Geats. In time, he becomes king of his people and is considered by all to be a just and generous ruler. One day, one of his war-

riors stumbles upon a treasure-trove belonging to a fierce DRAGON. The man steals a golden goblet to present to Beowulf; as a result, the enraged dragon devastates the kingdom. Although he is rather old, Beowulf leads his warriors in the attack on the dragon. At first, Beowulf's mighty sword seems to have no effect on the powerful dragon; all but one of his soldiers flee from the battle in fear. Only the brave Wiglaf remains, and with his help Beowulf kills the dragon. But Beowulf can not survive the wounds the dragon had dealt him, and so, in his last act on earth, he bestows upon his most loyal soldier the gold collar of a king. Beowulf's ashes are buried with the dragon's treasure, and all the Geats mourn their beloved protector and king.

For generations, the epic tale of *Beowulf* was preserved by BARDS through the tradition of oral storytelling. Certain Anglo-Saxon poetic conventions (including a particular form of alliteration) helped storytellers to memorize and then recite thousands of lines of the story to crowds of non-literate listeners. *Beowulf* is an important example of early English storytelling not only for its elements of Christian ALLEGORY, but also for the poet's portrayals of honor, fidelity, and courage (as well as cowardice) in battle. Through the story of *Beowulf*, modern readers can gain a better understanding of which character traits and behaviors were honored among the Anglo-Saxons and which were condemned. Among the most important of these were the sacred relationships between warriors and their lord, and between kinsmen. Further, some of the important cultural rituals of Anglo-Saxon life (feasts, celebrations, battles, funerals) come alive through the poet's depiction of the adventures of perhaps the greatest and certainly the earliest warrior-hero in the tradition of English literature.

For Further Reading

Clark, George. *Beowulf*. Boston: Twayne Publishers, 1990.

Fry, Donald K. *The Beowulf Poet: A Collection of Essays*. Englewood Cliffs, NJ: Prentice Hall, 1968.

Hill, John M. *The Cultural World in Beowulf*. Toronto: University of Toronto Press, 1995.

Raffel, Burton, trans. *Beowulf*. New York: Mentor Books, 1963.

BETHEL

Holy place in the Old Testament where GOD speaks to Jacob. In the Book of Genesis (*see* GENESIS, BOOK OF), Jacob is traveling when he stops for the night at a certain shrine. At this shrine are twelve stones, representing the twelve tribes of Israel. The twelve stones become one, and Jacob uses the stone as a pillow and goes to sleep. He dreams that he sees a ladder extending from the ground to HEAVEN, and angels of God ascend and descend the ladder. God speaks to Jacob, promising to give him and his descendants the land on which Jacob is lying. God says that Jacob's family will be very large, and all other families will wish to be blessed as Jacob's. He promises to protect Jacob and bring him back to that land. Jacob is astounded by this experience, and he realizes that he is at God's house and the entrance to heaven. In the morning, he uses the stone pillow on which he slept to construct a sacred pillar to the gateway to heaven. He names the place *Bethel,* meaning "house of God." Later, Jacob builds an altar to God at Bethel.

In storytelling traditions, ladders to heaven most often signify the center of the world and a place of communication with the divine (the *axis mundi)*; as such, they serve the same purpose as sacred mountains and are another version of the world navel (*see* MERU, MOUNT OLYMPOS, MOUNT PARNASSOS, MOUNT SINAI).

Likewise, the stone pillar that Jacob erects, marking "the house of God" and "the gate of heaven," is similar to the *ka'ba* at MECCA and the *omphalos* stone at DELPHI. All are sacred stones marking the center of the world and the entrance to heaven.

Other important stones in storytelling traditions include the Agdos Rock, ERATHIPA, the rock from which King ARTHUR pulls his sword, and the rock from under which THESEUS removes his sword and sandals. *See also* LADDER TO ANOTHER WORLD OR HEAVEN

BETTELHEIM, BRUNO (1903–1989)

Vienna-born Freudian analyst who contributed important work on the meaning of FAIRY TALES for children. After being held prisoner in the Nazi concentration camps of Dachau and Buchenwald, Bruno Bettelheim escaped from the Nazi-occupied portion of Europe and settled in the United States in 1939.

Bettelheim's *The Uses of Enchantment: The Meaning of and Importance of Fairy Tales* (1976) is a major contemporary contribution to understanding fairy tales and their influence on children and adults. He is also the coauthor with Karen Zelan of *On Learning to Read: The Child's Fascination with Meaning,* an evaluation of reading primers and their effects on children.

In *The Uses of Enchantment,* Bettelheim shows how fairy tales play a necessary role in allowing children to experience their emotional needs and helping them in the process of individuation. In his analysis of the story "The Fisherman and the Jinny," Bettelheim discusses the differences between fairy tales and FABLES, he explores Freud's concept of the "pleasure principle" versus the "reality principle" as it appears in "The Three Little Pigs," and he examines the frame story of *Thousand and One Nights* as well as one of its tales, "Sindbad the Seaman and Sindbad the Porter," along with "Tales of Two Brothers." Among the other themes Bettelheim explores are "The Youngest Child as Simpleton," "The Knight in Shining Armor and the Damsel in Distress," why fairy tales were outlawed, "Achieving Autonomy," "The Animal-Groom Cycle of Fairy Tales," and "On the Telling of Fairy Stories." His insights into "Hansel and Gretel," "Little RED RIDING HOOD," "JACK AND THE BEANSTALK," "Snow White," "Goldilocks and the Three Bears," "The Sleeping Beauty," and "CINDERELLA" reveal how these tales embody aspects of each stage of the child's psychological development. *See also* ANUBIS AND BATA, YOUNGEST BROTHER.

For Further Reading

Bettelheim, Bruno. *The Uses of Enchantment.* New York: Alfred A. Knopf, 1976.

Pollak. *The Creation of Dr. Bettelheim.* New York: Simon and Schuster, 1996.

BIBLE

Sacred books of Judaism and Christianity. Usually divided into the Old Testament, or

Hebrew Bible, and the New Testament, or Christian Bible, different versions and translations of the Bible exist, and there are significant differences between such versions as the King James Bible and the Jerusalem Bible. Depending on the religion, different formats of the Bible have been considered correct.

The Hebrew canon consists of twenty-four books, which are broken into three groups. The first group is called The Law, or Torah, and includes the Book of Genesis (*see* GENESIS, BOOK OF), EXODUS, Leviticus, Numbers, and Deuteronomy. The second group, called Prophets, consists of the books of the Former Prophets, Joshua, Judges, Samuel, and Kings, and the books of the Latter Prophets, Isaiah, Jeremiah, Ezekiel, and the Twelve Prophets. The third group is called the Writings, and consists of Psalms, Proverbs, Job, Song of Songs, Ruth, Lamentations, Ecclesiastes, Esther, Daniel, Ezra-Nehemiah, and Chronicles. Samuel, Kings, the Twelve Prophets, Ezra-Nehemiah, and Chronicles are each considered one book.

The New Testament, which focuses on the life and teachings of Jesus Christ, begins with the gospels of Matthew, Mark, Luke, and John, followed by Acts, Romans, I Corinthians, II Corinthians, Galatians, Ephesians, Philippians, Colossians, I Thessalonians, II Thessalonians, I Timothy, II Timothy, Titus, Philemon, Hebrews, James, I Peter, II Peter, I John, II John, III John, Jude, and Revelation. Many of the PARABLES that have become part of oral tradition appear in the New Testament's four Gospels: the parables of "The Good Samaritan" and "The Prodigal Son" are found in Luke (*see* PARABLES OF JESUS).

Many of the Hebrew Bible's stories have become part of the storytelling tradition; for example, the well-known stories of ADAM AND EVE and the Garden of Eden, Cain and Abel, the Great FLOOD and NOAH's Ark, Abraham's sacrifice of Isaac, and Joseph and the coat of many colors, all of which appear in Genesis Stories about Moses and the parting of the Red Sea, the Ten Commandments, and the Israelites' sojourn in the desert appear in Exodus. Later books recount the famous stories

of King David, King Solomon, Ruth and Naomi, Job, Jonah and the whale, and Esther. These biblical tales have encouraged many retellings, embellishments, and transformations. The Cain and Abel story engendered Tobias Wolff's short story "The Rich Brother" and John Steinbeck's novel *East of Eden*; the story of Noah's Ark provided the source for Isaac Bashevis Singer's children's book *Why Noah Chose the Dove* (see SINGER, ISAAC BASHEVIS) and Robert Coover's transformation of Noah into the short story, "The Brother." In Soren Kierkegaard's *Fear and Trembling*, different versions of the story of Abraham and Isaac are offered, and the singer, songwriter, and poet Leonard Cohen has composed a song called "The Story of Isaac." Similarly, many retellings and transformations of the New Testament can be found, such as Nikos Kazantzakis's novel *The Last Temptation of Christ*.

For Further Reading

The Jerusalem Bible. New York: Doubleday, 1966.

Metzger, Bruce M., and Michael D. Coogan. *The Oxford Companion to the Bible*. New York: Oxford, 1993.

Singer, Isaac Bashevis. *Why Noah Chose the Dove*. Translated by Elizabeth Shub. Illustrated by Eric Carle. New York: Farrar, Straus, Giroux 1979.

BIRTH *See* HIDING THE CHILD

BLACK ELK (c. 1860–1950)

Holy man of the Oglala Sioux. Black Elk was born in the 1860s and died in 1950. He participated in the victory of the Sioux at Little Big Horn in 1876, and was close at hand during their defeat at Wounded Knee in 1890.

Black Elk's life and thought were first brought to public attention with the 1932 publication of *Black Elk Speaks,* by John Neihardt. In it, Black Elk tells Neihardt his life story, revealing much about Sioux culture during the last half of the nineteenth century—village and family life, religious RITUAL, and philosophy. He also describes an extraordinary shamanic vision that he experienced as a young man (*see* SHAMAN). Historical figures such as Crazy Horse, Buffalo Bill Cody, and George Armstrong Custer all appear in the episodes of Black Elk's life. In addition, Black Elk describes the messianic Ghost Dance religion that Native Americans followed during the last part of the nineteenth century. He tells how this religion culminated in the destruction of Native American hopes during the massacre of the Sioux at Wounded Knee.

Sixteen years after *Black Elk Speaks* was published, author Joseph Epes Brown also sought out Black Elk. In Brown's book *The Sacred Pipe* (1953), Black Elk describes traditional ceremonies of the Oglala Sioux.

In Neihardt's and Brown's books, Black Elk is presented as a nineteenth-century figure, a tragic representative of a dying culture. But in the 1993 publication *Black Elk: Holy Man of the Oglala,* Michael F. Steltenkamp writes that in 1904, Black Elk converted to Catholicism. He began to serve as a missionary to his own people and felt that his spiritual agony was replaced by a new enjoyment of existence. *See also* NATIVE NORTH AMERICAN STORYTELLING.

For Further Reading

Brown, Joseph Epes. *The Sacred Pipe: Black Elk's Account of the Seven Rites of the Oglala Sioux.* Norman, OK: University of Oklahoma Press, 1971.

Neihardt, John G. *Black Elk Speaks: Being the Life Story of a Holy Man of the Oglala Sioux.* Lincoln, NE: University of Nebraska Press, 1961.

Steltenkamp, Michael F. *Black Elk: Holy Man of the Oglala.* Norman, OK: University of Oklahoma Press, 1993.

BLANKET LIZARD

Australian aboriginal tale about the man, Blanket Lizard, who was swallowed by the RAINBOW SNAKE and whose LEGEND explains the appearance of blanket lizards, known for the spectacular frill around their necks, in northern Australia today. This tale belongs to a tradition of stories that explains the appearance of certain animals (*see* JUST SO STORIES, AESOP, OSEBO'S DRUM).

A man named Blanket Lizard came from the southeast. As he walked, he planted trees. He ate kangaroos, yams, and wild honey.

Whenever he felt weak, he painted himself all over with red ochre. To stop headaches, he tied lots of soft, cold bush twine around his head. Blanket Lizard walked in the soft sand along the creeks because it didn't hurt his feet.

Finally he came to the place he sought, and he made his home in a cave. However, he had no water. He tried to dig a well, but with no success. Then he used a very long stick to dig, and water appeared in the hole. The water did not stop flowing, and it spread everywhere. The water was sent by the Rainbow Snake, who was angry because Blanket Lizard had poked her with his stick. Finally, she swallowed Blanket Lizard. All of his things were drowned, and eventually turned to stone.

Before he died, Blanket Lizard proclaimed that he would turn himself into stone. He would leave his spirit at that spot, which he named *Gundamen-bo-wurkmeng,* meaning "Blanket Lizard poked the ground for water." Blanket Lizard turned to stone, and left red ochre at the place where he put his spirit.

Australian blanket lizards have reddish skin like ochre. They also have magnificent frills splotched with pink, black, brown, and white around their necks, similar to the large bush twine dressings the legendary man Blanket Lizard tied around his head.

BLUEBEARD

Villain prominent in EUROPEAN STORYTELLING and FOLKTALES. Bluebeard is the literary creation of Charles Perrault (*see* PERRAULT, CHARLES), so named for the unusual blue color of his beard. Bluebeard is generally seen as a member of the nobility or of the wealthy merchant class of European society. Bluebeard is not a paragon of gentility but rather a misogynist created in the MOTIF of the murderous husband. In many of the Bluebeard tales, Bluebeard marries a number of women (usually sisters) who mysteriously disappear or die as the result of failing to resist the temptation of opening the door to Bluebeard's secret chamber. Eventually, Bluebeard marries the youngest and only remaining sister or eligible woman, who consequently discovers the corpses of his previous wives in the locked castle chamber. The last bride succeeds in vanquishing Bluebeard, either by means of deception or from the help she receives from her brothers.

Although Perrault is credited with the creation of Bluebeard, this character has ties to other villainous folk characters, including TROLLS and the DEVIL. The GRIMM BROTHERS, in the 1812 edition of *Nursery and Household Tales*, include the story of "Blaubart," perhaps wanting to emphasize the devotion between a sister and her brothers. However, deeming that the story was as a whole too gruesome for a children's audience, the Grimms replaced "Blaubart" with a tale about the Virgin MARY in later editions.

For Further Reading

Perrault, Charles. *Perrault's Fairy Tales.* Translated by Sasha Moorsom. Illustrated by Landa Crommelynck. Garden City, NY: Doubleday: 1972.

BLUES

Musical form of oral storytelling, uniquely African American in its origin. Blues music originated on the cotton plantations of the South during the 1890s, then came to fruition in the ghettoes of urban America over the following four decades. Illuminating the emotional life and social consciousness of African Americans, the Blues developed from black FOLKLORE and traditional song formats, revamping spiritual and secular folk songs, WORK SONGS, *arhoolies,* BALLADS, and tales of African American HEROES and ANIMAL TRICKSTERS.

By embracing a dissonance not found in European American songs, the Blues provide a subversive sound of cultural resistance, focusing on the lives of African Americans under oppressive conditions, chronicling the working and living conditions, prison experiences, travels, and relationships. Blues songs fall into two categories: cautionary folktales, which offer ways to survive in a hostile social environment, and songs of self-assertion, full of pride and heroic conquests.

Early rural pioneers in the Mississippi Delta, such as Robert Johnson and Son House; and in East Texas, such as "Ragtime Texas" Henry Thomas, Blind Lemon Jefferson, and Leadbelly, helped to establish the Blues' unique chord progression. Blues migrated with those fleeing exploitation into urban centers such as St. Louis, Memphis, Chicago, New Orleans, and Detroit, as early as the turn of the century. As the Blues rose in popularity, and with the advent of recorded music, many urban pioneers, such as Bessie Smith, Ma Rainey, W.C. Handy, Sonny Boy Williamson, the Memphis Jug Band, and Jelly Roll Morton, often faced exploitation by the white-owned recording industry. However, their efforts to record their music preserved it in its rawest, truest forms, providing a wealth of early Blues music still available today.

More modern artists, such as Muddy Waters, Junior Wells, Little Walter, John Lee Hooker, Etta James, and Howlin' Wolf brought the Blues into the electric age and even enjoyed "crossover" success into white American audiences, eventually allowing the Blues to achieve the mainstream, cross-cultural success it enjoys today.

BOAS, FRANZ (1858–1942)

Early twentieth century scholar who revolutionized the study of anthropology with the concept of cultural relativism. Boas believed that the strongheld theory of his day, Social Darwinism, was inherently ethnocentric in its hierarchical use of terms like "savage" and "barbaric." Boas's relativistic view promoted understanding each culture within its own unique context, not in relation to Western civilization. In this light, he felt that FOLKTALES could be read as cultural autobiographies. Boas also rejected the current emphasis on analysis rather than collection. Referring to Darwinists as "armchair fieldworkers" who theorized about cultures from afar, Boas entered the field directly and recorded as many tales as possible. He felt that the non-European cultures he studied were in danger of dying, and it was the race against time that made collection, not analysis, to be of utmost importance. Boas founded the first anthropology department in the United States at Columbia University and gave the American

Folklore Society an anthropological foundation for the first half-century of its existence. Called "Papa Franz" by his students, he taught the first generation of professional American anthropologists, including Margaret Mead, Zora Neale Hurston, and Melville, Herskivits (*see* HURSTON, ZORA NEALE; HERSKIVITS, MELVILLE). Studying the development and dissemination of folktales and mythology, Boas's lasting influence lies in the importance of systematically collected and accurately recorded objective fieldwork.

BODHI TREE

Sacred tree under which the BUDDHA attains enlightenment. Like the cross of the Christian tradition, the Bodhi tree represents the pinnacle of self-denial and the access point to higher consciousness. In fact, the parallels with the Christian "tree" extend to the practice of relic gathering and veneration. Pieces of the Bodhi tree are said to exist in temples throughout Asia, just as pieces of the true cross lend holiness to the Christian cathedrals. Similarly, Buddhist tradition holds that seeds from the original Bodhi tree have been planted and cultivated at other temples.

The veneration of the Bodhi tree emerges from its association with the purity and inner light of the Buddha. In the story of his enlightenment, the Buddha sits immovable beneath the Bodhi tree, refusing to leave until he has received illumination. Recognizing that the Buddha will soon attain his goal, the DEMON Mara takes three forms to move him from the tree. In the first, he assumes the form of the demon Desire. His beautiful daughters assemble to tempt the "Blessed One," but the Buddha reaches the stage at which all things merge into all others, and he can make no distinction between Mara's daughters and himself. In his second form, Mara becomes Death and assails the Buddha with fear. The Buddha is no more moved by fear than by lust, so Mara attempts an appeal to his higher nature as the demon of Duty (*dharma*). He calls upon Buddha to reject the selfish life of meditation and fulfill his obligations as a prince, a husband, and a father. Again, however, the Buddha recognizes that all things

are one, and he sees no need for family or political power. To confirm his state of enlightenment, the Buddha touches the earth, and the earth responds that the Buddha has so sacrificed himself that he no longer exists in the traditional sense. All creation, including the elephant Mara rides upon, bows down to the Buddha and the temptations end. Having removed himself from the world of illusions, the Buddha remains under the Bodhi tree for seven days, then stands for seven more days to meditate upon the place of his enlightenment.

In the temptation of the Buddha under the Bodhi tree, we see the cosmic and spiritual centers of the universe. Like Christ's temptation in the wilderness or in the garden of Gethsemane, the Buddha rejects the demon by recognizing a call higher than obedience to the fleeting, visible world. In the story of the Buddha's enlightenment, the Bodhi tree binds him to a spiritual center where he can transcend the movement of time.

For Further Reading

Cunningham, Sir Alexander. *Mahabodhi, or the Great Buddhist Temple under the Bodhi Tree at Buddha Gaya*. Varanasi: Indological Book House, 1961.

Dahlke, Paul. *Buddhist Stories*. Freeport, NY: Books for Libraries Press, 1970.

BOGEYMAN

Mischievous, scary, and, at times, dangerous spirits who enjoy tormenting mortals. The bogeyman, or bogey, usually travels alone and is expert at SHAPE-SHIFTING. Some are malicious and known for frightening children, and adults often caution children to behave lest the bogeyman come and get them. Yet the bogey can also be quite harmless, simple, and gullible. In the story "The Bogey's Field," from W. Sternberg's *Dialect and Folk-Lore of Northamptonshire*, for example, a bogey who has claimed a farmer's field is fooled by a TRICKSTER farmer who manages to keep all the produce from the gullible bogey.

The term *bogey* (also *bogie* or *bogy*), a nineteenth-century word, has its etymological roots in the Middle English *bogge* or *bugge*, which means terror and bugbear respectively. It is related to the Welsh term *bwg*, which means ghost or hobgoblin, as well as the German *bumann* or *boggelman*, the Irish *bocan,* the Bohemian *bubak,* the *boggart* of Lancashire and Yorkshire, and the Scottish *bogle,* all of whom appear in numerous folk tales.

For Further Reading

Briggs, Katharine. *An Encyclopedia of Fairies.* New York: Pantheon, 1976.

Sternberg, W. *The Dialect and Folk-Lore of Northamptonshire.* London, 1851.

BONTEMPS, ARNA (1902–1973)

African American poet, critic, novelist, playwright, and collector of folklore. Born Arnaud Wendell Bontemps in Alexandria, Louisiana, Arna Bontemps was to enjoy a professional literary career that spanned six decades. Bontemps's father was a third-generation brick mason and wanted his son to carry on the family tradition; his mother, however, taught young Arna to love books and to strive for a more intellectual lifestyle. Bontemps was particularly influenced by his uncle, a hard-drinking man who loved to tell stories. From his uncle's accounts of dialect stories, preacher stories, GHOST STORIES, and other FOLKTALES, Bontemps learned about the tradition of African American FOLKLORE. This tradition would fuel Bontemps's writing for the rest of his life.

Bontemps came to prominence as a writer late in the Harlem Renaissance (approximately 1920-1930), winning prizes for his poetry in 1926 and 1927. He had moved to New York in the mid-1920s to take a teaching job at Harlem Academy, and although he did not live there long, his years in Harlem put him in close contact with other major literary figures of the time, including Jean Toomer, James Weldon Johnson (*see* JOHNSON, JAMES WELDON), and Countee Cullen. He also met Langston Hughes (*see* HUGHES, LANGSTON), who became Bontemps's lifelong friend and frequent collaborator. In 1931 Bontemps left Harlem to teach at Oakwood Junior College in Huntsville, Alabama. That same year he released his first novel, *God Sends Sunday,* to moderate critical acclaim. Bontemps continued to write and publish his

poetry, and, believing that younger audiences might benefit from positive images of African Americans in literature, also began to write children's books. His first of many juvenile stories, *Popo and Fifina* (1932), was co-authored with Langston Hughes. His most popular and highly acclaimed novel, *Black Thunder* (1936), dealt with the theme of revolution in the context of an eighteenth-century slave insurrection.

Bontemps left the teaching profession in 1938 and spent much of the rest of his career as the librarian at Fisk University in Nashville, Tennessee. His efforts there to establish important collections of African American literary documents have made the Fisk University Library an essential source of information about African American culture and tradition. Critics suggest that Bontemps's most important contribution to literature is his remarkable ability to use language that accurately reflects the dialects, customs, and world views of the people in his stories, which likely stemmed from his familiarity with and understanding of the African American folkloric tradition. Bontemps's legacy of African American scholarship may be found in the many anthologies he compiled and edited (several in collaboration with Hughes). Still useful today is THE BOOK OF NEGRO FOLKLORE (1958), in which Bontemps and Hughes collected FABLES, sermons, prayers, folk songs, ghost stories, spirituals, superstitions, ANECDOTES, JOKES, rhymes, essays, and short stories that reflect or address the folk tradition. In spite of frequent financial instability and a hectic domestic life (he had a wife and six children), Bontemps managed to make steady contributions to African American literature and scholarship until his death in 1973.

For Further Reading

Bontemps, Arna, ed. *American Negro Poetry.* Rev. ed. New York: Hill & Wang, 1982.

———. *One Hundred Years of Negro Freedom.* Westport, CT: Greenwood Press, 1980.

Jones, Kirkland C. *Renaissance Man from Louisiana: A Biography of Arna Wendell Bontemps.* Westport, CT: Greenwood Press, 1992.

BOOK OF NEGRO FOLKLORE

Anthology of representative selections from African American FOLKLORE. Edited by Langston Hughes and Arna Bontemps (*see* HUGHES, LANGSTON; BONTEMPS, ARNA), the book's entries are arranged chronologically as the folklore developed, from the antebellum to the modern era, and capture a majority of the material comprising the oral tradition of AFRICAN AMERICAN STORYTELLING.

Included are ANIMAL rhymes and tales, such as those of Brer Rabbit, Brer Fox, Old Sis Goose, John and the Lion, the Rooster and the Chicken, and the TAR BABY; slave narratives and memoirs, such as "How Buck Won His Freedom," "Uncle Israel and the Law," "Abraham Explains His Master's Shot," and "Hold the Book Up Higher, John"; sermons, prayers, and testimonials; GHOST STORIES; and essays about black magic, black chance, and voodoo.

Additionally, prose and poetry in the folk manner contemporary to 1958, when the book was first published, anthologizes work from such writers as Langston Hughes, Paul Laurence Dunbar, Sterling Brown (*see* BROWN, STERLING), Ralph Ellison, Richard Wright, Alice Childress, Gwendolyn Brooks, and Dorothy Rosenberg. This volume also provides extensive selections of African American music styles, from spirituals and gospel songs to BALLADS, BLUES, WORK SONGS, street cries, play songs, Harlem jive, and songs in the folk manner, as well as essays by important jazz musicians.

Another important aspect distinct to this collection of African American folklore is Arna Bontemps's introduction, which provides valuable background information on the material contained in the book, explains its origin and development, and ultimately affirms the importance and influence of this folklore not only to and on African Americans, but to and on all Americans.

BOONE, DANIEL (1734–1830)

Folk HERO of the United States frontier. Daniel Boone, like his contemporary Davy Crockett, (*see* CROCKETT, DAVY) attained a high level of fame as a backwoodsman, explorer, and legendary figure in the frontier era of American history. Like many of the frontier LEGENDS in the early years of the United States, Daniel Boone began his career in the Southwest, specifically in the still uncolonized region of Kentucky, but he eventually moved further west, pursuing the expanding frontier and the adventure that accompanied it. Historically, Boone is known for the discovery of the Cumberland Gap. His discovery provided easier passage through the Appalachian Mountains, thereby encouraging white migration westward and opening new areas of trade. Boone was also instrumental in the creation of the first road from the eastern part of Virginia, through the Kentucky wilderness, and further into the frontier West.

In addition to his historical accomplishments, Daniel Boone gained fame as a hunter and an "Indian fighter." On two separate occasions he was taken captive by Native American tribes. On one of those occasions, his qualities as a woodsman resulted in Boone's adoption by the Blackfish chief, Shawnee. Boone's frequent encounters with danger enhanced his standing as an idealized figure of frontier masculinity. Like other folk heroes grounded in historical fact, Boone's heroic status became exaggerated and took on a life of its own. In one legend ascribed to Boone, he kept a premade coffin with him, and would frequently lie down in it to check for any changes in his size that might require adjustments. Such a cavalier notion of DEATH is characteristic of the frontier character and the public's perception of him. The American frontier of the late eighteenth and early nineteenth centuries was fraught with violence, and one method of dealing with the brutal requirements of American expansion was through the humorous tales of the courageous, sometimes bumbling exploits of the folk hero. Through heroic figures like Davy Crockett, Mike Fink (*see* FINK, MIKE), and Daniel Boone, the American public could witness the violence of the frontier through the imaginative humor of the TALL TALE.

For Further Reading

Faragher, John Mack. *Daniel Boone: The Life and Legend of an American Pioneer.* New York: Henry Holt, 1992.

BOTKIN, BENJAMIN A. (1901–1975)

Folklorist employed by the U.S. government as second editor for the Federal Writers Project (FWP) during the 1930s, and one of the first scholars to popularize the discipline of FOLKLORE and bring academic research into the public sector. The FWP, a division of the Works Project Administration, was a vehicle for Botkin to thrive as a folklorist outside of academia when he was hired to document "American life" through the writing of tour books. The depression era created a sense of national unity based on misfortune and hardship and Botkin saw the use of folklore as the perfect tool to honor the common person's life and strife during this time. Unlike FWP colleague John Lomax (*see* LOMAX, JOHN AND ALAN) who believed that folklore could only be found in rural areas, Botkin asserted that folklore was continually emerging in urban society and focused much of his fieldwork in occupational settings. Botkin's literary contributions lie in *A Treasury of American Folklore* (1944) and *A Treasury of Railroad Folklore* (1963). The lasting significance Botkin gave to folk scholarship is the public sector idea that folklorists should act as individual clearinghouses, gathering information from the folk, and disseminating it back to them, the rightful owners.

BRAHMA

Creator GOD of the Hindu triad. Along with VISNU, the preserver, and SIVA, the destroyer, Brahma represents the manifestation of physical reality from the unknowable. In other words, Brahma creates the real and visible out of the indescribable spirit of the universe. One must exercise caution, however, in employing the term "reality" to Hindu thought. In one of the Hindu CREATION stories, Brahma creates things from his position on the lotus flower emerging from the sleeping Visnu's navel. As Visnu sleeps, his dream appears through Brahma as our earthly reality. Life is, therefore, a dream or illusion that appears from the eternal breathing of the universe.

Brahma does not function like the gods of other creation stories. In Hindu religious practice, he is less an object of veneration than a vehicle through which the indescribable principle of the universe, or BRAHMAN, is revealed. *Brahma* is the masculine form of the neuter *Brahman,* and may therefore be viewed as the movement into time and space of the inexpressible continuity of life. Nonetheless, Brahma does have distinct characteristics. He is usually depicted in a seated position, with four heads, and he sometimes rides upon a swan or goose. The four heads, like the FOUR DIRECTIONS or the four WINDS, represent the universality of his creation. In another of the Hindu creation stories, Brahma creates from himself a woman and procreates with her in a parallel to the Book of Genesis description of Adam's rib (*see* ADAM AND EVE; GENESIS, BOOK OF). The story illustrates Brahma's creation of all reality from a single principle that is at once both nothing and all things.

For Further Reading

Beck et al., eds. *Folktales of India.* Chicago: University of Chicago Press, 1987.

Bhattacharyya, Tarapada. *The Cult of Brahm.* Varanasi: Chowkhamba Sanskrit Series Office, 1969.

Zimmer, Heinrich. *Myths and Symbols in Indian Art and Civilization.* New York: Harper, 1962.

BRAHMAN

Inexplicable principle of ultimate reality in Hindu thought. While Brahman is the cosmic force or idea from which all life flows, it cannot be described or theorized and it defies all categorization. It is immanent in that it encompasses and permeates all things; yet it is transcendent in that it is beyond speech or thought. Nonetheless, in Hindu thought, Brahman is viewed as the continuity of life from which emerges BRAHMA, the creator, VISNU, the sustainer, and SIVA, the destroyer.

The great philosophical value of Brahman is its reconciliation of opposites. As human beings, we comprehend the universe in terms of opposition: night/day, good/evil, female/male. In the neuter term *Brahman,* such distinctions break down, since, ultimately, all life springs from the same paradoxical, indescribable source. For this reason, the notion of Brahman contributed to the concept of zero in Indian mathematics, a number that exists in a liminal stage between the opposites of positive and negative. In storytelling, Brahman serves as a reminder that life is, at bottom, contradictory and indescribable.

This theme is carried through in a stock character in Indian FOLKTALES. Brahman, the character, is a Hindu priest whose hypocrisy usually provides humor in the stories. As priests, the Brahmans should exercise the self-disciplines of chastity, poverty, and fasting. In the folktales, however, they are often presented as lusty, greedy, and gluttonous. In this way, the tales become a subversive tool in Indian society by bringing base qualities to the higher castes and noble qualities to the lower ones. Frequently, however, a Brahman is presented as possessing the qualities to which the caste ideally aspires. In these cases, the tales teach moral lessons and enforce the status quo.

For Further Reading

Dowson, John. *A Classical Dictionary of Hindu Mythology and Religion, Geography, History, and Literature*. New York: Routledge & Kegan Paul, 1979.

Elwin, Verrier. *Myths of Middle India*. Oxford: Oxford University Press, 1949.

Upadhyay, Asha. *Tales from India*. Illustrated by Nickzad Nodjoumi. New York: Random House, 1971.

BRIGGS, KATHARINE MARY (1898–1990)

British historian, writer, and folklorist. Born in London, Briggs obtained an M.A. and a Ph.D. at Oxford in 1926 and 1952 respectively. She is considered the leading authority on the subject of fairies and related phenomena. Claiming agnosticism as to the existence of fairies, she believed in keeping an open mind. Her work consists of such seminal fairy studies as *The Legend of Maiden Hair, The Witch's Ride,* and *The Prince, the Fox and the Dragon*. She also wrote the four volume *Dictionary of British Folktales in the English Language* (1971).

As a historian studying primarily the seventeenth century, she wrote *The Anatomy of Puck: An Examination of Fairy Beliefs among Shakespeare's Contemporaries and Successors* and *The Fairies in English Literature*. A meticulous scholar, she brought rigorous canons of criticism to bear on fairy studies. Her obituary in the *New York Times* heralded her as "omniscient in airy realms."

BROWN, STERLING (1901–1989)

African American writer, folklorist, and critic. Born to a highly educated and professional family in Washington, DC, Brown was educated at Williams College in Massachusetts (B.A., 1922) and Harvard University (M.A., 1923). He insisted, however, that his most important teachers were the rural farmers and migrant workers of the South, who taught him the African American folkloric tradition within which he worked for the rest of his life. One of the most significant characteristics of Brown's work is his synthesis of the literary and folk traditions of European Americans and African Americans. Brown's interest in the folk tradition is particularly evident in his first collection of poetry, *Southern Road* (1932), in which he combines the styles of folk songs such as BALLADS and WORK SONGS with the idioms and dialect of rural African Americans to create poems that give voice to individual as well as social issues and problems. In 1931, Brown began writing monthly critical essays in *Opportunity;* through these essays he established his reputation as a serious critic of American life and literature, especially pertaining to African Americans. His two book-length studies of African American literature, *The Negro in American Fiction* (1937) and *Negro Poetry and Drama* (1939), remain important statements on the development and status of the African American literary tradition. He also coedited *The Negro Caravan* (1941), a classic anthology of African American writing, particularly of the Harlem Renaissance. Brown was a highly respected professor at Howard University for four decades (1929–1969), won numerous awards for his many publications (poetry as well as folklore and nonfiction), and was named the poet laureate of the city of Washington, DC, in 1984.

For Further Reading

Gabbin, Joanne V. *Sterling A. Brown: Building the Black Aesthetic Tradition*. Westport, CT: Greenwood Press, 1985.

BROWNIES

Solitary household fairies found in Northern Europe, especially in England and Scotland. If they are treated well, brownies will complete many household tasks, usually at night.

In early fairy lore, English brownies were the same size as or larger than humans. Later, they became small and wizened, and they can also be hairy. Often they wear brown rags, but some are naked. Some do not have separate fingers or toes, while others have nostrils but no noses. Brownies occasionally take an animal form, and they are generally grotesque in appearance. They are experts at hiding and lurking, and if need be, they have the power to make themselves invisible.

Brownies are eager to receive offerings of a meal or milk, but only if they are left quietly by the owners of the house in a favorite corner. The luck of the house depends on its brownie. If the brownie is happy, the household will run smoothly, but if the brownie is miserable, it may ruin the family. Brownies may stay attached to the same house for centuries, performing a variety of domestic chores. Brownies live in the house to which they give their services, but they often keep a special pool, stream, rock, or cave as their permanent home. When brownies are mistreated, they may do damage and can be dangerous. If they leave a household, the good luck attached to them leaves as well. Brownies are often associated with the dead. In some stories, they are thought to be the ghosts of servants who worked in the house. Brownies are characterized by their mobility and free will.

Many brownie stories, as well as the GRIMM BROTHERS's version of "The Elves and the Shoemaker," tell how brownies are "laid" by a gift of clothes—this means they depart from a household forever (and are often offended).

Juliana Horatia Ewing's book *The Brownies and Other Tales* (1870) began the practice of referring to helpful children as "brownies," a term eventually used for junior Girl Scouts. Ewing continued the brownie theme in *Lob Lie-by-the-Fire* (1874). Beginning in the 1880s, Palmer Fox wrote and illustrated brownie stories in verse for the children's magazine *St. Nicholas*. Other brownie stories appear in Thomas Keightley's *The Fairy Mythology. See also* HOUSE SPRITES; PIXIES; KEIGHTLEY, THOMAS.

For Further Reading

Arrowsmith, Nancy, with George Moorse. *A Field Guide to the Little People*. London: Macmillan, 1977.

Keightley, Thomas. *The Fairy Mythology*. 1850. Reprint, New York: Haskell House, 1968.

South, Malcolm, ed. *Mythical and Fabulous Creatures: A Sourcebook and Research Guide*. Westport, CT: Greenwood Press, 1987.

BRYAN, ASHLEY (1923–)

Art professor and author and illustrator of books for children. Bryan studied at Cooper Union and Columbia University and works as a professor of art at Dartmouth College. His writings for children work to preserve African traditions in America. He also creates prints and woodcuts to add flavor and authenticity to his books.

His writings include *The Ox with the Wonderful Horns and Other African Folk-Tales* (1971), and *Walk Together Children: Black American Spirituals* (1974). *The Dancing Granny* (1976) relates the SAGA of the villain Ananse and *Beat the Story Drum Pum Pum* (1980) comprises Nigerian FOLKTALES, which reveal the origins of hostilities between ANIMALS, such as the animosity between the elephant and the bush cow and the enmity between the snake and the frog.

BUDDHA

Meaning enlightened one; specifically Gautama Siddhartha (c. 563 B.C.–483 B.C.), founder of the Buddhist faith. Born in the Lumbini Grove of Nepal, Gautama Siddhartha was the son of a PRINCE of the

Sakya clan who ruled a small kingdom. His mother, MAYA, bore him after a dream in which she envisioned him descending from HEAVEN, circling her body, and entering her womb as a white elephant. His earlier existences and incarnations are chronicled in the various JATAKA TALES, and Buddhist LEGEND has it that at Siddhartha's birth, there were earthquakes and miracles, ocean water grew sweet, and his birth was heralded by DIVINE SIGNS. His status as DIVINE CHILD was signified by the 32 primary and 80 secondary marks on his body, his amazing tongue that was capable of reading to the world of BRAHMA, and the victory shout he yelled and the seven steps he took. His future wife, his horse and elephant, his charioteer, and the Bo tree were all said to be born at the same moment as he.

Siddhartha was raised in luxury, and since the prophecy states that he would become either a universal king or an enlightened Buddha whose purpose was to save humankind, his father tried to ensure for him a life as a monarch by preventing him from seeing the three—or in some accounts four—sights of suffering that he believed would sway his son to want to save humankind: a decrepit old man, suggesting that people age and become infirm; a diseased old man, signifying pain and illness in the world; a dead man, introducing the concept of DEATH; and a religious ascetic, representing one who had relinquished worldly pleasures for the spiritual life. But the sheltered life his father arranged failed to prevent Siddhartha from seeing these sights, and he began to question human suffering and to realize the impermanence of earthly goods. At the age of 29, he gave up his position and his kingdom, his family and his city, and, with the help of the GODS, stealthily left the city by night. Accompanied by five ascetics, he set out on a six-year course of discipline under a Bel tree. At the end of that time, he left the Bel tree to become a beggar, now sure that asceticism was not the correct path to truth. Like all HEROES, he had to undergo a period of trials. Mara, the prince of evil, and his daughters, threw stones and darts at him, but by the time the stones and darts reach Siddhartha, they were transformed into flowers. Mara and his daughters also tempted him with lust, fear, and his sense of duty, but Siddhartha withstood all. The trials of temptation over, Siddhartha became enlightened under the sacred BODHI TREE, where he remained for seven days, thus attaining Buddhahood.

After Siddhartha reached Buddhahood, he wondered whether or not he should teach people that existence involves suffering produced by desire. The answer came to him through Brahma, who reminded him that salvation is not attainable unless the people are aware of it. Beginning with his first sermon at Benares, for the next 45 years, Buddha wandered about preaching his doctrine and winning converts.

When he was 80 years old and knew that his death was near, Buddha rested under two Sala trees that were blooming out of season; he went into a trance and through various stages until he reached NIRVANA, dying in the arms of his beloved disciple Ananda. As at his birth, his death was accompanied by divine signs: his funeral pyre would not light until the arrival of his disciple Kasyapa—once he arrived , it burst into flames.

As E.A. Burtt writes in his introduction to *The Teachings of the Compassionate Buddha*, Buddha "was a man of rich and responsive human sympathy, of unfailing patience, strength, gentleness, and good will. His friendliness, to all who came to him in sincere search, was genuine and unreserved." Furthermore, "he was a thinker of unexcelled philosophic power" and "one of the giant intellects of human history, exhibiting a keenness of analytic understanding that has rarely been equaled."

For Further Reading

Burtt, E.A. *The Teachings of the Compassionate Buddha*. New York: Mentor Books, 1955.

Jaspers, Karl. *Socrates, Buddha, Confucius, Jesus*. Edited by Hannah Arendt. Translated by Ralph Manheim. Florida: HarBrace, 1962.

Khoroche, trans. *Once the Buddha Was a Monkey: Arya Sura's Jatakamala*. Chicago: University of Chicago Press, 1985.

BUDDHIST STORYTELLING

Oral tradition of Buddhism. Although various sects of Buddhism exist and Buddhism may differ in philosophy depending on its sources, masters, and country, storytelling as a means of teaching is a common thread joining them. These stories and lessons are drawn from a wealth of sources, including the JATAKA TALES, birth tales of the BUDDHA that are part of the vast store of Buddhist literature called the *Tripataka*, Zen *koans* and parables, and the Tibetan MILAREPA Tales. The oral tradition helped spread Buddhism over a vast area, from India in 500 B.C. to China in A.D. 500, and then to Japan and other countries of the Far East.

Buddhist teaching stories vary greatly in style and content. The "Birth Stories," known as the *Jataka Tales,* show the *Bodhisattva,* meaning "Being of Wisdom," in his previous incarnations before he had his final birth as Gautama Siddhartha, the Buddha. As Bodhisattva he performed many acts with great compassion and self-sacrifice, and he perfected his wisdom and virtue. The stories collected as the *Jataka Tales* were often adopted from popular legends and fables, and illustrations of them can be found in early Buddhist art. Often the Bodhisattva's incarnation comes in the form of an animal, as in the tale "The Crocodile and the Monkey," and the stories usually offer a kind of moral at their close, where the incarnation is made apparent.

Zen Buddhist storytelling includes stories that tell of the actual experiences of Chinese and Japanese Zen teachers over the last five centuries. They come from such sources as the *Shaseki-shu,* or *Collection of Stone and Sand,* written by Muju, a thirteenth-century Japanese Zen teacher, and from the anecdotes of Zen monks that began to be recorded and published in Japan in the beginning of the twentieth century. The stories tend to focus on self-discovery, and use paradox as a means to reach this end. In the story "The Tunnel," for example, Zenkai, a murderer and thief, repents by spending over thirty years cutting a tunnel through a mountain so people can avoid the dangerous road over the mountain.

However, the son of the man he has slain comes to kill him in revenge before the tunnel is completed. Zenkai asks only that he first be permitted to complete the tunnel. The son agrees, eventually begins to help Zenkai out of boredom, comes to admire him, and cannot kill him when the tunnel is finished for he has come to see him as his own teacher.

Koans, or problems, dating back to the thirteenth century, are another kind of story that Zen teachers have used to guide their students toward release. The *koans* were meant to be meditated on, and the right answer to the problem was that there were "many right answers and no right answer," as Paul Reps points out in *Zen Flesh, Zen Bones,* and "the *koan* itself is the right answer." These stories often use slang, and "make no pretense at logic." As Reps writes, "The whole intent [of the *koan*] was to help the pupil break the shell of his limited mind and attain a second eternal birth, *satori,* enlightenment." They date back to the early thirteenth century when the Chinese master, Ekai, also called Mu-mon, recorded forty-eight of the old *koans* in a collection he called *The Gateless Gate.*

Tibetan poet-ascetic Milarepa was believed to have written approximately 100,000 songs in his time, and tales about his life also became part of the storytelling tradition of Tibetan Buddhism.

For Further Reading

Evans-Wentz, W.Y., ed. *Tibet's Great Yogi Milarepa: A Biography from the Tibetan.* New York: Oxford University Press, 1928.

Reps, Paul. *Zen Flesh, Zen Bones.* Tokyo: Charles E. Tuttle, 1957.

BULFINCH, THOMAS (1796–1867)

American author of the storytelling classics *The Age of Fable, The Age of Chivalry,* and *Legends of Charlemagne.* Thomas Bulfinch was one of eleven children in a fairly prominent Boston family. He was educated at Boston Latin School, Phillips Exeter Academy, and Harvard University. A year after graduating from Harvard, Bulfinch embarked on a business career that never came to fruition. At age 41, he accepted a clerkship in the

Merchant's Bank of Boston, where he worked until his death.

Bulfinch's monumental contribution to storytelling includes three separate books of mythology. *The Age of Fable* (1855), more commonly known as *Bulfinch's Mythology*, retells in prose the great MYTHS of classical poetry. *The Age of Chivalry* (1858) retells tales from the chivalric ROMANCES. This work includes the legends of King ARTHUR and other Welsh folk tales. Bulfinch took his version of these stories from Malory's *Le Morte d'Arthur*. *Legends of Charlemagne* (1862) contains romances of the middle ages, including the epic fantasies of several Italian poets, the "Romans de Chevalerie" of the Comte de Tressan, and certain German collections of popular tales.

Some of Bulfinch's lesser-known works are *Hebrew Lyrical History* (1853), a short study of the Psalms; *The Boy Inventor* (1860), a memorial volume to a young friend, Matthew Edwards, who showed remarkable scientific ability; and *Poetry of the Age of Fable* (1863), a supplementary work to *The Age of Fable*.

A voracious reader, Bulfinch was a competent student of history, a devotee of poetry, and a good translator. His writing demonstrates a wide knowledge of the traditional classics, the contemporary poets, and European literature in general.

For Further Reading

Bulfinch, Thomas. *The Age of Chivalry and Legends of Charlemagne or Romance of the Middle Ages.* New York: New American Library, 1962.

——. *The Age of Fable or Beauties of Mythology.* New York: Tudor, 1935.

BUMBA

Boshongo (Bantu) god revered as first ancestor and creator of all. According to the mythology of the Boshongo of Zaire, Bumba was responsible for vomiting up the SUN, the MOON, the stars, and nine creatures—the leopard, the crested eagle, the crocodile, the fish, the TORTOISE, the lightning, the white heron, the beetle, and the goat. After that, Bumba, who was white, vomited up many human beings, though only one of them, Loko Yima,

was also white. The creatures and the sons of Bumba then went on to complete the creation of all other living things.

Like many CREATION myths, the presence of only a father creator suggests a largely patrilineal culture. That Bumba is white while almost all of humanity is not further suggests the influence of white colonialism in black Africa, which would date this MYTH as relatively recent.

BUNYAN, PAUL

Legendary character epitomizing a superhuman outdoors person. Although originally created as an advertising scheme, stories of Paul and Babe the Blue Ox (his equally super-sized companion) have surfaced in FOLKTALES and anecdotes as a symbol of northwoods identity. Various cities in Maine, Minnesota, and California claim to be the "Home of Paul Bunyan" and celebrate the gigantic duo with statues, museums, monuments, and children's amusement rides. Akeley, Minnesota, toasts annual Paul Bunyan days with fish fries, pie socials, and parades. Akeley was also the home to one of the largest sawmills in the world, owned and operated by the Red River Lumber Company. The advertiser of this company, W. B. Laughhead, created the Paul Bunyan icon and used him for propaganda between 1914 and 1916. Laughhead said his stories were based on his experiences of Minnesota logging camps between 1900 and 1908. Other sources report that Paul Bunyan stories began to circulate in print in the early twentieth century with the first stories written by James MacGillivray in the *Detroit News Tribune* in July 1910.

Thus the Paul Bunyan folktales are the creation of known writers, not the typically folkloric tradition of stories springing collectively from the minds of anonymous common folk. However, lumberjacks have always told LEGENDS about giant lumber men representing the strongest and best workers, so perhaps Paul Bunyan stories began as an oral tradition (albeit without a birth name), subsequently went to print with the name "Paul Bunyan" attached to this legendary lumber man, and then returned to traditional oral transmission with the adopted name. This story's origin and dissemination is similar to that of the Pecos Bill tales, put in print by Edward O'Reilly, and the John Henry legends, created by Roark Bradford (see HENRY, JOHN). Paul Bunyan tales still live on in oral tradition and written lore, with most people unaware of corporate America's involvement in the birth. People across the United States, especially those who live near his gargantuan statues or in rural forested areas, continue to both pass along old and invent new stories. Paul Bunyan and his stories epitomize the ideal outdoorsman and the hardiness required for frontier life.

For example, in one story Paul and Babe are able to break up a log jam by using their strength to redirect the river. Other stories poke fun at Minnesota's harsh natural environment; when the weather is very cold one day, the men's words freeze in mid-air and cause a terrible chatter when everything thaws. Another story involves snow so deep that Paul has to dig down to the trees to continue logging, and once the camp is infested with mosquitoes so large that Paul uses them to drill holes in the maple trees.

Other tales sought alternative explanations for the natural order of the earth; for instance, Minnesota's 10,000 lakes were said to be created from Paul's footsteps, and the Grand Canyon was created when Paul, in despair about losing Babe in a gambling incident, dragged his ax across the country. Contemporary stories are created to explain landmarks, such as identifying the Brainerd, Minnesota, watertower as Paul's knife handle thrown while he was playing the children's jackknife throwing game of "mumbledy peg."

Some more recent storytellers have modified Paul's profession, from northwoods lumberjack to scientific industrialist in the oil fields, with actions still typifying a TALL TALE HERO: incredible strength, superhuman capacity for labor, and a consequent ability to consume almost unbelievable amounts of FOOD. One tall tale about Paul's appetite claims that his stove was so large that men had to skate across the griddle with sides of bacon strapped to their feet in order to grease it.

In American FOLKLORE, there have been other hero legends manifested in frontier figures: Davy Crockett (see CROCKETT, DAVY), John Henry, and JOHNNY APPLESEED. Other Paul Bunyan characters created during this century include Johnny Inkslinger, Ole the Blacksmith, and Sourdough Sam the Cook. Similar legends to the Paul Bunyan stories are known to exist around the world, and there is both an Indian version and a European version of Paul.

BURTON, RICHARD (1821–1890)

British explorer, linguist, writer, and translator of the THOUSAND AND ONE NIGHTS (or *Arabian Nights*). In 1842, Burton began to work for the East India Company and was stationed in India, where he became fluent in Persian, Afghan, Hindustani, and Arabic. Determined to visit the forbidden cities of Mecca and Medina, he traveled to them in disguise in 1853; this visit was the source of his later work, *Personal Narrative of a Pilgrimage to El-Medinah and Meccah* (3 vols., 1855–56). He later traveled with John Speke to Somaliland, and disguised as an Arab merchant, he went alone to Harar, Ethiopia, where he managed to meet with the local ruler. Although he was determined to find the source of the Nile and traveled with Speke to the then uncharted East Central Africa with this goal in mind, he was unsuccessful in his pursuit. He did, however, find Lake Tanganyika in 1858. Later travels included a visit to Utah in the United States, where he visited the Mormon settlement and published a description of his visit in *City of the Saints* (1861); explorations of the Bight of Biafra, Dahomey in Benin, and the African Gold Coast, while he was consul at Fernando Po, off West Africa; and a visit to Santos, Brazil, in 1865, which generated his book *Explorations of the Highlands of Brazil* (1869).

In his last years Burton served as consul at Trieste, where he did literal translations of the Portuguese epic poet Luis Vaz de Camoes (1524–1580) and 16 volumes of the anonymous *Thousand and One Nights*, or *Arabian Nights* (1885–88). Originally written in Arabic, the *Thousand and One Nights* first appeared in Europe in Antoine Galland's 1704 French translation (*see* GALLAND, ANTOINE) and the stories collected in it are drawn from Persian, Arabian, Indian, Egyptian, and Jewish tales of all types. Burton's unexpurgated English translation with notes is considered the standard.

For Further Reading

Burton, Sir Richard, trans. *The Arabian Nights.* New York: Random House Modern Library, 1996.

————. *Tales from the Arabian Nights.* Illustrated by Steele Savage. Utah: University Publishing Press, 1992.

BUSK, RACHEL HARRIETTE (1831–1907)

British folklorist. Busk, an accomplished world traveler, is remembered for the two collections of Italian FOLKLORE she compiled during her residence in Italy. Heavily influenced by the collecting efforts of the GRIMM BROTHERS, Busk sought to assemble a compilation of Italian FOLKTALES. Although Busk originally intended to acquire these tales by selecting stories from the body of Italian literature, she abandoned this approach in favor of collecting stories from the storytellers themselves. In *The Folk-Lore of Rome* (1874), Busk succeeded in collecting a number of Italian FAIRY TALES (*favole*), religious tales (*ciarpe*), and humorous tales (*esempi*), as well as numerous ghost tales. Busk's other seminal work is a collection of Italian folk songs compiled with the assistance of Giuseppe Pitre, a renowned Italian folklorist. *The Folk-Songs of Italy* (1887) is an exemplary collection of folk literature, with Busk providing relatively accurate and rhymed translations of the Italian folk songs into English. Although this collection represents a minute number of the folk songs Busk collected, they touch on themes of ROMANCE, religion, and pastoral life. Busk's collections remain an important contribution to Italian folklore studies.

For Further Reading

Busk, Rachel Harriette. *The Folk Songs of Italy.* New York: Arno Press, 1977.

CALAMITY JANE

Nickname given to Martha Jane Burke, *nee* Canary, (1852–1903) because of her notoriously accurate shooting ability with both revolver and rifle, with which she could "guarantee to bring calamity" to anyone provoking her.

Born in Princeton, Missouri, Burke moved to Virginia City, Montana, at age eight with her parents, who separated when she was quite young. To survive the Wild West, she wore trousers and other "male" clothing and carried six-shooters, eventually becoming a well-known frontier character and scout and riding for pony-express companies. When South Dakota gained territorial status in 1861, she moved there, roving from one boom town to another to follow the gold rush. She finally settled in the Black Hills, where she died.

LEGENDS grew about Calamity Jane and her prowess with guns as early as the 1880s, some claiming she was a prostitute in Hays City, Kansas, some that she was the lover of Wild Bill Hickock, and others that she was a scout for General George Armstrong Custer and General Mills. The success of a series of dime-store novels by Edward L. Wheeler, such as *Deadwood Dick on Deck,* or *Calamity Jane the Heroine of Whoop Up* (1884), furthered the spread of her legendary exploits, cementing the image of a hard-hearted, tough woman of the frontier in the annals of oral storytelling about the American Wild West.

As a result of this notoriety, the term "Calamity Jane" is sometimes applied to a person who always has a dismal story to tell or dire forebodings to share. It is also applied to one who seems to bring trouble wherever he or she goes.

Several films, such as *The Plainsman* (1936), *The Paleface* (1948), *Calamity Jane and Sam Bass* (1949), and *Calamity Jane* (1953), depict Calamity Jane in all her rumored splendor, further cementing the myth of Martha Jane Burke as she may never have been.

For Further Reading

Faber, Doris. *Calamity Jane: Her Life and Her Legend.* Boston: Houghton Mifflin, 1992.

Muller, Ellen Crago. *Calamity Jane.* Laramie, WY: Jelm Mountain Press, 1981.

CALLING

Undeniable urge felt by a HERO to embark upon a journey, quest, or other adventure. A common motif in mythology in all cultures, the calling of the hero often takes the form of an unusual or even supernatural occurrence. Sometimes, the hero will refuse to heed a calling, which often leads to disaster.

The forms of callings are as diverse as the literature that describes them. JOAN OF ARC'S calling came in the form of inner voices and saintly visions, which commanded her to undertake her dangerous patriotic mission. Frightened but unable to resist this call, which she believed to be GOD speaking to her through the voices of Saint Michael, Saint Catherine, Saint Margaret, and others, the young peasant girl began her quest to save France from the English forces.

In Sophocles's tragedy *Oedipus the King,* the oracle of APOLLO provides Oedipus with the call to save Thebes from the moral plague that had befallen the city. Other heroes of Greek tragedy also receive their callings from oracles, a common device of the time. However, in a different play by Sophocles, Antigone's call to defy her tyrannical uncle, King Creon, arises not from an exterior oracle but from her inner sense of justice and religious propriety.

When still a very young man, ARTHUR receives his call to adventure by means of a magic sword, Excalibur, which can only be removed from a rock by the true KING. This is just one example of magical circumstances that often lead heroes to understand their calling. In another Arthurian legend, the calling to a great quest takes the form of vision of the HOLY GRAIL, which appears in the great hall of CAMELOT. PERCIVAL, one of King Arthur's knights, initially refuses the call to the quest for the Grail; his initial failure to obtain the Grail may be attributed to this reluctance.

An important calling in the Judeo-Christian tradition appears in the Old Testament story of Moses (*see* EXODUS). Moses is made aware of his call to lead the people of Israel on a journey to the Promised Land through his encounter with the burning bush. YAHWEH, in the form of an angel, speaks to him of his quest from a flaming bush, which, miraculously, is not consumed by the fire. Moses, like Percival, initially rejects then later embraces his calling.

Callings are not limited solely to the experiences of great heroes in mythology and legend. Religious people of all denominations often speak of their calling to their faith; others believe that they are called to perform specific duties or embark on particular careers. In storytelling and oral traditions, however, it is often the special calling of a particular person that leads to the adventure or the journey of the hero.

CALVINO, ITALO (1923–1985)

Prominent Italian author and collector of FOLKTALES. Calvino was born near Havana, Cuba, where his Italian scientist parents were doing field research, but he grew up in San Remo, Italy, and eventually settled in Paris.

Calvino's first fiction works reflect his participation in guerrilla warfare during the German occupation of Italy. As a writer, he soon became dissatisfied with the social realist style and developed his own blend of history and fantasy.

Calvino was preoccupied with the way in which a writer tells a story, as well as with storytelling itself. In *Cosmicomics* (1965) each of twelve stories begins with a scientific description of a stage in evolution. The opening citations are followed by the personal reminiscences of Qfwfq, who personally experienced each stage. *The Castle of Crossed Destinies* (1969)—a tale about the interpretation of signs and images—was written to accompany a pack of Tarot cards. Marco Polo reports on his travels to a series of *Invisible Cities* in Calvino's 1972 novel. Calvino also edited a two-volume set of fantastic tales from nineteenth-century Europe and America, *Racconti fantastici dell' ottocento.*

His 1956 *Italian Folktales* was widely popular and includes versions of fairy tales known throughout Europe, Asia, and Arabia, as well as some local Italian legends, animal FABLES, JOKES, and ANECDOTES. (*See also* GAMBLING.) The stories are selected from those narrated in various parts of Italy, though Calvino worked from materials already published rather than directly from the oral tradition.

Calvino's introduction to *Italian Folktales* refers to the collection as "hybrid"—three-quarters "scientific" and one-quarter the product of his own judgment. (Calvino notes that the GRIMM BROTHERS also added their own personal touch to old tales.) For example, Calvino's version of "BEAUTY AND THE BEAST," "Bellinda and the Monster," is a blend of tales told in various parts of Italy—and retold in his own lively style.

Calvino felt that folktales developed before MYTH, that those tales that resonated best with a people survived and took on the form of myth—and sometimes of ritual, religion, and taboo. In his introduction, Calvino says that as he worked on this collection he experienced "the confirmation of something I already suspected—folktales are real."

For Further Reading

Calvino, Italo. *Italian Folktales*. New York: Harcourt Brace, 1980.

CALYPSO'S ISLAND

Island of Ogygia, ruled by Calypso, one of the NYMPHS of the SEA. When Odysseus is shipwrecked there, Calypso holds him a virtual prisoner for seven years.

On his voyage home after the Greek war with TROY, Odysseus's ship is destroyed in a storm sent by ZEUS, and Odysseus is the sole survivor. He lashes debris together and eventually drifts to the shore of Calypso's island. The beautiful nymph welcomes the HERO as he staggers ashore. The island is rich with thickets of trees and wildlife. Four clear streams water a meadow covered with flowers. Calypso lives in a great cavern with a grape vine growing across its entrance.

The nymph falls in love with Odysseus and offers him immortality if he stays with her, but he refuses. She tries to make him forget ITHACA and his family, but Odysseus soon grows tired of her. He sits on the shore, hoping for a ship to pick him up.

Zeus sends the messenger of the GODS, Hermes, to Calypso with orders to help Odysseus on his way. The nymph tells the hero to build a raft, which she supplies with food, wine, and tools. Odysseus is finally free of Calypso's Island, but he faces other disasters on his long way home.

The story of Calypso represents an early use of the "enchanted island" MOTIF, which has been picked up again throughout the history of literature. Examples include Shakespeare's *The Tempest* and Jules Verne's *The Mysterious Island. See also* ANCIENT GREEK STORYTELLING, ODYSSEY.

For Further Reading

Graves, Robert. *The Greek Myths*. 2 vols. New York: Penguin Books, 1957.

Hamilton, Edith. *Mythology: Timeless Tales of Gods and Heroes*. New York: Mentor, 1969.

CAMELOT

In Arthurian legend, the sixth-century castle and chief city of King ARTHUR. Centuries of stories about KING Arthur, his legendary adventures, and his Knights of the Round Table have led to countless speculations regarding the actual whereabouts and history of the mythical Camelot. The site of Camelot is never explicitly identified in any of the Arthurian legends, although several sources suggest that it was annihilated after Arthur's death. As a result, a handful of areas in England claim the right to call themselves the modern keepers of Camelot. London, Winchester, and Carlisle, among others, are all possible candidates for this honor; however, the small village of South Cadbury, which found archaeological ruins, ancient ramparts, and Roman coins of gold, copper, and silver within its boundaries, may be the most likely site of the legendary city. It seems, though, that the precise location of Camelot matters far less to ancient storytellers (and to modern ones as well) than do the mythical implications of the place.

Camelot was first mentioned by name in CHRÉTIEN DE TROYES'S twelfth-century LANCELOT, and has enjoyed a strong literary presence ever since. The most marvelous of royal courts imaginable, Camelot is described in Arthurian legends as a large, magnificent castle surrounded by fields and not far removed from a forest and a river. It is there that the HOLY GRAIL appears in a vision, and from there that legendary quests for the Grail begin. Camelot houses the famous Round Table as well as all the noble knights who were a part of that Order. Camelot is King Arthur's favorite home, and for that very reason, the evil King Mark of Cornwall completely demolishes it after Arthur's death. In short, Camelot is Arthur's headquarters and, as such, contributes greatly to the continued popularity of the Arthurian stories.

Some legends compare Camelot to the Celtic paradise of Avalon—a kind of earthly paradise where immortal heroes dwell and where, some say, Arthur's wounded body was taken to be healed. Others liken it to a new JERUSALEM, nestled in the landscape of medieval western Europe. This connection between Camelot and Jerusalem is a common one, mostly due to the frequent association of the generous and compassionate Arthur with Christ.

Camelot appears in many children's stories of the twentieth century, including Rosemary Sutcliff's Arthurian stories *The Light Beyond the Forest* (1979) and *The Sword and the Circle* (1981). It also figures in Susan Cooper's five-volume fantasy novel sequence, *The Dark is Rising* (1965–77), a series of stories based on traditional Arthurian legends but set in modern times.

For Further Reading

Dunning, R. W. *Arthur: The King in the West*. Gloucester, England: Alan Sutton Publishing, 1988.

Fife, Graeme. *Arthur the King*. New York: Sterling Publishing, 1991.

CAMPBELL, JOSEPH (1904–1987)

Educator and comparative mythologist credited with popularizing the modern study of mythology. Campbell was born in New York in 1904. He developed an early interest in mythology from viewing totem poles at the American Museum of Natural History and from the performances of Buffalo Bill's Wild West Show. After a preparatory education at the Canterbury School in Connecticut, Campbell spent a year at Dartmouth College before transferring to Columbia University. His academic journey later led him to France and Germany, where he became increasingly compelled by the intellectual potential of comparative mythology. In 1934 Campbell joined the faculty of Sarah Lawrence College, a position he retained until his retirement from formal teaching in 1972.

Joseph Campbell's contributions to literature and comparative mythology is widespread and significant. His most influential book was also the first he published alone. In *The Hero With a Thousand Faces* (1949), Campbell seeks the psychological deep structures of what he terms (borrowing a phrase from James Joyce) the *monomyth*. The monomyth is the pattern through which a HERO attains self and communal understanding. Campbell argues that the stories of very diverse cultures from all historical periods bear similar patterns of heroic adventure. He views the pattern in the following, simplified terms: "A hero ventures forth from the world of common day into a region of supernatural wonder: fabulous forces are there encountered and a decisive victory is won: the hero comes back from this mysterious adventure with the power to bestow boons on his fellow man." One such boon of the hero's success is the sense of identity the culture receives vicariously through the hero. Heroes provide culture groups with a sense of origin and purpose. Furthermore, the hero's journey instructs the individual in the natural cycle of psychological growth. The adventure of the most common individual, from birth to marriage to death, finds expression in the hero's QUEST for meaning.

Campbell's other important works include the four volume *Masks of God* (1959–1968), *Myths to Live By* (1972), *The Mythic Image* (1975), and numerous other books and articles. At the time of his death in 1987, Campbell was completing the multivolume

Historical Atlas of World Mythology. While Campbell's work as a textual translator, educator, literary critic, and comparative mythologist earned him a scholarly reputation, it was his work with Bill Moyers on the PBS series *The Power of Myth* that gained him near cult-status in the final years of his life. His significance for storytelling emerged both from his investigations of the structural and psychological factors that permeate our myths, and from his gift for telling the stories that became his life's work.

For Further Reading

Campbell, Joseph. *The Hero with a Thousand Faces.* Princeton: NJ: Princeton University Press, 1990.

———. *Historical Atlas of World Mythology.* New York: HarperCollins, 1988.

Golden, Kenneth L. ed. *Uses of Comparative Mythology: Essays on the Work of Joseph Campbell.* New York: Garland, 1992.

Noel, Daniel C., ed. *Paths to the Power of Myth: Joseph Campbell and the Study of Religion.* New York: Crossroad, 1990.

Segal, Robert A. *Joseph Campbell: An Introduction.* New York: Garland, 1987.

CANADIAN STORYTELLING

French, English, and Native American oral tradition as it evolved in Canada's provinces. The history of the storytelling tradition in Canada mirrors the history of Canada itself, beginning with the prehistoric Inuit and Indian tribes who presumably moved across the Bering Strait into Canada followed by the Viking settlements in Newfoundland around A.D. 1000. In 1583 Newfoundland was claimed by the British, and Irish immigrants arrived in Newfoundland in the late eighteenth century. The French began to settle along the St. Lawrence River early in the seventeenth century. By 1759, French expansion into Canada had ended and England had triumphed, bringing the country under British rule.

As a result, Canada's storytelling tradition differs from region to region, depending on the backgrounds of its inhabitants. The stories and LEGENDS of many of Canada's Indian tribes were influenced by the French colonists and the stories they brought from France, and in the province of Quebec and in part of the province of New Brunswick, many of the stories can easily be traced to France. Scottish and English FOLKTALES are part of the storytelling tradition of the provinces of Nova Scotia, Ontario, Prince Edward Island, Manitoba, Saskatchewan, Alberta, and British Columbia. The Northwest Territories and the Yukon have many stories that evolved out of experiences of living in the harsh, Arctic climate and the courage it took to survive.

Because of its isolation from France, French Canada has been a preserver of many of the oral forms of French folk songs, folktales, and legends that have disappeared in France. Many of the folk songs were sung as people canoed or sailed up and down the rivers, and hundreds of folk songs have been collected. One famous folk-singer-storyteller of the early twentieth century, Louis L'Aveugle, was a blind itinerant who sang his songs on the boats that traveled the Saguanay River. The *Gargantua* legend, the subject of Francois Rabelais's *Pantagruel*, came to French Canada, and Point Gargantua can be found on the east side of Lake Superior. The French *Romans de la Table Ronde*, or *Arthurian Round Table Legends*, came very early to Canada, and are retold in the basin of the St. Lawrence at Vieilles Mines.

In English-speaking Canada, stories grew up around the weather, the search for gold and furs, Niagara Falls, and the midnight sun. The poet Robert Service told the tales of "The Shooting of Dan McGrew" and other "HEROES" of the midnight sun. American writer Jack London took the legends of the "oldtimers" and the *chechaquos*, or newcomers, of the Yukon and, along with his own experiences as a prospector, wove them into stories called *Klondike Tales* and such novels as *The Call of the Wild*. Tales grew up around the great waterfall, the Niagara, and its whirlpool, as shown in Jane Urqhart's recent novel, *The Whirlpool*.

For Further Reading

Berrong, Richard M. *Rabelais and Bakhtin: Popular Culture in "Gargantua and Pantagruel."* University of Nebraska Press, 1986.

Rabelais, Francois. *Gargantua and Pantagruel.* New York: Knopf, 1994.

Service, Robert. *The Shooting of Dan McGrew and Other Poems.* New York: Dover, 1993.

CANNIBALISM

Human consumption of human flesh, a theme that has a variety of implications in storytelling traditions. In practice, some cultures have used cannibalism as a RITUAL means of assimilating the strength or soul of another; consuming a body that has been sacrificed to a deity; or initiation into witchcraft.

Some NATIVE AMERICAN STORYTELLING includes threats of cooking and serving body parts, particularly testicles, and the Cannibal Spirit is a mythic figure among Northwestern groups. African Bantu stories warn of cannibalism by monsters who have magically taken human form.

In Europe, Hansel and Gretel escape an adversary with cannibalistic intentions (*see* ABANDONED CHILDREN), as does the hero of JACK AND THE BEANSTALK. OGRES, who are usually GI-ANTS with big teeth, are said to devour naughty children. Such stories may have served as warnings against bad behavior or perhaps against venturing too far on one's own.

In other tales, an evil parent eats the children or an adult prepares a child for others to eat. The GRIMM BROTHERS's collection includes "My Mother Killed Me; My Father Ate Me," in which a woman kills her stepson and serves him to the unknowing father for dinner. A bird singing the title line reveals the deed and drops a fatal stone on the wicked step-mother (*see* STEPMOTHER—WICKED). The boy is magically returned, alive and well.

In a Russian folktale, "The Cannibal Sister," a baby with ax-like teeth eats whole sheep and makes an attempt on her brother, but he escapes and kills her.

Being devoured also may have sexual implications in myths and stories. For example, Psyche becomes afraid that her unseen husband is actually a MONSTER who will devour her (*see* CUPID AND PSYCHE).

For Further Reading

Erdoes, Richard. *The Sound of Flutes and Other Indian Legends.* Illustrated by Paul Goble. New York: Pantheon Books, 1976.

Werner, Alice. *Myths and Legends of The Bantu.* London: Frank Cass & Co., 1968.

CASTLES—ENCHANTED

Castles with spells cast over them, the origin of which may be an evil force, an unknown agent, or a mysterious object, such as the HOLY GRAIL. Enchanted castles might randomly appear and disappear. They may once have been beautiful places that are now fortresses of evil. They might contain significant objects or be prisons. They frequently are in remote places or the otherworld. Stories with enchanted castles often include the theme of the hero who breaks the spell.

FAIRY TALES frequently contain enchanted castles. These are often places where PRIN-CESSES are kept under spells. One of the most well-known stories with an enchanted castle is the European LEGEND of "Sleeping Beauty." In this tale, a young princess pierces her hand with a spindle and, because of a curse put on her when she was a baby, falls into a deep sleep that lasts for one hundred years. An impassable forest of trees and brambles grows around the castle in which she and her court sleep. After one hundred years, a PRINCE de-termines to make his way to the center of this wood, and the trees and brambles allow him to pass. At the castle, he finds Sleeping Beauty, kisses her, and awakens her. The court gradually awakens as well, and after supper the prince and princess are married in the castle chapel.

The German fairy tale "The WATER OF LIFE," taken from oral tradition and retold by the GRIMM BROTHERS, tells of an enchanted castle with a fountain containing magic water. In this tale, the YOUNGEST SON of a KING sets out in search of the Water of Life for his sick father. A DWARF tells him where he can find the magic water, and he gives the prince an iron wand and two loaves of bread. The prince uses the wand to open the gate of the en-chanted castle, and he feeds the loaves of bread to the two ferocious lions inside the gate. In the castle, the prince sees a beautiful maiden who tells him that he has freed her from a spell. She will give him the whole king-dom if he returns in a year to marry her. Then she directs him to the fountain containing the Water of Life. On the way home, the young-est prince saves three kingdoms from ruin. After he returns home, his evil brothers replace the magic water with sea water while their younger brother sleeps. When the youngest son gives the sea water to the king, he becomes worse. The older brothers heal the king with the Water of Life. The angry king thinks his youngest son tried to kill him, and eventually the young prince hides in the forest. Later, the king receives precious gifts from the three kingdoms that the youngest son helped to save. The king realizes his mistake and proclaims that his son is welcome at home. Meanwhile, the two older brothers attempt to marry the beautiful princess. She builds a road of gold leading to her castle and announced that whoever rides straight up the middle of it is her true bridegroom. The older brothers fail the test. The third brother rides straight up the middle of the gold road, and the princess joyfully receives him.

In Arthurian legend, the castle of the Holy Grail is the primary enchanted castle, and it appears in many tales. In *Le Conte du Graal* (*The Story of the Grail*) or *Perceval* (*see* HOLY GRAIL, PERCIVAL), the earliest surviving story about the Grail, recorded by the French poet CHRÉTIEN DE TROYES at some time between 1160 and 1180, Perceval accepts shelter for the night in the castle of the Fisher King. While there, Perceval sees a youth carrying a white lance, from which falls a drop of blood, and a maiden bearing the Grail, but he asks no questions. In the morning, he finds the castle deserted and rides away. Later, he discovers that because he did not ask the right questions, the Fisher King will not be healed and there will be war in his kingdom. Perceval takes a vow to spend the rest of his life looking for lance and the Grail. The German poet WOLFRAM VON ESCHENBACH's *Parzival* (*c.* 1210), based on Chrétien de Troye's *Conte du Graal*, is considered to be the definitive grail story. In all stories, the grail is never found again and the knight spends the rest of his life searching.

In many Arthurian tales, Morgan and other tall, dominating, and seductively beautiful fairies or *fays* occupy enchanted castles. Such castles present an illusory promise of peace and pleasure, and knights are often imprisoned in these deceptive otherworld realms.

In the Hindu EPIC, the MAHABHARATA, the DEMON Maya builds a magnificent palace for the PANDAVAS. It takes fourteen months to build and can be compared only to the enormous, splendid, heavenly palaces of the gods. It is so brilliant with gems that it presents the illusion that it is on fire.

"The Tale of the Second Dervish" from "The Porter and the Three Girls of Baghdad," found in *Arabian Nights*, presents an enchanted castle where misfortune prevails. While digging in the forest, the second dervish discovers a stairway leading down to the courtyard of a magnificent palace. There, he finds a beautiful young princess who is a JINNEE's prisoner in the palace. The dervish and the princess spend a blissful night together. Then the brazen dervish summons the jinnee by kicking an enchanted dome. The furious jinnee suspects that the princess has been unfaithful to him. He tortures and then kills her.

Enchanted castles appear in the stories of many cultures. They frequently pose a challenge to the HERO, who meets forces of evil inside their walls. The success of the hero in overcoming the threats before him, and, in some instances, breaking the spell over the castle, depends on the time and the culture from which the enchanted castle story comes.

CAVE PAINTING

Ancient representations of animal life that served RITUALISTIC functions for prehistoric humans. Although cave paintings and engravings may be found in numerous cultural and historical epochs (including the rock pictures found throughout the world), the most prominent were created by the Magdalenians in the Upper Paleolithic period (25,000-15,000 B.C.). Over two hundred painted caves from this period have been discovered. Of these, the most frequently discussed is the Lascaux cave of Southern France. Although representations of humans are sometimes found in cave paintings and rock pictures, the Lascaux cave principally contains sophisticated depictions of large animals that were hunted for food. Frequently, the creators of the paintings employed the contours of the cave surface in their representations. For example, a bulge in the cave wall might be painted over to represent the shoulder or flank of a bull. Scientists have determined that the ancient painters used clay mixed with colored minerals to produce the pigments, and the elements were sometimes heated before application. The beauty and sophistication of the paintings have lead historians to rethink the traditional timeline of human artistic development. Purportedly, when Pablo Picasso emerged from a tour of the Lascaux cave, he proclaimed, "We have invented nothing!"

Despite Picasso's implication that the Paleolithic cave painters were self-conscious artists, there is no existing evidence to determine how they perceived their paintings. Since there is little to suggest that the painted caves were inhabited, most scholars assume that the caves served only ritualistic functions. The caves, with their physical danger and terrifying darkness, may have been used to initiate boys into the ritual of the hunt. The history of this era, however, is controversial, and little is known about the intended function of the paintings. Archaeologists, however, have conjectured that the cave paintings served as part of a fertility cult. Many paintings from this period bear scratches or chips that appear to indicate wounds inflicted upon the animal representations. This may suggest the use of "sympathetic magic": attempts to achieve on the symbolic level what the hunters desired on the physical level. Several paintings and engravings even bear holes in which arrows may have been placed to bring about success in the hunt. In order to have sufficient animals to kill, the Magdalenians also represented animals (and humans) giving birth. These paintings suggest that the early artists of the caves conceived of two worlds: the physical one and another, non-physical world through which the first is replenished. Since such a division is at the heart of every major mythological system, the Paleolithic cave painters represent a potential starting point for humanity's religious sensibilities. The caves are, in essence, graphic stories that convey the aspirations of early humans to survive in an inhospitable world.

For Further Reading

Berenguer, Magin. *Prehistoric Cave Art in Northern Spain*. Ciudad de Mexico: Frente de Afirmacion Hispanista, 1994.

Leakey, Mary D. *Africa's Vanishing Art: The Rock Paintings of Tanzania*. Garden City, NY: Doubleday, 1983.

Stone, Andrea. *Images from the Underworld: Naj Tunich and the Tradition of Maya Cave Painting*. Austin, TX: University of Texas Press, 1995.

CELTIC STORYTELLING

Myths and LEGENDS from the northwestern European Celtic regions, notably Ireland and Wales, that began as fluid oral traditions and eventually were written down. Elements of these stories include the heroic, superhuman warrior, the divine otherworld, and numerous elements of magic and the supernatural.

The Celts were the ancestors of the Irish, the Scots, the Welsh, the Cornish, the Bretons, and the Manx (natives of the Isle of Man). In the first millennium B.C., the Celts became the dominant people in non-Mediterranean Europe. During the first century B.C., they were overpowered by the Romans and began to assimilate. The Celtic tribes in Great Britain were driven back to Scotland, Wales, and Cornwall by succeeding waves of invaders: first, the Romans, then the Anglo-Saxons, and, finally, in the eleventh century, the Normans. Ireland, however, remained free of Roman colonization and did not change significantly until the introduction of Christianity in the fifth century A.D. There are six Celtic languages: Irish, Welsh, Scottish Gaelic, Manx, Cornish, and Breton.

Celtic MYTHS were transmitted orally by professional storytellers, who played an important role in Celtic society. They were employed by kings who used them, along with singers, musicians, and jugglers, to entertain chieftains and warriors (*see* MAN OF LORE). The earliest storytellers presumably memorized the outlines of traditional, well-known stories and filled in the details as they wished.

Although sources disagree about when Celtic stories were first written, it seems that Irish tales, for example, were first recorded in written form somewhere between the sixth and early seventh centuries, with a very few stories written before the eighth century. Most surviving manuscripts come from the twelfth century and were compiled by Christian monks. Irish stories invariably were written in prose, while Welsh tales, including the EPIC *Gododdin*, were told in verse.

Celtic kings and chiefs also supported BARDS, poets who sang their patrons' praises, memorized their genealogies, celebrated their victories, and mourned their deaths. Bards learned their art at special schools or from established poets. Bardic poetry reached its height in Ireland and Scotland between the thirteenth and seventeenth centuries, and in Wales between the eleventh and thirteenth centuries.

In the eleventh and twelfth centuries, traveling minstrels spread Celtic legends, including tales of ARTHUR and other HEROES, throughout Europe. Wandering minstrels earned their livings by traveling to courts, castles, fairs, and markets. They entertained their audiences with stories, poetry, and music. Minstrels sometimes remained at one court for several years. The effect of the dispersion of Celtic stories is clearly illustrated by the Bretons, who had links with the Cornish and the Welsh. The Bretons translated traditional Celtic stories into French. After the Norman conquest of England, the Bretons brought back tales of Arthur, for example, to England, their place of origin.

Important Celtic stories from Ireland include the *Tain Bo Cuailnge* (*Cattle Raid of Cooley*), which tells of the conflict between the ancient Irish provinces of Ulster and Connacht and contains many supernatural beings (*see* CUCHULAINN); the twelfth-century *Book of Invasions*, which sets the stage for the coming of the Gaels or Celts to Ireland; and the Fionn Cycle, which tells of the supernatural hero Finn and his heroic war-band, the Fianna. From Wales come the *Four Branches of the Mabinogi*, four stories about Pwyll, RHIANNON, and Pryderi; Branwen and Bendigeidfran; Manawydan; and Math, Lord of Gwynedd as well as the *Tale of Culhwch and Olwen*, a quest story in which Culhwch must complete a series of impossible tasks before he can marry Olwen. Although *The Mabinogion* and the *Tale of Culhwch and Olwen* are thought to have been written in the eleventh and tenth centuries respectively, the stories existed in oral tradition for many centuries before they were written down.

Many Celtic tales are about young, handsome, superhuman warriors. These heroes are fulfilled only when engaged in battle, and they exemplify those virtues valued in Celtic society: individualism, courage, and pride. Often there is a tendency toward exaggeration in these stories, and the impossible and the supernatural prevail.

Other Celtic stories include the popular theme of the love between two supernatural beings or between GODS and MORTALS. These stories may include the triangle of a young lover, a MAIDEN, and an unsuccessful, often older suitor. The jealousy that results has destructive effects on the land and the community. Irish myth includes the theme of sacral kingship, in which the union of a king and a GODDESS encourages the kingdom's prosperity.

The otherworld (or underworld) is another significant feature of Celtic storytelling. Irish myths and sagas are set in both historical Ireland and the mythic underworld of the *Sidhe*. It is not always clear whether the characters are divine or human; many are gods in the process of becoming mortals. The *Book of Invasions* details the activities of the fairy race, the Tuatha Dé Danaan, who inhabited Ireland and were driven into an underworld kingdom by the Gaels. *The Mabinogion* includes magic ANIMALS, SHAPE-SHIFTING, and Annwn, the pagan underworld.

Celtic otherworlds may be on an island or on a group of islands, under the ground, at the bottom of a lake, or in a hill or burial mound. They are not necessarily the land of the dead. Sometimes they are the home of the gods or they are inhabited by a fairy race. DEATH and time do not exist in these otherworlds. They often contain magic vessels of resurrection or regeneration. FOOD and drink come from such vessels. The inhabitants of the otherworld spend their time feasting and making love. They listen to beautiful music and smell wonderful scents. Flowers bloom constantly and fruit always hangs on the trees. The enchanted, uncanny beauty of Celtic otherworlds greatly influenced later western European storytelling traditions, notably medieval Arthurian legend and the genre of medieval ROMANCE.

The Celtic influence is also obvious in the plays, poems, and mythologies of the great modern Irish writer, W.B. Yeats (*see* YEATS, WILLIAM BUTLER), for instance, the play *The Countess Cathleen* and the collection of tales, *The Celtic Twilight*. The playwright John Synge also displays Celtic storytelling influence in plays like *Riders to the Sea* and *The Playboy of the Western World*. *See also* NORTHERN EUROPEAN STORYTELLING.

For Further Reading

Ebbutt, M.E. *Hero Myths and Legends of Britain and Ireland*. 1910. Reprint, UK: Blandford, 1995.

Gantz, Jeffrey. *Early Irish Myths and Sagas*. New York: Penguin, 1982.

Glassie, Henry. *Irish Folk History: Texts from the North*. Illustrated. Philadelphia: University of Pennsylvania Press, 1982.

Green, Miranda Jane. *Celtic Myths*. London: The Trustees of the British Museum, 1993.

CENTAURS

Creatures in Greek mythology, half-man and half-horse. The traditional image of a centaur is a horse's body with the torso and head of a man attached in place of the horse's head and neck.

The Centaurs were descended from a Thessallian mortal named Ixion, who unsuccessfully tried to seduce HERA, the queen of the GODS. Hera's husband ZEUS tricked Ixion with an image of Hera shaped from a cloud. This cloud, later named Nephele, bore a child named Centaurus, who mated with mares and produced the race of centaurs.

Centaurs are generally savage and unruly creatures. During the LABORS OF HERAKLES, the HERO fights off a gang of centaurs who want his wine for themselves. At the marriage of Pirithous, king of the Lapiths, a number of drunken centaurs get out of control and try to make off with the bride and all the other women in attendance. The Lapiths, aided by THESEUS, fight a battle against the centaurs and win.

One centaur, Chiron, was singularly wise and kind. He was the tutor of the warrior ACHILLES and the hunter Actaeon. Chiron's most famous pupil was Asclepius, the Greek god of healing. According to one story, Herakles accidentally kills Chiron during the centaur attack. According to another story, Chiron sacrifices his own life to save that of the Titan Prometheus (*see* PROMETHEUS AND THE THEFT OF FIRE).

It is possible that the mythical centaurs were inspired by an actual tribe in Thessaly, neighbors of the Lapiths. Robert Graves has suggested that their mythic image was derived from primitive rain dances in which men dressed as horses (*see* GRAVES, ROBERT).

The Babylonians designated the centaur as the constellation Sagittarius in the eleventh century B.C. Colorful male and female centaurs are featured in the 1939 Disney movie, Fantasia. The Gandharvas, Kimpurushas, and *Kinnaras* of HINDU STORYTELLING are also part horse and part human.

Other animal-human creatures abound in oral traditions—MERMAIDS in European storytelling; SATYRS, SIRENS, and the MINOTAUR in Greece; and the elephant-headed god GANESA in India. *See also* ANCIENT GREEK STORYTELLING.

For Further Reading

Graves, Robert. *The Greek Myths*. 2 vols. New York: Penguin Books, 1957.

Hamilton, Edith. *Mythology: Timeless Tales of Gods and Heroes*. New York: Mentor, 1969.

CENTRAL AND SOUTH AMERICAN STORYTELLING

History of the storytelling tradition in Central and South America. Because the region is so large and there are so many Native Central and South American Indian tribes, there is no one language used in storytelling. Many of the MYTHS have not yet been recorded, although certain MOTIFS exist among these varied peoples.

While there are not many CREATION myths across Central and South American folklore, there is often a "First Ancestor" or a CULTURE HERO, and some effort to explain the existence of the SUN, the MOON, and other special features of the world. The explanation for the existence of the world is often credited to a kind of "wandering magician" with the ability to transform things. This figure is called

Viracocha in Peru, *Bochica* in Colombia, *Maria* among the Tupi-Guarani, and *Keri* and *Kame* among the Bakairi. The culture hero is responsible for the present order of things, and he is the one who is seen as having taught the law, the social system, the arts, and the crafts to the people. As a result, they may be the HEROES of various EPICS.

In many South American mythologies, especially that of the Caribs, Bakairi, and Tierra del Fuego Indians, there is a pair of twins who are often even more important or powerful than the culture hero, and are credited with creating, transforming, and teaching. These twins can be regarded as personifying the sun and the moon, with the sun the elder and more powerful brother and the moon periodically having difficulties, dying, and in need of revival.

Both Central and South American tribes also believe that long ago a number of cataclysmic events occurred, during which various kinds of beings who had been created by the GODS were destroyed, until finally humankind was created and considered the most successful form of life. These cataclysms include "the Great Fire," "the Long Night," "the FLOOD," and a long period of intense cold. There are a number of variants on the flood or deluge motif caused by a punishing or angry GOD.

A number of myths also focus on the origin of fire, which may be attributed to the twins, the culture hero, or HELPFUL ANIMALS. The motif of the theft of fire is a common one; a culture hero might steal it from a MONSTER or an ANIMAL. The TRICKSTER figure, often in animal form (e.g., a fox or a turtle), is also very popular in the oral tradition, and he is variously described as stupid, greedy, aggressive, ambitious, and mischievous, and a subject of laughter. Sometimes the trickster convinces his adversary—another animal— to do foolish things such as jumping into a pond to retrieve a piece of cheese that is really a reflection of the moon or beating children who turn out to be dangerous wasps. Sometimes the major gods themselves have trickster characteristics. The Toltec/Aztec QUETZALCOATL created humankind by sprinkling his blood on the bones of dead beings from previous worlds. Quetzalcoatl's rival, Tezcatlipoca, drove Quetzalcoatl away by a series of destructive tricks.

Central and South America have had their storytellers—sometimes Indian, sometimes Spanish— who have passed tales on by word of mouth, mixing traditions of the Old and New Worlds. *See also,* CONIRAYA AND CAVILLACA, COADIPOP, COATLICUE.

CHAIN OF WORLDS

Myth from the Campa Indians of Peru, most likely with Incan origins, describing some aspects of CREATION, the LEGEND of the first god and all the GODS of the tribe that followed him, and the Scale of the Gods, or the sequence of planets. The Campa Indians' tradition of a highly-defined mythology is the special provenance of the chiefs and SHAMANS of the tribe. Following in this tradition, this story was told by Chief Kecizate Ashaninga.

Millions of centuries ago, the EARTH was in darkness. In some places were springs of muddy water, which began to grow and to form great masses of thick, soupy muck. The coolness turned into warmth, and the mire began to bubble. Then thick mud oozed its way into channels, and rivers were formed. One day, the first man, Mahonte, and his family left their home, a hole, in search of earth to eat. Mahonte's youngest daughter remained in the hole. She heard a voice and then spat to one side. Unknowingly, Mahonte's daughter had spat on Manchakori, the first god.

Manchakori formed fruits for the family to eat and instructed Mahonte's daughter to tell her family to take the fruits in an orderly fashion. When the family returned, they didn't listen and grabbed the fruits. Manchakori appeared and told them that they had disobeyed. He said that because the fruits were mixed with the other plants, the family would have to search for the fruits and choose among them. When some of the people tried to pick up the earth-FOOD they had brought, they turned into ants.

Mahonte's daughter realized that she had become pregnant by talking to Manchakori. The god later returned and gave the girl two plants. One was to stave off pain when her son was born. During childbirth, Mahonte's daughter held the wrong plant, and her son was born very hot. The baby's body continued to burn. Manchakori instructed Mahonte, now his father-in-law, to take the baby away and bury him. He was not to put any water on the child no matter how hot he was. As he traveled, Mahonte could not stand the heat from the baby, and he threw some water on the child. Then he buried him. When Mahonte returned, he lied and said he did not throw water on the baby. Time passed and the sun appeared. When Manchakori saw fog, he knew that Mahonte had put water on some, but not all, parts of the baby. As a result, some parts of the earth have rain and others do not.

Because the sun was there to accompany the people during the day, Manchakori moved high up into the SKY and became the MOON. He promised to return and keep the people company at night. The stains on the moon are Mahonte's daughter's spit, from when she heard Manchakori's voice for the first time.

Before he left and turned into the moon, Manchakori took the youngest son of Mahonte and made him his disciple. Likewise, Mahonte's son later took a companion, another god, and made him his disciple. This god also took a disciple; thus, down the scale come all the gods of the tribe.

The Scale of the Gods is comprised of the planets above and below the earth. The earth is called *Kamaveni,* referring to immortality. Below Kamaveni is a planet called *Kirinte*. The spirits of unconscious people go to Kirinte. They can choose to stay and die or to return to the earth and revive. Below Kirinte is the planet *Karanshaveni,* or HELL. This is where souls of those who failed in their tribal duties go. Above the earth is the moon. Above the moon is *Kamayrotagaro,* where human spirits go immediately after death. If they pass an examination about their conduct on earth, they learn about life in *Ozarite,* or HEAVEN. The spirits ascend to *Tzego* where the gods of the ANIMALS live in human form. They then go to Ozarite where life is eternal. *Katzirinkaytiri,* the SUN, is above Ozarite. The highest planet is *Ayninka,* where iron GIANTS live. When they come down to Ozarite, they cross in front of the sun and cause eclipses on earth and the other planets.

This specific MYTH of the Campa Indians includes various MOTIFS that appear in the mythologies and the tales of other storytelling traditions. The beginning of this myth, when the world is in darkness and defined by great masses of muck which eventually become rivers, is similar to other creation from chaos stories, such as BABYLONIAN CREATION, EGYPTIAN CREATION, NORSE CREATION, and JAPANESE CREATION. In these creation stories, some power or force gives form and reality to indeterminate, undifferentiated nothingness, thus turning it into cosmos.

Likewise, the family's disobedience of Manchakori's instructions about how to take the fruits can be compared to ADAM AND EVE's disobedience regarding the fruit from the tree of the knowledge of good and evil. In both stories, the people choose to disobey their god's specific instructions, and they end up enduring great difficulties.

Although the son of Mahonte's daughter is not a traditional HERO in this story, his unusual conception resembles that of many heroes from other traditions. Perhaps most similar to the Aztec QUETZALCOATL, who was conceived when his mother was breathed upon by the supreme being, the son of Mahonte's daughter is conceived when Mahonte's daughter talks to the first god, Manchakori. Other heroes who were conceived under miraculous or unusual circumstances include ATTIS, KUTOYIS, Jesus, the BUDDHA, KARNA, and Waterjar Boy (*see* WATERJAR BOY MYTH).

Finally, according to Campa tradition, everything that exists in the world has its own legend. While this myth does not provide the stories for all things, it does explain the origins of ants, fog, rain patterns, the moon, the spots on the moon, and eclipses. Other explanatory tales include the Australian story BLANKET LIZARD, explaining why this lizard is reddish in color and has a frill around its neck, and the Ghanese tale OSEBO'S DRUM, describing how the leopard got its spots and how the turtle got its shell. Rudyard Kipling's JUST SO STORIES also contains several explanatory tales, including another version of how the leopard got its spots (*see* KIPLING, RUDYARD).

For Further Reading

Ashaninga, Kecizate, as told to Fernando Llosa Porras. "The Chain of Worlds." *Parabola* 2.3 (1977): 58-62.

CHAIN TALE

Subgenre of folk literature. The chain tale is differentiated from other types of FORMULA TALES by the repetition of a series of NUMBERS, objects, events, and characters throughout the tale. The formulation of a sequence of the previously mentioned elements in interconnected relationships of cause and effect is the primary component of the chain tale's interior structure. Although the event that starts the linking process is often the final link itself in the chain tale, some stories incorporate a more traditional, linear narrative approach. While the chain tale may lack the ornate decoration of other folktales, its listener may benefit by developing an understanding of the relationships between seemingly disparate elements. In "Lazy Jack," Jack's mother orders him, one Monday, to find work or face being removed from the house. On Tuesday, Jack earns a penny working for a neighboring farmer, but clumsily drops his wage into a stream. On Wednesday, Jack works on a dairy, earning a bottle of milk. However, on his journey home, Jack spills all of the milk, and is chastised once again by his mother. The tale ends the following Monday, when Jack earns a donkey by working for a cattle man. Finding it impossible to move the stubborn creature, Jack hoists the donkey onto his back and carries the braying animal home. Passing by the household of a wealthy man with a daughter who is incapable of speaking, Jack causes the beautiful young woman to laugh at the puerile sight before her, thereby breaking her congenital silence. The wealthy man rewards Jack with his daughter's hand in marriage and a fine house to live in. Although the series of relationships is simplistic, this story simultaneously reveals the didactic and jocular elements common in many chain tales. *See also* JACK TALES.

For Further Reading

Dailey, Sheila. *Putting the World in a Nutshell.* New York: H.W. Wilson, 1994.

CHANCE AND FATE

Concepts prevalent in many stories suggesting that events surrounding the characters are predestined.

In stories and tales around the world, fate plays an important role. The "fatal look"— that is, the glance that brings on death or destruction is a theme in a number of stories. Also there are children who are fated to bring evil (e.g., Oedipus) and there is the "fatal imitation" of Brer Rabbit, which brings about his own death.

According to the philosopher Boethius's (c. 450–c. 525) model, Chance, the term we use when some action appears to be random or spontaneous, does not exist. GOD imposes order on all things, and so there is no opportunity for random events. Rather, Chance is defined as individual acts that appear to be random to humans. Chance, nonetheless, is the result of Providence, the divine plan. Fate moves the sky and the stars, governs the relationship between the elements, renews all things in the cycle of life, and controls the chain of causes that effects the acts and fortunes of humans. This chain of causes is directed by Providence. A knowing God acts while ignorant humans look on.

Human beings don't have the ability to understand the order of Providence, which is why things don't seem to make sense, why the fortunes of both good and bad people continually vary between adversity and prosperity, and why certain results appear unjust. Boethius's writings assert that all things that happen are planned and suited to those to whom they happen. Free will is the illusion of human beings' ability to choose. Boethius's writings make the most sense in a tradition that comprises an omnipotent deity, the medieval Christian God.

The wheel of fortune, symbolizing the precariousness of things in this life, and Lady Fortune, whose origins are found in Fortuna, the Roman goddess of fortune and good luck, have been favorite symbols in western European literature from the middle ages to modern times.

The Fates or goddesses of destiny in the northern European myths are three giant maidens called the *Nornir* (*Norns*). Their ancestors are those beings who also gave rise to the Greek goddesses of Fate, the *Moirae,* daughters of Zeus, who determined the course of life among humans. The Nornir determine the length of all lives and are said to be all-powerful. Even ODIN, the ruler of the Norse pantheon, is subject to the power of the Nornir. The tremendous power of fate is a prevalent theme in many of the Norse legends and is the main lesson in the story of BALDR. In spite of the protection of Frigg and the wisdom of Odin, Baldr cannot escape his destined fate. In the Norse tradition, gods and goddesses are subject to fate because there is no omnipotent, omniscient deity.

After the advent of Christianity, the Anglo-Saxons continued to believe in the power of Urd, the oldest of the three Nornir. In Old English, *Urd* becomes *wyrd*, meaning "fate," or the final destiny that no thing can evade. The term *wyrd* appears several times in BEOWULF with this meaning. *Wyrd* existed as such in English at least to Shakespearean days. In *Macbeth*, the Weird Sisters are three witches with the ability to foretell the future and to influence the course of events.

In later traditions that don't comprise a conception of God like the medieval conception of God, the use of the terms "chance" and "fate" becomes less technical, and often chance, fate, providence, and destiny are used interchangeably. J. R. R. Tolkien's *The Lord of the Rings* contains examples of heroes who are driven by chance and fate (*see* TOLKIEN, J.R.R.).

CHANGELINGS

Fairies who are exchanged for human babies. Generally, changelings are old fairies, but they can also be fairy children who are sickly and in need of human milk. Sometimes changelings are pieces of wood or roughly molded figures. The most common reason that fairies steal human babies and replace them with changelings is because the fairies desire golden-haired, beautiful children to improve their fairy stock, who are often dark and hairy. In some stories, however, the fairies owe a tribute to HELL, which they are reluctant to

pay with their own kind; in other stories, humans are taken as servants, particularly nursing mothers to provide milk for fairy babies and midwives to assist in the birth of fairy children. Changelings are commonly substituted for unbaptized children unless certain precautions are taken, including hanging an open pair of scissors over them, sticking a pin in their clothes, laying their fathers' trousers across their cradles, or placing a circle of fire around them. Changelings are usually deformed and ugly, and they often display a spiteful, malicious nature.

Changelings who are old fairies generally reveal themselves when they betray their age. One way they are tricked into doing so, found in the folklore of several European countries, is when a suspicious human brews beer or boils water in egg-shells. This unusual activity causes the changeling to laugh and say he has seen many things, but he has never seen anything like that before. Often, the true child is then returned.

Because fairies covet human children and steal them whenever they can, there are numerous tales about changelings as well as about fairies' thwarted attempts to carry off humans. Charlotte Mew's poem "The Changeling" is told from the changeling's point of view. Numerous other stories about changelings from storytelling traditions across Europe can be found in *The Fairy Mythology* by Thomas Keightley (*see* KEIGHTLEY, THOMAS).

For Further Reading

Briggs, K. M. *The Fairies in Tradition and Literature.* London: Routledge and Kegan Paul, 1967.

Carter, John Marshall. "Fairies." *Mythical and Fabulous Creatures: A Source Book and Research Guide.* Edited by Malcolm South. Westport, CT: Greenwood, 1987.

Keightley, Thomas. *The Fairy Mythology.* 1850. Reprint, New York: Haskell House, 1968.

McGraw, Eloise Jarvis. *The Moorchild.* New York: Margaret K. McElderry Books, 1991.

CHANGING WOMAN

Navajo and Apache GODDESS and important religious figure. Her name comes from the fact that she can change at will from baby to girl to woman to CRONE and back again. The Apaches believe that Changing Woman is one of the founders of their culture. A teacher and guide, she is present at the puberty rites of women, where Changing Woman enters the girl's body and stays there for four days, helping her transform into a woman. The reenactment of Changing Woman's own sexual intercourse with the SUN takes place during these puberty rites. The offspring of Changing Woman and the sun are MONSTER-slaying twin sons who are culture heroes for the Apache.

The Navajos consider Changing Woman the First MOTHER, creator of the four heads of the original clans, sustainer of life through the FOOD she produces, in the tradition of the Great Goddess or EARTH-MOTHER, such as CORN MOTHER or the Greek goddess Demeter (see PERSEPHONE MYTH). She is thought to have had a miraculous birth, found in the form of a small turquoise on a mountainside by Fire Man. Through a special ceremony, she was then changed into a female baby. The Navajos also tell the story of her sons, the twin monster-slayers called Monster Slayer and Child Born of Water. Eventually, Changing Woman settled in a great home in the West, made for her by the sun, who would join her each evening. For the Navajo women, Changing Woman represents the ideal role model and is much beloved.

For Further Reading

Gill, Sam D., and Irene F. Sullivan. *A Dictionary of Native American Myth*. New York: Oxford University Press, 1992.

CHAPEL PERILOUS

Strange and terrifying chapel in Arthurian LEGENDS where the HERO must overcome his fear in order to fulfill a QUEST. The Chapel Perilous is one of several places, including enchanted castles and foreboding forests, where the Arthurian hero is tested by forces, often supernatural, of evil and DEATH (see CASTLES—ENCHANTED). He must prove himself in order to leave the Chapel Perilous with what he has come for. The hero may encounter a corpse on the chapel's altar, a black hand that extinguishes the candles, eerie voices, or, as in the following tale, threatening black knights and a sorceress.

LANCELOT is riding in the forest when a maiden asks him to help a fellow knight of the Round Table. The knight is seriously wounded and will die unless Lancelot will go to the Chapel Perilous and bring back a sword and a piece of cloth that he will find there.

Lancelot goes to the chapel. In the graveyard, he sees thirty tall knights, wearing black armor and brandishing their swords. Lancelot is terrified, but he holds onto his own sword, and the black knights let him pass.

Once in the dimly lit chapel, Lancelot sees the dead body of a knight, covered by a silken cloth and with a sword resting by his side. Lancelot cuts a piece from the cloth. The ground seems to tremble beneath him, and he is afraid. He takes the sword and piece of cloth and retreats outside where the black knights order him to drop the sword. Lancelot does not.

Outside the churchyard, a beautiful young girl tells him to leave the sword or die. Lancelot refuses. The maiden is a sorceress named Hellawes who loves Lancelot. She has planned to capture him in the Chapel Perilous, murder him, and then embalm his body so that she can embrace it at will. Lancelot leaves behind the evil chapel and takes the sword and cloth to the injured knight whose wounds are then healed.

For Further Reading

Cavendish, Richard. *King Arthur and the Grail*. London: Paladin, 1985.

CHARLEMAGNE (742–814)

Ruler of the Frankish kingdom who was crowned Emperor of the Holy Roman Empire on Christmas Day A.D. 800. Two centuries after Charlemagne's death, numerous anecdotes depicting his greatness circulated throughout Europe and were particularly popular in France and Germany. It seems to be true that the historical Charlemagne was concerned with the well-being of his subjects and their descendants and that he promoted advances in his government's administration as well as in the area of arts and letters. The MYTH of Charlemagne, however, has greatly exaggerated his accomplishments.

In the late eleventh-century poem, the SONG OF ROLAND, Charlemagne is portrayed as a snowy-bearded KING who is 200 years old or more. He is the Sacred Emperor, the Father of all Christendom, and a champion warlord against the Moslem heathens. Angels converse with Charlemagne, and he is GOD'S primary agent on earth. As such, Charlemagne is closely associated with Moses and Jesus as well as many other Biblical HEROES. The precedent for Charlemagne's association with religious figures was set during his own lifetime when he was compared to King David.

Also in the *Song of Roland*, Charlemagne is presented as the ideal earthly king. He is stately, courteous, valiant, and deeply religious. He loves his army, and he rides and fights with his men as the greatest among them.

Other medieval Italian, French, German, and English romances extend the myth of Charlemagne and his knights. Many of these romances, including the EPIC fantasies of the Italian poets Pulci (b. 1431), Boiardo (b. 1434), and Ariosto (b. 1474); the "Romans de Chevalerie" of the Comte de Tressan; and certain German collections of popular tales, appear in Thomas Bulfinch's (*see* BULFINCH, THOMAS) *The Legends of Charlemagne* (1862). In these ROMANCES, ORLANDO, Rinaldo, Astolpho, and Gano are all various forms of the character ROLAND. The romances tell the adventures of Roland (Orlando, Rinaldo, etc.) and his peers or paladins. Common elements include Roland's confrontation with Farragus the GIANT, the power of Roland's sword, and Roland's horse, Bayard. The heroes in these stories fall in and out of love, fatally wield miraculous weapons, and usually survive the deadliest of blows. The element of war is prevalent throughout, and the Christian warriors are always victorious over the pagan enemy. Charlemagne is often presented as a weak, but passionate ruler. Frequently he is the victim of treacherous counselors and at the mercy of unreliable barons, on whose prowess he depends for maintenance of his throne.

The historical figure Charlemagne was canonized on December 29, 1165.

For Further Reading

Brault, Gerard J. *The Song of Roland: An Analytical Edition*. Vol. 1. University Park, PA: Pennsylvania State University Press, 1978.

Bulfinch, Thomas. *The Age of Chivalry and Legends of Charlemagne or Romance of the Middle Ages*. New York: New American Library, 1962.

Burgess, Glyn S., trans. *The Song of Roland*. New York: Viking Penguin, 1990.

CHASE, RICHARD (1904–1988)

Folklorist of the Appalachian region of the United States. Born in 1904, near Huntsville, Alabama, Chase received a B.S. from Antioch College in 1929. He worked his entire life as a writer, a lecturer on FOLKLORE, and a teller of tales at schools, colleges, universities, libraries, and clubs throughout the United States. Most of his time was spent in the Virginia, Alabama, and Carolina region, which he loved. He helped found an Appalachian craft industry and has convened folk festivals and folk art workshops, becoming recognized as one whose research renewed interest in Appalachian stroytelling.

Concerned with the preservation of Anglo American traditions, he edited *Old Songs and Singing Games* (1938), *The Jack Tales* (1943), and *Grandfather Tales: American-English Folktales* (1948). His adaptations of *Jack and the Three Sillies* (1950) and *Billy Boy* (1966) appeared as picture books and served to introduce JACK TALES to a new generation of children.

CHELM

In Jewish FOLKLORE, city of wise people. The city of Chelm was known for the wisdom of its inhabitants, but in the tale "The Wise Men of Chelm," the so-called wise people reveal their inability to recognize the obvious. In building the city, for example, they must resolve what to do with the dirt they have dug up for the foundation. They decide to put the dirt from the hole into a second hole that they have dug without realizing that this process would require them to continue digging holes forever.

Another instance of their inability to find the most sensible solution to a problem occurs when the rabbi and wise men of Chelm are looking for a way to keep the synagogue alms box from thieves. While it made sense to hang the alms box from the ceiling of the synagogue, out of reach of thieves' hands, they were perplexed as to how to reach the alms box themselves. Ultimately, they decide to place a ladder in the synagogue in order to reach the alms box, not noticing that a thief could use the ladder as easily as they.

In another case, the wise men of Chelm want to avoid having the beadle who calls them to morning prayer step on the untouched white snow, so they appoint two men to carry the beadle, oblivious to the doubling of footprints they would leave. When the beadle gets too old to knock on the shutters of each home every morning, the wise men have the shutters brought to the beadle.

The stories of Chelm suggest that sometimes the truth lies under our noses, that wisdom can be simple, and that the obvious can elude us if we look too hard. As in many of the stories of Jewish folklore, "The Wise Men of Chelm" reveals humor as well as a wisdom of its own.

For Further Reading

Sadeh, Pinhas. *Jewish Folktales*. Translated by Hillel Halkin. New York: Doubleday, 1989.

Singer, Isaac Bashevis. *The Fools of Chelm and Their History*. Illustrated by Uri Shulevitz. New York: Farrar, Straus, Giroux, 1973.

Tannenbaum, Samuel. *The Wise Men of Chelm*. Illustrated by Zevi Blum. New York: T. Yosseloff, 1965.

CHEROKEE CREATION

Cosmogonic CREATION myth of the Cherokee tribe. According to the Cherokee creation MYTH, the universe began as one enormous and continuous body of water. Present from the beginning of the universe are a number of creatures, including ANIMALS, who live in a region above the water, and the SUN. Due to a problem of overpopulation in the HEAVENS, the animals send scouts to the "water" world to determine if what is below the water is inhabitable. The water-beetle, who dives to the depths of the water, returns to the surface with a substance resembling mud, which begins to grow until an inhabitable island is formed (*see* EARTH-DIVER CREATION).

After the EARTH, which began as a great flat island floating in the water, is fastened to the heavens with four cords, various animals volunteer to prepare the new home for inhabitation. The Great Buzzard is accredited with creating the mountains and valleys of the earth, caused by the flaps of his enormous wings. The animals are responsible for establishing the track that the sun must follow as it circles the earth. After the great migration from the heavens to the earth, the animals and plants are ordered (by whom is unknown) to remain awake for seven nights. However, because only a few of the various species could remain awake for the duration of the TEST, they were given certain powers or qualities that are not possessed by other species.

Perhaps one of the most interesting episodes of the Cherokee creation myth occurs in connection with the creation of humankind. Initially, only a brother and a sister inhabit the earth (from whence they came remains unclear). However, the brother strikes the sister with a fish and orders her to reproduce. Every seven days the woman produces a child, until it is determined (again by whom remains mysterious) that woman should only reproduce once a year to avoid the overpopulation of the earth.

One last episode of the Cherokee creation myth involves the sun, who hates the people of the earth because they can not look directly at her brilliance without contorting their faces. Seeking revenge against the earth people, the Sun kills hundreds of earth people on a daily basis with her scorching rays. After acquiring assistance from the Little Men, who practice the arts of medicine and are revered for their wisdom, the earth people sent Rattlesnake to kill the Sun with its poisonous bite. However, Rattlesnake mistakenly attacks the Sun's daughter, who subsequently dies. The Sun, quitting her murderous attacks, grieves the loss of her daughter and refuses to leave her abode, leaving the earth people in perpetual darkness. Only after appeasing the Sun with a musical performance does light and heat return to the earth people.

In many respects, the Cherokee creation story remains incomplete; the most problematic of these ambiguities is that there is no recorded cosmogonic myth that details the first act of creation, prior to the existence of the animals. The Cherokee creation myth is similar to other creation stories of Native America. The Great Buzzard, for example, is a character found in many Native American mythologies, especially in the genesis myths of the Creek and Yuchi peoples.

For Further Reading

Erdoes, Richard, and Alfonso Ortiz. *American Indian Myths and Legends*. New York: Pantheon, 1985.

Mooney, James. *Myths of the Cherokee*, New York: Johnson Reprint Corporation, 1970.

Thompson, Stith. *Tales of the North American Indians*. Bloomington, IN: Indiana University Press, 1971.

Ywahoo, Dhyani. *Voices of Our Ancestors: Cherokee Teachings from the Wisdom Fire*. Boston: Shambhala, 1987.

CHILD IN THE REEDS

Tale from Basutoland (now known as Lesotho) in southern Africa, which includes the themes of a forbidden tree, a father casting off his children, a baby finding protection in or near water, a woman who lives under water, and a descent into and emergence from a form of the underworld (*see* DESCENT TO THE UNDERWORLD).

The story begins when a boy, Hlabakoane, refuses to herd the cattle unless his sister, Thakane, gives him a piece of the *kumonngoe,* an incredible tree that provides food for their parents but is forbidden to the children. Afraid that the cattle will remain in the corral, Thakane gives in to Hlabakoane's obstinacy and cuts a piece from the *kumonngoe*. Thick milk pours from the tree like a river and spreads to the gardens where the parents are working. Mahlabakoane, the mother, and Rahlabakoane, the father, run back to their hut, where Thakane blames her brother for her disobedience. Rahlabakoane decides to cast off Thakane because she has eaten of the forbidden tree, and he takes her to an OGRE to be eaten.

When Thakane and Rahlabakoane arrive at the ogre's village, the ogre eats Rahlabakoane instead, and Masilo, the ogre's son, marries Thakane. Thakane gives birth to a baby girl, Lilahloane. When girls are born in this village, the ogre eats them; only boys are to be born. Thakane says she will drown her child herself rather than have her eaten by the ogre. At the river, a CRONE emerges from a pool where reeds are growing and takes Thakane's baby. Thakane returns regularly to the river to visit Lilahloane, who grows into a beautiful maiden. One day, Masilo observes Thakane and his daughter together by the river. That evening, he tells Thakane what he has seen. He begs to see his child and promises that she will not be eaten by his father now that she is grown up. For the price of a thousand cattle, the old woman brings Lilahloane out of the water.

Thakane, Masilo, and their children travel back to Thakane's home, so that her mother and her brother might see her again, and they encounter a rock blocking the road. The rock is Rahlabakoane, lying in ambush for Thakane. The rock speaks, saying that he will eat Thakane and then her escorts. Thakane and Masilo try to appease the rock by giving it first many cattle, then people, to eat. Still the rock will not let them pass. Finally, Thakane gives herself and her family up to the rock.

Inside one of the men cuts a hole into the flesh of the rock's belly. He opens a door out of the belly, the rock dies, and all the people and cattle emerge from the rock. Later, Thakane and Masilo are joyfully received at Thakane's village.

This Basuto story contains numerous MOTIFS found in other storytelling traditions. Just as Thakane and Hlabakoane are forbidden to eat from the tree that nourishes their parents, ADAM AND EVE from Judeo-Christian tradition are forbidden by GOD to eat from the tree of the knowledge of good and evil in the Garden of Eden. Both sets of children disobey their parents with the consequence that Adam, Eve, and Thakane are cast off by their fathers. In a comparable fashion, ODIN, the father of the Norse pantheon, casts the GOD-DESS HEL to the underworld.

The motifs of a child's abandonment in water and ensuing adoption are also repeated in stories from various cultures. The Indian HERO KARNA from the MAHABHARATA is abandoned in a river and adopted by a member of the lower class. Moses is hidden in a basket of bulrushes and adopted by the pharaoh's daughter (*see* EXODUS). The German hero SIEGFRIED is left in a glass vessel in the river and adopted first by a doe and then by a blacksmith. The Polynesian demigod MAUI is thrown into the SEA and adopted by sea spirits. The Greek Oedipus is left to die in the wilderness but is saved by a shepherd (*see* SECRET SON).

Another example of a powerful female figure who resides under the water is the Lady of the Lake from Arthurian LEGEND, a fay or fairy who lives in an enchanted palace in the depths of the lake. It is the Lady of the Lake who gives King ARTHUR his famed sword, Excalibur. In some tales, it is also the Lady of the Lake who imprisons the magician MERLIN (*see* MARWE IN THE UNDERWORLD, CASTLES—ENCHANTED).

Finally, Thakane and her family's descent into the rock's belly is reminiscent not only of the Hebrew Jonah, who is swallowed by a great fish and remains in its belly for three days and three nights, but of the descent of many heroes to the underworld in their journeys or QUESTS. ODYSSEUS, GILGAMESH, Aeneas (*see* AENEID), THESEUS, Jesus, and INANNA are all characters from various storytelling traditions who undertake a journey to the land of the dead.

For Further Reading

Abrahams, Roger, ed. *African Folktales: Traditional Stories of the Black World*. New York: Pantheon, 1983.

CHIMERA

In Greek mythology, female MONSTER who is part lion, part goat, and part serpent. The word *chimera* means "she-goat." In the ILIAD, HOMER describes the chimera as a fire-breathing monster that takes the form of a lion in the front part, a serpent in the hind part, and a goat in the middle. HESIOD writes in the

Theogony that the chimera has three heads, one of a lion, one of a goat, and the third of a snake. She, too, is a fire-breathing monster, who is large, fast, and strong. In Greek art, the chimera is usually portrayed as a monster with a lion's body, with a goat's head projecting from the lion's back, and with a snake for a tail.

The chimera is said to be of divine origin. Her mother was the hideous monster Echidna, a beautiful girl to the waist and a monstrous, man-eating serpent below the waist. Her father was Typhon, a man-beast hybrid, who was taller than any mountain and had wings, eyes of fire, hands made of dragons, and the lower body of vipers. Some sources say that the chimera's mother was the many-headed Hydra, and her father was Orthus, the two-headed dog who guarded the cattle of Geryon. The chimera traditionally lives in Lycia.

The chimera plays a significant role in only one myth, the story of Bellerophon. In this legend, the HERO Bellerophon refuses the advances of Anteia, King Proetus's wife, who takes her revenge by accusing him of trying to seduce her. Proetus sends Bellerophon to Anteia's father, King Iobates of Lycia. Iobates gives Bellerophon a task that he believes will result in the young hero's death: he challenges Bellerophon to kill the chimera who is destroying Lycia with her fiery breath. The seer Polyeidus advises Bellerophon to capture the winged horse, Pegasus, and to use him in his battle with the monster. With the goddess ATHENA's help, Bellerophon is able to capture Pegasus. He flies to Lycia on Pegasus's back and shoots the chimera with arrows from a safe distance above her. During their battle, he throws a spear with a lead point into chimera's gaping mouth. The monster's fiery breath melts the lead which burns out her insides and causes her DEATH.

The chimera originates in a tradition of matriarchal religions where the she-monster is a devastator and eater of raw flesh. Other she-monsters in Greek mythology include the SPHINX, MEDUSA, and the Hydra. Tiamat, from Babylonian mythology, is another example of a she-monster (*see* BABYLONIAN CREATION). Today, the term CHIMERA has come to be used to describe any horrifying creature of the imagination.

For Further Reading

Evslin, Bernard. *The Chimaera.* Chelsea House, 1988.

Mode, Heinz. *Fabulous Beasts and Demons.* London: Phaidon, 1975.

South, Malcolm, ed. *Mythical and Fabulous Creatures.* Westport, CT: Greenwood, 1987.

CHINESE STORYTELLING

History of the storytelling tradition in China. Because of China's vast size and population, several languages and dialects, and its long written history, the evolution of Chinese oral tradition is complex to trace. As Padraic Colum notes, "There is not in China, as there is in India and there was in Greece, any dramatization of divine activities—at least not in literature; there is no Chinese HESIOD, nor HOMER, nor VALMIKI. . . . To literate Chinese, the universe has been created and sustained by impersonal forces; that which makes a mythology—personification of supernatural powers and their identifications with some of the interests in mankind—is not conceived by them." On the other hand, R.D. Jameson takes the position that "the MYTHS and LEGENDS of the Chinese have not been studied in a systematic sense because there are too many of them," and he adds, "The thousands of major and minor deities who constitute the bureaucracies of HEAVEN and HELL, the hundreds of stellar deities, the *Bodhisattvas,* the *arhats,* the *lohans,* and the many others referred to by the populace as spirits or GODS or *Pusas,* not to mention the tens of thousands of SHAPE-SHIFTING foxes, and other shape-shifting ANIMALS, plants, and stones, constitute an enormous population of which no census has been taken." Myths and legends that surround the important figures in Confucianism, Taoism, and Buddhism are also part of the oral tradition.

Stories and legends surround Confucius, who was born in 551 B.C.; supposedly a UNICORN appeared at this birth and spat out a piece of jade with writing that prophesied that the philosopher would one day be an "uncrowned emperor." Kuan Ti was the god of war in Confucian tradition and a popular figure in Chinese folklore. Stories also flourished about Lao-Tzu, who was born in 604 B.C. and was the founder of Taoism and author of the TAO TE CHING; Chuang tzu, Taoist philosopher and writer; Huang-ti, the "yellow emperor" and patron saint of all Taoists; and Lieh-tzu, a semi-legendary Taoist sage. When Buddhism spread to China around the time of the birth of Jesus, legends arose focusing on BUDDHA; Ta-mo, the founder of Ch'an Tsung (the Chinese name for Zen Buddhism); Hsuan-tsang, or Tripataka, the great Chinese pilgrim and Buddhist; and Mi-lo, the future Buddha and counterpart of the Indian MAITREYA.

Of the many gods and GODDESSES and myths of Chinese mythology, there is KUAN YIN, the all-compassionate MOTHER-goddess (Kwannon in Japan); Lung, the dragon of Japanese folklore; P'AN KU, the primeval man born of the COSMIC EGG; T'ai Shan, the most revered of the five sacred mountains of China; Tsao Chun, the Chinese Kitchen god; and Yi, the HERO and excellent archer, China's version of William Tell (*see* TELL, WILLIAM).

Many FOLKTALES and FAIRY TALES also exist. The story of "Yeh-Shen," the Chinese version of "CINDERELLA," first appeared in *The Miscellaneous Record of Yu Yang*, by Tung Ch'eng-Shih, and dates back to the T'ang dynasty (A.D. 618–907).The earliest European version of the story is an Italian tale from 1634. Another famous folktale that recalls the star-crossed lover MOTIF of Shakespeare's *Romeo and Juliet* is "Faithful Even in Death," dating back to about A.D. 1368 or earlier. It is the story of Yingt'ai Chu, who, with her father's help, disguises herself as a boy in order to study at the school in the town. During her years of studying with her friend, Hsienpo, he never guesses her identity, but she falls in love with him and wants to marry him. When Yingt'ai Chu is forced to leave school because of an arranged betrothal, Hsienpo, who still thinks she is male, misses her and comes to visit her only to learn the truth about her gender. He then pines away and dies for love, Yingt'ai jumps into his grave on the way to her own wedding, and they both are transformed into a rainbow, with Hsienpo the rainbow's red and Yingt'ai its blue. The motif of a female disguising herself as a male in order to be able to study, resulting in a friendship that ends in love, also appears in a more modern version in Isaac Bashevis Singer's Yiddish novel, *Yentl the Yeshiva Boy* (1983) (*see* SINGER, ISAAC BASHEVIS).

CHRÉTIEN DE TROYES (c. 1170)

Twelfth-century French vernacular poet. Chrétien is the author of some of the earliest surviving tales of King ARTHUR and the knights of the Round Table; for this reason he is often considered to be the founder of the medieval romance. However, scholars now understand that Chrétien is far from the first teller of these Arthurian legends. He drew on the stories passed down for centuries about the legendary king and court, and based most of his Arthurian tales on the previous works of GEOFFREY OF MONMOUTH (his *Historia regime Brittanniae*, written in Latin in the early twelfth century) and the Norman cleric Wace's translation of these tales into French. It is generally accepted, however, that Chrétien did raise the Arthurian romance to new levels of achievement, and many important and well-known details of the legends (including Arthur's beloved CAMELOT and the well-known knight LANCELOT) appear for the first time in his texts.

All that is known of Chrétien's life has been inferred from his works, which he (fortunately for us) was careful to sign, and from comments about him made by other writers. Chrétien's connection with the city of Troyes (in the Champagne region) and certain references in his works suggest that he was familiar with aristocratic, courtly life in the cultural center of Champagne. Furthermore, his dedications of *Lancelot* to the Countess Marie de Champagne and *Perceval* to Count Philip of Flanders indicate that he was a poet employed by the court (*see* PERCIVAL).

Five romances can be attributed to Chrétien (*Érec et Énide, Cligés, Lancelot, Yvain,* and *Perceval*), as well as translations of Ovid (only one segment survives) and a work on King Mark and Iseult, also lost. Each of the five romances are composed of octosyllabic (eight-syllable) rhyming couplets. *Érec et Énide* is the earliest extant romance about the Arthurian court; it examines issues of marriage, knight-errantry, and what happens when these two come into conflict. The story focuses on Érec, a young prince whose victory in a duel wins him the hand of the beautiful Énide. The couple is so blissfully happy together that Érec begins to ignore his chivalric duties; others in the court begin to criticize him. Énide is greatly saddened by this turn of events; Érec mistakes her sorrow for accusation. He then embarks on a series of dangerous adventures, fighting giants, bandits, and nobles. Énide accompanies him and convinces him of her complete fidelity and love. They return to King Arthur's court, where, upon the death of Érec's father, Érec and Énide are crowned king and queen of his father's kingdom in a splendid ceremony.

Cligés tells the story of Alixandre, the first son of the emperor of Constantinople, who leaves Greece for Britain in order to become a knight in the service of King Arthur. There, he meets and marries Arthur's niece, Soredamor, and they have a son named Cligés. When the emperor dies, Alixandre's brother Alis assumes the throne. Alixandre soon arrives in Greece with his family to assume his rightful position as emperor, but decides to make a deal with his brother that allows Alis to keep the crown so long as he names Cligés his heir and promises never to marry. The deceitful Alis breaks his promise, however, and marries Fénice, the princess of Germany. Fénice, who does not love her husband, falls in love with the handsome and charming Cligés. When their illicit relationship is discovered, they flee to King Arthur's court. Alis pursues them, but dies of spite; Cligés and Fénice return to Constantinople to reign happily ever after.

Lancelot is the first story to feature that famous knight of the Round Table. The romance details the abduction of Queen Guenevere (*see* GUINEVERE) (as a result of King Arthur's rash agreement to allow his Queen to leave the court accompanied only by the senechal Kay), Lancelot's many adventures during his search for Guenevere, his rescue of the Queen, and their passionate love affair.

Yvain, another Arthurian tale, relates the story of the knight Yvain, who leaves his blissful marriage for one year (with the reluctant permission of his wife Laudine) to embark on chivalric adventures. Yvain neglects to return after a year has passed, and so Laudine renounces her love for her perfidious husband. Yvain, stricken with grief at the news that he has lost the love of his beloved wife, goes mad. He is eventually cured of his insanity, and spends the next several years performing noble, chivalric deeds and preserving his fidelity to Laudine. In time, Yvain hears that Laudine needs to be protected from intruders into her land; he comes to her aid and the two lovers are reconciled.

Perceval, Chrétien's last work of romance, was left unfinished at his death. It relates for the first time in literature the adventures of the knight Perceval and the story of the quest for the HOLY GRAIL (a widely used theme in later literature).

In spite of the fact that Chrétien's stories were not entirely original, his unique conception of the Arthurian court was so popular that it has engendered countless imitations during his own time and ever since. Chrétien de Troyes must be regarded as a seminal figure, in the history of French literature specifically, and in the preservation of Celtic legend generally.

For Further Reading

Chrétien de Troyes. *Arthurian Romances*. Translated by William W. Kibler and Carleton W. Carroll. New York: Penguin Books, 1991.

Frappier, Jean. *Chrétien de Troyes: The Man and His Work*. Translated by Raymond J. Cormier. Athens, OH: Ohio Univerity Press, 1982.

Uitti, Karl D., with Michelle A. Freeman. *Chrétien de Troyes Revisited*. New York: Twayne Publishers, 1995.

CHRISTIAN STORYTELLING

Tradition of teaching Judeo-Christian religious doctrine through the telling of stories. Using the BIBLE as a source of stories, Christians through the ages, from preachers to mothers to Jesus himself, have related the Christian CREATION story of ADAM AND EVE, the stories of NOAH and Moses, as well as the PARABLES OF JESUS, stories told to his followers that contained a moral, such as the story of the Good Samaritan.

Jesus of Nazareth followed the traditions of his Jewish forebears when he told stories to illustrate his teaching. These stories, and those told about Jesus by the gospel writers of the Bible's New Testament, became the foundations of Christian storytelling. Stories that drive Christian faith come from numerous sources; Jesus and the writers of the New Testament make numerous references, for instance, to stories from the Old Testament.

Christian storytelling begins with the Old Testament's Book of Genesis (*see* GENESIS, BOOK OF), an account of the creation the garden of Eden, and humankind's fall from favor with GOD when Adam and Eve committed the sin of disobedience by eating the fruit of the tree of the knowledge of good and evil. In the New Testament, the virgin birth of Jesus in the humble manger of Bethlehem, his sinless exemplary life, and his DEATH by crucifixion are all meant to atone for humankind's sinful nature represented in the "original sin" of Adam and Eve's disobedience. These stories form the core of Christian tradition. Additionally, the story of the development of the Christian church is told in the Acts of the Apostles, the letters of St. Paul and other early church leaders, and finally in St. John's apocalyptic vision of the second coming of Jesus Christ in Revelation (*see* APOCALYPSE).

As Christianity spread and became "Christendom," stories of faith and miracles of faith were added to the tradition. A substantial portion of the literature of the world is based upon the Bible and Christian belief; themes such as that of the prodigal son, the fall from grace, sibling rivalry (Cain and Abel), and the sacrifice of one for the many have been found throughout literary history in many stories, novels, and, more recently, films.

CHUANG TZU (369–286 B.C.)

Taoist Chinese writer, author of *The Thirty-Three Books of Chuang Tzu*, a collection of narratives, ANECDOTES, FABLES, and discourses. Chuang Tzu, also known as Chuang Chou or Nan Hua Chen Ching, was born in Sung, which then belonged to the kingdom of Liang or Wei. Against the very ritualized and moralistic social order of Confucianism, Chuang Tzu was a follower of the teachings of Lao Tzu's *Tao Te Ching*, and, as Clae Waltham writes in his introduction to *Chuang Tzu: Genius of the Absurd*, he "advocated a nondirected participation in nature, a Way of learning the course of things, of developing a capacity to allow things to happen spontaneously, a living of life from one's subtle, inward guidance." Concerned with the fundamental problem of moral choice, he rebelled against "hypocrisy and self-seeking" and "advocated a return to simplicity in order to regain individuality." At the time that Chuang Tzu wrote about the principles of the Tao, its cultivation had fallen away, and his books encouraged its readers toward embracing the anarchistic philosophy of the Tao. With patience, humor, wit, the gift of storytelling, and a true sense of the idiom of the absurd, Chuang Tzu was a guide toward the state of enlightenment, or *samadhi*. Both early Buddhism and Chinese literature in general were influenced by Lao Tzu's and Chuang Tzu's philosophical Taoism, with its intrinsic mysticism and poetry.

Among the most famous of the anecdotes collected in *The Chuang Tzu* is the dream of the butterfly, which the author relates in Book II: "Formerly, I, Chuang Chou, dreamed that I was a butterfly flying about feeling that it was enjoying itself. I did not know that it was Chou. Suddenly I awoke and was myself again, the veritable Chou. I did not know whether it had formerly been Chou dreaming that he was a butterfly, or it was now a butterfly dreaming that it was Chou. But between a butterfly and Chou there must be a difference. This is a case of what is called the transformation of things." This conundrum became enormously famous, entering into the oral tradition and retold for centuries. Other narratives and fables focus on such topics as "Foolish Judgments of Smaller Creatures"; the Tao in different men: "The Perfect Man, the Spirit-Like Man, and the Sagely Minded Man"; "The Usefulness of the Useless"; "Nonaction and Action"; "Perfect Benevolence"; "The Influence a Ruler Should Exert"; "Moderation"; "The Fitness That Forgets What Is Fitting"; "Difficulty of Controlling External Things"; "On Wealth and Poverty"; and "The Story of the Man Who Tried to Run Away From His Shadow."

For Further Reading

Merton, Thomas. *The Way of Chuang Tzu*. New York: New Directions, 1965.

Waltham, Clae, ed. *Chuang Tzu: Genius of the Absurd*. Translated by James Legge. New York: Ace Books, 1971.

CINDERELLA

One of the world's most popular FOLKTALES with over 700 variants world wide. Though versions differ, most feature a HEROINE who is persecuted by a stepmother (*see* STEPMOTHER—WICKED) and stepsisters, receives magic help from a FAIRY GODMOTHER or the spirit of her dead mother, undergoes a TEST of identity (fitting into the magic slipper), and marries a PRINCE. A Chinese variant of the story was first written in the ninth century A.D. (which accounts for the emphasis on small feet), but the tale itself has been part of an even longer oral tradition and, like many popular folktales, continues to be reworked and retold in books, poetry, and film, remaining popular with adults and children alike.

Probably the most widely-known variant of the tale in Western tradition was written by the Parisian Charles Perrault (1697) (*see* PERRAULT, CHARLES). In 1949 Walt Disney adapted the story as an animated film, taking its cheerful heroine, fairy godmother, and warning to return at midnight from Perrault. Perrault is believed to have refined some elements of the oral tale to make it more acceptable to the French court. For example, the stepsisters are not punished as they are in most versions, but are instead forgiven by Cinderella and marry lords of the court. Perrault's story lacks the violence that characterizes many of the other variants, including "Ashenputtle," a German transcription by the GRIMM BROTHERS (1812). In "Ashenputtle," the stepsisters cut off parts of their feet to fit into the magic slipper and later have their eyes plucked out by birds.

A good deal of the folktale's appeal can be attributed to the heroine herself. Shunned, overworked, often physically beaten, Cinderella patiently endures her stepmother's mistreatment until her debut at the ball. All the variants of the tale depict the heroine as morally and physically superior to her competitors over whom she triumphs completely whether she forgives them or not.

Whether French, German, African, Chinese, or Native American, the long-suffering young woman whose merit is finally recognized has become a universal symbol of how fate can and will reward the good.

For Further Reading

Perrault, Charles. *Cinderella*. Retold by Amy Ehrlich. Illustrated by Susan Jeffers. New York: Dial Books for Young Readers, 1985.

———. *The Complete Fairy Tales of Charles Perrault*. Translated by Neil Philip and Nicoletta Simborowski. Illustrated by Sally Holmes. New York: Clarion Books, 1993.

Sierra, Judy. *Cinderella*. The Oryx Multicultural Folktale Series. Phoenix: Oryx Press, 1992.

CIRCE

Sorceress in Greek mythology, daughter of the SUN god Helios. Along with HECATE and Medea, Circe is one of the most famous characters in Greek mythology relating to the practice of witchcraft (*see* WITCH).

Circe is beautiful and skilled in magic but does not care much for humanity. She poisons her own husband, the king of Samaritans. She then exiles herself to Aeaea, the Island of Dawn. She builds a marvelous palace there, which is guarded by wild beasts.

When a young man named Glaucus happens by, Circe tries to seduce him. However, Glaucus is in love with a NYMPH named Scylla, and refused the enchantress. Circe takes her revenge on Scylla, poisoning the waters of her favorite bay. Scylla is turned into a MONSTER, or reef, that poses a threat to ships. Across the strait from Scylla is the whirlpool monster, Charybdis. Therefore, the often-used phrase "between Scylla and Charybdis"

is used to mean "between two equal problems or dangers."

When Odysseus and his men wander to Aeaea, some of the crew members go ashore They encounter wild wolves and lions, but find them friendly. The beasts are, in fact, human beings that Circe has transformed. Circe gives the crew drugged food—in some accounts at a banquet in her palace, in other versions, she gives them acorns in a pigpen. When the crewmen eat, they are turned into swine, though they keep their human minds and understand what has happened to them. One crewman escapes and tells Odysseus what Circe has done.

Odysseus sets out alone to rescue his crew. The god Hermes meets him and shows him an herb that will protect Odysseus from Circe's spells. Hermes advises Odysseus to use the herb, drink whatever Circe gives him, and then threaten to run her through with his sword unless she releases his men.

Circe is amazed when her magic does not work on Odysseus. She falls in love with him and changes his men back to their former selves, either to please him or to save her own life. Odysseus makes her give an oath to harm neither him nor his men, which she gives and keeps.

Circe then holds a great feast for Odysseus and his crew. She treats them so well that they stay for an entire year. Circe bears Odysseus three sons. When the adventurers are finally ready to leave, Circe gives them information that will help them along their way.

In his 1896 novel, *The Island of Dr. Moreau*, H.G. Wells makes use of a Circe-like figure, a mad scientist who changes people into animals for his experiments.

The theme of TRANSFORMATIONS is common in the works of the Roman poet Ovid as well as in worldwide oral traditions. *See also* ANCIENT GREEK STORYTELLING, ODYSSEY, QUEST FOR THE GOLDEN FLEECE.

For Further Reading

Graves, Robert. *The Greek Myths*. 2 vols. New York: Penguin Books, 1957.

Hamilton, Edith. *Mythology: Timeless Tales of Gods and Heroes*. New York: Mentor, 1969.

CLODD, EDWARD (1840–1930)

English banker and author. Born in a fishing community in Suffolk in 1840, Clodd rose to a position of prominence as a banker, folklorist, and popularizer of Darwin's evolutionary theories. He was friends with Thomas Huxley, Edward Tylor, John Tyndall, and other scientific luminaries of the day. His first book, *The Childhood of the World* (1873), ran to four editions and was translated into six European and two African languages. This was followed by *The Childhood of Religions* in 1875. In 1888, he wrote an evolutionary primer. From 1895–96, he was president of the FOLKLORE Society and in 1906 chairman of the Rationalist Press Association, in which capacity, he is satirized as Edwin Dodd in H.G. Wells's *Boon*. He continued to write extensively on folklore and occultism from a rationalist evolutionary perspective, arguing that FOLKTALES represent elements of savage society residual in civilized society. He died three months short of his 90th birthday in 1930.

CLOUSTON, WILLIAM ALEXANDER (1843–1896)

Scottish FOLKLORE compiler and orientalist. Born on the Orkney islands in Scotland into an old Norse family, Clouston spent his early life engaged in commercial pursuits in Glasgow and London. He relinquished these in favor of his interest in literature and journalism. He became passionately interested in Near-Eastern tales and folklore and contributed to Richard Burton's *Supplemental Arabian Nights* variants and analogues of some of the tales in Burton's earlier volumes (*see* BURTON, RICHARD). He compiled *Arabian Poetry for English Readers* (1878) and a collection of wise sayings, *Flowers from a Persian Garden* (1890), as well as *The Book of Scottish Stories* written earlier in his career. He did much to popularize Near-Eastern folklore and literature in Victorian Britain, and, as a significant orientalist, he argued for the origins of the oral European folktale in the written forms of much older Arabic and Persian literature.

CLOWN

Both a circus entertainer who performs JOKES, antics, and tricks, or ludicrous character in many Native American ceremonies. Clowns have existed in cultures worldwide, whether as the wild men of the medieval Carnival, as the African *Javara*, or the Portuguese *bugios*. Clowns, clowning, and clown societies have played an important role in the ceremonies of such Native American tribes as the Pueblo tribes of New Mexico and Arizona, Iroquois, Mayo-Yaqui, and Papago (Tohono O'odham), and have been incorporated into the oral and storytelling traditions as both subject matter and sources. Often masked and costumed, the clown, like the fool, is permitted to challenge sacred and vested authority and in rare cases even depose a chief. Depending on the tribe, the purpose of the clown might be to frighten, amuse, possess magical curing powers, control the weather, influence fertility, or punish.

Among the Pueblo tribes, Hopi "Delight Makers" and Zuni KACHINA clowns participate in scatological practices, and, according to their actions can consist of "gluttony, eating or drinking or drinking filth, drenching or being drenched with urine or water, begging, burlesquing, satirizing, distributing prizes or food, playing games, and so forth." (*Funk and Wagnalls' Standard Dictionary of Folklore, Mythology, and Legend.*) Certain Iroquois clowns participate in female impersonating and obscene miming. Because they impersonate chthonic beings, clowns are thought to have magical powers by sheer identification with the spirits of the dead, fire, ANIMALS, and natural forces.

DISGUISE is a part of clowning; paint or masks made of wood, cloth, or hide, and women's clothes are regularly used. Among the Yahgan, *kina* clowns paint their faces with black and white stripes; the Iroquois *Husk Faces* will dress as women in order to give them the magical power to increase the fertility of crops and babies.

Signs of the clown can be found in the masks, costumes, and performances of *Mardi Gras* and Halloween "trick or treat" activities and pranks. The Harlequin, as a form of clown, is sometimes a miming storyteller-entertainer. Today, circus clowns are the favorites of children everywhere, and they appear as characters in many stories, including Walt Disney's *Dumbo. See also* MASKS AND MASQUERADE.

COADIPOP

FEMALE CREATOR of the Tariana tribe in the Amazon basin of what is now Colombia, South America. According to the oral tradition of the Tariana tribe, Coadipop was a young virgin, also referred to as "grandmother of the days." By taking the two largest bones from her legs, she first made a cigar holder. She then made a cigar by extricating tobacco from her body. After placing this cigar in the cigar holder, she squeezed milk on the cigar, lit it, and puffed on it. Her first two puffs brought thunder and lightning and the brief image of a man, and the third puff that brought forth Enu, Thunder, who was both her son and her grandson, and also became her companion.

Coadipop was next responsible for the CREATION of the EARTH. After living with Enu, she decided they should create some companions, so she had Enu create three brothers, who also were called Thunder, and she created two female companions. The earth itself was created when Coadipop constructed a circle made by wrapping a cord around her head. She then laid the cord on the ground so she could squeeze the milk from her breast into it, thereby creating the earth. The two women Coadipop had created went to live on earth, first planting it, then peopling it when they became pregnant by the Thunders.

COATLICUE

In Aztec mythology, Great MOTHER figure representing both genesis and destruction. Like KALI, the Hindu GODDESS, Coatlicue, whose name means "the serpent lady," incorporates the opposites of birth and decay. In legends told by the ancient Aztecs, Coatlicue is the mother of all the stars. While she is sweeping one day, a ball of hummingbird feathers falls to her feet and she tucks it in her bosom; later,

when she can not find it, she realizes she has become pregnant without sin. Her elder children fear that the new offspring will be a monster, and they attempt matricide before the child is born. According to one version of the myth, the loveliest star, Coyolxauhqui, whose name means Golden Bells, luckily warns her mother, thus allowing the birth of Huitzilopochtli, the SUN. As the greatest of Coatlicue's offspring, Huitzilopochtli sends darts toward his attacking elder siblings, destroying them, and rewards his sister Coyolxauhqui by cutting off her head and giving it a new life as the MOON. In other VARIANTS, Coyolxauhqui is not the one to warn her mother, and she is punished by having her head cut off.

As destroyer, Coatlicue is often depicted in a skirt of swarming snakes, wearing a necklace of human hands and hearts from which hangs a pendant of a skull. With her head of double serpents on a human torso, clawed hands and feet, and flabby breasts, Coatlicue subsists on human corpses. As consort to Mictlantecuhtli, the prince of HELL, she is goddess of the earth, the womb, and the grave. Yet her dual nature also makes her a goddess of healing and medicine, especially for women, and she was also called "the flower-covered earth in spring" and "she from whom the sun is reborn each day."

For Further Reading

Johnson, Buffie. *Lady of the Beasts*. San Francisco: HarperSanFrancisco, 1988.

Larrington, Carolyne. *The Feminist Companion to Mythology*. London: Pandora/HarperCollins, 1992.

COCAIGNE

Imaginary country of luxury and idleness. The name *cocaigne* is etymologically connected with cakes and cooking, and in the old French, the expression *trouver cocaigne* means "to find the country where good things drop of themselves into the mouth," or "to meet with good fortune." Some say the Land of Cocaigne is in the west of Spain, and there, amidst the ease and contentment, "everything is allowed to be done twice over." It appears in many poems and stories of the Middle Ages, as in the poem "The Land of Cockaigne," which appears in *R.H. Robbins's Historical Poems of the XIVth and XVth Centuries* (1959). Here, Cockaigne is "fairer" than Paradise; the "FOOD is choice"; the weather is always pleasant; the rivers are made "of oil, of milk, of honey and wine"; and the abbey is constructed of pastry, "of flesh, of fish, of choicest meat" and all the monks have nuns as wives. In other versions, houses are made of barley sugar and the streets themselves are paved with pastry.

The GRIMM BROTHERS wrote that "the houses there were covered with cakes" in "The Story of Schlauraffen Land" and "The Ditmars Tale of Wonders." The term came to be humorously associated with London and the Cockneys who live there.

COMPETITION OF LIES

Storytelling practice of the Mende of Sierra Leone in West Africa. The "lies" are the stories told by competing storytellers for village entertainment. The storytellers are both men and women, and the first storyteller defines the boundaries of the competition by choosing the tale. The same tale is repeated by each rival, but the details and even the outcome of the plot change in each retelling. The competition offers the opportunity to best a rival as well as to explore the myriad ways of telling a story.

For example, in one competition, the initial plot described how a young woman, Yombo, was carried into the wilderness by a lover. The lover turns out to be a hideous spirit who has disguised himself by borrowing human features from an array of attractive men. Yombo watches in horror as he eats humans, and eventually she bears his child. The rest of the story was left up to the individual storyteller. In this particular competition, the first woman storyteller used the tale to caution young women about sexual promiscuity and stubbornness. In her continuation, Yombo is a great fornicator who remains promiscuous even after the *Sande* society that prohibits such behavior is initiated in her town. Because of her lust, she follows a spirit away from her family, even though he offers her money to return. As they journey, the spirit makes frequent stops to return his handsome features to the humans from whom he has borrowed them. Yombo is afraid of her transformed lover but has no choice but to remain with him. Then the spirit tells Yombo that he must sleep for one year. He provides her and their child provisions in a separate house. However, Yombo doesn't believe that he will really sleep that long and insists that she and the child remain in the same house as the spirit. Locked in the house with no food, Yombo and the child starve to death as the spirit sleeps. When he awakes, he sweeps their bones outside. The storyteller, before passing the tale to her rival, wraps up by stating, "Therefore, stubbornness isn't good . . . whenever a person says, 'Don't do this,' listen to him."

The storytellers who followed placed a different spin on the tale. The second teller expanded the plot. Yombo takes a lover who eventually rescues her from the spirit. Because Yombo has fed this lover, he gives her the gift of all wealth. She brings houses, food, and agricultural knowledge back to her village. The third teller continued by praising Yombo as the loving wife of the spirit. Living among the spirit's people, Yombo acts as a dutiful daughter-in-law, and eventually rejoins her own village and family.

In the competition, the storyteller's relationship to the audience is very important. The audience will voice displeasure at certain versions of old-time stories. The storytellers use a variety of skills—vivid description, voice intonation, and gestures—to capture the audience's attention. Stories in this tradition are fluid, changing to meet the demands of different audiences and different needs.

For Further Reading

Abrahams, Roger D. *African Folktales: Traditional Stories of the Black World*. New York: Pantheon Books, 1983.

CONIRAYA AND CAVILLACA

Incan male spirit and the virgin GODDESS he impregnates. According to the legends of the Incas and the South American Indians of the coastal regions, Coniraya Virachocha was a *huaca*, or spirit, worshipped until the Spanish colonists arrived. Although he was the creator of all things and the one who introduced the Indians' method of irrigation and agricultural terracing, he appeared on earth as a very poor man who wore rags. Cavillaca was a beautiful virgin goddess, and Coniraya fell in love with her.

As the legend recounts, one day when Cavillaca is sitting under a *lucma* tree, Coniraya transforms himself into a lovely bird, and he transforms his sperm into a *lucma* fruit, which Cavillaca picks and eats. Although she is a virgin, she becomes pregnant and bears a child without knowing who its father is. Still mystified as to the child's paternity, Cavillaca holds a meeting of all the *huacas* when the child reaches a year old, but no *huaca* comes forward as the child's father. In the spirit of King Solomon, Cavillaca then places the child on the floor, sure that he will crawl to his true father. Indeed, the child crawls straight to the threadbare Coniraya sitting in the lowest seat. Proud Cavillaca is terribly ashamed that the father of her child should be so poor, and she flees with the boy. When they arrive at the coast, the two of them enter the SEA and are transformed into rocks.

Meanwhile Coniraya goes in search of Cavillaca, and his meetings with various ANIMALS along the way provide explanations for how these animals came to have their particular traits. A condor gives him the good news that Cavillaca is not far away and Coniraya will soon overtake her, so Coniraya blesses the condor, bestowing upon it the power to fly high above the mountains, to build its nest high where it will not be bothered, to feed on that which is dead or neglected by others, and to receive immunity. When the fox gives Coniraya a negative message—that Cavillaca is far away—he punishes it by making it foul smelling and hated and tormented by humans. Since lions and falcons give Coniraya good news, they are blessed, while parrots, whose news displease Coniraya, are cursed and penalized by receiving raucous voices that endanger them and make them hateful to humans. Finally, Coniraya arrives at the coast only to find

Cavillaca and their son metamorphosed into stone.

Later Coniraya encounters the two daughters of Pachamac and Urpi-huachac. He desires sexual intercourse with both daughters but succeeds only with the elder one; the younger daughter flees by transforming herself into a pigeon. Enraged that their mother, Urpi-huachac, is off visiting Cavillaca, Coniraya steals the fish from her pond and lets them go in the sea, which has hitherto been absent of fish, and so Coniraya becomes the source of all the fish in the sea.

For Further Reading

Bierhorst, John. *Mythology of South America*. New York: Morrow, 1988.

Osborne, Harold. *South American Mythology*. London: Hamlyn, 1968.

CORN MOTHER

Native American GODDESS representing the nurturing, fertile Great Goddess, provider of the life-giving corn, central to Native American culture. Among the Pueblo, Apache, and Navajo tribes, the figure of the Corn Mother, who symbolizes the corn, cornmeal, and corn pollen, is goddess of planting and harvesting, much like the Greek goddess Demeter (*see* PERSEPHONE MYTH). For the Navajo, corn is an important element in all MYTH and RITUAL, being central to their subsistence, and it is considered divine. Since it was the task of women to plant, pound, and cook the corn, or maize, women performed the maize rituals from puberty on, corn being linked with their fertility as well.

Variants of the story of Corn Mother are told by the different tribes of the eastern and southwestern United States. In Penobscot LEGEND, a young man, the first, is born from the warmth of the SUN and the wind on the water and appears to Kloskurbeh, the CREATOR. Then a beautiful young woman, born of the earth plant, warmth, and dew, also appears. The young man and the young woman mate, and she becomes First MOTHER, and the population increases. But since the people live by hunting, there is eventually no more game. Pitying the people, First Mother tells her husband he must kill her to stop her weeping. He should then drag her body over an empty patch of earth until all her flesh is gone and there, in the center of the patch, he must bury her bones. Only after seven moons have passed should her family return to that spot where, she promises, her flesh will be growing, ready to provide nourishment. Indeed, when they return after the prescribed amount of time, they find a tall, green, tasseled plant—corn—which they eat with great delight, and they make sure to save some of the kernels to rebury in the earth for future harvests. In the place where Corn Mother's bones are buried is another new leaf, the tobacco plant, and the spirit of Corn Mother tells them it is a sacred leaf they should smoke to clear their minds, aid them in their prayers, and bring joy into their hearts.

Variants of the legend of Corn Mother occur among Native North Americans, and Japanese and Babylonian myths tell of a FOOD-goddess who is slain in order to provide food for her people from her body.

COSMIC EGG

In numerous CREATION stories, the form of the precreation void that became the source of life. The cosmic or world egg is a recurrent image in the mythologies of many cultures, though the medium of the egg and the creation narratives vary. The connection between the births of birds and reptiles from eggs, familiar to all early cultures in which these myths evolved, and the birth of the cosmos and all humanity is obvious; that science has also used the term "egg" as the name for the female contribution to human birth—despite the great difference between bird eggs and human eggs—suggests the power of the image in terms of its connection with birth.

In one version of Chinese creation, an enormous egg containing a chaotic mixture of opposites, or *yin-yang,* is present at the very beginning, and Phan Ku, who is at first nothing, yet exists within the *yin-yang,* becomes a giant who breaks from the egg, dividing the chaos into opposites such as HEAVEN and EARTH. Similarly, in one version of the Egyptian creation, a cosmic egg represents the soul of the maternal waters, and, in another VARI-

ANT, the SUN god first comes from a primeval mound located in the chaotic and undifferentiated primeval sea. Tahitian mythology has it that the great god TA'AROA first lived in an eggshell, eventually breaking out of it to form the sky with the shell and the world with his own body. In the creation MYTH that appears in the NIHONGI, "The Chronicles of Japan" (A.D. 720), heaven and earth are formed from an egg-like chaos. The Mande tribe of Mali tell of a world egg that houses all the seeds for creation, including the seed for the four elements, the FOUR DIRECTIONS, and the first people.

Finnish mythology transforms the one great cosmic egg into seven eggs, six of which are golden and one which is iron. These eggs are laid by a teal resting on the upraised knee of the sky's daughter, Ilmatar, as she floats on the PRIMEVAL WATERS. The heat of the teal sitting on her nest in order to hatch the eggs eventually burns Ilmatar's knee, so she cools it in the water, upsetting the nest in the process. Broken by the dashing waves, the eggs create the world from their parts: the bottom of one eggshell becomes land, the top of the eggshell becomes the sky, the egg whites are transformed into the moon and the stars, and the egg yolk is transformed into the sun.

In ancient Greece, the Orphic cult believed that Time created a silver cosmic egg from which the androgynous Phanes-DIONYSOS was born. As creator of the universe, Phanes-Dionysos contained the seeds of life and produced the first daughter, Nyx, or Night, and then GAIA and Uranos, parents of ZEUS. Another ancient Greek creation myth generated by its early peoples, the Pelasgians, tells of a great GODDESS, Euronome, who lays a world egg after mating with a serpent, Ophion, which she has made by rubbing the north WIND. Following Euronome's orders, Ophion surrounds the egg until it hatches, producing the sun, the moon, the stars, the earth, the creatures, and the plants.

Depending on the source, different cosmic egg variants can be found in the mythology of India. In the sacred text called the *Satapatha Brahmana,* first the heated waters generate a golden egg, then the egg breaks open and PRAJAPATI emerges after a year-long gestation period, and within another year the sounds of his breath produce first the earth, then the sky, then the seasons. In the later Hindu scriptures called the *Upanishads*, the cosmic egg breaks into a silver part—earth— and a gold part—the sky. BRAHMA, the sun, is born from the egg, and the parts of the egg form the rivers, mountains, lakes, and clouds. In a later text, *The Lawbook of Manu*, the self-existent BRAHMAN first creates the waters out of thought, then creates a golden egg from his seed in the waters, then after a year in the egg Brahman emerges to divide the egg into earth and heaven.

For Further Reading

O'Flaherty, Wendy, trans. *Hindu Myths*. New York: Viking Penguin, 1975.

COUNTRY MUSIC BALLADS AND SONGS

Tradition of songs of love, gunfights, family, and country popularized in the United States. The country music known today grew from influences of the Wild West, bluegrass, BLUES, spirituals, and rock and roll. Bluegrass itself derives from folk traditions in Europe, especially from the British islands.

Early recording artists include the Carter Family, whose "Wildwood Flower" and "Will the Circle Be Broken" demonstrate both the bluegrass heritage and the storytelling character that has always been a part of country music. Gene Autrey's "Silver-Haired Daddy of Mine" represents filial devotion.

So many distinct themes came to be associated with country music over time that David Allen Coe recorded "The Perfect Country Song"—a story that includes references to home, mother, family, trains, prisons, and trucks. Coe's song cleverly defines archetypal country music subject matter. Marty Robbins immortalized the BALLAD of the Old West of gunfighters. Chris Ledoux picked up the tradition and contemporized it in stories of the troubled sixties and seventies of the United States. Buck Owens insisted, "We don't smoke marijuana in Muskogee," while Tammy Wynette lamented, "Our D-I-V-O-R-C-E becomes final today," in a time when divorce took a significant rise in American

society. Kenny Rogers tells of losing a loved one as a result of wounds inflicted in "that old crazy Asian war," while a number of songs praise the U.S. role in Viet Nam. America's difficulties during the Watergate scandal brought a rash of patriotic songs.

Contemporary country and western music continues to treat the perennial themes of family, tradition, love found and lost, betrayal, and heartbreak. Many fans of this music cite these recurrent themes as the reason for their appreciation. As long as the human experience continues to involve these themes, country music will continue to tell its story.

COURLANDER, HAROLD (1908–)

African American folklorist, novelist, and music compiler. Born in Indianapolis, Indiana, in 1908, Courlander received a B.A. from the University of Michigan in 1931. His career path reveals him as a man of multiple interests. From 1933–1938, he was a farmer in Rome, Michigan. He then worked for an airline company in Eritrea, and during World War II was a historian and editor for the U.S. Office of War Information in New York and in Bombay, India. Later he worked for the U.S. Information Agency, the Voice of America, and the United Nations Review. From 1960–1974 he worked as a political analyst in Washington, DC.

Courlander was awarded Guggenheim fellowships for studies in African and African American cultures, completed FOLKLORE studies on the Dominican Republic and Haiti, and worked extensively with the Hopi Indians of the American Southwest in collating and recording their myths and traditions. His prodigious output of scholarly and popular works includes *A Treasury of African Folklore* (1975), *A Treasury of Afro-American Folklore* (1976), *Hopi Voices: Recollections, Traditions and Narratives of the Hopi Indians* (1982) and a novel, *The African* (1970), from which portions of Alex Haley's best-selling novel *Roots* were said to have been taken. (Courlander received a substantial court settlement in this matter.) Courlander sees his work as expressing his interest in bridging the worlds of fiction and nonfiction, in

123

exploring the relation between culturally specific narratives and lived experience.

COYOTE

Great TRICKSTER of many Native American cultures. Coyote appears in stories from coast to coast in North America and from Alaska to the southwestern deserts. The character is especially popular among Plains groups. Even when a culture has other local trickster figures, Coyote is often a fellow mischief-maker.

In true trickster fashion, Coyote is a CLOWN, rebel, and troublemaker, but he is also a creator or CULTURE HERO. In his HERO aspect, he may create the world or human beings, bring the gift of fire, teach handicrafts, or instruct people on how to live. On the other hand, he indulges in lechery, cheating, poaching game, and gleefully destroying his enemies.

Coyote talks and behaves like a human being and may take human or animal form or something in between. He usually has a companion, such as SPIDER, Fox, Wolf, Wildcat, Lynx, or other animals. His companions may play the roles of stooges or of pranksters. Coyote's plans sometimes fail, and he is often tricked by those on whom he plays JOKES. Coyote always gets his due sooner or later.

In the plains and plateau areas, Coyote's cleverness alternates with his foolishness. On the north Pacific coast, Coyote stories stress cleverness more than stupidity. Among the Navaho of the Southwest, there are actually two distinct Coyote figures. Coyote himself is the holy culture-bringer, while Trotting Coyote is the buffoon or trickster. Trotting Coyote stories are told to children to illustrate certain morals.

In a Crow CREATION story, the world is at first nothing but water. Old Man Coyote and two ducks with red eyes are its only inhabitants. Coyote get the ducks to dive and see what is beneath the water. They bring up a root and then a bit of mud. Coyote blows on the mud until it spreads and becomes the EARTH. He plants the root, then all kinds of plants and trees begin to grow (see EARTH-DIVER CREATION).

With a lot of advice from the ducks, Coyote makes people out of mud and brings them to life (see GILGAMESH, HOPI CREATION). Then Coyote makes more ducks. When he realizes that all his creations are male, he makes females. He goes on to create other birds and animals. When the bear threatens the smaller animals, Coyote sends him away to a den for the winter.

Coyote gives the people *tipis* to live in and weapons to hunt with. But the ducks insist that he also create different languages so there will be war, because only then will young men have the opportunity to do great deeds. At the ducks' insistence, Coyote also sets up the practice of mutual wife-stealing so that everyone will be happy.

In a Zuni story, Coyote is an inept hunter who generally can not do anything right. He steals the SUN and the MOON from the KACHINAS, but they escape from him and fly away into the sky. After that, the world is much colder than before.

In a Wasco story, Coyote creates a ladder to the sky by shooting arrows at it. When Coyote and some wolves climb the ladder, they meet with two fierce grizzly bears. Coyote thinks that the bears and wolves make a nice composition as they sit staring at each other. So Coyote leaves them there, removing the arrows as he goes back to earth. The bears and wolves are now the stars in the Big Dipper. Coyote arranges a lot more stars in pictures all over the sky, then makes the Milky Way with the stars he had left over.

In a Brule Sioux story, a canny white trader eagerly challenges Coyote to beat him in a deal. Coyote says that he must first go home and get his cheating medicine, but he will need to borrow the trader's horse to do so. Also he will need to borrow the trader's clothes, so the horse will let him ride. Of course, Coyote leaves the trader standing bare-bottomed and does not return.

In a White River Sioux story, Coyote and his friend IKTOME admire a pretty rock. Coyote takes off his blanket and covers the rock to keep it warm. But during a storm, Coyote begins to feel the cold and takes his blanket back. As Coyote and Iktome wander on, they hear a rumbling that seemed to be getting closer. It is the rock, which chases them across a river and through a forest. The rock finally runs over Coyote, mashing him flat. A rancher finds him and takes him home for a rug. The next morning, the rug comes back to life and runs away.

Many Coyote stories end with the death of the trickster, though his death never lasts. Sometimes Coyote pretends that he has merely been asleep. He is always alive and ready for the next adventure.

In *American Indian Myths and Legends,* Richard Erdoes and Alfonso Ortiz comment that "Coyote and his kin represent the sheerly spontaneous in life, the pure creative spark that is our birthright as human beings and that defies fixed roles or behavior. He not only represents some primordial creativity from our earlier days, but he reminds us that such celebration of life goes on today, and he calls us to join him in the frenzy. In an ordered world of objects and labels, he represents the potency of nothingness, of chaos, of freedom—a nothingness that makes something of itself" (*see* ERDOES, RICHARD; ORTIZ, ALPHONSO).

Coyote stories usually take place in the prehuman age of MYTH, although among some groups his escapades continue into the present time. The evocative character also still turns up in contemporary literature. For example, in *Buffalo Gals, Won't You Come Out Tonight,* Ursula LeGuin presents a delightful female Coyote with all the traditional trickster attributes. And in her collection of essays, *Dancing At The Edge of the World,* LeGuin quotes Coyote: "That's what myths do. They happen all the time."

For Further Reading

Bright, William. *A Coyote Reader.* Berkeley: University of California Press, 1993.

Erdoes, Richard, and Alfonso Ortiz. *American Indian Myths and Legends.* New York: Pantheon, 1985.

Haile, Berard. *Navaho Coyote Tales.* Lincoln: University of Nebraska Press, 1984.

Hynes, William J., and William G. Doty, eds. *Mythical Tricksters.* Tuscaloosa, AL: The University of Alabama Press, 1993.

Malotki, Ekkehart. *Hopi Coyote Tales.* Illustrated by Anne-Marie Malo. Lincoln: University of Nebraska Press, 1984.

CREATION

Stories of origin that explain the emergence of the world, the GODS, and humanity. These stories are termed *cosmological,* and they appear in every culture's collective imagination. Creation stories frequently serve both an explanatory and an instructional function; in other words, they offer a history of the world's creation as well as the human place within it, and they frequently provide guidelines for survival and proper moral conduct. Creation stories not only offer answers to metaphysical questions of existence, they also function as metaphors for human powers of creation. As imaginative, ambitious beings, we seek a source that defines who we are and why we operate in our own creative ways. In the Book of Genesis account (*see* GENESIS, BOOK OF), when Adam is given the task of naming all creation, he is partaking of the imaginative task begun by YAHWEH with the words "Let there be light." A sense of being made in the image of GOD at once explains and perpetuates the human creative function (*see* ADAM AND EVE).

In the stories of many cultures, creation is often the product of a thought or a spoken word. Speech has long been recognized as a creative, and divinely inspired, act. By speaking the word, the object to which it refers comes into existence, at least in the mind of the listener. In the *Brhadaranyaka Upanishad,* a Hindu story of origin, a single thought leads to an explosion of creation. Before the existence of any life, only a soul in the form of a man exists. Upon recognizing his solitude, he thinks "I," and, since an "I" must have a "thou," he immediately splits in two. When he sees the other and recognizes her as woman, he procreates with her to form the human species. The woman, disgusted that he would sexually pursue that which emerged from his own being, becomes a cow and attempts to escape him. The man turns into a bull and unites with her again. She continues to transform, and he continues to pursue until the entire creation has been formed. For the Hindus, this story reflects an emphasis upon the illusory nature of creation. The original soul falls into the realm of dualism from a state of oneness. When he ceases to recognize that the other is an extension of his own substance, the creation spins into being from a simple thought. The concept of the thought or word creation also helps to explain how life could be formed from the state of chaos or nothingness that existed prior to the creation. Creation out of nothing, or *ex nihilo,* illustrates the power of the divine to create the cosmos out of an incomprehensible state.

While the cosmos may be formed by words from the God or gods, the human creation usually involves the physical manipulation of matter. Frequently, the divine being forms humanity out of mud, clay, or dust. The human creation is completed by the inspiration of the divine breath, which gives life and spirit to the inanimate matter. In the Hopi story of SPIDER WOMAN's creation, humanity is formed out of clay and the thought of the sky-god, Tawa. After creating the other gods through an asexual division of themselves, Spider Woman and Tawa unite to form humanity. The masculine thought of the creation takes shape in the feminine act of manipulating the clay. Spider Woman's association with the EARTH-MOTHER is characteristic of creation myths in which the EARTH brings forth life after impregnation by the sky-god's ray of fertilizing light (*see* HOPI CREATION MYTH).

Ultimately, stories of creation reflect the concerns of their tellers. The storyteller sees in acts of human creation violence, pain, joy, and awe. The battles between gods that usually precede the fleeting peace of a Garden of Eden, indicate the chaos that must be synthesized before any act of creation, mundane or artistic, can take place. That the peace following the creation is almost immediately followed by a human fall illustrates that we remain but imperfect artists. Human aspirations will always surpass human powers to attain them in creation.

CROCKETT, DAVY (1786–1836)

Hero of the frontier era of the United States. Davy Crockett is perhaps best known as one of the fighters at the Alamo who was killed by the Mexican forces under Santa Ana. Before his death, Crockett gained fame as a purveyor of TALL TALES and as a member of Congress. Born and reared in Tennessee, Crockett's tall tales evolved from his extensive experiences as a hunter and his humorous method of spinning a yarn. In one case Crockett claimed that he had killed 105 bears in the course of a year. Crockett's exploits were further encouraged and exaggerated by a public greedy for the perpetuation of an American mythology. These stories earned him the label of a "homespun oracle" and "rustic CLOWN." In the middle decades of the nineteenth century, as the American frontier was almost fully explored, Crockett's stories became symbols of American ingenuity and simplicity. They also offered a nostalgic look at a fading past of paradoxical innocence and violence.

Crockett's tales encouraged others to embellish his history. An anonymous book entitled *Sketches and Eccentricities of Col. David Crockett of West Tennessee* (1834) prompted Crockett to set his own stories down in writing. He did little to diminish his mythical status as a simple-minded but highly skilled woodsman. As his LEGEND grew, his tales grew more outlandish. In fact, Crockett even claimed to have rescued the earth when it ceased rotating on a bitter cold day. He simply heated the oil from a small bear to loosen up the earth's axis.

Crockett's storytelling contributed significantly to the cultivation of the humorists' writings of the Old Southwest. Writers such as Thomas Bangs Thorpe and James K. Paulding drew from half-real, half-legendary figures like Davy Crockett, Mike Fink (*see* FINK, MIKE), and others to transform the tall tale into a popular American literary genre in the mid-nineteenth century. In fact, in Paulding's play *The Lion of the West* (1831), Crockett serves as the basis for the character of Col. Nimrod Wildfire.

Crockett's status as a frontier legend also gave him temporary popularity as a politician.

Known as the "coonskin Congressman" for his peculiar hat and a trick he devised of selling the same skin repeatedly, Crockett fought to defend the rights of the small farmer in an era when Andrew Jackson's industrialist policies were rapidly transforming the character of the American landscape. After losing his seat in Congress, Crockett began his ill-fated sojourn in Texas, which ended in defeat at the Alamo. His death marked the end of his status as a simple storyteller, but it made him a figure of mythical stature, a position Crockett continues to occupy in American folklore. *See also* HERO.

For Further Reading

Cody, W.F. (Buffalo Bill). *Story of the Wild West and Camp-Fire Chats*. 1888. Reprint, Freeport, NY: Books for Libraries Press, 1970.

Crockett, David. *A Narrative of the Life of David Crockett of the State of Tennessee*. E. L. Carey and A. Hart, 1834. Reprint, Knoxville, TN: University of Tennessee Press, 1973.

Shackford, James Atkins. *David Crockett: The Man and the Legend*. Chapel Hill: University of North Carolina Press, 1956.

CROKER, THOMAS CROFTON
(1798–1854)

Irish writer and FOLKLORE compiler. Born in Cork in 1798, Croker experienced a limited education and was apprenticed to a local merchant. He spent his spare time collecting songs and stories in the south of Ireland. In 1818, he secured a clerkship in the Admiralty in London. His most important contribution, *Fairy Legends and Traditions of the South of Ireland,* (3 vols., 1825–1828) ran to several editions and was translated into German by GRIMM BROTHERS. Subsequent works included *Legends of the Lakes* (1829), *The Popular Songs of Ireland* (1839), and *The Adventures of Barney Mahoney* (1852). He was registrar of the Royal Literary Fund for more than twenty years and a member of the Society of Antiquarians.

CRONE

Hag or old woman; part of the Great MOTHER triad of MAIDEN, mother, crone. In MYTH, FOLKLORE, and FAIRY TALES, the figure of the crone has a number of connotations. In fairy tales, a crone can be a WITCH-like woman who brings bad luck or difficulties to the hero or heroine. Yet as Joseph Campbell notes in *The Hero with a Thousand Faces*, "For those who have not refused the call, the first encounter of the HERO-journey is with a protective figure (often a little old crone or WISE OLD MAN) who provides the adventurer with amulets against the dragon forces he is about to pass" (*see* CAMPBELL, JOSEPH). This crone might be SPIDER WOMAN of the legends of Southwest Native Americans or the "helpful crone" and FAIRY GODMOTHER of European fairy tales. "What such a figure represents is the benign, protecting power of destiny," writes Campbell, and she is a kind of "promise that the peace of PARADISE, which was first known within the mother womb, is not to be lost"; in other words, "Mother Nature herself supports the mighty task."

In Greek mythology, the goddess HECATE is often referred to as a crone, functioning as the third member of the maiden-mother-crone triad of Persephone-Demeter-Hecate, since Hecate was the one to hear the cries of Persephone when she was abducted by HADES and to inform Demeter of the event (*see* PERSEPHONE MYTH). The three female figures represent the stages in a woman's life as well as the phases of the MOON, and like Persephone, Hecate is associated with the moon and the underworld.

Crones, or crone-like old women and hags appear in many fairy tales, such as the GRIMM BROTHERS's "The Robber Bridegroom," where a crone serves as a helpful guide to the miller's daughter when she pays a visit to her bridegroom's home only to learn that he is a robber and murderer. The crone hides the young woman and helps her escape before her bridegroom finds her. In "Mother Holle," Mother Holle is a crone with a fairy godmother-like beneficence when dealing with the pretty and industrious but unloved daughter of a widow and a more witch-like, punishing attitude with the ugly and lazy but favored daughter of the same widow. The figure of the *hag,* the term more commonly used in Celtic folklore, appears in tales about the "Hag of Beare" and the "Hag of the Cats."

For Further Reading

Evetts-Secker, Josephine. *Mother and Daughter Tales.* Illustrated by Helen Cann. New York: Abbeville, 1996.

Grimm, Jacob, and Wilhelm Grimm. *The Complete Grimm's Fairy Tales.* New York: Pantheon, 1945.

CROSSLEY-HOLLAND, KEVIN
(1941–)

Folklorist, translator, and poet. While Crossley-Holland has proven himself as an accomplished poet, producing several volumes of poetry, including *The Dream-House,* and as a well-respected translator of medieval literature, including a translation of BEOWULF, his work on Norse mythology has proven to be invaluable to the comparative folklorist. In *The Norse Myths,* Crossley-Holland retells the Scandinavian mythology commencing with the complex unraveling of the cosmology of the CREATION tale, tracing the story of the Aesir, the race of great GODS and GODDESSES, until the destruction of the world at RAGNAROK. Yet what is most important about Crossley-Holland's work is the detailed footnotes that accompany each tale, which provide for comparison to the Norse tales readings of the FOLKLORE and mythologies of various other cultures. In "The Binding of Loki," Crossley-Holland associates the captivity of LOKI, the god of mischief, to the Christian tradition of the antichrist's imprisonment in HELL, as well as to the fettering of Prometheus in Greek mythology, which ultimately reveals a theme of universality in the folklore and mythologies of these seemingly disparate cultures.

For Further Reading

Crossley-Holland, Kevin. *Beowulf.* New York: Oxford University Press, 1988.

———. *The Norse Myths.* New York: Pantheon, 1981.

CROW DOG, LEONARD (1942–)

Contemporary Sioux medicine man and storyteller. A resident of the Rosebud Sioux Reservation in South Dakota, Leonard Crow Dog is the fourth generation of medicine men in his family. He does not read or write English, but is an important keeper and transmitter of the Lakota folktales and traditions of his tribe. His unfailing loyalty to his native traditions has caused him many difficulties; he took part in the 71-day occupation of Wounded Knee in 1973 and for related reasons spent time in jail. His oral autobiography, *Crow Dog* (1995), was written with the help of Richard Erdoes (*see* ERDOES, RICHARD), a collector of Native American stories and legends. Erdoes has also helped to preserve some of Crow Dog's native stories in *American Indian Myths and Legends* (1984). These stories, including "The Vision Quest," "Sun Creation," "The Ghost Wife," "The Coming of Wasichu," and "Remaking the World" have been handed down for generations in Crow Dog's tribe, and offer modern listeners and readers a link between the present and the mythical past. Crow Dog is an important figure in Native American oral tradition because he can relate the traditional stories of his people from the perspective of an insider who is intimately familiar with the history and lore of the Brule Sioux nation.

For Further Reading

Crow Dog, Leonard, and Richard Erdoes. *Crow Dog: Four Generations of Sioux Medicine Men.* NY: HarperCollins, 1995.

CRUIKSHANK, GEORGE (1792–1878)

English political caricaturist, book illustrator, and temperance advocate. The son of a political caricaturist, George Cruikshank worked in his father's print shop and was contributing original sketches by age 13. In 1824, Cruikshank shifted from caricature to book illustration. His woodcuts for the first English translation of the GRIMM BROTHERS'S FAIRY TALES, *German Popular Stories,* were widely popular throughout the nineteenth century, both in England and Germany. These illustrations provided a strong visual element to the oral tradition. Cruikshank's comic vision virtually fixed the landscape of the fairy world in the imagination of the new audience. Throughout his life, Cruikshank would return to illustrate the fairy tales that had first propelled his career.

Cruikshank also illustrated Charles Dickens's early works. However, by the 1850s, their friendship had waned, mainly because Dickens disapproved of how Cruikshank's strong temperance stance influenced his work. The publication of *The Bottle* (1847), a set of eight plates outlining the progress of a drunkard's life, had signaled Cruikshank's creative shift to temperance themes. These themes were continued in Cruikshank's four contributions to *The Fairy Library*, a work that was supposed to encompass all nursery stories but was never completed. As editor and illustrator of the volumes, Cruikshank molded the stories into temperance tales. His rendition of *Hop-o'-my-Thumb* is especially infused with the anti-alcohol message. *The Fairy Library* was not well received, partly because of Dickens's scathing review of the first story.

Soon after the relative failure of *The Fairy Library*, Cruikshank's career declined. Reprints of his earlier works sparked a revival in the late 1860s, and Cruikshank continued illustrating until his death in 1878.

CUCHULAINN

Hero of many Irish stories, including the *Táin Bó Cuailnge*, one of the most important tales surviving from early Irish literature. Although the *Táin* existed orally long before it took literary form, the earliest manuscript of this story is dated to the eighth century A.D. The *Táin Bó Cuailnge* (the *Cattle Raid of Cooley* or the *War for the Brown Bull*) tells the story of a great cattle raid, a characteristic feature of Irish heroic literature. The armies of Ailill and Medb, the KING and queen of Connaught, invade Ulster in their quest to obtain the *Donn Cuailnge*, a magnificent brown bull that Medb desires. Single handedly, the 17-year-old Cuchulainn defends Ulster from the enemy warriors while Ulster's army lies sick.

Cuchulainn, an archetypal superhuman of the EPIC tradition, is said to have lived about the first century A.D. The story of this HERO's birth is an ambiguous affair. According to one version, the King of Ulster's daughter, Deichtine, becomes pregnant under mysterious circumstances. People in Ulster believe that King Conchobor is the father. During a dream, however, a the Celtic god Lugh (or Lug) speaks to Deichtine and says that she is pregnant by him. Then Conchobor betroths Deichtine to another man. Deichtine is ashamed to go to her husband's bed pregnant with someone else's child, and so she lies down and crushes the baby inside her. Later she becomes pregnant by her husband and gives birth to Setanta (later named Cuchulainn).

Other tales suggest that King Conchobor is Cuchulainn's uncle, his mother's brother. Like the Arthurian hero PERCIVAL, Cuchulainn was raised only by his mother.

Cuchulainn's extraordinary youth, including the development of his impressive abilities, is depicted in the *Táin*. Conchobor observes Cuchulainn, who is six, at the playing fields. Alone, he is able to defeat 150 boys in various games. Conchobor invites the boy to join him at a feast given by Culann the smith. Cuchulainn arrives at Culann's house by himself and is threatened by Culann's ferocious bloodhound. Cuchulainn throws his ball into the dog's gaping mouth, and the ball exits from the dog's other end, taking its entrails with it. Cuchulainn dashes the dog on a stone and scatters it into pieces. As retribution, Cuchulainn offers to guard Culann's sheep and cattle until he gets another bloodhound. Thus, he receives the name Cuchulainn, which means Culann's Hound; later, Cuchulainn is known as the Hound of Ulster.

When Cuchulainn is seven, he hears a druid say that a boy who takes up arms on that day will be splendid and famous, but will die young. Cuchulainn goes to Conchobor and requests to take up arms, and Conchobor grants the boy his request. During the Cattle Raid of Cooley, Cuchulainn resists the enemy army and relieves the ill Ulsterman by fighting single combat after single combat. Tragically, he must fight a close childhood friend, Ferdia mac Damian. Although each is reluctant to confront the other, honor and duty urge them on. Their combat lasts several days until Cuchulainn kills Ferdia. Cuchulainn grieves bitterly for his friend.

Some years later, Cuchulainn's DEATH is surrounded by a number of portents. As Cuchulainn prepares for battle, weapons fall from their racks, the brooch from his mantle falls and pierces his foot, and his horse, the Grey of Macha, resists being harnessed to the chariot and weeps tears of blood. On the battlefield, Cuchulainn yields his spear three times to three enemy satirists who threaten to revile him and his race. The first two times, Cuchulainn recovers his spear. The third time, his own spear strikes him in the bowels. Knowing that he must die, Cuchulainn fastens himself to a pillar so that he will die standing up. While he remains alive, the wounded Grey of Macha defends him. Eventually a raven perches on Cuchulainn's shoulder, signifying his death. As one of the enemy approaches, Cuchulainn's sword falls and severs the enemy's hand. Cuchulainn's right hand is cut off in revenge and is buried with his head in Tara.

Other tales in the *Ulster Cycle*, the group of stories from which the *Táin* comes, feature the hero Cuchulainn, but in a different context from that of the *Táin*. One story, "Cuchulainn's Sickbed and Emer's One Jealousy," includes the familiar motif of an alluring GODDESS who entices Cuchulainn to the underworld. More tales, some written centuries later, continue the action begun in the *Táin*.

For Further Reading

Kinsella, Thomas, trans. *The Tain*. Oxford: Oxford University Press, 1970.

O'Rahilly, Cecile, ed. *Tain Bo Cualnge*. Dublin: Dublin Institute for Advanced Studies, 1967.

CULTURE HERO

Benefactor who brings various aspects of culture to a people. The figure, who may be human or ANIMAL, appears in oral traditions around the world. He or she initially teaches human beings their skills, crafts, and magic spells. In addition, the culture hero may provide the people with land to live on, sunlight, warmth, food sources, and water. The HERO may also be a transformer, changing people into animals and vice-versa, and reshaping features in the landscape.

The institution of MARRIAGE is often introduced by the culture hero, complete with specifications to avoid INCEST. In fact, the gifts of the culture hero frequently include a set of rules for living. As Barbara Sproul comments in *Primal Myths: Creating the World,* "GODS and heroes of all sorts descend into time and space to instruct people in the way of proper, absolute being: 'Walk this way! Speak this way! Multiply in this manner! Organize yourselves in this way! Be like this!' From Babylonian to Chuckchi Eskimo myths, the gods reveal that the appropriate ways of personal and social being are the same as nature's. Just as various aspects of nature relate to each other harmoniously and fruitfully, so should aspects of society and aspects of the self."

The culture hero may also be the creator deity. In other cases, culture heroes steal from the gods for the benefit of human beings. The idea that power, knowledge, or tools will not be given willingly and must be stolen is probably why the culture hero is so often the local TRICKSTER. The thief sometimes pays a dear price for such gifts to humankind (*see* PROMETHEUS AND THE THEFT OF FIRE). However, thieving cultural heroes are generally treated positively by storytellers, with the notable exception of Eve and the serpent in the Biblical legend of ADAM AND EVE.

In NATIVE NORTH AMERICAN STORYTELLING the culture hero is usually an animal or can take both human and animal forms. He or she is often a trickster—COYOTE, RAVEN, Mink, Bluejay, GREAT RABBIT, SPIDER Man, or SPIDER WOMAN (*see* HOPI CREATION). According to the Cherokee, a female spider brought humanity a precious burning coal. Raven also stole fire for his people, as did Coyote, and Coyote was responsible for bringing seeds into the present world and giving them to each tribe.

The Native American GLOOSCAP brought warmth to the cold northern lands when he kidnapped Summer from her father, the chief of the little people. When winter had been melted away, he let her go home. WHITE BUFFALO WOMAN taught the Lakota how to use the holy pipe and how to pray, and she assigned specific jobs and responsibilities to the men, women, and children of the tribe.

The Polynesian trickster and culture hero MAUI created the islands for people to live on and also stole fire from the deity who kept it hidden. According to the Kayapo of central Brazil, a young man named Botoque was taught by a jaguar how to make bows and arrows and how to cook. Botoque killed the jaguar's wife when she threatened him, and returned home with his cooked meat, weapons, and a hot coal. Other men liked what they saw, and also stole from the jaguar's cave. The jaguar was so angry that he gave up cooking food and hunting with weapons. But everyone knows that the flame can sometimes be seen in the jaguar's eyes.

A blacksmith is the culture hero of some African stories. In Benin, the eldest son of the creator deity MAWU was Gu, the heavenly blacksmith. Gu was given the task of making earth habitable for humans, and he also taught them ironworking and toolmaking. In the DOGON CREATION story, the creator stole fire from the sun in order to forge tools. In Bantu legends, culture heroes brought livestock, taught the people how to dress hides, and cleared out dangerous wild beasts or MONSTERS. Some of the stories told about HARE feature him as this kind of benefactor. African mythology also features other animals as culture heroes and often as assistant creators. The Mantis brought fire to the Koisin and also invented language. Pale Fox invented agriculture for the Dogon by stealing seeds from the creator god. Antelope was sent by the creator god to teach the secrets of agriculture to the Bambara. On the Papua coast, a wandering culture hero, known as Sido and other names, is said to have created geographical features as he traveled—cutting a pass through the mountains, creating a lake when he urinated. His discarded hairs became dogs and pigs, and he also gave the people fish and vegetables.

The royal deities ISIS AND OSIRIS brought civilization to Egypt and then to neighboring lands. They taught their people agricultural and food storage methods, music, crafts, laws, and rites of worship, as well as how to make wine and beer and bake bread.

Sometimes there is competition between culture heroes. The Australian sisters of the beginning, or Dreamtime, were eventually subjugated by their two brothers (*see* DJANGGAWUL AND HIS SISTERS). In the New Hebrides, stories describe two culture heroes with the same name, Tagaro. One was wise and created useful things for the human beings; the other was foolish and spoiled much of what his brother had created. Coyote also has two distinct aspects in Navaho legend; one is culture hero and the other, trickster. When the job is completed, the culture hero often leaves to rejoin the gods, enter the underworld, or wait at some specific place for the end of our world.

For Further Reading

Erdoes, Richard. *The Sound of Flutes and Other Indian Legends.* Illustrated by Paul Goble. New York: Pantheon Books, 1976.

Sproul, Barbara. *Primal Myths: Creating the World.* San Francisco: Harper & Row, 1979.

Werner, Alice. *Myths and Legends of The Bantu.* London: Frank Cass & Co., 1968.

CUMULATIVE STORY AND SONG

Story or song in which the elements accumulate and are often repeated. Sometimes the elements are repeated in reverse order to complete the pattern. Cumulative songs and stories turn up in oral traditions around the world.

Well-known cumulative songs include "The Twelve Days of Christmas" and "There's a Hole in the Bottom of the Sea." Perhaps the best-known story is "The House that Jack Built."

Cumulative stories sometimes only link together a sequence of events, rather than repeating all elements. For example, in the GRIMM BROTHERS's collection, "The Nail" is about a merchant on the way home from a fair who repeatedly ignores warnings that his horse has a nail missing from a shoe. When the horse falls and breaks his leg, the merchant blames the nail. A similar story is told in the folk rhyme "Horseshoe Nail," in which a battle was eventually lost for want of a horseshoe nail. *See also* CHAIN TALE, FORMULA TALE.

For Further Reading

Grimm's Tales for Young and Old. Translated by Ralph Manheim. New York: Doubleday, 1977.

CUPID AND PSYCHE

Roman god of love (*Eros* in Greek mythology), and the mortal whom he loved. The written story of "Cupid and Psyche" first appears in the second century *Golden Ass* of the Latin author APULEIUS, but was probably based on earlier oral Greek tradition. The theme of the Cupid and Psyche story—the lover whose identity must remain secret— is a common one in FOLKLORE.

Cupid is the son of the GODDESS Venus and the god Mercury (the Roman equivalents of the Greek APHRODITE and Hermes). Psyche is the youngest and most beautiful of the three daughters of a KING. Some said that even Venus could not equal the mortal Psyche's beauty; in fact, people became so infatuated with Psyche that they began to neglect the temples of Venus. Jealous and furious, Venus asks Cupid to make Psyche fall in love with some vile creature. But when Cupid sees Psyche, he falls in love with her himself.

Although her sisters are married, Psyche shows no interest in any suitor. Worried, her father consults the oracle of APOLLO. Cupid, meanwhile, has already confessed his love for Psyche to Apollo. So the oracle orders Psyche to wait on a lonely hilltop for the creature destined to be her husband—a terrible dragon.

On the hilltop, Psyche is lulled into sleep by a gentle breeze. She wakes beside a great palace. Inside, she finds FOOD, wine, and riches, and is attended by invisible servants. Her new husband comes to her that night, and though she cannot see him, she knows that it is no MONSTER.

Cupid comes to her every night but leaves each night before sunrise. He warns her that she must not ever know who he is or see him. The reason for the taboo is the potential anger of Venus, who is jealous of the beautiful Psyche and will not easily tolerate her son's interest in her. Nevertheless, because of her sister's questions and her own curiosity, Psyche lights a lamp one night while Cupid sleeps next to her. But a drop of hot oil falls on Cupid's shoulder, and he awakens and flees.

Heartbroken, Psyche searches for her beloved husband, and in her desperation, offers to serve Venus. The goddess devises three dangerous jobs for her, including a DESCENT TO THE UNDERWORLD (*see also* NUMBERS). Eventually, Venus puts Psyche into a deep sleep.

Cupid finds and awakens her. He enlists the help of Jupiter (the Roman equivalent of the Greek ZEUS) to keep Venus from doing more harm to Psyche. Announcing that Cupid and Psyche are married, Jupiter makes her immortal. At that point, Venus can no longer object to the union.

In Apuleius' story, Cupid is an adult young man. His image was later transformed into the more familiar one of a cherubic child, as often portrayed on Valentine's Day cards in the United States, replete with wings, a bow and arrow, and sometimes a blindfold. The GODS or mortals shot by his arrows usually fall in love—either with a specific person or with the first being they see. On other occasions, Cupid uses his arrows to prevent his victim from falling in love at all.

Psyche means both *breath* and *soul* or *life* in ancient Greek, and she is often depicted with butterfly wings. Her image has appeared in advertising, as well as in the work of poets such as Milton and Keats—always as a symbol of the feminine soul or spirit.

Elements of the story of Cupid and Psyche turn up in such tales as "BEAUTY AND THE BEAST," "CINDERELLA," and "Sleeping Beauty." *See also* YOUNGEST DAUGHTER.

For Further Reading

Barth, Edna. *Cupid and Psyche: A Love Story.* Illustrated by Ati Forbert. New York: Seabury Press, 1976.

Hodges, Margaret. *The Arrow and the Lamp: The Story of Psyche.* Boston: Little, Brown, 1989.

CYBELE

Great Mountain GODDESS of Anatolia (the Greek name for Asia Minor, roughly present day Asiatic Turkey), who is also known as the *Magna Mater* of Phrygia. The Great MOTHER Cybele lives on Mount Ida, where she sits on a lioness throne, observing all. She wears a turret-like crown and holds a sacred cymbal. Her throne is flanked by lions. Her priestesses ride in lion-drawn chariots, and her priests are eunuchs, who have discarded their genitals to become like Cybele's son and lover, ATTIS. The mother of the deities, Cybele is also the protectress of all who live in the towns and the cities of Anatolia.

Cybele, as a baby, is exposed on a mountain, but grows up there and thus becomes the nurturing Mother of the Mountain. She sometimes takes the form of the Agdos Rock (*see* ATHENA). In her form as the virgin Nana, she is the mother of Attis.

The story of Cybele and her son-lover, Attis, comes from the vegetation-year MYTHS of the Fertile Crescent and the myths of the Mother and her sacrificial victim-KING-lover. In this LEGEND, Attis is a princely young shepherd who is set upon by a lustful monster. In order that he should remain faithful to his mother, he tears his GENITALS from his body and dies beneath an evergreen tree. Cybele takes Attis's mutilated body to a cave on Mount Ida. Every spring, she laments her dead son and lover. She reburies his body in the earth and performs the rites of mourning. According to Ovid, Attis is hardened into the trunk of the pine tree.

This myth exemplifies a pattern in the stories of the great fertility goddesses. In many stories, the great mother goddess figure mourns the loss of a loved one. She goes on a search and brings about a form of resurrection—associated with the planting and harvesting of crops—which establishes new religious practices or mysteries (*see* ISIS AND OSIRIS, LEMMINKAINEN, PERSEPHONE MYTH).

As with other fertility goddesses, Cybele's concern with planting and harvesting is evident in the myths surrounding her. Counterparts of Cybele in other cultures include ARTEMIS, DEVI, and INANNA or Ishtar, as well as Demeter and Isis.

For Further Reading

Green, R.L. *A Book of Myths*. Illustrated by Joan Kiddell-Monroe. New York: Dutton. 1965.

Stapleton, Michael. *The Illustrated Dictionary of Greek and Roman Mythology*. New York: Peter Bedrick Books, 1986.

CYCLOPES

Brutish, one-eyed creatures found in Greek and Roman mythology; in many MYTHS, the Cyclopes are depicted as GIANTS. The first three Cyclopes, named Arges, Brontes, and Steropes, were the children of Uranus (HEAVEN) and GAIA (the EARTH-MOTHER). They were storm spirits or powers of the air. They were wild and had a single eye in the middle of their foreheads. Known for their skill as smiths, the Cyclopes forged a thunderbolt for ZEUS, a magic helmet for HADES, and a trident for Poseidon.

According to HOMER'S ODYSSEY, the Cyclopes were a gigantic race of one-eyed shepherds and the descendants of the original three Cyclopes. They were wholly uncivilized creatures who lived in caves on the island of Sicily. In the ninth book of the *Odyssey*, Odysseus and his companions land on the Cyclopes' island and enter the cave of the Cyclops Polyphemus, who takes the men as his prisoners. He plans to devour them raw, two by two. Odysseus offers the greedy Polyphemus some strong wine, and eventually Polyphemus falls into a deep sleep. Odysseus and his remaining companions heat a sharpened stick and drive it into Polyphemus's eye, blinding him. By riding under the bellies of Polyphemus's sheep, Odysseus and his men are able to escape from the Cyclops' cave.

Polyphemus is also known for his pursuit of the sea NYMPH Galatea. In Ovid's version of this LEGEND, the Cyclops Polyphemus serenades Galatea while unbeknownst to him she lies nearby in her lover's, Acis's, arms. When Polyphemus spies the lovers, he hurls a rock that crushes and smothers Acis. With the help of the Fates, Galatea transforms Acis into a river god.

In other legends, the Cyclopes are the assistants of Hephaestus, the god of fire, who has his workshop in the volcanoes. They make metal armor and ornaments for GODS and HEROES. Other traditions say that the Cyclopes formed a tribe that was expelled from Thrace. They followed King Proetus and protected him by building gigantic walls.

In general, the Cyclopes belong to a storytelling tradition in which giants are evil, grotesque, and uncivilized beings, who must be overcome by their human adversaries.

For Further Reading

Evslin, Bernard. *The Cyclopes*. New York: Chelsea House, 1987.

Low, Alice. *The Macmillan Book of Gods and Heroes*. Illustrated by Arvis Stewart. New York: Macmillan, 1985.

DANCE

Rhythmic movements of body and feet often playing an integral part in the storytelling processes of cultures with strong oral traditions. Dances have always been performed to sung versions of specific tales (*see* BALLAD, MINSTRELSY). Folk dance in particular has always been an integral part of the community and not merely the property of an interested few. Historically, dancing was something one did rather than simply watched. Dancing is deeply connected to social rituals throughout the world and is often the pretext or the focal point for gathering to listen to tales. Dance is often viewed as a narrative art form, and many FOLKTALES have been choreographed as ballets, such as *Swan Lake, Coppelia,* and *The Nutcracker.*

Folk narrative dances or vernacular dances have not been as well recorded as their musical equivalents, because they rely on a live tradition in the absence of sophisticated choreographic notation. Although *labanotation,* a method of recording body movement by means of symbols, was used to record some folk dances in Europe, it has never really made much headway outside of that continent. As a result, numerous stories told through dance have been irrevocably lost.

Dance also serves as a MOTIF for many FAIRY TALES, sometimes representing both the pleasures and the dangers of a protagonist's inauguration into adult (sexual) pleasure. Hans Christian Andersen's "The Red Shoes" connotes the demonic aspects of dance, its connection with uncontrollable appetite and frenzy (*see* ANDERSEN, HANS CHRISTIAN). Commonly, dance can represent romantic fulfillment well regulated by community sanction, a famous example being the ball in "CINDERELLA."

DAT

Egyptian mythical underworld. The Egyptians, like most other ancient civilizations, believed in a place where the souls of the dead continued to exist. In the Pyramid Texts and the *Egyptian Book of the Dead,* the Egyptians told of a place, the *Dat,* that served as the site of REBIRTH for the once-dead souls. Through the intervention of the resurrection god,

Osiris, souls were properly prepared over time to resume another life in the world above (*see* ISIS AND OSIRIS, NEAR AND MIDDLE EASTERN STORYTELLING). The SUN, the ancient Egyptians believed, exemplified this process every day. As the sun disappeared into the Dat, it briefly lit up the totality of the underworld before it was once again regenerated enough to begin it ascent back into the living world. The world that the sun illuminated during its REBIRTH was not without an aspect of horror. DEMONS were thought to endanger this rebirthing process and therefore must be caged within the Dat. Huge, repulsive monsters alternatively described as poisonous fire-spitting serpents, lions, lakes of fire, or DRAGONS of all shapes guarded the gates of the Dat in to which no living soul could gain access. The exact location of the Dat varied according to difference sources; it may be beneath the EARTH, or in the HEAVENS, or even within the imagined water systems just below earthly land. *See also* DESCENT TO THE UNDERWORLD, HELL, TIBETAN BOOK OF THE DEAD.

D'AULNOY, MADAME (MARIE-CATHERINE LE JUMEL DE BARNEVILLE) (1650–1705)

French author of collections of FAIRY TALES. Little is known about the life of d'Aulnoy, who married young, disappeared for almost two decades (supposedly she traveled throughout Europe during this time), and later resurfaced in France in 1690 to commence an intense period of writing that terminated almost a decade later. Although d'Aulnoy has 28 volumes of literature to her name, she is probably most well-known for her two collections of popular fairy tales, *Les Contes des Fees* (*Fairy Tales,* 1697) and *Les Contes Nouveaux, ou les Fees a la mode* (*New Tales or Fashionable Fairies,* 1698). In these fairy tales, d'Aulnoy utilizes a number of MOTIFS, including interior and exterior metamorphosis and DISGUISE, enabling her to critique society on a number of issues, including the definition and elasticity of gender-specific roles. D'Aulnoy's fairy tales appear to have been aimed at the growing number of young ladies in French society, rather than children, as they often deal with issues of creating female identity and the experimentation of sexual pleasure. For example, in *"L'abeille et l'orangier"* ("The Bee and the Orange Tree"), Aimee, a princess, is metamorphosed into a bee, while her male lover, Aime, is changed into an orange tree. Aimee reverses traditional gender role identification as she protects her feminized lover with her phallic stinger, and engages in a sort of love-making as she rests within the confines of her lover's blossoms. Although d'Aulnoy is often overshadowed by the fairy tales of her contemporary Charles Perrault (*see* PERRAULT, CHARLES), critics such as Maya Slater and Amy DeGraff have argued that her tales are important because they often challenged the established patriarchal traditions of European society.

DAVY JONES

Evil spirit of the SEA. Among sailors, the MYTH of Davy Jones, the personification of the dangerous, malevolent aspect of the sea, arose as a way of speaking of and naming the fear of the sea that is always ready to threaten or claim a sailor's life. When a sailor dies, he is said to go to "Davy Jones' Locker," meaning his grave at the bottom of the sea, and at times the sailors simply call the spirit "Davy." One old LEGEND has it that "at the crossing of the line," i.e., the equator, the sailors call out "that Davy Jones and his wife are coming on board and everything must be made ready."

The etymology of the name seems to derive from *Duffy* or *Duppy Jonah*, with the West Indian name for "a haunting spirit or ghost" being *duffy* or *duppy,* and Jonah, transformed to Jones, the name of the prophet of the Hebrew BIBLE who took off on a ship instead of following GOD's directions to preach in the wicked city of Nineveh. As punishment, God sent a terrible storm that threatened the lives of everyone aboard. Jonah confessed that he was the cause of the storm, and the sailors threw him overboard, where he was swallowed by a "great fish" or whale. He lived in the belly of the whale for three days until he repented, was vomited by the fish onto dry land, and returned to preach in Nineveh. Despite his repentance, his name became associated with a bringer of bad luck, especially at sea.

DEATH

Archetypal end of life or stage before REBIRTH in MYTH and LEGEND. Death appears in stories everywhere, being a common experience to all humankind. In storytelling, tales exhibit explanations of the ORIGIN OF DEATH, as in the Native American tale, "COYOTE and the Origin of Death"; death as PUNISHMENT, as in the death of the wicked stepmother (see STEPMOTHER—WICKED) in the GRIMM BROTHERS'S FAIRY TALE "Snow White"; death as reversible or irreversible, as in the Christian story of Lazarus raised from the dead; death as a prelude to rebirth and RESURRECTION, as in the Native American BEAR MAN MYTH; death as the result of unrequited love or thwarted love, as in the Chinese fairy tale "Faithful Even in Death" (see CHINESE STORYTELLING); death of the HERO as a result of *hubris*, as in the case of the Hawaiian MAUI; death in childbirth or soon after so that the young HEROINE must learn to survive without a mother, as in the Grimm's fairy tales of "Snow White" and "CINDERELLA"; death postponed by substitution, as in the Greek story of Admetus and Alcestis; the loss of a loved one through death, as in the death of Cinderella's mother; death as a prophesy that the story's characters try to prevent from coming to pass, as in "Little Briar Rose" and "Two Brothers"; and death as the result of natural disaster, illness, or old age, as in all tales in which the KING dies and the PRINCE takes his place. In the oral tradition, the death of an important character may generate the story's conflict or constitute its resolution.

As a RITE OF PASSAGE, death is the last transition. Instructions for preparation for death and the stages immediately following it can be found in *The Egyptian Book of the Dead* and the TIBETAN BOOK OF THE DEAD.

DEGH, LINDA (1920–)

Hungarian American folklorist who, like Richard Bauman (see BAUMAN, RICHARD), recognized performance as a defining medium for FOLKLORE. Her most popular work is *Folktales and Society: Story-Telling in a Hungarian Peasant Community,* published in 1962 in Germany and in 1969 in the United States. This book was one of the first to present the new theoretical trends in 1960s and 1970s FOLKTALE research, utilizing fieldwork to examine the social function of storytelling and altering the focus of research from reconstructing the past to interpreting the present. Degh asserts that folklore research should move beyond the limited realm of recording texts to include all the cultural contexts surrounding the performance of narrators and the response of audiences. Degh studied the historical background of a transplanted *commun* of Szeklers in Kaksd, Transylvania, and looked at how the new social and economic realities after relocation affected their storytelling occasions. She concluded that the functions of folklore lay in, and change in respect to, social need. For instance, stories told by serfs of rich estates for entertainment were modified and told by the poorest class of peasants to express hopes and aspirations after the breakup of the estates. Degh's book also considered the contribution of industry on rural traditions. In addition to studying the effect of migration and urbanization of folklore's functions, Degh was engaged with individualism—exploring the ways in which each storyteller's unique language, style, and dramatic presentation shape narration. She believed that the status and personality of the narrator greatly affect tale texts. Both Degh and Bauman profess this individual performance theory, viewing the text as meaningless apart from a living performance. Degh's studies reflect an analysis of tellers' skills, tales' functions, and audiences' interactions.

For Further Reading

Degh, Linda. *Folktales and Society: Story-Telling in a Hungarian Peasant Community.* 1969. Reprint, Bloomington, IN: Indiana University Press, 1989.

———. *Indiana Folklore: A Reader.* Bloomington, IN: Indiana University Press, 1980.

DELARUE, PAUL (1889–1956)

French folklorist. Delarue is recognized by many critics as one of the most important collectors of French FOLKTALES in the twentieth century. In *The Borzoi Book of French Folk Tales* (1956), Delarue introduces the study of French FOLKLORE as a relatively new field of study. Delarue discusses the difficulty of collecting and developing a representative canon of French folklore that until the late nineteenth century was primarily composed of the works of Charles Perrault (*see* PERRAULT, CHARLES). Although Delarue acknowledges the universality of folktales, citing a number of variations on the "CINDERELLA" FAIRY TALE throughout the world, he argues that, in general, tales in French storytelling are different from those in other cultures: "The French story is all action, direct, without accessory details, without description, without lyricism; the style is sober and unadorned." For example, while BLUEBEARD may be a "cannibalistic monster" in the folktales outside of France, the French folktale depicts this character as a member of the bourgeois class. Delarue also says that French tales often substitute actions based on magical forces with dramatic narratives that explore the human psyche while simultaneously eliminating whatever is bloody, or a "survival of barbaric periods," such as decapitations.

DELPHI

Location of an ancient oracle (a place where deities are consulted) on the southern slope of MOUNT PARNASSOS. The site included caves, a spring, and a river. The vapor that rose from a cleft in the rocks was possibly intoxicating, and the raving convulsions of people who breathed the mist were thought to be inspired by GODS. Because of this, a temple was erected on the spot, which originally had been an earth-GODDESS shrine (*see* EARTH-MOTHER).

According to Greek legend, a serpent or DRAGON named Python lived in the shrine at Delphi. APOLLO killed Python and took over the shrine for his own cult. In the first volume of *The Greek Myths,* Robert Graves (*see* GRAVES, ROBERT) comments that this story may represent an invasion by Northern Hellenes. The invaders historically captured many oracular shrines and took them over for their own gods.

Apollo's shrine at Delphi became the most famous oracle in the Grecian world. In fact, Delphi was thought to be the center of the world, and was visited by travelers from many countries. A sacred stone there called the *omphalos* was considered the navel of the world.

The Delphic Oracle served as a direct link between gods and humans. A priestess, called the *Pythia,* sat on a three-legged stool called a *tripod.* The tripod was placed over a cleft in the rock from which the mist rose. She went into a trance and gave incomprehensible replies to questions posed by visitors, then her words were interpreted by a priest.

The message was usually so ambiguous that it was almost certain to prove correct, one way or another. Greek drama and myth feature many such prophecies that eventually came true in ironic or unpredictable ways. Sometimes, the oracle is not heeded by the unfortunate listener, and other times, the message is misunderstood.

Cadmus, the first KING of THEBES, consults the Delphic oracle while searching for his sister, Europa. After Herakles kills his wife and sons, the oracle recommends a purification that results in his undertaking the LABORS OF HERAKLES. The oracle gives Perseus a clue that turns out to be useless in his attempt to locate the Gorgons (*see* MEDUSA).

The oracle figures most famously in the LEGEND of Oedipus. It is from the oracle that Oedipus first learns that he is fated to kill his father and marry his mother. This prophecy causes him to flee his adopted home of Corinth to Thebes, where, ironically enough, he fulfills the oracle's prophecy.

The ruins of the oracle are still a great tourist attraction today. *See also* ANCIENT GREEK STORYTELLING.

DEMON LOVERS

Attractive, seductive men who turn out to be dangerous to women. The figure of the DEMON lover appears in FAIRY TALES, FOLKLORE, BALLADS, and contemporary literature. Associated with the DEVIL, the demon lover at first appears benign and loving, as in the case of BLUEBEARD in Charles Perrault's fairy tale (*see* PERRAULT, CHARLES). Although his wife has no idea that Bluebeard is dangerous, her curiosity when he is away causes her to try all the KEYS on the key ring with which he has entrusted her, including a small, forbidden key. When she finds the skeletons of his former wives, she recognizes the demon lover. In the

Irish ballad "The Daemon Lover," dating back to the sixteenth century or earlier, a man returns to find the woman he loved seven years earlier, but she now is married with children. He woos her with promises of his riches, until she leaves her husband and children to sail off with him. Once at sea, however, he turns into the devil, sinks the ship, and takes her to HELL. A later variant of this theme appears in Robert Browning's poem "Porphyria's Lover" (1836), where the jealous lover of Porphyria becomes her murderer. The figure of the VAMPIRE is a variant of the demon lover, and two well-known twentieth-century authors, Shirley Jackson and Elizabeth Bowen, each have written stories called "The Demon Lover," suggesting that the figure of the demon lover is still a familiar one. Canadian writer Margaret Atwood, also intrigued by this theme, has rewritten the Bluebeard fairy tale in her short story "Bluebeard's Egg" (1987).

While both Psyche in APULEIUS's story of "Amor and Psyche" and Beauty in Perrault's "BEAUTY AND THE BEAST" believe they are with a demon lover, in each tale the reverse is true (*see* CUPID AND PSYCHE). In Psyche's case, her lover forbids her to see him, and she—with the help of her sisters—assumes he is a demon rather than the splendid god he actually is. In Beauty's case, the Beast is only an external manifestation, not a reflection of the inner self.

For Further Reading

Atwood, Margaret. *Bluebeard's Egg and Other Stories*. New York: Fawcett, 1987.

Climo, Shirley. "Psyche." *Princess Tales from Around the World*. Illustrated by Ruth Sanderson. New York: HarperCollins, 1996.

The Complete Fairy Tales of Charles Perrault. Illustrated by Sally Holmes. Boston: Clarion Books, 1993.

DEMONS

Evil or destructive spirits to whom negative occurrences are attributed in most cultures. Although occasionally benevolent or protective, demons are generally considered dangerous spirits who are the enemies of humans. Illness and DEATH are often believed to be caused by demons, and in many cultures demonic spirits must be placated. The Australian aborigines of Arnhem Land fear the demons they call the *namarakains*, who steal the spirits of sick people, as well as the malicious *Nabudi* women, who are reputed to send invisible barbs into men traveling alone, thereby sickening them.

HEROES, HEROINES, and holy men and women have traditionally had to overcome the demonic in one form or another: in Christianity, Saint Anthony must overcome the frightening demons whose role is to shake his faith just as in Hinduism, the goddess Durga must destroy the evil demon Mahisasura, who has taken the form of a buffalo. The Persian hero Rustam is driven to fight the White Demon and the demon Akwan.

Demons also torment human beings in contemporary fiction, as in many of the stories of Yiddish writer Isaac Bashevis Singer, for example *Satan in Goray* (1935) (*see* SINGER, ISACC BASHEVIS).

As enemies of humankind, demons tend to represent darkness and temptation; the human battle against demons is, therefore, the age-old struggle for illumination and knowledge instead of ignorance and confusion.

For Further Reading

Mountford, Charles. *The First Sunrise: Australian Aboriginal Myths*. New York: Taplinger, 1972.

Narayan, R.K. *Gods, Demons, and Others*. New York: Viking, 1964.

O'Flaherty, Wendy D. *Hindu Myths*. New York: Penguin, 1975.

Sendak, Maurice. *Where the Wild Things Are*. New York: Harper and Row, 1963.

Singer, Isaac Bashevis. *Satan in Goray*. Translated by Jacob Sloan. New York: Farrar, Straus, Giroux, 1955.

DESCENT TO THE UNDERWORLD

Universal stage of the HERO-journey in MYTH. The stages of the hero's journey often involve a descent into the underworld, which can take place on both the physical and spiritual planes. There are many external reasons for this descent, such as the need of important information that only someone in the underworld can offer, the need to retrieve a loved one, or the need to complete a TEST. In most cases, the descent is successful, in that the hero is able to achieve what he or she set out to do and then ascend to daylight once again with the "Boon."

The descent to the underworld appears in the Sumerian story of the GODDESS INANNA, who is slain there and must be brought back to life; the Hawaiian story of Hiiaka, sister of PELE, who is searching to bring back her lover, Lohiau; the story of the warrior lover of the African WANJIRU, a maiden sacrificed to bring rain, in order to bring her back; the story of the Greek god DIONYSOS, who descends to bring his mother, Semele, back from the dead; stories of Jesus Christ, who was believed to have descended into HELL before his RESURRECTION; the stories of the Greek hero Herakles, whose twelfth labor involved descent, struggling with death, and freeing the hero THESEUS from its clutches (see LABORS OF HERAKLES); the story of the Blackfoot Indian KUTOYIS, whose descent is to the inside of a monster (see MONSTER KILLED FROM WITHIN); the Latin folktale, "CUPID AND PSYCHE," in which Venus sends Psyche to HADES to fetch a container with some of Proserpine's (Persephone's) beauty in it (see PERSEPHONE MYTH); the Greek story of Orpheus, who seeks his new wife, Eurydice, but fails to follow the directions of the GODS and therefore loses her before she can fully complete her ascent with him (see ORPHEUS AND EURYDICE MYTH); the story of the Comanche Indian known as Young Comanche, who brings his wife back from the dead but also fails to follow the RITUAL properly and therefore loses her once again; the story of the Icelandic Hermod, who unsuccessfully seeks to bring back his friend BALDR; the Japanese story of Izanagi who seeks to see his sister-wife Izanami once more (see JAPANESE CREATION); the story of the Hebrew Moses, whom GOD sends to visit Hell as a means of educating him (see EXODUS); the story of the Greek hero Odysseus, who speaks with the blind seer TIRESIAS as well as his mother during a visit to the underworld (see ODYSSEY); and the story of the Roman hero Aeneas, who gains important information from his father Anchises (see AENEID). The Italian Dante Alighieri's own "dark night of the soul" generates his descent into *purgatorio* in *The Divine Comedy*.

On one level, the descent to the underworld signifies the hero's return to the womb as symbolized by the inner earth. Like a seed, he or she must remain under the earth in darkness for a period of time before ascent is possible, signifying renewal and REBIRTH. The underworld is a place where a certain kind of knowledge can be gained that is not available otherwise, and once the hero has come to know this "higher truth" residing in the earth's dark recesses, emergence as a higher spiritual being is possible.

On another level, the descent to the underworld is the enactment of the descent into the self that each human being must embark upon in order to achieve self-realization and awareness. Turning inward is a necessary stage of meditation in the QUEST for enlightenment, or *samadhi*. Unless each person seeks to know his or her own shadow side, what is buried because it seems socially acceptable, it is impossible to be a fully individuated, self-actualized person. The dark forces within us must be reckoned with, and the symbolic night journey or the "dark night of the soul" is a universal experience of the hero within us all.

For Further Reading

Climo, Shirley. "Psyche." *Princess Tales from Around the World*. Illustrated by Ruth Sanderson. New York: HarperCollins, 1996.

The Odyssey. Retold by Robin Lister. Illustrated by Alan Baker. New York: Kingfisher, 1994.

DEVI

Hindu GODDESS, "MOTHER of the universe." In Hindu mythology, Devi symbolizes the female goddess in all her manifestations: fierce Chandi, inaccessible Durga, mountain-woman Parvati, light Uma, erotic Gauri, and the black one, KALI, are all manifestations of Devi. Sometimes she is a virgin; at other times she is associated with a great god, usually SIVA. Different MYTHS about Devi can be found in the individual PURANAS, and the *Devimahatmya*, a famous poem glorifying the goddess, can be found in the *Markandeya Purana*.

In the *Skanda Purana*, Devi is created for a specific purpose, to kill the buffalo DEMON Mahisasura. She is created from the anger of the other GODS, with her head coming from Siva's energy, her arms from VISNU'S anger, her feet from BRAHMA, her waist from Indra, her hair from Yama, her thighs from Varuna, her nose from Kubera, her fingers from the Vasus, her teeth from the nine Prijaptes, and her eyes from the Oblation-bearer. Nature, too, plays a role in Devi's creation, for her toes come from the SUN, her breasts from the MOON, and her hips from the EARTH. As her goal is to kill these buffalo demons, Devi appears in her fierce aspect as Durga. In another version that appears in the *Skanda Purana*, Devi already exists when the gods are confronted with the buffalo demon; they ask her to help them by transforming herself into a NYMPH in order to seduce and thereby weaken the demon.

The *Markandeya Purana* tells how Devi actually slays the demon. When Devi throws a noose over the demon, he transforms himself into a lion. After she decapitates him, he becomes a man with a sword. Her arrows pierce him, but he changes into a large elephant; when she cuts off his trunk, he becomes the buffalo demon again. By this time Devi is furious, so she intoxicates herself with celestial wine and attacks him, leaping upon him and putting her foot through his neck and decapitating him with his own sword.

For Further Reading

Coomaraswamy, Ananda K., and Sister Nivedita. *Myths of the Hindus and Buddhists*. New York: Dover, 1967.

Dimmitt, Cornelia, and J.A.B. van Buitenen. *Classical Hindu Mythology*. Philadelphia: Temple University Press, 1977.

O'Flaherty, Wendy Doniger. *Hindu Myths*. New York: Penguin, 1975.

Zimmer, Heinrich. *Myths and Symbols in Indian Art and Civilization*. New York: Harper, 1946.

DEVIL

Evil figure in religion, MYTH, and FOLKTALES, ruler of HELL. There are many names for the devil, who is considered the adversary of GOD. Whether he is called Samael, as in the fallen ANGEL who became the force behind the serpent in the Garden of Eden; Beelzebub; Lucifer; Satan; or the PRINCE of Hell, he is almost always male, demonic, part ANIMAL with horns and hooves, and representing the evil spirit, heresy, and black magic. He is believed to carry a hammer as a symbol of DEATH, and he is capable of possessing people and forcing them to do terrible acts. Known for enticing people to make pacts with him, in many European stories the devil buys the soul of a person or that person's son or daughter.

In the European fairy tale "The KING's Son and the Devil's Daughter," a man unconsciously sells his son to the devil, and the devil's daughter is the one who redeems the son. Women who live with the devil, such as the devil's daughter or grandmother, are generally friendlier to humans than the devil himself, and they represent his heart or love.

The figure of Robert the Devil was a hero of medieval legends. He had been using his strength to commit awful crimes when he learns that his mother had prayed to the Devil for a son when she was childless. He then visits a hermit to be purified and chooses to undertake severe penance, living at the court of Rome as a mute fool and managing to save the city from the Saracens on three different occasions. The end of his life, however, he spends at the hermitage. Variants of this legend appear in a French metrical ROMANCE of 1496, a fifteenth-century English metrical romance called *Sir Gowther*, a prose romance by Thomas Lodge written in 1591, and in an opera by Meyerbeer called *Robert le Diable*, with the libretto by Scribe and Delavigne.

DIFFUSION

Study of how FOLKTALES move from one place to another and how the tale modifies and changes during the process. Scholars such as Stith Thompson and Vladimir Propp sought to identify and define recurrent features in fixed corpus of folktales (*see* THOMPSON, STITH; PROPP, VLADIMIR). Thompson mapped the distribution of sequentially related MOTIFS or tale types. If there was a concentration of folktales with similar details, characters, plot structures, or motifs in one geographic area, and then a less dense concentration of a recognizably similar tale in an adjacent geographic area, Thompson assumed that this meant that the tale originated in the first area and then spread to the second. His theory of diffusion claims that the similar motifs and tale types found across the globe shared a common origin and then diffused across cultural boundaries, altering according to the influence of each culture.

Diffusion theory is opposed by POLYGENESIS, which claims that different cultures can and have produced very similar tales independently. Psychoanalytic accounts of FAIRY TALES can be used to support the polygenecists because they assert that folktales express many of the fundamental hopes and fears of early childhood, the experience of which is held to be universal.

A clear example of diffusion theory is found in the tracking of certain tales that have early recorded versions in Persia and India in Persian and Hindi. Corresponding tales are found in Arabic in the *Arabian Nights* and in the GRIMM BROTHERS's collections of German FOLKLORE. The strongest evidence for diffusion theory is the replication of details that are inessential to the plot-structure and characterization in different versions of a tale. For example, most versions, but not all, of "Little RED RIDING HOOD" portray the central character dressed in a red hood. However, this is not an essential component of the tale. Little girls in a dangerous forest, wearing other attire, could quite as easily undergo the same series of traumatic and redemptive experiences. The defining detail of the red hood is extraneous to the structure of the tale and resistant to explanation by theories of polygenesis. In such a case, diffusion of the tale from a central source would appear to be the only explanation. Franz Boas, the founder of modern anthropology, maintained that when a story that has the same combination of several elements is found in two separate regions, we must conclude that it is due to diffusion, not to independent invention (*see* BOAS, FRANZ).

DIONYSOS

In Greek mythology, the god of wine and revelry. The tales of Dionysos are, for the most part, ancient and preliterate in origin. Dionysos's stories have been transcribed in the works of Plutarch, HESIOD, and certain of the Homeric *Hymns*. He also appears in two classical Greek plays—Euripides' tragedy *The Bacchae,* and Aristophanes' comedy *The Frogs.*

In the most familiar story, Dionysos is born in THEBES, the son of the mortal woman Semele and the god ZEUS. When Zeus' wife HERA learns of her husband's love for Semele, she plots to have Semele killed. But at the instant of Semele's violent death, Zeus snatches their unborn child from her womb and sews it into his own thigh. There he protects Dionysos until he is born.

Even after his birth, Dionysos repeatedly falls victim to Hera's jealous rage. While he is still very young, Hera has Dionysos torn limb from limb. But Rhea, the mother of Zeus and the Olympians, resurrects Dionysos. Zeus places Dionysos in the protection of NYMPHS, and Dionysos invents wine while he grows to adulthood among them.

While Dionysos is still young, Hera drives him mad, sending him wandering the world as far as India. He acquires many followers along the way, most notably wild female worshippers known as *maenads* or *bacchantes*. When he nears Greece again, his grandmother cures him of his madness.

The wine god initially finds little respect or acceptance in Greece, especially in his home city of Thebes. There, the KING is a straitlaced young man named Pentheus—the son of Agave, Semele's sister. When Dionysos arrives in Thebes with his train of women followers, Pentheus tries to ban their frenzied ceremonies. Dionysos punishes his cousin by driving him mad. He then persuades Pentheus to dress in women's clothes and spy upon the bacchantes. The bacchantes—led by Pentheus' own mother, Agave—mistake Pentheus for a lion and tear him apart.

The Greeks gradually came to worship this strange new god who—like wine itself—had appeared mysteriously out of the east. The day even came when Dionysos was allowed to reign as one of the twelve Olympian gods— the only half-mortal in the pantheon.

Dionysos is very powerful; he can transform himself into a bull, a serpent, or a lion, and the innocent-looking wands wielded by his worshippers can prove the deadliest of weapons. It was believed that Dionysos perished every year along with the vine. Robert Graves (*see* GRAVES, ROBERT) suggests that in the oral tradition Dionysos began as a type of sacred king who was ritually sacrificed each year by a GODDESS. In this he resembles the Phrygian ATTIS and the Egyptian Osiris (*see* ISIS AND OSIRIS).

He is, then, a very ambiguous god—at once vulnerable and indestructible, gentle and brutal. The classical Greeks worshiped him and even held dramatic festivals in his honor, including those at Eleusis, but they did not seem to have been completely comfortable with him. They were more at ease, perhaps, with his fully immortal, highly rational half-brother APOLLO.

This tension between Dionysian and Apollonian thought is the subject of *The Birth of Tragedy,* an essay by Nietzsche. In it, Nietzsche traces the decline of the Dionysian influence in Greek drama and in civilization itself.

But today, there appears to be a resurgence of the Dionysian vision. When multiculturalism challenges Eurocentrism; when diversity displaces authoritarianism; and when new sciences are given names like Catastrophism, Chaos, and Complexity, the spirit of Dionysos and various "trickster" or "outlaw" figures seems very much with us. This is nowhere more evident than in popular culture. Singers like Elvis Presley, Mick Jagger, and Madonna, with their unabashed rebellion and sensuality, appear almost to be incarnations of Dionysos himself. *See also* ANCIENT GREEK STORYTELLING.

For Further Reading

Graves, Robert. *The Greek Myths.* 2 vols. New York: Penguin Books, 1957.

Hamilton, Edith. *Mythology: Timeless Tales of Gods and Heroes.* New York: Mentor, 1969.

Nietzsche, Friedrich. *The Birth of Tragedy.* Translated by Shaun Whiteside. New York: Penguin Books, 1993.

DISGUISES

MOTIF in MYTH and FAIRY TALE involving hiding or changing one's identity. Disguises are used by mythical and fairy-tale characters to aid them to achieve their goal, generally by fooling people into thinking they are other than their true identity. A disguise may be magical, such as a magic cloak, hood, or hat; it may cause a person to be invisible; it may involve transvestitism, wearing clothes of the opposite sex; it may be achieved through the use of a mask; it may be achieved by SHAPE SHIFTING, or it may involve wearing clothes to disguise one's true class, age, or race.

In the GRIMM BROTHERS's fairy tale "Snow White," the wicked stepmother (*see* STEPMOTHER—WICKED) uses disguises to trick Snow White into buying and tasting the items that are meant to destroy her. In the fourteenth-century Chinese FOLKTALE "Faithful Even in Death," a daughter, Yingt'ai, longs to be able to study in town, but girls are not allowed to do so. Yingt'ai's father finally agrees to let her dress as a boy, and she goes off to study with the son of a neighboring family, Hsienpo. Her disguise enables her to fool both Hsienpo, with whom she shares a bed, as well as all the other students. As they grow up, Yingt'ai falls in love with Hsienpo and swears to marry him, but after her father's death, she is forced to leave school to marry a doctor. Hsienpo finally learns Yingt'ai's true identity and of her love for him. Hsienpo pines away for Yingt'ai until he dies, and on the way to her wedding, Yingt'ai jumps into Hsienpo's grave and together they fly up to HEAVEN and become rainbows (*see* CHINESE STORYTELLING). Similar to "Faithful Even in Death," a more modern version of this tale is Isaac Bashevis Singer's Yiddish novel *Yentl the Yeshiva Boy* (1983), the story of an orphaned young woman who disguises herself as a man in order to study at a Yeshiva (*see* SINGER, ISAAC BASHEVIS). The recent Broadway musical *M. Butterfly* draws on the motif of the disguise when a man disguises himself as a woman and fools his male lover for many years.

Disguises are intriguing to children, for they offer one the opportunity to change one's identity, as in William Pene du Bois's story *Bear Party* (1951), where Australian koala bears overcome their fighting with each other by disguising themselves in a masquerade. *See also* INVISIBILITY, MAGIC CLOTHES, MASKS AND MASQUERADES.

For Further Reading

Du Bois, William Pene. *Bear Party*. New York: Viking, 1951.

Eberhard, Wolfram, ed. and trans. *Folk Tales of China*. Chicago: University of Chicago Press, 1968.

Singer, Isaac Bashevis. *Yentl the Yeshiva Boy*. Translated by Marion Magid and Elizabeth Pollet. New York: Farrar, Straus, Giroux, 1983.

DISMEMBERMENT OF PRIMORDIAL BEING

Form of creation MYTH involving the cutting up of a deity or MONSTER. In the mythology of some cultures, CREATION takes place when a primordial being, or monster, is dismembered, as in BABYLONIAN CREATION, Aztec Creation, Indonesian (Ceram) Creation, NORSE CREATION as depicted in the *Prose (Elder) Edda*, and Indian Creation as depicted in the *Rig Veda* (*see* EDDAS, ELDER AND YOUNGER; RIG-VEDA CREATION).

In Aztec mythology, the earth GODDESS COATLICUE is pulled down form the heavens by QUETZALCOATL, the Plumed Serpent, and Tezcatlipoca; they then rip her in half to form the EARTH and sky. The parts of her body are subsequently used to form different aspects of the earth and nature: her hair is the source of plants; her eyes and mouth become caves, springs, and wells; other bodily parts form mountains and valleys.

Similarly, in Babylonian Creation, the god MARDUK rides the waters of the goddess Tiamat, who takes the form of a monster or DRAGON, and he cuts her in half, forming the sky and the earth. Tiamat's stomach becomes the place of the SUN's path. From the blood and bones of the monster Kingu, Tiamat's lover, Marduk makes humans.

In the Indonesian creation myth of the Ceram people, HAINUWELE is sacrificed, dismembered, and planted. Where her body parts are planted grow the important plants of the Ceram culture.

In the Indian *Rig-Veda*, Purusa, the thousand-headed and -footed primal man, is sacrificed to become the universe, with each of his body parts forming another aspect: his bottom quarter becomes the world; his mouth becomes the god Indra and the wise Brahman priest (*see* INDRA AND THE ANTS); his arms form the warrior caste; his thighs become the common people; his mind is the MOON; his eye forms the sun; his breath becomes the wind; his head is transformed into the sky; his feet make the earth; his navel becomes the atmosphere; and from Purusa's sacrifice itself come plants, beasts, rituals, sacred words, and the *Vedas*.

DIVINE CHILD

Motif of child GODS in mythology. The MOTIF of the divine child appears in the mythologies of many cultures, generally following the pattern of a miraculous birth, subsequent ABANDONMENT or orphaning, exposure to extreme dangers, and ultimate triumph and evolution to become a mature god. In Greek mythology, Hermes, APOLLO, ZEUS, and DIONYSOS are each portrayed first as the divine child, as are the Hindu Narayana and KRISNA and the Polynesian MAUI.

As Carl Jung notes about the divine child in *Essays on a Science of Mythology: The Myth of the Divine Child and the Mysteries of Eleusis*, "Abandonment, exposure, danger, etc. are all elaborations of the 'child's' insignificant beginnings and of its mysterious and miraculous birth." Because *child* means something evolving towards independence, it must detach itself from its origins; thus, writes Jung, "abandonment is therefore a necessary condition, not just a concomitant symptom." That the child is "on the one hand delivered helpless into the power of terrible enemies and in continual danger of extinction" reveals its divinity all the more, for the divine child "possesses powers far exceeding those of ordinary humanity." Maui's ability to not only survive his premature birth when he is cast into the SEA wrapped in a knot of his mother's hair but also to return to his family, proclaim his status as rightful son, and be the only one of his siblings curious and clever enough to find out where his mother disappears to by day underline his extraordinary power.

The "classic Greek picture of divine childhood," according to C. Kerényi in the same work, can be found in the Homeric *Hymn to Hermes*, yet there is certainly something of the TRICKSTER in the child Hermes, as in Maui. Hermes, son of Zeus and the nymph Maia, is described in the *Hymn* as "Born in the dawn, by midday well he harped, and in the evening stole the cattle of Apollo the Far-Darter, on that fourth day of the month wherein lady Maia bore him." By creating the lyre out of the shell of a tortoise, the baby Hermes cleverly produces the item that will overcome Apollo's wrath and cause him to swear loyalty to Hermes forever after.

DIVINE SIGNS

Auguries of the future in MYTH and LEGEND. In all cultures and forms of storytelling, the prophecy of the future as indicated by divine signs holds great importance. Whether the indicator of the meaning of the signs be a prophet, an oracle, a *sibyl*, a seer, or a SHAMAN, "the indicator and the event are in some form of logical harmony; each is the cause or the reflection of the other," notes Maria Leach in *Funk and Wagnalls Standard Dictionary of Folklore, Mythology, and Legend*. The most widespread divine signs are DREAMS, the flight of birds, markings of the shoulder bone or entrails of an animal sacrifice, and the configuration of the stars at a precise moment. Accidental signs that are bad omens include the bearing of twins, the breaking of a mirror, sneezing, tripping and falling, a black cat crossing one's path, and meeting an old or cross-eyed woman first thing in the morning.

The dream as a divine sign is accepted almost everywhere, and dreams play an important role in the biblical narrative of Joseph, the ODYSSEY, and the conception of BUDDHA.

Maidens are supposed to dream of their future husbands on Saint Agnes's Eve.

The Greek oracle at DELPHI predicts the future for the parents of Oedipus as well as Oedipus himself: they are all told that the son will slay the father. The oracle also tells Creon that the city of THEBES must be cleansed of Laius's murderer if the plague is to end. The *sibyl*, or Pythoness, the priestess of APOLLO, would utter cryptic phrases that came to her from the god himself. A recent novel with this theme is Par Lagerkvist's *The Sibyl* (1956).

In the story of ANUBIS AND BATA, an ancient Egyptian tale, the formation of a river comes as a divine sign from the SUN god to protect Bata and prove his innocence. In the Greek story of King MIDAS, the divine sign comes in the form of ants gathering up grains of wheat and marching them to the infant Midas's lips, which presaged Midas's future wealth. In the BIBLE, GOD offers various divine signs such as the rainbow shown to NOAH after the FLOOD has receded and the parting of the Red Sea when the Hebrews are escaping from the land of Egypt (*see* EXODUS).

Astrology is another ancient form of reading divine signs and figures into the myths of various cultures. Jewish scholasticists relied on numerology and number symbolism as a form of divine signs.

For Further Reading

D'Aulaire, Ingri, and Edgar P. D'Aulaire. *Ingri and Edgar Parin D'Aulaire's Book of Greek Myths*. New York: Dell, 1992.

DIVISION OF WORLD PARENTS

Basic MOTIF in many MYTHS of CREATION characterized by the separation of HEAVEN and EARTH, symbolized by SKY-FATHER and EARTH-MOTHER. As David and Margaret Leeming note in *A Dictionary of Creation Myths*, "The world parents—the unified or coupled unity of earth and heaven or sky—are suffocating for the potential world caught within the potentially divisible unity." This separation of heaven and earth can be found in Aztec, the Celtic, Chinese, Greek, Hebrew, Mariana Islands, Mayan, Minyong, Navajo, Roman, and Zuni creation myths.

In Aztec mythology, QUETZALCOATL and Tezcatlipoca, both male, pull the female spirit, COATLICUE, down from the heavens and tear her in two to form the earth and sky. For the Chinese, a huge COSMIC EGG, which originally contained a chaotic mixture of all opposites, or *yin-yang*, is broken and a GIANT named P'AN KU separates this chaos into its many opposites. P'an Ku separates earth and sky by standing between them and growing ten feet each year, thus pushing them further and further apart until at last 30,000 miles separate them. In a version of the Maori story of RANGI AND PAPA, (the sky-father and earth-mother), Tane, their son, pushes them apart. Rangi's tears of loneliness become the rain; Papa's sad sighs become the mist that rises up to the sky.

The Celts saw Earth and Heaven as the original parents, but their closeness allowed little room for creation. Consequently, one of their children castrates the father, and from his skull is made the sky while the waters are made from his blood. Similarly, the ancient Greek cosmogony depicts GAIA, the Earth-Mother, as giving birth to Uranos, Heaven. Their mating produces the Titans who hate their father because he detests them and hides them in dark places. One of the Titans, Kronos, takes a sickle made by his mother and, thrusting it between his coupling parents, castrates Uranos, flinging his genitals into the sea, and out of the foam is born APHRODITE, GODDESS of love and desire. From the spilled blood of Uranos comes the FURIES, terrible giants, and graceful NYMPHS.

DJANGGAWUL AND HIS SISTERS

Divine trio of the Australian Aborigines of Arnhem Land, creators and ancestral beings who appeared in human shapes. They are Bildjiwuraroiju (or Bildiwuwiju), the Elder Sister; Miralaidj (or Muralaidj), the Younger Sister; and Djanggawul, the Brother. Their story is told in the *Djanggawul*, a song-cycle consisting of 188 songs that come to 2,921 lines in translation. According to the MYTH, the Djanggawuls live far out at SEA on the island of Baralku, or Bralgu, the Land of Eternal Beings. They leave Baralku to travel to the mainland of Australia, journeying by a bark canoe in which is stored the sacred objects and emblems. Accompanied by Bralbal ("another being"), their way is lit by the morning star. As they journey over the sea, they encounter many difficulties, including roaring waves, a whale blocking their path, "lines of sea eggs spreading across the sea," and driftwood that also blocks their way. Finally, they reach the shore of Arnhem Land at Yelangbara Beach at Port Bradshaw. The Aborigines believe their landing spot is marked with a sacred rock symbolizing the canoe, and a freshwater spring nearby is said to have sprung forth when Djanggawul plunged his walking stick into the sand.

After their arrival, the Djanggawuls travel across the land naming the ANIMALS and the places. They put sacred objects known as *ranggas* in the earth for future generations, they create wells by planting their sacred walking stick—the *mauwalan*—into the ground, and wherever they go they people the country. When they reach Elcho Island, Djanggawul is said to have tripped, inadvertently plunging the walking stick into the sand, which causes the seas to rise and flood the land, separating Elcho Island from the mainland.

Eventually, the sons of Bildjiwuraroiju and Miralaidj steal the sacred objects used in fertility ceremonies in order to give men control. Although the sisters are upset, they forgive the sons because they are still in possession of their own wombs. This aspect of the myth points to the Djanggawuls' connection with fertility and fecundity.

After many adventures, the three Djanggawuls return to their home on Baralku Island. To the Aborigines, they are important for their role in passing on language and culture and for giving them the origins of the Arnhem Land.

For Further Reading

Mudrooroo. *Aboriginal Mythology*. New York: HarperCollins, 1994.

DOGON CREATION

Cosmogony of the Dogon people of modern Mali. As David and Margaret Leeming note in *A Dictionary of Creation Myths*, the Dogon people have incorporated into their cosmogony both incest and the COSMIC EGG, in particular because such an INCEST STORY supports their kinship system. As the Dogon are patrilineal, the ideal MARRIAGE for a Dogon man is with the daughter of his maternal uncle, his first cousin, but first he is expected to have intercourse with the mother of his fiancée, his aunt, as a kind of replacement for the highly tabooed intercourse with his mother, "the ideal spouse."

The story the Dogon tell of their creation begins with a cosmic egg "shaken by seven huge stirrings of the universe." The egg is then divided into two birth sacs. Each sac holds a set of male and female twins, offspring of Amma, the supreme deity and fertilizer of the maternal egg. Each male and female twin is also androgynous, containing the essence of the other twin's gender within it. Creation comes after Yorugu, a male twin, breaks out of his sac before the right time, and the EARTH is formed from the broken piece of sac. Yorugu tries to return to his twin, but he cannot find her for she has been transferred to the other sac. Although Yorugu returns to earth and has intercourse with the earth, his mother, there is no creation of human beings. Instead, Amma sends the twins of the other sac to earth in order to beget human beings, which they do with the mating of brother, sister, and cousin twins.

For Further Reading

Griaule, Marcel. *Conversations with Ogotemmeli.* Oxford: Oxford University Press, 1975.

DRAGON

Serpentlike monster of tremendous size and power that usually breathes fire or poison and guards a treasure. The general features of dragons include wings, claws, large teeth, a crest, and a long tail. They usually live in remote areas, whether on land or in or near water, and they can fly. Many dragons are impervious to weapons unless they are struck in their soft spot which may be located below the belly, under the wing, or elsewhere. For thousands of years, dragons in one form or another have been antagonists to the HEROES

of many stories. Regardless of the cultures from which they come, many dragon stories follow the same narrative pattern: the dragon guards something valuable, the hero tries to steal the dragon's treasure, the hero and the dragon fight, the dragon is slain, and the hero wins the treasure.

Dragons are not always portrayed as terrifying monsters. In Asian dragon lore, the dragon is a primarily benevolent protector of people. It is a dispenser of life-giving water and a harbinger of fertility and good fortune.

Greek mythology greatly influenced the Western concept of dragons. Dragons in Greek MYTHS are often composites of many animals, and they may have several heads. They breathe fire and guard treasures. In the story THE QUEST FOR THE GOLDEN FLEECE, told in the *Argonautica* of Apollonius Rhodius, Jason must get the golden fleece in order to claim his father's kingdom. The fleece is guarded by a dragon, a writhing monster with sleepless eyes and scaly skin. Medea puts the dragon to sleep, and Jason takes the golden fleece. In a later version of the same story, the dragon has a three-forked tongue and golden teeth.

The interest in dragon stories was passed on to the Middle Ages. Dragons are prevalent in Old English literature where they are a portent of tragedy and representative of human greed. In the Anglo-Saxon work BEOWULF, the destructive rampages and physical appearance of the dragon are described vividly. The dragon is a hideous color and fifty feet long. It flies and slithers. Although it looks reptilian, it has smooth skin. A sentient creature, the dragon is poisonous as well as fire-breathing. It lives in a stone cave near the sea where it has guarded treasure for over 300 years.

In Christianity, the dragon represents spiritual evil and is equated with the DEVIL. The New Testament book of Revelations describes the WAR IN HEAVEN when Michael and the angels fight against the dragon, the devil or Satan, and throw him down to earth. During the Middle Ages, there are many accounts of Christian saints slaying dragons. The legend of Saint George is the most popular of these narratives. In one version, the dragon is fifty feet long, with scales as bright as silver and as hard as brass, and a gold belly. When Saint George plunges his spear into the monster, the weapon breaks into a thousand pieces. When the dragon lashes out with its poisonous tail, Saint George escapes to safety under a magic orange tree. Finally, Saint George strikes the dragon in its tender spot under the wing, and purple gore flows from the wound. The dragon loses so much blood that it dies, and Saint George beheads it.

In Arthurian legends, dragons are agents of chaos, destruction, and death. If a knight slays a dragon, he has achieved a victory over death. Yet, dragons also portend the coming of King ARTHUR (*see* MERLIN).

In the Renaissance poem *The Faerie Queene*, the Redcrosse Knight, a figure of Saint George, battles a horrible dragon for three days before he is able to kill it. Other famous dragon-slayers include Perseus, MARDUK, Hercules, APOLLO, SIEGFRIED, Beowulf, Arthur, and Tristan (*see* LABORS OF HERAKLES, TRISTAN AND ISOLDE).

After the Renaissance, stories of dragons and dragon-slayers became much less popular, although dragon lore has reemerged in the nineteenth and twentieth centuries. In 1898, Kenneth Grahame published the short story "The Reluctant Dragon" in his book *Dream Days*, and in 1899, *Book of Dragons* by E. Nesbitt appeared. Recent works in which dragons have an important role include J. R. R. Tolkien's *The Hobbit* (1937) and *Farmer Giles of Ham* (1949) (*see* TOLKIEN, J.R.R.); Rosemary Manning's *Green Smoke* (1957), the first in a series of books about a child named Sue and her friend R. Dragon; Margaret Mahy's *The Dragon of an Ordinary Family* (1969), a picture book in which a dragon is bought as a household pet; and *The Farthest Shoe* (1972), the last volume of Ursula Le Guin's Earthsea trilogy. *A Book of Dragons* (1964) by Ruth Manning-Sanders and *The Hamish Hamilton Book of Dragons* (1970) by Roger Lancelyn Green are examples of two modern anthologies of dragon stories.

For Further Reading

Shuker, Karl. *Dragons: A Natural History*. London: Aurum, 1995.

DRAMA

Storytelling through public performance. In most cultures, drama emerged from early oral traditions via religious songs, DANCES, and RITUALS. However, ceremonies in honor of deities or rulers are real-world activities, while drama, as the Greek philosopher Aristotle noted, is not the action itself, but an imitation of action. One might add, it is also possibly an imaginative act illuminating and surpassing real-life events, as all good storytelling can be.

The line between early theater and religious ceremony is sometimes indistinct. Egyptian pharonic plays dating to 3200 B.C. were highly ritualistic and specifically religious, even though they described the CREATION of the world and told the stories of ISIS AND OSIRIS and HORUS. Medieval European passion plays and MYSTERY PLAYS were quite similar to Egyptian drama in this respect.

In *The Theatre* (1985), Phyllis Hartnoll comments that, "For the theatre as we understand it today three things are necessary: actors speaking or singing independently of the original unison chorus; an element of conflict conveyed in dialogue; and an audience emotionally involved in the action but not taking part in it." Without these elements, she says, you may have ceremony but not theatre.

Drama in the Western tradition is generally considered to have begun in fifth-century B.C. Greece. According to many scholars, hymns sung around the altar of the wine-god DIONYSOS were gradually expanded into full-scale stories about deities and heroes and moved out of the temples into specially-built structures. Thespis of Attica was credited with being the first actor to detach himself from the chorus and engage in dialogue—thus acting is called the Thespian art. Both tragedy and comedy were first fully created by Greek authors, many of whose works are still performed today. The tragic dramatists Aeschylus, Sophocles, and Euripides portrayed familiar figures in Greek mythology, including Oedipus, AGAMEMNON, HELEN OF TROY, ODYSSEUS, and TIRESIAS, basing their plots on familiar sources like the works of HOMER. The comic playwright Aristophanes wrote about contemporary issues with a fantastic slant in plays like *Birds, Frogs,* and *Lysistrata.*

Roman drama began with the Greek tales, but eventually degenerated into bawdy mimes and farces dealing with the coarsest elements of everyday life. Medieval Europe returned drama to its religious roots, presenting the stories of the BIBLE to a largely illiterate population. After 1400, morality plays such as EVERYMAN focused on the struggle between good and evil in the human soul.

The Renaissance presented classical and humanist themes in drama, as it did in all the arts. In sixteenth-century Italy the *commedia dell'arte* drew on the traditions of mimes, of MINSTRELSY, and jesters. The actors used stock characters and standard scenarios but improvised the details of their stories as well as their dialogue.

William Shakespeare was the greatest dramatic storyteller of the Elizabethan period in England. Although he drew on both mythology and history, his plays are open to such a range of interpretation that their power has persisted through centuries of cultural change. His work includes comedies like *A Midsummer Night's Dream* and *Twelfth Night,* histories like the two parts of *Henry IV,* tragedies like *Hamlet* and *King Lear,* and romances like *The Winter's Tale* and *The Tempest.*

The seventeenth and eighteenth centuries in Europe and America saw an increasing emphasis on the actor, as did nineteenth-century melodrama. Near the end of that century, writers such as Shaw, Chekhov, Ibsen, and Strindberg demonstrated the power of story to engage with ideas. The shifting paradigms of the twentieth century have been reflected in drama that ranges from the subjectivity of expressionism and surrealism back to realism. In our own time, film and television drama both fuel and feed an apparently insatiable public demand for stories, though perhaps not for great variety in them.

In other cultures, drama also had its roots in ceremonial practices. In many cases, the style of theatrical storytelling remained more closely linked to its origins. In India, references to plays and actors are found in both the MAHABHARATA and the RAMAYANA, indicating that the dramas were based on history and mythology as well as on newly invented tales. Sanskrit drama emerged in India by the beginning of the sixth century A.D. perhaps influenced by Greek theatre and certainly by early Indian dance forms. India also has a long tradition of folk drama, popular plays also based on legends and myths.

As early as the fourth century A.D., music and dance were combined with storytelling in China. This developed into true theatre in the thirteenth century, with the Mongolian Yüan Dynasty. Like the *commedia dell'arte,* Yüan drama made use of stock characters, but the Chinese actors had much more leeway in the characterizations. Ming and Ch'ing Dynasties developed more variations of the traditional forms. The famous Peking Opera reintegrated music, dance, acrobatics, and story into a high art form.

Similarly, early Japanese theatre blended elements of dance, puppet shows, and mime to tell traditional stories. In the fourteenth century, *Noh,* a highly ritualistic and aristocratic form of drama, was defined and has been preserved since then. *Kabuki* drama, directed specifically toward the common people, appeared in the seventeenth century—as did *Bunraku,* which tells the same tales through PUPPETRY.

For Further Reading

Hartnoll, Phyllis. *The Theatre: A Concise History.* New York: Thames and Hudson, 1985.

Watson, Jack, and Grant McKernie. *A Cultural History of Theatre.* White Plains, NY: Longman Publishing, 1993.

Wikham, Glynne. *A History of the Theatre.* 2nd ed. New York: Cambridge University Press, 1992.

DRAUPADI

In Hindu mythology and the MAHABHARATA, wife of the PANDAVAS, five brothers. Many stories are told about Draupadi, especially how she becomes the wife of all five Pandava brothers even though ARJUNA is the one to win her in a TEST OF PROWESS set up by Drupada, father of Draupadi. Whoever can string his bow and shoot an arrow through a high ring will win the PRINCESS. Disguised—as are his brothers—like a BRAHMAN, Arjuna wins and expects to have Draupadi as his wife (*see* DISGUISES).

However, his mother, Kunti, insists that the brothers share all bounty, not realizing a wife is included, so they all have to share her.

In another tale concerning Draupadi and her husbands, the Pandava brothers have been warring with their cousins, the Kauravas, and little by little have lost almost everything. Still, the leader of the brothers, Yudhishthira, cannot stop trying to win, and his cousin Shakuni, the Kauravas leader, persuades him to bet the beautiful Draupadi, their wife. When Yudhishthira throws the dice and loses, Draupadi will be sacrificed and become the slave of the Kauravas. But Draupadi refuses, claiming that the Pandavas brothers were already slaves when they began the game and therefore they can have no rights or possessions or wife they can pledge. Enraged, Shakuni sends one of his brothers to fetch Draupadi by force, and she is finally dragged by the hair to the court of the Kauravas, where they force her to kneel. Undaunted, Draupadi rises up, explains that she is no slave, and scolds them. Her punishment is to be stripped naked in court, which will serve to humiliate both Draupadi and her husbands. Draupadi prays for help, and the god KRISNA causes new clothes to appear on Draupadi each time a garment is stripped away until the Kauravas give up. The huge pile of clothes on the floor around her disappears in flame, and outside a storm bursts. The old, blind uncle of the Pandavas, father of the Kauravas, is immensely embarrassed by what has transpired, and offers Draupadi anything, including her husbands' kingdom, which she refuses; all she wants is their freedom. Still, he perseveres and gives them back their kingdom. The Pandavas and Draupadi then live together peacefully for the next three decades.

For Further Reading

Coomaraswamy, Ananda K., and Sister Nivedita. *Myths of the Hindus and Buddhists.* New York: Dover, 1967.

Dimmitt, Cornelia, ed. *Classical Hindu Mythology: A Reader in the Sanskrit Puranas.* Philadelphia: Temple University Press, 1978.

O'Flaherty, Wendy Doniger. *Hindu Myths.* New York: Penguin, 1975.

Zimmer, Heinrich. *Myths and Symbols in Indian Art and Civilization.* Princeton, NJ: Princeton University Press, 1992.

DREAMS

Portents of the future or symbolic moments of great change in MYTHS, FAIRY TALES, and stories. All over the world dreams appear in mythology, LEGEND, FOLKTALES, and many of the sacred texts of different religions, often playing an important role in the story's outcome. As Diane Wolkstein notes in her commentary on "The Dream of Dumuzi" in INANNA: *Queen of Heaven and Earth,* "In ancient literature, Great Dreams often emerge at moments of intense confusion or turmoil; and the one who can interpret the dream and find direction for the dreamer then becomes invaluable to the dreamer." Wolkstein goes on to observe that "It often takes a person of opposite character from the dreamer to interpret the dream, for the dream speaks of the inner life that lies hidden away from the dreamer" (*see* WOLKSTEIN, DIANE).

In "The Dream of Dumuzi," Dumuzi, the husband of the Inanna, Queen of Heaven and Earth, has a "Great Dream" after Inanna chooses him to replace her in the underworld, and he attempts to escape the DEMONS that pursue him to take him there. For Dumuzi, "The message of the dream is devastating . . . for there is no escape from the forces that will carry him to his death. Yet buried within the dream, there is a small detail portending life and hope," writes Wolkstein. This small hope is what will save Dumuzi from going to the underworld permanently; instead he will end up spending only half the year in the underworld with his sister replacing him for the other half year.

In the ODYSSEY, PENELOPE, wife of Odysseus, has a "Great Dream." She has dreams from the Gate of Ivory and the Gate of Horn, which, "when understood, accurately describe the future." When Odysseus returns home disguised after his ten years at sea and his years at fighting at TROY, Penelope tells him her dream and he interprets it and is instrumental in making it happen.

In the BIBLE, the Hebrew Joseph, who has been enslaved by the Egyptian pharaoh, is freed because he is able to interpret the Pharaoh's dream. The conception of the future BUDDHA takes place when his mother,

MAYA, has a dream that symbolically portrays this conception.

The Interpretation of Dreams, by "the father of psychology," Sigmund Freud (*see* FREUD, SIGMUND), is of great importance in the understanding of dreams. The work of psychologist Carl Jung, which often focuses on the importance of the dream, has been a crucial influence in the studies of Joseph Campbell and Mircea Eliade (*see* CAMPBELL, JOSEPH; ELIADE, MIRCEA).

For Further Reading

Freud, Sigmund. *The Interpretation of Dreams*. New York: Avon, 1965.

Jung, Carl G. *The Basic Writings of C.G. Jung*. Reprint, New York: Random House, 1993.

———. *Dreams*. Translated by R.F.C. Hull. 1974. Reprint, Princeton, NJ: Princeton University Press, 1992.

Wolkstein, Diane, and Samuel Noah Kramer. *Inanna: Queen of Heaven and Earth*. New York: HarperCollins, 1983.

DWARFS

Short, powerful beings in stories from northern Europe, who have human shape and intelligence, live communally in underground kingdoms, and are known for their skill as smiths and craftsmen. Dwarfs often have long beards and wrinkled skin. Many are misshapen and hideous, with humpbacks, huge heads, flattened noses, and deformed arms, legs, and feet. Their feet may be those of a goat or another animal. However, some dwarfs are exceptionally handsome.

In Norse mythology, dwarfs were formed from the maggots that lived in the frost giant Ymir's flesh (*see* NORSE CREATION). Four dwarfs, North, South, East, and West, hold aloft the HEAVENS. The dwarfs in Norse mythology are ugly and misshapen. They represent greed and are quick to show malice. These dwarfs lust after beautiful women, power, and gold. They are magicians, and they fear sunlight, which turns them to stone. Like most other dwarfs, they are master smiths. Norse legends in which dwarfs figure prominently include those telling of FREYA's acquisition of the necklace of the Brisings, of ODIN and the mead of poetry, of the death of BALDR, and of the weapons of the GODS and the ornaments of the GODDESS, all of which the dwarfs created (*see* TROLLS).

German tales mention such dwarf-KINGS as Goldemar, Gibich, and Alberich. In the EPIC the NIBELUNGENLIED, Alberich guards the *Nibelung* treasure that SIEGFRIED wins. In the saga *Ortnit*, the dwarf Elberich helps the emperor Ortnit to gain the daughter of the Paynim Soldan of Syria.

Another example of Germanic dwarfs is found in the GRIMM BROTHERS's popular story "Snow White." In this tale, seven dwarfs live in a small cottage in the forest. They work in the mines, digging out precious metal. They are benevolent beings, who take care of and cherish Snow White.

The dwarfs of Switzerland have a lively, joyous disposition and are kind and generous. They are fond of strolling through valleys; unlike their Norse counterparts, sunlight does not turn them to stone. Dwarfs in Swiss lore are associated with agriculture and particularly the keeping of cattle. They make a magic cheese, which grows back in the spot where it is bitten or cut. If a hungry person eats all of his cheese, however, it will not be replenished.

The Isle of Rügen in the Baltic has a well-developed tradition of dwarfs, including white, brown, and black dwarfs. The white dwarfs are the most beautiful and delicate of all. They are innocent and gentle. In the winter, they stay in the hills, working with silver and gold. In the spring and the summer, they live above ground in the sunshine and the starlight. They dance at night to their own music. During the day, they travel alone in the form of little birds, butterflies, or doves. The brown dwarfs wear brown jackets and brown caps with silver bells on them. Generally, they wear glass shoes. They are very handsome, cheerful, and good-natured, although they do exhibit some roguish traits. They have unlimited power of transformation and can pass through a tiny keyhole. The black dwarfs are ugly creatures who wear black jackets and caps. They are expert steel craftsmen. They are malicious and delight in doing mischief to humans. They are unsociable beings and remain close to the hills where they live.

For Further Reading

Hayes, Sarah. "Snow White and the Seven Dwarfs." *The Candlewick Book of Fairy Tales.* Illustrated by P.J. Lynch. Cambridge, MA: Candlewick Press, 1985.

Keightley, Thomas. *The Fairy Mythology.* 1850. Reprint, New York: Haskell House, 1968.

DYING GOD

Motif involving the DEATH of a GOD-KING, associated with the cycle of vegetation and spiritual REBIRTH. The MOTIF of the dying god occurs in the mythologies of many cultures and continues in stories and literature over the centuries. It involves the death of a king or god who is then revived, usually through a Great GODDESS. As David Leeming writes in *The World of Myth,* "The dead god becomes the seed planted in the MOTHER." In the myths of ATTIS, ODIN, and Jesus, the dying god is hung on a tree—the cross symbolizes a tree; the myths of Adonis, Osiris, and DIONYSOS show them to be associated in some way with trees (*see* ISIS AND OSIRIS). Another aspect of this motif is the focus on the phallus or its loss, as in the cases of Osiris, Dionysos, and Attis, which also connects these gods with the idea of seed-bearing and the cycle of vegetation.

The dying god can also be seen as connected with the SCAPEGOAT motif, for he must somehow take on the sins of his society. His death then cleanses the society and it experiences REBIRTH. This scapegoat aspect of the dying god motif appears in the stories of Jesus, Attis, Osiris, and Dionysos, as well as in such stories of the tragic hero as Sophocles' *Oedipus the King* and Shakespeare's *King Lear* and *Hamlet.*

DYLAN, BOB (1941–)

American singer, songwriter, and poet. Born Robert Allen Zimmerman and raised in Minnesota, Bob Dylan entered the spotlight of American music in the early 1960s with his folk and folk/rock albums, *Bob Dylan* (1962), *Freewheelin' Bob Dylan* (1963), *The Times They are A-Changin'* (1964), and *Another Side of Bob Dylan* (1964). During a time of great political and social unrest, Dylan was heralded as a voice of protest against the establishment and a supporter of social change,

cultural revolution, and justice for all. He took many of the topics for his songs straight from the newspaper headlines of the times, singing the stories of the Civil Rights Movement and the tragic fates of, for example, Emmett Till and James Meredith. Many came to consider Dylan as the articulator of a new moral conscience for the nation. However, his controversial 1965 appearance at the Newport (Rhode Island) Folk Festival with an electric guitar and a rock music program marked the beginning of a new style of Dylan music, subsequently eliciting strong condemnation from many of his previous fans. Yet Dylan proved himself a success in the rock music genre, and his albums *Highway 61 Revisited* (1965) and *Blonde on Blonde* (1966) earned for him a whole new following. Never content to stay with one style of expression for too long, the end of the 1960s and the beginning of the 1970s found Dylan experimenting with country music. His albums *Nashville Skyline* (1969), *Self-Portrait* (1970), and *New Morning* (1970) caused as much consternation in his rock fans as his rock albums had caused in his folk fans.

Since then, Dylan has surprised his loyal followers with forays into many other musical styles and political approaches. He converted to Christianity in 1979 and released several albums with a strong evangelical flavor. Never afraid to tackle difficult social and national issues, Dylan uses his music to challenge the decisions of political leaders and question the morality of any powerful group. Above all, he infuses his music with images of personal consciousness and individual identity which encourage self-exploration and discovery.

Dylan has received considerable attention as a poet and storyteller as well as a musician. His lyrics have been studied as poetry in the tradition of the Beat poets of the 1960s. Dylan's *Tarantula* (1966) is an autobiographical novel of sorts composed of seemingly unconnected images which, when taken together, purport to suggest something of Dylan's life and philosophies. Other written works include *Approximately Complete Works* (1970), *Writings and Drawings* (1971), *Poem to Joanie* (1972), *XI Outlined Epitaphs and*

Off the Top of My Head (1981), *Lyrics, 1962–1985* (1985), and *Road Drawings* (1992). A popular figure in music around the world, Dylan's dozens of albums and many politically oriented contemporary BALLADS have carved for him a position as an important lyric storyteller of late-twentieth-century America.

For Further Reading

Herdman, John. *Voice Without Restraint*. New York: Delilah Books, 1982.

Thomson, Elizabeth M., ed. *Conclusions on the Wall: New Essays on Bob Dylan*. Manchester, England: Thin Man, Ltd., 1980.

EARTH

Personified MOTHER of humankind in the oral tradition of many cultures. Earth is usually seen as the EARTH-MOTHER, out of which all things grow. Because of the vegetation cycle, with its magical properties of disappearance and reappearance, Earth is likened to a deity that must be propitiated lest the seeds do not grow. That Earth is considered female is an almost universal concept—the Egyptian Geb is an exception—and this Great Mother can be either bountiful or withholding. In some stories, such as PERCIVAL and *Oedipus the King,* a SCAPEGOAT must be sacrificed in order to make the Earth fertile once again.

In CREATION myths, Earth is formed out of the void or chaos in various ways and then joins with sky or SKY-FATHER to produce the ANIMALS, plants, and humans that make up the living world. In some cases, such as the Maori story of "RANGI AND PAPA," earth and sky must then be separated. In EMERGENCE CREATION myths, common among such Native Americans as the Acoma and the Hopi, human beings live within the earth in dark-ness and must find a way to emerge out of a hole in the earth in order to reach daylight. At death, people return again into the earth, as the numerous stories of the DESCENT TO THE UNDERWORLD illustrate. *See also* DIVISION OF WORLD PARENTS.

EARTH-DIVER CREATION

Story in which a deity or CULTURE HERO asks a creature to dive through primeval or FLOOD waters to bring up a bit of EARTH. The god or SHAMAN then expands the mud into all the land of the earth.

In Siberian oral tradition, the earth-diver is sent by GREAT SPIRIT or by a shaman, and the diver is a water bird. In NATIVE NORTH AMERICAN STORYTELLING the creator-figure is OLD MAN, COYOTE, RAVEN, GREAT RABBIT, or some other TRICKSTER.

According to the Native American stories, the trickster is on a raft with the other ANIMALS. For a long time, they drift across the endless waters. When they all get tired of nothing but water, the trickster asks the animals to dive down and bring up some earth.

Several animals or birds (usually three) make the attempt but fail, returning exhausted and dejected. Finally, a powerful swimmer—Loon, Muskrat, Turtle, Beaver, Crawfish, Mink, or another—undertake the dive. After a long time, even several days, the diver floats back to the surface, practically dead but carrying a bit of mud. Then the trickster recites a charm over the mud, places it on the water, and it increases.

The earth-diver tales, like many creation stories, suppose that in the beginning there is only water. The creation of land is described as a matter of bringing order to chaos, as well as of giving people and animals a place to live.

In a similar story told among pygmies on the Malay peninsula, a dung beetle pulls mud out of the earth and brings order to a watery, chaotic world. In the JAPANESE CREATION MYTH a heavenly spear is dipped into the endless waters, and land forms from the brine dripping from its tip. *See also* CREATION, NATIVE NORTH AMERICAN STORYTELLING, WOMAN WHO FELL FROM THE SKY.

For Further Reading

Campbell, Joseph. *The Masks of God: Primitive Mythology.* New York: Penguin, 1987.

EARTH-MOTHER

Ancient representation of the primal deity and the embodiment of the natural forces that create and sustain life. The Earth-Mother ARCHETYPE existed from the earliest records of human history, thriving during the Upper Paleolithic era (30,000–10,000 B.C.), and still persists today. Although relatively little is known about the stories and mythology of very early human history, archeological evidence suggests a strong vision of the EARTH as a GODDESS from whom all life emerges and to whom all life returns. In the earliest periods of human existence, hunting and gathering were the sole means of survival, and the Earth-Mother emerged as the vehicle, not only of all life, but of all deities. Like the Greek GAIA or the Hindu DEVI-Shakti, she is the timeless mother of CREATION.

The Earth-Mother's primal status makes her guardian over all aspects of creation.

Thus, she does not only give birth and sustain; she also destroys. Evidence of the Earth-Mother's dominion over life and DEATH exists in the earliest CAVE PAINTING, sculpture, and burial practices. The caves, with their depictions of animal life and childbirth, represent the liminal region between the mystical otherworld and the physical plane of existence. Early figurines depicting exaggerated breasts and hips also suggest a strong connection between the goddess and fertility. Markings at the entrance and interior of the caves representing the vulva, indicate access to the sacred interior of the Earth-Mother. For this reason, burial in a cave or in the soil signifies a return to the womb/tomb.

One of the earliest recorded examples of the Earth-Mother appears in the Mesopotamian story of INANNA-Ishtar. Inanna-Ishtar descends below her domain of the heavens and earth, into the netherworld (*see* DESCENT TO THE UNDERWORLD). There she confronts her dark elder sister, Ereshkigal, who has her killed and hung upon a stake. Eventually, Innana-Ishtar rises from the dead and ascends to the world above. Her journey, as well as her death and resurrection, recall the DYING GOD stories common to FERTILITY STORIES. As the ruler of the netherworld, her sister may represent the side of her own divinity that requires death as a component of life.

Similarly, the HOPI CREATION story of SPIDER WOMAN depicts the goddess as the principle of earth who, in conjunction with Tawa, the SUN god, creates life. Although Tawa takes part in the creation, it is clearly Spider Woman who plays the more active role. She instructs her human creations in the proper RITUALS and activities of their lives, and her departure back into the earth through a sand painting indicates the ease with which she negotiates the realms of life and death.

While figures of the Earth-Mother do exist in the stories of ancient culture, quite often they are masked or converted to serve patriarchal ideologies. The ancient ARTEMIS of Ephesus, for example, bears dozens of breasts upon her body as symbols of a nourishing earth. However, in her development as a member of the Greek pantheon, Artemis takes on the roles of huntress and virgin. Her fertility functions are stripped away, and she assumes characteristics acceptable to a patriarchal culture. The rise of patriarchy nearly 10,000 years ago also brought the transformation of the Earth-Goddess into the more manageable form of the CORN MOTHER. As agricultural practices developed, the Earth-Mother's role became more sharply defined. Although her status remained enormous, the warring sky-gods of patriarchal power slowly eliminated the stories and rituals that gave her precedence over the other gods.

Despite her fall from the heights of religious power, the Earth-Mother has sustained a significant role in the history of storytelling. Feminine descriptions of earth and nature permeate the imaginative tales of all cultures, and her influence continues in the environmental consciousness of the modern era. In fact, recent scientific theories have drawn from the Earth-Mother concept to construct the Gaia hypothesis: the notion that the entire planet is an immense, but unified, organism that regulates itself like a human body. The theory holds that any disruption in the natural function of the organism will bring a corrective response. Thus, the rapid exploitation of resources could endanger humanity as Gaia attempts to eliminate a cancerous threat. The Earth-Mother concept, which could not be extinguished by millennia of cultural changes, will persist in the imaginative stories of the future.

For Further Reading

Campbell, Joseph. *The Masks of God: Primitive Mythology.* New York: Penguin, 1987.

Leeming, David Adams, and Jake Page. *Goddess: Myths of the Female Divine.* New York: Oxford University Press, 1994.

Larrington, Carolyne, ed. *The Feminist Companion to Mythology.* London: Pandora, 1992.

EDDAS, ELDER AND YOUNGER

Perhaps the two best known pieces of Nordic literature, one concerned with preserving and the other with analyzing Norse poetry. The *Elder Edda,* also known as the *Poetic Edda* or *Edda Saemundar,* is the written record of the traditional oral poetic lore of the Norsemen, the pre-Christian Scandinavian peoples of Northern Europe. The *Younger Edda,* also called the *Prose Edda* or *Edda Snorra Sturlusonar,* is a guide to the poetry of the *skalds,* the ancient Scandinavian poets, written by the medieval writer and historian, Snorri Sturluson.

The stories of the *Younger* and *Elder Eddas,* though separate in form and purpose, were both drawn from the Scandinavian people's own fundamental interest in their early Nordic ancestry. The history of Scandinavian oral tradition is indeed fascinating. A prowess for adventure and seamanship allowed early Viking pirates to extend their ancestrally Germanic culture not only along the northern shores of Europe—Denmark, Sweden, and Norway were those areas most predominantly settled by the Vikings—but also in Normandy, England, Sicily, and Russia, spreading a rich oral tradition in native mythology and religion across the continent. Iceland at the time of the *Elder Edda's* creation was an oligarchy of families proud of their Scandinavian ancestry. Even when, in A.D. 1000, the Icelandic peoples were converted to Christianity, Norse folklore was not forgotten. Scholar Lee M. Hollander believes that the memory of Norse mythology was preserved partly because of the absence of religious fanaticism and partly because of the isolation of the country, which allowed Icelandic people to resist the stricter enforcement of Church discipline in faith and living. Christianity, moreover, encouraged enthusiasm for writing, making written records of the ancient Norse verses possible—even popular. Wealthy freeholders often made a hobby of compiling the old Norse sagas, which had been perpetuated through oral tradition before the advent of Christianity. Gradually, most Icelandic families bore codices of ancient Norse verse, and were found by Danish historian Saxo Grammaticus to hold an "unflagging zeal" in the history of their people. It was at the height of what some have called an Icelandic Renaissance that Iceland discovered the work of poet and chieftain, Snorri Sturluson. In 1643, roused by the this discovery, the Danish King Fredric III, with the help of his bishop in Iceland, uncovered the second great work, the *Poetic* (or *Elder*) *Edda*.

The traditional Icelandic poetry found in the *Elder Edda* is distinguished from other forms of early European, and especially other Germanic, poetic lore in a number of ways. First, the poetry falls syntactically into stanzas, not stichic verse like other Germanic poetry. Second, the eddaic poetry uses dialogue far more and prose narrative far less than Old High German or Old English poetry, suggesting rather than describing. The author apparently relied on the reaction to allusion from the audience, though the allusions are lost on readers of this century.

The outcome of the Iceland poetic story was known to a thirteenth century audience as well, much like the European FAIRY TALE, and the narrator played on the audience's anticipation of the scripted outcome, not on dramatic suspense (*see* EUROPEAN STORYTELLING). Icelandic poetry often also contains a pedagogical theme of the domestic and heroic RITUALS of everyday life, evidence of the relationship between the priestly tradition and the poetic tradition.

A guide to the poetry of the *skalds* (the ancient Scandinavian poets whose works were compiled in the *Elder Edda)* the *Younger Edda* was written by the historian and writer of the thirteenth century, Snorri Sturluson. Snorri was born of an aristocratic family, becoming entranced with the politics of both Iceland and Norway by the early thirteenth century. As head of the highest Icelandic court in 1215, Snorri was invited to Norway by King Haakon IV to make peace between their countries in 1218. In fact, "Hattatal," the first poem compiled for The *Younger Edda,* was written in honor of Haakon IV. Snorri was killed by his son-in-law supposedly under orders of King Haakon in 1241 when he returned to Iceland after having fled in 1239 because of a precarious political situation.

In addition to the *Younger Edda,* Snorri is also probably the author of *Heimskringla,* or *Sagas*—stories extending from mythological Norwegian kings that are based on chronicles, tradition, and LEGEND—and perhaps the author of *Egils saga Skallagrimsonar,* a SAGA about an Icelandic Viking and *skald*.

Consisting of five sections, the *Younger Edda* was conceived with "Hattatal," a technical commentary on poetry written by Snorri in esteem of Haakon IV, King of Norway; a long poem that lacks the flair of the other works of his collection, "Hattatal" is read today only by specialists, and relegated to the back of most volumes because of its lack of popular interest. Despite this lack of popularity, the conception of "Hattatal" led the former historian and politician to begin a career as an educator, and eventually inspired Snorri to expand his work to include four other sections: "Formali," "Gylfaginning," "Bragaroethur," and "Skaldskaparmal." "Formali," the prologue, is both an account the biblical story of the CREATION and the FLOOD (*see* BIBLE, NOAH) and an introduction to the traditional Scandinavian GODS, chiefly ODIN and his wife, FREYA. "Gylfaginning," or "The Deception of the Gylfi," is the second chapter and the principal story of the prose *Edda*. The scholar Marlene Ciklamini believes that the "Gylfaginning" was inspired by the lack of structure, coherence, and general interest of the fourth section, "Skaldskaparmal" ("Poetic Diction" or "The Art of Poetry"), in which Snorri had modified a traditional wisdom poem in an attempt to explain the MYTHS and heroic legends of the *kennings*, the poetic circumlocutions that are the primary distinctive feature of skaldic poetic language. "Gylfaginning" is the only section in the collection to present Scandinavian mythology as cyclical, chronicling both birth and destruction of the cosmos. Structured in question and answer form, "Gylfaginning" intermingles the frame story and its main body to tell the story of Gylfi, the pagan god of Sweden, who sets out to find the source of the Aesir's power. The Aesir are three mysterious figures who are sit on high seats placed one above the other. Upon Gylfi's demand, the three talk of the mythic course of the world, traditional deities, and recount some of the major myths. Along with the next section, "Bragaroethur," "Gylfaginning" is the most important source for modern knowledge on the Scandinavian myths it chronicles.

Although Snorri Sturluson has not been well depicted in contemporary records, he is acknowledged to be one of the greatest medieval writers. His *Younger Edda* has been called a masterpiece of organization, wit, and irony, and other works ascribed to him have been similarly received. Snorri Sturluson was also a learned and accomplished man, and managed to be a poet, a historian, and chieftain in one lifetime. He is perhaps most noted for his devotion to the preservation of Viking lore, a devotion that rivaled that of his predecessors, the *Elder Edda* compilers.

For Further Reading

Ciklamini, Marlene. *Snorri Sturluson.* Boston: Twayne Publishers, 1978.

Hollander, Lee M. *The Poetic Edda.* Austin, TX: University of Texas Press, 1962.

Patricia Terry, trans. *Poems of the Elder Edda.* Philadelphia: University of Pennsylvania Press, 1990.

Snorri Sturluson. *Edda.* Translated by Anthony Faulkes. London: Everyman's Library, 1987.

Taylor, Paul B., and W.H. Auden. *The Elder Edda: A Selection.* New York: Random House, 1967.

EGYPTIAN CREATION

Cosmology of ancient Egypt. Because the civilization of ancient Egypt was so complex and long-lasting, there are various versions of Egyptian CREATION, based on the time period and particular religious center. The earliest creation MYTH reflects a matriarchal civilization with a great GODDESS figure, Nun, as the FEMALE CREATOR who, like the Greek GAIA who bore Uranos, gives birth to Atum, who then creates the universe. Later Egyptian creation myths reflect the evolving patriarchy that came to dominate. These myths all share certain aspects: they begin with PRIMEVAL WATERS, a symbol of the feminine principle, and then an Eye, symbolizing the SUN, brings order out of the chaos of the waters, thus creating the universe. The sun is related to the primal mound; this mound was later represented by the building of the pyramids.

The Egyptians at Heliopolis had Atum or Ptah as their original god. He was called *Khepri* or *Khoprer* in his manifest form, and *Ra* when seen as the sun. According to the Pyramid Texts, at first Atum is alone in the universe; by masturbating or expectorating,

he then creates Shu, his brother, who represents air-life, and Tefnut, his sister, who represents moisture-order. Shu and Tefnut mate, producing as their offspring the god Geb, the EARTH, and the goddess Nut, the sky. Their act of sacred incest became a model for Egyptian pharaohs, who practiced incest as a means of keeping their dynasties pure (*see* INCEST STORIES).

The original god, the Eye (Atum), is the one to oversee this creation and reproduction. Geb and Nut then produce ISIS AND OSIRIS, Seth, Nepthys, and the older HORUS, as well as all the people of Egypt. An important and famous aspect of this Egyptian creation myth is the DIVISION OF WORLD PARENTS, Geb and Nut. While Geb, the earth, lies prone, Nut, the sky, arches over him until their father, Shu, separates them. Creation occurs when they are separated at last.

For Further Reading

Hamilton, Virginia. *In the Beginning: Creation Stories from around the World.* New York: Harcourt Brace Jovanovich, 1988.

Leach, Maria. *The Beginning: Creation Myths around the World.* New York: Thomas Crowell, 1956.

EL CID

Soldier HERO of eleventh-century Spain and subject of EPIC poem, *El Cantar Del Mio Cid.* El Cid was also known as Roderigo or Ruy Diaz de Vivar, and El Cid Campeador. Diaz was a peasant who became skilled at arms. In civil wars following the death of Ferdinand I, Diaz supported Sancho II of Castile and helped ensure his success. When Sancho II was later assassinated, Diaz recognized Alfonso VI as king but swore allegiance to Castile. His own man, Diaz was frequently out of favor with the king and almost as often redeemed though coming to the monarch's aid in battle. At one point Alfonso sent Diaz to collect tribute of Seville, then accused him of stealing some of the funds and banished him.

After his banishment, Diaz wandered the Spanish peninsula with a few loyal warriors. Soldiers of fortune, they sought wealth and honor in battle. Diaz eventually gave his service to the Moslem king of Saragossa, winning fame throughout Spain from his victories against both Moslem enemies and Christian kings. His Moslem soldiers called him *El Cid,* an Arabic term for lord or master.

The epic poem *El Cantar Del Mio Cid* narrates the exploits of the hero. After his break with Spain, Cid and his men favor first one sovereign and then another, until Cid controls Valencia. When attacked by the Saracen Yussef and his army of fifty thousand, Cid and his four thousand warriors take the day, routing fifteen thousand fleeing Moslems. El Cid is severely wounded in battle, and while he recovers, Valencia comes under attack again as Yussef's brother Bucar retaliates. Valencia is saved, but Cid dies in his bed, just as prophesied forty years before by Saint Lazarus.

First thought to be composed shortly after the hero's death, scholars now place the poem with other medieval ROMANCES such as *The* SONG OF ROLAND. The character may actually be a composite of two different heroes. The first is "El Campeador," from legends of the Duero river area. This man was a harsh vassal of Alfonso VI, a conqueror of Andalusian Moors, and a man involved in monetary payments and tributes. The other figure is "El Cid," a Mozarab leader of minor separatist disputes in Valencia. The latter is remembered as tolerant and humane, and has become a sentimental and fabulous hero.

For Further Reading

El Cid. New York: Oxford University Press, 1989.

ELDER BROTHER

Great Pima Indian CULTURE HERO. In Pima LEGEND, Elder Brother is responsible for creating order out of primordial chaos. It is Elder Brother who fixes the feature of the land, brings culture to the Pima, and struggles against evil. The tales of the Pima are told in "a narrative chain, one incident suggesting the next, achieving an episodic progression with neither beginning nor ends," writes Richard Erdoes (*see* ERDOES, RICHARD).

In "A Tale of Elder Brother," told by Frank Russell and included in Richard Erdoes's and Alfonso Ortiz's collection, *American Indian Myths and Legends* (*see* ORTIZ, ALFONSO), El-

der Brother is attacked by Vulture, whom the people have gone to for help in destroying Elder Brother. In his anger, Elder Brother sets out to destroy the people who hate him and the miniature EARTH created by Vulture. Whatever and whomever he encounters—a voice from the darkness, Talking Tree, and the god Earth Doctor—he is asked why he looks like a ghost, and each time Elder Brother answers, "Despite all I have done for the people they hate me." Meanwhile, he has crushed "all mortal magicians; the orator, the warrior, the industrious, and the provident woman, and even ground his own house into the earth." Using his magic powers, Elder Brother violently destroys what has been wrought, and with the help of Earth-Doctor and Gray-Gopher, he gets the people of the underworld to make war on the people of the upper world. As the victorious people of the underworld conquer Elder Brother's enemies, "everything relating to the conquered" is swept "from the face of the earth." Thus Elder Brother vanquishes evil and creates the world anew.

This tale of Elder Brother can be compared to other "imperfect" CREATIONS in which the creator is for some reason dissatisfied with the people he or she has made. *See also* FLOOD, NOAH.

For Further Reading

Erdoes, Richard, and Alfonso Ortiz. *American Indian Myths and Legends.* New York: Pantheon, 1985.

ELIADE, MIRCEA (1907–1986)

Rumanian religious historian, mythographer, Orientalist, ethnographer, philosopher, and novelist. Influenced by Carl Jung, Mircea Eliade was an important interpreter of religious and mythical symbols, images, and ARCHETYPES, often telling the stories that came out of the oral tradition of various cultures as a means of illustrating his interpretations. He was a student of Indian philosophy and yoga, having taken his doctorate at the University of Calcutta, where he completed his dissertation on yoga in 1933. He began teaching at the University of Bucharest, where he remained until 1940 when he became the cultural attaché for the Royal Rumanian Legation in London, then Portugal. After World War II, he moved to Paris and taught at the Sorbonne until 1957 when he became a professor of the history of religions at the University of Chicago.

Interested in all aspects of early religions, MYTH, and symbols, Eliade was a prolific writer. As a novelist, Eliade drew on his knowledge of myth, psychoanalysis, archetype, religion, and the occult. Among his wide-ranging studies that discuss such topics as alchemy, the SHAMAN, HOMER, the DEVIL, DEMONS, and the myths of the modern world are *The Myth of the Eternal Return* (1954); *The Forge and the Crucible (The Origins and Structures of Alchemy)* (1956); *Images and Symbols: Studies in Religious Symbolism* (1952); *Myths, Dreams, and Mysteries: The Encounter Between Contemporary Faiths and Archaic Realities* (1957); *Myth and Reality* (1963); *The Quest: History and Meaning in Religion* (1969); *Rites and Symbols of Initiation: The Mysteries of Birth and Rebirth* (1958); *Shamanism: Archaic Techniques of Ecstasy* (1964); *The Two and the One* (1962); and *Zalmoxis, The Vanishing God: Comparative Studies in the Religion and* FOLKLORE *of Dacia and Eastern Europe* (1972). As Wendell C. Beane writes of Mircea Eliade, "Eliade, in sum, insists that behind and beyond the linguistic structure and pragmatic function of myth lies the conception, gestation, and birth of myth *out of the depths of a genuine religious experience.*"

In drawing on the oral tradition of so many cultures and collecting and interpreting their mythologies and religions, Mircea Eliade has profoundly influenced contemporary scholars in his field. As he writes of his encounters with Carl Jung, Joseph Campbell (*see* CAMPBELL, JOSEPH), Eugene Ionesco, Paul Tillich, Pierre Teilhard de Chardin, and Alan Watts, among others, in his journal *No Souvenirs* (1977), he reveals himself to be a brilliant thinker and a deeply spiritual man questing after the truth.

For Further Reading

Eliade, Mircea. *Myths, Dreams, and Mysteries: The Encounter between Contemporary Faiths and Archaic Realities.* New York: Harper, 1967.

———. *Rites and Symbols of Initiation: The Mysteries of Birth and Rebirth.* New York: Harper, 1965.

———. *Shamanism: Archaic Techniques of Ecstasy.* Princeton, NJ: Princeton University Press, 1964.

ELVES

Communal, fairy-like creatures, lately perceived as having a diminutive human physiognomy. Although *elf* is the Anglo-Saxon word for spirits of any kind, it later became a term to describe particular beings most like the Scandinavian light elves, exceedingly fair creatures who live in *Alfheim* (elf home), a part of Asgard, the home of the Norse GODS. Light elves are connected with the sun and are thought to be good. Scandinavian mythology also mentions dark elves who are extremely black. Unlike their light counterparts who live near to the gods, dark elves live in the crannies of the earth and have a hostile disposition. In some stories, dark elves are not differentiated from DWARFS. Both the light elves and dark elves of Norse mythology have a divine nature.

Later European legends portray elves as small, delicate creatures that live in the air, dance on the grass, or sit on the leaves of trees. Other stories depict them as malicious underground dwellers who inflict sickness and injury on humans. It was commonly believed that elves could cause wounds or illness by "elf-shot," an arrow or dart tipped with a flint arrowhead.

In more recent traditions, elves have become helpful creatures, similar to BROWNIES, who aid in domestic chores. In the well-known FAIRY TALE recorded by the GRIMM BROTHERS, "The Elves and the Shoemaker," a poor shoemaker is surprised to find that the leather he cuts in the evening is impeccably stitched into a pair of shoes the following morning. This fortuitous event occurs night after night. The shoemaker's customers are so satisfied that they pay a higher price than usual for the shoes, and the shoemaker soon becomes well off again. One evening, the shoemaker and his wife hide in a corner of the room to see who it is that comes and does the shoemaker's work for him. At midnight, two little naked elves appear. They quickly complete the evening's work and disappear again. As a gift of appreciation, the shoemaker's wife makes the elves suits of clothing. When they are finished, she and her husband lay them out on the table. The elves arrive about midnight. They dance, skip, and hop around the room. When they see the clothing, they chuckle delightedly, dress themselves, and dance out the door, never to be seen again.

In another Grimm Brothers tale, "The Three Little Men in the Forest," three small elf-men have magical powers. They use their magic to help an obedient young girl who is treated poorly by her wicked stepmother (see STEPMOTHER—WICKED). First, they help her in the seemingly impossible task of finding strawberries in the snow. Then each gives her a gift. The first elf-man's gift is that she will become more beautiful each day. The second elf-man's gift is that a piece of gold will fall from her mouth with each word that she speaks. And the third elf-man's gift is that she will become a KING's wife. In a similar fashion, the three elf-men give the obedient girl's jealous stepsister three curses. The first elf-man's curse is that she will become uglier each day. The second's curse is that a toad will jump out of her mouth with every word she speaks. And the third elf-man's curse is that she will die a cruel death. In the end, the obedient girl is happily married to a king, and the wicked stepmother and jealous stepsister are put in a barrel that is hammered full of nails and rolled downhill into the river.

In J.R.R. Tolkien's classic work *The Hobbit*, Bilbo Baggins and his companions are given shelter at Rivendell, an earthly paradise inhabited by benevolent elves akin to the fairies in *A Midsummer Night's Dream* (see TOLKIEN, J.R.R.; GOBLINS; PUCK). The elves in Tolkien's *The Lord of the Rings* are serious, introspective, and wise creatures.

For Further Reading

Arrowsmith, Nancy. *A Field Guide to the Little People.* New York: Hill and Wang, 1987.

Plume, Ilse. *The Shoemaker and the Elves.* New York: Harcourt Brace Jovanovich, 1991.

EMERGENCE CREATION

Type of CREATION myth in which human beings "emerge" onto the earth from the underworld. Popular among the Southwestern Native Americans and Mexican Indians, emergence creation MYTHS begin in the underworld, which functions as a kind of maternal womb where humans, ANIMALS, and plants grow in darkness like seeds until they are ready to "emerge" into the sunlight. This "emergence" generally takes place through a sacred opening, and the birth is often aided by a midwife such as SPIDER WOMAN or THINKING WOMAN. In some cases, the humans who emerge are still the animals who will eventually become their totems. Examples of emergence creation myths can be found in the Acoma, Hopi, Navajo, and Tewa creation myths (see HOPI CREATION, NAVAJO CREATION).

ENUMA ELISH See BABYLONIAN CREATION

EPIC

Long narrative poem about the deeds of HEROES, warriors, or divine figures. Epics are told in a formal, elevated style, and incorporate the MYTHS, LEGENDS, and histories of a people. Most often, the hero of an epic embodies the ideals most revered by a particular nation or group.

Epics are generally classified into two categories: traditional (or folk) epics, and literary epics. Traditional, folk epics belong to the oral tradition; they begin as oral narratives and are eventually written down by poets or anthropologists. Examples of traditional epics include the ODYSSEY and the ILIAD, the Anglo-Saxon BEOWULF, and the Indian MAHABHARATA, all of which were written down many years after the epic tales were created. However, not all traditional epics were transcribed ages ago; oral traditions of narration continue to this day in thousands of indigenous cultures around the world—even literate cultures. Many folk epics continue to be transmitted orally; only now are people beginning to preserve them in writing, and countless epics still exist only through the performances of the BARDS. These epics often play an important role in preserving the identity of a colonized culture, especially when native communities are faced with pressures to conform, at least outwardly, to the social conventions of the colonial forces.

Because of the nature of oral traditions, folk epics exist in many forms. The bards who relate the epics incorporate their own set of legends and myths, thus individualizing each telling of the tale. Epics are generally narrated in a series of distinct episodes, owing to the long length of the tales. Often, they are presented against a background of music, DANCE, or chanting. The most formal events of a culture often call for the narration of an epic poem; these occasions include important religious festivals, feasts, and battles. Epics sung for celebrations not only entertain the people, but also valorize the common ideals of that culture. Epics sung before battles are intended to encourage strength and bravery in the warriors; epics sung after war account for the actions of the warriors in battle. Sometimes bards would accompany a particularly brave warrior into battle, in order to create an epic poem recounting his heroic deeds.

Literary epics are highly conventional narrative poems which are deliberately conceived by one poet and are written down from the start. Sometimes these works were commissioned by a ruler in order to commemorate a particular event or person; other times, poets chose the epic form to tell a story on a grand scale. Examples of literary epics include Virgil's AENEID and John Milton's *Paradise Lost*. Epics may be categorized according to their adherence to certain features of both content and style.

The content of epic poems is always of grand scope, and has some sort of large-scale significance on a national or religious level. The heroes of epics are figures of great importance; Beowulf is a legendary warrior of the Geats, Aeneas (in the *Aeneid*) is the son of APHRODITE, ADAM AND EVE (in *Paradise Lost*) are the parents of all human beings. The setting of epic poems is also of a grand scale; such poems may take place across the world (as in *Odyssey*) or even across the universe (as in *Paradise Lost*). The plot involves perilous journeys, superhuman deeds, magnificent performances in battle, or some other remarkable achievements far beyond the capabilities of anyone but the mightiest, wisest, or most important figures. Frequently, supernatural forces such as GODS, spirits, angels, and DEVILS intervene or actively participate in the action of the story.

Epics also generally adhere to a basic set of stylistic conventions that order the episodes and contribute to the ceremonial importance of the genre. Epics often begin with a statement of the epic theme, or argument, which explains the topic of the poem and invokes the assistance of a guiding spirit to help the narrator tell the tale. Epics also tend to start in the middle of the story's action, picking up the narrative at a critical moment. Often, the narrator includes long catalogues of main characters, including descriptive details relevant to the story. Also featured in the style of epic poetry are long speeches, elaborate greetings, wide-ranging allusions, repetition of dialogue or other long passages, epic similes (an extended, elaborate comparison), and a general lofty style of language.

The term *epic* is also used to describe novels that endeavor to tell a story of great human importance on a grand scale, such as Herman Melville's *Moby Dick* and Leo Tolstoy's *War and Peace*. The term *epic theater* refers to dramas (such as Bertold Brecht's) which attempt to convey an ideological point of view by creating the objective distance between the audience and the subject. *Mock epic* is a term used to describe poems that adhere to the stylistic features of traditional literary epics, but which tell the story of an utterly trivial event or person. As a result, mock epics such as Alexander Pope's *The Rape of the Lock* make an unimportant subject seem completely ridiculous.

ERATHIPA

Fertility stone in Australian Aboriginal mythology. Certain cultures believe that stones or rocks have the power to bequeath fertility on a sterile woman. In the tale told by the central Australian aboriginal tribes, there is an enormous rock called *Erathipa* that has an opening on one side. Because the opening is suggestive of the female vaginal opening, the tribes came to believe if a woman walked by the opening she would become pregnant; the rock is actually a prison for the souls of children waiting to be reborn. Should a woman who did not wish to become pregnant walk by the rock, she might pretend to be an old woman in order to avoid Erathipa's power. *See also* FERTILITY STORIES.

ERDOES, RICHARD (1912–)

Compiler, biographer, and author of various books on the American West. Born in Frankfurt, Germany, and educated in Vienna, Berlin, and Paris, Richard Erdoes came to the United States and worked for many years as a free-lance artist, photographer, illustrator, and film-maker. While working on a portfolio for *Life* magazine, he was "befriended by an old and almost totally illiterate Sioux medicine man, Lame Deer," who chose Erdoes to write his life story. After that experience in 1970, Erdoes became a serious writer and continued to develop his interest in Native American lore and mythology.

Among his many self-illustrated books about the American West are *The Pueblo Indians* (1967); *Lame Deer, Seeker of Visions* (1971); *The Sun Dance People* (1972); *The Rain Dance People* (1976); *The Sound of Flutes* (1976); *Yuwipi* (1977), a novel; and *Saloons of the West*. He is the coauthor with Mary Crow Dog of *Lakota Woman*. He and Alfonso Ortiz compiled the important collection, *American Indian Myths and Legends* (1984), a number of which he recorded himself. He is also the author of *AD 1000: Living on the Brink of the Apocalypse*, and he has written and illustrated a number of children's books.

For Further Reading

Erdoes, Richard, and Alfonso Ortiz. *American Indian Myths and Legends*. New York: Pantheon, 1985.

ESCHENBACH, WOLFRAM VON (c. 1170–1220)

One of the greatest medieval German poets and singers of courtly love. Wolfram von Eschenbach is especially known as the author of *Parzival*, a brilliant 24,000 line retelling of the incomplete ROMANCE of CHRÉTIEN DE TROYES's, *Perceval, or the Grail* (*see* PERCIVAL). It remains uncertain whether Wolfram himself was the source of the ending of his version of *Parzival* or whether he had another, now unknown source. Many variations on the theme of *Parzival* were engendered by Wolfram's masterpiece, including opera *Parsifal* (*see* WAGNER, RICHARD).

Wolfram's *Parzival* presents the pattern of courtly knighthood as represented by the court of King ARTHUR. Pureness, passion, compassion, and love of GOD are all woven into his lyrics. Variants of the LEGEND of the HOLY GRAIL and the *Parzival* theme, including Wolfram's version, are explored in Jessie L. Weston's *From Ritual to Romance: An Account of the Holy Grail from Ancient Ritual to Christian Symbol*, the study that was to become the major source for T.S. Eliot's poem *The Waste Land* (1922) (*see also* VARIANT).

Wolfram von Eschenbach also left two incomplete works, *Willehalm* and *Titural*, both written around 1215. Though eventually transcribed, all his lyrics were meant to be sung, and, in the poet's own words, he introduces himself as someone who knows "a little about singing."

For Further Reading

Weston, Jessie L. *From Ritual to Romance: An Account of the Holy Grail from Ancient Ritual to Christian Symbol*. Cambridge: Cambridge University Press, 1920.

Wolfram von Eschenbach. *Parzival of Wolfram von Eschenbach*. New York: AMS Press reprint of 1951 edition.

ESHU *See* AFRICAN STORYTELLING

EULENSPIEGEL, TILL

Cunning and amusing peasant in medieval German FOLKTALES whose superior wit, demonstrated through his jests and pranks, gets the best of the typical townspeople, who are dull and smug bourgeoisie; tales about Till Eulenspiegel are pointed at certain class distinctions of the period and the region. In the numerous stories that chronicle Till

Eulenspiegel's adventures, he travels throughout Germany, often in disguise, tricking and deceiving those whom he encounters. Eulenspiegel, whose name means "owl-mirror" or "owl-looking glass," does not respect rank, nor does he ignore vice. He often puts priests and other learned men in ludicrous and humiliating positions. He is wise and sly, but clumsy and humorous. The satirical tales in which he appears are meant to be instructive and an occasion for moral reflection. Eulenspiegel is often depicted wearing a jester's costume.

Till Eulenspiegel, the son of a peasant, was born in Brunswick around the turn of the fourteenth century. The first tale is about his birth and how he is christened three times in one day. First he is christened in the church. Then, on the way home from the christening feast, one of Eulenspiegel's tipsy godmothers falls with the baby who gets covered in mud. Finally, he is washed in hot water. As with many folk HEROES, Eulenspiegel's unusual infancy foreshadows his future greatness.

Another tale describes how Eulenspiegel, when a young man, gets drunk and crawls into a beehive to sleep. Two thieves steal the heavy beehive, thinking it is filled with honey. Eulenspiegel wakes, sticks his hand out of the hive, and yanks the hair of one of the thieves. Because it is so dark, no one sees his hand. The thief assumes that his cohort has pulled his hair, and he becomes angry. Eulenspiegel waits a while, and then he grabs the hair of the other thief. The thieves put down the hive and begin to fight. Because of the darkness, they cannot see each other. They lose their way and flee. Eulenspiegel goes back to sleep in the hive, knowing that by his wit and wisdom he will lead a happy life.

In another typical tale, Eulenspiegel is low on money. He decides to disguise himself as a pardoner and travel about with a holy relic. He obtains a human skull and has it decorated by a silversmith. Then he travels to a place where the priests prefer drinking to preaching. Eulenspiegel promises to give the priests half the money if they will allow him to preach and to show his holy relic to the peasants. The priests agree. By telling the village parishioners that the skull belongs to Saint Brandonus, in whose honor a church is to be built, Eulenspiegel collects many offerings and earns respect for his piety.

Eulenspiegel died in Mölln in 1350. The story of his burial tells how the rope under his feet breaks as his coffin is being lowered into the grave. The coffin falls into the hole, standing on one end. The people take this as another sign of the clever peasant's marvels and decide to leave the coffin as is. An owl grasping a mirror in its claws decorates Eulenspiegel's tombstone.

Till Eulenspiegel comes from a tradition of clever little men who take advantage of the vices of their supposed superiors. The GRIMM BROTHERS'S "Bumpkin," "The Clever Little Tailor," and "The Valiant Little Tailor" also contain variants of this popular MOTIF. ROBIN HOOD is a parallel figure from English storytelling traditions, who, with his band of outlaws, gives the Sheriff of Nottingham, the clergy, and others who represent the corrupt law their just desserts.

In his symphonic poem *Till Eulenspiegel's Merry Pranks*, the German composer Richard Strauss (1864–1949) set to music some of the adventures of this famous German folk hero. *See also* TILL'S PANACEA.

For Further Reading

Janisch, Heinz. *Till Eulenspiegel's Merry Pranks*. New York: Children's Press, 1991.

EUROPEAN AMERICAN STORYTELLING

Oral tradition of FOLKTALES borrowed from European FOLKLORE and transplanted to America, which makes use of the ANECDOTE, LEGEND, BALLAD, and TALL TALE.

The nineteenth-century American story was highly influenced by European and British thought, but, at the same time, unique breeds of storytelling were being formed all across the country, each characteristic of and reliant on a specific geography and people. Many European folktales transplanted to the American continent were preserved in the French tradition of the Saint Lawrence and Mississippi river basins; others were indigenous to the Spanish tradition of the Southwest, in states such as California and New Mexico. The JACK TALES, a collection of European tales related to a narrative cycle known as "Jack the Giant Killer," became the tales of the Appalachian Mountain region, reliant on this earlier European form, but departing to reflect a growing American self-consciousness. Another kind of distinctly American story was the tall tale, a tale characterized by the boasts of its central character or narrator or the exaggeration of a character's tremendous feats, and told first by American pioneers, frontiersman, and workers.

The American frontier tale, and especially the tall tale, has offered popular American culture a wealth of folk heroes. Some of the most well-known legendary American characters include JOHNNY APPLESEED, a woods craftsman; Paul Bunyan and Tony Beaver, both legendary giant lumberjacks (see BUNYAN, PAUL); Mike Fink, a keelboatman (see FINK, MIKE); and Casey Jones, a railroad engineer. Men and women whose legends are merely exaggerated accounts of real deeds include the western heroes Daniel Boone (see BOONE, DANIEL), James Bridger, Kit Carson, Davy Crockett (see CROCKETT, DAVY), Billy the Kid, Jesse James (see JAMES, JESSE), CALAMITY JANE, and Annie Oakley. Animals heroes and figures of tall tales include Pacing Mustang, the legendary wild stallion of the western frontier; the Big Bear of Arkansas, the legendary bear who was able for years to evade trappers; and the FROG whose ability to win jumping contests prompted Mark Twain's account, *The Celebrated Jumping Frog of Calaveras County*.

The cowboy is one of the most prominent mythical heroes of the Western United States, his image grounded in ethics, integrity, loyalty, and rugged individualism. The ideals of the cowboy have been adopted, via the legacy of pulp fiction and the paperback novel (and more recently, through Hollywood and television images), as the American way. Hal Cannon describes the American cowboy mystique as "a jazz of Irish storytelling and lore, Scottish seafaring and cattle tending, Moorish and Spanish horsemanship, European cavalry, African improvisation, and a reluctant observation of Native American survival. . . ."

American folklore remains today a vital part of American culture, owing to both its preservation in print and, more recently, the mass media culture. Undoubtedly, commercialization of much of America's folklore has led to the evolution of shorter, catchier tales in place of the more highly developed form of story of previous eras, but mass media has also popularized many cultural icons that might otherwise be lost to isolated regions of the country.

For Further Reading

Becker, Jane S. *Folk Roots, New Roots: Folklore in American Life*. Lexington, MA: Museum of Our National Heritage, 1988.

Botkin, Benjamin Albert. *A Treasury of American Folklore, Stories, Ballads, and Traditions of the People*. New York: Crown, 1944.

Brown, Carolyn S. *The Tall Tale in American Folklore and Literature*. Knoxville, TN: University of Tennessee Press, 1987.

Brunvand, Jan Harold. *American Folklore: An Encyclopedia*. New York & London: Garland, 1996.

———. *The Study of American Folklore: An Introduction*. New York: Norton, 1978.

Dugaw, Dianne, ed. *The Anglo-American Ballad: A Folklore Casebook*. New York: Garland, 1995.

Emrich, Duncan. *Folklore on the American Land*. Boston: Little, Brown, 1972.

Great American Folklore: Legends, Tales, Ballads, and Superstitions from All Across America. Compiled by Kemp P. Battle. Garden City, NY: Doubleday, 1986.

Lee, Hector Haight. *Lore of Our Land: A Book of American Folklore*. Evanston, IL: Harper, 1963.

Mercatant, John J. *American Folklore and Legends*. New York: Globe, 1967.

EUROPEAN STORYTELLING

Telling of tales and stories handed down orally from generation to generation by the common people of Europe. Recognized as both the second smallest continent in the world— sometimes even considered merely a peninsula of the larger Asiatic continent—and the cradle of modern Western civilization, Europe has commanded economic and political power over nearly every neighboring region at some point in its history. Although it has not been united by government or language since the fall of the Roman empire, Europe continues to be recognized as a culturally-, geographically-, and historically-bound entity.

European storytelling is dominated particularly by the FAIRY TALE and the FABLE, the former a narrative commonly characterized by improbability and supernatural occurrence and the latter a didactic tale, the main characters of which are often ANIMALS endowed with human speech. The merry tale, charms, NURSERY RHYMES, BALLADS, and RIDDLES are also characteristic of European storytelling (see HUNDRED MERRY TALES). Characters commonly featured in the European folktale include the VAMPIRE of Slavonic Europe; religious characters such as the DEVIL, the virgin MARY, and sometimes the apostles; and WITCHES, seen chiefly in German and Scottish storytelling.

Throughout history, Europe's storytellers have been amateurs, especially country people. Unlike Near Eastern and African cultures, European culture never prohibited the telling of stories during certain times of the day or year.

Many FOLKLORE scholars, especially those who lived after 1700, recorded the early European FOLKTALES directly from oral tradition. Other tales have been preserved in literature, including those of Giambattista Basile's IL PENTAMERON, the earliest notable collection of the written fairy tale, and those recorded by the French writer Charles Perrault (see PERRAULT, CHARLES). These include such well known stories as "CINDERELLA," "Little RED RIDING HOOD," and "Sleeping Beauty." Perrault's work, which came closer to the folk idiom than had Basile's, first popularized the written folktale. From this impetus many such tales were written in Europe, particularly in France, including the *Contes Nouveaux* ("New Tales") in 1698 by the French author Madame d'Aulnoy (see D'AULNOY, MADAME).

The GRIMM BROTHERS first excited interest in the fairy tale in Germany in the early 1800s with the publication of the *Kinder- und Hausmarchen* ("Childhood and Household Stories") from 1812 to 1815. The Grimms had collected these German folktales both from the oral traditions of the common people and from books and manuscripts. This publication also may have brought about the writings of Danish author Hans Christian Andersen (see ANDERSEN, HANS CHRISTIAN) and Scottish classicist and folklorist Andrew Lang (see LANG, ANDREW).

Although there is no longer the same stress on oral storytelling, European literature, art, and music remain reliant on the cultural icons and themes established in the genres of European storytelling. Walter Scott, Charles Dickens, Thomas Hardy, and Henrik Ibsen, among others, have all drawn from this body of folklore.

For Further Reading

Briggs, Katharine. *A Dictionary of Fairies: Hobgoblins, Brownies, Bogies, and Other Supernatural Creatures.* London: Penguin Books Ltd., 1976.

Espinosa, Aurelio Macedonio. *Folklore in European Literature.* Palo Alto, CA: Stanford University, 1935.

McGlatherly, James M. *Fairy Tale Romance: The Grimms, Basile, and Perrault.* Chicago: University of Illinois Press, 1991.

EVERYMAN

Popular pageant of anonymous authorship (c.1495), probably translated from a Dutch play entitled *Elckerlijk.* It is the most famous of all the *moralities,* fifteenth- and sixteenth-century plays, based on sermons and presented in the vernacular, which dramatized the struggle of the human soul toward salvation. Like all moralities (and unlike MYSTERY PLAYS and miracle plays, which drew their stories directly from the BIBLE), *Everyman* is an ALLEGORY, its characters representing concepts and virtues.

GOD in HEAVEN, growing troubled by humankind's sinfulness and lack of piety, sends DEATH to summon Everyman to his final reckoning. Everyman, who has spent his life in sin and idleness, begs Death for some reprieve, but to no avail.

Desperate not to make his final journey alone, Everyman approaches his devoted friend Fellowship and asks if he would accompany him. Under the initial impression that Everyman is inviting him on a night of drinking and debauchery, Fellowship is at first quite willing. But when Everyman reveals the true magnitude of his situation, Fellowship abandons him.

Everyman turns to his relatives Kindred and Cousin, who react with similar horror to his appeal for traveling companions. Cousin complains of a cramp in her toe; Kindred lamely offers to send her maid along with him. Once again, Everyman finds himself alone.

Everyman asks his worldly Goods to accompany him. More forthright than Everyman's human friends and relatives, Goods explains that he would do Everyman more harm than good at his final reckoning. After all, it is to no small extent Everyman's immoderate love of Goods that makes his present situation so precarious. After hearing Everyman's curse, Goods abandons Everyman.

Then Everyman turns to his own Good Deeds, in whom, at last, he finds someone sympathetic enough to accompany him. Unfortunately, Good Deeds is weak and buried in the cold ground due to Everyman's long neglect, and simply not strong enough to make the journey. She advises Everyman to ask Knowledge for help.

Knowledge wisely counsels confession and penance. Following Knowledge's instructions, Everyman scourges himself, and Good Deeds instantly regains her strength. Then Everyman calls on Beauty, Strength, Discretion, and Five Wits for further assistance. Knowledge and Five Wits advise Everyman to go to a priest and take communion.

After he does so, Everyman and his companions approach the brink of his grave. There his friends abandon him one by one—all except Good Deeds, who remains willing to speak for Everyman at his final reckoning. Everyman and Good Deeds descend together into the grave while angels sing of his imminent salvation.

The DRAMA ends with a character called the "Doctor" directly advising the audience to look after spiritual matters during life, "For after death amends may no man make,/For then mercy and pity doth him forsake."

For several centuries after their composition and performance, medieval plays like *Everyman* were denigrated as two-dimensional, didactic, and ill-formed. This attitude changed at the turn of the twentieth century, when a few daring directors endeavored to stage the plays for modern audiences. The plays suddenly sprang to life.

What astonishes a modern-day audience about *Everyman* is the concreteness and reality of its ostensibly abstract characters. As Francis Edwards writes in *Ritual and Drama: The Mediaeval Theatre*, "So cunningly wrought is the theme of the play that it is rarely possible to separate the symbolical and the moral from the physical and psychological. It is upon the last two, however, that the theatrical pathos of the play mainly depends."

Audiences also sense in *Everyman* a precursor of still greater theatrical glories. Along with mysteries and miracle plays, moralities paved the way for England's richest dramatic period. As A. C. Cawley writes in his introduction to *Everyman and Medieval Miracle Plays*, "The staging of the miracles and moralities . . . and the freedom of the medieval playwrights in mingling KINGS and CLOWNS—all these things are a part of the heritage of the great Elizabethan dramatists." Thus a case can be made that the character of Everyman is a direct ancestor of Marlowe's Doctor Faustus (*see* FAUST).

The name Everyman has come down to our own time with reverberations that are tangential to the medieval original. Generically, an "Everyman" is a figure who appeals to common human sympathies (i.e., Charlie Chaplin's "Little Tramp" or Willy Loman in Arthur Miller's *Death of a Salesman)* or one whose experiences somehow represent a cross-section of our age (i.e., Winston Groom's Forrest Gump, or the performance persona of Spalding Gray).

For Further Reading

Cawley, A.C., ed. *Everyman and Medieval Miracle Plays.* New York: E.P. Dutton & Co., 1959.

Edwards, Francis. *Ritual and Drama: The Mediaeval Theatre.* London: Lutterworth Press, 1976.

Hartnoll, Phyllis. *The Theatre: A Concise History.* New York: Thames and Hudson, 1985.

Simon Eckehard, ed. *The Theatre of Medieval Europe: New Research in Early Drama.* Cambridge: Cambridge University Press, 1991.

EXODUS

Book of the Old Testament of the Hebrew
BIBLE describing the Israelites' plight in Egypt,
how the prophet Moses leads them out of
Egypt, and their ensuing experiences as they
journey to the Promised Land. The life of
Moses, also told in the book of Exodus, in-
cludes such well-known stories as his ABAN-
DONMENT in the Nile and adoption by the
pharaoh's daughter, the appearance of GOD
in the burning bush, the plagues visited on
Egypt, the parting of the Red Sea, and the
Ten Commandments (*see* CHILD IN THE REEDS).
Exodus also contains many Hebrew laws
given to Moses by God.

The book of Exodus is the second volume
of the *Pentateuch*. It opens with a description of the oppression of the Israelites by the
Egyptians and continues with an account of
Moses' birth. During the time Moses was
born, the pharaoh ordered that all newborn
Hebrew males were to be thrown in the Nile.
Because Moses' mother realizes he is special,
she puts him in basket and hides the basket
in the reeds along the banks of the Nile. The
pharaoh's daughter finds Moses and adopts
him.

After Moses is a grown man, he kills an
Egyptian for abusing two Hebrew slaves and
flees to Midian where he marries and becomes
a shepherd. While he is tending sheep one
day, an angel of God appears to him in a burning bush. God calls to Moses from the bush
and commands him to lead the Israelites out
of Egypt. God provides the reluctant Moses
with several signs to convince the Egyptians
of his presence and power: He turns Moses'
staff into a serpent, makes Moses' hand diseased and then heals it, and imbues Moses
with the power to turn water from the Nile
into blood. In addition, God reminds Moses
that his brother, Aaron has a powerful gift of
words, that he can be Moses' "prophet."

The pharaoh refuses Moses' initial request
to let the Israelites leave, and he increases their
work. Even after, at Moses' command, Aaron
turns his staff into a serpent and changes the
water of the Nile into blood, the pharaoh remains obdurate and unconvinced of the power
of the Hebrew God.

Then God sends plagues to Egypt: an
abundance of frogs, an infestation of maggots, swarms of flies, a pestilence that kills all
the Egyptians' livestock, festering boils on all
the people and animals, a violent hailstorm,
an invasion of locusts, three days of darkness, and turning the Nile red. None of these
portents affect the Israelites. During each
plague, the pharaoh promises he will let the
Israelites leave, but after Moses lifts each
plague, the pharaoh refuses to let them go.
Finally, God tells Moses to prepare the Israelites for the night when God will visit each
home in Egypt and take the life of the firstborn son, including the pharaoh's. Moses instructs the Israelites to put lambs' blood on
their door frames so that God will know to
pass over that door. After this, the pharaoh
orders Moses and the Israelites out of Egypt.

Pharaoh and his army then pursue Moses
and the Israelites. God commands Moses to
raise his staff and hold his hand out over the
Red Sea. As Moses does so, a strong wind
blows and divides the waters revealing a dry
path to the opposite shore. The Israelites escape from the Egyptians, who are destroyed
when the waters close over them. Moses leads
his complaining and unbelieving people into
the wilderness, consistently following God's
instructions and reassuring the Israelites of
God's presence. When the water is bitter,
Moses pleads to God for help, and God shows
him a log that makes the water sweet. When
there is no food, God tells Moses that he will
provide meat and bread. That evening a flock
of quails descend on their camp, and, in the
morning, manna (or bread) is left behind.
When the people are thirsty, God commands
Moses to strike a rock with his staff; and water
flows from the rock.

Moses takes his people to MOUNT SINAI.
There, God appears to him in the presence
of the terrified people so that their faith in
Moses would be unfailing. God comes down
to Mount Sinai in fire, and the mountain is
enveloped in smoke. A trumpet sounds. God
delivers the Ten Commandments and many
other laws to Moses, but Moses destroys the
tablets.

Moses returns to Mount Sinai for 40 days and nights. He receives instructions for the Israelites to construct a Tabernacle, or a Tent of Meeting. Because Moses stays away for so long, the Israelites doubt that he will return. Forgetting the faith they have placed in their prophet and in God, they make an idol of a bull-calf to worship. When he returns, Moses smashes in anger the stone tablets on which God had written the laws and commandments. Moses burns the idol, grinds it to powder, mixes it with water, and forces the Israelites to drink it. He orders those who believe in God to kill the others, and a massacre ensues.

The final chapters of Exodus describe Moses' second ascent to Mount Sinai where he again receives the Ten Commandments as well as the Israelites' construction of the Tabernacle and the Ark of Testimony, a receptacle for the stone tablets containing God's laws. Once the Tabernacle is completed, the pillar of cloud which God has used to protect the Israelites on their journey from Egypt, descends on it. Whenever the cloud lifts, the Israelites break camp and continue traveling; if the cloud remains, they stay at their current location. Because Moses does not uphold God's holiness in one instance when the Israelites were without water, God does not allow Moses to enter into the Promised Land.

Moses is a typical CULTURE HERO. Like Jesus he is saved from a massacre as a baby, and similar to the Indian KARNA, the German hero SIEGFRIED, the Polynesian demigod MAUI, and the son of the king in the Nigerian tale SE-CRET SON, Moses is abandoned in water and then adopted. He is called to adventure by God, just as the appearance of the HOLY GRAIL calls King ARTHUR's knights, and the BUDDHA is called by the "Four Signs" that appear to him as he rides about with his charioteer. Like many heroes, including Odysseus; Jonah, who tries to escape God's call and is returned to the true path while he is in the belly of a whale; and PERCIVAL, Moses initially refuses the call (*see* REFUSAL OF THE CALL). He is referred to in the Hebrew Bible as the meekest of men.

The theme of exile or banishment occurs in various forms in the ODYSSEY and the AENEID, in the stories of ADAM AND EVE, the Norse goddess HEL, and in many FAIRY TALES, including "Snow White" and "The WATER OF LIFE" (collected by the GRIMM BROTHERS), and the Scottish tale "KATE CRACKERNUTS."

The MOTIF of a sacred mountain like Mount Sinai is also an important element in many storytelling traditions. The Hindu god SIVA sits on the mountain MERU, the Greek gods live on MOUNT OLYMPOS, and the oracle at DELPHI delivers her prophecies at MOUNT PARNASSOS. The story of Exodus has been basic to the Judeo-Christian tradition, serving as a narrative source for many forms of oral story-making—especially songs and hymns celebrating release from oppression, African Americans have made particularly fruitful use of Exodus in spirituals such as "Go Down, Moses," in which the words "Let my people go" tie the plight of the ancient Hebrew slaves in Egypt to that of the African slaves in America.

For Further Reading

The Revised English Bible. Oxford: Oxford University Press, 1989.

Harris, Stephen. *Understanding the Bible*. 2nd ed. Palo Alto, CA & London: Mayfield Publishing, 1980.

FABLE

Short narrative tale, in prose or verse, intended to teach a specific moral or a mode of appropriate conduct. Often satiric and highly allegorical, fables point out the follies of human behavior with wit and precision. Fables have also been collected and told as religious exempla. The origin of fables is unknown; they appear in the ancient writings of both the East and the West. Frequently the main characters in fables are talking ANIMALS, although human characters and inanimate objects also may appear as central figures. Fables often draw upon material in FOLKLORE, and in some cases incorporate instances of the supernatural. The moral of the fable, which comes at the end of the tale, is often stated by the narrator or one of the characters in the form of an epigram or PROVERB.

The earliest known fable is found in *The Works and Days of* HESIOD, a Greek living in the eighth century B.C., AESOP, a Greek slave of the sixth century B.C., is perhaps the most well-known of the ancient fabulists, and the earliest surviving collection of fables in the Western world is ascribed to him. Aesop, like many other fabulists, told a specific type of fable called the "beast fable." Beast fables always have animals as their principle characters, who talk and act like the type of human that they are supposed to represent. For example, in Aesop's famous fable about the fox and the grapes, a fox who cannot manage to attain some delicious-looking grapes just above his reach, grumbles to himself that they are probably sour. The fox represents an ambitious, perhaps greedy person; the moral of the fable is that people disparage those things that they want but cannot have. Because animals play such important roles in fables, many animals have come to be generally associated with the trait that they allegorically portray in the stories. For example, the owl is often the embodiment of wisdom, the dog of loyalty, the fox of craftiness, and the rabbit of cleverness.

The fable is an important mode of both written and oral storytelling because through them the collective wisdom and morality of a culture are imparted. Fables have always been especially (though by no means exclusively) popular with children, who learn through the antics of the birds and bears and foxes and wolves who figure in these stories just what kinds of behavior are rewarded and punished. In this way, fables are cultural transmitters that help to preserve and record the identity of a people over time.

Fables have been a favorite style of storytelling throughout the centuries and around the world. Ancient Buddhists of India used fables to convey the moral messages present in the PANCHATANTRA, an ancient Sanskrit collection of animal tales. Geoffrey Chaucer incorporated a beast fable about a rooster and a fox into the *Nun's Priest's Tale* in his *Canterbury Tales*. In twelfth-century France, Marie de France composed 102 fables in verse. Jean de la Fontaine a French writer of the late seventeenth century, wrote popular, witty, highly satiric fables about the French court in particular and human nature in general (*see* LA FONTAINE, JEAN DE). The Russian writer Ivan Krylov published nine books of fables between 1810 and 1820 (*see* KRYLOV, IVAN). More modern works such as Rudyard Kipling's (*see* KIPLING, RUDYARD) JUST SO STORIES (1902), James Thurber's *Fables for Our Time* (1940), Joel Chandler Harris's (*see* HARRIS, JOEL CHANDLER), UNCLE REMUS *Stories* and George Orwell's *Animal Farm* (1945) have used the vehicle of the fable to expound moral messages as well as sharp political commentary. *See also* ALLEGORY.

FAIRY GODMOTHER

Supernatural being, especially prevalent in FAIRY TALES, who provides protection, assistance, or the fulfillment of a deserving character's desires. Although fairy godmothers are benevolent beings, these supernatural figures originate with the Fates (also called the *Norns*), a group of three crone-like beings who bestow good or ill fortune upon a child at birth. However, it has been suggested that fairy godmothers are somewhat of an anomaly, considering the volatile nature of the relationships held between fairies and humans found in many fairy tales. For example, fairies, like Tatiana in Shakespeare's *A Midsummer Night's Dream*, are more likely

to curse a unlucky victim rather than bestow benevolence and good fortune on a deserving human. Perhaps the most recognized fairy godmother character comes from the fairy tale, "CINDERELLA." In Charles Perrault's *Cendrillon*, the fairy godmother transforms Cendrillon's tattered garments into a dress crafted from gold and precious stones and provides the remaining necessary material accompaniments, thus establishing the young woman as a suitable candidate for the PRINCE's hand in MARRIAGE (*see* PERRAULT, CHARLES). Ralph Briggs's *The Halfchick Tale in France and Spain* involves a fairy godmother who magically animates two halves of a chicken that belong to a pair of orphaned brothers. The *demi-coq* (half-chicken) subsequently assists the destitute children in recovering money that their parents had lent to a neighbor who had become wealthy, yet had not made good on the loan.

For Further Reading

Perrault, Charles. *Cinderella.* Retold by Amy Ehrlich. Illustrated by Susan Jeffers. New York: Dial, 1985.

FAIRY TALE

Strictly speaking, a type of FOLKTALE that features the adventures of small beings, or fairies who possess supernatural endowments. With their extraordinary understanding, their ability to assume different forms, and other magical powers, these spirits are able to affect the lives of human characters for good or evil. Despite the name, however, the term, "fairy tale" has been broadened to include folktales that do not actually involve fairies.

An example of a classic fairy tale is "Sleeping Beauty," in which the fate of a young PRINCESS is determined by the fairies who attend her Christening. One fairy, angered at being excluded from the event, vengefully promises that the princess will someday prick her finger on a spinning wheel and die. Fortunately, another fairy is able to soften the impact of this spell; she changes the death sentence into a long sleep, to be broken only by the kiss of a PRINCE. In this, and in other fairy tales, supernatural and human characters interact casually, good is always rewarded with a happy ending, and evil is generally punished.

Like all folk literature, fairy tales stem from a long oral tradition, which explains the existence of several different variants of one tale. Most cultures have their own fairy tale traditions and a number of similar tales exist from one culture to another. As folklorist Stith Thompson writes in "The Universality of the Folktale" "[T]he same tale types and narrative MOTIFS are found scattered over the world in the most puzzling fashion. A recognition of these resemblances and an attempt to account for them brings the scholar closer to an understanding of the nature of human culture" (*see* THOMPSON, STITH). Like mythologists, some folklorists and scholars read fairy tales archetypally, seeing universal human concerns in the repetition of patterns (such as dark forests, WITCHES, step-parents, supernatural events, KINGS and princesses, etc.) in stories throughout the world.

The Freudian psychologist Bruno Bettelheim sees these patterns in psychological terms (*see* BETTELHEIM, BRUNO). In *The Uses of Enchantment: The Meaning and Importance of Fairy Tales*, he discusses why children usually respond so powerfully to fairy tales. He writes, "[T]he child preconsciously or even consciously knows what the 'truth' of the story consists of" and responds accordingly. For example, he explains the cross-cultural popularity of the "CINDERELLA" fairy tale as a story about sibling rivalry. He argues that many children identify with the HEROINE because they too may feel that their parents favor their siblings; Cinderella's happy ending provides hope that their own worth will someday be recognized: "It gives the child confidence that the same will be true for him, because the story relates so well to what has caused both his conscious and his unconscious guilt."

It is perhaps because of their psychological or archetypal appeal that fairy tales are continually adapted and re-adapted today. The Walt Disney Company is responsible for popularizing a number of fairy tales with American audiences in this century. Their versions of "Snow White and the Seven Dwarfs," "Cinderella," "Sleeping Beauty," and "The Little Mermaid," among others remain for many Americans classic examples of the fairy tale genre, despite the fact that Disney's versions take considerable liberties with the tales as they were originally written or transcribed (transcriptions that, themselves, often differ from the original oral telling). Fairy tale adaptations are not limited to an audience of children, but have also been rewritten for adults, often with a satirical twist or a social irony. For example, Anne Sexton (*see* SEXTON, ANNE), in her book *Transformations*, and Angela Carter in her short-story collection, *The Bloody Chamber*, reinterpret traditional fairy tales to confront issues of class, gender, and violence.

The GRIMM BROTHERS in Germany, Charles Perrault (*see* PERRAULT, CHARLES) in France, and Andrew Lang (*see* LANG, ANDREW) in England are among the more famous collectors and transcribers of fairy tales. Authors of original fairy tales include Hans Christian Andersen (*see* ANDERSEN, HANS CHRISTIAN) of Denmark, and John Ruskin, Oscar Wilde, and Rudyard Kipling (*see* KIPLING, RUDYARD) of England.

FALL FROM SKY

Theme of many CREATION MYTHS, in which a being falls from the sky or HEAVEN, usually into the PRIMEVAL WATERS below. Related to EARTH-DIVER CREATION MYTHS, the fall from the sky is often enacted by a woman. In Finnish Creation, for example, the sky's daughter, Ilmater, drifts to the waters below to rest, where she floats and swims until the stages of creation begin to take place. In Native American Huron mythology, a GODDESS falls from the sky toward the water, where two loons alert the Giant TORTOISE, who gives Sky-Woman a place to land and orders some earth to be placed on his back, which forms the land. Sky-Woman then gives birth to twins who are important to creation.

On an archetypal level, the fall from the sky can be seen as "The Fall into Time," notes William Irwin Thompson in *The Time Falling Bodies Take to Light* (1981) (*see* ARCHETYPE). This "Fall into Time" is not so much an event itself as the conditioning of time-space out of which all events arise. "The Fall" exists prior to the world of events, both logically and temporally, and so it seems as if it must be "The Event," the single action which echoes down throughout all ancient mythologies, children's NURSERY RHYMES, and modern stories: the Fall out of the One into the many, the emergence of the physical universe out of a transcendent GOD, the Fall of the soul into time," writes Thompson. Even the fall of Humpty Dumpty in the children's rhyme echoes this "Fall out of the One into the many": after Humpty Dumpty's fall, "All the King's horses and all the King's men/couldn't put Humpty together again." Valiska Gregory's story, *When Stories Fell Like Shooting Stars* (1996), also picks up on this theme.

For Further Reading:

Gregory, Valiska. *When Stories Fell Like Shooting Stars*. Illustrated by Stefane Vitale. New York: Simon and Schuster, 1996.

Thompson, William Irwin. *The Time Falling Bodies Take To Light: Mythology, Sexuality & the Origins of Culture*. New York: St. Martin's Press, 1981.

FALSE BRIDE

One of the most widespread FOLKTALE themes, in which a lovely young bride is replaced by another woman or a MONSTER. The bridegroom either has never seen his betrothed, is misled by a disguise, or sometimes just does not seem to notice. The true bride—even though she has been hidden, turned into an animal, or even killed—is always returned to her rightful place, and the impostor is usually put to death.

In some of the stories, a PRINCESS traveling to her betrothed PRINCE is replaced by her servant. An example is THE GOOSE GIRL, which is found in the GRIMM BROTHERS'S collection, throughout Europe, and on other continents as well. The deposed princess is put to work herding geese, but is later identified—sometimes by the decapitated head of her talking horse. In other stories, an evil sister takes the bride's place—as CINDERELLA's sisters had in mind.

Often, an animal or a wise CRONE gives away the secret. In other cases, the true bride is recognized because only she knows a magic word or her husband's true name. Sometimes she sneaks back to nurse her child or to spend the night with her husband, and is recognized.

Or she may disguise herself, search out her husband, and take some action that jogs his memory.

Other false bride stories appear in European, Arabian, Indonesian, Indian, and Lappish oral traditions. They are also found in all parts of Africa and in NATIVE NORTH AMERICAN STORYTELLING.

For Further Reading

Zipes, Jack, trans. "The Goose-Girl." *The Complete Tales of the Brothers Grimm.* Illustrated by John B. Gruelle. New York: Bantam, 1987.

FARO

Male twin in the CREATION myth of the Mende people of Mali in West Africa. Faro, the oral MYTH carried down from generations of the Mende people tells us, created the EARTH as we know it. Originally, Mangala (supreme god) made seeds that carried all the elements (including two sets of male and female twins) that would later organize creation. The seeds were placed within Mangala's egg to mature. One of the male twins, Pemba, decided to leave the egg early and fell through space. His placenta became the lifeless shape of earth. Unsuccessful in returning to the egg, Pemba nevertheless stole some of the male seeds and subsequently planted them in the earth's soil. Because this was a form of incest (the earth was Pemba's own placenta), the earth was contaminated. In order to appease Mangala, Pemba's male twin Faro (in the form of a fish) was sacrificed. He was cut into sixty parts which became trees on earth, symbolizing resurrection. Mangala later brought Faro back to life and sent him to earth in an ark made from a placenta. Much like the story of NOAH and the ark, Faro was responsible for keeping the ancestors and the first plants and ANIMALS safely within the ark. Faro flooded the earth in an effort to cleanse the world of Pemba's incestuous contamination. Since there are two Faros: the revived Faro and the originally sacrificed one, his "son," they are referred to as the "twin fish." Faro was later thought to be the Niger river itself with Lake Debo as his head. Faro also represents fertility because he embodies the male and female life forces originating in the primordial egg (*see* COSMIC EGG, FERTILITY STORIES).

For Further Reading

Sproul, Barbara C. *Primal Myths: Creation Myths around the World.* San Francisco: HarperSan Francisco, 1979.

FATHER

Symbolic figure representing supreme authority or divinity and the masculine principle. In MYTH, religion, LEGEND, and FAIRY TALE, the figure of the father appears in many forms as SUN, GOD, emperor, KING, SKY-FATHER or HEAVEN, Father Time, priest, *paterfamilias*, judge, and/or superego. In Judaism and Christianity, God is referred to as the Heavenly Father, and as the representatives of God, priests are called "father."

While MOTHERS represent the female principle and the intuitive side, fathers represent the masculine principle and the rational side. They figure far more prominently in fairy tales, where the dead mother often is replaced by a wicked stepmother (*see* STEPMOTHER—WICKED). In the GRIMM BROTHERS's tale "Hansel and Gretel," the children return to live with their father at the end of the tale; their wicked stepmother is the one who wanted to abandon them, not their weak father. In "The FROG prince," the King is the superego figure who tells his daughter she must keep her promise to the frog who saved her golden ball. In the Biblical story "The Prodigal Son," the father is the one to open his arms to his rebellious son and welcome him back into the fold. The Greek myth, "ICARUS AND DAEDALUS" portrays a father trying to save himself and his son; the father represents rationality and moderation—not to fly too high or too low—while the son represents passion and rebellion. Similarly, the Greek Helios represents fatherly strength and control as he guides the chariot of the sun across the sky each day while his son Phaethon, who is not strong enough to control the horses, represents youthful *hubris*.

At times the father figure is too strong and must be overthrown, as in the case of the Greek Titan Kronos having to overpower his father, Uranos, and Kronos's son ZEUS having, in turn, to overthrow Kronos. In Shakespeare's play *King Lear*, Lear symbolizes the father who cannot see the true worth of his daughter, Cordelia, and consequently brings about his own downfall and his daughter's death. In *The Merchant of Venice*, Shylock is the father who, despite his shortcomings, loves his daughter Jessica dearly.

For Further Reading

Berenzy, Alix. *A Frog Prince.* Illustrated. New York: Henry Holt, 1989.

Grimm, Jacob, and Wilhelm Grimm. "Hansel and Gretel." *The Complete Grimms Fairy Tales.* New York: Pantheon, 1945.

Jeffers, Susan. *Hansel and Gretel.* Illustrated. New York: Penguin, 1980.

FAUST

Astrologer and scholar of literary lore. He was modeled on the German magician Georg Faust (c. 1480–1540), whose life was exaggerated into the stuff of legend soon after his death. Faust's first name was mistakenly changed to Johann as his story gained popularity. Among his early chroniclers was the German theologian Philipp Melanchthon, who helped popularize the notion that Faust was somehow allied with the DEVIL. In his earliest literary incarnations, Faust was a reprobate who sold his soul to Satan in return for twenty-four years of unrestrained pleasure.

The oldest extant *Faustbuch* (a full written account of Faust's life) is the German *Historia von Dr. Johann Fausten,* published in 1587. This was probably the inspiration for the Elizabethan drama *The Tragical History of Dr. Faustus* (1588) by Christopher Marlowe (1564–1593), which focused on the theological aspects of the legend.

Marlowe's Faustus was a scholar who tired of traditional scholarly pursuits and signed his soul over to the devil in return for deeper knowledge. During the course of his adventures, Faustus was visited by such figures as the Seven Deadly Sins and HELEN OF TROY. Even after making his diabolical pact, Faustus had it in his power to repent and escape damnation. But his pride made it impossible for him to do so, and he was eventually carried away into HELL.

Marlowe's play is clearly influenced by didactic medieval DRAMA in its use of ALLEGORY, but it is nevertheless quite ambiguous.

On the one hand, it seems to take a clear stand in favor of piety and penitence. On the other hand, Faustus' craving for knowledge is treated sympathetically and even heroically, and the play is often read as a veiled criticism of religious constraints on human knowledge.

The German poet Johann Wolfgang von Goethe (1749–1832), who became enchanted by the Faust legend when he saw it enacted in a puppet show as a youth, penned its most ambitious treatment in his massive two-part verse drama *Faust* (1808 and 1832).

In Part I, a learned and elderly Faust craves to grasp the whole of experience, so he makes a pact with Mephistopheles. If the devil can grant Faust one moment of contentment so pure that he wished it to last forever, he would give up his soul to damnation. Mephistopheles rejuvenates the old scholar and conducts him on a tour of worldly pleasures, including the corruption of a young woman named Gretchen. Gretchen is redeemed by her faith in GOD moments before her execution for drowning her illegitimate child. But Faust does not find his moment of pure contentment in sensual delights, and Mephistopheles does not win Faust's soul.

In Part II of the drama, Mephistopheles leads Faust into the larger arena of worldly power and knowledge, but Faust still does not discover the satisfaction he seeks. Weary of Mephistopheles' efforts, Faust devotes himself to altruistic schemes to better human life. These at last bring him perfect contentment— and in his restless striving, he also achieved salvation. At the moment of his death, his soul is carried away by angels exclaiming, "Whoever strives in ceaseless toil,/Him we may grant redemption."

Thus Goethe completed the three-century transformation of the Faust legend from a cautionary tale of a reprobate's damnation to a soaring saga of human evolution. His version has inspired many creative talents ever since. Opera versions based on Goethe's drama include Berlioz's *The Damnation of Faust* (1893) and Gounod's *Faust* (1859). Thomas Mann's 1947 novel *Doktor Faustus* is not directly about Faust, but relates the life of a musician of Faustian intensity and ambitions.

In struggling with HEAVEN itself in his quest for knowledge, the Faust of legend is clearly a descendent of Prometheus, the Titan who stole fire from the gods to benefit humankind (*see* PROMETHEUS AND THE THEFT OF FIRE). He is also a close literary cousin to Don Juan. Like Faust, Juan was first portrayed as a degenerate profligate, then eventually came to symbolize humankind's evolutionary striving for perfection in such works as Bernard Shaw's play *Man and Superman* (1905).

Faust is also closely related to Mary Shelley's Victor Frankenstein (described in the subtitle of Shelley's novel as "the Modern Prometheus"). This connects Faust to today's sciences and technologies, with their intoxicating dangers and enticements, their alternating promises of universal destruction and universal redemption.

For Further Reading

Marlowe, Christopher. *The Tragical History of Dr. Faustus.* Purged and amended by A.D. Hope. Canberra: Australia University Press, 1982.

von Goethe, Johann Wolfgang. *Faust.* Translated by Walter Arndt. New York: Norton, 1976.

FEMALE CREATOR

Creation MYTHS that reflect the GODDESS as supreme being. While Jewish, Hindu, and Egyptian creation MYTHS reflect the emergence of patriarchal cultures by having a MALE CREATOR, the myths of some cultures underline the natural order of birth from the female. Huron, Fon, and Greek creation myths all provide examples of female creators.

In the Native American Huron creation myth, a goddess falls from the sky toward the primal waters below, where two loons see her and alert the Giant TORTOISE, who gives Sky-Woman a place to land and orders some EARTH to be placed on his back, which forms the land. Sky-Woman gives birth to twins—one good boy and one bad—who fight while still in the womb. The bad twin causes Sky-Woman's death when he will not be born in the normal way but bursts through her side instead. All vegetables and fruits are born from her buried body. The twins, however, continue to struggle, with the good one creating the helpful animals and the bad one making the threatening ones, the good one creating all that is positive in nature and his rival twin all that is dangerous or difficult, until finally the good twin slays his brother.

In Greek mythology, GAIA, the Great MOTHER or EARTH-MOTHER, is the first being. Born from chaos, she gives birth to her son, Uranos, who later becomes her husband and the father of their children, the Titans.

In the mythology of the Fon people of Dahomey, West Africa, MAWU, the MOON, is mother of all GODS and humans. As a fertility goddess and creator, Mawu is seen as the maker of the world. After arriving in the mouth of a great snake, she gives the earth its mountains, valleys, and rivers following the path of the snake, much as the RAINBOW SERPENT and the goddess KUNAPIPI do in Australian Aborigine mythology. Mawu then makes the SUN in order to see her work, and afterwards she makes people and animals. Once her creation is completed, Mawu retires to the HEAVENS and the snake coils underneath the earth, carrying the weight of all that Mawu has created. In one tale, Awe, a human being, attempts to create his own human being, boasting that he is as powerful as Mawu. However, his *hubris* only brings about his death, for Mawu uses him as an example to instruct the people that only she is capable of breathing life into mortals and sucking it away when she chooses, emphasizing the power of the female creator.

FERTILITY STORIES

Motif of regeneration in MYTH and FOLKLORE. From the earliest times, humankind recognized the need for the EARTH and its people, animals, and plants to be fertile. Many stories arose centering on the vegetative cycle, either literally or symbolically, and the need for fecundity. The Australian Aborigines, for example, have a myth about a fertility rock called ERATHIPA, where the rock has the power to cause a sterile woman to become fruitful if she passes close to the rock.

The myth of Persephone and Demeter can be seen as a fertility story, for angry Demeter causes the earth to become sterile as long as her daughter remains in the underworld, and

spring occurs each year when Persephone is reunited with her mother (*see* PERSEPHONE MYTH). The stories that surround the Native American CORN MOTHER, who is sacrificed and resurrected as corn, can be considered fertility stories. The Apache and Navajo goddess CHANGING WOMAN also belongs to the fertility MOTIF, as she said to be present in young girls during their puberty rites.

Myths and legends such as *Parsifal* (*see* PERCIVAL) and *Oedipus the King,* concerning the DYING GOD or KING who becomes a SCAPEGOAT, are forms of fertility stories—they signify a sterility that must be cleansed or purified before the land can resume its fruitfulness.

FIELD, RACHEL (1894–1942)

Novelist, playwright, poet, illustrator, children's author, and compiler of FOLKTALES. Although Rachel Field did not learn to read until after she was ten years old and died an untimely death at the age of forty-two, she was the author of numerous plays, volumes of poetry, and works of adult and children's fiction; she was also the editor of Madame D'Aulnoy's *The White Cat, and Other Old French Fairy Tales* (1967) (*see* D'AULNOY, MADAME) and *American Folk and Fairy Tales* (1929). Her famous children's novel, *Hitty: Her First Hundred Years* (1930) made her the first woman to win the Newbery Medal, and her novel *All This and Heaven Too* (1938), based on the life of her great-aunt, became a best-seller and a major motion picture. Her poems and stories draw on many of the motifs present in MYTH and folktale, including GYPSIES, ELVES, fairies, ANIMALS, and WITCHES.

For Further Reading

Field, Rachel. *Calico Bush*. New York: Dell, 1990.
———. *General Store*. Boston: Little, Brown, 1988.
———. *Hitty: Her First Hundred Years*. New York: Simon and Schuster, 1969.

FINK, MIKE (1770–1823)

American pioneer and boatman on the Ohio and Mississippi rivers who would become the subject of countless LEGENDS of courage and physical prowess. Fink is an actual historical figure born at Fort Pitt whose daredevil pranks, brutal fights, and skillful marksmanship made him famous throughout the Mississippi River region where he was known as "Snag," and in the areas surrounding the Ohio River, where he was referred to as "Snapping Turtle."

As with other frontier figures Daniel Boone (*see* BOONE, DANIEL), Billy the Kid, and Davy Crockett (*see* CROCKETT, DAVY), the Mike Fink that would be remembered was largely invented by storytellers who embellished Fink's stories or created new narrations about him. Not the least of these storytellers was Fink himself, who was known to be a braggart and took great pleasure in the telling and embellishing of his tales. Fink declared himself "king of the keelboatmen," and told numerous tales of his battles with the currents of the Ohio River as well as his brawls with other keelboatmen, who were referred to as "savages" for their reckless lifestyles.

A representation of the ideals of frontier style individualism taken to an extreme, whether portrayed as a boatman, Indian scout, or a trapper, Fink's triumphs, which were usually called "practical JOKES," often involved cruel and inhumane treatment of others, including considerable physical violence toward Native Americans and African Americans. He came to symbolize some of the best and worst qualities of Western frontiersmen. Among the many accounts of his death, one that seems to hold some historical veracity suggests that he was executed after he unintentionally killed a fellow trapper when missing his mark when trying to shoot a whisky cup off his friend's head.

Stories about Fink proliferated especially between about 1828 and the beginning of the Civil War.

For Further Reading

Blair, Walter, and Franklin J. Meine. *Half Horse, Half Alligator: The Growth of the Mike Fink Legend.* New York: Arno Press, 1977.

FLOOD

Motif of the deluge that cleanses and regenerates. Flood stories exist in many cultures, often generated by actual floods that over-whelmed a population, causing almost total disaster. Rivers such as the Nile might flood their banks each spring, leaving victims in their wakes. The MOTIF arose to explain why such disasters took place, and they often took the form of GODS punishing humans for their sins. On a symbolic level, the flood serves to cleanse evil from the EARTH, as in the story of NOAH in the Book of Genesis (*see* GENESIS, BOOK OF) and provides the opportunity for REBIRTH, with the surviving HERO functioning as the symbolic seed of the new life to come. The water is suggestive of the womb's amniotic fluid that breaks before the child is born, and the breaking of the water evokes the destructive side of the Great Mother ARCHETYPE, as seen in the actions of the Hindu GODDESS KALI and the Greek Demeter (*see* MOTHERS, PERSEPHONE MYTH). The purifying water of the flood is also related to the ritual of baptism and the sense that a person is reborn to a new life after being baptized.

The flood story that appears in the epic of GILGAMESH is based on an early Sumerian MYTH where humankind is destroyed by the gods. These in turn are sources of the Hebrew story of Noah, where GOD saves only the devout Noah and his immediate family and two of each of the other species of plants and animals.

In China, a flood myth dating back to 1000 B.C. appears in the *Shu Ching* of the Chou Dynasty, while in India, in the *Shatapatha-Brahmana*, the Noah-like Manu is the only one saved from a great flood with the help of the gods (*see* MANU AND THE FISH). In Ovid's *Metamorphoses*, with its collection of Greco-Roman myths, a flood sent by Jupiter (ZEUS) cleanses the earth of its sinful humans leaving only two righteous people, Deucalion and his cousin-wife, Pyrrha. In the Mayan POPOL-VUH, a flood appears to erase the wooden men God makes, for God feels they are a mistake. The Aztecs also had a sort of a flood used to cleanse the earth of sinful humans, where only one devout couple, Tatu and Nena, are saved. Many different flood stories belong to the various tribes of Native North Americans, and these are very often linked with CREATION myths. In Egypt, too, the SUN-god Ra sends a flood to punish the wicked humans, but when his instrument of punishment, the goddess Hathor, the Eye of Ra, goes too far in her destruction, killing thousands of people, Ra has to stop her by intoxicating her.

In contemporary literature, retellings of the story of Noah and the flood appear in Robert Coover's story "The Brother" (1969) and in Isaac Bashevis Singer's *Why Noah Chose the Dove* (1979) (*see* SINGER, ISAAC BASHEVIS).

FLYING CARPET

Magic carpet of Eastern tales and romances. The magic carpet is a stock device used to transport a character to whatever place he or she wishes. Sometimes it is referred to as "Prince Housain's carpet" for its role in the story of Prince Ahmed in the *Arabian Nights*. King Solomon was also said to have a magic carpet made of green silk, according to Islamic legend in the Koran. Whenever he traveled, King Solomon had his throne placed on this carpet, and it was so large that it could hold all his forces. Birds would then form a canopy over them with their wings to protect them from the heat of the sun. *See also* MAGIC OBJECTS.

For Further Reading

Burton, Richard, trans. *Arabian Nights*. New York: Heritage Press, 1962.

Mayo, Margaret. *The Prince and the Flying Carpet*. Illustrated by Jane Ray. New York: Penguin, 1993.

FLYING HORSE

Winged creatures, often found in Greek and Hebrew mythology, and symbol of the soaring spirit and poetic inspiration. Much symbolism exists concerning horses, yet the flying or winged horse has a symbolism all its own, connected with poets and creative imagination. Pegasus of Greek legend, arguably the most famous of the winged horses, and the winged horse Chrysaor spring fully grown from the blood of Medusa after Perseus cuts off her head. Their father is Poseidon, god of the SEA and horses. Pegasus always remains associated with the sea, wellsprings, and sources. Born at the source of the ocean, Pegasus is drinking from a well when Bellerophon captures him and tames him. If Pegasus kicks a mountain, a spring will gush forth. With Bellerophon on his back, he helps the man by flying above his enemies, allowing Bellerophon to hurl rocks on his enemies, and with Pegasus's aid, Bellerophon is able to slay the dreadful CHIMERA. Ultimately, however, Bellerophon suffers from *hubris*, as he tries to ride Pegasus up to the clouds above Mount Olympus, home of the gods. ZEUS hurls a thunderbolt their way to stop them, and Bellerophon is blinded and burned, falls off the flying horse, and tumbles down the mountainside, while Pegasus easily ascends the mountain and takes his place with the GODS. Thus he comes to symbolize the imagination objectified, which elevates human beings to the sublime regions. Both the wings of Pegasus and his connection with wellsprings represent spiritual creativity.

Besides Pegasus, such gods as Helios, Poseidon, and ATHENA are drawn by or ride winged horses. Many winged horses are present in the apocalyptic vision of St. John the Divine in the BIBLE's New Testament. The Hebrew prophet Elijah is whisked off to heaven by two flying horses. Writers have been inspired by the figure of Pegasus, and Nathaniel Hawthorne chose to retell the story of Pegasus, creating a "gentle child" who rides Pegasus to even greater heights than did Bellerophon. As Hawthorne ends his version, the child "grew to be a mighty poet!"

For Further Reading

Hawthorne, Nathaniel. *Pegasus, the Winged Horse*. Illustrated by Herschel Levit. New York: Macmillan, 1963.

FOLKLORE

Traditional artistic manifestations of a community: the spirit and essence of a culture. These performances, elements of material culture, and oral lore exist and persist because of, and through, human actions and interactions. They include music, song, DANCE, foodways, proverbs, RIDDLES, rhymes, games, tales, BALLADS, and a plethora of visual art forms. A term coined by William John Thoms (*see* THOMS, WILLIAM JOHN) in 1846, folklore is the accumulated traditions of a community (whether that community be familial, religious, tribal or ethnic, regional or occupational). A traditional art form is one that is pervasive, commonplace, based on known models, and repeated often in the community; reflecting both continuity and consistency through time and space. Folkloristic art forms must reflect and represent the culture from which it comes, acting as a badge of identity for community members. Through folklore community members demonstrate and reveal the qualities that link them together and distinguish them from others; including their attitudes, values, world views, artistic tastes, and history. These folkloristic forms, processes, and behaviors are customarily learned face-to-face, with the cultural element being passed from one person to another in a nonacademic format such as listening, watching, imitating, and apprenticing. Folklore is dynamic, often modifying due to new ideas, talents, technologies, materials, or the communities' social needs or situations. However, folklore is always formulaic, conforming to time-honored guidelines and aesthetic standards. For example, when folklore is created, the creator consistently chooses from and preserves a standard repertoire of culturally appropriate and accepted actions, words, construction techniques, and aesthetic norms.

FOLKTALE

Imaginative and magical tales from many cultures whose primary purpose is to entertain. Folktales differ from other traditional narrative tales such as LEGENDS, which often are told as truths but use fiction to highlight morals. Legends are thought of as folk history, while folktales are considered oral literature. Although folktales are told for entertainment, they often tend to be serious narratives of a hero or heroine who usually begins destitute and, after a series of adventures incorporating supernatural elements, reaches his or her ultimate goal. Other common features of folktales include settings of unnamed kingdoms in distant times, threefold occurrences, imaginary creatures, TRANSFORMATIONS, MAGIC OBJECTS, and HELPFUL ANIMALS.

Folklorists worldwide use the German word *marchen* when referring to folktales, as it is the term used by the GRIMM BROTHERS in their famous and influential 1812 collection, *Kinder- und Hausmarchen*. Today, the terms FAIRY TALE, *folktale,* and *marchen* are used interchangeably. In the Aarne-Thompson index, the category "Ordinary Folktales" includes a systematic classification of *marchen* and describes them as having formulaic language and structure, supernatural MOTIFS, and sympathy for the usually suffering protagonist. There is a noticeable uniformity in folktale structure across cultures, although content and style often vary. "CINDERELLA" is one such tale that has a similar structure but varying content and style among its different versions around the world.

FOOD

Source of nourishment, TRANSFORMATION, sustenance, life, and possibly DEATH. Since the earliest experience of food is connected to the breast of the mother, women are associated with the preparing, presenting, or withholding of food. When Demeter, Greek GODDESS of the grain and agriculture, is angry because no one will tell her where her daughter Persephone is, she withholds the growing of the crops and the earth lies fallow (*see* PERSEPHONE MYTH). Because Persephone eats some pomegranate seeds while in the underworld, she must spend a part of each year with her husband, HADES. The ancient mysteries celebrated at Eleusis involved the preparation of food and drink. As Erich Neumann writes in *The Great Mother*, "a transformation sequence leads from the fruit to the juice, thence by fermentation to the intoxicant, whose lunar-spirit character appears in such potions of immortality as soma, nectar, mead, and so on. Another sequence rises from the natural realm of plants to the essence of poisons and medicines." Food itself is transformed by fire.

Food in the form of a magic potion is responsible for transforming Lucius into a donkey in APULEIUS's *The Golden Ass*. In Greek mythology, the goddess CIRCE feeds the men who find their way to her island, and they are transformed into swine. In the Hebrew bible, ADAM AND EVE are expelled from the garden of

Eden after they have eaten the apple from the Tree of Knowledge of Good and Evil. The "apple of discord" ultimately causes the abduction of Helen by Paris and the start of the Trojan War (*see* TROY, HELEN OF TROY). In the FAIRY TALE "Snow White," a magic apple is responsible for Snow White's death-like sleep. In "Hansel and Gretel," the lack of food causes the ABANDONMENT of the children in the forest, and the WITCH they encounter entices them with her mouth-watering gingerbread house (*see* ABANDONED CHILDREN). The witch then attempts to "transform" Hansel by fattening him up, but Gretel manages to save him and kill the witch all at once. In Shakespeare's "Romeo and Juliet," a magic potion causes Romeo to believe Juliet is dead, thereby causing him to take his own life. In American Indian lore, CORN MOTHER dies in order to provide corn to feed all her people.

For Further Reading

Apuleius. *The Golden Ass, or Metamorphosis*. Translated by Robert Graves. New York: Farrar, Straus, Giroux, 1951.

Grimm, Jacob, and Wilhelm Grimm. "Hansel and Gretel." *The Complete Grimms Fairy Tales*. New York: Pantheon, 1945.

Jeffers, Susan. *Hansel and Gretel*. Illustrated. New York: Penguin, 1980.

FORMULA TALE

Genre of FOLKTALE characterized by its unique internal structure: the minimization of narrative detail, a playfulness with language and linguistic rhythm, and the prevalence and importance of repetition (*see* CHAIN TALE). The formula tale is often utilized to convey a moral lesson or demand the resolution of a proposed dilemma from the listening audience. For example, in the formula story "Otter's Revenge," Otter approaches King Solomon, demanding justice because Weasel has trampled her whelps. Weasel, in defense, says he accidentally trampled Otter's whelps because he heard Woodpecker announcing a battle. The story progresses through a number of interconnected narratives from different ANIMALS, until Lobster testifies that she was defending her children against Otter. King Solomon judges that Weasel is not guilty, citing that

the lives of the whelps are on Otter's head. While some folklorists see the formula tale as an effective epistemic tool, others employ this genre with the intent of relating a humorous or shocking experience to the audience. In one subgenre of the formula tale, the endless tale, the storyteller repeats the premise, usually a task to be performed indefinitely by a character, until the audience, recognizing that the story will never end, calls for its merciful ending. For example, in the formula riddle "Pete and Repeat," the storyteller relates that "Pete and Repeat are sitting on a fence. Pete falls off." When the storyteller asks, "Who's Left?" and the audience replies, "Repeat," the storyteller repeats the story at the "request" of the audience.

The formula tale is an important genre of folk literature not only for its epistemic and jocular elements but also for the opportunity it affords individual storytellers to construct a tale contingent upon their own language and personal experience.

FOUR DIRECTIONS

Both the origin and the personification of these four compass points are themes in many tales of different cultures. In most Native North American traditions, spirits and GODS are identified with the four directions. The directions, often associated with the four WINDS, are established at the four corners of the world. These winds and the directions are also tied to color symbolism. The story of the origin of the directions occurs as part of the CREATION stories of many Native American mythologies. In one Sioux story four brothers, Yata, Eya, Yanpa, and Okaga, are called upon by their father to journey to the four edges of the world to establish seasons, directions, and the length of one year. Yata, the eldest, proves mean and bitter, so his direction, symbolized by the magpie, is always cold and ice-like. DEATH will follow him, and people will retreat inside during his time. Yanpa, the lazy brother, learns that his direction is to be symbolized by the owl. His direction is one of discontent and complaint. Eya and Okaga, represented respectively by the swallow and the meadow lark, fix the sunny directions that herald summer and spring. Each brother becomes a season, wind, and direction. Tales from other Native American cultures show HEROES waging war on the south, east, or west winds, attempting to regulate the seasons.

In European tales, the directions take on a more standard personification. The North Wind is always the king of winds, the strongest and most fierce. In the Norwegian story "East o' the Sun and West o' the Moon," the HEROINE must call upon each wind to help her in her quest. She is sent first to the East Wind, but he is too weak to help her find her PRINCE. The West Wind is stronger, but unable to help. The South Wind is stronger still, but suggests that the girl must turn to the North Wind, the oldest and strongest of the four. His temper as blustery as his weather, the North Wind nonetheless agrees to aid the girl. But as he blows her to the castle that lies east of the sun and west of the moon, he wreaks havoc on those below. The storm that follows him knocks down houses and forests.

The winds and directions control weather and living conditions in all their manifestations. The human characteristics that the winds possess reflect the effects the winds have on the people who tell stories about them.

For Further Reading

Willard, Nancy. *East of the Sun and West of the Moon.* Illustrated. San Diego: Harcourt, Brace, Jovanovich, 1989.

FOUR DIRECTIONS TALE *See* FOUR DIRECTIONS

FRAZER, JAMES GEORGE (1854–1941)

British mythologist and anthropologist best known for his seminal study of comparative mythology, *The Golden Bough* (1890). Sir James George Frazer was born to conservative parents of the Free Church of Scotland, and his mother was descended from Oliver Cromwell as well as James I and II of Scotland. This family tradition appeared in his parents' deep religious faith, a faith he shared until his education at the University of Glasgow. At Glasgow, Frazer excelled in the

study of ancient Greek and Latin, and his exposure to ideas, old and new, wore away at his religious convictions. After his studies at Glasgow, Frazer earned another degree at Trinity College, Cambridge, in 1874. He continued at Trinity College, as a student and researcher for the rest of his academic career. As a student at Trinity College, Frazer was a voracious reader of classics, and he began his professional career with the intention of being a classicist or a philosopher.

Critics dispute the origin of Frazer's inspiration for writing *The Golden Bough*, but one influence was certainly his friendship with Robertson Smith. Smith had been embroiled in controversy when he supported the then radical tenets of German historical criticism of the BIBLE. The scandal made Smith more popular, and when he was chosen to select writers for the *Encyclopaedia Brittanica*, he asked Frazer to compose several on anthropological issues. These articles began Frazer's published work as an anthropologist, and much of his research would prove valuable for *The Golden Bough*.

The influences for *The Golden Bough* are extensive and varied. The tone of the work, at least, is indebted to the German biblical critics of the mid-nineteenth century. In order to "demythologize" the Bible, and thereby have a keener understanding of its truths, these critics attempted to dismiss the contradictions and violations of natural laws that the Bible contained. In theory, what remained would be the kernel of truth. Frazer, though he consistently avoided direct commentary on Christianity, did seek to deemphasize the almost religious reverence for Hellenic tradition amongst his contemporaries. By examining the stories and rituals of the Greeks along with cultures considered "savage" at the time, Frazer undermined the stereotype of the Greeks as civilized citizens in the midst of barbarians. His work was a critical step toward a more objective form of anthropology.

Early in his comparative examination of ancient stories, Frazer discovered patterns that seemed to link ostensibly disparate cultures. Most prominent of these in *The Golden Bough* is the theme of the sacrificial king.

Frazer discovered that the rituals of many cultures decreed that, after a set length of time, the KING must be murdered, either in person or by proxy. Frazer linked this curious practice to the mythology of the Greeks, particularly in the stories of DYING GODS such as DIONYSOS and ATTIS. The dying god serves the sacrificial function of maintaining the fertility of the land, and Frazer connected the stories to the political and religious workings of multiple cultures. The implications of this study for Christianity are clear, though Frazer resisted an explicit discussion of them. If the dying god and SCAPEGOAT figures appear in highly developed forms in many pre-Christian cultures, what are the grounds for the primacy and divine inspiration of the Bible? Frazer was perhaps too politically astute to directly ask the question, but he clearly points to the dilemma.

The Golden Bough has been critical to a number of academic disciplines and to the practice and analysis of storytelling as well. Sigmund Freud (*see* FREUD, SIGMUND) found Frazer valuable for his own study, "Totem and Taboo." Writers such as W.B. Yeats (*see* YEATS, WILLIAM BUTLER), James Joyce, T.S. Eliot, Joseph Conrad, and William Faulkner were also strongly influenced by Frazer's assertions, and much of the mythological emphasis in their works derives from Frazer. *The Golden Bough* is perhaps more important for its comparative method of analyzing stories. Frazer illustrates the value of seeking the deeply-embedded patterns and psychological motives behind stories. His work was influential almost from the time it was published, and it continues to have relevance today. Frazer never lost his fascination with the scope of his studies, and he died in 1941 while having his own writings read to him.

For Further Reading

Ackerman, Robert. *J.G. Frazer: His Life and Work.* Cambridge: Cambridge University Press, 1987.

Fraser, Robert. ed. *Sir James Frazer and the Literary Imagination: Essays in Affinity and Influence.* New York: St. Martin's Press, 1991.

Frazer, James George. *The Illustrated Golden Bough.* New York: Simon & Schuster, 1996.

FRENCH STORYTELLING *See* **EUROPEAN STORYTELLING**

FREUD, SIGMUND (1855–1939)

Austrian psychiatrist and founder of psychoanalysis. As one of the major influences on twentieth-century Western culture and thought, Sigmund Freud showed his brilliance from his earliest school days. Trained as a medical doctor, Freud began by doing research in physiology and revealed his interest in what would become psychoanalysis when his acquaintance, Joseph Breuer, began treating the hysterical symptoms of "Anna O." in 1880. Freud continued to explore hysteria and hypnosis when he studied with French neurologist Jean-Martin Charcot, and by 1888 he was publishing articles on neurological and psychiatric subjects. Eventually Freud turned away from hypnosis to DREAMS as a source of uncovering repressed emotions and the inner lives of his patients, for he believed that repression engendered neurotic behavior.

Among Freud's most important theories are his division of the forces that control an individual's psychic life into the id, the ego, and the super-ego, with the id referring to instinctual, uncontrollable, and unconscious behavior; the ego representing the mediating force that uses reason and common sense; and the super-ego referring to the force that controls the ego into those patterns of behavior that are socially acceptable. His theory of the Oedipus and Electra complexes, influenced by Greek mythology, was a way of explaining the stage of early childhood development characterized by an ambivalent attitude to the parent of the same sex on the part of the young child and "an object-relation of a solely affectionate kind" to the parent of the opposite sex. The publication of *The Interpretation of Dreams* in 1900, followed by the controversial *Three Theories of Sexuality* in 1905, helped Freud become a household name in years to come. The analyses of FAIRY TALES in *The Uses of Enchantment* by Bruno Bettelheim (*see* BETTELHEIM, BRUNO can be seen as the product of Freud's profound influence on Bettelheim.

Freud's interest in MYTH, dreams, the symbolic content of his patients' narratives and storytelling, FAIRY TALES, and creativity have made his books and essays essential to our understanding of twentieth-century literature. In particular, the essays "The Theme of the Three Caskets" and "The Occurrence of Material from Fairy Tales," that draw on such myths and literature as Shakespeare's *Merchant of Venice* and *King Lear*, the GRIMM BROTHERS's *Fairy Tales*, the Three Fates and "the apple of discord" in Greek mythology, the *Norns* of German mythology, and APULEIUS's *Amor and Psyche,* connect the oral tradition and storytelling with psychoanalysis.

For Further Reading

Freud, Sigmund. *Character and Culture*. New York: Macmillan, 1963.

———. *The Ego and the Id*. New York: Norton, 1960.

———. *A General Introduction to Psychoanalysis*. New York: Washington Square Press, 1952.

———. *The Interpretation of Dreams*. New York: Avon, 1965.

———. *On Creativity and the Unconscious*. New York: HarperCollins, 1958.

Wollheim, Richard. *Freud*. London: Collins, 1971.

FREYA

Beautiful, blue-eyed, and blonde Norse GODDESS, the foremost goddess in the Vanir, the race of Teutonic fertility GODS, who later became associated with the larger Teutonic PANTHEON, the Aesir. As a fertility goddess, Freya is associated with swine, a symbol of fecundity, and one of her nicknames is *Syr*, meaning "sow." Her connection to mother EARTH is further indicated by the pair of cats that pull her chariot. Freya is sexually alluring and portrayed as a goddess of love.

Freya is also associated with magic and war. When she joins the Aesir, Freya becomes a sacrificial priestess and teaches the gods witchcraft (*see* WITCH). Freya owns a falcon skin that enables her to transform into a bird and travel to the underworld from which she returns with prophecies. When she rides to the battlefield, she takes half of the corpses while ODIN, FATHER of the Norse pantheon, takes the other half to VALHALLA.

In one well-known myth about the Necklace of the Brisings, Freya is drawn, perhaps by her greed, to a cave where four DWARFS are smithing a beautiful gold necklace, a traditional symbol of fertility. Freya desires the necklace more than anything, and her longing is so intense that she finally agrees to pay the hideous dwarfs the price of her body over four nights. Unbeknownst to Freya, the mischievous god LOKI has followed the goddess to the dwarfs' cave, and he observes all. Loki reports to Odin, who orders him to get the necklace. In the shape of a flea, Loki stings the sleeping Freya, causing her to turn and expose the necklace's clasp. Loki changes back into his own form and steals the necklace. When Freya awakens, she suspects what has happened and demands the necklace from Odin. He says she'll receive it only if she incites war between two human KINGS, each with an army of twenty. Freya must use her magic, Odin orders, to give life back to any resulting corpses.

The myths that relate the rebuilding of the wall of Asgard, home of the Norse gods, Thor's duel with the GIANT Hrungnir, and the stealing of Thor's hammer demonstrate Freya's great appeal to giants. In the last of these, Freya's necklace is shattered. The myth in which the giantess, Hyndla, recites the lineage of Ottar (Freya's human lover who is disguised as a boar named Hildisvini), presents Freya as goddess of fertility (Hyndla refers to Freya's promiscuity and the boar is a symbol of fertility); goddess of war (Hildisvini means "battle-boar"); and goddess of witchcraft (she envelopes Hyndla in flames).

For Further Reading

King, Cynthia. *In the Morning of Time.* Illustrated by Charles Mikolaycak. New York: Four Winds Press, 1970.

FROGS

Highly symbolic amphibians associated with the MOON and appearing in MYTHS and FAIRY TALES around the world. Principally associated with water, frogs are connected with fertility, and their song coincides with the advent of springtime and rain. Many rites performed to invoke rainfall involve frogs. The Japanese believe that frogs bring happiness, and in the West, frogs symbolize resurrection, as they rise from the water with moist, alive skin as opposed to death's dry skin. For the Hindus, the Great Frog supports the universe, representing the undifferentiated primordial slime, and the nineteenth-century Indian sage Ramakrishna associated frogs with transcendence, given their ability to live in both water and air. The Celts believed the frog to be the Lord of the Earth, having the power of healing waters, and the Egyptians saw the green frog of the Nile as a symbol of abundance, fertility, regeneration, and longevity.

As Marie-Louise von Franz notes in *The Feminine in Fairy Tales*, the frog in FOLKLORE is seen as an unchaste animal that "was used in love charms in olden days in which its bones had to be worn in a certain form." Although much folklore suggests that the frog is "a maternal animal used to help women at childbirth and to bring fertility," writes von Franz, "in many countries the frog is believed to be poisonous and is called a WITCH's animal." In fairy tales, the MOTIF of the PRINCE who has been turned into a frog and awaits someone or something that will break the spell and return him to his human form is a common one, related to the fairy tale "BEAUTY AND THE BEAST." One of the most well-known of these fairy tales is "The Frog Prince," also called "The Frog KING," collected in the GRIMM BROTHERS's fairy tales but dating back in its earliest versions to the thirteenth century. As Bruno Bettelheim (*see* BETTELHEIM, BRUNO) notes in *The Uses of Enchantment*, here the frog is a symbol of sexuality: "The story of the frog—how it behaves, what occurs to the PRINCESS in relation to it, and what finally happens to both frog and girl—confirms the appropriateness of disgust when one is not ready for sex, and prepares for its desirability when the time is ripe." The metamorphosis of the frog from tadpole to frog represents the child's metamorphosis from child to sexual adult.

For Further Reading

Grimm, Wilhelm, and Jacob Grimm. *The Complete Grimm's Fairy Tales*. New York: Pantheon, 1945.

von Franz, Marie-Louise. *The Feminine in Fairy Tales*. New York: Spring Publications, 1972.

FURIES

In Roman mythology, the GODDESSES of vengeance. Known as the *Eumenides* or the *Erinyes* in Greek mythology, these goddesses are mentioned by HOMER and HESIOD, but these writers establish neither their numbers nor their names. Hesiod describes them as the daughters of GAIA (EARTH); they sprang to life from the blood of Coelus (Uranos) when his son Saturn (Kronos) castrated him with a sickle. Other MYTHS suggest that the Furies are the daughters of Night and Darkness. The works of Euripides establish that there are three Furies; later myths reveal their names to be Tisiphone ("avenger of murder"), Megaera ("the jealous one"), and Alecto ("she who rests not").

The role of the Furies is to punish crimes that escape public detection or justice, particularly those crimes that offend basic tenets of human society. They avenge murder, deception, betrayals of all kinds, all violations of family responsibilities, and various other forms of offense, regardless of whether or not the perpetrators are excused or forgiven for their crimes by society. Residents of the underworld, the Furies torture transgressors while they live on earth as well as after they die; they never show mercy and never forgive. These goddesses were worshipped in Athens as well as at several other shrines; the traditional sacrifice offered to the Furies was fresh water and a black sheep.

In appearance, the Furies are portrayed as ugly, bat-winged, serpent-haired women. Æschylus's description of them in the *Eumenides* is perhaps one of the most frightening; in this work the goddesses have bloodshot eyes, fierce teeth, and are every bit as terrifying as the Gorgons (*see* MEDUSA). Later myths temper this vision of the Furies, and make them appear as strict maidens, sometimes dressed like huntresses, with snakes wrapped around their arms or in their hair and torches or sickles in their hands. In spite of their complete lack of mercy for transgressors, the Furies are seen as essentially benevolent forces insofar as they punish evildoers and support both the good and the unjustly victimized. They function in storytelling as symbolic representations of vengeance and, in the case of Æschylus's *Eumenides*, as ancient powers of the earth.

GAIA

Mother EARTH in Greek mythology. As the first deity, Gaia forms out of Chaos, and in turn creates Uranos, the HEAVENS, to be her mate. However, once Gaia is impregnated, Uranos will not let their children, the first race known as the Titans, be born. Gaia grows fuller and fuller, until finally she creates a sharp-toothed sickle made of adamantine, which she gives to her son Kronos, or Time. With the sickle, Kronos castrates his FATHER, thus freeing his siblings. When he throws his father's GENITALS into the SEA, APHRODITE, GODDESS of sexual love, is born from them. The blood of Uranos falls to earth and forms the FURIES, the goddesses of retributive justice. Gaia's son Kronos marries her daughter, Rhea, who gives birth to many children; however, after each child is born, Kronos swallows him or her in order to prevent this child from acting upon him in the same manner as he acted upon his father, Uranos. Finally, Rhea cleverly manages to hide ZEUS, her son, and substitutes a stone for him, which Kronos swallows. Kronos then vomits up all the other children, is banished, and Zeus, Gaia's grandson, becomes the controlling god of MOUNT OLYMPOS.

Other children of Gaia include Agdistis, Ceto, and Charybdis, and some MYTHS say she was the mother of the three Moirae, the goddesses of fate: Clotho, Atropos, and Lachesis. Gaia has also been considered the mother of the nine Olympian Muses, although some versions give Mnemosyne, Antiope, or Moneta credit for their birth.

The Gaia principle, taken from the original EARTH-MOTHER, is a modern ecological theory proposed by the British scientist James Lovelock. As David Leeming describes Lovelock's theory in *The World of Myth*, "Earth . . . can best be seen as a living organism with the capability of organizing its own biosphere," with "the Earth's living matter, air, oceans, and land form[ing] a complex system which can be seen as a single organism."

GALLAND, ANTOINE (1646–1715)

French archivist, orientalist, and translator of A THOUSAND AND ONE NIGHTS. In 1661, he traveled to Paris to study at DuPlessis College. Following the completion of his course of study, he began instruction in oriental languages at the Sorbonne and in 1666 received a royal prize of 300 books. In 1670, he was appointed the secretary of Charles-Francois Olier de Nointel—a Jansenite—who was the ambassador to Constantinople. Galland went with him to Constantinople, ostensibly to study the evolution of the doctrine of the transubstantiation of the Eucharist in relation to the Greek Orthodox church. About this Galland knew very little, but he was able to familiarize himself with Turkish and Arab literature, making many translations of Arabic texts. He also began to buy manuscripts, art objects, and ancient coins for the king. Between 1673 and 1675, he visited Greece, Syria, Palestine, and Libya where he attempted several archaeological excavations. Returning to Paris, he began to write. In 1685, he was appointed Royal Antiquarian. In 1702 he embarked on his major lifework—the translation of *A Thousand and One Nights*. The translation was published in sections between 1703 and 1717—the last segments published posthumously after his death in 1715.

GAMBLING

Within a recreational and storytelling context, taking a risk or wagering something upon a game of chance. Gambling stories are found in all parts of the world and in every period of history. Huge bets—involving money, property, and even wives—have been made on card games, horse races, and trivialities of all kinds and have been related in stories.

Stories about wagers on a wife's fidelity appear in Boccaccio's *Decameron,* Calvino's *Italian Folktales* (*see* CALVINO, ITALO), Shakespeare's *Cymbeline,* and in stories from Chile, Germany, Great Britain, and Far Eastern and Middle Eastern countries. A traditional Turkish story about wagering against giving in to the impulse to scratch is also told by UNCLE REMUS. The GRIMM BROTHERS relate how Gambling Hansel gave shelter to the Lord and Saint Peter and in return requested cards and dice that would always win.

Gambling stories from life along the Mississippi River and the American frontier include legendary figures such as Jim Bowie, Deadwood Dick, Colonel Starr, and occasionally CALAMITY JANE. Both CENTRAL AND SOUTH AMERICAN STORYTELLING and NATIVE NORTH AMERICAN STORYTELLING featured gambling long before the Europeans arrived. For example, COYOTE wagered his hunting skills against a night with another creature's wife. Coyote lost, and his own wife enjoyed a night with someone else.

In a Hopi tale, a boy named Tsorwukiglö unwisely wagers on a dice game with an unsavory character. The boy loses all his clothes, wagers his life, and loses again. He is saved from death, however, by KACHINAS called up by his grandmother, SPIDER WOMAN. The kachinas rescue Tsorwukiglö by beating the evil gambler at dice and at a series of contests demonstrating both their ingenuity and their control over the natural world. *See also* CHANCE AND FATE.

For Further Reading

Botkin, B.A., ed. *A Treasury of Mississippi River Folklore: Stories, Ballads, Traditions and Folkways of the Mid-American River Country.* New York: Crown, 1955.

Erdoes, Richard. *Tales from the American Frontier.* New York: Pantheon Books, 1991.

Talashoma, Herschel. *Hopitutuwutsi/Hopi Tales: A Bilingual Collection of Hopi Indian Stories.* Translated by Ekkehart Malotki. Illustrated by Anne-Marie Malotki. Tucson: Sun Tracks and The University of Arizona Press, 1983.

GAME SONGS

Rhymes or songs that accompany childhood games. There are many children's games typically accompanied by folk rhymes that are chanted or sung as accompaniments to the game itself. The Swiss psychologist Jean Piaget classified children's games into three categories: practice games, symbolic games, and games with rules. As Francelia Butler notes in *Sharing Literature with Children,* RIDDLES, TONGUE TWISTERS and catches, counting-out rhymes, acting-out rhymes, and JUMPROPE SONGS can all be considered songs for practice games, where a new skill is acquired. Games with rules include circle games, DANCE games, hopscotch, and hide and seek, and have their own set of accompanying rhymes and songs. Some of these rhymes involve stories, and all of them are passed on from generation to generation of children.

Tongue twisters like "Peter Piper picked a peck of pickled peppers" tell a short story as well as testing a child's ability to manage the repetition and alliteration. A counting-out rhyme like "One, two, buckle my shoe" teaches a child to count. A game song like "Patty cake, patty cake, baker's man" accompanies a practice game or exercise for young children and the clapping of the small child's hands imitates the parent's bread baking. The short folk rhyme "The incey wincey spider, climbed up the water spout" involves both singing and the storyteller's acting out the spider's adventures. In "Ride a Cock-Horse to Banbury Cross," the storyteller sings the song while dandling the child on his or her knee to the beat of the song. Jumprope songs or rhymes require the jumper to keep the beat of the song and the rules of the game. Riddle rhymes or songs such as "Humpty Dumpty" encourage the child to guess the answer and lead to more sophisticated forms of literature.

For Further Reading

Butler, Francelia, ed. *Sharing Literature with Children*. New York: Longman, 1977.

Chase, Richard, ed. *Old Songs and Singing Games*. New York: Dover, 1974.

———. *Singing Games and Playparty Games*. Illustrated by Joshua Tolford. New York: Dover, 1967.

Lipman, Doug. *Storytelling Games*. Phoenix: Oryx Press, 1995.

———. *We All Go Together*. Phoenix: Oryx Press, 1994.

GANESA

Hindu god and son of Parvati and SIVA. With his one-tusked elephant head, pot belly, yellow skin, and four hands, Ganesa is indeed an unusual looking god. Known for bestowing wisdom and removing obstacles, he is invoked at the start of any significant undertaking, and his name means "Lord of the Hosts." A beloved god, Ganesa is also the bestower of prosperity and well-being. In representations of Ganesa, he is usually depicted riding a rat or with a rat in attendance. In each of his four hands he holds, respectively, a shell, a discus, a club, and a water lily. His specific role in the Hindu PANTHEON is to create and remove obstacles.

Indian storytellers offer VARIANTS of the birth of Ganesa. In one version, Parvati, the consort of Siva, is angry that Siva threatens the woman who guards her door and therefore make his way into the house. So Parvati creates a handsome young man (Ganesa) from the dirt of her own body, considering him her son and the person who will guard her. Unafraid of Siva, Ganesa guards his mother so well that he strikes blows on Siva when he arrives. Though Siva calls all the other guards, they are unable to withstand the fearless Ganesa. Finally, Siva and VISNU both battle against Ganesa, and Siva is able to cut off his head. The furious Parvati then creates hundreds of thousands of powers, or *saktis*, to destroy the world. After a million GODS are destroyed, the seers make every effort to propitiate Parvati, who at last agrees to stop her course of destruction if Ganesa is revived and made overseer of everything. Siva agrees to do this, and tells the gods to take the head of the first being they encounter, which is an elephant with one tusk. This they firmly attach to the body of Ganesa, and they bring him back to life, and Parvati is happy once again. Other MYTHS tell of how Ganesa wins two wives, Siddhi and Rddhi, and of his rivalry with his brother, Skanda.

The punishment that Parvati wields at the death of Ganesa can be connected with the punishment the Greek GODDESS Demeter inflicts on the other gods and human beings when her daughter Persephone is abducted by HADES (*see* PERSEPHONE MYTH). She causes the EARTH to lie fallow, preventing all agriculture from growing. Similarly, in the legend of the Great HARE, the earth is darkened and made cold when the brother of Hare is drowned by the Manitos. Only after the god or goddess is propitiated and the child or brother returned or at least honored will the world resume its equilibrium.

The symbolism of Ganesa can be associated with that of elephants in general, where the domesticated elephant exhibits both helpfulness and wisdom. Elephants are known to connote royal power, and various myths about the "universal monarch" portray him as riding a white elephant as he travels the world in watchfulness. The Hindu god Indra is carried by the great elephant Airavata (*see* INDRA AND THE ANTS). Jean and Laurent de Brunhof's children's stories of *Babar the Elephant* and Walt Disney's *Dumbo,* the flying elephant, also convey the positive connotation associated with Ganesa.

For Further Reading

Dimmitt, Cornelia, and J.A.B. van Buitenen, eds. and trans. *Classical Hindu Mythology*. Philadelphia: Temple University Press, 1978.

Zimmer, Heinrich. *Myths and Symbols in Indian Art and Civilization*. Edited by Joseph Campbell. New York: HarperCollins, 1946.

GARDEN OF THE GODS

Place where GILGAMESH seeks his dead friend, Enkidu. Gilgamesh, grieved at the death of Enkidu, journeys past the world of mortals through darkness to arrive at the Garden of the GODS. The garden is filled with sunlight. Fruit and flowers appear to be fashioned from jewels, rare stone and pearls. The gods who see Gilgamesh proclaim that no mortal has before, or will ever again, enter this sacred place. They tell Gilgamesh that he will not find Enkidu in the garden, but must travel over the water. Despite the beauty of the garden, Gilgamesh feels no pleasure.

This Garden of the Gods has its counterparts in other mythologies and religions. For instance, the idyllic beauty of the garden is reminiscent of the garden of Eden as well as the Greek Elysian Fields, where heroes spend their AFTERLIFE. Also, the DESCENT TO THE UNDERWORLD is a common QUEST, found in the ORPHEUS AND EURYDICE MYTH. *See also* ADAM AND EVE.

GARDNER, RICHARD A. (1931–)

Psychiatrist, writer, and storyteller. Gardner was born in New York, graduated from Columbia College in 1952, and became a medical doctor in 1956 and a certified psychoanalyst in 1966.

In the context of psychological treatment of children and in therapeutic practices, he is best known for his theorizing of the "mutual storytelling technique." He became a psychiatrist because he believed that "an inquiry into basic mechanisms of psychopathological disorders could be among the most fascinating of intellectual pursuits," and that an investigation into the process of storytelling could help illuminate this inquiry. Of his many publications, the following are most directly concerned with storytelling: *Therapeutic Communications with Children: The Mutual Storytelling Technique* (1971), *Dr. Gardner's Stories About the Real World* (2 vols., 1972, 1983), *Dr. Gardner's Fairy Tales for Today's Children* (1974), *Dr. Gardner's Modern Fairy Tales* (1977), *Dr. Gardner's Fables for Our Times* (1981), and *The Storytelling Card Game* (1988).

GENESIS, BOOK OF

First book of the BIBLE. Genesis begins with the Hebrew creation story (*see* ADAM AND EVE). This story is concerned primarily with the establishment of the human role in the universe, and it contains many similarities to the BABYLONIAN CREATION MYTH. Genesis also includes accounts of many well-known biblical characters, including Adam and Eve, Cain, Abel, Abraham, Isaac, Lot, Jacob, Esau, and Joseph as well as the stories of NOAH and the FLOOD and the Tower of Babel.

Abraham, the hero-patriarch of Judaism, Christianity, and Islam, is one of the primary figures in Genesis. His name means "Father of Many Nations." GOD makes an everlasting covenant with Abraham, promising that he will be Abraham's and his many descendants' (the chosen people) true god. He promises to make Abraham exceedingly fruitful and the ancestor of many kings. God gives the land of Canaan to Abraham and his descendants. This covenant is reiterated throughout Genesis.

The story of Abraham and Isaac demonstrates Abraham's unwavering faith in God. God orders Abraham to sacrifice his son, Issac. They travel to the place God specifies, and Abraham builds an altar. He binds Isaac and lays him on the altar. When Abraham is just about to slay his son with a knife, an angel of God calls to him and tells him to stop. God blesses Abraham abundantly because Abraham obeyed him and did not attempt to save his son. This story can be seen as a foreshadowing of Jesus' crucifixion and is paralleled in the legend of Athamas and Phrixus from Greek mythology.

The story of Lot's escape from Sodom is reminiscent of the ORPHEUS AND EURYDICE MYTH. Angels appear in Sodom and instruct Lot to depart with his relatives from the city because the angels were sent by God to destroy it. The next morning, the angels grab the hands of Lot, his wife, and their two daughters and lead them to safety outside of the city. The angels tell them to flee and not to look back or stop or they will be destroyed. God rains down fire and brimstone on Sodom and Gomorrah. He overthrows the cities and destroys all. Lot's wife looks back and turns to a pillar of salt. Like Adam and Eve, Orpheus, and characters from other storytelling traditions, including "Little RED RIDING HOOD" and Thakane and her brother from the Basuto tale CHILD IN THE REEDS, Lot's wife disobeys a strict command and suffers an extreme consequence.

Genesis presents several stories about the tumultuous relationships between brothers. Cain, a farmer, and Abel, a shepherd, are the sons of Adam and Eve. Their story contains the common biblical theme of the farmer versus the herdsman. Cain brings some seeds from his crops as an offering to God, while Abel brings the choicest of the firstborn of his flock. God regards Abel's offering with favor, but he dismisses Cain's offering. As a result, Cain murders Abel. God curses Cain by having the ground yield nothing in spite of Cain's effort to farm it, and he makes Cain a fugitive. God puts a mark on Cain so that no one will kill him.

Jacob and Esau are the twin sons of Isaac and Rebecca. Like Cain and Abel, they are very different. Esau has red, shaggy hair and is a skillful hunter. Jacob, who was born second, grasping Esau's heel, lives quietly among the tents. Isaac favors the oldest, Esau, and Rebecca favors Jacob. When Isaac grows old and blind, he calls for Esau and instructs him to make a savory dish for him to eat so that

he can give Esau his blessing before he dies. Rebecca overhears Isaac's words. She makes a savory dish and then dresses Jacob in Esau's clothes and puts goatskins on his hands and the nape of his neck. In disguise, Jacob takes the savory dish to Isaac so that he, rather than Esau, will receive his father's blessing. Isaac is deceived, and he bestows on Jacob grain and new wine and makes him lord over his brothers. When Isaac and Esau discover Jacob's deceit, Esau weeps bitterly and plans to kill his brother. Rebecca contrives a plan whereby Jacob is sent away. The brothers are eventually reconciled.

The well-known story of Joseph and his coat continues the theme of jealous brothers. Joseph's brothers hate him because he is Jacob's favored son. They throw him into an empty cistern and plot to sell him into slavery. Before the brothers can put their plan into action, Joseph is found in the cistern by some passing merchants and sold to Ishmaelites who take him to Egypt. The brothers put goat's blood on Joseph's robe, a gift from Jacob, and tell their father that he was eaten by a wild beast. Meanwhile, Joseph becomes known in Egypt as an interpreter of dreams, a power he attributes to God. He is summoned by the Pharaoh who has had two puzzling dreams. Joseph interprets Pharaoh's dreams to signify seven years of bumper crops followed by seven years of famine. Because of Joseph's skill, Pharaoh makes him ruler of Egypt.

Joseph's brothers came to Egypt from Canaan in search of food, and eventually Joseph reveals himself to his brothers. He sends them to get their father and families. Jacob on his deathbed, continues the blessing of the family line (the oath from God to Abraham, Isaac, and himself), telling Joseph that God had appeared to him, saying he would make Jacob fruitful and increase Jacob's descendants until they became a host of nations. Jacob's twelve sons represent the twelve tribes of Israel.

After Joseph and his brothers die and a new king ascends to the throne in Egypt, the Israelites are taken into slavery, and their story is told in EXODUS.

In general, the book of Genesis documents the family of Abraham, God's chosen people, and concludes by explaining their presence in Egypt and the stories about them that follow in the book of Exodus.

For Further Reading

Gauch, Patricia Lee. *Noah.* Illustrated by Jonathan Green. New York: Philomel Books, 1994.

Graves, Robert, and Raphael Patai. *Hebrew Myths: The Book of Genesis.* London: Cassell, 1964.

Segal, Lore. *The Book of Adam to Moses.* Illustrated by Leonard Baskin. New York: Alfred A. Knopf, 1987.

GENITALS

Reproductive organs that, for storytelling and mythology, are invested with symbolic value. The genitals, the *lingam* of the male and *yoni* of the female, are of particular significance for stories and RITUALS of fertility. Often a DYING GOD or HERO figure is emasculated and his genitals placed in the ground or a river as part of the fertility process, as in the story of the Phrygian ATTIS or that of the Egyptian Osiris. In many representations of DIONYSOS, the god holds a phallic pine cone staff.

In storytelling, the symbolic genitals also serve as the guide to a culture's sexual and political roles. In the Apache story of the "Vagina Girls," the female genitals are transformed from an active to a passive force, thus confirming a patriarchal order. The story begins with a creature named Kicking Monster whose four daughters are the only women in the world who possess vaginas, but those vaginas have teeth. The girls draw men to the cave where the men are kicked inside by their father and devoured by the teeth-armed vaginas. A young hero named, significantly, Killer-of-Enemies, gives the daughters a potion to eliminate the teeth from their vaginas, thereby transforming women forever into the passive half of the sexual equation. The story, like many mythic representations of the genitals, illustrates a male fear of female reproductive power as well as a subsequent attempt to control it. Another story of phallic power is that of the Egyptian god-king Osiris, models of whose phallus are "planted" in various sites in Egypt by this sister-wife, Isis. From the planting arises the fertile grain of which

the god is the symbol. *See also* ISIS AND OSIRIS, FERTILITY STORIES.

GEOFFREY OF MONMOUTH
(c. 1100–1154)

Twelfth-century writer believed to be the first to compile, in Latin, various oral and written tales about King ARTHUR into a comprehensive written form. It is thought that Geoffrey of Monmouth came from Monmouth on the Welsh-English border and was of Welsh or Breton descent. He taught at the scholarly center of Oxford from 1129–1151. He began the work for which he is best known, *Historia regum Britanniae* (*History of the Kings of Britain*), about 1130 and completed it around 1136. This work presents a "history" of Britain's legendary kings, including Brutus of TROY, the supposed founder of Britain; King Lear of Shakespearean fame; and Old King Cole of later nursery rhyme collections. Arthur's reign makes up the climax of the book and this heroic image of the king became the basis for many subsequent accounts of his life in the literature of France, England, and other parts of Europe. Geoffrey of Monmouth also introduced the characters of MERLIN and GUINEVERE. Although the *Historia* was taken as historical truth for many centuries, today the *History of the Kings of Britain* is considered a work of fiction, primarily the product of the Geoffrey's genius and imagination and clearly based on orally transmitted tales popular in Geoffrey's time.

For Further Reading

Barber, Richard. *The Arthurian Legends: An Illustrated Anthology.* New York: Dorset Press, 1985.

———. *King Arthur: Hero and Legend.* Woodbridge, Suffolk: The Boydell Press, 1986.

Cavendish, Richard. *King Arthur and the Grail.* London: Paladin, 1985.

Geoffrey of Monmouth. *The History of the Kings of Britain.* Translated by Lewis Thorpe. New York: Penguin, 1977.

GERVASE OF TILBURY (c. 1150–1235)

English author of the thirteenth-century work *Otia Imperialia* (*Imperial Trifles*). This work presents an impressive amount of FOLKLORE, including information and stories about fairies and King ARTHUR. Gervase of Tilbury presents the earliest record of diminutive fairies, specifically mentioning the *dracae* of Brittany and *portunes,* little creatures about half an inch high who come into the homes of farmers at night, warm themselves by the fire, and remove little FROGS from their bosoms, which they roast on the coals and eat. In addition, Gervase recorded the earliest version of a popular story about the necessity of human midwives to the birth of fairy babies, and he mentions the WEREWOLVES of England. Also in this work, King Arthur first appears in the popular folklore role of the sleeping warrior who, when the spell is broken, will awaken and reappear as a leader. According to Gervase of Tilbury, Arthur disappears to Avalon, but the author also tells of the groom of an Italian bishop, who, when recently on Mount Etna, saw Arthur in a garden reminiscent of Eden, accessed by a narrow opening in the rock. As is evident from this account, not all chroniclers of Arthur followed the tradition of Arthur at Avalon or his supposed burial at Glastonbury.

For Further Reading

Barber, Richard. *King Arthur: Hero and Legend.* Woodbridge, Suffolk: The Boydell Press, 1986.

————. *The Fairies in Tradition and Literature.* London: Routledge and Kegan Paul, 1967.

GESTA ROMANORUM

Tales of the Monks, probably the most popular stories of the Middle Ages, originally compiled as a manual for preachers. Nearly two hundred hand-lettered manuscripts of the *Gesta Romanorum* exist today in Latin and German. The printing press offered another avenue for publishing of the tales, and editions of the text were freely altered and revised. Four English versions remain today in manuscript. Wynkyn de Worde published the earliest edition between 1510 and 1515, and the work was refurbished by Richard Robinson, noted by Manual Komroff as "an extremely minor man of letters," who revised the work and printed six editions of *Gesta Romanorum* between 1577 and 1601.

The didactic tales, used to illustrate moral and religious vice and virtue, open upon colorful and romantic scenes that feature adventure, chivalry, mystical wonders, and the revival of classical heroes. The works also rely a great deal on oriental influence and imagery. The romance of the works did not go unnoticed by monks, who often found the stories a relief from their long and difficult religious works. The monks often ascribed religious imagery to Greek characters and read the works with an eye for double-meaning. Actaeon the Greek hunter, for instance, who is torn to pieces by his hounds, quickly became the symbol for the persecution of Christ.

Though it was the monks who studied and hand-lettered the bulk of *Gesta Romanorum* manuscripts, the stories had diverse origins, from the East—probably Palestine—to Greek and Latin historical legends to European FOLKLORE. It is probable that many of the works of Lucius Seneca—who lived in Cordova, Spain, and was known in Rome during its rise—were adapted to the *Gesta Romanorum.* Seneca wrote ten books of imaginary legal cases to be used in training Greek and Roman orators, and it is believed that the romantic element in his work was attractive to later readers. Ancient Eastern tales were similarly snatched up for their romantic elements by European pilgrims or soldiers who heard the stories in bazaars during long periods of inactivity.

While the stories of the *Gesta Romanorum* were originally drawn up to catch the attention of the monks—which they did for two hundred years—they also came to serve the greater purpose of the muse. However indirectly, the themes of *Gesta Romanorum* tales influenced the works of Boccaccio, Chaucer, Shakespeare, Schiller, Rossetti, and other, lesser-known, writers. References can definitely be traced to the *Gesta Romanorum* from these later works, including Shakespeare's *The Merchant of Venice.*

For Further Reading

Gesta Romanorum: A Record of Ancient Histories Newly Perused by Richard Robinson (1595). Delmar: Scholar's Facsimiles & Reprints, 1973.

GHOST STORIES

Tales of the supernatural. Most cultures have some form of ghost stories as part of their oral tradition, and the telling of ghost stories is meant to frighten and cause a chill, goosebumps, or the hair to stand on end. They are usually short stories or tales, and, according to author Roald Dahl, "The best ghost stories don't have ghosts in them. At least you don't see the ghost. Instead you see only the result of his actions."

Ghost stories have long been part of the oral tradition of Native North Americans, the Japanese, Chinese, Europeans, and Americans. Types of ghost stories include those with ghosts as protective spirits who warn the living of danger or even save lives, such as "The Phantom Stagecoach"; those meant to explain a supernatural occurrence, such as "The Light in the Window"; tales of vanishings of individuals, ships, planes, or towns, such as "The Man Who Fell Forever"; ghosts at SEA either as ghost ships or spirits aboard a ship, such as "The Mystery of the *Seabird*"; stories where the presence of ghosts is sensed by animals, such as "The Frightened Dog"; and the haunted house MOTIF, where a building is the home of a troubled and obsessive spirit, such as "The Baby Ghost."

As Marie-Louise von Franz notes in *The Shadow and Evil in Fairy Tales*, ghost stories often concern "people who have committed suicide, or have been killed or who died before their time." This is because they are jealous of the living, for they "have not had the time to detach naturally from the living and therefore [the dead person] now has a destructive and dangerous edge in the world of the living." Frustrated because they still have too much life energy in them "which has not been exhausted but has been unnaturally blocked before the proper time," they come back to cause trouble for the living. Such stories as "The Sound of the Drip" and "The Octagon Hauntings" illustrate this point.

Although ghost stories have existed for centuries, with Hamlet's father and the ghostly Banquo of *Macbeth* providing examples from Shakespeare, the nineteenth and early twentieth centuries saw a proliferation of ghost stories in the Gothic novel or RO-MANCE and in short stories by such authors as Henry James ("The Turn of the Screw"), Edith Wharton ("Afterward"), Washington Irving ("Ichabod Crane, or The Headless Horseman"), Edgar Allen Poe (*Tales of the Grotesque and Arabesque)*, George Eliot ("The Lifted Veil"), and Oscar Wilde ("The Canterville Ghost"), literary stories that have become part of the oral tradition. Historically, there is a great fondness of telling scary ghost stories at night around a campfire, where the atmosphere is evocative of the story's setting, or at bedtime, when one is prone to suggestion and the darkness tends to encourage the imagination.

For Further Reading

Charles Keeping's Book of Classic Ghost Stories. New York: Peter Bedrick, 1986.

Colby, C.B. *World's Best "True" Ghost Stories*. Illustrated. New York: Sterling, 1988.

Dahl, Roald. *Roald Dahl's Book of Ghost Stories*. New York: Farrar, Straus, Giroux, 1983.

Irving, Washington. *Rip Van Winkle or the Strange Men of the Mountains and Legend of Sleepy Hollow or the Headless Horseman.* Edited by Sandra Sanders. Illustrated by William Hogarth. New York: Scholastic, 1975.

Johnston, Tony. *Four Scary Stories.* Illustrated by Tomie de Paola. New York: Putnam, 1978.

McKissack, Patricia. *The Dark-Thirty: Southern Tales of the Supernatural.* Illustrated by Brian Pinkney. New York: Alfred A. Knopf, 1992.

GIANTS

Mythical humanoid beings of enormous stature who are usually malevolent. In stories, giants are usually an evil force that must be overcome by the superior wit, faith, or superhuman strength of their opponents, the HEROES of the tales in which giants appear. Giants are usually male, although various storytelling traditions also contain female giants.

Giants are portrayed in a variety of ways. They might have one arm, long teeth, long hair, no hair, or stone hearts. They have gargantuan appetites and often eat humans. They can travel huge distances in just a few steps. Giants often wear animal skins for clothes and use less sophisticated weapons, such as clubs, rocks, and tree trunks, signifying their crude nature. Giants usually live apart from civilized societies, sometimes in rocky caves or on islands.

In Greek and Norse mythologies, giants are a significant element in CREATION stories. They are primordial beings and the first race of people to inhabit the earth. In Norse legend, the earth is created from the giant, Ymir (*see* NORSE CREATION). There are three kinds of Norse giants: hill giants, fire giants, and frost giants. Hill giants are responsible for landslides and earthquakes. Fire giants cause volcanoes, lightning, and the northern lights. Frost giants make avalanches, glaciers, and frozen SEAS and rivers. With the giantess Angrboda, the Norse god LOKI fathers three evil and monstrous beings: Fenrir, the wolf who kills ODIN, Jormungand (the world serpent), and HEL, the queen of the dead.

In Greek mythology, the earth-born giants are the offspring of Uranos's blood. Other Greek giants, including the Titans, CYCLOPES, and Hecatonchires (hundred-handed monsters), are the result of the union between Uranos, the personified HEAVEN, and GAIA, or EARTH.

Giants exist in great numbers in ancient Hindu legends, as well as in Siamese, Indian, and Mongol legends. As in Western stories, there is a relation between these giants to creation myths in these cultures. In ancient Chinese legend, the giant P'AN KU named heaven and earth. Rivers were formed from his tears, the wind from his breath, and thunder from his speech. Parts of his body shaped the five holy mountains in China and the SUN and the MOON.

Giants appear frequently in Eskimo and North American Indian mythologies (*see* NATIVE NORTH AMERICAN STORYTELLING). In these tales, giants may be human, animal, or bird in form, and they are almost always cannibals. On the northern Pacific coast, stories of cannibal giants are especially popular. In one such tale, a giantess who abducts children is killed, but because her soul lives outside her body, she revives. The story of a giant bird (*roc*) who carries a boy to a cliff is common in Native North American storytelling traditions, as are stories about the giant Thunderbirds and about the giant MONSTER who sucks in his victims.

The most famous giant in Judeo-Christian legend is the Philistine Goliath whom David kills in battle with a slingshot. Like most of the giants in Greek and Norse myths, Goliath is associated with brute force and is a representation of evil. As in many stories depicting conflict with giants, the hero, David, uses his nimble skill to defeat Goliath and cuts off the giant's head as a trophy.

In medieval legends, giants continue to be an evil force that must be suppressed by warrior knights. The giant Grendel in BEOWULF can eat fifteen men or more at one time. It became conventional to link giants to the Biblical figure Cain, and thus, Grendel and his mother were conceived by a pair of monsters born from Cain. Beowulf, a Christian, vanquishes the evil and pagan Grendel and his mother.

In Arthurian romances, giants' characteristics of brute force, ignorance, destructiveness, greed, and lust are usually in direct contrast to the exemplary characteristics of the aristocratic heroes. In the fourteenth-century work SIR GAWAIN *and the Green Knight*, however, Gawain beheads the gallant Green Knight, "the largest man alive . . . and yet the seemliest for his size," who picks up his own head and must be overcome by the unwitting knight again. And there is Geoffrey of Monmouth's story of ARTHUR's defeat of the giant of Mt. St. Michel. Other famous legends telling of wicked giants include TOM THUMB, JACK AND THE BEANSTALK, and *Jack the Giant Killer* (*see* JACK TALES).

Not all giants are malevolent. The legendary Saint Christopher, to whom Jesus revealed himself by changing Christopher's staff into a palm tree, was said to be of gigantic stature. Likewise, giants in Renaissance literature lose their evil and brutish medieval associations. *Pantagruel* and *Gargantua* by Rabelais are works about two virtuous giant KINGS whose size contributes to many comical episodes. Paul Bunyan (*see* BUNYAN, PAUL), the mythical hero of American lumber camps, is another good giant. *See also* OGRE.

For Further Reading

Branston, Brian. *Gods of the North*. New York: Thames and Hudson, 1980.

Cavendish, Richard. *King Arthur and the Grail*. London: Paladin, 1985.

Giants! Giants! Giants! Selected by Helen Hoke. New York: Franklin Watts, 1980.

Stoutenberg, Adrien. *Fee, Fi, Fo, Fum: Friendly and Funny Giants*. Illustrated by Rocco Negri. New York: Viking, 1969.

Tolkien, J.R.R., trans. *Sir Gawain and the Green Knight, Pearl, and Sir Orfeo*. London: George Allen and Unwin, 1975.

GILGAMESH, THE EPIC OF

Ancient Babylonian EPIC poem. Gilgamesh was the fifth KING of URUK, two-thirds god and one-third mortal. Initially an uncontrollable tyrant who ruthlessly exploited his people and seized other men's wives for his own pleasure, he was transformed through his friendship with the wild man Enkidu.

Gilgamesh is the oldest epic poem known in any language, predating HOMER by more than 1500 years. It was completely forgotten until the 1800s, when archeologists began to make important discoveries in Mesopotamia. The most complete version of the epic was found in the library of Assurbanipal, the last great king of the Assyrian Empire, and dates from around 650 B.C. But versions of the Gilgamesh narrative can be found on much older tablets, and the story may have roots going back to the third millennium B.C.

There is evidence that Gilgamesh was a historical figure, the actual fifth king of Uruk. The poetic account of the battle against Humbaba is possibly an embellishment of a real expedition to seize timber from foreign tribes—timber that Gilgamesh would have needed for his grand architectural ambitions. In the hands of Sumerian storytellers, this historical Gilgamesh was transformed into the earliest known tragic HERO, making him a literary ancestor of such dramatic figures as Oedipus, King Lear, and Hamlet.

Given its antiquity, the poem's resemblance to subsequent works is often astounding, suggesting that it greatly influenced Western literature despite its obscurity for so many centuries. Utnapishtim's account of the FLOOD is extraordinarily like the later biblical story of NOAH. It has even been suggested that the Gilgamesh stories had a direct influence on the epics of Homer.

In the story, the citizens of Uruk pray to Aruru, the FEMALE CREATOR, for respite from the cruelties of King Gilgamesh. In answer, Aruru molds Enkidu out of clay to serve as the king's companion. Enkidu lives in the forest among the animals, knowing nothing of agriculture or civilization. A trapper encounters Enkidu and tells Gilgamesh about the man of the forest. When Gilgamesh hears rumors of this incredible creature, he sends a harlot into the wilderness to tame Enkidu and lure him to Uruk.

The harlot finds Enkidu and lays with him. She teaches him to drink wine and eat bread like a man. To his enormous grief, Enkidu soon finds that he has lost much of his animal prowess, and his friends the beasts are now afraid of him. But in place of his former wildness, Enkidu gains godlike wisdom and a talent for interpreting DREAMS.

The harlot brings Enkidu to Uruk, where he wrestles with Gilgamesh. Gilgamesh wins the match, but recognizes in Enkidu a kindred spirit—almost a brother. They become devoted friends. Under Enkidu's wise influence, Gilgamesh at last becomes a just and thoughtful ruler.

Though part god, Gilgamesh knows that he will eventually die, so he is anxious that his name live on. To increase his fame, he decides to slay Humbaba, the guardian GIANT of the mountain where the GODS live. Gilgamesh and Enkidu journey to the mountain together, where they kill Humbaba and cut down his grove of cedar trees.

Soon after that victory, Ishtar (or INANNA), the GODDESS of love and war, falls in love with Gilgamesh, and offers to become his bride. Gilgamesh refuses, bluntly reminding Ishtar of her heartless treatment of other lovers. Enraged, Ishtar persuades her parents, Anu and Antum, to send the Bull of HEAVEN to earth to wreak destruction on humankind. But Gilgamesh and Enkidu slay the bull in yet another heroic adventure.

By this time, the exploits of Gilgamesh and Enkidu had cause considerable consternation among the gods. Enkidu is a hero of many talents and gifts, but also has many frailties. These include overweening pride, a trait he shares with Sophocles' Oedipus and Shakespeare's Coriolanus. He counsels Gilgamesh to slay Humbaba despite the giant's pathetic promise to become Gilgamesh's servant. And he taunts the goddess Ishtar by throwing the phallus of the slain Bull of Heaven in her face. Such actions anger the gods, who meet in council and decide that Enkidu must die. He perishes not in heroic conflict but of a lingering illness, and Gilgamesh grieves the loss of his friend for the rest of his life.

Gilgamesh becomes more obsessed than ever with DEATH. He sets out in search of Utnapishtim, a mortal who has been granted eternal life by the gods. After a long journey, Gilgamesh finds Utnapishtim in Dilmun, an earthly PARADISE and the source of the sunrise. He asks Utnapishtim to grant him the secret of immortality.

Utnapishtim relates how Enlil, the god of the EARTH and WIND, had, many years before, become enraged with the human race. He decided to drown all earthly life in a gigantic deluge. But the god Ea warned Utnapishtim, instructing him to build a boat to save himself and every other kind of living thing. When the floodwaters receded, Enlil repented and granted Utnapishtim immortality.

Utnapishtim promises Gilgamesh immortality if he can stay awake for six days and seven nights. Instead, the exhausted adventurer falls into a long slumber. So Utnapishtim tells Gilgamesh about a sacred plant that grows at the bottom of the ocean. A taste of this plant will give any mortal eternal life.

Gilgamesh dives into the ocean and brings the plant back to the surface. On his way back to Uruk, he bathes in a well, awakening the serpent who lives in its waters. While Gilgamesh sleeps, the serpent emerges and eats the magical plant. So, Gilgamesh reluctantly accepts that immortality is not his destiny. But his fame is greater and more lasting than that of any other king of Uruk.

In *The Origins and History of Consciousness,* Erich Neumann suggests that the Gilgamesh stories reflect the overthrow of an earlier matriarchal culture by the Sumerians,

particularly in Gilgamesh's defiance of the goddess Ishtar. This argument casts an interesting light on the ambivalent role of goddesses and women in the Gilgamesh epic. For example, Ishtar is cruel and flighty, but Gilgamesh's mother, the goddess Ninsun, is kind and benevolent. And it is only at the urging of his wife that Utnapishtim tells Gilgamesh the secret of eternal life.

The harlot who tamed and civilized Enkidu also reflects this ambivalence. In a sense, she can be seen as the literary ancestor of the later *femme fatale,* a woman whose attractiveness proves dangerous to a male hero. The biblical Delilah, who destroys Samson's strength by cutting off his hair is such a woman. This character type also figures prominently in the novels of such figures as Balzac and Thackeray and even in American detective stories, most notably in Dashiell Hammett's 1930 novel *The Maltese Falcon.*

Many other themes from *The Epic of Gilgamesh* recur throughout world storytelling. These include the formation of a living creature from clay—also found in NATIVE NORTH AMERICAN STORYTELLING, including the HOPI CREATION and COYOTE stories. The golem of JEWISH STORYTELLING provides a cruder comparison. Even contemporary science has tapped into this theme; chemist Graham Cairns-Smith suggests that life first evolved from clay, a hypothesis discussed in his book *Genetic Takeover.*

The transformation of heroes through brotherly friendship is another common motif in the stories of the world. Friends of lore include David and Jonathan in 1 Samuel of the BIBLE, Ishmael and Queequeg in Herman Melville's *Moby Dick,* and Huck and Jim in Mark Twain's *The Adventures of Huckleberry Finn.* This transformative concept of friendship also crops up in countless Hollywood movies, including 1987's *Lethal Weapon.* The 1991 movie *Thelma and Louise* might be regarded as a feminist reworking of this same theme.

For Further Reading

Heidel, Alexander. *The Gilgamesh Epic and Old Testament Parallels.* Chicago: The University of Chicago Press, 1946.

Sandars, N.K. *The Epic of Gilgamesh: An English Version with an Introduction.* London: Penguin Books, 1972.

GLOOSCAP

Algonquin Indian HERO whose name means *Deceiver-with-Words.* MYTHS about Glooscap were commonly told among the Algonquins, and were first retold and recorded in 1884 by Charles Godfrey Leland, an American folklorist, in *The Algonquin Legends of New England.* Glooscap was a spirit, a TRICKSTER, and a medicine man, as well as a hero. The Algonquins believed that Glooscap was capable of everything: he had created all the ANIMALS to be peaceful and helpful to humans, and he had taught people hunting, fishing, and love-making. Capable of great power and rage to achieve his goals, he was also known for befriending a tiny elf of summer, whom he would hide in his deerskin robe (*see* ELVES).

In one tale, Glooscap sets off north on the longest night of the year until he comes to the home of Winter. With the tiny elf concealed, Glooscap appears to be under Winter's spell, totally frozen. But because the elf represents summer, he secretly causes Winter to cry salty tears, thereby dissolving both himself and his snowy home, and Summer replaces Winter as Glooscap laughs. *See also* ORIGIN OF SEASONS.

For Further Reading

Erdoes, Richard, and Alfonso Ortiz. *American Indian Myths and Legends*. New York: Pantheon, 1985.

GNOMES

Fabled beings that resemble grotesque-looking DWARFS and live beneath the earth, first mentioned by Paracelsus. Gnomes often have beards and humpbacks and wear gray or brown clothes with monastic hoods. They are said to move through the earth as easily as if it were air. One of their primary functions, like the griffins of Greece and the East and the DRAGONS of northern Europe, is to guard buried treasure.

Gnomes are distinct from the various creatures that are considered fairies because they are a product of science rather than of folk tradition. According to medieval thought, all mortal creatures are a blend of the four elements: earth, air, fire, and water. The Swiss physician and alchemist, Philippus Aureolus Paracelsus (1493–1541) popularized the term *gnome,* a Greek work meaning "earth-dweller." He, wrote in *De nymphus,* the first description of the gnome as one of the four beings representative of the elements. Paracelsus associated gnomes with earth, SYLPHS with air, salamanders with fire, and nereids with water.

In popular tradition, gnomes are frequently called dwarfs or GOBLINS. Such familiar tales as "Rumpelstilzschen" and "Snow White and Rose Red" depict gnomes as decidedly unpleasant creatures. The Germanic belief in "dark elves" popularlized the gnome in the early nineteenth century. A contemporary depiction of gnomes appears in the book *Gnomes* by Wil Huygen.

For Further Reading

Gag, Wanda. *The Earth Gnome.* Illustrated by Margaret Tomes. New York: Coward-McCann, 1985.

Huygen, Wil. *Gnomes.* Illustrated by Rien Poortvliet. New York: Harry N. Abrams, 1977.

GOBLINS

A wide range of beings or spirits of the fairy type, which are most often wicked and malevolent towards humans, but which may be friendly, honest, and useful, depending on the time period, the region, and the story in which they appear. Goblins are usually misshapen and grotesque-looking. They live in dark places. They may possess great strength and cunning. Some may have the features and attributes of cats, rats, wombats, and other beasts. Specific kinds of British goblins are *redcaps, kelpies, spriggans*, and *bugbgears*.

In Somerset folklore, there is a goblin called Bloody Bones who lives in a dark cupboard. This dreadful creature, with blood running down its face, crouches on a pile of raw bones that had belonged to children who told lies or said bad words. Bloody Bones also captures children who peek at him through the keyhole.

The Redcap lives in Scottish Lowland towers and re-dyes its red cap in the blood of travelers who shelter there. The Highland *Kelpie* is also bloodthirsty and hungry for human life. It usually has the form of a horse, but can disguise itself as a man. One popular story tells of seven girls who see a pretty horse and climb on its back. The horse lengthens itself so there was room for all the girls. Frightened by the horse, a little boy refuses to join the girls. Instead, he runs away and hides. The horse dashes into a loch with the seven girls on its back. Only the girls' entrails wash ashore.

The term *hobgoblin* is sometimes used synonomously with *goblin* in English folklore to refer to evil spirits. In the sixteenth and seventeenth centuries, when the English Puritans believed all fairy creatures were ghosts or DEVILS, John Bunyan wrote in *Pilgrim's Progress* (1678) that hobgoblins were forces of evil that must be resisted. They may be evil, grotesque, and terrifying creatures in later English tales.

Hobgoblins, however, are generally a better-natured class of fairy. They are rough and hairy, but amiable and honest spirits. They are usually about one or two feet tall and have dark skin. They may be naked or dressed in brown, tattered clothes. Like BROWNIES, they are solitary beings who often have connections with human families. They may live in houses and assist in domestic chores such as helping the bread to rise and caring for babies. Hobgoblins may also work on farms, guard treasure, and keep an eye on the household servants. They may act as guardian spirits of the home. Hobgoblins, as with other tutelary fairies, may have originated from the classical *lares,* deities associated with the welfare and protection of a household. Hobgoblins are not exclusively domestic, however, but are often associated with natural features such as streams, pools, and rocks. Hobgoblins are easily offended and can often be sly, cunning, and prankish. PUCK from Shakespeare's *A Midsummer Night's Dream* is perhaps the most famous example of a friendly, but mischievous hobgoblin.

Similar to hobgoblins, goblins in French folklore (*gobelins*) are household spirits like the English brownies. They perform various chores but also have a mischievous, rather than an evil nature.

Christina Rossetti's "Goblin Market" (1862) is a poem in which goblins take the shapes of various animals as well as sell seductive and dangerous fruit to unsuspecting human purchasers. In George Macdonald's novel *The PRINCESS and the Goblin* (1872), the goblins are grotesquely ugly subterranean creatures who have no toes and whose feet are the most sensitive parts of their bodies, as their heads are hard as stones. They are greatly contemptuous of humans. It is possible that Macdonald drew on the tradition of the earth-dwelling dark ELVES from Norse mythology. In *The Hobbit* (1937), J. R. R. Tolkien (*see* TOLKIEN, J.R.R.) included goblins similar to those in *The Princess and the Goblin* (a childhood favorite of Tolkien's) and who lurk in mines beneath the Misty Mountains. In his later work *The Lord of the Rings* (1954-56), Tolkien called his goblins "orcs." *See also* HOUSE SPRITES, PIXIES.

For Further Reading

Heller, Nicholas. *Goblins in Green*. New York: Greenwillow, 1995.

McCoy, Karen Kamamota. *A Tale of Two Tengu*. Illustrated by Koen Fossey. Morton Grove, IL: Albert Whitman & Co., 1993.

GOD

Single all-powerful deity in monotheistic religions; character in the stories of these religions. In the major monotheistic religions—Judaism, Christianity, and Islam—one figure referred to as God appears throughout, although Muslims refer to God as *Allah*. While the Hebrew God is also called YAHWEH or *Jehovah* in the Hebrew BIBLE, or Old Testament, depending on the version or translation, in most of the biblical stories and MIDRASHIM, the name God is used in such a way to suggest God as masculine. This use of the name God continues through to the Christian Bible, or New Testament, and the Holy Trinity of Catholicism is composed of the FATHER (God), the Son (Jesus Christ), and the Holy Ghost (the spirit).

In the Book of Genesis (*see* GENESIS, BOOK OF), the first book of the Hebrew Bible, God is creator of everything, including humankind. He is an active and prominent character in the early Biblical story of ADAM AND EVE, where he first warns Adam and Eve not eat the fruit of the Tree of Knowledge of Good and Evil, and then punishes them for doing so by exiling them from the garden of Eden and PARADISE. He is portrayed as mysterious and all-knowing in his encounter with the sons of Adam and Eve, Cain and Abel, where he is pleased with Abel's sacrifice but not with Cain's; when Cain and Abel then quarrel, because Cain is jealous and angry, and Cain slays Abel, God knows what has transpired and punishes Cain by exile as well.

Portrayed as a demanding deity in the Book of Genesis, God tests Abraham's faith by requiring that he sacrifice his beloved son Isaac, though God saves Isaac at the last moment. As in MYTHS of other cultures where the creator figure is dissatisfied with the human beings he or she has wrought, in the story of NOAH and the FLOOD, God destroys the entire human race except for Noah and his family.

For Further Reading

Metzger, Bruce M., and Michael D. Coogan. *The Oxford Companion to the Bible*. New York: Oxford University Press, 1993.

Segal, Lore, and Leonard Baskin. *The Book of Adam to Moses*. New York: Schocken, 1987.

Singer, Isaac Bashevis. *Why Noah Chose the Dove*. Illustrated by Eric Carle. New York: Farrar, Straus, Giroux, 1979.

GODDESSES

Female deities important in many cultures in both the East and the West; however, Native Americans generally consider their deities spirits. All goddesses represent aspects of the Great Goddess, or what the Jungian Erich Neumann calls "The Great Mother ARCHETYPE," symbolizing birth and DEATH, the EARTH, plants, and the positive and negative feminine principles. While the goddess/MOTHER figure begins as container in her elementary form, she becomes the source of spiritual TRANSFORMATION when she becomes the "good mother" and the source of negative transformation when she becomes the "terrible mother."

The "good mother" is symbolized by such goddesses as the Greek Demeter, the Egyptian Isis (see ISIS AND OSIRIS), the Phrygian CYBELE, the Sumerian INANNA, and the Babylonian Ishtar. In her younger form, she is virgin and maiden, as portrayed by the figure of Persephone and the Virgin MARY; in her older form she is Mary as mother of Christ and Demeter, mother of Persephone (*see* PERSEPHONE MYTH). The "terrible mother" appears in her younger form as the young WITCH, as exemplified by CIRCE or LILITH; in her older form she is exemplified by the Hindu KALI as destroyer, the old witch BABA YAGA, the Gorgon, or HECATE in her negative aspect. The good mother goddesses symbolize birth and REBIRTH, vision, inspiration, ecstasy, and wisdom, while the terrible mother goddesses symbolize rejection, deprivation, ensnaring, dissolution, madness, impotence, stupor, dismemberment, sickness, diminution, devouring, and death.

Depending on the culture, goddesses can be projections of the ideal feminine or can encompass all aspects of the feminine: while the Greek goddess APHRODITE and her Roman counterpart, Venus, have come to mean youthful beauty and sexuality, the Hindu Kali combines the three aspects of creator, preserver, and destroyer. In their book *Goddesses: Myths of the Female Divine*, David Leeming and Jake Page trace the evolution of the goddess, beginning with the archetype of the Earth Goddess, such as the Australian aborigine KUNAPIPI, the Native American Okanaga Earth Woman, and the Hindu DEVI-Shakti. In her next stage she is the Great Mother, and then she is seen as Fertility Goddess. Sometimes the goddess is "abused," as in the cases of Eve, Circe, and PANDORA, as patriarchy assumed a more powerful stance (*see* ADAM AND EVE). In other cases the goddess is disguised, with her feminine elements denied, as with ATHENA, born from the forehead of her father, ZEUS, and portrayed as the goddess of wisdom as well as the woman warrior. As Leeming and Page note, however, "Goddess has never died, and one of the major spiritual and psychological phenomena of our time has been her reemergence as a significant presence in our lives." Not only has she "found a central place in several of the great world religions—particularly, Catholicism and Hinduism," but "She has expressed herself politically and sociologically in the drive for a new wholeness—a new spiritual, psychological, and physical ecology— that is the power behind what we call the women's movement."

For Further Reading

Gimbutas, Marija. *The Language of the Goddess*. San Francisco: HarperSanFrancisco, 1989.

Johnson, Buffie. *Lady of the Beasts*. San Francisco: HarperSanFrancisco, 1988.

Neumann, Erich. *The Great Mother*. Translated by Ralph Manheim. Princeton, NJ: Princeton University Press, 1963.

GODS

Male deities who have power over mortals in cultures worldwide. Gods are part of the early pantheistic belief systems and mythologies of cultures everywhere. Many cultures, such as the Greek, Egyptian, Aztec, Norse, Hindu, and Hawaiian, have PANTHEONS that include major gods and in some cases minor ones as well. Male gods are generally representative of patriarchy, and they may personify the different ages of man.

Gods have power over each other as well as over mortals. In Greek mythology, for example, ZEUS is considered the most powerful of the gods, and wherever he is he can be privy to their conversations. Wars between the gods are not uncommon, and the death and dismemberment of the Egyptian Osiris is caused by his brother, the god Seth. Gods often marry their sisters, with Osiris marrying Isis, and Zeus marrying HERA (*see* ISIS AND OSIRIS). Depending on the culture, some gods are monogamous and others, like Zeus, are known for their adulterous liaisons. Again, depending on how closely modeled on human life the gods are in a particular culture, they can father children, shape shift, create and destroy humankind, mate with mortal women, bring culture to humankind, and be violent or benevolent, depending on will and whim (*see* SHAPE-SHIFTING). They may be the ones to determine a person's fate, whether it be punishing *hubris*, rewarding devoutness, or gratuitously wiping out cities by causing "natural" disasters. The personalities of the various gods are as numerous as the personalities of humans.

When pantheism gave way to monotheism in many cultures, the various gods who personified nature and aspects of humankind were blended into one, all-powerful GOD.

For Further Reading

Knappert, Jan. *Kings, Gods, and Spirits from African Mythology*. Illustrated by Francesca Pelizzoli. New York: Peter Bedrick, 1995.

GOLEM *See* JEWISH STORYTELLING

GOLGOTHA

Hill in JERUSALEM where Jesus is crucified. According to the BIBLE's New Testament gospels, Jesus is led by the Roman soldiers to Golgotha ("Place of a Skull"). In the book of John, Jesus carries the wooden cross himself, whereas in the other gospels, Simon of Cyrene is forced to carry the cross for him. Prior to the crucifixion, the soldiers offer Jesus either wine mixed with gall or drugged wine. Jesus refuses to drink. Two criminals are put to death at Golgotha at the same time as Jesus.

In Christian tradition, Golgotha is as close as the Christians can come to the place of the "sacrifice" of Isaac by Abraham (*see* GENESIS, BOOK OF), which prefigures the actual sacrifice of Jesus by his father. In addition, Golgotha is thought to be the place where Adam is created and buried, prefiguring the New Adam who is Jesus Christ (*see* ADAM AND EVE). As such, Jesus is the new apple of the new tree (the cross) on the cosmic mountain, pointing back to the old tree at the center of the world in Eden, where the old sinful fruit is consumed leading to Adam's death. According to this tradition, Jesus Christ, as the new Adam and the new fruit of life, overcomes death.

The motif of a sacred or cosmic hill or mountain is present in many storytelling traditions and includes the Hebrew MOUNT SINAI, the Greek MOUNT PARNASSOS and MOUNT OLYMPOS, and the Hindu Golden Mountain, MERU. In addition, the wooden cross on which

Jesus is hanged is also a sacred site of sacrifice and redemption; the MOTIF of the cosmic tree is similar to and often related with that of the cosmic mountain, particularly as world center symbols. The cross is reminiscent of YGGDRASIL, the World Tree on which the Norse god ODIN hangs himself, the tree on which ATTIS is hanged, as well as the BODHI TREE under which the BUDDHA receives enlightenment. *See also* CHRISTIAN STORYTELLING.

GOMME, GEORGE LAURENCE
(1853–1916)

British folklorist and anthropologist. Early in his career, Gomme attempted to establish FOLKLORE as a "science" that would assist him in tracing the influences of various cultures, including the Aryan, Celtic, Roman, and Saxon, in the formation of then current (late nineteenth-century) Britain. In 1889, Gomme, in his essay "Totemism in Britain," argued and produced evidence that early British cultures worshipped totems (*see* TOTEMISM). For the remainder of his career, Gomme would be under the attack of a group of social Darwinists, led by Alfred J. Nutt, who challenged Gomme's "disturbing" thesis that studies of "primitive" cultures would shed light on economic and social institutions in early British cultures. Gomme's work, however, operated as a precursor to comparative studies that focused upon the MOTIF analysis of the folklore of ethnically disparate cultures. Also of import is Gomme's attempt to amalgamate the study of history with that of folklore by recognizing folklore as an "historical science." In fact, in *Folklore as an Historical Science* (1908), Gomme argues that the study of folklore is more valuable than other "historical sciences" such as economics, sociology, and archaeology to the study of history because folklore has not been utilized in attempting to reconstruct history. Although much of Gomme's work was rightly criticized by other prominent folklorists of his time, his theories have elevated the importance of folklore studies to almost scientific proportions.

For Further Reading

Gomme, George Laurence. *Folklore as an Historical Science*. London: Methuen & Co., 1908.

THE GOOSE-GIRL

Fairy tale collected and rewritten by the GRIMM BROTHERS about a PRINCESS who is forced to tend geese. "The Goose-Girl" has many of the familiar ingredients of FAIRY TALES. As the tale opens, the beautiful daughter of an old and widowed queen is betrothed to a PRINCE whose kingdom is far away. When the time comes for the princess to marry, her mother sends her off with her dowry, a maid-in-waiting, a talking horse named Falada, and a white handkerchief with three drops of the mother's blood upon it. As the princess and the maid-in-waiting travel, the servant becomes emboldened, refusing to wait on the princess. At first the drops of blood on the handkerchief speak to the princess in her misery, but then the princess carelessly lets go of the handkerchief and it floats off in the stream where she has been drinking. Seeing this, the servant is further empowered, and she begins to ride Falada while the princess must ride the bad horse. By the time they arrive at the kingdom of her betrothed, the princess is presented as the maid-in-waiting, while the maid-in-waiting has taken full power and decided to pass herself off as the princess. The true princess is then sent off to tend the geese with a little boy named Conrad. Meanwhile, the maid-in-waiting has the young prince cut off the head of Falada for fear the horse might tell the true story, and she has the horse's head hung from the gate through which the real princess has to pass to tend the geese. Every time she goes through the gate, Falada speaks to her, saying the same words as the drops of blood had said. Then, while tending the geese, Conrad annoys her by trying to pluck some of the golden strands from her beautiful hair. But the princess will not let him, calling upon the WIND each time to blow away Conrad's hat, forcing him to chase it. Eventually, Conrad's own frustration with the goose-girl drives him to complain to the aged KING, who then manages to learn the truth, and puts the princess in her rightful place next to his son. Brutal retribution against the maid-in-waiting takes the very form the servant would have inflicted on the princess, and the maid dies. The young Prince then marries the princess.

As Bruno Bettelheim (*see* BETTELHEIM, BRUNO) writes in his analysis of "The Goose-Girl" in *The Uses of Enchantment*, the theme of this fairy tale is "the usurpation of the HERO's place by a pretender." He further notes that the topic of the tale is "Gaining autonomy from one's parents," and "To become himself, the child must face the trials of his life on his own; he cannot depend on the parent to rescue him from the consequences of his weakness." While the story underlines some of life's trials—"coming into maturity, gaining independence and self-realization," notes Bettelheim, "if one remains true to oneself and one's values, then, despite how desperate things may look for a while, there will be a happy ending." As soon as the princess begins to resist people taking advantage of her, as seen when she thwarts Conrad's efforts to grab her hair, she is on her way to victory. While many children's stories encourage "doing" as a means of coming "into one's own," one of the most famous and beloved is "The Little Engine That Could."

For Further Reading

Grimm, Jacob, and Wilhelm Grimm. *The Goose-Girl.* New York: Creative Ed., 1984.

———. *The Goose Maiden.* New York: Random House, 1990.

GOSPEL PARABLES *See* PARABLES OF JESUS

GRANDFATHER TALES

Tales about the CULTURE HERO of the Cariri Indians of Brazil. In the many tales about Grandfather told in eastern Brazil, Grandfather is the figure sent to EARTH by Touppart, the supreme deity of the Cariri tribe. He is credited with providing enough women for all the Cariri men, since in the beginning there was only one woman. Begging Grandfather for more women, the men are each given a piece of the one woman, whom Grandfather has cut up in enough parts to go around. Each man is then told to hang his piece of woman in his hut. Then the men go hunting, and when they return, each one finds a woman cooking his dinner in his hut, and they are glad.

In another tale, the people receive tobacco from Grandfather. Grandfather takes care of the children of the village while the adults are out hunting. He decides to transform all the children into peccaries, and then he takes them up a tree into the sky. Next Grandfather tells the ants to cut down the tree. By now the children are up in the sky with Grandfather, so their parents try to resurrect the tree but are unsuccessful. The children make a rope out of their belts and try to descend, but it is not long enough, and the children fall. Meanwhile, Grandfather remains in the sky; his gift to the people is tobacco, and they send him offerings in return.

GRAVES, ROBERT (1895–1985)

English poet, novelist, critic, and translator of Greek classics and MYTHS. Graves was badly wounded in the first World War, which is the subject of many of his early poems. He lived in Majorca for many years before and after his professorship of poetry at Oxford (1961–1966).

Between 1916 and 1975 Graves produced 55 collections of poetry, fifteen novels, ten translations, forty nonfiction books, an autobiography, and a biography of his friend T.E. Lawrence. His historical novels—which the author dismissed as potboilers—include *I, Claudius* (1934), *The Golden Fleece* (1944), and *Homer's Daughter* (1955). He edited a collection and also wrote a critique of English and Scottish BALLADS. His later poetry is humorous or focused on the nature of love.

Graves' *The Greek Myths* was published in 1955. In this well-researched and extremely valuable collection, Graves not only gives English renditions of the myths, but also lists their sources and interprets them in anthropological and historical terms. He points out when sites changed hands and describes the transformations of characters and stories after shifts in political power—for example, from matriarchal to patriarchal societies.

For Further Reading

Graves, Robert. *English and Scottish Ballads.* London: Heinemann, 1957.

———. *The English Ballad: A Short Critical Survey.* London: Haskell House, 1971.

———. *Good-bye to All That: An Autobiography.* Providence, RI: Berghahn Books, 1995.

———. *The Greek Myths.* 1955. Reprint, Mount Kisco, NY: Moyer Bell, 1988.

Seymour, Miranda. *Robert Graves: Life on the Edge.* New York: Henry Holt, 1995.

GREAT RABBIT

Powerful TRICKSTER figure in NATIVE NORTH AMERICAN STORYTELLING, especially in the eastern United States. Native American Rabbit tricksters also appear as Cottontail in the Great Basin area and as HARE. Rabbit is also a CULTURE HERO who steals fire or light for his people.

Great Rabbit has magic powers. He can sense what others are thinking from a long way off. He can jump as far as a mile. He has been known to disguise himself as a human being—though his long ears sometimes give him away.

In an Algonquin story, Wildcat swears by his tail that he will make a meal of Great Rabbit, also called Mahtigwess. Wildcat is a skillful tracker, but he is constantly fooled by the trickster's disguises and illusions. Finally, the persistent Wildcat is driven away by musket and cannon fire from a big ship, with Mahtigwess as captain. Though illusory, the gunfire is terrifying to Wildcat. And even worse, Wildcat has to forfeit the tail he has sworn on and so remains a bobcat to this day.

A Rabbit trickster is also found in African mythology, the various forms of which have been blended in the Brer Rabbit tales (*see* TAR BABY, UNCLE REMUS).

GREAT SPIRIT

Major deity of the Sioux Indians and other tribes. For the Sioux Indians, four colors were central to their mythology—red, symbol of the SUN; blue, symbol of the sky; green, symbol of the EARTH; and yellow, symbol of the rock. Using the analogy of the joining of colors to make a rainbow, the Sioux believe that everything is united in one Great Spirit, whom they call *Watanaka.* When the Sioux tell of what came first, they speak of the rock followed by the earth, then the sky followed by the sun, yet they are all the Great Spirit.

Sometimes the Great Spirit is personified by the character of OLD MAN, who appears in various legends.

In the Jicarilla APACHE CREATION MYTH, the Great Spirit is responsible for settling the Jicarilla near the hole from which they emerged and what they believed to be the center of the world. In *A Dictionary of Creation Myths,* David and Margaret Leeming note that the Arapaho Indians of the Great American Plains have a creation myth where the original creator is "a personified version of the flat pipe so important in their ceremonies," and "The Great Spirit is a formless projection of his thoughts." The Cherokees believe that the Great Spirit was responsible for the earth, the plants, and the first man and woman. The Omaha Indians called the Great Spirit *Wakonda,* and all plants, ANIMALS, and humans began as spirits in his mind.

GRIAULE, MARCEL (1898–1956)

French anthropologist, most noted for his work on African religions and mythologies. In *Abyssinian Journey* (1935), Griaule accounts his journey through Abyssinia as he attempts to uncover the traditions and customs prevalent among North African tribes. Griaule also records pieces of FOLKLORE from the indigenous peoples, including several tales of "miracle births" (*see* VIRGIN BIRTH) in which snakes impregnate unsuspecting virgin females—tales similar to some CREATION tales from Native American folklore, such as ALGON AND THE SKY MAIDEN. In Griaule's other seminal work, *Dieu d'eau* (1948), he explores the complexities of the Dogon religion through a series of interviews with a Dogon religious leader (*see* DOGON CREATION). Griaule's work showed a contradiction to what many Western anthropologists had considered to be a "primitive" religion, thus opening the floodgates for numerous subsequent works on African religions.

For Further Reading

Griaule, Marcel. *Abyssinian Journey.* London: John Miles, 1935.

GRIMM BROTHERS

Jacob Grimm (1785–1863) and Wilhelm Grimm (1786–1859), brothers whose repeatedly revised two-volume collection of FOLKTALES (Vol. 1, 1812 and Vol. 2, 1815) contains many of Europe's best-known and best-loved FAIRY TALES, including "Snow White and the Seven Dwarfs," "CINDERELLA" and "Little RED RIDING HOOD." Jacob and Wilhelm were raised in Steinau until the untimely death of their father, a respected magistrate, in 1798. They were then enrolled in the Lyzeum in Kassel. They studied law at the University of Marburg, where they became fascinated with old German literature. The brothers came to believe that language, rather than law, was the true bond that united the German people, and lost the desire to follow in their father's footsteps. Jacob worked briefly as KING Jerome's personal librarian during the French occupation of Hesse. Plagued by Wilhelm's asthma and the difficulty of supporting their siblings after their mother's death in 1808, the brothers set about collating and publishing the first volume of *Kinder- und Hausmarchen.*

After the collections appearance in 1812, people began to send the Grimms stories they had heard or read. The brothers themselves recorded numerous tales told by Dorothea Viehmann, a market woman from Zwehrn, who often stopped at their apartment on her way home from selling her wares in Kassel. Napoleon's defeat in 1813 and the subsequent return of the Hessian monarch to Kassel produced much nationalist sentiment, shared by the Grimms. Jacob was sent off in the train of Hessian troops chasing Napoleon's retreating army and later to the Congress of Vienna, while Wilhelm remained behind to edit the second volume of *Kinder- und Hausmarchen.* With alterations and additions, it appeared in seventeen editions between 1815 and 1858, gaining in popularity and increasing in sales over the years.

The Grimms saw themselves as collectors, adapters, and transmitters of existing stories, and their work represents a major attempt to capture in writing the European folk oral narratives. The relationship of the Grimms to the stories is hotly contested. Arguably, they were not simply collectors and editors of the tales, but shaped the form of the stories and in some cases may have authored tales or parts of them. Moreover, in many instances it is clear that the Grimms's collection of tales was heavily influenced, directly and indirectly, by earlier literary versions of the stories.

Interpretation of the tales is consequently a complex business. Fairy tales aspire to universal significance yet are clearly also context-bound within their moment of narration. The Grimms's interest in folktales in the early nineteenth century can be understood in terms of an emerging romantic German nationalism in the light of German cultural and political humiliation during the French occupation under Napoleon. The impulse to document the vanishing tales of the countryside developed at the time when a common language was understood to define a national identity, and the tales themselves could be seen as linguistic evidence of a common culture. Secondly, biographical data can be amassed to explain the importance of early childhood experiences in the Grimms's interest in fairy tales. The Grimm brothers suffered real material deprivation and loss of social status as a result of the early death of their father during their adolescence.

Several attempts have been made to have the stories transcend their contexts by reading them psychoanalytically. Freud discusses "Little Red Riding Hood" and "The Wolf and the Seven Little Kids" in a 1913 essay called "The Occurrence in Dreams of Material from Fairy-Tales," suggesting that the suppressed or displaced content of the story of the wolf that ate up the little goats and Little Red Riding Hood's grandmother may simply be infantile fear of the father. The little red cap has been read by Fromm, amongst others, as symbolic of menstruation, and fear of the wolf as disavowed desire for the father. However, many psychoanalytic readings of fairy tales run aground on structuring an interpretation around a detail that is only present in some VARIANTS of the basic folktale. Little Red Riding Hood is not always dressed in red in many versions of a story with very similar narrative content. Bruno Bettelheim's *The Uses of Enchantment: The Meaning and Importance of Fairy Tales* (1976) offers cogent, if controversial psychoanalytically driven readings of many of the Grimm stories (*see* BETTELHEIM, BRUNO). Bettelheim argues that fairy tales translate psychic realities into concrete characters, images and events, thus allowing internal processes to become externalized and comprehensible. In this respect, fairy tales are thought to resemble DREAMS.

The Grimms themselves had an interpretive slant on the varying meanings and versions of the stories. They did not believe in any one authentic original form of a tale but instead viewed the versions in rather idealistically neo-Platonic terms as attempts to approximate an inexhaustible primal form that exists only in the mind. The true story exists only as an idea, with any given version being only an attempt at its realization. They did, however, claim that their tales were authentically German, and not borrowed from Italian, French, or Eastern sources, though they acknowledged the profound similarities between them and stories found in Basile's IL PENTAMERONE, Perrault's fairy tales (*see* PERRAULT, CHARLES), and the Arabian Nights (*see* THOUSAND AND ONE NIGHTS).

For Further Reading

Grimm, Wilhelm, and Jacob Grimm. *The Complete Grimm's Fairy Tales*. New York: Pantheon, 1945.

———. *Selected Tales*. Translated by David Luke. Harmondsworth, Middlesex: Penguin, 1982.

GRIOT

West African folk singer. The *griots* of various West African countries such as Gambia and Senegal are considered storytellers, TROUBADOURS, public singers, poets, oral folk-historians, praise-singers, musicians, and genealogists. Their duties include reciting tribal and family histories and functioning as the local village storyteller. Often a head chief will have a band of musicians and dancing women called griots, or they might be attached to particular families. In West Africa they might play versions of the banjo, the fiddle, and the xylophone.

One notable *griot* was Griot Mamoudou Kouyate, a Malinke traditional historian who told the story of SUNDIATA to D.T. Niane, and whose family had kept the history of Mali's kings for generations.

In his popular book *Roots* (1976), Alex Haley tells of visiting Africa to attempt to trace his genealogy back through American slavery to his African origins. When he hears the oral folk history as it is told and sung by the local *griot*, he recognizes the names he has heard from his forebears and realizes at last his true family roots.

GUINEVERE

King ARTHUR's beautiful wife, whose love for LANCELOT leads to the end of Arthur's reign and the disintegration of the Round Table.

Guinevere and Arthur are wed in splendor at CAMELOT. As her dowry, Guinevere brings the Round Table. In some tales, the magician MERLIN warns Arthur that his marriage to Guinevere will be tragic. These accounts emphasize the passionate relationship between Guinevere and Lancelot.

In one version of the Arthurian tales Arthur demands Guinevere's execution by burning when he learns that she and Lancelot are in love. Lancelot rescues Guinevere and takes her to his castle. A civil war ensues, and the fellowship of the Round Table is divided. Arthur sends word that if Guinevere is returned, her relations with Lancelot will be ignored. Lancelot insists that she go back in order to preserve her honor. After Guinevere returns to Arthur, the king orders Lancelot to leave Britain forever. Lancelot goes to France where Arthur and his army follow him with plans for further attack, leaving Mordred (his illegitimate son by his half-sister or his nephew, depending on the source) in charge in Britain. Mordred attempts to seduce Guinevere, who escapes to the Tower of London. In Thomas Malory's *Le Morte D'Arthur* (1485), Arthur returns to England to fight Mordred. Guinevere flees to a nunnery. When she learns that Arthur and Mordred both are dead, she becomes a nun. Meanwhile, Lancelot returns to Britain to aid Arthur against Mordred. When he learns that he is too late, he travels to Guinevere. She pleads never to see him again, saying that she is devoting her life to religion. They part miserably, and Guinevere later dies at the nunnery. One tradition says that she and Arthur are buried together at Glastonbury.

The earliest existing account of Guinevere and Lancelot's passionate love was recorded in twelfth-century France by CHRÉTIEN DE TROYES. At that time, TROUBADOURS had brought romantic love and the idolization of women into fashion in the stories they told. Guinevere is the essence of a woman who is deeply loved and held in the highest esteem, both by her husband and by Lancelot. At the same time, she is the familiar obstacle of the *femme fatale*, and her attraction to Lancelot causes much suffering and the eventual demise of Arthur's kingdom. Other *femme fatales* from various storytelling traditions include APHRODITE, PANDORA, CIRCE, the SIRENS, INANNA, Dido, with whom the Trojan-Roman hero Aeneas falls in love (*see* AENEID), HELEN OF TROY, Eve (*see* ADAM AND EVE), and the biblical Delilah.

For Further Reading

Barber, Richard. *The Arthurian Legends: An Illustrated Anthology*. New York: Dorset Press, 1985.

Chrétien de Troyes. *Lancelot: Or the Knight of the Cart*. Athens, GA: University of Georgia Press, 1990.

Lister, Robin. *The Legend of King Arthur*. Illustrated by Alan Baker. New York: Doubleday, 1988.

Malory, Thomas. *Arthur and the Sword*. New York: Atheneum, 1995.

———. *Le Morte d'Arthur*. New York: Random House, 1993.

Perham, Molly. *King Arthur and the Legends of Camelot*. Illustrated by Julek Baker. New York: Viking, 1993.

GULLAH TALES

Creole FOLKLORE of the Gullah African Americans living on the Carolina Sea Islands. The African Americans who came to the Carolina Sea Islands from Liberia and Angola evolved a Creole dialect that is a mixture of sixteenth- and seventeenth-century English and such West African languages as Yoruba, Ibo, and Hausa (*see* YORUBA CREATION). The folklore of this region is also greatly influenced by the African tribes from which the Gullah came.

The figure of SPIDER, the animal TRICKSTER also known as ANANSI, appears in the tales of the Gullah, but there he is called "Aunt Nancy," an anglicized form of Anansi. Other trickster figures such as TORTOISE also appear in their tales. DuBose Heyward's novel *Porgy*, on which the Gershwin opera *Porgy and Bess* was based, was written in the Gullah dialect.

For Further Reading

Branch, Muriel Miller. *The Water Brought Us: The Story of the Gullah-Speaking People*. New York: Dutton, 1995.

Joyner, Charles W. *Down by the Riverside*. Urbana IL: University of Illinois Press, 1984.

GYPSIES

Legendary storytellers and fortune tellers. Although little is known of the actual origins of the gypsies, it is likely that their roots are Hindu. As Ruth Sawyer (*see* SAWYER, RUTH) notes, the gypsies "wandered from the east westward," "their language shows Sanskrit or Prakrit source," and "they claim descent from the first Pharaoh." The earliest legends of the gypsies occur in the Apocryphal Book of Adam, and they appear in many chronicles and manuscripts of the Middle Ages. In *The Way of the Storyteller*, Sawyer speaks of how the gypsies "were prized for their music, their storytelling and prophecies. . . . They have left their imprint on almost every country: Turkey, Afghanistan, Algeria, Spain, Finland, the British Isles, the Americas. In olden times KINGS feasted them, monasteries opened their doors to them, overlords granted them living-space among their serfs. Vagabonds always, but vagabonds with silver tongues and imaginations."

Sir James Frazer (*see* FRAZER, JAMES) speaks of the gypsies of Transylvania and Romania in *The Golden Bough*, describing how their chief celebration of spring was the festival of Green George. Here a young willow tree is "cut down, adorned with garlands and leaves, and set up in the ground." Various rituals are practiced with the willow tree as their focus, and the gypsies believed the tree then had the power to grant "an easy delivery to women and of communicating vital energy to the sick and old," all of which fits in with the European tradition of tree worship. In another ritual performed by the gypsies of Southern Europe on Easter Sunday, they take "a wooden vessel like a band-box" placing herbs and the dried carcass of a snake or a lizard that everyone had to have touched; it is closed up, SPELLS are performed over it, and it is supposed to expel all evils. Should anyone open the box, "he and his will be visited by all the maladies which the others have escaped." (*See also* PANDORA.)

Although the gypsies are legendary storytellers, they also figure in many stories, from George Eliot's *The Mill on the Floss* (1860), in which Maggie Tulliver runs away to the gypsies, or in D.H. Lawrence's novella *The Virgin and the Gypsy* (1930). In Sir Walter Scott's novel *Guy Mannering* (1815), Meg Merrilies, the half-mad queen of the gypsies, is the one to recognize the grown-up heir who was kidnapped when she was his nurse, and in 1820 Keats wrote a poem with her as its subject. The Spanish poet Federico Garcia Lorca became famous when he published eighteen ballads called *Romancero gitano* (1928), translated as *Gypsy Ballads*, where gypsies represent the freedom so repressed in Spain at that time. Marilyn Brown's *Gypsies and Other Bohemians: The Myth of the Artist in Nineteenth-Century France* discusses how artists have used gypsies as a metaphor for their own lives and aims.

For Further Reading

Hampden, John. *The Gypsy Fiddle, and Other Tales Told By the Gypsies.* Illustrated by Robin Jacques. New York: World Publishing, 1969.

Roth, Susan L. *Gypsy Bird Song.* New York: Farrar, Straus, Giroux. 1991.

HADES

Lord of the underworld in Greek mythology. The story of Hades and his realm combines several different views of the AFTERLIFE, taken from ancient oral traditions, including various locations in which ghosts might live after DEATH and various forms that the soul could take. Over time, Hades eventually came to represent the Hellenic concept of the inevitability of death.

Hades was the son of Kronos and Rhea, and the brother of ZEUS and Poseidon. After the three brothers overthrew their father, they drew lots to divide the universe among themselves. Hades drew the underworld, which was later known by his name. In Greek stories, Hades became the land where the dead were either punished or rewarded for their lives.

Hades was also regarded as the god of riches, due to the precious metals and stones to be found in his kingdom beneath the earth. He built a palace in the underworld and drove a black chariot drawn by four black horses.

Hades seldom left his kingdom. However, when he wanted a wife, he came to the world of the living to kidnap the virgin GODDESS Persephone (*see* PERSEPHONE MYTH). Eventually, he agreed to let her spend part of every year among the living.

In the ILIAD, Hades's kingdom is located directly beneath the earth. In the ODYSSEY, it is beyond Ocean at the edge of the world. Several rivers run through the land of Hades. The Lethe is the river of forgetfulness, Acheron is made of liquid fire, and the Styx has to be crossed on Charon's ferry by anyone who wants to enter the land of the dead. Even when this realm was reached by those bold enough to venture there, the gates were guarded by the monstrous, three-headed dog, Cerberus. *See also* ANCIENT GREEK STORYTELLING.

HAINUWELE MYTH

In Indonesian mythology, maiden GODDESS whose murder causes human life to exist. The MYTH of Hainuwele comes from New Guinea, where the Ceramese tell the story of a beautiful maiden who miraculously grew from the drops of Aneta, the night-man, when they fell on a coconut leaf. It took Hainuwele three days to grow, and three days later she becomes a bountiful and powerful Great MOTHER, producing wonderful gifts from her body. Not long after this, the people hold a festival, where they dance the *Maro* DANCE as they hold a long rope, forming a spiral around Hainuwele as she bestowed her gifts. As the men come closer and closer, they press in on Hainuwele till she is buried alive in a pit, and her anguished cries go unheeded. The next morning one of the men comes to dig up the body, which he cut into pieces, burying all the parts except for the arms in different places. From these body parts grow various new plants, including tubers, which became one of the major foods for human beings. But the arms he takes to another goddess, Satene. Out of the arms of Hainuwele she constructs a door, and then she calls all the murderers of Hainuwele to her, telling them that she will be leaving that place but first, the men must come with her through the door. Those who could advance through the door remained human beings, and those who could not became spirits or animals. From that point on, Satene was seen no more. In a VARIANT of this myth, it is Hainuwele herself who is angry after her murder, and she builds a gate in the shape of a huge spiral at one of the spots where the dance had taken place. Then, in order to see Hainuwele, people have to die and go through this gate to the Underworld. According to this variant, people could die and be born again only because Hainuwele had been murdered.

The myth of Hainuwele clearly connects the themes of DEATH and fertility, with Hainuwele belonging to the class of moon-maidens: "At the centre of the Ceramese mythological view of the world there is a connection between death and procreation, and this, as with so many people of the earth, is seen and experienced in the image of the *plant* as a form of being, and in the phenomenon of the dying and returning MOON," writes A.E. Jensen in *Hainuwele*. In *Essays on a Science*

of Mythology, C. Kerényi draws parallels between the abduction and rape of Persephone (*see* PERSEPHONE MYTH), noting that "Hainuwele's descent into the earth was made at the ninth of nine dancing-places, and during the ninth night of the great Maro Dance. The dance itself is the means of her descent. Men and women linked alternately form a huge ninefold spiral. It is a LABYRINTH, the primordial image and later the replica of that through which men have to pass when they die in order to reach the Queen of HADES and be ordained to human existence again. Hainuwele stands in the middle of the labyrinth . . . . The NUMBER on which the Maro dance is based—3 and 3 times 3—and probably the spiral as well, have their counterparts in the domain of Persephone."

In his essay "Myths and Mythical Thought," Mircea Eliade (*see* ELIADE, MIRCEA) points out that the Hainuwele myth belongs to "the myths recounting changes in man's condition," where its primordial deity, called *dema*, is killed by *dema* men. Eliade, drawing on Jensen's research, writes that "The murder of a *dema* divinity by the *dema* ancestors ended an epoch and opened that in which . . . *dema* became men, that is, sexually differentiated and mortal beings. As for the murdered *dema* divinity, she survives in her creations (FOOD, plants, animals, etc.) and in the house of the dead. . . . The violent demise of the *dema* divinity is not only a creative death; it is also a way of being continually present in the life of men, and even in their death. For by feeding on the plants and animals that sprang from her body, men feed on the very substance of the *dema* divinity."

Other correspondences can be drawn between the Hainuwele myth and the Native American CORN MOTHER myth. Shirley Jackson's story "The Lottery" (1948) offers a twentieth-century version of the myth by drawing on the connection between murder and fertility in a farming community.

For Further Reading

Eliade, Mircea. "Myths and Mythical Thought." *Myths*, edited by Alexander Eliot. New York: McGraw Hill, 1976.

Leeming, David, and Jake Page. *Goddess: Myths of the Female Divine.* New York: Oxford University Press, 1994.

HAITIAN STORYTELLING *See* MAGIC ORANGE TREE

HAMILTON, EDITH (1867–1963)

American scholar of the classics and collector of Greek and Roman mythology. The eldest of four sisters, Hamilton was born to American parents in Dresden, Germany, and was raised in Fort Wayne, Indiana. She attended Miss Porter's School in Farmington, Connecticut, and studied the classics at Bryn Mawr College. She earned a European Fellowship that enabled her to study for a short time in Leipzig; when she returned to the United States she accepted the position of headmistress at Bryn Mawr School in Baltimore, where she remained for 26 years. She published the first of her many books about the ancient Greeks, *The Greek Way,* in 1930 (revised 1942). Other notable publications include *The Roman Way* (1932), *Three Greek Plays* (1937), *Spokesmen for God* (1949), *Witness to the Truth* (revised 1957), and *The Echo of Greece* (1957). Her collected *Mythology* (1942) is still considered an important and useful text for students of the traditions of ancient Greece. *The Ever-Present Past* was published posthumously in 1964. Hamilton was a highly respected lecturer and writer who received numerous honorary degrees and national awards for her scholarship and service. She is remembered as a notable collector, translator of ancient mythology, and a reliable source to which storytellers have always turned.

For Further Reading

Reid, Doris Fielding. *Edith Hamilton: An Intimate Portrait.* New York: W. W. Norton, 1967.

HAPPY HUNTING GROUND

Name for Native American HEAVEN or burial ground in nineteenth- and early-twentieth-century American LEGEND. Although this term came to be used by European colonists to describe the place where Native Americans went after death, it was seldom used by Native Americans themselves. Rarely does this term occur in the many MYTHS and legends of Indian lore belonging to the various tribes of North America, yet in the storytelling tradition it has come to signify the place where the Indian warrior would go after death. Today Native Americans eschew this term.

HARE

Among various Native American tribes, a SUN god and TRICKSTER figure. For the Ojibwa Algonquin tribes and the Winebago Sioux of North America, the Great Hare, MANABOZHO, is both the chief god who created the water, the fish, and the deer and a trickster. Sometimes identified with North America's great Mississippi River, he is also known by such names as *Michabo, Messou, Menebuch,* and *Missibizi,* and also referred to as Great Rabbit. As the legends tell it, Manabozho came and put himself in the service of humanity, providing human beings with the manual arts, and combating MONSTERS to protect them.

In one tale of the Great Hare, Manabozho has a brother named Chibiabos. Manabozho does not want Chibiabos to leave his sight, and the one time he does, Chibiabos drowns, destroyed by the Manitos, ancestors of the Pawnee. In return, the furious Manabozho wages war by blackening his face and secluding himself in his dark lodge for six years, leaving the earth dark, cold, and frost-bitten, much as the Greek goddess Demeter makes the earth lie fallow as a form of blackmail to induce the other GODS to tell her where her daughter, Persephone, has been taken (*see* PERSEPHONE MYTH). Finally, the Manitos, preferring the rage of Manabozho to his melancholy, builds a lodge near him and coaxes him out with healing preparations and sacred liquor until Manabozho forgets his sorrow and dances, sings, and smokes with them, invoking the presence of Chibiabos (*see* DANCE).

The figure of Hare belongs to the ARCHETYPE of the HERO as well as that of the trickster. *See also* GREAT RABBIT, TORTOISE AND THE HARE.

For Further Reading

Bierhorst, John. *The Mythology of North America.* New York: William Morrow, 1985.

McGaughrean, Geraldine. Illustrated by Bee Willey. *The Golden Hoard: Myths and Legends of the World.* New York: Simon & Schuster, 1995.

HARPIES

Foul, predatory creatures in Greek and Roman mythology. A harpy has the head and breasts of a woman, the body of a vulture, long, curved claws, and a pale, starved complexion. Their name derives from the Greek "to snatch." The Harpies swoop down from the clouds and seize food in either their claws or in their long arms to satisfy their insatiable hunger. They vomit and excrete over everything, contaminating all they touch. Harpies are known for their loud screeches, their repulsive stench, and their invulnerability.

Originally, Harpies were associated with storm WINDS as wind spirits who carried away anyone whom the GODS wished. In the ILIAD, HOMER mentions Podarge, the Harpy who was impregnated by the wind Zephyrus and produced the horses of Achilles. In *Theogony*, HESIOD names the Harpies Aello and Ocypete, meaning *Storm-foot* and *Swift-wing*. In this work, they are winged divinities with long, flowing hair and are swifter than the birds and the winds. The Harpies were usually three in number, however, and they were most commonly named Celaeno, Nicotheon, and Thyella. Aeschylus, in his work *Eumenides*, was one of the first writers to depict the Harpies as ugly, misshapen, and monstrous. In some accounts, such as Virgil's AENEID, the Harpies are found at the entrance to the underworld.

The most famous Greek myth involving the Harpies is found in the stories of the Argonauts. In their QUEST FOR THE GOLDEN FLEECE, the Argonauts travel to Thrace where they meet the KING Phineus, who is being punished by the gods with blindness and premature old age for abusing his gift of prophecy. Phineus also is doomed never to eat from his own table because the Harpies swoop down and ravage his food, polluting everything with their disgusting smell. In return for advice on how to win the fleece, the Argonauts Zetes and Calais fight the Harpies and drive them across the sea to the Strophades in the Aegean where they promise never to torment Phineus again.

As the evolution of the Harpies indicates, Greek and Roman writers emphasized their negative role as cruel predators, as destroyers of life, and as the object of fear and hatred. The Harpies' breasts and oft-depicted flowing hair, however, point to their ancient role as a maternal figure, and in this way they share the dual role of many GODDESS figures as both creator and destroyer. *See also* SIRENS.

HARRIS, JOEL CHANDLER (1848–1908)

Author and folklorist of the American South, known primarily for his UNCLE REMUS stories. Harris was born in Eatonton, Georgia, and spent most of his adolescence there. His father was an itinerant Irish laborer who deserted the family some time around Harris's birth. At only thirteen years old, Harris apprenticed to *The Countryman*, the newspaper where he began his long career as a writer of humorous local-color sketches. By 1870, Harris had gained notoriety as a humorous writer for the *Morning News* in Savannah. He married in 1873 but had to remove his family to Atlanta in 1876 as the result of a yellow fever epidemic. Fortunately, the move helped Harris's career, as he earned recognition as the author of dialect stories for the Atlanta *Constitution*, a newspaper for which he would continue to write until 1900. After the appearance of his first *Uncle Remus* story in 1876, Harris's fame spread rapidly through the United States, and it continued to increase after the publication of his first book, *Uncle Remus: His Songs and Sayings* (1880).

Harris eventually published four other volumes of *Uncle Remus* stories as well as numerous collections of local-color sketches. The most noteworthy of these, "Free Joe and the Rest of the World" represents a departure from the humorous sketches that made Harris famous. Although Free Joe is "the humblest, the simplest" kind of person, he has no place as a free black man in a slave culture.

His status as an outsider extends even to the slaves who perhaps envy Joe his freedom. "Free Joe and the Rest of the World" demonstrates Harris's ability to go beyond the simpler tone of the *Uncle Remus* tales.

But it is for his humorous stories of Brer Rabbit, Brer Fox, and the TAR BABY that Harris is most well known. Throughout these talking ANIMAL tales, the format remains relatively constant: Uncle Remus tells a small white child stories of Mr. Fox's consistently failed attempts to capture and eat Mr. Rabbit. While the tales appear to be simple animal FABLES, the narrative structure of the stories is complex. Harris based the stories upon the African American storytellers (*see* AFRICAN AMERICAN STORYTELLING) he heard as a boy on his employer's plantation. It is significant, therefore, that he uses the narrative voice of Uncle Remus speaking to a white child about racially neutral animals. While Uncle Remus is a stereotyped character who holds no power in a white society, he does exercise an imaginative power over the child. Although modern readers may justifiably object to the stereotyped depiction of Uncle Remus, one must also recognize that the tales Remus recounts are far from simplistic. Through the clever figure of Brer Rabbit, the tales are subtly infused with a sense of the African American struggle to survive during the particularly hostile years of Reconstruction. For example, one may view Mr. Fox's persistent attempts to destroy Mr. Rabbit as a metaphor for the racial oppression of the post-Civil War era. Brer Rabbit sometimes reacts with flattery, sometimes with open deceit, but he always discovers something beyond physical power with which to thwart Brer Fox's attacks.

In two of the most famous of Harris's stories, "The Wonderful Tar-Baby Story" and "How Mr. Rabbit Was Too Sharp for Mr. Fox," Brer Fox tricks Brer Rabbit into striking a tar figure and rendering himself helpless. As Brer Fox howls with pleasure and contemplates his impending meal, Brer Rabbit pleads with the fox to eat him quickly but not to throw him in the briar patch. Brer Fox, whose cruelty outweighs his common sense, throws Brer Rabbit into the briar patch and soon spots the rabbit in the distance, combing the tar out of his fur. Brer Rabbit's only comment for Brer Fox is "Bred en bawn in a briar-patch, Brer Fox—bred en bawn in a briar-patch!"

In the history of American storytelling, Harris's work has been extremely influential. Apart from their enduring popularity as stories for children, Harris's work helped to define the conventions of Southern literature in the latter half of the nineteenth century. His use of dialect was adopted by those who attempted to justify the plantation tradition of the Old South through the image of the "happy slave." Others, such as African American writer Charles Chesnutt, employed an Uncle Remus-like figure who takes advantage of white fears and stereotypes for his own benefit. These two very different uses of Harris's style and characterizations attest to the complexity of his ostensibly simple tales. *See also* OLD SOUTH STORYTELLING.

For Further Reading

Brookes, Stella (Brewer). *Joel Chandler Harris, Folklorist*. Athens, GA: University of Georgia Press, 1950.

Cousins, Paul M. *Joel Chandler Harris: A Biography*. Baton Rouge: Louisiana State University Press, 1968.

Harris, Joel Chandler. *Free Joe and Other Georgian Sketches*. New York: Collier, 1887.

———. *Uncle Remus, His Songs and Sayings: The Folk-Lore of the Old Plantation*. New York: D. Appleton, 1881.

HARTLAND, EDWIN SIDNEY (1848–1927)

Folklorist and anthropologist. In 1890, Hartland published a collection of English folk literature gathered mostly from narrative sources. However, the tales he collected from periodicals and county collections reflect the presence of the oral tradition in the pastoral scene. In *The Science of Fairy Tales* (1890), Hartland explores the art of storytelling, the importance of time, and the character of the SWAN maiden in relation to the English FAIRY TALE. Hartland's work later shifted focus from FOLKLORE studies to the more anthropological study of institutions in uncivilized cultures. Hartland firmly believed that folklore studies and a vast majority of anthropological work was one and the same, as evidenced in his work on South American social systems and mythologies. Hartland is particularly important to the oral tradition because he believed in the notion of "cultural receptivity," which argues that folk literature is capable of migrating between disparate cultures. Although Hartland argues that a culture will appropriate a migratory folktale if the traditions and customs it values are similar to those from which the folktale originated, his argument does suggest the universality of folk literature. While some twentieth-century folklorists, including Richard M. Dorson, support Hartland's argument in favor for the universality of folktales, it must be acknowledged that a counter-movement that seeks to separate social anthropology and folklore studies is becoming increasingly accepted in academic folklore studies.

HAWAIIAN CREATION

Cosmology chanted in the long poem the *Kumilipo*, or "Genealogy of All Things." This 2,000-line poem tells the story of the Hawaiian CREATION; it was regularly chanted when a royal child was born. In its description of "creation from nothing," the *Kumilipo* depicts the various stages of the world's darkness gradually becoming light.

In the first stage, there is complete darkness. Night, the first male, Kumilipo, the "essence of darkness," and the first female, Po'ele, "darkness itself" were born from the original darkness. They parent "the children of darkness": the plants that emerge from seeds buried in the darkness of the earth, the insects that live in the dark soil, and the shellfish that live in the darkest depth of the ocean. Eventually there are more plants and animals and some light, but there are no humans beings and just one god, Kane-i-ka-wai-ola.

In the next stage, Pouliuli, a male representing "deep darkness," and Powehiwehi, a female representing "darkness with a little light," produce the various fish and more plants, but the EARTH is still quite dark. Then Po'el'ele, who is male and "dark night" and Pohaha, who is female and "night becoming dawn" are born, and they parent the night

insects, grasshoppers, flies, caterpillars, and an egg that cracks open to produce the first bird.

Now, dawn is close, but has not fully arrived. Another male and female, Popanopano and Polalowehi, are born and parent such animals as turtles and lobsters, which move from sea to land. The next male and female are then born, Po-kanokano and Po-lalo-uli. From them come the "dark and beautiful" pig, Kamapua'a, whose progeny—called "the ancient ones born at the end of the night"— cultivate the islands. Then "night ending" is born in the form of the male and female Po-hiolo and Po-ne'a-aku, and they give birth to the rat, Pilo'i, but the rats that follow scratch and eat the land, damaging it.

In the next stage, dawn, the WIND, and the dog are born to the male and female, Po-ne'e-aku and Poneie-mai, "night leaving and night pregnant." Humans are then born to Po-kinikini and Po-he'enalu. Finally, daylight comes to the world with the birth of the woman, "dark La'ila'a," and the man, dark Ki'i, and these two "knew the red-faced god Kane."

The story of the Hawaiian Creation is similar to other Polynesian Creation myths, though the names and stages of creation vary throughout Polynesia and Oceania.

For Further Reading

Leach, Maria. *The Beginning: Creation Myths around the World.* New York: Thomas Crowell, 1956.

HEAVEN

Place in the sky or above where the supreme deity or deities live and where people go after DEATH as a reward for earthly behavior. Because the sky is the source of light and warmth, and light symbolizes GOD or the GODS, the heavens began to take on religious meaning. The home of the supreme deity, heaven is imagined as a form of PARADISE where the blessed and faithful in life join the divine in the AFTERLIFE. Seen as a direct contrast to HELL, heaven might consist of several discrete heavens, each suited to a different human occupation.

Many stories tell of a heaven where the gods make their home. Sometimes a person can climb a ladder joining heaven and EARTH, symbolizing the connection between humankind and God. (*see* LADDER TO ANOTHER WORLD OR HEAVEN). The rainbow is also said to symbolize the bridge between heaven and earth, as in the Book of Genesis (*see* GENESIS, BOOK OF) when God causes a rainbow to appear to NOAH after the FLOOD recedes as a symbol of his promise to Noah that he will never again destroy humankind.

In Scandinavian mythology, Asgard is home of the gods and GODDESSES, and is reached by crossing the bridge, Bifrost. Divided into twelve realms, Asgard includes VALHALLA, the resting place of heroic warriors who have been killed in battle; Gladsheim, domain of ODIN and the chief gods; Thrudheim, home of Thor; Folkvang, realm of FREYA; Vingolf, realm of Frigga and the *asynjur;* Sokkvabekk, home of SAGA; Landvidi, home of Vidar; Breidablik, home of BALDR; Himinbiorg, home of Heimdall; Ydalir, the damp region of Uller; and Blitnir, the bright palace of Forseti.

For the Greeks, the Isles of the Blessed or the Elysian Fields, ruled by Kronos and located in the Western Ocean, are the destination of heroes and the blessed after death. ACHILLES is said to have been residing there since his death in the Trojan War. The Isle of Avalon, where the British King ARTHUR is said to have gone after his death, is similar to the Isles of the Blessed, and the Celts had Saint Brendan's Island, or the Island of the Blest, a joyful Otherworld much like the Christian Heaven. Eskimos call their heaven *Qudliven*, and it is described as a joyful place filled with pleasure and games. For Christians, the streets of heaven are paved with gold.

HECATE

Underworld GODDESS in ANCIENT GREEK STORYTELLING, associated with pathways and dark nights. Hecate is first mentioned in the *Theogony* by HESIOD. She is a synthesis of three goddesses: Selene, the goddess of the MOON; ARTEMIS, the goddess of the hunt; and Persephone, the queen of the underworld (*see* PERSEPHONE MYTH). Because of her tripartite nature, she is sometimes described as having three heads—one of a dog, one of a mare, and one of a lion. Robert Graves (*see* GRAVES, ROBERT) suggests that she was originally Hecuba, the Trojan queen who was transformed into a dog. Graves has also proposed that she may have been an early form of Cerberus, the three-headed dog who guards HADES.

Hecate is one of the Titans, the primordial deities who were overthrown by the GODS of MOUNT OLYMPOS. As such, one might guess her to be in bad stead among the Olympians, but this is not so. She is greatly respected by the gods for two services she performs for them. The first is when the GIANTS, brothers of the deposed Titans, rebel against ZEUS, the ruler of Olympos. Hecate sides with Zeus in the battle, and the victorious Olympian rewards her loyalty by allowing her to retain her talent of granting any gift she wishes to mortals.

The second service is when Persephone, the daughter of the goddess Demeter, is abducted by Hades and carried away into the underworld. Hecate and the SUN god, Helios, are the only witnesses to this crime; Hecate is the first to alert Demeter to her daughter's plight. She then leads Demeter on a torch-lit search for her daughter in Hades' realm. For this service, Hecate is rewarded with great powers in the underworld.

There Hecate remains as Persephone's companion; it is said that Persephone greatly prefers her company to that of her husband, Hades. Hecate holds the keys to the underworld and has the power to allow the ghosts of the dead to revisit the living. In the world of the dead, she is generally seen carrying a torch and accompanied by a pack of infernal hell-hounds.

Hecate is the mother of the once-beautiful Scylla, one of the NYMPHS. Scylla is transformed by the jealous sorceress CIRCE into a multi-headed monster rooted to a rock in the SEA, where she remains a danger to sailors ever afterward. Hecate also gives birth to the Empusae, fifty female DEMONS who run loose in the world at night and frightened travelers.

Despite her power to grant good luck, mortals are often wary of Hecate, because she became associated with WITCHES and black magic. She is the goddess of the crossroads, magical places frequented by ghosts. There mortals place triple-faced effigies of Hecate and offer her sacrifices of dogs, honey, and black lambs. Medea, the sorceress who marries Jason, is her priestess (*see* QUEST OF THE GOLDEN FLEECE). In her book *Hekate Soteira,* Sarah Iles Johnston suggests that post-classical scholars have over-emphasized these darker associations; Hecate is essentially a goddess of mediation between gods and humankind.

Hecate appears in Shakespeare's tragedy *Macbeth* (albeit in passages of disputed authorship) as the queen of the witches. At first, she excoriates the three weird sisters for speaking with Macbeth, then assists them in carrying out his doom.

The Hebrew LILITH is another version of Hecate.

For Further Reading

Johnson, Sarah Iles. *Hekate Soteira: A Study of Hekate's Roles in the Chaldean Oracles and Related Literature.* Atlanta: Scholars Press, 1990.

HEL

Name for both the Germanic underworld and its GODDESS, the queen of the dead. The precise location of the place Hel varies from legend to legend. In one Norse poem, men passed through Hel to die again in the vast depths of NIFLHEIM, nine worlds down. Generally, however, "Hel" is a broad term used to describe the infernal regions, while the names *Niflheim* and *Niflhel* emphasize the underworld's cold and fog (*nifl* means fog, mist, or murk). Often, in Norse mythology, the terms *hel, Niflheim,* and *Niflhel* are used interchangeably.

Hel is a dark, cold, and foggy region that one reaches by descending into the earth. The beginning of the road to Hel is an ominous black cave set among cliffs and ravines. In some stories, the cave is guarded by the hound, Garmr, who has blood on his chest from those who have attempted to escape. Garmr is chained at the entrance to Hel until RAGNAROK, the end of the world. The river Gjoll, meaning "howling" or "echoing," forms a boundary around Hel proper. Modgud, a mysterious maiden, guards Gjoll Bridge, which is roofed with gold. Beyond the bridge stands Hel Gate, barring the way to the hall of Hel, the queen of the underworld.

The parallels between Hel and the underworld of Greek mythology are evident: the descent into darkness; the hound Garmr and the hound Cerberus; and the crossing of a river watched over by a strange figure—in Greek mythology, the river Styx guarded by the ferryman Charon.

According to Norse legend, men who are not chosen for VALHALLA descend to Hel where they exist in miserable conditions until Ragnarok, at which point they will march out in legions and fight against the GODS. Some stories indicate that Hel is reserved for sinners, a possible influence of the Judeo-Christian mythological traditions of the underworld. Other Norse legends suggest that those who die of illness or old age reside in Hel. Niddhogg, the DRAGON who chews on one of YGGDRASIL'S roots, lives in Hel with a collection of serpents, and at least one passage from the existing sources for Norse mythology suggests that LOKI is a prisoner in the underworld.

The female monster Hel, the daughter of Loki and the giantess Angrboda, is the queen of the Norse underworld (*see* GIANTS). In order to avert disaster, ODIN, the ruler of the Norse pantheon, throws Hel down to the underworld and gives her absolute power over all who are sent there. Hel is hideous. Her upper body is that of a living woman, but, from the hips down, her skin is decayed and that of a corpse. Her expression is always gloomy.

The myth of the death of BALDR includes a vivid description of the journey to the Norse underworld. *See also* HADES, HELL, PURGATORY, SHEOL, TARTARUS, DESCENT TO THE UNDERWORLD.

HELEN OF TROY

In Greek MYTH, the daughter of the immortal god ZEUS and the mortal woman Leda. She is most celebrated as the cause of the Trojan War (*see* TROY).

Helen is the most beautiful woman in the world, and all the great men of Greece want to marry her. She is eventually won by MENELAOS, KING of Sparta, but only after all the other Greek leaders swear to defend the honor of Helen's future husband, whoever he might be.

Soon afterwards, the GODS hold a banquet to which Eris, the goddess of strife, is not invited. Eris avenges herself by tossing a golden apple, bearing the inscription "For the Fairest," into the scene of the banquet. The goddesses ATHENA, APHRODITE, and HERA all vie for the apple, each claiming to be the most beautiful.

The Trojan prince Paris, known for his appreciation for female beauty, is called upon to choose between the goddesses. He chooses Aphrodite, because she promises to reward him with the most beautiful woman in the world. This, of course, is Helen, whom Paris soon abducts while a guest in Menelaos's home.

Reluctant, but true to their oaths to Menelaos, the Greek leaders sail to TROY to win Helen back. The war they wage drags on for ten years, but the Greeks eventually prevail, and Menelaos brings Helen home to Sparta.

In the ILIAD of HOMER and two extant plays by Euripides—*Orestes* and *The Trojan Women*—Helen is portrayed unsympathetically as a vain and shallow woman indifferent to the vast suffering she inflicts upon two great cultures. In Homer's account, most of the Trojans and Greeks despise Helen, despite the fact that both sides were fighting for her.

There is, however, another version of the story that is much more sympathetic to Helen. This version reportedly originated with the Sicilian-born poet, Stesichorus, who was said by Plato to have been blinded by Helen for having maligned her. He repents and regains his sight by telling a very different story from Homer's. According to Stesichorus, Helen is faithful to Menelaos and never goes to Troy. Instead, she is kidnapped by Hermes and taken to Egypt, while a "phantom" Helen, created by Hera, is abducted by Paris. The real Helen virtuously resists the advances of

the Egyptian king, Theoclymenus, until she is rescued by her husband. This version of the Helen story is retold by Euripides in his fascinating and atypical tragicomedy, *Helen*.

In the post-classical world, Helen's image and reputation continued to be transformed. In Christopher Marlowe's Elizabethan play *Dr. Faustus,* she is portrayed as an ideal of feminine beauty, and her responsibility for the Trojan War is romanticized. And in the second part of his nineteenth-century poetic DRAMA, FAUST, Johann Wolfgang von Goethe carried this idealization of Helen still further. To Goethe, she was one personification (along with the Virgin MARY and Faust's betrayed lover, Gretchen) of a sublime but ultimately unattainable evolutionary goal, the "eternal feminine." Perhaps Goethe made reference to Stesichorus when he portrayed two different Helens in the second part of *Faust*— one illusory, the other real. *See also* ACHILLES, ANCIENT GREEK STORYTELLING.

For Further Reading

Euripides. *Helen.* Translated by Richmond Lattimore. Vol. 3, *The Complete Greek Tragedies.* Chicago: University of Chicago Press, 1959.

———. *The Trojan Women.* Translated by Richmond Lattimore. Vol. 3, *The Complete Greek Tragedies.* Chicago: University of Chicago Press, 1959.

Homer. *The Iliad.* Translated by Robert Fitzgerald. New York: Doubleday, 1974.

Treece, Henry. *The Windswept City: A Novel of the Trojan War.* Illustrated by Faith Jaques. New York: Meredith Press, 1967.

HELL

Domain of the DEVIL or the underworld of punishment. While the underworld of the Hebrews (SHEOL) and Greeks (HADES) was portrayed as an unappealing place, it becomes a place of punishment and suffering for sinners in the theology of Christianity as well as in other religions. The term "hell" is derived from HEL, the Norse GODDESS of DEATH, with its Germanic etymological roots meaning "hole," "hollow," and "conceal." The fiery hell with its sulfuric smell portrayed in so many stories comes from the image of volcanoes spewing lava as well as from the ravine outside of Jerusalem known as *Gehenna* in Latin and *Jehenna* in Arabic; this ravine was first used for sacrifices and later as a place for burning refuse.

In Hindu mythology, *Naraka* is a hell divided into 28 parts, each with its own name and form of punishment to fit the particular crime of the offenders sent there. These offenders must atone for their transgressions before they can be reincarnated on a higher or lower level, depending on each one's *karma*. In Norse mythology, NIFLHEIM is the name for the land of darkness and mist that is the lowest region of the underworld. Ruled by Hel, Niflheim is the place where those who died of age or disease went, as opposed to VALHALLA, the hall of specially chosen slain warriors. Hellfire for Moslems is supposed to be seven times hotter than fires on earth. The Etruscans, Japanese Buddhists, and Aztecs also have their own images of hell as a place of punishment.

The vision of hell described by Dante Alighieri (1265–1321) in *The Divine Comedy* gave rise to many later stories about the nature of hell and hell as a place of punishment. His work had an enormous influence on the way hell was imagined and described in all forms of storytelling and literature that followed. *See also* DEVIL.

HELPFUL ANIMALS

In MYTHS, FABLES, and FAIRY TALES, the ANIMALS that speak or understand and aid the HERO. Helpful animals come in all forms and can be found in the stories of most cultures. Some are able to speak, but others cannot, as in the case of the bear in the BEAR MAN MYTH of the Cherokee Indians of North America. Able to understand the hunter's thoughts, the bear feeds him throughout the winter and can communicate with him wordlessly through the mind; the tale offers a portrait of RESURRECTION as well as the connection between human beings and animals. In the Iroquois myth "HOW THE HUMAN RACE WAS SAVED," birds and animals pray to the GREAT SPIRIT to help the hero Nekumonta survive winter and sickness and save his lovely wife, Shanewis. Hanumat (or Hanuman), the MONKEY KING, serves as a forceful ally in Rama's fight against the demon Ravana in the Hindu myth in-

cluded in the RAMAYANA, and he helps Rama win back his wife Sita by leaping over the ocean and setting fire to Sri Lanka. As a reward, Rama bestows perpetual life and youth upon this helpful animal. In Greek mythology, Pegasus the FLYING HORSE is crucial in helping the human Bellerophon slay the dreadful MONSTER, the CHIMERA.

In more recent storytelling, the generous spider Charlotte helps both animals and humans in E.B. White's *Charlotte's Web*, the Christ-like lion, Aslan, helps the children of C.S. Lewis's *The Chronicles of Narnia*, wolves raise the Indian baby, Mowgli, in Rudyard Kipling's *Jungle Book* (*see* KIPLING, RUDYARD), and DRAGONS help the mage, Ged, several times in Ursula Le Guin's *EarthSea Quartet*. In Walt Disney's film version of the GRIMM BROTHER's fairy tale "Snow White," animals help Snow White clean the cottage of the seven dwarfs.

From a Jungian point of view, helpful animals represent the instinctual side of ourselves, and as Jungian psychoanalyst and author Marie-Louise von Franz writes in *Shadow and Evil in Fairy Tales*, "one must never hurt the helpful animal in fairy tales," for "if any animal gives you advice and you don't follow it, then you are finished." Von Franz notes that this is the "one rule which seems to have no exception" in hundreds of stories and fairy tales of all nations. For her, this means that "obedience to one's most basic inner being, one's instinctual inner being, is the one thing which is more essential than anything else."

For Further Reading

Denman, Cherry. *The Little Peacock's Gift*. New York: Bedrick/Blackie, 1987.

Kipling, Rudyard. *Jungle Book*. 1895. Reprint, New York: Penguin, 1987.

Le Guin, Ursula K. *A Wizard of EarthSea*. New York: Houghton, 1968.

Sax, Boria. *The Frog King: On Legends, Fables, Fairy Tales and Anecdotes of Animals*. New York: Pace University Press, 1990.

HENRY, JOHN

African American folk HERO featured in many American BALLADS. John Henry is an exceptionally strong railroad worker who pits himself against a steam drill and succeeds in crushing more rock than the machine, but dies from the effort, the hammer still in his hand.

The story originated during the construction of the Big Bend Tunnel of the Chesapeake and Ohio railroad through the rugged hills of West Virginia in the early 1870s. The steam drill was introduced during this project, and so comparative tests probably occurred. From this central incident the legend of John Henry spread through the Southern work camps, where he came to rival Paul Bunyan (*see* BUNYAN, PAUL) and Pecos Bill as a figure of extraordinary strength. As the story spread, more songs arose, containing details of his childhood—he weighed 44 pounds at birth and set out to seek work after eating his first meal. Songs about his enormous sexual prowess with shantytown women abounded; thus making him a symbol of double potency. Regional variations of John Henry arose. In Kentucky, he was white. Roark Bradford codifies the tales in his *John Henry* (1931). The figure of John Henry has been interpreted as a symbol of the oppression of black people by whites, and as indicative of the subjugation of human dignity by the machine. The principal song concerning John Henry is probably derived from a Scottish tune and was played on the banjo and the guitar. *See also* TALL TALES.

For Further Reading

Gianni, Garry. *John Henry.* New York: Kipling Press, 1988.

Lester, Julius. *John Henry.* Illustrated by Jerry Pinckney. New York: Dial Press, 1994.

HERA

Goddess of Greek mythology, one of the twelve Olympians. Hera is the daughter of the Titans Kronos and Rhea. She is sometimes portrayed as a jealous and independent figure, other times as a long-suffering wife in a stormy marriage with her brother ZEUS.

The worship of Hera, however, predated that of Zeus, with roots in the older matrilineal system. The Heracean Games for women were held at Olympia long before the Olympic games for men were established there. Hera was the pre-Hellenic Great GODDESS, the EARTH MOTHER. She was originally connected with the three stages of woman's life—maiden, fertile woman, and elder (*see* MAIDEN, MOTHER, CRONE).

In later patriarchal mythology, Hera became the unsympathetic wife of a philanderer and was designated the goddess of MARRIAGE. In *Goddess: Myths of the Female Divine,* David Leeming and Jake Page observe that in her new role, "she appeared to lend female approbation to the very institution by which the old matrilineal rights were most clearly usurped by the patriarchy that saw wives as belonging, like other valuable objects, to their husbands."

In the classical story, Zeus seeks out his sister Hera and courts her. She turns him down, but he persists. Finally, he uses the technique of DISGUISE that was to work so well for him with other women in the future. Zeus appears to Hera as a cuckoo bird, and she takes him to her bosom. He then resumes his true identity and rapes her. Hera is shamed into marrying Zeus, but they remain often at odds with one another.

With Zeus, Hera gives birth to Ares, the god of war; to Hebe, the goddess of youth; to Eilethyia, the goddess of birth; and to Hephaistos, the crippled god of fire and the forge. She is also stepmother to her husband's illegitimate children, including Herakles and DIONYSOS.

Many stories describe Hera taking revenge on the mistresses of her husband or on their children. For example, Hera is furiously jealous of her husband's affair with a mortal named Alcemena. The goddess becomes determined to destroy the child of that union, Herakles. She sends two great snakes to kill Herakles and his brother, but the year-old hero kills the snakes. Hera hounds Herakles throughout his life, visiting madness and other disasters on him. She finally reconciles with the hero after he is taken to HEAVEN, where he marries her daughter Hebe (*see* LABORS OF HERAKLES).

Hera can be quite beneficial toward those who gain her favor. She manipulates Medea in order to aid Jason, and she provides guides for the Argonauts along their voyage. During the Trojan War she takes the side of the

Greeks, opposing her husband even when he orders the other Olympians to stay out of the conflict. In fact, Hera uses the magic girdle of APHRODITE to enhance her own attractions and seduce Zeus, distracting his attention from the battle.

The sources of Hera's story include the ILIAD and the *Theogony* of HESIOD. *See also* ANCIENT GREEK STORYTELLING, APOLLO, CENTAURS, DELPHI, HELEN OF TROY, IO, NARCISSUS, QUEST FOR THE GOLDEN FLEECE, TIRESIAS, TROY.

For Further Reading

Graves, Robert. *The Greek Myths.* 2 vols. New York: Penguin, 1957.

Spretnak, Charlene. *Lost Goddesses of Early Greece: A Collection of Pre-Hellenic Myths.* 4th ed. Boston: Beacon Press, 1992.

HERCULES *See* LABORS OF HERAKLES

HERO

Archetypal figure in all forms of storytelling who overcomes a series of trials to arrive at a state of transcendence. In the words of Joseph Campbell, "The hero is the man or woman who has been able to battle past his personal and local historical limitations to the generally valid, normally human forms." In order to find himself or herself, the hero must undergo certain RITES OF PASSAGE, or events, that Campbell calls the *monomyth* of the hero, which forms a universal pattern, or archetype. These events can be divided into eight basic rites of passage.

The first phase of monomyth of the hero begins with conception and birth, and those events immediately succeeding birth. Often the conception of the hero is miraculous in that the hero's mother may be a virgin, as in the case of Jesus and KARNA. As soon as the hero is born, he or she must be hidden or abandoned, and may need to be reborn in a river or alone (*see* DIVINE CHILD, HIDING THE CHILD, REBIRTH.)

The second stage of the hero's journey involves initiation during childhood and the presence of DIVINE SIGNS that signify that this person is indeed out of the ordinary. The Hindu hero KRISNA, avatar of VISNU, was capable of slaying a demoness and still a whirl-wind caused by a DEMON while yet an infant in the cradle. The Greek hero Herakles succeeded in defeating evil serpents while a baby. These early TESTS or trials show that the child has heroic qualities.

The third stage involves a period of withdrawal or meditation on the part of the hero before he or she embarks on the QUEST in the fourth stage. This withdrawal may take the form of a period of time of isolation in a cave, the desert, or a mountain top, where separation from the world and resistance to temptation is accomplished. Only then can the hero set out to overcome the trials with which he or she is confronted. While the meditative stage symbolizes the inner trials, the quest symbolizes the outer trials. These trials continue into the fifth stage, or rite of passage, when the hero faces physical death and potential dismemberment.

In the sixth stage, the hero must face DEATH through a DESCENT TO THE UNDERWORLD, where the return or ascent from the underworld brings the hero to a higher plane of wisdom and awareness. The seventh stage, then, is the hero as SCAPEGOAT who rises from the dead. Resurrection here signifies rebirth and renewal. The final stage, in which immortality is achieved, is brought about through ASCENSION to HEAVEN, atonement, and APOTHEOSIS. Self-realization and a higher state of awareness, joined with a transformation to the status of a divinity, are all part of this final stage in the monomyth of the hero.

For Further Reading

Campbell, Joseph. *The Hero with a Thousand Faces.* Princeton: Princeton University Press, 1968.

Leeming, David. *Mythology: The Voyage of the Hero.* New York: HarperCollins, 1992.

Low, Alice. *The Macmillan Book of Greek Gods and Heroes.* Illustrated by Arvis Steward. New York: Macmillan, 1985.

Rank, Otto. *The Myth of the Birth of the Hero.* New York: Knopf, 1959.

San Souci, Robert D. *Larger Than Life*: *The Adventures of American Legendary Heroes.* Illustrated by Andrew Glass. New York: Doubleday, 1991.

HEROINE

Female HERO who undergoes a QUEST. Like the hero, the heroine has to have her own form of quest, which at times may take a more internal form than the journey-quest of the hero. The female quest make take the form of initiation through incubation into selfhood. As Marie-Louise von Franz notes, where the male hero "has to go into the Beyond and try to slay the monster, or to find the treasure, or the bride" and therefore "make more of a journey and accomplish some deed instead of just staying out of life," the heroine has to experience some form of isolation, and afterwards comes the return into life.

This incubation can be seen in such FAIRY TALES as "Snow White," where Snow White goes into the forest and then into the coffin; "Sleeping Beauty," where the heroine sleeps for one hundred years; "Rapunzel," who is isolated in a tower; and "The Seven Swans," where the sister's sewing and silence are signs of deep introversion that will lead to her brothers' renewal as human men. Von Franz sees this incubation as a form of internal quest even though it appears as if most of these heroines are, as Susan Cooper writes, "chosen for their beauty (*en soi*), not for anything they do (*pour soi*)," and "they seem to exist passively until they are seen by the hero, or described to him." On the surface the heroines are passive and helpless, waiting to be chosen, but inside they may be achieving selfhood as vigorously as the hero with his feats of physical prowess and his visible journeying.

Not all heroines appear passive, as exemplified by Gretel in the GRIMM BROTHERS's "Hansel and Gretel." She is the one to save Hansel by pushing the witch into the oven in his place. In "The Seven Ravens," the heroine must go on a long journey to the sun, moon, and stars to get help from the morning star. Von Franz writes that "In fairy tales on feminine psychology when the heroine makes the quest by such a heavenly journey, there is very often a reversal of values in which the sun is the most evil power, the moon rather evil, and the night with its teeming stars beneficial, in contrast to the usual interpretation by which the sun is the source of enlightenment and the night the darkening power to be avoided."

Another kind of fairy tale in which the heroine plays an active savior role is the "ANIMAL groom" MOTIF, where the heroine is kind to the animal, who then turns out to be a PRINCE or KING who has been under a SPELL. Her love—or anger—becomes the source of transformation, as in "Beauty and the Beast," "Snow-White and Rose-Red," and "The Frog King." In Norse mythology, heroines tend to be strong, as portrayed by the three Valkyries.

For Further Reading

Le Guin, Ursula. *The Tombs of Atuan*. New York: Houghton, 1971.

Riordan, Jane. *The Woman in the Moon and Other Tales of Forgotten Heroines*. Illustrated by Angela Barrett. New York: Dial, 1984.

Saxby, Maurice. *The Great Deeds of Heroic Women*. Illustrated by Robert Ingpen. New York: Peter Bedrick Books, 1990.

HERSKOVITS, MELVILLE JEAN
(1895–1963)

Anthropologist and Africanist, and founder of the first African Studies program in the United States at Northwestern University. Herskovits is attributed with providing scientific evidence that links the New World African-Americans to a specific geographic location in West Africa, and establishing an entire field of anthropological and sociological studies around the diaspora of millions of Africans to the West. Aside from being elected president of the American FOLKLORE Society (1945), Herskovits' interest in oral literature culminated in the publication of *Dahomean Narrative* (1958), which classifies the genres and subgenres of Dahomean folk literature. Dahomean oral tales are divided into two major categories, the *hwenoho* (MYTHS) and the *heho* (tales), which are then further divided into numerous other categories, including numerous tales about women and their dichotomous delineation as either "devoted wife" or "faithless woman." Herskovits's other studies of African and African-American folklore include Bulu tales, Trinidad proverbs, and pidgin English tales from both Nigerian and Ashanti peoples. *See also* AFRICAN-AMERICAN STORYTELLING, AFRICAN STORYTELLING.

For Further Reading

Herskovits, Melville J., and Frances S. Herskovits *Dahomean Narrative: A Cross-Cultural Analysis.* Evanston, IL: Northwestern University Press, 1958.

Simpson, George Eaton. *Melville J. Herskovits.* New York: Columbia University Press, 1973.

HESIOD (c. 800 B.C.)

Greek didactic poet, famous for two major works, *The Works and Days* and the *Theogony.* While *The Works and Days* is a sermon written to his brother, Perses, and deals with axioms concerning farming along with some autobiographical material, it is the *Theogony* with its depiction of the Greek cosmogony that has influenced so much of the oral tradition that followed it. Hesiod relied on HOMER, the oral tradition of the Greeks, and the mythology of the Ancient Near East in creating his *Theogony*, but he is to be credited as the first to establish such a pattern of the GODS and their various functions.

As a poem, the *Theogony* is divided into 12 sections, with the opening and closing sections focusing on ZEUS's monarchy and his distribution of rights and privileges over the other gods. Books II-V depict the basic structure of the physical and human cosmos, and Books VI-XI describe Zeus's emergence as the monarch who rules over all that is divine, human, and physical in the cosmos. The four appendices offer catalogues of the Muses, the Children of the Night, the Daughters of Nereus, and the Children of the Ocean. As Norman O. Brown notes in his introduction to his translation of the *Theogony*, "The direction of the cosmic evolution is not only from a natural to an anthropocentric order, but also from the primacy of the female to the primacy of the male." This movement toward male dominance can be seen in the way Zeus shows much more ingenuity and power than his mother Rhea, who had been more powerful than his father Kronos; in the birth of APHRODITE, "the divine counterpart of the prototype of womankind manufactured by Zeus," from the castrated sexual organs of her father, the Sky; and in the story of PROMETHEUS AND THE THEFT OF FIRE, which causes Zeus to inflict on mankind the curse of womankind. In the world of Hesiod, women are an unproductive luxury. Though often violent, Zeus's regime also strengthens the forces of good over evil.

For Further Reading

Hesiod. *Theogony.* Translated by Norman O. Brown. Indianapolis: Bobbs-Merrill, 1953.

HIAWATHA TARENYAWAGON

Iroquois LEGEND of the founding of the Five Nation Confederacy of the Iroquois. Although the story of Hiawatha is well-known through the poet Longfellow's poem of the same name ("Hiawatha," 1855), Longfellow was in fact writing about an Algonquin deity named Michabo. For the Iroquois of the land that is now upstate New York and who were the enemy of the Algonquin, Tarenyawagon was the deity who upheld the HEAVENS. He came to EARTH to help humankind when people were in despair from fighting and anarchy.

In the story, Tarenyawagon takes a little girl by the hand and leads the surviving humans to a cave, where they rest and regain hope. Then he has them build a great lodge where the sun rises, and eventually they flourish and proliferate. Tarenyawagon tells the people they must form five great nations, and taking the little girl by the hand, he separates them into the Mohawk nation, who speak differently, and to whom he gives squash, beans, tobacco, corn, and dogs for hunting; the Oneida nation, who have fine forests and their own language, too; the Onondaga who live on the mountain and speak their own language; the Cayuga who live by Lake Goyoga; and the Seneca, who are the sentinels of the five nations and live on Canandaigua mountain. Each nation is given special gifts: the Onondaga receive knowledge of special laws and the power to understand the Creator, the Mohawks receive prowess in hunting, and the Oneidas receive the ability to make both baskets and weapons. The girl whose hand Tarenyawagon holds as he makes each nation represents the matriarchal tradition of the Iroquois, whose most revered leaders are the old women who were once these girls.

All goes well until the Five Nations are attacked by the Algonquins. Joining together, they wait for Tarenyawagon to lead them. Now called Hiawatha, Tarenyawagon has been living among the Onondaga people, where he marries and has a daughter, Mnihaha. Hiawatha is able to bring peace to the Five Nations, but only in exchange for Mnihaha, who is carried away by the Great Mystery Bird of Heaven after her father gives her his blessing. After grieving deeply for three days, Hiawatha bathes in the lake to cleanse and purify himself. He then brings together each of the leaders of the Five Nations and tells them they must become one nation undivided, which will ensure their survival, and the wisest woman should be their ruler. Each nation has a particular role: the Onondagas become the warriors; the Seneca, the spokespeople; the Cayuga, the ones who guard the rivers; and the Mohawk, the hunters and farmers. The legend of Hiawatha Tarenyawagon ends with the formation of this powerful confederacy, as Hiawatha rides off in his magic birch canoe and ascends into the sky.

For Further Reading

Erdoes, Richard, and Alfonso Ortiz. *American Indian Myths and Legends.* New York: Pantheon, 1985.

HIDING THE CHILD

Aspect of the birth stage of the life and QUEST of the HERO. The birth of the hero usually involves a miraculous birth, and, in a number of cases, the subsequent hiding of the child to prevent him or her from coming to harm. The hiding of the child usually occurs in a place that can be seen as symbolic of the womb, such as a cave, a stable, a grotto, or in a river or the SEA. The MOTIF suggests that the DIVINE CHILD or hero is being reborn from the Great Mother, a universal symbol, just as the hero transcends the personal and represents the universal ARCHETYPE. The difficulties that the hero faces and cause him or her to be hidden represent the difficulties in life and the lack of protection from the negative forces both within and without. When the hero is placed in the river or sea, he or she experiences a purifying rite of passage or initiation, and the subsequent adoption makes the hero ultimately be adopted by everyone.

Many examples of the hiding of the child occur in storytelling and MYTH. In *The Myth of the Birth of the Hero*, Otto Rank traces the recurrent motifs present in these stories, beginning with the birth of Sargon, the founder of Babylonia, dating back to 2800 B.C. In Sargon's own words, he claims he was the son of a vestal, born in a hidden place, laid in a vessel made of reeds with the door sealed with pitch, dropped into the river, and found by Akki the water carrier and adopted and raised by him. When he grew up, he became a gardener for Akki until Ishtar (INANNA) the Queen fell in love with him and married him; he reigned as KING for the next 45 years.

Other heroes who are hidden at birth include the Hebrew Moses (*see* EXODUS); the Hindu KARNA; the Greek Oedipus, ZEUS, Telephus, Perseus, DIONYSOS, Herakles, and ATHENA; the Trojan Paris; the Polynesian MAUI; the Celtic TRISTAN; and the Norse SIEGFRIED. Moses is hidden in an ark in the bulrushes when the Pharaoh decrees that the sons of all Hebrews must be thrown in the river; the Pharaoh's daughter finds and adopts him, with his own sister, Miriam, serving as his nurse. Like Moses, Karna is hidden in a basket amid the rushes and placed in the river until he is found by Radha and her husband the charioteer, who raise him as their own. Oedipus is given at birth to a slave by his parents, Laius and Jocasta, who have been warned by the oracle that if they have a son, he will slay his father; however, the slave cannot bear to leave the baby exposed to die on the mountain (one VARIANT says he is supposed to be thrown over a cliff and another says he is exposed in a box on the sea) and instead gives him to another shepherd who brings him to King Polybus and Queen Merope of Corinth, who adopt him. Paris, too, is supposed to be exposed because of prophecies that say he will bring ruin upon his city, but when the slave Agelaos leaves him and Paris survives by being nursed for five days by a bear, Agelaos comes back and, finding Paris, adopts him as his own. In one version of the birth of Telephus, his mother Auge hides him in the temple. Athena is sewn into the thigh of her father Zeus and later born full-grown from his forehead. Maui's mother wraps her premature son in a piece of the top-knot of her hair and throws him into the sea; after he is raised by "the old man of the sea," he returns to his mother to establish his relationship with his family.

HINDU STORYTELLING

History of the storytelling tradition in Hindu India. In the small villages all over India, the *Pandit* was the official storyteller, and in some villages continues to be so. He is usually an old man who begins the session with a prayer. While he once had an accompaniment of musical instruments, now he uses only his voice. His stories come from the vast store of literature he has memorized, including every line and stanza of the RAMAYANA, the MAHABHARATA, and the *Bhagavad Gita*. While he may have a Sanskrit text in front of him, it is more for show since he is self-reliant in his knowledge of each work.

The nature of the Pandit's storytelling follows an oral tradition that has been in place for centuries and dictated everything from the tone of voice used for each word to the Pandit's dress. Gifts were brought to him in exchange for his storytelling. He practiced and perfected the pronunciation of every word, and his knowledge of Sanskrit was complete. The Pandit might interject an epigram when he felt that his audience's reaction to be excessive, for he believed in the dignity of his stories. For him, the VEDAS were created by GOD, and he treated them with reverence. What was important for him, whether the tales were drawn from the eighteen major PURANAS or any of the other texts, was the spiritual truths they embody. All the Hindu texts combine stories, ethics, philosophy, scriptures, moral codes, mysticism, semantics, astrology, and astronomy. Goodness always triumphs.

The major characters are always the same—the triumvirate of GODS formed by BRAHMA the creator, VISNU the protector and preserver, and SIVA the destroyer. They are central to every story, as is KRISNA, the *avatar* of Visnu, and the *shaktis* or female companions of the gods—the different forms taken by DEVI. All the tales have sages who live isolated in the woods, DEMONS (*asuras* and *rakshasas*), KINGS, and gods. Another common element is that of the PRINCESS who comes of age and is allowed to choose her own husband in the *Swayamwara* ceremony.

For Further Reading

Narayan, R.K. *Gods, Demons, and Others*. Chicago: University of Chicago Press, 1993.

HLAKANYANA *See* AFRICAN STORYTELLING

HOBGOBLINS *See* GOBLINS

HOLIDAYS

Days or periods of days that often serve as occasions for the telling of particular stories. As with the Jewish holiday of Passover, which celebrates the Jewish EXODUS from Egypt, and the Christian holiday of Easter, which celebrates the resurrection of Jesus Christ, each religious holiday serves as a celebration of a certain religious story. Thus, it is not surprising that celebrations often involve the retelling of the specific story that the occasion celebrates, as well other stories that that have become in some way tied to the celebration. Perhaps the most widely celebrated holiday, and the holiday with the most stories connected to it, is Christmas. Each yearly celebration of Christmas involves, of course, the retelling of the narration to which the day is dedicated: the birth of Christ. This tale, and those related tales, like the tale of the three wise men who give the Christ child gifts, is told through story and song each year. There are countless other stories that are retold upon each celebration of this holiday, like those involving the legend of SANTA CLAUS (also called SAINT NICHOLAS).

HOLY GRAIL

Powerful talisman, best known for its importance in the Arthurian cycle of medieval ROMANCES. Always mysterious and holy, the Grail is usually represented as a chalice, a dish, or a cup into which a lance drips blood. The Grail and the maiden who carries it are described as radiant with blazing light.

The Grail legend is woven from Irish and Welsh MYTH and may have originated in a pagan cult, in which the grail and bleeding spear were fertility symbols. The basic elements of the story appeared in an Irish tale before 1056.

The legend is also found in the fourteenth-century Welsh *Mabinogion,* which is based on earlier oral traditions. The Grail originally may have been one of the magic possessions of Bran, who never grew old. In one story, the Grail provides food and drink for an eighty-year feast. In later versions it remains connected with spiritual and physical sustenance and healing, as well as immortality.

The earliest surviving Grail story is CHRÉTIAN DE TROYES' 1180 *Perceval* or *Le Conte du Graal.* In that account, the would-be knight, PERCIVAL, meets the long-suffering Fisher King in his disappearing castle. Percival fails to ask a certain question of the king, and spends much of his career searching for a second chance to do so.

In thirteenth-century Christian legend, the Grail was a goblet or dish used by Jesus at the last supper. It came into the possession of Joseph of Arimathea, who caught some of the blood of Jesus in it at the crucifixion. Joseph took the Grail to England, where it provided him with lifetime food, drink, and spiritual nourishment. The Grail was handed down to Joseph's successors and finally to Sir Galahad, the most perfect Knight of the Round Table at King ARTHUR's court.

In most versions of the Arthurian romances, the Grail has vanished because the times had grown evil. The Knights of the Round Table swear an oath to find the holy object. The Grail is guarded by the Grail Keepers in a castle that is not always visible. Only the completely pure can see the holy vessel, and LANCELOT becomes disqualified because of his infidelity with GUINEVERE. SIR GAWAIN gives way to other distractions and adventures. Galahad has the ultimate experience of looking into the Grail, after which he abandons this life and is carried up to heaven. In some stories, Percival and Lancelot's cousin, Bors, also see the Grail.

The Grail stories are complex and inconsistent, switching back and forth between allegory and literal storytelling. The traditional legend appears in Sir Thomas Malory's *Morte d'Arthur* and Tennyson's *Idyls of the King,* and has been retold in Christian stories across the years. But the theme of a quest for the holiest of objects has also inspired the authors of related stories.

In T.S. Eliot's 1922 poem, *The Waste Land,* the Grail takes back its pagan fertility-symbol form. Grail-centered characters and quests appear in C.S. Lewis's 1945 novel *That Hideous Strength.* The basic elements of the Grail legend are integrated into a baseball story in Bernard Malamud's 1952 novel, *The Natural,* and the 1984 film based on the book. And there have, of course, been swashbuckling Hollywood film treatments of the legend. The 1975 film *Monty Python and the Holy Grail* is a parody of those efforts. *See also* CELTIC STORYTELLING.

For Further Reading

Cavendish, Richard. *King Arthur & the Grail: The Arthurian Legends and Their Meaning.* London: Weidenfeld and Nicolson, 1978.

Caxton's Malory: Morte d'Arthur. University of California Press, 1983.

Hopkins, Andrea. *Chronicles of King Arthur.* London: Collins & Brown, 1993.

Lagorio, Valerie M., and Mildred Leake Day. *King Arthur through the Ages.* 2 vols. New York: Garland Publishing, 1990.

Malamud, Bernard. *The Natural.* New York: Harcourt, Brace, 1952.

Scherer, Margaret R. *About the Round Table: King Arthur in Art and Literature.* The Metropolitan Museum of Art, 1945. Reprint, New York: Arno Press, 1974.

Tennyson, Alfred. *Idyls of the King.* London: Ticknor and Fields, 1866.

HOMER

Legendary author of Greek EPIC poems. The two most important works attributed to Homer are the ILIAD and the ODYSSEY. Traditional biographies of Homer dating from classical times are highly contradictory. At least seven cities have been claimed as his birthplace. According to one tradition, Homer was actually a woman. Most accounts agree that the poet was blind.

Whether or not there was ever any such person is impossible to determine. If a Homer really did exist, it would likely have been during the ninth century B.C., when the *Iliad* and the *Odyssey* were first compiled. For at least four centuries before then, BARDS or *aoidoi* developed these stories through the oral tradition, drawing on MYTH, FOLKLORE, and history. Did one person execute the compilations of the ninth century? The current scholarly consensus considers this unlikely. The *Iliad* and the *Odyssey* are highly individual poems; they appear to have been compiled by different hands at different times. The stylistic evidence for this has long been recognized. The *Iliad* is rough-hewn, contradictory, and archaic, while the *Odyssey* is well-constructed, harmonious, and even novelistic.

In recent years, psychological differences have been noted as well, especially by Julian Jaynes in *The Origin of Consciousness in the Breakdown of the Bicameral Mind.* The HEROES of the *Iliad* are volitionless and puppet-like, while Odysseus in the *Odyssey* is cunning and resourceful. That one poet was responsible for two such dissimilar works seems highly doubtful.

Such differences notwithstanding, the possibility still exists that the *Iliad* and the *Odyssey* were each executed by a single compiler. But there is neither evidence for nor against the supposition that one of these compilers was a blind poet named Homer.

Even after their composition in the ninth century B.C., the *Iliad* and the *Odyssey* were handed down by way of the oral tradition for several hundred years. They were edited and arranged by the Athenian ruler Pisistratus in the sixth century B.C. His versions were recited by performers known as *rhapsodes* at the Panathenaic festivals. The version that has been handed down to us dates from the second century B.C., and was edited by the critic and scholar Aristarchus.

In Classical Greece, the Homeric canon had a virtually religious status. These poems were considered invaluable receptacles of cultural identity, their heroes revered as the founders of Greek civilization. Much classical storytelling was derived from the two great Homeric epics and the related Epic Cycle. This is especially true of Greek tragedy in fifth-century B.C. Athens. Athenian dramatists frequently drew on Homeric lore to comment on current events, not always with blind respect. For example, Euripides's *Trojan Women* used the unheroic treatment of women after the Trojan War as a metaphor for war atrocities recently committed by his fellow Athenians.

The influence of the Homeric epics reverberates down to our own century. This can be seen not only in works of "high" literary art, like James Joyce's *Ulysses,* but in popular art as well. The movie creations of George Lucas represent a fine example. His *Indiana Jones* movies portray a cunning, courageous, Odysseus-like hero, while his *Star Wars* trilogy presents an *Iliad*-like conflict over the heart and soul of a civilization. *See also* ANCIENT GREEK STORYTELLING.

For Further Reading

Jaynes, Julian. *The Origin of Consciousness in the Breakdown of the Bicameral Mind.* Boston: Houghton Mifflin, 1990.

Latacz, Joachim. *Homer: His Art and His World.* Ann Arbor, MI: University of Michigan Press, 1995.

HOPI CREATION MYTH

Creation by deities who sang the world and human beings into life, from the Hopi oral tradition. In the beginning, the earth is nothing but water and only two spirits exist. Tawa, the SUN god, holds power in the Above. SPIDER WOMAN, the earth GODDESS, rules over the Below. They live together in the Underworld, the abode of the GODS.

When they decide to create other gods, Tawa and Spider Woman each divide into two deities. This produces Huzruiwuhti and Muiyinwuh, who become the first lovers and bring forth many other deities.

Then Spider Woman and Tawa decide to create a world between the Above and the Below. They stand together and sing the EARTH into being. Tawa forms strange images in his mind and Spider Woman shapes the first creatures out of clay. They put a woolen blanket over the figures and bring them into life with a powerful incantation.

Spider Woman and Tawa also create beings like themselves to rule over the ANIMALS. The blanket magic does not work on the new creatures, so the deities have to sing the humans into life. Then Tawa takes his place in the Above, so his light will shine down on the newly-populated world.

Spider Woman separates the people into tribes and tell them who they are. She leads the newly created animals and people out of the Underworld. They pass through an opening called a *sipapu* into the newly created world. To this day *kivas*—the underground chambers used for social and religious activities—have a small hole, or *sipapu*, in the floor.

Spider Woman assigns a different creature to lead each group to a special place where they will live. She gives them rules to live by, teaches them how to grow FOOD, and assigns them jobs to do.

In another version of the Hopi creation story, it is two goddesses called the Huruing Wuhti who cause the waters to recede and the dry land to appear. They sing the birds and animals and one human couple into life. Then Spider Woman creates a man and woman and teaches them Spanish. Spider Woman continues creating other couples and giving them other languages. But she forgets to complete the pair in two cases, which is why some men and women do not find mates.

In *The World of Myth*, David Leeming notes, "The dominance of Spider Woman, the female creative principle, befits a culture that remains to this day matrilineal."

Many Native American creation stories (including that of the Mayan POPOL VUH) emphasize the division of humankind into tribes. The JAPANESE CREATION MYTH describes the work of a pair of deities, and the Maya creation results from collaboration and conversation. The opening of the book of John in the New Testament of the BIBLE also suggests a creation that begins with divine vocalization: "When all things began, the Word already was." *See also* CREATION, NATIVE NORTH AMERICAN STORYTELLING.

For Further Reading

Erdoes, Richard, and Alfonso Ortiz. *American Indian Myths and Legends*. New York: Pantheon, 1985.

HORUS

Egyptian god, also known as Hawk the Avenger or the falcon-headed sky-god, son of ISIS AND OSIRIS. Like the stories of the birth of QUETZALCOATL, BUDDHA, MAUI, DIONYSUS, Jesus, and ZOROASTER, the story of Horus's birth belongs to the ARCHETYPE of the DIVINE CHILD and his or her miraculous conception. Although Osiris is dead, Isis manages to conceive when she takes the form of a hawk and flutters over her husband's corpse as he lies in a swamp. Like Moses, the infant Horus has to be hidden from his wrathful uncle, Seth, who is responsible for his father's death (*see* HIDING THE CHILD, EXODUS). One day Isis returns to find her son has died from a scorpion's sting. By praying to the SUN-god, Ra, Isis is able to save Horus: Ra sends the god, Thoth, to instruct her in performing a SPELL that will remove the poison from Horus's body.

Later MYTHS about the grown Horus tell of his efforts to avenge his father's death. He succeeds in capturing Seth, but while he is pursuing Seth's helpers, Seth manages to coax Isis to let him go. In his anger at finding Seth freed by his mother, Horus beheads Isis, whom Thoth then restores with the crown and head of the ancient goddess Hathor. Mother and son then pursue Seth once more, but Seth retaliates by tearing out the eye of Horus, which contains his soul. Horus successfully retrieves his eye, and he and Isis drive Seth into the SEA. Horus is then responsible for resurrecting his father by embracing Osiris's corpse, transferring his *ka* or spirit-double to Osiris, and feeding him the eye that Horus replaces with the divine serpent, thereafter the emblem of royalty. Horus's strength reaches Osiris, making him a "*ka*-in-harmony." Osiris, alive once more, ascends the LADDER TO HEAVEN, and there he proclaims Horus his son and earthly heir. As David Leeming notes in *The World of Myth*, this renewal reflects the "questions of pharaonic legitimacy and the AFTERLIFE," as the Egyptians believed that "A pharaoh dies as Osiris" and "his successor reigns as Horus," who is also seen as "the spiritual force behind the reigning pharaoh." Horus can also be regarded as the archetype of the dutiful son.

HOUSE SPRITES

Domestic spirits that act as family guardians and look after the welfare of a particular household; also known as tutelary fairies. House sprites appear in the lore of many European countries. The Germans call their domestic spirit *der Kobold*. When a kobold seeks to attach himself to a family, he makes a trial of the family by bringing wood chips and sawdust into the house and by throwing dirt in the milk vessels. If the master of the house ensures that the wood chips are not scattered about and that the dirt is left in the vessels after the milk is drunk, then the kobold will stay in the house as long as one of the family is alive.

The *nis* (or plural, *nisses*) is the house sprite of many Scandinavian countries. Nisses resemble DWARFS. They are the size of a year-old child, but have the face of an old person. Nisses usually wear gray clothing with a peaked red cap. As with the other tutelary fairies, nisses help a home to run smoothly, and it is said that no farm house goes on well unless a nis lives in it. They do domestic chores such as sweeping, bringing in water, and tending the cattle and the horses. They treat their favorite humans and animals particularly well. They also like to play tricks, laugh loudly, and frolic in the moonlight. In Norway, they may be seen in sleds in the wintertime. They are skilled in music and dancing. Like the English and Scottish BROWNIES, nisses are malicious and full of spite and revenge if they are treated poorly.

In the north Atlantic Faeroe Islands, the domestic spirits are called *niagruisar*. They are little creatures with red caps, and they bring luck to any place they decide to live. The Slavic *domovois* are covered with hair. They are amiable and live in the warmth near the hearth. When a family moves, they place a piece of bread beside the stove in the hopes that their *domovoi* will accompany them. The Irish BANSHEE is perhaps the most tragic tutelary fairy: he or she appears when someone is about to die.

The French domestic spirit is named the *esprit follet*. The English and Scottish tutelary fairy is the well-known BROWNIE, and sometimes hobgoblins will attach themselves to human families. The Spanish house sprite is called the *duende*, some of whose exploits are found in Torquemada's *Spanish Mandeville* and Calderon's comedy *La Dama Duende*.

Domestic spirits can be a nuisance. In many stories, they annoy the families with whom they live with a variety of pranks. They are known to throw objects such as stones, clay, sticks, and domestic utensils. They also might snatch away food, shake the curtains of a bed, and nearly suffocate children.

The tutelary fairies may have originated in the classical *lares,* domestic deities associated with the well-being of a household.

Thomas Keightley's *The Fairy Mythology* is a rich source for stories about house sprites (*see* KEIGHTLEY, THOMAS).

For Further Reading

Ackerman, Karen. *The Banshee.* Illustrated by David Ray. New York: Philomel Books, 1990.

Climo, Shirley. *Piskies, Spriggans, and Other Magical Beings.* Illustrated by Joyce A. dos Santos. New York: Crowell, 1991.

HOW EVIL BEGAN

Lakota Indian CREATION myth. As in most creation MYTHS, this tale is a means of explaining aspects of nature and the metaphysical world. In this Lakota tale, the original creator, Inyan, is the rock of the EARTH, who then creates Maka, the earth, who convinces him to create everything else, including the creatures and the Pte people. While creating, Inyan shrinks and becomes hard and powerless, while MAHPIYATO, the sky and the great judge who is the source of all wisdom and power, takes his place. Mahpiyato then begins the creation of the animals with clay, and he gives the other spirits this clay and tells them to make four-limbed shapes, but they cannot use hands and wings. While Wi, the SUN; Hanwi, the MOON; Wakinyan, Inyan's companion; Ksa, the spirit of wisdom; and Inyan create the various animals with claws, hooves, horns, and blunt teeth, the evil and mean Unk defies Mahpiyato and creates creatures without limbs, who eventually become the fish of the sea, for Mahpiyato refuses to let Wi warm them as Wi does the other animals who are then put on earth. Unk defies Mahpiyato more and more, until she and her companion and her sons separate themselves from the other spirits, ruling themselves and forming the circle of evil spirits. *See also* SIOUX CREATION.

For Further Reading

Bierhorst, John. *The Mythology of North America.* New York: William Morrow, 1985.

Walker, James R. *Lakota Myth.* University of Nebraska Press, 1983.

HOW SALMON GOT GREASY EYES

Coos-Coquille tribe myth about Old Mr. Coyote, the TRICKSTER. In this tale, Old Mr. Coyote makes all the Salmon girls pregnant, and, consequently, furious, chasing him till he finds a tree to hide in. Commanding the tree to grow tightly around him so as to avoid a hailstorm, Old Mr. Coyote can't get out. Finally he realizes that he can cut himself in pieces and push them through a small hole. Unbeknownst to him, however, RAVEN flies by and takes a piece of Old Man Coyote. So when Coyote is free of the tree and reassembles himself, he realizes that his rectum is missing and food can not stay in him but fell out. He tries different vegetables as a means of stopping himself up, but only pitch works; when the pitch catches on fire, he jumps into the ocean into a whale's mouth. Using his knife, Old Man Coyote cuts out the whale's heart, and when the dead whale drifts ashore, he cuts the side of the whale to let himself out, but the blubber gets in his eyes and blinds him. Still he manages to get back to Big Creek, home of the Salmon, where he manages to convince the Salmon to trade eyes with him, so they end up with the greasy eyes while the coyote has bright shiny eyes instead.

This tale belongs to the type that explains how things in nature came to be, a type typical of many cultures, and it also conveys the nature of the trickster.

For Further Reading

Bierhorst, John. *The Mythology of North America.* New York: William Morrow, 1985.

HUGHES, LANGSTON (1902–1967)

African American poet, novelist, essayist, short-story writer, playwright, editor, and translator. Langston Hughes's long career and diversified interests led him to dozens of literary projects in which he addressed, with both passion and compassion, the troubling racial issues and questions that characterized American life.

Hughes was born in Joplin, Missouri, to educated parents. Hughes's father, frustrated with the limited possibilities for a black man in America, left his wife and infant son and moved to Mexico in 1903. Hughes's mother traveled from city to city in search of work, leaving her young son in the care of his grandmother in Lawrence, Kansas. Throughout his childhood, Hughes visited with his mother periodically and, more infrequently, with his father in Mexico. In 1915, Hughes joined his mother and her new husband in Illinois; the following year they moved to Cleveland, Ohio. There, Hughes entered Central High School, became a successful student-athlete, began writing poetry, and was introduced for the first time to organized socialism. Hughes enrolled at Columbia University in 1921, but soon dropped out in order to participate more fully in the lively and exciting activities of the Harlem Renaissance. Hughes wrote and published poetry in the magazines *Crisis* and *Opportunity*, and experimented with what would become the unique blues poetry of *The Weary Blues* (1926), his first published collection.

Hughes enrolled in Lincoln University in Pennsylvania in 1926, but spent his vacations in Harlem. During these years he met and worked with many of the important figures of the Harlem Renaissance, particularly Arna Bontemps (*see* BONTEMPS, ARNA). In 1927 he met Charlotte Mason, an elderly white woman who was so impressed with Hughes that she offered to become his literary patron. Mason's financial support allowed Hughes to finish his first novel, *Not Without Laughter* (1930), which appeared not long after his graduation from Lincoln. Later that year, however, Hughes ended his relationship with Mason because her interests in African American art and literature were confined solely to the folkloric tradition; she would not accept a more racially progressive philosophy, and Hughes would not limit his art to please her.

The decade of the 1930s found Hughes traveling all over the world, including Russia, Japan, Mexico, Spain, and France. He was deeply embroiled in radical world politics and committed himself to facing and exposing fascism and racism wherever he went. He never stopped writing; in 1934 he released *The Ways of White Folks*, an acclaimed collection of satiric short stories about racial prejudice. The following year saw Hughes's dramatic debut; his sensational and highly controversial play, *Mulatto*, was produced on Broadway.

Hughes continued to produce writing of all kinds until his death in 1967. A highly lauded figure of the Harlem Renaissance, some critics suggest that his lasting contribution to African American literature is his celebration of the black folk tradition in America (including his popular folk stories about a black character named Simple). His lyric poems are infused with the rhythms of spirituals and blues, his fiction reveals the power of colloquial folk songs and FOLKTALES, and his nonfiction celebrates the experiences of African Americans struggling to overcome widespread race prejudice and oppression. Unfailingly dedicated to any movement that promoted freedom and creativity, Hughes remains a seminal figure in the evolution of African American literature, and especially the folktales derived from oral storytelling.

For Further Reading

Hughes, Langston. *Collected Poems of Langston Hughes*. New York: Random House, 1995.

————. *I Wonder As I Wander: An Autobiographical Journey*. Hill & Wang, 1993.

————. *Not Without Laughter*. New York: Macmillan, 1995.

————. *Short Stories*. Hill & Wang, 1996.

Miller, R. Baxter. *The Art and Imagination of Langston Hughes*. Lexington, KY: University Press of Kentucky, 1989.

Tracy, Steven C. *Langston Hughes and the Blues*. Urbana, IL: University of Illinois Press, 1988.

THE HUMAN RACE IS SAVED

Story of Iroquois warrior who finds healing waters. In this MYTH, a plague has killed most of the people, including the entire family of the warrior, Nekumonta, except for his beautiful wife Shanewis. Only a few other villagers are alive, and soon they and Shanewis fall ill as well. Determined to save his wife, Nekumonta sets off to search for a herbal cure in the deep snow of winter, first praying to the GREAT SPIRIT. After several days of searching to no avail, Nekumonta himself falls ill. The birds and ANIMALS see the dying Nekumonta and remember how he has always been so kind to them and only kills one when it is absolutely necessary for survival, so they pray to the Great Spirit to save him. While he sleeps, the Great Spirit sends him a message through a DREAM. In the dream the ailing Shanewis sings a mysterious and lovely song, and Nekumonta hears a waterfall that sings the very same song urging the warrior to find this waterfall that will heal his wife. Nekumonta then awakes, and though he can see no waterfall, he begins digging in the snow until finally a small stream emerges from the hole. As the stream grows, Nekumonta begins to feel healthy again. After thanking the Great Spirit, he makes a clay jar to carry some of the magical waters back to Shanewis and the other villagers. Luckily, Nekumonta arrives in the nick of time, and is able to save his wife, the villagers, and the human race, and is forever remembered for this. *See also* WATER OF LIFE.

A HUNDRED MERRY TALES

English jestbook printed by John Rastell in 1526. Collections of witty sayings and humorous tales, jestbooks entertained the English public from 1484 to 1584. Later Elizabethan literature drew upon this comic tradition. While some jestbooks are apparently based on actual conversation and capture the vernacular language of the time, jestbooks are also part of a literary genre that dates back to Ancient Greece. The tale of ODYSSEUS escaping from the CYCLOPES is one example of an early jest. Odysseus tells Cyclops that his name is "No Man," and later Cyclops repeats that "No Man" has blinded him. This play on language creates the jest.

A Hundred Merry Tales (also *A C. Mery Talys*), however, is unique in the English jestbook genre. Rather than relying on translations of other European and ancient texts, *A Hundred Merry Tales* is purely English. Its tales apparently derive from word-of-mouth stories current in sixteenth-century England. Though the form of the jest may date back to HOMER, *A Hundred Merry Tales* captures the concerns of its contemporary audience. In colloquial English, the tales both entertain and inform. Most stories offer "advice" that is as comical as the anecdotes. For instance, at the end of a story about the stupidity of a squire's Oxford-educated son, the reader is told, "By this tale men may see that it is great folly to put one to school to learn any subtle science which hath no natural wit."

Men do seem to be the avowed audience of *A Hundred Merry Tales,* and many tales warn readers of women's wiles. Women are depicted as adulterers and merry widows who quickly replace dead husbands with new. For instance, one story describes a woman sobbing at the funeral of her fourth husband. At the three previous burials, prospective husbands had eagerly presented themselves to the widow. However, this time, no suitor has called, and the widow cries: "I am sure of no other husband and therefore ye may be sure I have great cause to be sad and heavy." Other stories present women as lusty accomplices in romantic assignations who make elaborate plans to accommodate lovers and deceive husbands and fathers. The more bawdy tales do not shy away from explicit descriptions of women's bodies and sexual pleasure.

Many of the stories tell of monks, friars, priests, and nuns. But these stories, too, reveal the holy men and women as sexual beings prey to the same foibles of their lay contemporaries. A judgmental voice is missing from most of these stories that, to a degree, preach cultural relativism. For example, one story begins with two nuns, one old, one young, confessing their sins in a London church. The young nun admits that she made love with a young man in a garden. The confessor pardons her readily because as a beautiful young woman surrendering to love in the spring she "did but [her] kind." However, when the old nun describes her "sin in lechery," the priest is less lenient: "An old whore to lie with an old friar in the old cloister in the holy time of Lent—By cock's body! if God can forgive thee, yet will I never forgive thee—" The moral of this story is telling: "By this tale men may learn that a vicious act is more abominable in one person than in another." Sex and youth are pleasing topics to the priest, and presumably, to the readers, while decrepitude and lust are not.

The characters who inhabit *A Hundred Merry Tales* murder, fornicate, boast, and lie. MARRIAGE is seldom happy; young women are seldom virgins, and priests and nuns disregard their vows of chastity. However, the sin and follies of the characters provide the substance of the jests. These tales, collected bits of folk culture, resurface later in the rich literature of Elizabethan England. One can certainly imagine Shakespeare's Falstaff entertaining the tavern crowd with such stories.

For Further Reading

Zall, P.M. *A Hundred Merry Tales and Other Jestbooks of the Fifteenth and Sixteenth Centuries*. Lincoln, NE: University of Nebraska Press, 1963.

HURSTON, ZORA NEALE (1891–1960)

African American anthropologist, folklorist, and writer, and important figure of the Harlem Renaissance. Born in Eatonville, Florida, the first all-black incorporated town in America, Hurston was one of eight children in the family of Eatonville's former alderman, mayor, and founder. Her mother died when she was nine, and the child was shuffled between the homes of various relatives until she ran away. She found domestic work that took her to Baltimore; there, she enrolled in the high school division of Morgan State University. While working various odd jobs, Hurston earned her high school diploma and then an associate's degree from Howard University. She moved to New York, found work as an assistant to the novelist Fannie Hurst, wrote and published several short stories, and earned a scholarship to Barnard College where she studied anthropology under Franz Boas (see BOAS, FRANZ). Hurston completed her B.A. in 1928, Barnard's first African American student.

Boas helped Hurston to win a fellowship to collect black FOLKLORE in her native south; her travels to Florida and Louisiana led to the publication of MULES AND MEN (1935), her first full-length collection of folklore. A Guggenheim grant supported her fieldwork in Haiti, resulting in another collection of folklore, *Tell My Horse* (1938). Hurston is recognized as an important leader in the scholarly examination and appreciation of folkloric traditions; her interest in the African American oral traditions of folktales, songs, and sermons carries over into her canon of long and short fiction.

Hurston loosely based her first novel, *Jonah's Gourd Vine* (1934), on the lives of her parents. Hurston uses her extensive knowledge of folklore and her familiarity with rural southern black dialects to tell the story of John Pearson, a poor itinerant preacher who longs for a better life. Her second and most highly acclaimed novel, *Their Eyes Were Watching God* (1937), also fuses folk culture with poetic fiction and rural dialect to describe the life of Janie, a woman who learns to find happiness and fulfillment as an independent woman. *Moses, Man of the Mountain* (1939), retells the Old Testament story of Moses by connecting the experience of the ancient Hebrews with the lives of contemporary African Americans; Moses, an irreverent figure, speaks in African American dialect and practices "hoodoo." Hurston's final and least-favored novel, *Seraph on the Suwanee* (1948), has as its protagonist a rural southern white woman.

Hurston's work met with disfavor from certain critics who attacked her lack of racial militancy, her willingness to publish in politically conservative journals, and her support of certain aspects of segregation. Indeed, in her autobiographical *Dust Tracks on a Road* (1942), Hurston omits any serious discussion of racism or race prejudice. Defenders of Hurston point to her unusual upbringing in an entirely black community as a possible explanation for her reluctance to aggressively attack issues of racism in America.

Hurston's literary career peaked in the early 1940s; she was hailed as an important literary force in the worlds of fiction and folklore. But by the 1950s, she disappeared from the literary spotlight. She returned to Florida in 1951, took various short-lived jobs to support herself, and tried, for the most part unsuccessfully, to publish her articles. Her health failed her, her money ran out, and in 1959 she was forced to enter a welfare home in St. Lucie. Penniless, she died there of heart disease in 1960 and was buried in an unmarked grave in Fort Pierce. The literary establishment had forgotten about her, and her books had fallen out of print.

The early 1970s revival of Zora Neale Hurston was spearheaded by the African American writer Alice Walker, who searched for and marked Hurston's grave in 1973. An article that Walker published in *Ms.* magazine in 1975 catapulted Hurston back into the spotlight and garnered for her a new generation of fans. Hurston is now lauded as an important twentieth-century writer, a proto-feminist who preserved the vitality of the African American oral tradition through her fiction and her collections of folklore.

Among Hurston's most well-known stories suitable for storytelling are found in *Mules and Men*, including many animal stories (such as "How the 'Gator Got Black," "Why We Have Gophers"), "Ole Massa" stories grounded in the folklore of slavery (such as "Massa and the Bear," "Ole Massa and John Who Wanted to Go to Heaven"), and Hoodoo stories (which include the folk rituals "To Make Love Stronger," "To Help a Person in Jail," and "To Keep a Husband True"). Many of Hurston's individually published short stories, including "Spunk," "The Gilded Six-Bits," and "Sweat," are lively tales that are wonderfully appropriate for storytelling today.

For Further Reading

Hurston, Zora Neale. *Dust Tracks on a Road*. 1942. Reprint, New York: HarperPerennial, 1991.

———. *Folklore, Memoirs, and Other Writings*. New York: Literary Classics, 1995.

———. *Mules and Men*. Philadelphia: Lippincott, 1935.

Roses, Lorraine Elena, and Ruth Elizabeth Randolph. *Harlem Renaissance and Beyond*. Boston: G.K. Hall & Co., 1990.

ICARUS AND DAEDALUS

Tragic story from Greek and Roman mythology in which Daedalus makes wings for himself and his son, Icarus, who does not heed his father and plunges to his death in the ocean.

According to this LEGEND, Daedalus, the famous Athenian inventor, artist, architect, and craftsman, longs to escape from Crete, where he is imprisoned and in exile, and return to his homeland (see MINOTAUR, LABYRINTH). Because Minos, the KING of Crete, has strict control over the SEAS, Daedalus decides to attempt escape by flying to Sicily. He constructs wings by threading together quill feathers and holding the smaller feathers in place with wax. After completing a set of wings for himself and a set for his son, Icarus, Daedalus instructs his son not to fly too high as the sun's heat might melt the wax and not to fly too low as the water from the waves might weigh down the feathers. The tearful, trembling old man instructs his son to follow him. Daedalus and Icarus began to fly. Icarus so much enjoys the thrill of flight that he leaves his father and soars too high into the HEAV-ENS. The sun melts the wax that bind the feathers together, and Icarus drowns in the sea, later named the Icarian Sea. Daedalus curses his skill and buries his son on an island that now is called Icaria. Like many parents, he regretted the dangers inherent in a child's "growing up" and experimenting with life.

The ascent to heaven on eagle-back or in the form of an eagle is a common religious MOTIF. Etana, the Babylonian HERO, rides on eagle-back to INANNA's heavenly courts, but, like Icarus, he also falls into the sea and drowns.

For Further Reading

Farmer, Penelope. *Daedalus and Icarus.* Illustrated by Chris Connor. New York: Harcourt Brace Jovanovich, 1971.

Oldfield, Pamela. *Tales from Ancient Greece.* Illustrated by Nick Harris. New York: Doubleday, 1988.

IKTOME

Spider Man TRICKSTER in the NATIVE NORTH AMERICAN STORYTELLING oral tradition of the Sioux. Iktome is also called Ikto, Unktomi, and other variations. Sometimes he appears in stories as a companion to other tricksters, such as COYOTE.

Although Iktome is presumed to be a CULTURE HERO, the stories told about him are typical outrageous trickster tales, often obscene. In one, he pretends to be a woman with a strange growth between her legs in order to seduce an ignorant girl. In another, he makes love to his own wife by mistake. In yet another, he has a nightmare in which his enlarged penis is about to be run over by a wagon.

In the story of "Coyote and the Rock," Coyote and Iktome are together one day when Coyote annoys a boulder by first giving it a blanket and then taking the blanket back. When the angry rock is about to roll over both tricksters, Iktome decides that this isn't his quarrel. Abandoning Coyote, Iktome quickly changes into a spider and disappears down a mouse hole. *See also* SPIDER, SPIDER WOMAN.

For Further Reading

Erdoes, Richard, and Alfonso Ortiz. *American Indian Myths and Legends.* New York: Pantheon, 1985.

ILIAD

Greek EPIC poem attributed to HOMER. The *Iliad* relates a few days' events of the Trojan War, which begins when the Trojan prince Paris abducts Helen from her husband MENELAOS, the king of Sparta. The Greek leaders ally themselves with Menelaos and lay siege to TROY. The poem opens ten years into the siege.

There is as yet no decisive victor when a mysterious plague strikes the Greek army. An inquiry reveals that AGAMEMNON, the Greek commander-in-chief, has offended the god APOLLO by seizing a priest's daughter as his concubine. Agamemnon reluctantly returns the young woman to her father, but first, he demands another concubine, Briseis, who is the captive of his fellow-warrior ACHILLES.

Achilles gives up Briseis, but angrily protests this insult by refusing to fight in the war. So now the Greeks are deprived of their most valiant warrior. Achilles' mother, Thetis—one of the NYMPHS—seeks out the chief Olympian god, ZEUS. She persuaded Zeus to turn the

tide of the war against the Greeks until Achilles returns to battle.

Meanwhile, a truce is declared in hopes that Paris and Menelaos can decide the conflict once and for all in one-to-one combat. Just as Menelaos is about to win their fight, APHRODITE (GODDESS of love) spirits Paris away to safety. Then the goddess ATHENA goads a Trojan soldier to shoot an arrow at Menelaos, ending the truce. War rages again.

The tide of battle shifts back and forth between the Greeks and Trojans. Each side's fortunes depends largely upon alliances and quarrels among the Olympian GODS. But without Achilles, the Greeks are ultimately doomed to defeat. Agamemnon eventually realizes this, and offers to return Briseis to the brooding warrior. But Achilles refuses the offer and remains in his tent.

At last, the Greeks are nearly routed, and Agamemnon and many of his finest warriors are injured. Then Achilles allows his dear friend Patroclos to don his own armor and join the fray. They hope that the Trojans will mistake Patroclos for Achilles and withdraw in discouragement.

But Patroclos is soon killed by the Trojan, Hector. The grieving Achilles now has no choice but to return to battle and avenge his friend, despite his mother's prophetic certainty that he is doomed to die.

Achilles makes peace with Agamemnon and fights the Trojans until he and Hector meet for their fatal combat. Hector believes that the goddess Athena will fight by his side, but the goddess tricks and abandons him. Upon realizing this, Hector flees from Achilles and runs around the walls of the city three times. When he returns to fight, he is killed.

Still furious at Patroclos' death, Achilles dishonors the slain Hector by dragging his body from a chariot. But when the Trojan king Priam crosses enemy lines and offers Achilles splendid gifts in return for his son's body, Achilles relents. The poem ends with Hector's funeral.

There is no doubt that an actual Trojan War took place about 1230 B.C., although it was probably fought over trade routes, not over a beautiful woman. During the centuries that followed, BARDS known as the *aoidoi* retold, elaborated, and mythologized these real events through their oral tradition. Then, around 900 or 850 B.C., the poems were written down and collated to become the epic *Iliad.* The earliest extant manuscript version dates from the fourth or third century B.C. Whether there was ever an actual poet-compiler named Homer is unknown.

A synopsis of the *Iliad* cannot convey the archaic strangeness of this poem, particularly the psychology of its mortal characters. Today's reader, having heard it touted as a glorious story of valor and bravery, may find it mystifying. Its heroes are weirdly puppet-like, their decisions and fates almost always dictated by the gods. One is hard-pressed to think of one truly autonomous act on the part of any human character. How can valor and bravery exist without volition?

In *The Origin of Consciousness in the Breakdown of the Bicameral Mind,* Princeton psychologist Julian Jaynes proposes that the *Iliad* is a relic of a time when human experience was very different than it is today. People might even be said not to have been self-conscious at all. Their actions and decisions were determined by the schizophrenia-like voices of personal or collective deities. Perhaps most intriguingly, Jaynes holds that storytelling itself evolved out of the trance states of ancient bards and singers—that the great narratives of the ancient past were initially dictated by hallucinated gods and muses.

Even some of Jaynes's admirers find his claims a bit overstated. Regardless, his arguments about the *Iliad* (along with other works of ancient literature) are compelling, particularly his examination of the poem's original Greek diction. There are, for example, no words in the *Iliad* for *will* or anything pertaining to it (a peculiarity which is inevitably glossed over in translations). The self-awareness of the poem's authors seems to have been dramatically different than our own.

Given this interpretation, perhaps the greatness of the *Iliad* is not that it imparts eternal truths about courage and cowardice, loyalty and betrayal, but that it shines such a ruthless and vivid light on what human experience may have been like more than three millennia ago. It also may tell us much about

how western storytelling traditions came to be. *See also* ANCIENT GREEK STORYTELLING, HELEN OF TROY, ODYSSEY.

For Further Reading

Homer. *The Iliad.* Translated by Robert Fitzgerald. New York: Doubleday, 1974.

———. *The Iliad.* Translated by W. H. D. Rouse. New York: New American Library, 1950.

Jaynes, Julian. *The Origin of Consciousness in the Breakdown of the Bicameral Mind.* Boston: Houghton Mifflin, 1990.

INANNA

Ancient Sumerian GODDESS, Queen of HEAVEN and EARTH, called Ishtar by the Semites. In its written form, the story of Inanna, the Sumerian MOON goddess—like the Greek ARTEMIS, the Roman Diana, the Phrygian CYBELE, and the Egyptian Isis (*see* ISIS and OSIRIS)—dates back to 2000 B.C. It was discovered as part of the earliest writing of literature on various Sumerian clay tablets and fragments written in cuneiform. The MYTH of Inanna, daughter of the moon god Nanna and the moon goddess, Ningal, is actually a cycle beginning with Inanna as a maiden and ending with her as a mature woman.

The first section of the Cycle of Inanna, "The *Huluppu*-Tree," takes place in the earliest day of the world, when the GODS have recently divided the various domains, with the sky-god An, Inanna's great-grandfather, taking the heavens; the air god, Enlil, Inanna's paternal grandfather taking the earth, and the goddess Ereshkigal taking the underworld. Inanna's maternal grandfather, Enki, the god of wisdom, sets sail for the underworld, and a single tree that was planted by the Euphrates, the *huluppu*-tree, is uprooted by the South WIND. Inanna sees it in the river and brings it to her holy garden in URUK, where she tends it for over ten years, but the serpent, the *Anzu*-bird, and the "dark maid" LILITH build their homes in the tree. Inanna, who wants the tree for her "shining throne and bed," weeps with frustration at the three usurpers, and begs her brother Utu, the SUN god, to help her, but he refuses. Then she turns to her brother (really her cousin) GILGAMESH, Shepherd-KING of Uruk, and he comes to Inanna's aid, ousting the serpent, the *Anzu*-bird, and Lilith from the tree, and making a throne and bed from the tree-trunk for Inanna.

In the next section, "Inanna and the God of Wisdom," Inanna, still a virgin, has clearly become a woman ready to embrace her sexuality. She goes to Enki, the God of Wisdom, and he gives her many gifts representing "the attributes of civilization," such as "the high priesthood," "the throne of kingship," "the dagger and the sword," "the art of lovemaking," "the art of song," etc. Placing all the gifts on the Boat of Heaven, Inanna returns home only to find that Enki wants all the gifts returned, if necessary by force. Inanna refuses, calling on her servant Ninshubur, former Queen of the East for help, and together they withstand Enki's attack, until Enki gives in at last and the gifts are presented to the people of Sumer.

In one of the most powerful and moving sections, "The Courtship of Inanna and Dumuzi," Inanna's brother Utu wants her to marry Dumuzi, the Shepherd-King of Uruk, but Inanna prefers to marry a farmer. Dumuzi and Inanna argue, and "From the starting of the quarrel/Came the lover's desire." The section portrays a woman and man falling deeply in love with each other and enjoying their lovemaking. However, by the end of this section, there is foreshadowing for the final part of the cycle, for Dumuzi asks Inanna to set him free, meaning that now that he is king he cannot simply devote himself to being her "exclusive paramour," notes Diane Wolkstein in her commentary on the myth in *Inanna: Queen of Heaven and Earth (see* WOLKSTEIN, DIANE*)*.

In the final section of the cycle, "The Descent of Inanna," Inanna must visit the underworld in order to "know" and "understand" more fully, and she risks her life and her powers in this descent (*see* DESCENT TO THE UNDERWORLD). Inanna is killed by Ereshkigal, then saved and reborn thanks to her faithful servant, Ninshubur, and her grandfather, Enki, but in order for Inanna to leave the underworld, someone must replace her (*see* REBIRTH). Although Inanna will not let the *galla*, the DEMONS of the Underworld, take either Ninshubur or Inanna's two sons,

she does let them take the impassive Dumuzi, her husband, who is so involved in his role as king that he "refuses to acknowledge the ties of feeling and love that once bound him to his wife." Dumuzi is taken by the *galla*, forced to recognize that he, too, is not beyond DEATH, and is saved by his sister Geshtinanna, who will take his place in the Underworld for half the year, though he must spend the other half year there. Geshtinanna's compassion reawakens Inanna's compassion, and Inanna and Dumuzi are reconciled, united for half the year suggesting seasonal change and the annual renewal of love and the human life cycle of "budding, blooming, and dying."

For Further Reading

Wolkstein, Diane, and Samuel Noah Kramer. *Inanna: Queen of Heaven and Earth*. New York: HarperCollins, 1983.

INCA CREATION

Cosmogony MYTHS of early Peruvian Indian civilization. The Incas of what is now known as Peru had different versions of the story of their "creation from chaos," though similarities are shared in the following four VARIANTS.

In one version, the SUN-god, known as *Pachacamac* or *Viracocha*, emerges from Lake Titicaca to create the planets, the MOON, the stars, and humans. Pachacamac has a son and a daughter whose mother is the moon GODDESS, and they are sent to EARTH where the son becomes the Inca, or emperor, and the daughter becomes the queen. All Inca rulers thereafter are descendants of these first rulers. They are the teachers of the people their FATHER has made, and, following his orders, they place a golden rod at each point where the people are supposed to build a city or a temple. The Inca then goes north while his sister goes south, and he founds Northern Cuzco and teaches men to farm and build while she founds Southern Cuzco and teaches women to weave and cook.

In another version of the Inca Creation Myth, there are three caves on a hill called Tavern of the Dawn, and four brothers and their sister-wives emerge from these caves. These brothers and their wives journey throughout the world, inventing it. The brother who acts as their leader, Ayar-Manco, also has a golden rod that will provide a sign as to where the site for a new city should be. If the golden rod sinks far into the earth when thrust into the ground, a city should be founded, and this is the case with the founding of Cuzco, the Inca capital. The other three brothers are turned to stone, Ayar-auca becoming the cornerstone for Cuzco, Ayar-oco becoming the stone called Huanacari, and Ayar-cachi becoming the Traitor's Stone when the others seal him in a cave for being too strong. Ayar-Manco and his sister-wife Mama-occlo, like the son and daughter of Pachacamac in the other version, are the parents of the first Inca and the builders of the House of the Sun, the temple devoted to Pachacamac.

In a third version of the creation story, Con Tiqui Viracocha emerges out of Lake Collasuyu, bringing human beings with him and then creating Inti, the sun, and the moon and stars. Inti becomes the ancestor of the Inca, and Con Tiqui Viracocha creates more human beings out of rock. Although these people are sent out to populate the world, Con Tiqui keeps one woman and one man with him at Cuzco, which is considered the "navel of the world."

In yet a fourth variant, the Creator, Con, appears in human form but he has no bones. Con provides the first humans with all that they will need, but the people are rebellious and unappreciative. Con, like the goddess Demeter of Greek mythology (see PERSEPHONE MYTH) and the African god LITUOLONE, punishes the people by stopping the rain. The people suffer greatly until a new god, Pachachamac, comes and vanquished Con, turns Con's human beings into monkeys, and then creates his own new human beings.

For Further Reading

Sproud, Barbara. *Primal Myths: Creation Myths around the World*. New York: HarperCollins, 1991.

INCEST STORIES

Creation MYTHS where first parents are closely related. In many CREATION myths, the theme of incest is a common one, given that the first children are born of the same parents or only a father and a daughter or a mother and son exist. In the Egyptian and Incan creation myths, however, incest had another importance: it was symbolic, emblematic of the power of a dynasty, and the Egyptians practiced brother-sister incest in actuality as a means of insuring that the dynasty would stay pure (*see* EGYPTIAN CREATION, INCA CREATION). In general, however, incest in myths did not condone incest in most cultures, and the incest taboo remained strong.

In Greek creation, the Great MOTHER, GAIA, bears a son, Uranos, with whom she then incestuously couples, and their children are the first GODS, the Titans. The Titan Kronos then rapes his sister, Rhea, in a second act of incest, and she gives birth to six of the 12 gods who later make up the Greek PANTHEON and live on MOUNT OLYMPOS. ZEUS, their sixth child, and HERA, their fifth, are the next brother and sister to marry, thus committing incest once again with the birth of their two children, the gods Hephaistos and Ares.

In one Eskimo creation myth, a sister wants to discover the identity of the man who visits her bed each night, so she puts soot on her hands. The next day when she sees soot on her brother's back, she angrily realizes who it is and, taking a torch, she departs. Her brother, too, carries a torch, but his is not as bright as hers, and as they enter the sky, she is transformed into the SUN, while he becomes the MOON.

INDRA AND THE ANTS

Hindu story from the *Brahmavaivarta Purana*. In this story, Indra, an Aryan sky-GOD of immense power, battles a MONSTER who holds the waters of the EARTH in his stomach. The earth is made arid by the monster, and even the heavenly palaces of the GODS dry and crumble. To solve the problem, Indra hurls his thunderbolt at the monster's stomach. The ensuing FLOOD returns fertility to the earth, but the palaces of the gods remain in a state of decay. Indra calls upon Vishvakarman, the artisan of the gods, to build him a new palace. Year after year, Vishvakarman builds more splendid palaces, but Indra's ambitions grow loftier with each new creation.

Vishvakarman, concerned that his work could go on eternally without Indra's approval, seeks help from BRAHMA, the creator god. Brahma assures him that all will be settled.

The next morning, a beautiful, luminous boy (actually VISNU in disguise) appears at Indra's court. The boy states that he has heard of Indra's majestic palace and has come to see if it is more grand than that of any Indra to come before. Indra, somewhat disturbed by the boy's notion of previous Indras, asks him how he, in his youth, could presume to know of other Indras. The child responds that he has seen worlds and universes come and go. Brahmas create worlds upon worlds, then dissolve out of existence. For each day and night of a Brahma, twenty-eight Indras are born and expire. As the boy speaks, a parade of ants marches through the door. To Indra's dismay, the boy sees them and laughs. Upon asking to know the reason for the boy's laughter, Indra is told that the ants are all former Indras. Through the cycle of birth, DEATH, and REBIRTH they raise themselves from the lowest to the highest states, only to descend back to the level of the insects in moments of pride. Although Indra temporarily reacts with despair, he quickly accepts that he must fulfill his duties as a god with humility.

"Indra and the Ants" is actually a story within a story. By learning that he is a part of the infinite cycle of death and rebirth, Indra gains humility from the boy's tale. The listener also benefits from Indra's reaction, learning that good or bad *karma* can influence all beings. While Indra's tale may bring about a sense of satisfaction in the downtrodden, it should also convey a sense of justice and, ultimately, humility. All have experienced the highest and lowest stations in life, and all will experience them again. The story teaches that the fulfillment of one's duty, despite social station, generates good *karma* and is the only road to peace in life.

One finds parallels to this theme in many Indian FOLKTALES. In "The Elephant and the Ant," the ANIMALS of the jungle stage a revolt against the elephant. An ant suggests that he is best suited to lead the revolt, and, after scoffing at him, the other animals allow him to try. The elephant hears of the plot with amusement but no fear. When the elephant falls asleep the ant creeps up his trunk and into his head, causing him such great pain that he tires himself from running. A bullock informs the elephant that he must not utter insults about the ant and should rather pray for it. When the elephant complies, the pain disappears. Like Indra, the elephant perceives himself as lord over all. His pride gives way to pain in the face of his insignificance, and it is only through the counsels of another that he can recognize the universal fate, and inherent value, of all creatures.

For Further Reading

Beck, et al., eds. *Folktales of India*. Chicago: University of Chicago Press, 1987.

Jamison, Stephanie W. *The Ravenous Hyenas and the Wounded Sun: Myth and Ritual in Ancient India*. Ithaca, NY: Cornell University Press, 1991.

INVISIBILITY

In FOLKLORE, the ability not to be seen, usually as a result of a magic spell or potion. The MOTIF of invisibility can be found in cultures all over the world. In MYTH and FAIRY TALE, being invisible can endow power, giving the hidden person the ability to spy and overhear. Sometimes one becomes invisible through SPELLS, magic potions, or, depending on the belief system, DEATH. Symbols of invisibility are the cloak, the mantle, the veil, and the hood, for they are all able to hide a person's true nature and suggest DISGUISE, secrecy, darkness, and dissimulation. In some initiation rites, wearing a hat or veil that covers the head completely also suggests invisibility and connection with the spirits. King ARTHUR was said to have a cloak of invisibility, and the Greek god HADES possessed a hat. Other MAGIC OBJECTS that make one invisible include a ring or stone, such as the one possessed by Discordia; a serpent's crown; the heart of an unborn child; a fern seed; and shoes. GODS, GODDESSES, and angels often have the ability to become invisible without the aid of a magic object, but humans and DWARFS generally require help.

In Irish mythology, the cloak of invisibility belonging to the SEA-god Manannan Mac

Lir is used when his wife, Fand, falls in love with the hero CUCHULAINN, when he protects her during a period when her husband has left her. Cuchulainn's wife, Emer, is very jealous of their love and threatens to kill Fand, but when she realizes that Fand truly loves Cuchulainn, she offers to give him up to show her own love. Manannan, however, appears and insists that Fand choose between him and Cuchulainn; because Cuchulainn has Emer, she chooses Manannan. In order to make Fand and Cuchulainn forget each other, Manannan holds the magic cloak between them making them invisible to each other thereafter.

In the "Danced-Out Shoes," a central European tale with many variants, the HERO wears a cloak that renders him invisible, enabling him to spy on the PRINCESS (or princesses) who goes off to dance all night; thus he learns the secret of her worn-out shoes each morning. Plato relates the story of the ring that permits Gyges to become invisible and enter the queen's bedroom. In the OCEAN OF STORY, Gunasarman forces the KING, Vikramasakti, to make peace by pretending to be the gods' messenger and using the magic collyrium to appear and disappear before the king.

IO

Priestess of HERA in Greek mythology and the daughter of the river-god, Inachus. She appears as a character in Aeschylus's tragedy *Prometheus Bound*.

In perhaps the most famous story of an often-repeated scenario, ZEUS seduces Io. When Hera is about to catch the two together, Zeus takes drastic measures to protect Io—and himself—from his wife's fury. As a disguise, Zeus changes Io into a white cow. But Hera sees through the ruse, claims the cow as her own, and puts it in the care of a monstrous creature named Argus.

Unhappy that Io must live the life of a beast, Zeus asks Hermes to kill Argus, not an easy task, since Argus has a hundred eyes, none of which are ever closed at the same time. However, Hermes manages to put Argus to sleep by playing his reed pipe and telling stories. Hermes kills Argus, and Hera takes his hundred eyes and puts them into the tail of the peacock.

But Io is not yet free—she is still a white cow. Even worse, Hera now sends a gadfly to torment her. The fly drives Io nearly mad, sending her in a frenzy across Greece and much of Asia. She crosses a SEA, which is later named for her—the Ionian. In Egypt, Zeus is finally able to restore her to human form. She founds the worship of ISIS as a manifestation of Demeter.

Io marries a mortal, but gives birth to a son by Zeus. This is Epaphus, the ancestor of the people of the southern Mediterranean countries. Among her descendants are 50 sisters known as the *danaïds*, 49 of whom kill their husbands on their wedding nights.

According to Robert Graves (see GRAVES, ROBERT), Io is associated with the MOON. This is because the horns of the cow were held to be symbolic of the new moon, which was thought to be the source of all water. *See also* ANCIENT GREEK STORYTELLING, PROMETHEUS AND THE THEFT OF FIRE.

IROQUOIS CREATION

Cosmogony of the five American Indian tribes of the Iroquois league of nations. Although there are individual MYTHS of CREATION belonging to each of the five tribes of the Iroquois Indians—the Cayuga, Mohawk, Oneida, Onondaga, and Seneca nations, several VARIANTS of a general Iroquois Creation Myth exist. As David Leeming notes in *A Dictionary of Creation Myths*, these variants share with other Native American myths in having "earth-diver aspects" and "a creatrix who falls from the sky."

In one variant, the myth begins with PRIMEVAL WATERS, water birds, and the TORTOISE. The Ongwe, presumably the creator, inhabits the HEAVENS with his wife and his daughter, Star-Woman, whom he pushes out of a hole in the sky. Star-Woman falls for a long time, then the water birds find some EARTH for her to land on, which they put it on the back of the Tortoise. The Tortoise serves as the earth's foundation and the place where Star-Woman lands and begins creating the world and its people.

In a similar variant, human beings live beyond the sky and there is no earth. In order to cure the ailing daughter of a great chief, the people try to provide her with the healing roots of a magic tree by digging a huge hole around the base of a tree. Instead, the tree and the daughter fall through the hole to the SEA below, and when the girl hits the water, there is the sound of thunder. Two SWANS who swim in the sea come to investigate, and since they are perplexed, they go to the wise Great Tortoise for advice. The Great Tortoise tells the swans to find the tree and its magic roots with magic soil still attached. This magic soil is needed to make an island for the girl. Only an old toad succeeds in finding the soil, which she takes in her mouth, brings to the surface, spits out, and dies. The magic soil becomes a huge mass of land. Because there is still no light, however, the girl tells the Great Tortoise how there is light where she comes from. Great Tortoise creates light by having the burrowing ANIMALS make holes in the sky to allow the light to come through. As in the first variant, the girl is the mother of everything, including the human race, perhaps becoming impregnated by the sea or the combination of the magic soil mixing with the sea. *See also* EARTH-DIVER CREATION, FALL FROM SKY, HIAWATHA TERENYAWAGON.

ISIS AND OSIRIS

Egyptian Mother GODDESS and the god of vegetation and of the dead. Isis and Osiris were sister and brother, wife and husband, and the ruling CULTURE HERO partners who brought civilization to Egypt. They were worshipped from about 3000 B.C. until about A.D. 400. Both appear in ancient sculptures, relief carvings, paintings, and papyrus illustrations.

Osiris was originally an agricultural god, identified with natural cycles such as birth, harvest, DEATH, and REBIRTH; the rising and falling of the Nile; and the rising and setting of the SUN. He is depicted as dark-skinned or green-skinned in keeping with his relationship to the soil and to vegetation. He is sometimes identified with the jackal and in some areas it was thought that his soul was lodged in a ram. He is often shown with his body wrapped in mummy linen. As the ruler over death, he became the most important of the Egyptian GODS. Isis, the Egyptian Mother Goddess, is depicted in human form or sometimes as a hawk. She is also seen with cows' horns.

The story of Osiris and Isis, from ancient oral tradition, is recorded in hieroglyphic texts—the Pyramid Texts and *The Book of the Dead* (which was buried with mummies to identify the dead with Osiris and to serve as a guide through the AFTERLIFE). The most complete account was recorded by the Greek writer Plutarch in the first century A.D.

Osiris and Isis are both the grandchildren of Ra, the sun-god who created and ruled the world. Their parents are the earth-god, Geb, and the sky-goddess, Nut, Ra's wife. Their other siblings are Seth and Nephthys. Isis gains power when she tricks her grandfather, Ra, by taking some of his spittle and mixing it with soil to shape a serpent. When the snake bites Ra, he can not overcome the poison. Isis tells Ra that she can remove the pain with her magic, but only if he tells her his secret name, which is the essence of his spirit. He gives her the name, and she cures him. Ra makes her promise to tell the name to no one except HORUS, the son she will eventually bear. Isis keeps her promise.

Isis and Osiris together develop agricultural methods, crafts, laws, and rites of worship for the Egyptian people. Osiris shows his people how to pick wild fruit, make wine and beer, grow FOOD, and store grains in order to survive the seasons of drought. He is credited with ending the practice of CANNIBALISM in ancient Egypt. He builds towns, makes laws, organizes worship, and teaches his people to play music. Isis discovers grains growing wild and teaches the people to grind grain, bake bread, and weave.

After Osiris, a wise and gentle Pharaoh, has civilized Egypt, he decides to do the same for savages in other lands. His conquest and education of neighboring people is entirely peaceful. When he returns from his journeys, he finds that Isis had ruled well in his absence. However, their productive reign is soon interrupted by their jealous brother, Seth.

Seth invites Isis and Osiris to a banquet, and after the festivities, Seth displays a jeweled golden coffin. He announces that he will give the wonderful sarcophagus to whomever fits into it perfectly. Of course, it has been tailored exactly to Osiris's measurements. When Osiris tries out the sarcophagus, Seth slams the lid and seals it shut. He has the coffin thrown into the river Nile, where Osiris drowns. The river carries the golden box into the Green Sea—the Mediterranean—and onto the Phoenician shore. A tamarisk tree springs up around it, enclosing it completely. When the KING and Queen of nearby Byblos see the enormous tree, they cut it down and make it into a pillar in their great hall, not knowing what was inside.

Isis is inconsolable. To make matters worse, the Egyptians believe that they will spend eternity wherever they are buried. Isis has no idea where that means for Osiris. Finally, she disguises herself and searches until she finds the sarcophagus and her husband's body.

The sympathetic King and Queen of Byblos provide Isis with a ship and crew to take the body home. On the way home, Isis stops and searches for secret herbs to restore Osiris. But crocodiles inform the evil Seth that Isis is trying to return Osiris to life. While out hunting a wild boar, Seth finds the body of Osiris, chops it into pieces, and scatters it across the land.

Isis knows that if her husband's body remains scattered, his soul will have no place to rest. Her sister, Nephthys, Seth's wife, helps her search for the pieces. According to Plutarch, they find all the parts of the body except the penis. Seth threw that to the crocodiles.

Isis carefully puts all the parts of Osiris together again, rubs the dead limbs with oils and herbs, and wraps the body with linen strips. Osiris returns from the dead as an immortal, but he is no longer at home in the land of the living. After the growing season, he retires to the underworld. Ever since then, Egypt has had its green growing season and its bare season of rest.

In some versions of the story, Isis impregnates herself on the voyage home. In others, she takes the form of a hawk and flutters over the Pharaoh's body soon after his death. In either case, she impregnates herself while her husband is dead.

In addition to Isis, there are many manifestations of the mother-goddess in world mythology, including the Greek HERA, the Japanese AMATERASU, the Hindu KALI, and Babylonian Ishtar (INANNA). Osiris's death and resurrection are also echoed throughout the world of MYTH. Slain and resurrected gods range from the Greek DIONYSOS to the Hero Twins of the Maya POPOL VUH. In *Primitive Mythology,* Joseph Campbell (*see* CAMPBELL, JOSEPH) relates this aspect of the Osiris and Isis myth to the stories of Adonis (*see* APHRODITE), who is killed by a wild boar while out hunting, and ATTIS, who was gored by a boar. Both were also resurrected.

In *The Gods of Ancient Egypt,* Barbara Watterson notes, "The LEGEND of Osiris as a god of resurrection had its origins in the ancient custom of killing the king." In many primitive societies, when the king's fitness and virility were in doubt, he was ritually put to death. The Egyptians adapted the practice to magically renew the power of the Pharaoh.

David Leeming reminds us in *The World of Myth* that "the ancients thought of death as the essential prelude to life." Osiris is not only the god of death, but he is "the personification of coming into being of all things."

For Further Reading

Cashford, Jules. *The Myth of Isis and Osiris.* New York: Random House, 1994.

McDermott, Gerald. *The Voyage of Osiris.* Illustrated by Gerald McDermott. New York: Windmill Books, 1977.

ISOLDE *See* TRISTAN AND ISOLDE

ITHACA

Island kingdom ruled by the Greek HERO Odysseus, which he must reclaim upon return from his wanderings (*see* ODYSSEY). When Palamedes arrives in Ithaca to persuade Odysseus to join his fellow Greeks in what was to become the Trojan War, Odysseus is so reluctant to leave his home, his wife, and his son that he pretends to be mad (*see* TROY). He yokes an ass and an ox to a plow and begins to sow salt. The doubting Palamedes tests Odysseus's sanity by putting TELEMACHOS, Odysseus's infant son, in the path of the plow. Odysseus turns the plow aside, proving that he is not insane. Odysseus then must take part in the war against the Trojans.

After the war is over, Odysseus spends 10 years attempting to return to his island kingdom. When he finally lands on Ithaca, he does not recognize his own home (*see* RIP VAN WINKLE). Over one hundred nobles from Ithaca and neighboring islands have been pursuing PENELOPE, Odysseus's wife. The suitors have taken over Odysseus's palace and his kingdom. Odysseus and Telemachos are reunited, and they plan how to seek revenge and punish the suitors. Telemachos proceeds to the palace where the usual feast and party are in progress. Disguised as a beggar, Odysseus enters his own palace and is given some food. Only Odysseus's dog, Argus, who has been waiting for his master for 20 years, recognizes him. Argus then dies. The suitors treat Odysseus poorly, and one even hits him with a stool.

Believing that Odysseus must be dead, Penelope has agreed to choose the suitor who prevails in a trial of skill with a bow and arrow. Telemachos brings a bow that had been a gift to his father. All the suitors' weapons are removed from the hall. The first part of the trial is bending the bow to attach the string. Neither Telemachos nor a number of the suitors have the strength to complete this test. Odysseus suggests that he be given a chance. He succeeds in bending the bow and attaching the cord to its notch. He then shoots an arrow through the twelve rings arranged in a line for the contest. Before anyone can react, Odysseus quickly shoots and kills the most insolent suitor. Telemachos and other faithful followers jump to Odysseus's side. Odysseus announces that he is the long-lost KING, whose house the suitors have invaded, whose possessions they have squandered, and whose wife and son they have persecuted for many years. He and his followers kill them all. Once again, Odysseus is master of his palace and his kingdom, and he is reunited with Penelope.

For Further Reading

Homer. *The Odyssey*. Translated by Robert Fitzgerald. 1961. Reprint, London: Collins Harvill, 1988.

McCaughrean, Geraldine. *Greek Myths*. Illustrated by Emma Chilchester Clark. New York: Macmillan, 1992.

JACK AND THE BEANSTALK

English FOLKTALE popular in Britain and America. "Jack and the Beanstalk" is an important folktale not only because its popularity has inspired countless versions of the story, but also because it incorporates several common MOTIFS that appear in many such tales. These recurring themes include an apparently foolish bargain (which in fact turns out to be providential), a giant plant that leads to another world, a HERO who outwits his enemy by hiding from him, and the theft of MAGIC OBJECTS by the hero.

A common and traditional version of the story relates how Jack, the simple son of an impoverished widow, is commanded by his mother to sell their beloved cow. He exchanges the cow for some magic beans, which infuriates his mother. In her anger, she throws the handful of beans out the window. When Jack wakes up the next morning, he sees that an enormous beanstalk reaching to the sky has sprouted from the beans. He climbs the beanstalk and finds the castle of a GIANT amid a world of fairies. Frightened, Jack hides from

the giant who sings "Fee-fi-fo-fum/I smell the blood of an Englishman/Be he live or be he dead/I'll grind his bones to make my bread." Jack spies on the giant's wife as she prepares a giant-sized feast for her husband, and sees a hen lay a golden egg. Jack waits patiently for the giant to fall asleep, then he steals the hen and escapes down the beanstalk. The next day he returns to the land of the giant, and steals a bag of gold from him. On his third trip up the beanstalk, Jack steals the giant's magic harp, which cries for help and alerts the giant. The enraged giant chases Jack down the beanstalk, but Jack beats him down to earth and chops down the stalk. The giant crashes to earth and is killed, and Jack and his mother enjoy their new-found wealth. Other versions of the tale suggest that the fairyland at the top of the beanstalk was once owned by Jack's father, a noble knight who was killed by the evil giant. In this version, Jack and his mother resume their rightful ownership of the castle and reign over the kingdom of fairies.

Another version of this popular folktale appears in the storytelling tradition of Appalachia. In this version (written in the Appalachian dialect of the North Carolina mountains), Jack's mother finds a large bean while sweeping the house, and quiets her crying son by telling him to go outside and plant it. The "bean tree" grows magically, and within three days reaches high into the clouds. Jack climbs the bean tree and finds a giant and his wife living in a huge house in the clouds. On his first trip to this other world, Jack steals the giant's "rifle-gun" and quickly escapes down the bean tree. The next day, Jack returns to steal the giant's "skinnin' knife." On his third trip, Jack steals the giant's coverlet that has jingle bells sewn all over it. The bells ring loudly as Jack flees with the coverlet, waking up the angry giant. But Jack makes his escape down the bean tree, and swiftly cuts down the stalk. The giant, his wife, and their house crash to the ground about a half-mile from Jack's home; Jack and his mother pick through the shattered house and find many nice additions to their meager household.

A modern and radically different version of "Jack and the Beanstalk" is included in Toni Cade Bambara's collection of *Tales and Stories for Black Folks* (1971). This retelling of the traditional tale is an ALLEGORY of race relations in the United States. In this story, an impoverished African American boy named Jack, who lives in a Harlem ghetto, climbs forty flights of stairs to the penthouse apartment of Sam Giant, an evil white slumlord. Jack steals two bags of money from him, races down the stairs, and escapes from the wicked and greedy Giant. Jack uses the money to pay for medical attention badly needed by his ailing mother, and then helps his mother to organize the black people in his neighborhood to buy and then rehabilitate their crumbling buildings.

An even more contemporary, and sharply ironic, version of "Jack and the Beanstalk" appears in James Finn Garner's recent collection of *Politically Correct Bedtime Stories* (1994). In this tale, a magic vegetarian offers Jack three magic beans in exchange for his cow. When the beanstalk grows and Jack climbs up into the clouds, he encounters a kind (but somewhat dull-witted) vegetarian giant who pulls Jack's beanstalk up out of the ground. Stuck in this new world, Jack resigns himself to life in the giant's commune (where 13 other men had previously climbed up beanstalks and been stranded in the clouds), where there is plenty to eat, little work to do, and nobody is judged based on their stature. *See also* JACK TALES.

For Further Reading

Chase, Richard. *The Jack Tales*. Cambridge, MA: Riverside Press, 1960.

Garner, James Finn. *Politically Correct Bedtime Stories*. NY: Macmillan, 1994.

Spencer, Edward. "Jack and the Beanstalk." *Tales and Stories for Black Folks*. Edited by Toni Cade Bambara. New York: Doubleday, 1971.

JACK TALES

Collection of oral FOLKTALES based on the adventures of a young TRICKSTER-hero named Jack. These tales usually begin with Jack leaving home to seek his fortune, though sometimes his goal is to escape mistreatment by his mother. Using his own nonmagical skills, which may include anything from simple cunning to extraordinary physical skills (such as incredible climbing ability), Jack outwits physically or socially superior opponents, gaining either a MAGIC OBJECT or the hand of a nobleman's daughter. Jack's opponents might be mythological (a GIANT), supernatural (the DEVIL), or human (a nobleman).

The Jack tales can be traced to an international collection of folk narratives ranging from German tales about a young man named Hans to the more familiar English FAIRY TALE "JACK AND THE BEANSTALK." The North American Jack tale is particularly endemic to the southern and eastern regions of the United States, with a traditional origin credited to the Appalachian Mountain areas in Virginia, North Carolina, and Kentucky. The American Jack tales can be traced back to the mid-eighteenth century to the Hicks-Harmon families of Watagua and Avery Counties, North Carolina, to the Couch family in Harlan and Leslie Counties, Kentucky, and to folktales from Wise County, Virginia.

The protagonists of the European Jack tales are often characterized by naiveté and a general lack of intelligence, but the North American Jack is a self-reliant and cunning trickster figure. For example, in "Jack and the Devil," Jack agrees to combine his life-savings with the Devil's with the intent of creating a successful farm. Time after time, Jack tricks the Devil out of his share of the harvest or livestock, until the Devil eventually loses his entire original investment.

The American Jack tales also maintain a certain disparity from their European cousins through the incorporation of traditions and customs endemic to the Appalachian region. Instead of stealing the giant's gold or the mythical hen that lays golden eggs in the European version, the Appalachian Jack steals the giant's rifle and knife, which is indicative of the importance of these "real" objects to the American storytellers.

The Jack tales, perhaps better than any other collection of oral narratives, exemplify the universality of motifs and characters endemic to specific folk literature, while simultaneously maintaining a particular individuality contingent upon the localized cultural traditions and customs of different world folk cultures. *See also* HERO.

For Further Reading

Chase, Richard. *The Jack Tales*. Cambridge, MA: Riverside Press, 1960.

McCarthy, William B., ed. *Jack in Two Worlds: Contemporary North American Taletellers*. Chapel Hill, NC: University of North Carolina Press, 1994.

Perdue, Charles L. Jr. *Outwitting the Devil: Jack Tales from Wise County, Virginia*. Santa Fe, NM: Ancient City Press, 1987.

JACOBS, JOSEPH (1854–1916)

British folklorist and historian. Although Jacobs is primarily known as a historian of Jewish culture, his contributions to the study of FOLKLORE are of great import. Jacobs, who specialized in the FABLE, published two editions of AESOP's fables, *The Fables of Aesop* as first printed by William Caxton in 1484 with those of Avian, Alfonso, and Poggio (1889), which compared Greek FOLKTALES to those of Aesop, and *The Fables of Aesop, Selected, Told*

Anew, and Their History Traced (1894), a popular collection of the fables. Jacobs, in *The Most Delectable History of Reynard the Fox* (1895), discovered that this ANIMAL tale migrated from Finnish culture over a period of hundreds of years before finally being received into French culture. This discovery would lead Jacobs to make a comparison of European and Indian tales that emphasized the similar legends surrounding Buddha and Christian figures in *Barlaam and Josaphat, English Lives of Buddha* (1896), forcing other folklorists to acknowledge the importance of the migration of folktales between various cultures. Jacobs is also well known for his collection of Indian, English, and Celtic fairy tales, published under five separate titles, beginning with *English Fairy Tales* (1890) and ending with *More Celtic Fairy Tales* (1894). In publishing this series of books, Jacobs brought to the forefront of folklore studies the question of emphasizing the DIFFUSION and migration of folk literature.

For Further Reading

Jacobs, Joseph. *Celtic Fairy Tales*. New York: Dover Publications, 1968.

———. *English Fairy Tales*. New York: G.P. Putnam's Sons, 1968.

———. *Indian Fairy Tales*. New York: Dover Publications, 1968.

———. *More Celtic Fairy Tales*. New York: Dover Publications, 1968.

———. *More English Fairy Tales*. New York: Dover Publications, 1967.

JAMES, JESSE (1847–1882)

Infamous American outlaw. Born in Clay County, Missouri, the outlaw Jesse James began his notorious career as a member of "Quantrill's guerrillas," a pro-Confederate group seeking revenge against a local group of Kansas militiamen. In his relatively short life, Jesse and his brother Frank became two of the most feared and famous of all American outlaws. Accompanied by the James gang, a band of outlaws assembled by Frank and Jesse James during the mid-1860s, the brothers are credited with robbing numerous banks and railroad trains, as well as murdering several people involved in the robberies. Jesse

James, the victim of a murderous conspiracy, was assassinated by Robert Ford, a member of his own gang, in April 1882.

Although the number of railroad trains and banks robbed, as well as the numbers murdered, may be exaggerated by highly suspect reports, Jesse James epitomizes the American outlaw. Much of the FOLKLORE surrounding James draws comparisons between himself and the British folkloric figure ROBIN HOOD as one who "robbed from the rich and gave to the poor." Even though the James gang is credited with successfully stealing tens of thousands of dollars, it has not been proven that any of the money was distributed amongst "the poor." Part of the James legend includes the repeated denials made by both Jesse and Frank James concerning their respective roles in various robberies, even though Frank James himself acknowledged the brothers' involvement in a number of the escapades. Perhaps the most interesting piece of folklore attached to Jesse James centers upon the claims made by J. Frank Dalton who, in 1948, insisted that he was actually the outlaw himself, still living at the tender age of 101 years. However, much of the "evidence" that Dalton provided historians was proven false or inconsistent with the actual known events of James' life.

For Further Reading

Baldwin, Margaret. *Wanted: Frank and Jesse James.* New York: Julian Messner, 1981.

JAPANESE CREATION MYTH

Co-CREATION of the world and its deities in the Shinto tradition. The oldest Japanese text, the KOJIKI, compiled in A.D.712, and the NIHONGI, of A.D. 720, are the primary sources for the many variations of early Japanese stories.

At first, the cosmos was an unformed, egg-shaped mass. Eventually, the clearer parts separated and became HEAVEN, then the denser parts sank and became EARTH. A reed-shoot emerged from a spot of land still floating in the void and became the first god. Other deities followed, and the seventh generation consisted of a brother and sister, Izanagi and Izanami.

The two youngest GODS stand on the Floating Bridge of Heaven, the rainbow. They thrust down the Jewel Spear of Heaven—a phallus according to some scholars—and find the ocean. Brine dripping from the spear forms an island. In another version, the two are commanded by older gods to organize the floating islands. And in another account, the female—Izanami—gives birth to the Islands of Japan.

On the new land, Izanagi and Izanami build an elegant home. They marry by walking around opposite sides of a magnificent central pillar, but Izanami commits the blunder of speaking first when they met.

The two deities learn to make love by watching a pair of water birds called wagtails. But Izanami gives birth to a deformed leech child, Hiruko—the result of her impropriety at the wedding. They set Hiruko adrift in a reed boat. Then the god and GODDESS carefully repeat their MARRIAGE ceremony, making sure that Izanagi speaks first this time.

In Shinto tradition, everything in nature contains a deity. When Izanagi and Izanami produce the natural features of the earth—mountains, valleys, forests, meadows, waterfalls, streams, and the WIND—they create those deities. In some accounts, Izanami gives birth to them. In others, Izanagi produces several directly; for example, he exhales the wind.

Izanagi's and Izanami's most beautiful child is AMATERASU, the goddess of the SUN. Her brother SUSA-NO-WO, the storm god, is quite different. His temper tantrums and flowing tears wreak havoc on earth and in heaven. But the most difficult birth is that of the fire god, Kagu-Tsuchi. He burns Izanami so badly that she dies and goes to Yomi, the LAND OF THE DEAD.

Izanagi follows her, but Izanami says he is too late—she has already eaten food cooked in Yomi. Izanagi breaks off a tooth from the comb he wears in his hair and lights it for a torch. He sees Izanami's body decayed and infested with maggots.

Furious that Izanagi has viewed her horrible condition, Izanami calls forth the eight Ugly Females of Yomi. The monsters pursue

Izanagi back to the living world. To slow them down, he turns his headdress into a bunch of grapes then his comb into bamboo shoots. Each time, the Ugly Females stop to eat before resuming the chase. When he reaches the pass to the living world, Izanagi drives the monsters back by throwing peaches at them.

Izanagi blocks Yomi Pass with a great boulder. From that position of safety, he has one last discussion with his wife. Izanami threatens to kill one thousand of his subjects a day in retribution for shaming her. Izanagi counters that if she does, he will cause 1500 children to be born every day. Finally, Izanami urges Izanagi to accept her death. He enacts the ritual of divorce and never goes back to Yomi, not even when he dies.

After his escape from Yomi, Izanagi cleanses himself in the SEA. In doing so, he creates deities of the ocean, of good and ill luck, and others. In some variants, the gods of the sun, moon, and underworld are created from the washing of his eyes and nose.

In *The Hero with a Thousand Faces,* Joseph Campbell (*see* CAMPBELL, JOSEPH) notes the concept of a primordial COSMIC EGG in ANCIENT GREEK STORYTELLING, HINDU STORYTELLING, BUDDHIST STORYTELLING, as well as the mythic traditions of Finland and Polynesia.

Dual creator deities appear in Hindu and NATIVE NORTH AMERICAN STORYTELLING as well as in many other oral traditions The paired deities are often brothers, but sometimes a male and female are partners in creation—as in the case of Izanagi and Izanami. In Polynesia, for example, both male and female are contained in the Cosmic Egg. (*See also* HOPI CREATION).

Generally, one of the creators is constructive and the other destructive—one ruling the land of the living, the other ruling the underworld. A DESCENT TO THE UNDERWORLD in an attempt at RESURRECTION of the dead is a worldwide theme. The idea of being bound to the underworld after eating food there is also found in the Greek story of Persephone, as well as in many European, Maori, Melanesian, and Native North American sto-

ries. *See also* BALDR, COSMOLOGY, MAORI, PERSEPHONE MYTH, POPOL VUH.

For Further Reading

Aston, W.G. *Shinto: The Way of the Gods.* New York: Krishna Press, 1974.

Campbell, Joseph. *The Hero With a Thousand Faces.* Princeton, NJ: Princeton University Press, 1990.

Nihongi: Chronicles of Japan from the Earliest Times to A.D. 697. Translated by W.G. Aston. London: George Allen & Unwin, 1956.

Nomura, Noriko S. *I am Shinto.* New York: PowerKids Press, 1996.

Piggott, Juliet. *Japanese Mythology.* London: Paul Hamlyn, 1969.

JAPANESE STORYTELLING

The history of the storytelling tradition in Japan. The earliest Japanese stories concern the cosmogony, which is Shinto, and are recorded in the oldest Japanese book, the KOJIKI, written in A.D. 712. In it the world begins with the birth of seven deities, who pass away to high HEAVEN, followed by five couples of deities who are born, the last couple being Izanagi and Izanami (*see* JAPANESE CREATION). This is followed by the *Theogony* and the stories of Izanagi's DESCENT TO THE UNDERWORLD to bring Izanami back after she dies giving birth to the god of Fire. Izanagi then gives birth to three more deities: SUSA-NO-WO, the God of the WIND, who springs from his nose; the God of the MOON from his right eye; and from his left eye, AMATERASU Omikami, the GODDESS of the SUN, the main deity of Japan and the ancestor of the Imperial House of Japan. Stories about Amaterasu and Susa-no-wo form a cycle of MYTHS that also show the connection between these gods and the emperor of Japan.

Buddhist mythology also contributes to the stories told in Japan, including many new deities with their own LEGENDS. Numerous legends and tales surround the Buddhist figure of Jizo, who is believed to be a protector of all suffering people, especially small children; he also has the power to take sinners from HELL to PARADISE. Kwannon, formerly a male *bodhisattva,* or future BUDDHA, became a woman—KUAN YIN—in Chinese mythology, and in Japan is considered the Goddess of

Mercy. Japanese DEMONS, called *oni*, are regularly found in FAIRY TALES and legends.

Japan has many of its own fairy tales that are part of the oral tradition. Five of the most popular ones known to all Japanese children include the story of URASHIMA TARO, a Japanese version of RIP VAN WINKLE; the story of MOMOTARO, who was discovered sitting in a peach when he was a baby; the story of Kintaro, a warrior HERO; the story of the Mirror of Matsuyama; and the story of the Bamboo-Cutter and the Moon-Child. Popular ANIMALS in Japanese folk tales include the Fox and the BADGER. GHOST STORIES are also very popular.

For Further Reading

Hearn, Lafcadio, et al. *Japanese Fairy Tales*. Illustrated by Ruth McCrea. New York: Peter Pauper Press, 1948.

Lang, Andrew. "Urashimo Taro and the Turtle." *A World of Fairy Tales*. Illustrated by Henry J. Ford. New York: Dial, 1994.

Tyler, Royall, ed. and trans. *Japanese Tales*. New York: Pantheon, 1987.

JATAKA TALES

Indian birth tales of the BUDDHA. These tales of the Buddha in his previous incarnation, or birth, include characters who might be humans, ANIMALS, or *devas* (DEMONS). The situations in which the characters find themselves is related to their behavior in their previous existence, which is told in the *Jataka*. Thus the tales illustrate the law of *karma*, which states that actions in previous lives influence the conditions of the present life.

There are 547 of these tales in the Pali canon, part of the *Khuddaka-Nikaya* or *Sutra-pitaka*. The Chinese have several collections of *Jataka Tales*, taken from the Sanskrit or Prakrit, and VARIANT collections can be found in other Buddhist countries in Southeast Asia. A significant number of the tales were originally Indian; Buddhists later adapted them as a means of instruction by adding a prologue and an epilogue to the FOLKTALE. While the prologue sets the scene, the epilogue connects the characters with people who were important in Buddha's day. The verses, which sometimes offer the moral of the story and at other times part of the narrative and dialogue, are considered canonical.

One of the most well-known of the *Jataka Tales* is number 208, "Sumsumara-Jataka," the story of the monkey and the crocodile. In this tale, the future Buddha has been born a monkey who lives near the Ganges River at the foot of the Himalayas. A crocodile and his wife also live in the Ganges, and when the crocodile's wife sees the large and sturdy monkey, she has a craving to eat the monkey's big heart. Since the monkey lives on land, however, the crocodile and his wife have to figure out a way to catch the monkey. So the crocodile devises a strategy: when the monkey comes to drink from the river, the crocodile offers to give the monkey a ride on his back as a ferry to the other side of the river where delicious fruits and mango trees grow in abundance. Trusting the crocodile, the monkey climbs on his back, but as soon as the crocodile reaches the middle of the river, he dives down into the water, leaving the monkey thrashing about in the river. The monkey begs the crocodile to save him from drowning, but the crocodile has no intention of doing so, and he reveals the whole reason he has taken the monkey on his back to begin with—he wants his heart to eat. The clever monkey earnestly tells the crocodile that is impossible, for he does not have his heart with him lest it be broken while he leaps from tree to tree. The crocodile angrily asks where the monkey keeps his heart, and the monkey tells him it is hanging with the figs on the fig tree. The crocodile promises not to kill the monkey if he will show him his heart. So the monkey convinces the crocodile to ferry him back to the shore where the fig tree stands, but as soon as they arrive, the monkey leaps into the fig tree, chiding the crocodile for his lack of common sense. The humiliated crocodile then returns to his home. At the end of this tale, Buddha reveals that "the crocodile was Devadatta," his "life-long enemy, the lady Cinca was his wife," and he "was the monkey."

Other well-known *Jataka Tales* include "The Turtle Who Couldn't Stop Talking" and

"The Spirit that Lived in a Tree." Because the *Jataka Tales* appear in pictorial or bas-relief form on pagodas and monasteries, Buddhists of Southeast Asia are quite familiar with the tales and the virtues of Buddha they are meant to expose. Like the FABLES of AESOP in that both are beast tales used for moral purposes, the *Jataka Tales*, however, generally approach a higher moral level. Similarities can also be drawn between these tales and those found in the Brahmanical PANCHATANTRA and its Arabic counterpart, *Fables of Bidpai*.

For Further Reading

Ernst, Judith. *The Golden Goose King: A Tale Told by the Buddha*. Chapel Hill, NC: Parvardigar Press, 1995.

Galdone, Paul. *The Monkey and the Crocodile: A Jataka Tale from India*. Illustrated. Boston: Houghton Mifflin, 1979.

Hodges, Margaret. *Hidden in Sand*. New York: Scribners, 1994.

Khoroche, trans. *Once the Buddha was a Monkey: Arya Sura's Jatakamala*. Foreword by Wendy Doniger. Chicago: University of Chicago Press, 1989.

JERUSALEM

Holy city sacred to Jews, Christians, and Muslims, both as an actual historical place and a symbolic idea.

Jerusalem, an old Canaanite settlement, is first mentioned in the BIBLE when King David decides to make this city his capital (2 Samuel). David brings the Ark of the Covenant, containing the stone tablets given to Moses on MOUNT SINAI (*see* EXODUS), to Jerusalem, and he builds an altar to GOD on top of Mount Moriah, thus establishing the religious and cultural significance of the city.

The biblical books 1 Kings and 2 Chronicles describe the construction of a grandiose temple on Mount Moriah by King Solomon, David's son. The Temple of Solomon was an enormous structure. Outside it stood the great altar and within, in a curtained chamber called the Holy of Holies, was placed the Ark of the Covenant. The Temple was a unique site of Jewish sacrificial worship of God. The Temple of Solomon was destroyed by the Babylonians in 587–6 B.C. when they raided the city and took the Jews as prisoners. The significance of this devastating loss is poetically depicted by Jeremiah in the biblical book of Lamentations.

After 538 B.C., the exiled Jews were allowed to return to Jerusalem, and a smaller version of Solomon's Temple was built on the site of the original Temple. The biblical prophets Isaiah, Ezekiel, and others put forth the notion that the city of Jerusalem was a symbol of and identical with the Israelites—God's chosen people—as well as with the land of Israel itself. Jerusalem became a "heavenly" notion imbued with a significance that superseded the presence of the Temple. Through the prophets' teachings, the city became symbolic of the glory of the chosen people, and it served as a reminder of the presence of God.

In 20 B.C., the Jewish king Herod increased the size of Jerusalem by extending the street plan and by building an immense citadel at the western gate of the city, his own palace, and a reconstruction of the Temple of Solomon, which doubled the size of Solomon's original temple.

Jesus was born during the rule of Herod. He taught, performed miracles, died, and was buried in Jerusalem. He worshiped in Herod's Temple and predicted its destruction (Matthew 24, Mark 13, Luke 13:34), a prophesy that came true in A.D. 70 after a Jewish rebellion against the Romans, who had taken control of the city. Today, only the platform and some gates of Herod's Temple remain. For Jews, the Western Wall, a retaining wall of the platform, is a symbol of Jewish historical continuity. In A.D. 135, Jerusalem was razed by the Romans, and the Roman emperor Hadrian built a new city from which Jews were banned.

In A.D. 638, Muslims took Jerusalem from the Christian Romans. The Muslims built a mosque on the former site of the Jewish Temple. The mosque was called *al-Masjid as-Aqsa,* meaning the "distant sanctuary." The Quran tells how God carried his servant by night from the Sacred Sanctuary to the Distant Sanctuary. According to Muslim tradition, the servant is Muhammad, the Sacred Sanctuary is *al-Masjid al-Haram* and the *Ka'ba* at MECCA, and the Distant Sanctuary is identified as the Temple area in Jerusalem.

Later, the Muslims constructed in the middle of the Temple platform a shrine called the Dome of the Rock, an ornate octagonal structure over an outcropping of Mount Moriah. In Muslim tradition, the Dome of the Rock marked part of the foundation of Temple. To Muslims, Jerusalem is known as "the Holy" or "the Holy House," and their association with the sacred city runs through the Bible to the Temple and through the Quran to Muhammad. The significance of Jerusalem for Muslims centers exclusively on the Temple mount.

For the ancient Hebrews, Jerusalem was God's dwelling place. The Hebrews identified themselves with the city and the Temple; for them, the people, the city, and the Temple were united and linked in destiny. Eventually, the notion of a "Heavenly Jerusalem" emerged, an idea that persevered after the loss of the city and the destruction of the Temple; this Jerusalem is perennial. Historical Jerusalem had little meaning for early Christians; however, the notion of "Heavenly Jerusalem" as a symbolically charged place took hold. Jerusalem, as in the book of Revelations, became the newly discovered Kingdom of God and a symbol of the New Covenant. In Islamic tradition, the *Ka'ba* itself will travel from Mecca to Jerusalem for the Day of Judgment.

As with various cities in other storytelling traditions, Jerusalem is feminine in nature. The city is imbued with the properties of nourishment and protection. It must be guarded against potential invaders, and her corruption or destruction is a tragedy. *See also* THEBES, TROY, URUK, ZION.

For Further Reading

Vilnay, Zev. *Legends of Jerusalem: The Sacred Land.* Vol. 1. Philadelphia, 1973.

JEWISH STORYTELLING

History of the storytelling tradition of the Jews. Jewish storytelling comes from the many different countries to which Jews dispersed over the many centuries after they were expelled from Canaan, now Israel, and later from Spain at the time of the Spanish Inquisition (1478). While a large portion of the stories told by the Jews of Eastern Europe came from rabbinical writings, the *Talmud*, and MIDRASHIM, the stories told by the Jews who settled in Morocco, Tunisia, Turkey, Egypt, the Levant, Yemen, Iraq, Iran, Afghanistan, and the Caucasus often show similarities to the storytelling of other cultures. The influence of the THOUSAND AND ONE NIGHTS can be found in a number of the tales from North Africa, for example.

Many types of FOLKTALES belong to the Jewish storytelling tradition. Characters may be drawn from the Hebrew BIBLE, as in the numerous tales that illustrate the legendary wisdom of King Solomon, such as "King Solomon and the Jar of Honey," "King Solomon and the Old FROG," "Solomon and the Poor Man," "King Solomon and Queen Keshira," "King Solomon and the Stars," "King Solomon's Wager with Fate," and "King Solomon and the Three Brothers," where the youngest brother is the one who heeds Solomon's wisdom, which he prefers to gold (*see* YOUNGEST SON).

Others tell of rabbis and students, including "Rabbi Nissim the Egyptian," "The Talmud Student Who Wished to Study Magic," "Rabbi Judah the Pious and the Beardless Rich Man," "Rabbi Abraham ben Ezra and the Devil Worshipers," "Rabbi Yehiel and the King of France," and "Rabbi Isaac Luria and the Waverers." KINGS, PRINCESSES, rich men, poor men, DEMONS, and tailors are other typical characters in these stories.

In another cycle of folktales, the major character is the Ba'al Shem Tov, the folk name given to Rabbi Israel Ben Eliezer (1700–1760), the founder of *hasidism*, the religious and social movement that spread through Eastern Europe in the mid-eighteenth century (*see* BAAL-SHEM STORIES). As a young man, he was a miracle worker, a *ba'al shem*, who could cure the various ills of both body and soul by employing the medicinal herbs he had studied along with using vows, amulets, and prayer. The Ba'al Shem Tov was also known for being both gracious and talented as a storyteller, and people came to him for advice and guidance. From this group came his disciples, the *hasidim*, and he taught them his philosophy by using stories, FABLES, homilies, and shirt dialogues. Among the stories included in this cycle are "The Baal Shem Tov and the WITCH," "The Baal Shem Tov and the Frog," "The Baal Shem Tov and the Dybbuk," "The Baal Shem Tov's DREAM," "The Baal Shem Tov and the Sappatai Zevi," and "The Baal Shem Tov and the DEVIL."

Many Jewish tales depict the *golem*, or "homunculus legend in Jewish folklore," which dates back to Rabbinic times. As Nathan Ausubel writes in *A Treasury of Jewish Folklore*, "In its literal meaning the word 'golem' means lifeless, shapeless matter into which the one who has discovered the tetragrammaton (*Shem-Hamforesh* or God's Ineffable Name), can by its mystic means breathe the impulse of life." The golem was said to be created by great rabbis and miracle workers, who used them as automaton servants. Often the stories tell of the golem exceeding its orders and thereby causing difficulties. Among the most well-known of these tales of the golem are "The Golem or The Miraculous Deeds of Rabbi Liva," told by Yudl Rosenberg, "The Golem of Vilna," and "The Golem of Prague."

Other types of tales include the numerous Jewish mystical tales drawn from the *Talmud*, the Zohar, and Hasidic masters. Jewish tales of the supernatural include VARIANTS of the story of PANDORA, the PERSEPHONE MYTH, and the FAIRY TALES "The Fisherman and His Wife," "Bluebeard," and "The Sorcerer's Apprentice."

Modern Jewish storytelling shows both the influences of the various cultures that surround it as well as the melting pot of sources that can be found in contemporary Israel today. Because of this, the stories told by American Jews, North African Jews, and Israeli Jews may be vastly different though they share a religion.

For Further Reading

Ausubel, Nathan, ed. *A Treasury of Jewish Folklore*. New York: Bantam, 1980.

Neugroschel, Joachim, comp. and trans. *The Great Works of Jewish Fantasy and Occult*. Woodstock, NY: Overlook Press, 1986.

Singer, Isaac Bashevis. *Yentl the Yeshiva Boy*. Illustrated by Antonio Frasconi. New York: Farrar, Straus, Giroux, 1983.

Weinreich, Beatrice Silverman, ed. *Yiddish Folktales*. Translated by Leonard Wolf. New York: Pantheon, 1988.

JINNIE

Also *jinn, jinni, djinn,* and *genie* (and sometimes misconstrued as related to "genius")— a type of Arabian DEMON or spirit that lurks in the wilderness or roams the desert and has miraculous power. The jinnie is born of fire with the power of assuming the form of any animal, human, or supernatural being, often the snake (the household serpent is one of the only good jinn [the plural of jinnie is *jinn*; the feminine form, *jinniyah*] and the jinn that is most similar to the Roman *genie*); the goat (this common form suggests parallels to the goat-like SATYR); the GIANT; the beetle; the toad; the scorpion; and the being described as half hyena and half wolf. Jinn remain mostly unseen to humans, although they always retain an animal characteristic, often a paw, hoof, or tail. Humans are alerted to their presence by the crow of a rooster or the bray of an ass. The ass and the rooster are the only beings who can see the jinn (aside from Solomon, who was at first sight horrified by the jinn, but nevertheless went on to become their master and was able to command them at will with a magic ring). The jinn roam by night and disappear at dawn, riding abroad on foxes, ostriches, or other beasts.

The earliest concept of the jinn is of a malicious nature demon who is sometimes believed to be the earliest inhibitor of the EARTH. Often in animal shape, the early jinn lived only in deserted or impure places. Later, when Islam adopted the spirits, there were both good and evil jinn. This dualism evolved to accommodate five kinds of jinn: *jann, jinn, shaitan, ifrit,* and *marid,* though they are seldom distinguished in English translation.

The jinnie is seen most prominently in Arabian FOLKLORE, where he is often portrayed as the powerful antagonist or protagonist of the Arabian FOLKTALE. In the story "Bird of the Golden Feather," for instance, the jinnie takes the forms of a bird, a pomegranate, a girl, a horse, and a servant to ultimately reveal himself as the HERO of the tale. There is also probably a connection between the jinnie and the Genie of the THOUSAND AND ONE NIGHTS. (*See also* NEAR AND MIDDLE EASTERN STORYTELLING).

However, the jinnie is not exclusively Arabian. Outside of Arabian folklore, resemblance to the jinnie is seen in the Persian and Hindu *devas, divs, rakshasas,* and *yakshas*; in the Moroccan *jnun* (a toad-like demon); and in the Roman and European (chiefly French) *genie* (plural *genii*). *Jinnistan*, an Arabian transmutation of the word jinnie, is an Arabian fairyland.

For Further Reading

Muhawi, Ibrahim, and Sharif Kanaana. *Speak, Bird, Speak Again: Palestinian Arab Folktales.* Berkeley: University of California Press, 1989.

Surmelian, Leon. *Apples of Immortality: Folktales of Armenia.* Berkeley: University of California Press, 1968.

JOAN OF ARC (1412–1431)

Virgin saint who heard voices telling her to save France from the English during the Hundred Years War; later, she was tried for witchcraft and heresy and then burned at the stake (*see* WITCH). Joan of Arc is sometimes called the Maid or the Maid of Orléans.

Joan was born at Domremy in Champagne, the daughter of a peasant farmer, and grew up during the Hundred Years War. Joan first heard mysterious voices at about the age of 14. In the beginning, there was a single voice accompanied by a blaze of light. Later, the voices increased, and she identified them as Saint Michael, Saint Catherine of Alexandria, and Saint Margaret. The voices urged her to save France from its English and Burgundian aggressors. By May of 1428, the voices were insistent and explicit. Eventually, Joan secretly left her home and went to Vaucouleurs to see Robert Baudricourt, the commander of the royal forces in that town. His disbelief in Joan's message was undermined when he received confirmation of a French defeat that Joan had earlier predicted. Joan gained further credibility when other predictions and prophecies of French defeat were fulfilled, and, early in 1429, Baudricourt sent her with an escort of three men-at-arms to the Dauphin (later Charles VII). Joan dressed in male clothes to protect herself. The Dauphin was impressed by Joan's ability to recognize him in disguise; it is said that she gave him an unknown sign, proving the supernatural origin of her mission. She asked for troops to relieve Orléans. Before the Dauphin granted her request, theologians examined Joan for three weeks. They found no reason for disapproval and advised the Dauphin to make use of her special abilities. Joan was provided with white armor, a special standard, and a staff of attendants. She joined the French army at Blois. With Joan riding at the head, the French army saved Orléans and captured nearby English forts. Joan's presence was immensely successful in boosting the low morale of her compatriots. A wound to her breast by an arrow enhanced her reputation. She continued to lead other military victories against the English, which Joan had prophesied including their approximate dates.

In July 1429, the Dauphin was crowned Charles VII with Joan at his side. This event supposedly completed her mission, and Joan knew that she would not live for long. She continued to lead attacks with less success. In 1430, she was captured by the Burgundians at Compiegne. The duke of Burgundy imprisoned her, and Charles left her to her fate. The Burgundians sold Joan to the English, who declared her success the result of witchcraft and SPELLS. She was imprisoned at Rouen for nine months and tried on charges of witchcraft and heresy by the court of the bishop of Beauvais. During fifteen sessions of examination, Joan maintained a shrewd defense and refused to betray the origin of her mission. The judges declared her visions inauthentic and found her diabolical, a verdict supported by the University of Paris. Joan was forced into making some sort of recantation, and then she was imprisoned again. She resumed wearing the male clothes, which she had earlier agreed to abandon. After another visit from the bishop of Beauvais, Joan was declared a lapsed heretic and turned over to the civil authorities. She was burned at the stake in Rouen's market-place on May 30, 1431. She was less than twenty years old. She is said to have died while looking at a cross and calling Jesus' name. Her ashes were thrown into the Seine. In 1456, Pope Callistus III appointed a commission that declared Joan's innocence; she was canonized in 1920 by Pope Benedict XV.

Stories about Joan of Arc contain many elements of the universal HERO pattern or monomyth. Joan is born at a time when France needs a strong leader to save it from its political foes. Joan's call to adventure comes in the form of mysterious voices, compelling her to leave home to fulfill her mission. In other traditions, the voice of GOD calls to Moses from the burning bush (*see* EXODUS), and the young BUDDHA is summoned by the "Four Voices" that appear to him as he rides with his charioteer. Like Moses, Joan is equipped with special signs to convince skeptics of the urgency of her mission.

Joan's QUEST is marked by various trials, including a battle wound, and confrontations with those who don't believe in the validity of her mission. Throughout her quest, however, she is guided by the voices, just as many other heroes and HEROINES receive strength from various sources; in FAIRY TALES, for example, heroes and heroines are frequently by guided by a spirit who takes the form of a FAIRY GODMOTHER, a WISE OLD MAN, or a wise fool. Joan's condemnation as a heretic, her execution, and her eventual canonization contain elements of the MOTIF of the SCAPEGOAT, which is associated most strongly with Jesus, ATTIS, Osiris, DIONYSOS, and others from the DYING GOD tradition (*see* ISIS AND OSIRIS).

In addition, the fact that Joan was believed by many to be a witch is an important aspect of her LEGEND. Persecution of accused witches and the suspicion of witchcraft in intolerant societies are themes addressed in Arthur Miller's play *The Crucible* as well as in Nathaniel Hawthorne's novel *The Scarlet Letter*.

For Further Reading

Banfield, Susan. *Joan of Arc*. New York: Chelsea House, 1985.

Fadiman, Edwin Jr. *The Feast Day*. Illustrated by Charles Mikolaycak. Boston: Little, Brown, 1973.

Shaw, Bernard. *Saint Joan*. 1924. Reprint, New York: Penguin, 1946.

JOHNNY APPLESEED

Legendary character in American history, literary tradition, and FOLKLORE based on the American pioneer, John Chapman (1774–1845). Born in Massachusetts, Chapman became a devout follower of the Swedish scientist-philosopher and mystic, Emanuel Swedenborg; this influenced the rest of his life. Chapman began his travels in the 1790s across the East and the Midwest on foot, planting fruit trees and supplying frontier settlers with apple seeds. "Johnny Appleseed" planted orchards of fruit trees in Pennsylvania, Illinois, Indiana, and Ohio, but his legendary status has led to claims that he planted orchards from New England to California. The LEGENDS that surround the figure of Johnny Appleseed are various and sometimes contradictory. Stories commonly ascribe to him a devout reverence for life; he would harm neither animal nor human, and for years regretted killing in anger a rattlesnake that bit him. He is often described as a barefoot itinerant wearing tattered clothes, or even a mere sack over his body, using his cookpot as a hat, and tearing apart his Swedenborgian tracts in order to distribute them more widely to the people he met. Legend tells us that he was never harmed by Indians, but worked as a intermediary between them and the frontier settlements. Allegedly, his friends and acquaintances included Daniel Boone (*see* BOONE, DANIEL), John James Audubon, Abraham Lincoln, Generals George Rogers Clark and Anthony Wayne, and even the illustrious Paul Bunyan (*see* BUNYAN, PAUL).

The missionary-like character of Johnny Appleseed has been celebrated in BALLADS and works of poetry and prose throughout the last century. He is seen as a symbol of the pioneer, an individualist who is concerned with simple living and service to others. Lydia Maria Child's poem *Appleseed John* is one of the most popular "Appleseed" verses; its exact publication date is unknown, but the poem was in circulation before Child's death in 1880. Other important appearances of the figure of Johnny Appleseed in poetry include Denton J. Sniger's *Johnny Appleseed's Rhymes* (1894) and Vachel Lindsay's free verse poem

In Praise of Johnny Appleseed (first published in 1921 but subsequently condensed and revised). Many book versions of Johnny Appleseed's legend have also been published, which are appropriate for storytelling; for example, Reverend Newell Dwight Hillis's sentimental novel, *The Quest of John Chapman* (1904), is the first fully developed narrative of Chapman's life. Other novels about Johnny Appleseed include Eleanor Atkinson's *Johnny Appleseed, The Romance of the Sower* (1915), Louis Bromfield's *The Farm* (1933), and Harlan Hatcher's *The Buckeye Country* (1940). Playwrights have also adopted the story of John Chapman; perhaps the best-known stage version of this legend is Marc Connelly's and Arnold Sundgaard's *Everywhere I Roam* (1938). Although it seems that few contemporary writers are occupied with rewriting or revising the MYTHS surrounding John Chapman, his legendary identity as Johnny Appleseed is firmly established in American folklore and is perpetuated in contemporary children's literature and collections of TALL TALES.

For Further Reading

Hatcher, Harlan, et. al. *Johnny Appleseed: A Voice in the Wilderness: The Story of the Pioneer John Chapman.* 3rd ed. Paterson, NJ: The Swedenborg Press, 1947.

JOHNSON, JAMES WELDON (1897–1938)

African American novelist, poet, scholar, educator, and political activist. Johnson grew up in a middle-class family in Florida, then was educated at Atlanta University and Columbia University. His commitment to civil rights in the early twentieth century led him to write poetry examining the social status of African Americans, to publish investigative essays and editorials exposing American oppression in many forms, and to assume important leadership roles in the National Association for the Advancement of Colored People in the years between 1916 and 1930. Johnson's professional career was always characterized by a diversity of interests: he worked as the principal of Stanton, his former primary school in Jacksonville; founded a short-lived newspaper called the *Daily American,* which was intended to educate the adult black population in Jacksonville; and studied and practiced law (he was the first African American admitted to the Florida bar).

Johnson's creative abilities led him to explore certain other career possibilities as well. In 1897, Johnson began collaborating with his brother John in writing songs and poetry; in 1900 they wrote the celebrated poem "Lift Every Voice and Sing," which became known as the "Negro National Anthem." The two Johnson brothers teamed up with the musician Bob Cole and together produced dozens of hit songs. In time, though, James Johnson's reluctance to exploit commonly held stereotypes about black people (through such media as the popular "coon songs" and minstrel shows) led to his disillusionment with the music industry. He entered graduate school at Columbia University and began to try writing more serious literature.

Johnson's first novel, *The Autobiography of an Ex-Colored Man* (1912), was published anonymously, in hopes that the fictional story of a light-skinned black man who decides to live his life as a white person might be perceived as an authentic life story. The novel itself was by no means personally autobiographical, but the story was familiar to Johnson, and he himself had known black people who "passed" for white. The novel (which was re-issued in 1927 under Johnson's name) received little critical attention when it was released, but has since come to be considered an important and revealing examination of the psychology of "passing." Johnson continued to write poetry, and published his first collection, *Fifty Years and Other Poems*, in 1917. Ten years later he released the unique, creative, and highly praised *God's Trombones: Seven Negro Sermons in Verse* (1927).

A prolific writer, Johnson published numerous essays and several other books, including *Black Manhattan* (1930), a historical examination of black life in New York. However, many consider his most important literary accomplishment to be his pioneering work in the compilation of African American anthologies of literature and FOLKLORE. In 1922 he included the work of 31 poets and an extensive historical preface in *The Book of American Negro Poetry*, the first anthology of African American poetry ever published. This collection was revised in 1931 to include some of the Harlem Renaissance writers whose literary careers peaked shortly after the first edition was released. Two other anthologies, *The Book of American Negro Spirituals* (1925) and *The Second Book of American Negro Spirituals* (1926), offer historical and linguistic examinations of the African American spiritual; these collections of songs greatly contributed to the increased awareness and appreciation of this traditional genre. Johnson was deeply interested in examining and promoting specific contributions that African Americans had made to national American culture, and his work greatly increased the attention and respect paid by both white and black critics to African American spirituals, ragtime, and folklore. Johnson's work as a collector of stories and songs related to the African American experience furthered academic appreciation and analysis of these uniquely American genres of cultural expression.

For Further Reading

Fleming, Robert E. *James Weldon Johnson*. Boston: Twayne Publishers, 1987.

JOKES

Short and simple stories with a humorous conclusion, or "punch line." Jokes belong to a long oral tradition and VARIANTS of the same joke are often passed from one culture to another.

Many jokes take their humor from words that have more than one meaning, or from variations of familiar sayings. For example, one joke tells a long story of a midget knight who rides a shaggy and unkempt dog. Its punch line is "I wouldn't send a knight out on a dog like that!" Such stories became popular after World War II, but derive their origins from earlier sources such as Chaucer's *Canterbury Tales* and Laurence Sterne's eighteenth-century novel *Tristam Shandy*, with

their long digressions and delight in narrative and storytelling for its own sake.

Other jokes are told with the intention of mocking the attributes of a group of people. Such "jokes" are often amusing to one party only, a situation in which a joke is not just a joke, but has potentially damaging consequences. These jokes usually invoke racial, gender, or cultural stereotypes for their humor, often mimicking dialects or accents in order to emphasize the supposed ignorance, inferiority, or disagreeableness of the featured group. Often, their punch lines can be transferred from one group to another. For example, British stories about the simplicity of the Irish often turn up in Irish culture mocking the Welsh.

A number of stories about married couples derive their humor by mocking the stereotypical ill-tempered wife, often a popular theme in societies dominated by men. In one such joke, a wife drowns and her husband looks for her upstream, assuming that her body will obstinately drift against the current. Other family members, such as mothers-in-law, are also subjects for jokes. Other jokes make fun of a prominent person, such as a politician or celebrity, often exaggerating the person's famous characteristics, or of prominent events.

Like the similar RIDDLES and NURSERY RHYMES, jokes are part of a larger oral folk tradition, a tradition that is continually evolving as cultures shift and come in contact with one another.

JUMP ROPE SONGS

Form of folk rhyme or chant sung while skipping rope. All over the world children skip or jump rope, and it is common to chant a song that keeps the tempo of the turning rope and the jumper. The earliest jump rope songs that have been recorded date back to the seventeenth century, and while the domain of jumping rope in America belongs generally to girls, in the seventeenth and eighteenth centuries boys jumped rope as well. In Thailand, the skip-rope dance is an excuse for boys and girls to be allowed to go out to play together.

The jump rope songs sung by Vietnamese and Japanese children tend to be tamer than the ones sung by American children. The earliest American rhymes drew on English sources, which children passed on to one another. As jump rope chants evolved in America, drawing on both European and African American sources, the chants reveal a variety of subjects: they range from storytelling, to political, to bawdy or openly sexual. They are often humorous, generally rhyme, and have double meanings. Sometimes they tell stories, and it is possible to find variants of the same rhymes in different regions throughout America.

As Francelia Butler writes in *Sharing Literature with Children*, "The chants accompanying rope-skipping . . . are in the nature of charms—if the child can get through the ritual of skipping without stumbling and so breaking the magical circle created by the swinging rope, then maybe he/she can get through life, or at least that phase of life with which the chant is concerned." The songs have a way of conveying power to the children who sing them and tend to reflect the culture and concerns of children. They can magically reverse the power teachers or adults have over them by chanting satirical songs such as the following one about a teacher: "The DEVIL flew from North to South/With Miss Hooker in his mouth/And when he found she was a fool/He dropped her on the Cherrydale School." The jump rope song as a kind of charm is obvious in the following folk rhyme from Malaysia: "If I swing high/And touch the rooftop/Before my teeth grow/I can read a book." Wherever a jump rope song hails from, it reveals children's love of rhyme, chant, and storytelling.

For Further Reading

Abrahams, Roger D., ed. *Jump-Rope Rhymes: A Dictionary*. Published for the American Folklore Society. Austin, TX: University of Texas Press, 1969.

Chase, Richard, ed. *Old Songs and Singing Games*. New York: Dover, 1972.

JUST SO STORIES (1902)

Collection of children's stories written by Rudyard Kipling (*see* KIPLING, RUDYARD). These stories were part of a Kipling family oral tradition: Kipling told such tales as "The Sing-Song of Old Man Kangaroo" and "How the Camel Got His Hump" to his children during their winters in South Africa. Later, the written versions were published in various magazines between 1897–1902, before being collected as *Just So Stories for Very Small Children* in 1902. Kipling also provided the original illustrations and the sing-songy poems that follow each story.

The title for the collection comes from the first story, "The Elephant's Child." This child, with his " 'satiable curtiosity" asks why such diverse phenomenon as the ostrich's tail feathers and the taste of melons are "just so." The stories, all addressed to "Best Beloved," attempt to answer questions like these, presumably asked by small children who share the elephant's keen curiosity. Kipling answers with fantastical post-Darwinian CREATION myths.

Each story concentrates on how a particular ANIMAL or human trait came into existence. For instance, in "The Elephant's Child," the elephant begins the story with a "blackish, bulgy nose, as big as a boot," but by the end has acquired a proper trunk. This feat of evolutionary adaptation is acquired in humorous Kipling fashion. The elephant child's many questions lead him across South Africa to the bank of the Limpopo River. There, he seeks out a crocodile to answer his question, "What does the Crocodile have for dinner?" A crocodile readily agrees to answer and enjoins the elephant to put his head near the "crocodile's musky, tusky mouth." What follows is a veritable tug-of-war: the crocodile pulls the elephant's nose while a helpful Bi-Coloured Python Rock Snake wraps himself around the elephant's legs and pulls even harder. Finally free, the elephant child is embarrassed by his out-of-shape nose and tries to shrink it in the water of the Limpopo. The python eventually convinces him that the new nose is better, for the elephant can now spray himself with water, pick fruit off trees, swat flies, and best of all, spank all his relatives who once spanked him. The other elephants soon learn to value the long trunk as well.

One by one, they head to the Limpopo and the crocodile to undergo their own tugs-of-war.

All the *Just So Stories* are variations on this theme. In "How the Leopard Got His Spots," an Ethiopian hunter and a leopard change their skins to better chase the newly spotted and striped giraffes and zebras. To elude the painted jaguar, the hedgehog and tortoise miraculously become armadillos in "The Beginning of the Armadilloes." Kipling also provides mythic stories to describe the beginning of human literacy in "How the First Letter Was Written" and "How the Alphabet Was Made."

The stories share a landscape as varied as the British Empire itself. Set in South Africa, Australia, South America, India, and the Middle East, the tales paint an imaginative and mythic picture of the Empire. Given this setting, the stories also read as stand-ins for the oral traditions of indigenous people from these lands. Kipling's alternative myths represent, on one level, a westerner's sarcastic rendering of native creation tales. This effect is heightened by the exotic names of the human characters and the foreign words interspersed throughout the stories.

For Further Reading

Kipling, Rudyard. *Just So Stories for Little Children.* Harmondsworth, Middlesex: Penguin, 1987.

KA'BA *See* MECCA

KACHINAS

In Hopi Indian mythology, good spirits related to the AFTERLIFE. There are several meanings of the term *kachina* as used by the Hopi tribes. As Alice Marriott and Carol K. Rachlin note in *American Indian Mythology*, "a kachina may be one of the forces of nature: life, DEATH, fire, flood, or famine;" or it may be "the spirit of a much-loved ancestor," "a man dancing to impersonate one of these spirits," or "a doll carved and painted to represent a spirit." The Hopi kachinas live inside the San Francisco Peaks north of Flagstaff, Arizona, a sacred place to the Hopis. Their world is a kind of PARADISE, where corn, squash, melon, and beans are abundant, as is fresh water in real lakes, many important plants, and sacred trees.

As Hopi myth tells it, the kachinas spend the crop-growing months of February through July living side by side with the Hopis in their villages, but they are INVISIBLE except when they DANCE in the plazas. During this time they provide a sense of comfort and safety to the Hopis. At the end of July and the growing season, the kachinas perform a final dance for the people, distribute gifts to the children, and return across the desert to the San Francisco Peaks, appearing in the form of tall rain columns as they travel.

The Hopi goal is to live a good life, acting generously and kindly to others and keeping the heart pure. This will allow a person to join the kachinas after death. Those who act badly suffer the fate of going to the Two Hearts, the land of WITCHES, which is a desert. The kachinas are strong enough, however, to defeat the Two Hearts when a witch tries to take a good person.

Kachinas also belong to the Zunis, as well as many Rio Grande and New Mexican Pueblos, but the kachinas of these tribes do not live in the San Francisco Peaks. Zunis believe that when kachinas are killed they become deer.

The visit of the kachinas is celebrated in RITUAL dances performed by various pueblos at ceremonial times of the year. Men wear transforming masks to identify with the kachinas (*see* MASKS AND MASQUERADE). One must be an initiate in order to participate in these dances, led by medicine men, and many taboos exist concerning the impersonating of kachinas by the uninitiated. Initiates generally consist of all mature men and boys, who are members of the kachina societies, while most women and all children are considered among the uninitiated.

KALEVALA

National folk EPIC of Finland. The *Kalevala* is a conflation and concatenation of numerous traditional songs, sung by singers living mostly in Karelia, a large region on both sides of the Russo-Finnish border. Dr. Elias Lönrott (1802–1884) collected the songs during a number of trips to Karelia and compiled them in a book that was first published in 1835. He rearranged and expanded the poems and then published a second version of the *Kalevala* in 1849. Almost all of the verses in the *Kalevala* are the product of Finno-Karelian singers living in the first half of the nineteenth century. The songs were commonly performed by singers of both sexes to the accompaniment of a small harplike instrument called a *kantele*. Because the songs were gathered over many years from numerous singers, the poems in the *Kalevala* range dramatically in style and tone: some are lyrically tragical, some mere fun, while others depict warfare, magic incantations, or detailed observations of the daily lives of Finno-Karelian peasants. There is no particular unity of style in the 50 poems that comprise the *Kalevala*. The characters are peasants from an indefinite time in the past who rely on magic to carry out their roles.

The name *Kalevala* describes a completely legendary region, also called the Kaleva District, where much of the action in this epic takes place. The Kaleva District is thought to lie along the sea, and it features a misty headland and a foggy island. The Kaleva District is across the bay, or perhaps further, from North Farm (*Pohjola*), another center of action. A cold and gloomy place, North Farm is nonetheless a prosperous farm presided over by Louhi, known as the "mistress of North Farm."

In 1907, W. F. Kirby loosely translated "*Kalevala*" into "Land of the HEROES." Nearly 60 years later, Francis Peabody Magoun argued that such a "formula" was inadequate because the poems "do not designate any of their characters as a 'hero.'" In this sense, the *Kalevala* is not like national heroic epics such as the ILIAD, the ODYSSEY, the SONG OF ROLAND, or the NIBELUNGENLIED.

Similarly, Kirby wrote that the *Kalevala* "relates the history of four principle heroes": VÄINÄMÖINEN, Ilmarinen, LEMMINKAINEN, and Kullervo. Magoun prefers to refer to Väinämöinen, Ilmarinen, and Lemminkainen as the "Big Three," disregarding any "hero" status and Kullervo as a primary character.

The *Kalevala* begins with a description of how Ilmatar, the Air Spirit, descends into sea, is tossed about by WIND and waves, creates the EARTH, and finally gives birth to Väinämöinen, a son, who swims to shore. Even at birth, Väinämöinen is conceived of as being old; he is an eternal sage. The chief of the Big Three, he is a gifted singer and player of the *kantele*.

Once on shore, Väinämöinen clears and plants the country. He becomes pledged to Aino, who is distressed at having to marry an old man. Väinämöinen makes love to Aino in the forest. She returns home in grief and anger. Later Aino drowns. Väinämöinen captures her in the form of a salmon, but she escapes. His mother advises him to seek a bride in *Pohjola*, the North Farm.

Louhi, a gracious hostess and competent WITCH, receives Väinämöinen. She offers her beautiful daughter if he will forge the MAGIC OBJECT called the *Sampo*, a producer and symbol of prosperity. Väinämöinen replies that he will send his brother Ilmarinen to complete this task. The handsome Ilmarinen is a great smith and a skilled craftsman, but he declines to go to North Farm, so Väinämöinen causes a whirlwind to carry him there. Ilmarinen forges the Sampo, but Louhi's daughter refuses to marry him.

Next comes a group of poems relating the early adventures of Lemminkainen, a reckless ladies' man who is constantly getting into trouble. After he is slain, his mother rescues and revives him.

Väinämöinen and Ilmarinen travel to North Farm and agree that Louhi's daughter must choose between them. She chooses Ilmarinen. Everyone is invited to the wedding except for Lemminkainen, who is too quarrelsome and ill-mannered. Lemminkainen forces his way to North Farm and slays Väinämöinen in a duel. His mother sends Lemminkainen to hide on a distant island. Eventually he returns home and finds the whole country has been destroyed. He attempts to attack North Farm, but Louhi deters him with Frost.

The next group of poems tell of the Kullervo, a morose and wicked slave of great strength. He is mentally disturbed from having been rocked excessively as a baby. After a tragic life, Kullervo wanders into the forest and falls on his own sword.

In the last group of poems, Ilmarinen forges a new wife of gold and silver. He cannot give her life or warmth, and so he takes another of Louhi's daughters. She angers him so much that he turns her into a seagull.

The Big Three then make an expedition to North Farm to carry off the Sampo. Väinämöinen makes a *kantele* and lulls Louhi and her people to sleep. But Louhi pursues the robbers, and the *kantele* is lost overboard. Sampo is broken into pieces and disappears in the sea. Väinämöinen saves enough to secure the prosperity of the Kaleva District, but Louhi has only a small fragment. Väinämöinen makes a new *kantele*. Louhi brings pestilence on the Kaleva District, sends a bear against the country, and steals away the SUN and MOON. Väinämöinen drives away the pestilence and kills the bear. Ilmarinen terrifies Louhi into restoring the sun and moon.

In the final poem, the virgin Marjatta swallows a whortleberry and gives birth to a son, who is proclaimed King of Karelia. The angry Väinämöinen departs from his country, but he leaves behind his *kantele* and songs for the heritage of the people.

The *Kalevala* includes numerous MOTIFS found in stories from other traditions. The CREATION sequence with which the *Kalevala* begins contains elements of creation from chaos stories in which some power or force gives form and reality to indeterminate, undifferentiated no-thing-ness, thus turning it into cosmos. Other examples of creation from chaos myths include the BABYLONIAN CREATION, EGYPTIAN CREATION, NORSE CREATION, and JAPANESE CREATION. In addition, the creation story in the *Kalevala* also contains elements of creation from COSMIC EGG and EARTH-DIVER CREATION stories.

The character Väinämöinen resembles Adam, the first man in the Hebrew creation story and caretaker of the garden of Eden, as well as the Greek Orpheus, also a talented musician (*see* ADAM AND EVE, ORPHEUS AND EURYDICE MYTH).

The girl Aino's transformation into a salmon reminds us of the Norse god LOKI'S transformation into a salmon. Likewise, the rescue and resurrection of Lemminkainen by his mother parallels the ISIS AND OSIRIS myth, and Ilmarinen's creation of a wife from silver and gold is reminiscent of the Greek Pygmalion's creation of the beautiful woman Galatea from ivory.

The baby boy who becomes King of Karelia is discovered in a fen. The motif of a child's ABANDONMENT in water is repeated in the stories of Moses (*see* EXODUS), SIEGFRIED, and MAUI as well as the African tales CHILD IN THE REEDS and SECRET SON.

For Further Reading

Kirby, W.F., trans. *Kalevala: Land of the Heroes*. Vol. 1. London: J.M. Dent and Sons, 1907.

Magoun, Francis Peabody Jr., trans. *The Kalevala or Poems of the Kaleva District*. Cambridge: Harvard University Press, 1963.

KALI

Hindu GODDESS of CREATION, preservation, and dissolution. In Hindu mythology, Kali, consort of SIVA, is seen as one of the fiercer aspects of the Great MOTHER goddess, known as DEVI or Mahadevi by the Hindus. Other aspects of Devi are Uma, light; Gauri, the erotic; Parvati, the mountain woman; Durga, the inaccessible; Chandi, the fierce; and Bhairavi, the terrible. Called the Black one, Kali is known for her necklace of skulls, her fang-like teeth, and her long, lolling tongue, which symbolizes her voracious desire for drinking the blood of her victims. Dressed in black with her girdle of severed arms, she is portrayed as standing upon the corpse of Siva, who lies prostrate on a bed of lotuses. As in the case of the ISIS AND OSIRIS myth, Siva's phallus is erect, suggesting Kali's regenerative capabilities. Though her feet make her appear here as the conqueror, her right foot can be seen as protective, for it is placed on Siva's heart. Kali's four arms also suggest both her benign and frightening attributes, for while one right hand offers a blessing and the other assuages fear, one of her left hands holds a bloody sword and the other holds a head by the hair. Her paradoxical nature of both creator and destroyer is always apparent, as in the horrible features of her face in contrast with her beautiful and lithe body, with milk-filled breasts. Other depictions show Kali dressed in blood red drinking from a skull filled with boiling blood, stroking the cobras that wind about her neck or waist, representing a spider that beheads its victims, or appearing as sleep, night, DREAMS, or DEATH. In Indian terms, the wrathful, fearsome aspect of Kali is as necessary and beautiful as the gentler depictions of Parvati.

Of the many stories that surround Kali, one of the most famous in South India tells of a dance contest that is held between Kali and Siva. Kali challenges Siva's ability to dance better than she; however, it is Kali who loses. Siva's power or trickery outdoes Kali, and she is tamed of her wildness. The dancing is violent, and Kali loses not because she is an inferior dancer but because she is a woman: Siva lifts his leg in a way that Kali will not imitate because it offends her sense of feminine propriety.

The major sources for the various images and stories of Kali are the great Sanskrit texts known as the VEDAS, the MAHABHARATA, the RAMAYANA, and the PURANAS. Indian storytellers, known as *Pandits*, memorize all the verses of these texts and take great pride in their role in the villages where they are also commentators on the tales they recite with perfect intonation for each verse. Because Kali represents both positive and negative aspects of female divinity, she has continued to inspire major philosophers, sages, and authors. The great Vedantic philosopher of non-dual-

ism, Shankaracharya (c. A.D. 800), composed a famous hymn to Kali, where he describes her essence as "She who takes up her abode in all perishable beings under the form of energy." The Indian mystic Sri Ramakrishna (1836–1886), another important devotee of Kali, referred to her as his "Divine Mother" and "The Ferry across the Ocean of Existence"; Nobel Prize-winner Thomas Mann (1875–1955) gave Kali an important role in his novel of India, *The Transposed Heads* (1940).

For Further Reading

Harding, Elizabeth U. *Kali: The Black Goddess of Dakshineswar*. York Beach, ME: Nicolas-Hays, 1993.

Mookerjee, A. *Kali: The Feminine Force*. London: Thames and Hudson, 1988.

KARNA

Warrior and divine HERO of Hindu MYTH in the EPIC *Mahabharata*. As in the birth of various GODS and heroes such as BUDDHA and Jesus, Karna is miraculously born of the virgin Kunti. Kunti grew up the adopted daughter of Kuntibhoja. A kind and solicitous young woman, Kunti is pleasant to the sage Durvasa, who gives her a SPELL to make it easy for her to conceive sons, for he could tell she will have difficulty. Kunti tries the spell, and manages to call the SUN god to her, who becomes the FATHER of her son, Karna, who is born wearing earrings and armor. After the birth of Karna, Kunti is made a virgin once more by the Sun.

Kunti fears that her family will look badly upon her for having borne this son without a husband, so she throws Karna into the river. Rescued by a charioteer, Karna is renamed "Vasusena," and he becomes a skilled warrior and a generous man. When he is approached by the god Indra, who asks him for his armor and his earrings, he cuts them off his very body and gives them to Indra, though he bleeds everywhere (*see* "INDRA AND THE ANTS"). In return, Indra gives him "the Sakti weapon," able to kill any foe and Vasusena begins to be called Karna, "the cutter."

During these years, Kunti marries and bears three sons, again by divine conception. One of her sons, ARJUNA, is challenged by

Karna at a tournament. Arjuna thinks it is beneath him, however, to fight the son of a charioteer, but someone anoints Karna as if he were a KING, and Arjuna fights him. Kunti recognizes the anointed Karna by the marks of his divinity, and she tries to tell him the truth of his birth so he will not fight his brother. Karna can not believe the story, and Arjuna kills by Arjuna.

The myth of Karna embodies the recurrent themes of the miraculous birth, the DIVINE SIGNS, ABANDONMENT of the child in the water, and adoption by someone of a lower class, recalling the early years of the lives of the Hebrew Moses (*see* EXODUS), the German SIEGFRIED, the Hawaiian god MAUI, and the Greek Oedipus.

For Further Reading

Mahabarata for Children. Vol. 3. Cohasset, MA: Vedanta Center, 1994.

KATE CRACKERNUTS

Collected in the Orkney Islands, a FAIRY TALE about a girl named Kate who breaks an evil SPELL that has been cast over her stepsister and cures a PRINCE of a mysterious illness.

In this tale, a widowed KING with a daughter named Kate takes a new wife. The new queen also has a daughter named Kate, and the stepsisters love each other very much. The queen becomes jealous of her stepdaughter's beauty, and she devises an evil plan with a WITCH. As a result, Kate's head vanishes and is replaced by a sheep's head. Then Kate's stepmother (*see* STEPMOTHER—WICKED) turns her loose in the forest. The queen's Kate finds her stepsister and wraps her head in a cloth. They end up at a castle in a nearby kingdom, where the queen's Kate finds work. She learns that the elder prince is sickly and confined to his bed and that the king has offered a peck of silver to anyone who could watch the prince the whole night through; all who have tried thus far have vanished. Kate offers to sit up at night with the kingdom's ailing prince. At midnight, the prince suddenly rises from his bed, gets on his horse, and with the queen's Kate behind him, rides to fairyland. Along the way, Kate fills her apron with nuts from the trees' branches. The prince dances all night

with the fairies. At dawn, the prince and Kate return to the castle. The same thing happens the next night. This time, Kate learns that a magic wand a fairy child holds will restore her stepsister's pretty head. She rolls nuts across the floor, distracts the fairy child, and steals the wand. After she and the prince return to the castle, Kate cures her stepsister. The following night at the fairies' dance, Kate learns how to cure the prince. By rolling nuts to the fairy child, she is able to steal a magic bird from him. Kate cooks the bird for the prince. After the third bite, he completely recovers. In typical fairy tale fashion, the queen's Kate marries the prince, and the king's Kate marries his younger brother.

In similar tale, "The Twelve Dancing PRINCESSES," collected by the GRIMM BROTHERS, a king's twelve daughters mysteriously wear out their shoes every night, and the king offers a reward to anyone who can discover the cause. A number of princes try, fail, and are executed. An old soldier takes on the task, after having been warned by a CRONE not to drink the wine; she also gives him a cloak of INVISIBILITY. That night, the soldier pretends to be asleep, and then, wearing the cloak of invisibility, he follows the princesses through a trapdoor to fairyland, where they journey to a castle and spend all night dancing. For two more nights the soldier follows the princesses to fairyland. At last he tells all he has seen to the king, displaying tokens of proof that he has collected in fairyland. The princesses admit the truth, and the soldier chooses the eldest among them for his wife and becomes the king's heir.

For Further Reading

Briggs, Katherine Mary. *Kate Crackernuts.* New York: Greenwillow, 1979.

Greaves, Margaret. *Kate Crackernuts.* Illustrated by Francesca Crespi. New York: Dial, 1985.

KEIGHTLEY, THOMAS (1789–1872)

British folklorist. Keightley's major contributions to FOLKLORE center upon two books he authored in the first half of the nineteenth century. In *The Fairy Mythology* (1828), he acknowledges the importance of the oral tradition in the formation of a culture's folk literature. Working primarily with the FAIRY TALE, he theorizes that this genre originated in early Scandinavian-Germanic religions before eventually spreading to Celtic peoples of the British Isles.

Keightley appears to suggest the prevalence of a notion of community in the folk literature of disparate cultures. In his other major work on folklore, *Tales and Popular Fictions* (1834), Keightley divides folklore into three separate categories: one that migrated from the Middle East to Western Europe, one in which FOLKTALES resemble one another but appear to have developed independently of the others, and one that fits neither of the first two divisions. What is significant about this work is that Keightley recognizes the presence of different MOTIF groups in folklore. Keightley's comparative folklore studies paved the road for the work of other late nineteenth-century folklorists such as Edwin Sidney Hartland and William Alexander Clouston who would begin to classify stories and folktales according to motifs (*see* HARTLAND, SIDNEY; CLOUSTON, WILLIAM ALEXANDER).

KEYS

Symbolic of the double role of opening and closing, mystery or enigma, or of a task to be accomplished and the method for doing so. Keys are symbolically important in many cultures and in many forms of the oral tradition. Deeply connected with the two-faced Roman god Janus, who looks both backward toward the year's end and forward toward the beginning of the new year, the keys of Janus open the doors of the solstices, the ascending and descending phases of the annual cycle. Janus, god of initiation and binding and loosing as well as inventor of locks, is also considered the guide of souls because of his double face, one looking toward the sky and the other toward the earth. With a baton in his right hand and a key in his left, Janus guards all doors and governs all routes.

In FOLKLORE, LEGEND, and mythology, three keys often symbolize three secret chambers that hold valuable objects, representing initiation and knowledge. One key is made of silver, a second of gold, and a third of diamond, with the silver key representing the revelations attained through psychological awareness, the gold key representing philosophical wisdom and/or spiritual power, and the diamond key bestowing the ability to act. In the case of the HERO, finding a key precedes the discovery of the treasure. In the famous FAIRY TALE of "BLUEBEARD," the keys Bluebeard gives his wife before he leaves offers his wife the truth of her marriage just as it offers Bluebeard the sign of her insatiable curiosity.

For Further Reading

MacDonald, George. *The Golden Key*. Illustrated by Maurice Sendak. New York: Farrar, Straus, Giroux, 1967.

KIND AND THE UNKIND GIRLS, THE TALE OF THE

Title of the first FOLKLORE dissertation, written by Warren Roberts. Using the historic geographic method, Roberts analyzed the various tale types of this Native American story in order to graph the DIFFUSION and locate the original ARCHETYPE. Roberts was the first folklore Ph.D. candidate, in the first Ph.D. folklore program, under the direction of Stith Thompson at Indiana University (*see* THOMPSON, STITH). Roberts was awarded his degree in 1953, four years after the program's inception. In order to legitimize his degree in this still questionable new discipline, Roberts was required to take separate examinations in both the English and anthropology departments.

For Further Reading

Roberts, Warren E. *The Tale of the Kind and the Unkind Girls*. Detroit, MI: Wayne State University Press, 1994.

KING

Symbolic patriarchal figure of rule. The figure of the king functions as a symbol for law and order, integrity and ethics, the masculine principle, and divine power. Often equated with the creator GOD, the king is the earthly representative of God or the GODS in MYTHS and FAIRY TALES. He also represents the fertility of the land and is necessary for it to flourish. If his power wanes through age or illness, he must be sacrificed as a SCAPEGOAT in order to render the fallow land fertile once more.

The figure of the wise king is common in storytelling, as illustrated by the many tales in JEWISH STORYTELLING about King Solomon. The most well-known of these tells of how King Solomon was able to determine the true mother of a baby being fought over by two women. When Solomon suggested that the child be cut in half to divide him fairly, the true mother would not agree, for Solomon had wisely guessed that a mother would rather give up her son than have him killed.

The combination of wisdom and magical power is vested in the figure of the Celtic King ARTHUR, central to the many ROMANCES of the Arthurian cycle. Arthur's ability to pull the sword Excalibur from the stone signifies his supernatural power in the beginning of his life, and the hand that reaches out for the sword as it is thrown in the lake further suggests this as he is about to die; the boat of magical women who take him off with them at his death further corroborates this.

The aging king who is no longer at the height of his powers can be seen in the figure of Dhritarashtra, the aged monarch of the Hindu *Vedic* epics, and in the figure of Shakespeare's King Lear. King Amfortas of *Parsifal* symbolizes the sick king who represents sterility of spirit, as does the Fisher King of T.S. Eliot's *The Waste Land*. Oedipus of Sophocles' *Oedipus the King* is an example of a king who must be exiled from the city in order to cleanse and purify it, thus saving it from the plague that destroys it.

In fairy tales, the king may be the ethical king of "The FROG PRINCE," who insists that his daughter keep her promise to the frog who has saved her golden ball and happens to be a prince (or king) under a SPELL. In the tale of "Snow White," the king is an absent father whose daughter must find a way to cope with her wicked stepmother (*see* STEPMOTHER—WICKED) on her own. Becoming king also represents the end point of all the hero's trials and adventures on his journey-QUEST, and signifies maturity.

For Further Reading

Ausubel, Nathan, ed. *A Treasury of Jewish Folklore*. New York: Bantam, 1980.

Berenzy, Alix. *A Frog Prince*. Illustrated. New York: Henry Holt, 1989.

Morpurgo, Michael. *Arthur: High King of Britain*. Illustrated by Michael Foreman. FL: Harcourt-Brace, 1995.

THE KING'S DAUGHTER WHO LOST HER HAIR

African (Akamba) FOLKTALE that resonates with other classical stories told throughout the world. The story of *The King's Daughter Who Lost Her Hair* was one of many folktales transmitted orally in AFRICAN STORYTELLING sessions. The stories were sometimes told in DANCES accompanied by drumming. The themes in this story are familiar even to Westerners. The KING's daughter possesses luxuriant, floor-length hair that she is very proud of. When a mysterious talking bird asks the PRINCESS for a bit of her hair to build a nest with, the princess flatly refuses. The bird, angry over her refusal, chants a magical SPELL that causes the King's daughter to lose all of her hair the very next day. The King consults with the wisest men of his kingdom to find a solution that will replace his daughter's hair. After the princess dreams of a tree that grows a copious amount of hair, the King offers anyone in the kingdom a fortune if only they can locate this dreamed-of tree. A poor young man named Muoma is successful in locating the unusual tree, and this only after an arduous and dangerous journey into unknown lands. The tufts of hair brought back by Muoma are successfully replanted on the princess's head and all is well; Muoma is awarded the gold as well as the king's daughter as a wife.

For Further Reading

Abrahams, Roger. *African Folktales: Traditional Stories of the Black World*. New York: Pantheon, 1983.

KIPLING, RUDYARD (1865–1936)

British author, many of whose stories were based on his experiences in India. Kipling was born in Bombay of English parents. After a bleak childhood and an education in England, he began work as a journalist in India, writing for English newspapers. He also lived in or visited America, South Africa, and quite a number of other countries during his lifetime. He married Caroline Balestier in 1892, and for a time the couple lived in her hometown of Brattleboro, Vermont.

Kipling was acclaimed by English literary society after the publication of his semi-autobiographical *The Light That Failed* (1890). He was a prolific writer, producing stories, novels, and poems in a variety of settings. *Captains Courageous* (1897) was written after his stay in America. Today, Kipling is perhaps best remembered for his stories for children, especially *The Jungle Book* (1895), *Kim* (1901), and the JUST SO STORIES (1902). A number of his works have also been made into successful films.

Fortunately for Kipling, his children's works contain the least amount of racism and fascism, which has allowed them to endure. Kipling was inclined to be didactic, strongly advocating law and order, discipline, hard work, and the wisdom of age. Nevertheless, he also expressed a certain amount of ambivalence—admiring laughter, the vitality of youth, and even anarchical farce. His 1888 "The Man Who Would Be King" seems to parody his own admiration of men of action and of British imperialism. Kipling's autobiography, *Something of Myself*, was published posthumously in 1937.

Kipling was awarded the Nobel Prize in 1907, the first English writer so honored. In his writings, he glorified the British Empire and considered it necessary to rule over native peoples, but it should be remembered that he wrote in a time of extreme imperialism. However, his writing talents and genius for telling stories sustains his reputation. Kipling's storytelling, while firmly based in Anglo-imperialist views, is colored by a simplicity and "let me tell you a little story" technique that the author perhaps associated with his idea of an Indian telling a tale to his or her child.

For Further Reading

Harrison, James. *Rudyard Kipling*. Boston: Twayne Publishers, 1982.

Kipling, Rudyard. *Something of Myself: For Friends Known and Unknown*. Garden City, NY: Doubleday, Doran & Company, 1937.

KOJIKI

Oldest Japanese text, a chronicle of the earliest principles of Shinto nature worship. The *Kojiki (Record of Ancient Matters)* was compiled in A.D. 712 under the auspices of the royal court, probably to provide an authoritative statement of its own origins and verification of its claim to power. Even when they were recorded, the events were ancient history and had become overlaid with LEGEND and MYTH. The oldest actual manuscript is from A.D. 1371–72. The manuscript was kept by the Shinto priesthood until it was first printed in 1664.

The *Kojiki* is a collection of genealogical and anecdotal histories, begun at least a hundred years earlier than it was recorded. The preface states the aim of correcting falsehoods that had been allowed to creep into the historical and genealogical documents kept by the leading families. This was especially important to the ruling houses, since positions of power were based on ancestry and degree of relationship to the imperial family.

The bulk of the material in the *Kojiki* is made up of myths, legends, and songs. In addition to genealogies and what may be interpretations of early political events, the *Kojiki* includes a cosmology and a mythology, especially in the first of its three books. Some scholars have suggested that these stories are from an oral literature that had been memorized and recited verbatim over a long period of time. Both the *Kojiki* and NIHONGI were said to have been committed to memory by Hiyeda no Are, thought to be a woman. The original manuscripts may have been recorded from her recitation.

Other sources that have been suggested are early written records, the repertoire of court musicians, popular legends and rites, and the traditions of noble families and the court. Some of the myths contain elements that can be identified with southern Asia and Korea, while others reflect Chinese ideas.

The *Kojiki* relates a number of long and complex myths, including some not repeated in the *Nihongi*. Included are the JAPANESE CREATION MYTH, stories about Izanagi and Izanami, stories about the heavenly myth-world Takama-no-para, the home of the deities ruled by AMATERASU; and stories about EARTH and nature deities such as SUSA-NO-WO and his son-in-law, the god Oh-kuni-nushi.

For Further Reading

Kojiki. Translated by Daniel L. Phillipi. Princeton, NJ: Princeton University Press, 1969.

KRISNA

Hindu avatar of VISNU. Many MYTHS surround the life and DEATH of Krisna. Although he is hardly mentioned in the *Chhandogya Upanishad* (c. 500 B.C.), he is a prominent figure in the MAHABHARATA (A.D. 300-200) and the *Bhagavad Gita* (c. 500 B.C.). The numerous stories of the boy Krisna come later, in the tenth or eleventh centuries in the VISNU and *Bhagavata* PURANAS.

The birth of Krisna comes when Visnu plucks one black hair and one white hair out of his head and places them in the wombs of Devaki and Rohini; the black hair becomes Krisna. His birth is threatened by Devaki's uncle, Kansa, who learns that Devaki's son will destroy him, so Krisna is removed and carried to the home of Nanda, the cowherd.

Many stories surround the childhood and youth of the beloved Krisna, who has something of the TRICKSTER about him. While still an infant in the cradle, he manages to kill a demoness and calm a storm. The music of his flute is said to entice many women, and in one famous tale he steals the clothes of the *gopis*, or milkmaids, as they bathed.

He is the best friend and charioteer of ARJUNA in the *Mahabharata*, but he does not take sides between the PANDAVAS brothers and their cousins, the Kauravas. He is the source of important advice to Arjuna, which appears in the form of the *Bhagavad Gita*. When Arjuna has misgivings about fighting against his relatives, Krisna addresses both Arjuna's dilemma as well as the difficulties faced by the human soul. Krisna advises Arjuna to take the right action, *dharma*, with a detached commitment.

KROHN, KAARLE (1863–1933)

A Finnish folklorist known as the founder of the historic geographic method. Although Krohn gave this technique of analysis an international focus in the mid 1920s, his father and mentor Julius Krohn (1835–1888) was actually the first scholar to apply the method to FOLKTALE research in the late 1800s; Krohn focused his life's research on making geographical distribution maps of MOTIFS found in the KALEVALA, the national Finnish EPIC. Wanting to make accessible the growing archival treasury of traditional narratives, Kaarle Krohn created folktale classification. He deemed an index necessary when he struggled to gather from different countries variations of a particular story he was studying. The sheer number of folktales archived made research chaotic and nonsensical. Krohn put forth the most serious attempt to perfect a technique for the study of the folktale by counting frequency of occurrence of each possible handling of the trait. This process of mapping folktale DIFFUSION was removed from the confines of Europe and brought to America when Kaarle Krohn asked American scholar Stith Thompson to translate and complete Antti Aarne's tale type index. Krohn also proclaimed that stories can diffuse over great distances solely through oral tradition (*see* AARNE, ANTTI; THOMPSON, STITH).

KRYLOV, IVAN ANDREEVICH (1768–1844)

Russian author and fabulist. If Krylov is remembered for his work accomplished in the St. Petersburg Library system, then he is revered for the FABLES he composed in early nineteenth-century Russia. Although his early collections were merely translations of the fables of Jean de la Fontaine (*see* LA FONTAINE, JEAN DE), Krylov later composed collections of original work. Nothing is more characteristic of a Krylov fable than the harsh social and political criticism implicitly buried beneath his ANIMAL characters. In "The Bear among the Bees," Mishka the bear is elected Inspector of the Beehives for his seemingly trustworthy nature. However, Mishka abuses his position and steals all of the honey. Mishka, found guilty, is sentenced to spend the entire winter in his den. Although irony is present throughout the fable (bears usually hibernate during the winter), Krylov wrote this fable at a time when political extortion ran unabashed in Russia under Alexander I. Krylov's fables are important reminders of the difficulties and injustices encountered under the Russian regime of the eighteenth and nineteenth centuries. Furthermore, Krylov's fables, which bear a strong resemblance to those of AESOP, are important sources of children's literature due to the moral lessons inscribed within the tales—the above tale would presumably warn children about the negative effects of abusing one's power.

For Further Reading

Krylov, Ivan A. *Krylov's Fables.* Translated by Bernard Pares. Reprint, New York: Hyperion, 1987.

KUAN YIN

Compassionate Chinese mother GODDESS and bestower of children (*see* MOTHERS). Kuan Yin is the form taken by the *bodhisattva* Avalokitesvara, "the lord who looks down in pity," and she has the ability to take on different forms to ease suffering. Sent by the BUDDHA Amitabha, Kuan Yin is the goddess of mercy, protecting women and children. Yet because Kuan Yin is able to take on so many forms and sometimes appears as the many-armed male, Kwannon, in Japanese culture, she is also regarded as androgynous, neither male nor female.

In the Chinese Buddhist myth that recounts the story of Kuan Yin, Kuan Yin suffers when she must resist the cruelty of her father, whose home she has come to live in with her two sisters. As is typical in China, she is expected to marry. Although her sisters comply, Kuan Yin refuses to marry, desiring instead to live in the temple of the White Bird. However, her father makes sure the women of the temple mistreat Kuan Yin by forcing her to do the hardest work and eat the worst food. When the women sleep, Kuan Yin is helped in her tasks by a serpent, a tiger, birds, the fire spirit, and other HELPFUL

ANIMALS. This infuriates her father, who retaliates by setting the temple on fire. Kuan Yin extinguishes the fire by putting her hands over it, clearly showing her supernatural power. Next her father sends a servant to behead his daughter, but the sword cannot decapitate her and instead breaks into two pieces. Afraid of Kuan Yin's father, the servant then succeeds in strangling her. Kuan Yin is transported to the LAND OF THE DEAD on a tiger's back, but she transcends her own fear of death and begins to sing with a beautiful voice, and the shades are soothed of their sorrow by her song. Her ability to relieve suffering makes the KING of the Land of the Dead banish Kuan Yin, who now returns to EARTH and lives in solitude on an island in the northeastern SEA, continuing to bring peace and comfort to both the living and the dead.

KUNAPIPI

Great mother GODDESS of the aboriginal people of the Arhemland area of Australia. Kunapipi, translated as "MOTHER" or "old woman," (*see* CRONE) comes from across the SEA with the ancestors, preceded by the RAINBOW SERPENT who prepares the way for her. She creates the song lines from what the aborigines call "DREAM time," teaching the people to see and know the lines. These lines are to take the people to the sacred places on the body of Kunapipi, the sacred caverns carved out of the EARTH.

For members of the secret cult of Kunapipi, renewal of the original MYTH was part of their initiation, which took place after young men had already undergone their puberty initiation rites. The ritual practiced involved a reenactment of a return to the womb, from which they would then emerge, "reborn."

KUNIO, YANAGITA (1875–1962)

Japanese intellectual, diplomat, and pioneer FOLKTALE collector. Kunio, one of seven sons, battled illness throughout his childhood and was forced to leave elementary school. With the help of family and his own self-will, Kunio managed to overcome his early academic obstacles and graduated from the Tokyo Imperial University in 1900. He held several political positions, including a role as an observer to the League of Nations in 1921, but his first love was FOLKLORE. When Kunio began his work collecting the folk stories of Japan, he entered a field nearly nonexistent, at least as an academic pursuit. His first work, *Tono Tales* (1910), began a long series of published stories and criticism, and it was Kunio's work over five decades that brought respectability to the folk tradition in Japan. Kunio did not begin his full-time work on collecting tales until he was fifty-seven, but he had been wandering the country transcribing spoken stories since 1910. Kunio's critical works examine the differences in legend and folktale forms as well as the relationship between various Japanese tales. Kunio was a prolific writer, and his collected writings comprise 36 volumes.

For Further Reading

Kunio, Yanagita. *The Yanagita Kunio Guide to the Japanese Folk Tale.* Edited by Fanny Hagin Mayer. Bloomington, IN: Indiana University Press, 1986.

KUTOYIS

Savior, DYING GOD figure, and HERO of Native American mythology. In the Blackfoot story of Kutoyis, an OLD MAN allows a young warrior to marry his two daughters with the expectation that he will provide for him in his old age. The young man is generous for a time, but he soon refuses to give the old man and his wife any part of his kill. The old man even helps the warrior flush buffalo from beneath a log jam, but the warrior only grows more selfish. One day, when the warrior wounds a buffalo, the old man discovers a clot of blood on the ground and places it in his quiver. He sneaks it back to his lodge where he instructs his wife to place it immediately into a pot of boiling water. Almost immediately they hear screams coming from the pot, and they quickly remove a crying baby boy from the pot. Knowing that the warrior will murder the child if he discovers it is a boy, they trick the warrior into believing the child is a girl. They name the child Kutoyis which means "clot of blood."

After only four days, the child begins to speak, instructing the old couple to tie him between the lodge poles. When they comply, Kutoyis grows immediately into a man. He then learns of the warrior's cruelty and plans to cure the injustice. After an ineffectual attempt by the old man to kill the warrior, Kutoyis intervenes and shoots the warrior four times. Kutoyis kills not only the warrior but the old couple's two daughters as well. Since the daughters have let the love for their husband overcome compassion for their parents, Kutoyis must kill them.

Kutoyis then proceeds on a journey in which he encounters ANIMALS and MONSTERS who demonstrate their greed by not caring for the community's elder members. After criticizing their cruelty, Kutoyis kills the bear and snake people, sparing one female from each group to perpetuate the species. In his next adventure, Kutoyis comes to a realm where most of the people have been consumed by a monster named Wind Sucker. Kutoyis enters Wind Sucker's mouth and kills him from within, releasing the live captives through an incision in Wind Sucker's ribs. Shortly thereafter, he has two separate battles with women who attempt to destroy him. Upon defeating them both, Kutoyis conquers his final enemy, "Man-Eater," by allowing himself to be killed, cooked, and resurrected.

As a hero, Kutoyis fulfills many aspects of the QUEST theme. He has a miraculous birth, endures trials and monsters, fights off *femme fatale* figures, enters and departs from an underworld atmosphere, and brings benefits to his people. *See also* MONSTER KILLED FROM WITHIN.

For Further Reading

Grinnell, George Bird. *Blackfoot Lodge Tales.* Lincoln, NE: University of Nebraska Press, 1962.

Leeming, David. *World of Myth.* New York: Oxford University Press, 1990.

LA FONTAINE, JEAN DE (1621–1695)

French author known for his FABLES. *The Fables of La Fontaine* made this French poet and author of comedies, BALLADS, bawdy tales, and elegies world famous. Born at Chateau-Thierry, La Fontaine came from a bourgeois family and was a dilettante in his youth. He eventually settled in Paris, where he married in 1648. After his marriage ended in 1659, he lived in the home of a patron.

A libertine and lover of cultivated pleasures, La Fontaine passively avoided obligations and seemed to drift along as a kind of lazy dreamer. Yet he was a professional and prolific writer, with his major work, known in France as *Fables choisies, mises en vers* ("Selected fables, put into verse"), consisting of approximately 230 fables, mostly taken from AESOP, which appeared in 12 books. So popular were these fables that 37 editions appeared before La Fontaine's death. Although the main characters of each of these short fables are ANIMALS, they act with the flaws and foibles of human beings. While the fables appeal to children, they also work on a more sophisticated level as they were also written as a satire on French society at the time. Among the most well-known of the fables are "The Dove and the Ant," in which a dove saves a drowning ant and the ant, in turn, bites the heel of the hunter who would kill the dove and thereby saves the bird; "The Camel and the Floating Sticks," which reminds us that things that are frightening when they are far away are much less frightening close at hand; and "The Plowman and His Sons," which teaches us that "toil itself is a treasure."

La Fontaine was also known for his more scandalous *Contes and nouvelles en vers* (*Tales and Novels in Verse*), which appeared in four volumes between 1664 and 1674. Drawn from such writers as Boccaccio, Rabelais, and Ariosto, they reveal a sly licentiousness and produced a strong negative reaction in the Académie francaise and among the royalty and police.

Other works of La Fontaine include mythological poems retelling the stories of Adonis, CUPID AND PSYCHE, and the nymphs of Vaux.

For Further Reading

La Fontaine, Jean de. *Fables*. Translated by M.W. Brown. Illustrated by Andre Halle. New York: Harper, 1940.

Sewal, Roberta. *Five Fables of La Fontaine*. Illustrated by M. Boutet de Moneval. New York: Grolier Society, 1967.

LABORS OF HERAKLES

Greek MYTH that relates the adventures of Herakles, perhaps the most famous HERO in all of Greek mythology. The son of ZEUS and Alcmene, Herakles is relentlessly assaulted by the tricks of HERA, Zeus's jealous wife. After Herakles marries a PRINCESS and fathers children by her, Hera causes a fit of madness to descend upon him, leading him to murder his wife and children in an uncontrollable frenzy. When he returns to his senses, he realizes with horror what he has done. As penance for his sins, the oracle of APOLLO commands him to travel to MYCENAE to become the servant of the cowardly KING Eurystheus, Herakles's half-brother. If he accomplishes every task bestowed upon him, the oracle tells him, he will be received among the GODS.

Eurystheus, intimidated by and jealous of Herakles's physical prowess, devises a series of twelve seemingly impossible tasks that he is sure will destroy even his powerful kinsman. Herakles's first task is to slay the lion of Nemea, a troublesome and ferocious predator, and retrieve its body. Herakles travels to the forest where the lion lives, armed with a bow and arrows and an enormous wooden club. The arrows can not penetrate the lion's skin, so Herakles stuns the beast with a blow of his club and then strangles it with the immense strength of his hands. He returns to Mycenae with the carcass of the beast, and has its impenetrable hide made into a cloak for himself.

Eurystheus, terrified by Herakles's strength in battle, assigns him an even more difficult labor: to slay the deadly Hydra, a poisonous snake with many heads. Herakles, in the company of his friend, Iolaus, travels to the marsh where the Hydra lives. When they come upon the snake, Herakles begins crushing its many heads and then cutting them off. However, this approach proves fu-

tile, for where one head is severed, two spring up in its place. Herakles then adopts a different approach and commands Iolaus to sear the roots of each head with a hot iron as Herakles lops them off. This proves successful, and soon the headless MONSTER is dead.

The next task assigned to Herakles is to procure the hind of Arcadia, a stag sacred to the GODDESS ARTEMIS. Herakles pursues this fleet-footed animal for an entire year, never even approaching the wily creature. But eventually the stag becomes so exhausted that it can no longer out-distance Herakles, who captures the animal, binds its legs, and proceeds back to Mycenae. On his journey he encounters Artemis, who is deeply enraged at the capture of her precious animal. Herakles explains his situation and promises to return the stag to the forest after showing it to Eurystheus; Artemis allows him to continue on his way.

For his fourth labor, Herakles is required to kill a vicious wild boar that has been ravaging the area around Mycenae. He pursues the creature up into the mountains where the snows are very deep. The boar's short legs can not carry him easily through the snow, so Herakles soon catches up with the exhausted beast. He ties its legs, slung it over his back, and carries it down the mountain to Eurystheus.

Herakles's next task is to clean the stables of King Augeas in a single day. These stables house thousands of animals and have not been cleaned in ten years. Herakles asks the king for a tenth of his herds if he completes the apparently impossible task in one day; the king, of course, agrees. Then Herakles causes the river Alpheus to change course and clean the stables by gushing directly through them and then running into the SEA. When the task is completed, the river reverts back to its original course. King Augeas balks at rewarding Herakles for his accomplishment, because he claims that the labor had not been done by the strength of Herakles's own hands. In response, Herakles leads an attack on the kingdom, displaces King Augeas, places the former King's son on the throne, and returns to Mycenae with his reward.

The sixth labor assigned by Eurystheus is to kill the man-eating birds that live in the Stymphalian lake. There are so many of these dangerous birds that Herakles does not know how to drive them from their hiding places. To assist him, the goddess ATHENA gives him a brass rattle, which, when shaken, drives the birds into the air with its great noise. As they fly over the lake, Herakles shoots them with his arrows.

Herakles's seventh task is to capture alive the mad bull of Crete. He struggles with the mighty creature, and succeeds in subduing it with his bare hands. He carries the huge animal back to Mycenae, once again frightening his half-brother both with his trophy and with his enormous strength.

The next labor is to capture the man-eating horses of the savage King Diomedes. Herakles vanquishes the king in battle and feeds his body to his mares, then brings the mares back to Eurystheus. Terrified, the King commands the horses to be sacrificed to Zeus. Zeus rejects them as unnatural, and so they are eaten by wild animals.

The ninth labor of Herakles is to travel to the land of the Amazons and fetch the girdle of Hippolyte, their queen. He finds the queen quite willing to sacrifice her girdle to him, but to thwart his success in this labor Hera interferes and spreads a rumor among the Amazons that their queen is in danger. A fierce battle ensues, in which Herakles is forced to slay many Amazon warriors. He takes the girdle and returns to Mycenae.

The tenth labor is to destroy Geryon, a GIANT with three heads and three bodies, and steal his cattle. Herakles travels far to the west to find the giant and slay him. On his way back to Greece, he meets with many forces that try to steal the cattle; Herakles prevails, however, and drives the herd safely back to Eurystheus.

Herakles's next task requires him to retrieve some of the golden apples of the Hesperides. For this he needs the help of the immortals; only the gods know where the garden of the three NYMPHS called Hesperides is located. River nymphs tell him to force Nereus, the GOD of the sea, to reveal the location of the garden. After a long and difficult struggle, Nereus at last gives Herakles the needed directions, and Herakles eventually arrives at the remote garden. The guardian nymphs permit him to take a few of the precious golden apples to Eurystheus, and so the penultimate task is completed.

The twelfth and final labor assigned to Herakles is to descend into the underworld and retrieve Cerberus, the three-headed watchdog of HADES. Herakles travels down the path to the underworld, passing terrible sights, until he reaches Hades, the King of the Dead. He explains his mission to the King, who gives him permission to take the dog as long as he uses no weapons other than his hands. Herakles quickly subdues the ferocious creature with his great strength, carries him back to the world of the living, shows him to the terrified Eurystheus, and then returns him to Hades. Thus Herakles completes the twelve impossible labors, and is destined to live among the gods.

The myth of the Labors of Herakles resonates throughout many other storytelling traditions. The feats that Herakles accomplishes appear, in altered form and with different emphases, in other narratives of extraordinary courage, fearlessness, devotion, and strength. In this way, Herakles may be seen as "related" to other noble warriors and heroes found in mythology and FOLKLORE. Herakles's slaying of a giant, his destruction of several ferocious and magical wild animals, and his safe descent into and return from the underworld echo in other stories of valor. And Herakles's willingness to serve another man in order to achieve a higher goal appears also in the BIBLE, in the story of Jacob and his voluntary 14-year indenture to Laban in order to marry Laban's daughter, Rachel. The Labors of Herakles is an important and remarkable story for its synthesis of so many heroic adventures and courageous feats that appear in storytelling traditions around the world. This tale has even been adapted into many versions suitable for young listeners or readers, including the collection, *Greek Myths* (1993), retold by Geraldine McCaughrean and beautifully illustrated by Emma Chichester Clark. *See also* JACK AND THE BEANSTALK, ARTHUR, BEOWULF.

For Further Reading

McCaughrean, Geraldine. *Greek Myths.* Illustrated by Emma Chichester Clark. New York: Macmillan, 1993.

LABYRINTH

Maze-like structure in the palace of KING Minos on the island of Crete. In a Greek MYTH, Minos orders the Labyrinth to be built to house a half-man, half-bull monster called the MINOTAUR. It is designed by the master craftsman Daedalus. Later, Daedalus and his son, Icarus, are locked in the Labyrinth and escape on artificial wings (*see* ICARUS AND DAEDALUS).

In another story, the HERO THESEUS goes into the Labyrinth to kill the Minotaur. Ariadne, the king's daughter, lends Theseus a magic ball of thread given to her by Daedalus. Theseus uses it to find his way into and out of the maze.

The sites of the Minoan civilization were excavated by an English archaeologist, Sir Arthur Evans, beginning in 1900. At Knossos, he uncovered the actual ruins of the great palace of King Minos. The palace was called the house of the double ax, presumably implying a sacrificial weapon. The Greek word for ax was *labrys.* The palace was a highly complex maze of rooms and corridors. Robert Graves (*see* GRAVES, ROBERT) suggests that Athenian raiders may have had difficulty finding their way through it, giving birth to the LEGEND of the Labyrinth. Graves also mentions a maze pattern on a dance floor in front of the palace, which was used in an erotic spring rite. That pattern has also been called a labyrinth.

Labyrinths or mazes appear in the stories of many cultures. In *The Masks of God: Primitive Mythology,* Joseph Campbell (*see* CAMPBELL, JOSEPH) mentions labyrinthine spirals found on early Irish burial mounds, an ancient Egyptian structure known as the Labyrinth that was excavated in 1888, and the use of the image of the labyrinth in Melanesia by those who wished to enter the land of the dead.

Labyrinths generally represent difficult journeys into the unknown. Finding one's way through the labyrinth, escaping the MONSTER,

and returning, may imply REBIRTH. In *The Origins and History of Consciousness,* Erich Neumann suggests that the Greek legend of Theseus in the labyrinth is "the myth of the hero who conquers the symbol of matriarchal domination."

The Labyrinth of Solitude, by Octavio Paz, is an essay on Mexican history and the human condition. A selection from the work of Jorge Luis Borges has been published in English as *Labyrinths: Selected Stories and Other Writings.* In her novelistic versions of the Theseus stories, Mary Renault considers the nature of the Labyrinth and the Minotaur. And Jim Henson's 1986 movie, *Labyrinth,* features David Bowie as the monster in the center—in this case a GOBLIN King.

LADDER TO ANOTHER WORLD OR HEAVEN

Method for purified souls to reach HEAVEN. The idea of the ladder to heaven reaches far back into early mythology. Typically, the virtuous, the worthy, or the purified are able to climb the ladder while all others are pitched into HELL. Symbolizing both ascent and journey, the climb up this ladder has a purifying role, and, depending on the mythology, a SHAMAN, a monk, or a wise person would be portrayed as reaching heaven.

The belief that there was once a primordial connection between heaven and EARTH that was later broken is also embedded in this symbol. The ladder allows one to reestablish this connection, as in the case of AMETERASU, the Shinto GODDESS, who borrows the ladder to the sky. With its seven or twelve rungs, the ladder to another world or heaven takes the form of the rainbow in Native American FOLKLORE or a ladder with the footprint of BUDDHA on its bottom and top rungs in Buddhist LEGEND. For the Hebrews, the ladder is the means of communication between human beings and angels, and "Jacob's ladder" refers to the ladder with angels on it that Jacob envisions in a DREAM.

The ladder to heaven is also associated with the movement from darkness into light, from death to immortality, or the Cosmic or

World Tree and the pillar. Just as its verticality represents ascension and the spiritual journey, the ladder may also serve as a means for divinity to descend to earth.

LAGERLOF, SELMA (1858–1940)

Swedish novelist and short-story writer. As the first woman to receive the Nobel Prize in Literature in 1909, Selma Lagerlof is known for her stories and novels that draw on LEGEND and SAGAS and contain an epic flow found in some of the great EPIC poems. Unhappy with the realism of her day, Lagerlof turned to romanticism and the past, and her subject matter was often peasant life in her native Varmland. Among her novels are *Gosta Berlings Saga* (1891, trans. 1898), *Jerusalem* (1901, trans. 1901–2), and the trilogy *The Ring of the Lowenskolds* (1925–28, trans. 1931). Her collections of short stories, *The Wonderful Adventures of Nils* (1906–7) and *Further Adventures of Nils* (1911), tell of the adventures and escapades of a young boy who travels over Sweden on the back of a wild goose and are considered classics of children's literature to this day.

For Further Reading

Lagerlof, Selma. *The Legend of the Christmas Rose*. Retold by Ellin Greene. Illustrated by Charles Mikolaycak. New York: Holiday House, 1990.
———. *The Wonderful Adventures of Nils*. Illustrated. New York: Ingram, 1996.

LANCELOT

In Arthurian legend, heroic knight in King ARTHUR's court, best known for his love for Queen GUINEVERE.

During the twelfth century, when the first Arthurian ROMANCES were being written in French, the ideals of chivalry were tempered by softer influences than they had been in previous times. Although courage and superior skill in battle were still of paramount importance, graceful manners, elegance, wit, and refined taste were also demanded of a knight. In addition, he was expected to be in love. TROUBADOURS popularized romantic love and the idolization of women in storytelling circles, and the legendary Lancelot more than fulfills these chivalric requirements. He is the supreme HERO of the Round Table, and because he is the ideal knight, he is the ideal lover. Lancelot is in love with the king's wife, however, and his loyalty to Arthur and his prowess as a knight are marred only by his love for Guinevere. It is because of his relationship with Guinevere that Lancelot fails in his QUEST for the HOLY GRAIL and why Arthur's kingdom disintegrates.

The first account of Lancelot's love for Guinevere was written by CHRÉTIEN DE TROYES in *Lancelot* or *The Knight of the Cart* (c. 1170). In this story, Meleagant, evil prince of the land of Gorre, abducts Guinevere. Lancelot sets out to rescue the queen. Along the way, he finds a comb with Guinevere's golden hair. Lancelot presses the hairs to his eyes and his lips and then puts them into his shirt, near his heart. After several harrowing adventures, Lancelot arrives at the tower where Guinevere and others from Arthur's realm are held captive. Lancelot challenges and defeats Meleagant, and Guinevere and the other prisoners are soon to be released. Lancelot and Guinevere plan to meet secretly by Guinevere's prison window. Driven by desire, Lancelot pulls apart the iron bars guarding Guinevere's window, and they consummate their love.

In later romances, Lancelot and Guinevere's love begins when Lancelot arrives at King Arthur's court to be knighted. During the knighting ceremony, Arthur neglects to belt a sword on Lancelot. Instead, Guinevere gives Lancelot his sword, and they soon fall in love.

Lancelot and Guinevere's love is characterized by passion, jealousy, misunderstanding, and deception. In the thirteenth-century French prose *Lancelot*, King Pelles, the keeper of the Grail, tricks the knight into sleeping with his daughter, Elaine, by giving him a potion that convinces him that he is lying with Guinevere. Elaine gives birth to Galahad, who eventually surpasses his impure father in skill and obtains the Grail.

After Arthur learns about Guinevere's and Lancelot's relationship, the knights of the Round Table are irreparably divided between those who are loyal to Arthur and those who support Lancelot. Civil war breaks out, and eventually Lancelot goes to France. According to *Le Morte d'Arthur* (1485) by Thomas Malory (whose account of the demise of Arthur's kingdom is unrivaled), Lancelot returns to England to aid Arthur in his battle against Mordred, Arthur's illegitimate son. When Lancelot learns that the king has been killed, he goes to see Guinevere, who has become a nun. She begs Lancelot never to see her again, and he spends the rest of his life in a hermitage.

Lancelot is the hero of T. H. White's *The Ill-Made Knight* (1940), later incorporated into *The Once and Future King* (1958), which is a retelling of Malory's *Morte d'Arthur*.

For Further Reading

Barber, Richard. *The Arthurian Legends: An Illustrated Anthology*. New York: Dorset Press, 1985.
———. *King Arthur: Hero and Legend*. Woodbridge, Suffolk: The Boydell Press, 1986.
Carpenter, Humphrey, and Mari Prichard. *The Oxford Companion to Children's Literature*. New York: Oxford University Press, 1984.
Cavendish, Richard. *King Arthur and the Grail*. London: Paladin, 1985.
Chrétien de Troyes. *Lancelot: Or the Knight of the Cart*. Athens, GA: University of Georgia Press, 1990.

LAND OF MILK AND HONEY

Phrase that specifically describes the PROMISED LAND of the biblical EXODUS and generally refers to any potential land of great fertility. The phrase is located in several parts of the Pentateuch (the first five books of the BIBLE), but the first reference occurs in the book of Exodus, where YAHWEH makes a covenant with Moses to deliver the Hebrews from Egyptian bondage into "a good and broad land, a land flowing with milk and honey" (Exodus 3: 8). Following the departure from Egypt, the Hebrews sojourn in the wilderness of the Sinai desert for 40 years before entering the Promised Land, an event which Moses does not live to see. Moses, however, does obtain a glimpse of the land's fecundity when he sends scouts from the 12 tribes of Israel to spy out the land. The scouts return with a large cluster of grapes suspended from a pole, as well as figs and pomegranates to attest to the fer-

tility of the region. The eventual movement into, and conquest of, the land of milk and honey is accomplished by Joshua after the death of Moses.

Geographically, the region is located in present-day Israel, and the fact that it has been violently contested for millennia attests to its religious and strategic significance. In Judaism, the region and the struggle to reach it represent the pivotal moment in Jewish history. The land of milk and honey illustrates not only the search for a promised land but the story of a people and their enduring covenant with Yahweh. For Christians, the story recounts the same covenant and prefigures an AFTERLIFE of abundance. Parallels to the land flowing with milk and honey can be seen in many afterlife stories, particularly in the pure land of the Amida BUDDHA and in the Islamic vision of HEAVEN.

LAND OF THE DEAD

Mythological place to which human souls go after separating from the body. Human beings throughout the world and from all times believe in an existence after DEATH. Most versions of the underworld MYTH include certain common elements: a mountain barrier, a river, a boat and boatman, a bridge, gates and guardians, and an important tree.

The earliest literary fragment on Sumerian clay tablets discusses the descent of the GODDESS INANNA to "The Great Below." As she visits her sister Ereshkigal, the queen of the underworld, Inanna is stripped systematically of everything before being allowed through the gates. Inanna is eventually resurrected through a ransom that anticipates many dying-vegetation-god myths and Christianity (*see* DYING GOD).

The EPIC *of* GILGAMESH is a related story in which the HERO, having offended the goddess Inanna, loses his friend Enkidu to death. Afraid that he is next, Gilgamesh seeks the only man ever granted immortality, Ziusudra. Finding his QUEST to escape death a vain one after talking with the sage, Gilgamesh is given a plant that will restore youth, if not grant eternal life.

Another version of the story has Gilgamesh talking with his friend Enkidu, who claims that the underworld is too terrible for words. Vermin feed on his body, which is filled with dirt. All the early versions of the land of the dead give those souls a bleak and distressed existence.

The Egyptian Book of the Dead, recorded on papyrus rolls, demonstrates Egyptian concerns with the afterlife. The Egyptian dead led a bodily existence. Life force and soul board the boat, Ra (which is the SUN), to cross the sky river and arrive at night in the west. Leaving the boat, the dead must go through seven gates and greet the portals of the house of Osiris, god of the dead. In the Hall of Justice the soul pleads the case for its former and continuing existence. No matter how eloquent the speech, one's afterlife is determined by weighing the heart on the scales of justice against a feather from the headdress of the goddess of truth. Weighed down by sin, a soul is delivered to the jaws of the DEMON Ammit and devoured. If the soul survives, however, there are still other challenges, with the ultimate goal being transformation into a bird.

Hesiod wrote down the early Greek beliefs that included the Abyss that contains the mansion of HADES, GOD of the underworld, guarded by the hounds of HELL. HOMER'S Odysseus sees some of the most famous sights of Hades, and Virgil's Aeneas also visits the underworld the Romans borrowed from the Greeks (*see* AENEID, ODYSSEY).

The Hebrew words SHEOL and *Gehenna* are translated as "Hell" in the BIBLE, but generally refer to the place where the body is laid, literally the grave, and only metaphorically to torment in the form of despair.

The earliest Christian writers focused more on obtaining the kingdom of HEAVEN than on eternal damnation. The Gospel of Mark speaks of punishment for blaspheming the Holy Ghost, but mentions Hell only once. Most Christian notions of Hell come from the writings of Matthew, who tried to add eschatological warnings to the PARABLES OF JESUS. The apocalyptic vision of St. John from the Book of Revelations is filled with images of Hell and its torments.

Differing images of the underworld have inspired countless works of art and literature, including Dante's *Inferno,* the works of John Milton, and Goethe's *Faust. See also* DESCENT TO THE UNDERWORLD.

LANG, ANDREW (1844–1912)

Scottish folklorist, historian, poet, author, translator, and editor. After receiving a first class degree in classics at Oxford University's prestigious Balliol College, Andrew Lang went on to write, translate, and compile editions of MYTHS and FAIRY TALES. As a folklorist, he was one of the first to recognize the connection between mythology, anthropology, and ethnography. After writing such books as *Ballads and Lyrics of Old France* (1872), *Mythology and Fairy Tales* (1873), *Custom and Myth* (1874), the novel *The Mark of Cain* (1886), and *Perrault's Popular Tales* (1888), he became well-known for his 12 volumes of collections of children's fairy tales, beginning with *The Blue Fairy Book* (1889) and continuing for the next 23 years with subsequent volumes using different colors for their titles. In his introduction to the last volume, *The Lilac Fairy Book* (1912), he clarified for his readers that he was not the creator of these fairy tales but the reteller of them. He was also the author of two of his own fairy-tale influenced works of fiction for children, *The Princess Nobody: A Tale of Fairyland* (1884) and *Tales of a Fairy Court* (1907).

For Further Reading

Lang, Andrew. *The Blue Fairy Book.* New York: Penguin, 1988.

———. *The Green Fairy Book.* Illustrated by H.J. Ford and G.P.J. Hood. New York: Crown, 1929.

———. *The Rainbow Fairy Book.* Illustrated by Michael Hague. New York: William Morrow, 1993.

———. *The Red Fairy Book.* Illustrated. New York: Buccaneer Books, 1987.

———. *The Rose Fairy Book.* Illustrated by Vera Bock. New York: McKay, 1966.

LEGBA

West African TRICKSTER god in the Dahomean oral tradition, also known as Elegba, and as Eshu to the Yoruba (*see* YORUBA CREATION). His story is also found in African-based cultures in South American countries and Cuba, as well as in the voodoo cults of Haiti and New Orleans. Christian missionaries in Africa equated Legba with the DEVIL.

Legba is generally pictured as an old man who walks with a stick and is dressed in tatters. In Haitian voodoo rituals, he is called upon to open the gate so that the ancient GODS can merge with their followers in the new world.

In Africa, Legba is the youngest son of the High Deity—the androgynous though predominately female MAWU in the *Fon* tradition of the Dahomy. Legba knows all the languages of his brother deities, and therefore can communicate between the various tribes. He is also the messenger who communicates between gods and human beings and a god of entrances and crossroads.

Like all tricksters, Legba delights in subverting authority. He is often held responsible for quarrels among humans and between humans and gods. According to some stories, Legba was responsible for the creator deity's decision to move away from the world and its people.

Legba grows tired of being blamed for all that goes wrong in the world is even more annoyed that the High Deity, Mawu, takes all the credit for everything that goes right. So he warns Mawu that a thief plans to steal her yams. Legba slips into Mawu's house at night and steals her sandals. Strapping the sandals to his own feet, Legba sneaks into the High Deity's garden and steals all the yams. The next morning, Legba loudly reports the theft, pointing to the footprints in the garden as a sure way of identifying the thief. But when the people of the village check everybody's sandals, they discover that no one has feet as big as those footprints.

Then Legba suggests that perhaps the Mawu has stolen her own yams, perhaps while sleepwalking. Though Mawu denies it, her sandals—and only hers—match the prints exactly. The people cry out that Mawu had stolen from herself. Humiliated, Mawu withdraws from the world into the sky. But since the sky was only six or seven feet from the EARTH in those days, Legba still reported to

her every night on everything that went on in the world. That is how Legba became the messenger between people and the gods.

Stories from other African cultures, including those about the Ashanti's ANANSI, tell of a trickster who shames a deity into withdrawing from the earth. *See also* AFRICAN STORYTELLING.

For Further Reading

McGaughrean, Geraldine. Illustrated by Bee Willey. *The Golden Hoard: Myths and Legends of the World.* New York: Simon & Schuster, 1995.

Murphy, Joseph M. *Working the Spirit: Ceremonies of the African Diaspora.* Boston: Beacon Press, 1994.

Pelton, Robert D. *The Trickster in West Africa: A Study of Mythic Irony and Sacred Delight.* Los Angeles: University of California Press, 1980.

LEGEND

Traditional narrative handed down from the past, often concerning a particular historical figure or event. Originally, legends were the stories of saints' lives or church HEROES which might be read at religious services; the term eventually came to signify any collection of such stories from the past.

This sense of legend applies to Chaucer's collection of stories of famous women of ancient history called *The Legend of Good Women*. Today, a legend is any story that contributes to the traditional lore of a culture or nation. A legend is different from a MYTH in that legends tend to rely less on supernatural devices and often include a fair amount of historical fact. JOHNNY APPLESEED, King ARTHUR, Daniel Boone (*see* BOONE, DANIEL), and Jesse James (*see* JAMES, JESSE) are examples of common legendary figures who actually existed and around whom elaborate and unprovable stories have developed. Any famous folk character in any culture is likely to become the focus of various legends; these stories develop and expand over time and frequently survive through such oral traditions as folk songs and BALLADS. Eventually, many of the legends may be written down and added to the collection of folk literature of a people.

Legends are not specific to any one era or geographical location; every culture throughout history has created, preserved, and perpetuated their own legends about important heroes, warriors, leaders, or saints. For example, Chaka, the celebrated and feared East African Zulu king and warrior, has been immortalized in songs, stories, a novel, and even a film version of his life. And Indian FOLKLORE is full of legends about the BUDDHA and Buddhist saints such as Upagupta and Asoka. Indeed, legends are still being created and preserved (orally or in writing) about contemporary heroes and political leaders of today. Often, legendary stories endure that are grounded in virtually no historical fact, but which are found to be generally appealing. For example, the American legend that tells the story of George Washington chopping down his father's cherry tree as a young boy and then honestly confessing his deed, maintaining to his angry father that "I cannot tell a lie," is pure fabrication invented, no doubt, to impart a moral lesson. Nevertheless, this legend will, in all probability, continue to endure because the connection between a nationally important hero and virtue, however fictional, is universally appealing.

Legends from different time periods and different parts of the world often contain remarkable parallels, including common MOTIFS such as the supernatural births of heroes, fierce battles against evil figures (sometimes in the form of monsters and sometimes in the form of demonic men), wise KINGS, great lovers, marvelous magicians, and notorious criminals. Although the origins of many legends have been obscured by time, some can be traced back to their deliberate creation. For example, the American legend of Paul Bunyan (*see* BUNYAN, PAUL), the giant lumberjack, was deliberately invented by a lumber company in Minnesota in order to bolster sales. And some legends regarding genealogy have been used to reinforce the political position of a particular family, as the rulers of Ethiopia looked to King Solomon as their ancestor, and the kings of England in the Middle Ages looked to Aeneas as theirs.

LEMMINKAINEN

Young, arrogant, boastful figure in Finnish folk LEGEND (*see* KALEVALA). Stories about Lemminkainen come from traditional Karelo-Finnish songs. His epithet, a feature characteristic of traditional Finnish poetry, is "reckless." He is also known as a man with a far-roving mind. Lemminkainen is handsome, light-hearted, proud of his strength and knowledge, and lacking in foresight. A fickle and demanding lover, Lemminkainen's lustful ways get him into trouble.

One series of songs from the *Kalevala* relates how Lemminkainen woos the MAIDEN Kylliki. When the beautiful maiden shuns him, Lemminkainen abducts her. Kylliki weeps and condemns Lemminkainen for his warlike tendencies. Lemminkainen promises never to go to war, and Kylliki also promises to remain at home. Later, Lemminkainen learns that Kylliki has socialized and danced with the neighborhood maidens. He becomes angry, casts her off, and makes plans to woo the maiden of North Farm. Lemminkainen's MOTHER, who plays an important role in his life, unsuccessfully tries to dissuade him from going to North Farm, saying that he will die there. Lemminkainen asks Louhi, the mistress of North Farm, for her daughter. Louhi gives Lemminkainen several tasks to complete. During the third task, Lemminkainen is killed by a cattle herder and thrown into the river of DEATH's domain. Death's son cuts Lemminkainen's body into pieces. Lemminkainen's mother rakes the pieces of his body from the water and, with the help of charms and ointments, reassembles her son (*see also* ISIS AND OSIRIS).

In another group of songs, Lemminkainen is enraged because he is not invited to the wedding of Ilmarinen and Louhi's daughter. In spite of his mother's warnings and predictions of death, he sets out for North Farm. Along the way, he encounters a vicious, fiery eagle and plunges a flock of black grouse into its ravenous mouth. After surmounting several other obstacles, Lemminkainen arrives at North Farm and slays its master in a duel. Lemminkainen escapes to an island where he lives wantonly with the island's women. The men of the island decide to kill Lemminkainen, and he returns to his home only to discover that it is a wasteland, burned by the people of North Farm. Lemminkainen vows to take revenge and sets out for North Farm. Louhi invokes a severe cold spell, which freezes his ships in the sea. Temporarily defeated, Lemminkainen walks to shore on the ice and returns home.

The stories about Lemminkainen contain elements of the hero's QUEST journey, the DYING GOD MOTIF, and the theme of the brash, reckless lover. In addition, Lemminkainen's relationship with his mother, particularly when she resurrects him, suggests the relationship between the EARTH-MOTHER and her divine son and lover, and is reminiscent of the relationships between, among others, BALDR and Frigg as well as Jesus and MARY.

For Further Reading

de Gerez, Toni. *Louhi, Witch of North Farm.* Illustrated by Barbara Cooney. New York: Viking Kestrel, 1986.

LEPRECHAUN

Fairy creature in Irish FOLKLORE and mythology. Leprechauns are popular figures in the Irish folkloric tradition, and stories and descriptions of them abound. Leprechauns are generally described as tiny figures resembling old men; they haunt lonely places, make shoes continually, and guard fabulous caches of fairy treasure and gold. Mischievous and clever, they are often portrayed wearing a cocked hat, a leather apron, silver shoe-buckles, and spectacles. Some stories suggest that leprechauns possess the secret to brewing heather ale. And in spite of their humble trade as shoe-cobblers, many legends connect leprechauns to a more lofty mythological heritage in which they are considered to be not just artisans but artists. Most accounts of human interaction with leprechauns involve a person unexpectedly coming upon one of these tiny cobblers, grabbing him, and demanding to be led to his treasure. The quick-thinking leprechaun invariably outsmarts or distracts the person and escapes without ever revealing the whereabouts of his riches. Some stories, however, mention that occasionally the leprechaun will accidentally leave behind his tiny shoe, thus providing a small souvenir of the encounter for a lucky person.

For Further Reading

Arrowsmith, Nancy. *A Field Guide to the Little People.* Illustrated by Heinz Edelman. New York: Hill and Wang, 1977.

LILITH

Female DEMON in Jewish, Christian, and Islamic mythology. Islamic tradition says that Lilith is the wife of the devil and the mother of all demons. In the Hebrew tradition, Lilith was the first woman on EARTH and Adam's mate before Eve was created (*see* ADAM AND EVE). YAHWEH made both Lilith and Adam from clay, and they were meant to dwell together as husband and wife in the PARADISE of Eden. Some accounts explain that Adam, who is larger and stronger than Lilith, commands her to lie down so that he can couple with her. She refuses to lie beneath him, noting that they are created as equals. Adam insists and Lilith, in her anger, flies away to the Red Sea. Yahweh sends three angels, Sinoi, Sinsinoi, and Samengeloff, to Lilith, and they bid her to return to Adam. The angels threaten that if she does not obey Yahweh's command, she will live to see thousands of her children killed every day. Still, Lilith remains unmoved and will not obey her creator.

Lilith remains in her home far from Adam, and there couples with demons and becomes the mother of legions of evil spirits called *lilim*. These lilim are she-devils that she sends to suck the life force from men. They, like their mother, embodied the image of the *femme fatale*, the seductive, sensual, vengeful woman who tempts men to their downfall. These demonic female children seek revenge for their mother's ill treatment, but Lilith also exacts her own revenge. Legend tells that a jealous and angry Lilith returns to the garden after Yahweh creates a new, more accommodating wife for Adam. The serpent that tempts Eve and brings about the fall of humanity is really Lilith in disguise.

The MYTHS of Lilith often represent her as a night bird or owl; in the Old Testament she is referred to as a "screech-owl." Other texts call her a "night-hag"; she is both beautiful and horrifying. She seduces men with profoundly malevolent intentions and is therefore considered an infinitely hostile force. However, more sympathetic readings of the Lilith myth consider her a tragic female figure who serves to warn women of the terrible consequences of disobeying man. Lilith appears as a literary character in works that include Goethe's *Faust*, Dante Gabriel Rossetti's *Eden Bower*, and George MacDonald's *Lilith*. In Mexican folklore, she appears as *La Llovona*; the Penobscot Indian *Pskégdemus* is a related swamp spirit.

For Further Reading

Schwartz, Howard. *Lilith's Cave: Jewish Tales of the Supernatural*. Illustrated by Uri Shulevitz. San Francisco: Harper & Row, 1988.

LION AND UNICORN

Symbolically joined ANIMALS in Christianity, alchemy, and the arms of Great Britain. The magical UNICORN is often depicted in medieval tales and tapestries, and a thirteenth-century text describes the unicorn as brave enough to attack an elephant, but able to be caught if a young virgin is placed in his midst. He will lay his head on her lap and let himself be caught, and he is said to represent Jesus Christ. Similarly, the lion is often linked with Jesus Christ, for the way the lion erases its tracks with its tail is the same way Christ erases his spiritual tracks; that the lion sleeps in a cave with its eyes open is likened to Christ asleep on the Cross, though his divinity never sleeps. In alchemy, the unicorn symbolizes the primal essence, mercury, that is then joined with sulfur, symbolized by the lion, to create a higher unity.

In heraldry, the lion and the unicorn each stand on separate sides of the shield of arms of Great Britain. Since the unicorn represents Scotland and the lion Britain, together they allegorically represent the animosity that once existed between the two countries that now are joined. Lewis Carroll's *Through the Looking-Glass* (1872) satirizes this theme in its chapter called "The Lion and the Unicorn," in which Alice sings the song, "The Lion and the Unicorn were fighting for the crown/The Lion beat the Unicorn all around the town." Both the Lion and the Unicorn have never seen a child, and they call Alice a MONSTER. At one point the KING is forced to sit down between the two beasts, and they humorously suggest that maybe they will fight for the crown, with the allusion made to the many battles fought between Scotland and England.

LITUOLONE

Bantu African god-HERO and savior. According to an old Sesuto legend, a MONSTER feeds on humans until there is no one left on EARTH but one old woman who has carefully hidden herself. While in hiding, she miraculously becomes pregnant without having been with a man, and she gives birth to a child who is born decorated with amulets. Like BUDDHA, KUTOYIS, and Herakles, the child attains adult stature as soon as he is born. His mother names him Lituolone, and he immediately wants to know where the other men are to be found. When his mother informs him that the monster Kammapa has devoured everyone else, Lituolone takes a knife and goes to fight the monster. Although the monster swallows him, Lituolone is able to tear apart Kammapa's entrails, releasing thousands of humans from the monster's stomach. Thus Lituolone becomes the savior of humankind and the destroyer of evil. *See also* MONSTER KILLED FROM WITHIN.

LOKI

Spiteful and fickle Norse god of mischief and fire. According to the Icelander Snorri Sturluson (1179–1241), from whom we receive most of our information about this dynamic figure, Loki is a handsome but evil god who continually causes trouble and grief for the other GODS and GODDESSES in Asgard, the home of the Norse gods (*see* EDDAS, ELDER AND YOUNGER).

Loki's parents are GIANTS, enemies of the Aesir, the Norse pantheon. His father is Farbauti, whose name means "Dangerous Smiter." His mother is Laufey, whose name means "tree." Loki's birth occurs when fire meets wood and he represents the destructive aspects of fire. Loki is the father of three evil and monstrous beings, Fenrir (the wolf who kills ODIN, the ruler of the gods, at RAGNAROK, the end of the world), Jormungand (the world serpent), and HEL, the queen of the dead.

The story about the reconstruction of Asgard's wall after its destruction in a war demonstrates Loki's androgyny as well as his power to transform himself into other forms. A mysterious visitor says that he will rebuild the wall in eighteen months for the price of FREYA, the most beautiful goddess. Loki encourages the incensed gods and goddesses to consider the visitor's proposition, saying that they will lose nothing if they set the time limit to six months. The builder will be unable to finish the wall, forfeit his fee, and Asgard will have half a wall. The arrangement is made, but, when it becomes clear that with the help of his stallion the builder will complete his task in six months, Odin demands that Loki get the gods out of their trouble. Loki transforms himself into a mare and entices the builder's stallion away from him. The two horses spend the night in the woods, no stone is hauled from the quarry, and the builder is unable to finish the wall. Later, Loki presents an eight-legged colt, of which he is the mother, to Odin.

Although Loki is accepted in Asgard, he plans to destroy the gods and the universe, and he works toward this goal in sly and mischievous ways. Loki is responsible for the death of BALDR, the son of Odin. When Loki observes that Baldr is protected from harm by every thing that could possibly cause him to die, he turns himself into an old woman and visits Frigg, Baldr's mother. Frigg reveals to the CRONE that the only thing that can harm Baldr is mistletoe. Loki gets a branch of the mistletoe and shapes it into a dart. He gives it to Baldr's brother, Hod, at a party where the gods are making sport of testing the power of Baldr's safety. With Loki's help, Hod throws the dart at Baldr and kills him. There is no reason for this murder; it illustrates Loki's evil character.

After Baldr's death, Loki, in the form of a salmon, is captured by the other gods. In an image resembling that of Prometheus, the gods bind Loki to three rocks with his son Nari's entrails (*see also* PROMETHEUS AND THE THEFT OF FIRE). These were torn out by Loki's other son Vali whom the gods had transformed into a wolf. The gods tie a poisonous snake above Loki's head. The snake drips venom into his face. Sigyn, Loki's wife, stands beside her husband's body and captures the venom in a basin. Each time the basin fills and she turns away to empty it, the venom drips on Loki's face, causing him to shake and shudder with such force that the earth trembles and there are earthquakes. Loki remains a prisoner until Ragnarok, the apocalyptic end of the world in Norse mythology.

Loki appears in almost every Norse myth. His role in the stories of the Necklace of the Brisings and the stealing of Sif's long, golden hair demonstrates his skill at shape-changing and his prowess as a thief. In a myth about Thor, Odin's son, and the giant Geirrod, Loki is caught in the form of a hawk by Geirrod. He is locked in a chest for three months before promising to bring Thor, without his weapons, to the giant. In another tale, Loki kills an otter, the son of a magician-farmer. As retribution, Loki must pay a ransom of gold, which he gets from the DWARF Andvari.

Unlike the other deities in Norse mythology, Loki is unpredictable and his volatility disrupts the stable order of Asgard and brings fire and verve to the tales. Loki might be compared to the TRICKSTER figure of American Indian, African, and other mythologies.

For Further Reading

Climo, Shirley. *Stolen Thunder: A Norse Myth.* Illustrated Alexander Koshkin. New York: Clarion, 1994.

Crossley-Holland, Kevin. *Axe-Age, Wolf-Age: A Selection of Norse Myths.* Illustrated by Hannah Firmin. London: Andre Deutsch, 1985.

LOMAX, JOHN (1872–1948) AND ALAN (1915–)

Father-and-son team of folklorists who recorded and collected North American BALLADS. Alan Lomax, a public sector folklorist in the 1930s and first editor of the Federal Writers Project (FWP), was inspired to found the Archive of American Folk Song (housed at the Library of Congress). His desire to collect folk songs was fueled by his belief that the FOLKLORE in rural areas was disappearing due to ever-encroaching modern life. This was in opposition to the view of FPA colleague Ben A. Botkin (*see* BOTKIN, BEN A.), who believed that urban life only created new, and modified old, traditions. Alan and his mentor and colleague John are noted for discovering Huddie "Ledbelly" Ledbetter while doing fieldwork in a Louisiana prison in 1935. Giving recognition to previously unknown African American folk singers became family tradition when John's daughter, Bess Lomax Hawes, brought Bessie Jones to public attention in 1964. Like their scholarly predecessors George Lyman Kittredge and Francis James Child, the Lomaxes believed in the communal origins of ballads. This notion was dismissed by ballad scholar Louise Pound when she asserted the opposite; ballads are created by individual authorship. Although Pound's theory is accepted by scholars today, the Lomaxes contributed greatly to the study of ballads. John pioneered the study of occupational folklore with his publication of *Cowboy Songs and Other Frontier Ballads* in 1910, and Alan revolutionized ethnomusicology ideas in *The Folk Songs of North America in the English Language,* published in 1960.

For Further Reading

Brunvand, Jan Harold. *The Study of American Folklore: An Introduction*. New York: W.W. Norton, 1986.

Clements, William M., ed. *100 Years of American Folklore Studies: A Conceptual History*. Washington, DC: The American Folklore Society, 1988.

Lomax, Alan. *The Land Where Blues Began*. New York: Pantheon, 1993.

Lomax, John. *Cowboy Songs and Other Frontier Ballads*. Temacula, CA: Reprint Services Corp., 1993.

LORD RANDALL

Early English folk BALLAD. Part of the oral tradition, ballads are usually anonymous narrative songs that have many VARIANTS. While it is impossible to pin down the exact date of "Lord Randall," it most likely originated in the period between A.D.1200 and 1700, though it was not printed before the eighteenth century. Like many other ballads that belong to English FOLKLORE, "Lord Randall" has as its subject a tragic and mysterious DEATH. Lord Randall, a "handsome young man," returns home to his mother after having been in the "wild wood" where he dined with his "true love." However, the refrain for each four-line stanza suggests that he is ailing, for he says "make my bed soon/ For I'm weary wi' hunting and fain wald lie down." In the third stanza, Lord Randall tells his mother he has eaten eel broth, and in the fourth stanza he relates to her that his bloodhounds "swelled and they died," foreshadowing his own death, for in the fifth stanza he admits that he is poisoned and "sick at heart." The end of the ballad implies that he is about to die, but who his true love is or why she has poisoned him is never established.

The story of Lord Randall appears in variants all over Europe in both songs and tales. In America, Lord Randall's name appears as Johnny Randall, Johnny Ramble, Jimmy Randal, etc.

For Further Reading

Child, Francis J., ed. *"Lord Randall" and Other British Ballads*. New York: Dover, 1996.

LOST CHILD

MOTIF of disappearance symbolizing loss of soul. If the child symbolizes the formative powers of the unconscious of a beneficent and protective kind of soul, according to Carl Jung, then the lost child represents the lost soul or life force and parallels DEATH. The lost child, who may be an orphan, an abandoned child, or one who has vanished due to supernatural events, points to the need to find the child to restore order.

In the GRIMM BROTHERS's "Hansel and Gretel," the brother and sister are lost in the woods and cannot find their way home. They must defeat the wicked WITCH who would like to eat them before they are able to return to civilization and their father. The "lost boys" of J.M. Barrie's *Peter Pan* are lost because they are no longer with their parents but with Peter in Never-Never Land, and they no longer remember their families. In the Jewish FOLKTALE "The LOST PRINCESS," a variant of which appears in the THOUSAND AND ONE NIGHTS, a daughter is lost when her father loses his temper and yells, "May the Evil One take you!" Her disappearance causes him to search for her for many years, and the story centers on how she can be found and freed.

For Further Reading

Barrie, J.M. *Peter Pan*. Illustrated by Trina Schart Hyman. New York: Bantam, 1981.

Jeffers, Susan. *Hansel and Gretel*. New York: Dial/Penguin, 1980.

McCaughrean, Geraldine. *A Thousand and One Nights*. Illustrated by Stephen Lavis. New York: Oxford, 1996.

MAGIC CLOTHES

Garments that enchant or disenchant in MYTH and FAIRY TALE. Magic clothes may come in the form of a hood, a hat, gloves, a cloak, a shirt, or an ANIMAL skin or headdress. A SHAMAN will wear a robe or animal skin and headdress to help his or her performance, and an ANIMAL MASTER in some Native American tribes wears buffalo skins and horns. In the fairy tale "the SEVEN SWANS," the seven brothers are transformed into swans when their stepmother throws magic shirts over them, and they are transformed back into men when their sister throws shirts of nettle over them years later. Because the seventh shirt is missing a sleeve, the youngest brother retains one of his swan wings.

In *The Feminine in Fairy Tales*, Marie-Louise von Franz observes that, "Enchantment and disenchantment are often achieved in fairy tales by covering with a garment or an animal skin—the wolfskin, etc. There are also many fairy tales where the WITCH garment or animal skin has to be quickly grasped. The skin, or garment, indicates the modus, or the way, in which one appears, or it can be the mask, or the persona—the skin or garment under which you hide." *See also* MASKS AND MASQUERADE.

For Further Reading

von Franz, Marie-Louis. *The Feminine in Fairy Tales*. Rev. ed. Boston: Shambhala, 1993.

MAGIC JOURNEYS

In MYTH and FAIRY TALE, an enchanted voyage or trip. In every culture, the journey occurs at some stage in the QUEST of the HERO, and often this journey is magical. The method of travel itself may be magical, such as a magic ship, flying carpet, magic horse, etc., or the journey itself may be enchanted or sacred. Since the journey, as J.E. Cirlot notes in *A Dictionary of Symbols*, "is never merely a passage through space, but rather an expression of the urgent desire for discovery and change that underlies the actual movement and experience of traveling," all studying, seeking, or living "with intensity through new and profound experiences are all modes of traveling or . . . spiritual and symbolic equivalents of the journey." Cirlot adds that "Heroes are always travelers, in that they are restless." Thus, the DREAM, the SEA JOURNEY, and the DESCENT TO THE UNDERWORLD may all be, in a sense, magic journeys. Similarly, the path of the SHAMAN or the prophet may involve a magic journey. For example, the night journey of MUHAMMAD, *Laylat al-Miraj*, on his amazing horse Buraq, was a kind of VISION QUEST, where the angel Gabriel led the prophet through Jerusalem, past the seven celestial spheres in order to ascend to GOD.

In fairy tales, Lewis Carroll's *Alice in Wonderland* and *Through the Looking Glass* involve magic journeys, and a sprinkle of star dust enables Wendy, Michael, and John to join Peter Pan and fly with him to Never-Never Land in James Barrie's nostalgic view of childhood, *Peter Pan*. The children of C.S. Lewis's *Chronicles of Narnia* travel through a wardrobe door that brings them to Narnia. In Ursula K. Le Guin's *Earthsea Quartet*, when the mage Ged rides on the back of a DRAGON, he is partaking in a magic journey.

For Further Reading

Barrie, J.M. *Peter Pan*. Illustrated by Trina Schart Hyman. New York: Bantam, 1981.

Carroll, Lewis. *Alice's Adventures in Wonderland and Through the Looking Glass*. New York: Bantam, 1984.

Le Guin, Ursula. *A Wizard of EarthSea*. New York: Houghton, 1968.

Lewis, C.S. *The Lion, The Witch, and the Wardrobe*. New York: Collier, 1970.

MAGIC LAMP *See* MAGIC OBJECTS

MAGIC OBJECTS

In the MYTHS and FOLKTALES of many cultures, various objects that provide some kind of magical power. In folktales and LEGEND, certain objects—magic wands and cauldrons, for instance—have the ability to lend power to, transform, or weaken an individual. In Jewish FOLKLORE, for example, the tale of "The Baker's Apprentice and the Magic Cup" depicts a baker's apprentice who finds a gold cup that produces gold coins. Every time he drinks from the cup, it produces more gold coins, and because of it, he eventually wins marriage to the KING's daughter.

In such FAIRY TALES as the "Vasilisa the Beautiful," a Russian version of "CINDERELLA," Vasilisa is given a magic object by her dying mother, in this case, a doll. This object helps the girl perform difficult tasks and have the strength to overcome her wicked stepmother and the WITCH BABA YAGA (*see* STEPMOTHER—WICKED). In Malory's *Le Morte d'Arthur*, King ARTHUR's sword, Excalibur, has magical properties.

In many legends and in alchemy, gems are believed to have supernatural abilities. According to Paul Christian's *The History and Practice of Magic,* black agate protects "whoever wears it from all danger"; "crystal, worn as a necklace, increases the supply of milk in wet-nurses"; "diamond, with green tints, worn as a necklace, protects the fruit of a woman's womb"; and "pink amethyst prevents drunkenness if it is attached to the navel, . . . set in a silver plaque, . . . and engraved with a bear."

Magic mirrors that offer the ability to divine the future are mentioned by Spartianus, APULEIUS, Pausanias, Pythagoras, and St. Augustine. Eros of Greek mythology used magical arrows that could pierce the human heart, causing a person to fall in love (*see* CUPID AND PSYCHE). In the story of Aladdin of the THOUSAND AND ONE NIGHTS, both a magic lamp and a magical FLYING CARPET bestow power.

The significance of magical objects in myth and folklore suggests a supernatural explanation for mysterious events, the power of "magical thinking," the ancient belief in amulets, and the belief in REVERSAL OF FORTUNE being caused by concrete items that one finds by chance, as in "The Baker's Apprentice and the Magic Cup" or are purposely given to one, as in the case of "Vasilisa the Beautiful."

For Further Reading

Christian, Paul. *The History and Practice of Magic.* New York: The Citadel Press, 1969.

Givry, Émile Grillot de. *Illustrated Anthology of Sorcery, Magic and Alchemy.* New York: Causeway Books, 1973.

Sadeh, Pinhas. *Jewish Folktales.* Translated by Hillel Halkin. New York: Doubleday, 1989.

MAGIC ORANGE TREE (HAITIAN STORYTELLING)

Oral tradition of FOLKTALES that stem from both African and European (mainly French) origins. Storytelling is a popular pastime in the rural communities of Haiti. The storytelling ritual often begins in this way: a group of adults assemble outside on one of their porches to talk and gossip. As the night progresses, a member of the group might volunteer a story with the preface "Cric?" (pronounced "creek") to which, if they would like to hear the story, the group will respond with a resounding, "Crac!" This traditional opening comes from French written fairy tales, which traditionally began "Cric, Crac," and are followed by the text. In Haitian tradition, only when the group has given their assenting "Cracs!" will the storyteller be allowed to proceed.

The most popular storytellers usually demonstrate all the gestures and expressions appropriate for a particular story, and they may also improvise with dancing, singing, gesturing, and pantomiming. Each time a tale is told, the storyteller imparts much of his or her own personality and bearing to the story, and so it is bound to have a different reception each time.

There is also a tradition of professional storytellers in Haiti. The well-loved entertainers, called *maitre conte*, are sometimes elevated to nearly mythical proportions, but are very real. Since the eighteenth century, these men have wandered from plantation to plantation telling stories in exchange for food and lodging. In addition, they are often called upon to perform at festivals and wakes. For the death of a child, a simple story is appropriate, while for the death of an important man, an elaborate ROMANCE is expected.

"The Magic Orange Tree" is perhaps the best known example of Haitian FOLKLORE. In the story, a young girl is unhappy because her widowed father has married a cruel wife (*see* STEPMOTHER—WICKED). One day, the girl comes home to find three ripe oranges sitting on the table. Though she knows it is wrong, she eats one, and finding it delicious, shortly devours the second and the third or-

anges. When her stepmother arrives home to find that the child has eaten her three oranges, she cries out, "Whoever has [taken the oranges] had better say their prayers now, for they will not be able to say them later!" The child is so frightened that she rushes to her true mother's grave and cries and cries until she falls asleep. When she awakes and rises, an orange pit falls from the folds of her skirt. Entering the earth, it begins to sprout, as the child sings out triumphantly, "Orange tree/ Grow and grow and grow/Orange tree, orange tree/Grow and grow and grow/Orange tree/Stepmother is not real mother/Orange Tree." The orange tree grows to the size of the girl and blossoms and produces great ripe fruit. The girl fills her arms with oranges and returns home. When her stepmother sees the delicious oranges, she becomes jealous and demands that the girl guide her to the orange tree. Grudgingly, the girl leads the stepmother to the magic tree and again sings her song for the tree to grow. As it grows higher and higher, the stepmother becomes increasingly angry because she cannot reach the fruits. She orders the girl to lower it, and the girl complies, the stepmother climbs the tree "so quickly you might have thought she was the daughter of an ape," eating every orange she comes upon. The girl quickly orders the tree to grow again, and when the stepmother is high among the branches of the great tree, orders the tree to break, sending her stepmother to the ground to break into a million pieces. With the fall of the tree, the seed of a new orange arrives at the girl's feet.

Diane Wolkstein (*see* WOLKSTEIN, DIANE), a storyteller and songwriter who studied Haitian storytelling, believes that "Magic Orange Tree" is about the will to live "of a people who have not only survived but have done so with a creativity in art, song, DANCE, and story to rival Papa God."

Although many Haitian stories do not have titles, a few of the most popular do. "The Magic Orange Tree" is one and "Tayzanne," the story of a young girl whose friendship with a silver fish helps "hook" her into the spirit world, is another. In Creole, *tayzanne* is a combination of words for hook and hooked. The story tells of a young girl, Velina, who meets a silver fish at the pond from which she fetches water daily. The two become friends, but when Velina's mother learns of the friendship, she determines that the fish is an evil spirit that must be killed. The mother kills it, and Velina is devastated. Mourning and singing to the spirit while combing her hair before a mirror the same night, the girl is sucked into the ground—and thus is hooked into the realm of the spirits.

Many of the plots of the unnamed stories are of interest to note. One tale, for instance, closely follows the plot, seen both in European and Arabic tradition, of the pigeon who takes a turtle across the ocean only to see him fall to the water when he rashly opens his mouth to speak (*see also* AESOP). This tale is a fine example of the incorporation of modern details into traditional tales. Pigeon, who is going to New York, offers to carry his friend, Turtle, across the ocean if Turtle can hold on to a stick that Pigeon will keep in his mouth. Turtle does so, but while the two are over the ocean, Turtle turns back to wish his friends good-bye with the only English word he knows: "Bye-Bye." Opening his mouth to bid farewell, Turtle falls into the sea. This is why, the story goes, there are many pigeons in New York, but Turtle is still in Haiti.

For Further Reading

Diane Wolkstein, ed. *The Magic Orange Tree and Other Haitian Folktales*. New York: Knopf, 1978.

MAHABHARATA

Greatest EPIC of India and a primary source for Hindu mythology. Composed of nearly 100,000 couplets and divided into 18 books plus a supplement, the *Mahabharata* is the longest literary work in the world. Both written and oral versions of the *Mahabharata* appear throughout South and Southeast Asia and Kashmir. Composed some time between 200 B.C. and A.D. 200, it reached its present form, in its original Sanskrit, around A.D. 400. The *Mahabharata* has so many HEROES and LEGENDS folded into it that it may truly be considered the history of an entire culture. The *Mahabharata* has been published in India; it fills 11 volumes and about 5,000 pages of text.

It appears that certain elements of the *Mahabharata* may be founded upon actual historic events. Concerned largely with the struggle of generations to continue various dynasties of power, the *Mahabharata* may well be based in part on the Bharata war, which probably occurred between the years 1400 and 1000 B.C. This war was already firmly established in legend by the time the epic was composed. Therefore, it seems likely that the text's message that war should only be fought for religious or moral reasons may well find its origins in the stories of that ancient and famous battle.

The poem begins when VYASA, the poet who supposedly composed the epic, meets a young boy and offers to tell him the story of his people; a GOD named GANESA offers to write the story down as he tells it. Vyasa starts with the story of his own birth; he is the second son of a KING. One of his brothers vows never to have children, and the other brother dies, so Vyasa is left with the responsibility of continuing the family line. To this end, he is asked to sleep with two PRINCESSES and sire children by them. The women do not find him desirable; one shuts her eyes to him, and so her son Dhritarastra is born blind. The other woman blanches at his touch, and so her son Pandu is born pale. From these two sons (directly and indirectly) great dynasties of leaders, warriors, brothers, and lovers, mortal and semi-divine, arise. The adventures of these many descendants comprise the elaborate, complex, intertwined mythology of the Hindu tradition.

The complicated epic closes with the story of the heroic Yudhisthira, the son of Pandu's wife who was fathered not by Pandu (who was forbidden to sleep with his wives) but by Dharma, the god of earthly harmony and right conduct. Yudhisthira's faith is tested time after time, ending finally with his discovery that his enemies are in PARADISE while his family is in HADES. The gatekeeper of paradise explains to him that this situation is only an illusion, and Yudhisthira's family is returned to his side. The *Mahabharata* ends with Yudhisthira's realization that everything, including paradise and Hades, are mere illusions.

The *Mahabharata* includes many stories of great importance to the Hindu tradition. For example, part of book VI is called the *Bhagavad Gita*, the "Lord's Song." Considered by many to be one of the most beautiful of all Hindu scriptures, it is also the most important Hindu religious text. The 700 Sanskrit verses within it describe the events just prior to the central event of the epic, an important battle of cosmic proportions that must be waged between the family of Yudhisthira (the PANDAVAS) and their cousins (the Kauravas). In the context of this dramatic moral confrontation, the work details the three Hindu paths that lead to a mystical union with God. Indeed, the scope, vision, and importance of this extraordinary epic are perhaps best summed up by the proclamation found within its own pages: "What is not in the *Mahabharata* is not to be found anywhere else in the world."

The *Mahabharata* was published in its entirety in English by P.C. Roy and K. M. Ganguli in 12 volumes called *The Mahabharata of Krishna-Dwaipayana Vyasa* (1884–1896). Today, most people prefer the still-incomplete translation of the *Mahabharata* begun in 1973 by J. A. B. van Buitenen; only the first few volumes have been published thus far. Scholarly works on the *Mahabharata* tend to be fairly esoteric for general readers, but Alf Hiltebeitel's *The Ritual of Battle: Krishna in the Mahabharata* (1976) offers some important commentary on the work. This epic has also been cast into a nine-hour drama by Peter Brook and Jean-Claude Carriere, called *The Mahabharata: A Play Based Upon the Indian Classic Epic*. For commentary on this play, see David Leeming's *Mahabharata: The Great History of Mankind* (1987). Film adaptations of the *Mahabharata* have also been produced by Peter Brook—including an abridged version based on William Buck's shortened translation (1973).

For Further Reading

Buck, William. *Mahabharata*. Berkeley: University of California Press, 1981.

Carrière, Jean-Claude. *The Mahabharata: A Play Based Upon the Indian Classic Epic*. Translated by Peter Brook. New York: Harper & Row, 1987.

Dutt, Romesh C. *The Ramayana, and the Mahabharata, Condensed into English Verse*. New York: E. P. Dutton, 1910.

Hiltebeitel, Alf. *The Ritual of Battle: Krishna in the Mahabharata*. Ithaca, NY: Cornell University Press, 1976.

MAHPIYATO

In the Dakota and Lakota tribes, creator figure, the sky, source of all wisdom and power, and great judge. In Elizabeth Cook-Lynn's tale, "Mahpiyato," Mahpiyato as a character is considered one of the creators, and the CRONE of the tale refers to Mahpiyato as female. She explains to her grandchild that the word *mahpiyato* "is a Dakota word which tells us what we are witnessing right now, at this very moment." Since she is looking at the river, which looks part blue and part gray where a cloud passes over it, the tale suggests the paradoxical and immediate nature of CREATION for the old Dakota woman.

In "The Judgment of Mahpiyato," a Lakota tale retold by Paul Jordan-Smith, Mahpiyato is a MALE CREATOR who provides Wi, the SUN, with his companion Hanwi, the MOON. When Ite of the underworld wants to be more beautiful and take Hanwi's place, she is punished so that she ends up as Two-faced Woman, where on one side she has a beautiful face and on the other side, her face is hideous. Mahpiyato's punishments of IKTOME, the TRICKSTER; Wakanka and Wazi, rulers of the people of the underworld; and Wi, the sun, reveal a creator who is fair and metes out a judgment intimately related to the crime committed. Another Lakota tale that features Mahpiyato is "HOW EVIL BEGAN."

For Further Reading

Cook-Lynn, Elizabeth. *The Power of Horses and Other Stories*. New York: Arcade Publishing, 1990.

MAIDEN

First part of the triad symbolizing the phases of a woman's life. In the maiden-MOTHER-CRONE triad, suggesting the phases of the MOON, the maiden represents the first phase. In certain MYTHS, the maiden must DESCEND TO THE UNDERWORLD and then return, as in the Greek myth of Persephone (*see* PERSEPHONE MYTH). Persephone, also called Kore, which means maiden, is the maiden phase; her mother, Demeter, is the mother phase; and the older moon GODDESS, HECATE is the crone phase. Demeter is the goddess of the grain and agriculture, and the maiden's cycle, including her descent and return, is symbolic of the growth cycle of plants.

When Persephone is abducted by HADES, Demeter and Hecate hear her cries but cannot find her; her footprints have been trampled on by a herd of pigs. Demeter searches for nine days, but none of the GODS will help her until Helios, the sun god, finally informs her where her daughter is. Since Hades will not release Persephone, Demeter leaves Olympos, transforms herself into an old woman, and lets the earth lie fallow for a year until ZEUS relents and facilitates in Persephone's release. But Persephone has eaten a pomegranate seed while in the Underworld, and so she is forced to return to Hades for one third of the year.

When this myth was reenacted in the ancient Greek Eleusinian Mysteries, the women partaking in the rites would fast for nine days as a reminder of the nine days Demeter wanders about searching for some sign of her daughter, and they held an ear of grain symbolizing Persephone's return just as she did, suggesting the plant cycle and the seasons, for only in winter would Persephone remain in the Underworld. Like the corn, she rises in spring and summer. This ritual reenactment at Eleusis would also symbolize each woman's evolution from maiden to mother.

The "planting of the maiden" theme is found in other cultures as well. The moon maidens Rabie and Hainuwele are both "planted" in the earth to be reborn as the moon or food. The African maiden Wunjiru is also planted sacrificially. Her death brings needed water to her people.

For Further Reading

Evetts-Secker, Josephine. *Mother and Daughter Tales.* Illustrated by Helen Cann. New York: Abbeville, 1996.

Homer. *Demeter and Persephone: Homeric Hymn Number Two.* Translated and adapted by Penelope Praddow. Illustrated by Barbara Cooney. Garden City, NY: Doubleday, 1972.

Tomaino, Susan F. *Persephone, Bringer of Spring.* Illustrated by Ati Forberg New York: Crowell, 1971.

MAITREYA

Buddhist APOCALYPSE of Tibet, Mongolia, and Korea. In this PARADISE-like vision of the apocalypse, the world is utterly transformed. Because part of the ocean will dry up and become land, the subcontinent of India will be large enough to hold the people of the entire world. There will be enough FOOD for everyone, and sickness and war will no longer exist. All people will become kind, and although hunger, elimination of waste, and aging will still be problems, people will live much longer lives, marrying at around 150 and dying at around 500. Shankha will be the world's one ruler, and he will disseminate the law, the *Dharma* of BUDDHA, everywhere. While Shankha is ruler, Maitreya, the future Buddha, will be born, emerging absolutely clean from his mother's womb after her ten-month pregnancy (*see* MAYA). Maitreya, like the great Guatama Buddha who preceded him, will recognize life's illusory nature, will have 84,000 attendants, will preach for 60,000 years, and will be the last Buddha, leaving EARTH to go to his NIRVANA, the Buddhist term for supreme enlightenment and union with GOD. While Maitreya is Buddha, BRAHMA, the Eternal God, will communicate the truth of *Dharma*, and after Maitreya leaves, the *Dharma* will continue to rule for 10,000 years, and then everyone will reach Nirvana and Brahma himself will teach everyone the universal truth. During the period of Maitreya's preaching and the following period of Dharma, all selfishness, possessiveness, and illusion will disappear. People will no longer need to bear children because of their long lives, and instead will live chaste lives with no need to succumb to their passions. The only goal for all of humankind will be to achieve *samadhi*, or enlightenment.

For Further Reading

Eliade, Mircea, ed. *The Encyclopedia of Religion.* Vol. 2. New York: Macmillan, 1987.

MALE CREATOR

Patriarchal FATHER figure responsible for the cosmogonies of many cultures. Although some cultures have as their creator a female Great GODDESS figure, such as GAIA, reflecting the natural order or birth, a majority of cultures reflect their patriarchal basis by having a male creator as the original being responsible for creating order out of chaos. In many Native American creation myths, for example, there is a TRICKSTER-creator figure called OLD MAN, COYOTE, Old Man Coyote, or RAVEN. The Hebrew creator, YAHWEH, is generally considered to be male and a father figure, creating the universe in six days and resting on the seventh. He is responsible for making Adam, the first man, out of clay (see ADAM AND EVE).

In "creation by secretion" stories, the GOD who creates from expectorating, vomiting, masturbating, sweating, urinating, or defecating is almost always male. In Bantu and Boshongo Creation, the male god BUMBA creates the SUN, MOON, stars, and animals by vomiting. In Egyptian mythology, the male god, Atum, creates his brother and sister, Shu and Tefnut, by masturbating, or, in some versions, expectorating.

MAMADI THE MESSENGER

West African tale from the Soninke tribe, located in Senegal and in neighboring areas of West Africa, about a man who never tells a lie. When Bahene, the chief of the Soninke people, learns that Mamadi has never spoken an untruth, he decides to set a trap for him. Bahene instructs Mamadi to go to the village of Maftam and deliver a message to Bahene's wife. Mamadi must tell Bahene's wife that Bahene has gone antelope hunting, that he and his men will arrive in Maftam at noon that day, and that his wife should have a meal ready for the hungry men. Bahene, of course, decides not to go hunting or to travel to Maftam.

When Mamadi delivers the message to Bahene's wife, he says that it is possibly probable or at least not impossibly improbable that Bahene has gone hunting. Confused by Mamadi's words, Bahene's wife asks if there is any other message. Mamadi replies that if Bahene and his men did go hunting, then it might be prudent to prepare a meal for them, assuming they did go hunting and plan to eat afterwards. Finally, Mamadi tells Bahene's exasperated wife that it may have been Bahene's intention to arrive in Maftam before, or after, or even exactly at noon.

When Bahene and his men arrive the next day, they laugh uproariously at Mamadi. Bahene's wife, however, informs the chief that Mamadi had said that Bahene might go hunting, he might arrive at noon the day before, and it might be wise for her to cook a meal. Realizing that he has been put to shame in front of his own people, Bahene rewards Mamadi for his virtue, proclaiming that all Soninke people must remember that Mamadi will never lie. The tale ends with Mamadi saying that it is presumably true (or probably unlikely) that he *possibly* will never lie.

Another well-known LEGEND about a person who does not tell lies is the American myth about the boy George Washington, who cut down a cherry tree. When asked if he was the guilty one, the young George admits to it, saying, "I cannot tell a lie."

Many tales from various storytelling traditions include the MOTIF of a trap, which is often coupled with the clever use of language. In Greek tradition, Oedipus must solve the SPHINX's riddle, lest he be devoured like many others before him, before he can enter the city of THEBES. The Sphinx asks, "What being, with only one voice, has sometimes two feet, sometimes three, sometimes four, and is weakest when it has the most?" Oedipus correctly answers, "Man," causing the Sphinx to dash herself to pieces. In the European legend of "Little RED RIDING HOOD," the wolf finally traps Red Riding Hood when, disguised as her grandmother, he says, "All the better to hear/see/eat you with," in answer to the little girl's comments about her grandmother's big ears, eyes, and jaws. AESOP'S FABLES include numerous instances of the trap motif, notably in "The Dog, The Cock, and The Fox," when the dog and the cock work together to trap the fox; in "The Kid and the Wolf," when the kid convinces her captor, the wolf, to play his pipe for her, causing the dogs to hear the music and come and chase the wolf away; and in "The Fox and the Crow," when the fox flatters the crow, who holds a piece of cheese in her beak that he desires, by commenting on her beauty, but noting the lack of her voice; the crow opens her mouth to demonstrate her caw and loses the piece of cheese to the fox. Another famous trap is that of the TAR BABY from the UNCLE REMUS stories by Joel Chandler Harris (*see* HARRIS, JOEL CHANDLER).

A just reward for one's virtue is another popular storytelling theme, other examples of which can be found in the Igbo tale SECRET SON and in numerous FAIRY TALES with happy endings.

For Further Reading

Abrahams, Roger, ed. *African Folktales: Traditional Stories of the Black World*. New York: Pantheon, 1983.

Courlander, Harold, and George Herzog. *The Cow-Tail Switch and Other West African Stories*. New York: Henry Holt, 1947.

MAN OF LORE

Irish story about the poet Seanchan's search to recover the lost tale, *Táin Bó Cuailnge* (*see* CUCHULAINN). The story begins when King Guaire's brother, Marbhan, loses his temper because Seanchan and his company of poets, pupils, servants, and followers have worn out their welcome. After berating the guests, Marbhan chides the master poet to reveal his rumored mystical knowledge and tell the lost tale of the great cattle raid, *Táin Bó Cuailnge*. If Seanchan fails to meet Marbhan's challenge, he must forfeit his position and maybe his life.

Seanchan calls an assembly of poets and storytellers from the five provinces of Eire, but they are unable to reconstruct the tale. Seanchan and his son, Muirghein, travel throughout the country trying to find someone who might know the ancient story. Finally, they find Neidhe, the son of Seanchan's predecessor. Neidhe tells them that they might find what they seek at the Rock of Divisions on the Hill of Uisnech. The Rock of Divisions is an ancient holy place, the meeting point of the five provinces, the navel of Ireland.

At the top of the hill, Seanchan and Muirghein kneel by the rock. A storm arises, and in the wind Seanchan hears music and song, and he learns where they must go to find the tale. They travel to Eanloch where Feargus mac Roich, Cuchulainn's tutor in arms, is buried. When they reach the mound of Feargus's grave, Seanchan and Muirghein recite a praise song in honor of their ancestors as a mist rises around them. An immense apparition appears out of the mist. It is Feargus. He relates the missing tale to the poets and then vanishes.

The MOTIF of a rock as a holy place is common in storytelling traditions. Similar to the Rock of Divisions in "Man of Lore," the BETHEL stone in Hebrew tradition, the conical stone in APOLLO's temple at DELPHI, and the *Ka'ba* at MECCA mark the world navel (the *axis mundi*) and perhaps the gateway to HEAVEN. Some sacred stones, such as the Agdos Rock and ERATHIPA, are identified with the MOTHER and/or femininity.

Likewise, sacred hills or mountains, such as the Hill of Uisnech and Feargus's burial mound in this tale, are often sites of communication with the divine. Moses receives the Ten Commandments on MOUNT SINAI (*see* EXODUS), and the Hindu god SIVA sits on the mountain, MERU.

In addition to containing these familiar motifs, the story "Man of Lore" illustrates the importance of storytelling as a form of entertainment and as a profession in early Irish culture. The tale depicts with reasonable accuracy a particular setting, in this case a KING's court, in which stories in early Ireland were passed on by professional storytellers, whose livelihood depended on their ability to please their patrons. *See also* CELTIC STORYTELLING.

MANABOZHO

Algonquian (Native American) TRICKSTER, the Great HARE. Like most tricksters, Manabozho is powerful and benevolent, but also capable of deception and stupidity. He can give life to all beings and can also impersonate them. The Algonquian tale "Manabozho or the Great Incarnation of the North" was translated in the 1830s by Henry Rowe Schoolcraft (*see* SCHOOLCRAFT, HENRY ROWE). This translation was the source for Longfellow's Indian EPIC, "Hiawatha."

Schoolcraft's version of the story begins with Manabozho living alone in a wasteland with his grandmother. The pair are exiled, the grandmother having been cast to EARTH from her native planet. Her only child, a beautiful daughter, is kidnapped by the West WIND and dies giving birth to Manabozho. Learning of his parentage, the boy goes out to challenge his FATHER, the West Wind. Striding across the continent he becomes a giant, covering miles with every step. When he meets his father, Manabozho pretends to be reconciled but deviously learns his father's weakness. He uses his knowledge to fight his father, who eventually promises to give Manabozho a place with his other sons, but first requires fulfillment of certain tasks. Manabozho is sent to do good on earth, which is inhabited by monsters that cause trouble for people.

Manabozho's first job is to get oil for his grandmother's hair. To do so the boy goes fishing, only to be swallowed by the king of fish. Manzabozho kills the monstrous fish, which then washes ashore, and after three days, Manabozho returns to the world. He next battles the *manito* of wealth and then a serpent. He flees the serpents, which cause the water to rise, forcing him to cling to a tree. Three times he asks the tree to stretch to the sky, and each time the tree obliges. The water rises to the hero's chin, and just when he is about to despair the water begins to recede (*see* FLOOD).

Gazing at the flooded world while hanging from his tree, Manabozho determines to make the world new, and enlists the help of ANIMALS to bring mud from under the water with which to build a new earth. The loon and the muskrat try, but they both die in the attempt. Manabozho breathes life back into the muskrat, who returns to the bottom and brings up the tiniest bit of mud that does not wash from his paws during his ascent to the water's surface. From this little bit of mud and the body of the dead loon, Manabozho fashions a new earth. Because the serpent still

lives, however, Manabozho is not satisfied, and he goes out to kill his enemy. Only after he is successful will he return to his village.

To the Micmac and Passamaquoddy the Great Hare was know as *Mahtigwess*. This character also goes by the names *Winabojo* and *Nanabush* or *Nanabozho*; he is *Menapus* (Big Rabbit) to the Menominee, who say Menapus was fathered by the North Wind when a young girl ignored warnings against facing north. Some versions have the girl birthing triplets, Menapus and two brothers, Little Wolf and Flint Stone. The last son's delivery causes the mother to bleed to death, and the grandmother throws out the flint that then becomes a tool for people to start fires with. Little Wolf was killed, and Menapus sets out to avenge his death, enjoying many adventures along the way.

The Ojibway Winabojo has a brother called Wabosso. The two frequently challenge one another, until Wabosso turns up missing. Another story has Winabojo marrying a human woman and having children. When the family is attacked, Winabojo kills all his family but one to spare them from the attackers. He and his daughter join his grandmother in the sky.

Some cultures believed that Shawnee prophet, Tenskwatawa, was an incarnation of Manabozho. The character survives in contemporary Native American fiction among the characters of the Chippewa writer, Louise Erarion.

For Further Reading

Schoolcraft, Henry Rowe. *The Hiawatha Legends: Indian Folklore.* 7th ed. Avery Color, 1984.

————. *Schoolcraft's Ojibwa Lodge Stories: Life on the Other Lake Superior Frontier.* Edited by Philip P. Mason. Ann Arbor, MI: Michigan State University Press, 1996.

MANTICORA

Fabulous and frightening mythical beast of India. Like other mythical beasts that appear as a combination of several different creatures that might include human features, the manticora was believed to have a triple row of teeth set alternately in the face of a man with gleaming eyes and a ruddy complexion. It has the body of a lion, the tail of a scorpion, and its shrill voice is similar to the sound of pipes. Frightening because it likes to pursue and feed on human flesh, the manticora can travel great distances and is sure-footed.

For Further Reading

Payne, Ann. *Medieval Beasts*. New York: New Amsterdam, 1990.

South, Malcolm. *Mythical and Fabulous Creatures: A Sourcebook and Research Guide*. Westport, CT: Greenwood Publishing Group, 1987.

MANU AND THE FISH

FLOOD story from the Hindu *Shatapathat Brahmana*. In this MYTH, Manu discovers a fish in the palm of his hand as he washes. The fish speaks to Manu, requesting safety in exchange for Manu's salvation from an impending and disastrous flood. Since the greatest danger to the fish exists when it is small, it asks to be kept in a jar, and as it grows, to be transferred to a pit and then to the sea. Manu follows the fish's instructions, and, when it grows into a great fish, it informs Manu of the year in which the flood will occur. The fish also tells Manu to construct a ship to shelter himself from the flood waters. Manu complies, and when the time arrives for the fish to be taken to the sea, the floods begin and Manu enters the ship. The fish swims to Manu who fastens a rope to the large horn on its head. Guiding him to the lofty security of a mountain, the fish instructs Manu to fasten the rope to a tree and ease the ship down the mountainside as the flood waters recede. Manu does as instructed and is the lone survivor of all CREATION.

The story of Manu and the fish bears similarities to other flood myths, particularly those of the Hebrew NOAH and the Babylonian Utnapishtim. In all three stories, a remnant is saved from general devastation through supernatural assistance. In the Hindu belief system, the supernatural assistance is VISNU in the form (or *avatar*) of Matsyavatar: the fish. As the sustainer god of the Hindu PANTHEON, Visnu helps Manu survive the flood and start anew. Like Noah, in thanksgiving for his preservation, Manu sacrifices to the GODS, and he comes to be known as the founder of that practice. Either his devotion to the gods or his role as the founder of hu-

manity also associates Manu with the foundation of the Brahmanic legal codes of later Hindu culture. As a reflection of these associations, the story of Manu establishes for the listener a connection among tradition, sacrifice, and charity. As with the survivors of other flood stories, Manu stands as a model of obedience to the gods.

For Further Reading

Pratt, Jane Abbott. *Consciousness and Sacrifice: An Interpretation of Two Episodes in the Indian Myth of Manu*. New York: Analytical Psychology Club of New York, 1967.

MAORI COSMOLOGY

Creation MYTH of the Polynesian Maori people of New Zealand. Maori cosmology reflects both "CREATION from nothing" as well as the "DIVISION OF WORLD PARENTS" MOTIF.

In the beginning there is one Supreme Being, Io, or Iho. Io exists in a void where there is only darkness and water. Eventually, the words of Io bring the creation of day and night, and then the separation of the waters into heaven and earth. Rangi, the SKY-FATHER, and Papa, the EARTH-MOTHER, couple to produce many children, but their embrace is so strong that their children are crowded and cramped (*see* RANGI AND PAPA). Tane, the child who manages to separate them, becomes the GOD of life and creates the first Maori out of red clay. While Tane and his brother Rongo are responsible for creating the forests, the insects, and the plants, other children become the earthquakes, the WINDS, and the rains. One child, the warrior god Tu, is the father of the brave Maori people, and Tangaroa, the tenth child of Rangi and Papa, is known as the father of MAUI, the HERO. The sadness that Rangi and Papa feel at being separated causes Rangi's tears—rain—to fall on Papa, and her sighs at being torn from her husband causes the mists to rise.

MARCHEN *See* GRIMM BROTHERS

MARDUK

Mesopotamian god of the SUN, creator of the world, and god of the city of Babylon. Marduk was worshipped as a fierce and dynamic god who played a crucial role in shaping the world and its inhabitants. Each new year the Mesopotamians celebrated the CREATION of the world in rites that reenacted Marduk's fight with and ultimate victory over Tiamat, the female DRAGON of the primordial ocean. As god of the sun, Marduk arrives in his chariot and captures Tiamat in a net of light. First he prevents her jaws from seizing him by flinging a hurricane between them, and then he shoots her with arrows and slices her in half. The top half of Tiamat becomes the HEAVENS and the bottom half forms the EARTH. Finally, Marduk takes blood and bone to create nature and human beings, who are to serve as slaves to the GODS.

Tales of Marduk, which were undoubtedly part of the Babylonian oral tradition, were recorded in cuneiform on clay tablets found in the remains of the palace of Ashurbanipal, king of the Assyrians. Marduk's name meant "bull calf of the sun," and he had fifty additional names. Son of Ea and consort of Sarpanitu, the planet Venus, Marduk, with his double-head was a sun god of magic and incantation. Each spring his resurrection took place, signifying renewal. *See also* ORIGIN OF THE SEASONS.

MARRIAGE

MOTIF in MYTH and FAIRY TALE signifying the uniting of polar opposites. The purpose of marriage is to form a higher unity, with the two elements being joined to function as complements. Whether this takes place as the *heiros gamos*, the sacred wedding uniting HEAVEN and EARTH, male and female principles, SUN and MOON, or god and GODDESS or as the secular wedding of the KING and queen, PRINCE and PRINCESS, or man and woman, marriage represents fertility, wholeness, summer, and, in some cases, the goal of the QUEST of the HERO.

In many fairy tales that have courtship as their theme, marriage serves as the resolution that takes place after the story's climax, followed by the classic "And they lived happily ever after." As Marina Warner notes in *From the Beast to the Blonde*, "The weddings of fairy tale bring the traditional narratives to a satisfying open ending which allows the possibility to hope." Marriage tests may be part of the tale; the tests occur in the stories of Native North Americans as well as in the fairy tales of Europe and East Asia. A marriage test may be a TEST OF PROWESS or a test to see if the hero can correctly answer the riddle, make the right choice, etc. Marriage serves as the culmination of the conflict in all variants of such fairy tales as "CINDERELLA," "Snow White," "Sleeping Beauty," "Rose Red and Snow White," and "Rapunzel." As Susan Cooper writes, "Marriage is the fulcrum and major event of nearly every fairy tale; it is the reward for girls and sometimes their punishment." She also points out that "Marriage is associated with getting rich" and "the reward basis in fairy tales and folktales is overwhelmingly mercenary. Good, poor, and pretty girls always win rich and handsome princes, never merely handsome, good, but poor men." In Andrew Lang's *The Blue Fairy Book*, 18 of the stories end in marriage and in 12 others marriage is a component, although little is ever shown of married life after the marriage takes place (*see* LANG, ANDREW).

Some marriages involve an ANIMAL bridegroom, as in Charles Perrault's fairy tale "BEAUTY AND THE BEAST" (*see* PERRAULT, CHARLES). In his discussion of "Beauty and the Beast," Bruno Bettelheim sees Beauty's marriage to the former beast as "a symbolic expression of the healing of the pernicious break between the animal and the higher aspects of man—a separation which is described as a sickness" (*see* BETTELHEIM, BRUNO). Thus marriage can symbolize healing, wholeness, unity, and hope in storytelling.

MARWE IN THE UNDERWORLD

African tale from Kenya about the girl Marwe's suicide, experience in the underworld, and return to life on EARTH.

Marwe and her brother are responsible for keeping the monkeys from destroying their family's bean fields. One day, they go to a pool for a drink. When they return, the monkeys have eaten all the beans. Because Marwe fears her parents' wrath, she drowns herself.

Marwe sinks to the bottom of the pool and enters the LAND OF THE DEAD. For many years Marwe lives with a CRONE who is her guide in the underworld. Marwe becomes homesick, and the old woman knows that she desires to rejoin the living. The old woman has Marwe dip her limbs into a clay jar of cold water. When she pulls them out, they are covered with jewels. The old woman dresses Marwe in the finest robes. She tells Marwe that she will soon marry Sawoye, the best man in the world. Then she sends Marwe home.

After Marwe returns to her overjoyed family, word spreads that a rich, eligible woman is in the territory. Many suitors visit Marwe's home. Marwe ignores all of them except for Sawoye, who suffers from a terrible skin disease. Because she has been to the land of the dead, Marwe is able to read the hearts of all the men. She marries Sawoye, knowing that he is the best. After they consummate their MARRIAGE, Sawoye's disease disappears, and he is the most handsome man of all.

People begin to resent the wealthy couple. A group of neighbors attack and kill Sawoye. Marwe, knowing the secrets of the underworld, revives her husband, and Sawoye kills all their enemies. Marwe and Sawoye live in happiness and prosperity, and since they already have experienced death once, they fearlessly meet their ends.

The theme of children neglecting their responsibilities or disobeying their parents followed by an unpleasant consequence is a common one in storytelling traditions. ADAM AND EVE eat from the forbidden tree in the center of Eden and are banished by GOD from the garden forever. Thakane, in the Basuto story CHILD IN THE REEDS, is taken to be eaten by an OGRE for disobeying her parents and cutting a piece from the forbidden kumonngoe tree.

Likewise, the theme of jealousy is treated in many stories. KATE CRACKERNUTS, OSEBO'S DRUM, and SECRET SON are just a few of the many tales in which jealousy or envy figures as an important element.

A character's DESCENT TO THE UNDERWORLD is a MOTIF found in the journey QUESTS of most HEROES and HEROINES. These confrontations with DEATH help the characters to emerge in REBIRTH into a new individuated existence, a new wisdom, or wholeness. In Marwe's case, she is able to understand the true nature of all men. ODYSSEUS, GILGAMESH, Aeneas, THESEUS, Jesus, and INANNA are all examples of characters who journey to the land of the dead (see AENEID).

In addition, the motif of a powerful female figure who lives under water exists in stories from various cultures. The Lady of the Lake from Arthurian legend, a fay or fairy who lives in an enchanted palace in the depths of the lake, gives KING ARTHUR his famed sword, Excalibur. According to some sources, it is also the Lady of the Lake who imprisons the magician MERLIN. Similar to the old woman in Marwe in the Underworld, an old woman living beneath the river raises the baby girl Lilahloane into a beautiful maiden in Child in the Reeds.

The tale of Marwe also deals with the redemptive powers of a woman's love, as in the princess who transforms a FROG into a PRINCE with her kiss, a theme echoed in the well-known fairy tale "BEAUTY AND THE BEAST."

For Further Reading

Bierlein, J.F. Parallel Myths. New York: Ballantine, 1994.

MARY

Mother of Jesus Christ. Known as the Blessed Virgin Mary, Mary is the wife of Joseph although their marriage is not yet consummated when the angel Gabriel comes to her to prophesy the visit of the Holy Ghost and the subsequent birth of Jesus. At this time Mary is living in the city of Nazareth in Galilee. At first Mary is puzzled by Gabriel's announcement, known as the "Annunciation," but Gabriel explains that her son will be the "Son of GOD," with whom she has found favor, and that her barren cousin Elizabeth had also conceived a son, miraculously, who will become John the Baptist.

When Mary is almost ready to give birth, she and Joseph leave Nazareth for Bethlehem, his town of origin, because Caesar Augustus has decreed that each man must be taxed in his own town. All the inns at Bethlehem are crowded, and Mary and Joseph are forced to stay in a stable, where Mary gives birth to Jesus. Angels tell nearby shepherds of the birth of the Messiah, and they and the Three Wise Men visit him. Little is known about Mary from this point on, except that she and Joseph and their infant son return to Nazareth.

A multitude of stories have been told concerning Mary's "immaculate conception" and the subsequent birth of Jesus in the stable. Mary is always depicted as the archetypal "good mother" aspect of the Great GODDESS, the beatific Madonna, the second Eve or redeemer. The stories concerning her ASCENSION to HEAVEN at her death came at a later date and were a response to Catholic Church's exclusion of the goddess figure who had been so important to women and earlier religions. With her Assumption, Mary becomes Queen of Heaven, and is portrayed as having a crown on her head. The term "Mariology" has come to refer to the vast lore of songs, LEGENDS, FOLKTALES, MYSTERY PLAYS, and miracle cycles concerning Mary, the Mother of Jesus.

The story of Mary's virginity and the miraculous birth of Jesus is similar to the story of the MAYA and the birth of BUDDHA and reflects the archetypal miraculous birth of the HERO or god.

For Further Reading

Warner, Marina. *Alone of All Her Sex: The Myth and the Cult of the Virgin Mary*. New York: Knopf, 1976.

MASKS AND MASQUERADE

Disguise used in folk dances, initiation rites, tribal ceremonies, and in storytelling. Masks have been worn since primitive times to disguise, conceal, entertain, heal, frighten, fool, burlesque, and exorcise. Some of the earliest masks were worn by SHAMANS who impersonated natural forces and totemic spirits with the belief that they would be capable of taking on their powers by identification. Eventually masks became part of many rituals and ceremonies, and the CLOWNS of numerous American Indian tribes wear elaborate masks as part of their costumes.

Masks belong to the oral tradition in that they were and continue to be worn by storytellers and actors. The *shaman* of a tribe might wear a mask and tell a story, and ancient Greek actors performing the tragedies and comedies of Aeschylus, Sophocles, Euripedes, and Aristophanes always wore masks. Many Halloween stories depend on the wearing of masks as devices to fool and frighten. The costume ball or masquerade of FAIRY TALES has also provided many plots based on mistaken identity and deception. Edgar Allen Poe's short story, "William Wilson," has as its theme the confrontation with the double, or shadow, and its final scene involves the masked William Wilson killing what he sees in the mirror, unaware that it is himself.

The Dogon myth "The First Mask" is a story offering an explanation for how DEATH came to exist (*see* ORIGIN OF DEATH). As the Dogon recount, when people get old they become serpents, give up human language, and are supposed to speak only the language of the spirits. An old man who has done so and is now a serpent comes across some boys who have stolen the skirt of CREATION worn by women. Forgetting himself for a moment in his anger at their blasphemous act, the old man yells "Stop!" Because he speaks the language of the living, his soul leaves his snake's body, and all that is left is a corpse. The people have never seen a corpse before, and the elders take the snake corpse and put it in a cave, but they do not know where the soul has gone until a few months later when a baby is born with red circles on its skin like that of a snake. The elders believe that the baby has received the old man's soul. So they make a mask to look like the snake and sing the soul from the baby into the mask; as the soul comes to rest in the mask, death enters the world. The elders' dance becomes the first funeral and the mask the first mask, and masks become the place where the souls of the dead are housed.

In the stories and films of popular culture, the figure of the Lone Ranger, the "masked man," has been evocative in its suggestion of mysterious identity. Batman is another well-known masked popular culture HERO. In the children's story "Bear Party," written and illustrated by William Pene du Bois, Australian koala bears who cannot tell each other apart begin to quarrel and don masks for a masquerade where each one can at last tell who the other is and their quarrels are resolved.

MATAJURO THE SWORDSMAN

Famous Zen swordsman who learned through patience. In the Zen parable "The Taste of Banzo's Sword," Matajuro Yagyu longs to become a swordsman who will make his father, a famous swordsman, proud of him, but his father thinks he is incapable and, therefore, disowns him. Matajuro then goes to another famous swordsman, Banzo, and requests that Banzo teach him. Although Matajuro is prepared to work very hard, when he asks Banzo how long it will take to become an expert swordsman, Banzo is discouraging, saying at first it will take ten years, then thirty, then seventy. From this Matajuro learns that he must not be so impatient. When Matajuro comes to Banzo, he learns nothing of fencing for the first three years, and he is not allowed to speak of it to his master. Instead he cooks, cleans, and gardens. One day, his master surprises him from behind and strikes him with a wooden sword. The next day, Banzo surprises Matajuro again. From that point on, Matajuro must learn to defend himself from these unexpected thrusts. By becoming always prepared for Banjo's sword, Matajuro quickly grows to be the greatest swordsman in all the land.

For Further Reading

Reps, Paul, ed. *Zen Flesh, Zen Bones*. Rutland, VT: Charles E. Tuttle, 1957.

MAUI

Polynesian demi-god, CULTURE HERO, and TRICKSTER figure. Many MYTHS and LEGENDS surround Maui, the most well-known of the Polynesian HEROES. The story surrounding his birth reveals aspects of the birth of the DIVINE CHILD MOTIF and the ABANDONED CHILD motif, while his deeds reveal his mischievous, trickster aspect as well as his heroism and his *hubris*. Besides the story of his birth, Maui is known for forming language out of his grandmother's jawbone; for slowing the course of the SUN to make the day last longer; for stealing fire from his ancestor, the fire GODDESS, and then teaching humans how to kindle it; for fishing for islands, such as New Zealand; and for attempting to defy DEATH— the one deed at which he fails (*see also* THEFT OF FIRE).

In one VARIANT of the myth, Maui is the son of the wise woman and earth-goddess Taranga, and his father is Makea-tutara; in another version, his father is Tangaroa, or Kanaloa in Hawaiian, and his mother is a mortal woman; in a third variant, his mother is Mahuike, the earth-goddess, and his father is the creator god. Taranga has four other sons and a daughter, and when Maui is born prematurely as she strolls by the sea one day, she rolls him up in some hair cut from her topknot and casts him into the SEA. The sea god, or Old Man of the Sea, saves him and raises him then, teaching him the lore of his people. When he is still very young, Maui reappears to his family one evening, and his mother finds him sitting with her other four sons. After he introduces himself to her, she accepts him as her son and takes him to sleep in her bed that night, for night is the only time her sons can be with Taranga, since she disappears each day.

Maui's brothers have no idea where their mother goes during the day, and Maui's curiosity and the first signs of his trickster nature surface in his determination to find out. He notices that his mother rises at dawn and mysteriously leaves each day, so he cleverly covers all the openings in their house with rags so the dawn light cannot awaken her. When Taranga finally awakes, Maui is able to watch her disappear down a hidden tunnel into the earth. Transforming himself into a dove, he flies down into the tunnel that eventually opens onto a cavern and then countryside, where he sees his parents sitting with friends. At first they think he is a mischievous dove when he throws berries on them, but when his father hits him with a stone and he falls to the ground, he is suddenly transformed into a grown, godlike man in lieu of the baby or bird he has been.

During his stay with his parents in this country, Maui is able to trick Muri-ranga-whenua, his grandmother and queen of that land, into giving him her jawbone in return for food. This jawbone becomes the source of language and helps him in his later adventures. When he returns to earth with it, he convinces his brothers to make a very strong net in which to catch the sun. They then travel to the sun's home, cast the net over it while the sun sleeps, and stakes the net tightly, so when the sun tries to rise, the net pulls it to the ground. With his grandmother's magic jawbone, Maui then beats the sun, portrayed as a beast with a red belly and bushy tail. Maui persists, bruising the sun so badly that when he finally lets the sun out of the net, it is bloodied and limping and has to travel much more slowly, thereby giving the people longer days.

In another famous feat, Maui goes fishing with his brothers, but while they fish, he lazes; they do not realize that for days Maui has been fashioning a magical hook made from a splinter of his grandmother's jawbone while his brothers have been out fishing to feed their families. At the end of the fishing trip, Maui tells them he wants to make one effort at casting his line. His brothers refuse to give him bait for his beautifully carved, fancy hook, so Maui punches himself in the nose and rubs his blood on the hook. Much to his brothers' astonishment, he fishes up a large part of the island of New Zealand.

Again revealing his trickster side, Maui steals fire from Mahu-ika, "the Flaming One," his great-great-grandmother. First he puts out all the village hearths; then he goes to the fire goddess and asks for fire. She gives him her fingernail, ablaze with fire, and as soon as he is out of sight, he extinguishes the flame. He keeps going back to the woman, but every time she gives him a fingernail or toenail, he puts out the fire until she is left with only one toenail. Finally aware that Maui has been tricking her, Mahu-ika chases Maui to the Upper World and throws the toenail at him, thereby setting the world on fire. To escape the flames, Maui first changes himself into an eagle, but there is nowhere to land, then a fish, but the water is boiling; at last his prayers to his ancestors bring rain, and the only flames left are a few sparks in firewood. These become the fire sticks he gives to the people so they can begin fires themselves, and he teaches them that wood is the best fuel for burning.

In his final adventure, Maui's *hubris* becomes apparent. In one variant, Maui is to be punished by death for transforming his brother-in-law into a dog, but, at his father's suggestion, he tries to evade death by going to Hina, the goddess of death. In another variant, he simply wants to prove that he can conquer death. When Maui arrives in the underworld, Hina is asleep, so, magic jawbone in hand, he climbs up through her legs until he reaches her mouth. He has told the ANIMALS and birds that watch this remarkable feat to remain silent until he reappears, but one small bird laughs too soon, Hina awakens, and Maui is crushed to death between her jaws (*see* DESCENT TO THE UNDERWORLD).

As Alexander Eliot notes in *Myths*, bold Maui "recapitulated in his infancy the whole slow evolution of life from the sea. In boyhood, he traced his mother home to a place not in this world. In youth, he acted out the appropriation of new prerogatives for mankind as a whole. And finally, as a man, he attempted to overcome death itself, and failed—as we all must."

For Further Reading

Andersen, Johannes C. *Myths and Legends of the Polynesians.* Illustrated by Richard Wallwork. Rutland, VT: Charles E. Tuttle Company, 1969.

McCaughrean, Geraldine. *The Golden Hoard: Myths and Legends of the World.* Illustrated by Bee Willey. New York: Simon & Schuster, 1995.

MAWU

Fertility GODDESS and creator in the LEGENDS of the Dahomey tribe of Africa. Mawu is seen as the maker of the world. After arriving in the mouth of a great snake, she gives the EARTH its mountains, valleys, and rivers following the path of the snake, much as the RAINBOW SERPENT and the goddess KUNAPIPI do in Australian Aborigine mythology. Mawu then makes the SUN in order to see her work, and afterwards she makes people and ANIMALS. Once her CREATION is completed, Mawu retires to the HEAVENS and the snake coils underneath the earth, carrying the weight of all that Mawu has created. In one tale, Awe, a human being, attempts to create his own human being, boasting that he is as powerful as Mawu. However, his *hubris* only brings about his death, for Mawu uses him as an example to instruct the people that only she is capable of breathing life into mortals and sucking it away when she chooses.

The connection between the Great Goddess and the snake, or serpent, occurs in the legends of many cultures, and a snake often accompanies the Great Goddess as in the story of ADAM AND EVE. While scholars may argue whether the symbolism of the snake is feminine and lunar—with the snake shedding its skin likened to the waxing and waning of the moon and the female cycle—or masculine—with all the phallic symbolism associated with snakes—the connection between the two suggests birth, DEATH, and resurrection. As Buffie Johnson notes in *The Lady of the Beasts*, "As a universal symbol, the serpent, through its form, found direct access to our emotion."

For Further Reading

Herskovits, Melville, J. *Dahomey*. Vol 2. New York: J. J. Augustin, 1958.

Johnson, Buffie. *The Lady of the Beasts*. New York: HarperCollins, 1988.

MAYA

Mother of BUDDHA. Like many other enlightened, spiritual figures and HEROES, Buddha is miraculously conceived by Maya. As Buddhist legend tells it, Maya participates for six days before the full MOON in a summer festival in the city of Kapilavathu. Anointed in perfumes and draped in garlands, Maya drinks nothing strong throughout the festival. The day the full moon rises she awakens early, bathes and perfumes herself, dresses elegantly, gives away 400,000 coins, eats the best food, takes the eight vows, and goes into her chamber of state. There she falls asleep and dreams that four guardian angels transport her to the Himalayas and place her under a *sal*-tree. Then the angels' wives take her to Anolta Lake, bathing her to make her pure and dressing her in divine clothing. She is then taken to a golden mansion near Silver Hill, where her couch is placed with its head facing east. From the distant Gold Hill, the Future Buddha, in the form of a white elephant with a white lotus in his trunk, approaches Maya,

walking around the couch three times with his right side facing the couch. Striking Maya on the right side, he seems to enter her womb. When she awakens from her dream, Maya realizes she has conceived, and from the moment of the Future Buddha's conception, the earth shakes and all nature grows sweeter and more magnificent. Four angels guard Maya during her pregnancy, and after ten lunar months, Maya, while standing in a grove of *sal*-trees, gives birth to the Future Buddha. Four pure Brahma angels catch the Future Buddha in a golden net. As the legend describes, because the womb that housed the Future Buddha can never be occupied again, Maya dies seven days after giving birth and is then reborn in HEAVEN, recalling QUETZALCOATL's mother's death soon after he is born.

MECCA

The holiest site of Islam and focal point of the *Hajj*, the pilgrimage required of all Muslims. Mecca is significant in Islamic tradition for three principal reasons: 1) Like the holy cities or mountains of other religions, it is considered the central place in the universe, the point at which the voice of GOD can be heard most clearly; 2) Mecca is considered the site of the first temple (*ka' bah*) of Ibrahim (Abraham), patriarch of Islam, Judaism, and Christianity; and 3) most importantly for Islamic tradition, Mecca is the birthplace of MUHAMMAD who also received God's final revelation there.

As the holiest site of Islam, Mecca is also considered a safe haven for Muslims. All differences, from political disputes to family arguments, are to be set aside in honor of the Hajj. The rules of conduct for the Hajj also prohibit pilgrims from displays of individual wealth. Thus, the requirements for the pilgrimage to Mecca have a great leveling effect as Muslims of many nations and degrees of wealth converge with the single-minded purpose of the Hajj. The confluence of disparate voices and the rigors of a long journey have both provided a context for Muslim storytelling. Many stories of the Hajj can be found in Richard Burton's two volume *Per-*

sonal Narrative of a Pilgrimage to al-Madinah and Meccah (1893) (*see* BURTON, RICHARD). Although a tradition of stories surrounding the Hajj has emerged, a more formal context for creative expression existed in pre-Islamic Mecca when an annual poetry contest was held in connection with the Hajj.

For Further Reading

Foote, Mary. *A Touch of Sun and Other Stories*. New York: Garrett, 1969.

Peters, F. E. *Mecca: A Literary History of the Muslim Holy Land*. Princeton, NJ: Princeton University Press, 1994.

MEDUSA

One of the three hideous Gorgons in Greek mythology. Medusa was once a beautiful Serpent GODDESS who ruled Africa, but she is reduced to a Gorgon sister, a scaly, winged being with serpents for hair who would turn to stone any mortal who looked upon her face. Perseus, the son of ZEUS and a mortal woman, is dared by an evil KING to travel to the island of the Gorgons and capture one of their heads. Knowing the fatal consequences of looking directly at Medusa or her sisters, Perseus, who is armed with Athena's shield and Hermes's sword, looks only at the reflection of the creatures in the shiny bronze shield. Coming upon the sisters while they sleep, Perseus severs Medusa's head, puts it in a bag and, with his winged sandals, quickly flies away with it. Drops of blood fall from the head onto the African ground below and turn into poisonous snakes.

Perseus returns to the king who has dared him to challenge the power of the Gorgons and finds him and his men enjoying a great banquet. Perseus enters the hall and holds up Medusa's decaying head; the king and his men immediately turn to stone. Perseus turns over the head to Athena, who affixes it to her shield to increase her power in battle.

The figure of Medusa is just one of many female monsters who are destroyed at the hands of young male HEROES. Not merely a symbol of extreme ugliness, Medusa represents what cannot be seen, that is, DEATH itself. Her character appears in numerous literary texts including Hesiod's *Theogony*, HOMER'S ODYSSEY, Milton's *Paradise Lost*, and Dante's *Divine Comedy*. In each of these examples, Medusa guards the world of the dead. This connection between Medusa and death carries over into Christian symbolism, in which she is interpreted as the embodiment death, sin, and even of the DEVIL himself.

For Further Reading

Perseus and Medusa. New York: Troll, 1980.

MENELAOS

Legendary Greek chieftain, the KING of Sparta and brother of AGAMEMNON, the king of MYCENAE. Menelaos appears in both the ILIAD and the ODYSSEY, the two great poems by the EPIC poet HOMER. Robert Graves (*see* GRAVES, ROBERT) suggests that these stories came from older poems recited orally. Tale of Menelaos's wanderings in the Mediterranean may be derived from older stories of piracies and attempts at colonization in that area. Menelaos is also a character in three plays by the fifth-century dramatist Euripides.

Along with all the other leaders of Greece, Menelaos vies to marry HELEN OF TROY, the most beautiful woman in the world. Helen's stepfather forces all of her suitors to promise to defend Helen's husband, whoever he turns out to be. Menelaos eventually wins Helen's hand, but she is soon stolen from him by Paris, the prince of TROY.

True to their word, the other Greek leaders assemble a huge army and sail to Troy. After nine years of terrible fighting, the two armies elect to have Menelaos and Paris decide the war's outcome in man-to-man combat. Menelaos has almost defeated Paris when the GODDESS APHRODITE spirits the young prince away. After another year, the Greek army prevails, and Menelaos sets sail for home, accompanied by Helen.

Along the way, his ship gets caught in a storm which carries him to Pharos, an island off the coast of Egypt. There he struggles with the elusive and mutable SEA-god Proteus, who finally tells Menelaos how to get home. Menelaos lives happily with Helen for the rest of his life. *See also* ANCIENT GREEK STORYTELLING.

MERLIN

Mythical magician and prophet, best known for his role in Arthurian LEGENDS. Merlin's character may be based on a sixth-century Celtic BARD, and the earliest hint that we have of his existence as a legendary figure in the Celtic tradition may be dated as early as the seventh century. The first complete literary treatment of Merlin appears in the writings of the twelfth century Welsh cleric GEOFFREY OF MONMOUTH, in which Merlin (Myrrdin, in Welsh) transports the stones of Stonehenge from Ireland to England. Through the Middle Ages, the figure of Merlin became an important prophet for the Welsh and the Scots, and was adopted by the English during the fourteenth century.

It is through the English legends of KING ARTHUR and his Knights of the Round Table that Merlin endures in contemporary imagination. The Norman writer Wace's *Roman de Brut* (1155) includes the story of Merlin the magician in his account of British history, and the poet Robert de Boron (c. 1200) establishes Merlin as the founder of the Grail knighthood. Merlin's magical powers are a result of his unusual parentage; his father is a DEVIL and his mother is a virgin. From his father Merlin inherits a full knowledge of the past; from GOD Merlin is given a full knowledge of the future. This universal scope of knowledge establishes Merlin as an important prophet and strategic advisor. It is Merlin's power that allows Uther Pendragon, the king of England, to father Arthur through a secret union with the Duchess Igraine. Merlin, knowing the danger threatening the baby, raises Arthur himself and hides the boy's royal identity. When the time comes for Arthur to assume his rightful position, Merlin is instrumental in his succession, coronation, marriage to GUINEVERE, establishment of the Round Table, and Arthur's ultimate success as king. Stories also tell of Merlin's unfortunate love affair with an enchantress named Vivien. Accounts differ, but in essence Vivien casts a SPELL on Merlin, which removes his magic powers and imprisons him, variously, in an invisible prison in the air or in a stone tomb from which nobody can free him until, some say, the death of the sorceress.

Stories of Merlin abound from the twelfth to the fourteenth centuries in literature across Europe. In 1485, Sir Thomas Malory published his perpetually popular *Le Morte d'Arthur*, which immortalized the stories of Merlin and Arthur and which is still read as an extremely important and influential source of Arthurian legends. In these tales Merlin is a key figure in the protection of Christendom. From the fifteenth century until the present day, new stories and adaptations of Merlin's character frequently appear, both in retellings of the Arthurian tales and in other kinds of stories. For example, Merlin plays a role in early English versions of "The History of Tom Thumbe," in which he answers the wish of an impoverished and childless couple who desire a son even if he should be no bigger than a man's thumb. T.H. White also recreates the character of Merlin in the children's story *The Sword and the Stone* (1938), which remains popular through its transformation into an animated movie by the Walt Disney studios in 1963. In White's tale, Merlyn is an absent-minded magician for whom time goes backwards rather than forwards. As a result he can easily foresee the future, but has trouble remembering anything that has just happened.

Merlin also appears (as "Merriman") in *The Dark is Rising* (1965–1977), Susan Cooper's award-winning series of fantasy novels based on the legends of King Arthur. Peter Dickinson's children's novel *The Weathermonger* (1968) features Merlin as a character brought back to life; his horror at the modern world leads England to revolt (temporarily) against the mechanization of society. Rosemary Sutcliff's *The Sword and the Circle* (1981) also refigures Merlin as an important and powerful character. Merlin's mysterious origins and his role as the mythical author/dictator of Arthurian literature continue to fascinate and challenge both readers and writers of legend, and his recurring presence in children's literature attests to his enduring appeal in stories and legends of all kinds.

For Further Reading

Stewart, Mary. *The Crystal Cave*. New York: Fawcett, 1984.

Talbott, Hudson. *King Arthur: The Sword in the Stone*. New York: Morrow Junior Books, 1991.

Vinaver, Eugene, ed. *Malory: Works*. Oxford: Oxford University Press, 1971.

MERMAIDS

Literally, "Virgins of the Sea." Mermaids are mythical creatures, each possessing the tail of a fish and the head and torso of a woman; the HARPIES and the SIRENS are their ancestors. Mermaids are often depicted as versions of the GODDESS of DEATH, receiving the souls of men buried at SEA and frequently dragging living men down with them as well. Generally, encountering a mermaid during one's voyage was considered an ill omen. Norwegian mythology contains numerous accounts of such harbingers of bad fortune. In one story, a sailor who spots a mermaid lures her to his boat and cuts off her hand. A huge storm arises in consequence and the sailor nearly dies.

According to LEGEND, mermaids long to have human souls that they can acquire through union with men. Many fall in love with men, but this love can have dangerous repercussions. In a Swedish story, a knight named Gunnar falls in a lake and is rescued from drowning by a mermaid. They fall in love and meet one another weekly. One day, Gunnar fails to keep his appointment. The water rises and drowns him, and he sinks to the mermaid's underwater abode.

Legends of mermaids can be found in the FOLKLORE of cultures as diverse as Iceland and Asia. One of the most popular mermaid stories is Hans Christian Andersen's "The Little Mermaid," which features a mermaid who is willing to trade her voice for legs in order to marry her prince (*see* ANDERSEN, HANS CHRISTIAN). Unlike the Disney film version of the same story, Andersen's original tale does not have a happy ending. The prince marries another woman, and the mermaid dies and is taken to heaven and becomes an angel.

There are probably natural causes behind the perpetuation of mermaid myths. Walruses, manatees, and seals all have physical characteristics that have been attributed to mermaids; thus, a mermaid sighting is more likely a case of mistaken identity than an omen of doom. Nonetheless, legends of mermaids are part of a long storytelling tradition, comprising BALLADS, poems, songs, and oral and written tales, and they can be found in all cultures that have any contact with the sea.

For Further Reading

Andersen, Hans Christian. *The Little Mermaid*. Illustrated by Chihiro Iwasaki. Natick, MA: Picture Book Studio, 1984.

Blanco, Alberto. *The Desert Mermaid/La Sirena del Desierto*. Bilingual edition. Translated by Barbara Paschke. San Francisco: Children's Book Press, 1992.

MERU

Sacred mountain in Hindu mythology. As it is told in the MAHABHARATA, Mount Meru is a "shining mountain," and "its blazing golden peaks outshine even the light of the SUN." While GODS may live there, human beings cannot approach it. It is so tall that its highest peaks pierce the heavens. Divine herbs that shine in the dark illuminate the mountain, which is covered by trees and streams. It is on Mount Meru (also called *Sumeru*) that the gods take counsel and drink ambrosia, and where the god SIVA sits.

Mount Meru is central to various Hindu and Buddhist MYTHS, including one involving Vasuki, the KING of the serpents. Since a SEA of milk in which live a race of serpents surrounds the base of Mount Meru, Vasuki, their king, sleeps coiled about Meru with his head on the mountain's summit. When the gods decide to playfully seize and pull Vasuki one day, Vasuki pulls back. As a result, Mount Meru, caught in the serpent's coils, begins spinning like a butter churn. The sea of milk begins to curdle like cheese. Vasuki then vomits up the curdled milk along with his own venom, and from this emerges seven precious things, including Lakshmi, the GODDESS of beauty, a heavenly tree, and the mother stone of all gems.

In various mythologies, mountains such as Meru function as the center of the universe, the axial pole of the world. For the Hindu, Mount Meru connects HEAVEN and

EARTH, much as MOUNT OLYMPOS did in Ancient Greece. The construction of the Egyptian pyramids and the medieval Catholic cathedrals were attempts to create what might, in a sense, be called sacred mountains.

For Further Reading

O'Flaherty, Wendy D., trans. *Hindu Myths*. New York: Viking Penguin, 1975.

MEXICAN STORYTELLING

Synthesis of tales and storytelling techniques from indigenous and colonial Mexican cultures. From Mayan and Aztec oral and written traditions in Mexico and Central America come stories about origins, deities, magical ANIMALS, sacred objects, historical and legendary HEROES and events, and everyday life. These tales are told in language that is richly metaphorical and eloquent.

Most of the Mayan hieroglyphic books were destroyed by Catholic priests, who considered them works of the DEVIL. Some of the ancient mythology, history, RIDDLES, JOKES, and poetry survive in an alphabetic version of the POPUL VUH and in a few remnants of glyphic texts.

According to Mayan and Aztec CREATION MYTHS, we are now living in the fourth or fifth world, the previous ones having been destroyed. Like many cultures, these also have a FLOOD story. However, the Mayan GODS sent the flood to do away with an experimental human race that did not work out well, and to start anew. In some versions of the story, our own world is expected to end in drought.

The mythological Feathered Serpent is a powerful image in both Aztec and Mayan stories. The figure was known as QUETZALCOATL to the Aztecs and as Cuculcan or Huruacan (which became "hurricane" in English) to the Mayan. The Aztec identification of Cortés with the god Quetzalcoatl was a factor that both led to the Spanish conquest in 1591–1621 and facilitated the ensuing cultural convergence.

During the Colonial era, Christian stories were smoothly integrated into those of the native people, with "FATHER GOD" and "Jesucristo" replacing some of the earlier names. Some later Mexican stories also include marble palaces, PRINCES, KINGS, GIANTS, and other elements adopted from European tales.

Many stories from the ancient oral traditions have gone through various cultural transitions and are still heard in contemporary Mexico. For example, a well-known tale is told about *La Llorona*, a wailing woman in white. In the Aztec story, she was a GODDESS who sacrificed babies. In later versions, she became identified with a woman who had borne her lover several children out of wedlock, then murdered them when the man married a woman of his own station (a version which bears an uncanny resemblance to the story of Medea in the QUEST FOR THE GOLDEN FLEECE. Since La Llorona was originally said to appear near wells and bodies of water, her origins might well lie in the WILL-O'-THE-WISP phenomenon.

The veneration of Our Lady of Guadalupe is an example of the merging of indigenous and Spanish traditions. In 1531, an apparition of the virgin MARY appeared three times to Juan Diego, an Aztec converted to Christianity. Speaking Náhuatl, the Virgin bid him to have a church built on that spot. After several additional miracles, Juan was eventually able to convince the Catholic bishop to do so. A painting was made of the Virgin, picturing her as a dark-skinned Aztec princess. The site had previously been the shrine of an Aztec goddess called "Our Mother," and her worshippers easily made the transition.

Miracles continued to accrue at the spot, and the Spaniards incorporated Our Lady of Guadalupe into their religious rituals and processions. The story also entered into Indian oral tradition. Indian story-songs and ritual dances dramatizing historical events still incorporate both Juan Diego and Our Lady. Armies of the revolution carried her banner into the wars for independence from Spain.

In Mexico, a story may be enacted in a pageant or turned into a procession, carnival, or fiesta. Stories and dances are often enacted with masks, with the gringo-looking faces wearing especially stupid expressions.

A more specific emphasis on both performance and participation is deeply rooted in Maya traditions. In his foreword to Allan F. Burns's *An Epoch of Miracles,* Dennis Tedlock says that, "For the Yucatec Maya, even an asymmetrical genre such as narrative formally requires performance not only by 'the person who knows the stories' but by 'the person who knows how to answer,' the latter being much more than a mere member of an audience." Burns explains further, "It is not possible to say 'tell me a story.' Indeed the only way to bring a story into verbal expression is to ask someone to 'converse' a story with you."

At the very least, the one hearing a story is expected to interject affirmative responses such as "true" and "ahah" and "like that." In other cases, the conarrator may provide segments of the story itself. And the story is often told as if it is ongoing and includes the present-day participants. (*See also* MAGIC ORANGE TREE.)

In Charles Briggs's 1988 study of a group of Mexican Americans living in Northern New Mexico, *Competence in Performance,* he observed the same practice as a vital aspect of community life. Master storytellers explained to him that, unlike the European equivalent, even PROVERBS require a context. For example, a statement such as "it takes all kinds" was considered "just words" unless it was performed to illuminate the "sense, significance, or meaning . . . of a given situation."

Discussion, collaboration, and participation are such strong elements in the Maya tradition that even creation is not the act of a solitary deity. In the opening lines of the *Popul Vuh,* two gods create the world by talking together. And the work of the SHAMAN in Maya ritual is still done within a supporting group.

For Further Reading

Burns, Allan F. *An Epoch of Miracles: Oral Literature of the Yucatec Maya.* Austin, TX: University of Texas Press, 1983.

Davis, E. Adams. *Of the Night Wind's Telling: Legends from the Valley of Mexico.* Norman, OK: University of Oklahoma Press, 1946.

Freidel, David A., Linda Schele, and Joy Parker. *Maya Cosmos: Three Thousand Years on the Shaman's Path.* New York: William Morrow, 1993.

Paredes, Americo, ed. and trans. *Folktales of Mexico.* Chicago: University of Chicago Press, 1970.

MIDAS

In Greek mythology, the KING of Phrygia and the son of the GODDESS CYBELE and a SATYR. Many different versions of the MYTH of King Midas have arisen, although many of them include Midas's foolish desire for the "golden touch." One traditional version of the tale explains that when Silenus, a drunken follower of DIONYSOS, gets lost and wanders into Midas's rose garden, the king helps him find his way back to Dionysos. In gratitude, Dionysos offers to grant Midas any wish. The greedy king wishes that everything he touches will turn into gold. Midas soon realizes his folly; his food and drink turn to gold when he touches them, and so he can neither eat nor drink. He has to pray to Dionysos to take back this fatal gift. The god commands Midas to bathe in the Pactolus River in order to rid himself of the "golden touch;" as a result, the sands of the river turn to gold. Other versions of the tale show how the gift of the golden touch destroys Midas's family. One rendition of the story tells how Midas's beloved daughter, Iris, the joy of his life and his only family, is turned into a golden statue when she hugs her father. Another interpretation suggests that it is King Midas's wife and young son who are turned to gold. All of these tales, however, demonstrate that the suffering caused by Midas's foolish and greedy wish leads him to become a much wiser man.

In another popular story of Midas, the king is asked to choose the winner in a musical contest between Marsyas and APOLLO. He chose Marsyas, and an enraged Apollo punishes him by turning his ears into those of a donkey. Ashamed, Midas wears a hat to cover his ears. However, he can not manage to keep his secret for long. In desperation, he digs a hole and shouts his secret into the earth. Reeds grow up from the hole, and whisper Midas's secret to the whole world.

The stories of King Midas have proven to be perennially popular, and interpretations of these myths appear in many collections of Greek mythology and FOLKLORE.

For Further Reading

Osborne, Mary Pope. *Favorite Greek Myths*. Illustrated by Troy Howell. New York: Scholastic, 1989.

Philip, Neil. *King Midas*. Boston: Little, Brown, 1994.

MIDDLE EARTH

In Norse mythology, the home of humans; more recently, an imaginary world of the distant past created by the author J.R.R. Tolkien (*see* TOLKIEN, J.R.R.). In his works *The Hobbit* and *The Lord of the Rings*, Tolkien presents Middle Earth as our own world, complete with continents and oceans, at a remote time in the past called the Third Age. Middle Earth is inhabited by small, amiable, hairy-footed creatures called *hobbits*, the most famous of which is Bilbo Baggins; ELVES; DWARFS; men; and other wonders. Middle Earth has its own history, races, geography, customs, songs, and languages, notably Elvish. Numerous appendixes, providing specific details about Middle Earth, accompany *The Lord of the Rings*. These appendixes include annals of the KINGS and rulers, a chronology of the history of Middle Earth, family trees, calendars, maps, and notes on the writing, spelling, pronunciation, and translation of various languages used during the Third Age.

"Middle Earth" derives from Norse mythology. During the CREATION of the Norse universe, the three brothers ODIN, Vili, and Ve use the eyebrows of the slain GIANT Ymir to encircle the area known as *Midgard*, the home of humans (*see* NORSE CREATION). Midgard, meaning "middle enclosure," is also encircled both by the ocean and by Jormungand, the ocean-dwelling world serpent who is so long that he wraps around the earth and bites his own tail. Tolkien's Middle Earth, in contrast, is home to much more than humans and is surrounded by a mountain wall. In time, however, the creatures of Middle Earth give it up to humans.

Other popular fantasy stories containing imaginary worlds include Lewis Carroll's *Alice's Adventures in Wonderland* (1865), Frank Baum's *The Wonderful World of Oz* (1900), J. M. Barrie's *Peter Pan* (1904), C. S. Lewis's series of Narnia novels (1950 onwards), Madeleine L'Engle's *A Wrinkle in Time* (1962), and Ursula LeGuin's Earthsea trilogy (1967–72).

For Further Reading

Branston, Brian. *Gods of the North*. New York: Thames and Hudson, 1980.

Kocher, Paul H. *Master of the Middle-Earth: The Achievement of J. R. R. Tolkien*. London: Thames and Hudson, 1972.

Tolkien, J.R.R. *The Hobbit*. Boston: Houghton Mifflin, 1984.

———. *The Lord of the Rings*. 3 vols. 1954-56. Reprint, New York: HarperCollins, 1993.

MIDDLE EUROPEAN STORYTELLING
See EUROPEAN STORYTELLING

MIDRASHIM

Jewish commentaries on the BIBLE compiled from the Oral *Torah*. The Hebrew term *midrash* means "searching out," and the nature of midrash is explained through the image of the Torah as a rock that has been split into many pieces by a hammer. The texts of midrashim (the plural form of midrash) were compiled between A.D. 400 and 1200, and the commentaries themselves were based on PARABLES, *haggadic* LEGEND, and exegesis and have the feel of FOLKTALES. Some midrashim are bold in the claims they make about biblical characters and events, and, as a result, are not treated literally.

Numerous midrashim offer variations on events that take place in the BOOK OF GENESIS, such as the Fall, the CREATION of Adam's original wife, LILITH, and the DEATH of Adam (*see* TALMUDIC CREATION AND FALL, ADAM AND EVE). One midrash tells how GOD "asked the angels to bow down and honor His latest creation," Adam, whom he has just made, but Samael, or Satan, one of the highest archangels, refuses, believing that he is above this new being made of dust. God replies that Adam is greater than Samael in wisdom and understanding, even if he is made of dust. Furious at feeling slighted, Samael requests that God "test him against Adam." The TEST involves Samael descending to EARTH, lining up all the beasts and birds and creeping things that God has so recently created, and naming them. If Samael succeeds in giving them the name God would have given them, then Samael will indeed be above Adam in wisdom, and Adam must revere him; however, if he cannot and Adam can, then Samael must revere Adam's superior wisdom. When the time comes for Samael to name the animals, however, he cannot speak. Adam, on the other hand, is helped by God, for "God then planted understanding in Adam's heart and spoke in such a manner that the first letter of each question points to the beast's name." With God's helpful hints, Adam chooses the right name for each. Realizing that God has given Adam this enlightenment, the indignant Samael yells at God, who replies by asking Samael, "Do you yell?" Samael's response—"How should I not when you have created me from your Glory, and afterwards bestow understanding on a creature formed from dust?"—suggests not only his Cain-like frustration but the difference between angels that are created from light and man created from matter. As William Irwin Thompson points out about this midrash in *The Time Falling Bodies Take to Light*, "Language is the articulation of the limited to express the unlimited; it is the ultimate mystery which is the image of God, for in breaking up infinity to create finite beings, God has found a way to let the limited being yet be a reflection of His unlimited Being." As biblical commentaries, *midrashim* invite commentaries.

In "The Death of Adam," a midrash from Howard Schwartz and John Swanson's *Midrashim: Collected Jewish Parables*, Adam is nine hundred thirty years old and about to die. His many sons and daughters surround him, Lilith has long since left him and Eve has been dead for two hundred years. With his memory failing him, he has forgotten the years in the Garden of Eden, and this is when Eve died of grief, for the memory of the "lost splendor" was too large a burden to carry for one person. Now even some of his grandchildren doubt the story of the creation of Adam and Eve, doubt that this one couple can give birth to so many, though his sons

and daughters remember all the years their father has labored outside the gate guarded by the angel, and they remember the stories of Cain and Abel, the first two sons and the only ones who now are missing. As Adam comes close to death, he no longer hears his son Seth's words, for his gaze has turned inward. Just before he dies, his eyes become luminous and a bright glow circles his face. At the moment of his death, "even those who had been uncertain that he was, in fact, the first father, felt the past become a blank wall behind them, and knew that the first era was finally past."

For Further Reading

Schwartz, Howard, and John Swanson. *Midrashim: Collected Jewish Parables*. London: Menard Press, 1976.

MIEDER, WOLFGANG (1944–)

German folklorist and paremiologist. Mieder is a leading scholar on German and English PROVERBS and aphorisms. In his work in this field, Mieder has focused on both classical and contemporary proverbs and aphorisms, exploring the ways certain sayings originated, what they have been interpreted to mean, and how they have been used through time. Mieder's *A Dictionary of American Proverbs* (1993) contains more than 15,000 proverbs used in Canada and the United States, many of which originated in European literature or the BIBLE and have been integrated into American dialects. In *Proverbs Are Never Out of Season: Popular Wisdom in the Modern Age* (1993), he explores the power of proverbs, and in a section that focuses on the language of Nazi Germany, he investigates the danger of their misuse.

Meider has also published translations, including a translation of *Aphorisms*, a collection of nearly 600 aphorisms by nineteenth-century Austrian writer Marie von Ebner-Eschenbach. In addition, he edited *The Wisdom of Many: Essays on the Proverb*, a collection of essays from various academic disciplines, with each contribution focusing on proverbs from a different part of the world.

MILAREPA (c. 1025–1135)

Famous poet-saint of Tibet. Milarepa, also called Milarespa, whose name means "Mila who wears the cotton cloth of an ascetic," is said to have lived an exceptionally long life. Born in western Tibet in 1025, he was believed to have died at the age of 110 in 1135, although some sources say he was born in 1040 and died in 1143. When he was seven, his father died, and Milarepa and his mother were treated badly by greedy relatives. According to the tales that recount his life, Milarepa revenged these injuries by learning to control the destructive forces of nature and thereby killing a large number of people with a terrible storm. He later wanted to atone for these deaths, so he turned to the Nyingmapa teacher Rongton, and Rongton sent him to Marpa, who became his master when Milarepa was thirty-eight years old. For six years his role was that of a servant, and his training seemed so cruel at times that Milarepa was close to suicide. Finally, after Milarepa's evil actions were sufficiently cleansed through this harsh discipline, Marpa prepared him for a life of solitude, transmitting to him Naropa's teachings, especially the practice of "inner heat," so that Milarepa was able to survive in the icy caves of the Himalayan mountains wearing only a thin cotton cloth. There he lived alone and meditated; after nine years of total solitude, Milarepa began to accept students, to whom he taught the tenets of Tibetan Buddhism through his songs.

In his autobiography, Milarepa relates a tale illustrating his belief in the Buddhist concept expressed by Nagarjuna: "Like images seen in a DREAM, thus we must regard all things." His story takes place in a cave where he was living and in which he saw many DEMONS destroying his food and books. He tried to stop them with admonishments, and when this did not work, he apologized for not having made them an offering and promised to do so. It was to no avail, nor was any threat or argument or reasoning he could present to them. Finally, he spoke to himself, saying "Mila, was it really worthwhile to have spent so many years in meditation and still believe in the existence of demons? Do you not know that they are a product of your own creation and exist only in your mind?" He then told the demons to do whatever they wanted to do, and they disappeared.

Over the years, Milarepa's fame spread as a poet, and he wrote the Milarepa tales or *The Hundred Thousand Songs*, in which Milarepa's own life and spiritual pilgrimage are used as the basis for stories and songs related to the quest for spiritual awakening.

For Further Reading

David-Neel, Alexandra. *Initiations and Initiates in Tibet*. Berkeley, CA: Shambhala Publications, 1970.

MINOTAUR

Ferocious MONSTER in Greek and Roman mythology with the head of a bull and the body of a man. According to the legend of the Minotaur, Pasiphae, the wife of King Minos of Crete, passionately desires a white bull, which has been sent out of the SEA by Neptune to show his favor for Minos. The inventor Daedalus makes a wooden cow in which the queen can conceal herself and satisfy her desire (see ICARUS AND DAEDALUS). The Minotaur, sometimes named Asterius, is the result of Pasiphae's union with the white bull. Minos instructs Daedalus to build a LABYRINTH in which to conceal the monstrous Minotaur.

In some versions of the Minotaur myth, King Minos imposes on the city of Athens a yearly tribute of seven men and seven maidens, which he feeds to the Minotaur. The HERO THESEUS determines to free his country of this cruel burden when it becomes his turn to be sacrificed to the Minotaur. Ariadne, Minos's daughter, falls in love with Theseus and gives him a ball of thread, which he unwinds as he disappears into the labyrinth. Theseus kills the Minotaur and escapes from the maze, following the thread back to the entrance.

In the Middle Ages, the Minotaur was a popular subject in religious art, in encyclopedias, in commentaries on the classical authors, and in the works of the contemporary poets, where he often represents the DEVIL and where Theseus becomes a Christ-like figure. Perhaps the most famous literary representation of the Minotaur in the Middle Ages appears in Dante's *Inferno*, where the beast is the guardian of the seventh circle of hell. As Dante and Virgil descend into this circle, they approach the Minotaur, who becomes furious and begins biting himself. Virgil taunts the Minotaur, reminding him of his DEATH at the hands of Theseus and Ariadne. Enraged, the Minotaur leaps about and the two pilgrims slip by him.

More recently, in such works as Andre Gide's *Theseus* (1946) and Jorge Luis Borge's short story/monologue "The House of Asterion" (found in *El Aleph* and *Labyrinth*), this hybrid creature becomes an expression of the complexity of the contemporary human consciousness.

Another example of a creature resembling the Minotaur is the Chinese hero Shen Nung, also known as the "Earthly Emperor" (2838–2698 B.C.). He is eight feet, seven inches tall, has a human body and the head of a bull, and is miraculously conceived through the influence of a DRAGON. His ashamed mother exposes him on a mountainside, but the wild beasts protect and nourish him. Later, his mother brings him home. Shen Nung invents the plow and a system of barter. He is known to the Chinese peasant as the "prince of cereals." In one day, he discovered 70 poisonous plants and their antidotes—through a glass covering to his stomach, he observed the digestion of each herb. At the age of 168, Shen Nung became immortal.

The figure of the tyrant-monster appears in the mythologies, folk traditions, and LEGENDS of the world. He is almost always a greedy monster who wreaks havoc. Other examples of monsters that have a combination of human and animal features include DEVILS, angels, SATYRS, MERMAIDS, SIRENS, HARPIES, gorgons (*see* MEDUSA), SPHINXES, and CENTAURS.

For Further Reading

Evslin, Bernard. *The Minotaur.* New York: Chelsea House, 1987.

Hutton, Warwick. *Theseus and the Minotaur.* New York: Macmillan, 1989.

MINSTRELSY

BALLADS and lyrics sung by minstrels. Minstrels were professional musicians in the Middle Ages. They were either attached to a particular court or they wandered about, searching for an audience; they played and sang secular lyrics, folk songs, and ballads of their day. The songs and ballads that made up this minstrelsy became part of oral tradition and were sung for hundreds of years without ever being printed. Even after they began to appear in print, these songs continued to be sung even up to the twentieth century.

Collections of minstrelsy began to appear in Great Britain in the eighteenth century, and in 1802 Sir Walter Scott published his *Minstrelsy of the Scottish Border*. This was followed by Francis J. Child's five volumes, *English and Scottish Popular Ballads*, which appeared from 1882–1898, and the 305 songs he included have come to be called the *Child Ballads*. These songs tell of the common life of the community from feudalism to the industrial revolution, with ghosts, as in "The DEMON LOVER"; betrayed lovers, as in "The Twa' Sisters"; religious and historical figures, as in "The Bonny Earl of Murray"; and CULTURE HEROES, such as ROBIN HOOD, typical of the themes and subjects treated.

A more recent form of minstrelsy, the songs, dances, and comedy routines sung in minstrel shows by whites in blackface, became popular in nineteenth-century America. In 1828 Thomas Dartmouth Rice first performed in blackface, creating the *Jim Crow* act of song and dance (*see* RICE, THOMAS D). Later minstrel shows followed in the 1840s and continued into the twentieth century with the singer Al Jolson and the songs of Stephen Foster. *See also* TROUBADOUR.

For Further Reading

Child, Francis J. *"Lord Randal" and Other British Ballads.* New York: Dover, 1996.

Scott, Sir Walter. *Minstrelsy of the Scottish Border.* 4 vols. Edited by T.F. Henderson. 1802. Reprint, Detroit: Omnigraphics, 1968.

MOMADAY, N. SCOTT (1934–)

Poet, novelist, and FOLKTALE compiler of Kiowa Indian heritage. In all his writing, N. Scott Momaday draws on his Native American heritage, and his poetry, according to him, "in particular, grows from and sustains the Indian oral tradition." As the author of the Pulitzer Prize-winning novel *House Made of Dawn* (1968), he uses Native American culture, myth, and sensibility, while in *The Names: A Memoir* (1976), he explores his Kiowa heritage in autobiographical form.

Among his many books are a collection of retold Kiowa Indian folktales, *The Way to Rainy Mountain* (1969), *Angle Geese and Other Poems* (1974), and a volume of poems, *The Gourd Dancer* (1976).

For Further Reading

Momaday, N. Scott. *The Way to Rainy Mountain.* Albuquerque: University of New Mexico Press, 1969.

MOMOTARO

Ancient Japanese FAIRY TALE of the "Peach Boy." A poor elderly childless couple works hard to get by. The old man goes to cut grass for local farmers one day while his wife takes the laundry to the river for washing. She looks up and sees a large peach floating down the river. It is the largest peach she has ever seen, and anticipating how delicious it must be, she tries to reach it. The peach is too far away, and finding no stick nearby to aid her, she repeats a spell:

> Distant water is bitter
> The near water is sweet
> Pass by the distant water
> and come into the sweet.

Repeating this charm brings the peach easily into the woman's reach. Returning home with her prize, the old woman eagerly awaits the return of her husband, knowing how much the old man will appreciate the flavor of the peach.

When the old man finally arrives, his wife presents the peach and both anticipate its flavor. Just as the man brings down the knife to split the peach, the peach opens of its own accord, and a beautiful child steps out. The boy speaks, saying he is no demon or fairy, but rather the answer to the old couple's prayers: he is to be the son of their old age. The couple name the child "Peach Boy."

Years quickly pass, and at fifteen Momotaro (Peach Boy) has wisdom beyond his years as well as greater strength than the other boys his age. Momotaro asks his father to allow him to go to a far island to conquer the band of DEMONS that live there and trouble the emperor and the local people. The father agrees and Momotaro sets out.

Passing through a field, the boy is challenged by a dog. Upon learning Momotaro's name, however, the dog asks to join the hero. A monkey and a pheasant also join the group, and the four set out by ship to find the demons' island. When they arrive, Momotora sends the pheasant to the demon stronghold to issue a challenge.

As the pheasant engages the demons, Momotaro and the others land the boat, finding two MAIDENS crying as they wash laundry in a stream. They tell Momotaro that they are captives of the demon KING, who makes them work until the time he will kill and eat them. Momotaro promises to rescue them, and the maidens show him a back way into the castle.

After a long struggle, many of the demons are killed, and the demon king surrenders, giving up his iron bar and breaking the horns from his head. The maidens, daughter of nobles, return to their homes, Momotaro to his. The boy takes with him the treasure from the demon island, which enables him to care for his elderly parents with plenty until the end of their days.

The MONSTER-slaying theme is common to HERO stories of many cultures. See KUTOYIS for a Native American example and the many traditional European tales of the dragonslayer, such as SIEGFRIED and BEOWULF, who, like Momotaro, are rewarded by the discovery of treasure.

For Further Reading

Sakurai, Gail. *The Peach Boy.* New York: Troll, 1994.

MONKEY KING

Hanuman, in the Hindu epic RAMAYANA. Hanuman, the Monkey KING, is the son of a NYMPH and the WIND GOD, Vayu. He aids Rama in rescuing Sita, Rama's wife, for the DEMON king Ravana has her in his clutches. Hanuman is able to shape shift, and he has the power of flight. When he takes one leap across the strait separating India and Ceylon, a female demon, Surasa, tries to swallow him, but Hanuman cleverly distends his body so that Surasa has to elongate her own mouth. Immediately, he shrinks himself down to thumb size, shoots through her head and out her right ear, and then sneaks into Lanka, the demon city, in order to locate Sita. He then helps build a bridge across the strait to allow Rama and his troops to cross the water to save Sita. Later he uses magic herbs to bring those who fell in the battle back to life. His reward from Rama is the gift of youth and perpetual life.

The Monkey King also exists in Buddhist mythology, most prominently in the Chinese novel, *Pilgrimage to the West*, by Wu Cheng-en (1505–1580). It tells of Hanuman's aid to Tripitaka on his journey to India to procure the Buddhist scriptures.

For Further Reading

Wu, Cheng-en. *Monkey: Folk Novel of China*. Translated by Arthur Waley. Grove-Altantic, 1988.

MONSTER KILLED FROM WITHIN

Widespread MOTIF in which a HERO is swallowed by a monster then kills the monster to escape. The motif of the monster killed from within is one that appears in tales ranging from Africa to Siberia, and it appears in North America and Europe as well. In these tales, the hero is swallowed by an OGRE, ANIMAL, or fish—usually a whale or leviathan—and must in some way free himself. This might involve making a fire in the belly of the creature, cutting out its heart from within, or cutting a hole in its side or carcass. In some cases, the monster spews the hero forth; in other cases, the monster dies and then the hero cuts his way out.

This motif is apparent in the tale told by the Coos-Coquille tribe of Native America: "HOW SALMON GOT GREASY EYES." OLD MAN COYOTE is swallowed by a whale, cuts out the heart of the whale, the whale is washed ashore, and he cuts his way through the whale's side, although the blubber blinds him until he tricks the salmon into trading eyes with him. In one Bella Coola myth where a fire is made in the belly of a Grizzly Bear, the sparks fly up to become the stars.

Related to this motif are tales in which the hero is swallowed and then escapes or is vomited up, but the monster is not killed, such as in the biblical narrative of Jonah, who lives for three days in a whale before he is spewed out, and in Carlo Collodi's *The Adventures of Pinocchio* (1883), where the carpenter Geppetto spends two years in the belly of a shark until Pinocchio finds him there and they escape. In the Polynesian legend of the TRICKSTER and demi-GOD MAUI, Maui chooses to enter the body of the GODDESS of DEATH to show he can defy death, but before he can exit, she clamps her jaws on him, killing him.

MONSTERS

In MYTH and FAIRY TALE, fabulous, negative beings that must be overcome. Threatening monsters come in all forms, and in myth and fairy tale they are often composites of several ANIMALS creating one creature that is even more frightening than the sum of its parts. Among the most well-known monsters are the SPHINX, with a woman's head and breasts, a dog's or bull's body, a bird's wings, a dragon's tail, and a lion's claws; the DRAGON; the Gorgon, a mixture of the lion, eagle, bird, and serpent but with women's heads with hair of snakes (*see* MEDUSA); the CHIMERA, with a lion's head, a goat's body, and a dragon's tail; the MINOTAUR, half man, half bull; the hydra, a huge snake with fifty venomous heads; the basilisk, with a bird's head and claws and a serpent's body; Cerberus, the three-headed guard dog of the Greek underworld; the HARPY, with a woman's head and breasts and a vulture's claws; the griffin, with the front half like an eagle and the back half like a lion with a serpentine tail; the SIREN, a bird-woman or a fish-woman; Scylla, with six heads with triple rows of teeth; Charybdis, roaring whirlpool-monster; the leviathan, a huge fish and primordial ocean monster; the giant sea-serpent; and the winged bull.

As Stith Thompson (*see* THOMPSON, STITH) shows in *Tales of the North American Indi-*

ans, Native American mythology is replete with such monsters as Sucking-Monster, a giant known for sucking in his victims; Fire-Moccasins, an OGRE whose moccasins cause fire wherever he walks; and Burr-Woman, who attaches herself like a burr to the HERO's back and cannot be pried loose. Other monsters include a cannibal who kidnaps children and a GIANTESS who feeds her young by kicking people over a cliff to her children below.

As J.E. Cirlot notes in *A Dictionary of Symbols*, monsters symbolize "the cosmic forces at a stage one step removed from chaos." Monsters are viewed in the context of the hero who must overcome them, and they are thus "the antithesis—or adversary— of the 'hero' or of 'weapons.' For weapons are the positive powers granted to man by the deity, and this is the explanation of the mysterious, miraculous, or magical context of weapons wielded by heroes in myth and LEGEND. Weapons then are the symbolic antithesis to monsters." When a monster ravages the countryside in a myth or fairy tale, it symbolizes the "ill-fated reign of a wicked, tyrannical or impotent monarch." Conquering a monster suggests the mastering and sublimation of wickedness.

Many heroes receive their first fame after slaying a monster. In ancient Greek mythology, THESEUS, with the help of Ariadne, slays the minotaur in the LABYRINTH, thereby preserving the lives of the Athenian maidens and youths who were sacrificed to the minotaur. Oedipus saves THEBES from the Sphinx by correctly answering her famous riddle. Herakles must slay the Hydra (*see* LABORS OF HERAKLES), and BEOWULF must slay Grendel and his mother. The Creator, MARDUK, must slay Tiamat, monster of the deep, PRIMEVAL WATERS, who represents chaos. In later European mythology, knights are expected to slay dragons. In every case, the monster's jaws symbolize the gates of HELL or the threshold of the underworld, and slaying the monster represents the triumph of good over evil, of order over chaos.

Monsters are also known as the guardians of treasures, and the monster thus becomes the sign of something sacred, for where there is a monster there is a treasure. Grif-fins, dragons, tigers, serpents, etc. are often posted at the entrance to the treasure, and the tree of life is said to be under the surveillance of griffins. Whether the treasure is wealth, glory, knowledge, health, or immortality, a monster must be overcome for the heroic act to be accomplished. With the destruction of the monster, the hero becomes a new man and experiences rebirth and resurrection. When the biblical Jonah survives his punishment of being swallowed by a whale or leviathan, he understands GOD's message finally and is symbolically resurrected as he is now able to preach God's word in Nineveh.

Slaying the external monster in folklore can also signify slaying the monster within, where the inferior self must be slain in order to replace it with the superior self. Each person carries his or her own monster within, with which he or she must constantly struggle; the French expression *bete noire*, meaning black beast, signifies something internal or external that is to be avoided, as in one's nemesis.

For Further Reading

Gibson, Michael. *Gods, Men and Monsters: From the Greek Myths.* New York: Peter Bedrick Books, 1991.

Homer. *The Odyssey.* Retold by Robin Lister. Illustrated by Alan Baker. New York: Kingfisher, 1994.

South, Malcolm, ed. *Mythical and Fabulous Creatures.* Westport, CT: Greenwood Publishing Group, 1987.

MOON

Symbol of biological rhythms and cycles and DEATH in many cultures. Because the moon has different phases that repeat themselves in a monthly cycle, it is associated with the feminine principle in a variety of cultures. Similarly, because the moon disappears for a period of three nights each month and then is reborn, it has come to symbolize death and RESURRECTION. In many primitive societies, the moon is also regarded as an important fertilizing force, even responsible for causing pregnancy.

In Greek mythology, Persephone and HECATE, GODDESSES of the underworld, are also lunar goddesses, as is ARTEMIS, although Artemis represents the celestial role of the moon while Hecate represents the infernal role of the dark moon (*see* PERSEPHONE MYTH). Other moon goddesses include Ishtar (INANNA) of Babylon, CYBELE of Phrygia, the Celtic MOTHER Goddess Anu or Annis, the Greek Selene, Isis of Egypt (*see* ISIS AND OSIRIS), and Shing Moo of China.

In some ancient cultures, the moon was regarded as a man who was thought of as living in the moon, and this Moon Man was probably the source of "The Man in the Moon" of oral tradition. As M. Esther Harding notes in *Women's Mysteries*, "Many ancient KINGS wore a horned head-dress emblematic of the 'hornéd moon,'" and "horned animals, especially the bull and the cow, are among the animals associated with the moon," recalling the nursery rhyme "the cow jumped over the moon." The Egyptian GOD Osiris is a moon god, as is the Babylonian god, Sinn. For the Hindus, the sphere of the moon is the end point of the path of the ancestors, and it is linked with the transforming role of SIVA, whose emblem is the crescent moon. In the *Rig-Veda, soma*, the drink of the GODS, which bestows immortality, often means moon (*see* RIG-VEDA CREATION).

In certain cultures of Tibet, China, Ceylon, Africa, and North America, the markings on the moon are known as "The Mark of the Hare" or "The Hare in the Moon," and the HARE is an animal symbol of the HERO. The African American Brer Rabbit tales and the West African tales of the Great Hare correspond to the Great Hare of North American Indian mythology. Even the Easter Bunny is connected to the moon through "The Mark of the Hare," for Easter "was originally a moon festival and was connected with the resurrection of the Moon Man or Moon Hero, long before the dawn of Christianity," writes Harding.

For Further Reading

Ehlert, Lois. *Moon Rope/Un lazo a la Luna: A Peruvian Legend*. Bilingual edition. Translated into Spanish by Amy Prince. San Diego: Harcourt Brace Jovanovich, 1992.

Hall, Nor. *The Moon and the Virgin*. New York: HarperCollins, 1980.

Young, Ed. *Moon Mother*. New York: HarperCollins, 1993.

MORALITY TALE

Stories intended to teach the values of the Christian church, in which the forces of good and evil battle for control over a human soul. Highly allegorical and overtly didactic, morality tales often take the form of DRAMAS (*see* ALLEGORY); the origins of these plays probably lie in the miracle and mystery plays of the Middle Ages. Morality plays developed as a discrete, recognizable genre in the fifteenth century and continued as a popular literary form into the sixteenth century and beyond; the anonymous play EVERYMAN (c.1500) is perhaps the best known extant example. This morality tale portrays the temptations that befall every person on the journey from birth to death and the AFTERLIFE. The main characters include Everyman, GOD, DEATH, Fellowship, Knowledge, and Good Deeds. Everyman, a personification of every human being, must confront death and the possibility of damnation on his quest for eternal salvation.

A recurring theme in these religious morality tales is the ongoing battle between God and the DEVIL, which is waged in the hearts of human beings. Frequently, the forces of evil are personified as the Seven Deadly Sins, worldly riches, pleasures of the flesh, various other DEMONS and even the Devil himself. These forces endeavor to tempt the Christian, who must rely on God, angels, and moral virtue to escape damnation and succeed in the ultimate spiritual struggle.

Later, the form of the morality tale was adopted to suit the purposes of more secular writers. Often political, doctrinal, or pedagogical dogma became the topic for such works. These morality tales operate on a somewhat more limited and specific scale than the purely religious ones; instead of the battle between good and evil over a human soul, these tales address one particular vice or problem. For example, John Skelton's *Magnyfycence* (1516) deals with the vice of extravagance and may have been directed toward the immoderate habits of England's King Henry VIII. William Shakespeare, Christopher Marlowe, and Ben Jonson may be counted among other writers whose works demonstrate the influences of the morality tale.

MOSES *See* EXODUS

MOTHER GOOSE STORIES

FAIRY TALES and NURSERY RHYMES credited to a fictional elderly woman named "Mother Goose." Many of the tales associated with "Mother Goose" were little known French FOLKTALES that became popular in the court of Versailles near the end of the seventeenth century. In 1697, Charles Perrault (*see* PERRAULT, CHARLES), a French academic, created his own modernized versions of the tales, and published them as *Tales of Past Times, with Lessons,* but they became known popularly as *Contes de ma Mere l'Oye* ("Tales of Mother Goose"), adapting the narrator "Mother Goose" from the popular folk tradition of the tales. In 1729, Robert Samber would translate the stories into English, where they would be known as "mother goose stories." Of Perrault's "Mother Goose" tales, "RED RIDING HOOD," "The Sleeping Beauty," "PUSS IN BOOTS," "CINDERELLA," and "BLUEBEARD" are the most widely recognized. The success of Perrault's versions of these tales has often been credited to the simplicity of style with which he narrates them. Indeed, other than affixing a rhymed moral at the end of each tale, his version seems generally consistent with what is known of the oral versions that preceded him.

English and American translations and adaptations have also remained extremely popular through time, and long after Perrault, the number of tales credited to "Mother Goose" continues to grow. In 1781, with the publication of *Mother Goose's Melody; or Sonnets for the Cradle,*" "Mother Goose" first became associated with NURSERY RHYMES. Published by the successors of one of the pioneers of the children's book industry, John Newbery (1713–1767), and allegedly edited and composed in part by Oliver Goldsmith, this collection of tales purported to contain the songs and lullabies of British nurses. Included in the first edition were such famous nursery rhymes as "Jack and Jill," "Hey Diddle Diddle." Later, "Humpty Dumpty," "Little Jack Horner," and a myriad of others that continue to be popular became associated with "Mother Goose." Even today, new books of "Mother Goose" nursery rhymes appear in bookstores each year, often including new rhymes.

As "Mother Goose" stories gained popularity in the United States, after publisher Isiah Thomas printed the first U.S. edition of Newbery's book, so did legends about the existence of an actual "Mother Goose." Often depicted as a beak-nosed and sharp chinned elderly woman, "Mother Goose" was widely believed to have been a Boston woman named Elizabeth Goose who had written a book of rhymes in 1719, and whose grave is located in Boston's Old Granary Ground. However, there is no evidence that the book has ever existed, causing many historians to conclude that an actual "Mother Goose" never existed, but rather she was a fictional narrator based in a folk tradition that often depicted narrators as elderly women (*see* GRIMM BROTHERS).

For Further Reading

Cook, Scott. *Mother Goose.* New York: Alfred A. Knopf, 1994.

de Paola, Tomie. *Tomie de Paola's Mother Goose.* New York: G.P. Putnam's Sons, 1985.

Mother Goose's Fairy Tales. Illustrated by John Gilbert. Stanford, CT: Langmadour Press, 1995.

The Original Mother Goose. Illustrated by Blanche Fisher Wright. Philadelphia: Running Press, 1992.

MOTHERS

In all forms of storytelling, women who bear children. In the stories of many religions and cultures, Great Mother GODDESSES represent all mothers as well as the EARTH and fertility. In Greek mythology, GAIA is the first mother, followed by her daughter Rhea and her granddaughters HERA and Demeter (whose name means "the mother"). In the story of Persephone, the MAIDEN, and her mother, Demeter, it is the mother who is relentless in her search for her abducted daughter, making the earth lie fallow until Persephone is returned to her (*see* PERSEPHONE MYTH). This myth suggests the power, protectiveness, love, and nurturing provided by mothers.

Among the Pueblo, Apache, and Navajo tribes, the figure of the CORN MOTHER, who symbolizes the corn, cornmeal, and corn pollen, is goddess of planting and harvesting, much like the Greek goddess Demeter. The Navajos consider CHANGING WOMAN the First Mother, creator of the four heads of the original clans, sustainer of life through the food she produces, in the tradition of the Great Goddess or EARTH-MOTHER, such as Corn Mother or Demeter.

Other important mother goddesses are the Egyptian ISIS, the Assyro-Babylonian Ishtar, the Sumerian INANNA, the Phoenician Astarte, and the Hindu KALI. In the Christianity of Roman Catholicism, MARY is considered divine for being the mother of Jesus Christ.

The figure of MOTHER GOOSE, a type of mythical fairy "birdmother" who tells stories, RIDDLES, jingles, rhymes, TONGUE TWISTERS, and yarns to children seems to have originated among the French peasantry and suggests the role of the mother as storyteller and repository of those tales that are passed on from generation to generation. These tales first appeared in France in Charles Perrault's collection, *Histoires ou Comtes du Tems Passé, avec des Moralités* (*Stories or Tales from the Past, with Lessons*), subtitled *Contes de ma Mere l'Oye* (*Tales of Mother Goose*) (*see* PERRAULT, CHARLES).

Although they figure in various FAIRY TALES, such as the GRIMM BROTHERS'S "Snow-White and Rose-Red," mothers are glaringly absent from many FOLKTALES and fairy tales, having died in childbirth and been replaced by stepmothers who are often wicked, as in the Grimm Brothers's "Hansel and Gretel," "CINDERELLA," and "Snow-White" (*see* STEPMOTHER—WICKED). Presumably, if the real mothers were present, they would protect their daughters more successfully. However, their absence forces their daughters to learn how to survive on their own. In "JACK AND THE BEANSTALK," the mother "fails her son because, instead of supporting his developing masculinity, she denies its validity," notes Bruno Bettelheim in *The Uses of Enchantment* (*see*

BETTELHEIM, BRUNO). As in real life, the child of the fairy tale must undergo a series of trials that will allow him or her to mature to the point of individuation, which suggests that the mother figure is no longer required.

For Further Reading

Evetts-Secker, Josephine. *Mother and Daughter Tales.* Illustrated by Helen Cann. New York: Abbeville, 1996.

MOUNT OLYMPOS

Tallest mountain in Greece, lying on the eastern range of mountains separating Thessaly from Macedonia (not to be mistaken for the recently-declared Yugoslavian state of Macedonia). At 9,800 feet, the peak of Mount Olympos is snow-capped and frequently cloud-covered.

According to ancient Greek LEGEND, Olympos was the home of the GODS. A paradise of perfect weather and endless sunshine, this was the court of ZEUS and was filled with palace-homes of the other principal gods.

However, there is some confusion as to whether the legendary Olympos was actually a mountain or a heavenly abode. Even HOMER in the ILIAD sends mixed messages on this issue. But the story of the GIANT brothers Ephialtes and Otus, who made war upon the Olympian deities, seems to resolve this contradiction. According to some versions of this legend, the giants piled two mountains on top of one another to reach the heavenly abode of the gods, presumably creating Mount Olympos. This is an example of how storytelling is used to explain the unknown (how the mountain came to exist).

In ancient times, Mount Olympos was the home of the Olympic Games, a pan-Hellenic athletic event held once every four years in July. *See also* ANCIENT GREEK STORYTELLING.

MOUNT PARNASSOS

Mountain in central Greece. It was named after Parnassos, a son of Poseidon and the inventor of the art of divination. The slope of Mount Parnassos became the home of the oracle at DELPHI, where visitors heard the prophecies of APOLLO.

Mount Parnassos figures prominently in the Greek story of the FLOOD, which has many parallels with the biblical SAGA of NOAH (*see* BIBLE). When ZEUS decides to drown the world with rain, the Titan Prometheus warns his son Deucalion to build a ship in order to escape. Only the top of Mount Parnassos is left uncovered by the deluge. Deucalion and his wife Pyrrha land there and began the human race anew.

Mount Parnassos has two peaks. One of them is consecrated to DIONYSOS, the other Apollo and the Muses. Consequently, Mount Parnassos is often associated with poetic and artistic inspiration. *See also* ANCIENT GREEK STORYTELLING.

MOUNT SINAI

Sacred mountain in the BIBLE. Mount Sinai is best known as the place where the Hebrew GOD appears to Moses and to the Israelites and where God delivers his laws to the chosen people (*see* EXODUS, YAHWEH).

Mount Sinai is part of a tradition in which mountains play a significant symbolic role in storytelling and religious traditions around the world. Mountains and hills often signify the center of the world and a place of communication with the divine (the *axis mundi*); thus, they are a version of the world navel. Other examples of the sacred mountain motif include the Greek MOUNT PARNASSOS, where the oracle of DELPHI delivers predictions; MOUNT OLYMPOS, home of the Greek PANTHEON; the Hindu Golden Mountain, MERU, where the great god SIVA sits; the hill GOLGOTHA, on which Jesus was crucified; the heavenly mountain of ZION; Mount Moriah in JERUSALEM, which is sacred to Jews, Muslims, and Christians alike; and the Hill of Uisnech in the Irish story MAN OF LORE.

Specifically, Mount Sinai is a place of revelation. In the book of Exodus, God tells Moses to instruct the Israelites to sanctify themselves. In three days, God will descend on Mount Sinai for all the people to see in order that their faith in God will never fail. God appears to Moses and the Israelites amidst peals of thunder, flashes of lightning, loud trumpet blasts, and a dense cloud. God summons Moses to the mountain top and warns him not to allow the terrified Israelites, who are gathered at the base of Mount Sinai, to touch the holy mountain or they will perish. God also gives the Ten Commandments to Moses.

Later, God tells Moses to bring Aaron, Nadab, Abihu, and seventy Israelite elders to Mount Sinai. There they see God. Under his feet is a pavement of sapphire, which is as blue as the HEAVENS. God calls only Moses up on the mountain so that he can give to Moses the stone tablets with the laws and commandments. Moses ascends the mountain and a cloud, the glory of God, covers it for six days. On the seventh day, God speaks to Moses from the cloud. To the Israelites, God's presence looks like a fire devouring the mountain top. Moses enters the cloud where he remains for 40 days and nights and receives God's laws on two stone tablets.

As a place of revelation and where God's laws are specified to the Israelites, Mount Sinai symbolizes God's eternal covenant with his chosen people.

For Further Reading

Clifford, Richard J. *The Cosmic Mountain in Canaan and the Old Testament*. Cambridge: Harvard University Press, 1972.

MUHAMMAD (A.D. 570–632)

Founder of Islam. Born in the Arabian city of MECCA, Muhammad was orphaned at a young age, and his grandfather and his uncle became his guardians. Like other enlightened religious leaders and *avatars* such as BUDDHA and Jesus Christ, Muhammad was said to have had a miraculous birth, because his mother was ostensibly told of his birth by a heavenly voice and a powerful light that could be seen from afar was supposed to have shone from her womb while she carried him. Nevertheless, he grew up in poverty, though his clan, the Hashamites, belonged to the Quraysh, the dominant tribe of Mecca. Despite his poor upbringing, he was able to overcome his class by working industrially, having a pleasant personality, and marrying Khadija, a rich widow. Because he was a contemplative man, Muhammad began to question the source of his good fortune by actively involving himself in religious devotion. Influenced by Judaism and Christianity, he turned from the polytheism that surrounded him, adopting a monotheism that eventually spread rather rapidly.

Many stories are told of Muhammad, including one that recounts the opening of his breast so that the black dot on his heart could be removed and he be thereafter cleansed and an immaculate model for his people. He was in the habit of practicing a yearly religious withdrawal in the caves near Mecca, and it was on one of these withdrawals to Mount Hira that he received his first revelation from a figure identified with the angel Gabriel. Other stories say that Muhammad was able to feed all of the workers in Medina from a mere handful of dates, that he could dissolve a rock with his saliva, that he had a miraculous ride from Mecca to Jerusalem on the back of the amazing horse called Buraq, and that he ascended from Jerusalem to HEAVEN and the throne of GOD. The stories about Jerusalem are part of a collection entitled *Fadail al-Quds*, or *The Virtues of Jerusalem*.

Another famous tale of Muhammad begins with Muhammad and his followers journeying to Medina. With the threat of attacks from the people of Mecca, Muhammad and his first convert, Abu Bakr, hide in a cave to elude a raiding party. Miraculously, a SPIDER spins a large web across the entrance to the cave, thereby concealing the hiding place and fooling the raiders.

After many years as a religious leader and general, Muhammad laid out the path for Muslims and Islam. After his "Farewell Pilgrimage" to Mecca, Muhammad took sick and died in 632 in the arms of his favorite wife Aisha, the daughter of his beloved convert Abu Bakr.

MULES AND MEN

Ethnographic work on African American oral culture of the South by Zora Neale Hurston, first published in 1935 (*see* HURSTON, ZORA NEALE). An African American native of Florida studying at Columbia University, Hurston went back to the American South to collect folk stories at the urging of the eminent anthropologist Franz Boas, her professor and advisor (*see* BOAS, FRANZ). *Mules and Men*, the written outcome of her journey, is much more than a compendium of FOLKTALES: it includes songs, sayings, LEGENDS, cures, MYTHS, and descriptions of hoodoo (voodoo) rites. With its vibrant, patchy, and participatory narration, the book also surpasses standard anthropological studies.

Melding together the genres of ethnography, journalism, and travelogue, Hurston created a unique style. In social scientific fashion, there are footnotes throughout to explain local words and idiom, a glossary of key terms, and appendixes of songs and prescriptions. However, due to the lack of references to other relevant works of FOLKLORE (she did not think very highly of them, her critics tell us) and analysis, the book's scholarly legitimacy was questioned in her time. Her creativity and singular approach to collecting cultural material was to be better appreciated in later decades.

Part of what makes *Mules and Men* unique, critics have noted, is that Hurston defies the ground rules of ethnographic writing by disregarding the convention of the detached scientific observer who leaves scant trace of his or her own presence in the text. The narrator in this book relates vividly her own role in the wide range of circumstances she confronts as well as her extensive involvement in the communities she studies. She is collecting and recounting not only folk material but also her own striking experiences in this journey back to the South.

The text is divided into two parts: "Folk Tales" takes place in three communities in Southern Florida, including Eatonville, Hurston's hometown; "Hoodoo" details Hurston's initiation into magical religious ritual in New Orleans. Besides tales, the first part incorporates songs, rhymes, banter, and religious speech about many topics including the war of the sexes, slave-master relations ("Ole Massa" stories), ANIMALS (such as Brer Rabbit and Brer Dog), and divisiveness among the Christian churches. The telling and reciting of tales and verse takes place in social interaction: community members chime in with their JOKES and PARABLES in response to the social topic at hand. Hurston does not erase herself from the recording of these interactions. On the contrary, she is an integral part of the storytelling event (known as a "lyin' session"), many times initiating songs and tales through her participation and inquiries. For example, while sitting on the store porch (the site of many "lyin' sessions") with community members, she hears a prayer (reproduced in the text) from the church house. She asks why in such a small town like Eatonville there should be two churches, which prompts one man to tell a parable relating to the source of the Baptist and Methodist split. There is also much repartee (called "woofing") often of a sexual nature and always depending on very quick verbal wit, in which Hurston takes frequent part.

Many of the tales Hurston records are origin stories, inventing beginnings of the present social order. One storyteller attributes the reason for black people's skin color to a mishearing of GOD's command "get back!" as "get black!" Another tells the tale of how the white managed to end up with easier indoor work. A significant amount of the banter, repartee, and storytelling turn on male/female relations. Although there is much denigration of womanhood, Hurston records the forceful and witty responses of the women. One origin story relates how black women ended up at the bottom of the hierarchy of work distribution ("Why the Sister in Black Works Hardest"), while another tells of how woman took charge of her situation despite man's devious maneuvering to acquire superior physical strength ("Why Women Always Take Advantage of Men"). In one preacher's sermon, "Behold de Rib," the female creation story becomes the story of gender equality: "... God Almighty, he took de bone out of his side/Sod dat place de woman beside us/Hah! God knowed his own mind." Sexual politics and women's resilience, favorite Hurston themes, make up a significant part of both the verbal arts recorded and the book as a whole. Of all the characters who are named and described, it is one tough and autonomous woman, Big Sweet, who becomes Hurston's protector and friend and a central character in *Mules and Men*.

When she gets involved with violent trouble in the community, the narrator flees to New Orleans. There, Hurston is the subject of hoodoo ceremonies, undergoing many psychic experiences and becoming an acolyte of the powerful dead god/mother of hoodoo, Marie Leveau. Whereas folktales are communally engendered and performed, hoodoo, Hurston says, is private and secret. However, part of what fascinates her is hoodoo's origins in the culture common to black Americans, i.e. the African. The cures and malediction rites, detailed through Hurston's own experiences, link her with African ritual. She declares the BIBLE to be a hoodoo book and belief in magic to be "older than writing," thus privileging oral, folk culture.

With her finger on the pulse of black creativity, Hurston straddles the tale-telling world of Southern Florida and the conjure space of New Orleans with equal zest and skill. *Mules and Men* is not only a resource, but also, in its narrative originality and exuberance, a continuation in the storytelling culture and the verbal artistry of African Americans.

For Further Reading

Hurston, Zora Neale. *Mules and Men*. Philadelphia: Lippincott, 1935.

MÜLLER, MAX (1823–1900)

Ninteenth-century German solar mythologist. Solar mythology derives from the study of the Sanskrit language and implies that all MYTHS are linked to the solar cycle. Müller saw solar mythology as proof for POLYGENESIS. When Sanskrit was first identified as the original language of the Indo-European family, Müller studied the Sanskrit names of heavenly bodies and compared these to other names for gods in various bodies of myth. From this study, Müller concluded that solar phenomena were the origin behind the names of various principal GODS and furthermore that European FOLKTALES descended from these myths and contained similar symbolic messages.

Scottish folklorist Andrew Lang was a strong critic of Müller's interpretations and examined ethnology, rather than the HEAVENS, as the key to understanding tales' origins (*see* LANG, ANDREW). Unlike collectors Franz Boas and Henry Schoolcraft (*see* BOAS, FRANZ; SCHOOLCRAFT, HENRY ROWE), Müller was a theorist. Based on his background in linguistics, he professed another creative theory for seeking tales' origins. He called this theory "The Disease of Language" and believed that cultures created new myths for the basis of the Greek gods' names because the original myths had been forgotten over time.

While Müller was a professor of modern languages and comparative philology at Oxford in the mid-1800s he worked on translating an edition of the *Rig-Veda*, the *Sacred Hymns* of the Hindus and the 51 volumes of the *Sacred Books of the East* (*see* RIG-VEDA CREATION). He also traced several contemporary European tales back to Sanskrit collections, such as the PANCHATANTRA. Although Müller's views achieved little popularity and have not influenced contemporary study of tales, his knowledge of Sanskrit helped make accessible the traditions enshrined in the ancient language to those unable to read it themselves.

For Further Reading

Müller, Max, ed. *Sacred Book of the East: Vedic Hymns.* 2 vols. Krishna Press, 1975.

MURILÉ AND THE MOONCHIEF

African story from Kenya about the youth Murilé's success on the MOON and his ensuing demise, due to a broken promise, after his return to EARTH. In this tale, Murilé can no longer bear his MOTHER's incessant nagging and criticism. He sits on his father's stool and recites all the magic incantations he knows. Suddenly the stool flies from the earth to the moon. Murilé goes to the village of the Moonchief where he astonishes the backward people by building a fire. He becomes a HERO to the moon people and a favorite of the Moonchief. Murilé is given many cattle and many wives. He prepares to return to the earth and show his mother what he has become.

Murilé sends a mockingbird to announce his arrival, but returns announcing that Murilé's family thinks he is dead. Murilé does not believe his report. The mockingbird goes to earth a second time and returns with Murilé's father's walking stick as proof of his visit to Murilé's family. Murilé dresses his wives and children in their finest clothing and covers them with jewelry, and they set out to earth on foot. One of Murilé's finest bulls offers to carry his master on his back under the condition that Murilé will never kill or eat the bull. Murilé agrees. Murilé's family joyfully receives him, and his mother brags about her rich and powerful son. Murilé makes his parents swear never to harm the bull that carried their son home. After some time, Murilé's parents forget their promise, and they kill the bull. His mother prepares a dish seasoned with the bull's fat and broth. The meat speaks to Murilé, reminding him of his promise. When Murilé takes a bite of the bull's meat, the earth swallows him up.

The broken promise in Murilé's story is evocative of the story of ADAM AND EVE in Eden. Because they eat the fruit from the forbidden tree of the knowledge of good and evil, they are banished from the paradisiacal garden forever. Another form of this theme occurs in the poignant tale of Orpheus and Eurydice, in which Orpheus breaks his promise not to look back at Eurydice as he leads her from the underworld (*see* ORPHEUS AND EURYDICE MYTH). When Orpheus reaches the sunlight, he turns to see if Eurydice is still with him, she vanishes back to HADES, and he loses her forever.

As the giver of fire to the moon people, Murilé resembles the Greek GOD Prometheus (*see* PROMETHEUS AND THE THEFT OF FIRE).

For Further Reading

Abrahams, Roger D. *African Folktales.* New York: Pantheon, 1983.

Biebuyck, Daniel, and Kahombo C. Mateene, eds. *Mwindo Epic from the Banyanga (Congo Republic).* Berkeley: University of California Press, 1969.

MUSIC

In MYTH and FOLKLORE, the importance of the creation of music and its role in tales of cultures worldwide. Ancient mythology suggests that the creation of music is an important moment in the history of humankind, and many early stories underline the power of music to soothe, disturb, entice, ensnare, and delight, whether the music is sung or played upon an instrument. Presumably, ancient BARDS sang their EPICS, as did the medieval TROUBADOURS and minstrels (see MINSTRELSY). The music of BALLADS, folk songs, the BLUES, and ROCK SONGS have made their stories easy to transmit and memorable. The role of music is important in African and Hindu storytelling, where the storyteller often plays various instruments and the audience participates by singing.

In Greek mythology, Hermes is credited with creating the lyre from the shell of a tortoise, which he then bequeaths to APOLLO, who becomes the god of music. Of the nine Greek Muses, Euterpe is the Muse of music, especially wind instruments, and she is symbolized by a flute. The music of Orpheus is so beautiful that he is even able to descend to HADES to use his music to persuade the GODS to return his wife Eurydice to him (see ORPHEUS AND EURYDICE MYTH). In HOMER's ODYSSEY, the song of the SIRENS is so enticing that sailors who hear it forget everything and die of hunger or are dashed upon the rocks and brought to their deaths. Odysseus cleverly withstands their destructiveness by first putting wax in his sailors' ears and then lashing himself to the mast so he can hear the music without self-destructing. In the Hebrew BIBLE, David is able to soothe King Saul with his harp-playing. In Hindu mythology, KRISNA is often represented as playing on a divine flute, and the music he plays has a powerful effect on women, calling them to him. In Robert Browning's poem "The Pied Piper of Hamelin," based on popular LEGEND, the Piper's wonderful music has the ability to enchant the children of Hamelin, so that they follow the Piper into a door in the mountainside that shuts behind them forever.

As Edna Johnson and Evelyn Sickels note in *An Anthology of Children's Literature*, "hero stories and legends are always strengthened by music, and vice versa. . . . Rossini's music for *William Tell* can be appreciated only when the listener is familiar with the famous legend of that name." Like Rossini, many composers have drawn on the storytelling tradition for inspiration for their musical compositions. Serge Prokefieff drew on an old Russian FOLKTALE for his musical FAIRY TALE, *Peter and the Wolf*. The German composer Englebert Humperdinck created *Hansel and Gretel*, a famous opera based on the GRIMM BROTHERS's fairy tale of the same name. E.T.A. Hoffman's retelling of the old German fairy tale, *The Nutcracker and the Mouse*-King, inspired Peter Tchaikovsky's *Nutcracker*. Tchaikovsky also composed *The Sleeping Beauty*, an orchestral suite based on the fairy tale. French composer Maurice Ravel composed the orchestral suite MOTHER GOOSE as a musical interpretation of the fairy tales of Charles Perrault (see PERRAULT, CHARLES).

MUSICAL INSTRUMENTS

Flutes, lyres, lutes, drums, harps, zithers, and pipes that play important roles in various MYTHS and FAIRY TALES. Musical instruments are found in various mythologies, and can be symbols of the sound of CREATION, of shape, of ANIMALS, and of DEATH.

In Hindu mythology, KRISNA's flute is the magical cause of the creation of the world and later had the power to call women to him. Among the many stories about Krisna is one in which the usually modest and restrained wives and daughters of herdsman hear the flute of Krisna and follow him into the forest. In Vedic myth, the seer, Narada, invents the lute and is the patron of music.

The lyre, symbol of the harmonious union of cosmic forces, was considered the invention of Hermes, Greek god of travelers, messenger of ZEUS, and conductor of souls to the underworld. As legend has it, Hermes finds a tortoise and emptied it from its shell. He then stretches oxhide around it and places seven strings made of sheep gut over a bridge. The harmonious sounds of this first lyre so enchant APOLLO when Hermes presents Apollo with the lyre as a gift, that he is willing to forgive the mischievous Hermes for stealing his heifers. Thereafter, Apollo was known as god of song and the lyre, which he played for the other gods. Orpheus, son of Apollo, was also known for playing the lyre so beautifully that he would tame the wild beasts and enchant the GODS of the underworld (*see* ORPHEUS AND EURYDICE MYTH).

The pipes of Pan, the SATYR represent universal harmony in nature. The story of how Pan acquired his famous pipes tells of his pursuit of the NYMPH Syrinx, who is transformed into a reed when she begs her father, a river god, to save her from the satyr. To console himself, Pan cuts some reeds and ties them together, inventing a new kind of flute. In the tale of "The Pied Piper of Hamelin" the musician is connected with a fascination with death, as the sound of his piping seduces all the children of Hamelin to leave their homes and families and follow him into a door in the mountainside, which shuts behind them.

MWINDO EPICS

Heroic tale of Nyanga people of Zaire. *Mwindo* is a title given to Nyanga sons born after several daughters. There are four Nyanga EPICS in a series dealing with HEROES and chiefs, with a central character named Mwindo.

Mwindo's father declares that he does not want sons, but only daughters. After an especially long pregnancy, the preferred wife gives birth to the boy Mwindo. The unborn child manifests its future heroic qualities by fulfilling certain unsolicited tasks for its mother, such as bringing firewood, vegetables, and water. The hero himself decides the moment of birth and emerges from his mother's middle finger. He is born speaking and walking. Immediately after birth, Mwindo is attacked by his father and by lightning.

Mwindo is born with intrinsic capabilities and special objects that set him apart from the rest of humanity. Among those objects are a shoulder bag that contains a rope, an *adze* (an ax-like tool for trimming), and an ax. These tools respond to Mwindo's command, and in a fight, the MAGIC OBJECTS do the work for him.

Mwindo loves to sing and uses the power of the sung word effectively and continuously. He has numerous reliable allies among humans, divinities, and animals. His adventures take him throughout the earth, through the celestial realms, and into the subterranean world. When Mwindo's father learns of the hero's successes, the two are reconciled and return to the village, where the people greet them with drums and songs, presenting them with goats as welcoming gifts. Mwindo is eventually enthroned as chief and lives in glory among his people.

Throughout the lands of the Nyanga people there are numerous tales that spin off of the Mwindo epics. The names of the heroes are often different, but their births and exploits are very similar to those of the heroes in the Mwindo epics. These stories are told to Nyanga young people to train them in the values of Nyanga society.

MYCENAE

Ancient city near Corinth, Greece, and focal point of several major Greek stories. Mycenae is perhaps best known for its HEROES from the House of Atreus who go to the Trojan War in HOMER'S ILIAD. AGAMEMNON, the KING of Mycenae, sacrifices Iphigenia to appease ARTEMIS and gain favorable winds for the journey to TROY. Upon his return from the war, he is murdered by his wife, Clytemnestra, who is in turn murdered by their son Orestes. In fact, many of the stories set in Mycenae are concerned with murder, adultery, and even CANNIBALISM. In another famous story from Ovid's *Metamorphoses*, Herakles must perform 12 labors under the cowardly king of Mycenae, Eurystheus. In one such labor, Herakles must kill the Nemean lion and return it to Mycenae. Herakles completes his task, and the lions carved on the gates to Mycenae are still visible today as a testament to the significance of the Greek story.

In historical terms, the height of Mycenean power dates to the late Bronze Age (1600–1100 B.C.). The city was excavated by the renowned archeologist Heinrich Schliemann in the 1870s, and his discoveries confirmed a civilization of great wealth and power. The discovery, along with the excavations of Troy and Cnossus, did much toward establishing the historical basis of many Greek stories.

For Further Reading

Schliemann, Heinrich. *Mycenae: A Narrative of Researches and Discoveries at Mycenae and Tiryns.* 1880. Reprint, New York: B. Blom, 1967.

MYSTERY PLAY

Form of popular medieval religious DRAMA based on scenes from the BIBLE. Mystery plays seem to have developed from Latin liturgical drama that was performed by the clergy in church. As lay people and the vernacular became a part of these dramatizations, they physically moved from inside the churches to the streets of the towns where they became civic occasions. Mystery plays were performed throughout Europe from the thirteenth to the sixteenth centuries. In England, they were traditionally produced on or around Corpus Christi Day, a holy feast day that falls in late May or early June.

Mystery plays were performed as long series called "cycles." Cycles were comprised of individual episodes or "pageants." Each pageant was sponsored by a local trade or religious guild that was totally responsible for its production. An entire cycle dramatized the Bible from Creation to the Last Judgment with popular scenes including NOAH and the FLOOD, Abraham and Isaac, the shepherds' visit to the Nativity, Jesus' crucifixion and resurrection, and doomsday. Masons might present the Noah story, bakers acted out the Last Supper, and so on.

The pageants were usually performed on a procession of wagons. The lower portion of the wagon was enclosed with a curtain and served as a dressing room. The wagons stopped at prearranged stations where the performers acted. When the pageant was finished, the wagon moved to the next station. In theory, spectators could stand in one spot and watch an ongoing sequence of Bible stories. A cycle sometimes lasted an entire day or longer.

Pageants often included mechanical contrivances, elaborate costumes, sound effects, and spectacular lighting for evening performances. Some mystery play cycles were enacted in an open space surrounded by individual stages. In addition, some cycles seem to have toured the countryside.

Most of the existing English mystery plays are part of a few major cycles named for the places in which they were acted, including the *Chester Cycle*, the *York Cycle*, and the *Towneley* or *Wakefield* cycle. *The Second Shepherd's Play* by the anonymous "Wakefield Master" is perhaps the most celebrated of the mystery plays. This work consists of two episodes. In the first episode, Mak steals a sheep from three fellow shepherds. His wife dresses it as a baby and hides it in a cradle. When the shepherds come to Mak's cottage with gifts for the "baby," they discover Mak's deceit, toss him in a blanket, and return to the fields to sleep. In the brief second episode, the shepherds are awakened by an angel and directed to Bethlehem. The plot of *The Second Shepherd's Play*, like that of several other mystery plays that were produced by and for lay people, often contained comic and farcical elements.

Other famous European cycles include the thirteenth-century Cyprus *Passion Cycle*, a collection of Greek prose plays depicting the events of Holy Week, and the seventeenth-century Oberammeragau *Passion Play* still performed in Bavaria in Germany during Easter.

For Further Reading

Beer, Lisl, ed. *Second Shepherd's Play.* Boston: Branden Publishing, 1963.

Cawley, A.C., and Martin Skvens. *Towneley Cycle.* Huntington Library, 1976.

MYTH

Basic archetypal story to explain or celebrate the mysteries of human existence in all cultures. Myth can be seen, on one hand, as the stories and tales of GODS and GODDESSES in whom we no longer believe; on the other hand, myth is "a thread that holds past, present, and future together," writes J. F. Bierlein in *Parallel Myths*, for it is "a pattern of beliefs that give meaning to life," and the "basis of identity for communities, tribes, and nations." The psychologist Carl Jung saw myth as "the natural and indispensable intermediate stage between unconscious and conscious cognition," and used the term ARCHETYPE to refer to the recurrent patterns or MOTIFS that appear in the myths of cultures world-wide. For Jung, the "archetypes of the collective unconscious" were basic to all humankind.

In myth we see religion, philosophy, art, sociology, anthropology, history, and science coming together to give us a sense of the deepest truths and energies of humankind. That the patterns of myth are paralleled in different cultures, that the same basic story occurs again and again in the basic archetypes of myth, suggests the human need for myth and the connection between myth and language, myth and DREAM, and myth and human understanding of the mystery of the universe. At the center of each culture's mythologies lies the need to understand the ineffable, to answer the basic and essential questions of why are we here, how did we get here, and what is our purpose in being here? The journey-QUEST of the HERO symbolically answers that question, as the hero rises out of the personal to represent the universal human being.

NAINEMA

Creator in the mythology of the Uitoto Indians of Columbia. In the beginning, Nainema is only an illusion who has a vision, which is also an illusion. He examines the vision by holding it by the thread of a DREAM, but he can find nothing. With magical glue, he joins emptiness to the thread of the dream. He creates the EARTH by stomping on the bottom of the illusionary dream, and finally he is able to sit down on the earth. Continuing to hold on to the illusion, Nainema creates the sky by lying down on the earth, and the forests grow from his saliva.

As David and Margaret Leeming note in *A Dictionary of Creation Myths*, this myth is a good example of "creation *ex nihilo*, Creation from Nothing." It is also an example of "Creation by Thought" and "Creation by Secretion."

NARCISSUS

Beautiful youth of Greek mythology. The most well-known version of his story is told in the Roman poet Ovid's *Metamorphoses*. Narcissus is the son of Leiriope, one of the NYMPHS, and Cephisus, a river god. While Narcissus is still very young, the seer TIRESIAS assures Leiriope that her boy would grow to a ripe old age—as long as he never comes to know himself.

The loveliest youth in the world, Narcissus requites no one's love and breaks hearts wherever he goes. One of the saddest of his victims is a beautiful nymph named Echo. Echo can not speak her own words; she can only repeat the utterances of others. This is a punishment from HERA, queen of the GODS, for Echo's role in the dalliances of Hera's husband ZEUS.

Echo remains hidden in the woods and tries to speak with Narcissus, but she can only repeat the last words of every sentence he speaks. She finally shows herself to him, only to have Narcissus declare, "I shall die before you lie with me." Pathetically, Echo begs, "Lie with me." Ignoring her, Narcissus hurries on his way. Echo wastes away with grief until she becomes no more than a voice haunting caves and valleys.

Another of Narcissus's doomed suitors is a young man named Ameinius. In despair of unrequited love, Ameinius kills himself with a sword that Narcissus gave him—but not before praying to the GODDESS ARTEMIS to avenge him.

His vengeance comes to pass when Narcissus sees his own reflection in a pool and falls in love with it. He quickly realizes that the face he sees is his own, but that only makes his longing more unendurable. He stabs himself, calling out "Farewell!" to his reflection as he dies. Witnessing his suicide, the still-grieving Echo calls out "Farewell!"

Narcissus vanishes as he dies, and a white flower appears in that spot—a flower known today as *narcissus*. According to some stories, Zeus used a narcissus to help his brother HADES lure Persephone to the underworld (*see* PERSEPHONE MYTH).

Flowers play a role in many tales from the oral tradition, and stories were often developed to account for the properties of plants—such as the narcotic effects of narcissus-oil. The story of Narcissus may also be based on an earlier Cretan spring-flower-hero.

Narcissism is now a commonly used psychological term denoting vanity and self-obsession. In Freudian psychology, there are two kinds of narcissism. One of these, *primary narcissism,* is associated with the so-called "pregenital period" of child development and involves indulging oneself in physical pleasure. Another is *secondary narcissism,* in which the adult ego takes great pride in its ability to discern and follow the rules and regulations of the superego. *See also* ANCIENT GREEK STORYTELLING; FREUD, SIGMUND.

For Further Reading

Low, Alic. *Macmillan Book of Greek Gods and Heros.* New York: Macmillan, 1985.

NASREDDIN HODJA

Also called *Mullah Nassr Eddin* in the original Persian, a TRICKSTER character in traditional Middle Eastern FOLKLORE who is known for his foolish tricks. Unlike tricksters such as COYOTE and Brer Rabbit, however, Nasreddin Hodja is silly and illogical at best. Although he does lie and steal in some cases,

he is best known for riding his donkey backwards or mistaking his convoluted (but beautiful) echoing voice in the Turkish bath for his own real voice.

At the center of the irony about Nasreddin is his name: a *hodja* is the name for a wise Islamic teacher. Incidentally, Nasreddin's home town of Akshehir is very close to the city of Konya, where the Mevlevi Sufis (also called Whirling Dervishes) of the Persian mystic poet Jalal al-din Rumi (1207–1273), were first established. Coupling this fact with the implication of wisdom in the tales, it is tempting to assume that underlying Nasreddin's silly antics, there is representation of the spiritual meaning of the Sufi. According to the Sufi, true logic is not implicit in following conventions, but relies on overcoming conditioned responses. In the ceremonial *sema*, for instance, the Sufi whirls wildly in an effort to overcome the logic of gravity and ordinary fatigue. The wise Rumi did use the Nasreddin Hodja stories—but in fact, only as comical ALLEGORIES—to show the paradoxical nature of the mystical understanding. There is nevertheless convincing evidence of allegory ascribable to the Sufi in the tales.

In a popular story in which the *hodja's* donkey has strayed and the master is roaming the town, the silly Nasreddin continually cries out, much to the confusion of the townsfolk who are helping him search out the animal, "Allah be praised!" When some of the townsfolk venture to ask why he is praising Allah when his donkey is lost, Nasreddin answers, "I praise GOD because I was not riding the donkey when he got lost, for if I had been on his back then, we would without doubt both be lost." The possible levels of allegory are at least two fold here. First, the storyteller could actually be referring to the mystical path, especially as Nasreddin calls out "praise to Allah!" as he walks along among a group of baffled neighbors. Second, the donkey might be a representation of the *hodja's* animal nature and in this case, the *hodja* is praising God for not being attached to his animal nature when it is "lost" in sin.

The implied allegory in the tale of Nasreddin Hodja's grave in Aksehir is particularly remarkable and perhaps the most easily ascribed to the Sufi. A huge padlock secures an iron gate standing before Nasreddin's gravestone. Significantly, however, no fence adjoins the gate on either side to block the visitor's entrance to the gravestone. The Sufi's belief that the common man overlooks the deceivingly simple answer while the wise man discovers it by merely bypassing accepted logic is at the base of the gravestone's allegory. The common man will search for a logical way to unlock the gate, or, failing this, propose a bribe to open the lock, while those who understand the mystic and his illogical logic perceive the truth—that locked gates prevent only those who will not look around them from moving on. The people of Akshehir say that the *hodja* looks out from a small hole in his gravestone to observe the world. Perhaps he laughs at those who fret at the gate and welcomes those who walk around it to the truth.

For Further Reading

Downing, Charles. *Tales of the Hodja.* New York: H.Z. Walck, 1965.

Ekrem, Selma. *Turkish Fairy Tales.* Princeton, NJ: Van Nostrand, 1964.

Kelsey, Alice Geer. *Once the Hodja.* New York: David McKay, 1962.

NATIVE NORTH AMERICAN STORYTELLING

Oral tradition of narrative found among the indigenous peoples of the United States and Canada. This tradition is expressed not only in spoken MYTHS and LEGENDS but in song, chant, and prayer. Other forms of narrative within Native North American FOLKLORE include puns, PROVERBS, RIDDLES, and pantomime, which is most often performed in ceremony by tribe members dressed in costumes that represent ANIMALS and other figures.

Myths and legends are the most popular forms of Native American storytelling, and most closely resemble the oral traditions of other cultures, including the European FAIRY TALE and the European American TALL TALE (*see* EUROPEAN AMERICAN STORYTELLING, EUROPEAN STORYTELLING). Narratives serve to advise or entertain, though not always both. For instance, the legends of tribes in the Great

Basin are told primarily for entertainment, while among the Yokut tribe of California, and among some Apache tribes, tales are told with a moral undertone that serve to set a basis for how the tribe should act. The Navajo have a body of legend that serves to both instruct and to amuse—for while many Navajo myths are of a serious nature, the Navajo are also known for their "trotting or traveling" COYOTE stories, told to children as entertainment.

Narratives told for amusement usually center around the deeds of a TRICKSTER, such as the Raven, Mink, or Bluejay of North Pacific Coast legend. Other prominent characters include the Raven, OLD MAN, and the Coyote of the Plateau; the Raven, Beaver, and Crow of the northern area; the Coyote or Rabbit in the Great Basin and Southwest; the Coyote, Old Man, *Sen'deh*, and *Inktumni* in the Plains; the Hare, Raccoon, *Nanabozho, Wisaka, Tcikapis* in the Woodlands area; and the Opossum and Rabbit of the Southeast (*see* MANABOZHO).

The heroes of the Native North American story may be human, as in the nonfictional tales that belong to a somewhat recent trend in Native American storytelling, "historical" tales that revolve around tribal encounters and personal accounts of war and hunting experiences, or animal trickster, as in tales belonging to the prehuman "Mythical Age," where the animal trickster figures prominently. Although the trickster may serve, in serious culture tales, as the hero, he is often portrayed as the obscene, greedy, stupid, boastful antagonist.

There has been much dispute about whether spoken history is a reliable source of generational, or historical, truth. Robert Lowie, who studied the Crow Indians in the early to mid-1900s, argued that their oral tradition had no factual accuracy, even in those tales regarded as "historical." He formed this conclusion on the basis that the stories told to him were constantly changing. In 1910, for instance, he recorded a Crow account of a battle against the Dakota. The same storyteller years later (in 1931) told Lowie of the same battle, but then insisted the battle had taken place against the Cheyenne. Lowie's point was that the Native American storytelling communities relied less on detail than on the traditional form and style of the story—putting more weight on tale-telling itself than on fact or accuracy.

Just as the European American oral and literary folklore tradition was influenced by native tribes, Native American tribes were influenced by European *märchen* tales—or German fairy tales, most notably those recorded by the GRIMM BROTHERS—and noodle tales, a genre of silly tales told to children. The Southwestern, Plateau, Southeastern, Northern, and Northeastern tribes in particular borrowed tales such as the TAR BABY story, the biblical story of the FLOOD, John the Bear, and "CINDERELLA." Renditions of European-based tales show degrees of integration, some having been completely refurbished in setting, characters, cultural background, style, and theme and others narrated with few adaptations.

Storytelling is obviously and often informal: a grandparent may tell stories to children at home, men and women may sit about at home telling stories late into the night, or stories may be told at funerals, dances, and hunting trips. Many middle-aged and elderly men are especially esteemed for their ability to tell stories, and the most esoteric tales are reserved for telling in a more formal atmosphere—often to restricted audiences.

For Further Reading

Feldman, Susan, ed. *The Storytelling Stone: Traditional Native American Myths and Tales.* New York: Dell, 1991.

Henry, Jeannette, and Ruper Costo, eds. *A Thousand Years of American Indian Storytelling.* San Francisco: Indian Historian Press, 1981.

Kavasch, E. Barrie, ed. *Earth Maker's Lodge: Native American Folklore, Activities, and Foods.* Peterborough: Cobblestone Publishing, 1994.

NAVAJO CREATION

Emergence tale of Navajo people of American Southwest. Before the present Navajo world, a long and complex era takes place in worlds below the present earth's surface. There are usually four such lower worlds stacked one on the other.

The first pair to exist in the first world was First Man and First Woman. Some claim they were transformed from two ears of corn. After emergence the couple builds a sweat lodge, where they plan the world. Next they build a hogan, the traditional Navajo house, where they construct the world in microcosm, later transforming it into the Navajo world.

In the beginning, First Man and First Woman, and sometimes COYOTE, exist with various insect peoples who live according to Navajo customs. On each of the worlds they quarrel and are unable to mend their ways despite repeated warnings from the elders. Consequently water or fire destroys that world, and the people flee upward in search of a new home. In most versions of the story, the fourth world precedes the emergence and is the most complex of the lower worlds. Stories in this world account for the origin of witchcraft and the making of the medicine bundle from which First Man draws the powers to create the Navajo world.

CHANGING WOMAN is the daughter of Long Life Boy and Happiness Girl, but she is reared by First Man and First Woman. Keeper of the mountain soil bundle containing the powers of creation, Changing Woman represents life. She grows to maturity and old age and then begins again, endlessly repeating the cycle of life. She is the foundation for and the measure of time.

Changing Woman creates the Navajos by rubbing epidermal waste from her body into balls. From the waste balls, Changing Woman uses the powers of her mountain soil bundle to create four couples, the ancestors of the first four Navajo clans.

NEAR AND MIDDLE EASTERN STORYTELLING

Encompasses the FOLKTALES and storytelling of a people closely allied in ancestry, language, religion, and culture living in a wide area that includes Arabia, Mesopotamia (Iraq), Syria, Palestine, Egypt, Lebanon, Yemen, Armenia, Malta, and North Africa, as well as the non-Arab speaking country of Iran, formerly called Persia.

Before the eighteenth and nineteenth centuries, the pre-Islamic literature of Arabic speaking countries consisted primarily of poetry, which for a long time was transmitted by professional reciters whose memories were remarkable but who also caused great divergences in the ancient poems and in the subsequent written texts. The pre-Islamic poems fall into two groups: the occasional poems of 2-20 lines with themes of war or revenge and the elaborate odes, ranging from 60 to 100 lines, told by a poet on a supposed journey stopping at a deserted camping ground. The poet begins by recalling the sorrow of parting from his love, continues by describing his camel or horse and comparing it to a wild animal of the desert, which leads to an account of a chase, and ends with praise of his tribe, his own gallantry, descriptions of camp or desert life, or praise of a patron in whose honor the poet has composed the poem.

In the eighteenth and nineteenth centuries, after vast Arab conquests and the growing refinement of social life, prose literature found its way into Arabic literature. It is within this class of works that the popular romances and story cycles, originally transmitted through oral tradition, belong. Of these works of entertainment the most familiar is the THOUSAND AND ONE NIGHTS.

Because the Islamic world never regarded the tales as belonging to polite literature, they existed primarily as recitations in coffeehouses, with the result that not only are the origins of the tales elusive, but as a collection they have been highly fluid rather than stable and have consisted at different times of different stories. In fact, because of the number of storytellers who drew upon the treasury of popular tales to supply the number of stories necessary for a *Thousand and One Nights,* the only constant features of the many renderings of the tales are the introductory framework story and the division of the tales by nights. Despite the modifications that occurred to suit the role of the storyteller and the occasion of the storytelling through centuries of oral narration, it is still possible to identify three narrative groups as the sources of the tales that eventually emerged from Egypt in manuscript form. The first group, which includes the frame story, consists of those tales of Persian origin, which reach into the ancient Persian and Indian past, which were circulating both orally and in manuscript form in Arabic by the end of the tenth century. A second source derives from a group of tales that probably originated in Baghdad in the tenth to twelfth centuries. The third source includes stories that originated in Cairo from about the twelfth to the fourteenth century, some of which can be traced as far back as the stories and folktales of ancient Egypt. All three groups of stories circulated orally then began to be pulled together and written down in various forms from the twelfth to the fourteenth century. The stories accumulated over an extraordinarily lengthy period of time and over a wide area geographically and culturally. As a consequence, no standard text remains as the precursor of all others, although one text, originating in Egypt in the late eighteenth century, has attained the dignity of a Vulgate and has been widely translated.

The tales included in the *Nights* are among the most widely read and influential stories ever to be published in English. Swift, Pope, Johnson, Walpole, Gray, Goldsmith, Gibbon, Scott, Austen, Thackeray, Dickens, and Charlotte Brontë all admired and were influenced by the stories, and Sinbad, Aladdin, ALI BABA, and Scheherazade have become staples of our shared cultural mythology. The stories included in the *Nights* are FABLES, FAIRY TALES, travel adventures, crime stories, ROMANCES, and family anecdotes that, as the folklorist Jack Zipes has observed in *Arabian Nights: The Marvels and Wonders of the Thousand and One Nights,* are intended to socialize readers regarding Muslim custom and law. They are primarily lessons in etiquette, aesthetics, decorum, religion, government, history, and sex.

The folktales of the *Thousand and One Nights* do not, of course, comprise the only tales told in the vast area of the Near and Middle East, regardless of the commonalities existing in the region, for folktales continue to circulate orally long after distinct versions have been recorded in writing. Nor are folktales told in this area solely reliant on Islamic custom and law. Tales originating from Christian and Jewish communities survive as well and continue to be narrated by grand-mothers, aunts, and mothers to children in the private family setting and by men in the public coffee-houses. Among the recently re-corded oral narratives derived from the Near and Middle East are tales that are analogous to those in the *Thousand and One Nights* and tales that are not. The tales circulated over centuries continue to spread orally, and al-though they are often told to instill a moral truth, they nevertheless rely on PRINCES and PRINCESSES, on *djinn* (*see* JINNIE) and ghouls, on magic rings and hidden treasures and, just as with European tales, are often about younger sons and daughters despised and ill-treated who triumph in the end. We find in Turkey the tale of "NASREDDIN HODJA and Tamerlane"; in Egypt "The Falcon's Daugh-ter"; in Iraq "The Cruel Mother-in-Law"; and in Israel "A Dispute in Sign Language." For Moslem women, the Beduin tales have been traditionally told by the elderly in groups of women, children, and slaves who joined to-gether to sew in the evening at the end of a day's work. Titles of the tales include "The Last Camel of Emir Hamid," "The Price of Pride," "Two Mothers Mourning," and "The Jewel in the Sand."

Collections of stories also continue to be recorded far from the country of origin just as Antione Galland's version of the *Thousand and One Nights* includes tales that traveled from India, Persia, Bagdad, Cairo, and Syria before their retelling in translation in Paris (*see* GALLAND, ANTIONE). One such collection of tales emerged in the 1960s from a Detroit, Michigan, neighborhood, gathered by Susie Hoogasian-Villa, an American-born daugh-ter of Armenian immigrants who listened to her grandmother's and neighbors' village tales in Armenian, an Indo-European language, and recorded them in English. Just as in most countries of the world, folktales told in the Arab countries are about children and par-ents, siblings, sexual awakenings and court-ship, the quest for a spouse, brides and bride-grooms, husbands and wives, family life, so-ciety, environment, and the universe.

For Further Reading

Bushnaq, Inea, ed. *Arab Folktales*. New York: Pan-theon, 1986.

El-Shamy, Hasan, ed. *Folktales of Egypt*. Chicago: University of Chicago Press, 1980.

Hoogasian-Villa, Susie. *100 Armenian Tales and Their Folkloristic Relevance*. Detroit: Wayne State University Press, 1966.

Zipes, Jack, ed. *Arabian Nights: The Marvels and Wonders of the Thousand and One Nights*. Adapted from Richard F. Burton's unexpurgated translation. New York: Signet, 1991.

NENNIUS (c. A.D. 800)

Welsh antiquary who lived on the border of the counties Brecknock or Radnor, credited with writing or revising the *Historia Brittonum* (c. A.D. 830). Although there continues to be debate as to whether Nennius actually wrote the work attributed to him, or whether, in fact, he even existed, and few would ascribe the work much value as a history, the text does hold great significance for the history of storytelling. A miscellaneous collection of notes that mix legend and history, the *Historia Brittonum* provides the earliest known refer-ence to the legendary British King ARTHUR. Nennius offers, as an historical account, a narrative of 12 battles of the fifth or sixth cen-tury in which Arthur, described as a general or chieftain, led the Britons to victory against the Saxons.

The *Historia* summarizes and combines early traditions of Roman, Saxon, and Irish sources. It includes a section that explores and narrates Briton origin LEGENDS, includ-ing both the origin found in Latin sources as well as an alternative origin from native sources. The text also contains a lengthy nar-rative of St. Patrick's legendary exploits in Ireland. Approximately 30 of the manuscript versions of the *Historia* still exist today.

For Further Reading

Nennius. *History of the Britons*. Translated by J.A. Giles. British American Books, n.d.

Thomson R. L. *A Medieval Miscellany: Proceedings of the Leeds Philosophy and Literary Society*. Leeds: W. S. Maney & Son, 1982.

NIBELUNGENLIED

German heroic EPIC written about A.D.1200 by an unknown poet for performance at court in Austria. This lengthy work contains the familiar epic themes of love, war, revenge, and murder, and it contributes to the legend of the great Germanic HERO, SIEGFRIED. In the beginning of the *Nibelungenlied*, Siegfried, PRINCE of the Netherlands, Norway, and Nibelungland, arrives in Burgundy to woo Kriemhild, sister of King Gunther. Although Siegfried has never seen or spoken to Kriemhild, he wins favor with the Burgundians by defeating their enemies in battles, and finally he is allowed to meet the beautiful Kriemhild.

King Gunther desires Brunhild of Iceland, known for her superhuman strength. In order to win her, Gunther must vanquish her in contests far beyond his own power. Hagen, Gunther's vassal, tells him that that Siegfried can conquer Brunhild in the contests. In addition to possessing mighty strength, Siegfried has hardened his skin in the blood of a DRAGON that he has slain. Gunther and Siegfried make a deal: if Siegfried can win Brunhild for Gunther, then Gunther will give Kriemhild to Siegfried.

Brunhild is deceived twice. First, she is led to believe that Siegfried is Gunther's vassal. Then, Siegfried, wearing a cloak of invisibility, defeats her in the contests while Gunther only appears to participate.

Later, there is a double wedding at which Brunhild is dismayed and then suspicious to see that Kriemhild is marrying a man she thinks is Gunther's vassal. Brunhild refuses to sleep with Gunther until she learns why Kriemhild has married Siegfried. Brunhild ties up Gunther with her girdle and hangs him from a nail until morning.

The next night, Siegfried aids Gunther by slipping into their bedchamber in his cloak of invisibility. While Gunther remains to the side, Siegfried wrestles with the unrelenting Brunhild until, finally, his strength overcomes hers. Siegfried leaves the bed, but not before he takes a gold ring from Brunhild's finger and her girdle. Gunther sleeps with his virgin wife, thereby eliminating her incredible strength.

Siegfried and Kriemhild travel to Siegfried's country. After ten years, Brunhild invites them back to Burgundy. She wants to know how the wife of a vassal can be a queen,

and a quarrel develops between the two women. Brunhild says that she has heard Siegfried say that he is Gunther's vassal. Unaware of Siegfried and Gunther's schemes, Kriemhild is incredulous and insulted. She responds by entering the cathedral before Brunhild, the Queen of Burgundy. Brunhild challenges Kriemhild on another occasion outside the church. Kriemhild takes out the gold ring and the girdle, implying that Siegfried slept with Brunhild before Gunther did. The dispute is resolved when Siegfried either offers or actually takes an oath denying that he had ever boasted of taking delight in Brunhild's body (the text is ambiguous.) Gunther accepts Siegfried's word without question.

The result of the quarrel between Kreimhild and Brunhild is the plotting and carrying out of Siegfried's death by Gunther's vassal, Hagen. After Kriemhild loses her beloved husband, she remains in Burgundy and is convinced by her brothers to move her kingdom's treasure from Nibelungland to Burgundy. Hagen sinks the entire treasure in the Rhine, hoping to retrieve it for himself one day.

Kriemhild's anger toward Hagen increases. Kriemhild marries Etzel, King of the Huns, not out of love, but in an effort to exact the revenge she desires. Vicious fighting ensues between the Huns and the Burgundians, until Dietrich, one of Etzel's brave knights, fights and captures Hagen and then Gunther. Dietrich brings his prisoners to Kriemhild who orders Gunther's execution. She carries Gunther's head to Hagen, and then chops off Hagen's head with Siegfried's sword. In the end, Hildebrand, Dietrich's tutor and Master-at-Arms, executes Kriemhild.

Although some critics have argued that the *Nibelungenlied* is Kriemhild's biography, there is no scholarly consensus on this point. Theodore M. Andersson asserts in *A Preface to the Nibelungenlied* that "the story is not so much biography as family drama." A. T. Hatto, in his translation, takes another angle and champions "the clear-sighted and fatalistic heroism of Hagen," claiming that

Hagen's heroism "defeats her [Kriemhild] in the moment of her triumph."

The issue concerning whether Siegfried actually slept with Brunhild is a complicated one. A. T. Hatto writes that "we could be absolutely certain that our poet was . . . refashioning an incident in which Siegfried deflowered Brunhild because that is what taking a ring and a girdle means in ancient poetic language." In the interest of propriety, particularly because this work was originally performed at a royal court, it is possible that the poet revised and refined his source. Likewise, Andersson observes that the poet "eliminates [from his source] the sexual act without eliminating the sexual accusation. . . . At the same time [the poet] is eager to exculpate his hero publicly as well as in fact; hence the oath. But he realizes that if the exculpation is complete there will be no further reason to proceed against Siegfried and no justification for his murder. He therefore aborts the oath in order to leave the impression . . . that Siegfried may indeed have made the boast. For the reader the sequence of events becomes obscure."

The evolution of the Nibelung story, as it appears in the *Nibelungenlied*, took centuries and is exceedingly complex. The barest outline suggests that a historical event, several lays, and an epic were the sources for this great poem. As has been assumed for the ILIAD and as is certain for the SONG OF ROLAND, the prime source for the Nibelung LEGEND was a historical occurrence. At some point during the fifth and sixth centuries, using material already incorporated into heroic lays, a poet composed a lay about the actual facts of the demise of the royal house of Burgundy and of the death of Attila in revenge. It is thought that this lay was composed among the Burgundians or Franks in Northern Burgundy of the Merovingian period.

Later in the sixth century and again in Northern Burgundy, a poet composed a lay on the wooing of Brunhild and the death of "Sigifrid" (it cannot be proven that the hero's name was in fact Sigifrid). This second lay was associated with the first lay in a cyclic sense, as is often the case in the growth of oral literature.

Indirect evidence suggests that the lay of Siegfried and Brunhild was expanded into longer lays—now lost, while the ruin of the Burgundians was worked up into a great Austrian epic poem known to scholars as *Diu Nôt* (c. 1160)—also lost. The second part of the *Nibelungenlied* derives from the lost epic, and it is thought that the first part conflated two divergent lays about Siegfried and Brunhild, including perhaps information from other lays concerned with Siegfried's youth. "The final poet" took one or more lays of young Siegfried, two parallel lays of Siegfried and Brunhild, and the epic poem *Diu Nôt*, and out of them composed the *Nibelungenlied*.

For Further Reading

Andersson, Theodore M. *A Preface to the Nibelungenlied*. Stanford: Stanford University Press, 1987.

Hatto, A. T., trans. *The Nibelungenlied*. Harmondsworth, Middlesex: Penguin, 1978.

NIFLHEIM

Norse underworld, a freezing region of fog, glaciers, mountains of ice, and darkness. It existed long before the creation of the earth. Hvergelmir, the bubbling, seething source of all rivers, surges up from the center of Niflheim.

In Norse mythology, the frost GIANT Ymir, from whom the EARTH is created, is formed when warm air from Muspellheim, the infernal region to the south, meets the ice of Niflheim in the chasm called Ginnungagap (*see* NORSE CREATION).

Niflheim is ruled by HEL, the monster daughter of LOKI and the giant Angrboda. In an effort to avert disaster, the GODS cast Hel down to Niflheim where she became queen of the dead. The dead over whom Hel presides include those who die of illness or old age. Warriors who die a courageous death in battle are taken to VALHALLA.

The queen Hel lives in hel. Sometimes the terms *Niflheim* and *hel* are used interchangeably. In one Norse poem, however, men passed through hel to die again in Niflheim. It is suggested that hel is a part of Niflheim. Nidhogg, the DRAGON who gnaws on one of the World Tree YGGDRASIL's roots, lives in Niflheim. Hel will lead legions of the dead out of Niflheim to fight the gods at RAGNAROK, the end of the world.

Descriptions of Niflheim appear in the Norse CREATION MYTH, in the account of the gods banishing Hel to rule over the dead, in the dreams that precede BALDR's death, and in the myth about Baldr's death, when Hermod journeys to the underworld. Another myth relates how Svipdag, a human, goes to Niflheim to tell his dead mother, the seeress, Groa, that his father's new wife has put a dangerous task before him. Groa agrees to guard her son by singing charms.

HADES, TARTARUS, SHEOL, PURGATORY, and HELL are examples of "underworlds" or realms of the dead from other storytelling traditions.

NIHONGI

Ancient Japanese text, completed in A.D. 720 under the auspices of the royal court, also known as the *Nihon Shoki.* Like the KOJIKI, the *Nihongi* is an expression of the Shinto belief in the divinity and power of nature. Though it includes variations of many of the same MYTHS as the *Kojiki,* the *Nihongi* is more focused on historical events than the earlier text. Some scholars believe that both the *Kojiki* and *Nihongi* were committed to memory by Hiyeda no Are, thought to be a woman, who held them in memory for twenty-five years.

In an apparent sign of Chinese influence, the *Nihongi* begins with a state of chaos, rather like a COSMIC EGG. A stirring in the center of this mass marks the beginning of the division into yin and yang, HEAVEN and EARTH. The serene and clear part of the chaotic mass becomes heaven. Later, the thick and cloudy material solidifies and becomes earth.

Like the *Kojiki,* the *Nihongi* includes the tale of Izanagi and Izanami, the deities who were the ancestors of all things; the JAPANESE CREATION MYTH; stories about the heavenly myth-world Takama-nö-para, the home of the deities ruled by AMATERASU; and stories about earth and nature deities such as SUSA-NO-WO.

For Further Reading

Kojiki. Translated by Donald L. Philippi. Princeton, NJ: Princeton University Press, 1969.

Nihongi: Chronicles of Japan from the Earliest Times to A.D. 697. Translated by W.G. Aston. London: George Allen & Unwin, 1956.

NINIGI

Japanese god and grandson of AMATERASU, GODDESS of the SUN. Ninigi plays an important role in Japanese mythology when his grandmother, Amaterasu, sends him to EARTH with three precious items: the sword Kusanagi, found in the tail of an eight-headed snake by Amaterasu's brother Susanoo (*see* SUSA-NO-WO); the heavenly jewels created by all the GODS to help bring Amaterasu out of the cave in which she was hiding from her brother Susanoo, thereby causing the world to be dark; and the mirror also used to lure Amaterasu out of her hiding place. These three items that Ninigi takes with him to earth become the three emblems of Imperial power.

Once on earth, Ninigi and his entourage build a palace on cape Kasasa in the province of Hyuga. He marries Kono-Hana-Sakuya-Hime, daughter of the mountain god. Because she conceives on their wedding night, Ninigi is suspicious of his wife's fidelity. His wife's response is to build herself a doorless house, swearing that if the child is not Ninigi's, it will perish in the fire she sets to the house immediately following the birth. She then bears three sons, though later tales refer to only two sons, Hosuseri and Hikohohodemi. The grandson of Hikohohodemi, who is posthumously known as Jimmu-Tenno, is renowned as the founder of Japan's Imperial line.

For Further Reading

Leeming, David, and Jake Page. *Goddess: Myths of the Female Divine.* New York: Oxford University Press, 1994.

NIRVANA

In Hinduism and Buddhism, transcendent state of illumination. Used slightly differently by Hindus and Buddhists, Nirvana literally means "extinction." For Hindus, Nirvana is characterized by a state of liberation in which there is the merging of the individual, transitory "I" into BRAHMAN, and one is freed from the cycle of suffering, DEATH, and REBIRTH, and is equated with the highest consciousness. Buddhist Nirvana also means a departure from the cycle of rebirths, *samsara*, and it necessitates complete defeat of desire, hatred, and delusion, and the end of active volition. With the achievement of Nirvana, one is past the effects of *karma*, or one's acts in a previous life. All branches of Buddhism see as their spiritual goal the achievement of Nirvana. At times Nirvana is equated with a state of bliss, yet this is not an accurate definition, for it more closely means the cessation of suffering, though language cannot aptly express its true nature.

For Buddhists of the branch called *Hinayana*, there are two types of Nirvana: the kind that can be attained before death, which has a remainder of conditionality, and the kind achieved at death, with no conditionality. In Zen Buddhism, Nirvana is not separated from this world, but is seen as "the realization of the true nature of the mind (the mind's essence), which is identical with the true nature of human beings." This is only possible with wisdom, or *prajna*, and a person who has attained this wisdom and insight into his or her mind can be said to have achieved the goal of Nirvana. The term *pragna* refers to the wisdom of he or she who has attained Nirvana. Many of the stories, PARABLES, and *koans* of Zen Buddhism focus on the attainment of the wisdom that leads to Nirvana. *See also* JATAKA TALES, MILAREPA.

NISHAN SHAMANESS

Heroine of a FOLKTALE originating in China during the Manchu dynasty, in the seventeenth century. The story tells of an incident involving a female SHAMAN, a mythic individual who has access to the supernatural and can restore life. After the DEATH of a young boy, the boy's parents hire the shaman to reclaim their son from the underworld (*see* DESCENT TO THE UNDERWORLD). While the shaman is rescuing the boy from the underworld, she encounters her deceased husband who demands that she also bring him back, but she rejects him, asserting her desire to live among women. When she returns with the boy she is rewarded and praised, until others learn of her rejection of her husband. The story concludes as her mother-in-law charges her in court for these actions and the official, who is the father of the boy she saved, punishes her by having all of her shamanist implements taken from her.

Like the TRICKSTER character of Native American oral tradition, the shaman of Nishan challenges the conventional social order in her actions, often through comic deception.

NOAH

Biblical figure whom GOD chooses to build an ark and survive the FLOOD that he sends to destroy humankind. The story of Noah is told in Genesis (*see* GENESIS, BOOK OF). When God becomes displeased with the wickedness of humans, he resolves to wipe out the human race with a vast flood. God decides to spare Noah and his family, however, because Noah is righteous. God apprises Noah of his plan and instructs him to build an ark. He tells Noah to take his wife, his sons and his sons' wives, and one male and one female of every kind of living creature onto the ark with him. Seven days after Noah boards the ark, it begins to rain and continues for 40 days and 40 nights. Every living thing on earth perishes, except for those in the ark.

After 150 days, the flood begins to subside, and eventually the ark grounds on Mount Ararat. Noah sends out a dove, which is unable to find a place to land because the earth is still under water. After seven days, he sends the dove out again, and she returns with an olive leaf in her beak. Noah sends the dove out after another seven days, and she does not return. After Noah emerges from the ark, he builds an altar to God and burns animal offerings. God pledges never to send another flood to destroy the earth, giving the rainbow as the sign of his covenant.

Noah was also a farmer, inventing the hoe, scythe, and plow. In another story, he plants a vineyard, gets drunk from the wine, and sleeps with his daughters. His son Ham sees him naked. When Noah learns this, he condemns Ham's descendants to be slaves, while blessing the descendants of his other sons, who have not looked at their drunken, naked father.

A source for the story of Noah and the flood is found in the EPIC of the legendary king GILGAMESH. According to this epic, the hero Utnapishtim builds a boat to save himself, his family, a few other people, and animals from a great flood sent by the GODS. The flood story from *Gilgamesh*, however, is based on an earlier MYTH of the Suzerains, the HERO of which is the worthy man Ziusudra.

The Indian story of MANU AND THE FISH also recounts a tremendous flood from which Manu alone is saved by receiving supernatural help and by remaining on a ship until he is able to go ashore on a mountain.

For Further Reading

Geisert, Arthur. *The Ark.* Boston: Houghton Mifflin, 1988.

Hogrogian, Nonny. *Noah's Ark.* New York: Alfred A. Knopf, 1986.

NORSE CREATION

Nordic myths describing the beginning of the world. The most common Norse account of CREATION begins with a chasm or tremendous emptiness called *Ginnungagap*. North of Ginnungagap is a freezing region of fog, ice, and darkness called NIFLHEIM. To the south lies a fiery realm called *Muspellheim*, ruled over by the GIANT Surt who brandishes a flaming sword (*see* RAGNAROK). When warm air from Muspellheim meets ice from Niflheim in the middle of Ginnungagap, the ice begins to melt and the evil frost giant, Ymir, is formed from the drops of water. From Ymir comes a whole family of frost giants. More ice melts, and the drops form a cow, called Audumla. Ymir drinks Audumla's milk, and she licks the ice. At the end of the first day, a man's hair emerges from the ice that Audumla licked. Audumla continues to lick, and at the end of the second day, a man's head appears. At the end of the third day, a whole man, named Buri, is formed.

Buri has a son named Bor, who marries the frost giant Bestla, and with her, he fathers three sons: ODIN, Vili, and Ve. Bor's three sons attack and kill Ymir. So much blood comes from his wounds that it drowns all the frost giants except for two who continue to propagate the giant race.

Odin and his two brothers form the world from Ymir's body. His flesh becomes the earth. They shape his unbroken bones into mountains. His teeth, jaws, and shattered bones become rocks, boulders, and stones. The brothers use Ymir's blood to make lakes and the ocean, and they create the sky from his skull.

From the maggots that live in Ymir's flesh, Odin and his brothers make DWARFS. They place the dwarfs, named North, South, East, and West, at the four corners of the sky. Using sparks of fire from Muspell, the brothers form the sun, the moon, and the stars. They create regions specifically for the rock giants and for the frost giants. Out of Ymir's eyebrows, they make *Midgard*, home of humans. They make the first man, Ash, and the first woman, Elm, from two fallen trees and give them Midgard. The brothers throw Ymir's brains into the air, forming the clouds.

Odin takes the dark-haired, dark-eyed, and dark-skinned giant, Night, and her son, Day, and places them in horse-drawn chariots in the sky, where they ride around the world. Night leads the way. Day's horse's brilliant mane lights up the earth and the sky. Then the brothers take two children from Midgard, a boy called Moon and his sister, Sun, and put them in the sky to guide the chariots.

Finally Odin and his brothers build the kingdom of Asgard, a realm of plains and palaces. They link Asgard to the earth with a magic rainbow bridge called Bifrost. Asgard became the home of the gods.

The story of Norse creation belongs to a tradition of creation myths in which the universe is formed from the dismemberment of a sacrificed being, usually a primordial being. *See also* BABYLONIAN CREATION, DISMEMBERMENT OF PRIMORDIAL BEING, RIG-VEDA CREATION.

For Further Reading

Crossley-Holland, Kevin. *The Norse Myths.* Harmondsworth, Middlesex: Penguin Books, 1982.

NORTH AFRICAN STORYTELLING

See NEAR AND MIDDLE EASTERN STORY-
TELLING

NORTHERN EUROPEAN STORYTELLING

Oral tradition as it originated in the preliterate culture of northern Europe. Many northern European stories were transmitted orally, often for centuries, before they were preserved in writing. The original, oral forms of these stories depended on the oral-formulaic technique. Unlettered singers or storytellers did not memorize the poems and stories that they learned or composed themselves; instead they employed a wide-ranging body of formulas—a preexisting language—of themes, plots, and proper names, which they used to compose their own versions of traditional poems and stories. These formulas were the creation of innumerable generations of singers and storytellers. Oral tales varied with each performance, and these stories continued to be fluid until they were fixed in writing. Often these formulas were transmitted to the written form of poems, and the recurrence of a significant number of formulas indicates the originally oral nature of a given tale. Modern studies of oral singers and storytellers show that the length of a performance largely depends on how much time a singer has on a given occasion; in other words, singers can adjust the length of their tales to accommodate the situation.

One group of oral storytellers were the Norse *skalds*. They were popular in the courts of Scandinavian KINGS and in the halls of cultured men, particularly during the twelfth century. Skalds relied on pre-Christian MYTHS as the primary source of imagery for their poems. In addition, they often performed eulogies and elegies, celebrating their contemporaries. A prominent characteristic of the skalds' method was their use of *kennings*, or condensed metaphors, to describe their subjects.

Our primary source of information about Norse LEGENDS, however, comes from the *Poetic* or *Verse Edda* and the *Prose Edda* (*see* EDDAS, ELDER AND YOUNGER). The *Poetic Edda*

is a collection of poems from different poets, times, and places. Composed from about the tenth century onward, the *Poetic Edda* is of special importance because most of the poems were written before the end of the pagan period in Scandinavia.

The *Prose Edda* was written about 1200 by the Icelander Snorri Sturluson (1179–1241), poet, writer of SAGAS, chieftain, historian, and critic. From this work, we receive most of our knowledge about Norse mythology. The *Prose Edda* also might be considered a handbook for skalds as it contains a treatise on conventional vocabulary, phraseology, and figures of speech, including kennings, to be used in the creation of poems.

Sagas were a particularly popular form of storytelling in Iceland in a period beginning in the early part of the twelfth century. Sagas tell of the adventures of Icelandic settlers, Norwegian kings, and heathens.

A second group of northern European storytellers were the Anglo-Saxon *scops*, the English equivalent of the Norse skalds. Scops told cycles of tales, some of which in a static form have been rendered into what we know as the text of the EPIC BEOWULF, recorded in writing in about A.D. 1000. This poem, important for the information it contains about the way of life in pre-Christian northern Europe, also depended on the oral-formulaic technique.

In the eleventh and twelfth centuries, traveling minstrels, another representative group of northern European storytellers, spread tales, notably the Celtic legends of King ARTHUR, from Ireland and the west to England and the continent (*see* MINSTRELSY). These professional storytellers earned their living by traveling to various public and private forums (castles, fairs, markets) and entertaining their audiences with poetry, music, and tales of love and adventure. These oral traditions became an elaborate set of literary traditions in English, French, and other languages.

The Germanic storytelling tradition includes the heroic epic, the NIBELUNGENLIED. Written about A.D. 1200 for performance at court by professional storytellers, this work contains the familiar epic themes of love, war, revenge, and murder as well as the important figure SIEGFRIED. The legend of Siegfried the DRAGON-Slayer has a long, complex tradition, deriving from the early Germanic HERO, Sigurd the Dragon-Slayer. The legend of Sigurd spread to Scandinavia where he became the hero of the *Volsunga Saga* and other Norse tales.

Today, the best known German storytellers are perhaps the GRIMM BROTHERS. Jacob and Wilhelm Grimm published their volume of tales, *Kinder- und Hausmarchen*, in 1812. Many of the stories they collected for their first volume, including "RUMPELSTILZCHEN" and "Hansel and Gretel" came from Dorothea Wild, a Grimm family neighbor. Apparently, Dorothea's sisters, mother, and housekeeper were also sources for stories. Frau Katharina Dorothea Viehmann, who lived in a village close to the Grimms's, was the primary source for the second volume of tales (1815), narrating such stories as "The Master Huntsman" and "Faithful John." When Wilhelm Grimm died in 1859, he had been preparing an eighth edition of the tales for publication. At that time, he and Jacob had collected two hundred stories. Many of their most famous tales are concerned with wish-fulfillments and magic events; they contain themes and elements common to FOLKTALES from regions all across Europe as well as from around the world.

Hans Christian Andersen is another example of a relatively modern northern European storyteller who gained success by retelling traditional folktales and nursery stories (*see* ANDERSEN, HANS CHRISTIAN). Born in Odense, Denmark, in 1805, Andersen wrote his best-known works, including "The Ugly Duckling," "The Snow Queen," "The Little Match Girl," and "The Princess on the Pea," in the mid-nineteenth century. Andersen strove to present tales as though he were telling them to children; he was acutely aware of how they would sound when read aloud. Many of Andersen's stories focus on the home and its immediate, familiar environs. In his allegorical tales, he translates recognizable human types into ANIMALS, plants, or insects and describes the world from their points of view. The quest theme is prevalent in his work. In addition to composing fables ("The Snail and the Rosebush" and "The Butterfly") and retelling myths ("The Garden of Paradise"), Andersen wrote drama, short stories, lyrical sketches, and science fiction.

Finally, the Finnish national epic, the KALEVALA, offers an illuminating modern example of the oral-formulaic storytelling tradition. Until captured in written form by the Finnish doctor Elias Lönrott (1802–1884) in the 1820s, 1830s, and 1840s, this "epic" was a heterogeneous collection of disparate tales and traditions. The *Kalevala* as we know it is a static, cogent narrative. Although much more appealing to a modern, literate audience, the *Kalevala* would have been entirely alien to an earlier, oral storytelling culture.

NUMBERS

Symbolic amounts that recur throughout MYTH, LEGEND, and religious tales. Certain numbers have come to take on a symbolic or archetypal significance in oral tradition and the storytelling of different cultures. For example, while zero represents the COSMIC EGG and the number one stands for unity, the number two always stands for duality, as in the Chinese yin-yang.

The number three appears very often, whether in the three Magi (or wise men) and the Christian Holy Trinity or in FAIRY TALES and myths where one is chosen out of three: in the fairy tale "CINDERELLA," Cinderella is chosen over her two stepsisters; in the myth of CUPID AND PSYCHE, Psyche is more beautiful than her two sisters; in the Greek story of the Apple of Discord, Paris must choose the most beautiful of three GODDESSES; in Shakespeare's *King Lear*, Lear wants to choose the most loving of his three daughters; and in *The Merchant of Venice*, the choice of the correct one of three caskets is related to the winning the hand of a woman.

Besides the three Fates of Greek mythology, many of the GOD-like creatures born of GAIA and Uranos came in groups of three: the Furies, three avenging female deities whose job was to relentlessly pursue those guilty of shedding a relative's blood; the Greae, three

CRONES who shared one tooth and one eye; the CYCLOPES, three one-eyed, lawless giants and cannibal shepherds; the Gorgons, three serpent-haired females who turned those who looked upon them to stone; and the invincible Hecatoncheires, three male deities each with 50 heads and one hundred arms.

HEROES of fairy tales often must prove themselves by passing three tests or accomplishing three feats. The three stages of womanhood as personified by the MAIDEN, the MOTHER, and the crone—as in Persephone, Demeter, and HECATE (*see* PERSEPHONE MYTH)—and the three stages man as depicted in the answer to the riddle of the SPHINX also suggest the power of three. Similarly, Hindu deities occur in trinities as in BRAHMAN, SIVA, and VISNU.

The number four occurs frequently in Native American myths, where the FOUR DIRECTIONS play an important role. The four seasons, four winds, four rivers of PARADISE, four points of the cross, four quarters of the MOON, the four sides of a square, and the four elements of the West all suggest completion, wholeness, and order.

The number seven symbolizes the seven original planets. There are frequent references to the seven days of the week, and the seven seas.

The number 10, also associated with completion, occurs in all cultures based on the fact that humans have ten fingers and ten toes. The Ten Commandments of the Bible and the 10 divine manifestations of the *Cabala* correspond to 10 secret names for God.

The number 12 also occurs frequently and can be found in the 12 GODS of the Greek PANTHEON, the 12 signs of the Zodiac, the 12 tribes of Israel, and the 12 Apostles of Christ.

The number 40 is associated with fasting, tests and trials, and seclusion. The biblical FLOOD lasts for 40 days and 40 nights (*see* GENESIS, BOOK OF); Moses waits 40 days on Mount Sinai for the Ten Commandments; 40 years are spent in the desert before the Israelites can enter the PROMISED LAND (*see* EXODUS); after his baptism, Christ fasts for 40 days; the Greeks held their funeral banquets 40 days after a person's death.

The fascination with numbers can be attributed, therefore, to the almost endless opportunity for symbolism.

NURSERY RHYMES

Children's folk rhymes, including but not limited to the famous rhymes of MOTHER GOOSE. Although generally grouped together under the term "nursery rhymes," these jingles, which exist worldwide, cover a wide range of subjects. Most children hear their first nursery rhymes as infants, often accompanied by amusing actions such as clapping or tickling, such as in "Pat-a-Cake" or "This Little Pig Went to Market." As children grow older, they learn to accompany some rhymes like "Eensy Weensy Spider" with their own gestures and use rhymes to help learn NUMBERS and letters. Nursery rhymes are an integral part of childhood play, becoming more advanced as children age. Game rhymes accompany bouncing balls, are found in JUMP-ROPE SONGS, and other regular motions. Counting out rhymes such as "Eeny, Meeny, Miny, Mo" single out a child to be "it."

Nobody knows how many centuries nursery rhymes date back, or whether some rhymes have "hidden" meanings, whether political, religious, or sexual. We can never be sure whether "Mary, Mary, quite contrary" refers to Mary, Queen of Scots, or whether "Little Tom Tucker [who]/Sings for his supper" was an obscure attack on the selfish Cardinal Wolsey, as some have speculated. Certainly some rhymes seem more appropriate for adults than children. As early as the seventeenth century, people were protesting the bawdy references in certain nursery rhymes, and by the early twentieth century, efforts were well under way to purify the content of these rhymes. In 1952, Geoffrey Handley-Taylor of England pointed out that in an average volume of two hundred nursery rhymes, approximately one hundred rhymes contain "unsavoury" material for children, including murder, racial discrimination, cruelty to ANIMALS, lost children, and body snatching. Nonetheless, despite efforts to censor some of these references, nursery rhymes continue to be passed on to children in much the same form as they existed centuries ago.

NYMPHS

Minor female nature deities in Greek mythology. They are young and beautiful maidens who are usually friendly toward humankind. Nymphs are not immortal, but can live for several thousand years. They are often pursued by lustful SATYRS.

There are several categories of nymphs, corresponding to various facets of the natural world. The *oceanids* are sea nymphs, the daughters of the Titan Oceanus and his wife, Tephys. The most famous of these are Aphitrite, the wife of the SEA-GOD Poseidon, and the "gray-eyed" Doris.

Doris and her husband Nereus, the OLD MAN of the Sea, are the parents of fifty more sea nymphs known as the *nereids*. The most famous of these are Thetis, the mother of ACHILLES, and Galatea (not to be confused with the Galatea of the Pygmalion legend), who loathed but was loved by the CYCLOPES Polythemos.

The *dryads* or *hamadryads* are tree nymphs who perish when their trees die. The most famous of these is Eurydice, the wife of Orpheus (*see* ORPHEUS AND EURYDICE MYTH). The *oreads*—such as Echo—are nymphs of the mountains, and the *naiads* are nymphs of lakes, fountains, rivers, and streams.

Images of nymphs have turned up in the paintings of artists as varied as Cellini, Corot, and Picasso. They were especially popular during the nineteenth century Art Noveau period. *See also* ANCIENT GREEK STORYTELLING.

For Further Reading

Hamilton, Edith. *Mythology: Timeless Tales of Gods and Heroes.* New York: Mentor, 1969.

OCEAN OF STORY

Eleventh-century Indian EPIC, also translated as *Ocean of Stories,* by SOMADEVA. The *Ocean of Story* is a collection of tales, some of which antedate its composition. One of its cycles of stories, the *Vetalapanchavimshati,* or TWENTY-FIVE TALES OF A VETALA, contains "Tales of a DEMON," 24 RIDDLE stories used for Buddhist instruction.

In his recent novel *Haroun and the Sea of Stories* (1990), Salman Rushdie draws on the *Ocean of Stories* for his title, and his main characters are the storyteller Rashid Khalifa, called "the Ocean of Notions" by his admirers, and his only son Haroun.

For Further Reading

Ness, Caroline, et al. *The Ocean of Story: Fairytales from India.* New York: Lothrop, Lee & Shepherd, 1996.

Rushdie, Salman. *Haroun and the Sea of Stories.* London: Viking Penguin, 1990.

ODIN

One-eyed ruler and FATHER of GODS in the Norse PANTHEON, the Aesir. According to the Icelander Snorri Sturlson (1179–1241), who recorded much of the information we have about Odin in the *Younger* or *Prose Edda* (c. A.D. 1220), Odin is the highest and oldest of the Norse gods (*see* EDDAS, ELDER AND YOUNGER). Odin is known as *Wodan* or *Wotan* to Germanic peoples. "Wednesday" is contracted from *Wodan's Tag* (Wodan's Day).

Odin's father is Bor, and his mother is the giantess Bestla. With his two brothers, Odin creates the HEAVENS, the EARTH, the sky, and humans (*see* NORSE CREATION). Odin and his wife, Frigg, parented the race of gods called the *Aesir.*

Odin is a formidable, and perhaps terrifying deity whose warlike aspect is emphasized. One of his many nicknames is "god of Battle." He is also lord of VALHALLA, leader of the souls of the dead. He sits in a high seat in Asgard, the Norse MOUNT OLYMPOS, and surveys his worlds. Two ravens, Huginn (Thought) and Muninn (Memory) perch on his shoulders and whisper news of the kingdom in his ears. They are the source of much information. He also has two wolves named Geri and Freki. Gungnir, Odin's magic spear, is a symbol of his power. Once its thrusting motion begins, it never stops. Odin frequently travels through his kingdom in disguise, and he is a shape-changer.

Odin is often characterized by his relentless search for wisdom and knowledge. In order to discover the secret of runic wisdom, Odin crucifies himself on YGGDRASIL, the World Tree. According to the *Havamal*, a poem from the tenth century *Elder* or *Poetic Edda*, Odin hangs on Yggdrasil for nine nights. He is pierced with a spear, and no one offers him FOOD or drink. In the process of his suffering, Odin's wisdom increases. He eventually returns to life from this DEATH experience, which recalls both Jesus' crucifixion and the DYING GOD MOTIF.

Odin gives his eye to Mimir, guardian of the well of wisdom located under one of Yggdrasil's roots, as payment for a drink from the magic well. After that, Odin is able to foresee the world's doom in RAGNAROK.

In another story, Odin transforms himself into a GIANT and goes to Jotunheim, the home of the giants, in order to get the mead of poetry from the evil giant, Suttung. He coerces Baugi, Suttung's brother, to drill a hole through a mountain to the room where Suttung's daughter guards the mead. Odin changes into a snake and slithers through the hole. When he reaches Gunnlod, Suttung's daughter, he changes again, this time into a handsome giant. After seducing Gunnlod, Odin drinks all the mead. Then he changes into an eagle and flies to Asgard where he spits the mead into crocks. For gaining possession of the divine mead, one of Odin's many names is "God of Poetry." Odin will be finally killed by Fenrir, LOKI's evil wolf son, at the end of the world, Ragnarok.

For Further Reading

Branston, Brian. *Gods and Heroes from Viking Mythology.* New York: Schocken, 1982.

ODYSSEY

Greek EPIC poem of the ninth century B.C., attributed to HOMER. It began as an oral tale, recited by bards called *rhapsodoi*, before emerging in written form around 535 B.C. The poem, which relates the elaborate story of Odysseus as he attempts to return to his home in ITHACA after the end of the Trojan War, is over 12,000 lines long and is divided into 24 books. Drawing together a conglomeration of many ancient FOLKTALES from various traditions, the *Odyssey* is considered to be one of the most important epics in the history of Western literature.

Beginning in the middle of the story's action, as epics typically do, Homer starts his tale by revealing that Odysseus has been stranded on the island of Ogygia for seven years, a prisoner of the SEA NYMPH, Calypso, as punishment for offending Poseidon, the god of the sea (*see* CALYPSO'S ISLAND). Back in Ithaca, where Odysseus's wife, PENELOPE, and son, TELEMACHOS, have been waiting for 10 years for Odysseus to return from the Trojan War, many suitors are pressuring Penelope to accept a new husband. ATHENA appears to Telemachos, informs him that his father still lives, and encourages him to remove the suitors from the palace and to begin a QUEST to find Odysseus. The suitors refuse to leave, but are pleased to see Telemachos depart.

Meanwhile, ZEUS orders Calypso to release Odysseus; he leaves her island on a raft but is soon shipwrecked by Poseidon. He washes ashore on a Phaeacian island, where he is befriended by a PRINCESS and her family. They promise to help him return to Ithaca, and he tells them of his adventures leading up to that point.

After the Trojan War, Odysseus and his men had left Troy and sailed to Ismarus, the city of the Cicones, which they plundered. They next arrived in the land of the Lotus Eaters, where Odysseus's men ate some of the sweet lotus food which made them forget their homes and their past. Odysseus had to drag them forcefully away from this land. The next stop on their journey was at the land of the one-eyed monsters called CYCLOPES. Odysseus and a dozen of his men were captured by a Cyclops called Polyphemos, who began eating the men one by one. Odysseus tricked him by first intoxicating him with wine and then blinding his one eye with a sharp stick. As Odysseus sailed away from the enraged and wounded monster, he rashly revealed his identity to him. Polyphemos called upon his own father, Poseidon, to avenge him by thwarting Odysseus's journey home; this is the aforementioned offense for which Odysseus had been suffering these many years.

Odysseus and his remaining men next sailed to Aeolia, the island where dwelt Aeolus, god of the WINDS. Aeolus gave Odysseus a bag containing all the unfavorable winds; as long as they stayed tied up, all the good winds would be free to push him toward Ithaca. But the men, believing the bag to be full of treasure, untied it just as they were nearing Ithaca. These contrary winds blew the ship all the way back to Aeolia, where the angry Aeolus refused to help them any further. They sailed away to the land of the Laestrygonians, a race of GIANT cannibals, who plucked many of Odysseus's men from their ships and ate them. Odysseus's ship managed to escape; he and his crew sailed to Aeaea, the island home of the enchantress CIRCE. She transformed most of Odysseus's men into swine, but with the help of Hermes, Odysseus forced her to change them back into human form. Circe tells Odysseus that he must consult the blind prophet TIRESIAS in the Land of the Dead if he wishes to return safely to Ithaca. From Teiresias, Odysseus learns of Poseidon's grudge against him and also how he might reach his home.

Next, Odysseus and his men sailed passed the island of the SIRENS, enchantresses who lured sailors onto the rocky shore with their beautiful voices. Odysseus stopped his crew's ears with wax and had himself bound to the ship's mast to prevent them all from falling under the bewitching spell. They also sailed past Scylla, a six-headed monster, and Charybdis, a whirlpool-monster, but Scylla managed to swipe and devour six crew members. They landed next on Thrinacia, an island belonging to the SUN god, Hyperion. Against Odysseus's orders, some of the starving crew butchered and ate one of Hyperion's sacred cattle. Angered, Hyperion caused their ship to be wrecked in a storm; every man perished except for Odysseus, who was rescued by Calypso and then held prisoner by her for seven years. So ended Odysseus's account of his adventures to the Phaecians.

The generous Phaecians provide Odysseus with a ship laden with treasure to take him back to his homeland. He arrives safely on the shore of Ithaca, but Poseidon then turns his ship and all its contents into stone. Odysseus consults with Athena about how to avenge himself on the overbearing suitors to his wife; they decide that he should return to the palace disguised as a beggar. Athena arranges a meeting between Odysseus and Telemachos (whom the goddess fetched back to Ithaca). Odysseus reveals his identity to his son, and the two make plans to punish the suitors. They arrive at the palace shortly before a contest among the suitors intended to decide which of them might marry Penelope. The winner must string Odysseus's great bow and then shoot an arrow through 12 axes. None of the suitors even manage to string the bow, until the disguised Odysseus steps to the front. Amid scorn and derision, Odysseus strings the bow, shoots the arrow through the axes, and then shoots Antinous, a particularly arrogant suitor. Odysseus reveals his identity, and a raging battle ensues in which all the suitors are killed and 12 women servants who had sympathized with the suitors are hanged. A suspicious Penelope is finally convinced that this man is really her husband, returned to her after 20 years. They are joyfully reunited, Odysseus is reinstated as the KING of Ithaca, and through the intervention of Athena, peace settles over the kingdom.

Odysseus is often portrayed as the archetypal wise man. According to Greek myth, Odysseus was the son of Laertes, king of Ithaca, and Anticlea; he married Penelope and fathered Telemachos. He figures prominently in Homer's ILIAD, particularly in the ninth and tenth books, and is represented as resourceful, diplomatic, tactful, energetic, and at times cunning. In the *Odyssey*, Odysseus's primary characteristics are his deep desire to return to his home, his willingness to endure great suffering and face grave danger in order to reach it, and his strong sense of self-control that allows him to wait until just the right moment to exact revenge on Penelope's suitors. Homer depicts Odysseus as a great HERO; however, certain of the Attic tragedies portray him less favorably. For example, Euripides creates an Odysseus more ruthless and unscrupulous than Homer's in *Iphegenia in Aulis* and *Hecuba*. Later writers, though, reinvent Odysseus more positively, as in Shakespeare's *Troilus and Cressida* and Tennyson's *Ulysses*.

One of the best poetic translations of the *Odyssey* into English is Robert Fitzgerald's *The Odyssey of Homer* (1961); an important prose translation, written more colloquially and appropriate for younger readers, is E. V. Rieu's *Odyssey*. David H. Millstone's *An Elementary Odyssey: Teaching Ancient Civilization Through Story* (1995) offers an interesting explanation of how epics such as the *Odyssey* may be used in primary school classrooms. *See also* ILIAD.

For Further Reading

Fitzgerald, Robert, trans. *The Odyssey of Homer*. Garden City, NY: Anchor Press/Doubleday, 1961.

Rieu, E. V., trans. *The Odyssey*. Harmondsworth, Middlesex: Penguin, 1991.

OGETEMMELI

Dogon holy man who related story of Dogon belief to European scholar Marcel Griaule. Ogetemmeli was from Lower Ogol in Mali, West Africa. A hunter, he lost his sight when a gun exploded in his face. This accident led to Ogetemmeli's application of his keen intellect to understanding the natural world. In 1946 he told Griaule about his understanding of Dogon cosmology. This exchange was published as *Conversations with Ogetemmeli*. Griaule's description of his first encounter with Ogetemmeli includes references to the many deaths in the African man's family, saying, "All the tragedy of African mortality was in his words, and the deep questionings of these men about death and their defenselessness in the face of it." Griaule conversed with Ogetemmeli for 33 days to record the stories that represent Dogon cosmology (*see* DOGON CREATION).

OGRE

Common figure in African and European FOLKLORE. The ogre appears primarily in stories for children, but is not absent from adult tales. The ogre is a kind of mythical MONSTER, often closely associated with the DEVIL and the underworld. The term *ogre* appeared for the first time in print in the tales of Charles Perrault in 1697 (*see* PERRAULT, CHARLES). The GRIMM BROTHERS did not adopt the specific image of the ogre in their tales, but their portrayals of WITCHES, wolves, GIANTS, and devils echo the most common characteristic of the ogre: an enormous appetite, especially for the bodies of children. Ogres in folklore and FAIRY TALES are magical, monstrous creatures that often possess an acute sense of smell, imperfect eyesight, dull intellect, large teeth, and an insatiable hunger for raw prey (usually in the form of humans). These characteristics suggest that ogres are more like fierce ANIMALS than they are like humans, although their physical form is often approximately human. Ogres frequently live within deep forests, possess fantastic wealth, and own MAGIC OBJECTS that allow them, for example, to travel very quickly or to continually increase their riches. Many versions of common folktales include ogres or ogresses, including "The Three Billy Goats Gruff," "JACK AND THE BEANSTALK" and "PUSS IN BOOTS." The ogre's popularity in storytelling traditions seems to demonstrate a continued and widespread fascination with threatening, bloodthirsty monsters; however, in most tales the ogre is either vanquished by the HERO or is converted into the more positive role of rescuer or watchman. The MYTH of the ogre has enjoyed a recent revival in adult literature, as in Jacques Chessex's prize-winning novel *L'Ogre* (1973).

For Further Reading

de Paola, Tomie. *Favorite Nursery Tales*. New York: G.P. Putnam's Sons, 1986.

OLD MAN

Creator, HERO, or TRICKSTER figure of Native American myth. The figure of Old Man appears in the oral tradition of the Blackfoot, Arapaho, western Algonquian, Sioux, and Salish tribes. In some myths he is portrayed as a creator or personification of the GREAT SPIRIT, and in others he reveals more of his trickster-transformer roots. Among the Arapaho, he is depicted as "the hero of raft stories and diving animals."

In "The Blackfoot Genesis," the LEGEND that tells of the creation of the Blackfoot people, Old Man is the creator of the birds, the ANIMALS, and the people, all of whom can understand him when he speaks to them. He also makes the rocks and the rivers, the mountains and the grass, the fruit and the vegetables. This MYTH depicts the ORIGIN OF DEATH as well, for Old Man and the woman he has created use a stone thrown in the river to decide whether people will die and come alive again in four days, will live forever, or will die. When the stone the woman throws sinks in the river, it means that there will be DEATH. Old Man is the teacher of the first people, showing them how to find FOOD and make clothing, how to make bows and arrows to kill the buffalo, how to cook the meat of the buffalo, and how to know the power of their DREAMS. As Old Man travels through the land, he creates more and more people until finally he rests.

In another legend with Old Man depicted as a creator, Old Man focuses on how to make women and men mate. Men and women live apart, and little by little, the men come to want what the women have to offer and vice versa, but until each group bathes and makes itself attractive, neither one wants the other. Finally, the women approach the men, the men are smitten, and Old Man is drawn to the chief of the women, and they try sexual intercourse for the first time and decide it is very pleasurable. When they go to tell the people of their discovery, they find that all the men and women have already paired off, and thus love, MARRIAGE, and procreation are begun.

Portrayed as more of a trickster figure in the legend "The Theft from the SUN," here Old Man pays a visit to the lodge of the sun. Sun invites Old Man to go deer hunting, for they are running out of meat. Sun dons a beautiful pair of magical leggings, which sets the brush on fire and drives out the deer, and Old Man covets the Sun's leggings. That night, when the Sun is sleeping, Old Man steals the leggings and leaves. After traveling for a long time, he lies down to sleep using the leggings for a pillow, but when he awakens, he finds himself back in Sun's lodge. When Old Man tries this the second night, he again finds himself back in Sun's lodge, and it is then that he realizes that the whole world is the Sun's lodge. Sun then decides to make Old Man a gift of his leggings, but when Old Man wears them to hunt, the brush that catches fire also ignites the leggings, causing them to burn and sending Old Man into a river to extinguish the flames. The legend suggests that this is Old Man's PUNISHMENT for attempting to steal the leggings of the sun and is related to the theme of theft of fire and the Greek myth of Phaeton, the sun's son, who is not strong enough to guide properly his father's chariot of the sun (*see* PROMETHEUS AND THE THEFT OF FIRE).

For Further Reading

Erdoes, Richard, and Alfonso Ortiz. *American Indian Myths and Legends*. New York: Pantheon, 1985.

Feldmann, Susan, ed. *The Storytelling Stone*. New York: Bantam, 1965.

OLD SOUTH STORYTELLING

Oral tradition from a region with a rich storytelling culture. Although the region of the Old South of the United States was far from homogenous, encompassing slaves, both African- and American-born, as well as masters and laborers with European roots, the region produced a storytelling tradition that is distinct from other regions of the country.

Popularized by the writings of Georgian journalist Joel Chandler Harris (*see* HARRIS, JOEL CHANDLER), the Brer Rabbit, Brer Fox, and Brer Alligator tales have achieved the widest recognition of stories of the Old South; indeed, to many they serve as a full representation of the tales of this region. These tales, which Harris had heard and been fascinated by as a child, had their roots in old-world TRICKSTER tales. Retold frequently by African Americans during slavery and after, these ANIMAL FABLES suggest that an individual in a position of little or no power can achieve small triumphs over the powerful through verbal tricks and general cunning. Harris' written versions of these stories employs a dialect for the UNCLE REMUS, the African American narrator of these tales, in an attempt to capture some of the oral flavor of the tales.

Another type of tale common in the Old South was the mountain JACK TALES. Like the tales popularized by Harris, these can also be traced to the Old World, where the main character is known as "Hans" in Germany, "Jake" in Scotland, and "Jack" in England. These tales focus on a young trickster HERO who leaves home or escapes mistreatment and finally succeeds. In the Old South, the tales became most commonly told in the Appalachian region, centered in Kentucky, Virginia, and North Carolina. The Old South version of the "Jack" stories depicts the hero as more cunning, self-reliant, and amoral than versions of other countries, reflecting the hardedged vision of the folk people of the region. The stories were popularized in America by Richard Chase in the 1930's with his publications of *The Jack Tales* (1943) and *The Grandfather Tales* (1948) (*see* CHASE, RICHARD).

OLD WIVES' TALES

Derogatory term for gems of information long handed down orally, especially concerning herbal medicines and healing techniques. The concept is English and European in origin. A related expression is "old wives' FABLE," implying a trivial story.

The term "old wife" was not originally derogatory and the lore once contained the most valuable treatments available for injury and illness. With the advent of more scientific medicine, home remedies often were disregarded. However in some cases—the most famous being the use of foxglove (containing digitalis) for heart disease—the old wives' tales actually led scientists to a modern-day cure.

Another reason that old wives' tales fell into disrepute was the inclusion of pagan charms and incantations that became identified with WITCHES. In turn, the notion of witchcraft was kept alive by the repetition of a stock of old wives' stories about village SCAPEGOATS.

A similar oral tradition among sailors is sometimes categorized as "old salt's yarns." However, the practitioners of shipboard superstitions and cures were generally not demonized in the way that their village counterparts sometimes were.

For Further Reading

Chamberlain, Mary. *Old Wives' Tales*. London: Virago, 1981.

Maple, Eric. *Old Wives' Tales*. London: R. Hale, 1981.

OLD WOMEN *See* CRONE

OLLANTAY AND CUSICOLLUR

Inca love story. Since the main characters of this story actually lived in the twelfth or thirteenth century A.D., it is equally possible that the story of Ollantay and Cusicollur really took place. Like Shakespeare's *Romeo and Juliet*, Ollantay and Cusicollur love each other but are not permitted to marry. Because Ollantay, a brave warrior, is a commoner, it is against the law for him to marry Cusicollur, the daughter of the Inca, or emperor. Although they beseech a kind old priest to marry them, he sadly refuses. Nevertheless, Cusicollur becomes pregnant and is sent by her father to the priestesses at the temple of the SUN, where she gives birth to a daughter, Yma Sumac, who is taken from her to be cared for in another section of the temple. Meanwhile, the Inca declares that Ollantay must die, and eventually Ollantay is captured.

On the way to the center of the empire, where he is to be executed, Ollantay learns that the old Inca has died and that his son, the brother of Cusicollur, is to become the next Inca. This brother, Tupac Yupanqui, has also been Ollantay's childhood friend, and Ollantay hopes that his old friend will save his life. When Ollantay arrives at Cuzco and meets with Tupac Yupanqui, his friend is immensely sympathetic but feels he cannot revoke his father's orders. Ollantay explains that he is not a traitor to the Inca or the empire, but that the law itself is "a traitor to love." Ollantay convinces his old friend that the GODS themselves choose who loves whom, and therefore he and Cusicollur should marry. Because he is a compassionate and wise ruler, Tupac Yupanqui saves Ollantay's life, permitting him to marry Cusicollur and bring their daughter to live with them, and from that time on Ollantay serves as chief general and adviser to his brother-in-law, the great Inca Tupac Yupanqui.

So popular was this love story that it inspired a famous sixteenth-century Peruvian play that is performed to this day.

For Further Reading

Gifford, Douglas. *Warriors, Gods & Spirits from Central and South American Mythology.* Illustrated by John Sibbick. New York: Schocken, 1983.

OLODE THE HUNTER BECOMES AN OBA

African story from Nigeria about a poor hunter who becomes a KING and then loses his good fortune. At the beginning of this story, Olode (meaning "hunter") is a very poor man. He lives in a hut on the edge of the village, and his only possessions are his gun and his loincloth. He has no relatives. One day, when Olode is hunting, he goes deeper into the forest than he has ever been before. He sits down to rest and closes his eyes for a minute. When he opens them, he sees a fierce, manlike creature in front of him. The creature is Oluigbo, King of the Bush. Olode explains his miserable plight to Oluigbo. The King of the Bush instructs Olode to follow him, and he leads the hunter to a great tree. Oluigbo tells Olode to throw down his gun and his loincloth, and then he strikes the tree with his hand. A door opens, and Olode enters. Olode finds himself at the gate of a town where people are waiting for him. They welcome him and bring clothing for his naked body. They place him in a carrying chair and carry him into town, shielding his body from the sun with a red parasol. Olode is the *Oba*, or king, for whom the people have been waiting. The elders give Olode his instructions as their new Oba. They forbid him to enter the room behind the carved door in the third house. For a while, Olode is a good king. Then he remembers what it was like when he could not even buy palm wine. He orders palm wine and drinks all of it. Then he calls for more. Olode forgets about being king, and he continues to drink. One day he enters the third house and decides to open the carved door. When he crosses the threshold, the door closes. Olode finds himself back in the forest. He is naked, and his gun and ragged loincloth are at his feet. Olode the hunter found good fortune and lost it.

This story is an example of a MORALITY TALE that illustrates the evils of drinking and of forgetting one's responsibilities. In spite of his rise to riches, a title, and fame, Olode's irresponsibility and drunkenness results in his return to poverty. The Russian folktale "How Much Land Does a Man Need?" is another example of a morality tale from a different culture that also contains the theme of the rise to riches and subsequent loss of fortune (*see* TOLSTOY'S FAIRY TALES AND PARABLES). In this story, the peasant Pahóm loses his considerable fortune and his life in an attempt to acquire as much land as possible. Just as Olode's love of palm wine results in his loss of everything, Pahóm's vice of greed is the cause of his downfall. The Ghanese tale OSEBO'S DRUM is yet another morality tale. The leopard Osebo is excessively proud of his drum, and because of his tremendous pride, he eventually loses the drum to the Sky-God.

Many stories from various traditions include the creative TRICKSTER figure, for example COYOTE, TAR BABY, and Brer Rabbit, whose antics, like the actions of Olode, Pahóm, and Osebo, often illustrate human failings: ego, lack of responsibility, vanity, pride, and so on (*see also* LOKI). Likewise, AESOP tells many FABLES in which ANIMAL characters are thwarted by their own weaknesses. A more humorous account of the evils of drinking appears in Jean de la Fontaine's fable "The Drunkard and His Wife" (*see* LA FONTAINE, JEAN DE).

The story *Olode the Hunter Becomes an Oba* also contains the common theme of disobeying a strict command and suffering the consequence. In numerous tales from a variety of traditions, characters often are given explicit instructions that they ignore, resulting in loss, banishment, or even DEATH. ADAM AND EVE eat from the forbidden tree of the knowledge of good and evil and are banished from Eden for eternity. Similarly, Thakane from the Basuto tale CHILD IN THE REEDS eats from the forbidden kumonngoe tree and is cast off by her father, who takes her to be eaten by an OGRE. In Greek tradition, Orpheus looks back as he leads Eurydice out of HADES and loses her forever (*see* ORPHEUS AND EURYDICE MYTH). Likewise, Lot's wife looks back on the burning city of Sodom, and she turns into a pillar of salt (*see* GENESIS, BOOK OF). In the Kenyan tale MURILÉ AND THE MOONCHIEF, Murilé's parents kill the sacred bull, and Murilé is swallowed up by the EARTH.

For Further Reading

Courlander, Harold, and Ezekiel A. Eshugayi, retold by. "Olode the Hunter Becomes an Oba." *African American Literature: Voices in a Tradition.* Austin, TX: Holt, Rinehart & Winston, 1992.

OPIE, PETER (1918–1982) AND IONA (1923–)

Important folklorists and archivists. Both Peter and Iona Opie are considered specialists in the literature and tradition of childhood FOLKLORE. Born in Cairo, Egypt, Peter Opie was an avid folklorist who served as president of the Folklore Society. He and his wife, Iona, who was born in England, became the authors of numerous books on childhood and folklore, and their collection *The Classic Fairy Tales* not only includes some of the most important Western FAIRY TALES but gives a well-researched introduction to and history and examination of each. Their publications include the *Oxford Dictionary of Nursery Rhymes, The Oxford Nursery Rhyme Book, Children's Games in Street and Playground, The Oxford Book of Children's Verse,* and *Lore and Language of Schoolchildren.*

For Further Reading

Opie, Peter, and Iona Opie. *The Classic Fairy Tales.* New York: Oxford, 1980.

———. *Tale Feathers from Mother Goose.* Illustrated. Boston: Little, Brown, 1988.

ORIGIN OF CORN

As explained in stories, the source and use of the staple FOOD of many North, Central, and South American Indians. Archeological evidence suggests that corn was cultivated as a food source for the natives of North and South America as early as 6000 B.C. As these cultures moved from hunting to agriculture for subsistence, the increasing dependence upon corn made it an object of veneration. Stories were composed to explain its role as a sacred gift of divine origin. In North America, as agriculture replaced hunting as the primary means of survival, stories indicated a shifting cultural emphasis.

Although the personified source of corn could be either male or female, it was frequently the product of a CORN MOTHER. In a story from the Penobscots of the northeastern United States, a young MAIDEN becomes a figure of the EARTH-MOTHER as well as the DYING GOD. The young maiden is born from a drop of dew and marries a youth who was conceived from the foam of the ocean. They live off the game of the land and are prosperous until the increase in population makes food scarce. The Corn Mother weeps at the people's misfortune and tells them that she can only be comforted in death. She explains that, in order to save the people, she must be killed and dragged across the face of the EARTH. Eventually, her people comply, and after several months pass, the earth sprouts with corn, saving the people from starvation. At the place where Corn Mother's bones are buried, tobacco grows, and the people realize that the corn was her body and the tobacco was her spirit.

The story's apparent CANNIBALISM teaches two important facts about Native Americans and the Corn Mother: she gives of herself in the cycle of death and rebirth of seasons; and the nature of life, as the consumption of other life, must be understood and embraced. All life enters into a sort of contract of renewal, and veneration for the divine origin of that contract is a principal facet in stories of corn's emergence.

For Further Reading

Erdoes, Richard, and Alfonso Ortiz. *American Indian Myths and Legends.* New York: Pantheon, 1985.

Fussell, Betty. *The Story of Corn.* New York: Knopf, 1992.

ORIGIN OF DEATH

In MYTHS and LEGENDS, an explanation of how DEATH entered into being. Stories concerning the origin of death begin with the premise that death did not always exist. Just as the world, the EARTH, the SUN, MOON, and stars, plants, ANIMALS, and human beings had to be created out of the void, as depicted in the various CREATION myths, so too did death need to be "created." Many of these stories suggest that death came to be because of some human trespass or "fall" from grace. That death did not always exist suggests a belief system that sees human beings as formerly immortal or more connected to the GODS and therefore seeks to explain how this split between immortality and mortality occurred.

For the ancient Hebrews, the creation of ADAM AND EVE in the Book of Genesis (see GENESIS, BOOK OF) soon leads to their fall from grace and their expulsion from the PARADISE of the Garden of Eden. Because Eve then Adam eat of the fruit of the Tree of Knowledge of Good and Evil expressly disobeying GOD's orders, they are punished by the kinds of labors they would each have to suffer, ending ultimately in death.

In the Dogon story, "The First Mask," at first there was no death; aged people became serpents and were not supposed to utter human speech again. For the Dogon, when the soul went to rest in the mask, death entered the world.

Other stories that tell of the origin of death include the Native American Caddo tale, "COYOTE and the Origin of Death," and the Blackfoot tale "Woman Chooses Death." In the Caddo version, coyote is the only one who believes death should last forever when overpopulation is a threat, so when the whirlwind comes to return the spirits of the dead to a large grass house so they can live again, Coyote shuts the door and death becomes eternal. The Blackfoot tale tells of the time when OLD MAN created the first woman and child, and when the woman asks if they would live forever, Old Man tells her to throw a buffalo chip into the water, saying that if it floats, people will die and come back four days later. However, the woman suggests she throw a stone for fear the chip will dissolve too quickly. When the stone of course sinks, Old Man tells her that she had made the choice, and people will henceforth die.

In Japanese mythology, death comes to the world after the gods Izanagi and Izanami marry and bring the natural world into creation (see JAPANESE CREATION MYTH). When Izanami dies of a terrible fever and goes to Yomi, the land of the dead, her husband Izanagi pursues her there; because she has already eaten the food of Yomi, however, she cannot return from the land of death and Izanagi flees in horror at what he sees there. Izanami then pursues him in return, and Izanagi places a boulder between Yomi and the land of the living, with husband and wife on either side. Izanami then threatens to strangle 1,000 people each day if Izanagi continues to flee, and Izanagi in return threatens to build 1,500 birthing huts each day, to signify that many births. Thus the "divorce" of the two gods brings death to mortals.

The Genesis, Blackfoot, and Japanese origin of death tales all place women as the cause of death, and this idea is connected to the image of woman as both creator and destroyer, the one who gives life and takes it away. The Hindu GODDESS KALI and the ancient Greek "Three Fates," who were women, also embody this belief. *See also* MASKS AND MASQUERADE, MIDRASHIM.

For Further Reading

Erdoes, Richard, and Alfonso Ortiz. *American Indian Myths and Legends*. New York: Pantheon, 1985.
Whittaker, Clio. *An Introduction to Oriental Mythlogy*. New Jersey: Chartwell Books, 1989.

ORIGIN OF THE SEASONS

In MYTHS and LEGENDS, an explanation of how seasons came to be. Just as different cultures have CREATION myths, so they have stories to explain how certain aspects of nature first occurred. The mystery of the changing seasons has fascinated different peoples, especially those of lands where the TRANSFORMATION is most pronounced. Like the phases of the MOON, the changing seasons are linked with the growth cycle of plants; youth, ripeness, old age, and DEATH; and the MOTIF of death and RESURRECTION found in many religions.

The Native American Tahltan myth, "Determination of the Seasons," tells of the quarrel between Porcupine and Beaver over the appropriate number of winter months: Porcupine wants five, the same amount as he has claws, while Beaver wants the same amount as the scratches on his tail. Porcupine gets so angry that he bites off his thumb, frightening Beaver into settling on a four-month winter, for from that moment on, Porcupine has only four claws on each foot.

For the ancient Greeks, the Homeric *Hymn* of Demeter, which recounts the story of Demeter and Persephone, not only focuses on the relationship between the mother and daughter and the cycle of the daughter becoming the mother, but also offers an explanation for the origin of the seasons (*see* PERSEPHONE MYTH). That Demeter is the GODDESS of the corn and grain is significant, for when she finally finds Persephone and arranges for her return, Persephone will be allowed to emerge from the underworld, where she has been abducted by HADES, for two thirds of the year—spring and summer when the plants emerge, grow, and ripen—and must return to her husband Hades when the plants die back to the EARTH and winter covers the land. Though her return to the underworld is ostensibly the result of her having eaten a pomegranate seed while she was held there, the myth's connection with cycle of growth and harvest produced by the seasons suggests Persephone's profound link with early rites practiced to encourage a healthy harvest. Moreover, in the Eleusinian Mysteries, ancient rites practiced largely by women enacting this myth, when Persephone emerges from the underworld, she is holding an ear of grain.

Similarly, in the Native American BEAR MAN MYTH, the hunter stays with the bear in a cave all winter, and the bear provides him with food such as nuts. In the spring they emerge, and the bear knows he will be killed by other human hunters who will come to seek him, but he tells the hunter to look and see what happens after the hunters leave. The bear's res-urrection suggests a link with the seasons and the coming of spring, REBIRTH, and renewal.

The fact that the resurrection of Jesus Christ at Easter happens to coincide with the beginning of spring suggests links with ancient beliefs about the origin of the seasons.

For Further Reading

A Children's Treasury of Mythology. Illustrated by Margaret Evans Price. New York: Barnes and Noble, 1994.

Evetts-Secker, Josephine. *Mother and Daughter Tales*. Illustrated by Helen Cann. New York: Abbeville Press, 1996.

ORLANDO

Charlemagne's nephew and one of his Paladins, also called ROLAND. In the French *Chanson de Roland*, from the mid-eleventh century, Roland is depicted as the devoted and courageous knight who will sacrifice himself for his KING. In a great battle against the Saracens, Roland dies when he sounds his horn when he can no longer save his men. Other tales about Roland appear in the *chansons de geste* of the time. By the fifteenth century, Roland became known as Orlando among the Italian minstrels, and stories about his loves and his adventures can be found in Boiardo's *Orlando Immarato* (1487) and Ariosto's *Orlando Furioso* (1532). *See also* SONG OF ROLAND.

For Further Reading

Bulfinch, Thomas. *Legends of Charlemagne*. Illustrated by N.C. Wyeth. New York: David McKay, 1924.

Burgess, Glyn S., trans. *The Song of Roland*. New York: Viking Penguin, 1990.

Collier, Virginia, and Eaton, Jeanette. *Roland the Warrior*. Illustrated by F.E. Schoonover. New York: Harcourt Brace, 1934.

ORPHEUS AND EURYDICE MYTH

Ancient Greek and Roman MYTH of doomed love which, like the Mesopotamian QUEST of GILGAMESH, represents the human wish for immortality. Orpheus, whose mother had been one of the muses, was distinguished among mortals for his gift of music. Growing up in the musical city of Thrace, Orpheus was able to inspire animals, rocks, and rivers with his remarkable talent. Sailing with Jason and the Argonauts, Orpheus's music saved the heroes a number of times. If they were tired, quarrelsome, or tempted by the songs of the SIRENS, Orpheus's music would soothingly return them to their heroic mission.

Orpheus's musical talent was probably responsible for his winning the love of Eurydice. The two are married, with Hymen, the god of MARRIAGE, attending the wedding. Yet the god's attendance is not accompanied by the hoped-for luck. As Eurydice walks with her bridesmaids after the wedding, she is bitten on the ankle by a serpent and dies. Orpheus, inconsolable at the loss of his bride, determines to go to the underworld himself and win her back.

Orpheus crosses the river Styx, passes the shades of the dead, and seeks out HADES, lord of the underworld, and his bride Persephone, hoping to charm them with his song and win their sympathy. Accompanied by his lyre, Orpheus begins to sing. He sings of his grief and his unsuccessful struggle to overcome it, he sings of Hades's famous love for his own bride, and he sings of their eventual and inevitable return to the underworld for eternity.

No one who hears his song is unmoved; ghosts, FURIES, and even Hades and Persephone weep at his words. Unable to refuse his request, they summon Eurydice and give her back to her husband on one condition: Orpheus must not look back at her as he leads her out of the underworld. The pair set out on their return to earth, a long, gloomy, and arduous journey. Toward the end, just as the darkness of Hades gives way to the light of earth, Orpheus turns to his bride in joy. As he does so, she slips back to the world of the dead with a faint "Farewell."

All of Orpheus's effort to retrieve Eurydice again are fruitless. He grieves passionately, and for the rest of his life, avoids the company of women. He wanders through Thrace, playing melancholy tunes, comforted only by the trees. One day, a group of *maenads* kill and violently dismember him. His head is buried on the island of Lesbos, and his limbs on the foot of MOUNT OLYMPOS, where the nightingales sing most sweetly.

Orpheus's quest to retrieve his bride, his journey into the underworld to confront mortality, and his eventual dismemberment and "planting" into the earth are part of the mythic cycle of death and renewal found in many FOLKTALE themes. Most famously told by the Roman poet Ovid in *Metamorphoses,* the myth has captivated the attention of artists and writers for thousands of years. Artistic renderings and retellings of the tale include the medieval narrative poem, "Sir Orfeo," *Orpheus and Eurydice,* the famous painting by the Victorian artist George Frederic Watts, and "Eurydice," a poem by the modern American poet H.D. (Hilda Doolittle).

A related tale is the biblical story of Lot's wife, who was turned to a pillar of salt when she looked back at the doomed city of Sodom after being admonished not (Genesis 19:26). *See also* GENESIS, BOOK OF.

For Further Reading

Hieatt, Constance B. *The Minstrel Knight.* Illustrated by James Barkley. New York: Crowell, 1974.

Nye, Robert. *Out of This World and Back Again.* Illustrated by Bill Tinker. Indianapolis, IN: Bobbs-Merrill, 1977.

ORTIZ, ALFONSO (1939–)

Native American author and compiler. Alfonso Ortiz was born in the San Juan Pueblo of New Mexico and educated at the University of New Mexico and the University of Chicago, where he received a doctorate in anthropology. Active in Native American rights, Ortiz is the author of *The Tewa World* (1969) and *New Perspective on the Pueblos.* He is the coeditor with Richard Erdoes of the important collection, *American Indian Myths and Legends* (1984), which has become one of the standards in the field of recording the most important legends of the Native American oral storytelling tradition (*see also* ERDOES, RICHARD).

For Further Reading

Erdoes, Richard, and Alfonso, Ortiz. *American Indian Myths and Legends.* New York: Pantheon, 1985.

Ortiz, Alfonso. *The Tewa World: Space, Time, Being, and Becoming in a Pueblo Society.* Chicago: University of Chicago Press, 1969.

OSEBO'S DRUM

Tale from Ghana explaining how the leopard got its spots and how the turtle got its shell. In this story, Osebo, the powerful leopard, has a great drum that is admired by all the ANIMALS and GODS. When Nyame the sky god's mother dies, Nyame decides to get the drum for the funeral. He calls together all the earth animals, except for Osebo, and asks who will get the drum for him. Many strong animals attempt to get the drum, but Osebo drives them all away. Then the turtle, who at that time has a soft back, says he will get the drum. Everyone laughs because the turtle is small and weak. After the turtle arrives at Osebo's home, he tells the leopard that Nyame has built a drum that is so large that he can enter into it and be completely hidden. The turtle tells Osebo that Nyame's drum is greater than his. Osebo does not believe that there is any drum greater than his own, and he crawls into his drum to prove his point. When Osebo pulls the tip of his tail into the drum, the turtle plugs the opening with a cooking pot. Because of the turtle's cunning, he can be considered a TRICKSTER figure.

In spite of the leopard's cries, the turtle slowly drags the drum to Nyame. When the turtle finally removes the pot from the drum's opening, Osebo comes out backwards and falls into the Sky God's fire. His hide gets burned in many little places, and that is why leopards have dark spots. As a reward for getting the drum for his mother's funeral, Nyame gives the turtle a hard shell to wear on his back.

Osebo's Drum is an example of an explanatory tale because it provides an explanation for natural occurrences. Other explanatory tales include the Australian story "BLANKET LIZARD," explaining why this lizard is reddish in color and has a frill around its neck.

Rudyard Kipling's JUST SO STORIES (*see* KIPLING, RUDYARD) contains several explanatory tales, including another version of how the leopard got its spots.

Osebo's Drum is also an example of a moralistic tale. Osebo is excessively proud of his drum and, because of his tremendous pride, he eventually loses the drum to the sky god. The Nigerian story OLODE THE HUNTER BECOMES AN OBA is another moralistic tale, illustrating the evils of drinking and of forgetting one's responsibilities. The Kenyan tale MURILÉ AND THE MOONCHIEF describes what happens when Murilé's parents break an important promise that they have made to their son. In addition, AESOP tells many FABLES in which animal characters are thwarted by their own weaknesses, such as vanity or pride.

For Further Reading

Berry, Jack. *West African Folktales.* Evanston, IL: Northwestern University Press, 1991.

O'SULLIVAN, SEAN (1903–)

Collector of FOLKTALES and archivist of the Irish Folklore Commission. O'Sullivan was born in County Kerry and began his career as a school teacher. Since joining the Irish Folklore Commission in 1935, O'Sullivan has been a pivotal force in the preservation of ancient Irish stories, transcribing them from a waning oral tradition. His books include *A Handbook of Irish Folklore* (1942), *Types of the Irish Folktale* (1963), and *Irish Wake Amusements* (1967). In the latter part of his career, O'Sullivan turned his attention from folktales to LEGENDS. In *Legends from Ireland* (1977), he argues for the preservation of Irish legends. Since the legend "thrives best where social change comes slowly. . . and is kept alive by constant repetition," the threat from the modern world is evident.

OUR LADY'S TUMBLER

Medieval French miracle tale. In this story, a minstrel who has tired of his wandering and worldly life joins a monastery. However, as his only skills are tumbling and dancing, he fears that he has no way to serve GOD or the Virgin MARY. Watching the other monks and priests fulfill their duties, his despair grows. After fervently praying to the Virgin for guidance, he decides to display his skills in front of her altar. Deep in a crypt, he somersaults and dances naked for the Virgin every day. The abbot and another monk, curious about the tumbler's activities, follow and observe his performance. They watch him dance until he falls down exhausted. At that moment, the Virgin and attendant angels descend to comfort the tumbler.

This story has been connected to the medieval chivalric tradition. The story demonstrates the humanity of the Virgin, a common theme of many such tales. Different towns and cities will claim these stories as true events that occurred in their churches; however, VARIANTS of the same tales spring up in different places, and, ultimately, the origins of the LEGENDS are lost. Some have also argued that miracle stories are transmutations of Eastern tales, perhaps brought to Europe by the Crusaders.

For Further Reading

Kemp-Welch, Alice, trans. *Of the Tumbler of Our Lady and Other Miracles*. New York: Cooper Square Publishers, 1966.

OUTCAST CHILD *See* ABANDONED CHILDREN

OYA

Black GODDESS of the EARTH from the Nigerian Yoruba culture (*see* YORUBA CREATION). Oya, meaning "she tore," takes a variety of forms. She can be a mountain, a river, an earthquake, or an ANIMAL. Oya also can be evident in various aspects of human behav-

ior. She gives individuals the ability to use the spoken word as a weapon. Like many goddesses, including the Indian goddess KALI and the Polynesian goddess PELE, Oya is both constructive and destructive. In her good aspect, Oya is the goddess of water and fertility, the bringer of justice, the truth who opposes the wicked. In her terrifying aspect, she is the whirlwind, the fire, and the flood. She is the instrument of DEATH as she carries the dead on her back.

Oya is the chief wife of the Yoruba god, Schango, a lover of war who conquers his foes with a magic thunderbolt. Oya steals the secret of Schango's magic from him, and so she shares Schango's power and personifies violent rainstorms. When Schango becomes tired of life, he goes into the forest to hang himself. His body is never found. After Schango's disappearance, Oya turns into the river Niger and becomes known as the mother goddess of the Niger.

The patroness of childbirth, Oya is the mother of children as well as the mother of corpses. She is particularly associated with female strength and with feminine leadership.

For Further Reading

Gleason, Judith Illsley. *Orisha, the Gods of Yorubaland*. Illustrated by Aduni Olorisa. New York: Atheneum, 1971.

PAINTING

Visual form of storytelling. The prehistoric cave and rock paintings found in France and Australia, as well as other locations, suggest the need to tell stories of animal hunts, shamanistic visions, aboriginal RAINBOW SERPENTS, and aspects of early ceremony and RITUAL. Just as human beings have had the need to relate the stories of their GODS, tribes, and HEROES verbally, they have also needed painting to help them remember and visualize their physical and spiritual experiences. Sand painting plays an important role in various Native American ceremonies.

Face painting may be part of the costumes or DISGUISES of the CLOWNS of different Native North American tribes, and the painting of masks is common in cultures everywhere (*see* MASKS AND MASQUERADE). Face painting as a form of concealing one's identity occurs in FAIRY TALES such as the GRIMM BROTHERS'S "Snow White," where Snow White's wicked stepmother paints her face in order to transform herself into an old peddler woman or peasant, thereby tricking Snow White into buying her wares or tasting her apple (*see* STEPMOTHER—WICKED).

For Further Reading

Halifax, Joan. *Shaman: The Wounded Healer*. London: Thames and Hudson, 1982.
———. *Shamanic Voices*. New York: Dutton, 1979.

PALEY, VIVIAN (1929–)

Writer, educator, and astute observer of childhood development and storytelling. Paley's works examine childhood perceptions of the world, as seen through story. As Courtney Cazden notes in the forward to *Wally's Stories* (1981), Paley teaches us to "explore the ideas that flow from the children's own premises." In children's perceptions and constructions of stories, she finds a thriving world of imaginative coping strategies. Paley's writing also reflects her own love of the story as she weaves together fields of education and psychology within her descriptions of childhood imagination. In *The Boy Who Would Be a Helicopter*, Paley says that a "day without storytelling is, for [her], a disconnected day." Paley's work is important for its examination of storytelling as an act of cognition. Children's stories reveal not only the manner in which children construct the reality of the story but the way in which these stories inform and shape life.

For Further Reading

Paley, Vivian. *Bad Guys Don't Have Birthdays.* Chicago: University of Chicago Press, 1988.

———. *Boys and Girls: Superheroes in the Doll Corner.* Chicago: University of Chicago Press, 1984.

PANCHATANTRA

Hindu collection of FABLES and tales, composed between 200 B.C. and A.D. 1199. In his translation of *The Panchatantra*, Arthus W. Ryder notes that not only does the collection contain "the most widely known stories in the world," but they are also, to his mind, "the best collection of stories in the world." Historically, some of the fables were written around 200 B.C., but the complete version and standard text dates from A.D. 1199; by the seventeenth century it had been translated into the major European languages.

The Panchatantra is divided into five books, ostensibly composed by a BRAHMAN priest, Vishnusharman, who is asked by the KING, called "Immortal Power," to educate his three "blockhead" sons, called "Rich Power," "Fierce Power," and "Endless Power," and ready them for their future duties. Vishnusharman promises the king that in six months his sons will be wise and intelligent. His method of teaching them is to have them learn "by heart" the five books of fables that he has written: *The Loss of a Friend, The Winning of Friends, Crows and Owls, Loss of Gains,* and *Ill-Considered Action.* The main characters in many of the tales are the typical animals of FOLKLORE, and they behave in keeping with the stereotypes that prevail in the oral tradition and storytelling, as in the case of the lion who is strong but lacking in intelligence.

More than 30 fables can be found in *The Loss of a Friend,* and they are told by Rusty and Cheek, two jackals. The book centers on the jackal Rusty, a lion, and Lively, a bull, whose friendship is suffering. The framing story of *The Winning of Friends* is a tale depicting the friendship of Swift, a crow; Gold, a mouse; Slow, a TURTLE; and Spot, a deer. War between crows and owls is the subject of the book *Crows and Owls.* Of the 12 tales in *Loss of Gains,* the most well-known is "The Ass in the Tiger Skin," called "The Ass and the Lion" in collections of AESOP'S FABLES and "The Ass in a Lion's Skin" in *Bennett's Fables.* The fifth book, *Ill-Considered Action,* includes 11 tales pertaining to the theme of the title.

In the story "The Ass in the Tiger Skin," a young Ass is not content with being an ass; he prefers to be a tiger. Believing it will be possible to disguise himself by wearing a tiger's skin, he prevails upon his parents to obtain one for him, which they do at great cost to themselves. For a while he is able to fool people into thinking he is a tiger, and they run from him in fear. Nevertheless, his long ass's ears and his bray, which, try as he may, he cannot turn into a roar, eventually give him away. The real tigers attack him, and the ass flees, leaving his tiger skin behind him and lucky to have his life. As he runs, everyone laughs and throws things at him, disgracing him even further. The fable teaches that clothes or costumes are not enough to "make a man," or, as Bennett puts it, "It is not the cocked hat that makes the Warrior."

The Panchatantra has been widely influential on the various collections of fables drawn from Aesop. At least 200 versions exist, translated into more than 50 languages. In England, it is known as *The Fables of Bidpai,* while in Arabic it is the *Kalila wa Dimnah* and the *Anwar-u-Suhaili* in modern Persian. Hans Christian Andersen's short fairy tale about what is required to be a "real" PRINCESS, "The Princess and the Pea" (*see* ANDERSEN, HANS CHRISTIAN), was inspired by one of its tales; in turn, Andersen's tale influenced the Broadway musical, *Once Upon A Mattress.*

For Further Reading

Jacobs, Joseph, ed. *Indian Fairy Tales.* Illustrated by J.D. Barren. New York: Putnam, 1892.

Sharma, Pandit V. *Panchatantra: The Complete Version.* South Asia, 1991.

The Tortoise and the Geese, and Other Fables of Bidpai. Retold by M.B. Dutton. Illustrated by E. Boyd Smith. Boston: Houghton Mifflin, 1908.

PANDAVAS

In Sanskrit literature, the five sons of Pandu—Yudishthira, Bhima, ARJUNA, Nakula, and Sahadeva. The Pandavas are raised in the palace of their uncle, the blind king Dhrita-rashtra, after their father's DEATH. When Dhrita-rashtra makes Yudishthira, his eldest nephew, heir apparent instead of the eldest of his own 100 sons, the evil Duryodhana, his act engenders between the cousins a terrible rivalry ending finally in a war won by the Pandavas. But the Pandavas brothers, especially Arjuna, are unhappy about fighting with their cousins, relatives, and teachers. In despair, Arjuna enters into a series of dialogues with the god KRISNA, which forms the content of the *Bhagavad Gita*. Krisna reassures Arjuna that he should fight with all his strength for "the Spirit is beyond destruction" and "the Eternal in man cannot die." Not to fight when it is one's righteous duty is a transgression, Krisna tells him.

Other stories concerning the Pandavas appear along with that of the 18-day war in the Sanskrit epic, the MAHABHARATA, of which the *Bhagavad Gita* is a part. The five Pandavas all married the same woman, DRAPAUDI, because their mother, Kunti, mistakenly hearing that Arjuna has won alms, insists that he share them among all the brothers. Unbeknownst to her, what he has won in a competition is his bride, Drapaudi. Because a mother's word is sacred, Drapaudi is shared between the five brothers.

The Pandavas are still worshipped in south India, where five stones may be placed in a field to guard the crops. They are also linked with the Himalayas, where legend mentions they retired after World War I.

PANDORA

Woman of Greek myth who looses illness and vice upon the world. The story of Pandora has several variants. In the earliest tradition, Pandora was made of EARTH and water by Prometheus, who made humankind (*see* PROMETHEUS AND THE THEFT OF FIRE). In this version, she also was animated by Prometheus with the fire that he stole from HEAVEN. In HESIOD'S version, Pandora was made by the god Hephaistus at ZEUS'S instigation, for Zeus wanted to avenge Prometheus's act of stealing fire from MOUNT OLYMPOS. Athena is credited with animating her, according to Hesiod, and while all the GODS perfected her and gave her gifts, Hermes and APHRODITE gave her harmful gifts so she became a "beautiful evil." Pandora was then brought to earth by Hermes, and she married Epimetheus, the brother of Prometheus, although he had been warned by Prometheus to accept no gifts from the gods. As his wife she became the mother of all women, but she brought evil to the world because, overwhelmed by curiosity, she opens a jar (or, in some versions, a box) she carries from the gods, who have forbidden her to open it. Out fly all the vices and ills that have since afflicted humankind: only Hope remains in the jar.

Similarities can be drawn to Eve and her desire to taste the fruit of the Tree of Knowledge of Good and Evil in Eden: The story of Pandora allowed the Greeks, as did the story of Eve for the Hebrews, to blame all of the ills of humankind on a woman. Hesiod wrote, "She is the mother of hordes of women who have become the ruin of mortal man." She is supposed to be the mother of Pyrrha, the first mortal woman born and the sole survivor of the great FLOOD with her husband and cousin, Deucalion.

The story of Pandora eventually entered the oral tradition as well as the world of art, and reappeared in the work of Erasmus in the early sixteenth century, by which time she had gained certain similarities to Psyche. She later appeared in the works of du Bellay, Goethe, and Calderon.

For Further Reading

A Children's Treasury of Mythology. Illustrated by Margaret Evans Price. New York: Barnes and Noble, 1994.

Panofsky, Dora, and Erwin Panofsky. *Pandora's Box.* Princeton, NJ: Princeton University Press, 1956.

Wells, Rosemary. *Max and Ruby's First Greek Myth.* Illustrated. New York: Penguin, 1993.

P'AN KU

Chinese CREATION story. In the beginning there was nothing. After a very long time, nothing became something, and after an even longer time, this something divided itself into two parts, male and female. These produced two lesser somethings, and the resulting two pairs working together produced the first real being, who was named P'an Ku. A VARIANT version of the MYTH has P'an Ku emerging from the COSMIC EGG. He is furnished with a hammer and chisel with which he fashions the mountains and the sky. Chinese prints portray him in the company of the TORTOISE, the PHOENIX, and a DRAGON-like being who may represent the primeval "somethings"—the symbols of water, EARTH, and air.

In one version of the story, P'an Ku arrives when there is no world and begins chiseling out the earth with his tools. Each day P'an Ku grows six feet in height, and the earth grows just as fast. P'an Ku's head pushes the sky farther away as he makes the earth larger and larger. From the sky comes four beasts, a UNICORN, the phoenix, the tortoise, and a dragon that reached across the sky. When the world is finally finished, there is no living thing on it until P'an Ku dies and his spirit goes to HEAVEN. This DEATH gives life to the world.

Another version of the myth represents P'an Ku as a GIANT who is destroyed in order to form the material universe. His flesh becomes the soil, his bones the rocks, his blood the waters of the world, his hair vegetation. The wind is P'an Ku's breath, thunder his voice, rain his sweat, dew his tears, the heavens his skull, his right eye the MOON, and his left eye the SUN. His body is covered with vermin, which become the races of humankind.

This animistic approach to creation also is found in Sumerian myth and is particularly prevalent among Native American peoples (see MARDUK).

PANTHEONS

Major GODS of a pantheistic culture are considered to form a pantheon, literally meaning "all gods." This pantheon will usually include those gods who are also prominent characters in the mythology of that culture. Among the most familiar and important ones are the Greek, Roman, Norse, Hindu, Egyptian, Hawaiian, and Aztec pantheons.

The Greek pantheon has 12 chief gods and GODDESSES who sit on MOUNT OLYMPOS and two gods who are earth-bound. (The many other minor gods and goddesses who appear in Greek mythology are not considered members of the pantheon.) The Roman pantheon follows the Greek very closely, with Latin names replacing the Greek names for the gods and goddesses, although the attributes of each are much the same. The 12 who sit on Olympos and the two earth gods are led by ZEUS, called Jupiter or Jove by the Romans. Known for his thunderbolt, his power, and his many adulterous love affairs, Zeus is considered the KING of the gods, the sky god who had overthrown the Titans. His brother HADES, Pluto to the Romans, is king of the underworld, where he presides with his wife Persephone, also known as Kore, and called Proserpina by the Romans (see PERSEPHONE MYTH). The third brother, Poseidon, or the Latin Neptune, is god of the SEA. The goddess HERA, or the Roman Juno, is the wife and sister of Zeus, and her role is to serve as patroness of brides and MARRIAGE. Included in the pantheon are two other sisters, Hestia to the Greeks (Vesta to the Romans), goddess of the hearth, and Demeter, or the Roman Ceres, goddess of the grain, corn, and agriculture. The war god Ares (Mars to the Romans) is the son of Zeus and Hera, as is Hephaistus, or Vulcan, the god of the forge and the patron of smiths. APOLLO, the god of the SUN and patron of the arts, and his twin sister ARTEMIS, or Diana in Latin, the virgin MOON goddess and huntress, are the children of Zeus by Leto. ATHENA, or Minerva, is the daughter of Zeus and Metis, and goddess of wisdom, justice, and war, and bringer of culture in the form of numbers, mathematics, cooking, weaving, and spinning, and many other inventions such as the plow. APHRODITE, or Venus, the goddess of love, was born from the foaming sea that formed when the GENITALS of Uranus were cut off by his son Kronos and flung into the ocean. DIONYSOS, or Bacchus, son of Zeus and Semele, is the god of the vine, grapes, and wine.

The Norse pantheon includes ODIN, the wise one-eyed ruler of the gods; Frey, god of agriculture, trade, and peace; FREYA, goddess of beauty and love and sister of Frey; Frigga, wife of Odin; Tyr, or Tiw, the god of war;

LOKI, the TRICKSTER god; and HEL, sister of Odin and goddess of the Underworld.

The principal Egyptian gods are Ra, or Re, sun-god and ruler of the gods; Shu, son of Ra and god of the air; Tefnut, daughter of Ra and goddess of moisture and the world order; Geb, earth god and son of Shu and Tefnut; Nut, daughter of Shu and Tefnut, wife of Geb, and goddess of the sky; Osiris, son of Geb and Nut and god of the dead; Isis, daughter of Geb and Nut, wife and sister of Osiris, and goddess of wisdom and beauty (see ISIS AND OSIRIS); Set, the evil desert god; Nephthys, the goddess of dusk; Horus, son of Isis and Osiris and patron of pharaohs; Bast, the cat goddess; Hathor, the goddess of vengeance; Maat, the goddess of justice; and Ernutet, patroness of women in childbirth.

The Hawaiian pantheon is comprised of Ao, the masculine principle, day, and the sky, personified by Ku, god of agriculture; PO, the feminine principle, night, and the earth, personified by Hina, goddess of the Underworld; PELE, the volcano goddess; the sea god Kanaloa; the trickster god, MAUI; and Lono, an agricultural god.

The principal gods of the Aztec pantheon are Onteotl, the supreme god; Tlaloc, the rain god; Ehecatl, the wind god; Xipe Totec, god of spring; Xochipilli, god of flowers; Tlatzoteotl, goddess of sexual desire; and Huitzipochtli, sun and war god. Among the lesser Aztec gods is COATLICUE, a goddess of fertility and childbirth.

Although Hinduism has a pantheon, it can also appear monotheistic, with all gods being seen as aspects of the one eternal god, BRAHMAN. The three major male gods, BRAHMA the Creator, VISNU the Preserver, and SIVA the Destroyer, are incarnations of Brahman. The female counterparts, or *shaktis*, of these three are Sarasvati for Brahma, Lakshmi for Visnu, and DEVI, the great goddess who takes many forms, for Siva. Other Hindu gods include Brihaspati, priest of the gods; Indra, the sky god (see "INDRA AND THE ANTS"); Varuna, source of all created things; Kubera, god of wealth; Rudra, the storm god; Pushan, the guardian of the flocks; GANESA, god of wisdom; and Skanda, god of war.

While similarities exist between these pantheons, each reflects the particular vision of the culture to which it belongs. The division of the physical and the metaphysical world into representative gods and goddesses was common until the advent of the monotheistic religions. The various members of each pantheon were the subjects of hundreds of stories that played an important part in the oral tradition for centuries.

PARABLES

Short narratives about human nature, used to illustrate a moral point or answer a question. Parables are closely related to FABLES, since they both point to a moral or spiritual truth. But while fables tend to include ANIMALS as characters and have a moral that is made perfectly obvious by the end of the tale, parables tend to have human characters and a more ambiguous or complex lesson to teach. The more enigmatic message of a parable suggests that such tales are intended for a specific, perhaps elite, audience that can appreciate the moral embedded in the story.

Parables are also closely related to ALLEGORIES; indeed, parables are sometimes considered a subcategory in the genre of allegory. Parables, like allegories, invoke characters which represent another, more profound level of meaning. This other level may be purely secular, but oftentimes religious truths or morals are the motivation behind the telling of parables.

Parables have been incorporated into the teachings of many religions; the most famous parables in Christian societies are those of the BIBLE. Old Testament prophets such as Ezekiel tell parables to awaken their audiences to religious issues; the books of PROVERBS and Kings also relate religious parables. The New Testament includes the well-known PARABLES OF JESUS. An example of a religious parable is the brief story that Jesus tells his followers about the "Good Samaritan." A man is traveling from Jerusalem to Jericho and is attacked by robbers. They beat him severely and leave him for dead on the side of the road. A priest soon passes by, but does not assist the injured man. Later, a Levite passes by; he too does nothing to help. Eventually, a Samaritan walks down the road. When he sees the beaten man lying bleeding and helpless, he is filled with compassion and stops to offer his assistance. He binds the man's wounds, takes him to an inn, and pays the innkeeper to take care of him. The message implicit in the parable is that we all should act as the Good Samaritan does, showing mercy, generosity, and love toward those who are more helpless and unfortunate than ourselves.

Other examples of well-known parables may be found in the Chinese TAO TE CHING. For instance, in the 80th section of the book, Lao Tsu explains the parable of a small country in which the people possess machines, boats, carriages, and the tools of war, but will not use them. These people return to the use of knotted cords instead of written characters, and they find pleasure and enjoyment in their plain food, their coarse clothes, their humble dwellings, and their simple lifestyles. Even though adjoining communities are within sight of this country, and barking dogs in one place can be heard in the other, the people of this small country live their entire lives without ever communicating with the neighboring states. One message implicit in this parable suggests that happiness may be found neither in technology nor in combat, but in the simplest of sources.

Parables have been used to great effect in nonreligious literature as well. For example, Franz Kafka and Søren Kierkegaard, two secular writers, employed the form of the parable in their works in order to illustrate particular moral truths.

For Further Reading

French, Fiona. *King of Another Country.* New York: Scholastic, 1992.

Lau, C. D., trans. *Tao Te Ching.* Hong Kong: Chinese University Press, 1982.

Stoddard, Sandol. *The Doubleday Illustrated Children's Bible.* Illustrated by Tony Chen. Garden City, NY: Doubleday, 1983.

PARABLES OF JESUS

Brief analogies, examples, and narratives related by Jesus to his followers to demonstrate theological and/or moral lessons. The parables appear in the Synoptic Gospels— i.e., the first three books in the New Testament of the BIBLE: Matthew, Mark, and Luke.

In his book *The Parables of Jesus* (which serves both as an excellent anthology of the parables and a collection of carefully considered theological interpretations), Simon J. Kistemaker divides Jesus' parables into three categories:

True parables use simple facts of everyday life to illustrate their lessons; for example, "The Leaven" (Matthew 13:33 and Luke 13:20–21) describes the kingdom of HEAVEN in terms of the action of yeast upon a batch of flour. Such parables are usually very brief and told in the present tense.

Story parables use narratives in an allegorical manner. For example, "The Judge and the Widow" (Luke 18:1–8) deals with a widow who, through sheer persistence, successfully appeals to a hard-hearted judge for justice. Her efforts are used to symbolize the power of steadfast prayer. Story parables are more elaborate than true parables and typically are told in the past tense.

Illustrations resemble story parables in their use of narrative, but are not necessarily allegorical. These portray examples of behavior either to be emulated or rejected. For example, "The Good Samaritan" (Luke 10:30–37)—which describes a man's kindness toward a stranger who had been attacked by robbers—clearly illustrates the virtues of generosity and hospitality. Like story parables, illustrations typically are told in the past tense.

From a purely aesthetic standpoint, many of the parables are extremely poignant and powerful, their extreme brevity notwithstanding. In "The Prodigal Son" (Luke 15:11–32), one farmer's son leaves home to live a wasteful and dissolute life while another son stays at home and devotes himself to farm and family. When the prodigal son at last comes home, his long-grieving father rejoices and celebrates his return, much to the dismay of the other son, who feels slighted for his loyalty.

Indeed, the most striking of Jesus' parables are those that demonstrate their lesson in a surprising, counterintuitive way. Perhaps the most startling is "The Shrewd Manager" (Luke 16:1–9). It tells the story of a rich man who discovered that his financial manager was wasting his money. When the manager realized that he would soon lose his job, he decided to curry influence among his master's debtors by drastically reducing their debts. His master soon discovered this borderline embezzlement, but far from being dismayed, decided that his manager was far more capable than he had previously thought—he truly understood the use of worldly wealth! The seeming amorality of this story appears in the wit and paradox in stories of Oscar Wilde, who often declared himself much indebted to Jesus' artistic and narrative genius.

The influence of Jesus' parables has resounded down through the centuries in such allegorical stories as the anonymous EVERYMAN and John Bunyan's PILGRIM'S PROGRESS. Parabolistic techniques have even found their way into such markedly secular works as Bertolt Brecht's Marxist dramas *Mother Courage* and *The Good Woman of Setzuan*.

But the true spirit of the parable is brevity, and perhaps their closest contemporary equivalents are political cartoons and television commercials. The latter often rely on analogy and even ALLEGORY, particularly in the case of political advertisements. A notorious example appeared during the 1988 U.S. presidential election campaign, when the George Bush campaign used the parole of an African American felon as a metaphor for liberalism run amok.

Nevertheless, the parables of Jesus are really quite distinct from subsequent didactic or instructive storytelling, which has generally tried to clarify lessons for as large a public as possible. Although Jesus' parables may appear to do the same, he himself described them in surprisingly undemocratic terms—as if they were more designed to conceal divine truth than reveal it. Generally, Jesus only explicated the meanings of his parables to his disciples. And as he told them in Mark 4:11–12, "To you the secret of the kingdom of God has been given; but to those who are outside everything comes by way of parables, so that [as Scripture says] they may look and look, but see nothing; they may hear and hear, but understand nothing; otherwise they might turn to GOD and be forgiven."

Thus a Christian parable tended to be a kind of RIDDLE that was answerable only by the faithful or the elect. Or as Jesus himself put it with characteristic succinctness in Matthew 13:9, "If you have ears, then hear." *See also* PARABLES, AESOP.

For Further Reading

Hendrickz, Herman. *The Parables of Jesus*. San Francisco: Harper & Row, 1983.

Joint Committee on the New Translation of the Bible. *The New English Bible with the Apocrypha*. New York: Oxford University Press, 1970.

Kistemaker, Simon J. *The Parables of Jesus*. Grand Rapids: Baker Book House, 1980.

PARADISE

In various religions, the place where one lives in a divine condition without suffering from the human condition. While Paradise may take different forms in art, daydreams, sleeping DREAMS, and religion, there has always been a nostalgia for Paradise, where one lives without troubles, sickness, or DEATH. Two concepts of Paradise prevail. The first is characterized by the belief in a "Golden Age" on EARTH, usually harkening back to the earliest state of the human race. Indian and Greek myths of this "Golden Age" are similar to the era of the "Golden Emperors" in China, the Garden of Eden in the Hebrew BIBLE, and traditional Babylonian and Persian MYTHS. The second concept of Paradise emphasizes a coming PROMISED LAND, a renewed connection between GOD and the human race, and the final redemption of human beings. Examples of this second concept are the Mahayana Buddhist splendid "western paradise," known as *Sukhavati*, which is reigned over by the Buddha Amida; the Nordic VALHALLA; the Happy Fields of the Egyptians; and Aztec and Muhammadan paradise.

Characteristically, in Paradise FOOD is abundant, often symbolized by a luxuriant garden; there is usually a fountain at its center, symbolizing the source of all water and the origin of life and knowledge; ANIMALS roam about freely and peacefully, and their language is understood by humans. In many religions and mythologies, human beings once lived in Paradise but were thrust from it at some point, as in the story of ADAM AND EVE's original home in the Garden of Eden in the Book of Genesis (*see* GENESIS, BOOK OF) of the Hebrew Bible. There Eden has a river with four branches. Adam names the peaceful animals, representing the dominance of the intellect over the senses and the instincts. Clothes are unnecessary either for warmth or for modesty, suggesting the idyllic state of early childhood, where all needs are met and shame has not yet been learned. By disobeying God, they are cast out of Paradise forever. In Jewish belief, when the Messiah returns, the world will end and Paradise will then be eternally restored.

Paradise is seen as the spiritual center of the world, the supreme region, the heart of the world, and the point of communication between HEAVEN and earth. In Christianity, after the fall, represented by Adam and Eve's exile from Eden, this connection between heaven and earth is broken. In Islamic tradition, the entrance to Paradise has eight doors, and each floor of Paradise has a hundred degrees. The highest floor is the seventh sky or heaven. To open the door to Paradise, a three-toothed KEY is needed, with one tooth signifying unity, the second representing obedience to God, and the third symbolizing the abstention from all illicit acts. As in the example of Edén, in Islamic tradition there is always spring and eternal light in Paradise, and one day in Paradise is equal to one thousand earthly days. Four rivers flow from mountains of musk between banks of pearls and rubies, and there are four mountains. Angels, hills, trees, and birds together create a universal melody of marvelous music.

The desire to find the "lost" Paradise is a common theme in oral tradition and literature, from the quest for Paradise on another planet (a popular theme in science fiction) to James Hilton's novel *Lost Horizon*, where human beings never age. Hans Christian Andersen's fairy tale "The Garden of Paradise" also deals with this theme and place (*see* ANDERSEN, HANS CHRISTIAN).

For Further Reading

Heine, Helme. *One Day in Paradise*. Illustrated by Helme Heine. New York: Macmillan, 1986.

PAREDES, AMERICO (1915–)

Prolific literary critic and compiler of Mexican American FOLKTALES. Paredes grew up in Brownsville, Texas, where he sang family folk songs as a child. By the age of 20, Paredes was working as a journalist and publishing poetry, but his work as a student at the University of Texas led him to the literary study of FOLKLORE. His skill and interest in a diverse range of topics has provided him with a valuable perspective for comparative studies of culture and folklore. In particular, Paredes draws from his extensive knowledge of folklore and Mexican American history to examine the cultural forces which inform many folktales. Paredes examines the ways in which Mexican and Mexican American folk stories communicate the traditions and frustrations of cultural conflicts. He has published extensively on the topics of machismo, folk medicine, and the representation of Anglo-Americans in Mexican folklore. He has also published a collection of folk songs as well as collections of Mexican folktales.

For Further Reading

Paredes, Americo. *Folklore and Culture on the Texas-Mexican Border*. Austin, TX: CMAS Books, 1993.

———. *Folktales of Mexico*. Chicago: University of Chicago Press, 1970.

———. *The Hammon and the Beans and Other Stories*. Houston: Arte Publico, 1994.

PEASANT

In storytelling, the poor, simple person who toils to make a living. In MYTH and LEGEND, the peasant represents the unsophisticated, simple man or woman who works the land and has no great wealth. Depending on the tale, a peasant may be praised for virtuousness in the face of poverty or may be depicted as greedy or stupid. Because FAIRY TALES were so often passed on as a form of entertainment among the peasantry, the figure of the peasant is a common one in every culture. In some popular MOTIFS, the handsome son or the beautiful daughter of the peasant becomes a HERO or marries royalty. Many tales focus on the way the peasant manages to overcome hardship, and follow the archetype of the QUEST. Such stories as "The Peasant and the

DEVIL," "The Peasant in HEAVEN," "The Little Peasant," and "The Peasant's Wise Daughter," found in the *Grimm Brothers's Fairy Tales*, depict the role of the peasant in FOLKTALES.

In the later stories of Leo Tolstoy, such as "The Death of Ivan Ilych" (1886) and "Master and Man" (1895), the peasant is extolled as a pure, healthy, and worthy person in comparison to the landowner or bourgeois, whose values bring him or her no happiness. The figure of the peasant most commonly appears in the stories of cultures where class division is prevalent.

THE PEASANT AND THE SHEEP

Russian FABLE told by Ivan Krylov (*see* KRYLOV, IVAN). This characteristically short Krylov fable takes place in a courtroom. A peasant accuses his sheep of killing his livestock. Two of the peasant's fowls are devoured in the night, and the sheep is the only one in the yard. The judge, a fox, immediately decides that the sheep must be guilty, despite its pleas of innocence. The fox ignores the sheep's claim that it never eats meat. Arguing that all thieves seek to hide their true motives, that fowls are known to be delicious, and that the sheep had opportunity, the fox pronounces his sentence. The sheep is to be killed, his body given to the court and his fleece to the peasant. Obviously the fox speaks of himself when he outlines the cleverness of rogues and expounds upon the savoriness of birds. The fox has, in effect, killed two birds with one stone: he has in all probability eaten the fowls himself and now will get to eat the sheep.

The stock figures of an early folk oral tradition are thrust into a modern courtroom in this Krylov fable. The legal language used at the beginning serves to make this story more than just another tale of the fox's cleverness. "The Peasant and the Sheep" functions as a commentary on a court system that benefits neither defendant nor plaintiff.

For Further Reading

Ralston, W.R.S. *Krylov and His Fables*. London: Strahan and Co., 1869.

PELE

Polynesian fire and volcano GODDESS. Pele is associated with the flow of lava, a physical feature of the Polynesian landscape. She is supposed to have been very beautiful, with breasts round like the moon and a back straight like a cliff. Legend has it that she wandered a great deal searching for her husband, Wahieloa, until finally settling on Hawaii. In the many MYTHS and LEGENDS that surround Pele, one reoccurring theme is her tempestuous nature, which represents both the unexpected and inexplicable nature of divinity as well as the mystery, surprise, and wrath suggested by the image of the fire- and lava-spewing volcano.

One of the most famous of the Pele myths is the story of how she takes the form of a young maiden and wins over the handsome young chief, Lohiau. They are married, but Pele leaves him to return to her home on their wedding night, telling him she will be making ready for him and will send for him. However, it takes so long for Pele's sisters to come and get him that Lohiau pines away and eventually dies of grief. When the sisters arrive, they are able to restore Lohiau to life, and set off with him to return to Pele. Again, the journey is lengthy, and now Pele grows more and more impatient, disliking her sister's attraction to Lohiau, until she bursts forth in a fury, setting fire to them all. The family then disperses, with the spirit of Lohiau set to wandering. In another VARIANT of the myth, Lohiau is restored to life and becomes the husband of Pele's favorite sister, Hiiaka.

Numerous variants exist of the myth of Pele and Kamapua'a, a demi-god in the form of a pig, who is said to have entered into a battle of insults with Pele. In some versions, Kamapua'a ends up swallowing everything with Pele barely escaping; in others Pele and Kamapua'a have a sexual relationship or marry but decide to live separately by dividing Hawaii into two parts, with Pele taking the lava-covered areas and Kamapua'a taking the areas of moist earth.

As Elizabeth Diab notes about the many tales concerning Pele, "The body of myth and legend . . . are told originally in the sacred chants and dances of the *hula*."

For Further Reading

Frierson, Pamela. *The Burning Island: A Journey through Myth and History in the Volcano Country, Hawai'i.* San Francisco: Sierra Club Books, 1991.

Kalakaua, David. *The Legends and Myths of Hawaii.* Boston, MA: Charles E. Tuttle, 1972.

Knipe, Rita. *The Water of Life: A Jungian Journey through Hawaiian Myths.* Honolulu: University of Hawaii Press, 1989.

PELLOWSKI, ANNE (1933–)

American storyteller, children's book writer, librarian, and historian of storytelling. In her book, *The World of Storytelling* (1977), Pellowski argues that the storytellers are as important as the FOLKTALES and FAIRY TALES themselves. She indicates that in many cultures, stories "belonged" to one particular teller and were only passed on to other storytellers by inheritance or direct permission. Pellowski also seeks to preserve the histories of great storytellers, as well as their stories. Her book offers a comprehensive guide to all sorts of storytellers, from BARDS of many different countries to modern librarians. Pellowski has observed the myriad forms of storytelling still alive throughout the world. She notes that most compilations of folktales and fairy tales today do not emphasize how the stories were told originally. It is the entire experience of storytelling, the way tales are told, how music or visual aids are employed, and how an audience is taught to respond, that Pellowski seeks to capture.

For Further Reading

Pellowski, Anne. *Made to Measure: Children's Books in Developing Countries.* Paris: UNESCO, 1980.

PENELOPE

In Greek mythology, the wife of Odysseus and the mother of TELEMACHOS. She figures prominently in the ODYSSEY of HOMER. Her story has archaic roots, in which she is connected with matriarchal customs and rites. In those versions, she is the mother of Pan, either by Hermes or by all of her suitors.

Sailing home after the end of the Trojan War, the Greek chieftain Odysseus is lost in a storm. Penelope and her son patiently await his return, although everyone else in the city of ITHACA believes him dead. Day and night, Odysseus's house is full of suitors vying for the presumed widow's hand. They are an ill-mannered gang who eat and drink everything in sight.

To forestall these suitors, Penelope promises to marry one of them as soon as she finishes weaving a funeral shroud for her father-in-law. But every night she unravels whatever work she has done during the day. She eventually is caught, and her suitors become all the more belligerent.

After 20 years, Odysseus finds his way back to Ithaca. But since he is in disguise as a beggar, Penelope does not know of his return. To further delay her suitors, she poses a test: she will marry the suitor who can string Odysseus' bow and shoot an arrow through 12 lined-up rings. Of course, the bow is too strong for any of them to bend. At last, the disguised Odysseus strings the bow and shoots an arrow through the 12 rings. Then he and Telemachos slay all the suitors.

Penelope was a feminine ideal to the ancient Greeks—long-suffering, faithful, and patient. But she also displays traces of her husband's wiliness. For example, she encourages expensive gifts from the uncouth men she has no intention of marrying. Doubtless, she and Odysseus relish these belongings when they settle back down to domestic life. *See also* ANCIENT GREEK STORYTELLING.

For Further Reading

Graves, Robert. *The Greek Myths.* 2 vols. New York: Penguin Books, 1957.

Hamilton, Edith. *Mythology: Timeless Tales of Gods and Heroes.* New York: Mentor, 1969.

IL PENTAMERONE

Giambattista Basile's "masterpiece in dialect," originally *Lo Cunto de li Cunti Overo lo Trattenemiento de li Peccerille* (*The Story of Stories or the Entertainment of the Little Ones*). This set of fifty stories for children, written by the Neapolitan author Giambattista Basile, perhaps elicits more attention today than when the piece was originally written in 1675. An important Italian translation by Benedetto Croce in 1932 brought *Il Pentamerone* into greater view most recently, but

Basile's *Pentamerone* also reached a European audience through the GRIMM BROTHERS and Charles Perrault (*see* PERRAULT, CHARLES), the noted German and French fairy-tale recorders who admittedly borrowed many story themes from Basile's original (*see* EUROPEAN STORYTELLING). Basile's plots were overwhelmingly popular among children, perhaps because many possessed exotic Eastern antecedents. In 1812 (and with the publication of a second, more widely read edition in 1822), the Brothers Grimm confirmed in an introduction to their tales that many of their stories shared similar plot elements and characters with those that had first appeared in *Il Pentamerone*. Not only "CINDERELLA," but Neapolitan versions of "BEAUTY AND THE BEAST," "BLUEBEARD," "Hansel and Gretel," "JACK AND THE BEANSTALK," "PUSS IN BOOTS," "Rapunzel," "RUMPELSTILTSKIN," "Sleeping Beauty," and "Snow White," as well as many other popular and well-known FAIRY TALES, all appear in Basile's *Lo Cunto de li Cunti*, later known as *Il Pentamerone*, before they appear in writing anywhere else.

The Greek title *Pentamerone*, paralleled to Boccaccio's *Decameron*, refers to the five days of storytelling in the narration, set forth by the frame story, in which Battista tells of the Moorish slave girl who has gained by deceit the place of a PRINCESS. After the marriage, the couple is entertained by ten women who tell one story on each day for a total of fifty. On the last day, the rightful princess tells her own story, exposing the Moorish girl's wrong and her own rightful place as princess. The true princess, the storyteller, is restored to her rightful position while the imposter is punished.

Critics of *Pentamerone* (as noted by scholars Peter and Julia Conaway Bonadella) recognize its interest in magic, the aforementioned use of Eastern elements, the representation of reality, the use of dialect, the use of parody and paradoxical metaphor and simile, the concern for justice, and the happy ending of the tale typical of the Baroque period style.

For Further Reading

Basile, Giambattista. *The Pentamerone of Giambattista Basile*. Translated from the Italian of Benedetto Croce. Edited by Norman M. Penxer.
2 vols. London: John Lane the Bodyley Head Ltd., 1932.

Calvino, Italo. *Italian Fables*. Translated by Louis Brigante. New York: Collier, 1961.

PERCIVAL

Valiant, but unlikely knight in King ARTHUR's court. Percival is the HERO of *Perceval* or *Le Conte du Graal* (*The Story of the Grail*), written by CHRÉTIEN DE TROYES about 1180. The primary theme of this unfinished work is the progress of a naive and uncouth boy towards the chivalrous and spiritual ideals characteristic of the best knight in the world.

Percival is raised by his mother deep in the forest. As a result of his sheltered life, Percival is unaware of knights, chivalry, and the Church, and he does not know his own name. One day he sees five knights from King Arthur's court, and so he decides to become a knight. He leaves his tearful mother fainting with grief, and departs.

After several misadventures, Percival arrives at Lord Gornemant's castle where he is knighted. Gornemant advises Percival not to talk so much as this habit is sinful and impolite. Now that he is a knight, Percival intends to return to his mother. On his way home, he comes to a river where a crippled fisherman offers him shelter at his castle.

At the castle, the fisherman gives Percival a sword. A young man enters the hall carrying a white lance by its shaft; a drop of blood runs from the lance's head to the man's hand. Next, a lavishly dressed girl enters carrying the golden Grail (*see* HOLY GRAIL). Last, another girl enters carrying a silver carving dish. Remembering Gornemant's advice not to talk too much, Percival does not ask any questions about what he sees, in spite of his curiosity.

The next morning, Percival finds that no one is in the castle. He and his horse leap from the closing drawbridge. He sees a young girl in the forest grieving over the headless corpse of a knight. The girl, whom Percival learns is his cousin, tells him that he has just spent the night at the Fisher King's castle, and that he has erred by not asking about the procession he observed. The girl asks his name, and suddenly, he knows that his name is Percival of Wales. Unlike many other heroes, Percival discovers his identity after a failure, instead of in victory. The girl tells Percival that if he had asked the right questions, the Fisher King would have been healed and good would have come to his kingdom. Instead, there now will be misery.

Percival next goes to King Arthur's court where a hideous MAIDEN enters and says that because Percival did not inquire about the lance or the Grail, war will erupt in the Fisher King's realm. Percival takes a vow to discover why the lance bled and whom the Grail serves.

Five years pass during which Percival leads the life of a courageous and chivalrous knight, except that he does not enter a church or worship GOD. He is totally self-reliant, but he comes no nearer to his goal.

Percival consults a hermit (who turns out to be his uncle) for advice. The hermit explains that Percival's troubles originate in the grief he caused his mother, which has led to her death. This sin made it impossible for him to ask questions at the Fisher King's castle. The hermit reveals that two kings live in the castle: the Fisher King himself and his father, the Grail King. The old king, Percival's uncle, is served by the Grail, which gives him a single Mass wafer at each meal. He has eaten nothing else for fifteen years. Percival's relation to the Grail King suggests that he is the rightful heir. The hermit instructs Percival to love and worship God and to respect the priesthood, and reminds him of his chivalrous duties. Finally, the hermit teaches Percival a prayer.

Chrétien de Troyes's account of Percival ends here. Other versions of Percival's adventures include the German *Parzival* (c. 1210) by WOLFRAM VON ESCHENBACH and two French works, *Perlesvaus* and the Didot *Perceval*, also from the early thirteenth century. In later works, LANCELOT's son, Galahad, replaces Perceval as the hero who wins the Grail.

The nineteenth-century German composer Richard Wagner's last and perhaps finest work, the opera *Parsifal*, was staged in 1882. Also in the late nineteenth century, Lord Alfred Tennyson helped to reestablish the popularity of Percival and the other Arthurian LEGEND with his immensely successful epic poem, *Idylls of the King*.

For Further Reading

Barber, Richard. *King Arthur: Hero and Legend*. Woodbridge, Suffolk: The Boydell Press, 1986.

Cavendish, Richard. *King Arthur and the Grail*. London: Paladin, 1985.

Chrétien de Troyes. *Arthurian Romances*. Translated by William W. Kibler and Carleton W. Carroll. New York: Penguin Books, 1991.

PERRAULT, CHARLES (1628–1703)

French poet, prose writer, and storyteller. A prominent member of the Académie francaise who played a major role in the literary controversy known as "the quarrel between the ancients and the moderns," Perrault is best remembered for a collection of FAIRY TALES for children, which he published under the name of his son, Pierre. Titled *Tales of Past Times, with Lessons* but known popularly in French as *Contes de ma Mere l'Oye*, these tales were translated into English in 1729 as MOTHER GOOSE STORIES by Robert Samber.

Consistent with his position in the academy's debates, where he argued that modern literature was superior to literature of the past because civilization progresses, most of Perrault's fairy tales were modernized versions of little-known French FOLKTALES of the past. Perrault's alterations to the tales, however, were not very extensive. Even as he converted these oral tales into a literary form, the form in which most future audiences would experience them, he nevertheless preserved much of the oral quality of them through his use of a simplistic style. Further, the content of his versions of the tales is believed to be relatively consistent with the oral versions that were experiencing a resurgence of popularity at that time in the French courts at Versailles, shortly before he published *Contes de ma Mere l'Oye*.

Among the eight Mother Goose stories in *Tales of Past Times, with Lessons*, seven have achieved international recognition: "RED RIDING HOOD," "SLEEPING BEAUTY," "PUSS IN BOOTS," "BLUEBEARD," "Diamonds and Toads," "Hop o' My Thumb," and perhaps the best-known fairy tale in the world, "CINDERELLA." Although Perrault's literary versions of these

"Mother Goose" tales would become the best-known versions, most of the stories had long folk traditions before Perrault, and had been known in cultures throughout the world.

Although there are no earlier versions established for "Bluebeard" or "Red Riding Hood," most scholars believe that Perrault did not create them, but borrowed from the folk tradition of the tales for his versions. "Bluebeard" is a variation on a common theme in storytelling—the fatal effects of curiosity, especially for a female character, as seen with Lot's wife in the BIBLE. Perrault's version of "Red Riding Hood" also depicts the demise of a female character, as she is devoured by the wolf; however, she is not punished for curiosity, but for naiveté. Yet, later versions of this tale, and many that are common in England and America today, have substituted happier endings. For example, in many modern versions, the young girl is saved by her father.

"Puss in Boots," a tale involving a TRICK-STER cat, can be traced back to Giambattista Basile's IL PENTAMERONE (1634), which depicts a similar cat con-artist. Perrault's version, though, has reached a much greater audience and is perhaps the best known of all tales that involve animals providing help to humans (see also HELPFUL ANIMALS). "Diamonds and Toads" also appears in *Il Pentamerone*. The theme of this story, which involves the trading of places between a privileged person and a poor person, has been popular nearly worldwide, as it has been paralleled in at least 20 countries. The tale also employs the frequently used MOTIF of contrasting sisters, one kind and courteous, the other rude, with the kind sister being rewarded for her goodness in the end. Popular in European fairy tales, this motif has appeared in the GRIMM BROTHERS's tale "The White Bride and the Black," and of course in Shakespeare's *King Lear*.

"Hop o' My Thumb" is similar in some ways to the British tale "TOM THUMB," as it takes for a central character a young boy of diminutive size. But the plot more closely resembles "Hansel and Gretel," as it deals with the issue of ABANDONED CHILDREN.

Perrault's two most famous fairy tales are "Sleeping Beauty," and "Cinderella." *Il Pentamerone* includes a version of "Sleeping Beauty," as do the Grimm Brothers. The Grimm Brothers also offer one of the many versions of "Cinderella," in their story "Aschenputtel." "Cinderella" has also been found in the folk traditions of Scandinavia, Great Britain, and China. The earliest version may be the Chinese version, which dates from about A.D. 850–860. Of the many versions, however, few include a HEROINE as passive as Perrault's Cinderella. Yet, they do all seem to offer the same message—that virtue is self-evident, apparent in the size of a shoe or ring, and thus can be discovered if it has been for some reason obscured.

For Further Reading

Perrault, Charles. *Charles Perrault: Memoirs of My Life*. Edited and Translated by Jeanne Morgan Zarucchi. Columbia: University of Minnesota Press, 1989.

———. *The Complete Fairy Tales of Charles Perrault*. Translated by Neil Philip and Nicoletta Simbrowski. Illustrated by Sally Holmes. New York: Clarion Books, 1993.

———. *Perrault's Fairy Tales*. Translated by Sasha Moorson. Illustrated by Landa Crommelynck. New York: Doubleday, 1972.

PERSEPHONE MYTH

Popular tale among the Greeks and the Romans about the earth GODDESS DEMETER (also known as Ceres) and her beautiful daughter Persephone (also known as Proserpine or Kore). Demeter is the source of EARTH's natural abundance. She is the sacred mother of the fruits of the earth. Her wonderful daughter is her constant companion; however, one day the dark god of the underworld, HADES, takes the maiden unaware and carries her off to his murky kingdom. Demeter bemoans the loss of her daughter and searches the world for her. Helios, the ever-watchful sun, tells her what happened. He explains that ZEUS himself gave permission for the outrageous abduction.

Demeter makes her way to Eleusis, where she poses as a poor old woman who agrees to take on the care of the prince's son. To give the boy immortality, Demeter bathes him in the fire of the hearth until one night she is observed doing so by the boy's horrified mother. When the mother screams and tries to remove her son, Demeter explodes in anger; she throws the child down, revealing her true identity, crying out that the boy could now only be mortal. She demands that a temple be built for her in Eleusis. She remains in Eleusis grieving for her daughter, and she allows the earth to become parched and unproductive. Even Zeus cannot persuade the goddess to bring life back to earth. Only when he arranges for his brother Hades to release Persephone does Demeter relent. However, since before Persephone left Hades, she ate the Pomegranate, the fruit of the Underworld, she is thus destined to return there to her husband for half of each year. Therefore, Demeter brings life back to the earth for only half the year, spring and summer.

In this MYTH, recorded by the ancient Greeks in the Homeric *Hymns* and later by Ovid in his *Metamorphoses,* it is a female figure, Persephone, who makes the DESCENT TO THE UNDERWORLD that so many ancient male heroes make. This fact suggests the power of women in ancient agricultural and sometimes matrilineal cultures (*see also* INANNA). But the power of Demeter and her daughter have been greatly diminished by that of the male sky gods of the Greek religion—a situation that reflects the social arrangements of the Greeks. Persephone's descent, after all, is the result of a rape, and Demeter—the embodiment of the old once powerful great goddess, must beg for justice and retribution. Still, Demeter can destroy the world if she chooses to do so, and even in patriarchal Greece she is a being to be reckoned with.

By the time of the establishment of the Persephone myth, Demeter and her daughter were the center of a popular mystery cult with its headquarters at Eleusis near Athens. Demeter was the grain GODDESS of the agricultural mysteries and her daughter was the menarcheal corn maiden or "seed of life."

The three stages of the goddess—MAIDEN, MOTHER, and CRONE—represented in the Demeter-Persephone story speak to the realities of nature's and the woman's life cycle. Persephone's journey can also refer to any individual's descent into the unconscious world, a descent that can result in a spring of rebirth in self-knowledge.

In connection to the Demeter-Persephone story, are the mysteries of Eluesis. These sacred rites of Demeter remain just that, a mystery. We know the story told about the mother and her daughter, but we know little of the ritual acts that told the story in another way. There are indications of an underground womb-sanctuary in which fertility objects were placed in and then removed from baskets and chests. Scholars have surmised that these objects might have been phallic symbols—snakes or long loaves of bread. The baskets and chests, then, would have been womb symbols.

Of course, the Demeter-Persephone story also served the ancients as an explanation for the mysterious movement from one season to another. Spring was the time of Persephone's return; spring came about because of her presence in Demeter's home; summer was the result of Demeter's happiness. Fall reflected her sadness at her daughter's departure, and winter was her despair of ever finding her again. Whatever the meaning of the story, it was one of the most popular narratives in the ancient classical world.

For Further Reading

Waldherr, Kris. *Persphone and the Pomegranate: A Myth from Greece.* New York: Dial, 1993.

PHOENIX

Magical bird in world mythology that is perpetually reborn out of its own ashes. The story of the phoenix has been traced as far back as the eighth century B.C., and has appeared, in various forms, in the iconography or texts of the Egyptian, Roman, Greek, Indian, Arab, Russian, and Judaic traditions. The most common ancient account of the phoenix appears in Herodotus's sixth century B.C. *Histories.* This story tells of the magical bird who, upon the death of its father, carries his body in an egg of myrrh to the Temple of the SUN in Heliopolis, Egypt. Later versions of the story link the phoenix to the most popular element of the MYTH of the phoenix: its cremation and subsequent REBIRTH.

Proponents of various ideologies during the first seven centuries A.D. adopted the myth of the phoenix to represent resurrection in any number of capacities. The rebirth of the phoenix was interpreted, among other meanings, as a symbol of the resurgent influence of the Roman Empire of the first century, the superiority of ANIMALS over humankind, and the divine power of the Christian GOD. In time, the myth of the phoenix came to be understood in the Christian tradition as an ALLEGORY of Christ's RESURRECTION.

Numerous renderings of the story of the phoenix naturally have led to many contradictory versions. Generally, the phoenix is understood to eat otherworldly food, such as sunbeams or manna and dew, and is closely associated with the sun which gives it life. It exists in a paradisiacal place until a very old age (upwards of 500 years by most accounts), and reproduces asexually (since most versions of the myth explain that only one phoenix can live at a time). Stories differ regarding the details of the phoenix's death and rebirth. Some texts suggest that the bird rises out of the ashes of the previous phoenix, others explain that the young phoenix is born out of the decomposing remains of the old phoenix, and still others declare that a worm grows out of the decaying remains of the old and forms a new phoenix. Some Christian versions of the myth suggest that this resurrection of the new phoenix takes three days, indicating a connection between the bird and the story of Christ. Another version of the myth portrays the phoenix as a bird that never dies at all, but travels with the sun across the sky each day and protects EARTH from the harmful rays. One fourth century text is unique in that two phoenixes live together; it depicts the old phoenix crashing to the ground and the young phoenix springing from the blood of the old bird's wounds.

An eighth-century Anglo-Saxon poem called *The Phoenix* is an important example of the allegorical uses to which the story of the phoenix has been put. In the poem, the phoenix represents Christ and also the souls of every true Christian who, like the phoenix, will be reborn in Christ. "The Golden Phoenix," a French-Canadian FAIRY TALE uses the figure of the phoenix to signify immortality; according to the tale, anyone who lives within the sound of the golden phoenix's voice will never grow old. This image of rebirth, resurrection, and immortality has also made the phoenix a popular image in love literature across the centuries. However, the British short story writer Sylvia Townsend Warner brings an entirely new meaning to the legend in her revisionary story "The Phoenix." In this 1940 tale, the phoenix is caged in a zoo and subjected to all sorts of abuse by scheming profiteers until it finally bursts into flames, destroying the zoo and killing everyone in the area.

For Further Reading

Barbeau, Marius. *The Golden Phoenix and Other French-Canadian Fairy Tales*. Retold by Michael Hornyansky. Illustrated by Arthur Price. New York: H. Z. Walck, 1959.

Silverberg, Barbara. *Phoenix Feathers: A Collection of Mythical Monsters*. Illustrated. New York: Dutton, 1973.

PILGRIM'S PROGRESS

Prose ALLEGORY written by John Bunyan in 1678. *The Pilgrim's Progress from This World to That Which Is to Come*, published first in 1678 and followed by a sequel, Part II, in 1684, was one of the most popular books written in English. Based on a DREAM that the author ostensibly had, Part I is the story of Christian and his QUEST to avoid the destruction of his family, town, and himself predicted by the BIBLE. Part II, less powerful than Part I, focuses on Christian's family's journey toward the Celestial City.

Christian's quest begins when the Evangelist warns him to flee the City of Destruction. He does so, heading for the Celestial City, but first he wanders into the Slough of Despond from which he cannot extricate himself because of the burden of sin weighing on his back. Help rescues him, and Mr. Worldly-Wiseman tells him to give up his quest and settle in the village of Morality, where Mr. Legality will remove his burden. Ready to do so, Christian is once more warned by the Evangelist, and he sets out again on his journey to the Celestial City. First he comes to the Cross, where his burden of sin rolls off his back. As he continues on his journey, he encounters such characters as Simple, Sloth, Presumption, Hypocrisy, Formalist, Timorous, and Distrust. When resting at the House Beautiful, he meets with the four damsels, Charity, Piety, Prudence, and Discretion, and they send him toward the Delectable Mountain. Further trials include a fight with the fiend Apollyon in the Valley of Humiliation and a journey through the frightening Valley of the Shadow of DEATH filled with Hobgoblins, DRAGONS of the Pit, and SATYRS.

In the next stage of his quest, Christian meets a fellow pilgrim, Faithful, and they continue their journey together, stopping at the town of Vanity Fair, where Faithful is burned at the stake for not wanting to buy anything; when Faithful is carried off by a heavenly Chariot, Christian continues on his way with Hopeful, another pilgrim inspired by Faithful's example. They travel past the plain of Ease and the tempting Hill of Lucre; are caught by the GIANT Despair at Doubting Castle; manage to free themselves with Christian's key called Promise; meet the shepherds Knowledge, Experience, Watchful, and Sincere at the Delectable Mountain; withstand the sleep caused by the Enchanted Ground; reach the country of Beulah in view of the Celestial City; cross the River of Death to get to the Celestial City; and are led by angels to the gate of HEAVEN.

Pilgrim's Progress grows out of the ancient and universal tradition of the quest story. What once had been the story of the quest for the HOLY GRAIL or the Golden Fleece (*see* QUEST FOR THE GOLDEN FLEECE), now becomes the story of the quest for eternal life or spiritual rebirth. Other such allegorical tales in the literary traditions include Dante's *Divine Comedy* and Spenser's *The Faerie Queene*. Bunyan's allegory, inspired itself by such allegories as *Everyman*, in turn inspired and influenced many writers and storytellers in the years following its publication. Louisa May Alcott's famous novel, *Little Women*, opens with the four March sisters reading *The Pilgrim's Progress* for guidance in their behavior.

For Further Reading

Bunyan, John. *The Pilgrim's Progress*. Edited by Roger Sharrock. New York: Penguin, 1965.

PIXIES

Mischievous fairies in Northern European FOLKLORE. Pixies are prevalent in the English regions of Somerset, Devon, and Cornwall. There are varying accounts of their size, appearance, and origin, but all accounts agree that they are dressed in green and that they have the habit of misleading travelers, or "pixie-leading" them. Although it is generally thought that pixies are small, they can inflate their bodies to large sizes. Like BROWNIES, pixies are sometimes kind and will help their favorite people. They too are appeased by a gift of clothes—they will leave a home forever if given garments to wear. More often, pixies are malevolent, and they enjoy playing tricks. In addition to leading travelers astray, they disrupt humans' well-ordered lives by displacing furniture and exchanging property. Spriggins are Cornish pixies who harm crops, steal newborn babies, and commit evil acts. Knockers, another kind of Cornish pixie, are more friendly to humans. They live in mines and make knocking noises to warn miners of imminent danger.

In Cornwall, most pixies are thought to be the souls of the area's prehistoric inhabitants. Knockers, however, are supposed to be the souls of Jews deported there by the Romans for their part in the crucifixion. Others believe that pixies are the souls of unchristened children, the souls of the Druids, or the souls of heathen people before the coming of Christ. A nice collection of tales about pixies can be found in Thomas Keightley's *A Fairy Mythology* (*see* KEIGHTLY, THOMAS). In addition, stories about Cornish pixies are told in *Traditions and Hearthside Stories of West Cornwall* (1870) and *Stories and Folk-Lore of West Cornwall* (1880) by William Bottrell and *Popular Romances of the West of England* (3rd ed., 1881) by Robert Hunt. Ruth Tongue gives recent descriptions of pixies in *County Folklore* (vol. VIII, 1965) and tells a story about pixies in *Somerset Folklore* (F. L. S., 1965). *See also* WILL-O'-THE-WISP.

For Further Reading

Arrowsmith, Nancy. *A Field Guide to the Little People.* Illustrated by Heinz Edelmann. New York: Hill and Wang, 1977.

Cohen, Daniel. *The Magic of the Little People.* Illustrated by Dale Payson. New York: JulianMessner, 1974.

PO

Polynesian creator of the earliest stages of CREATION. According to Polynesian LEGEND, first there was Po, representing the void, a time without light or heat or sound. From this evolved light, heat, matter, sound, the Heavenly FATHER, and EARTH-MOTHER, who were in turn the parents of the GODS, humans, and nature. The Ngaitahu of southern New Zealand see Po as the creator of light.

In Oceanic mythology, Po can also refer to the underworld or land of darkness, a black and gloomy place. Like the underworld of the Ancient Greeks, few mortals could visit Po and ever return.

POLYGENESIS

The folkloristic theory that FOLKTALES with similar form and content can simultaneously be created in different geographical regions. Scholars with an anthropological background advocate this cultural evolutionist theory which reasons that similar tales can exist concurrently in many places because the people who created them were at the same evolutionary level. The basic premise of polygenesis is that the developmental level of all human societies, while occurring at various historical moments, follows similar patterns. Timeless and universal preoccupations such as birth, DEATH, sex, and family interact with the developmental stages, resulting in similar folktales around the world. This theory was criticized by many scholars due to the presupposition of a parallelism in culture development. Opposing this doctrine of independent invention is the monogenetic theory of DIFFUSION, which asserts a common origin from which similar folktales spread and has often been studied via the historic geographic method. Finding independent invention an overly extreme explanation, many folklorists take positions between polygenesis and diffusionism, believing that a common center exists from which certain motifs and other elements diffuse and become a part of subsequent tales in various cultures.

POPOL VUH

Epic of the Quiché, a Mayan tribe of the Guatemala highlands. Many of the stories are found in the oral traditions of other Mayan groups.

The extant version, told in the Quiché language transcribed in European alphabetic script, probably dates between A.D. 1554 and A.D. 1558. But it is clearly based on an earlier work written entirely in Mayan hieroglyphs and based on ancient lore. The glyphic *Popol Vuh* possibly was destroyed by Catholic priests, along with innumerable other glyphic books.

Much of the *Popol Vuh* deals with the adventures of HERO deities and takes place before the CREATION of human beings or the appearance of the SUN. The most prominent of these heroes are two sets of twins.

The first of these twins were One Hunahpu and Seven Hunahpu. They were the sons of Xpiyacoc and Xmucane, the oldest of the GODS. One Hunahpu and Seven Hunahpu loved to play an ancient Mayan ball game somewhat resembling soccer. Unfortunately, their ball court was directly above Xibalba, the Mayan underworld and realm of the dead. Their games disturbed two lords of Xibalba, One Death and Seven Death.

One Death and Seven Death invited the twins down to Xibalba to play ball with them. But before they were allowed to play, One Hunahpu and Seven Hunahpu were forced to spend a night in a dangerous place called Dark House. They failed to survive the night, and One Hunahpu's head was placed in the fork of a tree in Xibalba.

One day, a MAIDEN named Blood Woman walked by the tree and mistook One Hunahpu's head for a gourd. The disembodied head spit into her hand, and she became pregnant. She fled the wrath of the lords of Xibalba to the surface of the EARTH, where she gave birth to another set of twins—Hunahpu and Xbalanque.

Hunahpu and Xbalanque were considerably more adept as heroes than their father and uncle. They successfully fought minor deities who presumed too much earthly power. These included Seven Macaw, a bird who falsely claimed to be both the sun and MOON, and Seven Macaw's two sons, who claimed to create and destroy mountains.

These twins' greatest adventure led them in the footsteps of their father and uncle. One day, a rat showed them their forebears' ball-playing gear. Hunahpu and Xbalanque began to play ball in the very same court as One Hunahpu and Seven Hunahpu, once again angering the lords of Xibalba. Like their uncle and father before them, Hunahpu and Xbalanque were invited to play ball in Xibalba by One Death and Seven Death.

But Hunahpu and Xbalanque cunningly endured their initiatory night in Dark House and a number of other deadly trials. Hunahpu survived his own beheading, and the two brothers even managed to resurrect themselves after being burned to powder. Eventually, the twins tricked One Death and Seven Death into dying themselves. This ended the tyranny of Xibalba over the world of the living (*see also* DESCENT TO THE UNDERWORLD). After their adventures in the underworld, the twins tried to resurrect their father, One Hunahpu, with only partial success.

Stories such as these are structured into a vast narrative frame which begins with the creation of the world and ends with the transcription of the poem itself.

In the beginning, there was only an empty sky and a calm SEA. The gods of these two realms carried on a dialogue which brought into existence the earth, plants, and people. Human beings were unusually difficult to bring into existence. The gods made four unsuccessful attempts before satisfactory humans were created from corn flour and water. Their third attempt had to be destroyed by a FLOOD.

The earliest humans of the fourth creation wandered through a dark world. They separated into tribes which spoke different languages. Eventually, the morning star appeared, followed by the sun. Humankind found a new unity in a world of sacred light.

The *Popol Vuh* concludes by following the history and generations of the Quichés through the Spanish conquest. With its extraordinary frame extending from earthly creation to the moments of its own transcription, a case can be made that the *Popol Vuh* boasts a grander conceptual sweep than anything in the European epic tradition. In his introduction to his own translation, Dennis Tedlock considers this vision to be broader and deeper than either MYTH or history—perhaps best described by the word *mythistory*.

But what is the relation of the surviving alphabetic *Popol Vuh* to its glyphic original? Tedlock finds many clues in the text itself. The transcribers describe their own work as less an act of literal transcription than interpretation. The glyphic *Popol Vuh* was probably too dense, multi-layered, and nonlinear to permit an adequate transcription into European script. Like other sacred Mayan books, it is much more than just a story. It also is an almanac filled with valuable calendrical information, as well as a magical text with divinatory properties.

The loss of such a document is a great cultural tragedy, but no greater than the destruction of many other Mayan texts. Though often described as the "Maya BIBLE," the epic is but a tiny sampling of what Mayan literature must have been during its richest period; it is one of only four surviving Mayan books. As Michael Coe put it in *The Maya*, it is "as though all that posterity knew of ourselves were to be based upon three prayer books and *Pilgrim's Progress*."

Even so, the *Popol Vuh* tells us a great deal about the civilization that created it. The sacredness of the maze plant and human blood are frequent themes. And in its nonlinear structure, we get a glimpse of the Mayan vision of time as recurrent and cyclical. To the Maya, these stories were not events of some distant past, but ever-present realities.

For Further Reading

Coe, Michael. *The Maya*. 5th ed. London: Thames and Hudson, 1993.

Popol Vuh: The Mayan Book of the Dawn of Life. Translated with commentary by Dennis Tedlock. New York: Touchstone, 1985.

POURRAT, HENRI (1887–1959)

French collector of FOLKTALES from the Auvergne region of central France. After a yearlong battle with a severe case of tuberculosis, Pourrat began to write stories and poems. He found inspiration for his work in the folktales he heard throughout the region in the language of Provencal. By 1910, Pourrat had begun a love for collecting tales that would span five decades. Pourrat sought to capture the rich language and custom of his region, thereby capturing something revealing about humanity at the same time. Although Pourrat meticulously recorded Auvergne's folktales, he was less concerned with accurate transmission than with the spirit of the tale. This compelled him to rewrite many of the stories he gathered, and the liberties he took with them led to the indignation of academic folklorists. But it was with the sense of the tale that Pourrat was concerned, and he dedicated his energies to preserving what he perceived as a precariously enduring national heritage. Remaining his entire life in the region of his birth, Pourrat painstakingly gathered tales, and his life work culminated in the publication of over 1,000 stories. The first part of his masterwork, the massive 13-volume set of French folktales entitled *The Treasury of Tales*, appeared in 1948.

For Further Reading

Pourrat, Henri. *French Folktales.* Reprint, New York: Pantheon, 1994.

———.*The Roquefort Adventure*. Translated by Mary Mian. Roquefort sur Soulzon, 1956.

PRAJAPATI

In Hindu mythology, the primeval FATHER of creatures. Prajapati, the father of Dawn, wished to commit incest with his daughter, according to Indian legend, but during the act of intercourse, his seed spilled on the ground, thus generating living beings. Indeed, the name Prajapati means "lord of offspring." In later legends, Prajapati is identified with BRAHMA. In the RIG-VEDA CREATION story, the divine Prajapati heats himself from within, "sweating out" the world. He is a father figure, protector of those who father. His children are both GODS (*devas*) and DEMONS (*asuras*) who engage in great rivalry.

PRIMEVAL WATERS

In MYTHS OF CREATION, the earliest stage when everything is endless water. The primeval, or primal, waters appear as a feature of many creation myths, especially those of the "earth-diver" type (*see* EARTH-DIVER CREATION). In this type of myth, the primeval waters are all there is, though in some cases several waterfowl like loons or swans swim on the waters. Something or someone then falls from the sky, usually Sky-Mother or SKY-MAIDEN, and this being requires something hard—a rock or a mound—on which to land. Through one means or another, land is created out of the primeval waters and often the waters then dry up with the help of a SUN god.

Primeval waters appear in many Native American creation myths, such as those of the Algonquin, Altaic, Arapaho, Cherokee, Huron, Iroquoian, Onondaga, Seneca, Yakima, and Yuma tribes.

PRINCE

Symbol of the potential of royalty. As J. C. Cooper notes in *An Illustrated Dictionary of Traditional Symbols*, the figure of the prince suggests "the power and vigor of youthful royalty." Like the figure of the KING, the prince is associated with "the fertility of the people and the land." The figure of the prince plays an important role in many MYTHS and FAIRY TALES, often in his role of suitor to a PRINCESS. "Winning the hand of a Princess, in myth and LEGEND," writes Cooper, "is to aspire to the superior or highest state, a situation fraught with danger which can either kill the aspirant or raise him to a higher and more noble state, as in psychic and spiritual aspirations and QUESTS."

The prince often functions as a HERO in myths and legends, and J. E. Cirlot points out that "his great virtue is his intuition and it is by no means rare for him to possess the powers of a demiurge." The prince is the idealization of man, in his handsomeness, love, youth, heroism, and charm. Therefore, it is fitting that it is the prince, or "the King's son," who awakens Briar-Rose, more commonly called "Sleeping Beauty," after she has slept 100 years in the GRIMM BROTHERS's fairy tale "Little Briar Rose." Similarly, it is the prince who pursues CINDERELLA in the Grimm Brothers's "Cinderella." In their story "Little Snow White," the prince's love for Snow White is so strong that he must kiss her in her glass casket, which causes the bit of poison apple lodged in her throat to come loose. For all three princes, MARRIAGE is their prize.

In some tales, the prince is the victim of WIZARDS or WITCHES, and he has been transformed into a MONSTER or an ANIMAL; his only hope for recovering his princely form is a heroic love. This is seen in Charles Perrault's fairy tale "BEAUTY AND THE BEAST," in which the Beast is transformed into a handsome prince when Beauty's love frees him from a SPELL (see PERRAULT, CHARLES). In the Grimm Brothers's fairy tale "Snow-White and Rose-Red," a talking bear visits their home each evening, and their kindness to him and their involvement with the DWARF who has put him under a spell eventually bring the bear in contact with the dwarf, so that the bear kills the dwarf, is returned to his princely shape, and marries Snow-White while his brother marries Rose-Red. On a symbolic level, the young woman who is the catalyst for this transformation from beast to prince, thus winning a husband through her kindness and love, is also participating in the "taming" of the wilder, less civilized side of man. She prepares him for marriage, a more socially acceptable form of existence; indeed, she brings out the "prince" in him.

For Further Reading

Berenzy, Alix. *A Frog Prince*. New York: Henry Holt, 1989.

Lang, Andrew. "Snow White and Rose Red." *The Rainbow Fairy Book*. Illustrated by Michael Hague. New York: William Morrow, 1993.

Sierra, Judy. *Cinderella*. The Oryx Multicultural Folktale Series. Phoenix: Oryx Press, 1992.

PRINCESS

Symbol of potential royalty, youth, beauty, and privilege in MYTHS and FAIRY TALES. While the role of the princess often is passive as she waits to be found or won by the PRINCE, she is central to the dreams of young men. She is an idealized woman (as the prince is an idealized man), in her beauty, youth, love, and courage. A "real" princess must have special qualities, as in Hans Christian Andersen's fairy tale, "The Princess and the Pea," inspired by a FABLE from the Hindu PANCHATANTRA (*see* ANDERSEN, HANS CHRISTIAN).

Sometimes the princess's role—unbeknownst to her—is to free the bewitched prince, who appears in the form of an ANIMAL or beast, from his SPELL, as in the GRIMM BROTHERS's fairy tale "The FROG Prince." In this story a frog retrieves the princess's golden ball, which has rolled into a well, in exchange for her promise that he can eat and drink from her dishes and sleep in her bed. She agrees, but when the frog comes to the palace to exact his payment, she is repulsed by his ugliness. However, her father, the king, makes her keep her promise, but when the frog comes to sleep in her room, she is so disgusted that she flings him against the wall. Suddenly, he is transformed into a handsome prince who marries her the next day.

In another Grimm Brothers's fairy tale, "THE GOOSE GIRL," a princess is sent off on a journey to marry a prince, but her lady-in-waiting overpowers her and claims that she is the true princess. Here the qualities of the princess—her golden hair, her ability to make the WIND blow, her connection with the decapitated talking horse, Falada—outshine those of her servant, and eventually the truth surfaces and the true princess marries the king's son. This tale suggests that a true princess's beauty and inner qualities transcend what at first appears to be true.

For Further Reading

Andersen, Hans Christian. *The Princess and the Pea*. Translated by Anthea Bell. Illustrated by Eve Tharlet. New York: Picture Book Studio, n.d.

Berenzy, Alix. *A Frog Prince*. New York: Henry Holt, 1989.

Climo, Shirley. *Princess Tales from around the World*. Illustrated by Ruth Sanderson. New York: HarperCollins, 1996.

Lewis, J. Patrick, retold by. *The Frog Princess*. Illustrated by Gennady Spirin. New York: Dial/Penguin, 1994.

PROMETHEUS AND THE THEFT OF FIRE

Profoundly influential story based upon the Greek Titan's loyalty and kindness to humanity. Prometheus, whose name means "forethought" or "forethinker," has captured literary imaginations from the time of the ancient Greeks to the present day. The lineage of Prometheus is unclear, but several stories suggest that he was the son of the Titan Iapetos and either GAIA or Themis. Although a Titan, Prometheus sided with ZEUS in the war for supremacy, and he formed a fleeting allegiance with the chief of the GODS of Olympos.

The principal cause of the animosity between Prometheus and Zeus is their debate about the inherent worth of the human race. Prometheus defends humanity against Zeus's charge that they are irredeemably flawed. When the gods meet to decide upon the level of sacrifice to be demanded from humanity, Prometheus attempts to trick Zeus into choosing a lesser burden. After dividing a sacrificial ox in half, he wraps the meat and organs inside of the less-desirable skin and places the worthless bones beneath rich pieces of fat. Zeus chooses the disguised bones as the sacrifice required of humanity, though whether he sees the deception of Prometheus and acts in the hope of revenge against humanity, or whether he does so out of foolishness, varies from story to story. In either case Zeus places heavy burdens upon humankind, denying them the gift of fire that would mitigate their suffering.

Upon seeing humanity's misfortune and wishing to relieve it, Prometheus conceals embers from the forge of Hephaistos and gives them to the human race. Enraged, Zeus orders Hephaistos to chain Prometheus to a cliff. Prometheus remains there for 30,000 years, and each day an eagle arrives to peck out his liver, only to have it grow back during the night. Eventually Prometheus is freed when Herakles, the son of Zeus, destroys the eagle and breaks the Titan's bonds (see LABORS OF HERAKLES). One story holds that Zeus allows Herakles to free Prometheus in order to increase his own fame, while another suggests that Prometheus purchases his freedom with a secret that Zeus desired.

The gift of fire, and its cost for Prometheus, creates a bond between the god and humanity rarely seen in the Greek tradition. Generally, the gods of the Greek PANTHEON are petty and quarrelsome, giving of themselves only with the expectation of compensation or to offend another god. Prometheus's self-sacrificial gift of fire undermines the relationship of authority that Zeus desires, and it allows humanity the technology to pursue goals beyond the basic requirements of survival. The fire represents not only a tool for mollifying life's hardships, but the gift of divine inspiration.

Significantly, Prometheus also is credited with forming humanity out of clay, and he adds the divine fire to complete the creation. It is this imaginative, fiercely independent element of human nature that creative minds have found so compelling. Since Hesiod's eighth-century B.C. version of the Prometheus story in the *Theogony*, writers have examined the relationship between the Titan's tragic affinity for humankind as well as humanity's own promethean potential. The Aeschylus tragedy *Prometheus Bound* laid the foundation for the explosion of interest in the Prometheus myth by writers of the Romantic Age. Goethe and Byron, as well as Mary Wollstonecraft Shelley and Percy Bysshe Shelley, returned to the Prometheus myth over and over again in their work. The promethean fire-theft serves as a particularly apt metaphor for the Romantic artist's struggle for creative independence in the midst of social restraint.

Percy Bysshe Shelley examined the individual's tragic aspiration for creative and political liberty in *Prometheus Unbound* (1820), a lyrical drama which adopts the theme of the Aeschylus tragedy. In form and content, *Prometheus Unbound* is an unconventional work. Shelley connects Prometheus to Satan as a figure who defies the ruling power and suffers the consequences of his ambition. For Shelley, there is honor in the tragic aspirations of figures like Satan and Prometheus. Not surprisingly, poets of the

Romantic era supported the French Revolution, and the loss of their initial hopes for a bloodless, noble struggle recalls the promethean movement from idealistic ambition to tragic recognition. Mary Wollstonecraft Shelley, writing two years before her husband, realized the tragic consequences of the Prometheus myth in her novel *Frankenstein*. Dr. Frankenstein, the scientist whose complex mixture of ambition and benevolent sentiment ends with tragedy, cannot recognize the weight of his actions as he creates life. Aspiring to god-like status without the divinity to control it, Frankenstein becomes, for Mary Wollstonecraft Shelley, the "modern Prometheus." The evil brought about by the promethean hero is not malevolent, but it is brought about by ambitious defiance. The story of Prometheus and the theft of fire speaks, not only to all that is benevolent and self-sacrificial in human nature, but to the often tragic consequences that accompany ambition.

For Further Reading

McCaughrean, Geraldine. *Greek Myths.* Illustrated by Emma Chichester Clark. New York: Macmillan, 1992.

PROMISED LAND

Land of Canaan, which GOD promised to Abraham in the Book of Genesis of the Hebrew BIBLE (*see* GENESIS, BOOK OF). In his covenant with Abraham in Genesis, God promised him land, specifically the land of Canaan. This promise was reaffirmed to Isaac, Jacob, and Joseph and his brothers, the descendants of Abraham. It was later reaffirmed to Moses, although Moses himself was denied entry after 40 years in the desert (*see* EXODUS). Not until the time of David, in the tenth century B.C., was the land completely seized by the Hebrews. When the nation of Israel was split into the two kingdoms of Israel and Judah around 921 B.C., prophets began predicting exile of the people from Israel and Judah because of their practices of idolatry. Israel in the north was conquered by Assyria in 721 B.C.; Judah fell to Babylon in 587 B.C. Once the people were exiled from Israel and Judah, they longed to return to the "Promised Land."

Only in Jerusalem were the Jewish people allowed to perform animal sacrifice, yet they performed other rites to maintain their identity. When King Cyrus of Persia conquered Babylon in 538 B.C., he permitted the Jews to return to the Promised Land and Jerusalem to rebuild their temple, though some chose to remain in exile. The destruction of the Temple by the Romans in A.D. 70 caused further dispersion of the Jews, and not until the nineteenth-century Zionist movement began, culminating in the formation of the state of Israel in 1948, was there a real return of the Jews to the Promised Land.

Christians also refer symbolically to the Promised Land, seeing Abraham's QUEST for his new faith as a paradigm for Christians "who should seek the heavenly country or city that God is preparing for them." The Promised Land, or a "new Canaan," was a symbol for the Puritans in the "New World" as well as for the Boers in South Africa. On a metaphorical level, images of the Promised Land are linked with those of PARADISE and the kingdom of God.

PROPP, VLADIMIR (1895–1970)

Russian folklorist of German descent who explored the structural similarities between different types of FOLKTALES. Propp's pioneering work in FOLKLORE began while he was a student at the University of Petrograd, where he majored in Russian and German philology. He graduated from the university in 1918, but the chaos of the times made a secure position as a student or teacher difficult. After World War I, the newly born Soviet Union was in disarray, and political affiliation became an increasingly important factor in one's success. Through the course of his life, Propp experienced firsthand the requirements for conformity set upon the intellectual elite of the Soviet Union. It was a requirement he resisted, but to which he ultimately submitted. Somehow, in the midst of the revolutionary reforms of communism, Propp found work as a high school teacher of German. By 1932 Propp was conducting folklore courses at Leningrad University, and he earned a reputation as an exceptional teacher. He was promoted to professor in 1938, and he went on to serve as chair of the folklore department.

Vladimir Propp's first book (and first publication) was almost universally ignored. *Morphology of the Folktale* appeared in 1928, and only a few Russian critics acknowledged it. Originally titled *Morphology of the Wondertale*, Propp's book was renamed by editors, apparently to broaden its appeal. The change could not alter the book's fate; Propp would have to wait 30 years before realizing his important contribution to critical theories of folklore. It was only with the 1958 English translation that the work earned widespread critical acclaim.

In *Morphology of the Folktale*, Propp attempts the very ambitious project of connecting all Russian tales under a category of numerous structural components. Propp argues that, while Russian tales vary widely in particulars, they share a detailed plot structure which remains consistent from tale to tale. This plot, which consists of 31 separate elements, not only appears in each Russian tale, but each element of the plot also occurs in the precise order that it appears in other tales. While the tales also contain diverse characters, Propp contends that these can be reduced down to seven stock figures. Although the allegorical structures of folktales had been noted before Propp, he was the first critic to formulate a complex pattern of structural similarities.

Propp's theories, which eventually brought him widespread recognition from scholars in the West, were dangerous for his career in the Soviet Union. In applying theories that connected the Russian folktale to those of other countries through deep structural patterns, Propp offended the sensibilities of those who wanted the tradition of Russian storytelling to stand alone. As the influence of the Russian Formalists waned after the Communist shift in power during the 1930s, Propp found his loyalties to Marxist theory under suspicion. During the 1940s, Soviet authorities condemned *Morphology of the Folktale* as an elitist book which drew too heavily from theorists of Western Europe, particularly from the French Structuralist critics. During the

latter half of the 1940s, Propp was also compelled to defend his other works as well as his association with other scholars who did not meet the political requirements of the Central Committee. When his 1946 book, *Historical Roots of the Wondertale*, was also condemned for its foreign influences, Propp submitted and apologized for his failure to consistently promote a Marxist agenda. To what extent Propp was committed to Marxist theory is not known, but he was deeply shaken by the threat to his career, and he rarely deviated from the party line afterwards.

While Propp was defending his work in Russia during much of his career, critics in Europe and the United States were unaware of his theories. When Propp was finally introduced to the West, his fame spread quickly, and his status as a world-renowned Russian scholar earned him respect in the Soviet Union. His importance for storytelling is not confined to the Russian tale, since his theories explore the structures of language which are inherent to any story. Propp spent the remainder of his career examining these structures and engaging in dialogues with structuralist critics of the West. His other important works include *Russian Heroic Epic Poetry* (1955), *Russian Agrarian Festivals* (1963), and *Problems of Laughter and the Comic* (published posthumously in 1976).

For Further Reading

Propp, Vladimir. *Theory and History of Folklore.* Edited by Anatoly Liberman. Translated by Ariadna Martin and Richard Martin. Minneapolis: University of Minnesota Press, 1984.

PROVERBS

Short sayings that embody a generally accepted and widely known truth. The origins of proverbs are usually impossible to determine with any degree of certainty, although certain proverbs may be attributed to particular stories or FABLES. For example, certain proverbs such as "don't kill the goose that lays the golden eggs" may be traced back to a specific fable of AESOP. Proverbs are an ancient form of expression; they appear in the oldest existing writing and therefore often employ archaic language. An example might be "time and tide wait for no man"; the word "tide" in this sense probably means "season," a rare construction in contemporary English.

Proverbs are often based on a metaphor, such as "fish or cut bait," or "you can lead a horse to water but you can't make him drink." Others may rely on clever plays on words, as in "forewarned is forearmed," or "put up or shut up." Still others remain in the collective folk memory through their pattern of rhyme, as in "a friend in need is a friend indeed," or "when the cat's away, the mice will play." Antithesis ("man proposes, God disposes," or "young saint, old devil"), alliteration ("all that glitters is not gold") and parallelism ("for the want of a nail the shoe was lost; for the want of a shoe the horse was lost; for the want of a horse the rider was lost; for the want of a rider the battle was lost; and all for the want of a horseshoe nail") all find their way into many common and uncommon proverbs.

Proverbs exist in all languages, and translate from culture to culture fairly freely (which also makes tracing the origin of proverbs difficult). Perhaps the best-known collection of proverbs in the Western tradition is the Book of Proverbs in the Old Testament of the Hebrew BIBLE. Proverbs have been created and perpetuated to deal with diverse topics and sets of circumstances, including medicine, weather, agriculture, superstitions, childbirth, intoxication, history, customs, and racial or cultural stereotypes.

Proverbs are embedded in storytelling traditions in a number of ways. A particular work may take a proverb as a title (such as Shakespeare's *All's Well That Ends Well*) in order to indicate a message or attitude that surfaces in the work itself. Proverbs may also appear as common similes used to describe particular behaviors, such as "sly as a fox" or "wise as an owl." Traditional beast fables and FAIRY TALES perpetuate these proverbs; even the modern Winnie the Pooh stories include a scholarly owl who believes himself to be the wisest creature in the forest. Fables and fairy tales also may connect closely to a proverb that provides "the moral of the story." For example, a story in which a character is disappointed after depending too much on one specific event or outcome may illustrate for a child the relevancy of the proverb "don't put all your eggs in one basket." In this way, young listeners or readers of proverbial stories receive instruction in certain lessons in life.

PUBERTY STORIES

Type of story told at initiation ceremonies at puberty or tales depicting puberty as a rite of passage. Storytelling has been a part of various puberty ceremonies in cultures around the world. Depending on whether the subject of puberty is male or female, puberty stories will reflect the gender difference.

In Native North American FOLKLORE, stories of the VISION QUEST depict this initiatory rite of passage. In the Brulé Sioux tale "The Vision Quest," a young man wants to go on a vision quest in order to become a great medicine man, but he does not have enough humility, wisdom, and patience to receive the vision he seeks; thus the story instructs other young men in what is needed to succeed in a vision quest and reflects the nature of puberty and the period immediately following it.

In a White Mountain Apache puberty story, CHANGING WOMAN is sent to EARTH to initiate menstruation. In a Chiricahua Apache tale, White Painted Woman initiates puberty rites for girls.

FAIRY TALES such as "Snow White" suggest that even before Snow White hides in the forest, she has reached puberty, which is why she poses a threat to her stepmother (*see* STEPMOTHER—WICKED). Her stay in the forest, followed by her deathlike sleep in the glass coffin, suggests a period of incubation where Snow White must achieve selfhood before she can move on to the next stage, MARRIAGE. Since female puberty comes at the onset of menstruation, puberty stories about maidens suggest that once they menstruate, they are ready to marry and bear children.

For Further Reading

Evetts-Secker, Josephine. *Mother and Daughter Tales*. Illustrated by Helen Cann. New York: Abbeville, 1996.

Snow White and the Seven Dwarfs. Illustrated by Chihiro Iwasaki. New York: Picture Book Studio, n.d.

PUCK

Fairy of the hobgoblin type, the most famous of which appears in Shakespeare's *A Midsummer Night's Dream*, although other hobgoblins named Puck appear in English literature.

Shakespeare's character Puck is a Robin Goodfellow, the best-known of all English hobgoblins; Robin Goodfellows are mentioned frequently in Elizabethan literature. Puck is mischievous and shrewd, but also a friendly and comical spirit. He frightens MAIDENS and plays tricks on them as they go about their domestic chores. He causes them to churn in vain and makes their ale bear no froth. If he does people's work, however, they will have good luck (*see* BROWNIE).

Puck calls himself "that merry wanderer of the night." He enjoys misleading night travelers and then laughing at them. He is capable of moving at great speed and can travel from Athens to England and back again in a few minutes.

Puck is a SHAPE-SHIFTER. For the pleasure of Oberon, the KING of the fairies, he beguiles a fat horse by neighing like a filly. Sometimes he changes into a roasted crab apple and lurks in an old woman's bowl of ale. When she drinks, he bobs against her lips and pours the ale on her. Other times he transforms into a stool, and then causes the unlucky person who sits on him to topple over. Puck also turns himself into a headless bear and a WILL-O'-THE-WISP.

Although it is not clear exactly what Puck looks like, an illustration from the seventeenth-century ballad *Robin Goodfellow: His Merry Prankes and Merry Jests* represents Robin Goodfellow as a SATYR.

A more modern rendition of Puck is found in Rudyard Kipling's *Puck of Pook's Hill* (see KIPLING, RUDYARD). He is a small, brown person with broad shoulders and pointy ears. He has a snub nose, blue eyes, and freckles. He is ageless and lives in Pook's Hill. Puck appears before the children Dan and Una in a fairy circle. He introduces them to a legendary history of both Sussex and England. He is the voice of the fairy folk, or the "people of the hills," all of whom, except for Puck, have departed from England.

The character Puck originates in a tradition of hobgoblin types that includes the Irish *Pooka* or *Phooka* and the Welsh *Pwca*, all of which enjoy misleading night travelers and changing into various forms to trick others.

For Further Reading

Briggs, K.M. *The Anatomy of Puck*. London: Routledge and Kegan Paul, 1959.

———. *The Fairies in Tradition and Literature*. London: Routledge and Kegan Paul, 1967.

Kipling, Rudyard. *Puck of Pook's Hill*. 1906. Reprint, London: Macmillan, 1983.

Shakespeare, William. *A Midsummer Night's Dream*. Edited by Wolfgang Clemen. New York: Signet, 1963.

PUNISHMENTS

Usually a symbol of good overcoming evil in all aspects of storytelling, whether MYTH, LEGEND, FAIRY TALE, or FOLKLORE. Punishment by those in higher authority (GOD, a KING or queen, a HERO, etc.) who represent the forces of good over those who are evil, have sinned, or have exhibited *hubris*, is a common theme in the oral tradition, meant to convey to listeners that culpability always is recognized. Punishment may take a physical or psychological form and can involve dangers that must be overcome, torture that must be experienced, or DEATH as the ultimate form of punishment.

In the Hebrew BIBLE, God (YAHWEH) punishes ADAM AND EVE for daring to eat from the forbidden Tree of Knowledge of Good and Evil; their punishment takes the form of being cast out of PARADISE forever, where Eve must labor to give birth to her children and Adam must labor in tilling the soil. Their first son Cain is later punished for murdering his brother Abel when God exiles him. Later on in the Book of Genesis (*see* GENESIS, BOOK OF), God punishes the entire human society except NOAH and his family by submitting the earth to an annihilating FLOOD. Demeter, the Greek GODDESS of agriculture whose name means "The MOTHER," punishes the other gods as well as humans when she forces the earth to lie fallow until her daughter Persephone is returned to her (*see* PERSEPHONE MYTH). When the Greek Titan, Prometheus steals fire from the gods, he is punished by ZEUS by being chained to a rock where an eagle pecks away at his liver (*see* PROMETHEUS AND THE THEFT OF FIRE). In Sophocles' play *Oedipus the King*, based on the myths surrounding Oedipus, first the city of THEBES is punished with a plague for not having rid itself of the murderer of its former king, Laius. King Oedipus decrees that the murderer will suffer exile from Thebes, not realizing due to his own *hubris* that he himself is responsible for Laius's death. When he eventually learns of his culpability, exacerbated by the fact that Laius was his father and his wife Jocasta his mother, he punishes himself by blinding himself. Both Medea and Procne of Greek mythology punish their unfaithful husbands by killing their children, cooking them, and serving them to their husbands to eat. In the fairy tale "Snow White," retold by the GRIMM BROTHERS, the wicked stepmother is punished by being forced to dance in red-hot iron shoes until she drops dead (*see* STEPMOTHER—WICKED). Generally, the form of punishment reflects the belief system of the culture to which the story belongs.

For Further Reading

Evetts-Secker, Josephine. *Mother and Daughter Tales*. Illustrated by Helen Cann. New York: Abbeville, 1996.

Hogrogian, Nonny. *Noah's Ark*. Illustrated. New York: Knopf, 1986.

Hutton, Warwick. *Adam and Eve*. Illustrated. New York: M.K. McEldery Books, 1987.

Snow White and the Seven Dwarfs. Illustrated by Chihiro Iwasaki. New York: Picture Book Studio, n.d.

PUPPETRY

Manipulation of a doll or other object used to play a role. The word is derived from the Latin for a female "little child" or "doll." Puppets have been used for storytelling around the world and throughout history. Major types include directly operated hand or glove puppets; marionettes, manipulated from above by strings; rod puppets, manipulated from below by long rods; and shadow puppets, backlighted figures that cast images upon a screen.

The best-known storybook puppet character is Pinocchio—a wooden marionette who was freed from his strings. Pinocchio's nose grew longer every time he told a lie, but eventually his behavior improved and he was transformed into a real, live boy. The children's classic by Carlo Collodi was published as a magazine serial in 1880 and as a book in 1883. Collodi was the pseudonym of Carlo Lorenzini (1826–90), an Italian journalist who also translated the fairy tales of Charles Perrault (*see* PERRAULT, CHARLES). *The Adventures of Pinocchio* was made into an animated film by Disney in 1940.

The earliest uses of puppetry were often religious in nature, though puppets have always been enjoyed for their entertainment or artistic value, too. The Bunraku puppet theater of Japan dates from the seventeenth century and is still considered a serious art form. The same is true of East Asian shadow-puppet performances, particularly those of Bali and Java.

Many countries have their favorite puppet characters. The nineteenth-century English Punch and Judy slapstick figures originated in Europe in the seventeenth century. Petrushka came from Russian carnival puppet theater. And in the 1920s and early 1930s, Garcia Lorca wrote several puppet plays based on the Spanish *Don Cristóbal*.

Puppet theater in Europe gradually became mass entertainments, though not without satirical power. Puppetry was a regular feature of cabaret performance in Vienna and Germany in the early twentieth century. That period also saw a renewal of interest in puppetry among artists and writers.

In this country, puppetry has often been regarded as only for children or family entertainment. Edgar Bergen's Charlie McCarthy was followed by a number of ventriloquist acts, and the hand puppets on *Sesame Street* have taken on a life of their own. Electronically operated puppets have been created for films such as *Labyrinth* and *The Dark Crystal*. Today storytellers often use puppets, and many FOLKTALES and MYTHS are available in puppet-play form.

For Further Reading

Collodi, Carlo. *Pinocchio*. Adapted from M.A. Murray's translation of C. Collodi's story. Illustrated by Ed Young. New York: Philomel Books, 1996.

Mahlmann, Lewis, and David Cadwalader Jones. *Folk Tale Plays for Puppets*. Boston: Plays, Inc., 1980.

Segal, Harold B. *Pinocchio's Progeny: Puppets, Marionettes, Automatons, and Robots in Modernist and Avant-Garde Drama*. Baltimore: Johns Hopkins University Press, 1995.

Shershow, Scott Cutler. *Puppets and "Popular" Culture*. Ithaca, New York: Cornell University Press, 1995.

VanSchuyver, Jan M. *Storytelling Made Easy with Puppets*. Illustrated by Ellen Kae Hester. Phoenix: Oryx Press, 1993.

PURANAS

Sanskrit texts of FABLES, songs, LEGENDS, and tales dealing with all aspects of ancient and medieval Indian beliefs. The oldest of the 18 *Puranas* was written in about A.D. 600, and the most recent ones were probably composed in the fifteenth or sixteenth century. Each one is written in verse in the form of a dialogue, with stories and comments by other people embedded in the text. All of them have been revised over time, and the stories resemble some of those in the MAHABHARATA, although their narratives are by no means the same.

Five subjects are discussed in the *Puranas*: CREATION, or *sarga*; dissolution and recreation, or *pratisarga*; the periods of the Manus, or *Manvantara*; geneologies, or *vamsa*; and the history of the Solar and Lunar races spoken of in the *Vamsa*, or the *vamsyanucharita*. Besides these five areas of discussion, the four phases of human activities are also considered: love, or *kama*; wealth, or *artha*; righteousness, or *dharma*; and the final emancipation from REBIRTH, or *moksa*.

The chief GODS of the *Puranas* are BRAHMA, the creator; VISNU, the preserver; and SIVA, the destroyer. Together, the three are really aspects of the GOD, with Visnu not involving himself at all in human affairs although Siva lives among humankind practicing human asceticism.

Numerous stories and legends are collected in the *Puranas*, including at least three different versions of CREATION; the tale of "Matsya, the Fish"; "The Churning of the Ocean"; stories of KRISNA's conception, birth, youth, and adulthood; the birth of Parvati; the betrothal and wedding of Siva and Parvati; other stories of Siva and KALI; the tale of "Indra and the Ants"; and tales of kings and supernaturals.

For Further Reading

Coomaraswamy, A.K., and Sister Nivedita. *Myths of the Hindus and Buddhists*. New York: Dover Publications, n.d.

Dimmitt, Cornelia, and J.A.B. van Buitenen, eds. and trans. *Classical Hindu Mythology*. Philadelphia: Temple University Press, 1978.

Fischer-Schreiber, Ingrid, Franz-Karl Eberhard, Kurt Friedrichs, and Michael S. Diener. *The Encyclopedia of Eastern Philosophy and Religion*. Boston: Shambhala, 1989.

O'Flaherty, Wendy D., trans. *Hindu Myths*. New York: Viking Penguin, 1975.

PURGATORY

An intermediary otherworld, or third place, between HEAVEN and HELL, developed by the Catholic church during the course of the Middle Ages. In medieval Catholic thought, there were three possibilities for the souls of the dead: heaven for the good, hell for the wicked, and purgatory for those who were neither entirely good nor entirely wicked. Purgatory offers a second opportunity for souls to attain eternal life in heaven. In general terms, purgatory is a place where venial or less severe sins might be expiated. The souls of the dead must endure one or more trials, usually torture by fire, fire eventually becoming the dominant symbol for purgatory. The fire of purgatory brings about salvation through purification, after which souls go to heaven. The length of time that souls spend in purgatory may be shortened by the prayers of the living as well as by God's mercy and personal merits collected during the souls' lives. Dante's *Divine Comedy* contains perhaps the most well-known literary description of purgatory.

Examples of "underworlds," realms of the dead, or the AFTERLIFE from other storytelling traditions include HADES, TARTARUS, SHEOL, NIFLHEIM, and the "pure land," most of which are, at least in part, purgatorial as opposed to hell-like. *See also* KACHINAS.

For Further Reading

Le Goff, Jacques. *The Birth of Purgatory*. Translated by Arthur Goldhammer. London: Scolar Press, 1984.

PUSHKIN, ALEKSANDR (1799–1837)

Prolific Russian writer of fiction, poetry, verse FAIRY TALES, lyrics, and DRAMAS. Born in Moscow to a prominent Russian family, Pushkin was educated first by tutors and governesses and then at the newly established Lyceum at Tsarskoe Selo (where students prepared to assume important state positions). Pushkin's liberal political views caused him to chafe under the strict control of the government; in 1824 his comments regarding religion led to his dismissal from government service and his exile for two years. He married Natalia Goncharov in 1831, who was so beautiful that even an admiring Tsar Nicholas I arranged for her attendance at court balls. In 1834 Madame Pushkin met George d'Anthès-Heeckeren, a Frenchman who ardently pursued her for years. His behavior was so scandalous (even after he married Natalia's sister) that Pushkin challenged him to a duel. D'Anthès-Heeckeren shot first and wounded Pushkin, who died two days later on January 29, 1837.

Pushkin's literary legacy is vast and varied; although he is known for producing works in diverse styles and genres, he must be considered above all a poet. He first received notice for his unique romantic EPIC *Ruslan and Lyudmila* (1817–1820), and composed many other long and original verse narratives. Pushkin's most popular, enduring, and critically acclaimed work is the innovative *Eugene Onegin* (1823–1831), a novel in verse, which he developed and revised over eight years. The HEROINE, Tatiana, remains one of the most beloved female characters in Russian literature, and the work itself is considered by many to be the first great Russian novel. Pushkin's lyric poetry and dramas have inspired musical scores and even operas.

Pushkin's verse fairy tales, all of which first appeared in the 1830s, remain popular with audiences of both adults and children. "The Golden Cockerel," the story of an enchanted bird given to a lazy and idle KING by an evil sorcerer, became the inspiration for an opera by Rimsky-Korsakov in 1909. "The Fisherman and the Fish" relates the story of how a magical fish grants unlimited wishes to a poor fisherman. However, the fisherman's greedy wife abuses the gift in her selfish endeavor to gain power and riches for herself. "Tsar Saltan" is a long fairy tale that explains the life story of an exiled PRINCE who was cast away upon a barren island when he was just an infant. These enchanting stories (and many other Pushkin tales) continue to figure as an important part of Russian storytelling traditions generation after generation.

PUSS IN BOOTS

Popular FOLKTALE. Puss in Boots is a clever cat who aids his somewhat less clever master by executing a number of ingenious ruses against the master's enemies. The story of *Puss in Boots* appears around the world in many different versions but always includes the common MOTIF of the HELPFUL ANIMAL. The animal helper in most Western European versions of the tale is a cat, but in Eastern European stories the cat is often replaced by a fox, in India by a jackal, and in the Philippines by a monkey. *Puss in Boots* is a type of beast FABLE, which includes a moral at the end of the tale.

A common European version of "Puss in Boots," told by Charles Perrault (*see* PERRAULT, CHARLES), involves the three sons of a poor miller. When the miller dies, the eldest son inherits his father's mill, the second son inherits his father's donkey, and the youngest son inherits his father's cat. This youngest son is discouraged by his patrimony, for he realizes that he cannot earn a living with only a cat. The cat, however, conceives an elaborate plan to provide for the security of both his master and himself; to this end, he asks his master to provide him with a pair of boots to protect his feet and a sack. The cat catches rabbits, partridges, and other game in the sack, and sends them to the KING with the compliments of the Marquis of Carabas (the noble name the cat chooses for his master). The cat then stages a sequence of encounters between the king, the king's beautiful daughter, and the so-called Marquis of Carabas. Ultimately, the king is fooled by the machinations of the clever cat and marries the Marquis to his daughter. The moral of the tale is that cleverness and ingenuity may often be more useful than a monetary inheritance.

Various interpretations of the adventures of this clever cat abound in collections of children's stories; one particularly charming American version, accompanied by beautiful illustrations, has been recently retold by Lincoln Kirstein in *Puss in Boots* (1992).

For Further Reading

Galdone, Paul. *Puss in Boots*. New York: Clarion, 1976.

Kirstein, Lincoln. *Puss in Boots*. Boston: Little, Brown, 1992.

Perrault, Charles. *The Fairy Tales of Charles Perrault*. London: Victor Gollancz Limited, 1977.

PYRAMID TEXTS *See* EGYPTIAN CREATION, ISIS AND OSIRIS

QUEST

Basic MOTIF, or ARCHETYPE, of the HERO-journey. The hero's quest takes many forms, but at the center is the search to achieve a greater level of awareness and wisdom. Whether the quest involves the search for the HOLY GRAIL, the courtship of the bride, the freeing of the animal bridegroom, the need for the water of life, or the Golden Fleece, trials must be overcome before the quest can be completed.

Although the goal of the quest differs depending on the MYTH or FAIRY TALE, there can be no quest without the hero or HEROINE, and no hero or heroine without the quest. Inextricably linked, the hero will always have to move through the different stages of the quest, symbolized by the journey. The stages of the monomyth of the hero are, in effect, the stages of the quest, for early on the hero is faced with trials and tests that must be successfully passed before the next stage of the quest can be undertaken. The hero must unite the conscious with the unconscious, must come to know his or her "shadow," before the quest can be completed. Ultimately, the goal of the quest is wholeness, which may be symbolized by integration, MARRIAGE, REBIRTH, or RESURRECTION.

All storytelling is thus the relating of the individual quests that speak to humankind in every culture. Just as the cycle of life is exemplified in the expression, "The KING is dead. Long live the King!" so the quest begins again after it is successfully completed, for the end of the quest signals the beginning of a new quest, as every storyteller knows.

QUEST FOR THE GOLDEN FLEECE

Common English title of the *Argonautica*, a third-century B.C. EPIC by Apollonius of Rhodes. The most complete extant account of Jason's voyage with the Argonauts, the story is based on the work of HOMER, who took it from an older BALLAD cycle.

Pelias, the unrightful ruler of Iolcos, is told by a prophet that he will be killed by a visitor wearing one sandal. When a young adventurer named Jason arrives in Iolcos with one bare foot, Pelias is anxious to make him disappear for good. Pelias challenges Jason to undertake a presumably fatal mission. He is to voyage to the warlike land of Colchis and retrieve the Golden Fleece of a sacred, flying ram.

Jason gathers together a band of hearty warriors, and they set sail in a 50-oared ship called the *Argo*. Throughout their journey, the Argonauts are aided by Jason's patron goddess HERA, the queen of the Olympian deities.

The ship first puts in at Lemnos, an island where women have previously killed off all the men. The Argonauts are warmly welcomed there and they stay for a few months; they prove to be a great help in repopulating the island.

Adventures and mishaps pursue them the rest of the way to Colchis. Hylas, an armor bearer for the demi-god HERO Herakles, is drowned by one of the water NYMPHS. Searching for his beloved companion, Herakles wanders away from the *Argo*. The Argonauts have no choice but to sail on without him.

They next visit the blind soothsayer Phineus. The old man has angered ZEUS by delivering unambiguous predictions, and as punishment, he is repeatedly visited by the HARPIES. These hideous winged creatures either eat his food or defile it to the point of making it inedible. But two of the *Argo's* heroes, Zeles and Calais, drive the harpies away once and for all. In gratitude, Phineus gives the Argonauts valuable advice for their journey—including how to sail past the notorious Clashing Rocks, which otherwise would certainly destroy the *Argo*.

The Argonauts see many extraordinary sights and wonders as they travel on. These include the Amazons, a race of women warriors with whom the Argonauts wisely avoid doing battle. They also see the Titan Prometheus chained to a rock while his entrails are endlessly devoured by an eagle—his punishment for having given fire to humankind (*see* PROMETHEUS AND THE THEFT OF FIRE).

At last, the Argonauts reach Colchis. Initially, they are warmly greeted by King Aeetes. But Aeetes seethes when Jason tells him of his QUEST for the Golden Fleece. Like Pelias, Aeetes decides to challenge Jason to fatal tasks.

Aeetes orders Jason to yoke together two fearsome, fire-breathing bulls and use them to plow a field. Then Jason has to sow the soil with the teeth of a DRAGON, which causes the earth to sprout forth into a multitude of warriors. If Jason fights these warriors successfully, says Aeetes, the Golden Fleece will be his.

Hera knows that Jason needs magical help to escape Colchis alive with the Golden Fleece. So she conspires with APHRODITE to make Aeetes' daughter, Medea, fall in love with Jason. Medea is a beautiful WITCH with extraordinary powers, and her magic allows Jason to carry out his tasks.

Then Medea helps Jason to steal the Golden Fleece by lulling the serpent guarding it to sleep. Hopelessly in love with Jason and having completely betrayed her father, Medea then flees Colchis with the Argonauts.

The voyage back to Greece is scarcely less eventful than the voyage to Colchis. Medea prevents a sea-bound army from pursuing the Argonauts by brutally murdering her own brother, Apsyrtus. She also saves the Argonauts from Talus, the last of a race of gigantic bronze men.

The *Argo* survives a passage through the Wandering Rocks with the aid of the sea nymph Thetis. And when the SIRENS try to lure the crew to certain destruction, the Argonaut Orpheus sings and plays his lyre so beautifully that the siren song is rendered harmless. At last, the Argonauts reach Iolcos, where they disband and go their separate ways.

This is where Apollonius' poem ends. Primarily interested in the voyage itself, he was rather sketchy about such matters as Pelias' treachery. In fact, Jason was the true heir to the throne of Iolcos, and went on his voyage on the condition of regaining his kingdom if his quest were successful.

When Jason returns to Iolcos, Medea arranges Pelias' murder at the hands of his own daughters. This part of the story was told by the fifth-century poet Pindar. Jason's eventual betrayal of Medea and her terrifying retaliation was recounted by Pindar's contemporary Euripides in his tragedy *Medea*.

The *Argonautica* was ridiculed when it first appeared in Apollonius' home city of Alexandria. Apollonius then went to Rhodes, where a new version of the poem was much more favorably received. Eventually, the *Argonautica* was honored throughout the ancient world, and it had a great influence on the Roman poet Virgil.

Today's reader is likely to find Apollonius' version more akin to a novel than an ancient epic. Even the narrative voice has a personal quality completely lacking in Homer; Apollonius is not shy about commenting directly on the events of the story.

Particularly powerful is Apollonius' vivid and sympathetic portrayal of Medea. By contrast, Jason is drawn rather unsympathetically—not particularly dependable and decisive, either as a warrior or as a lover. Today's reader is likely to recognize him as a prototype of the literary antihero.

The story of the Argonauts is a classic example of a quest, one of the most enduring themes in world storytelling. For this reason, the story continues to be retold in the popular culture. An example is Charles H. Schneer's imaginative and surprisingly faithful 1963 film *Jason and the Argonauts. See also* ANCIENT GREEK STORYTELLING.

For Further Reading

Apollonius of Rhodes. *The Voyage of Argo.* Translated with an introduction by E. V. Rieu. London: Penguin Books, 1986.

QUESTIONS OF KING MILINDA

Pali text that records a supposed actual dialogue between the Buddhist monk Nagasena and the Greek KING Meander (known in India as Milinda). Many different stories in this series explore the ideological differences between these two. Their story, however, true to the Buddhist belief in reincarnation, begins centuries before their births, in a different incarnation.

A monk, angered at a novice's refusal to follow directions, beats the intractable man. Later, the monk overhears the novice pray that in each successive REBIRTH he be blessed with the power to say the right thing. The monk then prays that in each of his lives he will follow the novice and will be able to answer each of his questions and problems. The

two wander together through successive incarnations, questioning each other. The BUDDHA predicts that 500 years after his own death the two will reappear engaged in discourse. Through their endless questioning, they will unravel the difficulties inherent in Buddhist doctrine.

Five hundred years later, King Milinda puts to shame all the teachers and sages in India with his questions which threaten the foundation of Buddhism. The monk Nagasena, as penance, is ordered by his teacher to engage Milinda in argument until his doubts are overcome. A series of tales then relate the encounters between these later incarnations of the original monk and novice. For example, in their first meeting Nagasena tells Milinda that though his name is Nagasena, "there is no permanent individuality implied by [names]." This puzzles the king who then asks what the name Nagasena is if not a permanent individual. Milinda wonders if "Nagasena" is hair, skin, bones, organs, bodily functions, or consciousness. When Nagasena replies, "No," then Milinda asks if "Nagasena" is the sum of these parts. Again, Nagasena answers, "No." Milinda finally concludes that as Nagasena can be nothing more than his body or thoughts, Nagasena must not exist at all. To answer, Nagasena questions the king. After ascertaining that the king was brought to court in a carriage, Nagasena asks if a carriage is its wheels, framework, yoke, shafts, or axle. Milinda answers that the carriage is none of these things. Nagasena concludes that "'carriage' is a mere empty sound denoting nothing." As the king could not have arrived at court in "nothing," Nagasena surmises that the king must not be in court at all. Milinda, undaunted by Nagasena's verbal trickery, explains: "It is on account of its having all these things— yoke, traces, axle, wheels, and frame—and because of its purpose and use as a conveyance, that it is called by the generally understood designation of 'carriage.'" But Milinda has fallen into Nagasena's trap: "Just so, O king, is 'Nagasena.'" In each subsequent debate, Nagasena manages to quell a new doubt raised by Milinda.

For Further Reading

Milindapanha. *The Questions of King Milinda.* Translated from the Pali by T. W. Rhys Davids. 2 vols. New York: Dover, 1963.

Pesala, Bhikkhu. *The Debate of King Milinda: An Abridgement of the Milinda Panha.* Delhi: Motilah Banarsidags Publisher, 1971.

QUETZALCOATL

Plumed serpent and major Aztec god and CULTURE HERO of ancient Mexico. Originally a vegetation god, Quetzalcoatl is the son of the EARTH-MOTHER and SKY-FATHER, and he represents the Spirit of Duality. Among his many attributes, Quetzalcoatl is a bringer of culture, crafts, weaving, and fine arts; discoverer of maize; patron of crops and priests; inventor of learning and calendars; protector of craftsmen; and symbol of DEATH and RESURRECTION. The MYTHS pertaining to Quetzalcoatl can be found in five fragments in the *Annals of Cuauhtitlan,* the *Florentine Codex,* and *Codex Vaticanus 3738.*

The story of Quetzalcoatl's birth and childhood fits into the ARCHETYPE of the DIVINE CHILD, for he is conceived when the virgin Chimalma swallows an emerald that is transformed into a child and she dies soon after his birth (*see* VIRGIN BIRTH). Aztec CREATION myths say that Quetzalcoatl and the god of night, Tezcatlipoca, help create the EARTH and sky by pulling COATLICUE, earth GODDESS and Lady of the Serpent Skirt, from HEAVEN and tearing her in two to create earth and sky. According to Aztec belief, Quetzalcoatl comes to earth as a man in the Toltec period (A.D. 600–1000) where he serves as ruler, reformer, and priest.

Of the many myths surrounding Quetzalcoatl as both god and man, there is one called "Restoration of Life," wherein he and Xolotl, the dog-headed god, descend to the underworld to gather the bones of the dead. First Quetzalcoatl carries the bones to PARADISE and puts them in Earth-Mother's womb. By inseminating the bones with his blood, he becomes the father of the human race. Other myths tell of how Tezcatlipoca is jealous of Quetzalcoatl and schemes to make Quetzalcoatl drunk and licentious, so that he will commit incest with Quetzalpetatl, his sister. Depending on the variant of the myth, Quetzalcoatl is then driven away or he leaves in humiliation. He subsequently dies by fire either on a funeral pyre or on a boat of serpents, and his heart rises through the ashes till it becomes the god of the morning and evening star, with the promise that one day he will return to earth as KING. In a VARIANT of the myth, he sails away to the Yucatan where he becomes the Mayan equivalent of Quetzalcoatl, Kukulkan. *See also* ARTHUR.

RAGLAN, LORD (1885–1964)

English historian, FOLKLORE expert, and myth-ritualist. In his book, *The Hero*, Raglan argues that there is no such thing as "folk-history" or "race-memory." Historical events, he claims, are forgotten so quickly, that it is impossible to imagine that folk traditions can be actual history.

If folk tradition cannot be classified as history, it can be classified as MYTH. For Raglan, myth is the story that explains ritual. Raglan was particularly interested in the myth of the HERO, whom he equates with the KING. Raglan argued that numerous hero myths follow a similar pattern. This pattern roughly follows the story of Oedipus: The hero is born to royal parents, but he also is said to be the son of a god. Often, the child's father tries to murder him. The child survives and, after being reared by foster parents, returns to his homeland. The hero then performs some amazing feat and marries a royal PRINCESS. As king, he rules successfully for a number of years until he loses favor with the GODS or his subjects. He dies mysteriously, and his children do not succeed him. To Raglan, this pattern of the hero's life and death corresponds to the myth of the death and REBIRTH of the god of vegetation. This myth, in turn, is accompanied by the ritual killing of the king to ensure the survival of the community. Raglan's theories have been linked to those of James Frazer (*see* FRAZER, JAMES).

For Further Reading

Raglan, Lord. *The Hero. A Study in Tradition, Myth, and Drama.* New York: Vintage, 1956.

Segal, Robert, ed. *In Quest of the Hero.* Princeton: Princeton University Press, 1990.

RAGNAROK

Apocalyptic end of the world in Norse mythology. At the time of Ragnarok, the forces of evil, led by LOKI and Surt (*see* NORSE CREATION), will march against the GODS and the slain warriors from VALHALLA. The demons will destroy the gods and the world.

According to Norse mythology, several significant events will precede Ragnarok: the DEATH OF BALDR; a three-year war in Midgard, home of the humans; and three brutal winters without summers in between. In addition, the wolf Skoll will seize the SUN and swallow her. Skoll's brother, Hati, will capture the MOON and destroy him. The stars will disappear, the EARTH will tremble, trees will be uprooted, the world tree, YGGDRASIL, will moan and shiver, and avalanches will occur. Fenrir, Loki's evil wolf son, will run free, and Jormungand, Loki's monstrous serpent son, will emerge from the SEA. Naglfar, the ship made from dead men's nails, will launch and carry the giants to Ragnarok.

On the morning of Ragnarok, three cocks will crow: one for the GIANTS, one for the warriors in Valhalla, and one to raise the dead in HEL (see NIFLHEIM). Loki, Surt, Fenrir, Jormungand, the giants, HEL and her prisoners, and other DEMONS will assemble on Vigrid, a plain in Asgard, the home of the gods. All the gods and the dead warriors in Valhalla will arm themselves and ride to Vigrid. They will be led by ODIN, ruler of the Norse PANTHEON. He will wear a golden helmet and a gleaming war coat and carry his sword, Gungnir.

During the battle, Fenrir will swallow Odin, only to be destroyed by Odin's son Vidar, who will tear the wolf's throat apart. Thor will slay Jormungand but then die from the serpent's poison. Loki and Heimdall, watchman of the gods, will kill each other. After this vicious battle, Surt will cast fire over the whole world. Almost everything will die. The sun will be dark and the stars will cease to shine. The earth will disappear into the sea.

But the earth will rise again from the waters. Some gods, including Baldr, will return to HEAVEN. Two humans, Lif and Lifthrasir, will survive Ragnarok by hiding in Yggdrasil. They will repopulate the earth.

The idea of a catastrophic end to the world appears in many storytelling traditions. In many instances, the apocalypse emphasizes an end to the current order of things and the establishment of a new order. The apocalyptic theme is common in the Old Testament, where the Hebrew prophets speak in dire terms of the Day of YAHWEH, when the dead will return to be judged and the enemies of GOD will be destroyed before the new Kingdom is established. In Christian tradition, the apocalypse is described in the last book of the New Testament, the Book of Revelations, and predicts the coming of the Kingdom, the raising of the dead, and the final judgment. According to Indian texts, apocalypse is the natural ending of the world in the fourth age, the KALI Age. It is but one of a series of apocalypses. VISHNU, the preserver god, is the central figure in this apocalypse story. In Hopi tradition, the apocalyptic prophecy says that the United States will be destroyed by atomic bombs and radioactivity and that only the Hopis and their homeland will be preserved. The ancient village of Oraibi, the center of the world, eventually will be rejuvenated with Hopi faiths and ceremonies. The establishment of a new order will occur in the Emergence of the Fifth World.

RAINBOW SERPENT

God of CREATION and rainbringer in the myths of various cultures. Among some Australian tribes, Julunggul, the Rainbow Serpent, is honored as the creator god and the cause of civilization. Members of these tribes perform magical rituals to convince the Rainbow Serpent to bring rain after a drought. Initiation of the SHAMAN into his or her art might involve "a journey to the sky on the back of the Rainbow Serpent," notes Roslyn Poignant in *Oceanic Mythology*, and only the shaman "would dare to venture into a pool sacred to a Rainbow Snake."

For some Australian aboriginal tribes, the Rainbow Serpent is responsible for preparing the way for KUNAPIPI, a Great MOTHER figure and their creator, by descending to EARTH and creating streams, rivers, mountains, and paths as its serpentine form slithered across the earth. In Peru, a jaguar god is believed to hold up the arch of the sky in the form of a Rainbow Serpent. The Benin tribe in Africa have as their queen a GODDESS who is patroness of the waters and appears in the form of a Rainbow Serpent with the name "All-Bringing-Forth."

The recurrence of the Rainbow Serpent in the oral tradition of so many diverse cultures suggests its importance on a metaphorical level. The snake or serpent has long been connected or joined with mother goddesses, yet its phallic nature also lends itself to being associated with masculine gods. The serpent also symbolizes "the impenetrable manner in which our lives change, twist, and renew themselves," writes Buffie Johnson in *Lady of the Beasts*, while the rainbow symbolizes a bridge between HEAVEN and earth.

For Further Reading

Johnson, Buffie. *Lady of the Beasts*. New York: HarperCollins, 1988.

Robinson, Roland. *Aboriginal Myths and Legends*. Illustrated by Roderick Shaw. London: Paul Hamlyn, 1969.

RALSTON, WILLIAM (1828–1889)

Compiler and author of Russian FOLKLORE and histories. Educated at Trinity College, Cambridge, William Ralston later taught at the University of Oxford and became a member of several Russian societies that were concerned with preserving Russian folklore and traditions. Ralston was determined that Europeans and Americans be exposed to Russian culture, "that, whether they like it or not, English readers shall be forced to read about Russian songs and stories. I intend . . . to 'force them down their throats,'" (from an 1872 letter). *Songs of the Russian People* (1872) related Slavic mythology and Russian social life, while *Russian Folktales* (1873) and *Early Russian History* (1874) attempted to bring to life the early history of Russia. *Early Russian History* actually was delivered as four lectures before it was published. In addition to his scholarly lectures, many times Ralston read his translations of Krylov's FABLES before an audience of rapt children (*see* KRYLOV, IVAN). He also made numerous trips to Russia to hear "byliny," traditional narrative poems, being recited by storytellers. Remarkably, Ralston's tireless writings and research on Russia was done in his spare time while he continued to work as a librarian for the British Museum.

RAMA *See* RAMAYANA

RAMANUJAN, A. K. (1929–1993)

Author of Indian poetry and FOLKTALES. Attipat Krishnaswami Ramanujan was considered the leading scholar of Tamil, the oldest living Indian language. Born in Mysore, India, Ramanujan spoke Tamil on the main floor of his family home, according to family custom, while he and his family spoke English and Sanskrit upstairs. Ramanujan's primary exposure to the Indian oral tradition of FOLKLORE was derived from his grandmother as she told stories at family meals. Ramanujan, concerned with preserving Tamil and other Indian language folklore, set to work translating the ancient stories and poems. He published many volumes including *Proverbs* (1955), *Fifteen Poems from a Classical Tamil Anthology* (1965), *The Literature of India: An Introduction* (1975), *Another Harmony: New Essays on the Folklore of India* (1986), and *Folktales from India: A Selection of Oral Tales from Twenty-Two Languages* (1991). The folktales gathered by Ramanujan reflect the diverse Indian society. Critics consider *Folktales from India* to be a valuable anthology, especially to readers approaching Indian folklore with its myriad languages and cultural traditions for the first time. Credit also is given to Ramanujan for advancing the importance of Tamil and other Indian languages as distinct from the previously venerated Sanskrit language.

RAMAYANA

Sanskrit EPIC of ancient India. The *Ramayana* was composed by the poet VALMIKI, probably between the years 200 B.C. and A.D. 200. Over the course of its 24,000 couplets and seven books, it tells the life story of Rama, an Indian PRINCE and popular character in Hindu FOLKTALES.

The first book, the "Book of the Boyhood of Rama," relates the remarkable details of the birth of Rama in the kingdom of Ayodhya. On the same day that Rama is born to the KING's first wife, two sons are born to the king's second wife, and another son is born to the king's youngest wife. As these four princes grow up together, Rama and his brother Laksmana form a special bond between them; likewise, the other two brothers, Satrugha and Bharata, become particularly close. When the boys are 16 years old, a Brahmin sage comes to the court and tells the king that Rama must go into the forest to battle the demon king who lives there. Rama and Laksmana go into the forest together, and spend the next 13 years battling against the evil king and learning from the wise man. During this time Rama performs a difficult task which wins him the hand in MARRIAGE of the beautiful demi-GODDESS Sita. Rama's three brother's marry three of Sita's sisters at the same time, and the king begins to hand over responsibility for the kingdom to Rama.

The second book, the "Ayodhya Book," begins after Rama and Sita have been married for 12 years. Rama's father wishes to turn his crown over to Rama, but his wife Kaikeyi, to whom he owes two wishes, begs him to make her son Bharata the king and to send Rama back to the forest for 14 years. The king is saddened by this request, but feels compelled to honor it. Rama, Sita, and Laksmana (ever loyal to his brother) leave the kingdom for the forest; the king tries to stop them at the last minute, but he does not reach them in time. Once the three exiles are gone, the king loses his sight. Realizing that he has made a terrible mistake, the old man dies of grief.

Bharata, after learning of Rama's exile and his father's death, refuses to become king under such circumstances. He travels into the forest with a huge entourage to find Rama and convince him to return to the kingdom. He soon finds his brother and pleads with him to accept their father's crown. Rama refuses, citing his promise to their father to remain in the forest for 14 years. Bharata agrees to rule the kingdom for those 14 years, but threatens to kill himself if Rama does not return to take over as soon as his pledge is fulfilled. Rama and his companions remain in the forest for 13 years; the second book ends during their 14th and final springtime of exile.

The third book, the "Forest Book," describes the further adventures of Rama, Sita, and Laksmana in the forest. The hideous sister of the demon king of the forest spies Rama one day and, charmed by his handsome looks, tries to take him for her husband. Rama's refusal angers her so much that she attacks Sita. Laksmana intercepts her, cuts off her

ears, and sends her screaming back to her people. There, she rallies an army of 14,000 troops to attack her offenders. Rama hides his wife and brother in a cave, then defeats the entire army with his golden arrows. The demon sister is the only survivor. She, her brother, and their uncle hatch a plan to avenge Rama's massacre by stealing his beloved Sita. The uncle, in the form of a stag, lures the men away from Sita while the brother kidnaps her and takes her to his palace. Rama and Laksmana return to find Sita gone; a hermit woman tells them that the secret of Sita's whereabouts lie with the monkeys who witnessed her abduction.

In the fourth book, the "Book of Kishkindhya" (the land of the monkeys), Rama and Laksmana meet Sugriva and Hanuman, two monkeys who are trying to recover Sugriva's stolen wife. The four agree to help each other. Sugriva's wife is quickly rescued, with the help of Rama's well-aimed arrow, and the monkeys promise that after the rainy season they will all search for and find Sita. Sure enough, after the rains subside, the monkeys, with the help of the vultures and the bears, begin their search for Sita.

The fifth book, the "Sundara Kanda" (The Book Beautiful) opens with Hanuman the monkey's journey to Lanka Island, where Sita is being held prisoner. He approaches Sita on her morning walk and offers to fly her back to Rama on his back. She declines, wishing to be rescued by Rama himself. Hanuman returns to Rama with the good news of Sita's survival, and requests of Rama that when he goes to Lanka Island to retrieve his wife that he kill the demon king who keeps her there.

The sixth book, the "War Book," opens with Rama, Laksmana, the monkeys, the vultures, and the bears all planning their invasion of Lanka Island. A magical monkey builds a bridge over the ocean to the island, and Rama's forces march across it in search of Sita. A bloody battle ensues, during which a terrible GIANT attacks Rama's motley army. Rama slays the giant, then shoots an arrow through the demon king, killing him and ending the fight. Sita is brought before Rama, who rejects her because he believes she has been defiled by her captor. A grieving Sita tries to immolate herself, but Agni, the god of fire, refuses to burn her body since she is without sin. Agni rebukes Rama for questioning his wife's virtue, and the couple is reunited. Meanwhile, Hanuman is given the secret to restoring life to the slain animals. He restores them, the 14-year exile ends, and the entire company flies back to Ayodhya in a giant chariot. There, they are greeted with great celebration. The next day, Rama and Sita are crowned king and queen, and Rama begins his prosperous 11,000 year reign over the kingdom.

The seventh and final book, the "Uttara Kanda" begins one month after Rama's coronation, as all their animal friends begin their journey back to their respective homes. Then the action quickly shifts to 10,000 years later. Sita, who is pregnant, requests permission to go to a retreat along the Ganges. After learning that some of his subjects still believe that Sita might have been ravaged by her evil captor so many years ago, Rama commands Laksmana to abandon Sita at the Ganges. Unhappily, Laksmana obeys.

Sita roams into the forest where she encounters Valmiki, the composer of the *Ramayana*, who shelters her during the birth of her two sons. The three live with Valmiki in his hut for 12 years while he composes the *Ramayana* and teaches it to them. Sita and her sons returns to the kingdom during a great festival; the boys recite the *Ramayana*, and Sita comes forward with her father. She asks permission of Rama to prove to him once again her purity, and calls upon her own mother, Mother EARTH, to embrace her if she has been faithful to her husband. Mother Earth rises up, takes Sita onto her lap, and then returns into the ground. All the creatures in the world rejoice at this happy ending.

The *Ramayana* is an old and popular epic and has spread widely throughout southeast Asia. Various versions of the tale exist in the cultures of Indonesia, Burma, Thailand, and the Philippines, and often the figure of the local ruler would be inserted in Rama's place. The *Ramayana* incorporates themes of transformation, raging battles, demonic kings, family loyalty, and spiritual purity, which inform our modern understanding of ancient Indian culture. However, the value of this epic in storytelling traditions has not waned in modern times for it continues to signify, allegorically, personal battles which still wage today. Historically, the *Ramayana* is an important work because it, along with the MAHABHARATA, exposes the root of ancient Hindu tradition; Rama, Sita, and Laksmana represent the ideal king, wife, and brother, and their adventures provide the basis for generations of FOLKLORE and LEGEND which are still evolving and expanding.

Most folk and oral versions of the *Ramayana* exist primarily in India and Indonesia, including puppet versions and comic book versions (both of which are highly popular with children). Stories of the flight and salvation of Sita are particular favorites, and often are sung by women. Further, many Asian cultures perform ritual dances which reenact Sita's adventures. These dances, called "ketchak," or "monkey dances," are especially common in Bali; film versions of these rituals are available.

A major three-volume prose translation of the *Ramayana* into English, *The Ramayana of Valmiki*, was published by Hari P. Shastri in 1962. An interesting satiric recreation of the story, *The Ramayana* (also called *Rama Retold*) was written in English by Aubrey Menon in 1954. An important source of further information for scholars and others is *The Mircea Eliade Encyclopedia of Religion* (1987).

For Further Reading

Buck, William. *Ramayana: King Rama's Way.* Berkeley: University of California Press, 1976.

Dutt, Romesh C. *The Ramayana, and the Mahabharata.* Condensed into English verse. New York: E.P. Dutton, 1910.

Shastri, Hari P. *The Ramayana of Valmiki.* 3 vols. London: Shanti Sadan, 1952-1959.

RANGI AND PAPA

Maori GODS of HEAVEN and EARTH. In Maori mythology, first there is Io, creator of light. Io then makes Rangi, SKY-FATHER, and Papa, EARTH-MOTHER, who embrace each other so tightly that their offspring are locked in Papa's womb and cannot be born. In one variant, two of their offspring, Rongo and Tane, create the forests, plants, and insects. Tane, the god of life, then separates his parents, but Rangi is so unhappy to be apart from Papa that his tears become the rain; Papa, in turn, is equally sad, and her sighs become the mist that rises up to the sky. In another variant, Rangi and Papa give birth to their offspring in darkness. In order for CREATION to take place, however, the offspring have to do something about their parents. Although Tumatauenga wants to kill his parents, Tane-mahutu, the forest god, advocates separating them. Rongo-ma-tane, the god of cultivation, and Tangaroa, the ocean god, both try and fail, until finally Tane-mahutu stands on his head and use his powerful legs to push his father off his mother as his parents yell in pain. Then there is light at last and the people on earth can be seen.

As Sky-Father, Rangi is the equivalent of the Greek god Uranos. Papa also is known in Hawaiian mythology as the earth GODDESS who was the ancestress of the Hawaiian people, mother of the gods, and queen of the underworld. Her name means "foundation," and she personifies that which is hard and broad, such as flat rock or floor.

For Further Reading

Alpers, Anthony. *Maori Myths and Tribal Legends.* Boston: Houghton Mifflin, 1966.

Te Kanawa, Kiri. *Land of the Long White Cloud: Maori Myths, Tales, Legends.* Illustrated by Michael Foreman. New York: Arcade Publishing, 1989.

RAP SONG

Music genre. Although the coining of the name " rap song" traditionally is credited to H. "Rap" Brown, a 1960s African American nationalist whose highly stylized manner of speech came to be known as "rappin'," this musical genre can be traced from African bardic traditions to the southern African American religious sermons and FOLKTALES to the mid-twentieth-century creation of jive talk, a manner of speech that reinterpreted the traditional definitions of English words from an African American perspective. The rap song became a popularized musical genre in the early 1970s after the words of Brown's political speeches, which contained elements

of rhyme, signifying, and double entendre, were put to music in the late 1960s. The spectrum of topics addressed in rap music includes the harmonious "funk" sounds of rap pioneer George Clinton and his group Parliament, the highly politicized messages from artists like Public Enemy and Arrested Development, as well as a sub-genre resulting from inner-city gangster lifestyles, "gangsta rap," as shown in the work of the late Tupac Shakur and N.W.A.

A particular element of rap songs called "playing the dozens" bears a striking resemblance to the storytelling contest; instead of winning for telling the best-judged story, the participants of "playing the dozens" attempt to insult the familial relations of the other competitors. The applause of the audience consequently determines the winner of this contest, which is often viewed as a RITE OF PASSAGE in the maturation of the victorious individual.

RAVEN

Symbol of ill-omen in MYTH and FOLKLORE; TRICKSTER figure and CULTURE HERO in Native North American story cycles. The figure of the raven appears in almost every culture. Common themes include etiological stories that explain why ravens croak, are black, are bald, or clap their wings. The belief that they possess supernatural, fearsome powers is widespread, as exemplified by Edgar Allen Poe's famous nineteenth-century poem, "The Raven," with its haunting refrain, "Quoth the Raven, 'Nevermore.'"

The Ancient Greeks believed the raven was a sacred, prophetic bird, associated with APOLLO. The Arabs consider the raven "Father of Omens," and believe, as in Europe, Great Britain, India, and the Slavic countries, that to see a raven flying on the left means bad luck.

In Genesis in the Hebrew BIBLE, NOAH first sends a raven from the ark to see if the waters of the FLOOD have dried up (*see* GENESIS, BOOK OF). The raven flies back and forth until there is land to rest upon, but does not return with the message. His PUNISHMENT is to suffer thirst, be black, or eat carrion.

In Norse mythology, ODIN has two ravens, Hugin and Munin, that are sent out to scout the world each day and return to Odin with their news. These ravens are responsible for revealing to Odin the location of Odhroerir, the magic cauldron.

In Old Irish mythology, the three battle GODDESSES Morrigan, Badb, and Macha, all appear in raven form. Like Apollo, the mythological Bran was associated with the raven as an oracular bird. King ARTHUR of Celtic mythology, LEGEND, and ROMANCE, is said to live on as a raven. Legends also recount how Owen Glendower had a pet raven who provided him with a magic stone that could render him invisible (see INVISIBILITY).

The GRIMM BROTHERS's "The Raven" tells of a person who is transformed into a raven (see TRANSFORMATION). Here a queen grows impatient with her daughter and wishes she would become a raven. Her wish comes true, and the little PRINCESS is transformed into a raven and flies away. After many trials, including overcoming a glass mountain with a magic stick and horse and a cloak of invisibility, a young man finally succeeds in breaking the SPELL, and he marries the princess.

The figure of Raven appears in many of the tales of the Pacific Northwest and the Arctic. He is often the one responsible for stealing light and bringing it to the world, for the CREATION of different parts of the world, and for naming plants and teaching ANIMALS. He is reputed to be insatiable regarding food and sex, and his trickster nature makes him cunning, deceptive, and untrustworthy. Depending on the particular culture, Raven is said to come from GHOSTS, be the son of "Flood-Tide Woman," marry Bright-Cloud Woman, have a brother named Logobola and a sister named Whut, or be able to shapeshift (see SHAPE-SHIFTING). The Tsimshian believe that Raven not only brought light to the world but also created human beings.

As a benefactor, according to the mythology of the Quillayute people, Raven is the one to bring the blueback salmon to the rivers of Washington. In their tale "How Raven Helped the Ancient People," he is also the bringer of daylight and fire, which are hidden from people when Gray Eagle is guardian of ev-erything. Raven, however, falls in love with Gray Eagle's daughter, and although he is a handsome man, he transforms himself into a snow-white bird in order to please her. Grey Eagle's daughter then asks him to stay in her father's lodge. While he is there, he manages to steal the SUN, MOON, stars, fresh water, and fire. He then places the sun, moon, and stars in the sky; drops the fresh water to the ground where it then serves as the source of all of the earth's freshwater rivers and lakes; and finally has to drop the fire for it is burning his beak and blackening his feathers. Thus, fire is said to leap out of two rocks rubbed together because Raven drops the fire on rocks, and Raven is said to be black from the smoke of the fire he carried away from Grey Eagle's lodge.

The Tlingit people of the Northwest Coast tell a VARIANT on this myth, called simply "Raven." Here Raven is promised by his father that when he grows up he will be given enough strength to make the world, which has no light. When Raven learns that a rich man with a daughter is the one with the light, he makes himself into a small piece of dirt that the daughter swallows, making her pregnant. The baby that is born is Raven. As a baby, Raven crawls about crying so hard that his grandfather has to give him the various bundles hanging on the walls. In one bundle are the stars, which Raven lets go up the smoke hole so that they spread through the skies; next Raven manages to get the grandfather to give him the bundle with the moon, which he lets up the smoke hole till it reaches the sky; finally he manages to get the box holding the daylight, and he escapes. He flies on to the man who has the freshwater, and he tricks him as well until he drinks all the water and flies up through the smoke hole. This time he is caught in the hole by the man's spirits, and the soot from the fire beneath blackens him. Eventually, he gets free, spitting out the water, thus making the rivers and streams, and finally he lets the sun out of the box and there is daylight.

Similarities can be found among the Native North American Indian tales of Raven, COYOTE, OLD MAN, IKTOME, and the Polynesian culture hero MAUI, all trickster figures.

For Further Reading

Erdoes, Richard, and Alfonso Ortiz. *American Indian Myths and Legends*. New York: Pantheon, 1985.

REALISTIC TALE

Type of complex tale that avoids references to the supernatural. In the realistic tale, the action focuses on the character's cleverness. The character, unaided by MAGIC OBJECTS or invisibility, still must win the PRINCESS, solve the RIDDLE, or cheat others. The realistic tale usually has a complicated plot. The types of stories differ only slightly from those that employ fantastical devices.

Realistic tales fall into five categories. In the first, the HERO is able to win a princess through his clever trickery. The hero must find a way to solve a princess's puzzle or to make her laugh, as in "The Golden Goose." While in this story a magic object, the goose that causes people to stick to it, is employed, such tales are generally more concerned with the hero's ability to trick and blackmail. Another type of realistic tale revolves around a character's ability to answer seemingly impossible riddles. In a Russian example, "The Tsar's Riddles, or the Little Wise Girl," a small child must appear before the Tsar both dressed and undressed, not empty-handed but not with a gift, and not on foot but also not on horseback. To fulfill these strange requests, the girl covers herself in a fish net, rides to court upon a hare, and carries a quail that flies away as soon as she unclasps her hands. These stories tend to end with some sort of reward for the riddle-solver. In this case, the Tsar, amazed by the little girl's cleverness, decides to wed her when she grows up. A third type of tale depicts clever counsels offering sound advice. For instance, in "The Three Words of Advice," a tinsmith is told to mind his own business, to stay on the highway, and to think before he acts. By following this advice, the tinsmith saves his own life and that of his son.

Cleverness is not used for good in all types of realistic tales. The story of a swindle is common to Europe, Asia, Africa, North and South America. Often, in these tales, a cheat pretends that an ordinary object or ANIMAL possesses magic power. A pot is said to provide its own food; a horse supposedly defecates gold. By sticking a gold piece in the horse's dung, the cheat proves his claim. The lie is generally discovered and the villain punished, though sometimes he escapes unscathed. In "Peter Ox," for instance, a sexton convinces a peasant that he can teach a calf how to speak. The peasant showers money upon the sexton, and the sexton's trickery is never discovered. The last type of realistic tale depicts robbers consistently outwitting those from whom they steal. In an enduring example, "The Treasure Chamber of Rhampsinitus," an architect who designs the KING's treasure house leaves a secret entrance for his own use. Either the architect or his sons continually steal from the treasure house. When the king notices that his gold supply is dwindling, he sets a trap for the thieves. One thief is caught, but the other cuts off his head so that his identity remains hidden. The king, through his daughter or through the headless body, tries again to trick the remaining thief into revealing his identity. The thief, however, outwits the king in each attempt. Finally, the king gives up and marries his daughter to the thief.

All of these realistic tales have magical counterparts. In other stories, animals truly do produce gold. Princesses are won by magical or supernatural intervention. However, realistic tales emphasize the power of an intelligent mind.

For Further Reading

Daniels, Guy. *The Tsar's Riddles, or the Little Wise Girl*. Illustrated. New York: McGraw Hill, 1967.

Shulevitz, Uri, ed. *The Golden Goose*. Illustrated. New York: Farrar, Straus, Giroux, 1995.

REBIRTH

Progression of the HERO from death or non-life to life. Similar to RESURRECTION, rebirth can take place on the spiritual or physical plane in MYTHS and FAIRY TALES. In a way, rebirth repeats the theme of the miraculous birth by symbolizing this event once again. The hero undergoes a reincarnation, and may be reborn as a human, a god, or a part of nature. Connected with the fertility cycle in many religions, the pieces of the god (or hero as representative of the god) might be planted in the earth and reborn the following spring. The return of the Greek Persephone (*see* PERSEPHONE MYTH) and the Hittite TELIPINU symbolize the end of the earth lying fallow. The Ancient Greek Eleusinian Mysteries were a celebration of the cycle of birth and rebirth depicted in the story of Persephone. Similarly, in the Native American BEAR MAN MYTH, the bear is killed but then reborn in the spring.

The Greek hero Herakles is "reborn" when ZEUS wants him to join the 12 Olympian GODS, and he cannot displace any of the gods from their positions. Zeus then asks HERA to adopt Herakles as her own son in a rebirth ceremony, so she goes to bed in mock labor, producing Herakles from beneath her dress.

Rebirth also can take place at different stages of life, as human beings undergo trials that take them to the next plane of awareness. As David Leeming notes in *Mythology: The Voyage of the Hero,* "Psychologically the rebirth myth is the culmination of the process of self-realization and individuation which produces the new, whole man [or woman]. The hero has faced and overcome death" and has now returned to "the MOTHER's cycle" representing humankind collectively. When reborn, the hero comes to represent all humanity. In the GRIMM BROTHERS's fairy tales, rebirth can be said to occur when Snow White comes back to life after the apple is dislodged from her throat and when the FROG is changed into a PRINCE in "The Frog-Prince."

RED RIDING HOOD

Popular FOLKTALE that serves as a warning to children to be self-disciplined and obedient. Although the French storyteller Charles Perrault (*see* PERRAULT, CHARLES) created the literary version of the tale (1697), many of the basic elements date back to a tradition of warning stories in the late Middle Ages in France, Tyrol, and northern Italy. Scholars have been able to reconstruct a version of the oral tale similar to the one Perrault would have been familiar with and on which he probably based his tale. In the oral version, a little girl is accosted by a WEREWOLF on her way to her grandmother's. The werewolf arrives at the grandmother's house before the girl does, kills the grandmother, and puts her meat and blood in the cupboard. When the girl arrives, she eats the meat until a cat informs her that she is eating her own grandmother. The wolf then invites the girl into bed with him, compelling her to remove her clothes item by item and throw them in the fire. The girl climbs into bed with the wolf, but grows suspicious after noticing and commenting on "how hairy you are," "what big ears you have," and other oddities. As the wolf becomes more threatening, the girl becomes more suspicious; she finally manages to escape by pretending she has to urinate.

Perrault, who wrote for children and adults of the French middle and upper classes, added the red riding hood and "refined" the original story considerably to emphasize the importance of virtuous behavior. Perrault eliminated the eating of the grandmother, comments about "her" hairiness, and toilet references. One of the most significant changes is in the HEROINE herself. While the girl in the oral folktale cleverly saves herself by outwitting her predator, Perrault's Red Riding Hood is spoiled, disobedient, and completely helpless, ultimately falling victim to the wolf's designs and being eaten. Another famous update comes from Germany. The GRIMM BROTHERS added a happy ending to their "Little Red Cap," but unlike in the original folktale, the girl escapes not through her own resources, but through the heroism of a passing hunter, who fills the wolf's belly with stones.

Victorian and twentieth-century adaptations of the story often combine elements of the Perrault and Grimm stories. In all versions, there is a lesson to be learned about obedience, as well as about sexual promiscuity. Had she not ignored her mother's injunction not to talk to strangers, Red Riding Hood would never have encountered the wolf at all. The red hood worn by the heroine is symbolic of her sinful sexuality, a sexuality later emphasized by her crawling in bed with the wolf. For her disobedience to her mother as well as her gullibility to her ravisher, Red Riding Hood's death or near-death reinforces the lessons of female self-control and passivity.

For Further Reading

Galdone, Paul. *Little Red Riding Hood.* New York: McGraw Hill, 1974.

Marshall, James. *Red Riding Hood.* New York: Dial, 1987.

REFUSAL OF THE CALL

In MYTHS and FOLKTALES, whereby the potential HERO does not respond to the call to adventure, initiation, change, or the QUEST. The call to adventure for the hero, male or female, may come in many forms ranging from an animal that one must chase, drawing one farther and farther away from the world that is known and safe, to a human guide in the form of a WISE OLD MAN or a CRONE. But not everyone heeds the call that will transform the hero and transport him or her to the next stage of life's journey. Some are too frightened to budge, or do not notice the possibility of divinity awaiting them. In the case of the nymph Daphne, pursued by APOLLO, her fright overwhelms her, and she runs from the god while praying to her father to destroy her beauty. Her well-known metamorphosis into a tree is the result. As Joseph Campbell observes in *The Hero with a Thousand Faces*, "The girl retreated to the image of her parent and there found protection." Campbell goes on to say that by being "bound in by the walls of childhood," one "fails to make the passage through the door and come to birth in the world without." Another example of this refusal is the story of Lot's wife, in Genesis of the Hebrew BIBLE: when she is called by GOD to leave her city but pauses to look back, she is turned into a pillar of salt (*see* GENESIS, BOOK OF). In T. S. Eliot's poem "The Love Song of J. Alfred Prufrock," Prufrock's "paralysis" can be seen as a kind of refusal to heed the call to adventure or the quest.

Refusal of the call can lead to stagnation. In order to grow and individuate, one must leave the "safe" world and move outside of what is known.

RESURRECTION

Act of rising from DEATH and ascending to HEAVEN (*see* ASCENSION). In a number of MYTHS and religious texts, HEROES and GODS are resurrected. As David Leeming notes in *The World of Myth*, "In the stories of the Great GODDESS, a pattern emerges in which the Goddess figure mourns the loss of a loved one, goes on a search, and, in bringing about a form of resurrection—clearly associated with the planting and harvesting of crops—establishes new religious practices or mysteries for her followers." The connection is made between "death, planting, sexuality, and resurrection or immortality, on the one hand, and physical as well as spiritual renewal, on the other." Thus the Egyptian Isis seeks Osiris, who is resurrected (*see* ISIS AND OSIRIS), and Demeter seeks her daughter Persephone, who returns from the underworld (*see* PERSEPHONE MYTH). Jesus Christ dies and is resurrected before his subsequent ascension into HEAVEN. In the Native American BEAR MAN MYTH, the bear dies, arises, and is resurrected in the spring. Likewise, the great mortal Greek hero Herakles (the Roman Hercules) is resurrected from the devouring flames and reborn with an even stronger, more beautiful body; he then ascends to Heaven in the chariot of ZEUS and becomes immortal.

REVERSAL OF FORTUNE

Peripeteia, or an unexpected change for better or worse in the protagonist's life. In comedy and tragedy as well as in MYTH and LEGEND, HEROES, HEROINES, and important characters sometimes undergo what is known as a reversal of fortune: a parent may die suddenly, leaving an unexpected inheritance; what appears to be good news may, in fact, be the opposite; good luck may suddenly turn bad or vice versa. In his *Poetics*, Aristotle describes reversal of fortune, *peripeteia*, as the result of *anagnorisis*, a discovery or recognition made by the protagonist of a comedy or tragedy.

A famous example of reversal of fortune comes in the story of Oedipus as depicted by Sophocles in his play *Oedipus the King*. When the Corinthian comes to inform Oedipus that his father, Polybos, is dead and that he will now be king of Corinth as well as THEBES, the Corinthian expects that he is bringing good news: although Oedipus has lost his father, he has gained a throne. At first Oedipus himself regards the news as positive, for now he no longer has to fear the oracle's prophecy that he would kill his father. However, as the Corinthian and Oedipus talk, the Corinthian reveals that Polybos was not Oedipus's real father to begin with. Before long, Oedipus discovers the truth about his parents' identity, and he recognizes that he has indeed killed his father, Laius, and married his mother, Jocasta, after all. Since his goal has been to find Laius' murderer and thus cleanse his city of a plague by exiling the murderer, he experiences reversal of fortune: since he is the murderer, he must sacrifice his throne and himself be exiled from Thebes. What he once considered his good fortune and luck have been reversed and instead bring about his downfall.

For Further Reading

Sophocles. *Oedipus the King*, from *Three Tragedies by Sophocles*. Translated by H. D. F. Kitto. New York: Oxford University Press, 1962.

REYNARD

The fox, a TRICKSTER of the medieval EPIC, *Roman de Renart*. Like other medieval stories in which ANIMALS talk and behave like people, the stories satirize human behavior.

The Reynard stories date from about 1150 to 1500. They were developed from the beast FABLES of oral and written tradition, including those of AESOP. An anonymous fox is a character in many early stories. In 1148, he was named Reinardus in a collection of aphorisms by Nivardus. After 1175, the Reynard stories became the most popular of the animal fables in French, Flemish, and German literature. (In France, the word *renard* came to mean *fox*.) In the fourteenth century, Chaucer used some of the material in *The Nun's Priest's Tale* of *The Canterbury Tales*. The Reynard stories were translated and published in English by William Caxton in 1481. By the fifteenth century they were heavily used to make political points. In 1794, Goethe published a German version, *Reineke Fuchs*, in which he stressed the resourcefulness—therefore usefulness to society—of the immoral man. Jacob Grimm also published a German version in 1834 (*see* GRIMM BROTHERS).

Reynard struggles constantly to outwit other animals: the physically stronger wolf, Isengrim; King Noble the lion; Sir Bruin the bear; Chanticleer the cock; and others. Reynard persists in playing the rebel, coward, seducer, and liar.

An early anti-HERO, Reynard is a progenitor of many contemporary characters in novels and film, such as Yossarian in Joseph Heller's *Catch-22* and the "Man With No Name" in Sergio Leone's "spaghetti" westerns from the 1960s starring Clint Eastwood (*A Fistful of Dollars; For a Few Dollars More;* and *The Good, the Bad, and the Ugly*).

For Further Reading

Best, Thomas W. *Reynard the Fox*. Boston: Twayne Publishers, 1983.

Chaucer, Geoffrey. *Chanticleer and the Fox*. Adapted and illustrated by Barbara Cooney. New York: Crowell, 1958.

Hastings, Selina. *Reynard the Fox*. Illustrated by Graham Percy. New York: Tambourine Books, 1990.

Reynard the Fox: The Epic of the Beast, Consisting of English Translations of the History of Reynard the Fox and Physiologus. London: Caxton, 1481. Reprint, New York: E.P. Dutton, 1924.

RHIANNON

Beautiful figure in the *Mabinogion*, a collection of Welsh tales written in the early twelfth century, who possesses mysterious powers and is identified with the ancient mother GODDESS and Celtic horse goddess. Rhiannon first appears in magnificent clothing riding her white horse. Pwyll, the King of Dyfed, orders several of his men to follow her. Although Rhiannon's horse appears to move at a constant pace, the king's swiftest horses cannot overtake her. Finally, Pwyll calls out to Rhiannon who stops. She tells Pwyll that she is being given a husband against her will, and she wants to marry him. They plan to marry one year from that night.

One year later, Rhiannon and Pwyll are married and she gives birth to a boy. While Rhiannon and the six women who sit with her are sleeping, the baby disappears. Rather than be punished, the women kill some pups, smear the blood on Rhiannon, and throw the bones near her. When she wakes, the women tell Rhiannon that she has destroyed her son. For her penance, Rhiannon sits outside the court's gate and tells everyone who comes how she has killed her child. She offers to carry the visitors, like a horse, on her back to the court.

Meanwhile, a lord discovers an infant boy in his barn when his mare is foaling. He and his wife raise the child and name him Gwri, for his golden hair. When the lord notices the resemblance between the child and Pwyll, he realizes whose son Gwri actually is and returns the boy to his parents.

Rhiannon's association with fertility and the mother goddess, specifically Demeter, is plain when she attempts to rescue her son, renamed Pryderi (meaning "Trouble"), from a SPELL which has made him immobile and mute. At this time, Dyfed is also under a spell which has rendered the kingdom a wasteland. Both Rhiannon and Pryderi become prisoners in the otherworld, but when the spells are broken, they return to Dyfed which is fertile once again.

For Further Reading

Caldecott, Moira. *Women in Celtic Myth*. Rochester, VT: Destiny Books, 1992.

RHYS, JOHN (1840–1915)

Professor of Celtic studies at Oxford University and collector of Welsh folk knowledge. After graduating from Oxford, Rhys became interested in linguistics, which eventually led him to study the language of his own region, Wales. As the foremost expert in this field, he was the first appointed professor of Celtic studies at Jesus College, Oxford. His early work on grammar was followed by his exploration into the religion and folklore of ancient Wales. In *Celtic Folk-lore: Welsh and Manx* (1901) he collected and translated a number of little-known stories. These tales and bits of folk knowledge were gleaned from the memories of various Welsh storytellers. As one such orator notes, "The grey old man in the corner of his father heard a story, which from his father he had heard, and after them I have remembered." In *Studies on the Arthurian Legends* (1889), Rhys wrote about the more familiar LEGENDS connected to Celtic lore. His scholarship helped to preserve the fading traditions of Wales, an area drastically changed by the Industrial Revolution.

For Further Reading

Jones, Gwyn. *Welsh Legends and Folktales*. Illustrated. New York: Henry Z. Walck, 1955.

RICE, THOMAS D. (JIM CROW)

Nickname for Thomas D. Rice, the creator of minstrel character "Jim Crow." A generally unknown actor, Rice first performed as "Jim Crow" in 1928 and was quickly propelled to international fame. Some of his most popular performances were burlesques of the tragedies *Othello* and *Uncle Tom's Cabin*, the farces *Jumbo Jum* and *The Virginia Mammy*, and the songs "Lucy Long" and "Jim Crow." Each of these performances consisted of Rice performing in blackface, while acting out a story through a song-and-dance comic routine. Rice's performances were caricatures of African Americans; he employed and perpetuated extreme stereotypes by depicting African Americans as unintelligent, indolent, and sexually irrepressible. As "Jim Crow," Rice employed a ludicrous and incongruous speech permeated by malapropisms, the unstated message being that African Americans were "simple" and needed to be slaves for their own benefit. Indeed, Rice portrayed slaves as content with their situation, bemused by the movements to end slavery. This message, historians have argued, was the force behind the popularity of "Jim Crow" and other minstrel performances. Many white Americans looked to Rice's caricatures to reaffirm their own views of slaves. In fact, Rice was lauded by many for the "authenticity" of his portrayals.

Although Rice was not the first to portray an African American on stage for comic effect, his portrayal of "Jim Crow" had an instant impact on popular comic performances, as MINSTRELSY would continue to be popular for years to come. More significantly, though, Rice's character would have a lasting impact on American society. Since this "comic" character embodied many racist beliefs held by many whites at the time, it is certainly not surprisingly that the term promptly filtered into common usage as a derogatory epithet for African Americans. Yet, more than just an epithet, the term "Jim Crow," or "Jim Crow Laws," became a simple way to describe the system of racial segregation in the United States and the racism inherent in this system.

THE RIDDLE PRINCESS

Russian FAIRY TALE with VARIANTS. Called "The PRINCESS Who Wanted to Solve RIDDLES" in Aleksandr Afanas'ev's (*see* AFANAS'EV, ALEKSANDR) collection, *Russian Fairy Tales*, this is the story of a Tsar's daughter, a princess who says she will marry the man who propounds a riddle she can not answer. If she can answer the riddle, the man who poses it is put to death, and, indeed, many men die.

At this time there is a man who has three sons, the youngest of whom is called Ivan the Simpleton (his name suggests he is something of a fool). He is taken with the idea of going to the tsar's court to pose a riddle, and on his way he devises a riddle from what he sees. When he gets to court, his riddle stumps the princess, so she begs for more time. That night she sends her chambermaid to offer money to Ivan the Simpleton, but he will not take it; he will give the princess the answer only if she stands all night in his room, which she does. The next day she knows the answer, so he poses a second riddle, and the same thing happens again. The third day he poses a riddle concerning the princess's inability to solve his riddles and the bribes. Since this is done in front of all the senators of the court, the princess does not answer the riddle, and that night, when she stands all night in Ivan the Simpleton's room, she realizes that she cannot say the answer because she will be found guilty, so she marries Ivan. This tale suggests that the simpleton is often the wisest one of all.

For Further Reading

Afanas'ev, Aleksandr. *Russian Fairy Tales*. New York: Pantheon, 1976.

RIDDLES

Form of wordplay that poses a question, the answer to which depends upon the recognition of unexpected relationships between things or between words. Riddles were developed in the oral traditions of cultures worldwide and may represent one of the earliest forms of structured thought. One of the oldest known riddles was found on a tablet believed to date to Babylonian times.

The Ancient Greeks were especially fond of riddles. Although Aristotle pointed out the relationship between riddles and metaphor, Western culture has often considered them mere simplistic games. Nevertheless, some riddles have been incredibly long-lasting, with origins predating their use in Hellenic, Semetic, and Vedic cultures. Japanese *koans* are a form of riddle central to Zen Buddhism.

Riddles are often based on parts of the body or on images in nature. For example, the "30 white horses upon a red hill" are recognized as the teeth. And riddles about similar subjects are found in widely separated cultures. In his *Dictionary of Riddles,* Mark Bryant quotes riddles about shadows from fourth-century B.C. Greece and sixteenth-century Germany, among others. And in *An Epoch of Miracles: Oral Literature of the Yucatec Maya,* Allan F. Burns also mentions a number of shadow riddles, such as "You see it but you can't grab it. It goes with you but you can't grab it." In addition to more casual wordplay, the Maya still use riddles ritually, including during wakes.

Riddles play a part in many stories. Samson, Solomon, and others in the BIBLE asked or answered riddles, as did Herakles and many heroes of Greek mythology. The riddle posed by the deadly SPHINX finally was answered by Oedipus, but the storyteller HOMER is said to have died in frustration at being unable to answer one. *See also* MEXICAN STORYTELLING.

For Further Reading

An Epoch of Miracles: Oral Literature of the Yucatec Maya. Translated by Allan F. Burns. Austin, TX: University of Texas Press, 1983.

Schwartz, Alvin. *Unriddling: All Sorts of Riddles to Puzzle Your Guessary.* New York: J.B. Lippincott, 1983.

RIG-VEDA CREATION

Oldest Hindu MYTHS of CREATION as they appear in the first of four *Vedas*, or collections of hymns. The *Rig Veda* was originally composed by Indo-Europeans, known as Aryans, who invaded India around 2000 B.C. Vedism, based on the four *Vedas*, was an early, polytheistic form of Hinduism. Three different creation myths can be found in the first and tenth books of the *Rig Veda*.

In one of these creation myths, "the phallus of HEAVEN," the male principle, has sexual intercourse with his daughter, EARTH. The god of fire, Agni, is the creator of this passion that has occurred, and he is also responsible for making "the seed of Heaven." When some of this seed spills on Earth during their lovemaking, it becomes words, rituals, and the Angirases, distributors of the gifts of the GODS and the mediators between gods and mortals. This myth is an example of creation caused by incest (*see* INCEST STORIES).

In a second creation myth based on DISMEMBERMENT OF A PRIMORDIAL BEING, Purusa, the thousand-headed and -footed primal man, is sacrificed to become the universe, with each of his body parts forming another aspect: his bottom quarter becomes the world; his mouth becomes the god Indra and the wise Brahmin priest; his arms form the warrior caste; his thighs become the common people; his mind is the moon; his eye forms the sun; his breath becomes the wind; his head is transformed into the sky; his feet make the earth; his navel becomes the atmosphere; and from Purusa's sacrifice itself come plants, beasts, rituals, sacred words, and the *Vedas*.

In yet a third creation myth, the nature and necessity of opposites plays a crucial role. Being requires non-being; there cannot be one without the other, says the hymn. Non-being and Being are then united and chaos becomes order.

For Further Reading

Zachner. R.C., trans. *Hindu Scriptures*. London: J.M. Dent, 1966.

RIP VAN WINKLE

Hero of Washington Irving's (1783–1859) legend, first published in *The Sketch Book* (1819–20). Set in Sleepy Hollow (North Tarrytown, NY), the famous story concerns the magical sleep of Rip Van Winkle, a henpecked, obedient husband, with an aversion to profitable labor. Rip is out shooting squirrels in the Catskill Mountains one day, when he encounters a strange-looking man, dressed in old-fashioned Dutch clothes, carrying a keg of liquor. Rip helps him and is then cajoled into playing bartender for the man and his motley crew of friends. True to form, he sneaks a few drinks and falls asleep. When he awakes, he finds his dog gone, an old gun next to him(which he assumes to be a replacement for the new one the strange men must have stolen from him), and a very long beard sprouting from his chin. Surprised that he might have slept all night, Rip discovers on his return to the village that he in fact has slept for 20 years. His domineering wife is gone. The American War of Independence has taken place. No longer subject to his wife or to George III, Rip is pleased to discover that he is also too old to work, and lives a happy, idle existence with his daughter and a namesake grandson.

The inhabitants of the village associate Rip's explanation of his 20-year absence with a local legend concerning Henry Hudson, after whom their river is named and who had opened up the country in which these people live. Every 20 years, the ghost of Hudson was said to return with his crew to revisit scenes of his exploits and keep a guardian eye on the river.

Rip represents the desire of all lazy, henpecked husbands to escape domestic tyranny. The magic sleep MOTIF, for example, in the GRIMM BROTHERS's "Sleeping Beauty" and "Snow-White," is a popular one in the oral and folk traditions of numerous cultures.

For Further Reading

Irving, Washington. *Rip Van Winkle*. Illustrated by Arthur Rackham. New York: Dial, 1992.

RITES OF PASSAGE (LIFE CYCLE)

Rites of transition that accompany every change of place, status, and age. The typical stages of the life cycle—birth, baptism or naming, puberty, MARRIAGE, becoming a parent, and DEATH—each involves what Arnold Van Gennep called *rites de passage,* or "rites of passage," and the stories told as part of the oral tradition can be viewed through this lens. Each stage is marked by a form of initiation, which may take the form of TESTS, RITUALS, ceremonies, or VISION QUESTS.

The birth stage appears in the many MYTHS of the DIVINE CHILD as well as in FAIRY TALES where a queen wishes for a child, as in "Snow White," who is then named because she has what the queen wished for: "hair as black as ebony and skin as white as snow." The period of puberty appears in the fairy tale as "Little RED RIDING HOOD" as well as the myth of Persephone, who is abducted by HADES because she has now reached puberty (*see* PERSEPHONE MYTH). Between puberty and marriage, the HERO, PRINCE, HEROINE, or PRINCESS must undergo a series of trials as a rite of passage, such as the "12 labors" of the Greek hero Herakles (*see* LABORS OF HERAKLES) and the feats Burd Janet must perform to save her betrothed, Tamlane, from Elfland in the English fairy tale "Tamlane." Marriage is the stage following puberty, and many fairy tales end with union, as in Perrault's "CINDERELLA" (*see* PERRAULT, CHARLES) and the GRIMM BROTHERS'S "Snow-White and Rose-Red." The bearing of children is a rite of passage for women, and many of them in myth and fairy tales lose their lives in the process. Death is the final rite of passage, with the funeral signifying the passage from one state to another, and the cycle begins again, as in, for example, the death of QUETZALCOATL.

For Further Reading

Lang, Andrew. *The Rainbow Fairy Book.* Illustrated by Michael Hague. New York: William Morrow, 1993.

Sierra, Judy. *Cinderella.* The Oryx Multicultural Folktale Series. Phoenix: Oryx Press, 1992.

RITUALS

Social or community performances related to the cycles of human life, usually religious or superstitious in origin. Rituals are ceremonies, a kind of community theater during which participants act out certain roles, speak scripted lines, and perform certain gestures to mark the passage from one state of exist-

ence to the next. The primary rituals in contemporary Western culture center around these transformatory passages from pre-life to life at birth, from childhood to adulthood at puberty, from single to coupled at MARRIAGE, from life to AFTERLIFE at DEATH.

Precapitalist societies had a greater diversity of rituals, through which they defined their relationship to the natural world and with other neighboring groups. Ritual feasts to celebrate the bringing in of the harvest are common among agricultural peoples, as are rain DANCES—ritualized movement and MUSIC, believed to encourage rainfall. Rituals such as donning certain clothing and performing certain acts are closely associated with hunting and battle among nomadic peoples.

Arguably any form of human behavior can become ritualized through repetition and the attribution of meaning to it that exceeds its appearance. Carl Jung claimed that the deepest levels of the unconscious can be discovered only through MYTH and ritual. Similarly, people with obsessive compulsive disorders need to repeat certain behaviors such as the endless washing of hands, in a way that can only be described as ritualistic, to ward off evil. Both private and public rituals tend to contain a narrative element that allows human beings to act out and express many of their most private and collective joys and sorrows, anxieties, and hopes.

ROBERT THE DEVIL *See* DEVIL

ROBIN HOOD

Outlaw figure in English FOLKLORE. The earliest surviving written tales or BALLADS of Robin Hood are dated to the early fifteenth century, although the legend of Robin Hood most likely began two centuries earlier. Robin Hood, a yeoman, lives outside the law in the forests of Sherwood and Barnsdale in northern England. A band of outlaws, including the important character Little John, accompanies Robin. They wear green livery and carry longbows, although, in the earliest tales, they often fight their enemies with swords. Robin Hood is one of the great archers in storytelling traditions as well as a superlative swordsman. Robin and his men are engaged in an ongoing battle with the Sheriff of Nottingham and others who come to represent the corrupt law, such as monks, abbots, and clerics. Robin and his men, the outlaw HEROES of these tales, inevitably prevail.

Many attempts have been made to prove that Robin Hood was a real person, but the evidence is inconclusive. According to some "historical" accounts, he was born as Robert Fitzooth in 1160 at a place called Locksley or Loxley. Other accounts say he was one Roger Godberd, an outlaw in Sherwood Forest in the 1260s, who was notorious for robbery and for murdering travelers. Both "Robert" and "Hood" were common names in thirteenth-century England, and the frequency with which "Robin Hood" is used as a place name suggests that this character may have originated in a primitive mythological figure.

The earliest Robin Hood LEGENDS are simple adventure stories. Robin and his men disguise themselves, enter various contests, and engage in bloody battles. They steal from travelers, but only those who lie about how much money they have. As it happens in these tales, the rich always lie and the poor tell the truth. Robin Hood is masterful at outwitting his foes. He is devoted to the Virgin MARY and swears by her name. Robin is honest, generous, courteous, and devout. In short, he is an honorable criminal. In the early tales, Robin does not attempt to overturn social conventions; instead, he merely obtains justice through cunning and violence.

The foremost of these tales, the *Gest of Robyn Hode*, printed at some time between 1492 and 1534, is a long poem of 456 four-line stanzas by an unknown author. The tale begins with Robin Hood delivering the outlaw code to his band of men, including Little John, Scarlock, and Much the Miller's son. Robin tells his band to do no harm to the poor, but to give bishops, archbishops, and the Sheriff of Nottingham their just desserts. Robin's charge to his men sets the tone for the remainder of this particular story as well as for many others.

The *Gest* contains recurring scenes which help to underscore its moral lesson: Robin Hood refuses to eat without a guest, he sends his men to find a guest, they participate in the RITUAL of dinner, Robin Hood requests payment for the meal, and the guest's bags are opened, revealing whether or not he has told the truth about how much he can pay. The knight in the *Gest* tells the truth, and Robin Hood helps him. Conversely, the monk lies, and Robin Hood steals from him. However, the modern stereotype of Robin Hood as a noble robber who steals from the rich and gives to the poor does not become prevalent for several more centuries.

Another typical story is that of *Robin Hood and Guy of Gisborne*, which begins with a common celebration of the forest. Robin and Little John encounter a stranger in the forest. Robin and Little John quarrel, and the latter departs. Robin and the mysterious man, Guy of Gisborne, talk politely. Robin offers to be Guy's guide, and Guy tells him that he is hunting an outlaw named Robin Hood. Once Robin's identity has been revealed, they fight a vicious battle. Robin kills Guy, cuts off his head, and sticks it on the end of his bow. Then he slashes Guy's face beyond recognition with a knife. Robin returns to find that Little John has been captured by the sheriff. Through guile, Robin is able to free Little John who then cleaves the sheriff's heart in two with an arrow.

In another early tale, *Robin Hood and the Monk*, Robin and Little John set out to church in Nottingham. After a quarrel, Robin strikes Little John, who leaves. A monk sees Robin entering the church. He locks the town's gates and alerts the sheriff. The sheriff's men descend on the church and attack Robin who manages to kill twelve of them. Then Robin loses his weapon. At the same time, Little John learns of Robin's plight. He and Much the Miller's son find the monk and his page. John cuts off the monk's head while Much does the same to the boy. In the end, John releases Robin from Nottingham's jail, and they return to Sherwood.

Other early tales include *Robin Hoode his Death*, *Robin Hood and the Potter*, and a dramatic fragment dated to c.1475. The prevalent themes are Robin's escapades in the forests of Sherwood and Barnsdale, his enviable prowess with the longbow, and his enmity for the Sheriff of Nottingham and his men, the villains in many Robin Hood tales. The heroes are the outlaws. Often their victory is bloody and violent.

Early on, these BALLADS may have been recited by traveling minstrels who performed for both peasants and townspeople as well as the gentry. By the sixteenth century, Robin Hood was one of the most popular figures in the May Games, a traditional springtime festival with DANCES, competitive sports, pageants, and plays. The tales of Robin Hood were turned into plays, and new characters, notably Maid Marian and Friar Tuck, appeared. With the introduction of Maid Marian, romance became a part of the Robin Hood legend.

Later, several Elizabethan and Jacobean dramatists, including Anthony Munday, elaborated greatly on the Robin Hood legend, and it may have been during this period that his character was imbued with the status of an unfairly dispossessed nobleman.

During the seventeenth and eighteenth centuries, the legend of Robin Hood was transmitted primarily by broadsides, cheaply produced sheets of text, and garlands, little books also cheaply printed on coarse paper. Although a few new tales appeared, these broadsides and garlands mostly contained adaptations of the already familiar verse narratives. Tales recorded during this time include *Robin Hood and Little John*, *Robin Hood and Allen A Dale*, and *Robin Hood and Maid Marian*. At this point, Robin becomes something of an urban hero. He engages in contests with tanners, tinkers, and butchers. His foes increasingly outwit and outfight him, and the tales are more lighthearted and comic than their medieval sources. Despite the fact that young people had enjoyed the legend of Robin Hood for generations, it wasn't until the nineteenth century that tales about the famous outlaw were written specifically for children. The second edition of Joseph Ritson's collection, *Robin Hood* (1820), was printed as a single volume in a size appropriate for little hands. In America, the most popular example was Howard Pyle's *The Merry Adventures of Robin Hood* (1883). It was at this time that Robin became the benevolent patron of the poor, the hero figure we know best today.

More modern versions of Robin Hood tales include Carola Oman's *Robin Hood* (1937), Anne Malcolmson's *Song of Robin Hood* (1947), Rosemary Sutcliff's *The Chronicles of Robin Hood* (1950), Roger Lancelyn Green's *Adventures of Robin Hood* (1956), and Ian Serraillier's verse-narratives, *Robin in the Greenwood* (1967) and *Robin and His Merry Men* (1969), a rendering of the *Gest* into modern English. Although children's literature continues to be an important vehicle for the perpetuation of the Robin Hood legend, movies have also contributed to Robin's story and to our modern conception of this long-lived hero.

For Further Reading

Dobson, R.B., and J. Taylor. *Rymes of Robin Hood: An Introduction to the English Outlaw*. London: Heinemann, 1976.

Holt, J.C. *Robin Hood*. London: Thames and Hudson, 1982.

Keen, Maurice. *The Outlaws of Medieval Legend*. London: Routledge and Kegan Paul, 1961.

Knight, Stephen. *Robin Hood: A Complete Study of the English Outlaw*. Cambridge, MA: Blackwell, 1994.

ROCK SONG

Dating from the 1950s, a type of music that incorporates some of the themes of MYTH and FAIRY TALE. As Robert Palmer notes in *The Rolling Stone Illustrated History of Rock and Roll*, "It is possible, with the help of a little hindsight, to find rock roots at almost every stratum of American folk and popular music during the mid-Thirties." The myths and LEGENDS that are so much a part of storytelling have worked their way into both folk songs and the music of rock and roll. MOTIFS such as that of the temptress or her counterpart, the DEMON LOVER, appear frequently, just as the theme of star-crossed lovers like Romeo and Juliet are also familiar. The HERO—or the anti-hero—may be thwarted and have to overcome difficulties in his or her journey through life. Figures such as the DEVIL may appear in rock songs, as in *Sympathy for the Devil* by the Rolling Stones, while the madonna aspect of the Great GODDESS is present in the Beatles' song "Lady Madonna," among others.

For Further Reading

Palmer, Robert. *The Rolling Stone Illustrated History of Rock and Roll*. Edited by Jim Miller. New York: Random House/Rolling Stone Press, 1980.

RÖHRICH, LUTZ (1922–)

Researcher and compiler of European FOLK-LORE. After returning from his tour of duty in World War II, Lutz Röhrich began his university studies in his Swabain birthplace of Tübingen. In Tübingen, Röhrich gained a solid preparation in European folklore research by studying German, folklore, history, music, and Latin. His dissertation, "The Demonic Figures in Swabian Folklore," launched him further into the world of folklore research (*see* EUROPEAN STORYTELLING). His first publication, *Folktales and Reality: A Folkloristic Investigation* (1956), established Röhrich as one of Europe's leading folklorists while at the University of Mainz. Röhrich later accepted a position at the Freiburg School as a professor of folklore and Germanic philology, where he also became chair of the department. In subsequent years, Röhrich's department became known as a center of folklorist achievement, especially in its concentration on oral forms of storytelling. Röhrich himself is considered to be an authority on the oral genre in the Germanic languages. His published works include *Medieval Literature and Folklore* (1962), *Folktales, Legends and Jokes* (1967), and *Proverbs and Proverbial Phrases* (1972). The translation of *Folktales and Reality*, published in 1991, provides a large sampling of European folk narrative that supports Röhrich's theory that distinct folkloric genre such as LEGEND and MYTH arise from particular cultural contexts that dictate the narrative elements of the genre. Röhrich examines this relationship between the fictive world and reality by turning to the degree of belief held by the members of the culture. In this volume, Röhrich also posits the relationship between folklore and the rectification of social problems. Scholars in many areas of research besides folklore consider *Folktales and Reality* an important work in the study of culture.

ROLAND

Romantic HERO of the medieval French EPIC, the SONG OF ROLAND. A great warrior, the possessor of supernatural strength, and the epitome of French chivalry, Roland belongs to the medieval storytelling tradition of superlatively noble and valiant knights (*see* PERCIVAL, SIEGFRIED, SIR GAWAIN). Roland is the Christian CHARLEMAGNE's nephew, and thus is considered the great king's "right hand." He is extremely brave and self-confident. Roland's stepfather, Ganelon, says that, after a victory, Roland gave Charlemagne a golden apple, boasting that he would give his uncle the crowns of all the kings on earth. In spite of his arrogance, Roland is unswervingly loyal, innocent, and even simple in character.

Roland's relationship with Ganelon is reminiscent of the jealous relationship between step-parents and stepchildren in many stories (*see* CINDERELLA, KATE CRACKERNUTS). Ganelon plots to have Roland killed by the Saracens, the enemy Moors. After the Saracens attack the Twelve Peers, a chosen group of valorous knights including Roland, and an army of 20,000 Franks, Roland refuses to blow his horn to summon help from Charlemagne and the rest of the Frankish army. He prefers to rely on his prowess and his sword called Durendal. Ultimately, as in many heroic epics, Roland's pride is his downfall. It is not until his army is almost completely destroyed that he finally blows his horn and alerts Charlemagne. The last to survive the Saracens' ferocious attack, Roland dies a magnificent death beneath a pine tree. Displaying his essential Christianity, he pleads for GOD's mercy and asks that his soul be saved.

The story of Roland contains elements of the DYING GOD or the dying hero MOTIF. Like many dying gods from other stories, the brave, young, and heroic Roland dies for the good of his society. He fights all of his battles, including his final one, in the name of the Christian God against the heathen Moors.

Although the character Roland may be based on the eighth-century figure Roland, Duke of the Marches of Brittany, nothing is known about this historical figure except for the legendary status he has achieved in the *Song of Roland*.

For Further Reading

Burgess, Glyn S., trans. *Song of Roland*. New York: Viking Penguin, 1990.

ROMANCE

Narrative genre of the courtly and chivalric age. The chivalric or medieval romance first developed in France in the twelfth century, eventually spreading to the literatures of other countries. Originally the term "romance" meant a work written in French, which had evolved from a dialect of Latin, the language of Rome. Later it came to mean a tale that represented the Age of Chivalry with its courtly manners instead of the heroic age of tribal wars represented by the EPIC form. Soon the romance replaced the epic in popularity.

The typical plot of a romance involves a knight on a QUEST to gain the favor of a lady, with the theme of courtly love central to the action, and might consist of tournaments fought to win a lady and DRAGONS or monsters slain for her sake. The heroic knight must uphold the chivalric ideal of acting with courage and honor, of showing mercy to an opponent, and of always behaving with excellent manners. While the epic relies on supernatural events caused or controlled by the GODS, the romance focuses on the presence of magic, SPELLS, enchantments, and the workings of fairyland.

Romances are divided into four groups of subjects. The first group, called "The Matter of Britain," draws on Celtic sources and includes all the stories about King ARTHUR and the Knights of the Round Table. The second group, "The Matter of Rome," takes for its subject matter stories drawn from classical antiquity, such as the adventures of Aeneas and other HEROES of the Trojan War or Alexander the Great (*see* AENEID). The third group, "The Matter of France," includes the stories about CHARLEMAGNE and his knights, while the fourth, "The Matter of England," consists of stories about heroes like King Horn and Guy of Warwick.

Romances that belong to the Arthurian cycle were immensely popular and continue to play a part in storytelling. Many of the early romances, such as *Erec and Enide*; *Yvain, or the Knight of the Lion*; LANCELOT, *or the Knight of the Cart*; and *Perceval, or the Story of the Grail*; were written by the twelfth-century French poet CHRÉTIEN DE TROYES. Marie de France of Breton also produced fine narrative verse romances collected as *The Lais of Marie de France*, also written in the twelfth century. The fourteenth-century English romance SIR GAWAIN AND THE GREEN KNIGHT, written by the mysterious Pearl Poet, and Malory's *Morte d'Arthur*, written in the fifteenth century, are two of the most important romances in this cycle. Although some romances feature Gawain or Galahad as the Grail hero, many versions of the story of the quest for the HOLY GRAIL, which belong to this cycle, feature Arthur's knight PERCIVAL, with the most famous one being WOLFRAM VON ESCHENBACH's Parsifal. The Percival versions always center on "the sickness and disability of the ruler of the land, the Fisher King," and "the task of the Quester becomes that of healing the King," writes Jessie L. Weston in *From Ritual to Romance* (*see* DYING GOD, SCAPEGOAT). T.S. Eliot drew on this theme more recently in his long poem *The Waste Land* (1922), while the entire Arthurian cycle is the source for T.S. White's *The Once and Future King* (1958) and the Broadway musical *Camelot*.

Beginning in the late eighteenth century and continuing into the nineteenth century, romance came to mean a fictional prose narrative in which the plot involved mystery, strangeness, and adventure rather than the commonplace. Gothic romances such as Horace Walpole's *The Castle of Otranto* and Maria Edgeworth's *Castle Rackrent* became popular in England, and in America Nathaniel Hawthorne considered his novel *The House of the Seven Gables* to be a romance. Contemporary versions of romances based on the Arthurian legends continue to be popular among both adults and children.

ROOTABAGA STORIES

Children's stories written by poet Carl Sandburg (1878–1967). Rooted in the style and rhythm of FOLKLORE, Carl Sandburg's *Rootabaga Stories* first appeared in 1922, and a second volume, *Rootabaga Pigeons*, was published the following year. The stories are both poetic and humorous, with long titles such as "Three Stories about the Finding of the Zigzag Railroad, the Pigs with Bibs On, the Circus Clown Ovens, the Village of Liver-and-Onions, the Village of Cream Puffs" and "Two Stories about Corn Fairies, Blue Foxes, Flongboos and Happenings that Happened in the United States and Canada."

In the story "How They Broke Away to Go to the Rootabaga Country," the language and the name are meant to surprise and amuse children. A man named "Gimme the Ax" lets his children name themselves, so "The first words they speak as soon as they learn to make words shall be their names." Thus his son's name is "Please Gimme" and his daughter's name is "Ax Me No Questions." When his children begin to grow up, the three decide to sell all their belongings and leave their home where everything is always the same. They buy a railroad ticket and travel "to where the railroad tracks run off into the blue sky and then forty ways farther yet." As they travel, they pass through Over and Under country, the country of the balloon pickers, the country of the circus CLOWNS, and, finally, they come to Rootabaga Country "where the big city is the Village of Liver-and-Onions," the train tracks change to zigzags, and the pigs wear bibs.

Another often anthologized and especially poetic story is "The White Horse Girl and the Blue Wind Boy." It tells of a girl who loves to ride horses "white as snow," "white as new washed sheep wool," and "white as silver" and a boy who loves the "blue wind of day time," "a night wind with blue," and "a blue wind of the times between night and day, a blue dawn and evening wind." When the boy and the girl meet, they eventually run off "to go where the white horses come from and where the blue winds begin." Where they end up remains a mystery in Rootabaga Country, until one day many years later "a Gray Man on Horseback" appears and tells of having seen the boy and girl at the very place they were searching for. The end of the story suggests that the White Horse Girl and the Blue Wind Boy have become LEGENDS in stories told to the young people of Rootabaga Country, while the story itself has the feel of a FOLKTALE.

For Further Reading

Sandburg, Carl. *Rootabaga Stories*. Illustrated by Maud and Miska Petersham. New York: Harcourt Brace, 1922.

RUMPELSTILZCHEN

German FAIRY TALE, recorded by the GRIMM BROTHERS, about a DWARF who spins gold from straw. In this tale, a boastful miller tells the KING that his beautiful daughter can spin straw into gold. The greedy king locks the miller's daughter into a room piled with straw and tells her she has one night to spin the straw into gold; otherwise she will die. A funny-looking little man, sometimes referred to as a hobgoblin, a DWARF, or a "mannikin," appears and offers to spin the straw into gold for the price of the girl's necklace. The next night, the pleased king gives the girl a larger pile of straw to spin into gold. Again the little man appears, and this time he spins gold for the price of the girl's ring. On the third night, the greedy king offers to marry the miller's daughter if she can spin an even greater pile of straw into gold. The girl has nothing more to give the dwarf when he arrives. He asks for her first child, and the girl reluctantly agrees. A year later, after the miller's daughter has married the king and given birth to their first child, the dwarf suddenly reappears and demands the baby. He gives the stricken queen three days to guess his name; if she guesses correctly, she may keep her baby. For two days, the queen guesses incorrectly. On the third day, a messenger reports that he saw a hut high on a hill in the forest. In front of the hut, a little man was dancing around a fire and shrieking a song in which he said, "Rumpelstilzchen is my name." When the dwarf arrives for the baby, the queen guesses that his name is Rumpelstilzchen. The dwarf becomes so enraged that he stamps his right foot so hard that he drives his whole leg into the ground; in his fury, he seizes his left foot with both hands and tears himself in two. In some versions, Rumpelstilzchen flies off on a spoon.

Variations of this tale exist in other European countries. In an English version, a king marries a girl on the condition that she spin five skeins each day for the last month of the year; otherwise, he will kill her. Tom Tit Tot, a black creature with a long tail, offers to spin the skeins. He allows the girl three chances each night to guess his name. If she doesn't guess it by the last night of the month, then the girl will be his. Each night when Tom Tit Tot delivers the skeins, the girl is unable to guess his name. On the second to the last day of the month, the satisfied king eats supper with his wife. He tells her that while he was hunting in the woods, he saw a funny little black thing spinning and singing, "My name's Tom Tit Tot." The next night, the girl correctly guesses Tom Tit Tot's name. When he hears his name, the long-tailed creature shrieks and disappears into the dark. Other British versions name the Rumpelstilzchen figure Terrytop and Whuppity Stoorie, and he is known on the Continent as Titeliture, Ricdin-Ricdon, and Dancing Vargaluska. Ireland's version of Rumpelstilzchen is named Trit-a-Trot.

In a similar Irish FOLKTALE, a fairy woman named Gírle Guairle takes on the task of spinning and weaving flax for a mortal woman, under the condition that the woman remember her name. The woman forgets the fairy's name and dreads the penalty. Then, one day, she overhears a voice singing, "If you knew my name to be Gírle Guairle . . ." When the time comes, the woman greets the fairy with her correct name. The fairy gives the woman the finished cloth and departs in a rage.

A folktale from Haiti, "The Name," tells the story of a servant girl whose employer, a mean woman, demands that the girl tell the woman her name in order to get something to eat. The girl says nothing because she does not know the woman's name, and thus she does not eat. One day as the girl is washing turkey intestines by a river, a crab finally tells the girl the old woman's name. When the old woman learns who told the girl her name, she lunges after the crab and disappears under the water.

"Rumpelstilzchen" and other similar stories contain the name-tab MOTIF. One element of this complex motif is the notion that guessing the name of a supernatural being, for example, gives one power over that being.

For Further Reading

Carter, Angela, ed. *The Virago Book of Fairy Tales*. London: Virago Press, 1990.

Grimm, Jacob, and Wilhelm Grimm. *Selected Tales*. Translated by David Luke. Harmondsworth, Middlesex: Penguin, 1982.

Taylor, Edgar, trans. *German Fairy Tales and Popular Stories as told by Gammer Grethel*. London: H. G. Bohn, 1863.

SACHS, HANS (1494–1576)

Prolific German writer who composed an amazing number of songs, plays, and FABLES in the sixteenth century. Sachs was born to middle-class parents who instructed him in religious values and secular ambitions. According to Sachs, both of his parents contracted the plague near the time of his birth. While this was not uncommon for the time, the fact that all three survived is notable. When he was seven years old, Sachs was sent to school. There, he became proficient in Latin, was given moral training, and fell in love with the disciplines of poetry and music. At the age of 15, Sachs was apprenticed as a shoemaker, and he quickly advanced to a five-year trial as a journeyman. It was during this period that Sachs conducted most of the travels in his life. He visited Vienna, Munich, and Frankfurt, but he chose to make Nuremberg his permanent home. Although he succeeded in his time as a journeyman shoemaker, Sachs was not content to abandon his intellectual pursuits, and he continued to write throughout his life. In 1519, he began a 41-year marriage to Kunigunde Kreutzer. When she died in 1560, Sachs married Barbara Harscher, who was 40 years younger than he.

Hans Sachs lived during one of the world's most fascinating historical epochs. Radical transformations in politics, the arts, technology, and theology took place during his life, and his location in Nuremberg placed Sachs in the center of many important intellectual movements. By the time of his death, Sachs had witnessed the major struggle between the Emperor and the church for power, the sweeping changes in theology brought by the Reformation of Luther and Melancthon, the widespread use of the printing press, and the start of a general intellectual renaissance. As a German free city of the Empire, Nuremberg allowed Sachs to keep his finger on the pulse of cultural trends.

Sachs participated vigorously in these trends, writing dialogues in support of Luther's teachings and resisting the popular notion that "high art" could be expressed only in Latin. In 1524 he composed a *Disputation between a Canon and a Shoemaker*, in which he defended the reforms Luther had inaugurated and emphasized the role of the individual in matters of faith. Sachs's religious writings point to his concern for the "common man" and his disdain for the sixteenth century's elitism in matters of church, art, and politics. Although Sachs was proficient in Latin, he wrote almost all of his work in German, preferring the language of the masses over the language of the church. In fact, it is as a pioneer in the use of the German vernacular that Sachs is most highly regarded as a storyteller. Sachs's role as a shoemaker and artist must have compelled him to sympathize with the reforms in the church and in society generally.

As a storyteller, Sachs worked in many forms and produced a remarkable number of texts. In an autobiographical poem from 1567, Sachs mentions having written 208 comedies, tragedies, and farces; 13 musical pieces for the Guild of *Meistersinger*; and 1,700 poems. These include *Lucretia* (1527), *The Tragedy of King Saul* (1557), and *David and Bathsheba* (1557). Many of Sachs's works fall under the category of *Meisterlieder*, stories in prose or verse that conveyed anecdotal material or the moral lesson of a fable. In his plays and tales, Sachs drew upon his broad knowledge of theology and classics, but his works preserve a distinctly German flavor and a persistent concern with social issues.

Hans Sachs's role as a simple artist and proponent of German vernacular literature did not secure him fame in the two centuries following his death. However, by the late eighteenth century, Goethe had written a poem in praise of Sachs, and Wagner, composing operas nearly 100 years later, made Sachs the hero of *Die Meistersinger von Nürnberg* (1868). Wagner saw in Sachs an emblem for the German artist, and he depicts him as an example of German artistic superiority. As Frank Shaw has noted, there is little of the historical Hans Sachs in Wagner's opera. However, Wagner succeeded in presenting Sachs as a model artist, and the opera secured Sach's status as an important artist and storyteller.

SAGA

Prose narratives from medieval Iceland and Scandinavia. Sagas are tales of famous families, of the bold and daring settlers of Iceland, and of heroic leaders such as early Norse KINGS or thirteenth-century bishops. The stories recorded in many sagas were transmitted orally until the twelfth century when authors began to give them written form. There are no fewer than 700 known sagas.

Sagas are divided into several generally accepted groups. The "kings' sagas" tell primarily of the lives and deeds of early Norwegian kings, but also include tales about Danish kings, the earls of Orkney, and Faroese chieftains. The Icelandic sagas, including the well-known *Njal's Saga*, describe the period in which Iceland was first settled (c. 850–1030) and vividly portray the Norsemen's insatiable appetite for exploration and settlement. The "family sagas" tell of the lives, loyalties, dilemmas, and feuds of both individuals and families in Iceland's Heroic Age, around A.D. 1000. The *fornaldar* sagas are about legendary times in Iceland and have little historical foundation. Their action takes place before the settlement of Iceland; thus, they are more fantastic and less realistic than the other groups of sagas. The "bishops' sagas" are historical in content like the kings' sagas and present the reign of several bishops in the time period c.1000–1340. The *Sturlunga* saga is a collection of sagas about the Sturlungs, a family of ruling chieftains. The broader term, "contemporary sagas," is sometimes used to classify the *Sturlunga* saga, the bishops' sagas, and some of the kings' sagas. Contemporary sagas focus on the period from the beginning of the twelfth century, and their authors were contemporaries of the people about whom they wrote.

Though often recast by the sensibilities of their Christian authors, sagas nevertheless reflect the religious beliefs and attitudes of their protagonists, making available to a modern audience a great deal of information about pre-Christian belief and practice.

For Further Reading

Sorensen, Preben Meulengracht. *Saga and Society: An Introduction to Old Norse Literature*. Translated by John Tucker. Odense: Odense University Press, 1993.

SAINT NICHOLAS (c. A.D. 300)

Fourth-century bishop of Myra in Lycia (southwestern Asia Minor), whose cult spread throughout Europe in the middle ages; the LEGEND of Saint Nicholas is the origin of the MYTH of SANTA CLAUS. Although very little is known of his personal history, Nicholas has been one of the most popular Christian saints. He is the patron saint of children, sailors, merchants, pawnbrokers, unmarried girls, apothecaries, and perfumiers as well as of countries (Russia), provinces, dioceses, and cities. What we know of Saint Nicholas today is based entirely on oral tradition. The first written stories were recorded about five hundred years after his death.

The legend of Nicholas includes a story of three daughters whom he gave bags of gold as their marriage dowries; some versions say he saved the girls from prostitution with his gift. Another tale describes how he brought back to life three boys who were murdered in a brine tub by a butcher. Nicholas is also said to have saved three unjustly condemned men from death as well as three sailors in distress off the Lycian coast. Clearly, the number three is important in Nicholas's lore, and his emblem is variously three gold balls or three bags of gold (see NUMBERS).

In addition, it is said that Nicholas saved his region during a famine when he acquired enough grain from ships bound for Alexandria to feed the population for two years. He promised the sailors of the ships that they would find the original quantity of grain on board when they arrived at their destination. After this miracle, the sailors became converts of Saint Nicholas.

Nicholas's shrine is at Bari in Apulia. When Myra and his original shrine were taken by Moslems (c.1087), the relics were moved to Bari where a new church was built to house them. In 1095, Pope Urban II was present at the inauguration of the new shrine. After this time, the cult of Nicholas was prevalent in the West, and so Saint Nicholas is sometimes called Nicholas of Bari.

In Europe and Asia Minor from the sixth century onward, Nicholas has been represented in innumerable paintings, carvings, frescoes, and stained glass cycles of his life. He is perhaps the most frequently represented saint for centuries. Nicholas also has been celebrated in custom and FOLKLORE. The origin of Father Christmas is found in Nicholas's patronage of children. In many countries, including Holland and Belgium, presents were and still are given to children on his feast day, December 6.

Saint Nicholas' took on his present form of Santa Claus in North America when Dutch Protestants of New Amsterdam joined legends of Saint Nicholas to Nordic legends of a magician who rewarded good children with presents and punished naughty children. Santa Claus is derived from the Dutch dialect form of his name, *Sinte Klaas* or *Sinterklaas*. Our contemporary conception of Saint Nicholas, or Santa Claus, most likely arose with the 1823 publication of the well-known poem *A Visit from Saint Nicholas* (also known as *The Night Before Christmas*) by Clement Clarke Moore in a New York newspaper. Moore was the first storyteller to describe in print the flying sleigh, the eight reindeer, and Nicholas's method of entering houses by the chimney.

SAM SLICK

Comic depiction of a New England "Yankee" clock peddler created by Canadian writer Thomas Chandler Haliburton (1796–1865). Due to the popularity of the character, Haliburton published his first collection of Sam Slick stories, *The Clockmaker; or The Sayings and Doings of Samuel Slick of Slicksville* (1836), only a few years after he had created him in sketches. Slick would appear again in the following years in several works, including *Sam Slick's wise saws and modern inventions; or what he said, did, or invented* (1853). As a representation of mechanism and progress, the loquacious Yankee travels through the traditional agrarian society of Nova Scotia (and later to New York and England) offering his philosophies, generally in the form of pithy comments and homespun metaphors. While reproaching the habitants for not developing their potential and boasting of the United States's mechanized progress, he exposes the guile and greed that may accompany that progress.

The influence of various humorous traditions in storytelling are apparent in the character of Sam Slick. Much of the humor derives from Slick's own ability as a storyteller, especially in his use of TALL TALES. In addition, Haliburton employs regionalism for comic effect by giving Slick an exaggerated regional dialect and eccentric customs. Yet even as Slick clearly descends from an established tradition of regional comic figures, his own influence can be seen in later characters, such as Davy Crockett (*see* CROCKETT, DAVY). Furthermore, Slick's linguistic influence can still be heard even today, as it is not uncommon to hear such "slickisms" as "barking up the wrong tree."

For Further Reading

Laird, Matthew R. "Nativist American Humour: Sam Slick and The Defense of New England Whig Culture." *Canadian Review of American Studies* 23, no. 4 (1993): 71-88.

SANDMAN

Nursery story character. The LEGEND of the Sandman is found throughout western Europe and in North America as well. He is the man who comes each night to sprinkle sand in the eyes of the children to make them fall asleep. In the oral tradition of storytelling, mothers sing or croon or simply tell their children, "The Sandman is coming, the Sandman is coming" as a way of getting them ready to fall asleep and as an explanation for the heaviness of their sleepy eyelids, and many young children believe there is indeed a real man called the Sandman. While no actual MYTHS or legends exist about the Sandman, he is a well-known imaginary figure who is a product of the FOLKLORE of mothers everywhere, like the East Frisian Finger-Biter and other imaginary creatures, and the children who have heard it in the nursery remember the Sandman when they sing lullabies to their own children. Various contemporary stories about the Sandman exist in children's literature, but they are generally the creations of the authors as opposed to retellings of one FOLKTALE.

SANTA CLAUS

Mythical Christmas gift-giver, also known as SAINT NICHOLAS. Saint Nicholas, a bishop in fourth-century Asia Minor and patron saint of children, was associated with a European children's holiday that took place on December 6. The origins of Saint Nicholas are murky. He was transformed in different cultures into various gift-giving manifestations. In Germany, Kriss Kringle ("Christ-child") brings gifts to small children. In New Amsterdam (now New York City), the Dutch settlers gave the name Sinter Claes to their version of Saint Nicholas. Later, English settlers in New York adopted Sinter Claes as their own and changed his name to Santa Claus. Santa Claus was popularized in 1823 when Clement Clarke Moore published *A Visit From Saint Nicholas* (also known as *The Night Before Christmas*), a Christmas poem. This poem relates how Santa, driven by flying reindeer, alights on rooftops, slides down chimneys, and delivers presents. In 1866, a drawing by Thomas Nast in *Harper's Weekly* definitively illustrated Santa Claus for the American public. Santa is an old man with red cheeks, a white beard, a red, fur-lined suit, and a pot belly in the songs, literature, television shows, and movies that have filled out his story. In American cultural mythology, Santa resides in the North Pole and runs a toy workshop serviced by ELVES. On Christmas Eve, he loads up his sleigh, and takes his gifts all over the world. Traditionally, children leave milk and cookies by the fire for Santa and hang stockings on the mantle to be filled with presents. However, Santa delivers toys only to good children while bad children receive lumps of coal in their stockings. Children are warned that Santa keeps a list, and many songs and illustrations depict Santa squinting through wire-frame glasses at a long tally of children's names, divided into columns of "naughty" and "nice." The tradition of Santa seems to grow with time as more and more stories seek to fill in the details of his MYTH. Small children are still taught to believe that Santa brings them presents on Christmas.

For Further Reading

Giblin, James Cross. *The Truth about Santa Claus.* Illustrated. New York: T.Y. Crowell, 1985.

Glover, William, ed. *Christmas Drawings of Thomas Nast.* New York: World Publishing, 1970.

Luckhardt, Mildred Madeleine Corell. *The Story of Saint Nicholas.* Illustrated. New York: Abingdon Press, 1960.

Moore, Clement Clarke. *Twas the Night Before Christmas: A Visit from Saint Nicholas.* New York: Random House, 1975.

SATYRS

Creatures in Greek mythology, half man and half goat. The traditional image of a satyr has the back legs and tail of a goat with a man's upper body. Their faces are only semi-human, with horns, flat noses, and pointed ears. They bear a physical resemblance to Pan, the god of the woodlands—although, according to Aristotle, satyrs were actually mortal. Worshippers and devotees of DIONYSOS, satyrs were frequently portrayed as chasing and lusting after NYMPHS. They were generally mischievous, drunken, and cowardly.

The most famous satyr was the elderly Silenus, a heavy drinker. Silenus tutored Dionysos and later became his most devoted worshipper. Once, in a particularly debilitating drunken stupor, Silenus wandered away from Dionysos' train of followers into the garden of King MIDAS. Midas was kind enough to return Silenus to Dionysos, and in gratitude, the god offered to grant him a wish. Midas' wish was to have everything he touch turn to gold—a wish which came true, much to his eventual dismay.

According to LEGEND, the satyrs held ritual processions featuring dithyrambs—verses and songs devoted to Dionysos. These processions were said to be the beginnings of drama itself.

Indeed, during the fifth century B.C., the trilogy of tragedies performed at a dramatic festival was capped off with a fourth play known as a "satyr play," an irreverent and comic piece in which satyrs formed the chorus. True to the intentions of the mythical satyrs, the satyr play filled the audience with the spirit of Dionysian revelry after a long afternoon of intense and serious DRAMA. The only complete surviving satyr play is Euripides' *Cyclops,* in which Silenus is a principal character.

Other animal-human creatures in oral traditions include the CENTAURS, MERMAIDS, SIRENS, the MINOTAUR, and GANESA. *See also* ANCIENT GREEK STORYTELLING.

For Further Reading

Euripides. *Cyclops.* Translated by William Arrowsmith. Vol. 3, *The Complete Greek Tragedies.* Chicago: University of Chicago Press, 1959.

Homer. *The Odyssey.* Translated by Robert Fitzgerald. New York: Doubleday, 1963.

SAWYER, RUTH (1880–1970)

Storyteller and collector of tales. Ruth Sawyer was born in Boston where she was fortunate to have a spell-binding Irish storyteller for a nurse. Joanna, her nurse, gave Sawyer her love of storytelling, and as an adult she traveled through Ireland, Spain, and America collecting wonderful and strange tales, which she then retold in her various books. Her versions were well-researched and authentic, and she was known throughout the United States as speaker and storyteller.

In one of Sawyer's most well-known books, *The Way of the Storyteller,* she discusses storytelling as a folk-art: "All folk-arts [sic] have grown out of the primal urge to give tongue to what has been seen, heard, experienced. They have been motivated by simple, direct folk-emotions, by imagination; they have been shaped by folk-wisdom," writes Sawyer. According to her, "The art of storytelling lies within the storyteller, to be searched for, drawn out, made to grow." An effective storyteller needs experience, background, creative imagination, and a gift for selection, "But the secret of the gift lies in the sixth sense of the true storyteller. This true storyteller has "that intense urge to share with others what has already moved him deeply." It is her belief that "the best of the traditional storytellers. . . live close to the heart of things—to the earth, the sea, the wind and the weather. They have been those who know solitude, silence. . . . They have come to know the power of the spoken word."

Among Ruth Sawyer's many books are *Journey Cake, Ho!*, *Roller Skates*, *The Year of Jubilo*, *The Long Christmas*, *The Christmas Anna Angel*, *The Enchanted Schoolhouse*, and *The Year of the Christmas Dragon*.

For Further Reading

Sawyer, Ruth. *The Christmas Anna Angel*. Illustrated by Kate Seredy. New York: Viking, 1944.

————. *The Least One*. Illustrated by Leo Politi. New York: Viking, 1941.

————. *Picture Tales from Spain*. Illustrated by Carlos Sanchez. New York: Frederick A. Stokes, 1936.

———— *Roller Skates*. Illustrated by Valenti Angelo. New York: Viking, 1936.

————. *This Way to Christmas*. New York: Harper, 1916.

————. *Tono Antonio*. Illustrated by F. Luis Mora. New York: Viking, 1934.

————. *The Way of the Storyteller*. New York: Penguin, 1962.

————. *The Year of Jubilo*. Illustrated by Edward Shenton. New York: Viking, 1940.

SAYERS, PEIG (1873–1958)

Irish storyteller and folklorist. Peig Sayers is known for her two-volume autobiography, *Peig: The Autobiography of Peig Sayers of the Great Blasket Island* (published in 1936), and *Machtnamh Seana Mhna* (or *An Old Woman's Reflections)*, published first in 1939, then again in 1962. Sayers did not write the books herself, instead her son Mícheál wrote as she dictated her compelling life story. Part of Sayers' story concerns her immediate family; nine of her brothers and sisters died young; only four of a family of 13 survived. After first leaving home at the age of 14 to work as a servant-girl in the house of a shop-keeper, Sayers continued to work in the homes of others to earn enough money to survive. Eventually Sayers left for the Great Blasket Island to marry a man that was chosen for her. She lived on the Great Blasket Island for over 40 years experiencing the death of four of her 10 children and also the death of her husband. Even before her son wrote down the story of his mother's life, the islanders on the Great Blasket Island considered Peig Sayers a remarkable storyteller of Irish folklore and her own place in it.

SCANDINAVIAN STORYTELLING

The oral and literary tradition of MYTHS and LEGENDS from the time of the pre-Christian Scandinavian peoples, called Norsemen, who occupied the peninsula of Norway and Sweden, to the present, which, like most FOLK-LORE, is shaped by geography and peoples, often used anthropomorphism to portray the arctic scene. However, some characters in the mythology, many of them minor GODS, were often merely used as props in a story, and had no other significance (*see* NORSE CREATION).

Scandinavian mythology is generally regarded as one of the most historically prominent folklores, tantamount in influence to the mythologies of Greece and Rome. The bulk of Nordic mythology is contained in Norwegian literature, in the *Younger* and *Elder Eddas* (*see* EDDAS, ELDER AND YOUNGER) and later SAGAS, and in the commentaries of Danish historian, Saxo Grammaticus, and the German writer, Adam of Bremen. Legend is also preserved in old inscriptions and in later folklore. Norse storytelling was immortalized by the medieval Christian historians, but because the legends were also altered by these later historians, it is difficult to consider accurately the original religious beliefs, attitudes and practices of the Norsemen. It is known that Scandinavian mythology evolved slowly, and its gods and HEROES varied at different times and places. For instance, ODIN, chief of the gods, may have become popular just before the legends were recorded, replacing older deities such as Ull, Njord, and Heimdell, who were relegated to the status of minor gods. In addition, although he is the god of war, and associated with learning and wisdom, Odin is also represented as having acquired his wisdom from others.

Major deities include Odin, god of war, and his wife Frigga, GODDESS of the home; Thor, who protected men and other gods from the GIANTS; Frey, a god of prosperity; and FREYA, sister of Frey, a fertility GODDESS. Minor gods and goddesses include BALDR, Hermod, Tyr, Bragi, Forseti, Idun, Nanna, and Sif. Most of the minor deities did not occupy roles as the major deities did, an important distinction from Greek mythology, which is often cited as a counterpart to Scandinavian mythology. Instead, these minor characters merely appeared in the legendary tales, seeming to have no special functions. Heroes, some of whom may have been derived from real figures, were believed to be the descendants of gods. They include Sigurd (SIEGFRIED), the DRAGON-Slayer; Helgi Thrice-Born; Harald Wartooth; Hadding; Starkad; and the Valkyries, a band of warrior maidens that served Odin as choosers of slain warriors. Scandinavian mythology also included DWARVES, ELVES, and the Norns, who distributed fates to mortals. Personal spirits called *fylgja* or *hamingja* were also allotted to the Norsemen, and have been cited as precursors to the idea of the Christian soul or spirit. LOKI the TRICKSTER, was the representation of evil among the gods; there is no record that the Norsemen worshipped Loki.

Scandinavian mythology revolved primarily around storytelling, but ceremonial ritualism was also important; worship of deities was first conducted outdoors under guardian trees, near sacred wells, or within a sacred arrangement of stones. Later, wooden temples replaced these primitive arrangements. The most important temple was at Old Uppsala, Sweden, where ANIMALS and occasionally human beings were sacrificed.

The gods are collectively called the *Aesir*, but are really an alliance of two formerly warring divine tribes, the Aesir and the *Vanir*, who lived together in the divine city, Asgard. Ordinary men were received after DEATH by the goddess HEL in an underground world that may be paralleled to the Greek underworld, or even the Christian idea of HELL—for the Scandinavian underworld was indeed desolate (*see* DESCENT TO THE UNDERWORLD). The Eddic poem "Volsupa" ("Prophecy of the Seeress") defines the Scandinavian belief of CREATION, from which realms, such as those of heat and cold, were created. "Volsupa" portrays a chaos, followed by the creation of giants and gods, and at last, mankind. *Ginnungagp* was the yawning void, *Jotunheim* the home of the giants, *Niflheim* the region of the cold, and *Muspelheim* the realm of heat. The great world-tree, YGGDRASIL, reached through all time and space, but it was perpetually under attack from Nidhogg, the evil serpent. The fountain of Mimir, source of hidden wisdom, lay under one of the roots of the tree.

From this vast body of mythology grew a more modern Scandinavian oral tradition. The Middle Ages hailed a compendium of histrionics, clowns, jugglers, singers, and dancers to entertain a grateful northern audience. During this time, the most vital genre was folk poetry, especially BALLADS, which were composed in the vernacular and sung as an accompaniment to dance. The ballads—which become more loved than the ancient skaldic poetry—were most popular in the thirteenth and fourteenth centuries, but remained prevalent in throughout the seventeenth century. In fact, Scandinavian literature still esteems these medieval folk ballads, the amalgam of short lyrical songs and narrative verse.

Although recent Scandinavian culture has been dominated more by literature than by oral tradition, the sung ballad of medieval times was not replaced by the written poem until the nineteenth century. Carl Michael Bellman, an esteemed Swedish man of letters, is evidence to this. In the late 1700s, Bellman was still putting his poetry to music in Swedish taverns.

In the nineteenth century, three authors brought acclaim to the Scandinavian folktale. First, the celebrated master of the FAIRY TALE, Hans Christian Andersen, began writing—a man who, though lonely and unhappy while alive, was famed after his death for bringing a wealth of folklore to the center of Scandinavian tradition (*see* ANDERSEN, HANS CHRISTIAN); and in the mid-1800s, P.C. Asbjornsen and Jorgen Moe collected and edited numerous folk- and fairy tales (*see* ASBJORNSEN, PETER CHRISTEN).

For Further Reading

Clausen, Adler C. *Treasures of the Northland: A Compendium of the Literature, Art, Science, Poetry, Folk-Lore, and Ancient Myths of the Scandinavian Race.* Spokane: Cole, 1919.

Craigie, William A. *Scandinavian Folk-Lore: Illustrations of the Traditional Beliefs of the Northern Peoples.* Detroit: Singing Tree Press, 1970.

Hallmundsson, Hallberg, ed. *An Anthology of Scandinavian Literature: From the Viking Period to the Present.* New York: Collier Books, 1965.

SCAPEGOAT

Any material object, animal, bird, or person upon whom the misfortune or sins of the people are symbolically placed. In MYTH, religion, and FOLKLORE, the scapegoat is often a person who must, either by choice or decree, receive in a symbolic RITUAL the bad luck, diseases, or sinful acts committed by an individual or group. This person—or animal— is then let loose, driven off with stones and rocks, cast into a body of water, thrown over a cliff, or burned on a pyre. The scapegoat then takes with it all the evil and misfortune, thereby purifying the people. The transference of this evil to a scapegoats occurs all over the world, often in an annual ritual, and it dates back to all primitive people. The term's etymology comes from The Book of Leviticus in the Hebrew BIBLE, where Aaron symbolically laid the people's sins upon a goat on Yom Kippur, the Day of Atonement. The goat was then led away and let loose in the wilderness.

In Ancient Greek ritual, a scapegoat would often be a slave or someone who volunteered, was decorated and led around the city, then brought outside the city's walls to be stoned to death. In Sophocles's play *Oedipus the King*, the tragic HERO Oedipus functions as a scapegoat, for presumably his exile from the city as a punishment for his regicide/patricide will end the plague from which the city of Thebes suffers. In Nikos Kazantzakis's modern Greek novel, *Zorba the Greek*, the attractive widow who refuses all the men of the village is eventually stoned to death, functioning as a scapegoat for their unbridled male desire and lust.

In many religions, the theme of the scapegoat was linked to the MOTIF of the DYING GOD, as seen in the crucifixion of Jesus Christ who saw his death as a means of taking the sins of the people upon himself. This figure may be the sick KING, who has sterility of spirit and must therefore be sacrificed as a scapegoat

in order that renewal take place, as in the case of King Amfortas of *Parsifal*.

The Incas believed that diseases could be expelled by transferring them to a scapegoat, and a black llama was made to take all the clothing of the sick people on its back before it was driven from the village with the belief that the diseases went with it.

For Further Reading

Sophocles. *Oedipus the King. Three Tragedies by Sophocles*. Translated by H. D. F. Kitto. New York: Oxford University Press, 1962.

SCHENDA, RUDOLF (1930–)

Researcher and collector of European FOLKLORE (*see* EUROPEAN STORYTELLING). Rudolf Schenda, working at and for the University of Zürich, primarily is known for his work collecting and analyzing popular literature and the rise of literacy in Germany, Italy, and France (for which he received the Pultizer Prize in 1988). His published works include *Social History of Literature and Reading* (1972), *Popular Medical Attitudes and Practices, Folklore and Everyday Life* (1970), *Folk Narrative Research* (1970), *Social Gerontology* (1972), and *Sagenerzähler und Sagen der Schweiz* (1988). *Sagenerzähler*, a "treasury of Swiss legend research," contains a biographical and critical account of Swiss LEGEND collectors and writers. The focus in one part of the volume is an examination of the way in which storytellers rely on oral accounts as the basis for their literary creations; in a sense Schenda looks for the actual origin of orality and literacy itself. The book also explores the legendary characters of Swiss MYTH, including *Lavater* and *Cysat*. Although Schenda compiled the volume, much of the contributions to the book are from his students as they participated in his seminar on the subject. Schenda told critics he felt it was important to showcase the research efforts of his students. Because of the diversity and critical approach of the volume, other researchers in folklore believe Schenda's book to be invaluable as a new method of folklore research that goes beyond the scope of Swiss legend.

SCHEUB, HAROLD (1931–)

Author of African FOLKLORE. As an expert in African literature and languages, Harold Scheub has made many research trips to southern Africa to record African oral storytelling among the XHOSA, Zulu, Swazi, and Ndebele peoples (see AFRICAN STORYTELLING). Scheub is author of *African Images* (1971), *The Xhosa Ntsomi* (1975), and *The World and the Word: Tales and Observations From the Xhosa Oral Tradition* (1992). While Scheub primarily concentrates on African verbal storytelling, he also is intrigued by African nonverbal communication as manifested in DANCE and/or the written word as he outlines in his published article "Translation of African Oral Narrative-performances to the Written Word" (*Yearbook of Comparative and General Literature*, 1971). In *The Word and the World*, Scheub has recorded the tales and observations of Nongenile Masithathu Zenani (see ZENANI, NONGENILE MASITHATHU), a traditional Xhosa storyteller and healer in the Transkei region of South Africa. It is Zenani herself who interprets and analyzes the tales as Scheub faithfully records them. Some of the tales are highly symbolic, in which each tale conveys a moral lesson according to Xhosa society, with themes ranging from birth to DEATH or from puberty to MARRIAGE.

SCHOOLCRAFT, HENRY ROWE (1793–1864)

American Indian agent who is known as the father of American FOLKLORE. His 1839 recordings of Ojibwe narratives became the first devised and implemented systematic concept for a "folkloristic" study. He demonstrated to other scholars the manner in which to study Native American oral literature. From this venture, he concluded that a discipline should be created that would study a "total science of man." He asserted that studying a people from four different perspectives—physical type, material culture, oral traditions, and surrounding geography—would provided a complete and holistic construction of a particular culture. Although he believed that both field observation and library investigation were required for this holistic reconstruction, he focused on collecting living narratives in the field. A precursor to Franz Boas (see BOAS, FRANZ), the two scholars both undercut the evolutionary theory of culture and each believed folklore was no longer being created. Hence any tales still in circulation were remnants of the past, much like museum artifacts. Despite the connotation of the title, "Father of Folklore," Schoolcraft's contributions lie not in theory but in a collection of information. His work was pioneering in that he demonstrated the diversity of Native American cultures and the vitality and significance of native folklore. Schoolcraft's work led his colleagues and future folklorists to examine and focus on language and mythology. In addition to his influential fieldwork, Schoolcraft helped to establish the American Ethnographic Society.

SCHWARTZ, ALVIN (1927–1992)

Author of children's storybooks. Schwartz is best known for his fanciful and sometimes frightful characters. While some parents feel his scarier books are perhaps too alarming for small children, Schwartz's stories are a favorite among school-age children. In books such as *In a Dark Room and Other Scary Stories* (1984) and *Ghosts: Ghostly Tales from Folklore* (1991), Schwartz highlights WITCHES, ghosts, and zombies. Schwartz is interested in the way FOLKLORE plays an integral part in a person's life; substantiating a sense of place and a sense of self through tradition. Schwartz is concerned with the onset of new technologies and the part they play in distancing people from a tradition of reliance on one's self and one's family. Schwartz realizes that American folklore gave his own early life structure and continuity. In this spirit, Schwartz is careful to note and utilize the compelling games, songs, JOKES, tales, and customs created in the distant past through oral or written storytelling. Besides his good-natured horror stories, Schwartz delighted in creating many books of TONGUE-TWISTERS, JOKES, RIDDLES, and superstitions for children that were accompanied by his own brand of absurdist humor; *A Twister of Twists, a Tangler of Tongues* (1972) is one such example.

SCHWARTZ, HOWARD (1945–)

Jewish American writer of fiction and poetry. Schwartz's retelling and compilation of ancient Jewish FOLKTALES and FAIRY TALES help to perpetuate the Jewish tradition of oral and written storytelling (*see* JEWISH STORYTELLING). Through the sometimes familiar archetypal characters, Schwartz hopes to create a sense of proud heritage in his readers, whether they are of Jewish descent or not (*see* ARCHETYPE). At times Schwartz's subject matter is almost reverential, creating a sense of benign beneficence within the world of his poems or stories (he often turned to biblical and other religious sources). At other times Schwartz may create a dark and foreboding presence. Schwartz's tales often combine familiar traditions with his own highly imaginative style. In addition, Schwartz's writings usually are amply illustrated. In *Elijah's Violin and Other Jewish Fairy Tales* (1983), Schwartz consulted poems, fragments, and oral sources from 40 countries in more than 20 different languages for the final versions contained within the volume. Schwartz created his own unique interpretation of the ancient stories from the sometimes conflicting or incomplete versions. *Elijah's Violin and Other Jewish Fairy Tales* and Schwartz's other anthologies of Jewish lore are said to be some of the most comprehensive collections of Jewish mythology available.

SCOP *See* BARDS, NORTHERN EUROPEAN STORYTELLING

SEA

Body of water symbolizing the dynamic of life. The sea is the place of birth and DEATH—everything comes from the sea. In many mythologies, the sea is the primordial site before the EARTH is formed. As the home of monsters that emerge from its depths, the sea is symbolic of the unconscious.

As a place of potential danger, the sea provides a challenge to the HERO in his or her travels. Heroes such as Odysseus in the OD-YSSEY (*see also* HOMER) and Aeneas in Virgil's AENEID must journey across the sea to return home or make a new home. The Celtic GODS came by sea to Ireland.

The sea has mystical qualities as a place of birth, as in the tales that say the sorcerer MERLIN of Arthurian legend was born from the sea. The power of Poseidon, god of the sea to the Ancient Greeks, is central to many MYTHS, and the NYMPHS that come from the sea are often the mothers of heroes. *See also* SEA CHANTEYS, SEA JOURNEYS.

For Further Reading

Connolly, Peter. *The Legend of Odysseus*. Illustrated. New York: Oxford, 1986.

Le Guin, Ursula. *A Wizard of Earthsea*. New York: Houghton, 1968.

Lister, Robin, retold by. *The Odyssey*. Illustrated by Alan Baker. New York: Kingfisher, 1994.

Riordan, James, comp. *Stories from the Sea*. Illustrated by Amanda Hall. New York: Abbeville Press, 1996.

SEA CHANTEYS

Traditional WORK SONGS sung by sailors. Originally from the French verb *chanter*, to sing, the chantey is a kind of chanting song with a leader and a chorus. Sailors would sing chanteys while performing tasks such as hoisting sail or dropping anchor. Often there would be a solo stanza sung by the leader, or chantey-man, followed by a chorus repeated after each stanza by the entire group. The solo stanzas would often tell a story, and VARIANTS were passed on among the sailors who worked on different ships. Like the songs chanted by working men all over the world, be they shore gangs or lumbermen, the chanteys are noted for their rhythms and repetition, for the tempo and beat of the song enabled the men to work better as a team. With everyone chanting "Yo Heave Ho," for instance, the sail would be raised or the cargo hoisted. Some of the songs reflected the melancholy mood of sailors long at sea.

Many of the world's sea chanteys are of American origin, such as "Way, Haul Away" and "Wide Missouri." West Indian shoremen have their own traditional sea chanteys, and the barcaroles of the Italian boatmen and the Oriental rope songs are related. The British chantey, "For He's A Jolly Good Fellow" has found its way through the famed "seven seas" of the chanteys themselves. By their very nature, sea chanteys are part of the world's oral tradition.

SEA JOURNEY

Symbol of the sea of life which must be crossed. The sea journey is a common aspect of the QUEST, where the HERO must cross the waters of the sea as either part of his or her trials or as an initiation rite. J. E. Cirlot in *A Dictionary of Symbols* notes that "The Night Sea-Crossing" is "equivalent to the Journey into Hell" (*see* DESCENT TO THE UNDERWORLD).

Many heroes must journey by sea in order to attain their goal, whether it be to return to hearth and home, as Odysseus attempts to do in the ODYSSEY, or to found a new city, as Aeneas does in Virgil's AENEID, when he flees TROY and eventually becomes the founder of Rome. The Greek hero THESEUS must travel by sea to slay the MINOTAUR in the labyrinth, and he also departs by sea with Ariadne and her sister Phaedra. That one must navigate through the often treacherous and unpredictable sea is a perfect symbol for life's unpredictability, and the waters of the sea can be seen as a symbol of the unconscious.

Many journeys by sea appear in literature. Ursula K. Le Guin's *Earth-Sea Quartet* offers good examples of the sea journey of the hero/mage, Ged, and Mark Twain's *Huckleberry Finn* can be seen as having a sea journey when Huck "voyages" on the river.

For Further Reading

Connolly, Peter. *The Legend of Odysseus*. Illustrated. New York: Oxford, 1986.

Le Guin, Ursula. *The Farthest Shore*. New York: Houghton, 1971.

————. *Tehanu*. New York: Houghton, 1990.

————. *The Tombs of Atuan*. New York: Houghton, 1971.

————. *A Wizard of Earthsea*. New York: Houghton, 1968.

Lister, Robin, retold by. *The Odyssey*. Illustrated by Alan Baker. New York: Kingfisher, 1994.

Riordan, James, comp. *Stories from the Sea*. Illustrated by Amanda Hall. New York: Abbeville Press, 1996.

SEARCH FOR THE FATHER

Recurrent MOTIF in MYTH and LEGEND when the HERO's father is unknown, lost, disappeared, or even dead. The search for the FATHER can be seen as an aspect of the QUEST or, in some cases, the actual goal of the quest, and the son's search comes as part of the theme of regeneration. On one hand, the age-old pattern of "The KING is dead. Long live the King," which depicts the normal scheme of generational evolution, involves the son becoming his father and, in some cases, improving on him.

In some stories, the search for the father involves finding a surrogate father who will help the hero until he or she is strong enough to stand alone. This surrogate father may be a relative, such as an uncle, a family friend, an adviser, or even a servant. The search for the father comes when the father is missing, as in the case of Telemachos's search for Odysseus in the ODYSSEY; when the father is unknown, as in the Native American Tewa myth, "WATERJAR BOY," and the Pueblo tale, "The Arrow to the SUN"; or when the father is dead, as in the case of Aeneas's DESCENT TO THE UNDERWORLD to see his father Anchises in the AENEID.

In the *Odyssey*, Telemachos begins his search when he is finally grown to manhood and feels the need to calm the chaos in his father's palace caused by Odysseus's 20-year absence. His father's trusted friend and teacher, Mentor, serves as a surrogate father, and with the help of the GODDESS ATHENA, Telemachos sets sail to learn whether his father still lives and what has become of him. When he returns home and finds his father has reached home before him, he joins with his father in destroying his mother's suitors.

The Tewa story of "Waterjar Boy" involves a boy born first as a waterjar from which he then emerges as an actual boy. Although his mother does not know his father's identity, Waterjar Boy somehow knows where to find his father, so he goes to a spring where he meets a man whom he recognizes as is his father. He enters the spring to live with his father, but he eventually returns to his mother and tells her he has found his father. She soon dies, and Waterjar Boy returns to the spring, finds his mother there as well, and learns that his father is really Red Water Snake. Rejoined, the family lives in the spring from that point on.

In the *Aeneid*, Aeneas's descent to the Underworld comes at the advice of the Sibyl, who functions as a helping figure in the hero's quest. He must find his father, Anchises, and this involves overcoming the trials involved in descending to and returning from the LAND OF THE DEAD. His encounter in the underworld with his father teaches him all he needs to know and how he will be the founder of Rome.

The motif of the search for the father appears in Gerald McDermott's adaptation for children of the Pueblo Indian tale *Arrow to the Sun* (1974). A fatherless boy goes on a search to find his father, who happens to be the SUN.

For Further Reading

McDermott, Gerald. *Arrow to the Sun: A Pueblo Indian Tale*. New York: Penguin, 1974.

SECRET SON

African tale from Igboland in eastern Nigeria about a KING's desire for a son and his surprise at the unlikely mother of the special child. In spite of all his riches and his many wives and daughters, the king is not happy because he does not have a son. The king visits the Land of Women to seek their help. The eldest of the women tells the king that he will get a baby from where he least expects it, and this should be a lesson against further mistreatment of womankind. The women give herbs to the king and tell him to include one alligator pepper in their brew; the wife who swallows the pepper will bear his son. After the king prepares the herbs, he assembles all his wives, except for Carrier of Wood Ashes, whom he hates and whom the other women treat unkindly. As each wife tastes the dish, she pretends that she has swallowed the alligator pepper. One wife feels pity for the rejected wife and takes the remains of the dish to her. Carrier of Wood Ashes swallows the pepper. As the result of a trick, Carrier of Wood Ashes becomes pregnant by the king.

Later, all the favored wives give birth to daughters, and then the midwife, Mother of All Women, is called away. The other wives blindfold Carrier of Ashes. She does not know that she gives birth to a healthy boy. One of the jealous wives throws the baby boy in the river. They tell Carrier of Wood Ashes that she had a stillborn female. Mother of All Women does not believe the story of the stillborn girl, and she discovers that the boy is being cared for by the King of the River GODS. Mother of All Women takes the boy home with her and raises him. Then she sends a message to the king, telling him of his son. The day comes when Mother of All Women presents the boy to the king in front of the entire kingdom. The boy has a charm hidden in a little gourd that he carries on his head. A trial begins during which each of the royal wives throws a twig at the charm; only the twig thrown by the true mother of the boy will strike the charm. Each wife's twig fails to strike the charm. Finally, Carrier of Wood Ashes is summoned. In actuality, she is a beautiful woman, but a spell had been cast on her by the evil, most favored wife. The spell has lost its power. Carrier of Wood Ashes throws her twig, and the gourd falls to the ground. The king embraces his son and his long-rejected wife. They return to the palace to begin a new life. The wicked wife is convicted of treason and sacrificed, and Mother of all Women is given a position in the palace. Each year, gifts are given to King of the River Gods.

This tale contains the common MOTIF of an innocent woman who is treated unfairly by other jealous women. "CINDERELLA," "KATE CRACKERNUTS," and "Sleeping Beauty" are examples of tales from other cultures with this theme. The name "Carrier of Wood Ashes" is synonymous with the name "Cinderella," further emphasizing a strong connection between these two characters.

Another common motif found in this story is that of an infant who is abandoned in or near water and then adopted soon after. The Indian hero KARNA from the MAHABHARATA is abandoned in a river and adopted by a member of the lower class. Moses is hidden in a basket of bulrushes and adopted by the pharaoh's daughter (*see* EXODUS). The German HERO SIEGFRIED is left in a glass vessel in the river and adopted first by a doe and then by a blacksmith. The Polynesian demigod MAUI is thrown into the SEA and adopted by sea spirits. Likewise, in the Basuto tale CHILD IN THE REEDS, Thakane leaves her baby daughter, Lilahloane, with an old woman who emerges from a pool in a river. Eventually Lilahloane is reunited with her parents just as the king's only son is reunited with his parents. *See also* ABANDOMENT, HIDING THE CHILD.

Like many tales, *Secret Son* presents a moral. Carrier of Wood Ashes's gentle characteristics of humility, patience, and loyalty win their just rewards: in the end, her beauty is restored, and she is happily reunited with the king (albeit a problematic figure) and with her son. In addition, the kind works of Mother of all Women and King of the River Gods are recognized, while the wicked wife is executed. Other examples of instructive stories include MURILÉ AND THE MOONCHIEF, which describes what happens when an important promise is broken, OLODE THE HUNTER BECOMES AN OBA, which illustrates the evils of drinking and of forgetting one's responsibilities, and OSEBO'S DRUM, in which Osebo's pride gets the best of him.

SEDI AND MELO

EARTH-MOTHER and SKY-FATHER of northern Indian Minyong mythology. The non-Hindu Minyong people have a CREATION myth in which Sedi, the EARTH, and Melo, the sky, are to marry. However, the creatures who live between earth and sky are frightened that this union will crush them, so a creature called Sedi-Diyor strikes Melo with great force. In return, Melo withdraws upward, leaving Sedi and their two daughters. Miserable at her husband's departure, Sedi will not care for her daughters but hires a nurse. When the nurse dies, however, the two daughters soon die of grief, causing darkness to fall upon the world.

The people want the girls to return so there will be an end to this darkness, so they dig up the corpse of the nurse, but all they find is the nurse's shining eyes. When they wash the eyes, the last images the nurse saw are still in them. A carpenter creates models based on these images, and the people see that they are of the two girls.

Once again the girls grow, shining brighter and brighter as they each leave their home to set out on their journeys. The intense light from both girls causes the crops to wither, so the people kill the second daughter, Bong. Although they succeed in making the light and heat diminish, the people do not anticipate the response of Bomong, the first sister. Grief-stricken, she hides her head under a stone; once again there is darkness. The people respond by having the carpenter revive Bong, only this time with less light, so she becomes the MOON and Bomong the SUN. Thus this myth can also be grouped with explanations of the origin of the sun and moon. *See also* DIVISION OF WORLD PARENTS.

For Further Reading

Hamilton, Virginia. *In the Beginning: Creation Stories from around the World.* New York: Harcourt Brace Jovanovich, 1988.

SEKI, KEIGO (1899– ?)

Compiler and writer of Japanese FOLKLORE. Keigo Seki, a professor who teaches Japanese folklore, first published a three-volume set entitled *Nihon no Mukashi-banashi (Japanese Folktales)* in 1956 (*see* JAPANESE STORYTELLING). Selecting 240 stories from a total of over 15,000 possible FOLKTALES and versions, Seki researched the chosen stories by listening to the stories firsthand. The only changes Seki deemed appropriate for the final published versions (as taken from the informants) was the transformation of rare Japanese dialects to standard Japanese. Later Robert Adams chose 63 of Seki's 240 stories to translate into English under the title *Folklores of Japan* (1963). Seki took a scientific approach to the study of Japanese folklore, developing elaborate numbering systems and ranks of each story as did his mentor, Yanagita Kunio (*see* KUNIO, YANAGITA) before him. The tales include some of the most popular and best-known Japanese tales, including stories of ANIMALS, tales of the supernatural, and JOKES and ANECDOTES. Although there are some surprising matches to be found between highly Japanized oral tales and common Western folktales, most of the stories and cultural phenomena are completely unfamiliar to the Western reader. While translators do their best to bring Japanese folklore (as collected by Seki) to life, the task is somewhat hindered in that the Japanese language itself is rich in onomatopoeia; some of the morality of the original stories is inevitably lost.

THE SEVEN LITTLE KIDS

German fairy tale in the GRIMM BROTHERS's collection. In this fairy tale, a wolf masquerades as the mother goat of the seven little kids. He swallows chalk to soften his voice and sprinkles flour on his paws to make them appear white. The kids, deceived by the wolf's disguise, allow him into their house. The wolf promptly swallows six of the seven little kids, but the last escapes by hiding in the clockcase. When the mother goat returns, the seventh little kid relates the sad event. Together, they find the wolf snoring in the meadow. With her scissors, the mother cuts open his stomach, and all six kids jump out, unharmed. The greedy wolf had apparently forgotten to chew. The goats place stones in the wolf's stomach, and their mother sews him up. These stones make the wolf thirsty. But, when he attempts to drink at the well, the weight of the stones propel him into the water, and he drowns.

The MOTIF of docile ANIMALS overcoming violent ones by trickery and of stronger creatures devouring and regurgitating weaker ones are common to many cultures. The presence of the clock-case, however, shows that modern elements had been incorporated into the ancient themes. This particular tale also proved relevant to modern psychoanalysis. Sigmund Freud (see FREUD, SIGMUND) found similarities between a patient's dream and "The Wolf and the Seven Little Kids." He theorized that the wolf in this tale symbolized the child's fear of the father and thus castration. A modern rendition of this tale by author Irving Fetscher, however, takes issue with the dangerous image of wolves perpetuated by this and other fairy tales. In his story, "The Goat and the Seven Small Wolves," it is the goat who is by nature wrong-headed and ignorant, and the wolves who are innocent victims.

For Further Reading

Fetscher, Irving. "The Goat and the Seven Small Wolves." *German Fairy Tales*. Edited by Helmut Brackert and Volkmar Sanders. New York: Continuum, 1985.

Grimm, Jacob. *About Wise Men and Simpletons*. Translated by Elizabeth Shub. Illustrated. New York: Macmillan, 1971.

THE SEVEN SWANS

European FAIRY TALE of seven brothers turned into SWANS and the sister who tries to save them. In this much loved fairy tale with several VARIANTS, a widower KING has seven sons and a lovely daughter. To soothe his grief over his wife's death, he remarries, but his new queen is jealous of his love for his children. Knowing some magic and SPELLS, she makes magic shirts and throws them over the heads of her stepsons, who are instantly transformed into swans (*see* MAGIC CLOTHES). The daughter tries to find them, and learns that they become human only after nightfall. The swan brothers decide to flee that country, carrying their sister along with them in a woven net. There she learns that the only way to free her brothers from the spell is to weave seven shirts of painful nettles, never speaking a word all the while. The brothers then fly off, and the sister begins weaving the shirts, always silent.

One day a king finds her, falls in love with her, and marries her, though she never speaks and continues to weave the shirts. The people find her strange, especially when she goes to the graveyard to find more nettles. They accuse her of being a WITCH, and she is condemned to be burned at the stake. At the last minute the seven swans swoop down, she throws the almost completed shirts on them, they are transformed, and she speaks and proclaims her innocence.

As Marie-Louise von Franz notes in *The Feminine in Fairy Tales* (in a discussion of a variant of "The Seven Swans," the Grimms's "The Six Swans"), the silent sister is involved in "the great task of getting a bewitched person back into human life, the redemption MOTIF which you find in all human mythologies." Like the creative person or artist, she is "working for many years in the deepest introversion and concentration, in order to find the human way to let these irrational contents—swans—reappear in human life in a way which does not shock or disintegrate the conscious world."

For Further Reading

Silverman, Maida. *Anna and the Seven Swans.* New York: William Morrow, 1984.

SEXTON, ANNE (1928–1974)

American poet who rewrote a number of FAIRY TALES by the GRIMM BROTHERS in story poems. Born in Massachusetts, Anne Sexton lived there until her suicide in 1974. She began writing poetry as a way to recover after suffering a nervous breakdown. Her poetry includes *To Bedlam and Part Way Back* (1960); *All My Pretty Ones* (1962); *Selected Poems* (1964); *Live or Die* (1966), which won a Pulitzer Prize; *Love Poems* (1969); *Transformations* (1971); *The Book of Folly* (1972); *The Death Notebooks* (1974); and the posthumously published *The Awful Rowing Toward God* (1975). A complete edition of her poems appeared in 1981.

Sexton's poetry is generally confessional, mirroring the unhappiness and estrangement in her life. She is important for her imaginative and witty way of breaking taboos that have faced women poets. Attracted to fairy tales and mythic MOTIFS, Sexton rewrote 17 of the most famous Grimms's fairy tales in her book *Transformations*, including "Snow White and the Seven Dwarfs," "RED RIDING HOOD," "Rapunzel," "RUMPELSTILTZCHEN," "CINDERELLA," "Hansel and Gretel," and "Briar Rose," more commonly known as "Sleeping Beauty." Her versions of these tales look at them through a dark lens, and they become metaphors for human behavior and relationships between women and men.

For Further Reading

Sexton, Anne. *The Complete Poems.* Boston: Houghton, 1981.

———. *Transformations.* Boston: Houghton, 1971.

SHAMAN

Healer, medicine man or woman, ceremonialist, or visionary in many cultures. Shamans have existed from the earliest prehistoric times, and, while their RITUALS may differ from culture to culture, they are connected by a common thread: "an awakening to other orders of reality, the experience of ecstasy, and an opening up of visionary realms as their mission," writes Joan Halifax in *Shaman*. They have been the repositories of the culture's traditions, lore, and rituals, the reciters of the chants, and the guardians of the myths for thousands of years.

One of the earliest roles of the shaman was to try to control the ANIMALS of the hunt and "become the master of wild game and the summoner of beasts." The shaman might dress up as in the costume of the hunted animal and then go into a trance or DANCE as a means of attaining this control (*see* ANIMAL MASTER). Every shaman would have an animal familiar to assist him or her, and each would have an animal-mother or origin-animal.

Another role of shamans is to "transmit to their people in sign, song, and dance the nature of the cosmic geography that has been revealed to them in the process of initiatory trances and soul journeys," notes Halifax. This might be done in ground-painting during the puberty ritual for boys, or it might be painted on a drumhead.

Initiation for a shaman might be private, thus invisible, or publicly displayed, depending on the culture. For many, the journey of the spirit is an "entry into the abyss of the mysteries," often symbolized by the labyrinth. Sometimes aided by hallucinogens like peyote, the shaman goes temporarily mad and his or her spirit seems abducted. Yet, as Joseph Campbell (*see* CAMPBELL, JOSEPH) writes in *The Masks of Primitive Mythology*, "the shamanistic crisis, when properly fostered, yields an adult not only of superior intelligence and refinement, but also of greater physical stamina and vitality of spirit than is normal to the members of the group." Through DREAMS and visions, the shaman comes to attain the "purely sacred" and function as "the wounded healer."

For Further Reading

Eliade, Mircea. *Shamanism: Archaic Techniques of Ecstasy.* Translated by Willard R. Trask. Princeton: Princeton University Press, 1972.

Halifax, Joan. *Shaman.* New York: Thames and Hudson, 1988.

———. *Shamanic Voices.* New York: Dutton, 1979.

SHANACHIE

Professional Irish storyteller and historian, also known as *seanchai*. The shanachie, who can be either male or female, tells stories as much by gesticulation and tone as by his or her actual words. Like an actor, he or she conveys emotion through movement and intonation. The stories told are not easily classifiable. History, heroic poems and BALLADS, and ROMANCE are all fair game for the shanachie. The "pant" or TALL TALE derived from a true experience is the most commonly found type of story told by modern-day shanachie. Shanachie still meet to spin their tales at *ceili*, a social gathering, in parts of Ireland. By the fireplace, they recount, in either Gaelic or English, stories such as "The Selkie Girl" and "The Irish Cinderlad." The shanachie is classified as a folkteller rather than a BARD.

For Further Reading

Climo, Shirley. *The Irish Cinderlad.* Illustrated. New York: Harper Collins, 1996.

Colum, Padraic, ed. *Treasury of Irish Folklore.* New York: Crown Publishing, 1954.

Cooper, Susan. *The Selkie Girl.* Illustrated. New York: Macmillan, 1986.

McGowan, Hugh. *Leprechauns, Legends and Irish Tales.* Illustrated. London: Victor Gollancz Ltd., 1988.

SHAPE-SHIFTING

Ability of certain spirits, fairies, WIZARDS, sorcerers, mages, and WITCHES to take on different forms. Some fairies only can change into two different forms, that of a young man or a horse, and others can only change into bird. True shape-shifting must be distinguished from the illusion caused by a kind of hypnotism that affects the senses of the viewers in such a way as to make them believe they are seeing a particular shape. While mischievous BOGEYMEN can shape-shift, the true shape-shifters are wizards and supernatural wizards, who even can transform fairies. In Mallory's *Morte d'Arthur*, the story of King ARTHUR and the Knights of the Round Table, the wizard MERLIN is capable of shape-shifting.

Shape-shifting is common in many FAIRY TALES, such as the Celtic tale "The Wizard's Gillie." Contemporary writers of fantasy have granted some of their characters the ability to shape-shift, as in Peter S. Beagle's novel *The Inn-Keeper's Song* (1993) and Ursula K. Le Guin's *Earthsea Quartet.*

SHEOL

Ancient Jewish concept of the Underworld. Sheol can be thought of as a metaphor for the nothingness or void that comes with DEATH. The Old Testament says, "Whatever task lies to your hand, do it with might; because in Sheol, for which you are bound, there is neither doing nor thinking, neither understanding nor wisdom" (Ecclesiastes 9:10). As such, Sheol is frightening and undesirable. The Book of Psalms evokes the themes that Sheol is both a place to which one descends and a fitting punishment for sinners: "May death strike them,/may they go down alive into Sheol;/for their homes are haunts of evil!" (Psalms 55:15).

According to Jewish tradition, the dead in Sheol were revived when the Hebrew GOD appeared to the prophet Moses and the Israelites on MOUNT SINAI (*see* EXODUS). This revelation was meant to take place in the presence of the living as well as the dead.

In another story, Samael, the Angel of Death, went to find Moses, not knowing that God had already taken the prophet's soul from his body. Samael searched Moses' house, the land of Israel, the shores of the sea, and many other places, including Sheol.

When the tyrannical Babylonian king Nebuchadnezzar died and descended to Sheol, LEGEND says that the inhabitants of this underworld trembled, fearing that the evil king would be able to rule over them.

According to the Old Testament, Jonah prayed to God from the depths of the whale's belly and equated his experience there to being in Sheol: "In my distress I called to the

Lord,/and he answered me;/from deep within Sheol I cried for help" (Jonah 2:2). Another version of the Jonah story says that the fish who swallowed Jonah, and whose eyes served as windows, showed his captive Sheol and many other mysterious and wonderful places.

HADES, HELL, NIFLHEIM, PURGATORY, and TARTARUS are just a few examples of the many "underworlds" from other storytelling traditions. In each case, as with Sheol, one must descend to this most unpleasant realm of the dead.

For Further Reading

Ginzberg, Louis. *The Legends of the Jews*. Philadelphia: The Jewish Publication Society of America, 1909.

SHUNDI AND THE COCK

African (Bondei) TRICKSTER folktale told primarily for entertainment. Often African FOLKTALES such as "Shundi and the Cock" were told in succession with many other stories in one storytelling session. The trickster figure in AFRICAN STORYTELLING was often represented as childish, yet destructive—if not actually malevolent; however, the trickster most often elicited laughter. In the story of "Shundi and the Cock," however, the trickster's actions lead to death when a *shundi* (a cockatoo) wishes to befriend the cock. The crafty cock agrees to this friendship but subsequently tricks the shundi into cooking himself in a pot over an open fire after a couple of exchanged visits to each other's homes. Because of the cock's instruction to his wife to tell the shundi that he was within his own hot pot, the shundi assumed the cock survived such a feat and tried it at his own home. In the same way, the cock tricks a ferocious leopard that also wants to befriend him. This time the cock hides his head under his feathers to look as if he had been beheaded. The leopard, later seeing the cock alive and well, attempts to imitate this behavior at his own house; of course, the leopard instantly dies. Eventually all of the animals realize that the cock is not to be trusted. Leopards most of all, carry an extreme hatred toward fowls of any kind to this day. This is why, the story tells us, leopards immediately eat fowls as soon as they lay eyes on them.

For Further Reading

Abrahams, Roger. *African Folktales: Traditional Stories of the Black World*. New York: Pantheon, 1983.

SIEGFRIED

Hero in Germanic and northern European storytelling traditions, best known for having slain a DRAGON when he was a boy. Siegfried is the central figure in the thirteenth-century Germanic EPIC, the NIBELUNGENLIED, but this HERO also appears with other names, notably Sigurd, in many other stories.

The character Siegfried evolved from the Sigurd LEGEND, which came from the area around the Rhine and from land occupied by the Franks. The character Sigurd is continental German in origin but appears in numerous Scandinavian sources, including the *Volsunga Saga*. There is no way of knowing what date the Sigurd legend migrated to the north. According to Norse legend, Sigurd killed the dragon Fafnir and won both his gold and his wisdom. He was the greatest of all Germanic heroes and could claim divine descent. Sigurd became the center of many, unrelated stories, and it is possible that this literary figure had historical origins. As such, he is a King ARTHUR of the northern world.

The old Norse *Thidreksaga*, recorded about the year 1250 by an Icelander, based on oral traditions and ancient songs, tells the story of the birth and the youth of Siegfried (Sigurd). According to this source, Siegfried is the son of King Sigmund and his wife Sisibe. Because Sigmund suspects his wife of unfaithfulness, she is banished and ends up giving birth to a remarkably beautiful boy in the forest. She places him in a glass vessel which is kicked into the river. The queen sees what happens to her son and dies soon afterwards. The glass vessel is carried to the sea and then lands on a rocky cliff where it breaks and the boy begins to cry. The boy's cries are heard by a doe, who raises the child with her own young. The boy attains enormous stature and strength and eventually is taken home by a smith, who names him Siegfried. Because of Siegfried's strength and willfulness, the smith tries to get rid of him by arranging for his brother, the dragon Regin, to kill the boy. Instead, Siegfried conquers the dragon. He smears his body with the dragon's blood, except where he cannot reach between his shoulders, and his skin grows horny so that no weapon can pierce him. Then he kills his foster father. After much time, Siegfried is murdered by his brother-in-law, Hogni, who plunges a spear between Siegfried's shoulder blades, his only unprotected spot.

In the *Nibelungenlied*, the gallant knight and dragon-slayer Siegfried, ruler of the Netherlands, Norway, and Nibelungland, is known for his great strength which he has tested in many kingdoms. In his youth, Siegfried vanquished the Nibelung PRINCES, Schilbung and Nibelung, and subdued 700 of their men. Fearing Siegfried, a host of young warriors gave the Nibelung land, castles, and treasure to Siegfried as their lord. The DWARF Alberich tried to avenge the princes' DEATHS, but Siegfried defeated him and won the cloak of invisibility.

Later, Siegfried's wife, Kriemhild, unwittingly reveals to the spiteful Hagen the location of Siegfried's vulnerable spot. Kriemhild asks Hagen to look after Siegfried in battle and even goes so far as to mark the unprotected place between his shoulders with a silk cross sewn on his outfit. During a hunting expedition, as Siegfried stoops to drink from a stream, Hagen hurls Siegfried's own spear at the vulnerable spot and pierces him. The mighty knight dies in a bed of flowers.

The legend of Siegfried the Dragon-Slayer contains several MOTIFS found in other storytelling traditions. Like Moses (*see* EXODUS), the Indian hero KARNA, the Polynesian demigod MAUI, the son of the KING in the Nigerian tale SECRET SON, and Lilahloane in the Basuto tale CHILD IN THE REEDS, Siegfried is abandoned near water and then later adopted. Siegfried's mother dies soon after his birth as do the mothers of the heroes QUETZALCOATL and Waterjar Boy (*see* WATERJAR BOY MYTH).

As his immense strength and stature indicate, Siegfried is possessed of adult qualities almost from birth. As such, he is included in the tradition of CUCHULAINN, KUTOYIS, LITUOLONE, Quetzalcoatl, and Waterjar Boy.

Like ACHILLES, Siegfried is a mighty hero with a vulnerable spot and dies young. In addition, the young, handsome, courageous knight's dramatic death is similar to that of the Frankish knight ROLAND specifically and reminiscent of the DYING GOD motif in general.

Siegfried is the hero of Richard Wagner's operatic cycle, *Der Ring des Nibelungen* (*see* WAGNER, RICHARD).

For Further Reading

Evslin, Bernard. *Fafnir.* New York: Chelsea House, 1989.

Trubshaw, Bob. *Dragon Slaying Myths Ancient and Modern.* Wymeswold: Heart of Albion Press, 1993.

Updike, John. *The Ring.* Illustrated by Warren Chappell. New York: Alfred A. Knopf, 1964.

SINGER, ISAAC BASHEVIS (1904–1991)

1978 Nobel Prize-winning American Yiddish author. Isaac Bashevis Singer was born in Poland and emigrated to the United States at the age of 31. One of the greatest Yiddish writers of New York City, he did not see his work translated into English until he was 46. A prolific writer, he was the author of many short stories for both adults and children, novels, and memoirs. His stories often include such supernatural characters as DEMONS and GIANTS. Among his most well-known short stories and novels that include folkloric elements are *Gimpel the Fool and Other Stories* (1978), *Short Friday and Other Stories* (1964), *Stories for Children* (1984), ZLATEH THE GOAT *and Other Stories* (1966), *Satan in Goray* (1935), and *The Golem* (1982).

For Further Reading

Farrell Lee, Grace. *From Exile to Redemption: The Fiction of Isaac Bashevis Singer.* Southern Illinois University Press, 1987.

Singer, Isaac Bashevis. *The Fools of Chelm and Their History.* Illustrated by Uri Shulevitz. New York: Farrar, Straus, Giroux, 1973.

———. *Gimpel the Fool and Other Stories.* Trans. by Saul Bellow and others. New York: Farrar, Straus, Giroux, 1978.

———. *The King of the Fields.* New York: Farrar, Straus, Giroux, 1988.

———. *The Penitent*. New York: Farrar, Straus, Giroux, 1983.

———. *The Power of Light: Eight Stories for Hanukkah*. New York: Avon, 1980.

———. *Why Noah Chose the Dove*. Illustrated by Eric Carle. New York: Farrar, Straus, Giroux, 1982.

SIOUX CREATION

Cosmogonic CREATION myth. Inyan (whose name, translated into English, means "rock") is the beginning of a Sioux creation MYTH. His spirit was *Wakan Tanka* (the Great Mystery); he was the first of the superior GODS. Inyan, who desired to exercise his creative powers, performed a "bloodletting," from which the EARTH (*Maka*) was created. However, Inyan lost control of the amount of blood that flowed from his veins (his powers of creation resided in his blood), resulting in a complete loss of his creative powers. The creative powers, which could not be contained within the flowing waters of the earth, separated themselves from Inyan's blood to assume another shape, which was called *Skan* (the Almighty).

The creation myth further develops as Skan attempts to appease the earth GODDESS (Maka-akan) on several occasions. First, Maka, recognizing her superior position over an essentially powerless Inyan, demands that she be allowed to see herself. Skan, in order to pacify Maka, creates light (Anp). However, Maka complains that Anp does not provide the warmth necessary to make herself beautiful, which results in Skan's creation of the SUN (Wi) and the sun spirit (Wi-akan). After the creation of Wi (the last of the superior gods), a bitter argument results from Maka's complaint that the sun should become subservient to her desires. Skan, the mediator of the superior gods, installs a hierarchy amongst the gods themselves, placing himself between Wi, the new chief of the gods, and Maka.

After these initial struggles for power amongst the superior gods, the Sioux universe is developed in more detail. Each god is allowed to create a companion. Inyan creates wisdom (Ksa), Skan creates the WIND (Tate), Maka creates passion (Unk) and Wi, the MOON (Wi-win); however, these lesser

spirits soon operate as servants rather than as companions to the gods. Ksa, arguing that Skan's daughter (Wohpe) should not live a life of servitude, suggests the creation of a pair of beings that would function as Skan's servants. Taking various body parts from the superior gods (bone from Inyan, blood from Maka) and the primary attributes of the lesser gods (Ksa's wisdom, Wohpe's beauty), Skan imbued each being with a spirit (*nagi*) and an energy force that would enable these creatures faithfully to serve the gods. This heteronormative pair (named Ate and Hun) in turn reproduced, resulting in the creation of an entire race of people (the Pte), who began to populate the earth.

This Sioux creation myth shares a number of universal MOTIFS found in the FOLKLORE and mythology of other cultures. Gnas, the god of plots, schemes, and persuasive speech, is similar to LOKI in the Norse mythology, as well as to Satan in the Christian mythology (*see* DEVIL). The Sioux creation also tells of a prelapsarian and postlapsarian inhabitation of the earth, analogous to the Christian tale of ADAM AND EVE.

For Further Reading

Bierhorst, John. *The Mythology of North America*. New York: William Morrow, 1985.

Eastman, Mary H. *Dahcotah, or Life and Legends of the Sioux around Fort Snelling*. Afton, MN: Afton Historical Society Press, 1995.

Walker, James R. *Lakota Myths*. Lincoln, NE: University of Nebraska Press, 1983.

SIRENS

Creatures from Greek mythology, half woman and half bird. They lived on an island not far from Sicily and—like MERMAIDS—were notorious for luring seamen with their beautiful songs. None of their victims ever returned to describe their fates, and it is assumed that they died of forgetfulness and hunger.

Jason and his fellow adventurers, the Argonauts, narrowly escaped the sirens with the aid of Orpheus's lyre; the musician's song was more beautiful than that of the sirens, and it has been said that they committed suicide out of sheer discouragement. This seems unlikely, however, as they were ready and waiting to torment Odysseus and his crew a generation later.

Odysseus prepared for this encounter by stuffing the ears of his crew with wax, then tying himself to the mast. At the sound of the sirens's song, Odysseus threatened to kill his men unless they turned him loose. But in obedience to his previous orders, they only tied him tighter. The words of the song Odysseus heard were even more enticing than the melody, promising infinite wisdom and knowledge of all future events.

As in the story of Jason, it is said that the sirens committed suicide after their encounter with Odysseus. One of the sirens, Parthenope, threw herself into the sea out of frustrated love for the adventurer and washed up in the Bay of Naples. Hence, the ancient Greeks knew the island of Naples by the name Parthenope.

Although HOMER only mentions two sirens, their number increased as more stories were told about them. In *The Greek Myths,* Robert Graves (*see* GRAVES, ROBERT) lists the names of 11 sirens.

Stories of animal-human creatures include those about CENTAURS, SATYRS, the MINOTAUR, and GANESA. *See also* ANCIENT GREEK STORYTELLING, ODYSSEY, QUEST FOR THE GOLDEN FLEECE.

SIR GAWAIN

Well-known knight in King ARTHUR'S court, as well as the legendary KING'S nephew. Gawain first appears in GEOFFREY OF MONMOUTH's *History of the Kings of Britain,* where he is called *Gualganus* and has a relatively unimportant role, and in the twelfth-century historian William of Malmesbury's well-known reference to the discovery of Gawain's grave at Walwyn's Castle in Pembrokeshire.

Early Welsh LEGENDS, in which Gawain is known as *Gwalchmi,* celebrate his fearlessness, unfailing courtesy, and persuasive speech. In these tales, Gawain resembles the Irish hero CUCHULAINN. Gawain is King Arthur's nephew, his sister's son; likewise, Cuchulainn is the nephew of Conchobar, the King of Ulster. In some societies, a nephew

is regarded as more important than a son. This tradition arises from early Celtic and Germanic kinship systems. Cuchulainn's father is the god Lugh, who is connected with the SUN and whose feast day falls at the height of the summer. Gawain's father is Loth of Lothian, whose name may be a corruption of Lugh. Like Cuchulainn, Gawain is associated with the sun-god or sun-HERO: Gawain's strength grows steadily during the morning, reaches its peak at noon when he is most dangerous, and declines in the afternoon.

Gawain's character rises to fame in French Arthurian ROMANCES. In the early French romances, Gawain possesses tremendous knightly skill and is the ideal of courage, gentleness, and courtesy. CHRÉTIEN DE TROYES's last, unfinished work, *Perceval* or *Le Conte du Graal* (*The History of the Grail*), written about 1180, is the earliest surviving tale which describes Gawain's adventures in detail (*see* PERCIVAL). In one part of *Le Conte du Graal,* Gawain comes to a garden where he sees the beautiful woman, Orgueilleuse. Gawain is captivated by Orgueilleuse and determined to win her. They arrive at the Castle of Wonders which has been put under a SPELL (*see* CASTLES—ENCHANTED). The castle is guarded by magic and inhabited by fatherless girls, elderly widows, and young men who have not yet been knighted. They all wait for a hero to break the spell. Gawain enters the splendid castle and sits on a bed. Arrows suddenly begin to attack him, and a lion leaps on him. Gawain defends himself from the arrows, beheads the lion, and then cuts off its paws. In doing so, he breaks the spell of the castle. After other adventures, Gawain eventually wins the love of Orgueilleuse. Another well-known early account of Gawain and his adventures is the German romance *Parzival,* written in the early 1200s by WOLFRAM VON ESCHENBACH.

In later French romances, Gawain's character becomes lascivious, cruel, and treacherous, and he acquires an evil reputation for merciless ferocity. The noble aspect of Gawain's character declines in the French romances as his position as the first knight of the Round Table is usurped by LANCELOT.

In English Arthurian romances, however, the superlative knight Gawain continues to represent the epitome of virtue, as exemplified in the famous Middle English poem, *Sir Gawain and the Green Knight*. In this late fourteenth-century poem, Gawain chops off the head of a gigantic green knight with the understanding that one year later he would have to submit to a return blow from the green warrior. After a year, Gawain rides in search of the Green Chapel and comes to a castle where he is welcomed by Sir Bercilak, his beautiful wife, and a hideous CRONE, who is later revealed as the enchantress Morgan le Fay. Gawain remains at the castle for three days. He and Bercilak make an agreement whereby each day Bercilak gives Gawain any game he catches while hunting, and Gawain gives Bercilak anything he acquires in the castle. Bercilak's wife repeatedly attempts to seduce Gawain, who courteously resists in spite of the kisses she bestows on him. On the first day, Gawain gives Bercilak one kiss in exchange for several deer. On the second day, he gives Bercilak two kisses in exchange for a boar. And, on the third day, Gawain gives Bercilak three kisses in exchange for a fox's skin. Bercilak's wife also gives Gawain a magic girdle of green silk which she claims would protect him from harm; however, Gawain keeps the girdle. On New Year's Day, Gawain meets the green knight at the Green Chapel and bows his head to accept the blow. He flinches when he sees the blade descend. The knight reproaches Gawain, raises the ax again, and lowers it without striking. The third time he raises the ax, the knight slightly nicks Gawain's neck. The green knight reveals that he is Bercilak, and the whole test was conspired by Morgan le Fay in hopes of frightening GUINEVERE and shaming Arthur's court. Gawain's life is spared because his virtue saved him from making love to Bercilak's wife; his neck is cut because he concealed the gift of the girdle. Gawain resolves to wear the girdle as a badge of shame. Gawain is joyfully received at CAMELOT, and all the knights wear green baldrics in honor of the heroic Gawain.

The story *Sir Gawain and the Green Knight* contains several common FOLKTALE MOTIFS, including a green man, a beheading game, and a magic girdle. Although the reason for the green knight's greenness is not clear, it is possible that this character derived from either the Celtic fairy tradition, as the color green is often associated with fairies; from the tradition of vegetation GODS; or, because of the green knight's castle in the mysterious forest with its sensuous woman, from a Celtic ruler of the Underworld. The beheading game came originally from Celtic legend and appears in several earlier stories, including the Irish story "Bicriu's Feast," in which the hero Cuchulainn beheads a GIANT. When the giant's turn comes, he does not return the blow; instead, he gently lowers the ax, blunt side downwards. For his bravery, Cuchulainn is recognized as the champion of champions. Finally, the motif of a magic girdle also appears in the Vulgate *Merlin* when the enchantress Vivien uses her girdle to draw a magic circle nine times around the sleeping MERLIN, thereby imprisoning the magician in a tower of mist.

Like his fellow knights Percival and Lancelot, Gawain is actively involved in the quest for the HOLY GRAIL. In many legends, he is accompanied by his warhorse, Gringolet, a Welsh otherworld horse which was originally white and had red ears. According to the thirteenth-century French work *La Mort le Roi Artu*, Gawain dies after he receives a wound to his head during an excruciating battle with Lancelot. Because the battle is fought in France where Lancelot has been banished, Arthur takes the dying Gawain back to England, and this great knight dies in Dover.

For Further Reading

Chrétien de Troyes. *Perceval: Or the Story of the Grail.* Athens, GA: University of Georgia Press, 1985.

Hastings, Selina. *Sir Gawain and the Green Knight.* New York: Lothrop, 1981.

———. *Sir Gawain and the Loathly Lady.* Illustrated by Juan Wijngaard. New York; Lothrop, Lee & Shepherd, 1985.

Talbott, Hudson. *King Arthur and the Round Table.* New York: Morrow Junior Books, 1995.

SISYPHUS

Evil mortal in Greek and Roman mythology who is famous for his punishment in the underworld, where he is condemned to roll a boulder uphill forever. In some accounts, Sisyphus is the father of Odysseus.

In spite of the fact that Sisyphus founded the city of Corinth and was recognized for promoting Corinthian commerce and navigation, he was known for his unscrupulous cunning and was considered a terrible knave. He made a career of robbery and often murdered unsuspecting travelers, one possible reason for his unique punishment.

When Salmoneus, Sisyphus's brother, usurped the Thessalian throne from him, Sisyphus seduced Tyro, Salmoneus's daughter. When Tyro discovered that Sisyphus's true motive was not love for her, she killed the two sons that Sisyphus had fathered. Sisyphus falsely accused Salmoneus of incest and murder, and had him expelled from Thessaly. One version of the Sisyphus story says that he received his punishment in the underworld for the vengeance he took on Tyro and the injury he gave to Salmoneus.

Although MYTHS vary as to the specific reasons for Sisyphus's punishment, one common story derives from ZEUS's abduction of the young girl Aegina. According to this version, Asopus, Aegina's father, arrived in Corinth in search of his daughter. Sisyphus would not reveal what happened to Aegina unless Asopus supplied the citadel of Corinth with perennial spring; Asopus complied, and Sisyphus told him all he knew. Zeus narrowly escaped Asopus's vengeance and ordered HADES to take Sisyphus to TARTARUS and punish him eternally for betraying divine secrets. After deceiving both Hades and Persephone, Sisyphus finally was brought to remain in Tartarus where he was ordered to roll a block of stone up the brow of a hill and topple it down the other slope. Each time he tries, the boulder nearly reaches the summit and then bounces to the bottom of the hill.

The Norse TRICKSTER figure, LOKI, is another example of a mythological character who is eternally punished by the gods for his wicked ways.

SIVA

One of the three GODS of the supreme triad of Hindu deities. Siva is the god of nature, learning, dancing, the arts, revelry, destruction, and reintegration. He is portrayed as being fair-skinned, with five faces, three eyes, and four arms. His third eye is enormously destructive; it can destroy all human beings with one look. Like KALI, he wears a necklace of skulls along with an animal skin; he has a blue neck from the poison he drank to prevent the world from being poisoned. One of his symbols is the *lingam* (phallus), for Siva is the god of reproduction.

Siva lives on earth with humankind as a master *Yogi*, practicing a life of asceticism. Because he is the destroyer, he is also associated with ghosts and cemeteries. He is known for dancing with Kali in a competition which he ultimately wins, called "The DANCE of Siva." As Emily Kearns notes in her essay "Indian Myth," "The taming or attempted taming of the GODDESS by a male god or DEMON is a recurrent theme, often with erotic associations." One version of this is the contest between Kali and Siva, where Kali challenges Siva's ability to dance better than she; however, it is Kali who loses. Siva's power or trickery outdoes Kali, and she is tamed of her wildness. The dancing is violent, and Kali loses not because she is an inferior dancer but because she is a woman: Siva lifts his leg in a way that Kali will not imitate because it offends her sense of feminine propriety.

Siva's wife is Parvati, and their marriage is not an easy one. Parvati wants children and Siva does not. GANESA is born from dirt that is washed from Parvati's body. Ganesa has the head of an elephant because Siva cut off his original head in a fit of anger over Parvati's having produced a child and then replaced it with the first head that he saw.

For Further Reading

Nagar, Shanti L. *Siva in Art, Literature, and Thought.* South Asia, 1995.

O'Flaherty, Wendy Doniger. *Hindu Myths: A Sourcebook Translated from the Sanskrit.* Harmondsworth, Middlesex: Penguin, 1975.

SKILLFUL COMPANIONS

Motif in which a number of companions create or argue over a woman. The MOTIF is most notably used in the FOLKLORE of India, Indonesia, Japan, and Africa. In these tales, a woman is created when a woodcarver carves her shape, a tailor fashions her clothes, and a gardener gives her speech. Often the skillful companions will then fight over to whom the woman belongs. In Indian and Japanese stories, skillful companions resuscitate a woman, then fight over who will be married to her. This "divided bride motif" parallels King Solomon's proof, in that the revived bride is threatened to be cut in three if the men cannot decide who will have her; when the threat is made, the true lover is discovered. Sometimes the appearance of a father, mother, or husband solves the dilemma and claims the woman. This theme is highly patriarchal and reinforces an oppressed feminine role in that a woman is created by men for their own use and has no say in whom she will marry. It has similarities to the Christian cosmogonic tale ADAM AND EVE, in that Eve is created by the Christian GOD for Adam, and is formed with Adam's rib.

SKY-FATHER

Complementary figure to EARTH-MOTHER in various CREATION MYTHS. In many creation myths, there is a Sky-Father or Sky-Man who represents the sky or HEAVEN. Often Sky-Father is connected with a mate who is his equal or whom he dominates, Earth-Mother or the Great MOTHER. As primal couple, they are WORLD PARENTS, symbolizing HEAVEN and EARTH joined together to perform the act of creation. This original divine couple has to be separated to allow their offspring to flourish, for example in cases such as the Maori Sky-Father and Earth-Mother, RANGI AND PAPA, and the Egyptian Geb and Nut. Other creation myths with the Sky-Father and Earth-Mother MOTIF are the Navajo and Zuni Sky-Father and Earth-Woman, the Japanese Izanagi and Izanami, the Hopi SUN god and SPIDER WOMAN.

In some myths, Sky-Father is the sole creator, called OLD MAN or the GREAT SPIRIT by different Native American tribes, An or Anu in the Sumerian-Babylonian epics GILGAMESH and *Enuma Elish*, GOD in the monotheistic religions of Judaism and Christianity, and *Allah* in the Moslem religion. Myths that show Sky-Father creating alone tend to reflect the influence of patriarchy, with Sky-Father functioning as the Supreme Being, sun-god, fecundator, giver of life to all things, as in the Hindu concept of BRAHMAN. *See also* DIVISION OF WORLD PARENTS.

SKY-MAIDEN

Melanesian GODDESS whose wings were stolen by a man. Like the SWAN-maiden of Northern Europe, Sky-MAIDEN is a swan goddess who is bathing with a group of other sky-maidens who have removed their wings. Qat, a Melanesian TRICKSTER god similar to the Polynesian MAUI, hides one pair of wings, preventing the Sky-Maiden from returning to the sky while the other maidens fly away. In this way the Sky-Maiden becomes Qat's wife.

In one Melanesian version of the story, Qat's mother scolds her new daughter-in-law, who bursts into tears and inadvertently washes away the earth that has been hiding her wings, which she puts on and flies away. In order to pursue her, Qat shoots an arrow chain into the sky with a banyan root winding around it, thereby providing himself with a ladder to climb to reach the sky world (*see* LADDER TO ANOTHER WORLD OR HEAVEN). There he meets a man who is gardening, and begs him to leave the banyan root alone until Qat and his wife have descended, but as they begin their descent, the root snaps and Qat falls to his death while the Sky-Maiden flies to safety and is free once more.

The tale suggests that swans and their sky-maiden counterparts should be free to come and go as they please, and even the trickster can be tricked.

For Further Reading

May, Charles Paul. *Oceania: Polynesia, Melanesia, Micronesia*. Nashville, TN: T. Nelson, 1973.

Strathern, Marilyn. *The Gender of the Gift*. Berkeley: University of California Press, 1988.

SLEEPING BEAUTY *See* FAIRY TALE

SOMADEVA

Eleventh-century Jain teacher of India known for his aphorisms and for compiling the OCEAN OF STORY. The Jainest Somadeva was a *Digambara* (a Jainist monk who wears no clothing) teacher who wrote the *Nectar of Aphorisms on Polity*, or *Nitivakyamrta*, a collection of gnomic sentences on politics and good conduct, written in Sanskrit prose. These aphorisms concerned the ideal king from a Jainist point of view, which did not differ greatly from that of the Hindus. Moral behavior was very important, as exemplified in the following aphorisms, "A true lord is he who is righteous, pure in lineage, conduct and associates, brave, and considerate in his behavior"; "He is a true KING who is self-controlled whether in anger or pleasure, and who increases his own excellence"; "If the king does not speak the truth all his merits are worthless. If he deceives, his courtiers leave him, and he does not live long"; "Laziness is the door through which all misfortunes enter. . ."; "The king who thinks only of filling his belly is abandoned even by his queen"; "He is dear to the people who gives of his treasure"; and "The king is the maker of the times. When the king rightly protects his subjects all the quarters are wishing cows [legendary divine cows that granted all the wishes of the people who milked them], INDRA rains in due season, and all living things are at peace."

While Indian rulers and thinkers believed warfare was legitimate, as typified by the attitudes in the MAHABHARATA, Jainism tended to see war as a last resort, and this is reflected in Somadeva's aphorisms on the subject: "The force of arms cannot do what peace does. If you can gain your desired end with sugar, why use poison?"; "For when water is drained from the lake the crocodile grows as thin as a snake [meaning that even if the enemy wins, he may be so weakened as to make it possible to overcome him]"; "A lion when he leaves the forest is no more than a jackal"; and "a snake whose fangs are drawn is a mere rope."

Somadeva was also the compiler of the *Ocean of Story*, a collection of tales, including RIDDLE stories. *See also* PANCHATANTRA.

For Further Reading

Bary, William. Theodore. *Sources of Indian Tradition.* Vol. 1. New York: Columbia University Press, 1864.

SONG OF ROLAND

Old French EPIC poem about the betrayal of the heroic knight ROLAND and the emperor CHARLEMAGNE's ensuing revenge of his nephew's death. The *Song of Roland*, as it exists today, was composed by a man known as Turoldus who lived in France around 1100. The LEGEND of Roland began centuries earlier, however, and Turoldus takes it for granted that his audience knows all about Roland, Charlemagne, Ganelon, Oliver, and so on. It is not known how the legend of Roland was passed on before it was written in the form we know it, but it is generally assumed that this story was transmitted orally, perhaps for the entertainment of the French court, and that it went through many revisions.

The historical basis for the poem is found in the ambush of Charlemagne's rearguard by a party of Basques as the emperor's army crossed the Pyrenees in 778. All of the Franks in the rearguard were killed. Loaded with booty, the Basques escaped into the night. When the poem was written over three centuries later, this small historical event was imbued with HEROES, traitors, and religious significance.

At the beginning of the poem, the Saracens, the enemy Moors, agree to convert to Christianity if Charlemagne and his troops leave Spain immediately. Charlemagne decides to appoint someone to go to Marsilion, the Saracen king, to learn his true intentions. Roland nominates his stepfather, Ganelon, who believes that Roland's nomination is an affront to his manhood and calls his courage into question. Because of his loyalty to Charlemagne, Ganelon knows that he must go to Saragossa, the Saracen stronghold. On the way, Ganelon and Blancandrin, the Saracen messenger, pledge to kill Roland.

At Marsilion's court, it becomes clear to the king that Ganelon is willing to betray the Franks and Roland. Marsilion and Ganelon devise a plan. Ganelon tells the king that Roland, another great knight named Oliver, and 20,000 Frenchmen will be guarding the mountain pass at Roncevaux as Charlemagne's army leaves Spain. Marsilion should send 100,000 Saracens to attack the rearguard. Ganelon guarantees Roland's death.

Ganelon reports to Charlemagne that the Saracen army refuses to be baptized. The Saracens flee to the sea where their boats are caught in a storm and they all drown. Marsilion, however, will journey to France and convert to Christianity. Charlemagne prepares to leave Spain, and Ganelon appoints Roland to the rearguard. Twenty thousand Franks and the Twelve Peers, a chosen group of extremely valorous knights, also remain behind. The Saracens attack, and, in spite of Oliver's urging, Roland refuses to blow his horn to alert Charlemagne. A ferocious battle ensues, and it is not until after almost all of the Franks have been killed that Roland sounds the *oliphant* until his mouth bleeds and his temples burst. When Charlemagne hears his nephew's horn, Ganelon tries to convince him that there is no battle. Charlemagne arrests Ganelon and turns him over to the cooks, who pluck his beard, beat him with sticks, and fasten a chain around his neck. Before Charlemagne returns to his army's aid, they all die magnificent deaths, including Oliver, the Archbishop Turpin, and finally Roland.

The second half of the *Song of Roland* tells of Charlemagne's revenge. He pursues the Saracens and prays for GOD to extend the day. The sun remains fixed in the sky, and Charlemagne destroys Marsilion's army. Emir Baligant, the lord of all Islam, arrives with his army from Alexandria. After a grueling battle, Charlemagne, the great Christian king, finally prevails over the pagans and kills Baligant. After destroying all the synagogues and mosques in Saragossa and baptizing its residents, Charlemagne's army retreats to France with the Saracen queen, Bramimond. There, Ganelon is executed and Bramimond is baptized. At the end of the poem, the weary King Charlemagne is called by the angel Saint Gabriel to fight another battle in the name of Christianity.

The *Song of Roland* contains the familiar epic themes of love, loyalty, jealousy, war, revenge, and murder, and Roland's dramatic death is a fine example of the MOTIF of the DYING GOD. In addition, this poem contains several elements found in the legends of King ARTHUR. The group of special knights, the Twelve Peers, can be compared to the Knights of the Round Table. Roland's sword, Durendal, a highly significant aspect of his persona, is like Arthur's sword, Excalibur. Finally, the extremely important code of knightly conduct, emphasizing bravery, unswerving loyalty, and keen battle skills, reflects a common medieval conception of appropriate aristocratic cultural values. *See also* ILIAD, NIBELUNGENLIED, ODYSSEY.

For Further Reading

Brault, Gerard J. *The Song of Roland: An Analytical Edition*. Vol. 1. University Park, PA: The Pennsylvania State University Press, 1978.

Sayers, Dorothy L., trans. *The Song of Roland*. Harmondsworth, Middlesex: Penguin, 1978.

SOPHIA

Biblical personification of wisdom. The figure of Sophia, the Greek word for wisdom, appears first in the Hebrew scriptures, and though there are more pages about her than such figures as ADAM AND EVE, NOAH, Abraham, or Jacob, she remains a far more confusing figure. As Susan Cady, Marian Ronan, and Hal Taussig note in *Sophia: The Future of Feminist Spirituality*, "she was not clearly GOD and was so clearly not human [that] she was confusing to the dogmaticians." In the Book of Wisdom (7:25,27), she is described as "a breath of the power of God," present at the time of God's CREATION of the world. As an integral part of the creative process, "Her radiance never sleeps" (7:10–11). She is "the process of learning or knowing," both teacher and what is taught. As lover, she loves both the Lord and humanity. Sometimes she is portrayed as a tree providing both abundance and shelter. In later books of the BIBLE, Sophia is connected with the Law that is fundamental to Hebrew belief. In relation to God,

Sophia can be seen as "a co-creator with the Hebrew God," "a heavenly queen," "a messenger from God," and "God's lover," write Cady, Ronan, and Taussig.

In the early Gnostic cult of Christianity, Sophia was seen as a Great GODDESS who bore two spirits: Christ, a male, and Achamoth, a female. As David Leeming describes in *Goddess*, Achamoth "bestowed existence and life to the elements and the earth" and "brought forth a new god named Ildabaoth," associated with Jehovah. While Ildabaoth prohibited humans from eating the fruit of the Tree of Knowledge of Good and Evil, Achamoth sent the snake Ophis, also called Christ, to convince the humans to disobey Ildabaoth. In later Christianity, Sophia is associated with Jesus Christ and in some versions is believed to have received the soul of Christ into heaven.

For Further Reading

Cady, Susan, Marian Ronan, and Hal Taussig. *Sophia: The Future of Feminist Spirituality*. New York: HarperCollins, 1986

SOUTH PACIFIC STORYTELLING

The storytelling tradition in the South Pacific, an area that covers all the islands of Polynesia, including the triangle of the Hawaiian Islands to New Zealand and Easter Island to Samoa and Tonga. The language spoken in this area generally consists of different Malayo-Polynesian dialects. The storytellers of these islands were BARDS who sang and told the stories of GODS and HEROES and the history of the ancestors. Songs of praise for the great chiefs were also part of their repertoire. Priests were the ones to guard the RITUAL words. Wherever Polynesians settled, the oral tradition was their form of communication, and poets, priests, and narrators drew from the mythological past called "The Night of Tradition."

Favorite stories all through these islands have the same characters with slight variations on their names and feats. The CREATION comes about through the coupling of RANGI AND PAPA, whose offspring must separate their parents in order to have room for themselves. Of their offspring, TA'AROA is the god of the ocean and fishermen, while Tane, or Kane in

Hawaii, is the lord of the forest and the creatures. Hina is the first woman, the one who beats "tape-cloth" in the MOON. In many ways she is similar to the ancient Greek figure of HELEN OF TROY, while Kaupeepee, son of King Kamauaua, plays a role similar to Paris.

The demigod and TRICKSTER Maui is the one who fishes up the islands and snares the SUN. DEATH comes when MAUI fails to provide immortality to humankind, and since then people have died and their souls have gone to the "leaping place."

Other favorite figures include Tinarau, who has a pet whale who is murdered by Kae, Tawhaki, who visits the sky, and Rata, who has a canoe that is burnt by the little people of the forest. The dark Underworld is called PO. The volcano and fire goddess PELE can show her anger at any time, and many tales surround her love life and her wrath.

Mythological references were and are part of everyday life, and chiefs are able to trace their genealogical references back to the gods. Hula dance troupes of Hawaii were and still are a means of telling dramatic tales.

For Further Reading

Andersen, Johannes. *Myths and Legends of the Polynesians*. Boston: Charles E. Tuttle, n.d.

Kalakaua, David. *The Legends and Myths of Hawaii*. Boston: Charles E. Tuttle, 1972.

Westervelt, William D. *Hawaiian Legends of Ghosts and Ghost-Gods*. Rutland, VT: Charles E. Tuttle, 1964.

———. *Hawaiian Legends of Old Honolulu*. Rutland, VT: Charles E. Tuttle, 1963.

———. *Hawaiian Legends of Volcanoes*. Rutland, VT: Charles E. Tuttle, 1964.

SPEECH, POWER OF

Both the use of speech in storytelling as well as the presence or absence of speech in a specific tale. Part of the role of the storyteller is to engage his or her audience through speech and intervening silence. The eloquence of the storyteller, his or her deep knowledge of the story, and how the storyteller's voice is used to best convey the story's nuances is all part of the art of the oral tradition.

Speech may play a role in stories themselves. While the HERO Odysseus is often eloquent in his speech, thereby persuading others, the silent daughter of Shakespeare's *King Lear*, Cordelia, is far more eloquent in her refusal to speak and her choice of silence. When language is used inauthentically, it is emptied of meaning and silence conveys more power than actual speech. In some cases a character may be silent not out of choice but out of necessity, as in the case of the mute sister in "THE SEVEN SWANS," where the freeing of her brothers depends on her silence and the completion of the shirts made of nettles.

The power of gentle and eloquent speech can be seen in the sermons of BUDDHA, Jesus, and MUHAMMAD.

For Further Reading

Lang, Andrew. *The Rainbow Fairy Book*. Illustrated by Michael Hague. New York: William Morrow, 1993.

Shakespeare, William. *King Lear. The Complete Works of William Shakespeare*. Edited by William Aldis Wright. Illustrated by Rockwell Kent. New York: Doubleday, 1936.

SPELL

Magical act of transformation or controlling power cast by WIZARDS, WITCHES, sorcerers, and SHAMANS. Spells of all kinds exist in the oral tradition, particularly in FOLKTALES and fantasy stories. Two kinds of spells exist— the harmful and the useful. As Emile Grillot de Givry notes in *Illustrated Anthology of Sorcery, Magic, and Alchemy*, "the 'double' life of the sorcerer" involved "a personage all-powerful in the countryside, hated and feared in his one aspect on account of the misfortune he could bring upon a household or family, but resorted to in his other when it was a matter of avoiding misfortune or ensuring success." Thus a sorcerer can cast a spell to "work mischief" or provide a cure, "prevent windmills from working" or make the wind blow, start or stop a famine, raise or stop a storm, etc. Sorcerers and witches can also give themselves special powers like the ability to walk on water or become invisible (*see* INVISIBILITY).

In many FAIRY TALES, the plot centers on a creature who has been put under a spell. For example, Sleeping Beauty falls under a spell when she pricks her fingers and sleeps for 100 years. Other fairy tales focus on the sexual partner who has been turned into an ANIMAL unbeknownst to those who surround him or her. For example, the Beast of Charles Perrault's "BEAUTY AND THE BEAST" is really a PRINCE under a spell (*see* PERRAULT, CHARLES), as is the bear of the GRIMM BROTHERS's "Snow-White and Rose-Red" and the FROG in "The Frog Prince." As Bruno Bettelheim notes in *The Uses of Enchantment*, most fairy tales do not provide the reason for the spell and do not necessarily punish the sorceress responsible for the spell. Common to almost all of these stories, however, is the requisite true love and devotion of the HEROINE or HERO necessary to transform the beast back to his or her human self. Such tales belong to the "animal groom" or "animal husband" cycle.

For Further Reading

Grillot de Givry, Émile. *Illustrated Anthology of Withchcraft, Magic, and Alchemy*. Translated by J. Courtenay Locke. New York: Dover, 1971.

Le Guin, Ursula. *A Wizard of Earthsea*. New York: Houghton, 1968.

SPHINX

In Ancient Greece and Egypt, a mythical, fantastic being, part human, part ANIMAL, symbolic of that which is enigmatic. Like the MANTICORA and UNICORN, the Sphinx can be considered a symbol of a projection of human fears drawn from the strange and often terrifying tales transmitted by travelers. For the Greeks, the Sphinx was female, with a woman's head and breasts, a dog's or bull's torso, a lion's claws, a dragon's tail, and a bird's wings. She was enigmatic and cruel, and, according to LEGEND, would devour those who could not answer her famous riddle: "Who walks on four feet in the morning, two feet at noon, and three feet in the evening?" By successfully answering the riddle, Oedipus was able to destroy the Sphinx that ravaged the countryside surrounding THEBES, and legend has it that she threw herself from a cliff to the sea below when she was outwitted. But the destruction of the Sphinx by Oedipus, which caused both Oedipus himself and the Thebans to believe him a HERO worthy of marrying the newly widowed queen, was not so much a sign of Oedipus's heroism as a portent of the perversity that his marriage and reign would engender, for the Sphinx represents the Terrible MOTHER and perverted femininity.

The Egyptian Sphinx possesses a human head and the body of a crouching lion. With an enigmatic look on its face, it lies near the great Egyptian pyramids, casting its long shadows as it guards the mummies of the pharaohs buried in the pyramids. Positioned to face the rising sun, the mysterious Sphinx at Giza appears to embrace both HEAVEN and earth. Tuthmosis IV (1425–1412 B.C.), when he was a prince, was promised by the Sphinx that if he were to clear away the sand covering its paws, he would eventually gain the throne.

SPIDER

Trickster HERO and god called ANANSI or Mr. Spider in West Africa; also a TRICKSTER god for the Pueblo Hopi, Sioux, and Iroquois Indian tribes of North America. Anansi the Spider is believed to be the creator of the first human beings, the SUN, the MOON, and the stars. Then the god of the sky, Nyamé, breathed life into the people Anansi created. Continuing to function as intercessor between the gods and humans, Anansi the Spider introduced the hoe and grain to humankind.

As the great trickster god, his adventures and exploits are told in many popular stories in both Africa and the West Indies. In one such tale, Anansi can be outsmarted only by Wax Girl, for when she refuses to answer him, he kicks her and sticks to her. Trying to strike her with his chest, he also sticks to her. Even his sweet talk and apologies are to no avail, for she never replies and he never escapes.

Among the Iroquois, Hopi, and Sioux tribes of North America, the wicked trickster Spider man is known as IKTOME, close friend of the trickster COYOTE. In such tales as "What's This? My Balls for Your Dinner?," "Coyote, Iktome, and the Rock," "Iktome Sleeps with His Wife By Mistake," and "Iktome Has a Bad Dream," the bawdy and lascivious side of Iktome emerges, although he tends to be tricked in return by the women he believes he is deceiving or overwhelming.

For Further Reading

Haley, Gail E. *A Story—A Story*. Illustrated. New York: Macmillan, 1971.

McDermott, Gerald. *Anansi the Spider: A Tale from the Ashanti*. New York: Holt, Rinehart & Winston, 1972.

SPIDER WOMAN

FEMALE CREATOR and EARTH goddess of Southwest Native American tribes. Sometimes called Spider Grandmother or Red-Spider-Woman, Spider Woman plays a very important role in many Native Americans MYTHS either as sole creator or assistant to the supreme power. In Chukchee CREATION, for example, Spider Woman appears as the maker of women, although RAVEN and his wife are the first creators of men.

In the Hopi creation myth, Spider Woman is the earth GODDESS controlling the magic of Below while Tawa, the SUN god, controls the power and mysteries of the Above. They created other GODS by dividing themselves—Tawa makes Muiyinwuh, God of All Life Germs, and Spider Woman makes Huzruiwuhti, Woman of the Hard Substances, or hard ornaments of wealth, including turquoise, coral, silver, and shell. Tawa and Huzruiwuhti are the First Lovers, producing the Magic Twins, the Ancient of Six, Man-Eagle, the Great Plumed Serpent and others. Then Sun God and Spider Woman make the Earth to exist between Above and Below, using the First Magic Song in their creation. While Tawa thinks of birds and fish, Spider Woman forms them out of clay, but they do not breathe for they do not as yet have spirit. Next Tawa and Spider Woman make Magic by placing a fleecy woven wool blanket over the figures, which gives them life and breath. Spider Woman then shapes a man and a woman out of clay, following the Thoughts of Tawa, but they do not move even with the magic blanket. Only when Tawa and Spider Woman sing the Song of Life over them do they come to life.

In the next stage of Hopi creation, Tawa, as Sun God, dries the Endless Waters to make Dry Land, and he makes all living things multiply. Now Spider Woman leads all the people to the land Tawa has created, divides them into tribes, leads them through all the Four Great Caverns of the Underworld to the Colorado River, and chooses a creature to take each group to the place where they should build a house. She establishes a matriarchal structure, with women of each clan in charge of building the house, having the family name descend through her, and being the home-maker; the men are in charge of making the *kivas*, the underground caves used for wor-shipping the gods, with sand paintings as al-tars. According to Spider Woman, men also are responsible for weaving the blankets. Af-ter this Spider Woman disappeared from the people.

In the Anasazi-Pueblo creation myth, Spi-der Woman is the first supreme being. Through thought, breath, and song, she spins a thread that stretches across the entire uni-verse between north and south, and another thread between east and west. She creates the sun from red and yellow rock, white shell, and turquoise, and then places it in the sky. She then makes the moon, the stars, birds and animals, and the first man and woman, who are made from spinning a bit of her own being, "a web of wisdom and thought." These two produce all the people, whom Spider Woman then has to lead through four worlds, each world reflecting a stage in the process of becoming fully human. In the fourth world, they can live happily and draw on Spider Woman's wisdom.

Other myths about Spider Woman include the Cherokee myth, "Grandmother Spider Steals the Sun" and the Hopi tale, "Son of Light." Many myths about Spider Woman are related to those of THINKING WOMAN of the Rio Grande Pueblo peoples.

For Further Reading

Mullett, G. M. *Spider Woman Stories: Legends of the Hopis*. Tucson, AZ: University of Arizona Press, 1990.

SPRETNAK, CHARLENE (1946–)

American feminist, spiritualist, fiction writer, and environmentalist. Charlene Spretnak, who received her bachelor's degree from Saint Louis University and her master's from the University of California at Berkeley, was the director of Berkeley's writing program and has been Visiting Professor of Philosophy and Religion at the California Institute of Inte-gral Studies in San Francisco. Spretnak ex-plores a prepatriarchal GODDESS tradition to find a spiritual and psychological base for modern feminism. In her influential *Lost Goddesses of Early Greece* (1978), Spretnak retells the stories of the Greek goddesses. Drawing upon the few threads from a pre-Classic oral tradition, Spretnak finds more compelling role models for women today. These MYTHS are compared to their more well-known, Classic versions. For instance, in the classic tradition, PANDORA brings DEATH and disease. Spretnak shows that this is a patri-archal rendering of a goddess who, in an ear-lier EARTH-goddess tradition, brought signifi-cant gifts, such as fruit and flint, to people.

Spretnak also uses these myths to take on Jungian psychology's uses of Greek goddess mythology. She indicates that by basing theo-ries on the negative, patriarchal images of the Greek goddess, these psychologists replicate a patriarchal world view.

In these myths, Spretnak finds the possi-bility of spiritual awakening. She argues that the Judeo-Christian religion no longer sup-plies the means of spiritual growth for many. Retelling the early goddess myths has pro-vided Spretnak with spiritual fulfillment. Her technique has been to meditate upon the sto-ries of each goddess until she has, in some sense, become that goddess.

In another of Spretnak's works, *The Poli-tics of Women's Spirituality: Essays on the Rise of Spiritual Power Within the Feminist Move-ment* (1982), she seeks to bring this spiritu-ality to bear on the political world.

For Further Reading

Spretnak, Charlene. *Lost Goddesses of Early Greece*. Boston: Beacon Press, 1984.

———. ed. *The Politics of Women's Spirituality: Essays on the Rise of Spiritual Power Within the Feminist Movement*. Garden City, NY: Anchor Books, 1982.

———. *States of Grace: The Recovery of Meaning in the Postmodern Age*. San Francisco: Harper San Francisco 1991.

STAND-UP COMIC TALE

Popular form of storytelling performed by a comedian for an audience, often based on the humor of everyday life. The stand-up comic tale is a recent phenomenon, having its most definite origins in the 1960s and 1970s and reaching its greatest popularity in the 1980s and 1990s. The break from the literary tradition to the oral tradition in humor occurred in vaudeville (a variety show of short acts or routines) in the 1920s, though vaudeville was still reliant upon and deemed less sophisticated than the art of humorous writing practiced by S.J. Perelman, Ring Lardner, and James Thurber, among others. In the 1930s, as radio became the new popular medium, spoken humor became more of a norm as Eddie Canton, Jack Benny, Edger Bergen, George Burns, and Gracie Allen entered the scene. But it was not until the late 1960s and early 1970s that comedians began performing the kind of stand-up comedy most popular today. Stand-up comics are often called our modern social philosophers, their art reflecting the popular culture. Lenny Bruce is cited as the first comedian to break from the old humor to a humor based on reality, which he often revealed in obscenity. Other noted comics who have made stand-up comedy a distinct form of entertainment include Woody Allen, Mel Brooks, Shelly Berman, George Burns, Jimmy Durante, Richard Pryor, Milton Berle, Sid Caesar, Bill Cosby, Billy Crystal, Phyllis Diller, Groucho Marx, Steve Martin, Lily Tomlin, Robin Williams, Jay Leno, Paul Reiser, and Jerry Seinfeld. In the 1970s and 1980s, Andy Kaufman and Sandra Bernhardt followed Lenny Bruce in pushing the limits of stand-up, often transforming comedy into performance art.

Although comics have differing relationships to a straightforward narrative style, stand-up comics perform the function of defining what is normal in a society and calling attention to its problems, via laughter-inducing ridicule. It could be said that comics perform the role of TRICKSTER, by subjugating larger, more powerful entities than themselves with their wit and quick thinking.

STAR HUSBAND TALE

Ojibwe story that FOLKLORE scholar Stith Thompson (*see* THOMPSON, STITH) used as a model for proving the use and effectiveness of the historic-geographic method in DIFFUSION analysis. He chose to study this particular tale as it remained solely a part of oral tradition and had not been influenced by European cultures. This study was an oppositional response to critics who claimed the historic-geographic method ignored crucial elements impacting a story's diffusion, especially the role of the storyteller. The storyline consists of two young girls who, while sleeping outside one night, saw and fell in love with two stars. Each of the girls made a wish that she could be married to one of these stars and when they awoke in the morning their wishes had come true—they were now star wives, living forever in the sky. The star husbands warned the girls not to return to their home on EARTH; however, the girls disobeyed the orders. One night they dug a hole in the sky, climbed down a rope and returned safely to their homeland. Thompson recorded 86 versions of this story from Native American tribes in regions including Alaska, California, New Mexico, the Great Lakes area, Texas, and Louisiana. He noted that the recorded stories differed at certain points, including the number of girls, how they ascended to the HEAVENS, how they escaped, and the description of the star husbands. Looking at the various versions across the continent, Thompson reconstructed the ARCHETYPE, on which all versions were based, and concluded that this tale most likely originated in the central plains before the eighteenth century, and that the role of the teller did not influence the diffusion.

For Further Reading

Erdoes, Richard, and Alfonso Ortiz. *American Indian Myths and Legends*. New York: Pantheon, 1985.

STEPMOTHER—WICKED

Evil, WITCH-like figure who appears in many FAIRY TALES. The familiar wicked stepmother plays a crucial role in such well-known fairy tales as "CINDERELLA," "Hansel and Gretel,"

"Snow White," and "The Beautiful Wasilisa." Her goal is to destroy the HERO or HEROINE, but eventually good triumphs over evil and the wicked stepmother is destroyed. In some fairy tales (for example, "Hansel and Gretel" and "Snow White"), she is childless herself but refuses to function as a mother figure to the child or children of her spouse; instead she is in competition with them over food or beauty. In fairy tales such as "Cinderella" or "The Beautiful Wasilisa," the stepmother has daughters of her own, and her goal is to displace her beautiful, kind stepdaughter with her own, less attractive offspring. Whether the stepmother engages in trying to kill the stepdaughter, as in "Snow White," or contrives impossible tasks for the stepdaughter to complete, as in "The Beautiful Wasilisa," the stepdaughter manages not only to survive but to conquer, either through marrying a PRINCE or overseeing the stepmother's own demise.

Many of the tales involving wicked stepmothers were passed on through generations over a period of time where mothers often died in childbirth and fathers remarried to provide their children with caretakers. From the point of view of the child, however, the stepmother can never replace the missing MOTHER, who is glorified in her absence. Furthermore, if the stepmother has children of her own, she is generally perceived as putting them first, whether true or not. According to Bruno Bettelheim, in *The Uses of Enchantment: The Meaning and Importance of Fairy Tales*, the child splits the mother into her good and bad aspects, with the negative traits belonging to the evil stepmother. "While the fantasy of the evil stepmother thus preserves the image of the good mother, the fairy tale also helps the child not to be devastated by experiencing his mother as evil" (*see* BETTELHEIM, BRUNO).

The wicked stepmother MOTIF is central to the centuries-old story of Snow White, which appears in many versions throughout Europe, always focusing on resolution of the Oedipus complex, according to Bettelheim. In the GRIMM BROTHERS'S version of the FOLKTALE, it is only when she reaches adolescence that the competition between step-

mother and daughter begins, presumably over the "absent" father. According to Bettelheim, "The story of Snow White warns of the evil consequences of narcissism for both parent and child. Snow White's narcissism nearly undoes her as she gives in twice to the disguised queen's enticement to make her look more beautiful, while the queen is destroyed by her own narcissism." The efforts the wicked stepmother/queen makes to murder Snow White represent her jealousy of Snow White's youth and beauty, yet Snow White also projects her own jealousy of the usurping stepmother onto the queen. In the end, both Snow White's and the Queen's destructive aspects of their personalities have been brought under control. When the Queen must dance in red-hot shoes at Snow White's wedding, the "fiery red shoes" symbolize "untrammeled sexual jealousy, which tries to ruin others" and ends up ruining itself.

Many VARIANTS of the wicked stepmother motif appear in literature and popular culture. Anne Sexton's volume of poetry, *Transformations* (1972), offers new interpretations of wicked stepmothers in various fairy tales (*see* SEXTON, ANNE), and the Disney retellings of the Grimms's fairy tales have made the wicked stepmother a household term. Stephen Sondheim's musical *Into the Woods* also reworks Cinderella and her wicked stepmother.

For Further Reading

Jeffers, Susan. *Hansel and Gretel*. Illustrated. New York: Dial/Penguin, 1980.

Maglin, Nan Bauer, and Nancy Schneidewind, eds. *Women and Stepfamilies: Voices of Anger and Love*. Philadelphia: Temple University Press, 1989.

Sierra, Judy. *Cinderella*. The Oryx Multicultural Folktale Series. Phoenix: Oryx Press, 1992.

STORY IN SEARCH OF AN AUDIENCE

Hindu tale of a woman blessed by the story she hears while in her mother's womb. This Hindu tale, which belongs to the category of those that explain the etiology of a custom or ritual, begins with an old woman who takes a ritual bath on the seventh day of the month of Magha, a Sunday, and then, in observance of the day's ritual, takes some sanctified rice and looks for someone to whom she can tell the story of the SUN god.

Everywhere the old woman goes, no one wants to listen, and they are all punished with some form of misfortune. Finally, a lower-caste pregnant woman agrees to listen, but wants food first. She eats the food and falls asleep, but the child in the womb cries out and asks the old woman to tell it the story instead, so she fills the woman's navel with the rice and tells the story, followed by a lullaby telling the baby what good luck she will have.

When the pregnant woman gives birth to a daughter, the old woman comes with gifts and makes a hammock for the baby to stay in, in the nearby forest; this way the mother can work and the birds and trees will care for the child. One day, the KING passes by the baby, and the birds tell him, "This little girl is your wife and our mother. Take her home with you, and marry her when she grows up." So the king takes her home and, everywhere she passes, good things happen. When the girl grows up, the king marries her, making her his younger wife, although his older wife is not pleased. In her anger, the older wife then throws all the palace jewels into the sea, but a fish swallows them, is caught by a fisherman, and is brought to the palace. The young wife manages to find the jewels in the fish, and the king finally realizes her powers. Still, he wants to test her, so he poisons himself to see if she can bring him back from the dead (see TESTS).

When the young wife is on her way to her husband's cremation, where she and the older wife will commit *sati* or *suttee* (the ancient Hindu practice of a faithful wife burning themselves on her husband's funeral pyre), a BRAHMAN comes to her and gives her RITUAL instructions. This Brahman is the sun god in disguise, and when he identifies himself, he gives her rice to throw on her husband's body. When she does so, the husband comes back to life, and from then on the upper castes perform the ritual celebrated in the story to bring good fortune.

For Further Reading

Ramanujan, A.K., ed. *Folktales from India*. New York: Pantheon, 1991.

STORY KNIFING

Genre of storytelling practiced by girls among the Yuks, Napaskiaks, and several other Eskimo groups in southwestern Alaska. Told almost exclusively by females, usually between the age of five and the early teenage years, this type of story requires the use of a knife to carve visual illustrations for the narrative into the snow or mud. The story knives, which were usually provided by the parents or elders, were traditionally made from bone or ivory, but kitchen knives are commonly used today.

While there are variations on story knifing, the telling and the knifing of these stories usually follow certain conventions. To begin each story, the narrator draws the opening scene, often using the accepted symbols for a house and furnishings. As the story progresses and characters enter, they also will be knifed into the picture. For each new scene, and when the story comes to a conclusion, the illustration is wiped away in order to begin anew.

Like sand storytelling, practiced by certain indigenous peoples in Australia, story knifing is seen as "play" to the children who practice it, but it also serves some important functions for the community, and for that reason it is encouraged by adults. Since the girls usually tell stories passed down to them from their mothers, story knifing provides an opportunity for them to connect with the attitudes and beliefs of the community that are usually expressed in the narratives.

STORY SCROLLS

Rolls of parchment, paper, or other material on which stories are told through text or pictures. In Japanese and Chinese art, scrolls were painted to show pictures or text on silk or paper. The scroll either was displayed on a wall or held by the viewer and rolled up when not in use. Chinese artists, the first to use scrolls, used not oil but a colored ink or mineral medium mixed with a light glue;

scholar painters preferred to paint in black ink with washes of clear water. Chinese artists did not use a vanishing paint or a single focus of perspective as artists might for a flat, open picture because the scroll was to be rolled, either from right to left or from top to bottom. Thus, the viewer could see the painting unrolled in successive sections. In addition, unlike European paintings, the Chinese scroll painter did not use dark and light to create shading, but was interested in the flexible lines that could be created with the Chinese brush. The painter's goal was to convey the feel and texture of a subject, and be able to show its movements. Japanese artists followed the Chinese in adopting scrolls for use in art and storytelling.

STORYTELLING STONE

Mythological stone of the Native American Seneca and Iroquois Tribes and tale that explains the sacred and mysterious origin of stories. In the MYTH of "The Storytelling Stone," an orphan boy named Poyeshao is brought up by a foster mother who encourages him to learn to hunt as soon as he is old enough. Each day he is more and more successful in hunting birds, and his foster mother is pleased. One day, however, while he is deep in the forest, his arrow needs repair and he sits on a large, smooth, flat round stone that he sees in the center of a clearing. The stone speaks to him, asking "Should I tell you stories?" The boy has no idea what a story is, and the stone explains that it is "telling what happened a long time ago." In exchange for the birds, the stone tells Poyeshao stories until sunset, and each day the boy returns to the stone to hear more. The foster mother, however, grows suspicious, for her son returns with fewer and fewer birds. First she sends another boy to follow him, but the follower becomes equally engaged in listening to the stories. Then two men are sent to follow, and they, too, end up listening to the stories. At the end of that day's storytelling, the stone instructs the four of them to tell their chief that every man in the village should come the next day with something to eat for the stone. The next day the whole village comes to hear the stone's stories, and they are told that some will remember everything, some will remember parts of the stories, and others will remember nothing. Those who remember everything and become the ones to tell stories to the others must always be brought something to eat in exchange for the stories of the world before this. The stone tells them everything it knows, and thus all knowledge comes from the storytelling stone and is passed to those who become the storytellers of the village.

For Further Reading

Feldmann, Susan, ed. *The Storytelling Stone: Traditional Native American Myths and Tales*. New York: Dell, 1965.

STRING FIGURES

Patterns formed by passing string around and between the fingers. String figures are often used by storytellers, producing images to illustrate a story. There are many variations on string stories, and they are told in most parts of the world.

In a story found in Guyana, New Caledonia, and Ghana, the storyteller forms a mosquito. With the final words of the story, "and the mosquito was gone," the string slips back into its original single loop. A Ugandan version is called "the locust."

Other string stories also describe disappearing acts, such as a farmer's stolen yams or a mouse being chased by a cat. Some stories wind up by handcuffing the teller or trapping a finger.

One of the best known string figures is the European four-hand version of "cat's cradle." The storyteller illustrates and tells the history of a little boy who slept in a cradle, then grew up to be a soldier and slept on a soldier's bed. On the way home, he slept in a manger, found a diamond, and adopted a one-eyed cat who ended up sleeping in the cradle.

String figures often illustrate natural elements—stars, lightning, animals—or important tools and equipment, such as —fishnets, kayaks, and teepees. Some string stories have magic overtones. For example, Eskimos use a string figure at the summer solstice to en-tangle the sun and keep it with them during the winter.

For Further Reading

Haddon, Kathleen. *Artists in String.* 1930. Reprint, London: Metheun, 1979.

Pellowski, Anne. *The Story Vine: A Source Book of Unusual and Easy-to-Tell Stories from Around the World.* New York: Macmillan, 1984.

SUFI TALES

Stories told by Sufi dervishes to impart knowledge. Sufi tales are an important part of the thought and wisdom of the Sufi. They are a mystical set of ideas over one thousand years old, originating in the Arabic world with followers from all over the world still pursuing its spiritual path to this day. "Teaching-stories," notes Idries Shah in *The Way of the Sufi*, are "told in public and form part of the outer activity of dervishes," devout Sufi mendicants known for their acts of ecstatic devotion and for their dancing and whirling.

Each plane of a Sufi tale is meant to impart more and more significance, although the tales are not didactic. In the tale called "The King and the Wolf," for example, a KING, in his ignorance and desire for admiration, decides to tame a wolf and make it his pet, so he has the wolf taken from its mother at birth and he hand-raises it among tame dogs. Because the grown wolf then behaves like a dog, people indeed admire the king and they believe he possesses great power. The king himself is convinced that this is so, but one day when he takes the tame wolf hunting, it hears a pack of wolves and runs off to join them. The story ends with the proverb, "A wolf-cub will always become a wolf, even if it is reared among the sons of man."

Among the major Sufi storytellers and poets are Omar Khayyam, Jalaludin Rumi, Rabi'a, and El-Halaj. As Idries Shah notes, the influence of Sufi tales, LEGENDS, and poetry can be seen in "the phenomenon of the TROUBADOURS, in the William Tell legend of Switzerland, in the Near Eastern cult of the 'Peacock Angel,' in Gurdjieff and Ouspensky, in Maurice Nicoll, in the Swede Dag Hammerskjold, in Shakespeare . . . in the tales of the Dane Hans Christian Andersen, in the works of Sir Richard Burton (himself a Qadiri dervish). . . in contemporary children's books, in the religion of the 'WITCHES' . . . in tales and techniques of supposedly Japanese Zen origin . . . in Chaucer and Dante Alighieri" (*see* TELL, WILLIAM; ANDERSEN, HANS CHRISTIAN; BURTON, RICHARD).

For Further Reading

Shah, Idries. *Tales of the Dervishes.* New York: Viking Penguin, 1993.

———. *The Way of the Sufi.* New York: Dutton, 1970.

SUN

Supreme deity in many MYTHS. Usually seen as a masculine force, the sun as deity can appear as the son and heir of the god of HEAVEN. Able to see all and know all, the sun symbolizes the Eye of Heaven in some cultures; for example, as Surya, the eye of Varuna in Hindu mythology, as the eye of ZEUS for the Greeks, as the eye of Ra for the Egyptians, as the eye of ALLAH in Islam, and as the eye of the supreme god for the Pygmies and Bushmen. In some cases, the sun and MOON are the eyes of heaven, with the sun representing good and the moon, evil.

The sun also represents the moment when the heroic principle shines its brightest, notes J.E. Cirlot. The sun's association with the HERO can be seen in the sword of fire associated with the hero, while the heavens tend to represent the father, with the weapon the net of stars that binds. Heroes, too, are promoted to solar eminence, and the sudden disappearance of the sun on the horizon can be equated with the sudden DEATH of heroes such as Samson, Herakles, and SIEGFRIED. The connection with the hero also stems from the sun's invincibility, for while the moon experiences fragmentation in its waning and total disappearance for three days each month, the sun does not need to die or dissolve to descend below, implying resurrection and life.

Many Native North and South American tribes worshipped the sun as their supreme deity. In North America, the Plains Crow, the Yuchi of the Southwest, the Southeastern Natchez, the Southwestern Pueblos, and the White Mountain Apaches all made the sun an object of worship. In Navajo legend, sun is married to CHANGING WOMAN. In Mexico and Peru the cult of the sun was practiced by the Incas and the Mayans.

Numerous tales of the oral tradition explain the CREATION of the sun or the placing of it in the sky, including the Jicarilla Apache tale of Holy Boy, who is credited for procuring the sun as a tiny object from White Hactcin at the suggestion of Whirlwind. The Caraja Indians of Brazil and the Polynesians of Oceania have similar tales of CULTURE HEROES finding a means to slow down the speed of the sun so the day lasts for a longer time. *See also* MAUI.

For Further Reading

McDermott, Gerald. *Arrow to the Sun: A Pueblo Indian Tale*. New York: Penguin, 1977.

SUNDIATA

Story from Mali of a HERO who unites his people. Sundiata was recorded by the scholar D.T. Niane from the words of the GRIOT Mamoudou Kouyate. The griot's telling begins by placing the EPIC in its oral context as he reminds his audience of the long history of the story as it has been passed down over the centuries by word of mouth.

The ruler Maghan Kon Fatta governs Mali with power and grace. Two hunters arrive at his home with a hunchbacked maiden between them. This had been foretold, so Maghan is not surprised by the visit. The hunters identify the woman as Sogolon Kedjou, and she is said to possess the spirit of buffalo. Maghan marries Sogolon and grows to love her. She gives birth to a boy a year later, but Maghan's first wife resents the new child. The new PRINCE, Sundiata, proves unable to speak or walk. He says his first words in response to his father's gift of the griot, who will teach the boy his family history. Maghan Kon Fatta dies, and the elders ignore the late ruler's desire to install Sundiata as leader, choosing instead the son of the first wife. Sundiata pulls himself to his feet with an iron rod. The first wife enlists the help of WITCHES to destroy Sundiata, but the magic will not work without the victim's anger. Sundiata is so slow to anger that he helps the

witches pick the herbs, and the magic is useless against this kindness. The evil first wife of Kon Fatta sends the griot away, which leaves the young Sundiata without guidance.

Sundiata, his mother, and her other children are forced to flee, traveling in exile for seven years before Sundiata is taken under the care of the ruler of Mema, who teaches the young man the arts of war and governing. Word comes to Sundiata that Mali has been invaded, and Sundiata gathers a vast army to return to his home. He is reunited with his griot who teaches him how to defeat his enemy, a sorcerer, liberates Mali and is hailed as its greatest hero.

For Further Reading

Wisniewski, David. *Sundiata: Lion King of Mali*. Boston: Houghton Mifflin, 1992.

SUSA-NO-WO

Impetuous male principle among the deities described in the Shinto JAPANESE CREATION MYTH. Sometimes described as the storm god, sometimes the MOON god, Susa-no-wo is generally considered troublesome.

Susa-no-wo is the son of the creator deities, Izanagi and Izanami. In some accounts, he was born from Izanagi's right eye. Susa-no-wo is dark and unruly, in contrast to his sister AMATERASU, the shining GODDESS of the SUN. His story is told with several variations in the KOJIKI, compiled in A.D. 712 and the NIHONGI of A.D. 720. This theme of division of the world into material and spiritual realms appears in oral traditions around the world.

Susa-no-wo wants to marry Amaterasu, but she finds him repugnant. Finally, Susa-no-wo convinces Amaterasu that he wants to make peace, and they exchange tokens of their trust. From those tokens are born several GODS.

After that, Susa-no-wo keeps to his own realm, the SEA, for a while. But eventually he returns to the land, where his tears and temper tantrums raise havoc with people, crops, and shrines. Offended, Amaterasu hides in a cave, plunging the world into darkness. When she is finally lured out, the other gods seize Susa-no-wo and send him wandering powerless upon the EARTH.

Susa-no-wo planted mountains and forests from the hairs of his beard. He also killed a number of DRAGONS and took a MAIDEN he rescued for his wife. When their daughter was courted and kidnapped by another god, Susa-no-wo tracked them down. But Susa-no-wo admired the craftiness of the kidnapper and accepted him as son-in-law after all.

Some scholars include Susa-no-wo among the TRICKSTER figures (see Robert Ellwood's essay in *Mythical Tricksters,* edited by William J. Hynes and William G. Doty).

For Further Reading

Aston, W. G. *Shinto: The Way of the Gods.* New York: Krishna Press, 1974.

Hynes, William J., and William G. Doty, eds. *Mythical Tricksters.* Tuscaloosa, AL: University of Alabama Press, 1993.

Kojiki. Translated by Donald L. Philippi. Princeton, NJ: Princeton University Press, 1969.

Nihongi: Chronicles of Japan from the Earliest Times to A.D. 697. Translated by W.G. Aston. London: George Allen & Unwin, 1956.

Piggott, Juliet. *Japanese Mythology.* London: Paul Hamlyn, 1969.

SWAHILI CREATION

Belief of origin held by the inhabitants of Eastern Africa combining Christian, Islamic, and mythical motifs.

The Swahili CREATION story stems from Swahili culture and history, which in itself is elusive. Scholars have for some time agreed that a common language, culture, and territory bind the Swahili people, but that the Swahili have no common historical background, even as the Kiswhali language has become the lingua franca of Eastern Africa. The Swahili descended from both the sailors and traders from Arabia, Persia, India, and Madagascar who settled in the coastal territory of Eastern Africa and the native people of that region. Today, the Swahili territory spans thousands of miles along the seaboard and includes the adjacent islands of Mogadishu and Mozambique. Groups of people living in the Swahili region have long described themselves, not as Swahili, but as Mombasan, Patean, Kilwan, Arab, Persian, or even Portuguese. It is this sense of identity true to the ancient past, as well as the division of the Swahili language into many different dialects, which divides the Swahili and perpetuates the idea that the Swahili have no common historical identity.

Because the Swahili people come from many different cultural backgrounds, Swahili belief is a mixture of many religious backgrounds as well. Primarily, however, it is a marriage of Christian and Islamic elements. This marriage of MOTIFS and ideas from two religious traditions is most evident in the Swahili creation story, which also forms the basis of the faith. The creation story includes the accounts of "The Light and the Souls," "HEAVEN and EARTH," "How Man Was Molded," "Satan: Prologue in Heaven," "ADAM AND EVE in PARADISE," "Adam and Eve on Earth," and "Habili and Kabili," the story of Cain and Abel.

The story begins with a description of GOD as omnipotent and immortal, a reflection of the Islamic conception that God, or Allah, is Almighty and Merciful, Omnipresent and Invisible, Eternal and Everlasting, and so on according to the list of 99 "most beautiful names" of God found in the Koran. Descending from this tradition, the Swahili Creation Story holds that all God must say is "Be!" and what he wishes to exist will exist. In the story, God first creates light, and lets it shine in his hand. Pleased with his fistful of light, God declares that he will extract the soul of his prophet MUHAMMAD from the light; and finding so much joy in Muhammad's soul, God decides to create all mankind so that Muhammad can walk among them as their prophet. Muhammad's word will teach the peoples of the earth good and evil; and God will judge all souls and allow a chosen few to follow Muhammad.

The theme of destiny runs throughout Swahili folklore. In the creation story, we learn that all life is destined by God, whose first three creations—after the creation of Light and the spirit of the prophet Muhammad—included a Throne on which he would sit on Judgment Day, a Carpet under whose shadow lay heaven, and a Tablet which held the record for all past and present knowledge. God also created a Pen, which had a mind of its own, to record the deeds of men. The Pen, which was the length of the distance between heaven and earth, wrote whatever Allah commanded it to. God could change the future, though he had already conceived of a plan for its course.

God commands the archangel Serafili to hold a Trumpet and to blow through it when he commands him. The Trumpet announces Doomsday, when all earth will crumble. In addition, God creates the Garden of Delights, where rivers of milk and honey flow. To counterbalance this paradise, God creates the fire, with an evil smell and loud roar. God then creates the angels, pure spirits who proclaim his praise. Among the spirits are Gabriel (Jiburili), the Trustworthy Spirit who carries God's word; Michael (Mikali), who doles out destiny and decides under God's command who will starve and who has plenty; Azeral (Zeraili), the angel of death; Maliki, the guardian of fire; and the angel with a thousand heads, each head with a thousand mouths, each mouth proclaiming scripture in a different tongue.

When God had created these things, he decided to create man. When he informed the angels of his plan, they were baffled that God would wish to create such a lumpy, disobedient creature who yielded to desire and lust, while the angels, who could not conceive of disobedience, were so superior. God replied that his plan would be revealed in thousands of years when Serafili blew his horn, and the angels were content. In fact, the angels willingly submitted to Adam, the man made of clay, when God orders them to prostrate themselves at his feet, except one. Satan, a stubborn and disobedient angel, would not bow down, and so was banished from the realm of heaven, though God granted him the freedom to punish those humans who were evil and allowed him to roam the earth. Satan's three flaws were pride, rebelliousness, and doubt.

The next part of the story follows more closely the traditional biblical story of Adam and Eve than the Islamic Koran. According to the story, Adam was feeling lonely in Paradise. After sleeping, he awoke to find one of his own kind and, rejoicing, called the woman "Life." God warned the two that they could eat from any tree in the garden except the Tree of the Knowledge of Procreation, though he knew what was to happen. Eve, instinctively feeling a need to bear children, was immediately attracted to the shade of the Tree of Knowledge. While she sat there quietly, Satan the serpent dropped a juicy delicious fruit into her lap. Calling Adam over, Eve presented her case for motherhood. Being a devoted and pious worshipper of God, Adam was resistant to her pleas, but as a second fruit dropped into her lap, Adam realized that he was more devoted to his wife than to God's word. He allowed her to take a bite of the fruit, then took a bite himself to join in her banishment from Paradise.

The two were banished from Paradise to live on earth. Eve bore many twins, each pair a boy and a girl. God ordered each twin to procreate with any brother or sister other than his own twin. When one boy asked another for his female twin, the latter refused, and falling into argument, one beat the other to death. Because of this incident, Eve found that not only could she make life but she also could make DEATH, and she wept.

Similar creation myths—in which a single god is the creationist—are seen in many cultures around the world. The most obvious parallels are those to the monotheistic religions Christianity, Islam, and Judaism, though creation by one being is seen in other cultures, for example in the religion of the Australian Aborigines.

For Further Reading

Allen, James de Vere. *Swahili Origins.* London: James Currey Ltd., 1993.

Knappert, Jan. *Myths and Legends of the Swahili.* Nairobi: Heinemann Educational Books, 1970.

SWAN

Symbol in many cultures of light, power, grace, beauty, mystery, and androgyny. The figure of the swan appears in worldwide FOLKLORE and mythology. It is a living epiphany of light, incarnating both the solar male and the lunar female, while the black swan is often a symbol of the occult. The swan's song can be seen as the eloquent sermon of the lover, and that the swan dies singing and sings while dying can also be seen as a symbol of sexual desire.

The most frequently named bird in Celtic texts, swans travel mostly in twos, joined by a chain of gold or silver, symbolizing a superior or angelic state. In Mongolia, the swan's whiteness is the symbol of purity, beauty, elegance, nobility, and courage. In Ancient Greek mythology, the male swan is the inseparable companion of the SUN god APOLLO, and in the Eleusinian Mysteries celebrating the bond of Demeter and Persephone (see PERSEPHONE MYTH), the swan symbolizes the power of the poet and poetry and is the emblem of an inspired poet. When the god ZEUS desires the mortal woman Leda, he takes the form of a swan, and from their union are born HELEN OF TROY, Clytemnestra, and the Dioscuri, Castor and Pollux. In Hindu mythology, the creator BRAHMA rides on a swan called Hamsa.

The Bouriate people of the Altai Mountains of Northwest China and Mongolia tell the story of a hunter who one day comes upon three beautiful women bathing alone in a hidden lake. They are swans who have removed their mantle of feathers to enter the water. The hunter steals one of their costumes and hides it; thus, only two of the swans can don their wings and fly away. The hunter takes the third and marries her, and she bears him 11 sons and 6 daughters, but then flies away, telling him that he is of the earth but she is of the sky and she must return to it. However, when he sees the swans flying north each spring and south each fall, he is to celebrate their passage with special ceremonies.

Swans are common in the fairy tales of both Hans Christian Andersen (see ANDERSEN, HANS CHRISTIAN) and the GRIMM BROTHERS. In Andersen's "The Ugly Duckling," the transformation of the unaccepted duckling into a beautiful swan signifies the hidden beauty and belonging each of us is capable of achieving, while in the Grimms's "The Wild Swans," 11 brothers have been transformed into white swans until their young sister can finally break the SPELL under which they are held.

For Further Reading

Andersen, Hans Christian. *Andersen's Fairy Tales.* New York: Grosset and Dunlop, 1945.

————. *The Ugly Duckling.* Illustrated by Lorinda Bryan Cavley. New York: HBJ, 1979.

————. *The Wild Swans.* Retold by Amy Ehrlich. Illustrated by Susan Jeffers. New York: Dial,1976.

White, E. B. *The Trumpet of the Swan.* New York: HarperCollins, 1973.

SYLPHS

Female spirits of the air that appear in mythology and folklore. The sylphs were said to be deceased virgins. Paracelsus (1493–1541) gave the sylphs their name, presumably after the Greek *silphe,* a kind of beetle that becomes a butterfly, although they may have a connection with female tutelary spirits revered in Ancient Gaul. It was said that only those mortals who have been chaste could be intimate with the gentle sylphs. In Rosicrucian philosophy, sylphs, as well as NYMPHS, GNOMES, and salamanders, were able to be enslaved by mortals and bound to service by imprisoning them in a ring, a mirror, or a stone. Sylphs play a significant role in Alexander Pope's *Rape of the Lock* (1714).

TA'AROA

Creator of EARTH and SEA in various legends of Polynesia. For the people of the Society Islands of Oceania, Ta'aroa first lived within an egg in the so-called primeval darkness, from which he eventually emerges. In one LEGEND, Ta'aroa's effort at CREATION cause him to sweat, which is the origin of the sea. On Tahiti, Ta'aroa is the supreme deity, creator of life and DEATH, source of all growth, builder of the first temple. As in the Society Islands, Tahitians believe that Ta'aroa first exists within a COSMIC EGG. Parentless, he then develops until he cracks out of the shell and creates the world using parts of the shell. VARIANT legends say he created the world out of the parts of his own body, excluding his head. *See also* SOUTH PACIFIC STORYTELLING.

TALAYESVA, DON (1890–?)

Hopi autobiographer. Don Talayesva, or Sun Chief, was born in Oraibi, Arizona, and lived the first 10 years of his life as a traditional Hopi Indian. Between the ages of 11 and 20, Talayesva was educated in white schools and incorporated into white culture. Later disenchanted with the white ways and Christianity, Talayesva returned to Oraibi at the age of 20, hoping to preserve traditional Hopi ways. Together with the Yale anthropologist and sociologist Leo Simmons, Talayesva endeavored to record the Hopi life through his own experiences and those of his people. The result was: *Sun Chief: The Autobiography of a Hopi Indian* (1942). Written in the first person, Talayesva brings the magical and seemingly improbable legends of the Hopi Indians into full and vivid detail. In *Sun Chief*, the non-Indian reader becomes acquainted with figures such as the SPIDER WOMAN and the KACHINA clowns (*see* HOPI CREATION). The reader must temporarily put aside his non-Hopi mind-set to begin to understand the world of the Hopi. Included in Talayesva's first-person account are the particular problems inherent in the clash of white and Indian culture. Talayesva employs his own conflicting experiences of living in and between both the white and Indian worlds. Because of its fascinating account of Talayesva's own experiences as well as the experiences of his people, *Sun Chief* continues to be one of the most authoritative and oft-cited texts on Hopi tradition.

TALKING TURTLE

Story in the FOLKTALE tradition of the American South. This story appears in a collection of Ozark folktales but is primarily linked to AFRICAN AMERICAN STORYTELLING. Lissenbe, a tattle-tale, has frightened his entire community with the power of his tongue. As unofficial town crier, Lissenbe tells his townspeople of the preacher's drinking, a woman's flirting, and of any other transgressions he hears about. Since Lissenbe is known never to tell lies, his words are given credence. All of this changes after Lissenbe meets a large talking turtle in the road one day. The turtle warns that Lissenbe talks "too damn much." Amazed, Lissenbe returns to town to spread the news of the miraculous talking turtle. However, when the townspeople return to see the turtle, it remains dumb. Lissenbe is kicked in a ditch and left to his turtle. At this point the turtle retorts, "Didn't I tell you?... You talk too damn much." Even after this experience, Lissenbe remains a "blabbermouth," but he has lost all credibility with his audience.

Another VARIANT of this story features a singing, banjo-playing turtle; in others the turtle is replaced by a bullfrog or mule. The tale is believed to be African in origin, though the African stories have more serious endings. In a Gold Coast version, the main character is put to death after a tortoise does not perform. All versions drive home the moral that talking too much leads to trouble.

For Further Reading

Randolph, Vance. *The Talking Turtle and Other Ozark Folk Tales*. New York: Columbia University Press, 1957.

TALL TALES

Humorous and deliberately exaggerated story told as fact. The tall tale has its roots in both FOLKLORE and humor.

Oral yarn-spinning occurs in most cultures and is probably the source of such LEGENDS as the ODYSSEY, BEOWULF, and ALI BABA. The eighteenth-century Baron Münchhausen, a great teller of tales, became the subject of

them in *Baron Münchhausen's Narrative of his Marvellous Travels and Campaigns in Russia*—an account written by R. E. Raspe and later elaborated on by others.

However, tall tales have become particularly identified with American frontier humor. Even Benjamin Franklin was an occasional practitioner. Comic tales of local HEROES were swapped on stagecoaches, river boats, and railroads, in barrooms, and around campfires. Over time, they were embellished and sometimes attributed to a different, more famous protagonist.

Like Münchhausen, the riverboatman Mike Fink (*see* FINK, MIKE) and the frontiersman and senator Davy Crockett (*see* CROCKETT, DAVY) were storytellers, heroes of their own tall tales, and finally heroes of tales others told about them. Other tall-tale heroes include Daniel Boone (*see* BOONE, DANIEL), John Henry (*see* HENRY, JOHN), Pecos Bill, and JOHNNY APPLESEED. The early twentieth-century Paul Bunyan (*see* BUNYAN, PAUL) stories did not come out of an oral tradition and are alternately considered tall tales or satires of the genre.

In the nineteenth century, American frontier tales moved from the oral tradition into written humor via almanacs, newspapers, and plays. Mark Twain (*see* TWAIN, MARK) surely remains the best known of such literary yarn-spinners.

Perhaps tall tales help us all to cope with life's absurdities. The traditional heroes still turn up on TV and film, as do impersonations of Mark Twain spinning his yarns. And new tall tales appear in the routines of stand-up comics, monologues of Garrison Keillor, and novels such as Thomas Berger's *Little Big Man* and John Barth's *The Sot-Weed Factor* (*see* STAND-UP COMIC TALE).

For Further Reading

Blair, Walter. *Tall Tale America*. New York: Coward-McCann, 1944.

Botkin, B. A., ed. *A Treasury of Mississippi River Folklore: Stories, Ballads, Traditions and Folkways of the Mid-American River Country*. New York: Crown, 1955.

Brown, Carolyn S. *The Tall Tale in American Folklore and Literature*. Knoxville, TN: University of Tennessee Press, 1987.

Erdoes, Richard. *Tales from the American Frontier.* New York: Pantheon Books, 1991.

TALMUDIC CREATION AND FALL

Version of the Book of Genesis (*see* GENESIS, BOOK OF) found in the Judaic Talmud. The Talmud was created during the post-biblical era, when Jewish rabbis were engaged in analysis of the questions and difficulties raised in the Hebrew BIBLE. Through this analysis came the Talmud, a repository of rabbinical commentary, theology, FOLKLORE, and wisdom. Much that is included in the Talmud grew out of centuries of oral tradition and storytelling.

The Talmudic version of the CREATION begins with GOD's decision to create the world. With this decision comes the appearance of the 22 letters of the Hebrew alphabet, with each letter vying to be the first spoken by God. Since the first word spoken is *baruch*, or "blessed," the letter Beth is chosen, and the creation begins with a blessing. Then, God makes the HEAVENS, EARTH, light, darkness, day, and night on the first day. The core of the earth comes into being when God throws a stone into the void. Angels are created on the second day; plants, iron ore, and PARADISE on the third; the SUN, MOON, and stars on the fourth; sea creatures and birds on the fifth; and beasts and human beings on the sixth.

There is controversy over the creation of human beings on the part of the angels, and those who are most impudent are consumed by fire from God. Though God asks the angel Gabriel to bring earth from all four corners of the world for the making of man, the earth does not want to contribute its soil because it knows that some day humankind will ruin its splendor. Finally, God takes the earth himself, creates Adam, the first man, and joins the soul, which he has created the first day, to Adam. The angel Samael is outraged and competitive over God having created another sentient being, and God punishes him and his followers by condemning Samael and his followers to HELL.

When Adam is created, God first breathes life into his nostrils and then makes him LILITH as a female companion. Lilith, however, does not want to be subordinate to man in any way

but wants to be his equal, especially when he expects to be on top of her in lovemaking. In anger, she pronounces the name of God, which is forbidden, and she disappears to become a DEMON and plot with Samael. In the meanwhile, Eve is then created as a better companion for Adam. While Adam rules over the plants and male animals in the east and north of the Garden of Eden, Eve rules over the female animals in the south and west. There they live innocently, naked but for the sacred name of God inscribed on a band they wear over their shoulders.

The Talmudic Fall comes about when Samael, or Satan, rides into the Garden of Eden on a serpent's back and seduces Eve by singing the heavenly songs he has learned while still in God's favor. Then the serpent climbs into a tree and bites its fruit, imbuing it with evil intention. Samael then convinces Eve to eat of it, and she convinces Adam in turn. Thus the venom of evil intention is introduced into the blood of humankind, their eyes are dimmed to God whom they can no longer look in the eye, the band over their shoulders with God's name falls off, they feel shame at their nakedness, and they hide. Adam and Eve are then cast out of Eden, and God places the cherubim to guard its gates. The earth now grows weeds and poisonous plants and requires rain to keep her fertile. *See also* MIDRASHIM, PUNISHMENTS.

For Further Reading

Steinsaltz, Rabbi Adin. *The Talmud: The Steinsaltz Edition: A Reference Guide.* New York: Random House, 1989.

TAO TE CHING

One of the primary sacred texts of Taoism, the equivalent of the BIBLE or Koran. It was ostensibly written down in the sixth century B.C. by Lao Tsu, an older contemporary of Confucius and the keeper of the Imperial Archives at Loyang in the province of Hoonan. He maintained through much of his life that the *Tao* that can be taught is not the eternal *Tao*. However, according to ancient legend, as he was riding off into the desert to die, sick at heart at the wicked ways of men, he was persuaded by a gatekeeper of the city to write down his teachings for posterity. The

Tao te Ching contains the essence of Taoism, and for 2,500 years has provided one of the major underlying influences in Chinese thought and culture. It is the source for many PROVERBS and FOLKTALES. The sayings of Confucius provide the rules of day-to-day conduct. The *Tao* offers a guide for the spirit. It is filled with philosophical speculation and mystical reflection, reading the life-force as a series of harmonious flows and urging humanity to find affinity with it.

Its 81 chapters have been translated more often than any other book except the Christian Bible. No other Chinese text has attracted as much attention in the West and there have been many attempts at translation in the last 100 years, the most definitive being German scholar Richard Wilhelm's 1910 translation. It is notoriously difficult to translate as many of its concepts have no linguistic equivalents in the major European languages.

For Further Reading

Wilhelm, Helmut, and Richard Wilhelm. *Understanding the Tao Ching: The Wilhelm Lectures on the Book of Change.* Princeton, NJ: Princeton University Press, 1995.

TAR BABY

Character who catches the TRICKSTER in one of the best-known UNCLE REMUS stories, created by Joel Chandler Harris (*see* HARRIS, JOEL CHANDLER). Brer Fox creates a figure made of tar and places it in Brer Rabbit's path. When Brer Rabbit hops by and greets the tar baby, he is met with silence. Upset by this response, Brer Rabbit makes further attempts at conversation and acknowledgment. Continuing to be greeted with a blank face, Brer Rabbit considers tar baby smug and punches him. Angered by tar baby's lack of retaliation and of the inability to retract his arm, Brer Rabbit strikes again. After both of Brer Rabbit's fists become stuck in tar baby, he uses his head and feet and is eventually completely stuck and subsequently captured. Brer Rabbit then tricks Brer Fox into throwing him into a briar patch. Brer Rabbit uses the briars to comb the tar from his hair, then escapes, outwitting Brer Fox once again.

The tar-baby story is documented in Antti Aarne's and Stith Thompson's tale type index (*see* AARNE, ANTTI; THOMPSON, STITH). Versions of the tar-baby story can be found all over the globe: Argentina, Chile, Columbia, Cuba, France, India, Japan, Latvia, the Philippines, Spain, Puerto Rico, and in the United States, including in the Navajo and Apache tribes. However, the widest dispersal of the tale is found in western Africa.

This tale has been studied extensively by those seeking answers to questions of old world tale DIFFUSION and the widespread use of ANIMAL tales in African oral tradition. The survival of the tale in modern URBAN FOLKLORE demonstrates its enduring popularity; for instance, this tale survives in "super glue tales," stories in which an adulterer is tricked by the intended victim and left humiliated and compromised.

For Further Reading

Parks, Van Dyke. *Jump Again! More Adventures of Brer Rabbit.* Illustrated by Barry Moser. San Diego: Harcourt Brace Jovanovich, 1987.

TARTARUS

Underworld, or home of the dead, in Greek and Roman mythology. In many stories, Tartarus is called "HADES," or, it is considered to be a place in Hades. In one Greek CREATION story, Tartarus is born from the union between Air and Mother EARTH. The main entrance to Tartarus is said to be in a grove of black poplars beside the ocean stream, although Tartarus has a few back entrances in caverns which are sometimes used by the living who journey to the Underworld. The ghosts of the newly buried dead descend to Tartarus on a gloomy path. They have a coin under their tongue which they use to pay Charon, the miser who ferries them across the sluggish river Styx, a tributary of which is Lethe, the river of forgetfulness. Penniless ghosts must wait forever on the near bank. Cerberus, the vicious three-headed, or, in some accounts, 50-headed, dog, guards the opposite shore. Each head is maned with serpents. He is prepared to devour living intruders or ghosts who attempt to cross. Tartarus is ruled by Hades and his wife, Persephone (*see* PERSEPHONE MYTH). Other inhabitants include the Gorgon MEDUSA, the FURIES, and HECATE.

The ghosts of the dead are judged by Minos, Rhadamanthys, and Aeacus at a place where three roads meet. If the ghosts are neither virtuous nor wicked, they are sent on the road to Asphodel Meadows, a cheerless place where souls stray without purpose. If the ghosts are virtuous, they are dispatched to Elysium, a happy land of perpetual day where snow and cold do not exist. Games, music, and revels never cease. The inhabitants of Elysium may elect to be reborn on earth at any time. If the ghosts are evil, they are sent to the punishment field of Tartarus, the place of everlasting torment where several well-known criminals suffer for crimes they committed on earth.

The eternally hungry and thirsty Tantalus hangs from the bough of a fruit tree which leans over a marshy lake. When he bends to drink, the waves of the lake retreat and black mud remains at his feet. Whenever he reaches for a piece of fruit, a gust of wind whirls the branch out of his reach. An enormous stone hangs over the tree and threatens to crush Tantalus's skull. Vultures continually tear pieces from the giant Tityus's liver. Ixion is tied to an eternally revolving wheel. The daughters of Danaus must forever draw water in leaking jars or sieves. SISYPHUS endlessly heaves a boulder uphill.

Many Greek and Roman MYTHS, including those about Demeter, Persephone, and Orpheus (see ORPHEUS AND EURYDICE MYTH), tell of a living figure journeying to the underworld in order to bring a loved one back to earth. The tales also relate heroic feats that characters accomplish in the LAND OF THE DEAD, as when Herakles captures Cerberus (see LABORS OF HERAKLES). A few stories, like that of THESEUS and Peirithous, describe the plight of those who are imprisoned in the underworld. Others tell of the inhabitants of Tartarus and the punishments given to wicked souls. See also AFTERLIFE, HEL, HELL.

TELEMACHOS

Son of Odysseus, whose QUEST to find his long-absent father is told in the ODYSSEY. The story of Telemachos is possibly the most famous example of the SEARCH FOR THE FATHER motif in Western mythology, a MOTIF which can also be found in the Native American MYTH of WATERJAR BOY.

Telemachos and his mother, PENELOPE are the only two who refuse to accept that Odysseus will not be returning home from the Trojan war after a 20-year absence. Numerous suitors invade their home on the island of ITHACA, trying in vain to convince Penelope to consider her husband dead and remarry one of them. They treat Telemachos contemptuously, and both mother and son find their situation intolerable, all the more so because they were unable to change it.

The GODDESS ATHENA, however, had always admired Odysseus, and now she sees many of the same qualities in his son. She determines to help Telemachos find his father; disguised as a sailor, she inspires him to leave his home and set sail to find Nestor, who had fought with Odysseus in TROY. The meeting with Nestor leads him to Menelaos in Sparta, where he heard of some of his father's misfortunes following the end of the war.

He promptly returns home, and, at the advice of Athena, stops at the home of the swineherd before returning to his mother. There he finds an old beggar who soon revealed himself to be Odysseus himself. The two weep for joy at being reunited and soon come up with a plan to reclaim control of their house. After killing the suitors, Penelope is summoned to greet her returned husband, and the family is reunited after 20 long years.

For Further Reading

Homer. *Odyssey.* New York: Viking Penguin, 1950.

TELIPINU

Hittite god of agriculture, son of the weather and fertility god. As the MYTH of Telipinu has it, this god of agriculture grows angry and disappears in a terrible temper, leaving the EARTH barren, much as the Greek GODDESS Demeter does when her daughter Persephone disappears (see PERSEPHONE MYTH). The trees and the plants all wither, the waters dry up, the humans and animals cease to bear their young, and there is famine and death. First the SUN god sends an eagle to find the missing Telipinu, but the eagle is unsuccessful.

Then the MOTHER goddess Hannahanna begs Telipinu's father, the weather god, to search for his son, but he goes to Telipinu's city and cannot find him. Hannahanna then sends a bee to sting Telipinu on his hands and feet and then smear him with wax and bring him home, but the bee is unsuccessful. Finally, the goddess of SPELLS, Kamrusepas, is able to mollify Telipinu's anger through a magical ceremony, and, astride the back of the eagle, he returns to his temple. Then an evergreen is set before Telipinu from which is hung a fleece with mutton fat in it, and offerings of wine, oxen, and corn are made to the god.

In another variant of the same myth, the goddess Kamrusepa is the one to send the eagle and the bee and "high magic" to bring back Telipinu. Thunder and lightning and loud cries can be heard by all the GODS, and finally Telipinu appears on the eagle. Then Kamrusepa practices her magic on Telipinu by putting a spell on the fruit and cream and honey set before him upon his return, and Telipinu's wrath disappears and the more he eats, the more he becomes kinder and more benevolent. The gods then celebrate, surrounding Telipinu, and the mortals sing to him, for they have no food to offer him. The prayers and the petitions of the people, who are emptying the garbage they have collected all winter, are actually magic spells, and suddenly winter disappears and is replaced by the first spring breezes. Everything on earth begins to breathe new life, and a tall pole is set before Telipinu in his honor, with the white fleece of a newborn lamb hung from it.

The myth of Telipinu suggests the themes of DEATH and REBIRTH, the changing of the seasons, the phases of the MOON, RESURRECTION, and the later importance of the lamb in Christianity.

For Further Reading

Gaster, Theodor. *The Oldest Stories in the World.* New York: Viking, 1952.

TELL, WILLIAM

Legendary Swiss HERO, famous for shooting an apple off his son's head with an arrow. As a national hero, William Tell stands for courage and defiance of tyranny. His story, set in the fourteenth century during the Swiss independence movement, is complete with dates and many other details. For many years it was considered to be true. However, the tale has parallels in other countries and recent scholarship indicates that no such historical figure existed. The story appeared in Swiss BALLADS before the sixteenth century.

The LEGEND tells of the Austrian Hapsburg governor, Gessler, who places his cap in a town marketplace as a symbol of authority. The townspeople are ordered to bow to the cap every time they pass by. Many people simply avoid passing it, even though they have to take the long way around town to do so. They are plotting to rise up against their tyrannical rulers.

A renowned hunter and marksman named William Tell lives in the nearby hills. When he visits the town market with his son, Tell refuses to bow the cap. Gessler orders Tell to demonstrate his famous marksmanship by shooting an apple off his son's head from 50 paces away. If he succeeds, both would go free, but if he fails, they would be put to death.

Even for a master marksman, such accuracy could not be guaranteed. But William Tell suppresses his anger and takes two arrows from his quiver. Putting one inside his vest, he puts the other on his crossbow, aims carefully, and releases the arrow. It pierces the apple without touching the boy beneath.

Annoyed, Gessler demands to know what Tell's second arrow was for. "If I had missed, and killed my son," the marksman replies, "that arrow was for your heart." Gessler has Tell arrested and taken by boat to prison. But along the way, the marksman escapes by leaping from the boat.

Later Tell ambushes and kills the tyrant, so that no others would be so ill-treated. The people celebrate, tear down the prison they had been forced to build, and ultimately rise in revolution against their rulers. The William Tell legend is the subject of an 1804 play by Schiller and an 1829 opera by Rossini.

The theme of the bold hero of the common people who will not endure tyranny and inspires rebellion is a common one, including the often-told historical story of the Roman gladiator Spartacus and the numerous tales about ROBIN HOOD. Similar tales to that of William Tell have been told in Denmark, Norway, Germany, Iceland, and England.

For Further Reading:

Bawden, Nina. *William Tell*. New York: Lothrop, Lee & Shepard, 1981.

Early, Margaret. *William Tell*. Illustrated. New York: Harry N. Abrams, 1991.

Small, Terry. *The Legend of William Tell*. New York: Bantam, 1991.

TESTS

Group of FOLKTALE incidents involving tests, contests, tasks, and QUESTS. The test MOTIF is one of the most widespread in the world, and most HEROES and many HEROINES must prove themselves through tests. The test may involve slaying a DRAGON, answering a RIDDLE, pursuing a dangerous quest, or conquering something that threatens the community in order to win the PRINCESS. Recognition tests might involve the hero picking out from a group of children his own child whom he has never before seen. In order to pass the test, the hero very often encounters or seeks out a supernatural adviser: a CRONE, a WISE OLD MAN, or a HELPFUL ANIMAL.

In the Greek MYTH "Oedipus the King," Oedipus manages to solve the riddle of the SPHINX, thereby freeing his community from her tyranny. His prize is the newly-widowed Queen Jocasta of THEBES. Only when Oedipus tries to solve a second riddle, "Who was the murderer of Laius?" does he almost fail. In another Greek myth, "Jason and the Golden Fleece," the enchantress Medea helps Jason find the fleece. The Greek hero Theseus must find a way to kill the MINOTAUR and escape from the LABYRINTH, and he succeeds with the help of Ariadne's thread. In the BIBLE, Abraham is tested by GOD when he is asked to sacrifice his son Isaac.

Tests are common motifs of North American Indian tales, where the hero is often tested by his prospective father-in-law or mother-in-law. The hero may have to eat burning food or catch a dangerous bird, kill rare game, or pass through a difficult door. In some cases, the hero is a TRICKSTER figure.

Some tests seems impossible, and it is the task of the hero to overcome these impossibilities. Herakles most overcome insurmountable odds in the 12 LABORS OF HERAKLES. In the myth of CUPID AND PSYCHE, Psyche also must do the impossible to pass the tests her mother-in-law, Venus, has given her, which involves a DESCENT TO THE UNDERWORLD and returning with some of Persephone's beauty balm. Although Psyche succeeds, she cannot resist trying a little, but she is instantly overcome by it, and only Cupid, with the help of Jupiter, can revive her. In FAIRY TALES such as the European "THREE GOLDEN SONS," the YOUNGEST SON is the one who succeeds at passing the tests that his older brothers fail. By passing the difficult test, the often unpromising hero or heroine proves his or her ultimate worthiness.

For Further Reading

Climo, Shirley. "Psyche." *Princess Tales from around the World*. Illustrated by Ruth Sanderson. New York: HarperCollins, 1996.

Evetts-Secker, Josephine. *Mother and Daughter Tales*. Illustrated by Helen Cann. New York: Abbeville Press, 1996.

Sierra, Judy. *Cinderella*. The Oryx Multicultural Folktale Series. Phoenix: Oryx Press, 1992.

TESTS OF PROWESS

In MYTH and LEGEND, feats of strength or accuracy the HERO must accomplish. Just as the MOTIF of TESTS of all kinds are a staple of storytelling, the particular type of testing called "tests of prowess" are a common motif in myths and FAIRY TALES. In order to free himself or win the prize, the hero must show he can outdo everyone else in his physical strength, agility, accuracy, and stamina.

The Greek Herakles, known as Hercules to the Romans, was considered one of the greatest of the HEROES. He performed 12 tests of prowess, the famous 12 LABORS OF HERAKLES, in order to expiate himself from the sin of having murdered his family when the GODDESS HERA drove him mad. These labors included killing the Nemean lion with his bare hands, killing the nine-headed Hydra monster, capturing the Arcadian stag, killing the Erymanthian boar, cleansing the Augean stables, killing the vicious Stymphalian birds, capturing the bull sent to King Minos of Crete by Poseidon, capturing the flesh-eating Thracian horses, seizing the girdle of the Queen of the Amazons, capturing the oxen of the monster-king Geryon, fetching the golden apples of the Hesperides, and bringing forth the three-headed dog Cerberus from the underworld (*see* DESCENT TO THE UNDERWORLD). Succeeding in these tests of prowess made Herakles a hero.

Many heroes of fairy tales must pass tests of prowess, either through stamina or cleverness. Jack of "JACK AND THE BEANSTALK" must find a way to kill the GIANT, and the young man of the GRIMM BROTHERS's "The Raven" must find a way to scale the glass mountain in order to reach the golden castle of Stromberg, where the little PRINCESS who has been transformed into a RAVEN is imprisoned. Only when the hero's prowess has been demonstrated does he or she earn the title of hero and win the accompanying prize.

THEBES

City of ancient Boeotia, in the eastern part of Greece. Still an important center in Classical times, Thebes figured prominently in ANCIENT GREEK STORYTELLING. The House of Thebes, along with the houses of Atreus, Athens, and TROY, was one of the principal royal families of Greek mythology.

The oracle at DELPHI commanded Cadmus to follow a wandering cow until it lay down to rest. At that spot he founded Thebes, but only after killing a DRAGON and planting its teeth, which sprouted into a multitude of soldiers. All of these soldiers killed each other except for five, who helped Cadmus to build his city. Robert Graves (*see* GRAVES, ROBERT) has suggested that Cadmus killing the dragon, like APOLLO killing the Python, represents a takeover of the territory.

Cadmus became the first KING of Thebes, with Harmonia as his queen. He was a just ruler, and is credited with bringing the alphabet to Greece. But like many of his descendants, Cadmus was doomed to suffer through no fault of his own. Particularly heartrending

to him were the fates of his children and grandchildren.

Cadmus's daughter Semele perished when her lover, the god ZEUS, revealed himself to her in a thunderbolt. Zeus rescued their unborn son, who grew up to be the wine god DIONYSOS.

When Dionysos returned to Thebes, Semele's sister Agave joined his throng of female worshippers. But Agave's son Pentheus disapproved of the Dionysian rites and tried ban them. Dionysos drove Agave mad, and she tore her own son to pieces, thinking he was a lion.

By this time, Cadmus and Harmonia were demoralized and decided to leave Thebes. They went to Illyria, where they were transformed into serpents. Their bloodline continued through their son Polydorus and Pentheus's son Menoeceus.

Polydorus's grandson King Laius was told by the Delphic oracle that his newborn son would grow up to murder him. Determined to keep this prophecy from coming true, Laius gave the infant to a shepherd to leave in the mountains to die. The shepherd did not have the heart to do this, and the child grew up in Corinth as the adopted son of King Polybus. His name was Oedipus.

Oedipus had no idea that he had been adopted. So when the Delphic oracle told him that he would one day murder his father and marry his mother, he fled Corinth in order to evade the prophecy. During his travels, he encountered Laius in his chariot, accompanied by soldiers. Laius demanded that the young stranger get out of the road, and Oedipus angrily slew Laius and most of his guard. Oedipus did not realize that he had fulfilled half of the oracle's prophecy.

During this time, Thebes was being persecuted by a SPHINX who asked every traveler she met a RIDDLE. Failure to answer it meant death—and no one knew the answer.

Fearing the Sphinx, Thebes closed its seven gates, rendering it helpless against famine. But Oedipus, known for both his bravery and intelligence, confronted the Sphinx and answered her riddle. The Sphinx then killed herself, and Oedipus became the celebrated savior of Thebes. He was made king and promptly married Laius's widow, Jocasta. Oedipus had no idea that the other half of the oracle's prophecy had now been fulfilled.

Oedipus and Jocasta had children and reigned happily for many years, until a mysterious plague came to Thebes. Oedipus learned from the Delphic Oracle that the plague would only be lifted when Laius's killer was punished. When the seer TIRESIAS told Oedipus that the king himself was the sought-after killer, Oedipus did not believe him. But Oedipus soon discovered the awful truth—that he had murdered his father and married his mother.

Jocasta committed suicide. Oedipus punished himself by putting out his own eyes. Jocasta's brother Creon reigned as regent, and Oedipus was eventually sent into exile. He wandered the countryside for years, accompanied by his loyal daughter Antigone. Oedipus died at Colonus, a grove near Athens. As a reward for his sufferings, the gods granted him a mysterious blessing, and the site of his death became sacred.

But his fate scarcely ended the troubles of the House of Thebes. His two sons, Eteocles and Polyneices, quarreled over the Theban throne. The younger of the two, Eteocles, became king, and the exiled Polyneices gathered an army to attack Thebes. Polyneices and six other chieftains each attacked one of the seven gates of Thebes.

The war reached a stalemate, so Polyneices and Eteocles agreed to decide the outcome in one-to-one combat. But the brothers died in each other's arms, and the battle raged again. Eventually, the Thebans drove away their attackers, killing all but one of the chieftains who had attacked their gates.

Now Thebes' king, Creon refused to bury Polyneices and the other dead chieftains. He was resisted in this blasphemous decision by his niece Antigone, but he would not change his mind. Creon's stubbornness led to the deaths of his son Haemon, his wife Eurydice, and Antigone. Creon at last relented and buried Polyneices, but not the other chieftains.

The chieftains' wives and children appealed to THESEUS, the ruler of Athens, for assistance. This led to a brief war between Athens and Thebes, which Athens won. Theseus wisely refrained from destroying Thebes; his goal had only been to bury the chieftains. But the chieftains' sons, known as the Epigoni, swore vengeance against Thebes. Ten years after the burials of their fathers, they warred against Thebes and won. This time the city was destroyed.

These stories were often dramatized in Greek tragedy, most notably in Aeschylus' *Seven against Thebes,* Sophocles's *Oedipus the King,* and Euripides's *The Bacchae.*

The House of Thebes has proven a rich mine of ideas and metaphors down to the present age. For example, Sigmund Freud dubbed the male child's attraction to his mother and hostility toward his father the "Oedipus Complex" (*see* FREUD, SIGMUND). And in his 1942 drama *Antigone,* Jean Anouilh used Oedipus's daughter as a symbol of French resistance against the Nazi occupation.

For Further Reading

Anouilh, Jean. *Five Plays.* Vol. 1. New York: Hill and Wang, 1960.

THEFT OF FIRE/LIGHT

Theme explaining how a culture first received daylight and fire for cooking and heat. The theme of the theft of fire and/or light occurs in many MYTHS and LEGENDS of different cultures, including those of the Native North Americans, the Polynesian, the Greek, the Jivaro tribe of Peru, the Aztecs of Mexico, and the aboriginal Djuan of northern Australia. These stories seek to explain how these two supernatural and most magical and necessary things were given to humankind. While light is a requirement for all forms of life, the harnessing of fire for warmth, cooking, and forging is something only human beings are capable of; indeed, the ability to use fire has contributed to the nature of human evolution.

The Ancient Greeks believed that humankind received fire from Prometheus the Titan, who, according to myth, first steals its secret from MOUNT OLYMPOS, home of the GODS. Hiding the spark of fire in the stalk of a fennel, Prometheus brings it to the human beings he likes to help. ZEUS, however, is furious at Prometheus for helping humankind, and when Prometheus refuses to reveal to Zeus the name of the woman whose still unconceived child with Zeus will bring about Zeus's downfall, Zeus punishes Prometheus severely. Prometheus is chained to a rock where an eagle will peck out his liver each day, and each night the liver regenerates, only to be pecked at the following day; however, he never loses his dignity or capitulates to Zeus (*see* PROMETHEUS AND THE THEFT OF FIRE).

For many of the tribes of the Pacific Northwest, RAVEN is the source of fire and light, and the sooty color of ravens is attributed to the theft and carrying of fire in Raven's bill. Among the Plains tribes, COYOTE is the one to bring fire. The Peruvian Jivaro tribe tells the story of the first man to make fire by rubbing together two sticks—*Takkea*—but he will not share his knowledge with the birds; he roasts them instead. One day, Takkea's wife allows Himbui the Hummingbird to come inside to warm up, and when her back is turned, Himbui puts his tail in the fire, flies off, lights a tree, and thus shares the gift of fire with all people. Similarly, among the Djuan of Australia, a sullen man named Koimul knows how to make fire from two sticks, but he, too, keeps this knowledge to himself. Wirrit-wirrit the Hummingbird steals these two sticks from under the arm of Koimul and shares them with humankind. The Aztecs also identify the gift of fire with the hummingbird, personified by their war god Huitzilopochtli.

The Polynesian TRICKSTER, demi-god, and culture hero MAUI is credited with stealing fire from his great-great-grandmother, Mahui-Ike, who keeps fire in the underworld. With his unfailing charm and cunning, Maui continually asks her for fire, and each time she gives him one of her fingernails or toenails, which is a burning fire, but he brings it up from the underworld and extinguishes it. Finally catching on, Mahui-Ike flings her last flame at Maui, setting the earth on fire. When Maui cannot escape the flame by transforming himself into an eagle and then a fish, he begs his father to make it rain, which his father does, and Maui then puts the fire in the one tree where the rain does not fall, and this becomes the source of all fire.

For Further Reading

A Children's Treasury of Mythology. Illustrated by Margaret Evans Price. New York: Barnes and Noble, 1994.

THESEUS

Hero of Greek mythology. Theseus's exploits and adventurers are recounted in the works of Ovid, Plutarch, and Apollodorus. He also appears in several tragedies by Sophocles and Euripides.

Theseus's father was Aegeus, the KING of Athens. But Theseus was raised by his mother Aethra far to the south of Athens. Before leaving his newborn son in Aethra's care, Aegeus placed a sword beneath an enormous rock. He told Aethra that Theseus would be ready to come to Athens and claim his birthright when he could lift the stone and take the sword in his hand.

Theseus grew to be a daring and athletic youth, and one day he lifted the stone and wielded his father's sword. The time had come for him to go to Athens. The shortest and easiest route was by sea, but this was not enough of a challenge for the ambitious young HERO. He took a difficult land route, fighting victoriously against dangerous foes along the way.

Theseus soon was renowned throughout all Greece. Aegeus welcomed Theseus to Athens without knowing that the youth was his son. But Aegeus' queen, the sorceress Medea, knew the truth and plotted Theseus' death. Theseus narrowly escaped poisoning when he showed his sword to his father, revealing himself as Aegeus's son.

From that time on, Theseus was the acknowledged heir to the Athenian throne. But those were hard times in Athens. Minos, the king of Crete, was exacting a cruel tribute from the city. Every nine years, seven young men and seven young women of Athens were sent to Crete, where Minos would sacrifice them to the MINOTAUR—a monster which was half human and half bull. This tribute came due not long after Theseus arrived in Athens.

Theseus decided to prove his worthiness to the throne by slaying the Minotaur. To do so, he volunteered to be one of the sacrificial victims. He assured Aegeus that he would give a sign of his safe return. The ship which carried the sacrificial victims had a black sail. If Theseus was on that ship when it returned, he would put up a white sail instead. That way, his father would know that he was still alive before he even reached Athens.

Ariadne, the daughter of King Minos, fell in love with the prisoner Theseus the moment she set eyes on him. After getting Theseus to promise her to marry her and take her back to Athens, she set about helping him to survive his encounter with the Minotaur.

The Minotaur roamed a gigantic maze called the LABYRINTH, designed by the legendary architect Daedalus. Ariadne gave Theseus a spool of thread so he could find his way through the Labyrinth. This allowed Theseus to find the sleeping Minotaur, kill him, and then escape.

Theseus, Ariadne, and the 13 other intended victims fled on the ship by which they had arrived in Crete. But Theseus heartlessly abandoned Ariadne on the island of Naxos. Then, when the ship approached Athens, Theseus forgot to change the black sail to white as he had promised his father. Thinking his son was dead, Aegeus threw himself into the sea with grief.

Theseus was promptly declared king of Athens, but renounced his royal power to declare a democratic form of government. For most of his reigning years, he guided his city with wisdom and compassion. He was particularly insightful when the neighboring city of THEBES suffered from civil turmoil. It was Theseus who gave sanctuary to the Theban outcast Oedipus during his last day on earth. And Theseus also saw to the burial of fallen warriors denied internment by the Theban king Creon.

He also went forth on many more adventures, including an expedition to the country of women warriors known as the Amazons. He took home the Amazonian queen Antiope (sometimes known as Hippolyta) and married her. Antiope's subjects sent an army to Athens bring her back, but the Athenians drove the Amazonians away.

Antiope died, but not before she bore Theseus a son named Hippolytus. After Hippolytus grew to manhood, Theseus remarried, this time to Phaedra, Ariadne's sister. Most improperly, Phaedra fell in love with her stepson. But Hippolytus, being rigidly celibate and more than a little misogynist, furiously rejected Phaedra's advances. Phaedra committed suicide after writing a slanderous letter to Theseus accusing Hippolytus of having tried to rape her.

Convinced of the truth of Phaedra's letter, Theseus sent his son into exile. Hippolytus was killed soon afterwards when a MONSTER rose up out of the sea and frightened his chariot's horses. Theseus learned of Phaedra's falsehood from the goddess ARTEMIS and bitterly grieved his injustice toward his son.

In later years, Theseus fell out of favor with Athens and was sent into exile. He was eventually murdered by King Lycomedes while a guest in his court.

Because Theseus was the patron hero of Athens, stories about him were carefully tailored to fit the classical city-state's image of itself. This is especially true of the account of Theseus bringing democracy to Athens. In *The Greek Myths,* Robert Graves (*see* GRAVES, ROBERT) describes this as "fifth-century propaganda." He also notes at least three mythological characters called Theseus, who were not unified into a single character until the sixth century B.C.

But there is also archeological evidence that some of the Theseus stories have a basis in truth. For example, the Cretan palace of Knossos actually was a maze. And Minos's sacrifices of prisoners to the Minotaur may have been inspired by primitive bullfighting rituals portrayed on Cretan frescoes.

The twentieth-century novelist Mary Renault took up such evidence as the basis of two historical novels about Theseus—*The King Must Die* and *The Bull From the Sea.* In these books, Renault strips the Theseus lore of its fantastic and supernatural elements to give a plausible account of how the legends may have originated. *See also* ANCIENT GREEK STORYTELLING, ICARUS AND DAEDALUS.

For Further Reading

Graves, Robert. *The Greek Myths.* New York: Viking Penguin, 1992.

Renault, Mary. *The Bull From the Sea.* New York: Pantheon Books, 1962.

———. *The King Must Die.* New York: Pantheon Books, 1958

Theseus and the Minotaur. New York: Troll, 1980.

Walker, Henry Jr. *Theseus and Athens.* New York: Oxford University Press, 1995.

THINKING WOMAN

FEMALE CREATOR in the LEGENDS of the Native American Rio Grande Pueblo tribes. As the first being in the lower world, Thinking Woman, Sus'sistanako, is alone, sometimes in the form of a SPIDER. She draws a cross on the ground so that there are four lines pointing in each direction. Then Thinking Woman puts a parcel north of the crossing lines on both sides of the north-south line. These mysterious parcels begin to shake when Thinking Woman starts to sing, and from each parcel emerges a woman. These two women begin to walk around, and they create all living things as Thinking Woman continues her song.

THOMPSON, STITH (1885–1976)

American literary folklorist known for introducing the historic geographic research method from Finland to American scholars. Trained at Harvard, Thompson joined the English faculty at Indiana University in 1921 and taught the first FOLKLORE course there in 1923. Thompson believed that when a particular tale has variations in many places, an original birthplace exists from whence the tale spread. In this birthplace, the tale has an original form, called the "ur" form, or ARCHETYPE. Thompson wrote an essay about the Native American STAR HUSBAND TALE to exemplify a study of folklore type sets accomplished using the historic geographic method. Thompson was inspired by the DIFFUSION studies of Kaarle Krohn and Franz Boas and was concerned with both variation and similarity occurring with tale diffusion (*see* BOAS, FRANZ; KROHN, KAARLE). Thompson utilized Boas's voluminous collections of FOLKTALES but, unlike Boas, Thompson looked solely at texts and did not take any social influences (such as the role of the storyteller) into account

when looking at tale diffusion. After the death of Finnish scholar Antti Aarne (*see* AARNE, ANTTI), Thompson completed, translated, and published Aarne's index of tale types work as *Antti Aarne's Verzeichnis der Marchentypen* in 1928. He revised this work in 1961 as *The Types of the Folktales: A Classification and Bibliography.* He also published the six-volume *Motif Index of Folk Literature* in the 1930s and revised it in the 1950s. Both of Thompson's books are standard reference material for folklorists around the world. Indeed, the *Motif Index of Folk Literature* is considered one of the most comprehensive general reference books in folklore studies. These two works of Thompson's are similarly systematized and cross-indexed in great detail, but retain distinct differences. The type index classifies whole plots and the MOTIF index classifies narrative elements (actions, actors, objects, and settings). Another well-known work by Thompson is *The Folktale*, a handbook of the historic geographic method of folktale studies, which is now considered dated due to its Freudian psychological approaches to folklore. *The Folktale*'s goal is to present folktales as important art form to be studied, to acquaint readers with many great folktales from around the world, and to highlight goals of future folktale scholarship.

For Further Reading

Thompson, Stith. *The Folktale.* Berkeley: University of California Press, 1977.

———. *Motif Index of Folk-Literature: A Classification of Narrative Elements in Folk Tales, Ballads, Myths, Fables, Mediaeval Romances, Example, Fabliaux.* Indiana University Press, 1993.

THOMS, WILLIAM JOHN (1803–1885)

English scholar who coined the term FOLKLORE. In 1846 Thoms published a letter in a weekly publication of art, literature, and science reviews, proposing that the word "folklore" be used in lieu of the common nomenclature of the day, "popular antiquities." This new terminology was quickly embraced by scholars as it bestowed the examination of traditional tales, sayings, music, customs, and beliefs with a suitable title that reflected and described the content of study. In this letter Thoms also solicited his readers' assistance in documenting such folklore genres as superstitions, BALLADS, and PROVERBS as he believed that these "antiquities" were in the process of not only becoming antique, but extinct. Thoms's literary contribution to folk scholarship lies in the three-volume set *A Collection of Early Prose Romances*, published in 1828, and *Lays and Legends of Various Nations,* published in 1834.

THOUSAND AND ONE NIGHTS

Collection of tales also known as *The Arabian Nights' Entertainment.* The stories are from Persian, Indian, and Arabian oral traditions. Although elements of the *Thousand and One Nights* can be traced to A.D. 850, the present version was assembled by an unknown writer toward the end of the eighteenth century, probably in Cairo, Egypt.

All the tales are framed by the story of the consummate storyteller, Scheherazade, and the Sultan Schahriah. Schahriah's first wife proved unfaithful, as did the wife of his brother. The Sultan then decided that women were never to be trusted. He vowed to marry a different woman every day, spend the night with her, then have her strangled the next morning.

One day, it was the turn of Scheherazade, the Vizier's daughter, to become Schahriah's one-night bride. Despite her father's objections, she went to Schahriah's bed quite willingly—but only on the condition that her sister, Dinarzade, sleep nearby.

Shortly before daybreak, Scheherazade began to tell her sister a story. Schahriah could not help but overhear and was overcome with suspense when Scheherazade left her story unfinished at dawn. He decided to delay strangling her until the following morning. But when the next dawn approached and Scheherazade began another story without finishing it, Schahriah delayed her execution again. During the many nights that followed, Scheherazade told many of the most beloved and enduring tales of world literature.

"The Seven Voyages of Sinbad" recounted the travels of a wealthy Baghdad merchant.

The Sinbad of the title told an impoverished porter, also named Sinbad, the stories of his adventures in order to illustrate the profitability of perseverance and risk.

During his first voyage, Sinbad mistook a whale for an island and was almost drowned. During his second, he hitched a ride on a gigantic bird known as a roc. During his third, he confronted a fearsome cyclops. During his fourth, he married a noblewoman in a distant land, only to be faced with the local custom of burning the husband alive on the funeral pyre in the event of the wife's death. During his fifth, he thwarted an alarming character known as the Old Man of the SEA. During his sixth, he visited the mountain where Adam fled after being expelled from PARADISE. During his seventh, he was caught by pirates and became a slave. Sinbad not only survived all these ordeals but profited by them. He returned to Baghdad and retired to a life of luxury.

Before becoming part of the *Thousand and One Nights,* "The Seven Voyages of Sinbad" probably constituted an independent work. These adventures bear a striking resemblance to those of Odysseus recounted in the ODYSSEY of HOMER, particularly Sinbad's adventure with the CYCLOPES. This resemblance is probably no coincidence. Although the authors who created Sinbad had no direct knowledge of Homer, they would certainly have heard the legends of Odysseus.

"Aladdin and the Enchanted Lamp" told of a good-for-nothing young man who was visited by a wicked magician pretending to be his uncle. After giving Aladdin a ring for protection, the magician sent the boy into the depths of a cave in search of a lamp. Aladdin refused to throw the magician the lamp until he was released from the cave, and the magician angrily shut him up inside.

Aladdin soon discovered that both the ring and the lamp contained powerful genies willing to fulfill his every desire. After escaping from the cave, Aladdin had a wonderful palace built for himself in China and married a sultan's daughter.

At the end of these and many other stories, a thousand and one nights had passed between Scheherazade and the Sultan Schahriah. Far from wanting to have Scheherazade killed, Schahriah realized that he had fallen in love with her. He renounced her death sentence and declared her the savior of her sex.

In his introduction to his own translation of a selection of *Arabian Nights* stories, N. J. Dawood argues that, notwithstanding their flights of fancy, they give a detailed and accurate portrait of medieval Islam. He also points out how anomalous these often amoral, bawdy, and even scatological stories seem in context with other Eastern writings.

Writes Dawood, "They can be regarded as the expression of the lay and secular imagination of the East in revolt against the austere erudition and religious zeal of Oriental literature generally." As a result, the *Thousand and One Nights* has never been accepted as a legitimate part of Arabian literature. But the Western world has embraced it wholeheartedly.

There are numerous versions of the stories available, many of them for children. Judith Gorog's *Winning Scheherazade*, written for young people, deals with the storyteller's adventures after Schahriah's reprieve. And of course, the stories have been made into many films, including Walt Disney's 1992 animated feature *Aladdin*. Scheherazade is also the subject of a popular orchestral suite by the Russian composer Rimsky-Korsakov. *See also* ALI BABA.

For Further Reading

Gorog, Judith. *Winning Scheherazade*. New York: Macmillan International, 1991.

Tales from the Thousand and One Nights. Translated with an introduction by N.J. Dawood. London: Penguin, 1973.

THREE GOLDEN SONS

Famous FOLKTALE of outcast triplets searching for their father. There are at least 600 VARIANTS of this folktale from all over the world, and its appeal has always been great. The plot draws on the oral tradition and appears in Arab and European versions. While various MOTIFS can be traced in this story, the importance of the number three—three sisters, three brothers, three things that must be obtained—is obvious.

The tale opens with a KING who overhears three girls predicting the future should he marry one of them, and the king chooses to marry the youngest, who has foretold that she would bear him golden-haired triplets with stars on their foreheads and chains around their necks. When she bears these children, her older sisters substitute an animal in their place, throw the children into the river, and make sure the guilt falls on the wife, who is imprisoned or exiled.

The children are found by a fisherman or a miller and raised by him until they are ready to search for their father and obtain "the bird of truth, the singing tree, and the WATER OF LIFE." The eldest sets out first, but fails in his QUEST and is turned to stone, and the second brother fails as well. The YOUNGEST SON then sets out and, with the amulets of a wise CRONE, causes his brothers to be released from their SPELL. The king then hears from the bird of truth the story of his three children and vilified wife, he and his family are rejoined, and his wife's sisters are punished. *See also* NUMBERS, ABANDONED CHILD, SEARCH FOR THE FATHER.

THREE WORLDS .

Universe divided into three "towns" comprised of the EARTH, middle space or the atmosphere, and the sky or firmament, according to ancient Indian Vedic belief. DEVI, Great GODDESS of the Hindus, is known as "The Fairest of the Three Towns" because she personifies this "total energy of creation." SIVA, the great Hindu god, is sometimes depicted as Tripurantaka, "He Who Puts an End to the Three Towns or Fortresses," for, according to Hindu legend, Siva conquers a tyrant, Maya, who has managed to acquire the three worlds. Maya has built a mighty fortress on each one. He then manages to combine these three fortresses into one, almost impregnable center of DEMONS, chaos, and world tyranny. What makes Siva's undertaking so extraordinary is that Maya, with his *yogic* power, has made it come to pass that this terrifying fortress will fall only if it is pierced by one single arrow. Since from earliest times Siva has been a hunter, he is known for the amazing deeds he has accomplished with his bow. Thus, Siva manages with one shot of his bow to pierce the fortress with his arrow, free the world of its evil, and regenerate the cosmos.

For Further Reading

Zimmer, Heinrich. *Myths and Symbols in Indian Art and Civilization.* Edited by Joseph Campbell. New York: Harper & Row, 1946.

TIBETAN BOOK OF THE DEAD

Sacred book of the science of DEATH and RE-BIRTH dating back to the eighth century A.D. "Buddhists and Hindus alike believe that the last thought at the moment of death determines the character of the next incarnation," writes W. Y. Evans-Wentz in his preface to his compilation of the Tibetan *Bardo Thodol*, otherwise known as *The Tibetan Book of the Dead or The After-Death Experiences on the Bardo Plane, according to Lama Kazi Dawa-Samdup's English Rendering* (1927). Relating it to comments made in such works as the *Bhagavad Gita*, the PROVERBS of the Hebrew sages, *The Egyptian Book of the Dead*, the *Metamorphoses* of APULEIUS, and the autobiography of Tibetan poet-saint MILAREPA, Evans-Wentz writes that the message of the *Bardo Thodol* is "that the Art of Dying is quite as important as the Art of Living (or of coming into Birth), of which it is the complement and summation; that the future of being is dependent, perhaps entirely, upon a rightly controlled death, as the second part of this volume, setting forth the Art of Reincarnating, emphasizes." As the avatar KRISNA tells ARJUNA in the *Bhagavad-Gita*, "only the Awakened Ones remember their many deaths and births." This is born out by the Buddhist JATAKA TALES, stories of BUDDHA in his previous incarnations.

In his "Psychological Commentary on *The Tibetan Book of the Dead*," Carl Jung notes, "Like *The Egyptian Book of the Dead*, it is meant to be a guide for the dead man during the period of his *Bardo* existence, symbolically described as an intermediate state of forty-nine days' duration between death and rebirth." The first part of the book, the *Chikhai Bardo*, is a description of what is happening psychically at the moment of death. The second part, the *Chonyid Bardo*, focuses on the DREAM-state that supervenes right after death and the accompanying "*karmic* illusions." The third part, the *Sidpa Bardo*, deals with the beginning of "birth-instinct" and of "prenatal events." The entire text of the *Bardo Thodol* is meant to be read by a *lama* in the presence of the corpse with the purpose being, in Jung's words, to "fix the attention of the dead man, at each successive stage of delusion and entanglement, on the ever-present possibility of liberation, and to explain to him the nature of his visions."

Links to the oral tradition of many cultures are revealed in each section of *The Tibetan Book of the Dead*. As Evans-Wentz notes, "Occidental occultists have contended that the hieroglyphical writings of ancient Egypt and of Mexico seem to have been, in some degree, a popularized or esoteric outgrowth of a secret language" and "that a symbol-code was sometimes used by Plato and other Greek philosophers, in relation to Pythagorean and Orphic lore; that throughout the Celtic world the Druids conveyed all their esoteric teachings symbolically; that the use of PARABLES, as in the sermons of Jesus and of the Buddha, and of other Great Teachers, illustrates the same tendency; and that through works like AESOP'S FABLES, and the miracle and MYSTERY PLAYS of medieval Europe, many of the old Oriental symbols have been introduced into the modern literatures of the West."

For Further Reading

Evans-Wentz, W.Y. *The Tibetan Book of the Dead or the After-Death Experiences on the Bardo Plane, According to Lama Kazi Dawa-Samdup's English Rendering.* London: Oxford University Press, 1968.

TILL'S PANACEA

Medieval German story in which Till Eulenspiegel (also Tyl Ulenspiegel) devises a plan to outwit the greedy governor of a hospital for the poor in Nuremberg (*see* EULENSPIEGEL, TILL). The hospital's governor often releases sick patients before they are well, making beds available so that he can receive the required entrance fee from the new patients who arrive. When Till learns of this evil practice, he disguises himself as a doctor and advertises throughout the town that he can cure any illness known to man. The unsuspecting hospital governor visits Till who says that he will clear the hospital of all its patients in a single day for the price of 200 guilders. If even one patient remains, then the hospital governor will owe nothing. The governor agrees and officially seals the bargain with a payment of 20 guilders to Till.

Till visits the hospital and whispers a secret message to each of the patients. He tells them that the only way to cure their illnesses is by taking a pill made from the ashes of the sickest amongst them. Therefore, the sickest person must be burnt. He says that all but the sickest should leave the hospital the next day when he and the governor make their rounds. If they return in three days, the pill to cure their illnesses will be available.

The next day, with the governor watching, Till throws open the hospital doors and instructs the sickest to stay behind and all others to leave the hospital. Immediately all the patients leave the hospital. Till demands the balance of his fee and departs. For three days at least, Till had cured all the sick in Nuremberg.

This tale contains the popular MOTIF of a cunning little man who takes advantage of the credulity and cupidity of his would-be superiors. The GRIMM BROTHERS's "Bumpkin," "The Clever Little Tailor," and "The Valiant Little Tailor" also contain VARIANTS of this motif. Likewise, ROBIN HOOD is an excellent example of a humble character who outwits the clergy and the law in the forests of northern England.

For Further Reading

Janisch, Heinz. *Till Eulenspiegel's Merry Pranks.* New York: Children's Press, 1991.

TIRESIAS

Seer of Greek legend. Although the stories pertaining to Tiresias vary, most agree that he was transformed into a woman for a time. According to some accounts, this happened when he came upon two snakes copulating. He struck them and killed the female, and paid for this deed by becoming a woman. Tiresias lived for some years in this condition—a celebrated harlot, according to some storytellers. Eventually, he happened upon two copulating snakes again, and this time killed the male. This transformed him back into a man.

It then came to pass that ZEUS and HERA, the king and queen of the Olympian GODS, quarreled over the question of whether men or women more greatly enjoyed the act of sexual intercourse. Zeus insisted that women felt greater pleasure than men, while Hera claimed the opposite. Due to his breadth of experience, Tiresias was chosen to arbitrate, and proclaimed without question that women experienced 10 times more erotic pleasure than men.

This infuriated Hera, who promptly blinded Tiresias. But Zeus compensated by giving Tiresias the gift of prophecy, particularly the power to interpret birdsong. He also granted Tiresias a vast earthly lifetime of seven generations.

Soon afterward, Tiresias predicted that the youthful NARCISSUS would live to be a ripe old age, as long as he "never knows himself." This prophecy came to poignant fulfillment when Narcissus fell in love with his own reflection in a pond and subsequently starved himself to death. Tiresias also prophesied the greatness and celebrity of the infant demi-god Herakles (*see* LABORS OF HERAKLES).

These feats established Tiresias as a seer, and he settled down to a long career counseling the leaders of THEBES. His prophecies were always accurate—if often enigmatic—but the Theban kings seldom heeded him.

He advised the youthful King Pentheus to take part in the rites of the wine god DIONYSOS. Pentheus refused, and was consequently torn to shreds by Dionysos' female followers—among whom was Pentheus's own mother.

Later, when King Oedipus promised to find the killer of Thebes's previous ruler, Tiresias assured Oedipus that the king himself was the criminal he sought. Oedipus angrily dismissed Tiresias as a charlatan, only to put out his own eyes when he discovered that Tiresias was correct.

Oedipus's successor, Creon, also had an unfortunate tendency to ignore Tiresias's advice. After Oedipus's son Polyneices died leading an unsuccessful invasion against Thebes, Creon refused to bury the young warrior's body, despite Tiresias's dire warnings. This resulted in the deaths of Creon's niece Antigone, his son Haemon, and his wife Eurydice.

The end of Tiresias's Theban career approached when the city was about to be sacked by warriors known as the Epigoni. Tiresias warned Thebes's inhabitants of the attack and successfully persuaded them to evacuate the city. Although he knew of his own impending death, he escaped along with the other Thebans. Soon after this flight, Tiresias drank from the spring of Tiphussa and died.

But death did not end Tiresias's role in Greek mythology. In the underworld, he was allowed the unusual privilege of remembering his earthly life. So when the wandering adventurer Odysseus found himself among the dead, Tiresias was able to advise him on how to get home again.

Few characters appear as frequently in Ancient Greek literature as Tiresias. The story of the seer advising Odysseus in the underworld appears in the ODYSSEY of HOMER. Tiresias's failure to persuade Pentheus to worship Dionysos is told in Euripides' drama *The Bacchae*. His attempt to counsel Creon regarding the body of Polyneices is described in Sophocles' drama *Antigone*. Tiresias also appears in Euripides' *The Phoenecian Women*.

Perhaps the most skillful dramatic treatment of Tiresias is to be found in Sophocles' *Oedipus the King*, which brilliantly captures the paradox of Tiresias's blindness. At the play's outset, only the blind Tiresias can "see" the truth about Oedipus, who himself only becomes wise through his own blindness.

More intriguing than either Tiresias's blindness or his longevity is his androgyny. In *The Greek Myths*, Robert Graves (*see* GRAVES, ROBERT) mentions a belief held in Southern India that the sight of two copulating snakes can bring on homosexuality. Perhaps the Tiresias legend builds on this folkloric notion.

It is likely that Tiresias' gender-switching has deeper significance, however. In *The Hero With a Thousand Faces,* Joseph Campbell (*see* CAMPBELL, JOSEPH) places Tiresias in the company of various androgynous and hermaphroditic figures in world mythology. And in *The World of Myth,* David Leeming suggests that the Tiresias story has "its roots in the archetype of the androgyne, the person of both sexes who becomes another version of the yin-yang/lingam-yoni unity, which carries with it the powers of prophecy."

The traits of blindness and longevity often reappear in the characters of the world's stories. Many North American TRICKSTER stories involve the blinding of a mischievous character (including COYOTE) for some misdeed. And the BIBLE relates the lives of many long-lived characters—especially Methuselah, who died at the age of 969.

Longevity has also become a major theme in both the science and science fiction of the twentieth century. Bernard Shaw's massive science fiction DRAMA, *Back to Methuselah,* focuses on the evolution of people able to live hundreds of years. Real-life attempts to increase the human lifespan include dieting and cryonic suspension; the latter technique is discussed in Ed Regis' book *Great Mambo Chicken and the Transhuman Condition.*

The Tiresian themes of longevity and androgyny were combined in Virginia Woolf's 1928 novel *Orlando,* about a handsome young Elizabethan courtier who mysteriously becomes a woman and lives until the present day. *Orlando* achieved new popularity through a successful 1992 film version directed by Sally Potter. *See also* ANCIENT GREEK STORYTELLING.

For Further Reading

Regis, Ed. *Great Mambo Chicken and the Transhuman Condition.* New York: Addison-Wesley, 1990.

Shaw, Bernard. *Back to Methuselah.* London: Penguin, 1987.

Sophocles. *Antigone.* Translated by Elizabeth Wyckoff. Vol. 2, *The Complete Greek Tragedies.* Chicago: University of Chicago Press, 1959.

———. *Oedipus the King.* Translated by David Grene. Vol. 2, *The Complete Greek Tragedies.* Chicago: University of Chicago Press, 1959.

TOLKIEN, J.R.R. (1892–1973)

Author of the popular works *The Hobbit* and *The Lord of the Rings*. John Ronald Reuel Tolkien was born in South Africa, but he spent most of his childhood in or near Birmingham, England. His experiences in the Midlands countryside as well as his taste for Nordic FOLKLORE and literature inspired much of his later work. He was also greatly influenced by his early reading of Andrew Lang's *Fairy Books* and George MacDonald's "Curdie" stories (*see* LANG, ANDREW). Tolkien's great interest in historical languages led him to study English Language and Literature at Oxford University. By the time he graduated in 1915, he had created two complete languages, supposedly spoken by ELVES. During World War I, Tolkien served as a signaling officer in the Lancashire Fusiliers. He taught at the University of Leeds before returning to Oxford in 1925 as Professor of Anglo-Saxon and English Language and Literature, a position he held until 1959. His scholarly work is well-known to students of English philology and medieval literature and includes *A Middle English Vocabulary* (1922), *Sir Gawain and the Green Knight* (1925), and BEOWULF: *The Monsters and the Critics* (1937).

Tolkien's renowned work *The Hobbit or There and Back Again*, first told to entertain his children, was published with the author's illustrations in 1937. The HERO of this story is a small, amiable, hairy-footed creature, the hobbit Bilbo Baggins, who lives in MIDDLE EARTH. He becomes involved in a dangerous expedition to recover treasure stolen by the DRAGON Smaug. Bilbo discovers his heroism and gains possession of a magic ring forged by the evil sorcerer Sauron. This story is continued in *The Lord of the Rings*, an EPIC trilogy comprising *The Fellowship of the Ring* (1954), *The Two Towers* (1954), and *The Return of the King* (1956). In the trilogy, Bilbo's nephew, Frodo, must protect the magic ring from those who would misuse it. He takes it to be destroyed in the mountain furnace where it was created. One theme explored in these works is the absurdity of conventional heroism. During the lengthy process of writing *The Lord of the Rings*, Tolkien received encouragement from C. S. Lewis, a colleague and close friend. Tolkien read chapters of his work to Lewis and a group of Lewis's friends called "The Inklings."

In his lecture titled "On Fairy-Stories" (1939), Tolkien spoke of the importance of secondary worlds in fantasy literature. A work of fantasy is successful, he claims, if the reader's mind can enter the secondary world and believe it. In spite of the elaborate, fantastical stories he created, Tolkien was always primarily interested in linguistics. He wrote that he began *The Lord of the Rings* trilogy to explain the history of the Elvish languages that he had invented.

Other works by Tolkien include *Farmer Giles of Ham* (1949), a children's book which, like *The Hobbit*, shows the absurdity of conventional heroism; *Smith of Wootton Major* (1967), a story about old age and the necessity of saying good-bye to the lands of the imagination; and *Mr Bliss*, a comic picture book about an eccentric driver, published posthumously in 1982. During the last years of his life, Tolkien was working on *The Silmarillion*, a "prequel" to *The Lord of the Rings* which was completed by his son, Christopher, and eventually published in 1977.

For Further Reading

Tolkien, J.R.R. *The Hobbit*. Boston: Houghton Mifflin, 1988.

———. *The Lord of the Rings*. Boston: Houghton Mifflin, 1991.

TOLSTOY'S FAIRY TALES AND PARABLES

Tales created or retold for children by Russian author Leo Tolstoy (1828–1910). Leo Tolstoy not only was responsible for writing such novels as *Anna Karenina* and *War and Peace* but also for several hundred FAIRY TALES, PARABLES, stories, and realistic ANIMAL tales, which he wrote for children. As a young unmarried man, Tolstoy became concerned with the education of children, and as he traveled in Europe, he became acquainted with and impressed by the French philosopher Jean Jacques Rousseau's theories of early childhood education. When he returned to his estate in Russia, he opened a school for the peasant children, which he then administered and taught in. During this time, he decided to write readers for children of all classes, as he became aware that in order to interest children in reading, their earliest readers must be well-written and engaging. His goal was to write what he called his *New Alphabet*, which would include tales written "beautifully, with brevity, simplicity, and above all, with clarity." Because children would receive their "first poetic impressions" from these books that would be used to teach generations of Russian children, he hoped they would forever love literature and their lives would be enriched.

Many of the stories Tolstoy wrote involve morals or appear to be parables. In "The Hen and Her Chicks," for example, a hen is having trouble taking care of her chicks and she encourages them to crawl back into their shells, where she knows how to sit on them as before they were born. Although the chicks try to do this, they cannot, for their wings become crushed. At the end of this short tale, one chick says to his mother, "If you now want us to stay in our shells all the time, you shouldn't have hatched us." The tale works for both children and adults, suggesting to children that they have to grow up and cannot crawl back into the womb for safety and suggesting to parents that they must let their children grow and learn how to care for them at each new stage.

In the tale called "The Bat," a war is being waged between the birds and the beasts. When the birds are winning, the Bat, who can also fly, goes over to the side of the birds and calls itself a bird. When the beasts are winning, the Bat claims to be a beast as it, too, has paws, teeth, and teats. When the birds win, however, they are disgusted with the Bat and will not let it join them. As a result, the Bat has to live in caves and tree hollows and only fly at night when the birds sleep. The tale's moral teaches children to be what one is, not to switch sides simply to be on the winning side. The Bat's disloyalty causes it to be ostracized. In a similar tale of the California Modoc Indian tribe, also called "The Bat," the birds and the beasts confer at the end of their battle, and both sides choose to ostracize the Bat, who will never have any friends thereafter.

In the fairy tale "The Two Brothers," two journeying brothers come upon a stone that gives written directions for finding one's luck. While the younger brother is eager to set off at the stone's bidding, believing in the proverb "no water flows under a sitting rock," the older brother is skeptical and believes in choosing a safer path, for "a bird in the hand is worth two in the bush." The brothers part ways, and the younger brother fortuitously becomes a KING for five years until his land is invaded. Meanwhile, the older brother has been quietly living in a village where he is neither rich nor poor. After losing his throne, the younger brother rejoins his elder brother, who is now more certain than ever that he has chosen the right path, given all the trouble his younger brother has experienced. But the younger brother still believes he has chosen the right path and that at least he has something worth remembering. This story may be seen as an example of the younger brother responding to the HERO's call to action, and the elder brother exemplifying the REFUSAL OF THE CALL.

For Further Reading

Tolstoy, Leo. *Fables and Fairy Tales*. Translated by Ann Dunnigan. New York: New American Library, 1962.

———. *Twenty-Two Russian Tales for Young Children*. Selected and translated by Miriam Morton. Illustrated by Eros Keith. New York: Simon and Schuster, 1969.

TOM THUMB

Diminutive HERO of FAIRY TALES. The GRIMM BROTHERS included a version in their collections (usually translated as "Thumbling" or "Thickasathumb"). In Charles Perrault's more violent 1697 story, the thumbling tricks a GIANT into beheading his seven daughters— as illustrated by Gustave Doré (*see* PERRAULT, CHARLES). A Danish story, "Svend Tomling," may be the basis for the English version.

The History of Tom Thumbe, the Little, for his small statue surnamed, King Arthurs Dwarfe was published as a chapbook in London in 1621 by Richard Johnson, a writer of popular literature. Probably printed earlier, it was certainly based on earlier oral tradition and drawn from multiple LEGENDS. Johnson made King ARTHUR central to the tale, a common addition at that time. He also included Gargantua—a character from François Rabelais's sixteenth-century satire *Gargantua and Pantagruel*—in his story.

Children's stories such as this were frowned upon by the British aristocracy and pious people as too vulgar for young minds. Nevertheless, the peasantry and children of all classes loved fairy tales and they endured.

Soon after the publication of Johnson's chapbook, the Tom Thumb character appeared in Ben Jonson's *The Fortunate Isles and their Union* (1624) and in Michael Drayton's *Nimphidia, the Court of Fayrie* (1627). Henry Fielding's satirical *Tom Thumb* was produced in London in 1730. And an American collection of NURSERY RHYMES entitled *Tommy Thumb's Song-Book* was published in 1794.

Children of the early eighteenth century read unexpurgated versions of books such as Swift's *Gulliver's Travels*. In his preface to *Tom Thumbe* in *Classics of Children's Literature,* Michael Patrick Hearn suggests that perhaps "Gulliver among the Lilliputians" owes something to Johnson's chapbook. For example, Gargantua boasts that he can drown a town with his urine, and Gulliver puts out a fire and nearly drowns a palace the same way.

Under the force of nineteenth-century Victorian progressive education, Tom Thumb stories, like other fairy tales, were made kinder and gentler. Tom was rescued by his mother before he could be swallowed by her cow and the giants were generally left out altogether.

In the basic story, a woodcutter and his wife longed for a child, even if it was no bigger than a thumb. Their wishes were soon granted—in Johnson's version by MERLIN himself. Enduring various adventures due to his small size, the child nevertheless prospered. On one occasion he was eaten by his mother's red cow. On another, he was carried away by a raven and dropped into the chimney of a giant. Escaping there, Tom became a courtier at the court of King Arthur, was made the godson of the Queene of Fairies, and spoke with Gargantua.

In the Grimm Brothers's version, Thumbling's father was offered a good price for his tiny son by two strangers he met in the woods. Thumbling told him to take the money, promising that he would soon be back. Though he was swallowed by a cow and had other adventures, he eventually returned home in the belly of a wolf. His father killed the wolf and the family was reunited.

A 1958 MGM movie musical of *Tom Thumb* starred Russ Tamblyn, and children's books continue to expand on the adventures of the tiny hero. Charles Sherwood Stratton, a midget and sideshow attraction at P. T. Barnum's circus, was called "General Tom Thumb."

Tiny people in other stories include Lewis Carroll's Alice during part of her adventures in Wonderland, Hans Christian Andersen's *Thumbelina* (*see* ANDERSEN, HANS CHRISTIAN), and Mary Norton's *The Borrowers. See also* DWARFS, LEPRECHAUNS.

For Further Reading

Andersen, Hans Christian. *Thumbelina.* Kansas City, MO: Andrews and McMeel, 1991.

Grimms' Tales for Young and Old: The Complete Stories. Translated by Ralph Manheim. New York: Doubleday, 1977.

Hearn, Michael Patrick. Preface to "The History of Tom Thumbe." *Classics of Children's Literature, 1621-1932.* Selected and arranged by Alison Lurie and Justin G. Schiller. New York: Garland Publishing, 1977.

Johnson, A.E., et al., trans. *Perrault's Complete Fairy Tales.* New York: Dodd, Mead, 1961.

Norton, Mary. *The Borrowers.* San Diego: Harcourt Brace Jovanovich, 1991.

Tatar, Maria. *The Hard Facts of the Grimms' Fairy Tales.* Princeton: Princeton University Press, 1987.

TONGUE TWISTER

Genre of FOLKLORE. The goal of the tongue twister is to pronunciate perfectly while simultaneously rapidly articulating and repeating alliterative words and phrases. Although there are no established "rules" for the creation of tongue twisters, a challenging paradigm of this genre will employ words or phrases that share an alliterative relationship, such as "she sells sea shells by the sea shore" or "Peter Piper picked a peck of pickled peppers . . ." Tongue twisters generally function as entertainment or pranks; the case of the latter is to make the victim mispronounce the tongue twister, usually resulting in the utterance of a profane or embarrassing word. Tongue twisters are also repeatedly employed by those who wish to improve pronunciation and articulation skills. For these reasons, the tongue twister is a popular genre of speech play in many cultures, especially amongst children.

TORTOISE

One of the main characters of West African and African American FOLKLORE. As an animal TRICKSTER figure like HARE and SPIDER, Tortoise figures in the myths and tales of Calabar, Ikom, and Yorubaland (Nigeria). He always is described as weak and slow but clever, as in the tales "The Elephant, the Tortoise, and the Hare," which is similar to the Western FABLE "The Tortoise and the Hare"; "Tortoise and the Singing Crab"; and "Tortoise Buys a House." His association with music, especially hypnotic magical music, is illustrated in the Ga tale of Ghana, "Why Singing Tortoises are Solitary" and the Yoruba "How Tortoise Got Water," as well as the above-mentioned Vane Avatime tale from Ghana, "Tortoise and the Singing Crab."

One of the most well-known tales featuring Tortoise as clever trickster is the Nigerian Igbo tortoise tale, "Tortoise and His Creditors." It is the story of how an old Tortoise who is too poor to get married has to manage somehow to find money for a bride price, since in his village any male who has not married by the age of 50 is put to death. Tortoise has little time left, so he manages to convince his closest friends, the Cockroach, the Fox, the Cock, and the Hunter, to lend him the money, which he will repay with interest at a set date. He then finds a bride, pays the price, marries her, and settles into his new life.

When the day comes for Tortoise's four friends to be repaid, Tortoise is busy gardening. First Cockroach arrives, and Tortoise asks him to wait inside the house. A bit later the Cock arrives, asks to be repaid, and is told to wait inside the house as well. However, when he sees the Cockroach, he immediately eats him. When Fox arrives and is also sent to wait in the house, he sees Cock and has a feast. Then the Hunter appears, is directed inside, sees the Fox, and shoots him dead.

Just then Tortoise enters, and he realizes what has transpired. Hunter is so pleased with killing the fox, for he has been yearning for a fox skin, that he ends up offering Tortoise money for the Fox's skin. Cleverly, Tortoise suggests that they split the carcass and that the Hunter can have the Fox's skin in repayment for the loan. The Hunter thinks it is a generous exchange indeed. Thus Tortoise triumphs. *See also* ANIMALS.

For Further Reading

Abrahams Roger. *African Folktales*. New York: Pantheon, 1983.

Berry, Jack. *West African Folk Tales*. Evanston, IL: Northwestern University Press, 1991.

Stevens, Janet. *The Tortoise and the Hare: An Aesop's Fable*. New York: Holiday House, 1984.

THE TORTOISE AND THE HARE

One of AESOP's most famous FABLES, adapted by Jean de la Fontaine, who used Aesop as his major source (*see* LA FONTAIN, JEAN DE). As in all of La Fontaine's fables, ANIMALS take the part of humans, and a moral is presented at the end of the story.

In La Fontaine's "The Tortoise and the Hare," the tortoise challenges the HARE to a race to a tree in the distance. The tortoise is certain he will win, which the hare finds extremely amusing, convinced that he can reach the tree in one hop. So sure of his ability to win, the hare even lets the tortoise get a head start. As the tortoise slowly plods along, the hare nibbles some grass and takes a nap. When the hare awakens, the tortoise is about to reach the tree. Quickly, the hare hops to the tree but he is too late. The tortoise is indeed the winner, and the moral of the story is "Slow and steady wins the race." As a lesson in focus, concentration, and perseverance, "The Tortoise and the Hare" is an appealing fable even today.

For Further Reading

Sewal, Roberta. *Five Fables of La Fontaine*. Illustrated by M. Boutet de Monevel. New York: The Grolier Society, 1967.

Stevens, Janet. *Tortoise and the Hare: An Aesop's Fable*. New York: Holiday House, 1984.

TOTEMISM

System of beliefs centering upon a mystical relationship. Totemism is not in itself a religion, although it may include the observance of certain rituals, practices, and prohibitions. (See, for example, the Ojibwa word *ototeman,* which roughly translates into "he is a relative of mine.") Rather totemism "is a system of beliefs and practices predicated upon the principle that there exists a kinship between an individual or clan and various natural objects, usually ANIMALS or plants. This natural object, called a totem, is regarded as a protective and generous mythical ancestor of the individual or tribal community. The relationship between the individual and the object is often at the center of oral tales from numerous cultures. It is considered taboo to touch, eat or kill the totem outside of certain sacrificial ceremonies. Totemism is found on a widespread scale throughout North and South America, Africa, Asia, and Australia.

It has been suggested that totemism is a stage in all cultural development, even in traditionally Western Christian religions, as exemplified by the reverence of such animals as the lamb and cattle by early Christian followers. It has also been suggested that individual totemism, which produced an intimate relationship between the individual and the totem, gave rise to totemism on a communal level, with individuals who shared similar totemic relationship being brought together.

The significance of totemism has been questioned by many twentieth-century theorists and anthropologists. Sigmund Freud (*see* FREUD, SIGMUND), from a psychoanalytic perspective, suggested that the taboo involved with the killing and eating of the totem, coupled with the endogamous or exogamous practices of the totemic community, are analogous to the Oedipal dilemma. Claude Levi-Strauss, writing from an anthropological point of view, questioned the validity of totemism as a unified practice (calling it a manifestation of hysteria), noting that the various behavioral patterns and practices associated with totemism varied between societies.

Perhaps the greatest misconception concerning totemism are the "totem poles," which are found primarily among American Indian communities. Totem poles do not represent the totem, but rather are grave markers which usually commemorate important events.

For Further Reading

Lang, Andrew. *The Secret of the Totem*. New York: AMS Press, 1970.

Levi-Strauss, Claude. *Totemism*. Boston: Beacon Press, 1963.

TRANSFORMATIONS

In MYTHS and FAIRY TALES, the act of metamorphosis from one form into another. The theme of transformation from one species or shape to another occurs in many mythologies and in FOLKLORE. Related to SHAPE-SHIFTING, transformations often happen not at will, whereas shape-shifters are generally WIZARDS, sorcerers, WITCHES, or fairies. In Greek mythology, the GODS of Olympos can transform themselves at will to appear as mortals or animals; in Polynesian mythology, MAUI—TRICKSTER, demi-god, and CULTURE HERO—transforms himself into a dove, an eagle, and a fish when he chooses.

Ovid's *Metamorphoses* focuses on transformation of gods and mortals in Greek and Roman mythology. Of the many cases of transformation that he includes, some of the most famous are the transformation of Daphne into a tree when she prays to the gods to be saved from APOLLO's pursuit; the NYMPH Syrinx's transformation into a reed after she prays for relief from the god Pan's pursuit; the transformation of ZEUS into a bull, a panther, then a serpent in his seduction of Semele; and the transformation of the aged, devoted husband and wife, Baucis and Philemon, into entwined trees in their death. In HOMER'S ODYSSEY, CIRCE transforms men into swine when they arrive on her island, and

ATHENA transforms Odysseus into a god-like man when he encounters his wife PENELOPE again after a 20-year hiatus.

In fairy tales, it is not uncommon to see a PRINCE transformed into a beast or animal, as in Charles Perrault's "BEAUTY AND THE BEAST" (*see* PERRAULT, CHARLES) or the GRIMM BROTHERS's "Snow-White and Rose-Red" and "The RAVEN." Often the love of a woman or man has the power to transform the beast back into his or her true self.

One of the most important recent treatments of this theme is Franz Kafka's *Metamorphosis*, where one morning Gregor Samsa awakens to find himself transformed into a cockroach. As in myths and fairy tales, Kafka's story suggests that the form into which one is transformed is some way related to some aspect of that person's personality or behavior.

For Further Reading

Ovid. *Metamorphoses.* Translated by Horace Gregory. New York: NAL Dutton, 1960.

Sax, Boria. *The Frog King: On Legends, Fables, Fairy Tales, and Anecdotes of Animals.* New York: Pace University Press, 1990.

TRAVERS, P. L. (1902–1996)

British author of *Mary Poppins* (1934) and its sequels as well as books on MYTH, FAIRY TALES, and stories. Pamela Lyndon Travers was born in Australia where she lived on a sugar plantation with her family, who encouraged reading and the life of the imagination. In her own words, she "grew up enthralled with fairy tales, myths, FOLKLORE, and LEGENDS" along with Shakespeare, Dickens, and the BIBLE, and she began writing at a very early age. In the 1920s she moved to England, where she lived on and off for a number of years. There she became a close friend of George William Russell—whose pseudonym was A.E.—and William Butler Yeats (*see* YEATS, WILLIAM BUTLER). Russell introduced her to the great Hindu epics, the RAMAYANA and the MAHABHARATA. Travers's poems and articles were published in *The Irish Statesman,* edited by Russell.

In 1934 Travers began writing about Mary Poppins, the famous magical British nanny, and her series of Mary Poppins books has always delighted children. When asked how she created such a character as Mary Poppins, she always claimed that Poppins discovered her, although in one account she claims that in telling stories to children, the figure of Mary Poppins emerged, and she began to write the stories down. One can recognize the influence of Zen Buddhism—of which Travers was a serious student—in the character of Mary Poppins.

Travers wrote many other books and articles, focusing on myth, fairy tale, and storytelling, and she served as a consulting editor and frequent contributor to *Parabola: The Magazine of Myth and Tradition* from 1976 until her death. In her poetic article "Lively Oracles," for example, she draws on NURSERY RHYMES; fairy tales such as "Sleeping Beauty," "THE GOOSE GIRL," "The Juniper Tree," and "RUMPLESTILZCHEN"; and mythology such as the semi-mythical Welsh BARD Taliesin; the Babylonian and Sumerian myths of INANNA and GILGAMESH; the Egyptian ISIS AND OSIRIS; the Hindu myths of DRAPAUDI, KRISHNA, ARJUNA, Rama, and Sita; the Japanese myths of AMERATSU; the Chinese myths surrounding Lao-Tzu; the Greek myths of Persephone and Demeter (*see* PERSEPHONE MYTH), HELEN OF TROY, and Odysseus (*see* ODYSSEY); and myths from the Norse, Mexico, the Australian Aborigines, Hawaii, Ireland, and England. By joining them all together using the archetype of the shadow as a thread running through this oracular narration, Travers shows the connection between the myths and stories of all cultures as well as her ability to tell a story. The first "children's writer" to be awarded the Order of the British Empire, Travers is also the author of the fictional *Friend Monkey* (1971), based on Hanuman, the Hindu MONKEY KING and *Two Pairs of Shoes* (1980), a retelling of two Middle Eastern tales. Her nonfiction includes *In Search of the Hero: The Continuing Relevance of Myth and Fairy Tale* (1970), *About the Sleeping Beauty* (1975), and *What the Bee Knows: Reflections on Myth, Symbol, and Story* (1989). The Walt Disney film version of *Mary Poppins,* which Travers felt included little of her original material, appeared in 1964.

For Further Reading

Travers, P. L. *Mary Poppins*. Rev. ed. New York: Dell: 1991.

————. *What the Bee Knows: Reflections on Myth, Symbol, and Story*. New York: Viking Penguin, 1991.

TRICKSTER

Dual-natured figure prevalent in oral traditions around the world. The trickster is usually male, lecherous, a cheat, careless about taboos, amoral, and outrageous. He can be human, semi-human, or take on an ANIMAL form which varies with the fauna of the area.

Tricksters clearly represent chaos and disorder. However, tricksters are also inventive and creative CULTURE HEROES who are often a great help to human beings.

Especially well-known trickster images include: the god Hermes and the Titan Prometheus in Greece; KRISHNA in India; LOKI in Northern Europe; REYNARD the Fox in medieval France; LEGBA, Eshu, ANANSI and SPIDER in West Africa; MAUI in Polynesia; and COYOTE, GREAT RABBIT or HARE, IKTOME, MANABOZHO, OLD MAN, RAVEN, and many others in Native American cultures.

The *Funk & Wagnalls Standard Dictionary of Folklore, Mythology, and Legend* states that "psychologically the role of the trickster seems to be that of projecting the insufficiencies of man in his universe onto a smaller creature who, in besting his larger adversaries, permits the satisfactions of an obvious identification to those who recount or listen to these tales." And Carl Jung describes the trickster as the epitome of the inferior traits of individual character.

However, in *The Masks of God: Primitive Mythology*, Joseph Campbell (*see* CAMPBELL, JOSEPH) observes that the "ambiguous, curiously fascinating figure" was the ARCHETYPE of the HERO, firebringer, and teacher in Paleolithic cultures. Campbell also notes that Prometheus was neither condemned nor mocked by Greek playwrights, "but offered, rather, as a tragic pattern of man's relationship to the governing powers of the natural universe." Judgment begins with the BIBLE, Campbell says, which "stands on the side of GOD and breaks not only man's will but the serpent's too."

Many tricksters are credited with such positive feats as creating the world or the people on it and giving fire to humanity. Prometheus, for example, stole fire from the GODS to give to the human beings he had created (*see* PROMETHEUS AND THE THEFT OF FIRE). In Native American stories, CREATION of the world and humanity is frequently credited to a trickster figure such as Coyote.

The trickster-hero often suffers for his gifts to humanity. Coyote and his kin die many times, though such DEATHS are never permanent. Sometimes Coyote pretends that he's merely been asleep, and he always returns, full of life, for the next adventure. Prometheus had to endure a more permanent sentence. Zeus had him chained naked to a pillar, where a vulture tore at his liver all day, every day. Prometheus healed every night, but he remained chained and was tormented again the next day.

In various stories, Coyote and friends stole fire or a fire-stone and gave it to human beings. In one case, seeing that the Fire People had fire, Coyote made a special headdress and visited them. He managed to set the headdress ablaze and ran away with it. He passed the blazing thing to Antelope, who passed it off to another animal, and so on in a relay. The Fire People caught and killed all the animals except Coyote, who gave the fire to a tree. Since then, people have been able to make fire-sticks from wood.

In another version, a little bird stole the fire-stone from Bear and passed it off to other animals in a similar relay. In fact, the same adventure is told all across North America, sometimes with Raven, Rabbit, or another trickster as the hero. A similar story—in which Kingfisher is the usual thief—is found in the myths of the Andamanese on a chain of remote islands in the Bay of Bengal.

In Native American stories, the trickster is often tricked and his attempts at practical jokes may fail, especially if they involve breaking taboos. The Native American trickster usually has a companion, such as Fox, Wolf, Wildcat, Porcupine, Badger, or Lynx. Sometimes the companion is a stooge, sometimes he outwits the trickster.

Many Native American tribes have taboos against the telling of trickster tales, especially at particular times of the year. There is generally no taboo against erotic trickster tales for mixed company, except in cases of later European influence.

In *American Indian Myths and Legends,* Richard Erdoes and Alfonso Ortiz quote the Sioux medicine man Lame Deer: "Coyote, IKTOME, and all CLOWNS are sacred. They are a necessary part of us. A people who have so much to cry about as Indians do also need their laughter to survive" (*see* ERDOES, RICHARD, ORTIZ, ALFONSO).

The trickster survives today in such figures as clowns, ELVES, and fools. Related figures are found in the animal FABLES of AESOP and Jean de la Fontaine (*see* LA FONTAINE, JEAN DE). An African rabbit-trickster became Brer Rabbit in the Southern United States.

Later tricksters range from Davy Crockett (*see* CROCKETT, DAVY) to Inspector Clouseau in "The Pink Panther" movies, and include a multitude of characters in animated cartoons. The DEVIL or Satan is sometimes regarded as a trickster figure. And in *Mythical Trickster Figures,* William J. Hynes and Thomas J. Steele describe the appearance of the Apostle Peter as a trickster in the Christian FOLKLORE of The Yaqui, Spanish, Mexican, and New Mexican cultures of the American Southwest. A story featuring the apostle-as-trickster also appears in Italo Calvino's *Italian Folktales* (*see* CALVINO, ITALO).

Some view the trickster as an example of how not to behave, thus a supporter of cultural norms. However, in *Mythical Trickster Figures,* Robert Pelton questions the assumption of a return to order after the trickster's antics. Instead, he says, "tricksters can prepare the way for adaptation, change, or even total replacement of the belief system. They are in this manner potential preludes to social change." *See also* SUSA-NO-WO.

For Further Reading

Ammons, Elizabeth, and Annette White-Parks, eds. *Tricksterism in Turn-of-the-Century American Literature: A Multicultural Perspective.* Hanover, NH: University Press of New England/Tufts University, 1994.

Basso, Ellen. *In Favor of Deceit: A Study of Tricksters in an Amazon Society.* Tucson, AZ: University of Arizona Press, 1987.

Bennett, Martin. *West African Trickster Tales.* Oxford University Press, 1994.

Roberts, John W. *From Trickster to Badman: The Black Folk Hero in Slavery and Freedom.* Philadelphia: University of Pennsylvania Press, 1989.

Welsch, Roger L. *Omaha Tribal Myths and Trickster Tales.* Chicago: Swallow Press, 1981.

TRISTAN AND ISOLDE

Arthurian SAGA featuring a conflict between love and honor, similar to that of LANCELOT and GUINEVERE. The LEGEND springs from Celtic oral tradition and was embellished during the medieval period. Malory included it in his *Morte d'Arthur.* The story has been retold through the ages, and Edward Arlington Robinson's *Tristam* won a Pulitzer prize in 1927.

A favorite at the court of his uncle, King Mark of Cornwall, Tristan was injured by a poisoned sword when he fought and killed an Irish GIANT. By chance, Tristan made his way to the only one who could cure him, Princess Isolde of Ireland—sister of the dead giant.

Cured, Tristan returned to the Cornish court. Later he is sent to persuade Isolde to become the bride of King Mark. But on the way back to Cornwall, the two young people mistakenly drink a love potion intended for the bride and groom. Under a powerful spell, Tristan and Isolde become lovers.

Isolde marries King Mark, but the two lovers keep in touch through various intrigues. Finally, Tristan travels abroad and marries a woman named Isolde of the White Hands. But unable to forget his true love, he refuses to consummate his marriage.

When Tristan again receives a poisoned wound in battle, he knows that only Isolde of Ireland could cure him. He sends a secret message to her by a ship captain. Upon his return, the captain is supposed to use white sails if Isolde is with him and black sails if she is not.

When the ship arrives, Tristan's wife lied, saying the sails were black. Heartbroken, Tristan dies before the ship landed. On seeing his corpse, Isolde of Ireland dies also.

The white/black sail confusion also appears in the Greek myth of THESEUS. *See also* ARTHUR, CELTIC STORYTELLING.

For Further Reading

Barber, Richard. *King Arthur: Hero and Legend.* Woodbridge, Suffolk: Boydell Press, 1986.

Bédlier, Joseph. *The Romance of Tristan and Iseult.* Translated by Hilaire Belloc and Paul Rosenfeld. Garden City, NY: Doubleday, 1956.

Eisner, Sigmund. *The Tristan Legend: A Study in Sources.* Evanston, IL: Northwestern University Press, 1969.

TROLLS

Hideous, hairy cannibals from northern European mythology that live in caverns or subterranean dwellings and are known for their propensity for stealing women, exchanging human children for their own offspring, and indulging in petty theft (*see* CHANGELINGS). In Norse LEGENDS, trolls are originally gigantic in size and have tremendous strength. One tale tells of a man on horseback who cannot reach with his whip to the bend of a female troll's knees while she is laying on the ground. Norse trolls appear only at night because sunlight either bursts them to pieces or turns them to stone. They have huge noses for smelling out human flesh and blood, which they crave. Because they are dimwitted, human beings often are able to outfox them. The Norse GODS frequently engage in battle with trolls.

In later storytelling traditions, trolls become small, DWARF-like beings. They characteristically have humped backs and red caps. They are not bloodthirsty, nor do they have great strength. They are, however, more intelligent than giant trolls, and can be equally as dangerous. They are skilled craftsmen and expert dancers. Trolls often possess beautiful wives and great riches.

One of the most famous trolls appears in the Norwegian folktale "Three Billy-Goats Gruff." In this story, three goats cross a bridge, beneath which lives a troll. The troll demands to know who is crossing his bridge. The youngest goat tells the troll not to eat him, but to wait for the next goat, who is fatter. The second goat says the same, but the third goat announces that he is the Big Billy-Goat Gruff and kills the troll.

TROUBADOUR

Lyric poet-musician, especially in the Provence region of southern France during the eleventh through the thirteenth centuries. Troubadour compositions were among the earliest forms of secular MUSIC.

Troubadours sang or chanted to tell stories. Their BALLADS celebrated chivalry and courtly love and made satirical commentaries on politics and morals. They also composed songs for special occasions. The language of romantic love was largely invented by troubadours, who addressed the objects of their affections in extravagant and even religious terms.

The ballad singers had a major effect on the development of European lyric poetry. Some scholars indicate that they changed European poetry forever by popularizing the subject matter, bringing new life to vernacular poetry, and creating complex new verse forms.

Troubadours were popular in the courts of Spain, Italy, and France. Similar wandering singer-storytellers were called *skalds* in Scandinavia, *minnesingers* in Germany, and *minstrels* in the British Isles (*see* MINSTRELSY).

The legends of CHARLEMAGNE, ROBIN HOOD, and ARTHUR were passed down in the ballads of troubadours and minstrels. Taillefer, an eleventh-century troubadour and soldier, was the first famous singer of the SONG OF ROLAND. He was killed when he led the Norman attack at the battle of Hastings. Other leading troubadours were Bertran de Born and Bernard de Bentadour, who appeared at the court of Eleanor of Aquitaine. *See also* ROMANCE.

For Further Reading

Akehurst, F. R. P., and Judith M. Davis, eds. *A Handbook of the Troubadours.* Los Angeles: University of California Press, 1995.

Bogin, Magda. *The Women Troubadours.* New York: Paddington Press, 1976.

Kendrick, Laura. *The Game of Love: Troubadour Wordplay.* Los Angeles: University of California Press, 1988.

Paterson, Linda M. *The World of the Troubadours: Medieval Occitan Society, c. 1100–c. 1300.* New York: Cambridge University Press, 1993.

TROY

City in the ancient world. It was situated on the coast of the Aegean sea in what is now Turkey. The war between Troy and Greece inspired much storytelling in classical times. The most notable of examples are the ILIAD and the ODYSSEY of HOMER; a number of Greek tragedies, particularly those of Euripides; and the EPIC AENEID by the Roman poet Virgil. In *The Greek Myths*, Robert Graves (*see* GRAVES, ROBERT) suggests that the subject matter is at least three centuries older than the *Iliad* and grew out of a recited poem called "The Wrath of Achilles."

According to legend—representing a blend of at least two oral traditions—Troy's first KING was Teucer, the son of the river Scamander. The Trojan War broke out several generations later, when Priam was king. Priam was married to Hecuba, and their children included the prophetess Cassandra, the HERO Hector, and the young PRINCE, Paris.

The war was instigated by an event known as "The Judgment of Paris." According to the story, Paris is called upon to decide which GODDESS is the most beautiful—HERA, ATHENA, or APHRODITE. Paris chooses Aphrodite, in no small part because she promises to give him the most beautiful woman in the world, HELEN OF TROY. Unfortunately Helen is already married to the Greek leader MENELAOS.

Paris kidnaps Helen while she is a guest in Menelaos's house. Menelaos forms an alliance among all the Greek cities, and their army sets sail to Troy.

The war rages for 10 years with neither side victorious. At last, the Greeks build a gigantic wooden horse, leave it outside the gates of Troy, then pretend to set sail for home. The Trojans, convinced that it had the power to make their city invincible and not knowing that its belly was filled with Greek soldiers, take the horse inside their walls. When night comes, the soldiers emerge and unlock the city gates. The Greek army pours in, and Troy quickly falls.

The behavior of the victors is hardly noble. To make certain there would be no heir to the Trojan throne, they throw Hector's wife, Andromache, and his young son from the walls of Troy. Then the Greeks divide up all the women of Troy—including those of the royal family—to serve as slaves and concubines. Finally, they burn the city to the ground.

From Homer on, Greek poets and storytellers treated the Trojans with remarkable sympathy. The blame for the war was placed firmly on certain individuals—Paris, Helen, and the goddesses who vied for Paris's favor. As a rule, the behavior of the Trojans throughout the war was portrayed as more exemplary than that of the Greeks. This is especially true in the works of Euripides, whose tragedy *The Trojan Women* was an undisguised protest against recent Athenian war atrocities.

This sympathetic treatment made it desirable for later civilizations to trace their lineage from Troy. In Virgil's *Aeneid,* the Trojan hero Aeneas escapes Troy's destruction to found the civilization of Rome. And as late as the Elizabethan Age, the British also claimed their origins in the bloodline of Aeneas.

By the nineteenth century A.D., few scholars really believed that Troy had existed. All this was changed by the archeologist Heinrich Schliemann (1822–90), who discovered ancient ruins on the Turkish coast of the Aegean. Subsequent excavation has proved that this was, indeed, the site of Troy. Moreover, a massive war between this city and Greece actually took place during the twelfth century B.C. The history of these discoveries is the subject of Michael Wood's book *In Search of the Trojan War. See also* ANCIENT GREEK STORYTELLING.

For Further Reading

Graves, Robert. *The Greek Myths.* 2 vols. New York: Penguin Books, 1957.

Hamilton, Edith. *Mythology: Timeless Tales of Gods and Heroes.* New York: Mentor, 1969.

Wood, Michael. *In Search of the Trojan War.* New York: New American Library, 1985.

THE TURKEY AND THE ANT

Poetic FABLE by John Gay (1685–1732). Fable 38 of the two-volume collection, *Fables*, published by John Gay in 1727 and 1738, "The Turkey and the Ant" treats the theme of finding fault with others but not ourselves, where "Each little speck and blemish find,/To our own stronger errors blind." Gay illustrates the theme with the story of a Turkey who gets tired of "common food," leaving the barn and heading toward the wood with her infant turkeys trailing behind her. As she comes upon an anthill, she tell her baby birds to feast on the ants. With that, she breaks into a complaint, saying that their lives would be blessed if they could escape "the poult'rer's knife." In a somewhat humorous passage, the mother Turkey complains how Christmas "shortens all our days" and goes on to describe the ways turkeys are cooked at Christmas. In her mind, the worst of the seven deadly sins is gluttony. However, the Ant who has climbed up out of the heap then speaks, chastising the Turkey: "Ere you christmas another's sin,/Bid thy own conscience look within./Controul thy more voracious bill/Nor for a breakfast nations kill." The Turkey has not seen her place in the food chain, nor has she considered the biblical advice, "Do unto others as you would have them to unto you." Ultimately, the small and lowly Ant teaches the proud Turkey a lesson.

TWAIN, MARK (1835–1910)

Pen name of Samuel Langhorne Clemens, journalist, story writer, novelist, and lecturer. Steeped in American dialects and FOLKLORE, Twain's writings were the first to accurately reflect the sounds and rhythms of American speech.

Twain grew up along the Mississippi River and traveled widely during his youth, working as a printer, miner, and steamboat pilot. His famous short story "The Celebrated Jumping Frog of Calaveras County" (1865) established him as a humorist. Other early works include *Roughing It* (1872), reminiscences of Twain's western adventures, and *The Adventures of Tom Sawyer* (1876), inspired by his own childhood.

Twain's mature works embrace larger themes. *The Adventures of Huckleberry Finn* (1884), told from the viewpoint of an outcast boy helping a runaway slave, is a ruthless critique of human society. *A Connecticut Yankee in King Arthur's Court* (1889), *The Tragedy of Pudd'nhead Wilson* (1894), and *The Man that Corrupted Hadleyburg* (1900) are also powerful and penetrating. Personal tragedy, financial misfortunes, and keen understanding of his own time made Twain's later works increasingly pessimistic.

Young readers should be encouraged to read Twain's writings for a true sense of the man and his work. Far from the commonly portrayed sentimental old eccentric, Twain became a cultural incendiary, bent on nothing less than the abolition of conscience, morality, and civilization—in favor of a decent human heart.

For Further Reading

De Voto, Bernard, ed. *The Portable Mark Twain*. New York: Penguin, 1997.

Emerson, Everett. *The Authentic Mark Twain: A Literary Biography of Samuel L. Clemens*. Philadelphia: University of Pennsylvania Press, 1984.

Kaplan, Justin. *Mark Twain and His World*. New York: Simon & Schuster, 1974.

Rasmussen, R. Kent. *Mark Twain A to Z: The Essential Reference to His Life and Writings*. New York: Facts on File, 1995.

Twain, Mark. *The Notorious Jumping Frog and Selected Works*. Des Moines, IA: Perfection Learning, 1991.

TWENTY-FIVE TALES OF A VETALA

Also known as *Vetâla-pañcavimsatika*, one of a number of seventh- and eighth-century A.D. Sanskrit texts derived from the traditional PANCHATANTRA, compiled by Vishnusarman for the enlightenment of a king's sons, and the most famous Sanskrit collection of stories.

The *vetala* in Hindu belief is an evil spirit that haunts cemeteries and animates dead bodies. Represented with hands and feet turned backwards and hair standing on end, the vetala stands in human form guarding the Deccan villages. There he occupies either a stone smeared with red paint or one of the stones in prehistoric stone circles scattered over the hills. He makes his appearance in the FOLKTALES as a mischievous DEMON, continually ready to play a practical joke on the unsuspecting.

Considered to be the "chief source of the world's fable literature," the *Panchatantra,* from which the *Twenty-Five Tales of a Vetala* originate, exists today in more than 200 different versions and in 50 languages. Similar tales, in fact, appear in The THOUSAND AND ONE NIGHTS, in Boccaccio's *Decameron,* and in the FAIRY TALES of Hans Christian Andersen (*see* ANDERSEN, HANS CHRISTIAN) and the FABLES of Jean de la Fontaine (*see* LA FONTAINE, JEAN DE).

The tales journeyed to the West through Persian, Arabic, Syrian, Hebrew, and Latin translations while also making far-reaching excursions to Southeast and East Asia. The Arabic version of the *Panchatantra* is the *Kalila wa Dimnah.* The modern Persian tales are the *Anwar-u Suhaili* and the *Iyar-i Danish;* and the English version is known as the *Fables of Bidpai.* Similar Sanskrit texts that are derived from the original *Panchatantra* include *Sukasaptati* or *The Seventy Stories of a Parrot* and *Simhasana-dvatrim-satika* or *Thirty-two Stories of a Royal Throne.*

The *Panchatantra* itself and its versions, including collections of tales such as the *Twenty-Five Tales of a Vetala,* are the chief mediums in the transmission of stories and MOTIFS from India to the oral traditions of Ceylon, Burma, Malaya, Thailand, Cambodia, Indonesia, Tibet, central Asia, China, Iran, Arabia, and Europe.

As A. K. Ramanujan (*see* RAMANUJAN, A.K.) has explained, roughly speaking, there are two separate bodies of FOLKLORE from India. The first derives from the ancient Sanskrit texts, which first existed in oral form. These works consist of the Vedic texts and sacrificial rituals, the EPICS, and the mythologies of the pan-Indian divinities like VISHNU, SIVA, and the GODDESS. The second category of literature comes out of the hundreds of regional languages and dialects with their own literatures, folk traditions, local gods, and sacrifices, which are often assimilated or connected by new MYTHS to the pan-Indian ones.

The two traditions often are versions of each other, however, and are constantly interwoven, one with the other. For one thing, Sanskrit authors were bilingual, able to write formal Sanskrit but also able to speak a regional dialect. For this reason, they not only created original Sanskrit works but also transferred the stories they heard in their own dialect into Sanskrit to be saved for posterity and for others outside their regions. Clearly, as one of the greatest early collections, the *Panchatantra* came into existence in this way. What's more, coming out of oral tradition as they had, the tales, though written down at some point in the seventh or eighth century, remained alive, as stories to be told rather than read, and continued to be carried by the people of the villages and retold from generation to generation.

The earliest collection and translation of these oral tales still circulating in India began over a hundred years ago with Mary Frere's *Old Deccan Days,* published in England in 1868 and soon translated into several European languages. Since then, a multitude of books and tales have been published, reflecting a zeal for folklore collection that began with travelers, missionaries, civil servants, and their wives and daughters, and moved on to philologists and comparativists and finally became a part of ethnographic research and a separate discipline called "folklore." The tales of India, including *The Twenty-Five Tales of a Vetala* now appear in both scholarly and popular versions. Among the collections of scholarly versions of the vetala tales are *Vetalapancavimsati: Vikram and the Vampire or Tales of Hindu Devilry,* a Hindi version translated into English by Sir Richard Burton; and *Vetalapancavimsati: Tibetan Fairy Tales of the Vetala.*

For Further Reading

Frere, Mary. *Old Deccan Days: Or Hindu Fairy Legends Current in Southern India.* 1868. London: John Murray. Reprint, New York: Dover, 1967.

TWO-HEADED SNAKE

Moralistic Iroquois tale of a thankless serpent. This tale belongs to the Seneca and Mohawk tribes of the Iroquois, and an early version of it is set on New York's Canandaigua Lake, where in the late nineteenth century a sea serpent hoax occurred, probably based on a mixture of this MYTH and the tales of the Scottish Loch Ness MONSTER.

The tale relates the story of a boy named Hahjonah who finds a beautiful, two-headed snake that is ill. Hahjonah takes the snake to his home, feeds it and cares for it, and considers it a friend. But as the snake grows to its full enormous size, it begins to hypnotize the children of the village who come to look at it while Hahjonah is out hunting for food for the snake. When it then swallows one of the children whole, the snake disappears. Hahjonah hardly notices because the village is preoccupied with a more upsetting event: each day children are missing, and the other children seem as if they are sleep-walking. Hahjonah then dreams that a great water bird, his spirit protector, speaks to him, saying "Beware the eyes of false friends" (see DIVINE SIGNS).

Hahjonah leaves the next morning and finds the serpent, who is indeed the devourer of the children. The stockade surrounding the village is closed to prevent the children from leaving, the serpent surrounds the village, and everyone tries to kill him but fails. Finally, Hahjonah is instructed by his great water bird spirit in a second dream the way to slay the serpent, which involves dipping his arrow point in magical medicine. He then confronts the snake, who ignores Hahjonah's questions as to how the snake can betray them. Hahjonah then knows what to do and slays the monster with his magic arrow. All the children's heads fall out of his mouth and become the fish of the lake.

This tale teaches the moral that "you must remember to treat with gratitude those who helped you when you were weak." *See also* MONSTER KILLED FROM WITHIN, TRANSFORMATIONS.

UCHIDA, YOSHIKO (1921–1992)

Asian American author of children and adult books. Uchida is best known for her Japanese FOLKTALES that allude to her family's incarceration after the bombing of Pearl Harbor. While many of her children's stories do not explicitly dramatize her own experience in the guarded camps, they do encourage young Asian American readers to heighten their self-esteem and self-knowledge. Volumes such as *The Dancing Kettle and Other Japanese Folktales* (1949), *New Friends for Susan* (1951), *The Magic Listening Cap—More Folk Tales from Japan* (1955), and *The Full Circle* (1957) convey Uchida's desire to break stereotypical images long held by non-Asians about the Japanese and instead provide realistic portrayals of Japanese life. Most of Uchida's books are richly illustrated, often by the author herself. Some of Uchida's stories, for example, *The Old Man with the Bump* (1973), are recorded on cassette tapes to further enhance the storytelling experience.

UNCLE REMUS

Fictional storyteller. Uncle Remus is the name given to the storyteller of the African American FOLKLORE compiled by Joel Chandler Harris during the nineteenth century (*see* HARRIS, JOEL CHANDLER). Folklorists consider Harris's interpretations, taken from international FOLKTALES, to be the first compilation of authentic African American folklore. Harris created Uncle Remus from a composite sketch of the slaves he knew while working as an assistant editor of the *Atlanta Constitution*. Originally, Uncle Remus was a voice only, describing the conditions encountered by the freedmen living in the postwar South. However, Uncle Remus was soon transformed into a plantation storyteller, specializing in telling FABLES with ANIMALS to the son of the plantation owner.

Uncle Remus is a wise, humorous narrator who has encountered and survived the hardships of Southern slavery. In many of his tales, the animal protagonist, usually Brer

Rabbit, outwits his nemesis, most often Brer Fox, as the weak triumph over the strong. In "Brother Rabbit's Laughing-Place," Brer Rabbit tells the other animals about a place he visits when he needs a good laugh. The other animals, led by Brer Fox, want to acquire a laughing-place of their own. Brer Fox is selected by the other animals to be the first to discover his laughing-place, which Brer Rabbit has promised to show him. However, the TRICKSTER Brer Rabbit, intent upon gaining revenge against Brer Fox for a previous act of malevolence, leads the unsuspecting party to a briar patch, inhabited by colony of bees. Brer Fox jumps into the patch, only to have the beehive fall onto his head. It is at this point that Brer Fox learns that this is Brer Rabbit's laughing-place. Explaining the importance of such themes as revenge, cunning, and self-preservation, Uncle Remus defends Brer Rabbit's often malicious and violent behavior. Perhaps the most famous of these tales include the fables of "The Big Wind," "Brer Rabbit and the Briar Patch," and "Brer Rabbit and the TAR BABY."

Because he lacks the traditional attributes of power within the animal kingdom—size, strength, excessive speed, or large jaws—Brer Rabbit relies upon the skillful manipulation of language as his principle asset. While the rabbit pretends to be obsequious and respectful, he constantly undermines the enslaving practices of the larger animals.

Historians suggest that the Brer Rabbit tales can be read as a representation of the slave community. Like the slaves, Brer Rabbit is disempowered by the mainstream culture and is forced to subvert this cruel power structure to his own ends.

Although Harris's collections of the Uncle Remus stories are revered as the first authentic collections of African American folklore, Harris's characterization of the Uncle Remus character has received sharp criticism, especially among African America critics. In *The Journey Back* (1890), Houston A. Baker, noting that many proslavery advocates argued for the eternal enslavement of Africans because they were apparently trapped at an in-

fantile stage of development, argues that Harris "continued this impulse by making his Uncle Remus a childlike figure whose designated audience was white plantation children." In this sense, Harris's Uncle Remus was not an authentic "black voice"; rather, he was an infantilized fictional creation to perpetuate proslavery ideologies.

In recent years, Brer Rabbit has intrigued a number of contemporary novelists: Most notably, Toni Morrison's *Tar Baby* (1981) plays overtly with this theme. References can also be found in the works of Ralph Ellison, Paule Marshall, and Ishmael Reed, and critic Henry Louis Gates, Jr. has addressed the topic at some length, as has historian Sterling Stuckey. Brer Rabbit remains a vital force in both folk culture and in AFRICAN AMERICAN STORYTELLING.

For Further Reading

Harris, Joel Chandler. *The Complete Tales of Uncle Remus.* Boston: Houghton Mifflin, 1955.

Lester, Julius. *Tales From Uncle Remus: The Adventures of Brer Rabbit.* Illustrated by Jerry Pinkney. New York: Dial, 1987.

UNICORN

Mythical creature that has many forms depending on the culture in which it is found; in the West, the unicorn is most often depicted as a small, white horse with the beard of a goat, cloven feet, and a spiraled horn projecting from the middle of its forehead.

Unicorns are rare creatures that live in distant lands. They are independent and fond of solitude. They are also noble and possess great strength and speed. Their horns have miraculous powers. When attacked, unicorns are extremely fierce and very difficult, if not impossible, to catch. Only virgins may capture unicorns. Elephants and lions are their traditional enemies.

Unicorns were included in certain translations of the BIBLE, thus becoming imbued with important symbolic meanings. In eight different passages found in the King James Version of the Bible, the unicorn is pictured as an untamable ANIMAL of great strength and fierceness.

The unicorn's inclusion in *Physiologus*, an allegorical bestiary probably written between the second and fourth centuries, also increased its importance. In *Physiologus*, the unicorn is described as a small animal that resembles a young goat and has a single horn in the center of its head. This work was translated into a variety of languages and profoundly influenced the literature and the art of the Middle Ages. The earliest known story of a virgin's capture of a unicorn appears here. According to the various versions of *Physiologus*, the hunters take a virgin to the place where unicorns are supposed to be. Unicorns become meek and gentle in the presence of a virgin. The unicorn approaches the virgin and climbs into her lap. Then the unicorn is taken to the palace of the king. If the woman is not a virgin, the unicorn will know and will kill her with its horn.

In western cultures, unicorns traditionally have had both negative and positive associations. They symbolize courage, nobility, and virtue, as well as chastity and purity. They are likened to Christ, and their horns symbolize his power and the oneness of the FATHER and the Son. In addition, unicorns were associated with kings. Perhaps the best-known use of unicorns in this context appears in the British Royal Arms. Yet, unicorns also represent lust, pride, wrath, and destructive forces. The unicorn is a virile animal whose horn is a phallic symbol. Unicorns might also represent the DEVIL, DEATH, and infernal regions.

In some legends, a unicorn can purify water by dipping its horn into it. The horn also can detect poison and counteract it; this is why people drank from cups or goblets made of unicorn horn. In addition to acting as a general cure-all, the horn is said to prolong youth and stimulate sexual desire.

Unicorn traditions are considerably different in non-Western cultures. The Chinese have several kinds of unicorns. The *ki-lin* is the most popular. Its body is usually that of a deer, but may be that of a horse or another creature. The head may be like that of a deer, a lion, or another animal. The ki-lin might have an ox's tail or one from another crea-

ture. It may or may not have scales. It may have one or two horns, which might be fleshy or have a fleshy tip. The ki-lin is supposed to combine both male and female attributes, although it can exist in the male form (*ki*), or in the female form (*lin*). The ki-lin is always benevolent and is associated with wisdom, justice, and rectitude. Like its Western counterpart, the ki-lin likes solitude and cannot be caught by hunters. Unlike the Western unicorn, the ki-lin's horn has no special powers. Along with the DRAGON, the PHOENIX, and the TORTOISE, the ki-lin is considered one of the four intelligent creatures.

The Japanese have two types of unicorns: the *kirin*, which is based on the ki-lin, and the *sin-you*, which has lionlike features and can distinguish innocence from guilt.

In Muslim traditions, the unicorn is known as the *karkadan*, a fierce creature. The karkadan often has bovine form, although it can have other forms. It is sometimes winged. The literature of ancient Persia tells of the three-legged ass, which has a white body, six eyes, nine mouths, and a hollow, golden horn. This creature can use its horn to purify any uncleanliness in water. Sea unicorns may have the body of a large fish or a whale.

Unicorns often appear in works of modern fantasy and in children's literature. They are usually linked with enchantment and magic, and they often appear suddenly and unexpectedly to humans. Frequently, they create feelings of wonder and astonishment. Relatively modern works that contain the unicorn in some way include the GRIMM BROTHERS's "The Brave Little Tailor," Lewis Carroll's *Through the Looking-Glass*, Lord Dunsay's *The King of Elfland's Daughter*, C. S. Lewis's *The Last Battle*, Alan Garner's *Elidor*, Peter S. Beagle's *The Last Unicorn*, whose main character is a female unicorn, Madeleine L'Engle's *A Swiftly Tilting Planet*, and James Thurber's tale "The Unicorn in the Garden." *Unicorns!* is a 1982 anthology containing 16 stories about unicorns by modern writers.

For Further Reading

Ada, Alma Flor. *The Unicorn of the West*. New York: Atheneum, 1994.

Preussler, Otfried. *The Tale of the Unicorn.* New York: Dial, 1989.

URASHIMA TARO

Fisher boy in Japanese FOLKLORE. Urashima Taro marries a MERMAID and goes to live in a beautiful palace far below the waves. Despite his pleasure in his married life, Urashima Taro yearns to see his parents once again. In order to do this, his wife gives him a casket, which he is not to open if he wants to return safely to his home beneath the sea. When he returns to his home, he is greatly upset to find that many centuries have passed. In his dismay, he disobeys his wife and opens the casket. Immediately, a puff of white smoke comes out of the casket and floats toward the SEA. Urashima Taro is overcome by a cold WIND, and he is transformed first into a very old man and then into a corpse. To this day, a shrine dedicated to Urashima Taro can be found on the coast of Tango. This tale shares a similar MOTIF with Washington Irving's "RIP VAN WINKLE." *See also* JAPANESE STORYTELLING.

For Further Reading

Sakade, Florence, ed. *Urashima Taro and Other Japanese Children's Stories.* Boston: C.E. Tuttle, 1958.

URBAN FOLKLORE

Stories passed around orally about fantastic or quirky events in contemporary life, told as if the story was true. The term "urban LEGENDS" is also used for these persistent tales told in virtually all parts of the United States, England, and in many other countries as well. Similar apocryphal stories are sometimes called contemporary legends, modern MYTHS, mercantile legends, corporate legends, and by other names according to their setting. Author John McPhee coined the term *asmut* or "apocryphal story much told" for similar sailors' tales.

Like other FOLKLORE, urban stories are made pertinent to the specific community in which they are told. The themes reflect urban life and attitudes, though the events may take place in rural settings as well as in cities. Descriptions may be highly detailed and an actual location is usually identified. The storyteller claims that the events happened to a relative, a friend, or a friend of a friend—often mentioned by name. Sometimes the stories feature famous people, whose identities are likely to be updated from time to time. Although convincing, urban folklore generally cannot be verified. Some of the stories, however, may begin with vivid elaborations of actual events.

Urban legends are sometimes referred to as "dead cat stories"—referring to the many tales of cats poisoned by nibbling on an entree or boxed for burial and stolen by unwitting thieves. Other persistent themes include the VANISHING HITCHHIKER and the alligator in the sewers.

Urban folklore might be thought of as contemporary TALL TALES—but without the HEROES. These are stories about bizarre things happening *to* people rather than about people undertaking great adventures.

For Further Reading

Brunvand, Jan Harold. *The Baby Train and Other Lusty Urban Legends.* New York: W.W. Norton, 1993.

———. *The Vanishing Hitchhiker: American Urban Legends & Their Meanings.* New York: W.W. Norton, 1981.

URUK

Ancient city, which lay between the Tigris and Euphrates river in Mesopotamia, founded in the fifth millennium B.C., or shortly after the quasi-mythic, quasi-historical FLOOD. It is mentioned in the BIBLE by the name of Erech. Its most famous KING was the title character of the EPIC *of* GILGAMESH. In a Sumerian list of kings—and also in the epic—Gilgamesh is cited as Uruk's fifth ruler.

Uruk was particularly famous for its massive walls and temples, which Gilgamesh was credited with building. These were destroyed when the Semites invaded the region and displaced the Sumerian civilization in c. 2000 B.C.

As the setting for Gilgamesh, the oldest surviving epic poem in any language, Uruk holds a unique and honored place in the history of Western storytelling.

For Further Reading

Sandars, N.K. *The Epic of Gilgamesh: An English Version with an Introduction.* London: Penguin Books, 1972.

VÄINÄMÖINEN

Wise, old figure from Finnish FOLKLORE, known for his skill at singing and playing the harp (*see* KALEVALA). The LEGEND of Väinämöinen comes from traditional Karelo-Finnish songs. Väinämöinen is depicted as a prophetic old man—he is conceived of as being old even at birth—as well as a gifted minstrel (*see also* ORPHEUS AND EURYDICE MYTH). His epithets, features characteristic of traditional Finnish poetry, are "steadfast old" and "eternal sage" (*see* WISE OLD MAN). Väinämöinen is mighty, clever, and a CULTURE HERO.

In the myth of Finnish CREATION, Väinämöinen, the first man, is born of Ilmatar, the virgin air spirit. His FATHER is the SEA. He swims on the sea for years until he lands on a treeless land. A young boy sows the seeds of various plants all over the land. An oak tree grows so large that it blocks the light of the SUN and the MOON. After Väinämöinen's plea for help, Ilmatar sends a water spirit, a tiny man who transforms into a GIANT, to fell the oak tree and restore light to the land.

Väinämöinen clears a tract of land, leaving one tree standing for birds to perch on. As a gift of appreciation, an eagle gives fire to Väinämöinen, who burns the land and sows barley seeds.

One famous song about Väinämöinen describes his courtship of Aino. After Väinämöinen is challenged to a duel by Aino's brother, Joukahainen, he sinks Joukahainen in a swamp with his magic songs. Joukahainen offers Aino in MARRIAGE to Väinämöinen. Aino is distressed at the prospect of marrying an old man. She wanders into the woods and drowns in an unfamiliar lake. Väinämöinen searches for Aino in the lake and catches her in the form of a fish. The fish escapes back into the water and announces who it is. Väinämöinen tries in vain to capture the fish again. This story illustrates his consistent failure to find a wife.

Another series of songs tell how Väinämöinen, Ilmarinen, and LEMMINKAINEN set out to get the Sampo from North Farm. Forged by Ilmarinen, the Sampo is a MAGIC OBJECT and a producer and symbol of prosperity. It grinds out grain, salt, and money in unlimited amounts. As they sail to North Farm, the voyagers' boat gets stuck on a pike's back. They kill the pike and Väinämöinen makes a harp from its jawbone. No one but Väinämöinen can make music from the harp. Once at North Farm, he plays the harp and puts all the people to sleep. He and his companions take the Sampo and sail away. Louhi, the mistress of North Farm, wakes after three days and creates a dense fog and other obstacles to delay Väinämöinen and the others. Väinämöinen loses his harp in the sea, and the Sampo is destroyed. Eventually, Väinämöinen makes a new birchwood harp with which he delights everyone and everything. Väinämöinen saves his land from curses and disease cast on it by Louhi.

At the end of the *Kalevala*, a baby boy is discovered in a fen and christened King of Karelia (*see* EXODUS). Väinämöinen gets angry and departs forever, but he leaves behind his harp and his songs. Presumably he is somewhere between heaven and earth.

VALHALLA

Huge hall in Asgard, home of the Norse GODS, where dead warriors are taken to feast, fight, and wait for the end of the world, or RAGNAROK. The name *Valhalla* derives from the Old Icelandic word meaning "hall of the slain." The dead fighters are brought to Valhalla by attractive young women called Valkyries (the choosers of the slain). ODIN, the ruler of the Norse gods, sends the armed Valkyries on horseback to the battlefield to select the men who are destined to die. At Valhalla, the Valkyries serve mead and food to the dead warriors. Each day, the same magical boar is cooked in a cauldron. The mead comes from the teats of a goat named Heidrun who grazes outside the hall.

Valhalla is guarded by a treacherous and noisy river through which the warriors must wade. Next they confront Valgrind, a barred gate that is difficult to open and the only door through which the men can enter. Valhalla has 540 doors. Its rafters are made of spears, and it shingles are shields. War coats clutter its benches. A wolf with an eagle above it

hangs over the western door. Valhalla and its many doors are so enormous that 800 can march abreast through each door.

In the MYTH telling of Thor's duel with the giant Hrungnir, the latter is invited by Odin into Valhalla. After several horns of mead, the drunk GIANT threatens to pick up the hall and carry it to Jotunheim, home of the giants. In other tales, Valhalla is mentioned as a geographic point of reference, as when Frigg, BALDR's mother, tells LOKI of a mistletoe bush growing to the west of Valhalla that can harm her son. The myth of Ragnarok also contains a vivid description of Valhalla.

VALMIKI

Author of the important Hindu EPIC, the RAMAYANA. Considered the inventor of poetry, Valmiki was born a Brahmin, or member of the priestly and meditative highest caste in Hinduism, which is comprised of four castes. Nevertheless, Valmiki was believed to have stolen to make a living until the semi-divine sage Narada, adviser of the GODS, helped him to find the right way. One legend claims that Valmiki wrote the entire *Ramayana* somewhere between 200 B.C. and A.D. 200 in one single burst of inspiration that occurred when he saw a hunter shoot an arrow and bring down a mating bird: "From *soka* (sorrow) flowed *sloka* (poetry)." Drawing on various well-known FOLKTALES and LEGENDS about Rama, one of the nine avatars, or incarnations, of the GOD, VISNU, Valmiki embellished these tales by adding supernatural incidents to create seven books comprised of approximately 24,000 couplets.

Valmiki's *Ramayana*, along with the MAHABHARATA, is one of India's two great Sanskrit epics. The story of the life of Rama, heir to the throne of a north Indian kingdom, it begins with Rama's birth and then focuses on his banishment to a forest by his father where he then lives for 13 years with his devoted wife Sita who, against Rama's wishes, has insisted on joining him in his exile. Sita, however, is eventually kidnapped by Ravana, a DEMON who symbolizes lust. Rama is finally able to save Sita with the help of Hanuman, the monkey god, who assists Rama in raising an army. To this day, monkeys are revered among Hindus because of Hanuman. Of the many incidents that follow, Rama comes to believe that his wife has been defiled, and wants his half-brother to accompany her and abandon her when she is pregnant and takes a trip to the Ganges. Sita then wanders in the forest where she encounters Valmiki, the sage and poet, who shelters her when she gives birth to the two sons of Rama, Kusa and Lava. Valmiki then composes the *Ramayana* and teaches it to the two boys during the 12 years they live together. Finally, Sita, with the help of EARTH-MOTHER, proves she has been faithful to Rama, and they are rejoined. To this day, both Rama and Sita are considered the perfect models of righteousness and are, in turn, considered the ideal man and the ideal woman.

For Further Reading

Valmiki, Shri. *Ramayana*. 3rd ed. Greenleaf Books, 1980.

VAMPIRE

Reanimated corpse which needs blood for nourishment; the spirit of a dead person inhabiting its own body. A vampire is neither dead nor alive; it is considered undead.

The most popular depiction of a vampire today is that of Dracula, a Transylvanian count with a pale face, long canine teeth, dark hair, and formal dress. He can transform himself into a bat, a wolf, or a wisp of smoke. This image of vampires derives Bram Stoker's 1897 novel, *Dracula*, as well as from the Bela Lugosi film of 1931.

The Dracula LEGEND originates in the fifteenth-century historical figure, Vlad Dracula, who ruled Wallachia, the southern half of modern Romania. He was known to torture and to execute people by impaling them on long stakes. On one occasion, he attacked the Transylvanian city of Sibiu, killing over 10,000 inhabitants. Dracula was eventually defeated by King Matthias of Hungary. With the aid of the printing press, the Dracula legend appeared in Germany and then spread throughout Europe. There are several other accounts of actual vampires, people who delight in taking human blood, including those of the Hungarian Countess Elizabeth Bathory and Gilles de Laval, Baron de Rais.

Stories of vampires have been around for much longer than the Dracula legend, and they appear throughout the world. It is possible that belief in vampires originated in the Himalayan Mountains, where over 3,000 years ago the earliest vampire lived in a variety of forms, including that of KALI, the bloodthirsty MOTHER GODDESS. The second-century story of the female vampire Philinnion, from Phlegon's "Concerning Wonderous Things" (found in *Fragmenta Historicorum Graecorum),* and the third-century account of vampirism in Philostratus's *Life of Apollonius of Tyana* also suggest the ancient history of vampire tales.

Vampires are almost always depicted as creatures with tremendous hungers. They lust after blood and sex. Male vampires search out young women, while female vampires crave young men. Vampires' violent quest for blood and the sexual connection between them and their victims are the two most consistent elements in vampire stories. Other common elements in vampire tales include their inability to experience DEATH, their foul odor, and their lack of need for food. In many stories, vampires are pallid before drinking blood.

Vampires can also be SHAPE-SHIFTING, and they may assume the form of a bat, a wolf, a dog, or a cat. In some stories, particularly in Eastern Europe, vampires escape from their graves in the form of smoke, mist, or fog.

There are many ways to become vampires and numerous ways to destroy them. The most common method of destruction is to drive a stake through its heart, chop off its head, and finally burn the body. The universal repellent for vampires is garlic. Vampires will also flee from or be destroyed by the crucifix, relics of the saints, the sign of the cross, holy water, and a consecrated host.

In general, however, there is little consistency in vampire lore, and specific aspects of vampire stories arise from the cultures in which they are told. In India, female vampires haunt crossroads and drink the blood of elephants. Japanese lore includes a medieval FOLKTALE about the Vampire Cat of Nabeshima, a large cat that attacks people and sucks blood from their necks. In Malaysia, female vampires attack people and have a fondness for fish.

Vampires did not become widespread figures until the eighteenth century, when they began to appear in DRAMA, poetry, and prose across Europe. In April 1819, the first vampire story in English prose, *The Vampyre* by John Polidori, appeared in *New Monthly Magazine*. This novella established the conventions of the modern vampire story in which vampires are adult sexual predators who mingle unnoticed with humans while killing young women.

The modern vampire story may retell vampire legends from Eastern Europe. The vampires are masked by wealth, intelligence, and culture. The setting is often a fancy social event. The vampires are then discovered and hunted. The first vampire novel to be published in English was the 1847 work *Varney the Vampire or the Feast of Blood*. Bram Stoker's *Dracula* inspired hundreds of ensuing plays, films, novels, and stories.

Twentieth-century works containing vampire lore include Richard Matheson's novel *I Am Legend* and his short story "Drink My Red Blood," Raymond Rudorff's *The Dracula Archives*, Jeff Rice's *The Night Stalker*, Theodore Sturgeon's *Some of Your Blood*, John Rechy's *The Vampires*, Fred Saberhagen's *The Dracula Tape*, Desmond Stewart's *The Vampire of Mons*, Colin Wilson's *The Space Vampires*, and Chelsea Quinn Yarbro's *Hotel Transylvania*. Perhaps the most successful twentieth-century vampire novels are Stephen King's *Salem's Lot* and Anne Rice's *Interview with the Vampire*.

Paul Barber's scholarly work *Vampires, Burial, and Death* contains tales about and accounts of vampires. The children's book *Monsters* includes a condensed version of *Dracula*. Donald Glut's *The Dracula Book* is an excellent source for vampire stories in magazines and comic books.

THE VANISHING HITCHHIKER

Urban LEGEND that has been adapted to fit technological advancements (*see* URBAN FOLKLORE). The story of a passenger who mysteriously disappears originally involved a carriage or a horseback rider. It took on new life with the advent of the automobile.

In the basic story, someone offers a ride to a stranger. Upon arriving at the stranger's destination, the driver is amazed to discover that the passenger is no longer in the vehicle. The driver makes inquiries and learns that the passenger has been dead for some time. In some versions, the passenger has beneficial intentions, such as saving a life. Sometimes he or she turns out to be an angel or other religious figure.

In most versions, the hitchhiker gives a destination to the driver; the hitchhiker chooses to sit in the back seat; the driver is concerned at the disappearance and makes inquiries; the identity of the hitchhiker is revealed by someone who knew the hitchhiker when he or she was alive. Sometimes a portrait or photograph supports the identification. And sometimes the hitchhiker borrows a coat, which the driver later finds draped across the appropriate tombstone.

Like most urban legends, "The Vanishing Hitchhiker" is customarily told as if it were true. The teller claims that it happened to a relative, a friend, or a friend of a friend—often mentioned by name. An actual location is identified. The legend appears in the oral tradition of virtually all parts of the United States and in many other countries. Since the 1930s, the story occasionally has been reported in newspapers.

"The Vanishing Hitchhiker" has been retold in the popular media—most notably in the song "Laurie," recorded by Dickey Lee. It is also discussed in Jan Harold Brunvand's book, *The Vanishing Hitchhiker: American Urban Legends & Their Meanings* (1981).

VARIANT

Alternate version of a MYTH, LEGEND, FAIRY TALE, or story. Because storytelling is part of the oral tradition, and storytellers have always liked to put their individual stamp on the story they are telling, we have variants. Some have occurred as stories pass from one culture to another either through war, colonization, domination through religion, or simply the movement of one people to a new place. Throughout Polynesia, for example, CREATION myths are very similar, with variants reflecting adaptation of some names and actions and modification of others. The fairy tale "CINDERELLA," believed to have originated in China, has a number of variants, for example the Russian fairy tale "Vasilisa the Beautiful." Charles Perrault's version of "Cinderella" is a variant of the GRIMM BROTHERS'S version (*see* PERRAULT, CHARLES). The popularity of Walt Disney's adaptation of "Cinderella" has made this version the most well known in North America and parts of Europe, but adaptations and variants are not synonymous, as variants arise in a more natural, less deliberate way from the nature of adaptation, which involves a conscious purpose in changing the story for a particular audience.

For Further Reading

Evetts-Secker, Josephine. "Vasilisa the Beautiful." *Mother and Daughter Tales.* Illustrated by Helen Cann. New York: Abbeville, 1996.

Sierra, Judy. *Cinderella.* The Oryx Multicultural Folktale Series. Phoenix : Oryx Press, 1992.

VEDAS

Sacred texts of Hinduism, the earliest of which is believed to be from about 2000–1700 B.C. The *Vedas* consist of four books, which include prayers, hymns, and directions for RITUAL. The oldest is the *Rig-Veda,* a collection of hymns. The *Sama-Veda* includes many of the same hymns with the addition of musical notation. The *Yajur-Veda* is made up of prayers and spells, and the *Atharva-Veda* is made up of popular material and stories. Also considered part of the Vedi literature are the *Brahmanas,* prose interpretations; the *Aranyakas,* treatises on meditation; and the speculative literature of the *Upanishads.*

Like other early mythologies, the *Vedas* celebrate a polytheistic belief system focused on nature. There are 33 *devas*—shining ones or GODS. The supreme position is attributed to each deity in turn. In the later books their identities become blurred, giving rise to the concept of a single divine principle, which takes many forms.

The metaphor of sacrifice is potent in the *Vedas* and may be considered a creative act. In one of the stories, a primal entity was dismembered, and the beings of the universe— including the gods, natural elements, humans, and ANIMALS—were produced from the parts of his body.

Vedic literature struggles with the limitations of language and rational thought in dealing with profound questions about the nature of reality. Concepts viewed as polar opposites are seen as each requiring and implying the other. In the Vedic view, the world was created from neither being nor not-being. Originally a germ of life, like a COSMIC EGG, was floating on the unmanifested waters of chaos. From that embryo PRAJAPATI arose, and took on the responsibility of making order out of chaos. However, the transformation of the potential into the actual is seen as a continuous process.

The *Vedas* include the stories of Indra, BRAHMA, and VISNU. Some of the stories are retold or continued in other Hindu literature. SIVA may be a later form of a malevolent storm god in the Vedic material. *See also* HINDU STORYTELLING, INDRA AND THE ANTS, KALI, KRISNA, MAHABHARATA, RAMAYANA.

For Further Reading

Miller, Jeanine. *The Vision of Cosmic Order in the Vedas.* London: Routledge & Kegan Paul, 1985.

van Nooten, Baron A., ed. *Rig Veda: A Metrically Restored Text.* Cambridge, MA: Department of Sanskrit and Indian, Harvard University, 1994.

Verma, Rajendr. *The World of Vedic Life and Culture: The Vedic Poetry.* Delhi: Sharada Prakashan, 1990.

VERSE STORY

Narrative poem or BALLAD, often with variants. Narrative verse, or verse stories, has existed since the earliest times, when primitive BARDS sang their chants in EPIC verse, glorifying heroic battles and courageous acts. Verse stories always have had wide popularity. They originated among the common people and continue to this day to move and stir us, whether in poems or folk songs or even ROCK SONGS. The older verse stories were sung in the marketplace for crowds of people or recited in taverns as a form of entertainment. They were also a form of communicating the news of the day.

Among some of the most well-known verse stories are ballads such as "LORD RANDALL,"

"Barbara Allen," "Sir Patrick Spens," "The DEMON LOVER," "The Two Sisters of Binnorie," and "John Barleycorn." Some famous nineteenth- and early twentieth-century verse stories include Tennyson's "The Charge of the Light Brigade," Alfred Noyes's "The Highwayman," Robert Browning's "The Pied Piper of Hamelin," Robert W. Service's "The Cremation of Sam McGee," Henry Wadsworth Longfellow's "Paul Revere's Ride," and Lord Byron's "The Prisoner of Chillon."

For Further Reading

Untermeyer, Louis. *Story Poems.* New York: Pocket Books, 1957.

VIRGIN BIRTH

Folkloric MOTIF. Virgin birth is a motif prevalent in cosmogonic CREATION myths, as well as MYTHS announcing the genesis of a divine religious figure. One of the problems concerned with this motif centers upon the ambiguous definition of virginity itself. While in most Western civilizations a "virgin" generally is someone who abstains from sexual intercourse until MARRIAGE, in other cultures a virgin may be defined simply as an unmarried woman. On the one hand, there is MARY, the virgin and mother of Jesus in the Christian tradition, who, while still unmarried, was impregnated by the spirit of GOD. Conversely, Ishtar, the Babylonian goddess of love and procreation, was called the "Holy Virgin" or the "Virgin Mother" by her worshippers, even though she was the wife of the MOON god.

What is common about the virgin birth is the notion of a magical, mystical, or divine impregnation of an unmarried woman, which culminates with the birth of a child. The virgin birth is exceptional from other births in the sense that the result is often the physical birth of a great religious leader or other divine figures. There are numerous variations on this motif—some of the more interesting include impregnation by eating a woman's heart (Norse), drinking a medicinal or magical substance, or eating stones (North American Indian). In the Algonquian tale "ALGON AND THE SKY MAIDEN," it is the west WIND that impregnates the daughter of the sky chieftain as she faces the wrong direction while performing gardening duties. *See also* SKY MAIDEN.

VIRGIN MARY APOCRYPHA

Non-canonical writings concerning the life of MARY, mother of Jesus. Much has been written about Mary that is not included in the New Testament of the BIBLE. Considered apocryphal, meaning "secret" or "hidden," these writings were inspired by the *Book of James* and the later *Gospel According to the Pseudo-Matthew.*

In the *Book of James,* Mary is portrayed as the daughter of Joachim and Anna. Joachim, a wealthy and charitable man, would always give away some of his worldly goods to the poor and the temple. Because his wife Anna is barren, Joachim goes to the temple to make an offering, but the High Priest tells him that he has caused the Lord displeasure, so Joachim flees to the desert to do penance for 40 days. The distraught Anna is wandering about the garden in her bridal dress when an angel announces to her that she will conceive. Meanwhile, in the desert, Joachim also is visited by an angel. He returns to his wife to celebrate, and Anna promises to dedicate the child to the temple and GOD.

After Mary is born, her infancy is supposedly attended by prodigies, she is able to walk seven steps when she is six months old, and when she is three her parents take her to the temple, where she dances on the steps, she is loved by all of Israel, and angels bring her food from HEAVEN. When the time comes for Mary to marry, Zacharias the High Priest announces that God will give a sign choosing her husband. The DIVINE SIGN comes in the form of a dove flying from Joseph's rod and perching on his head, or, in a VARIANT, the rod is left in the temple overnight and it bursts into flowers. Joseph is depicted as an old man who already has sons, and later, during the census, he is unsure whether to register Mary as his wife or his daughter.

When Mary is pregnant, Joseph reproaches himself, for Mary is a consecrated virgin of the temple and should not be defiled. A priest arraigns them, and they must drink "the bitter waters of conviction," which is supposed to poison them if they are lying, but they emerge triumphant. The birth of Jesus then follows much the same as in the Gospels; however, on the journey, notes Marina Warner in *Alone of All Her Sex*, "Mary is saddened by a vision of 'two peoples,' one weeping, the other exulting: allegories of the Jews, who will reject Christ, and the Gentiles, who will accept him." Mary then descends from her donkey and gives birth in a cave, attended by a midwife, and "a cloud of light" overshadows the cave as a sign of the miraculous birth. When a skeptical woman named Salome doubts the midwife's tale of this miracle, she goes to the cave and examines Mary, but fire withers her hand. Immediately, Salome begs forgiveness, promising to heal in the name of Jesus if her hand is restored. Then an angel advises her to hold up the baby in her arms, and Salome's hand is made whole once more.

For Further Reading

Warner, Marina. *Alone of All Her Sex: The Myth and the Cult of the Virgin Mary*. New York: Alfred A. Knopf, 1976.

VIRTUES

Prevalent theme in many tales from many cultures. Moral lessons are often taught through oral folk traditions. The values of a culture are transmitted through MYTH and story. In *Parallel Myths*, J. F. Bierlein wrote that morality tales functioned as "a means of conforming the behavior of the individual to that of the group." In many FOLKTALES, specific virtues are praised. In others, specific vices are condemned. Characters who exhibit virtuous behavior tend to be rewarded. This is demonstrated in the Indian tale from the MAHABHARATA, "The Virtue of Compassion." A parrot risks his life to stay with an old and dying tree. Refusing to abandon his old friend, the parrot eventually begins to wither with the tree. The GOD Indra, noting the parrot's extreme loyalty and compassion, restores life to the tree. In this, as in other morality tales, the main character sacrifices his or her own well-being for the sake of others. One extreme example of sacrifice is found in the German story, "Faithful John." In this tale, the servant John demonstrates his faithfulness. He is turned to stone so that his master and mistress remain unharmed. Later, they, in turn, must show their gratitude for John's loyalty. They chop off the heads of their sons to restore life to the stone John. This sacrifice is rewarded, however, when John places the heads back on the children.

The treatment of ANIMALS is another measure of a character's virtue. In the Greek story, "The Grateful Animals and the Talisman," Cinderello is repeatedly kind to animals. He saves a puppy, kitten, and little snake from the cruelty of other children. This kindness does not go unrewarded. Later, the animals work together to save Cinderello from the treachery of his wife. In the Indian story, "The KING, the Hawk, and the Pigeon," the king willingly feeds his own flesh to the hawk in order to save the pigeon.

In recent years, some, such as the former U.S. Secretary of Education, William Bennett, have linked escalating crime to the decline in moral storytelling. To counter what he sees as a lack of ethics in modern society, Bennett compiled *The Book of Virtues*. This book attempts to transmit such virtues as truthfulness and courage through folktales. In September 1996, public television in the United States began an animated series entitled "Adventures from the Book of Virtues." Each show highlights a separate virtue through myths and stories such as "George Washington and the Cherry Tree."

VISION QUEST

Native American ritual in pursuit of wisdom and power. The vision quest is a ritual practiced by different Native American tribes, usually when a boy reaches puberty. In some tribes it involves fasting, and the questing person may be taught songs, dances, and healing knowledge. At times the search for wisdom and power in the form of a vision may involve the acquisition of a helping spirit; in other cases the soul of an ANIMAL might appear in the vision to grant the boy its power and make him into a successful hunter. Once an animal's soul appears to him, it will continue to guide him for life.

While most vision quests are undertaken at puberty, they may also come at other life stages, either as a preparation for war or some other important transition. For the Plains Indians, the vision quest is a tradition for a man or a woman seeking the right path in his or her life or searching for enlightenment. The person will then remain alone on a hilltop or in "a vision pit," fasting for up to four days or nights. Ideally, the "spirit voices" will "reveal or confer a vision that shapes a person's life," write Richard Erdoes and Alfonso Ortiz in *American Indian Myths and Legends* (*see* ERDOES, RICHARD; ORTIZ, ALFONSO).

In "The Vision Quest," a Brulé Sioux story recorded by Erdoes, a young man wants to go on a vision quest to seek "a dream that would give him the power to be a great medicine man." The medicine men and his family prepare him for months, feeding him to make him strong. Just before he leaves for the vision pit, he visits the sweat lodge to purify himself. Although he is told by the medicine men that he must be humble in his request for "a gift which would make him into a medicine man," he is too arrogant. He cries out, he is afraid, he is told by a voice representing the creatures that he is keeping them awake, he is attacked by a boulder, and he is bruised and shaken but determined to persevere till the four days and nights have passed. Finally, when the medicine men come to get him, he has to admit that he has not had a vision. The medicine men tell him that he has gone after his vision quest in the wrong way: he has gone like a hunter, believing that suffering, courage, and will power will bring him the vision that is his due. Instead, "A vision comes as a gift born of humility, of wisdom, and of patience." This is the lesson to be gained from the vision quest.

For Further Reading

Erdoes, Richard, and Alfonso Ortiz. *American Indian Myths and Legends.* New York: Pantheon, 1985.

VISNU

One of the three supreme deities of Hinduism. Visnu is considered the most important of the solar deities, and he embodies some aspects of PRAJAPATI and Indra. His wife is Lakshmi or Sri, and he lives with her in Valkuntha, his HEAVEN. In paintings he is portrayed as a handsome young man with four hands holding a conch shell, a club, a lotus, and a *chakra* (wheel or SUN disk). He carries a bow and a sword, and travels on the back of a huge bird called Garuda. Visnu is the embodiment of mercy and goodness in the PURANAS.

Many stories are told about Visnu both as supreme deity and avatar. In one MYTH, he takes three strides and creates the THREE WORLDS. In another, the GODS unite against Visnu and cut off his head with the tip of his bow. In the cosmogonic myth of the *Puranas*, Visnu is seen lying on the serpent Sesa, who is coiled upon the ocean. A long-stemmed lotus emerges from his navel, and in its petals it holds a four-headed BRAHMA, representing the first stage of the CREATION of the world. His wife Sri lies at his feet.

As preserver and restorer, Visnu is also seen in the form of 22 avatars such as Rama and KRISNA, whose purpose is to help humankind. Other avatars of Visnu include the DWARF, the fish, and the boar. Visnu is also associated with sacrifice as the source of all prosperity in the world.

For Further Reading

Kearns, Emily. "Indian Myth." *The Feminist Companion to Mythology.* Edited by Carolyne Larrington. London: HarperCollins, 1992.

VYASA

Sage who in ancient times composed the great Hindu EPIC, the MAHABHARATA. According to Indian tradition, Krisna Dwaipayana Vyasa composed the work with the idea that his best pupil, Vaisampayana, would recite it at a ritual presented by Janamejaya in honor of his great grandfather, the *Mahabharata*'s primary HERO, ARJUNA. In fact, nothing is known of Vyasa. His first name and the fact that he is sometimes called the "Island-Born Krisna" suggest the belief that he was close to the god-hero KRISNA. The *Mahabharata* is also known as the "Veda of Krisna," or the "Fifth Veda" (*see* VEDAS), emphasizing the belief in that connection. In some versions of the Vyasa

LEGEND, he was the son of a hermit and a KING's daughter, who was herself born miraculously of a fish. Some say that Vyasa begat the ancestors of both the PANDAVAS and the Kauravas, the rival families of the *Mahabharata*. It is likely that the legendary figure of Vyasa is representative of the collective authorship of the great Hindu epic, much as the legendary HOMER is likely the collective author of the Greek epics, the ILIAD and ODYSSEY.

For Further Reading

Buck, William. *Mahabharata*. Berkeley: University of California Press, 1981.

WAGNER, RICHARD (1813–1883)

German composer of operas who used Norse and Germanic mythology for subject matter. Wagner was drawn to the interaction of art forms that opera offered and began composing both music and librettos while still in his teens. After an early period of poverty, Wagner achieved success in his homeland. However, his revolutionary activities forced him to flee to Switzerland in 1849, an exile that lasted until 1860. Wagner's later work was strongly influenced by the philosophy of Schopenhauer, especially concerning the power of love, will, and genius.

A primary Wagnerian theme is the conflict between a man of genius and the world in which he lives. Wagner considered genius all-important, requiring unquestioning loyalty from others. That motif appeared in his early works, notably *The Flying Dutchman* (1831), *Tannhauser* (1845), and *Lohengrin* (1848).

During the first half of the nineteenth century, a German EPIC poem, the NIBELUNGLIED, was popular. A medieval story of love, loyalty, and revenge, it was based on the earlier Norse *Eddas* (*see* EDDAS, ELDER AND YOUNGER). Wagner saw this story as a wonderful vehicle for his own ideas.

In 1853 he began work on *The Ring of the Nibelund* (*Der Ring des Nibelungen*), which eventually included four operas: *The Rhinegold*, *The Valkyrie*, SIEGFRIED, and *Twilight of the Gods*, in which VALHALLA, the home of the GODS, is destroyed by fire. During this time he also composed TRISTAN AND ISOLDE. His last opera was *Parsifal* (*see* HOLY GRAIL, PERCIVAL).

Wagner's work was appropriated by Adolf Hitler and the Nazis due in part to the anti-Semitic undertones. Consequently, his operas have been a source of ongoing debate concerning the relevance of the storyteller's underlying beliefs and agendas to the ultimate value of their work.

WANDJINA

Primal being of the Australian Aborigines (also called *Wondjina*). According to Australian Aborigine mythology, out of Wandjina comes the first inhabitants of the Kimberley region of northeast Australia. For these aborigines, the term Wandjina can be used in the singular to refer to the one creator GOD or in the plural to refer to many GODS. As Aborigine storyteller Daisy Utemorrah relates in Harvey Arden's *Dreamkeepers*, "There's many Wandjina and there's one Wandjina. Just like Jesus and God in HEAVEN and that Holy Ghost. Three, but still they're one. So that's like Wandjina, too. Many, but he's still one. He's in Heaven now with the one God. They're the same. Just the same. Wandjina and the one God. They're the same."

For the Australian Aborigines, Wandjina still live in the caves of central and west Kimberley, where Wandjina figures were painted 8,000 years ago. The paintings are haunting, unique, but not primitive. Halos representing clouds and lightning surround the faces of these figures, who stare out from the rock painting with wide, mysterious eyes. Each area of Australia has its own particular Wandjina, and the sum of all these Wandjinas is the Creator Wandjina. According to elder, philosopher, and mystic aborigine David Mowaljarlai, "Wandjina came from the wind and traveled the land and made this earth, and the sea, and the mountains, the rivers, the water holes, the trees, the plants, the animals, the language, and the people. . . . Wandjina then gave us the Law to follow and gave us the land to keep forever. . . . Wandjina see all things at all times no matter where we are on land. All that they created . . . is spiritual, possessing a powerful energy. . . . Wandjina spiritual presence is in all living things. It's in the land itself." *See also* AUSTRALIAN AND NEW ZEALAND ABORIGINAL STORYTELLING.

WANJIRU

African MAIDEN whose story illustrates several elements of the HERO QUEST. When the rain will not fall for three years and a severe drought threatens the people, the Medicine-Man declares that all men of the community must bring a goat to the meeting place as the purchase price of Wanjiru. The men comply, and Wanjiru is placed in the center of the meeting place. As the men stand in a circle around her with their goats, Wanjiru begins to sink into the ground. The EARTH has almost entirely covered her body when the rains begin to fall. Wanjiru cries out for her family, and they move to save her. They are prevented by the sudden presentation of the goats, which they accept as Wanjiru descends into the earth. A warrior who loves Wanjiru despairingly goes to the place where she disappeared into the earth, and he begins to sink as well. He travels far in the underworld until he finds Wanjiru and returns her to the surface. Upon seeing their resurrected family member, Wanjiru's relatives crowd around her, only to be pushed away by the warrior who claims that they have dealt treacherously with Wanjiru. Eventually they are reconciled, and the warrior marries the maiden Wanjiru.

The story of Wanjiru owes much to the hero quest, though to whom the quest principally belongs is not entirely clear. The warrior, in his descent into and return from an underworld space, undergoes a miniature version of the quest. Wanjiru's quest is that of the dying hero, the sacrificial figure who submits to DEATH for the benefit of the community. *See Also* DESCENT TO THE UNDERWORLD.

WAR IN HEAVEN

Motif in world mythology made most famous by British poet John Milton in *Paradise Lost* (1667), in the first, fifth, and sixth book. Numerous other writers had dealt with this theme before Milton (*see* MOTIF). The EPIC of Babylonian CREATION, the *Enuma Elish*, expresses the fall of the GODS and the primeval alienation among them in a story that resembles the tales of battles between elder and younger gods found in so many other religions. The *Enuma Elish* tells the story of Apsu and Tiamat, the primordial pair, whose progeny become rebellious. Ea kills Apsu, and Tiamat plans revenge, but he is killed by MARDUK.

In the BIBLE the story of warfare in heaven is hinted at in three passages, Isaiah 14:12–14, Luke 10:18, and Revelation 12:7–9. The passage in Revelation says:

And there was war in heaven: Michael and his angels fought against the dragon: and the dragon fought and his angels, and prevailed not; neither was their place found any more in heaven. And the great dragon was cast out, that serpent, called the DEVIL, and Satan, which deceiveth the whole world: he was cast out into the EARTH, and his angels were cast out with him.

Milton's famous description reads:

Hurl'd headlong flaming from th' Ethereal Sky
With hideous ruin and combustion down to bottomless perdition, there to dwell
In Adamantine chains and penal Fire.

The Christian story concludes with final warfare with Satan and his angels in which the rebellious ones are finally defeated for all time, ushering in the period of peace known as the "Great Millennium."

WARD, ARTEMUS (1834–1867)

American newspaper editor, humorist, lecturer, and author, born Charles Farrar Browne. Originally a newspaper man in New England, in 1858 Browne began contributing letters under the name of Artemus Ward to the Cleveland *Plain Dealer*. These humorous letters, written in Yankee dialect with purposefully misspelled words to make the tales seem more authentic and "spoken," related the adventures and escapades of his own traveling museum of wax figures. He quickly became well-known for the "Artemus Ward Letters," and was promoted to city editor for the newspaper. In 1860, he resigned from the *Plain Dealer* and moved to New York, where he began writing for *Vanity Fair* magazine. By this time, he was better known as Artemus Ward, and in 1862 his first collection, *Artemus Ward, His Book*, was published, selling over 40,000 copies almost immediately. By this time his fame was widespread, and even President Abraham Lincoln knew his work, for Ward had created a fictitious interview with Lincoln that had been published and amused the President. After six years in New York, Ward left for London in 1866 to become an editor of *Punch*, the famous British magazine of humor, but he soon died of tuberculosis. By this time, *Artemus Ward, His Travels*, had appeared in 1865; *Artemus Ward in London* (1869) and *Artemus Ward: His Works Complete* (1875) were posthumously published.

As an American humorist, punster, absurdist, and collector of stories, Artemus Ward was an influence on Mark Twain, whom he had met in his travels. His lectures, with their particular brand of deadpan humor and unexpectedness, charmed his audiences.

WARNER, MARINA (1946–)

English novelist, essayist, and editor of FAIRY TALES. Much of Warner's work has focused on the significance of female symbolism in MYTHS, both classic and contemporary. Her work includes book-length studies of the myths surrounding JOAN OF ARC, *Joan of Arc: The Image of Female Heroism* (1976), and the Virgin MARY, *Alone of All Her Sex: The Myth and the Cult of the Virgin Mary* (1981). She has also lent her feminist perspective to a broader discussions of some of the myths of women past and present in her study *Monuments and Maidens: The Allegory of Female Form* (1985), where she explores the symbolism in such figures as Boadicea, the Statue of Liberty, and former British Prime Minister, Margaret Thatcher. And in *Managing Monsters: Six Myths of Our Time* (1994), the 1994 Reich Lectures for BBC, she uses her knowledge of myths and fairy tales to reconsider some myths of today, especially those concerning gender, that are disseminated through different medias of storytelling, like film and video games. Warner's discussions of both classic and contemporary myths, described by Margaret Ann Doody as "clearheaded but subtle," have been praised for their contribution to the study of mythology.

In addition to her critical work, Warner edited *Wonder Tales: Six Stories of Enchantment* (1994), a collection of fairy tales by the great women storytellers of the seventeenth and eighteenth centuries. She has also written several novels, including *The Lost Father* (1989) and *In a Dark Wood* (1977).

WATER OF LIFE

In FOLKTALES, the magic liquid that bestows immortality, brings the dead to life, cures the blind or sick, and restores youth. Water of life is used in several FOLKLORE motifs. First, it appears in numerous QUEST tales in which the HERO is sent to get the water of life from a well, spring, lake, or river at a great distance, such as in the GRIMM BROTHERS's tale, "Water of Life." Sometimes the water of life MOTIF is combined with the magic helpers motif wherein the helper sees someone in need of help and magically produces the water of life to revive the dying person, often a KING or PRINCESS. The water of life is also connected to the source of the SUN's daily rebirth in fountains, rivers, and SEAS. Divine drinks imbibed by GODS hoping to retain their eternal youth (for example, ambrosia and soma) are an extension of the symbol of the water of life.

The water of life is featured in the mythologies of many cultures. One interesting example is the Babylonian myth of Ishtar's descent to the underworld. Ishtar seeks Tammuz to restore him with the water of life. But she, too, having once passed into the region of DEATH, has to be sprinkled with the water of life before she can return. The water of life is also featured in the European tradition. In the Grimm Brothers's story, a dying king has three sons, the eldest of whom are haughty and cruel, who set out to find the water of life for their father. The YOUNGEST SON finally finds the magic elixir, which springs from a fountain in the courtyard of an enchanted castle. In American tradition, author Nathaniel Hawthorne used the motif in *Dr. Heidegger's Experiment*.

Many mythical fountains provide the water of life. These include Caesar's Well, Czar's Well, Living Waters, Ponce de Leon's Fountain of Youth, Reviving Cordial, Vessel of Cordial Balsam, Well of Virtues, Well Beyond the World, and Well of the World.

For Further Reading

Grimms' Complete Fairy Tales. Garden City, NY: Nelson Doubleday, n.d.

WATERJAR BOY MYTH

Tewa Native American MYTH. The story of Waterjar Boy is an unusual QUEST that features such ARCHETYPE elements as the VIRGIN BIRTH, which sets the hero apart from his conception, and the SEARCH FOR THE FATHER, a MOTIF which represents the HERO'S (and our own) search for identity and life's meaning.

One day a young girl was making clay water jars, mixing the clay with her feet. Apparently, some of the clay made its way into her while she was making the jars, for she soon discovered she was pregnant. However, instead of giving birth to a baby, she gave birth to a water jar. The girl's father was especially fond of the little jar, which grew, walked, talked, and played like other children, though it had no arms, legs, or eyes.

As winter approached, Waterjar Boy, as he was called, begged his grandfather to take him rabbit hunting with the other men, pointing out that the old man would be unable to kill anything himself. Despite his reluctance, the grandfather complied. The two spotted a rabbit and began chasing it. Waterjar Boy threw himself against a rock; the jar broke, and a handsome, well-dressed boy emerged who turned out to be a fine hunter.

The boy easily convinced his family who he was, and spent a normal childhood until one day he decided to find his father. His mother pointed out that as she was a virgin, he had no father. But the boy was convinced that he did, and moreover that he knew who he was. He headed to a place called Horse Mesa Point where there was a spring. Nearing the spring, he saw a man headed toward him. The man asked him where he was going and the boy told him he was looking for his father who lived in the spring. After a short conversation, the two determined that they were father and son. They embraced and journeyed into the spring where the boy was welcomed by his relatives.

Soon after, the boy's mother died, and Waterjar Boy returned to the spring to live permanently. He found his mother there, and discovered that his father, who was Red Water Snake, had arranged his mother's illness so that they could all live together.

The story of Waterjar Boy is a story of adolescence. The hunting expedition is part of a rite of passage from boyhood to manhood, and the breaking of the waterjar represents the identity changes we all undergo as we shed our childhood selves to emerge as adults, ready to embark on our own hero quests.

For Further Reading

Bruchac, Joseph. *Iroquois Stories.* Illustrated by Daniel Burgevin. Trumansburg, NY: The Crossing Press, 1985.

WEREWOLF

Person who has been changed into a wolf or a creature in lupine form. Werewolf stories appear in Western European storytelling traditions, particularly in Brittany, but such stories are even more prevalent in Eastern European FOLKLORE, the origin of most of the essential elements of werewolf tales. In many werewolf stories, a wolfskin garment, a belt, or a salve causes the metamorphosis. Sometimes another person brings about the TRANSFORMATION, or a person sometimes transforms himself. A full moon also can trigger the change. If a full moon is the agent of transformation, a werewolf resumes its human form when the moon sets and the sun rises. Usually, the metamorphosis is involuntary. If a wolfskin garment or a special belt is the agent of transformation, the werewolf will return to its human form when it removes the garment or the belt. If a salve causes the change, the werewolf assumes its human shape when the salve is washed off.

Werewolves are larger and stronger than ordinary wolves, and they crave human flesh. Often, they brutally kill and then eat their victims. They may have longer hair than ordinary wolves, and their hair may be silvery.

Werewolves have two forms, one human and one wolf. Certain features evident in the human form can betray a werewolf: bristle-like hair on the palms, index fingers that are longer than middle fingers, a sign of a crescent or half-moon on the thigh. Sometimes a werewolf in its human form has scabby legs or sunken eyes that glow in the dark. Wounds suffered in the lupine form are usually carried over to the human form. In some cases, the transformation into a wolf is complete, and in other cases it is partial.

Werewolves commonly spread their condition by biting humans. In some Eastern European traditions, the power of werewolves is difficult to evade. In certain regions, werewolves cannot be warded off with religious items, while in other areas, crucifixes and garlic are effective. In France especially, SPELLS and pointed sticks repel werewolves.

There are various ways to eliminate werewolves, including using a stick with a metallic point to pierce a vital area, clubbing the creature with a silver object, or shooting it with a silver bullet. Burning at the stake and decapitation are other methods of destruction.

Petronius's *Satyricon* contains the most well-known werewolf story from classical antiquity. In this novel, the freedman Niceros, on the night of a full moon, observes his traveling companion change into a wolf. The wolf attacks some sheep and is stabbed in the neck by one of the farmhands. Later, Niceros sees his companion, in his human form, bleeding profusely from a deep gash in his neck.

In the twelfth-century poem *William of Palerne, or the Romance of William and the Werwolf,* translated into English about 1350, the HERO has become a Roman emperor with the help of a werewolf. A helpful and benevolent werewolf appears in another twelfth-century work, *Lay of the Bisclavaret* by Marie de France.

In general, werewolves were seldom used in literature before the nineteenth century, when many werewolf stories were published in British and American magazines as well as monthly literary journals. The first definitive werewolf story published in English was "Hugues, the Wer-Wolf" by Sutherland Menzies, which appeared in 1838 in the British publication, the *Court Magazine and Monthly Critic.* A more famous tale is Captain Frederick Marryat's "White Wolf of the Harz Mountains," published in the 1839 novel *The Phantom Ship.* Robert Louis Stevenson's 1886 novella, *The Strange Case of Dr. Jekyll and Mr. Hyde,* contains certain elements of traditional werewolf stories. Dr.

Jekyll discovers a liquid which can change him into the bestial Mr. Hyde and another liquid to change him back again. These liquids resemble the salve used in other werewolf tales. Dr. Jekyll's metamorphosis is rather lupine. His eventual loss of control over the transformation process is similar to the werewolf's inability to prevent its own metamorphosis.

Werewolf stories written in the twentieth century include Peter Fleming's 1931 short story "The Kill," Guy Endore's 1933 classic novel *The Werewolf of Paris*, James Blish's 1950 short story "There Shall Be No Darkness," Gary Brandner's 1977 novel *The Howling*, and Whitley Strieber's 1979 novel *The Wolfen*.

Werewolf stories resembling the warrior-werewolf traditions of the Indo-Europeans appear in North American Indian tribes. At least one Chinese tale, found in Robert Eisler's *Man into Wolf: An Anthropological Interpretation of Sadism, Masochism and Lycanthropy*, parallels European werewolf tales (*see also* BAAL-SHEM STORIES).

For Further Reading

Cheilik, Michael. "The Werewolf." *Mythical and Fabulous Creatures: A Source Book and Research Guide.* Edited by Malcolm South. Westport, CT: Greenwood, 1987.

WHITE BUFFALO WOMAN

Important story of the Sioux Nation in which a sacred woman/GODDESS shows the people how to live and hunt. At the beginning of the story, the chief of the tribe sends out two young warriors to hunt for food. They see a strange apparition floating toward them, and, when the first warrior recognizes it as a beautiful woman and looks lustfully on her, the woman reduces him to charred bones with a lightning bolt. To the other warrior, who held her in proper esteem, she describes the benefits she brings to the people. At the camp, Ptesan-Wi, or White Buffalo Woman, instructs the Sioux to build an altar of red EARTH in the center of the medicine lodge and traces a large ring in the earth to represent the great circle of life. She also initiates the people in the RITUAL use of the pipe and tells them the proper roles for men, women, and children in the culture. After she has instructed the people and departed, large herds of buffalo appear and offer themselves to be killed.

The story of White Buffalo Woman represents the center of the Sioux Nation's continuing oral tradition. The story, with its symbolic images and explicit ceremonial directions, functions as a guide for viewing, and experiencing, life as a unity. In fact, the repetition of the story itself functions as a ritualistic act, invoking the memory and spirit of the force which sustains life. The repetition of red images suggests an emphasis on life-blood and FERTILITY while the pipe stem and bowl symbolize the unity of the male and female principles. White Buffalo Woman explains that, like the four legs of the buffalo, the FOUR DIRECTIONS, and the four ages of CREATION, all aspects of the community's life must form a unity to support itself. After speaking to all the people, White Buffalo Woman addresses the women and children separately, telling them that their roles are sacred and no less important than the men's. The story teaches that, since all living things are of the earth, all are important. The life-giving earth, through its incarnation in White Buffalo Woman, must be respected. As the first warrior of the story demonstrates, failure to offer the earth respect will bring destruction upon the people.

For Further Reading

Crowl, Christine. *White Buffalo Woman.* Tipi Press, 1990.

THE WHITE STAG

Hungarian mythic story of the migration of the Huns and the Magyars from Asia to Hungary. The story, in effect, gives a fanciful account of how the Huns, with the famous Attila, finally came to settle in Hungary. The LEGEND begins with Nimrod, who like Moses (*see* EXODUS), has led his people into the wilderness in search of a PROMISED LAND. His GOD, Hadur, has urged him to move westward, but the search has proved fruitless. As the people lie starving, a white stag appears that only Nimrod and his sons, Hunor and Magyar, can see. The stag leads the sons to fertile ground in the west. Upon his sons' return,

Nimrod dies, knowing that his sons have found a temporary place for his people. However, through a vision he knows that neither he nor his sons will reach the promised land, but that the son of one of their sons will lead the final way.

Hunor and Magyar, known as the twin eagles, capture and marry moon maidens. Hunor's son, Bendeguz (White Eagle) leads the Huns in a bloody progression that moves continually west, defying the more peaceful Magyars. Bendeguz marries a Cimmerian when he learns that they too believe a white eagle will lead them to freedom and prosperity in the west. Their son, Attila (Red Eagle), leads the Huns to further battle, but leaves the Magyars behind. Finally, trapped in mountains, Attila and Bendeguz pray again to Hadur for direction. The White Stag appears and brings them to Hungary and peace.

"The White Stag" is essentially a story of racial origins. One compiler of the story, Kate Seredy, notes that only MYTH can connect the Hungarians to the Huns, that the legends "cannot bear the weight of facts and dates."

For Further Reading

Seredy, Kate. *The White Stag*. Illustrated. New York: The Viking Press, 1944.

WHITE WAVE

Tao FOLKTALE. This tale of oral CHINESE STORYTELLING tradition focuses on a young farmer, Kuo Ming, who discovers a generous GODDESS living in a snail shell. The discovery of this MAGIC OBJECT and the beautiful MOON goddess housed within it brightens up Ming's otherwise lonely life. But after Ming violates his pact with the goddess by reaching out and trying to touch her hair, the goddess leaves him, giving him the shell as a gift and insisting that he call for her if ever he is in need. When a poor harvest leaves Ming near DEATH from starvation, she does save him, as she delivers to him an abundance of rice. Although the goddess is never to return again, Ming marries, has children, and lives a comfortable life.

This story underscores the importance of a tradition of oral storytelling with its closing; the end takes readers beyond the death of Ming and his children, and explains that, in time, they will all pass, but the story of Ming and the moon goddess will live on, as it is passed from Ming to his children and from generation to generation. Stories are, the tale insists, all that one has to show for one's existence. "White Wave" continues to be told today; storyteller Diane Wolkstein has narrated it in recent years. In 1979, Wolkstein published the story in English (*see* WOLKSTEIN, DIANE).

For Further Reading

White Wave: A Chinese Tale. Illustrated by Ed Young. New York: Harcourt Brace, 1996.

WHY WOMEN ALWAYS TAKE ADVANTAGE OF MEN

One of many African American FOLKTALES recorded by Zora Neale Hurston in MULES AND MEN (*see* HURSTON, ZORA NEALE). Mathilda Moseley, a rare woman teller of "lies" among the men who frequently gather in front of a storefront in Eatonville, Florida, explains how women came to control the battle of the sexes. As Mathilda relates, the first man and woman were equally strong. Since neither could "whip" the other, their fights were endless. The man asks GOD to remedy the situation by giving him more strength than the woman. God complies, and the man immediately proves his physical prowess by beating up the woman. Angered, the woman marches straight to God to ask him for equal strength. However, God refuses her request on the grounds that he cannot take back what he has given. The woman finds the DEVIL more willing to help. He tells her to ask God for a set of keys. God gives them, but does not explain their power. The woman returns to the Devil who teaches her how to use the keys. One is the key to the kitchen, the second, the key to the bedroom, and the last, the key to generations. The woman learns quickly to lock each away from the man. So, the man, desperate for food, sex, and children, must use his strength to benefit the woman.

This tale follows a familiar African American motif: the Devil outsmarts God just as Brer Rabbit outsmarts the "massa" (*see* UNCLE REMUS). However, here the woman is aligned with the perennial TRICKSTER. But the tale ultimately supports a traditional role for women: Women can find power only through the kitchen, sex, and their ability to bear children.

For Further Reading

Hurston, Zora Neale. *Mules and Men.* Philadelphia: Lippincott, 1935.

WILD MAN

Creatures resembling humans as well as animals. In medieval storytelling literature, the wild man (or woman) lived within the deepest recesses of the forest. The wild people were described as part human in that they had human faces and walked upright, yet they were part animal because they were covered with hair or fur. According to most wild man LEGENDS, the wild people avoided humans, preferring to live among the animals. One example of a wild man is Spencer's Sir Satyrane (*see* SATYRS), a character in the EPIC poem *The Faerie Queen.* This wild man, along with other satyrs, discovered the virgin Una in the forest, the victim of an attempted rape. Because Una taught Sir Satyrane and the others "true sacred lore," they worshipped her instead of attacking her. The association of the wild man with the satyr (half human, half goat) is thought to have originated with Christianity. The actions of the wild man/satyr were deemed satanic.

Frequently one may find illustrations of the DEVIL as a satyr. The list of offenses against the wild man/satyr were woeful: mischievousness, cowardliness, drunkenness, lustfulness, and a host of other contemptuous activities. The modern-day stories of the sasquatch and the yeti echo the earlier versions of the wild man as a hairy, part human, part animal creature living in the dense forestland.

WILDE, JANE (1826–1896)

Irish nationalist poet and editor of two significant volumes of Irish FOLKLORE: *Ancient Legends, Mystic Charms, and Superstitions of Ireland* (1888) and *Ancient Cures, Charms and Usages of Ireland* (1890). Born Jane Francesca Algee and claiming descent from

Dante, Lady Wilde first achieved fame as a writer and poet for the Irish nationalist cause in the 1840's with the publishing of her work in *The Nation* (edited by Gavan Duffy) and writing under the names John Fanshawe Ellis and Speranza. Upon marrying Sir William Wilde in 1851, she set up the leading literacy salon in Dublin. After his death in 1876, she followed her brilliant younger son, Oscar, to London, where she embarked on a second literary career editing her late husband's collections of Irish FOLKTALES. Sir William Wilde, a leading urologist, had assembled a vast and unsorted collection of stories and LEGENDS told to him by his country patients, from whom he would accept a story in lieu of a fee. The two resulting volumes were very important for the Irish Literary Revival. William Butler Yeats, among others, borrowed source material for his plays from these stories (*see* YEATS, WILLIAM BUTLER).

WILLIAMSON, DUNCAN (1928–)

Scottish writer and traditional storyteller. As a member of the nomadic group of Scottish Highland people known as the "Travellers," Williamson grew up immersed in the ritual storytelling practices of the group. Williamson continued to retell the LEGENDS orally to the Travellers while his wife, Linda Williamson, taped and transcribed the narrations for the rest of world. The first of the books produced by Linda Williamson, *Fireside Tales of the Traveller Children,* was published in 1982. Both Williamson and his wife took pains to record the stories of adventure, enchantment, and the supernatural exactly as they were spoken. Of the stories themselves, critics have remarked on the richness of the narratives as manifested in their uniquely provincial style. To provide a wider understanding of the intimate characteristics of Williamson's FOLKTALES, Linda Williamson felt impelled to provide insightful footnotes to the Travellers stories. Williamson wholeheartedly supported and assisted in this transfer from oral storytelling to the written page because he believed the "great wealth of lore [of the Scottish Travellers] stood to be lost or misunderstood." Williamson wrote that it was imperative to impart the "cherished ideals of our ancestors" to children, in order to form a better future. Other Williamson volumes include *The Broonie, Silkies, and Fairies* (1985), *A Thorn in the King's Foot* (1987), and *Tell Me a Story for Christmas* (1987).

WILL-O'-THE-WISP

Phosphorescent light, also call Jack-o'-lantern, foxfire, corpse light, St. Elmo's Fire, *Ignis Fatuus,* and by other names. In FOLKLORE, the lights are variously identified as the souls of the dead who have been condemned to wander the earth, omens of DEATH, a ghostly funeral procession, and DEMONS or DRAGONS.

Will-o'-the-wisp or *Ignis Fatuus* is seen moving over marshy places. The swamp-lights appear to recede from those who try to reach them, sometimes vanishing and reappearing behind the person. Some who try to follow the lights drown in the marshes, leading to tales of a spirit who leads travelers astray—or who guides them on their way. Such lights are sometimes considered the souls of unbaptized children.

The electrical discharge that lights up ship masts during storms is called St. Elmo's Fire, after the patron saint of Mediterranean seamen. It may be considered a warning or a good omen. The light has also been associated with other saints and GODS and with the ghosts of drowned seamen.

Will-o'-the-wisps, Jack-o'-lanterns, or corpse lights can be seen in cemeteries at night, and are usually considered damned souls. There are many different superstitions about them; they can be driven away by swearing at them or by throwing a knife or a key at them; if you put a needle on the ground and run away, the souls will escape through the eye of the needle. Corpse lights are also said to float directly over a corpse and are thought to be the soul of the deceased seen rising from the body.

For Further Reading

Rhys, Ernest. *The English Fairy Book.* Illustrated by Frederick C. Witney. New York: F.A. Stokes, 1900.

WIND

Character who appears in many world mythologies, but is especially prevalent in many North American Indian tribal mythologies. The wind as a character often operates as a malevolent spirit or as a beneficent (super)natural force: in the Pueblo mythology, the wind is a spirit that brings smallpox and other epidemics to the people; in the IROQUOIS CREATION story ALGON AND THE SKY MAIDEN, the wind magically impregnates the daughter of the sky chieftain, resulting in the CREATION of humankind. In many mythologies, there are multiple wind characters who have been assigned a specific geographic location from which they emanate; this directional determinant often defines the relationship between the wind character and humankind. Also, in some mythologies, the various wind characters are assigned a color—the Apache mythology has a Black, White, Blue, and Yellow wind, each representing one of the FOUR DIRECTIONS—which signifies a relationship between the wind character and some aspect of tribal life or nature itself.

WISE OLD MAN

Protective figure who provides aid to the HERO as he or she departs. After the hero receives "the call to adventure," the first stage of the hero-journey or QUEST often involves an encounter with a wise old man or a helpful CRONE who plays a protective role. Whether the wise old man provides wisdom, encouragement, useful information, or an amulet, his role is to help the hero arrive at the next stage of the journey. This guide may be a WIZARD, hermit, teacher, shepherd, seer, or priest.

When TELEMACHOS, son of the long-absent Odysseus in HOMER's ODYSSEY, reaches manhood, he wants to rid the palace of his mother's suitors and find his father, Mentor, whose name means teacher, guides him (*see* SEARCH FOR THE FATHER). Tiresias, the blind seer of the Sophocles's *Oedipus Cycle* of plays, attempts to be a guide to both Oedipus in *Oedipus the King* and Creon in *Antigone;* however, neither one hears his wisdom and both of them are destroyed by their own *hubris.* As young men, the Greek heroes

Herakles and Jason are both taught by the wise centaur Chiron, who was part man and part horse.

Carl Jung saw the figure of the old man of special powers as the symbol of the spirituality of the personality which emerges when consciousness is overburdened with "clarified, apprehended and assimilated matter welling up from the unconscious."

WITCH

Images of the negative aspect of women appearing in MYTH, LEGEND, and FAIRY TALE. The witch as she appears in FOLKLORE must be differentiated from the widespread persecution and murder of witches in Europe and Salem, Massachusetts in the fifteenth to seventeenth centuries. The witches of folklore are represented as sorceresses, temptresses, murderers, cannibals, or simply as malevolent CRONES with special powers. Witches are said to be nocturnal, and familiar imagery has them accompanied by black cats and riding on broomsticks; other ANIMALS associated with witches are snakes, toads, and owls. They are often portrayed as dressing in black, living in a hut hidden in the woods, and stirring a boiling cauldron where magic potions are brewing. Witches generally are associated with the DEVIL and evil, yet occasionally there are good witches, such as Glenda in *The Wizard of Oz*. Although we tend to think of witches as hags or crones, they are also portrayed as seductive beauties. In fairy tales, wicked stepmothers are sometimes witches in disguise (*see* STEPMOTHER—WICKED). Witches are able to SHAPE-SHIFT and transform humans into animals, and they can affect the weather, sexuality, and fertility.

As destroyer, the witch appears in the fairy tales of many cultures. She is Ragana in Lithuanian folklore, with her name etymologically related to the verb "to know, see, foresee" and to the noun for "horn, crescent," connecting her to the Greek GODDESS and crone, HECATE, and to the MOON. In Russian fairy tales, she is BABA YAGA, a witch who will often eat her victims. The name "Baba" means "grandmother," while the roots of the name

"Yaga" connect it to "disease," "fright," and "wrath" in Russian, Polish, and Proto-Slavic.

The witch of the GRIMM BROTHERS's fairy tales is "a crooked Old Woman, yellow and lean, with a large hooked nose, the point of which reached her chin," writes Marija Gimbutas in *The Language of The Goddess*, and, "The nose is hooked like the beak of a bird of prey. She is none other than the goddess Holle degraded to a witch." She appears in "Hansel and Gretel," where she lives in a tempting cottage made of candy, but she would prefer to eat Hansel, whom she tries to fatten up and then cook. The wicked stepmother of "Snow White" has a magic mirror and can create poison to kill her stepdaughter; she is also able to transform herself into an old hag.

Common in British folktales, witches are present in stories such as "The Blacksmith's Wife of Yarrowfoot," where a blacksmith's apprentice is married to a witch; "The Elder-Tree Witch"; "The Witch of Berkeley," the story of a witch at the time of the Norman Conquest; and "Witches at Halloween."

Witches also appear in Shakespeare's plays, most notably *Macbeth*, and in modern fairy tales such as Frank L. Baum's *The Wizard of Oz* and C. S. Lewis's *Chronicles of Narnia*.

For Further Reading

Gimbutas, Marija. *The Language of the Goddess*. San Francisco: HarperCollins, 1989.

Hansel and Gretel. Illustrated by Susan Jeffers. New York: Dial, 1990.

Johnston, Tony. *Alice Nizzy Nazzy: The Witch of Santa Fe*. Illustrated by Tomie dePaola. New York: Atheneum, 1995.

Snow White and the Seven Dwarfs. Illustrated by Chihiro Iwasaki. New York: Picture Book Studio, n.d.

WIYOT

Creator of humans in the Shoshonean (Luiseno) creation MYTH. When the Shoshonean Indians dance to the rising moon, they are retelling the story of their CREATION. According to legend, before the world was created there existed only Kevish-

Atakvish (space void), also known as Omai-Yamai (nothingness). Kevish-Atakvish first created Turkmit and Tomaiyovit, the male sky and the female EARTH respectively. They in turn gave birth to the many topographical elements on earth. From earth itself came Takwish, a fearsome meteor, his son, Towish, the immortal soul of humans, and finally Wiyot, who created corporeal humans. The humans multiplied and moved with Wiyot to a place called Temecula. It was here where the EARTH-MOTHER Tomaiyovit finally decided to bring out the SUN she had hidden to light the earth. The people placed the sun in the sky. Apparently Wiyot also created ANIMALS because Frog complained of the legs Wiyot had given her. To spite Wiyot, Frog spit poison into Wiyot's water. Wiyot knew he would soon die and proceeded to teach the people everything they needed to know before he had to leave. From within Wiyot's burial ashes, a tree began to grow that became the great tree of YGGDRASIL. To this day Wiyot returns to his people most every night in the form of the MOON.

WIZARDS

Powerful magicians or sorcerers, commonly found in Druidic and Celtic FOLKLORE. Wizards were usually men capable of performing magic and SHAPE-SHIFTING after extensive experience and training. Not all wizards were bad, as the wizard MERLIN of Arthurian legend proves (*see* ARTHUR). Wizards would be hired to train boys to become wizards and learn to transform, shape-shift, and cast SPELLS.

Supernatural wizards were those who had an inborn aptitude and started as a god. Two such supernatural wizards are Gwydion, Wizard and Bard of North Wales, son of the Welsh GODDESS Don, and Bran the Blessed, a primitive god and GIANT whose story is told in the *Mabinogion*, a collection of 11 stories drawn from the ancient books of Wales. Supernatural wizards were capable of using a magical strategy called "the separable soul," where a wizard or giant removed his life, or soul, from his body, placing it in an egg that was then

hidden in various places for protection. In oral tradition, the separable soul is linked to invulnerability limited by one vulnerable spot, such as the heel of Achilles in Ancient Greek mythology.

Contemporary tales of wizards can be found in Frank L. Baum's famous novel, *The Wonderful Wizard of Oz* (1900); Ursula K. Le Guin's *Earthsea Quartet*, which opens with the novel *A Wizard of Earthsea* (1968); and in Peter Beagle's novel, *The Inn-Keeper's Song* (1993).

For Further Reading

Baum, Frank L. *The Wizard of Oz*. Illustrated by Michael Hague. New York: Henry Holt, 1982.

Brenner, Barbara. *The Color Wizard*. Illustrated by Leo and Diane Dillon. New York: Bantam, 1989.

Lehane, Brendan. *Wizards and Witches*. Alexandria, Virginia: Time-Life Books, 1984.

WOLF AND THE SEVEN LITTLE KIDS *See* THE SEVEN LITTLE KIDS

WOLKSTEIN, DIANE (1942–)

American storyteller, folklorist, and writer. An accomplished folklorist and storyteller, Wolkstein uses a vivid modern verse or prose to effectively reconstruct for modern audiences tales from various cultures ranging from Ancient Sumer to Eskimo. Wolkstein has published many of these stories, including *Squirrel's Song: A Hopi-Indian Story* (1975), *The Red Lion: A Persian Sufi Tale* (1977), *The Banza: A Haitian Folk Tale* (1980), and *Innana: Queen of Heaven and Earth: Her Stories and Hymns from Sumer* (1983). The 6,000-year-old Sumerian tales of Innana include many myths common to an oral tradition of storytelling, such as the sacred MARRIAGE, DESCENT TO THE UNDERWORLD, and the DEATH and REBIRTH of GODS.

Wolkstein's career as a storyteller began in 1967 with the New York City Department of Parks and Recreation, where she created her position of "storyteller" and told between 40 and 50 stories a month. Since then, she has been become one of the most highly regarded storytellers of her time. She has told stories at major storytelling festivals, including the John Masefield Storytelling Festival in Toronto, Canada (1972), and the Fifth National Association for the Preservation and Perpetuation of Storytelling Festival in Jonesboro, Tennessee (1977). In 1967, she hosted her own radio show "Stories from Many Lands with Diane Wolkstein," which featured her as the teller of stories from around the world and across the ages. She has received numerous awards for her storytelling, including an American Library Association Notable Book Citation for her narration of "WHITE WAVE: A Tao Tale."

WOMAN WHO FELL FROM THE SKY

Iroquois deity considered First Woman, creator and destroyer of life. Also known as Aataentsic to the Iroquois of northeast North America, Woman Who Fell from the Sky is the mother of Gusts of WIND and the grandmother of Iouskeha and Tawiskaron. Like the Hindu GODDESS KALI, she is a creator and destroyer, and in her malevolent aspect she is believed to cause fatal diseases and then serve as the keeper of the dead. In one LEGEND, Aataentsic learns from the spirit of her dead father that she is to marry Earth-Holding Chief. In her journey to reach him, she undergoes many difficulties, including TESTS created by Earth-Holding Chief. Finally, she returns to her village where she gives birth to a daughter, Gusts of Wind. Aataentsic falls to a blue lake below (although whether the people of the village throw her or she falls inadvertently is unclear) and her daughter returns to her womb as she is falling. Because she has to give birth once more, the ANIMALS and birds of the lake make land from the mud to give her a place to rest from her fall and bear Gusts of Wind. In another legend, Woman Who Fell from the Sky gives birth to twins, one good and one evil, but the evil twin kills her when he bursts from her armpit.

Equivalent goddesses to Woman Who Fell from the Sky are the Iroquois Awehai, the Seneca goddess Eagentci, the Huron sky goddess Ketq Skwayne and the Huron Yatahéntshi, and Navajo First Woman. In one myth about Awehai, she is thrown from the skies by her husband, who believes she has betrayed him. While she falls, she catches animals and seeds and takes them with her toward the water below. With the help of winged creatures who guide her descent, she lands on the back of Great Turtle, where they form the earth by gathering dirt on Great Turtle's back. Then Awehai frees the animals and scatters the seeds, which grow everywhere, beautifying the earth. Inspired by the earth's splendor, Awehai creates children who become the Iroquois tribe.

A WOMAN'S QUEST

African Wala tale involving TRANSFORMATION. A very handsome young man, whom all of the women are in love with and want to marry, decides that the only woman he will marry is the one who knows his private birthname. He devises a plan: He will pretend he is dead and have his father tell all the young women that if one can find out his private birthname, he will arise from the dead and marry her. Although young women come from everywhere, only one who is on her way finds out, for as she is traveling, an old woman taking a bath asks her to scrub her back. The young woman agrees, and the CRONE then informs her that in Busa is a man named Dzerikpoli. This happens to be the handsome man's private name, and as the young woman walks toward Busa, she keeps singing that she will marry Dzerikpoli. As she sings, one by one the seven doors of the seven-room compound where Dzerikpoli is kept begin to open. Dzerikpoli hears her singing and sings back, and by the time she arrives at the compound, Dzerikpoli comes out and embraces her and says he will marry her. On the way to get married, they see the same old woman in the bath, and once again she asks the young woman to scrub her back. This time the young woman is more arrogant, so she refuses. Shortly afterwards, she is changed into a leper, and Dzerikpoli no longer wants to marry her. He runs away, but she chases him; he turns into a reed and she becomes the fiber used to weave reeds together to form a mat. Just then a weaver cuts the reed and the fiber and weaves them into a mat that a new mother buys; the mat, however, makes little noises as she lies on it, showing that the leper has not stopped running after the man and man has not stopped running from the leper.

This story includes the MOTIF of the TEST and suggests that both the young man and the young woman are punished for being arrogant and they deserve each other and their transformations.

For Further Reading

Abrahams, Roger D. *African Folktales.* New York: Pantheon, 1983.

WOODS—ENCHANTED

Symbol of the threshold, the realm of the spiritual world or DEATH. The enchanted woods or forest is a place of peril, testing, initiation, darkness, the secrets of nature, and the realm of the psyche and the female principle. Carl Jung maintained that the enchanted forest and "its sylvan terrors that figure so prominently in children's tales symbolize the perilous aspects of the unconscious, that is, its tendency to devour or obscure the reason." That the woods obscure sunlight makes them a wild and mysterious place filled with dangers and DEMONS, far from what is safe, tame, and cultivated.

For the Ancient Greeks and Romans, the woods were a sacred place, consecrated to a particular god, symbolizing the mysterious abode of the god. Like the LADDER TO HEAVEN, the trees of the enchanted forest reach deep down into the EARTH on one end and high up toward heaven on the other, thereby connecting the earthly with the spiritual.

In the GRIMM BROTHERS'S FAIRY TALE "Hansel and Gretel," the children are lost in the woods and come upon an enchanted place with a gingerbread cottage; what seems to be PARADISE, given their hunger, becomes a place of danger and trials, forcing them to use their ingenuity to survive. In fairy tales in general, the enchanted woods or forest is "inhabited by WITCHES, dragons, GIANTS, DWARFS, bears, and the like—symbols of all the dangers with which young people must deal with if they are to survive their rites of passage and become mature, responsible adults," writes Hans Biedermann in *A Dictionary of Symbolism.*

WORK SONGS

Song or chant sung while working. Work songs often set the rhythm—as well as relieve the tedium—of repetitious motion. They may be sung by individuals or by groups and are usually accompanied only by the sounds of the tools or the bodies at work. Occasionally an instrument such as a bagpipe, drum, or rattle enlivens the pace.

Laborers around the world and in every period of time have developed work songs—Ancient Greeks, West Africans, African American slaves and prisoners, Korean coolies, and many others. Such songs are still heard today in cultures that do not use power tools and equipment.

Many songs are about the work itself, but others are about the food, drink, or other pleasures to be enjoyed after the work is done. For example, cumulative or counting songs may mark off rows mowed, shovels lifted, or the drinks to be consumed later.

Work songs and BALLADS also tell stories. The medieval French songs that accompanied weaving or spinning describe a woman's sad life and loves. African American work songs include stories about everyday life and about heroes such as the remarkable railroad worker, John Henry (*see* HENRY, JOHN). *See also* CUMULATIVE STORY AND SONG, SEA CHANTEYS.

WORLD PARENTS

Figures in MYTHS of CREATION based on the EARTH-MOTHER and SKY-FATHER motif. World parents occur in the cosmogonies of many cultures such as the Fon, Polynesian, Egyptian, Minyong, Yoruba, Yuma, and Greek creation myths. In general, the sky or HEAVENS is represented by the FATHER figure and the EARTH and matter is represented by the MOTHER figure. In EGYPTIAN CREATION, however, the female Nut is portrayed as the sky arching over her prone brother, Geb, who symbolizes the earth. Sometimes the parents are originally one and are then divided or separated (*see*

DIVISION OF WORLD PARENTS). In some myths the mother is seen first as the PRIMEVAL WATERS.

While the temptation is to envision world parents as humans, in many myths they are more correctly seen as the male and female principals, as in the world parent creation myth of the Shilluk people of the Sudan. There the male creator, Jo-Uk, first created the Sacred White Cow, symbol of the female, and then impregnated her. She gave birth to a son, and his grandson became the founder and first ruler of the Shilluk. In Babylonian creation, the primordial parents are Apsu, the freshwater ocean, and Tiamat, the saltwater ocean, whose "commingling" eventually produces the major gods. In Hindu mythology, "the phallus of Heaven," which symbolizes the male force, makes love to his young daughter, Earth. From some of the seed that spills onto Earth come words and rituals as well as the Angirases, who are "the mediators" between humans and gods. In the creation myth of the Minyong people, non-Hindus of India, Sedi symbolizes the earth and Melo the sky, and the creatures who live between them are fearful that they will be squashed to death by the love-making of these world parents (*see* SEDI AND MELO). In Greek mythology, GAIA, the Great Mother who represents Earth, is the first to emerge from chaos, and she is the mother of Uranos, who personifies Heaven. Out of their mating come the first gods, the Titans.

All world parents myths are archetypal in that they illustrate primitive people's intuitive sense of the need for both male and female forces to produce ANIMALS, vegetation, and human life. Because the birth process was so obviously connected with women and female animals, the female force was more likely to be connected with matter or the primeval waters, as the waters were connected with the womb and its amniotic fluid. The connection between the male force and the sky or heaven relates to the less obvious but no less necessary role played by the father figure in reproduction.

WULARBI

Male HEAVEN featured in the CREATION MYTH of the Krachi people of Tongo in Africa. In the beginning, it is said, Wularbi, representing a male-gendered heaven, slept on top of the female EARTH, Asase Ya. Mankind lived in the small space between them. Wularbi eventually moved to a higher place in the sky because the human movement irritated him. If the humans were not wiping their dirty hands on Wularbi after a long day's work, then they were blowing smoke from fires into his eyes. One older woman was said to repeatedly whack Wularbi with her grinding pestle. Another older woman was rumored to occasionally season her soups with cut-off bits of Wularbi.

For Further Reading

Radin, Paul. *African Folktales*. Princeton, NJ: Princeton University Press, 1970.

XHOSA

African people whose ancestors moved into southern Africa in the sixteenth century. Like the Zulu, Swazi, and Ndebele, the Xhosa are well known for their long tradition of oral narrative. Performers, such as Nongenile Masithathu Zanani (*see* ZANANI, NONGENILE MASITHATHU), who learned her storytelling techniques from different generations of her family, will interpret Xhosa tales and perform them using exaggerated movements and inviting audience participation. The tales themselves tend to involve a moral lesson taken from Xhosa life, with many having been recorded by folklorist Harold Scheub (*see* SCHEUB, HAROLD). *See also* AFRICAN STORYTELLING.

YAHWEH

Hebrew creator and originator of the universe; the patriarchal and monotheistic deity of the Semitic peoples; the GOD of Israel. Yahweh is one of the early versions of what in monotheistic religions, particularly Judaism, Christianity, and Islam, is thought of as God. Our understanding of Yahweh originates from a composite of many individual writers and is a reflection not only of Israel's varied history, but of an ancient tradition of patriarchal gods. In the BIBLE, Yahweh is depicted as a creator, a provider, and a lawgiver (*see* ADAM AND EVE; GENESIS, BOOK OF; EXODUS; MOUNT SINAI). Yahweh generally is considered to be just. He cultivates a unique relationship with the people of Israel, and he listens to prayer. Yahweh is not defined by time, space, form, or by moral and ethical categories.

The Bible presents two different occasions indicating when the worship of Yahweh began. According to Genesis 4, Eve knew God by the name "Yahweh," and thus the story suggests that Yahweh was worshipped as soon as a human community existed. By contrast, the author of Exodus 6 asserts that the name "Yahweh" was first revealed to Moses. Nevertheless, biblical writers and modern scholars agree that the Bible requires that the Israelites serve Yahweh exclusively, a fact which is made clear in the covenant formed between Yahweh (God) and Moses at Mount Sinai. In spite of Yahweh's reminders, the Israelites insisted on worshipping other gods. According to the biblical authors, the fall of JERUSALEM in 587–6 B.C., for example, was caused by the Israelites' early failure to honor their covenant with Yahweh.

Yahweh frequently is referred to as a jealous god, most often because of the worship of other gods, for which he might dole out punishment. However, it is also believed that he is slow to anger.

As the Israelites became increasingly monotheistic, Yahweh absorbed many of the functions and attributes of older gods. From El, the head of the Canaanite pantheon, Yahweh assumed the traits of wisdom and beneficence. From BAAL, Yahweh acquired a thunderous voice, evident in his appearances on Mount Sinai, as well as the title "cloud rider": "Sing the praises of God, raise a psalm to his name;/extol him who rides on the clouds./[Yahweh] is his name" (Psalms 68:4). In the book of Job, Yahweh reveals himself in a tempest or whirlwind, the appropriate element of the sky-storm god of whom he is one manifestation. Like Indra, Thor, ZEUS, and others, Yahweh also is described as a bull (Genesis 49:24; Isaiah 1:24; Psalms 132:2, 132:5).

Yahweh is often depicted as humanlike. The Hebrew creation story states that "[Yahweh] created human beings in his own image" (Genesis 1:27). Other biblical passages show that Yahweh has a face, a back, arms, and legs. Daniel describes Yahweh as an OLD MAN with white hair: "and the Ancient in Years took his seat;/his robe was white as snow,/his hair like lamb's wool" (Daniel 7:9).

Yahweh is sometimes presented as a warrior who bears a bow, arrows, and a sword. Several biblical passages describe Yahweh's combat with a sea monster, during which he defeats his enemy in a manner similar to MARDUK and Baal (Isaiah 27:1, Psalms 74:12–13). Just as Marduk is commonly referred to as a KING over his own peoples and the rest of the world, Yahweh is king of Israel and the world.

YEATS, WILLIAM BUTLER (1865–1939)

Modern Irish poet, dramatist, and author who first preserved traditional Irish FOLKLORE in Modernist fashion. Yeats was born in Dublin, the eldest son of J. B. Yeats and brother of Jack Yeats, both celebrated painters. Educated first at the Godolphin School, Hammersmith, and the High School, Dublin, Yeats later studied art in both London and Dublin, where he eventually developed an interest in mystic religion and the supernatural, abandoning his study of art at the age of 21 to pursue a career in literature.

Although his reading and interests were quite worldly, he nevertheless clung to Ireland as the main source for his imagery, center of his local allusions, and the locale for most of his activities. To better serve this in-terest in his country, he published *The Wanderings of Oisin and Other Poems* in 1889, in which, for the first time, Irish LEGENDS were expressed with a modern consciousness, and he also edited various anthologies of traditional Irish folklore in the oral tradition. Additionally, he founded an Irish Literary Society in London in 1891, and another in Dublin in 1892. He also helped create the Irish National Theatre, opening the Abbey Theatre in 1904 in Dublin to showcase his own dramatic works, as well as those by other Irish playwrights, including Lady Augusta Gregory and John Synge.

Eventually Yeats developed an intense interest in symbolism and the French symbolist movement, claiming that most poets wrote within schemes of systematic images, tracing such recurrent symbols in the works of Shelley and Blake. This work found its way into his own poetry, so that images such as the rose, lily, or star began recurring with double meanings, emblematic of human activities, as did less conventional ones, such as the two trees and the valley of the black pig; to all, Yeats gave a decidedly Irish inflection, always remaining ultimately concerned with symbolism and how art may represent nature, and vice versa. He also thought that consciousness arose out of a conflict of opposites, which he represented by interpenetrating cones, or gyres, the top of one in the base of the other.

Yeats was highly influenced by two occultists of the time, Madame Helena Petrovna Blavatsky, founder of the Theosophical Movement, and MacGregor Mathers, founder of the Golden Dawn, influences often evident in his symbolism.

In 1917, Yeats married an Englishwoman, Georgie Hyde-Lees, with whom he had a son and daughter, immortalizing them, as well as the Norman tower in which they lived on and off for years, Thoor Ballylee, in his poems. Yeats was also active in politics, not only serving six years in the senate after the Irish Free State was formed, but also remaining, after completion of that term, devoted to finding new ways to turn Ireland into a nation free of imaginative constraint, where people could cultivate their artistic talents without fear of reproach. He died on January 28, 1939, in southern France, just before World War II began; when the war was over, his body was exhumed and returned to Ireland.

The Wind Among the Reeds and *A Vision* are two of his more famous collections of poetry, while *The Celtic Twilight* and his edition of *Irish Fairy and Folk Tales* more thoroughly concentrate on the folklore he so painstakingly sought to preserve and modernize.

For Further Reading

Donoghue, Denis. *William Butler Yeats*. New York: Viking, 1971.

Hone, Joseph Maunsell. *William Butler Yeats: The Poet in Contemporary Ireland*. New York: Haskell House, 1972.

Seiden, Morton Irving. *William Butler Yeats: The Poet as Mythmaker, 1865-1939*. East Lansing, MI: Michigan State University Press, 1962.

Yeats, William Butler. *The Celtic Twilight: Men and Women, Ghouls and Faeries*. London: Lawrence and Bullen, 1893.

———. *Collected Works*. Edited by Richard Finneran and George Mills Harper. New York: Macmillan, 1989, 1994.

———. *Fairy and Folk Tales*. 3rd ed. Gerrard's Cross, Ireland: Smythe, 1988.

———. *Irish Fairy and Folk Tales*. New York: Modern Library, 1994.

YELLOWMAN

Navajo storyteller and informant for anthropologist Barre Toelken. Yellowman lived on the Navajo Northern Reservation, located in southern Utah, before he, his wife, and their 13 children moved to Blanding, Utah, in 1956. It was in Blanding that Toelken, a longtime friend of Yellowman's, would regularly visit him and listen to his tales and theories about storytelling, providing Toelken with considerable material on the style and significance of Navajo COYOTE tales.

Yellowman firmly believed in the value of using the coyote stories, and storytelling in general, as a way to introduce children to the Navajo culture and belief system. In fact, he claimed that most of his stories, such as the tale of coyote and his role in creation, were primarily intended for his own children, though adults also become emotionally involved. The stories, however, do not offer a simple moral, but rather they introduce listeners to all different experiences and possibilities.

According to Toelken, each of Yellowman's performances were slightly different, and the type of audience, whether made up of adults or children, played a major role in the style and intonation of his delivery. Yet Yellowman insisted that though the words and gestures may change, the content of each story, and its ultimate message, always remains consistent.

For Further Reading

Toelken, Barre. "The 'Pretty Languages' of Yellowman: Genre, Mode, and Texture in Navaho Coyote Narratives." *Genre* 2.3 (September 1969): 211-235.

YEP, LAURENCE (1948–)

Chinese American author of children's and adult fiction. Yep is best known for his detailed portrayals of Chinese and Chinese American characters (*see* CHINESE STORYTELLING). Often Yep's characters reflect the author's own childhood experiences growing up Chinese American in a multicultural neighborhood. Just under the surface of Yep's highly imaginative stories lies the struggle for identity and the problems of racism as they affect a minority individual. For instance, in Yep's first book, *Sweetwater* (1973), a young man belonging to a minority group on the planet Harmony must struggle to survive in a hostile world that seeks to alienate the protagonist. *Sweetwater* has been praised for its brilliant combination of rich imagery and thought-provoking themes. Yep, however, was not limited to one period or genre; he also wrote *The Serpent's Children* (1984), a historical novel set in nineteenth-century China, and *The Mark Twain Murders* (1982), a mystery set in the nineteenth century featuring a young Mark Twain as its main character (*see* TWAIN, MARK). Yep's self-described method of storytelling involves the adult's return to a child-like sensibility—to a time when they still viewed the world with a sense of wonder. This method, according to Yep, was the only way to write for children in a truly empathetic way.

YGGDRASIL

Mythological ash tree that gives structure and protection to the Norse universe. According to Norse LEGENDS, Yggdrasil seems to have had no beginning and will continue to survive after the end of the world, or RAGNAROK. Its branches hang over the nine worlds and reach above the HEAVENS. Yggdrasil has three roots and one spring beneath each root. One root goes to Asgard, home of the GODS. Beneath this root is the Well of Urd, where the gods assemble each day. The second root leads to Jotunheim, the home of the giants, and beneath it lies the Spring of Mimir, whose waters are a source of wisdom (*see* ODIN). The third root connects to NIFLHEIM, a frozen region of snow and darkness. The Spring of Hvergelmir, the source of 11 rivers, is found under this root.

A variety of creatures inhabit Yggdrasil, some of which perpetually are destroying the tree. A wise eagle sits on Yggdrasil with a hawk perched between its eyes. A squirrel runs up and down the tree carrying malicious tales between the eagle and Nidhogg, a dragon who lives with a collection of serpents in Niflheim and continually gnaws the nearest root. Four deer leap within Yggdrasil's branches and nibble its bark. The tree drips dew which bees use to make honey. Three Norns, goddesses of destiny, take water and clay from the Well of Urd and place a mixture of them on the tree to heal and to protect it.

In spite of the suffering Yggdrasil endures from malevolent forces, it continues to nourish itself and is associated with childbirth and the CREATION of life. In the NORSE CREATION myth, the first man was made from a tree and was named Ash. During Ragnarok, Lif and Lifthrasir hide in Yggdrasil and survive to repopulate a newly created EARTH. As such, Yggdrasil is a phallic symbol and a Tree of Life.

In order to acquire wisdom, Odin, the ruler of the Norse gods, hanged himself from Yggdrasil, also known as a Tree of Knowledge. Yggdrasil means "Odin's horse," a fitting name as Old Norse poets referred to the gallows tree as the "horse." Likewise, in Christian mythology, the cross of Jesus' crucifixion is a tree.

Yggdrasil belongs to a tradition in mythologies of a world tree as the axis or center of the universe. According to Indian mythology, BRAHMAN, the fully developed cosmos, is represented in the form of a giant tree, Asvattha. Asvattha's roots are buried in the sky, and its branches are spread over the earth. In the story of Hebrew creation, the Tree of Life and of Knowledge stands in the middle of Eden. ADAM AND EVE eat fruit from this tree and thus are banished from the garden. This world tree is both a source of knowledge and of death.

In other traditions, the BUDDHA finds enlightenment under the BODHI TREE, Osiris is found in a tree (*see* ISIS AND OSIRIS), and Adonis, from Greek mythology, is born of a tree.

YOLEN, JANE (1939–)

Children's author as well as a folksinger, playwright, poet, and editor. Yolen is best known and acclaimed for her writing of beautiful, and sometimes abstract, literary FOLKTALES. Many of Yolen's stories are conceptual reconstructions of ancient MYTHS, employing, for example, elements of the Greek myth of Daphne and APOLLO. Other stories by Yolen might resonate with seasoned NURSERY RHYMES or a modern-day historical event. Most of Yolen's stories, however, are an amalgam of these earlier echoes into more generalized symbols and illusions of FOLKLORE. Yolen's concern for the perpetuation of folklore, FABLES and MYTHS in either traditional or nontraditional modes is paramount. In *Touch Magic: Fantasy, Faerie, and Folktale in the Literature of Childhood* (1981), Yolen writes extensively on what she sees as the recent problematic move away from traditional storytelling, "the most basic element of our education." Yolen's own self-professed writing method involves reading each sentence out loud as she writes it before moving on to the next, then reading each paragraph out loud, and finally reading the entirety of the book out loud until the story has been thoroughly retold. Yolen revels in each reader's individual response to her stories because she considers storytelling to be ever dynamic and personal to both its tellers and listeners. In

The Girl Who Loved the Wind (1972), for example, Yolen created the story out of her own experience, yet one child who read it gleaned a measure of solace from reading the book. Other books, such as *The Devil's Arithmetic* (1988), explain a tragedy such as the Holocaust to its young readers. Yolen's published fiction and nonfiction writing is voluminous, beginning with *The Witch Who Wasn't* published in 1964.

YORUBA CREATION

Creation of the world, according to Yoruba oral tradition. Olorun, the Supreme Being, orders Orisha Nla, or Obatala, to make a world from Chaos, a watery and shapeless mass. Orisha Nla takes, or is given, a shell, some EARTH, a pigeon, and a five-toed hen to complete the task (minor story VARIANTS sometimes add iron to this list or change the bird to a rooster). As Chaos is below the sky in which Olorun and other GODS live, Orisha Nla has to descend on (what some say) is a chain extending downward towards Chaos. When he arrives, Orisha Nla throws the small amount of "magic" earth into a patch. The pigeon and hen immediately begin scratching the patch until land and sea are separated. A chameleon inspects the work done by Orisha Nla and pronounces a job well done to the Supreme Being. In some versions, lesser gods first live on the newly created earth before mortals eventually do. Orisha Nla later returns to earth and creates the city of Ifé, or Ifé-Ilé as it is known today. The Yoruba people, formed from earth by Orisha Nla, are actually given life by Olorun, the Supreme Being. Orisha Nla attempts to discover the secret of giving life by hiding in Olorun's workshop, but is put into a deep sleep by Olorun before he can see a thing. *See also* CREATION.

For Further Reading

Ogumefu, M.I. *Yoruba Legends.* New York: AMS Press, 1985.

YOUNG, ELLA (1867–1956)

Compiler and author of Irish FOLKLORE. Young had always been fascinated by the tales of BANSHEES, sprites, GIANTS, and other creatures from Irish folklore. After learning Gaelic, Young traveled throughout the Irish countryside to gather obscure Celtic stories (*see* CELTIC STORYTELLING). At times she wrote down the stories of the peasants exactly as they themselves had heard them throughout generations. Other times Young varied her stories according to her own humorous and suspenseful style—yet she always remained true to the spirit of Irish folklore. Most of Young's storytelling books are geared towards children in their employment of fascinating, magical detail, and other-worldly nuances. Young's first book published in America, *The Wonder-Smith and His Son* (1927), for example, tells of Wonder-Smith, the Gubbaun Saor, maker of the universe and the GODS. The stories within the volumes, sometimes frightful, all involve the principal character, Wonder-Smith. Young's two other children's books based on Irish Folklore, *The Tangle-Coated Horse* (1929), and *The Unicorn With the Silver Shoes* (1932), were regarded by critics as inferior to the Wonder-Smith stories. In addition to her children's books, Young incorporated Irish folklore into several books of original poetry that again evoked the fairyland and mystery of Irish LEGEND, such as *Poems* (1906) and *The Coming of Lugh* (1909). To explain her ability to capture the essence of the old Irish spoken language with all its subtleties, Young once said that she had talked with ELVES and understood the language of the forest and the SEA.

YOUNGEST DAUGHTER

In many MYTHS and FAIRY TALES, the most beautiful, the kindest, or the daughter chosen to perform a feat. Myths and fairy tales are replete with examples of the youngest of three sisters being far more beautiful than the others, as in the case of the Greek Psyche, who marries Cupid, the god of love. Her older, jealous sisters are the ones who persuade Psyche to learn the identity of her mysterious husband, which results in causing much grief and many trials for Psyche.

Like Psyche, CINDERELLA of the GRIMM BROTHERS's fairy tale is also the youngest and most beautiful of the three daughters, even if the older two are her stepsisters. Cinderella is the one chosen by the PRINCE to dance with him, and only her foot is small enough to fit in the glass slipper. In William Shakespeare's play *King Lear*, the youngest of Lear's three daughters, Cordelia, is the one who remains silent when her father questions his three daughters as to their love of him, for Cordelia is wiser and more sincere than her sisters, and she knows that no language can express her feelings. With Cordelia's death at the play's denouement, Lear finally recognizes the truth about Cordelia. *See also* APULEIUS, CUPID AND PSYCHE.

For Further Reading

Porazinska, Janina. *The Enchanted Book: A Tale From Krakow.* Translated by Bozena Smith. Illustrated. San Diego: Harcourt Brace Jovanovich, 1987.

Va, Leong. *A Letter to the King.* Translated by James Anderson. New York: HarperCollins, 1991.

YOUNGEST SON

In MYTHS and FAIRY TALES, the one who is singled out as the HERO, the good one, the simpleton, or the lucky one. In mythology and FOLKLORE, the youngest son is often "chosen" in one way or another. In Greek mythology, for example, ZEUS is the youngest son of the Titans Kronos and Rhea, and he is hidden from his father to protect him until he becomes the greatest of the GODS to sit on MOUNT OLYMPOS. The Polynesian TRICKSTER, demigod, and CULTURE HERO, MAUI, is the youngest of five sons and in all ways the cleverest and closest to a god in his feats. In the GRIMM BROTHERS's fairy tale "The Three Brothers," the youngest son proves the cleverest and the one to receive his father's house when all three sons are sent out to find a trade. The youngest son returns a fencing-master while his brothers have become a barber and a blacksmith; when it rains, the youngest son impresses his father most because he can wield his sword so quickly above his head that he prevents the rain from falling on him. The youngest son also triumphs in the Grimm Brothers's fairy tale "The Poor Miller's Boy and the Cat." *See also* YOUNGEST DAUGHTER, "THREE GOLDEN SONS."

For Further Reading

Isele, Elizabeth. *The Frog Princess.* Illustrated by Michael Hague. New York: Crowell, 1984.

Medearis, Angela Shelf. *The Singing Man.* Adapted from a West African folktale. Illustrated by Terea Shaffer. New York: Holiday House, 1994.

ZENANI, NONGENILE MASITHATHU

Female creator and teller of XHOSA narratives. Residing on the southeast coast of Africa, 30 miles from the Indian Ocean, Zenani is considered one of the finest living performers of Xhosa oral narratives. Zenani learned her trade from the many performances she observed when she was young, including those of her aunt, her grandmother, and her parents' friends. Folklorist Harold Scheub (*see* SCHEUB, HAROLD), who filmed many of Zenani's performances between 1968 and 1973, explains that she does use most storytelling techniques commonly observed in Xhosa performances, such as an exaggerated body language and emphasis on audience participation, but she employs them with a greater subtlety than most. Like other Xhosa storytellers, Zenani involves her audience in the performance, but she does not use an amiable approach to engage them. Instead she creates tension between herself and her audience by first using repetitions of words, phrases, and images, but then intentionally breaks from the patterns to frustrate the audience's expectations.

Although she is a frequent storyteller, and certainly has created hundreds of tales, most of her tales center around themes that are common to storytelling worldwide: birth, PUBERTY, MARRIAGE, and adulthood. In his recent book, *The World and the Word* (1992), Scheub collected over 20 of the tales he had recorded during his visits to Africa.

For Further Reading

Scheub, Harold. *The World and the Word: Tales and Observations from the Xhosa Oral Tradition.* Madison, WI: University of Wisconsin Press, 1992.

ZEUS

Patriarch of the Olympian dynasty in the ancient Greek PANTHEON. Zeus comes to power after he and the other Olympian GODS overthrow the Titans, establishing a patriarchal religious and social hierarchy. He and his brothers, Poseidon and HADES, draw lots to determine the realms over which they will rule. Poseidon becomes ruler of the SEA; Hades, lord of the Underworld; and Zeus, supreme ruler of the skies.

Zeus's daughter ATHENA, GODDESS of wisdom, is born directly from her father's forehead, but she is the only one of his children who is not the result of a sexual encounter. Though married to the jealous goddess HERA, who is also his sister, Zeus is famous for his many adulterous relationships with other women. A constant source of humiliation for Hera, Zeus's many love affairs are responsible for some of the most compelling and memorable stories about the Greek pantheon. His famous liaisons with mortal and immortal women often spawned gods, goddesses, HEROES, and HEROINES who figure prominently in Greek mythology. Disguised as a swan, he seduces Leda, a mortal woman, producing HELEN OF TROY, the woman whose kidnapping causes the Trojan War. An affair with Alcmene, another mortal, produces the famous hero Herakles. Zeus's seduction of Semele leads to the birth of the DIONYSOS, god of wine. One story holds that Zeus is the father of APHRODITE, goddess of love, by the nymph Dione. Zeus also has children with his wife: Hebe (cupbearer for the gods), Eileithyia (goddess of childbirth), Ares (god of war), and Hephaistos (god of fire and crafts and husband to Aphrodite).

Like other Olympian gods, Zeus frequently involves himself in the lives of mortals, often to gratify his sexual desires, and often because his loyalties or prejudices compel him to do so. He blinds Lycurgus, KING of Thrace, because the king insults Zeus's son, Dionysos. Sisyphus, king of Corinth, meets an even worse fate. Sisyphus tells the river god that he has seen Zeus, disguised as an eagle, carry off the god's daughter. For this betrayal, Zeus ensures that Sisyphus spends eternity rolling a rock up a hill only to have the rock roll back down every time. During the Trojan War, Zeus aides the Trojans by sending false dreams to Greek warriors, influencing battles, and ordering the other Olympians not to assist the Greeks. Years later, moved by the grief of Odysseus, he convinces the other gods to help assist the wandering hero on his journey home (*see* ODYSSEY).

As ruler of the sky and possessor of the thunderbolt, Zeus is the Greek version of the SKY-FATHER. He is the most powerful of all the deities who resided on MOUNT OLYMPOS, though his power is limited; he is neither omnipotent nor omniscient. His attempts to interfere in the lives of mortals and immortals often fail, and even he could not overcome the power of Fate. Still, he is awe-inspiring, and in the tradition of a true patriarch, he was worshipped and feared by both humans and gods.

For Further Reading

Low, Alice. *Macmillan Book of Greek Gods and Heroes.* New York: Macmillan, 1985.

ZION

From the Old Testament, Hebrew name for Jerusalem, Israel itself, and GOD's home. KING David captured Zion (Jerusalem) from the Jebusites and made it his home. As such, Zion is imbued with particular significance as the chosen place for the Hebrews, who become the people of Zion: "For the Lord has chosen Zion,/desired her for his home" (Psalms 132:13).

In addition, Zion is a spiritual or metaphorical place, the heavenly Jerusalem. It is the splendid home of God and, therefore, a refuge and defense for the Hebrews. The richness of Zion reflects the glory of its ruler: "Go round Zion in procession,/count the number of her towers,/take note of her ramparts,/pass her palaces in review/that you may tell generations yet to come/that such is God" (Psalms 48:12–14). Similar to sacred places in other stories, Zion is a mountain: "His holy mountain is fair and lofty,/the joy of the whole EARTH./The mountain of Zion, the far recesses of the north/is the city of the great King" (Psalms 48:1–2).

In Christian mythology, Zion is the place where the King or Messiah appears. Prior to entering Jerusalem, Jesus sent two of his disciples to bring him a donkey and her foal. He instructed the disciples to tell anyone who questioned them that "The Master needs them" (Matthew 21:3). Jesus' words fulfilled the Old Testament prophecy that said, "Tell the daughter of Zion, 'Here is your king, who comes to you in gentleness, riding on a donkey'" (Matthew 21:5). Thus, Zion is an important geographic and spiritual place in the Judeo-Christian tradition. *See also* GOLGOTHA, MAN OF LORE, MERU, MOUNT OLYMPOS, MOUNT PARNASSOS, MOUNT SINAI.

ZLATEH THE GOAT

Children's story written by Isaac Bashevis Singer (1904–), a Polish-born Yiddish author who emigrated to America in 1935 (*see* SINGER, ISAAC BASHEVIS). The story focuses on a young boy, Aaron, who must sacrifice his goat, Zlateh, to the slaughterer in order for his family to celebrate Hanukkah, which they otherwise cannot afford to do. Aaron is emotionally attached to Zlateh and does not want to take her to the slaughterer, but, like Abraham who must sacrifice his son in the story from the BIBLE, Aaron chooses to obey his father's request without question. Further paralleling the story of Abraham, the sacrificial offering, in this case Zlateh, is saved, presumably because of Aaron's willingness to sacrifice her.

In addition to the parallel to the Abraham story, "Zlateh the Goat" borrows from several FOLKLORE traditions, especially Jewish folklore. In Jewish folklore goats appear frequently, usually with positive associations. Most often, the goat has functioned as a sacrificial ANIMAL, but the goat figure has also appeared as a "nurse" in Yiddish literature, and even in Greek mythology (Zeus's goat-nurse Amalthea). The structure of Singer's story is also borrowed from FOLKTALES, and closely resembles numerous GRIMM BROTHERS'S tales. Singer's is a story of personal growth for the HERO, Aaron, as he goes on a journey, encounters a mystical experience, and returns altered by his experience because he possesses a greater understanding of his love and need for Zlateh.

For Further Reading

Singer, Isaac Bashevis. *Zlateh the Goat and Other Stories.* Translated from the Yiddish by Isaac Bashevis Singer and Elizabeth Shub. Illustrated by Maurice Sendak. New York: Harper & Row, 1996.

ZOROASTRIAN CREATION

Cosmogony of Zoroastrianism, a Persian religion founded by Zarathustra, or Zoroaster. Zoroastrianism dates back to the sixth century B.C., when the prophet Zoroaster wrote the sacred text of the AVESTA in the ancient Avestan language, although the present form of the Avesta was completed at least 200 years after Zoroaster's death.

According to the *Avesta*, Light is present before anything else, and within light are the power of the Word and the power of Nature. The formation of the universe came about when the Creator joined these two spirits. The "ideal" creation contains "the Spirit of the Power of the Words," while the material creation contains the Spirit of the Power of Nature. The nature of the Avestan material world begins with the "mass or conglomeration in the language of the world." Then comes conception and "hollowing" and "the language of men." This is followed by "formation and expansion in the language of men." At this stage, the Spirit of the Power of Nature unites with the Spirit of the Power of the Word and there is the firmament, with the SUN, MOON, and stars controlling "all creation under them." Then comes "the Wheel" and "becoming," the heat and moisture that makes the air, the "seeds of seeds," the elements, and, finally, living things such as cattle and men.

Zoroastrianism saw Ahura Mazda, also called Ohrmazd, as the creator, and he is opposed by Angra Mainyu, or Ahriman. Ohrmazd is responsible for having created Finite Time (12,000 years) from Infinite Time, with the stars placed to measure the passing of time. During the first 3,000 years of Finite Time, Ahriman is weak, but after the next 3,000, the period during which the world and ADAM AND EVE are created, Ahriman becomes strong and pollutes creation, so he has to be held in HELL.

For Further Reading

Boyce, Mary. *The Zoroastrians: Their Religious Beliefs and Practices.* London: Routledge & Keegan Paul, 1989.

———. ed. *Zoroastrianism.* Totowa, NJ: Barnes and Noble, 1984.

Zaehner, R.C. *The Teachings of the Magi.* New York: Oxford, n.d.

SELECTED BIBILIOGRAPHY

Abrahams, Roger, ed. *African Folktales: Traditional Stories of the Black World*. New York: Pantheon, 1983.

Abrams, M. H. *A Glossary of Literary Terms*. 6th ed. Forth Worth, TX: Harcourt Brace, 1993.

Adler, Sara Maria. *Calvino: The Writer as Fablemaker*. Potomac, MD: José Porrúa Turanzas, 1979.

Ammons, Elizabeth, and Annette White-Parks, eds. *Tricksterism in Turn-of-the-Century American Literature: A Multicultural Perspective*. Hanover, NH: University Press of New England/Tufts University, 1994.

Ashaninga, Kecizate, as told to Fernando Llosa Porras. "The Chain of Worlds." *Parabola* 2.3 (1977): 58-62.

Ashe, Geoffrey. *Guidebook to Arthurian Britain*. London: Longman Group Limited, 1980.

Ashliman, D. L. *A Guide to Folktales in the English Language*. Westport, CT: Greenwood, 1987.

Attwater, Donald. *The Penguin Dictionary of Saints*. Harmondsworth, Middlesex: Penguin, 1973.

Aylett, Robert, and Peter Skrine, eds. *Hans Sachs and Folk Theatre in the Late Middle Ages*. Lewiston: Edwin Mellen, 1995.

Baldick, Chris. *The Concise Oxford Dictionary of Literary Terms*. Oxford: Oxford University Press, 1990.

Barber, Richard, and Anne Riches. *A Dictionary of Fabulous Beasts*. London: Macmillan, 1971.

Barzun, Jacques, ed. *European Writers: The Romantic Century*. New York: Charles Scribner's Sons, 1985.

Basso, Ellen. *In Favor of Deceit: A Study of Tricksters in an Amazon Society*. Tucson: University of Arizona Press, 1987.

Bennett, Martin. *West African Trickster Tales*. New York: Oxford University Press, 1994.

Bettelheim, Bruno. *The Uses of Enchantment: The Meaning and Importance of Fairy Tales*. New York: Alfred A. Knopf, 1977.

Bierlein, J.F. *Parallel Myths*. New York: Ballantine, 1994.

Blackburn, Stuart. *Oral Epics in India*. Berkeley: University of California Press, 1989.

Boethius. *The Consolation of Philosophy*. Transcribed by V.E. Watts. Harmondsworth, Middlesex: Penguin, 1980.

Bondanella, Peter, and Julia Conway Bondanella, eds. *Dictionary of Italian Literature*. Westport, CT: Greenwood, 1996.

Bonnerjea, Biren. *A Dictionary of Superstitions and Mythology*. Detroit: Singing Tree Press, Book Tower, 1969.

Borges, Jorge Luis, with Margarita Guerrero. *The Book of Imaginary Beings*. Translated by Norman Thomas di Giovanni. London: Jonathan Cape, 1969.

Brackert, Helmut, and Volkmar Sander, eds. *German Fairy Tales*. New York: Continuum, 1985.

Branston, Brian. *Gods of the North*. New York: Thames and Hudson, 1980.

————. *The Lost Gods of England*. London: Thames and Hudson, 1974.

Briggs, Katharine. *A Dictionary of Fairies*. London: Allen Lane/Penguin, 1976.

————. *An Encyclopedia of Fairies: Hobgoblins, Brownies, Bogies, and Other Supernatural Creatures*. New York: Pantheon, 1976.

————. *The Fairies in Tradition and Literature*. London: Routledge, 1967.

Briggs, Ralph S. *The Halfchick Tale in France and Spain*. Helsinki: Academia Scientiarum Fennica, 1933.

Bulfinch, Thomas. *The Age of Fable or Beauties of Mythology*. New York: Tudor, 1935.

Burns, Allan F., trans. *An Epoch of Miracles: Oral Literature of the Yucatec Maya*. Austin, TX: University of Texas Press, 1983.

Burton, Richard F. *Supplemental Nights to the Book of the Thousand Nights and a Night*. Vol 3. Benares: The Kamashastra Society, 1886.

Briggs, Charles. *Competence in Performance: The Creativity of Tradition in Mexicano Verbal Art*. Philadelphia: University of Pennsylvania Press, 1988.

Calvino, Italo. *Italian Folktales*. New York: Harcourt Brace Jovanovich, 1980.

Campbell, Joseph. *The Hero with a Thousand Faces*. Princeton: Princeton University Press, 1968.

————. *The Masks of God: Primitive Mythology*. New York: Penguin Books, 1959. Reprint, Arkana, 1991.

Carpenter, Humphrey, and Mari Pritchard, eds. *The Oxford Companion to Children's Literature*. New York: Oxford University Press, 1984.

Carter, Albert Howard, III. *Italo Calvino: Metamorphoses of Fantasy*. Ann Arbor, MI: UMI Research Press, 1987.

Carter, Angela, ed. *The Virago Book of Fairy Tales.* London: Virago Press, 1990.

Cavendish, Richard. *King Arthur and the Grail: The Arthurian Legends and their Meaning.* London: Paladin, 1985.

Cirlot, J.E. *A Dictionary of Symbols.* Translated by Jack Sage. London: Routledge, 1971.

Coe, Michael. *The Maya.* 5th ed. London: Thames and Hudson, 1993.

Colum, Padraic. *Myths of the World.* New York: Grosset and Dunlap, 1930.

Coomaraswamy, A.K., and Sister Nivedita. *Myths of the Hindus and Buddhists.* New York: Dover Publications, n.d.

Cooper, Susan. "On Fairy Tales." *Sharing Literature with Children.* Edited by Francelia Butler. New York: Longman, 1977.

Cotterell, Arthur. *A Dictionary of World Mythology.* New York: Oxford University Press, 1986.

Couchaux, Brigitte. "Lilith." *A Companion to Literary Myths, Heroes and Archetypes.* Edited by Pierre Brunel. London and New York: Routledge Press, 1992.

Craigie, William A. *Scandinavian Folklore: Illustrations of the Traditional Beliefs of the Northern Peoples.* London: Alexander Gardner, 1896.

Crocker, Thomas. *Fairy Legends and Traditions of South Ireland.* London: John Murray, 1825-1828.

Crossley-Holland, Kevin. *The Norse Myths.* Harmondsworth, Middlesex: Penguin Books, 1982.

Cuddon, J.A. *A Dictionary of Literary Terms.* London: Andre Deutsch, 1977.

———. *The Penguin Dictionary of Literary Terms and Literary Theory.* 3rd ed. London: Penguin Books, 1991.

Dailey, Sheila. *Putting the World in a Nutshell.* New York: H.W. Wilson, 1994.

Daly, Lloyd W. *Aesop Without Morals: The Famous Fables and a Life of Aesop.* New York: Thomas Yoseloff, 1961.

Damon, James H. "The Strange Career of Jim Crow Rice." *Journal of Social History* 3.2 (Winter 1969-70): 109-122.

d'Aulnoy, Marie-Catherine. *Contes des Fees.* 2 vols. Paris: Plon, 1956.

Davidson, H.R. Ellis. *Gods and Myths of Northern Europe.* Harmondsworth, Middlesex: Penguin, 1964.

Davis, H.W. C., and J.R.H. Weaver, eds. *Dictionary of National Biography, 1912-1921.* Oxford: Oxford University Press, 1927.

Dawood, N.J., trans. *Tales from the Thousand and One Nights.* London: Penguin Books, 1973.

DeGraff, Amy. *The Tower and the Well.* Birmingham, AL.: Summa, 1985.

Delarue, Paul. *The Borzoi Book of French Folk Tales.* New York: Alfred A. Knopf, 1956.

Dobson, R.B., and J. Taylor. *Rymes of Robin Hood: An Introduction to the English Outlaw.* London: Heinemann, 1976.

Donoghue, Denis. *Thieves of Fire.* New York: Oxford Columbia Press, 1974.

Dorson, Richard M. *The British Folklorists: A History.* Chicago: University of Chicago Press, 1968.

———. *Folklore and Folklife: An Introduction.* Chicago: The University of Chicago Press, 1972.

Dorson, Richard M., ed. *Folktales Told Around the World*. Chicago: University of Chicago Press, 1975.

Eliade, Mircea. *Australian Religions: An Introduction*. Ithaca: Cornell University Press, 1973.

————. *The Forge and the Crucible: The Origins and Structures of Alchemy*. Chicago: University of Chicago Press, 1979.

————. *From Primitives to Zen. A Thematic Sourcebook of the History of Religions*. New York: Harper, 1967.

————. *Images and Symbols. Studies in Religious Symbolism*. New York: Sheed and Ward, 1969.

————. *Myth and Reality*. New York: Harper, 1963.

————. *The Myth of the Eternal Return*. Princeton, NJ: Princeton University Press, 1954.

————. *Patterns in Comparative Religion*. New York: Sheed and Ward, 1958.

————. *The Quest: History and Meaning in Religion*. Chicago: University of Chicago Press, 1969.

————. *The Sacred and the Profane: The Nature of Religion*. New York: Harcourt, 1959.

————. *The Two and the One*. New York: Harper, 1965.

————. *Yoga: Immortality and Freedom*. Princeton, NJ: Princeton University Press, 1970.

————. *Zalmoxis. The Vanishing God. Comparative Studies in the Religion and Folklore of Dacia and Eastern Europe*. Chicago: University of Chicago Press, 1972.

Eliade, Mircea, ed. *The Encyclopedia of Religion*. 16 vols. New York: Macmillan, 1986.

Eliot, Alexander. *Myths*. New York: McGraw-Hill, 1976.

Ellmann, Richard, and Robert O'Clair, eds. "William Bulter Yeats." *Norton Anthology of Modern Poetry*. 2nd ed. New York and London: W.W. Norton, 1988.

Erdoes, Richard, and Alfonso Ortiz. *American Indian Myths and Legends*. New York: Pantheon Books, 1985.

Evans, Ivor H., ed. *Brewer's Dictionary of Phrase & Fable*. 14th ed. New York: Harper & Row, 1989.

Farmer, David Hugh. *The Oxford Dictionary of Saints*. 2nd ed. Oxford: Oxford University Press, 1987.

Fischer-Schreiber, Ingrid, Franz-Karl Eberhard, Kurt Friedrichs, and Micheal S. Diener, eds. *The Encyclopedia of Eastern Philosophy and Religion*. Boston: Shambhala, 1989.

Gabbin, Joanne V. "Sterling Brown." *Afro-American Writers from the Harlem Renaissance to 1940*. Edited by Trudier Harris. Detroit: Gale Research Company, 1987.

Gantz, Jeffrey. *Early Irish Myths and Sagas*. Harmondsworth, Middlesex: Penguin, 1981.

Gassner, John, and Edward Quinn, eds. *The Reader's Encyclopedia of World Drama*. New York: Thomas Y. Crowell, 1969.

Gerould, Gordon Hall. *The Ballad of Tradition*. 1957. Reprint, New York: Gordian Press, 1974.

Gill, Sam D., and Irene F. Sullivan. *A Dictionary of Native American Mythology.* New York: Oxford University Press, 1992.

Ginzberg, Louis. *The Legends of the Jews.* Philadelphia: The Jewish Publication Society of America, 1909.

Glassie, Henry. *Passing the Time in Ballymenone; Culture and History of an Ulster Community.* Philadelphia: University of Pennsylvania Press, 1982.

Graves, Robert. *The Greek Myths.* London: Cassell, 1969.

Green, Miranda Jane. *Dictionary of Celtic Myth and Legend.* London: Thames and Hudson, 1992.

Grimal, Pierre, ed. *Larousse World Mythology.* London: Hamlyn, 1973.

Grimm, Jacob, and Wilhelm Grimm. *Selected Tales.* Translated by David Luke. Harmondsworth, Middlesex: Penguin, 1982.

———. *The Complete Grimm's Fairy Tales.* New York: Pantheon, 1945.

Gruffydd, W. J. *Folklore and Myth in the Mabinogion.* Cardiff: University of Wales Press, 1958.

———. *Rhiannon: An Inquiry into the Origins of the First and Third Branches of the Mabinogi.* Cardiff: University of Wales Press, 1953.

Hamilton, Edith. *Mythology: Timeless Tales of Gods and Heroes.* New York: Mentor, 1969.

Hartland, Edwin Sidney. *The Science of Fairy Tales: An Inquiry to Fairy Mythology.* London: Meuthen, 1925.

———. *The Legend of Perseus: A Study of Tradition in Story, Custom and Belief.* New York: AMS Press, 1972.

Hatto, A. T., trans. *The Nibelungenlied.* Harmondsworth, Middlesex: Penguin, 1978.

Hearn, Michael Patrick. "Preface to the History of Tom Thumbe." *Classics of Children's Literature, 1621-1932.* Selected and arranged by Alison Lurie and Justin G. Schiller. New York: Garland Publishing, 1977.

Holman, C. Hugh. *A Handbook to Literature.* 3rd ed. Indianapolis: The Bobbs-Merrill Company, 1972.

Holt, J.C. *Robin Hood.* London: Thames and Hudson, 1982.

Hunt, Robert. *Popular Romances of the West of England.* 1916. Reprint. Salem, NH: Ayer, 1968.

Hynes, William J., and William G. Doty, eds. *Mythical Trickster Figures: Contours, Contexts, and Criticisms.* Tuscaloosa, AL: University of Alabama Press, 1993.

Ivor H., ed. *Brewer's Dictionary of Phrase & Fable.* 14th ed. New York: Harper & Row, 1989.

Jackson, Guida M. *Encyclopedia of Traditional Epics.* Santa Barbara, CA: ABC-CLIO, 1994.

———. *Traditional Epics.* New York: Oxford University Press, 1994.

Jackson, Kenneth Hurlstone. *A Celtic Miscellany*: Translations from the Celtic Literatures. Harmondsworth, Middlesex: Penguin, 1986.

Joint Committee on the New Translation of the Bible. *The New English Bible with the Apocrypha.* New York: Oxford University Press, 1970.

Jones, Alison. *The Larousse Dictionary of World Folklore.* Edinburgh: Larousse, 1995.

Jones, Glyn E. "Early Prose: The Mabinogi." *A Guide to Welsh Literature*. Vol 1. Edited by A. O. H. Jarman and Gwilym Rees Hughes. Swansea: Christopher Davies, 1976. 189-202.

Jones, Gwyn, and Thomas Jones, trans. *The Mabinogion*. London: J. M. Dent and Sons, 1974.

Jones, Kirkland C. "Arna Bontemps." *Afro-American Writers from the Harlem Renaissance to 1940*. Edited by Trudier Harris. Detroit: Gale Research Company, 1987.

Jordan, Michael. *Encyclopedia of Gods: Over 2,500 Deities of the World*. New York: Facts on File, 1993.

Jordan-Smith, Paul. "The Questions of King Milinda." *Parabola 3,* no. 2 (1978): 70-75.

———. "The Questions of King Milinda." *Parabola 3,* no. 3 (1978): 56-59.

———. "The Questions of King Milinda." *Parabola 3,* no. 4 (1978): 70-73.

Jung, C.G., and C. Kerényi. *Essays on a Science of Mythology: The Myth of the Divine Child and the Mysteries of Eleusis*. 1949. Reprint, Princeton: Princeton University Press, 1963.

Kamenetsky, Christa. *The Brothers Grimm and Their Critics*. Athens: Ohio University Press, 1992.

Kearns, Emily. "Indian Myth." *The Feminist Companion to Mythology*. Edited by Carolyne Larrington. London: HarperCollins, 1992.

Keen, Maurice. *The Outlaws of Medieval Legend*. London: Routledge, 1961.

Keightley, Thomas. *The Fairy Mythology*. 1850. Reprint, New York: Haskell House, 1968.

Kemp-Welch, Alice, trans. *Of the Tumbler of Our Lady and Other Miracles*. New York: Cooper Square Publishers, Inc., 1966.

Kerenyi, Karl. *Prometheus: Archetypal Image of Human Existence*. Translated by Ralph Manheim. New York: Bollingen Foundation, 1963.

Kirby, W. F., trans. *Kalevala: The Land of the Heroes*. Vol. 1. London: J.M. Dent and Sons, 1907.

Knapp, Bettina Liebowitz. *The Prometheus Syndrome*. Troy, NY: Whitston, 1979.

Knight, Stephen. *Robin Hood: A Complete Study of the English Outlaw*. Cambridge: Blackwell, 1994.

Lacy, Norris J., ed. *The Arthurian Encyclopedia*. New York: Garland, 1986.

———. *The New Arthurian Encyclopedia*. Chicago: St. James, 1991.

Lagorio, Valerie M., and Mildred Leake Day. *King Arthur Through the Ages*. 2 vols. New York: Garland Publishing, 1990.

Lasne, Sophie. *Dictionary of Superstitions*. Englewood Cliffs, NJ: Prentice-Hall, 1984.

Lau, C. D., trans. *Tao Te Ching*. Hong Kong: Chinese University Press, 1982.

Leach, Maria, ed. *Funk & Wagnalls Standard Dictionary of Folklore, Mythology, and Legend*. San Francisco: Harper & Row, 1984.

Leeming, David Adams. *Mythology: The Voyage of the Hero*. New York: HarperCollins, 1981.

———. *The Peter Brook/Jean-Claude Carrière Mahabharata, the Great History of Mankind*. Lewiston, NY: Edwin Mellen Press, 1988.

———. *The World of Myth*. New York: Oxford University Press, 1990.

Leeming, David, and Kathleen Drowne. *Encyclopedia of Allegorical Literature*. Santa Barbara, CA: ABC-CLIO, 1996.

Leeming, David, with Margaret Leeming. *A Dictionary of Creation Myths*. New York: Oxford University Press, 1994.

Leeming, David, and Jake Page. *Goddess: Myths of the Female Divine*. New York: Oxford University Press, 1994.

———. *God: Myths of the Male Divine*. New York: Oxford University Press, 1996.

Lewis, C. S. *The Chronicles of Narnia*. 7 vols. (1950-56). New York: HarperCollins, 1994.

Lewis, Jayne Elizabeth. *The English Fable: Aesop and Literary Culture, 1651-1740*. Cambridge: Cambridge University Press, 1996.

London, Jack. *To Build a Fire and Other Stories*. New York: Bantam, 1986.

Magoun, Francis Peabody, Jr., trans. *The Kalevala or Poems of the Kalevala District*. Cambridge: Harvard University Press, 1963.

Mainiero, Lina, ed. *American Women Writers*. Vol. 2. New York: Frederick Ungar, 1980.

Mascaro, Juan, trans. *The Bhagavad Gita*. New York: Penguin, 1962.

Matejka, Ladislav, and Krystyna Pomorska, eds. *Readings in Russian Poetics: Formalist and Structuralist Views*. Cambridge: MIT Press, 1971.

McCaughrean, Geraldine. *Greek Myths*. New York: Macmillan, 1993.

McKendry, John J. *Aesop: Five Centuries of Illustrated Fables*. Washington: The Metropolitan Museum of Art, 1964.

McLeod, Glenda K. "Madame d'Aulnoy: Writer of Fantasy." *Women Writers of the Seventeenth Century*. Edited by Katharina M. Wilson and Frank J. Warnke. Athens, GA: University of Georgia Press, 1989.

Mercatante, Anthony S. "Lilith" and "Phoenix." *The Facts On File Encyclopedia of World Mythology and Legend*. New York: Facts On File, 1988.

Miguet, Marie. "Phoenix." *A Companion to Literary Myths, Heroes and Archetypes*. Edited by Pierre Brunel. London and New York: Routledge, 1992.

Millman, Lawrence. *Our Like Will Not Be There Again: Notes from the West of Ireland*. Boston: Little, Brown, 1977.

Mode, Heinz. *Fabulous Beasts and Demons*. London: Phaidon, 1975.

Moon, Beverly, ed. *An Encyclopedia of Archetypal Symbolism*. The Archive for Research in Archetypal Symbolism. Boston: Shambhala, 1991.

Muhawi, Ibrahim, and Sharif Kanaana. *Speak, Bird, Speak Again: Palestinian Arab Folktales*. Berkeley: University of California Press, 1989.

Neumann, Erich. *The Origins and History of Consciousness*. Princeton: Bollington, 1954.

O'Donnell, Elliot. *Werewolves*. 1912. Reprint Royston, Hertfordshire: Oracle, 1996.

O'Flaherty, Wendy D., trans. *Hindu Myths*. New York: VikingPenguin, 1975.

———. *Siva: The Erotic Ascetic*. New York: Oxford University Press, 1981.

One Feather, Vivian, ed. "The Four Directions." *Parabola 3*, no. 1 (1978): 62-70.

Ousby, Ian, ed. *The Cambridge Guide to Literature in English*. Cambridge: Cambridge University Press, 1993.

Ovid. *Metamorphoses*. Translated by A.D. Melville. New York: Oxford University Press, 1986.

Pellowski, Anne. *The Storytelling Handbook: A Young People's Collection of Unusual Tales and Helpful Hints on How to Tell Them.* New York: Simon & Schuster Books for Young Readers, 1995.

———. *The World of Storytelling.* 2nd. ed. New York: H.W. Wilson Co., 1990.

Pelton, Robert D. *The Trickster in West Africa: A Study of Mythic Irony and Sacred Delight.* Los Angeles: University of California Press, 1980.

Perrault, Charles. *Charles Perrault: Memoirs of My Life.* Edited and Translated by Jeanne Morgan Zarucchi. Columbia: University of Missouri Press, 1989.

———. *The Complete Fairy Tales of Charles Perrault.* Translated by Neil Philip and Nicoletta Simbrowski. Illustrated by Sally Holmes. New York: Clarion Books, 1993.

———. *Perrault's Fairy Tales.* Translated by Sasha Moorson. New York: Doubleday, 1972.

Poignant, Roslyn. *Oceanic Mythology.* London: Hamlyn, 1967.

Potter, Robert R., and H. Alan Robinson. *Myths and Folktales Around the World.* New York: Globe Book Company, 1963.

Pritchard, James B., ed. *The Ancient Near East, Vol. I: An Anthology of Texts and Pictures.* Princeton: Princeton University Press, 1958.

Propp, Vladimir. *Morphology of the Folktale.* Translated by Laurence Scott. Edited by Louis A. Wagner. Austin, TX: University of Texas Press, 1968.

Radford, Edwin, and M. A. Radford. *Encyclopedia of Supersitions.* Edited by Christina Hole. London: Hutchinson, 1961.

Radhayrapetian, Juliet. *Iranian Folk Narrative.* New York: Garland, 1990.

Radin, Paul. *The Trickster: A Study in American Indian Mythology.* New York: Schocken, 1955.

Raglan, FitzRoy. *The Hero: A Study in Tradition, Myth, and Drama.* 1956. Reprint, Westport, CT: Greenwood, 1975.

Rank, Otto. *The Myth of the Birth of the Hero and Other Writings.* Edited by Philip Freund. New York: Vintage Books, 1959.

Rappoport, Angelo S. *Myth and Legend of Ancient Israel.* 3 vols. London: Gresham, 1928.

Reeder, Roberta, ed. *Down along the Mother Volga: An Anthology of Russian Folk Lyrics.* Philadelphia: University of Pennsylvania Press, 1975.

The Revised English Bible. Oxford: Oxford University Press, 1989.

Roberts, John W. *From Trickster to Badman: The Black Folk Hero in Slavery and Freedom.* Philadelphia: University of Pennsylvania Press, 1989.

Roy, P.C., and K.M. Ganguli. *The Mahabharata of Krishna-Dwaipayana Vyasa.* 12 vols. Calcutta: 1970.

Rosenberg, Donna. *World Mythology.* Lincolnwood, IL: National Textbook Company, 1987.

Rowland, Beryl. "Harpies." *Mythical and Fabulous Creatures: A Source Book and Research Guide.* Edited by Malcolm South. Westport, CT: Greenwood, 1987. 155-161.

Sachs, Hans. *The Book of Trades.* New York: Dover, 1973.

———. *The Early Meisterlieder of Hans Sachs.* Edited by Frances H. Ellis. Bloomington: Indiana Universtiy Press, 1974.

————. *Merry Tales and Three Shrovetide Plays.* Translated by William Leighton. Westport, CT: Hyperion Press, 1978.

Segal, Robert, ed. *In Quest of the Hero.* Princeton: Princeton University Press, 1990.

Seyffert, Oskar. "Erinyes" and "Midas." *Dictionary of Classical Antiquities.* New York: Meridian Books, 1957.

Shakespeare, William. *Macbeth.* New York: Bantam, 1988.

Siepmann, Katherine Baker, ed. *Benét's Reader's Encyclopedia.* 3rd ed. New York: HarperCollins, 1987.

Singer, Isaac Bashevis. *Zlateh the Goat and Other Stories.* Illustrated by Maurice Sendak. New York: Harper and Row, 1966.

Siporin, Stephen Charles. "Story Versus Movie: Comments on I. B. Singer's 'Zlateh the Goat.'" *Studies in Jewish Folklore: Proceedings of a Regional Conference of the Association for Jewish Studies.* Cambridge, MA: Association for Jewish Studies, 1980.

Sophocles. *The Oedipus Cycle.* Translated by Dudley Fitts and Robert Fitzgerald. New York: Harcourt Brace, 1949.

South, Malcolm, ed. *Mythical and Fabulous Creatures: A Source Book and Research Guide.* Westport, CT: Greenwood, 1987.

Spretnak, Charlene. *Lost Goddesses of Early Greece: A Collection of Pre-Hellenic Myths.* 4th ed. Boston: Beacon Press, 1992.

Sproul, Barbara C. *Primal Myths: Creating the World.* New York: Harper & Row, 1979.

Stuart, L. Astor, and Leonard R.N. Ashley, eds. Englewood Cliffs, NJ: Prentice-Hall, 1968.

Surmelian, Leon. *Apples of Immortality: Folktales of Armenia.* Berkeley: University of California Press, 1968.

Taylor, Archer. *The Proverb.* Cambridge, MA: Harvard University Press, 1931.

Tedlock, Dennis. *Popol Vuh: The Mayan Book of the Dawn of Life.* New York: Touchstone, 1985.

Thompson, Stith. *The Folktale.* New York: AMS Press, 1979.

————. *One Hundred Favorite Folktales.* Bloomington, IN: Indiana University Press, 1968.

————. *Tales of the North American Indians.* Bloomington, IN: Indiana University Press, 1971.

Thompson, Stith, and Jonas Balys. *The Oral Tales of India.* Wesport, CT: Greenwood Press, 1976.

Thompson, William Irwin. *The Time Falling Bodies Take To Light.* New York: St. Martin's Press, 1981.

Thylmann, Karl, trans. *Gulistan: Tales of Ancient Persia.* Boston: Shambhala, 1977.

Tolkien, J.R.R. *The Fellowship of the Ring.* 1954. Reprint, Boston: Houghton Mifflin, 1988.

————. *The Hobbit.* 1937. Reprint, Boston: Houghton Mifflin, 1989.

————. *The Lord of the Rings.* Boston: Houghton Mifflin, 1991.

————. *The Return of the King.* 1956. Reprint, Boston: Houghton Mifflin, 1988.

————. *The Two Towers.* 1954. Reprint, Boston: Houghton Mifflin, 1988.

Toor, Frances. *A Treasury of Mexican Folkways.* New York: Crown Publishers, 1947.

Urquart, Jane. *The Whirlpool*. Canada: MeClelland and Stewart, 1987.

Vadé, Yves. "Merlin." *A Companion to Literary Myths, Heroes and Archetypes.* Edited by Pierre Brunel. London and New York: Routledge, 1992.

van Buitenen, J. A. B., trans. & ed. *The Mahabharata*. Chicago: University of Chicago Press, 1973.

Varadpande, M. L. *Mahabharata in Performance*. New Delhi: Clarion Books, 1990.

von Franz, Marie-Louise. *The Feminine in Fairy Tales*. Rev ed. Boston: Shambhala, 1993.

Wakeman, John, ed. *World Authors 1950-1970*. New York: H. W. Wilson, 1975.

Warner, Marina. *Alone of All Her Sex: The Myth and the Cult of the Virgin Mary*. New York: Knopf, 1983.

———. *From the Beast to the Blonde: On Fairy Tales and Their Tellers*. New York: Farrar, Straus, Giroux, 1995.

———. *Joan of Arc: The Image of Female Heroism*. New York: Vintage Books, 1982.

———. *Monuments and Maidens: The Allegory of the Female Form*. New York: Atheneum, 1985.

———. *Wonder Tales: Six French Stories of Enchantment*. Illustrated by Sophie Herxheimer. New York: Farrar, Straus, Giroux, 1996.

Wallis, Diz. *Something Nasty in the Cabbages: A Tale from Roman de Reynard*. Honesdale, PA: Boyds Mills Press, 1991.

Watson, Jack, and Grant McKernie. *A Cultural History of Theatre*. White Plains, NY: Longman Publishing, 1993.

Watterson, Barbara. *The Gods of Ancient Egypt*. New York: Facts on File, 1984.

Welsch, Roger L. *Omaha Tribal Myths and Trickster Tales*. Athens, OH: Swallow Press, Ohio University Press, 1981.

Wendell C., and William G. Doty. *Myths, Rites, Symbols: A Mircea Eliade Reader*. New York: Harper & Row, 1976.

White, T. H., ed. *The Book of Beasts*. 1954. Gloucestershire: Alan Sutton, 1992.

Wilkins, Ernest Hatch. *A History of Italian Literature*. Cambridge: Harvard University Press, 1974.

Willis, Roy, ed. *World Mythology*. New York: Henry Holt, 1993.

Wolkstein, Diane. *The Magic Orange Tree and Other Haitian Folktales*. New York: Schocken Books, 1978.

———. *White Wave: A Chinese Tale*. New York: Crowell, 1979.

Younes, Munther A. *Tales from Kalila wa Dimna*. New Haven, CT: Yale University Press, 1989.

Zimmer, Heinrich. *Myths and Symbols in Indian Art and Civilization*. Edited by Joseph Campbell. New York: Harper and Row, 1946.

INDEX

by Virgil Diodato

Note: Bold page numbers refer to main entries in the encyclopedia.